DATE DUE

DEMCO 38-296

The sixth volume of *The New Cambridge Medieval History* covers the fourteenth century, a period dominated by plague, other natural disasters and war which brought to an end three centuries of economic growth and cultural expansion in Christian Europe, but one which also saw important developments in government, changes of emphasis and concern in religious and intellectual life, giving greater weight to the voice of the laity, and new cultural and artistic patterns, not least with the rise of vernacular literature.

The volume is divided into four sections. Part I sets the scene by discussion of general themes in the theory and practice of government, religion, social and economic history, and culture, including discussions of art, architecture and chivalry. Part II deals with the individual histories of the states of western Europe; part III with the Church at the time of the Avignon papacy and the Great Schism; and part IV with eastern and northern Europe, Byzantium and the early Ottomans, giving particular attention to the social and economic relations with westerners and those of other civilisations in the Mediterranean.

The New Cambridge Medieval History

Volume VI *c.* 1300–*c.* 1415

St Louis of Toulouse crowning Robert of Anjou, by Simone Martini (*c.* 1284–1344),
Naples, Museo nazionale di Capodimonte

THE NEW
CAMBRIDGE
MEDIEVAL HISTORY

Volume VI c. 1300–c. 1415

EDITED BY

MICHAEL JONES

Professor of Medieval French History
University of Nottingham

CAMBRIDGE
UNIVERSITY PRESS

PUBLISHED BY THE PRESS SYNDICATE OF THE UNIVERSITY OF CAMBRIDGE
The Pitt Building, Trumpington Street, Cambridge CB2 1RP, United Kingdom

CAMBRIDGE UNIVERSITY PRESS
The Edinburgh Building, Cambridge CB2 2RU, United Kingdom
40 West 20th Street, New York, NY 10011-4211, USA
10 Stamford Road, Oakleigh, Melbourne 3166, Australia

© Cambridge University Press 2000

First published 2000

Printed in the United Kingdom at the University Press, Cambridge

Typeset in 10.5/12.5 Garamond   [SE]

A catalogue record for this book is available from the British Library

ISBN 0 521 36290 3 hardback

CONTENTS

PLATES

FIGURES

MAPS

GENEALOGICAL TABLES

CONTRIBUTORS

DAVID ABULAFIA: Reader in Mediterranean History, University of Cambridge, and Fellow of Gonville and Caius College

FRANÇOISE AUTRAND: Professor, Ecole Normale des Jeunes Filles, Paris

MICHEL BALARD: Professor, University of Paris IV

CAROLINE M. BARRON: Reader in Medieval History, Royal Holloway and Bedford New College, University of London

PAUL BINSKI: University Lecturer, Cambridge, and Fellow of Gonville and Caius College

A.D. CARR: Professor of Welsh History, University of Wales, Bangor

JEREMY CATTO: Fellow of Oriel College, University of Oxford

PAUL CROSSLEY: Reader, Courtauld Institute of Art, University of London

PETER EDBURY: Reader, University of Wales, Cardiff

ALAN FOREY: Sometime Reader in History, University of Durham

ROBIN FRAME: Professor of Medieval History, University of Durham

PAUL FREEDMAN: Professor of History, Yale University

ALEXANDER GRANT: Senior Lecturer, University of Lancaster

LOUIS GREEN: Professor of History, Monash University

NICK HAVELY: Senior Lecturer, University of York

PETER HERDE: Emeritus Professor of History, University of Würzburg

IVAN HLAVÁČEK: Professor of Auxiliary Historical Sciences and Archivistics, Charles University, Prague

MICHAEL JONES: Professor of Medieval French History, University of Nottingham

HOWARD KAMINSKY: Professor of History, University of Florida, Miami

MAURICE KEEN: Reader, University of Oxford, and Fellow of Balliol College

CHRISTIANE KLAPISCH-ZUBER: Professor, Ecole des Hautes Etudes en Sciences Sociales, Paris

NANCY SHIELDS KOLLMANN: Professor of History, Stanford University

ANGELIKI E. LAIOU: Professor, Harvard University

JOHN LAW: Senior Lecturer, University of Wales, Swansea

JEAN-PIERRE LEGUAY: Professor of History, University of Rouen

PETER LINEHAN: Lecturer, University of Cambridge, and Fellow of St John's College

I. METIN KUNT: Faculty Member, Sabancı University, Istanbul

CLAUDE MICHAUD: Professor of History, University of Paris I

W. MARK ORMROD: Professor of History, University of York

WALTER PREVENIER: Professor of History, University of Ghent

ALBERT RIGAUDIÈRE: Professor of History, University of Paris II

S.C. ROWELL: Institute of History, Vilnius

PETER SPUFFORD: Sometime Reader in Monetary History, University of Cambridge, and Fellow of Queen's College

JACQUES VERGER: Professor of History, University of Paris II

P.N.R. ZUTSHI: University Archivist, University of Cambridge, Fellow of Corpus Christi College

PREFACE

My first vicarious experience of the tribulations and triumphs of an editor of a Cambridge *History* came as I watched my remarkable tutor, J.P. Cooper, struggling for more than ten years to bring to birth his volume *The Decline of Spain and the Thirty Years War 1609–48/59* (1970), in the *New Cambridge Modern History*. Perhaps I should have learnt then that collaborative ventures call for more than usual editorial skills and patience, above all that they need much wielding of iron fists in velvet gloves, if the project is to be kept within reasonable word and time limits and the editor is to remain on speaking terms with contributors who first produced their chapters while cajoling those still some way behind into making the final effort! In the circumstances although, as with other volumes in this series, there has been slippage in the originally proposed schedule, the time from conception to birth is only just verging on the elephantine for works of this scale. It is thus with great pleasure (as well as a strong sense of relief) that I can now say how grateful I am to all those who have contributed. Particular thanks are due to those who replaced others, first chosen but unable to produce their chapters. Among these we may sadly note two fine American scholars, David Herlihy and John Boswell, both of whom died before they could write any part of their proposed pieces. In the case of the former, an ideal replacement, Christiane Klapisch-Zuber, who collaborated with Herlihy in the ground-breaking work, *Les Toscans et leurs familles* (1978), willingly undertook to write in his stead, whilst at an even later stage Alan Forey kindly supplied a chapter on the kingdom of Aragon which Boswell had originally agreed to do. Another late replacement to whom I am immensely indebted is Stephen Rowell, who not only provides a wide-ranging survey of Baltic history, but also made helpful suggestions with regard to other chapters touching on the Slav world. It is important to add that Paul Freedman was an even later recruit since the eleventh hour had already struck when he generously agreed to write the section on rural society (for which Guy Bois had originally contracted), without which the section on the Economy would have been sadly inadequate. It is certainly through no fault of these scholars that I have to apologise here to those colleagues who so speedily and efficiently discharged their obligations within a brief time after the launch of this volume only to see their chapters delayed for several years; they have been given some opportunity to revise their texts, though naturally some would now approach the task in a different fashion if asked to do so again in the light of their own maturer experience and continuing advances in their respective fields. An attempt has been made to note major additions to bibliographies compiled some years ago, though it has seemed best to allow them mainly to represent the work on which the individual chapters were then based.

As editor of a large and international team I have been immensely encouraged over the time this volume has been in production by the friendship shown me by busy scholars in many countries and by their unstinting co-operation as I edited their work for the final text. Many who were simply names to me when the project began, I now know much better and I am happy to acknowledge my debt to them. I think it also fair to say that for many, if not all contributors, the challenge of condensing what in most fields has become an enormous modern literature of their respective subjects often proved more taxing than they had first imagined. Few of the chapters that follow make any claim to be comprehensive; all contributors have had to make invidious choices about what to include or exclude (some of which are explained in the Introduction below); all have accepted editorial guidance with remarkable patience even where that may have been wrong-headed. Some have chosen to annotate their chapters fairly extensively; others have simply provided bibliographies which reflect their own reading and provide guidance to some of the most useful literature in their area. I hope that failure to standardise in this respect will be accepted as a reasonable compromise since I was anxious not to cram all contributors into the same procrustean mould.

Among those without whom the volume would have been very different, mention may especially be made of Juliet Vale who has been responsible for translating chapters **2, 4, 6, 7, 14(b), 22** and **25** from French, and **16(a)** from German, while Paula Kennedy translated **16(b)** from Czech; both were meticulous in their efforts to convey the sense of the original and in ensuring that the appropriate conventions have been used for transliterating names of people, places and offices to make the chapters accessible to an English-speaking audience, performing indeed much of the work of a general editor, for which I am very grateful. Likewise I have received valuable assistance in processing the bibliographies from Claire Taylor. The help of the volume's copy-editor, Linda Randall, and its indexer, David Atkins, have been invaluable in improving the consistency and accuracy of the text. My thanks must also go to fellow editors of this *History*, especially Rosamond McKittcrick, David

Abulafia and Christopher Allmand, as well as to other members of the Editorial Board, for their help and encouragement over the last decade. For his forbearance and unfailingly supportive advice and help through good days and bad, a special mention must be made of William Davies of the Press, whose 'worst-case scenario' I hope we have just collectively avoided.

MICHAEL JONES

ACKNOWLEDGEMENTS

Permission to reproduce pictures and photographs of buildings or of other objects in their care has been acknowledged above (pp. xi–xiii); the sources of figures 1–8 are also acknowledged appropriately, while the genealogical tables have been prepared in house at the Press. We are grateful to Reginald Piggott for expert preparation of the maps from difficult copy and in accord with the sometimes exigent demands of authors.

Finally, but by no means least, the editor would also like to place on record the enormous help that he has received from Dr Elizabeth Jones, latterly for proof-reading and stylistic suggestions, but also for support of every kind over many more years than even this volume has been in production.

ABBREVIATIONS

AAPH	*Anais de Academia portuguesa da historia*
AASS	*Acta Sanctorum*, ed. J. Bollandus *et al.*
AB	*Analecta Bollandiana*
ABret	*Annales de Bretagne*
ABSHF	*Annuaire-bulletin de la Société de l'histoire de France*
ABurg	*Annales de Bourgogne*
ACNSS	*Actes du Congrès national des Sociétés savantes*
ADH	*Annales de démographie historique*
AE	*Annales de l'Est*
AEM	*Anuario de estudios medievales*
AESC	*Annales: économies, sociétés, civilisations*
AFH	*Archivum Franciscanum Historicum*
AFP	*Archivum Fratrum Praedicatorum*
AgHR	*Agricultural History Review*
AHC	*Annuarium Historiae Conciliorum*
AHDE	*Anuario de historia del derecho español*
AHP	*Archivum Historiae Pontificiae*
AIBL	*Académie des inscriptions et belles-lettres*
AIPHO	*Annuaire de l'Institut de Philologie et d'Histoire Orientales*
AK	*Archiv für Kulturgeschichte*
ALKG	*Archiv für Literatur- und Kirchengeschichte des Mittelalters*
AmHR	*American Historical Review*
AMi	*Annales du Midi*
AN	Archives nationales, Paris
ANo	*Annales de Normandie*
APAE	*Anciens pays et assemblés d'état*
APH	*Acta Poloniae Historica*
ArtB	*Art Bulletin*
ASF	Archivio di stato di Firenze

ASI	*Archivio storico italiano*
ASL	*Archivio storico lombardo*
ASP	Archivio di stato di Pisa
AV	*Archivio veneziani*
BAE	Biblioteca de autores españoles
BAR	British Archaeological Reports
BB	*Byzantino-Bulgarica*
BBA	*The Black Book of the Admiralty,* ed. T. Twiss, RS, 1, London (1872)
BBCS	*Bulletin of the Board of Celtic Studies*
BBHS	*Bulletin of the Business Historical Society*
BCRH	*Bulletin de la Commission royale d'histoire*
BEC	*Bibliothèque de l'école des chartes*
BEFAR	Bibliothèque des écoles françaises d'Athènes et de Rome
BEP	*Bulletin des estudes portugaises*
BF	*Byzantinische Forschungen*
BG	*Bijdragen tot de Geschiedenis*
BH	*Bulletin hispanique*
Bib. mun.	Bibliothèque municipale
BIDR	*Bolletino dell'Instituto di diritto romano*
BIHR	*Bulletin of the Institute of Historical Research*
BJRL	*Bulletin of the John Rylands Library*
BL	British Library
BMGM	*Bijdragen en Mededelingen voor de Geschiedenis der Nederlanden*
BN	Bibliothèque Nationale de France, Paris
BPH(1715)	*Bulletin philologique et historique (jusqu'à 1715)*
BRAH	*Boletín de la Real academia de la historia*
BS	*Byzantine Studies/Etudes byzantines*
BSAF	*Bulletin de la Société des antiquaires de France*
BSBS	*Bolletino storico-bibliografico subalpino*
BSOAS	*Bulletin of the School of Oriental and African Studies*
BSPS	*Bolletino storico pisano*
BSPSP	*Bolletino della Societa pavese di storia patria*
BST	*Biblioteca storica toscana*
BZ	*Byzantinische Zeitschrift*
CAXI	*Crónica de Alfonso XI,* ed. C. Rosell, BAE, 66, Madrid (1875)
CBHB	Corpus Bruxellense Historiae Byzantinae
CEFR	Collection de l'Ecole française de Rome
CEHE	*The Cambridge Economic History of Europe,* ed. J.H. Clapham, M.M. Postan *et al.,* 8 vols., Cambridge (1941–89)

CEIII	*Crónica de Enrique III*, ed. C. Rosell, BAE, 68, Madrid (1877)
CFIV	*Crónica de Fernando IV*, ed. C. Rosell, BAE, 66, Madrid (1875)
CFan	*Cahiers de Fanjeaux*
CH	*Cuadernos de historia*
CH(E)	*Cuadernos de historia (de España)*
CHCA	*Congresso de historia de la corona de Aragón*
CIEB	*Congrès international des études byzantines*
CJI	*Crónica de Juan I*, ed. C. Rosell, BAE, 68, Madrid (1877)
CJII	*Chronique des règnes de Jean II et de Charles V*, ed. R. Delachenal, 4 vols., Paris (1917–20)
CMCS	*Cambridge Medieval Celtic Studies*
CMH	*Cambridge Medieval History*
CMRS	*Cahiers du monde russe et soviétique*
CNRS	Centre national des recherches scientifiques
Cortes	*Cortes de los antiguos reinos de León y de Castilla*, ed. Real Academia de la Historia, I, II, Madrid (1861–3)
CPI	*Crónica de Pedro I*, ed. C. Rosell, BAE, 66, Madrid (1875)
CPIII	*Pere III of Catalonia (Pedro IV of Aragon) Chronicle*, trans. M. Hillgarth, with introduction and notes by J.N. Hillgarth, 2 vols., Toronto (1980)
CRC	*Crónicas de los reyes de Castilla desde Don Alfonso el Sabio*, ed. F. Cerda, I, Madrid (1781)
CRH	*Commission royale d'histoire*
CSHB	*Corpus Scriptorum Historiae Byzantinae*, 50 vols., Berlin (1828–91)
CT	Geoffrey Chaucer, *Canterbury Tales*
DA	*Deutsches Archiv für Erforschung des Mittelalters*
DBI	*Dizionario biografico degli Italiani*, ed. A.M. Ghisalberti *et. al.*, 49 vols. continuing, Rome (1960–97)
DDG	*Dukhovnye i dogovornye gramoty velikikh i udel'nykh kniazei XIV–XVI vv.*, Moscow and Leningrad (1950)
DOP	*Dumbarton Oaks Papers*
DR	*Downside Review*
DVE	Dante Alighieri, *De vulgari eloquentia*, ed. A. Marigo, 3rd edn, Florence (1957)
DVL	*Diplomatarium Veneto-Levantinum*, I: *1300–1350*; II: *1351–1454*, ed. G.M. Thomas, Venice (1880–99)
EB	*Etudes balkaniques*
EcHR	*Economic History Review*

EETS	Early English Text Society
EHH	*Etudes historiques hongroises*
EHR	*English Historical Review*
EO	*Etudes orientales*
FC	Jean Froissart, *Chroniques*, ed. S. Luce *et al.*, 15 vols. continuing, Paris (1869–1975)
FHS	*French Historical Studies*
FOG	*Forschungen zur osteuropäischen Geschichte*
FS	*Franziskanische Studien*
GAKGS	*Gesammelte Aufsätze zur Kulturgeschichte Spaniens*
GBA	*Gazette des beaux arts*
GDGSO	M. Hayez (ed.), *Genèse et débuts du grand schisme d'occident*, Paris (1980)
GG	*Geschichte und Gesellschaft*
Gli Scaligeri	G.M. Varanini (ed.), *Gli Scaligeri*, Verona (1988)
GP, ed. Failler	George Pachymeres, *Relations historiques*, ed. A. Failler, 2 vols., Paris (1984)
GP, ed. Bekkerus	George Pachymeres, *De Michaele et Andronico Palaeologis Libri Tredecim*, ed. I. Bekkerus, 2 vols., Paris (1855–7)
Gregoras	Nicephorus Gregoras, *Byzantina Historia*, I–III, ed. L. Schopen and I. Bekker, *CSHB*, Bonn (1829–55)
HEMP	*Historia de España*, general ed. R. Menédez Pidal, 18 vols., Madrid (1957–90)
HF	Geoffrey Chaucer, *The House of Fame*
HG	*Hansische Geschichtsblätter*
HID	*Historia. Instituciones. Documentos.*
HJb	*Historisches Jahrbuch*
HL	Cl. Devic and J. Vaissete, *Histoire générale de Languedoc*, ed. A. Molinier *et al.*, 16 vols, Toulouse (1872–1904)
HMGOG	*Handelingen van de Maatschappij voor Geschiedenis en Oudheidkunde van Gent*
HR	*Historical Research*
HT	*History Today*
HUS	*Harvard Ukrainian Studies*
HZ	*Historische Zeitschrift*
IARP	Index Actorum Romanorum Pontificum ab Innocenti III ad Martinum V Electum
IC, *Hist.*	Ioannis Cantacuzeni, *Eximperatoris Historiarum Libri IV*, ed. L. Schopen, 3 vols., *CSHB*, Bonn (1828–32)
IESH	*Irish Economic and Social History*
IH	*L'information historique*

IHS	*Irish Historical Studies*
IJTS	*International Journal of Turkish Studies*
IMU	Italia medievale e umanistica
IZ	*Istoricheskie zapiski*
JBAA	*Journal of the British Archaeological Association*
JBaS	*Journal of Baltic Studies*
JBS	*Journal of British Studies*
JEEH	*Journal of European Economic History*
JEH	*Journal of Ecclesiastical History*
JG	J. and P. Zepos (eds.), *Jus Graecoromanum*, I, Athens (1931)
JGF	*Jahrbuch für Geschichte des Feudalismus*
JGO	*Jahrbücher für Geschichte Osteuropas*
JHI	*Journal of the History of Ideas*
JHP	*Journal of the History of Philosophy*
JIH	*Journal of Interdisciplinary History*
JItH	*Journal of Italian History*
JMH	*Journal of Medieval History*
JMRS	*Journal of Medieval and Renaissance Studies*
JÖB	*Jahrbuch der Österreichischen Byzantinistik*
JRAS	*Journal of the Royal Asiatic Society*
JRSAI	*Journal of the Royal Society of Antiquaries of Ireland*
JS	*Journal des Savants*
JSAH	*Journal of the Society of Architectural Historians*
JThS	*Journal of Theological Studies*
JWCI	*Journal of the Warburg and Courtauld Institutes*
JWH	*Journal of World History*
JZCH	*Jerónimo Zurita. Cuadernos de Historia*
KQS	Kirchengeschichtliche Quellen und Studien
LJ	*London Journal*
LS	*Lusitania Sacra*
MA	*Le moyen âge*
MAHEFR	*Mélanges de archéologie et d'histoire publiés par l'Ecole française de Rome*
MCV	*Mélanges de la casa de Velazquez*
MED	*Middle English Dictionary*, general ed. Hans Kurath, 11 vols. (continuing), Ann Arbor (1956–)
MEFRA/M	*Mélanges de l'Ecole française de Rome*
MGH	*Monumenta Germaniae Historica*
MH	*Mediaevalia et Humanistica*
MHR	*Mediterranean History Review*

MIÖG	Mitteilungen des Instituts für österreichische Geschichtsforschung
MKVA	*Medelingen van de Koninklijkse Vlaamse Academie*
MPG	J.-P. Migne, *Patrologia e Cursus Completus, Series Graeca*, 161 vols., Paris (1857–66)
MS	*Mediaeval Studies*
MSHAB	*Mémoires de la Société d'histoire et d'archéologie de Bretagne*
MSHP	*Mémoires de la Société de l'histoire de Paris et de l'Ile de France*
(N)AV	*(Nuovo) Archivio veneto*
NCMH	*New Cambridge Medieval History*
NMS	*Nottingham Medieval Studies*
NRHDFE	*Nouvelle revue historique de droit français et étranger*
NRS	*Nuova rivista storica*
OCA	*Orientalia Christiana Analecta*
OCP	*Orientalia Christiana Periodica*
ODB	*Oxford Dictionary of Byzantium*, 3 vols., Oxford (1991)
OESA	Order of Augustinian Canons
OFM	Order of Friars Minor (Franciscans)
OMCTH	Ordines Militares. Colloquia Torunensia Historica
OP	Order of Friars Preacher (Dominicans)
OSP	*Oxford Slavonic Papers*
Part.	*Las Siete Partidas*, ed. Real Academia de la Historia, 3 vols., Madrid (1807; repr. 1972)
PBA	*Proceedings of the British Academy*
PBSR	*Papers of the British School at Rome*
PER	*Parliaments, Estates and Respresentation*
Poly.	Ranulph Higden, *Polychronicon,* ed. C. Babington and J.R. Lumby
P&P	*Past & Present*
PP	William Langland, *Piers Plowman by William Langland: An Edition of the C-Text*, ed. D.A. Pearsall, London (1978)
PrAPS	*Proceedings of the American Philosophical Society*
PRIA	*Proceedings of the Royal Irish Academy*
PRO	Public Record Office
PS	*Population Studies*
PTEC	*Positions des thèses de l'Ecole des chartes*
PU	*Preussisches Urkundenbuch*, ed. M. Hein, E. Maschke, K. Conrad *et al.*, 6 vols., Königsberg and Marburg (1882–1986)
QAMK	Quellen und Abhandlungen zur mittelrheinischen Kirchengeschichte

QDHG	Quellen und Darstellung zur Hansische Geschichte
QFIAB	*Quellen und Forschungen aus italienischen Archiven und Bibliotheken*
QFGG	Quellen und Forschungen aus dem Gebiet der Geschichte
QSBG	Quellen und Studien zur baltischen Geschichte
QSGDO	Quellen und Studien zur Geschichte der Deutschen Ordens
RAH	Real academia de la historia
RBPH	*Revue Belge de philologie et d'histoire*
REB	*Revue des études byzantines*
REG	*Revue des études grecques*
RF	*Romanische Forschungen*
RH	*Revue historique*
RHDFE	*Revue historique de droit français et étranger*
RHE	*Revue d'histoire ecclésiastique*
RHGF	*Recueil des historiens des Gaules et de la France*
RIS	*Rerum Italicarum Scriptores*, ed. L.A. Muratori, 25 vols., Milan (1723–51); new edn G. Carducci and V. Fiorini, Città di Castello and Bologna (1900–)
RLR	*Revue des langues romanes*
RMAL	*Revue du moyen âge Latin*
RN	*Revue du Nord*
RPH	*Revista portuguesa de história*
RPV	*Registres du trésor des chartes*, III: *Règne de Philippe de Valois*, pt 1: *JJ 65A à 69*, ed. J. Viard, Aline Vallée and J. Favier, Paris (1978)
RQ	*Römische Quartalschrift*
RQH	*Revue des questions historiques*
RQly	*Renaissance Quarterly*
RS	Rolls Series
RSCI	*Rivista di storia della chiesa in Italia*
RSH	*Revue des sciences humaines*
RSJB	*Recueils de la Société Jean Bodin*
RStds	*Renaissance Studies*
RuH	*Russian History*
SAO	*Studia et Acta Orientalia*
SB	*Studia Byzantina*
SCH	*Studies in Church History*
SDECH	S.B. Chrimes and A.L. Brown, *Select Documents of English Constitutional History 1307–1485*, London (1964)

SEER	*Slavonic and East European Review*
SF	*Südost Forschungen*
SFGG	*Spanische Forschungen der Görresgesellschaft*
SG	*Studia Gratiana*
SH	*Studia Hibernica*
SHF	Société de l'histoire de France
SHR	*Scottish Historical Review*
SJ	Society of Jesus
SJH	*Scandinavian Journal of History*
SL	*Standen en Landen*
SM	*Studi Medievali*
SMGBO	*Studien und Mitteilungen zur Geschichte des Benediktineordens und seiner Zweige*
SMRT	*Studies in Medieval and Reformation Thought*
SR	*Slavic Review*
SRP	*Scriptores Rerum Prussicarum*, ed. T. Hirsch *et al.*, 5 vols., Leipzig (1861–74); repr. with a sixth vol., Frankfurt am Main (1965)
ST	*Studi e Testi*
SV	*Studi veneziani*
SVen	*Storia di Venezia*
THSC	*Transactions of the Honourable Society of Cymmrodorion*
TM	*Travaux et mémoires*
TODL	*Trudy Otdela drevnerusskoi literatury*
TRHS	*Transactions of the Royal Historical Society*
UTET	Unione tipografico-editrice torinese
VF	Vorträge und Forschungen
VKAWLSKB	Verhandlingen Koninklijke Academie voor Wetenschappen, Letteren en Schone Kunsten van België
VMGOG	Verhandlingen van de Maatschappij voor Geschiedenis en Ouheidkunde van Gent
VQHF	Vatikanische Quellen zur Geschichte der päpstlichen Hof- und Finanzverwaltung
VSW	*Vierteljahrschrift fur Sozial- und Wirtschaftsgeschichte*
VV	*Vizantiiskii Vremennik*
WF	Wege der Forschung
WHR	*Welsh History Review*
ZHF	*Zeitschrift für historische Forschung*
ZKG	*Zeitschrift für Kirchengeschichte*
ZR	*Zeitschrift für Rechtsgeschichte*
ZRVI	*Zbornik Radova Vizantoloshkog Instituta*

PART I

GENERAL THEMES

CHAPTER 1

INTRODUCTION

Michael Jones

THIS volume replaces the seventh volume of the *Cambridge Medieval History*, which was seen through the press in 1932 by C.W. Previté-Orton and Z.N. Brooke.[1] That volume, subtitled *Decline of the Empire and Papacy*, dealt with 'roughly speaking, the fourteenth century', though that was interpreted generously – from 1252 in the case of Spain, and from *c.* 1270 in the accounts of England, France and Germany, while terminal dates for some chapters ran well into the fifteenth century. Moreover, in a significant proportion of the volume, especially in thematic chapters devoted to the Jews, medieval estates, peasant life, the early Renaissance and medieval mysticism, discussion was set in a broader context, often covering the whole period from 1100 to 1500, with a consequent diminution of specific information on the characteristics of the fourteenth century itself, a period recognised by all scholars, then as now, as amongst the most turbulent, even apocalyptic, of the entire Middle Ages or, as one well-informed contemporary, Filippo Villani, starkly put it, 'this shipwreck of a century which is going from bad to worse'.[2]

Not that there was any lack of information in *Decline of the Empire and Papacy* in other respects: approximately three-quarters of the volume was devoted to traditional political history within a strong narrative framework, above all the deeds of popes and emperors, kings and princes, parliaments and estates. Some chapters can still be mined with profit although there are many new sources and, in most cases, a huge modern secondary literature now available to reconstruct the sequence of events or to reinterpret the role of individuals. It simply is not possible, nor is it desirable, here to attempt the same kind of detailed narrative for the whole of Europe provided there. In geographical spread, too, there are differences of emphasis between that volume and the present one.

Then, whilst some notice was taken of eastern and northern Europe, with chapters on the Hansa, the Teutonic Order, Bohemia and Russia, the vast bulk

[1] *CMH*, VII, Preface. [2] Filippo Villani, *De . . . Famosis Civibus*, cited by McLaughlin (1988), p. 135.

of the narrative concerned the heart of medieval Catholic Europe: Italy, France, Germany and the British Isles, with lesser attention being given to other regions, though it is interesting to note that the development of Switzerland from the thirteenth to fifteenth centuries was allowed more space than the chapter on Spain from the mid thirteenth century to 1410. In this latter case there has been an especially large explosion of historical research since the 1930s both within Spain itself and elsewhere, particularly amongst Anglo-American historians. The same is true of late medieval Italy where native historians have been joined by armies of foreign scholars ransacking the rich archives of cities like Florence, Venice, Genoa and Siena as well as those drawn to Rome and the papacy. Indeed it is characteristic of the period in general that there are few fields in which research has not become more 'archive' orientated in recent generations, especially since improved technical means for processing burgeoning quantities of historical data in whatever form it is presented are now so widely available both to individual scholars and to teams of researchers.[3]

Some areas least covered in *Decline of the Empire and Papacy* did, of course, receive modest attention elsewhere in the original *Cambridge Medieval History*, but treatment was deliberately uneven: chapters on south-eastern Europe, the Mediterranean world and relations with Islam were largely omitted from 'Decline' and gathered together in a single volume devoted to the whole history of the Byzantine empire.[4] If the current volume is more coherent in chronological terms than its predecessor, keeping largely within the framework *c.* 1300–*c.* 1415, it is also more comprehensive in its territorial coverage with eastern and northern Europe and the Mediterranean world, including Byzantium, the Balkans and the rise of the Ottomans, receiving significant attention (chapters **21–7**). Occasionally, even wider vistas are briefly glimpsed: the still-overshadowing influence of the Mongols on the political development of the principalities of Rus' is noted (**23**), the cultural impact of the Golden Horde (seen emblematically in the allusion to the khanate in the adoptive name of the lord of Padua, Cangrande della Scala, d. 1328),[5] Timur the Lame's defeat of Sultan Bayezid at Ankara in 1402, bringing the apparently inexorable rise of the Ottomans to a juddering halt (**26**), and the economic significance of markets in, and products from, the east (**8, 25**), not to mention the trajectory of the Black Death, reveal different aspects of the distant yet palpable impact of Asia on fourteenth-century Europe.[6] Whilst within

---

[3] Herlihy and Klapisch-Zuber (1978) for a pioneering example of this trend.

[4] Soon recognised as inadequate, the original volume was subsequently revised and expanded by Hussey (1966–7).   [5] Below p. 464.

[6] Abu-Lughod (1989) places late medieval European economic performance in a sobering world-wide perspective.

Christendom, the century saw a much closer symbiosis of the Mediterranean, North Sea and Baltic worlds, developments graphically displayed, for instance, in the expanding geographical knowledge revealed by makers of successive portolans, marine charts, as Italian and Iberian mariners established regular contact with the Atlantic seaboard and northern Europe from around 1300 (cf. **8**).[7]

However, this addition to territorial coverage has inevitably to be made at the cost of sacrificing some of that depth of treatment accorded to individual countries in 1932. For example, Italy and Germany then claimed just under 10 per cent and France just over 10 per cent of the available space, while Britain had almost 20 per cent, Wyclif and the Lollards alone getting more than that devoted separately to Wales, Ireland and Scotland. In the present volume only the British Isles gets over 10 per cent, and no other region claims more than 5 or 6 per cent.

Another obvious difference between Previté-Orton and Brooke's volume and this one (and others in the new series) is that the proportion of narrative history to analytical and thematic chapters is now more equitable, resulting in a third of the volume being devoted to 'General themes' (**2–12**); though it is fair to point out that the focus of many of these chapters is firmly centred on the heartlands of the medieval west, above all those regions that looked to Rome (or Avignon) for spiritual leadership. Thus in place of McIlwain's famous survey of 'Medieval estates', representative institutions are here largely subsumed within a more general discussion of the 'Theory and practice of government in western Europe', or make their appearance as appropriate in chapters devoted to individual states, notably those on England, Scotland, the Low Countries and Spain (**13(a,b,d)**, **17**, **18**).[8] The problem in this respect is, as in so many others, as Albert Rigaudière shrewdly notes, 'Western Europe in the fourteenth century was as diverse as the states of which it was composed',[9] a remark that is also equally applicable to social conditions as well as political structures in eastern and northern Europe as chapters **21–3** demonstrate.

While there are contemporary historians drawn to the exciting grand panoramic sweep – the recent appearance of two highly successful one-volume surveys of European history in its entirety shows what can be done when an extraordinary capacity to digest and synthesise is combined with a high degree of intellectual rigour, vision and organising skill[10] – the nature of the exercise here is different, the scale and ambitions more modest. There are, of course, thought-provoking general patterns to be drawn out as the thematic chapters

---

[7] Mollat and La Roncière (1984).

[8] See also Blockmans in *NCMH*, VII, pp. 29–64 for 'Representation'.   [9] Below, p. 17.

[10] Roberts (1996); Davies (1996).

illustrate but the particular continues to excite. Many chapters thus essay a lighter touch, one which is not so relentlessly factual but rather impressionistic and interpretive, though one which at the same time aims to set out any current historiographical disagreement in a balanced way.

Political affairs inevitably continue to bulk large, though it is hoped that in most chapters where they predominate, there is also recognition of wider social and cultural issues. For instance, the growth of bureaucratic institutions and routine administrative procedures in many more advanced polities had implications not only for the development of government, but for changing relationships between rulers, their servants and their other subjects, as well as for education, the spread and character of literacy, and so on (cf. **2–4, 12, 14(a),(b)**, etc.). Naturally, attention is paid to the ideology and symbolism of kingship or to that of republicanism in particular political contexts, alongside the claims of the universalist powers of empire and papacy. These latter especially affected the history of those geographically imprecise and fragmented regions, Germany and Italy, and gave rise to some of the most remarkable political treatises of the period on the nature of royal and ecclesiastical power like Marsilius of Padua's *Defensor Pacis*, so especially subversive of traditional papal views.[11]

Economic and social history was not absent from the *Decline of the Empire and Papacy*, but it is a reflection of the greater importance accorded to them in modern studies, that two of the longest sections here are devoted to 'Plague and family life' (**7**) and 'Trade' (**8**). But there are few nominally 'political' chapters where social and economic matters are completely ignored. The fact that many historians, even political ones, see the century as one of two halves (to borrow a cliché usually associated with a popular sport), hinging on the Black Death, inevitably reflects their taking into account (whether to confirm or to deny its importance for their own special concerns) of that quite unprecedentedly dramatic event, with all its multifarious resonances on which a huge literature has developed. More generally, in comparison with the thirteenth century, the fourteenth witnesses an age of expansion and consolidation being succeeded by one of contraction and upheaval as we shall see in more detail below.

Major institutional developments in the world of learning are reflected generally in chapter **4** on 'The universities', and in other chapters on particular regions (cf. **16(b), 21, 22**) where the growth in numbers and changing characteristics of centres of higher learning, as well as of schools, is traced. The novel part of secular authorities in encouraging these developments is made very evident in many instances, while the interplay between academic, theological and philosophical speculation, and the religious thinking and

---

[11] Below pp. 20 and 541.

spiritual practices of other ranks in society receives treatment particularly in chapter **3**, but is also touched upon at many other points (cf. **16(b)**, **23**, **24**). The relations of Christians with those of other faiths or beliefs is clearly important in discussing many regions – most obviously, perhaps, Iberia, the Balkans, central and northern Europe. The breakdown of *convivencia* in Castile (**18(b)**), growing brutality towards the Jews (cf. **18(a)**), only occasionally offset by signs of Christian and Jewish co-operation, as in trading partnerships in the eastern Mediterranean (**25**), and the survival or recrudescence of slavery (**8**, **18(a)**, **21**, **26**) shows an increasingly intolerant side of Christendom in this period. The Ottomans, on the other hand, appear to have displayed a greater sympathy towards (or acceptance and tolerance of) religious or racial differences in their rise to power than has been traditionally recognised (**26**). The themes of growing 'nationalist' or 'ethnic' feelings and their character-istics (perhaps most famously and concretely expressed in the Declaration of Arbroath, 1320 (**13(d)**), are taken up at other points too (cf. **13(c,e)**, **15(a)**, **16(b)**, **22**) in a century which sees major advances in both the institutions and ideology of states as lay powers grew in confidence and shook off ecclesiasti-cal restraint.

In chapters **19** and **20**, developments affecting the western Church hierarchy and the relations of Church and state are especially addressed from the point of view of the papacy and the cardinals, though ecclesiastical affairs in partic-ular states is also a theme properly considered elsewhere, with regard to the Statutes of Provisors or Praemunire or the Lollards in England (**2**, **13(a–b)**), the background to Hus and his followers in Bohemia and the empire (**16(b)**, **22**), or in the relationship of the Roman and Orthodox Churches in eastern Europe (**23**, **24**), for example. As is well known, the century also saw the official eradication of paganism from European soil, with the agreement of Jogaila (Jagellon), grand duke of Lithuania, to convert to Roman Catholicism in 1386 and to marry Jadwiga (Hedwig) 'king' of Poland, the culmination of an extended political evolution that brought a society still very primitive by western standards at the beginning of the century (the parallel with Merovingian Gaul is drawn) into full communion with Christendom (**21**).

In contrast to practice in the old *Cambridge Medieval History*, inclusion here of photographic plates allows illustration of some key examples in the chap-ters devoted to art and architecture (**10**, **11**), where a major theme is the evolu-tion of various expressions of the predominating Gothic style, an 'international language of extraordinary formal diversity'.[12] At the same time the century sees some breakdown or diminution of the hegemony which French cultural traditions and values had exercised in this field as in so many

---

[12] Below p. 234 and cf. p. 222.

others in the previous two centuries. These changes in art and architecture can be well demonstrated, convincingly perhaps for the first time, from non-ecclesiastical evidence, especially from study of secular court art as well as that patronised by leading urban communities. Considerable attention is paid to this material evidence of princely and oligarchic patronage – manuscripts, paintings, tapestries, jewelry, buildings – not only in these chapters but at other points – notably with reference to Emperor Charles IV's Prague, Edward III's Windsor ('the Versailles of its age'), Charles V of France's Paris, Robert of Anjou's Naples. But similar ideas and fashions pervade the Baltic north and stretch even to the urban republic of Novgorod; nor are the 'Maecenas' attitudes of popes like Clement VI and his immediate successors in transforming the townscape of Avignon overlooked (**19**). Less frequently recognised, perhaps, is a remarkable 'renaissance' in Byzantine culture in the first half of the century which also depended heavily on secular, notably imperial, patronage (**24**).

With regard to life in towns, the century, so often portrayed in cataclysmic fashion, saw an increasingly rational approach to the problems of urban living by many authorities with more evidence of town planning, building regulations, a concern with hygiene, water supplies and the health of townsmen becoming (perhaps not surprisingly in an era dominated by plague) an important concern of many town councils, and not just those in Italy. Defence was likewise a major priority for most towns and cities, a source of expenditure certainly but also one that stimulated the growth of municipal institutions and brought associated social change.[13] Elsewhere among urban communities, besides describing growing secularism and sophistication in government, particular attention is given to the ideology of Florence, a major industrial as well as cultural centre, where traditional communal values were significantly reshaped towards the end of the century by a new appreciation amongst the cultivated elite of classical concepts of republican liberty, an essential stage in the emergence of 'Renaissance' ideas and ideals (**15(b)**).

If emphasis in chapter **12** on burgeoning Italian, French and English literature, one sign of the Renaissance to come, is on some of the key figures – Dante, Petrarch, Boccaccio, Machaut, Deschamps, Chaucer – in the rise of vernacular writing in Europe (one of the very distinctive cultural achievements of the century), and on contemporary debate over concepts concerning 'authors' or 'poets', the work of other writers (academic, polemical, imaginative, historical, didactic, descriptive), including that of the first humanists, is drawn upon at many other points. While the wider political, social and literary significance of vernacular languages to individual 'states' or 'polities' is a theme

---

[13] Below pp. 117–18 (**6**), and cf. Contamine (1978); Rigaudière (1993), pp. 417–97.

which recurs in several chapters not only in those relating to the 'heartlands' of western Europe but also to areas well beyond: for instance, in Bohemia (**16(b)**, **22**), in the Baltic (**21**), as well as in the Slav, Orthodox and Byzantine worlds (**23, 24**). For private individuals too, as Caroline Barron remarks, by the end of the century the vernacular, allied to the spread of literacy, also sometimes allows us to hear ordinary people's voices, including those of women (**13(b)**).

All contributors have been under tight constraints with regard to space; difficult compromises have had to be made over content. Some overlap between individual chapters is inevitable when the same theme or political circumstances have to be sketched from different angles, though every effort has been made to keep repetition to a minimum. In practice, it was pleasing to note how modest such duplication was in the original draft chapters received by the editor, thanks to the co-operation of colleagues and the exchange of ideas and plans before chapters were written. Where overlap has been allowed to remain, this is normally because it is felt that the differing perspectives of the respective authors complement each other. Overall, the general aim has been to summarise the best of recent research and critical thinking rather than to provide a comprehensive account of the ever-increasing secondary literature.

A principal consequence of this has been, as already noted, to emphasise the diversity and particularity of experience across Europe. Another, incidental, one is to make a general editor cautious about making sweeping or lofty statements that have general applicability, because (*pace* the Introduction to *Decline of the Empire and Papacy*) it is very evident how such views so easily date and reflect our blind spots and misconceptions in understanding the past. Such caution is further encouraged since we are dealing with a century which in some respects has no obvious parallel in recorded European history. This is perhaps clearest in demographic terms.

The loss within three or four years, from 1347 to 1351, of at least a third of the population (and in some regions the figure is much higher), followed by a period of a hundred years or more in which the total continued to fall in most parts of Europe by another third, resulted in an unprecedented regression of human population, by as much as two-thirds or even more, in most economically developed regions. Where there had been three people in 1300, by 1450 there was usually only one, though as Christiane Klapisch-Zuber points out, the late fourteenth century did witness a marked recovery from the mid-century trough (**7**); it was the return of plague and war in the early fifteenth century that once more reversed this upward trend, intensifying and prolonging the late medieval demographic crisis, ensuring its unique and enduring character.[14] Many of these facts were known (or at least suspected) in 1932, even if Previté-Orton and other contributors were not sure what kind of weighting to give to the impact of the Black Death in other spheres, a situation that in some respects, though for very different reasons, still obtains today despite our immensely more detailed knowledge of demographic patterns, the range of diseases and rates of fertility, nuptiality and mortality prevalent in the late Middle Ages (cf. 7 especially). There is certainly no lack of information now available on these matters for most regions (only a few authors are unable to advance broad estimates because of a dearth of appropriate evidence),[15] much debated and uneven though many statistical findings remain. Without quite becoming a leitmotif, it is nevertheless true that few authors in this volume ignore the practical or psychological implications of the Black Death and its recurrences, whether dealing with political, social, economic or financial matters, or even considering cultural ones. The contrast may be crudely highlighted simply by comparing the handful of references for 'Black Death' and 'Plague' in the index of *Decline of the Empire and Papacy* with the substantial comparable entries for them in this volume.

It is easy to see how other significant omissions or emphases in the 1932 volume reflect the expectations and concerns of that generation and how fashions in historical research have changed in the interim: the relatively modest contribution of economic and social history and of cultural and intellectual matters, which perhaps made up at most 10 per cent of that earlier book, underlines how diplomacy, warfare, constitutional developments and changes in state administration and institutions were the predominant, even obligatory, themes. In turn, they were set within an already old-fashioned and procrustean framework of assumptions – an all-embracing but ill-defined 'feudal mould' – which despite the evidence of change and development still appeared to the principal editor to leave things at the end of the century very much where they were at the start. His overall assessment was deeply pessimistic: it is perhaps no coincidence that Huizinga's influential *Waning of the Middle Ages* had appeared in English translation in 1924.[16] Thus in the fourteenth century, there was allegedly 'a decadence, not so much retrogression, but that ossifying of regnant ideas which are slowly losing their vitality', a characterisation which finds some echoes, though with very different nuances, in Sir Richard Southern's recent magisterial description of the transformation of scholastic humanism by 1320.[17] As is pointed out below, it is not so much a case of the 'decline of scholasticism' in a time of vigorous intellectual debate but rather a

---

[14] Below pp. 133 and 135; Jones (1994) for a brief summary of work on the recovery in France in the latter part of the fourteenth century.

[15] Below p. 821 for cautious comment on the effects of the Black Death in Byzantium and p. 750 for a sanguine view of its impact in Poland.   [16] Huizinga (1924).   [17] Southern (1995).

shift of interest to questions of morality and the role of the individual that characterises much academic discussion at this point.[18] More generally in religion, fourteenth-century monasticism was dismissed in 1932 as 'static' and the friars as in decline; the ideals of crusading were deemed 'obsolescent', the military orders negligent, too wrapped up in mundane matters, and the only area of spirituality which showed originality and promise for the future was mysticism, 'the immediate search of the individual soul for God'.[19]

There is, of course, more than a grain of truth in such views, but as chapters 3 and 4 particularly show, a more positive assessment can be made of the processes and nature of change which affect all human institutions and organisations with the passage of time. There were many new beginnings as well as the decay of the old in the fourteenth century. We are now much better informed on the thought patterns, behaviour and practice of people in this period at all levels of society and these reveal rich and rewarding seams of human activity, experience and achievement that were significant in their own day and have a lasting importance for all those interested in the European past. To cite a couple of examples only, Jeremy Catto highlights aspects of improving pastoral care in this period, while the encouragement of personal paths to salvation through the use of a growing and original body of contemplative literature is one of the most original religious achievements of the century (3).

The same is true in secular affairs. If chivalry 'had become conventional and showy, a "gilded pale" to keep the vulgar out which too frequently hedged round the vulgar within' and the 'feudal age moves slowly towards its setting',[20] as chapters 9 and 10 demonstrate, there was also a creative, adaptable side to chivalry that had implications for developments elsewhere than simply in the circles of court or castle. More general discussion of the 'art of war' in the later Middle Ages has been assigned to volume VII of this series,[21] but attention can be drawn here to the significance of links between the theory and laws of war and the practice of chivalry, not merely with regard to their application in the great conflicts of the age, notably the Hundred Years War with all its many ramifications, but to the role of war in general as a stimulant to change in many fields during the century.

This is seen most obviously in the institutional, administrative and financial developments prompted by war (for instance, the establishment in advanced polities of innovative and regular taxation especially, with all the social consequences that flowed from that during this period). But there was also some limited technological progress. For example, there was the spread of gunpowder artillery, slowly from the 1320s, more rapidly after 1370 and, by 1400,

---

[18] Below pp. 43–4 and 55.   [19] *CMH*, VII, p. xx.   [20] Ibid., p. xvii.
[21] Allmand in *NCMH*, VII, pp. 161–74.

modest architectural adaptations to meet the new threats posed by cannon, as well as the evolution of new tactics on the battlefield itself, thanks above all to the massed use of the long bow.[22] Everywhere the costs of war were escalating, losses of men and *matériel* could be severe, even before manpower was reduced from the mid century by plague, an exception apparently being the battle of Tannenberg between the Teutonic Order and the Polno-Lithuanian state in 1410 when massive forces were involved.[23] If recruitment of troops by traditional feudal means was not completely superseded by new methods in even the most advanced states during this period, nevertheless in this respect also the practice of warfare was rapidly evolving. The omnipresence of war in the fourteenth century is one of the darkest but most evident hallmarks of this volume whether it is great international conflicts, civil wars or crusades against the Moors in Spain, Ottomans in the Balkans or pagans in the Baltic, where the events of 1386 did not automatically nor suddenly bring the activities of the Teutonic knights and their western *confrères* to an end. At the same time, modern historians of the later crusades now assess in a more positive and sympathetic fashion crusading efforts and achievements during this period as chapters **9, 19** and **27** especially show.

In political affairs, there were similar forlorn and negative judgements of the fourteenth century in 1932: 'the novel ferment in these creations [i.e. early bureaucratic and administrative developments, especially geared to furnishing war needs] strained, but did not break the feudal mould. . . . The century ends with Church and Feudalism and the accepted philosophy of life standing where they did' (pp. vii–viii), 'the fourteenth century [was] only the commencement of a transitional age' (p. xx). Despite the 'striving and stirring' of the century, especially in the great revolts and rebellions of maritime Flanders (1323–8), the Jacquerie in France (1358), Ciompi in Florence (1378) and Peasants in England (1381), 'the tide rose . . . against feudalised chivalric monarchy and its hide-bound bureaucratic instruments' only to be 'repelled' (p. xi). Though there was some acknowledgement that the Hundred Years War and Black Death 'hastened incipient decay and stimulated natural growth' and some 'harbingers appear of the Renaissance and even very dimly of modern times', the general mood was bleak indeed.

Many of these judgements are reformulated in what follows. The passage from 'feudal' forms of government to those of 'modern times', even if only 'dimly' perceived in Previté-Orton's account, finds confirmation in the considerable attention that has recently been paid to the critical period *c.* 1280–1360 in the search for the origins of the 'early modern state' in modern historiography.[24]

---

[22] Contamine (1984); Allmand (1988); Prestwich (1996).   [23] Below p. 755.
[24] Genet (1990); Blockmans and Genet (1993).

If England and France were once seen as 'the most advanced of feudal monarchies' in this period, the perspective has largely shifted to analyse the way in which notions of sovereignty, based on a renewed study of Roman law in France and Naples in particular, changed the nature of royal power from the late thirteenth century and provided kings, princes and their advisers, at least in western Europe, with powerful new conceptual tools to enforce their authority.[25] Rather than simply seeing the fourteenth century as the tail-end of an earlier 'feudal' age, it is now usually and surely more correctly envisaged as a formative stage in a longer continuum in the advance of governmental practice extending into the early modern period. In turn, these developments, especially by promoting social change through allowing the emergence of professional elites, lawyers, financial advisers, bureaucrats and so on, who made themselves indispensable to their rulers by staffing the essential institutions of state (courts, *parlements*, exchequers, *chambres des comptes*, secretarial and conciliar positions) and obtained a secure social place for themselves, gave form to a period which certainly lasted in many parts of the continent well into the seventeenth century, if not to the end of the *ancien régime* itself.[26]

At the same time, the remarkable ability of the old 'feudal' nobility to adapt to changing circumstances is another characteristic which has been much studied recently (cf. **9, 14(b), 22**); like chivalry, 'feudalism' took a long time to die and, if anything, this period sees the nobility in many parts of the continent reinforcing their social and political superiority despite occasional setbacks or crises in their political or economic fortunes; certainly the ideals of 'nobility' exercised a continuing fascination as 'a focus for social aspiration' for other groups in society.[27] Or take the shifting social relationships of townsmen, movements once summed up in blanket-descriptions of the 'rise of the bourgeoisie' or 'the growth of democracy'. Here too closer analysis has revealed the many cross-currents and clashing interests that complicated urban politics, fragmenting as well as uniting families, crafts, guilds and other corporate bodies in every town and city, creating patterns which cannot easily be resumed in simple catchphrases. Among the 'rising bourgeoisie', for instance, there were winners and losers: in some towns oligarchic rule was strengthened, in others there was a widening of the franchise, whilst the experience of town life in northern Italy or Flanders, the Rhineland or southern Germany, the regions most heavily urbanised, contrasted sharply both with each other as well as with municipal structures and society elsewhere, in Iberia under Christian or Moorish rule, in the Balkans under the Ottomans, or in northern and

---

[25] Below pp. 25–9; Ullmann (1949); for recent consideration of these developments see Coulet and Genet (1990). [26] See Jones in Bulst, Descimon and Guerreau (1996).

[27] Below, especially pp. 218–21, 431–5, and cf. Contamine in *NCMH*, VII, pp. 89–105.

eastern Europe where in some parts likewise 'oriental' patterns of urban structure existed.[28]

It is sobering for western European historians of this period to be reminded of the scale of Byzantine wealth, at least at the beginning of the century when Constantinople and Thessaloniki both had populations of *c.* 100,000 and when, in 1321, Emperor Andronikos II could collect 1,000,000 gold coins in tax (a sum representing only a seventh of what Michael VIII had been able to collect a few decades before!) (**24**). Peter Spufford similarly and arrestingly contrasts the relative scales of wealth and commercial dynamism of the regions dominated by the towns of northern Italy with those of the Hanseatic north, which he calculates as being at the very least five or six times greater in favour of the Mediterranean world in this period.[29] It is partly for this reason that special attention has been directed to the economic relations of Italian powers (notably Genoa and Venice) with Byzantium, which from the mid century witnessed the spectacular political collapse of the latter (**24, 25**). For in Mediterranean urban studies as in so many other areas there has been a plethora of detailed accounts of individual cities revealing differences that are both structural and temporal, reflecting different stages of economic and social development, as well as the haphazard incidence of such contingent factors as war, plague, famine and other natural or man-made disasters in a period of rapid economic change.[30] Thus recent pessimistic views of deteriorating urban conditions in the post-Black Death west through much of the remaining Middle Ages may be contrasted with the more up-beat conclusions of some contributors here dealing with central, eastern and northern European towns after the mid-century crisis (**16(b), 21–3**).

As for another contemporary historiographic concern, the part played by women in medieval society, it is a crude measure that of nearly five hundred chapter subtitles, which acted as a rough index to the themes treated in *Decline of the Empire and Papacy*, less than ten specifically mention women in general or a particular woman, and of those, four appear in the chapter on medieval mysticism: Hildegard of Bingen, Julian of Norwich and Saints Catherine of Siena and Genoa. Such key figures (Hildegard apart) naturally find their place at appropriate points in the chapters which follow, while the role of women generally in fourteenth-century society is extensively discussed in the section on 'Plague and family life' (**7**), though they find a minor but integral place at other points; for example, their position in Byzantine society is surveyed.[31] Of those who made a significant political mark, like the queen-mother Maria de Molina (d. 1321) in Castile (**18(b)**), or the much-married Queen Joanna of

---

[28] Below pp. 118–23, 565–7, 778–82; Nicholas (1997) provides a good survey of late medieval town life.
[29] Below pp. 205–6 and 802.   [30] See also Nicholas (1997).   [31] Below pp. 807, 809–10.

Naples (d. 1382) (**15(c)**), and Margaret 'lord of Sweden' (**21**), even Princess Joan of Kent (**13(b)**), not to mention Jadwiga (Hedwig) 'king of Poland' (**21, 22**), all warrant serious discussion. The prominent part played by royal mistresses and favourites in the political intrigues that especially wracked the Iberian peninsula is a characteristic of the age made abundantly clear (**18(b)**), though their influence elsewhere cannot be ignored as the example of Edward III and Alice Perrers shows (**13(a)**). It is a reminder that, at least for 'high politics', individual personality and temperament is a critical factor in this period which it would be wrong to underestimate in explaining the course of events, the success or failure of rulers, dynasties or governments, however much we should also take impersonal economic or social forces into consideration.[32] The promotion of dynastic interests by exploiting the family's own members, *Hausmacht*, as Sandy Grant reminds us in the case of late fourteenth-century Scotland, was not simply limited to the medieval empire but is characteristic of most ruling families in this century (**13(d)**).

Discussion of other groups who, along with women, were often largely overlooked by earlier historiography but who are now part of mainstream research – Jews, heretics, criminals, the poor (though regretfully not here the insane, apart from the occasional unbalanced ruler like William V of Holland (**17**) or Charles VI of France (**14(b)**) – is also mainly integrated into the chapters dealing with individual states rather than given thematic treatment. The existence of slavery in many parts of fourteenth-century Europe has already been mentioned: it is found in the Mediterranean, in some Baltic states and also in parts of central Europe but not apparently in Novgorod.[33] And, of course, the peasantry (already accorded a special place in 1932), who still comprised in most parts of the continent 90 per cent or more of the total population, are to be found not only in the specific discussion of western rural society (**5**) or their role in Byzantium (**24**), but elsewhere. Here again the diversity of legal status, customary laws, inheritance practices, economic fortunes or political significance defies easy generalisation apart from a cautious comment on the improvement in the living standards and conditions of many western peasants in the post-Black Death period, and ominous signs of the declining liberties and fortunes of their equivalents in northern and eastern Europe, where serfdom was to become oppressive in later centuries.

Naturally the current volume reflects, then, as did the *Decline of the Empire and Papacy*, some contemporary historical fashions and prejudices, some arbitrary choices and preferences on the part of the editor and editorial board. In summary, although there is still much political narrative, which forms the core

---

[32] See below pp. 316–25, 331–3 and 423–6 for the cases of Richard II of England and Charles V of France.   [33] Below p. 781.

of most chapters in parts II–IV, these are preceded by a long analytical section, part I, 'General themes', in which an attempt is made to survey some of the main governmental, religious, intellectual, economic, social, cultural and artistic patterns that are characteristic of the century. Music, that most difficult of the arts to recreate from historical evidence, amongst cultural achievements, gets short shrift though its echoes are occasionally heard.[34] I am conscious that there are other gaps, some of which might have been plugged by better planning: Scandinavia, among regions, perhaps fares less well than it deserves, Switzerland certainly does not get the attention it received in 1932, Serbia receives only passing mention, Bosnia, too, gets little; omissions which sad events, in part the still-enduring legacy of the fourteenth-century advance into the Balkans by the Ottomans, since the conception of the volume in 1987 make all the more poignant. The concept of Europe itself could have received more discussion.[35] Among outstanding figures, too, more attention might have been paid to individual thinkers, writers or artists, but the time has come to launch the volume, so that readers may finally judge whether it accords with Villani's view of the century or avoids going from 'bad to worse'.

---

[34] Below p. 733 for the gift of a clavicord and portative organ from the grand master of the Teutonic Order to Grand Duchess Anna and for flautists in the service of Vytautas, Grand Duke of Lithuania in 1398–9. Curtis in *NCMH*, VII, pp. 319–33, discusses late medieval music at more length.

[35] See Moore (1996).

CHAPTER 2

THE THEORY AND PRACTICE OF GOVERNMENT IN WESTERN EUROPE IN THE FOURTEENTH CENTURY

Albert Rigaudière

WESTERN Europe in the fourteenth century was as diverse as the states of which it was composed. It followed the rhythm of a history dictated by its capricious geography, imposed by frequently divergent traditions and which men, whose reflexes gradually freed themselves from feudal constraints, wrote down. But beyond this diversity, in the fourteenth century there was also unity; the medieval west was deeply rooted in a common religion and a common culture. Christendom and Latinity made a unified zone, even if papacy and empire still disputed a supremacy which the slow but sure assertion of states shattered into pieces. They all shared the same adventure, all reacting as Christian princes in the construction of their political systems. In this century, when feudalism died, absolute monarchy everywhere took its first steps. But still very cautiously, propagandists, philosophers and jurists occupying a position of prime importance in the life of these young states, as if to devise their architecture and focus their birth. They thought out, each in their own way, a theory of politics (see section 1, below) which princes, councillors and administrators slowly assimilated to construct a true art of government (section 2, below).

I A THEORY OF POLITICS

In the fourteenth century, the desire to establish the study of politics as a branch of knowledge (*science*) was not new. For a long time already, all the distant heirs of Aristotle had set out on this path. The lawyers themselves had not remained outside this movement, such as the author of the *Summa Coloniensis* (1169), who even saw in the slow birth of a *sciencia de regimine civitatis, castri et villae seu regni et orbis* (science of the government of the state, castle and village or of the kingdom and the world), an effective means of resolving the political problems of his day. Two centuries later, Nicolas d'Oresme presented political science as a discipline that was both noble and autonomous. Should it not be considered among 'all the fashionable branches of knowledge', 'as the very principal, the most worthy and the most profitable'? And for that reason why not treat it as an 'architectonic' science, that is 'queen over all'? But, in his eyes, lawyers could no longer have sole control of it, as the harsh name of 'political idiots' which Giles of Rome had reserved for them around 1300 already testified.

This is what attests to the profound evolution which the fourteenth century experienced in the domain of political theory and the science of government. Without neglecting the contribution of civil law which they assimilated perfectly, philosophers, theologians and propagandists, by extending the often narrow field, saw to it that their reflections resulted in a true political construct (1.1, below). Centred on the imperial *dominium mundi* (world supremacy) whose ascendancy constantly decreased to promote the assertion of the young states (1.2), from the study of princely power it resulted in the theory of *ministerium regale* (1.3).

1.1 From learned law to political science

Whether it was rejected or adapted, learned law dominated the whole of political thought in the fourteenth century. Even though it had never provided an exposition in the form of a complete political construct, it had always provided a means of access to political reflection and constituted the structural axis around which the statist society of the fourteenth century was built.

At no point was it possible to disregard the models transmitted by the Roman law of the glossators which, having crossed the Alps at the end of the twelfth century, dominated all the thought of the great continental jurists in the following century. It was partly through them that Henry Bracton (d. *c.* 1268) built his vision of common law and that, in France, in the schools of Toulouse, Montpellier and Orléans, the bases of an entire political system, shaped by Roman law slowly took root. That Jean de Blanot wrote on the powers of the empire in the middle of the thirteenth century, or, later, Jacques de Révigny (d. 1296), Pierre de Belleperche (d. 1308) and Pierre Jacobi (d. 1350) endeavoured to revive an entire political system by means of Roman law, was not the result of chance. Bearers of an inheritance bequeathed by an empire which had far exceeded in size the Europe of their own day, they attempted to decode all its messages in order to reconstruct, around the Roman model, renascent states. This was why all these jurists were led, in their commentaries or in the consultations that they gave, to devise solutions that were always capable of resolving the problems of their time.

It was above all with the school of the Postglossators that Roman law, once more rediscovered and the subject of commentaries, asserted its authority throughout the west in the first half of the fourteenth century, if not as a directly usable system, at least as a model bearing a new dynamic calculated to stimulate the political imagination. Leader of the new school, Bartolus (1314–57) dominated it with his innovatory genius. More concerned with practice than his predecessors, he always focused his political reflections on key themes. Having a presentiment of the ruin of the medieval order, he constantly wrote about the relationships between empire (*imperium*) and priesthood (*sacerdotium*), examined the subtle relations which were establishing themselves beneath his very eyes, between the monarch and the law (*loi*), denounced tyranny, unjust war and the violation of law (*droit*). For him, and for all those who followed the path he marked out, in particular Baldus (1327–1400), law (*droit*) constituted the cardinal axis of political reflection. Wisdom (*sapientia*), appropriate for encouraging an understanding of the divine, was also, simultaneously, both a branch of knowledge (*sciencia*) which should make it possible to master the complexity of political mechanisms and an art (*ars*), intimate knowledge of which could only foster a better practice of authority.

It was not only to Roman law that he attributed all these virtues. Bartolus adopted a similarly favourable attitude towards canon law in assigning it a task of the first importance in the political society of his time. At a point when princes everywhere were endeavouring to withdraw the Church's right to all temporal influence in order to promote the birth of the state, Bartolus exercised his wits to underline the part which had devolved to it in the ordinary course of things in the construction of new state entities, even going so far as to assert that, in many cases, *jura canonica prevalent legibus* (canon laws prevail over other laws). This was nothing more than a highly normal vision of things to the extent that civil society and ecclesiastical society still constituted in the fourteenth century two parallel structures built on common bases. Whether they were Italian such as Giovanni Andrea (d. 1348), in whom his contemporaries saw the 'source and trumpet of canon law', and Panormitanus (d. 1453, called *lucerna juris* or the light of law), or French, such as Jean le Moine (d. 1313), and Pierre Bertrand (d. 1349), the great canon lawyers of the fourteenth century, inheritors of their predecessors, made an incomparable contribution through their glosses to the political theories of their time. Although, just like the Roman lawyers, they never had a total vision of the statist society, the solutions which they suggested, based on the problems which they treated for the Church, were of the first importance for the development of the civil society of their period. Their conception of the organisation of ecclesiastical society through the slow maturation of rules, such as the *sanior et major pars* (the wiser and greater part) or the *quod omnes tangit ab omnibus approbari debet* (what concerns all ought to be approved by all), was valuable as a model for the secular states which could benefit from them to resolve the problems posed them by the positioning of new political mechanisms. There was wholesale transfer of structures and effective juridical skills from the Church – a highly organised society – to the state whose structures were still feeling their way.

Thus for much of the fourteenth century, jurists, whether Roman or canon lawyers, made a substantial contribution, by means of their thought to the enrichment of both political theory and government practice. But they were not the only ones. Often judged too rigid and unadaptable, their contribution long threatened by that of theology, philosophy and rhetoric, was also threatened by that of a political science whose dynamism was ceaselessly asserted each time there was any discourse on power. In his *De Monarchia*, Dante (1265–1321) already asked three fundamental questions. Was the empire, that 'unique principality', useful to the well-being of the world? Were the Roman people right to assume the function of the monarchy? And, finally, did the authority which that monarchy exercised come directly from God, or from some other minister and vicar of God? To the two first questions, the author of the *Divine Comedy* replied in the affirmative, before laying down as a fundamental principle that temporal and political authority, completely independent of the vicar of God could only be subordinate to God himself. Thus, kings and emperor were released from all allegiance to the pope. Envisaging the doctrine of the divine right of princes, Dante, a political exile and refugee in northern Italy, turned to the emperor to ask him to free from papal ascendancy an 'Italy enslaved and the home of grief'.

A further step along this path was taken by Marsilius of Padua (1275/80–1343). The product of *artiens* and *physiciens*, the *enfants terribles* of the university and confirmed opponents of tradition, he carried with him the entire inheritance of the turbulent politics of the Italian cities. Rector of the university of Paris, close to the political ventures of the Ghibellines, then the valued councillor of Lewis of Bavaria whose vicar imperial he became, he preferred Aristotle to Thomist theology and Roman law. This was why his *Defensor Pacis* (1324) was deeply opposed to the political order born of Christianity under the control of the papacy. The sworn enemy of sacerdotal hegemony, he denied the Church all power to transfer it to the state, thus empowered to supply its members' spiritual needs. And in the state it was to the people that the main part of power returned, in particular that of legislating in the general assembly of citizens. This was to construct a completely new system of powers from which the religious sphere was excluded to promote an absolutism of the state which, just as radically conceived, could only end in a totalitarian system.

Espousing these theses, but in a more moderate form, William of Ockham (1270–1347), product of the faculty of theology, represented the tradition, more than a century old, of the Franciscan Order. With a smattering of philosophy, this Oxford graduate also proved himself a resolute opponent of sacerdotalism, while maintaining papal power in all its integrity. From it, the imperial dignity stemmed directly. It was held *immediate a solo Deo* (directly from God alone) and it was through the agency of the emperor, from the moment when he was elected by the majority of the prince-electors, that God governed the world. This was to acknowledge in the emperor a true *dominium mundi* (world-wide authority) for which the young states were to challenge him for a long while to come.

1.2 From the dominium mundi to the assertion of the states

With the collapse of the empire after the death of Frederick II, then the Great Interregnum (1250–73), the thirteenth century marked the end of the imperial *dominium mundi*. Everywhere, civil and canon lawyers made a case for the redis-covered sovereignty of their own country and made the famous formula, *rex in regno suo imperator est* (the king is emperor in his kingdom), victorious from Sicily to England. Then began a threefold evolution which dominated the reorganisation of the states of the west. The empire did not disappear, but it fragmented while the national monarchies triumphed a little everywhere, except in the Italian peninsula where the city-states secured their success to varying degrees. From this profound remodelling of the states three political systems and three very different types of government were to be born.

Even diminished, the myth of *imperium mundi* in the hands of the emperor remained firmly anchored in the minds and political practices of the four-teenth century. Although Bartolus himself accepted the idea that the greater part of the world no longer recognised imperial authority and that the *regna* and *civitates* which were subordinate to the *imperium romanum* were fewer and fewer, there were also those who, with some nostalgia, thought that the emperor should still reign over all kings and all nations. In their eyes, the independence which they acquired was only a *de facto* independence, and not *de jure*. Moreover, there were still many canon lawyers who, in the fourteenth century, besides those who had encouraged the autonomy of the *regna*, believed that the pope remained the only true emperor and that, the emperor being his vicar, no *regnum* could ultimately escape imperial authority. This suffices to explain why, after his coronation at Rome (1312), the emperor Henry VII addressed a letter to all the princes of the west in which he recalled his claims to the universality of the empire. He did not lack arguments to justify them. He preserved a very powerful tool, Roman law, which was universally applicable. His justice should be acknowledged everywhere, so it was always possible for a subject to appeal from his king to the emperor and so the crime of *lèse-majesté* always seemed a crime essentially imperial in nature.

But the political events of the fourteenth century did not come to the aid of juridical argumentation. Even within the limits of the Holy Roman Empire of the German nation alone, the emperor was no longer the sole holder of power. Always a butt for the papacy, he had also to secure his own existence in relation to the territorial princes. If the dispute with the papacy was engaged on spiritual ground rather than on that of sovereignty, it was none the less true that the emperor found himself in a difficult situation of dependence in relation to the pope who always demanded, through the imperial coronation, the right to legitimate every imperial election. The struggle with imperial universalism was thus openly declared. It had to fail because the confusion of notions of empire, Church and Christendom, too intimately bound to the Germanic idea of empire, had led the emperor to overstep his competences, usurping the acknowledged prerogatives of the pope. In the aftermath of the death of Henry VII (1313), it was to the people of Rome that Lewis of Bavaria turned to secure his power and to whom he declared in 1328: 'in this town, by the grace of providence, we have legitimately received the imperial diadem and the sceptre from our Roman people particularly dear to us and, thanks to the invincible power of God and of ourselves, we govern the city and the world'. It was also to combat this situation of dependence in relation to the pope and to affirm the autonomy of the empire that he received among his councillors Franciscans in dispute with the pope, such as William of Ockham or philosophers like Marsilius of Padua.

This desire to escape from all subjection to the Holy See found its institutional expression in two constitutions of Lewis of Bavaria and one declaration of the prince-electors assembled at Rhens in 1338. They proclaimed that the king of the Romans, elected unanimously or by majority vote, had no need, for his power to be effective, to have recourse to any confirmation by the Holy See. This meant, thanks to the support of the princes, the end of dependence on papal power, but it also meant, at the same time, placing imperial power more securely under their control, to make the empire a dualist state whose mastery was henceforth shared between the electoral college of the princes and the emperor. This development was enshrined in the imperial code (*Kaiserliches Rechtsbuch*) of 1358, called the 'Golden Bull' from the beginning of the fifteenth century. This famous text fixed the order in which the prince-electors (*Kurfürsten*) cast their vote and stipulated that the election must be established by majority vote. Thus the elective principle triumphed and the thorny problem of relations between Church and empire was finally regulated. The empire freed itself from the Church but, strengthening the authority of the princes, it fostered the breakup of power and accelerated the triumph of the

Germanic territorial principalities in transferring almost all regalian rights to the prince-electors. This act therefore institutionalised the weakness of the emperor and his government who was not remotely endowed with the institutions which he needed to make himself obeyed. Without – or virtually without – a domain, a fiscal system and, consequently, without financial resources, the emperor could not equip himself with a professional army. The judicial mechanisms remained identical. Justice, most of the time granted as a fief, always eluded the emperor, which made peace constantly dependent upon regional alliances. As for the towns, to which the central authority owed part of its revenues through the harsh taxation it imposed upon them, they found themselves constantly exposed to the greed of the princes, particularly to that of the prince-electors, henceforth invested with a veritable territorial sovereignty.

Such an evolution could only favour the rise of the national monarchies. The more the century passed, the more their governments had to give themselves a structure to face the immense needs which sprang from the modern state, for which they were responsible. Admittedly, no word yet existed for 'state' as we understand it, and the term *status*, often used, was always followed by a complement: *status republicae, status regni, status coronae. Status*, then, designated more a state, a way of being, than 'the state'. But this was not because the state did not yet exist, endowed as it was with its principal component parts and with a government whose smooth running did not cease to hold the attention of the theorists. Throughout western Europe in the fourteenth century, except in Italy, the nation-state became reality every day and secured its own sovereignty. Bartolus himself agreed that all these *regna* were no longer actually subordinate to the imperial *dominium*, but that they were henceforth holders of the sovereign rights which they most frequently held *de facto*, and not *de jure*. The evolution which made them national sovereign monarchies was complete, even if no author had yet succeeded in defining a coherent theory of sovereignty. The essential was that the fully independent exercise of the great prerogatives traditionally devolved to the emperor, *imperium, potestas, juridictio* and *administratio*, be granted them.

Bartolus agreed to this, while insisting on the idea that the emperor preserved a permanent right, by reason of his *auctoritas principis vel superioris* (authority of prince or sovereign) of confirming the legitimacy of these new power-holders and of deposing them each time they behaved like tyrants. But that was more attachment to the past than an objective description of present reality. The turning-point had passed in the 1270s, the date when Jacques de Révigny (d. 1296) in his *Lectura* on the *Institutes* strove to demonstrate that the king of France *in temporalibus superiorem non recognoscit* (does not recognise any superior in temporalities) and when Guillaume Durand the Elder (d. 1296) echoed him in pounding out the formula, *Rex Franciae princeps est in regno suo* (the king of France is prince in his own kingdom). Everywhere else the same wind of independence blew, whether it was in Sicily where Marianus de Caramanico (d. 1288) endeavoured to establish the independence of the king of Sicily in his Preface to the *Liber Constitutionem Regnum Siciliae*, or in Castile, where *Las siete partidas* of Alfonso X took up the same plea on behalf of their sovereign. There was no longer any doubt that kings were emperors in their kingdoms in the fourteenth century. All the political literature bears ample witness to this. Finally freed from imperial power, all these young states also wanted to be free of the *plenitudo potestatis* (plenitude of power) of the pope, this unlimited power which had authorised him to intervene up to this point in the life of the states, as much to depose a king as to exempt the subjects from obedience to their prince. But to the extent that, at the beginning of the fourteenth century, the destinies of the Church and papacy were closely linked, it was no longer conceivable that all these national states set free from the empire would continue to accept a temporal dependence upon Rome. This was why they rejected it vigorously, as much because of the serious difficulties which the Church was experiencing at that time as because of their constantly advertised desire definitively to secure their total independence. Even in Italy, papacy and empire scarcely succeeded in maintaining their tutelage.

In the fourteenth century, the old rivalry between Guelfs and Ghibellines, which had until then torn the peninsula so violently apart, gradually dwindled away. The supporters of the two clans, once so violently opposed, came to an agreement to admit that their common interest was to do everything to safeguard their autonomy, in respect of both pope and emperor. From then on, setting aside Venice, which had always been able to preserve its autonomy, what should be done so that the kingdom of Naples, traditionally the vassal of the Holy See, and almost all the other cities of the peninsula – except for the Papal States – should succeed in freeing themselves from the pontifical or imperial yoke in order to achieve the status of city-state with their own institutions and government? There was, of course, imperial privilege from which Venice and other Lombard towns had benefited. But this concession *de jure* was rare. For a long while, a whole, very old doctrinal movement, started mainly by the canon lawyers then also supported by Roman lawyers, had opened the way to a *de facto* autonomy of the cities. Asserting that they had left the pontifical and imperial orbit, they had hammered out the theory of the *civitas sibi princeps* (the city a prince unto itself) which Bartolus systematised and generalised. But there should be no mistake about it. The *civitas* which Bartolus envisaged was still only an autonomous city, admittedly the depository of all the powers exercised by the emperor, but not a veritable city-state whose institutions gradually constructed themselves. Almost all of them had to reckon with the imperial vicariate which, although it still checked the road to complete autonomy, no less favoured the birth of particular institutions. That towns like Florence and Pisa sought to obtain – and succeeded – the imperial vicariate after taking an oath to the emperor is significant. Thanks to the vicariate, they often succeeded in legalising their power over the *contado* which they controlled and in strengthening their institutional structures. These constituent parts allowed them, slowly, to secure their accession to the rank of city-state and better to define the powers of those to whom they entrusted the responsibility of administering them.

1.3 From the authority of princes to the rights of the state

Throughout fourteenth-century Europe the state made its entry in force. The distinction, founded on scholarly juridical thought, between what was public and what was private, between *jus publicum* and *jus privatum*, made a substantial contribution to shaping the state and giving its government autonomous existence. King and state were henceforth separate, increasingly subject to a specific judicial regime. This was why the king now had the role of incarnating the state, representing it and acting in its name. To the extent that this new vision triumphed, there was a complete transfer of competences from a prince, whom evolution wrested from feudalism, to a king accountable for the government and the destinies of the state. It was better to discern all these competences that jurists and theoreticians of government applied themselves. In this sphere, the fourteenth century simultaneously combined maturity and novelty. Maturity because it did no more than consolidate the gains of the previous centuries each time the portrait of the king and lover of justice had gradually to be refined to make it a legislating king in the face of the crises and troubles of the time. Novelty because the doctrine defined to the advantage of a prince responsible for the peace, security and prosperity of the country, the element of power which he lacked to bring his task to a successful conclusion: the right to tax.

It was first the empire, then, where the sovereign still appeared, in the fourteenth century, as an ambiguous figure, at the same time both public authority and private authority because he was a chosen feudal lord and brought to power thanks to the consensus of the great princes. Despite this persistent duality in the nature of his function, the sovereign led with constancy an obstinate struggle for public opinion to assemble in a sort of supreme lordship, a veritable sanctuary of the state, all the prerogatives once devolved to the Roman emperor. Among their number featured, in the first place, judicial power. Always shared with the great feudal lords, but claimed by the prince, its exercise appeared as the product of a policy of conciliation. From the reign of Lewis of Bavaria onwards, the imperial German court (*Deutsches königliches Hofgericht*), which had until then been peripatetic, became sedentary and thus contributed to giving the empire its characteristic of 'justice-state'. Thus the authority of a central imperial jurisdiction was asserted, simultaneously a high court of justice with responsibility for hearing the most important cases and an ordinary supreme tribunal before which all final appeal procedure had perforce to end. Nevertheless, the sovereign could not succeed in imposing control of justice and public order unless he succeeded in keeping feudal law (*Lehnrecht*) apart from authority and constantly separating it from territorial law (*Landrecht*). However, this is what happened. Relying on this *Lehnrecht* conceived as an effective means of legal appropriation, the princes supported by a whole shift in commentary on the *Mirrors*, particularly the *Abridged Gloss of the Lehnrecht of the Saxons* in 1386, increasingly controlled all spheres of social life and arrogated to themselves the right of stating the law. Then a veritable *de facto* division of the power of justice occurred. The emperor had justice in his court; the prince other cases. Thus justice became less the apanage of state government than a veritable right granted to those who governed states whose structure began to stabilise around princely powers. It was therefore by means of feudal law that justice gradually became an integral part of the competence of states.

Elsewhere, the opposite development was taking place everywhere. All the sovereigns of the west recovered their judicial power by triumphing over feudalism. The image of the king as judge, whether he exercised his justice personally or delegated it, was sketched by the pen of all the theoreticians. Witness, for fourteenth-century France, the admiration with which Christine de Pisan (1365–1430) described Charles V dispensing justice in person and the acerbic criticism of delegated judges made by all the defendants of royal power. Jean Gerson (1363–1429) did not cease to abuse all those who 'sell their sentences, sacrifice the rights of a party, refuse to judge the poor or the innocent', while Philippe de Mézières (1327–1405) saw them as none other than 'pillagers and tyrants' (*pillars et tyrans*) who 'rule like lords in the kingdom in opposition to the king'. Incontestably, there was confidence in the justice of the king whom Philippe de Mézières even advised to draw inspiration from the Italian tribunals to reform the entire French judicial system. But this was too much to ask of a sovereign all of whose powers in this sphere now hardly experienced any check. Once seigneurial jurisdictions were almost completely subordinated by means of the appeal, committal for trial and cases reserved to the crown, and ecclesiastical justices strictly controlled by means of 'privileged cases', the prince naturally found himself compelled, to secure this success, to have recourse to the delegated judges, although they were of limited competence and impartiality. From *bailliage* tribunals to the *parlement* of Paris, the kingdom's supreme judicial authority since the last decades of the thirteenth century, the hierarchy became stricter, competence better defined under the control of a king who, with his council, constituted the capstone of the judicial edifice.

At the same time, England experienced a comparable evolution, even if the intervention of royal judges encountered greater resistance on the part of both ecclesiastical and secular lords. They were reluctant to accept that their competence should be limited and that the judgements they made should be controlled. They also rejected the constant obligation of proving the secure foundation of their autonomy to which the crown wanted to subject them. Nevertheless, by the end of the fourteenth century, the final triumph of royal justice was secured in the three essential domains, which were landed property and personal estate with the court of common pleas, royal finance with the court of the exchequer, and crimes against the state with the court of King's Bench. As this royal power of justice was secured everywhere, so also it experienced everywhere its natural extension in the right of *condere legem*.

Since the glossators, debate had been the order of the day. Natural corollary of judicial action, the power to make law found itself to some extent without any immediate holder in the aftermath of the check on the *dominium mundi*. A very vigorous demand followed, as much on the part of the city-states as the nation-states, throughout the thirteenth century. In the following century, their cause was understood but what authority did they possess, empowered to decree the law? A many-sided reply was given to this question.

Since a fair number of the Italian cities had complied with the statute of *civitates liberae*, their councils could freely decree *statuta* often surpassing the legislation of the nation-states in volume and quality. In the fourteenth century, the problem remained of the co-existence of these *statuta* with Roman law which progressively constituted a true *ius commune* whose power was soon to limit their legislative freedom just as – but to a lesser extent – that of other states.

In those of the Iberian peninsula, as in France, the prince's legislative capacity was acknowledged henceforth. Everywhere the tags *quod principis placuit legis habet vigorem* (what is pleasing to the prince has the force of law) and *princeps legibus solutus est* (the prince is not bound by laws) had made their way by sheer force. Often voluntarily given a wide interpretation, they made it possible to grant the prince a large normative capacity, at least in theory. In reality, there was absolutely no need to look in these two poorly understood formulae for a sort of clause justifying the absolute power of the prince to *condere legem*, since his legislative action could always be justified, in all circumstances, from the moment when he declared that he acted *ex certa scientia principis* (from the certain knowledge of the prince). There was nothing surprising, then, in the fact that all these kings were granted the 'right to make laws and constitutions . . . or to reduce them or entirely revoke and repeal them', as the author of the *Songe du Vergier* put it for the king of France. But nowhere was this capacity of the legislative prince to make a contribution, through the action of his courts, to the unification of laws and local customs, established so quickly as in England, a procedure which was to give birth to the 'common law', rapidly hoisted to the rank of the Roman *lex*. To this substantial capacity granted to the prince was added the power he had to judge, in his council, all miscarriages of justice, a power which Edward III officially delegated to his chancellor in 1349. Thus 'equity' gradually began to grow by means of the case law of the king's council, then that of the court of chancery. This demonstrates well how much judicial power constituted, in all circumstances, the surest foundations of normative power.

Judges and legislators, the sovereigns of the fourteenth century, also made insistent demands to be able to exercise undivided the right to tax whoever they wanted. If they did not completely succeed, and if the vision which the *Songe du Vergier* presents us for the whole of Europe, of 'kings . . . who can levy such extraordinary aids, salt taxes, hearth taxes and impositions on their subjects' is slightly idealised, it had to be acknowledged that royal power to levy taxation had become a reality everywhere. Feudal taxation was slowly replaced by state taxation, because, of course, throughout the century, profound changes took place as much at the level of mentalities as at that of the relations binding prince and country. Henceforth, taxes were no longer thought of as a due which the sovereign levied, but, quite the contrary, as a tax which subjects should bring him in order to participate in the defence of the kingdom. Taxation was thus progressively legitimised, a development which commanded attention all the more forcibly as a beneficiary other than the king emerged. This was the state which, in the sphere of fiscality, as in many others, had just transcended the person of the sovereign. Admittedly, it still often had to negotiate with the representatives of regions and towns, but this negotiation was always made easier because taxation was henceforth levied for the *utilitas regni* or the *necessitas republicae*. It was a condition for the exercise of royal power to levy taxes, not an obstacle to it.

Take France *c.* 1350, a period in the course of which the estates, although a very heavyweight force in political life, never made any real objection to the levying of taxation. Or take, at the same time, Castile with its sovereign whose exemplary fiscal system hardly suffered from the consent which he had to obtain from the *cortes* and the towns for levying taxes. Their representatives never succeeded in limiting or sharing institutionally the royal right to levy taxes. And, finally, take England, where there was a comparable development. Throughout the thirteenth century, the kings had acquired the habit of regularly levying a tax on the personal goods of subjects, and parliament, which had not opposed it, continued to respond favourably throughout the following century to their demands, in relation to both direct and indirect taxation. It was more from the people that opposition to the royal right to levy taxes came with the revolt of 1381, in the aftermath of the creation of a new poll tax.

This was enough to remind the sovereign, there as elsewhere, that it was always necessary to adjust the theory of power to the reality of facts. From a political science in full gestation necessity compelled a shift, more modestly, towards an art of government.

2 AN ART OF GOVERNMENT

While the thirteenth century had marked the triumph of the ideas of Aristotle, so significant for a new political science, the fourteenth century was characterised more by their being put into concrete practice in the daily exercise of powers. Solutions for them were often sought to attempt to resolve the political crises with which different governments were confronted. Everywhere a concern for national adaptation of this Aristotelian scheme showed through. A theorctician like Nicolas d'Oresme (1325–82) proclaimed aloud this necessity, affirming that 'according to the diversity of regions, complexions, inclinations, and the customs of peoples, it was fitting that their positive rights and their governments should be different'. It was above all to apply oneself to defining and making state structures operate which henceforth dominated the professional governing classes (2.1, below) and an increasingly structured government whose links tightened across the country (2.2) to lead it towards a contest which most often ended in a fruitful dialogue (2.3).

2.1 Government specialists

The entire history of the states of the west in the fourteenth century reflects their constant concern to place at their head government specialists experienced in the practice of power. This was first true of the sovereign whose dominant preoccupation was, always, to surround himself with the best-educated councillors.

From the states of the Iberian peninsula to England, passing through all the European capitals, the sovereign appeared henceforth as a veritable political expert. To be king became a profession which was learnt, which was exercised within the framework of strict rules and, additionally, which could be lost if one did not show oneself worthy and capable, or if one went beyond the limits fixed by law and practice in the exercise of the royal office.

In the Iberian states, much was demanded of the kings, a high proportion of whom, in the fourteenth century, were child-kings and often even also came from foreign countries or had been brought up far from the throne. Then they had to be taught everything about their new country, its customs and laws. The destiny of Philip, count of Evreux, to whose lot the throne of Navarre fell by right of his wife Jeanne in 1328, is particularly significant in this respect. In a few months, while continuing to sit on the council of Philip VI of Valois, the new king of Navarre had to come to know everything about his country, whose men, language and institutions became familiar to him in a short space of time. Or take Ferdinand of Trastámara of Antequera who, coming from Castile where he secured the regency, was chosen in 1412 to govern Aragon. Straightaway, he had to fathom all the secrets of the Crown of Aragon and of that northern province whose Mediterranean and continental policy had no connection with that of Castile. Take, too, the throne of Castile, perfect reflection of the need to train in a short time princes called to reign too young. Ferdinand IV was one year old in 1295, Alfonso XI had scarcely reached his second year in 1312, while Pedro I was called to ascend the throne at the age of fifteen in 1350. For these very young princes, a rapid and intensive education was indispensable so that they could take up the reins of the country as quickly as possible.

To educate the king and train him in the art of government appeared an urgent necessity everywhere. The fashion was for *Mirrors* which made it possible, at one and the same time, to make the prince an expert in government and to inculcate in him the idea that his primordial role was, above all, to lead his people towards a certain end. A providential man, sent by God and endowed with the noblest qualities, he should be able to practise all the virtues of the statesman without difficulty. In fourteenth-century France, numerous authors, such as Gerson, Christine de Pisan, Philippe de Mézières or the author of the *Songe du Vergier*, lingered long to describe, through an ideal portrait of the prince, how he should govern with love, make himself loved, without flattering, all the while making himself respected without tyranny, always practising 'the virtue of truth' which, alone, made it possible to govern prudently. But it was also expected that the prince be humble, pious, chaste, sober, generous, magnanimous, open and just. The ideal was thus composed of asceticism, exemplariness and of surpassing oneself. But appearing as a model of virtue was not enough, the prince had also to be able to make his image shine and present all his majesty. Familiar and open to the requests of his subjects, he was also to be admired, obeyed and feared. These were qualities which authorised him to assume with dignity his office entirely directed to the triumph of peace and justice.

This portrait of the ideal prince which the French authors of the fourteenth century present in such minute detail was to be found in very similar fashion beyond the Pyrenees in the Iberian peninsula. Alfonso XI the Justiciar, king of Castile (1312–50), following the example of all the kings of Christendom, had translated into Castilian the *De Regimine Principum* of Giles of Rome. At the same time, and based on this treatise, his cousin, Don Juan Manuel, formulated an entire system of government in his *Libro de los Estados*, where he delivered a careful reflection on royal sovereignty, the law, the *Fueros* and the participation of the people in the exercise of power. The bishop of Viseu, Alfonso Pais, followed this movement, in composing a *Mirror* entirely concerned with an analysis of royal function, while a little later it was the Castilian chancellor himself, Pedro de Ayala, who conducted, in the course of his works, a similar political reflection. All these authors were in agreement on the need for a king strong in the exercise of his power. The acclamation by the *cortes*, at the moment of his accession to the throne, legitimated his power which crowning had almost always just strengthened, but very rarely anointing, the rite of which had been virtually lost since the Visigothic period. It was then in one of the towns such as Saragossa, Pamplona, Burgos, Lisbon or Santiago, designated capital cities since the fourteenth century, that the king was anointed by the primate of his state. This king chosen by God and acclaimed by his people had henceforth a better-founded power but one which, in any case, could not become absolute under pain of sinking into tyranny which all Spanish authors of the century were agreed in condemning. In France, a whole current of thought also attached great value to limiting the powers of a king, who, although always anointed and Most Christian King, occupied a place apart in the world of the kingdoms of the west in the fourteenth century. Nicolas d'Oresme took the lead as spokesman for these authors in making a stand against the *plénitude de posté* too often granted the king. Against this concept he opposed that of *posté modérée*, in order to redress the perverse effects of an absolutist ideology which he ostentatiously denounced and which, in his eyes, appeared truly devastating, most particularly in the sphere of fiscality.

Little heard in France at this period, there seems to have been more discourse of this kind across the Channel throughout the fourteenth century. This was undoubtedly because Edward II, Edward III and Richard II had gradually drawn all the consequences of an affirmed absolutist monarchy whose harsh setbacks they had endured, as is well known. Deeming themselves above the law and released from all obligation, seeing their subjects only as individuals forced to obey them and the kingdom as their private property, they went counter to the common law and the statutes, pardoned criminals and bypassed the need for authorisation by parliament to levy taxes. This is why Edward II was forced, from 1308, to take a new coronation oath full of consequences for the future. In addition to the traditional undertakings made by the king on this occasion, he promised to observe the just laws and customs which the community – principally that of the barons – was to establish. And these barons set down loud and clear, in their declaration of 1308, the distinction between crown and royal person, affirming that homage and allegiance were owed to the crown and not to the king.

Such were certainly the harbingers of the deposition of Edward II by the parliament of 1327, immediately followed by the proclamation of Edward III as king. Too inclined to strengthen his authority and to control both his council and his chancellor with too heavy a hand, the new sovereign made ready the serious crisis of 1341. It came to an end only with a compromise at the end of which royal prerogatives were further diminished. Edward III acknowledged the supreme value of Magna Carta and undertook not to dismiss any official without the judgement of parliament. Even though he went back on all his promises in 1343, the crisis of 1341 was a no less destabilising element in royal power and a powerful factor strengthening the role of parliament, henceforth held to be the only institution capable of resolving conflicts between the king and his officials, a contentious issue which was no longer considered as being private in nature, but public. Under Richard II, relations between crown and parliament were constantly strained. Throughout the serious crisis of the years 1386–8, the authority of the sovereign was seriously challenged. Parliament truly set itself up as a supreme court, demanded a very strict control of expenditure and wanted to arrogate to itself the right to dissolution when the king was absent for forty days. Quite simply, it wanted to demonstrate that it was subordinate in no way whatsoever to royal authority. The sovereign had finally to accept the creation of a commission invested for a year with power to reform the state. Positions hardened and ended with the Merciless Parliament of 1388 which made parliament the ultimate legal arbiter and attributed to it supreme authority. The rupture was accomplished between a king which refused to submit and an all-powerful parliament. The final attempts of the sovereign, throughout the years 1397–9, to strengthen his absolutism were the direct cause of his deposition by parliament to which part of the royal prerogatives were transferred on the accession to the throne of Henry IV, who now held his power simultaneously from God and by the consent of the kingdom, expressed through parliament. Better advised, the English kings would doubtless better have controlled the absolutist tendency of their power.

This necessity for the prince to surround himself with constant and enlightened council, always stressed by theorists, was broadly applied in the government practices of all states in the fourteenth century. And this was so true in France that Charles V himself asserted that the duty for a king who did not want to be taxed with tyranny was to govern 'by the council of a large number of wise men, clerical or lay'. Doing this and following the demonstration of Aristotle, he also proved very open to an entire current of thought and to the pressing entreaties of his entourage. All the authors judged that the councillors constituted a cog in the government which the sovereign could not bypass. Gerson exhorted Charles V to follow this path, writing 'do all by council and you will not repent of it', while Christine de Pisan asserted that the sovereign always chose his councillors with *science et preudomie* (skill and judgement) from among *gens propices et convenables* (suitable and fitting persons). They all had to show sufficient qualities and guarantees, whether it was a question of their love of the public good, their sense of the truth and their indestructible attachment to the sovereign who, everywhere, appeared to retain control of both the composition and the convening of the council. The key piece in the political game, he shared with the chancellor the most important part of government tasks.

In France as in England, the chancellor was the only one of the great officers to survive in permanent form, which led him to play a decisive role in the mechanism of the state after the break-up of the *curia regis*. While the household was restricted to the service of the prince, chancellor and councillors were in the front line for taking charge of all tasks of drafting, justice, council and decision making. This was why, from the mid-thirteenth century onwards, and throughout Europe, princes surrounded themselves with men who they could trust and who they rewarded and who took an oath to them to serve the state by guarding all its secrets. Similar developments piecemeal – in England from before 1257, in France from before 1269 and throughout the second half of the thirteenth century in the German principalities – made the king, his chancellor and his councillors henceforth veritable pillars of the state.

Fluid in its composition since the sovereign summoned to it whoever he wanted, the council's competence was also flexible and constantly evolving towards an increasingly marked specialisation, principally confined within the function of council and, subsidiarily, of justice. The evolution was particularly clear in England in the fourteenth century, where the court of the exchequer, court of common pleas and the court of the King's Bench, which had long been gradually detached from the council, constituted, since the reign of Henry III, a complex judicial ensemble in which each of these courts (which now had only distant contacts with the council) had its own area of jurisdiction. In France, a similar evolution occurred, but it was later, since it was only in the last decades of the thirteenth century that the *parlement* began to secure an autonomy which did not become definitive until the 1340s. Then the council fully assumed its principal function, that of advising the king and participating with him in the exercise of justice reserved to the crown. In the Iberian states, the role of the council in the fourteenth century was undoubtedly still more fundamental. The main part of royal power originated in it. This is why directing the council meant directing the country, and why, too, the king's court was nothing other than a centre of intrigue in which all the candidates competed in the direction of the council which was a meeting of princes or intimates of the king.

In this way, therefore, at the end of the Middle Ages, whether it was a question of the great or continual council of England, of the *conseil étroit, conseil privé, conseil secret* or *conseil grand* in France, of the secret council or sworn council of the German princes or the secret council of Milan, all were in part detached from the tasks of finance and justice, which they had looked after at the time of their earliest history, so that they could dedicate themselves better to advising the prince in secret matters of the state and exercising, with him, that part of justice which he did not intend to delegate. This was why few members – some dozen at the most – were admitted to it, to make of them, at the sovereign's side, the veritable masters of the state. Noble or bourgeois, lawyer or financier, it was always from them that decisions came and the impulses fitted to stimulate an administration right in the middle of a complete transformation.

2.2 *An oppressive administration*

The complexity of the administrative structures of states of the west in the fourteenth century is explained, principally, by the incomparable rise of government bureaucracy throughout the previous centuries. Its development was the direct consequence of the increase in central administrative departments. Its rigidity, inertia and sometimes its inability to adapt to the new demands of the modern state necessitated the creation of local administrative departments increasingly diversified and capable of resolving at once and on the spot all the problems which a central government could not settle, too often lacking the information and the means of action to intervene rapidly and effectively. Priority was thus given to the administration and to its departments, whose actions, increasingly autonomous in relation to the impulses of central government, often also became as inclusive as they were burdensome for the governed. This was particularly true of fourteenth-century France but much less so for England, while the systems retained by the Iberian countries corresponded to a middle path.

In France, the corollary of the constant inflation in the personnel of central administrative departments throughout the fourteenth century – four councillors at the *requêtes du palais* in 1314 and twenty-nine in 1343, twenty councillors at the *parlement* in 1314 and sixty-two in 1343, thirty notaries in the chancery in 1316 and fifty-nine in 1361 – was the ever-greater complexity of local administration. One has the impression that the increase in offices and agents of the king in the capital was matched, throughout the country, by a necessary increase in both the number of local departments and staff. Since the mid-thirteenth century, the *bailli* became, from a peripatetic official without a fixed area, a sedentary administrator responsible for administering an area with well-defined limits, the *bailliage*. At the beginning of the fourteenth century, he was all-powerful in it and cut the true figure of a viceroy. In part, the full representative of the sovereign, he exercised there all the delegated prerogatives. Head of the judicial administration, he presided over the assizes, whose court he composed as he wished, mixing there representatives of the populace with *probi homines* (worthy men) chosen on account of their good legal knowledge. Responsible for the receipt of all royal funds, he organised the farming out of the *prévôtés* and drew the revenues from them, securing the collection of all levies, taxes and fines. Responsible for the maintenance of public order, he was invested with a veritable power of law and order, strengthened further by the obligation which was incumbent upon him to publish and observe all the royal ordinances that he could, by virtue of his statutory power, adapted to local necessities. Judge, tax collector, legislator, this was the picture of the *bailli* in the first decades of the fourteenth century. Remunerated by the king, he was directly responsible to him. Released from all ties to his *bailliage*, of which he could not be a native and where he could not possess any property and which it was compulsory for him to leave at the end of three years, he compelled recognition like a veritable agent of the state whose status and career were perfectly defined.

But it would be to concentrate too many problems in the hands of a single individual to make the *bailli* the only interlocutor of the state at a point when the latter was multiplying and diversifying the departments of its central administration. A similar development could, inevitably, only be planned within the entirety of the kingdom as a whole. Often the initiative came from the *baillis* themselves who, without being invited to do so by the central authority, surrounded themselves, from the 1320s onwards, with collaborators whose action would finally rebound against them. Chosen by them at the outset, these officials progressively arrogated a certain autonomy to themselves before being nominated by the king himself who made them his veritable agents. This was certainly the case with the receivers of the *bailliage*. Responsible since the last years of the thirteenth century for the collection and handling of funds under the control of the *bailli*, they became, in 1320, authentic royal receivers, following an ordinance of Philip the Fair which forbade all *baillis* to interfere with the handling of funds. A similar evolution made the lieutenants of the *baillis*, entrusted with assisting him in his judicial tasks since the end of the thirteenth century, veritable royal judges. Despite the opposition of populations, systematically denying that the *bailli* could delegate any of the areas of his jurisdiction, the crown had to ratify this development in 1389. It then profited from it to make these lieutenants of justice true royal judges whom it nominated and directly controlled. In the fiscal and financial sector, finally, the institution of the *bailliage* experienced the same curtailment of power. The collection of heavy hearth taxes (*fouages*) which the war imposed from 1355 onwards was to escape the *baillis* completely to the profit of officials at first appointed by the Estates General then, afterwards, nominated by the king, the *élus*. Their district was not remotely the *bailliage*, but the *élection*.

In the Iberian kingdoms, the distant life of the localities, of which the government often knew little, forced the monarchs to devise a complex administration responsible for extending their action on the spot. A general scheme, which could always be adapted, dominated the organisation of local administration. In the states as a whole, the responsibility for managing the province was entrusted to a *merino* or *adelantado*, who sometimes received the title of *mayor* if he was placed at the head of an area of acknowledged economic or strategic importance. All these agents received authority delegated from the king in the form of a charter which listed their powers in detail. Full legal authority was thus also conferred on them to administer their *merindad*, to strengthen its safety, law and order, and justice. All these powers were increased if the king were a minor, or in his absence, as in Navarre at the beginning of the fourteenth century, when the *merino* was empowered to appoint the *alcaytes* of the royal castles and receive their oath of allegiance in the name of the king, from whom alone this power to appoint, in theory, depended. Thus conceived, the *merindad* constituted a truly autonomous unit in which the *merino* exercised his powers with a whole group of officers who were subordinate only to him and who were found a post on his recommendation. This was especially the case with his *justicia* and his receivers. These were agents who sometimes forgot that they represented the central government and who were thus tempted to abuse their power.

Most fortunately, the men of the lordships and towns recalled them to their duty and never failed to do so in the presence of the sovereign at the assemblies of the *cortes*. This was why the kings of Aragon travelled a great deal. They considered it important to demonstrate that they were close to their subjects in order to hear their grievances, whether at Denia, Minorca or Teruel. As for the kings of Navarre, they adapted the Capetian system of requests, which allowed them to be constantly informed about what was happening in their kingdom as a whole. To these regional administrative structures fitted to extend the action of the sovereigns, moreover, the institution of the *baylle* came to be added, an agent entrusted with representing the king in his towns, facing the council, and with communicating to the central government all the city's grievances. If his action was well handled, it was always the opportunity for starting a true dialogue between the king and his subjects. In this way, therefore, in Spain as in France, complexity undoubtedly dominated the structures of local administration in the fourteenth century.

It was the same in England, but undoubtedly to a lesser extent. Dominated since the tenth century by the all-powerful sheriff, the territorial administration was progressively diversified to make of this official, in the fourteenth century, a representative of the king who had slowly lost the major part of his powers, just like the *bailli* of the kings of France. Since 1242, the escheators had deprived him of the main part of his powers in financial matters. Moreover, the policy of reducing the areas of his judicial authority, undertaken since the reign of Henry II, had not ceased to bear fruit in that direction. The increase in judicial circuits in the counties at the courts of which judges from Westminster presided in place of the sheriff at the sessions of the shire courts, and the gradual institution of the coroners, whose primary task was to hold an inquest, if a man died, designed to enable a grand jury to present the accused to the itinerant judges. It was in the same perspective of the reduction of the sheriff's powers that the sovereigns of the thirteenth century had progressively set up the institution of the 'keepers of the peace', officials whose role, both in the military field and that of law and order, was to make them, in the reign of Edward III in 1362, veritable justices of the peace. They had the appearance of permanent judges simultaneously endowed with powers of decision and execution, as much in the field of justice as that of administration. Called to become the most important officials in their area, they progressively emptied of its content all the power of the sheriff, whose essential competence remained the transmission of the king's writs in the county. This was still an important prerogative, in so far as the size and development, ceaselessly increasing, of the central bureaucracy produced an ever-greater number of written documents.

In this way, as in the other countries of the west in the fourteenth century, the dominant characteristic of the English administration lay in the great number of its officials. Whether appointed by the king but not paid by him, like the sheriffs, escheators and justices of the peace, or chosen by the shire courts like the coroners, they all contributed to give the impression of a very great independence in local administration. This sentiment was in addition

considerably strengthened by numerous franchises (exempt jurisdictions) and
the highly autonomous functioning of the courts of justice, in particular the
jury system. Reality was more nuanced. Although the English sovereigns had
granted some autonomy to all these local authorities, it was above all because
they expected from them unpaid services, whose exact bounds they stipulated
strictly. But it did not end there. The role of these authorities designated by the
prince or chosen by the local populations was above all to execute orders sent
from Westminster. Since none of these offices were remunerated, they could
only be assumed by well-to-do individuals, most frequently landholders,
whether knights or not, who always showed themselves concerned to maintain
the established order and, by the same token, to ensure royal orders were
respected. Thanks to them, too, and through their agency, a fruitful dialogue
was set afoot between the prince and the country, a dialogue destined to be
continued within the framework of parliament. In France, on the contrary, this
dialogue could scarcely be engaged other than by means of representative
assemblies; local administrative officials – paid by the sovereign and increasingly career administrators – had neither the inclination nor the qualifications
to engage in a similar dialogue.

2.3 A necessary dialogue

Representative institutions dominated the entire history of the relations of
those who governed with the country throughout the fourteenth century. This
century was everywhere a period of dialogue which was realised through the
intermediary of the estates general and the provincial estates, or, in England,
within the framework of parliament. Why was such a dialogue established and
how was it able to continue?

It was not by chance that these institutions of dialogue strengthened their position in the fourteenth century. Many of them had their origins in the previous
century, while others saw the light of day with feudalism but all, without exception, experienced their apogee in the fourteenth century. Quite simply because
in this century of crises and difficulties, the country felt more need to make its
voice heard, facing a prince and an administration whose power was constantly
asserted. In France, war and financial difficulties; in the Low Countries, the
death of princes without male heirs; in the German principalities, successive,
constantly repeated divisions of inheritance; in Hungary, the crisis of the state
of 1382, following the death of Louis the Great – these were the factors which
help explain the irresistible development of assemblies of estates.

Over and above their differences, they all obeyed a common model in their
organisation which was very broadly based on the assemblies of the Church.

Synods and councils constituted henceforth assemblies whose maturity made it possible to put to the test all the methods of representation and deliberation. The saying, *quod omnes tangit ab omnibus approbetur* (what concerns everyone should be approved by everyone), compelled recognition so that it was progressively adopted by all the political assemblies, whether by the English parliament in 1295 or, gradually, by all the assemblies of estates on the whole continent. To agree with this rule implied that the problem of representation was to be compulsorily resolved, since not all the deputies of different estates could attend the sessions of the assemblies. It was because methods of proxy had progressed throughout the thirteenth century that representatives could be gradually appointed to whom their constituents delegated first a limited power, that of *ouir et rapporter* (hearing and reporting) then, slowly and with many reservations, a *plena potestas* (full authority) which authorised them, in theory at least, to act with full liberty.

Parallel to this development of juridical methods, the fourteenth century saw a considerable enlargement in the composition of assemblies of estates. Until the mid-thirteenth century, representatives of the nobility and clergy were mainly summoned. From that time onwards, slowly and little by little, the delegates of the towns made their entrance. This was particularly true of France. After several attempts in this direction by St Louis, the policy of fourteenth-century sovereigns was to extend, as broadly as possible, representation to the deputies of the towns. There was a very similar, but later, development in the empire, where, in 1362, the representatives of the towns sat for the first time in the estates of the Tyrol. Thus these assemblies – increasingly referred to as the 'three estates' since the appearance of this expression in Burgundy at the end of the thirteenth century – became widespread throughout continental Europe in all the regions, as well as at the level of the state. In England, evolution was different because of the fact that parliament simultaneously possessed the same powers as the assemblies of estates on the continent but also, and above all, a considerable judicial and legislative power.

This was the problem set by the role devolved to these institutions of dialogue, whether they were assemblies of estates or parliament. After a period of trial and error, it was fairly well defined in the fourteenth century. Beyond the desire of the prince to communicate with the country and the desire to meet him evinced by the representatives of his subjects, these assemblies were always convened to resolve specific problems. They appeared then as veritable organs of government, adapted to suggesting solutions to questions which the prince would not or, most often, could not solve alone. Problems with the coinage seem to have lain at the very heart of the preoccupations of these first assemblies. They dominated their activities in the thirteenth century. Henceforth, the coinage was no longer the concern of the prince, as it had been in the feudal period. This was why clergy, nobility and bourgeois meant, through the agency of their representatives in the estates, to control a good part of monetary policy, especially in the area of mutations of the coinage. They had a very real influence everywhere. There was Edward III, who in 1352 agreed not to do anything without the agreement of the Commons, and John the Good, who made a similar commitment to the estates in 1355, while Jeanne and Wenceslas of Brabant promised, the following year, to do nothing without consulting the country.

More acute still, the problem of war and its financing in the fourteenth century made jurisdiction over the currency fade into the background. It was undoubtedly to the permanency of war that the representative assemblies owed the main part of their success. It was financial aid – rather than advice or counsel on the conduct of operations – that the sovereigns of the fourteenth century demanded from their estates, or their parliament, while attempting to convince them that necessity and emergency always justified their consent to the levy of new taxes. And since the war continued, they also had to continue. But the principle of permanent taxation was still a long way off. For the time being, the sovereigns had to admit that a tax could only be levied if there was need and with the consent of their subjects' representatives. Often the estates and parliament even imposed still stricter regulation on the ruler. For did not parliament appoint, in 1340, commissioners to control the levy of tax to which they had consented and the estates of the Languedoïl set up, from 1355, the entire administration of the *élus* with a view to controlling the complete management of the *aides* from assessment to collection?

This was an important decade for the role played by the assemblies. The middle of the fourteenth century marked, in fact, the period of their apogee. Although the English parliament succeeded in establishing its victories permanently, things were different with the estates in other countries. Those which it has become traditional to call 'the estates general' lost some of their weight and it was henceforth more with the provincial estates that the princes discussed the defence of their territory and the grant of the subsidy. This thus provided an opportunity for their deputies to present the grievances which the prince might sometimes, after careful scrutiny, transform into ordinances. This was a frequent occurrence in France, and also in Spain where the *cortes* played a role of the first importance in the formulation of the Constitutions of Catalonia and the *Fueros* of Aragon. In England, strong as a result of the role it played henceforth in financial matters, parliament had a clear tendency to lose sight of its powers in judicial matters to strengthen its normative capacity. To the individual petitions which it received until the end of the thirteenth century were added the collective petitions which it sent to the king if it judged it opportune. Thus in 1327 a common petition gave birth, for the first time, to a statute decreed by the king in parliament. This procedure grew to such an extent that parliament received fewer and fewer individual petitions for judgement, saw its court become empty and thus became, in the mid-fourteenth century, a true legislative body. This was a unique evolution, not experienced by any other country of the west even though the estates were, to some extent everywhere, the instigators of important ordinances suggested and, sometimes, imposed by means of their grievances.

But they were not convened with sufficient regularity for their activities to become truly institutionalised. The sessions were in general short, a few days at the most, and their rhythm subject to the goodwill of the prince except, perhaps, in Catalonia or Aragon, where the practice of convening the *cortes* annually became established at the beginning of the fourteenth century. But there, too, theory was very far from reality. In England, by contrast, the average duration of a parliament was about three weeks and it met practically annually in the fourteenth century. Since, additionally, the same peers were almost always summoned to the upper house and numerous knights and burgesses often sat in several successive parliaments in the House of Commons, it can better be understood how such continuity could make of parliament an institution which was rapidly able to consolidate its power against that of the sovereign. Nothing comparable occurred with the estates, even if some, such as those of Aragon, succeeded in developing, throughout the fourteenth century, permanent commissions responsible for extending their activities between the sessions able to force a constant dialogue on the prince.

'Dialogue' – this is the key word dominating both the theory and practice of power during the whole of the fourteenth century. A state which strengthened its grip everywhere faced a country which was starting to organise itself. Progressively freed from feudalism, it was no longer prepared to fall back into subjection and made its voice heard over and against a prince whose power nobody disputed, but which everyone wished to see regulated and its exercise limited. Two strong periods dominated this political evolution of the fourteenth century. Until around the 1340s, carried by the rapid expansion imparted it by the lawyers, royal power continually grew stronger. Everywhere, the great bodies of the state and its officials, whose numbers ceaselessly increased, assured its success. But with the arrival of war and the crises that accompanied it, then this fine enthusiasm was shattered. From Spain to England, from Hungary to France, a wind of democracy arose to remind the princes that they had to listen, in this game of politics, to the voice of their subjects and to reckon with those who represented them.

CHAPTER 3

CURRENTS OF RELIGIOUS
THOUGHT AND EXPRESSION

Jeremy Catto

THE main determinant of religious thought in the fourteenth century, which would eventually affect every aspect of public worship and private prayer, was the concentrated effort, in the previous century, to marshal, state logically and resolve questions according to an agreed theological language, establishing thereby a coherent method of religious education. The enduring issues of God's relation to the world, the human soul and the nature of redemption were not resolved, but they had been successfully contained within an abstract and largely Aristotelian language, and were generally discussed by a trained and conscious elite at Paris or its satellites in Oxford, Cambridge and the schools of the friars. The attempt to resolve them had created and continued to create philosophical syntheses of greater or less cohesion. That of Thomas Aquinas, promoted by the Order of Preachers and universally known after his canonisation in 1323, was matched in the first decades of the century by the more amorphous body of ideas associated with the Franciscan doctors Duns Scotus, Peter Auriol and François de Meyronnes: among whom the influence of current logic brought about, some twenty years later, a critical reexamination of theological language, associated with William of Ockham, and as the moral and social aspects of religious thinking began to dominate debate, a vigorous return to Augustinian ideas. These bodies of ideas did not create distinct schools of thought: virtually all theologians of the fourteenth century were independent thinkers who can be classified as Augustinians, Thomists, Scotists or followers of the *via moderna* – only in a broad sense. They were united by a common inheritance of terms and concepts and a common analytical training, to which the rich religious literature of the century owed the bulk of its conceptual structure: Ramon Lull's contemplation through memory, understanding and will, Meister Eckhart's 'ground of the soul', the unity of essence of Jan Ruysbroeck and the concept of naked love of *The Cloud of Unknowing* were all, or were derived from, ideas of theologians.

In the course of the fourteenth century the learning of theologians both proliferated across Europe, through new theology faculties in universities and innumerable cathedral, monastic and friars' schools, and came to focus more directly than before on the moral and pastoral questions which confronted individuals. Theologians began to play an active role in the government of the Church: in contrast to the work of teaching and speculation which filled the lives of thirteenth-century doctors like Aquinas, Henry of Ghent or Peter John Olivi, the experience of their successors in secular and ecclesiastical affairs and the work of the missionary and the inquisitor profoundly modified their thinking. Pierre de la Palud OP, for instance, left the Paris schools to argue the case of Pope John XXII against Franciscan poverty, and then as patriarch of Jerusalem to promote the crusade (1317–42). Richard Fitzralph, a secular doctor of Oxford, served Benedict XII and Clement VI in debate with Greek and Armenian churchmen, ending his career in 1360 as archbishop of Armagh and bitter opponent of the friars; the Czech theologian Adalbert Ranconis (d. 1388), who had studied at Paris and Oxford, served Emperor Charles IV as clerk and court preacher and gave support to the Bohemian reform movement; Peter Philargi (of Candia) OFM, a Cretan friar who studied at Padua, Oxford and Paris, promoted Catholic teaching in Lithuania, was made bishop of various Lombard sees, acted as an envoy of the duke of Milan, and was eventually elected Pope Alexander V (1409–10). In each case practical experience refocused these theologians' interests and ideas, bringing to the forefront aspects of their subject which had an immediate bearing on the pastoral work of the clergy. Not surprisingly this sometimes led to sharp controversy which involved canonists as well as theologians and in some cases judicial processes before the Roman curia. The question of the poverty of Christ and the apostles, for instance, which touched the vocation of Franciscans, provoked crisis in the order in the pontificate of John XXII, while in mid-century the relation of friars to secular clergy touched off a parallel debate on ecclesiastical property and its scriptural warrant which reverberated from 1350, when Fitzralph first raised it at Avignon, for the rest of the century and beyond.

Less dramatic but of equal import for the religion of the laity was the slow advance of theological education among the European clergy. In 1300 it was exceptional for a bishop, and *a fortiori* for a parish priest, to have attended the schools, even in England where a learned clergy had probably made most progress; in the province of Vienne, for instance, neither the archbishop nor his five suffragans is known to have done so, and only one of their recent predecessors, Henry of Geneva the elected but unconfirmed bishop of Valence, had studied in a university – in his case Bologna.[1] On the other hand many cathedral chapters and some monasteries had begun to appoint trained friars as

[1] Boisset (1973), pp. 116–25.

lectors, and in many European towns, the schools of the mendicant orders were attended by secular clergy and even the laity. The work of Remigio del Girolami OP as lector at Santa Maria Novella (*c.* 1275–1315) was valued by the commune of Florence, and it is probable that the friars' schools at Erfurt and Cologne were able to diffuse theological learning among the Germans and eastern Europeans in the absence of early universities. As the century progressed the schools of the friars multiplied, and in due course new theological faculties in universities began to turn out parish priests, cathedral canons and bishops, as well as friars. By 1414, when the Council of Constance was assembling, doctors of theology constituted a large minority of bishops, and a more substantial number were doctors of decrees; and among the effective leadership of the Council, the proportion of university-educated clergy was overwhelming.

Jurists therefore as well as theologians participated in the work of defining the pastoral mission of the clergy. The early success of Bologna as a centre for the study of Roman and canon law had been imitated during the thirteenth century by faculties of canon law in Paris, Oxford, Orléans, Montpellier, Salamanca and many other places; the strong sense of evangelical purpose which many of their *alumni* shared – whether exercised in missionary work beyond the borders of Christendom, or the defence of Orthodox belief and practice and the propagation of Christian teaching within them – was typified by Dr Jacques Duèse, bishop of Fréjus (1300) and Avignon (1310), who became Pope John XXII in 1316. The canon law, as a living law responsive to current ecclesiastical problems and preoccupations, had been fashioned by the thirteenth-century decretalists to implement the pastoral ideals of the Fourth Lateran Council, and by the end of the century a body of simple practical literature for the guidance of preachers, confessors and parish priests was taking shape. Among the summaries popular during the fourteenth century were the two great works of the elder Guillaume Durand, bishop of Mende, his *Speculum Iuris* (*c.* 1274) and *Rationale Divinorum*, which served as handbooks of the canonical and liturgical duty of priests respectively; the use of John of Freiburg's *Summa Confessorum*, a digest of legal, theological and practical guidelines for parish priests (1295–1302), was even more widespread. This practical literature both influenced the practice of priests and was modified by experience; and at the end of the century a new synthesis, more sensitive though no more indulgent to human weakness, was made in the *Opus Tripartitum* and other pastoral tracts of Jean Gerson, chancellor of Paris. These held the field throughout the fifteenth century and beyond.

The substance of this body of teaching was imparted to the laity through two main channels. The broadest was probably the medium of the sermon, an increasingly frequent event in the life of townsmen and even rural communities. Innumerable sermons survive from the fourteenth century: their form, originally an academic exposition of a biblical text, was constantly modified to conform to unlearned ears, and their content popularised with *exempla* or anecdotes with simple morals. The friars were the pacesetters of the popular sermon: their styles, ranging from the elaborate classical stories of Robert Holcot OP to the 'raw homilies for the benefit of simple folk' of Cardinal Bertrand de la Tour or the elegant rhetorical turns of Filippo di Montecalerio OFM, were honed to the capacities of varying congregations. Though the vast majority of sermons have been preserved in Latin, it is clear that they were generally delivered in the vernacular, often with powerful effect. Itinerant preachers like the Catalan Dominican Vincent Ferrer, who between 1399 and 1419 travelled through France preaching to great crowds in the open air, were believed to have a profound effect on public opinion, and the same was feared of Lollard preachers in England and Hussites in Bohemia.

The sermon at its best was a potent instrument of persuasion, and its influence upon the development of vernacular literature was profound. Yet the second medium through which the religious thinking of the schools reached the laity was arguably effective at the deeper level of the individual conscience: the growing practice of private confession. This too had been developed by the friars, and in the course of the fourteenth century it became common for at least the more substantial of the laity to make individual confessions at regular intervals, frequently though not universally to the mendicants. Literature for the guidance of confessors abounded; *Summae Casuum*, collections of cases before ecclesiastical courts and of other material, like the *Summa Pisanella* of Bartholomew of Pisa OFM, provided detailed advice and plans for the questioning of penitents. Where the influence of the confessional can be traced, it promoted, through the practice of private examination of conscience, independent religious thinking on the part of the penitent; the *Livre de Seyntz Medicines* of Henry of Grosmont, duke of Lancaster, a fresh and original discourse on sins and their remedies, was one fruit of the sacrament of penance. In the second half of the century it was becoming common among the European *noblesse* to have a personalised prayer-book or book of hours; originating in the Psalter, the book of hours developed into a compendium of private devotions, offices of favourite saints and prayers derived from contemplative works, according to individual taste; a late fourteenth-century example from the diocese of Rodez, for instance, now in a Glasgow library, contains a nativity mass and vespers with penitential psalms and litanies in Provençal, presumably for a lay owner.

Traditionally, the most public and communal aspects of religious devotion had focused on local saints, innumerable examples of which, originating in the late antique or early medieval eras and generally canonised only by popular acclaim, still attracted devotion in the fourteenth century. St Cuthbert, for instance, the patron of Durham, at whose tomb the 'inhabitants of the diocese swore their most solemn oaths or took the cross';[2] or St Eulalia the patron saint of Barcelona, round whose tomb the kings of Aragon rebuilt the crypt (completed in 1339) to accommodate pilgrims, placing a gothic statue of the saint in the church above. A regional cult might also focus on a newly recognised saint and his relics: one of the most bizarre was the cult of Thomas Aquinas at the Cistercian monastery of Fossanova in the kingdom of Naples, where long before his canonisation in 1323 the monks and lay devotees, including the saint's family, vied with the Dominican friars over possession of parts of his dismembered body: one result of which was the preservation of some of his autograph writings as relics in the convent at Naples.

The cult of local saints achieved greatest definition in stable, well-recognised communities which looked to a single, unshared intercessor. The careers of a growing number of Europeans, however, made them mobile and therefore less inclined to look to a cult bound to particular places and shrines. Their religious needs were sometimes satisfied by pilgrimage cults like that of St James the Greater at Compostela or St Thomas Becket at Canterbury, or at the end of the century by devotion to the hermit St Roch (d. *c.* 1380), whose cult became a prophylactic against the plague. The most potent of these unlocalised spiritual patrons was, of course, the Virgin; her cult, already well established in eastern Christianity, adopted from the twelfth century onwards a personal and intimate note in the west, partly from association with the humanity of Christ and partly from the ideal of courtly love. Spread throughout Europe with the blessing of St Bernard, and through the active propagation of Franciscan and especially Carmelite preachers, the various feasts and private devotions dedicated to Mary gained in popularity in the fourteenth century: the Annunciation, portrayed in innumerable altarpieces; the Holy Family, with its secondary cults of St Anne and the Presentation of Mary; the Assumption; the Angelus, by 1400 often observed at noon as well as in the evening; and the rosary, a personal aid to prayer which grew in popularity with the advent of the *devotio moderna*.

Marian devotion could as well be expressed privately as in the public liturgy, and its growth is one aspect of the proliferation of personal religion among the laity. It was paralleled by numerous devotions, often originating as personal cults and evolving into public feast, to facets of the incarnation or passion of Christ, such as the Transfiguration, the Crown of Thorns, the Five Wounds and the Holy Name. In contrast the cult of Corpus Christi, deriving as it did from the canon of the mass, retained a public and communal character while appealing equally to personal compassion for the suffering of Christ, and was

---

[2] Dobson (1973), p. 28.

therefore uniquely placed to be, in the following century, a channel through which the offices of the liturgical year could be refreshed by the reviving waters of inward devotion. Originating among the beguines of Liège before 1240, it finally achieved universal status in 1317, and was rapidly taken up by lay religious fraternities everywhere, especially in towns; eucharistic processions, rituals of unity associated with civic pride and sometimes enacted in hope or remembrance of a local eucharistic miracle, proliferated. The procession in turn, in the fifteenth century, became the focus of locally composed dramatic reenactments of the Passion. At every stage the personalisation of the Eucharist which the cult embodies touched a sensitive nerve, stimulating a widespread personal response, and it is not surprising that differing notions of its proper observance prompted violent controversy in the years around 1400.

Corpus Christi guilds were only one category among a bewildering variety of confraternities, ranging from trade guilds, most developed in the great manufacturing towns of Italy, which usually had a religious aspect, through societies dedicated to mutual insurance or to particular charities, to bodies bound by a common rule, religious practice or even belief, which might attract official disapproval. Originating long before the fourteenth century, they proliferated after 1300 and their purposes came to be more precisely defined, as increasing numbers of the laity of both sexes sought a specific form for their charitable or devotional aspirations. The establishment and running of hospitals was probably the commonest activity of confraternities, for instance that of La Scala at Siena, where St Catherine had nursed the sick, or the hospital of St Bénézet at Avignon. The *disciplinati* or flagellants formed a further species originating in the thirteenth century, dedicated to performing public penance on behalf of the community by mutual flagellation in the towns of southern Europe; organised locally in numerous confraternities, their members were largely artisans, who often combined flagellation with the cult of the Eucharist, as in Siena, or the Holy Name, like the fraternity of Barcelona. Attracting a good deal more suspicion than encouragement from Church authorities, they grew in numbers because they had widespread lay support. Nevertheless the idea of assuming public penance for the sins of a body of Christians derived from monastic discipline, and its popularity is one of many indices of the active development of earlier monastic religious thinking at the hands of the fourteenth-century laity.

The fraternity probably served as a model for the many bodies of enthusiasts whose unorthodox beliefs and practices had singled them out, in the thirteenth century, for condemnation and suppression by Church authorities. The cohesion of these groups of heretics is a matter of dispute. Most of them had originated in the religious ferment of the late twelfth century, but the Cathars or Albigensians, whose dualist principles and hierarchy of *perfecti* had made numerous converts in Italy and southern France, survived persecution by 1300 only in a few mountain villages, and may have disappeared entirely a few years later. The Waldensian congregations of the fourteenth century, heirs of an earlier wave of enthusiasm for the ideals of apostolic poverty and spiritual simplicity, are a different matter. They too persisted in upland villages, mainly in the Alps, though to what extent they were conscious of belonging to a separate sect is uncertain. In addition, they had penetrated into Germany, where small groups were to be found in some of the western and southern towns and in villages in the eastern borderlands, served evidently by secretive itinerant 'masters'. Their distinctiveness, limited though it was, seems to have made them generally unpopular with their neighbours, and the concerted effort made to root them out of every part of Germany between 1392 and 1401 rested on solid public support. It was not completely successful; some Waldensians survived to be greeted by the Hussites as torchbearers of true religion. But in general they and other enthusiasts for poverty, such as the Fraticelli in Italy, had little impact on popular religious practice.

Fraternities, being public bodies, did not in themselves provide spiritual sustenance for the many laymen and especially women who sought individual religious experience in these years, though they probably made private initiative easier. There is evidence from several parts of Europe, especially in the later fourteenth century, of earnest deliberation on the part of both laity and clergy on the right outward form of religious life, whether a monastic vocation, the evangelical life of a friar, the solitary calling of the anchorite or recluse or a contemplative life in the world, the 'mixed' life. While the considerable literature on the subject comes from the trained pens of the clergy, it was frequently evoked by lay need of advice: Walter Hilton wrote a tract on the utility of the religious life to guide the Carthusian vocation of the controller of the great wardrobe, Adam Horsley and Gerson addressed a series of tracts on meditation to his sisters. The question whether to enter a religious order, and if so which rule or community was appropriate to a particular vocation seems to have been posed especially sharply to trained men already embarked on a career. Within the monastic and mendicant orders it was becoming clear that some justification of the various orders' ways of life was necessary in general religious terms, and that justification might imply reform. Benedict XII had issued new constitutions for all the major orders, and their implementation, imperfect as it was, encouraged reflection on the mendicant and monastic rules. Bartholomew of Pisa's work in defence of Franciscan conformity to the life of Christ was written about 1385; somewhat earlier, a series of tracts on the instruction of Benedictine novices had been composed anonymously at Bury St Edmunds. Outside their orders of origin, these works were probably not widely read, but they indicate their authors' awareness of contemporary opinion and aspirations.

Both within and outside the established orders, however, the variety of spiritual experience and the informality of the groups in which a religious life was developed is striking. One such informal group was the *famiglia* of the Dominican tertiary Catherine Benincasa, later canonised as St Catherine of Siena, which she formed about herself, and extended in her correspondence, between 1367 and 1380. It included her spiritual director Raymond of Capua OP, later a reforming master-general of his order, the English hermit of Leccato, William Flete OESA, and the Vallombrosan monk Giovanni dalle Celle, all of whom, in spite of Catherine's somewhat imperious tone in her correspondence, were highly individual figures and spiritual advisers in their own right. They respected her personal experience of God, which arose from introspection: 'my cell', wrote Catherine, 'will not be one of stone or wood, but that of self-knowledge'.[3] Her influence was all the greater for not flowing through established channels. The informal and voluntary communities established by her contemporary Gerard Groote in the towns of the Ijssel valley in Holland seem to have been similar associations of independent minds, whose private devotions looked to no corporate support from the group beyond common manual labour. Known therefore as Brethren of the Common Life (as distinct from any special way of life), in the suspicious society of northern Europe they needed to fight for the right to live together without a rule. Perhaps a third contemporary group was that of John Wyclif's 'poor preachers', originally it would seem a body of university-trained radical preachers; but no evidence of any corporate activities, beyond preaching and producing vernacular books, now survives. Both within established communities or religious orders and outside them, in informal groupings or in the virtual isolation of some hermits and recluses, the spiritual life of the age was determined by individual choices and private forms of devotion.

In this context the debate on the relative merits of the active and the contemplative life conducted by Italian intellectuals, a line of thought to which Petrarch contributed by implication and Coluccio Salutati more explicitly, was part of a wider choice faced not only by humanists but by the whole of the educated European world, both laity and clergy, both men and women, in the later fourteenth century. Petrarch, by temperament a man of the world, was constantly and perhaps increasingly attracted by the monastic life, as he made clear in his *De Ocio Religiosorum* and *De Vita Solitaria*. His admirer Salutati, as chancellor of Florence, was professionally committed to public affairs, and proposed to justify them, in 1372, in a book provisionally entitled *De Vita Associabili et Operative*; but after the painful crises of the 1370s he was less sure, and by 1381 he could write a book of advice for a friend who had entered a

---

[3] Fawtier and Canet (1948), p. 60.

monastic order, *De Seculo et Religione*, in which the monastic life is praised as the highest ideal. The question continued to trouble him with 'tensions and frequent alternations between opposing attitudes'.[4] It is the same question which Walter Hilton considered, though with rather less hesitation, and which Gerson expounded to his sisters. If authors came to different conclusions, and if many of them even failed to maintain a consistent answer, the choice which it posed must have been real.

Amid the bewildering variety of religious aspirations expressed during the century, it is possible to discern the outlines of a body of ideas, or themes, which had been exposed by the ceaseless erosion of the immediate issues in the ebb and flow of academic debate. As Aristotelian logic was absorbed and then rapidly developed in the Paris schools, the earlier cosmologies and light-metaphysics gave way to more fundamental questions: first of all, in the 1270s, the question of the unity or plurality of forms, on which the whole status of life on earth, whether natural to man or merely a provisional state, or half-life, seemed to depend; and then the great issues of God's relation to creatures: divine omnipotence and human freedom, God's knowledge of creatures and human knowledge of God, whether the Incarnation was merely a consequence of the Fall of Man, and finally the relation of God's grace to human merit. These questions dominated the theology schools of Paris, Oxford and the provinces of the orders of friars from about 1280 onwards, and even after two generations of debate, which somewhat exhausted original thinking on them, they remained the standard diet of academic theological exercises up to the sixteenth century. In the process of arguing the questions, the role of the theologian significantly altered: whereas thirteenth-century theologians, including Aquinas, proposed to lay a solid, logically unassailable intellectual ground for the Christian faith, on which sound pastoral or missionary work, or speculative mystical thought, might be based, Henry of Ghent, Duns Scotus and Peter Auriol, acutely conscious of the systemic limits of human knowledge of God, seemed to regard speculation itself as their task. Eventually, after William of Ockham's demolition of numerous accepted abstract concepts and the anti-intellectualism of some neo-Augustinian theologians, the logical limits of human knowledge came to be so well established that theological speculation began to lose credit, leaving space for neoplatonic bodies of thought like that of John Wyclif, or more generally for various forms of mystical theology. Logic, first disciplining and then in effect strangling speculative theology, in this last stage withdrew from the field.

The harbinger of the culminating phase of speculative religious thought, between 1280 and 1320, was the Parisian secular master Henry of Ghent

---

[4] Baron (1966), p. 109.

(d. 1293), whose great series of quodlibets and disputed questions circulated rapidly and widely. Here under various headings he addressed himself to the fundamental nature of being as presented to the human intellect, bringing into juxtaposition on a general level ideas innate in the mind, like potentiality or being, and material realities apprehended by the senses. Taking these quite familiar notions to a new level of abstraction, he posited two wholly distinct orders of being, the world of existences as presented to the senses, which originated in creation, and the world of essences as known innately to the mind, which owed their origin to the procession of the divine intellect. He thus proposed, but did not resolve, a series of stimulatingly indeterminate distinctions: between the eternity of essence and the eternity of God; the abstraction of essence and the concrete nature of individual substances; the indifference of essence and the determinate properties of singularity and universality. His successors and especially Duns Scotus sought to bridge the chasm he had created between essence and existence; in the form of a stark contrast between the possible and the actual worlds, it would provoke theologians of the fourteenth century to explore the logical limits of God's omnipotence. The increasing sense of tension between God's overwhelming power and human contingency was not, however, confined to the schools, as much devotional literature of the fourteenth century shows. Henry merely stated in the language of logic, and theologians after him tried to resolve, questions which had come to dominate religious thinking at several levels of sophistication.

Henry of Ghent's formulation of these questions provided a text for the leading theologians who followed him, most notably and influentially, of course, John Duns Scotus, the Oxford-trained Franciscan theologian who also taught in Paris and Cologne in the decade of activity before his early death in 1308. Scotus sought to bridge the disjunction of essences and existences posited by his predecessor with the notion of being as such, *ens in quantum ens*, as the object of knowledge. Human knowledge of God was limited: there was a distinction between *theologia nostra*, God as conceived by man, and *theologia Dei*, God as he really was. Aware then of the limits of human reason in apprehending God, but following Augustine and Anselm 'who believed that they laboured meritoriously in trying to understand what they believed',[5] he attempted to grasp something of the nature of God's freedom of the will through the notion of human free will. Human will was free in regard to opposite acts, to burn or not to burn for instance, tending to opposite objects and producing opposite effects. Mutable in itself and therefore imperfect, it nevertheless carried a vestige of the divine will in its character as an active potency

---

[5] 'Augustinus et Anselmus crediderunt se meritorie laborare ut intelligerent quod crediderunt.' John Duns Scotus, *Ordinatio* II d. 1. q. 3, cited by Wolter (1986), p. 5.

or a causal principle, a principle of creativity. But the human will is subject to rational and natural inclinations, to love what is good for its own sake; and such love is perfected by God's gratuitous grace, making the well-ordered will truly and innately free. God's perfect freedom of will lacks human mutability, having instead the *firmitas* or steadfast will which is the perfection of its rational inclinations; it is thus both perfectly determined and perfectly free. Like creation itself, the incarnation of Christ is an absolutely free act of God's love, independent of human causality; it could not be merely a consequential remedy for original sin. Scotus defended the Franciscan doctrine of the immaculate conception of Mary by the priority of the incarnation to any human action, which placed her relationship with Christ, her motherhood, outside the inheritance of Adam's sin.

Among a wealth of perceptions characteristic of Scotus's thought, including univocity, the being-ness of beings, and *haecceitas*, their this-ness – itself a development of the Franciscan preference for arguing that things were knowable in their irreducible singularity, which he defended emphatically – the idea of the freedom of the human will as a perfection sharing in God's perfect freedom was perhaps the most potent religious idea. Like much of his thought, it was rooted in Franciscan theology and spirituality with its strong and concrete sense of the individual, its concentration on the notion of divine and human will perfected in charity or love, and its interpretation of theology as a practical rather than a speculative science; for Scotus, theology was the science of freedom and its perfection in charity, as distinct from philosophy, the science of nature, the realm of cause and necessary effect. His achievement was to reinterpret them in the light of Henry of Ghent's refinement of the notions of actual and possible being and of what was free and what necessary to God, giving them the intellectual coherence and strength to endure, even to absorb the effects of the new logic of the fourteenth century. Had he lived longer, he might have emerged from the disciplined professionalism of his theological teaching. There are some signs even in his most technical works that his analysis of the nature of God rested on a contemplative vision: in the prayer to God with which he closed his late tract *De Primo Principio*, he invoked God's formal qualities first in the language of the schools, and then in more mystical terms 'communicating the rays of your goodness most liberally, you are boundless good, to whom as the most lovable thing of all every single being in its own way comes back to you as its ultimate end'.[6]

In the republic of academic theology, the solutions of Scotus to these

---

[6] 'Tu bonus sine termino, bonitatis tuae radios liberalissime communicans, ad quem amabilissimum singula suo modo recurrunt ut ad ultimum suum finem.' Scotus, *De Primo Principio*, p. 144, cited by Wolter (1986), p. 8.

current questions were discussed, modified and developed by numerous independent thinkers; 'Scotism' never achieved more than a modest degree of coherence as a body of doctrine. They were most effective in maintaining a measure of human freedom and individuality in the many discordant responses to the question of God's omnipotence in relation to creatures and to the laws of nature, a question which involved the moral problem of God's gratuitous grace and human merit. These questions presented themselves first and most sharply to theologians, but in some form they concerned a far wider body of believers: laymen and old women, according to William of Ockham, badgered theologians on questions of contingency and free will,[7] and they were in the mind of the author of the English religious poem *Pearl*. A further stage in defining them was reached shortly after Scotus's death with the effort of largely English logicians and theologians to simplify the terms of theological debate and subject them to a more rigorous logic; this task was primarily, though not exclusively, undertaken by William of Ockham, another Franciscan theologian, shortly before and after 1320. The use of 'terminist' logic, the analysis of the properties of terms, and the introduction of the measure language of physics, concentrated attention on epistemological questions such as the limits of human knowledge of God and of the truths of faith; and with every new application of modern logic, the agreed body of theological propositions open to logical demonstration diminished, leaving a theology increasingly divorced from the natural order and saved from indeterminacy only by accepted Christian doctrine. By the 1320s, first in Oxford and soon also in Paris, where 'English' logic was increasingly fashionable, the metaphysical issues which had concerned Scotus, like essence and existence, were in retreat.

Nevertheless theology, in the middle third of the fourteenth century, did not lose sight of the great religious issues which Henry of Ghent and his contemporaries had clarified. In the hands of Franciscan theologians like Adam Woodham, Austin friars such as Gregory of Rimini or secular masters such as Thomas Bradwardine and Richard Fitzralph, debate focused on two main, interrelated issues: how divine foreknowledge could be reconciled with future contingents, events determined by human will, and how God's gratuitous grace, uncaused by any human agency, could be related to the meritorious acts of man without undermining the notion of free will. The necessity of retaining a place for human choice in a theology dominated by the idea of God's omnipotence brought some theologians to adopt 'semi-Pelagian' views, justifying the efficacy of human merit for salvation, such as Adam Woodham or the Parisian theologian John of Mirecourt. But the tide of opinion was flowing

---

[7] William of Ockham, *Contra Benedictum*, III, *Opera Politica* III, p. 231.

strongly in the opposite direction, and the statement of such views merely provoked their 'Augustinian' opponents to condemn opinions which were no longer seen as mere academic differences, but as challenges to faith itself. The defenders of human participation in the task of salvation were, to Bradwardine, ingrates and enemies of grace, and their appeal to reason and experience in justification of free will was a form of derangement.[8] Though in his great defence of the doctrine of predestination, *De Causa Dei contra Pelagianos*, published in 1344, he attempted to reconcile his view that every event happens of necessity with at least the form of human free will, his deep conviction that God's grace was utterly gratuitous and that it caused, rather than responded to, meritorious acts broke out from the restraints of an academic issue.

In the wake of Gregory of Rimini and Thomas Bradwardine the theologians of the second half of the century, Hugolinus of Orvieto and Dionysius of Montina in Paris and John Wyclif in Oxford generally maintained a predestinarian view of grace and salvation. The gradual reformulation of the question as one of individual justification reveals something of its religious significance. It was discussed by theologians who were themselves, or were close to, preachers and confessors involved in the pastoral work of the Church. The revival of biblical scholarship and its constant application in preaching, missionary work, the reformulation of doctrinal points through discussion with theologians of the separated Churches of eastern Christianity, and the practice of confession broadened the scope of their thought, as the vast range of non-philosophical and non-theological authorities cited by Bradwardine goes to show. He and his contemporaries, acutely aware of the constant human decisions which men of the world – to whom many of them were confessors – had to make, seem to have seen the doctrine of God's gratuitous grace and predestination of the saved as a source of consolation and steadfast faith, not of despair. For Bradwardine, the realisation of this truth was almost a religious revelation, 'a mountain of inaccessible truth';[9] and in varying degrees, theologians were beginning to recoil from 'useless' speculation and to take refuge in what they regarded as solid or simple verities. Bradwardine's Oxford contemporary Richard Fitzralph contrasted the light of scripture with his earlier theological speculations, as vain as the 'frogs and toads' croaking in his native Irish bog: a perspective which Wyclif also shared. At the end of the century the Parisian theologian Jean Gerson would condemn the questions discussed in the schools as useless, fruitless and insubstantial. These opinions were not entirely fair to the debates in Paris, Oxford and many

---

[8] Bradwardine, *De Causa Dei contra Pelagianos*, p. 309.

[9] 'Ipse me deduces in montem huius inaccessibilis veritatis.' Ibid., p. 808.

of the theological faculties in the new universities of the empire, where the
limits of the possible universe and God's omnipotence continued to be
explored with truly remarkable freedom; but they accorded with the outward-
looking, pastoral aspect of theologians' work, and were echoed in the awak-
ening interest in religious questions of the world outside the universities.

This common rejection of the speculations of earlier theologians has come
to be seen, by historians of medieval thought and by students of the early
humanists alike, as clear evidence of the decline of 'scholasticism', the supposed system of thought of the thirteenth- and fourteenth-century universities. In the light of the impressive though extremely various intelligence
of many religious writers of the century after 1350, however, such an interpretation seems doubtful. It is, rather, the effect of a general shift of interest
in religious questions towards the moral perspective of the individual, bringing into focus questions of personal justification and salvation and, more
broadly, questions of conscience. It would be a mistake to exaggerate the
abstraction or unworldliness of even the most remote philosophers of the
early fourteenth century; and in the following generations the concerns of a
wider world would come to the fore. At the hands of the educated men of the
world, active clergy or laity who concentrated on these questions, the unchang-
ing philosophical problems of theology, the problems brought to light by the
application of rigorous logic to religious truths, gave ground to historical and
ecclesiological speculations on the stages of the Christian dispensation, the
origin, destiny and constitution of the community of the faithful, and the character of public religious cult and personal devotion. At the beginning of the
fourteenth century, numerous accounts of Christian history and eschatology
were widely current. Many Franciscans, notably St Bonaventure, had seen
the appearance of St Francis as a work of divine mercy, restoring the virtue
of the primitive Church and, in some eyes, preparing for the imminent end of
the world; and Peter John Olivi, the champion of rigorous Franciscan poverty,
had developed this notion in the light of the theories of Joachim of Fiore into
an account of Christian history in seven ages, ending with the final age of the
spirit ushered in by the conversion of the whole world by the friars. An alternative Joachite view was that of the visionary Fra Dolcino, who was burnt in
1306, dividing history into four states on the basis of the Apocalypse. These
views appealed primarily to fanatics on the fringes of the educated world; but
for Dante, who was much more widely read, the decline of ancient virtue, of
the rational principles of Roman law and of the pure religion of the Apostles
was part of a providential pattern of history, which would be reversed in an
imminent *renovatio mundi* when true Roman rule would be restored.

These accounts of pagan and Christian history circulated among a
European laity and clergy increasingly aware of the spatial as well as the

temporal frontiers of the Christian world. Much had happened in the
thirteenth century to bring into focus not only the world of Islam, but the
Mongol empire and the remote civilisations of the far east. The translation of
Muslim and Jewish philosophical works, familiar to most theologians, had
shown that not all wisdom had been transmitted through the Latin or even the
Greek fathers; and the first missionaries to reach the Mongol khans and make
contact with the network of Nestorian Christians in central Asia offered some
hope, in their reports, of immeasurably widening the frontiers of Christendom.
Among scholars who hoped to bring Muslims to accept Christianity by rea-
soning, the Majorcan Ramon Lull, a Franciscan tertiary, was perhaps the most
influential with his various 'arts' or guides to the conversion of non-Christians;
his knowledge of Islam and of Muslim philosophy, as well as of the Jewish
intellectual tradition, encouraged him to found his efforts on the common
ground of the three monotheistic religions. His projects for teaching oriental
languages were adopted by the Council of Vienne in 1312, and his plans for a
crusade, together with his reflections on conversion, had some influence in the
milieu of the French court. Here for the rest of the century educated laymen
with some knowledge of the Orient, like the Venetian merchant Marino Sanudo
Torsello or the knight and publicist Philippe de Mézières, tried to fire crusading enthusiasm with intelligence and specific information. Knowledge of non-
Christian cultures was widespread, if limited, in the fourteenth century, and the
discussion of points of doctrine in which the papal curia engaged with various
Armenian prelates between 1320 and 1350 resulted in the work of Richard
Fitzralph, *De Questionibus Armenorum*, which considered several aspects of doctrine outside the framework of the schools. The question of the salvation of
heathen peoples, including those who had lived before the Christian era and
unbaptised infants, was raised by the Oxford theologian John Uthred of
Boldon and had some currency in the later part of the century. By 1415,
although Christian missions in the east had diminished and Islam was in the
ascendant in the Balkans, the intellectual frontier of Christendom had notably
expanded, and awareness of other religious traditions was widespread. The
groundwork for the heroic, if ultimately doomed, attempt to reunite
Christendom at the Council of Florence in 1438–9 had already been laid.

These lines of thought, modifying abstract philosophical speculation, had
been stimulated largely by external circumstance. They were further modified
by events within the Christian west. In 1302 Philip IV of France brought his
quarrel with Boniface VIII to a head with a violent outrage on the pope's
person at Anagni. The drama of the event provoked urgent thought on
the nature of ecclesiastical authority and of the Church as a corporate
body: the theologian John of Paris, who analysed the Church as a community,
and the varying views of the canonists John Monachus and Guillaume Durand

the younger, who applied the same principles to the Roman curia and to the body of bishops, looked to natural law and Aristotle to provide a general solution; and papal apologists such as Augustinus Triumphus of Ancona shared their opponents' approach. But by the 1320s and 1330s, when John XXII's assault on the Franciscan claim to a unique place in the Christian dispensation caused dissident friars to speculate on the problem of an heretical pope, William of Ockham, exiled at the court of Emperor Lewis at Munich, redefined the question as one for the individual conscience of theologians or others in places of responsibility, whose duty it was to question and ultimately to judge public authority. Ockham's perspective was shared by the protagonists of the controversy over the nature of dominion launched by Richard Fitzralph at the curia in 1350: originally fuelled by his objections, as archbishop of Armagh, to the interference of the friars in his clergy's pastoral work, it developed into a critique of their claims to poverty and practice of mendicancy, and then into speculation on the nature of ecclesiastical dominion, in which the thesis was propounded both by Fitzralph and some of his opponents that legitimate dominion depended on its possessor being in a state of grace, and was therefore, for practical purposes, exposed to the subjective judgement of conscience. Proponents of these ideas could be found both at Paris and at the new university of Prague; but their most eloquent advocate was the theologian John Wyclif at Oxford in the 1370s. Originally a supporter of Fitzralph's friar critics, Wyclif took further than his contemporaries the notion of personal conscience and judgement in his great tract *De Civili Dominio* (1375–7); finding the only earthly expression of the eternal ideas inherent in God in the word of scripture, he left its specific meaning to the interior judgement of its readers.

The immediate reaction to Wyclif's opinions on authority, which he extended into a wide-ranging rejection of both ecclesiastical hierarchy and popular religious practices, including the cult of the Eucharist, was hostile. Nevertheless his ideas found favour in varying degrees among numerous Oxford masters and some of the *bien-pensant* opinion of the English court, among whom plans for the disendowment of the Church circulated; a group of his followers executed, in semi-secrecy, an ambitious project of evangelisation which included a scholarly translation of the Bible into English, a body of model English sermons and texts and a campaign of preaching tours designed to bring the authority of bishops and priests into question. Their independent stance was echoed elsewhere in Europe. In Paris, reforming university masters like Pierre d'Ailly, Gerson and Nicholas de Clamanges gave only qualified support to Benedict XIII, the Avignonese claimant to the papacy; in Rome, the papal secretary Dietrich of Niem was even less enthusiastic about the Roman or eventually the Pisan claimants; and in Prague a succession of reformers, culminating in Dr Jan Hus, took up Wyclif's call to action and challenged the authority of the Church. Though the Bohemian schism which followed falls outside the present chapter, the opinions from which it sprang were widespread, and were reinforced by the schism in the papacy and the consequent necessity for a personal judgement on authority. The crisis imposed even on bishops and secular princes who prided themselves on their orthodoxy the obligation to make their own judgement; contemporary canonists such as Antonio de Butrio came to their rescue with the idea of *epieikeia* or necessity obliging private conscience. Public issues, when the Council of Constance opened in 1414, had moved firmly into the arena of the *forum internum* or individual judgement.

The recourse to conscience opened up to those who 'stand in activity by outward form of living' a logic of internal spirituality, a personal path to justification and grace; and by the closing years of the fourteenth century the idea of the spiritual development of the *viator*, the pilgrim through life, had taken sufficient shape to allow for a specific literature of contemplation. The practitioners of the art, themselves often members of religious orders, addressed their work, which was often written in a vernacular language, to nuns, anchoresses or, increasingly, to the laity. In the hands of Meister Eckhart, Catherine of Siena and Walter Hilton the literature of contemplation reached new levels of insight and perception, and taken as a whole remains one of the most original achievements of the fourteenth century.

The art or practice of contemplation did not, of course, originate in this period. Its origin, in the western tradition, lay in the Augustinian idea that the love of God was the basis of understanding, and in its division by the pseudo-Dionysius into purgative, illuminative and unitive phases; germinating in the solitude idealised by monks and anchorites, and taking form from the prayers and meditations of St Anselm, it had reached explicit expression in the monastic school of St Victor in twelfth-century Paris. Hugh of St Victor may well have been the first to give the term its first distinct religious meaning, and seems also to have sketched out the stages by which the pilgrim mounts to God. The idea of a journey of the soul towards God had been elaborated by his successor Richard of St Victor, for whom the love and knowledge of God were ultimately identical and, since he did not distinguish natural understanding from mystical knowledge of God, theology and contemplation were in essence the same. His 'speculative' mysticism was the basis of the intellectual approach taken by the Rhineland mystical writers of the fourteenth century to the contemplative experiences of the nuns and beguines under their direction. A century after Richard, the Franciscan theologian Bonaventure had defined the object of contemplation more specifically, by focusing it on the incarnation and passion of Christ, aspects of his humanity on which

Franciscan devotion turned. By making it a subject of the spiritual direction which the friars were developing, he broadened its appeal beyond the monastic world of the Victorines, and opened it to communities of nuns and anchoresses who were bound by a less formal rule; the purgative, illuminative and unitive stages of contemplation which, following the pseudo-Dionysius, he made its framework, marked out what was beginning to be at once a more widely popular and a more deeply individual way of spiritual progress.

At the same time, perhaps under the influence of the friars, loose religious communities or confraternities, whose distinctive mark was devotion to the life and passion of Christ, were springing up especially in the towns of Italy and the Rhineland. Women were prominent among them, particularly in Germany and the Low Countries, and in many of their surviving utterances the language of secular love poetry is adapted to contemplation: this *brautmystik* or bridal imagery was characteristic of the poetry of the Dutch contemplative Hadewijch of Antwerp, whose note of ecstatic union with God seems to show that her idea of the return of fallen man to his creator by means of love was derived from her own religious experience, though possibly given form, through the friars, by the literary tradition of the Victorines. Guided by spiritual directors though she and her contemporaries probably were, their religious experiences were certainly not mere literary devices in the autobiographical writings, letters and notes which many of them composed, and testify to a widespread and autonomous movement. Occasionally enthusiasm outran the limits of orthodoxy among the loosely controlled communities of beguines, beghards or flagellants, and antinomian tendencies emerged from time to time in groups like the Brethren of the Free Spirit in Germany or the Fraticelli in Italy. In one expression of such emancipation from the pursuit of virtue, *The Mirror of Simple Souls* evidently written by Marguerite Porète of Valenciennes, who was burned in 1310, contemplation replaced the moral life altogether. More frequently, however, the influence of friar directors like Henry of Halle OP, the adviser of the contemplative Mechtilde of Magdeburg, was strong enough to maintain the link between the teaching of the schools and spirituality. Though the religious experience of the contemplatives was authentic, it was increasingly expressed through theological concepts, and sometimes in the very words of their confessors or directors.

One of these spiritual directors, who clearly shared in the contemplative life and experience of his flock, was the Dominican friar Meister Eckhart (d. 1327), the leading figure of the Rhineland school of spirituality. Eckhart belonged by training and vocation to the small elite of theologians educated at Paris who carried their Thomist interpretation of religious truth into the heartland of Germany in sermons, guides to the spiritual life and commentaries on scripture. Much of his work, like that of his Dominican or Franciscan contemporaries engaged in pastoral activity, was uncontroversial. But he went further: he perfected an intellectualist and indeed metaphysical interpretation of the *wesen-mystik* or notion of contemplative union with God, which owed something to Aquinas, and more perhaps to the Neoplatonist inspiration of the Jewish and Arabic philosophers whose works were known in the universities of the west. The germ of this idea had already been expressed, though not in philosophical language, by Hadewijch of Antwerp. It was now given a speculative gloss at the hands of a theologian, and taught to Dominican nuns, and possibly to the laity, in sermons and treatises. Eckhart took the earlier notion of purgation or spiritual stripping away on to a metaphysical plane, seeing creatures as nothingness, seeking their very being from their return to and participation in God. Putting aside all created things, the 'ground' of the soul emerges as an uncreated being, part of God himself where the divine life can take root in a human individual. For Eckhart, the path of contemplation thus transcends the moral and sacramental life, transforming its pilgrim into the 'noble' man, one with the Godhead. Eckhart's spiritual direction therefore took the *wesenmystik* further than ever before, making it a coherent process of spiritual growth, and giving it a solid theological explanation in more or less Thomist terms. At his hands contemplation became a distinct art, independent of the life of prayer and moral progress for which the religious vocation had come to be formed.

In the atmosphere of controversy in which the friars moved during Eckhart's later years, it was inevitable that his teaching should come under suspicion of antinomian and pantheistic tendencies. He was forced to explain and defend his position, and died at Avignon before he could clear his name; some though not all senses in which his doctrine could be understood were condemned in 1329, though Eckhart himself was spared. One feature of his writings which probably intensified opposition was their vernacular language: in spite of the subtlety of his doctrine, his sermons and some expositions were written in German – almost the first abstractions to appear in that language – for the Dominican nuns under his direction, and were therefore open to the use and abuse of the laity. His brethren continued the spiritual direction of Dominican nuns and other communities of women, giving rise to a Rhineland 'school' of speculative mysticism; younger colleagues of Eckhart, the preacher Johann Tauler, Henry Suso and Henry of Nördlingen influenced other teachers outside the order, like the Flemish Augustinian canon Jan Ruysbroeck, the anonymous Teutonic knight who wrote the *Theologia deutsch*, and the 'Friend of God of the Oberland', who may have been the Strasburg visionary Rulman Merswin. They were the confessors and guides of a growing company of largely female disciples, many of whom described visions and revelations or wrote mystical poetry: the Dominican convents at Colmar and Töss, the Johannites of Isle-Verte near Strasburg, and the Augustinians of Groenendael in Brabant were active centres of Eckhart's art of contemplation. Perhaps the most perceptive mentor of these communities was Eckhart's younger confrère Henry Suso (d. 1366), whose life of ascetic contemplation and spiritual counselling, largely at Ulm, became a model for many of them, and whose writings, which presented the *wesenmystik* without the excesses attributed to Eckhart, were very widely read. In his *Horologium Sapientiae*, of which there is also a German version, he combined the determined introspection of the Rhineland school with the simple and universally popular devotion to the Virgin and to the Passion of Christ, which looks forward to the *devotio moderna*. Suso recognised the individuality and variety of religious experience and the growing body of practical literature on the subject; and he was perhaps the first to state explicitly that the stony path of contemplation was open to all.

It was certainly open to non-religious who did not wish to live in organised communities with a rule: to Catherine of Siena, for instance, who about 1367 chose to live in the world as a Dominican tertiary among a various body of disciples and associates, though she evidently had the services of Raymond of Capua OP as her spiritual director. Both his account of her, the *Leggenda Maiora*, and some of her own writings survive; among the latter, which includes a large collection of her letters and some prayers, her *Dialogo* of 1377–8 was particularly widely read and often translated. The absence of speculative language in her works may not especially distinguish her from her German and Dutch contemporaries, since the works of nuns such as Margaret Ebner and Suso's biographer Elizabeth Stägel are equally free from it: speculative mysticism was the province of their mentors, theologians like Suso himself and Eckhart. In fact Catherine's theme of the soul's ascent from sin through various grades of discernment and love to eventual union with God, and the identification of God with what is and the sinner with nothingness are stressed in the *Dialogo*, the fruit perhaps of her Dominican instruction. What was more particularly her own was her assertiveness and confident association of her individual vision of God with the need to reform the evils of the world: like John Wyclif, her contemporary, she identified these evils with the failure of the clergy to give a moral lead, and more specifically with the absence of the papal court from Rome. Interior spirituality or 'self-knowledge' must be associated with the apostolate of the Church, and with a reformed and ordered public religion, a theme taken up in the fifteenth century. For Catherine, the recall of lost sheep to conformity with God's will was a work of charity, by which the genuine life of contemplation would be known.

Catherine of Siena combined humility with the authority of holiness, an authority which seems to have been respected even by Gregory XI when she admonished him for residing at Avignon. It was one sign of the diffusion of spiritual leadership in the course of the century; in parallel with and in some ways as the result of the proliferation of theological learning, the spread of knowledge of the art of contemplation at the hands of the friars allowed local spiritual counsellors to emerge, to influence a restricted clientele or even, in time and through their disciples or writings, a larger body of devotees. One such was Rulman Merswin (d. 1381), the Strasburg banker whose community at Isle-Verte had some influence on the upper Rhine; another was Gerard Groote. The most influential, however was the English hermit Richard Rolle (d. 1349), whose followers and writings gradually made him known, first in his native Yorkshire and then throughout England and even beyond. Though Rolle was evidently at Oxford about 1320 and must have had some exposure to the teaching of theologians, he had no obvious spiritual mentor, and looked back to the monastic precedents of the twelfth century. Like the German nuns of his own time, he described, in Latin and English, his own experiences; using the physical analogues of heat, sweetness and harmony and the popular language of love, he tried to convey the essence of an early spiritual crisis when he 'knew the infusion and understanding of heavenly, spiritual sounds, sounds which pertain to the song of eternal praise, and to the sweetness of unheard melody'.[10] Rolle set up his hermitage near Pickering and then at Hampole; gradually, and not without opposition, he managed to diffuse his concept of the contemplative life, through personal contacts, sermons and guides like his *Form of Living*, among his neighbours. His work bore fruit: besides disciples like the recluse Margaret Kirkby and the nuns of Hampole, after his death the burgeoning Carthusian houses of northern England took up and proliferated his works, and the circle of clerics round Thomas Arundel, archbishop of York (1388–96), used them as a part of pastoral instruction to instil a habit of domestic devotion among the laity. This was in accord with the direction taken by Gerard Groote and Catherine of Siena, from the intense speculative mysticism offered by Eckhart and the German Dominicans to nuns enclosed and under a religious rule, to experiences which were less intellectual and more direct, which might be achieved not only in corporate or solitary enclosure but in the world, by the interior detachment of active laymen in what Walter Hilton called the 'mixed life'.

The two English spiritual writers who developed the theme of a contemplative life in the world, Hilton and the anonymous author of the *Cloud of Unknowing*, were writing north of the Trent in the last two decades of the fourteenth century, and evidently knew and influenced each other. Writing in the wake of Richard Rolle, they aimed to correct the excesses of his physical,

---

[10] 'Flagrante autem sensibiliter calore illo inestimibiliter suavi usque ad infusionem et percepcionem soni celestis vel spiritualis, qui ad canticum pertinet laudis aeterne et suavitatem invisibilis melodie.' Rolle, *Incendium Amoris*, p. 189, trans. Wolters (1972), p. 93.

rather unrestrained language, and to bring the practice of contemplation into the sphere of approved devotional exercises. Both of them wrote their principal works in English for disciples under religious vows, and Hilton also counselled educated friends in Latin. The author of *The Cloud*, who was perhaps a Carthusian of Beauvale, learnt from the pseudo-Dionysius and the Victorines the idea, congenial to fourteenth-century theologians like Bradwardine and Gregory of Rimini, of the absolute incomprehensibility of God; and developed further than his predecessors the concept of the soul's progress through the darkness of unknowing, the emptying of the mind of sense. Unlike Eckhart, but like Richard Rolle, he saw the contemplative life as a process of the will culminating in the love of God, rather than an intellectual progression. Walter Hilton (d. 1396) was a Cambridge canon lawyer who abandoned his secular life to enter the Augustinian house of canons at Thurgarton in Nottinghamshire, after a brief and unsatisfactory experiment with solitude. Perhaps for this reason he went further than his contemporaries in defining the tasks of the active and the contemplative life; he conceived both, like his contemporary Coluccio Salutati, in positive terms, advising one friend, John Thorpe, to live virtuously in the world, and another, Adam Horsley, to become a Carthusian monk. His *Scale of Perfection* was written for an anchoress, though its precepts were more widely relevant. Like his predecessors, he distinguished three grades of contemplation, all of them characterised as forms of burning love, though he attributed a special understanding to the highest grade; but he rejected the idea that it removed the contemplative from the moral sphere or from religious obligations. In principle contemplation and the struggle of the ordinary Christian against sin were the same, and in various forms the contemplative life was open to all.

Hilton, like Catherine of Siena and other spiritual writers of the later fourteenth century, extended the concept of the contemplative life from a special vocation for individuals living under a rule to encompass, albeit less completely, the life of the laity. Their precepts were probably most influential among recluses; though Julian of Norwich had evidently not read Hilton's works or the *Cloud* when she wrote her *Book of Showings or Revelations* about 1393, it is their equal in penetration and learning, and she was probably formed by similar counsellors; she in turn through her unrivalled clarity and simplicity of expression powerfully influenced others in a wider devotional world. Religious orders dedicated to the contemplative life flourished, particularly the Carthusian communities, whose numbers multiplied considerably in the course of the century, the Celestines and a few houses of nuns and priests of the new Brigittine Order, founded by the Swedish recluse and visionary St Brigit (d. 1373). One of the primary activities of these houses came to be the copying and dissemination of contemplative literature, often in the vernacular, for lay devotion, and it is largely due to them that so many copies exist of the works of Suso, Catherine of Siena, and other spiritual authors.

It was equally one of the tasks undertaken by the loosely organised followers of Gerard Groote in the Low Countries, who were sometimes known as the Brethren of the Common Life; they too embraced the less exalted, intense and speculative form of contemplation, or *devotio moderna*, which in a general sense was characteristic of Catherine of Siena or Julian of Norwich. The first brethren grouped round Gerard Groote owed something to the example and spirituality of Ruysbroeck at Groenendael; but Ruysbroeck's *De gheestelijke brulocht*, spiritual espousals, developed a personal form of speculative mysticism in the tradition of Eckhart which failed to influence them. For them, as for Groote, contemplation was the perfection of charity, a state of mind from which pastoral work, especially preaching and spiritual counsel, stemmed. After Groote's death in 1384, his disciple Florent Radewijns founded a house of canons at Windesheim which served as a focus for the communities of brethren, and eventually, either in itself or through its many daughter houses, came to be identified with them. The greatest work of fifteenth-century spirituality, Thomas à Kempis's *Imitation of Christ*, was written at the daughter house of Zwolle.

Ruysbroeck's work with its occasionally pantheistic phrases was sharply criticised by a theologian whose spiritual counsel nevertheless was akin to, if more intellectual than, the *devotio moderna*: Jean Gerson (d. 1429). It was a sign of the maturity of the genre that Gerson, chancellor of the university of Paris and heir of its long engagement with theological questions, should have read the principal contributions made to spiritual writing during the century, and have added to it himself repeatedly in his long literary career. The main body of his work was in the pastoral field, to which he brought not only the insights of a theologian but the perspective of a leading churchman and, above all, the psychological understanding of a confessor and preacher; and as a pastor, he firmly placed the starting-point of the mystical way in humble penitence, declaring, in his French tract of 1400 for lay use, *The Mountain of Contemplation*, that it was open to any believer. Moreover he meant what he said, pouring out a stream of homely images to express a sophisticated mystical theology: to pray should be like a beggar going cap in hand to the Virgin, to the saints, to Christ; the relation of love and knowledge in contemplation is like that of honey to the honeycomb which gives it form; the love of the world is a cage which the bird only sees when he tries to fly away; knowledge by negation, which the soul must acquire, is like watching a sculptor create a beautiful image by chiselling material away. This last Dionysian image indicates his return to the ultimate source of contemplative thought; at his death he was working on a commentary on the mystical theology of the pseudo-Dionysius.

Gerson's reflections on the work of his predecessors indicate his scholarly sense of the achievements of the past. Indeed he may be seen as the beneficiary of both the intellectual and the spiritual inheritance of the fourteenth century: as a pastor and writer on penitence he carried the programme set out at the Fourth Lateran Council and initiated by the friars beyond the pulpit, beyond the sphere of public morality into the realm of inner spiritual life, encouraging his contemporaries in self-knowledge, prayer and hope. He was therefore able to formulate, for the French clergy and court and eventually, through the Council of Constance, for a wider body of believers, a public religion which accommodated the conscience and devotions of the laity within an ordered, authoritative but responsive Church. His theology brought the great religious issues of the fourteenth-century schools, grace, predestination and human merit, to bear on the salvation of souls and the call of individual conscience, and thus united theological and spiritual precepts in a coherent body of ideas on the cure of souls, on which his practical advice ranged from episcopal visitation to the schooling of children. In this, though much of his thought touched on issues such as justification and Church order which would become acute in the sixteenth century, he was a child of his time. In the course of the fourteenth century, the formidable and now highly professionalised bodies of theological thinking, canon law and systematic spirituality made room for lay religious aspirations and for the lay conscience. Gerson, though a pioneer in this process, was only one of a host of figures, lay and clerical, whose personal religion and private conscience created the new religious landscape of the fifteenth century.

CHAPTER 4

THE UNIVERSITIES

Jacques Verger

THE UNIVERSITY NETWORK

ALTHOUGH there were still relatively few universities in western Europe in the fourteenth century, they occupied an unchallenged and powerful position in the development and diffusion of learning. The major centres of the university network remained the oldest universities, which had been founded at the beginning of the thirteenth century at Bologna, Paris and Oxford. Their prestige was unrivalled, and they attracted the largest numbers of students. They were both bench-marks for teaching standards and models for the institutional framework of newer foundations.

A dozen other universities appeared in the course of the thirteenth century, but their influence was much smaller. Although some, such as Cambridge or the faculty of medicine at Montpellier, were almost as old as those already mentioned, others were more recent foundations, dating above all from the 1250s and 1260s, amongst them Padua in Italy, Toulouse in France and Salamanca in Spain. Others (such as Lisbon, Lérida and the law faculty at Montpellier) dated from the very last years of the thirteenth century, and heralded the new foundations of the fourteenth.

These testified to the success of the university, which was an established institution from this date onwards. Nevertheless, the rate of foundation remained modest. In some cases, this was simply done by papal confirmation of the status of *studium generale* in schools which had already operated on a university level for varying periods of time: this happened, for example, to the law school at Orléans (1306), whose privileges were extended to those at Angers in 1364, as well as for the *studium* of Valladolid (1346) in Castile. Elsewhere, there were genuinely new foundations. Here, civil or ecclesiastical initiative was almost always crucial; henceforth, this increasingly replaced regroupings by university masters and their students in the quest for communal autonomy. Success was variable. In some places, above all where there were already schools of some importance, the *studium generale* developed, although at different speeds. But elsewhere, notably when the ruler arbitrarily insisted upon a site where there was no scholarly tradition, the planned university either never saw the light of day or collapsed rapidly.

These new foundations continued, especially in southern Europe, until the beginning of the Great Schism (1378). In Italy, the universities of Rome (the *studium Urbis*, distinct from the *studium Curiae*, 1303), Perugia (1308), Pisa (1343), Florence (1349) and Pavia (1361) were established by papal bull confirming initiatives taken by municipal authorities or (at Pavia) by the duke of Milan. But there were also a large number of unsuccessful attempts to transform urban schools for the study of grammar and law into *studia generalia* by means of a papal or an imperial bull. This was the case at Treviso (1318), Verona (1339), Cividale del Friuli (1353), Arezzo (1355), Siena (1357), Lucca (1369) and Orvieto (1378). Similarly, although the long-established schools of medicine at Salerno remained active, it proved impossible to transform them into a true university in the course of the Middle Ages. In southern France, the university of Avignon emerged as a result of the combined efforts of the count of Provence and the pope (1303). In 1332, the consuls of Cahors obtained permission from their compatriot, Pope John XXII, to found a small university in his native town. On a still smaller scale was the foundation of the university of Orange by the Emperor Charles IV in 1365, at the behest of both town and ruler. As for the university set up in Grenoble in 1339 at the request of the dauphin, it disappeared after a few years. Finally, in the Iberian peninsula, when there were disturbances at the Portuguese university of Lisbon, it was temporarily transferred to Coimbra (1308–39 and 1355–77). The kings of Aragon (who had already established the university of Lérida in the county of Catalonia in 1300) founded small universities in the two other parts of their kingdom, Roussillon and Aragon, at Perpignan (1350) and Huesca (1354).

All these universities were founded in areas where Roman law prevailed, and they were chiefly concerned with the study of law. Their statutes were based on those of Bologna, modified according to local context. University foundations in northern and central Europe were much less common before 1378. The reasons for this delay are undoubtedly to be sought in the relative social and political archaism of these regions and the slow development of towns. Of course there had been German, Polish and Hungarian students since the thirteenth century, but they all went to study at Paris and Bologna. These individuals were often wealthy nobles, who had no particular interest in encouraging native universities in their own lands, which would greatly have improved access to university education. Nevertheless, in 1347–8, Emperor Charles IV, a ruler with a passionate interest in French culture, decided to create, with the help of the pope, an entirely new university at Prague, comprising eleven

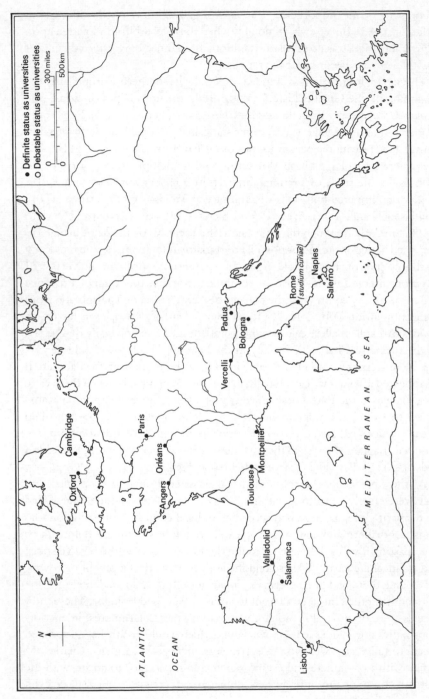

Map 1 Universities active in 1300

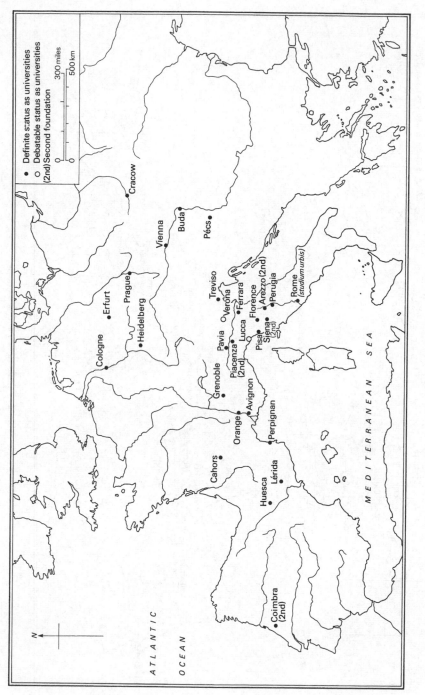

Map 2   University foundations, 1300–1400

Definite status as universities

Debatable status as universities

(2nd) Second foundation

300 miles

500 km

Cracow

Vienna

Buda

Pécs

Erfurt

Prague

Heidelberg

Cologne

Treviso

Verona

Ferrara

Arezzo (2nd)

Florence

Perugia

Rome
(studium urbis)

Pavia

Lucca

Pisa

Siena
(2nd)

Piacenza
(2nd)

Grenoble

Avignon

Orange

Perpignan

Cahors

Lérida

Huesca

Coimbra
(2nd)

ATLANTIC

OCEAN

MEDITERRANEAN   SEA

N

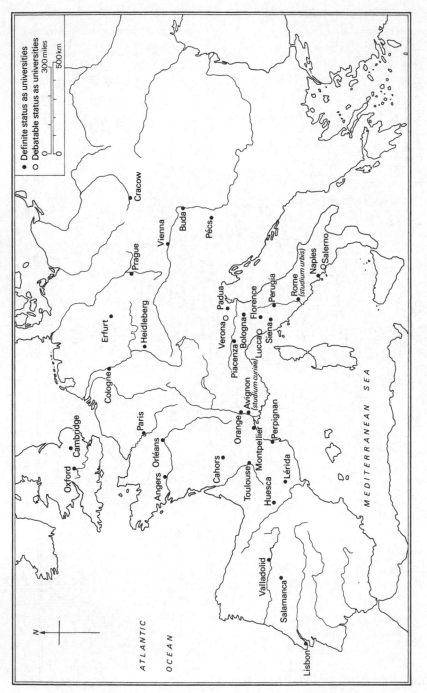

ATLANTIC

OCEAN

N

Oxford
Cambridge
Paris
Angers
Orléans
Cahors
Toulouse
Huesca
Montpellier
Perpignan
Lérida
Valladolid
Salamanca
Lisbon

Cologne
Heidleberg
Erfurt
Prague
Orange
Avignon *(studium curiae)*
Verona
Piacenza
Padua
Bologna
Lucca
Florence
Siena
Perugia
Rome *(studium urbis)*
Naples
Salerno

Vienna
Buda
Pécs
Cracow

MEDITERRANEAN SEA

Map 3   Universities active in 1400

faculties on the Paris model; the first decades were fairly difficult, however. Still more arduous were the attempts of neighbouring rulers, who wanted to imitate Charles IV. In 1365, Duke Rudolf IV of Habsburg founded a university at Vienna, but it languished totally until the 1380s. The universities of Cracow (1364) and Pest (1367) founded by the kings of Poland and Hungary were even less successful and disappeared very quickly, casualties partly of unfavourable circumstances and partly of the absence of continued royal support.

This all changed after 1378, as a result of the Schism. While the university of Paris remained loyal to the pope at Avignon, the German towns and princes, together with the sovereigns of central Europe, declared their support for the pope at Rome. The crisis of the Schism reinforced the sense of national identity in these relatively young states; it made their rulers still more determined to control the training of their clergy and officials and to provide it in their own lands. The masters of the Anglo-German 'nation' were in a difficult position at Paris, and they listened readily to the appeals of their fellow-countrymen. It was to a considerable extent thanks to these men that the universities of Prague and Vienna were reinvigorated (with the arrival in 1383 of the famous Parisian theologian, Henry of Langenstein) and those of Erfurt (1379–89), Heidelberg (1385) and Cologne (1388) were founded. Although the new Hungarian university foundation at Buda in 1389 was little more successful than the previous one, the reopening of Cracow university (1397–1400) as a result of the initiative of King (Jogaila) Ladislas Jagellon, saw the dawn of what was to become one of the principal centres of European culture in central Europe in the fifteenth and sixteenth centuries. All these new universities in northern Europe modelled themselves more or less on Paris, where many of their first masters had been trained; they adopted both the institutional framework of the university at Paris (with its rector, faculties and four 'nations') and its intellectual focus, teaching above all the liberal arts and theology. In southern Europe, by contrast, foundations ceased. The only exception is the foundation of the new university of Ferrara in 1391, for which the marquis of Este obtained a papal bull from Rome; but it was not really active until after 1430.

No picture of the universities of western Europe in the fourteenth century would be complete without some mention of the expansion of some old foundations by the addition of new faculties, in particular faculties of theology. The papacy was very vigilant on this point. Originally, its policy had been to impose a strict limit on the number of faculties of theology entitled to bestow the prestigious title of 'doctor of sacred theology' (*doctor in sacra pagina*), restricting this to a few centres of excellence, whose influence was incontestable and orthodoxy guaranteed. In practice, since Cambridge was still a minor university, this meant that Oxford (whose students came almost entirely from within the British Isles) and, above all, Paris had a monopoly of theological teaching at the highest level, although it was understood that the pope always retained the right to grant doctorates by papal bull, either directly or by means of the *studium Curiae*.

The situation changed in the mid-fourteenth century. Paris and Oxford were torn apart by quarrels over doctrine which weakened their claims to a monopoly. There was a whole range of local and national pressures for universities to be complete in themselves, each with the full range of faculties. The papacy thus adopted a new policy, whereby theological teaching was not concentrated in particular centres. Prague had had a theological faculty since its inception. After 1360, such faculties proliferated, especially in southern universities, where there was admittedly a general readiness to elevate local, mendicant *studia* to the status of university faculty with the right to grant degrees. The popes thus established a theology faculty at Toulouse and at Bologna from 1360 onwards, at Padua in 1363, Pavia in 1369, Salamanca in 1396 and Lisbon in 1400. During the Schism, the pope at Rome, who had no reason to have anything to do with Paris, followed a similar line in the new German universities (Vienna, Heidelberg, Cologne, Erfurt) and at Cracow; the first regents were often masters trained in a secular discipline at Paris.

Finally, we need to remember that the network of the *studia generalia* only represented the upper level of a whole range of educational institutions which probably expanded in the course of the fourteenth century. This is not the place to discuss domestic and professional apprenticeship, undoubtedly the most common form of education at the period. Nor can we examine the private tutoring found amongst the aristocracy and some *bourgeois* families. But there were undoubtedly also schools that were not universities. In towns and even certain rural settlements, small grammar schools, financed privately or by the municipality, taught the rudiments of education to children and adolescents. Of course there were also parish schools and others endowed by religious foundations. Cathedrals and some collegiate foundations still had active chapter schools, indeed some were boarding schools. In some cases, the level was comparable with that of some faculties of arts. Still closer to the university model were the innumerable *studia* (of the arts, philosophy, biblical studies and theology) run by the orders of friars for the use of their own members throughout Christendom.

These institutions – as yet relatively little studied, except schools in England – will not be examined in detail in this chapter. We know little about their organisation, the origins of their masters (some were master of arts), the numbers of students or the content of their teaching. Nevertheless, it is very likely that all these institutions, and in particular the urban schools, became more numerous in the course of the fourteenth century. Such schools provided future university students (notably future civil lawyers who frequently went straight to a faculty of law without any training in an arts faculty) with an essential foundation in Latin and logic. Even for those who did not go on to further education, they at least transmitted – in simplified form – some echo of the scholarly education developed in the universities. In short, the trend towards new university foundations in the fourteenth century seems to have been sustained by a generally increased demand for education in a much broader context.

INSTITUTIONAL STABILISATION

The university was a stable institution in the fourteenth century, fully recognised by the different actors on the political and social stage and accepted as an integral part of the mechanisms of law and government. University autonomy had sometimes been the focus of great conflict in the thirteenth century, but after that it was not challenged. The foundation documents (*Habita* of 1158, *Parens scientarum* of 1231) to which everyone referred were amplified in each university by a multitude of privileges and confirmations issued by the ruler or by the pope, who controlled the actual working of the scholarly community (*libertas scholastica*). Fiscal exemption and judicial immunity, independent organisation of teaching and examinations, internal control of doctrinal orthodoxy, control of the production and sale of university books were rights that had gradually been acquired or formally granted everywhere.

Naturally, there was no reduction in the tensions between the student population – a mass of young, turbulent foreigners – and the inhabitants and authorities of university towns, who quickly lost patience with their lawlessness and arrogance. Spectacular conflicts between 'town and gown' punctuated the history of fourteenth-century universities with brawls, murders, expulsion and voluntary exile. At Bologna in 1321, Toulouse in 1332, Oxford in 1355, Orléans in 1382 and 1387, the scenario was always identical: a chance brawl, speedy intervention by the local authorities under pressure from the population at large, a response from the university supportive of the students and characterised by a strike or 'secession', with order finally restored through the intervention of higher authorities, largely sympathetic to the universities. As a result, not only was there no further challenge to university autonomy, but the privileges of masters and students were generally confirmed and strengthened by such incidents. At Oxford, they ended by exercising a kind of tutelage over the town.

There was also very considerable economic support for the universities from secular and ecclesiastical institutions in the fourteenth century. This not only facilitated the development of the universities but also affected the way in which their members lived, and it raised their social status. As a result of the ever-increasing number of papal reservations and provisions, the papacy had a constantly growing number of ecclesiastical benefices at its disposal and distributed them with tireless generosity to masters and students, accompanied by dispensations from residence. Income from such benefices was a regular source of subsistence for many. Towns and rulers also sometimes made contributions towards the living expenses of some students, but most importantly they began to assume responsibility for the salaries of teachers. The earliest examples go back to the thirteenth century but, generally, masters who did not have access to ecclesiastical revenues at this period were subject to the hazards of student fees (*collectae*). The earliest recorded instance of a salary paid by a municipal authority to a teacher of law comes from Bologna in 1279. This system became widespread after 1320, when it became standard practice in all Italian universities, as well as in the Iberian peninsula. In the latter case, teaching salaries were assigned on the ecclesiastical revenues (*tercias*) traditionally granted to the king. At Paris and Oxford, on the other hand, where the clerical character of the university remained much more distinct, the regents continued to live from the revenues of ecclesiastical benefices. In any case, the increasingly high level of fees (*collectae*) and examination dues paid by students, often matched by private legal and medical consultations, remained important sources of additional revenue everywhere.

The generosity of authorities and eminent individuals towards the universities was displayed even more through the foundation of colleges in the fourteenth century. This, too, was a phenomenon which had first appeared in the thirteenth century, but was fully developed in the next. The first colleges were small religious foundations designed to lodge a few poor students and the earliest date from before 1200, but establishments of some importance appeared after 1250, such as those at Paris (Sorbonne, 1257), Oxford (Merton, 1264; University College, 1280; Balliol, 1282) and Cambridge (Peterhouse, 1284). These were not only lodgings but also (as a result of the careful recruitment of fellows (*socii*), the presence of a library and a teaching organisation that complemented that of the faculties) real centres of intellectual life. The phenomenon expanded enormously in the fourteenth century: thirty-seven colleges, many of them tiny, were founded at Paris; five and seven were founded at Oxford and Cambridge respectively, but they were considerably more substantial. The institution even won acceptance in southern universities, with seven colleges founded in Toulouse in the fourteenth century, four at Montpellier and four at Bologna, including the prestigious Spanish College (1367).

College founders were sometimes high-ranking ecclesiastics (pope, cardinals, bishops, canons of chapters), sometimes rulers (witness the College of Navarre founded by the queen of France at Paris in 1304, King's Hall at

Cambridge, The Queen's College in Oxford) and sometimes important royal officials. Merchants and citizens showed much less interest in these institutions, which were of very little use to their cultural and religious preoccupations, and did not serve their political aims.

Although the social position of the universities was strengthened in the fourteenth century, there was no change in their essential structures. The two main institutional types which had appeared in the thirteenth century – the Parisian 'university of masters' and the 'university of students' of Bologna – remained classic models for reference, with all their essential cogs (chancellors, rectors, faculties, 'nations'). Nevertheless, the fourteenth century was the great period of university statutes. The crystallisation of university institutions meant that henceforth detailed statutes could be drawn up, and they were much more specific than the general privileges or circumstantial texts of the thirteenth century. Statutes of this kind were promulgated at Toulouse in 1311–14, at Oxford and Bologna in 1317, at Padua in 1331, Montpellier in 1339–40, Paris in 1366; Salamanca apparently had to wait until 1411. As for new universities, they had a complete corpus of statutes from the very outset, drawn from those of an older university (Toulouse was a model for Cahors) or, more frequently, combining features from both Paris and Bologna.

There were also few innovations in the range of subjects studied, or in the teaching programmes and the methods employed. The list of 'authorities' (Aristotle, the *Sentences* and so on) remained virtually immutable, while lecture and disputation remained the two essential forms of both teaching and examination. Should we infer from this relative lack of development in both teaching and institutional structures that the universities were already starting to ossify in the fourteenth century? This complex question requires a careful reply.

The most important universities, those which attracted the great majority of students and the most remarkable teachers (Paris and Oxford for philosophy and theology; Bologna for law, but facing increasing competition from Padua, Perugia, Pisa and Pavia; Montpellier, Bologna and Padua for medicine), seem to have been characterised by remarkable intellectual energies in the fourteenth century. The two previous chapters in this volume give some indication of the great numbers of new doctrines and texts which were developed in a university setting at this period. The lively debates to which they gave rise show that intellectual passion and – despite a few instances of official condemnations – considerable freedom of discussion continued to be the rule in faculties of arts and theology.

Without repeating what has already been said, we need to remember that criticism of Thomist and Aristotelian thought was the central point of all philosophical and theological debate in the fourteenth century. This criticism was essentially Augustinian in origin and took very diverse forms. The product of theologians (such as Duns Scotus or Ockham) who were either Franciscans or secular clergy, it aimed to eliminate all determinist tendencies, simultaneously acknowledging both divine omnipotence and man's agonising freedom of choice: grace and free will, predestination and salvation became the key themes of Christian anthropology and were to remain so for a long time.

This challenge to the syntheses of the thirteenth century undoubtedly enabled, at least indirectly, the expansion of truly philosophical and even scientific disciplines, such as those which appeared at Oxford with the Merton 'calculators' and the brilliant logicians of the first half of the century (Walter Burley, Robert Kilvington, Richard Swineshead) and slightly later at Paris, with Jean Buridan and Nicolas d'Oresme, commentators on Aristotle's *Physics*.

The teaching of law in the first decades of the fourteenth century was equally dazzling. The 'glossators' were succeeded by the 'commentators'. Mastering all the resources of dialectic, these writers combined a synthetic and rational concept of law with a stronger desire to express the intangible teachings of the *ius commune* on the concrete realities of contemporary cities and states. In civil law, Cino da Pistoia (*c.* 1270–1336), Bartolus da Sassoferrato (1314–57) and Baldo degli Ubaldi (1327–1400), who taught at Bologna, Siena, Perugia, Pisa, Pavia, Naples and Florence; for canon law Giovanni Andrea (*c.* 1270–1348), founder of a veritable professorial dynasty at Bologna – these men all represent the zenith of medieval law which was reached at this period. Although they were less renowned, the French schools made famous by both the professors at Orléans and the doctors of Toulouse (*doctores Tholosani*) also produced a substantial body of works whose inspiration was close to that of the great Italians.

Finally, this period was the golden age of the medieval faculties of medicine, both at Padua and Bologna (where human dissection appeared under Mondino dei Liuzzi (1276–1328)), and at Montpellier. The medical faculty here saw distinguished doctors such as Arnau de Vilanova (*c.* 1240–1311), whose return to Galenism reflected a desire to create an essentially rational medical discipline, but which did not, nevertheless, lose sight of its therapeutic purpose. Guy de Chauliac (*c.* 1300–68), the famous author of *La grande chirurgie*, was another member of the Montpellier faculty of medicine.

These brief outlines are sufficient to demonstrate that the intellectual creativity of the great universities was in no way diminished in the fourteenth century. Moreover, it is important to emphasise that these new doctrines were generally in profound agreement with the social and mental expectations of the period in a wide range of disciplines (preaching, political science, etc). They brought their authors great rewards. Bradwardine (one of the great Oxford 'calculators') became archbishop of Canterbury, Emperor Charles IV made Bartolus da Sassoferrato his councillor and gave him permission to add the imperial arms to his own coat. Oresme worked closely with Charles V of France, while Guy de Chauliac was doctor to three popes. On a broader scale, it could be said that the innovatory value of university teaching was clearly discerned by contemporaries and undoubtedly contributed to the success and the social advancement of university studies and those who had pursued them.

However, this intellectual brilliance should not be allowed to conceal darker aspects. Everywhere, there were also uninspired teachers who followed traditional doctrinal teaching. These sometimes even became official doctrines, such as Thomism with the Dominicans after 1309, or Scotism (admittedly susceptible to various interpretations) amongst the Franciscans. Prudence led other regents to a simple eclecticism.

On the other hand, the successes just mentioned took place above all in the oldest and most important universities. In the less important universities, in particular new foundations, there was only a distant echo of these great debates, partly because of the influence of largely local recruitment. Less distinguished teachers and students concerned above all to obtain the degrees which were essential for a successful career were easily satisfied with an unimaginative and undemanding curriculum. At the most, we can assume that the prescribed courses were still fairly well respected in the fourteenth century and that, as a result, graduate competence corresponded by and large to the criteria laid down in the statutes.

This relatively optimistic overall picture of the education disseminated by the universities of the period should, nevertheless, not obscure the fact that they were unable to free themselves from the limits and constraints inherited from previous centuries. These limits operated especially in relation to the stress placed on authorities, the scholastic method and the narrow framework of traditional systems of classification in academic disciplines, as well as the social prejudices of the students (*scolares*). There is consequently as much reason in the fourteenth as in the thirteenth century to deplore the stifling of biblical exegesis by the primacy of speculative theology, the marginalisation of sciences proper, the continued exclusion of technology, history, the classics, vernacular literature and oriental languages (despite the canon *Inter Sollicitudines* of the Council of Vienne, 1312), as well as customary law. It is true that direct criticism of the university system was still rare, despite the reservations of the earliest humanists (Petrarch) and the disappointment sometimes expressed by mystics from Master Eckhart to Gerard Groote. But no one risked a radical challenge to an institution whose intellectual fertility seemed far from exhausted and whose social and political importance was more evident than ever before.

UNIVERSITY AND SOCIETY

It is difficult to be exact about the composition of student populations in the west in the fourteenth century. It has nevertheless been possible to assess the size of particular universities. From around 1300, Bologna had well over 2,000 students. Elsewhere, there have been estimates above all for the end of the century, when source material becomes somewhat richer (with the earliest matriculation registers and rolls of papal petitions). The Black Death of 1348 and the epidemics that followed do not seem to have resulted in any lasting reduction in numbers, because the social need was so strong. Around 1380–1400, there were as many as 4,000 students at Paris (three-quarters of them in the faculty of arts), with 1,500 at Oxford, and well over 1,000 at Prague, Toulouse and Avignon (the last largely because of the presence of the papacy). But elsewhere, numbers dropped to well below this figure: 500–700 is probably a reasonable estimate for the universities of Cambridge, Montpellier, Angers and Orléans. And the *studia generalia* which were still smaller (for example, Cahors in France) had to be content with a few dozen students.

We know just as little about the composition of these groups of students. This was self-evidently a mobile population. Geographical mobility should not be overestimated, however. The major currents were those which brought students from the German lands and central Europe to Italy on the one hand (Bologna, Padua) and to Paris on the other. With much lower numbers, the medical university at Montpellier seems to have had a very wide area of recruitment. But elsewhere student mobility rarely went beyond national boundaries. The influence of Oxford and Cambridge extended essentially over the British Isles, that of Salamanca and Valladolid in Castile; Lisbon and Coimbra in Portugal. Italian students virtually never crossed the Alps, and the universities of southern France drew their students principally from the south of the kingdom and from neighbouring Catalonia and Aragon, where the national universities (Lérida, Huesca, Perpignan) remained very small.

Social mobility is still more difficult to define. Noble students (mainly from the lower and middle nobility) are the best-documented group, but their percentage varied considerably. There were not many of them (fewer than 5 per cent) in Mediterranean regions where they were in competition with the urban patriciate, nor in the famous arts faculties of Paris and Oxford, which seem to have had a significant intake with rural and relatively lowly origins. On the other hand, it seems that they represented up to 20 per cent of the students from the empire who were prepared to travel to France or Italy to study; the German 'nation' had a fairly aristocratic cast everywhere.

University education offered real opportunities for social advancement. At least it did for those with a minimum of finance who had obtained a degree, for in the fourteenth century there was still a significant proportion of students – possibly the majority – which undoubtedly failed to graduate. We are largely ignorant of the destiny of these individuals. For graduates, on the other hand, and especially for licentiates and doctors of higher faculties, fine career prospects opened up, leading to prestigious and lucrative posts. When one member of a family gained a university qualification, it was often a decisive stage in their social ascent, sometimes the first step on the road to nobility. Nevertheless, we must be cautious in talking of the 'professionalisation' of university qualifications. Rather than any specific technical competence, they endorsed the mastery of a relatively theoretical and socially prestigious body of knowledge (Latin, dialectic, Aristotelian philosophy, Roman law, scholastic theology), while at the same time, there were networks of useful contacts, where former graduates and benevolent protectors combined their efforts to support the promotion of their young colleagues and protégés.

The Church was especially well disposed, substantially financing their studies and then opening the door to an ecclesiastical career to graduates. At the curia, the higher echelons of the papal administration were practically controlled by some forty doctors and licentiates, mainly qualified in civil or canon law. The episcopate was also very often composed of graduates and civil lawyers: it has been calculated that they constituted at least 50 per cent of the Avignon curia and as many as 70 per cent of the English episcopate in the reign of Edward III (1327–77). It was the same with cathedral chapters: around the middle of the century, 43 per cent of the canons of Laon and 64 per cent of those at Tournai were graduates, of whom more than half were from a higher faculty. These figures varied from country to country and were much higher in northern France and in England (where it was not unusual even to find graduates amongst the parish clergy) than in the Iberian peninsula or the empire. Fewer than one third of the canons of German chapters had followed any form of university study in the fourteenth century.

Service with individuals, with towns or rulers also offered an increasing number of openings to graduates, masters of arts and, above all, law graduates. In the fourteenth century, central law courts (such as the *parlement* of Paris) were in the hands of professional civil lawyers from the universities. Even in the provinces, the middle ranks of the royal administration employed some doctors or licentiates. The position was the same in the tribunals and chanceries of Italian towns. And doctors of medicine who did not teach had no difficulty in finding employment in the entourages of princes, great men and prelates.

Fourteenth-century academics were perfectly aware of the social dignity of their work and titles (well established from this date onwards) and gave it visible expression. Their taste for grandeur and precedence, together with a highly developed sense of hierarchy, infiltrated every aspect of university life. It was articulated in the continual increases in examination fees and the ostentatious pomp of university ceremonies. Some of the most substantial colleges founded in the fourteenth century, such as the Collège de Navarre at Paris (1304), the Spanish College at Bologna (1367) or New College at Oxford (1379) expressed this new attitude in their luxurious buildings, important libraries and avowedly 'elitist' recruitment.

We should not anticipate events, however. Although, as we have seen, fourteenth-century universities still had great intellectual energies, it is important not to exaggerate either their professionalism or their social exclusiveness. Exceptional individual achievement, such as that of Jean Gerson at Paris or William of Wykeham in England were evidence that university education remained generally accessible to those with the necessary intellectual abilities. There was still something of the universalism that had determined the shape of these studies in the thirteenth century. Here, as in many other areas, it was the Great Schism which divided the west in 1378, precipitating a latent crisis.

EPILOGUE: UNIVERSITIES AND THE GREAT SCHISM

In one sense, the Schism undoubtedly gave new life to the old universalism. Faced with the collapse of papal authority and the unrest of the faithful, academics, led by Parisian theologians and canon lawyers, believed that they had been appointed to the task, if not of assuming power in the Church themselves, then at least of advising prelates and rulers, putting forward solutions and advocating means by which the crisis might be overcome. Despite pressure from the crown, the university of Paris took several months to rally to the Avignonese pope, Clement VII, and there were intense discussions between ardent 'Clementists' and advocates of a general council and those who advocated the resignation of both popes, possibly underpinned by a policy of neutrality or withdrawal of obedience. The debate spread from Paris to the universities of southern France, where there was unwavering support for the Avignonese cause. It also spread to universities in continued obedience to Rome, such as Oxford, Bologna, Prague and, above all, the new German universities where Henry of Langenstein (who had gone from Paris to Vienna) had great authority. While the claims of Clement VII and his supporters were rejected, there was also insistence on the urgent need for reform and the possible advantage of a council. Stilled for a while, this debate was energetically resumed after 1392, in response to the intransigence of the rival popes. In 1398, members of the university of Paris were largely responsible for the 'withdrawal of obedience' of the kingdom of France.

Within France, only the university of Toulouse opposed this move. Since it was not followed by any other universities or rulers in the west, this premature decision had to be rescinded in 1403. Many members of the university of Paris greeted the 'restitution of obedience' with relief; they sent to Avignon the long roll of petitions (requests for papal dispensation), which they had foresworn in 1394 in order to demonstrate their reservations about the accession of Benedict XIII. In fact, an increasing number of university members realised that, although the need to combat the Schism was undiminished, the university itself could only profit from the conflict.

Bishops and rulers still undoubtedly sought advice from the university, but they did not have either the financial resources (in the form of ecclesiastical benefices) or the guarantees of autonomy assured by the papacy before 1378. The division of Christendom into two rival obediences resulted, as we have seen, in the creation of new universities and faculties; Paris in particular lost some of its clientele and its international influence. Recruitment there became more regionalised (as it was in smaller or more recent universities) drawing largely on the northern half of the kingdom of France. Everywhere, the collapse of papal power left the way open for increasing pressure from secular states and towns on universities. At Oxford, for example (despite the privileges of immunity that had been renewed once more in 1395), the university was unable to withstand the authoritarian interventions of the archbishop of Canterbury and, through him, of the crown. In 1411, after twenty-five years of vain resistance, all forms of Wycliffite teaching was decisively banned on the order of Archbishop Arundel.

Thus, like many other institutions at this period, without perhaps being fully aware of it, the universities were irresistibly caught up in the movement which, benefiting from the Schism, placed national churches and the modern secular state at the forefront of the political stage.

CHAPTER 5

RURAL SOCIETY

Paul Freedman

A S with nearly every other aspect of fourteenth-century history, the most important event affecting the medieval countryside was the Black Death along with the plagues that succeeded it periodically in the latter half of the century. Viewed from the safe distance of 650 years, the Black Death is usually presented in agrarian history as a demographic-economic event: a sudden radical diminution of population that produced a series of dislocations in the structure of medieval society. There are two contradictory ways that scholars have come to terms with this staggering example of historical accident. The first is to relate all subsequent developments to the plague. The agricultural depression, peasant revolts and ruin of much of the aristocracy can be seen as consequences of the epidemic and its renewed visitations. To what extent long-range changes can be ascribed to the Black Death (such things as the decline of servitude in England and its strengthening in eastern Europe, or the crisis of the Church) remains unclear, particularly as one moves into the fifteenth century.

Another approach is to minimise the impact of the Black Death by pointing to other factors that independently affected society. Population decline, agricultural stagnation and widespread peasant discontent, according to this view, antedate 1348 and so the 'crisis' of the fourteenth century was already manifested in its early decades. The Black Death would thus confirm or forward developments already underway, as opposed to destroying violently a stable economy and social structure.

These two interpretive tendencies are significant because they influence how the century and its upheavals are viewed, particularly whether or not the undoubted crisis in agrarian society of the late fourteenth century has an organic connection with what transpired earlier (and if so, how much earlier). Moreover, attempts to deal with the impact of the Black Death are intertwined with differences of opinion about the causes of the agrarian and social crisis, particularly between those who emphasise demographic shifts as the fundamental origin of social change versus those who identify frictions within the economic system that operated independently of how many peasants there were to work or to be fed. Impersonal factors such as population decline, caused by forces external to the economy such as disease or climate shifts, need to be compared with factors *within* the medieval economic system such as inheritance customs or the relations between peasants and their landlords.[1]

BASIC FEATURES OF THE AGRARIAN SYSTEM

The agrarian economy of the Middle Ages was more diverse than was once thought. Rather than a mass of undifferentiated peasants universally dedicated to the cultivation of wheat, the picture now seems to vary by region and time period. Within the villages themselves peasants differed considerably in status, size of holdings and what they owed in obligations to their lords. The textbook model of the medieval manor as a self-contained unit with a single lord controlling villagers governed by uniform manorial custom is even less valid for the fourteenth century than for the high Middle Ages. Residents of the same village were often tenants of different lords, and there were tremendous differences among villagers with regard to how much (if any) land they held. Moreover, the tendency was for lords to withdraw from the active supervision of their estates and for rents to be converted from labour and produce obligations to money, further distancing reality from the image of the self-sufficient seigniory.

The lives of the peasants were influenced by the nature of the family unit, customs and other solidarities inherent in the village community, and the impress of the seigneurial regime. There was considerable regional variation, but most European agriculturalists of the fourteenth century were subsistence farmers who also produced for a market and to pay a seigneurial rent. The interaction between the family's subsistence, the market for agricultural produce, land and labour and the obligations of tenants affected the fortunes of peasants along with the obvious fundamental considerations such as the soil's fertility and extent of their holdings.

Everywhere in Europe there were words used to describe an ideal concept of a peasant holding. The *mansus*, hide, virgate, *Hufe*, did not usually have a standard size in practice but conformed to a notion of what a full peasant tenement meant. For most of Europe a figure of perhaps thirty to forty hectares seems to be what was regarded as a full holding, but a much smaller parcel (as little as four hectares) was sufficient to support a family given the average quality of the land, the tools available to peasants and their obligations to apply their surplus to a seigneurial rent. Even before the fourteenth century, a rising

[1] Harvey (1991), p. 3.

population, partible inheritance and the dwindling inventory of uncultivated land meant that most peasants had to make do with a less-than-standard holding and supplement their income by seasonal labour or the production of some commodity other than cereals. For the high Middle Ages as a whole, Robert Fossier believes that 40 to 50 per cent of peasants had less than the four-hectare minimum.[2]

Peasant households were generally small, essentially a conjugal family. Better-off peasants might have a larger household including poorer relatives, labourers and elderly parents no longer able to work. It was not uncommon for ageing parents to arrange lifetime maintenance contracts with their children in return for ceding to them the familial property in advance of their decease. Because of the high rate of mortality and short life expectancy, the number of households with three generations was not very great.

The degree to which husbands legally controlled the property of their wives varied. In Mediterranean regions it was more likely that peasant women might own and retain property of their own distinct from that of their husbands and not part of their dowry. In general throughout Europe, the wife was seldom recognised as economically independent in law, while at the same time her exclusive rights to dower lands was generally recognised.

Husband and wife were both involved in the production of food and income. It is common to observe that peasant men tended the fields in what is called the 'outer economy' while women were more concerned with the immediate surroundings of the dwelling, the 'inner economy'. Ploughing, clearing land, herding were generally male activities while the tending of dairy animals and poultry, the vegetable garden, brewing and cloth making were women's work, along with the raising of children, providing meals and cleaning the house. In harvest time particularly, however, women were involved in the fields and certain tasks (gleaning, for example) were regarded as their peculiar responsibility.[3]

This household economy fits into a network of relations within villages in those areas of Europe in which settlement was relatively concentrated. The degree to which the village exerted a significant influence on peasant families differed with the human geography of European regions, but also with the nature of relations between lords and tenants. In south-western Germany, for example, village customs were set out in often elaborate bye-laws (*Weistümer*), but these were not purely spontaneous expressions of immemorial folk habits but resulted in part from the instigation of lords and for their convenience.[4]

---

[2] Fossier (1988), p. 146. See also Rösener (1992), pp. 125–6; *Agrarian History of England and Wales* (1988), II. pp. 594–714; Freedman (1991), pp. 36–8.   [3] Bennett (1987), pp. 115–17.

[4] Rösener (1992), pp. 159–60.

Historians have at times been inclined to exaggerate the solidarity of the late-medieval village, seeing it as exemplifying the tyranny of rural custom and conformity, or more favourably in opposition to modern anomie. More recently the divisions within the village have been demonstrated in cases such as that of Montaillou in Languedoc and the differentiation among different classes of villagers has been emphasised.[5] In England, manor court rolls reveal a select group of village leaders whose relative affluence gave them power over local enforcement.[6] Throughout Europe rural communities regulated ploughing, common areas like pastures and forests, and the informal resolution of disputes.

The fourteenth century witnessed considerable dislocation of both families and communities by reason of the tremendous mortality caused by disease and epidemic and the ensuing economic instability. One measure of a weakening of communal bonds is increased movement of peasants from familial property, an increase in mobility.[7] Another is the growing market in buying and selling land. Demographic decline and economic stagnation after 1350 may have frayed the ties holding villages together, thus the accelerating land market might indicate a stronger assertion of private interest. On the other hand, such transactions may not indicate the dissolution of village and family ties but merely amount to arrangements within families or between neighbours.[8] An active market for land is not necessarily incompatible with the survival of communal institutions. The dichotomy between individualism and communal bonds is by no means clear for rural European societies.[9] Long after the end of the fourteenth century, its upheavals notwithstanding, rural communal sentiment would manifest itself in continued and effective demands, especially with regard to the chief external factor affecting peasants, the seigniory.[10]

LORDS AND PEASANTS

There were allodial farmers in fourteenth-century Europe, and many more whose connection with a landlord was vague, or based on rights of usufruct (such as the medieval Mediterranean adaptation of the Roman law of emphyteusis) that gave the nominal tenant effective possession. There were even a few areas, usually in difficult terrain such as mountains or marshes, that were able to form independent peasant republics (such as the Swiss Forest Cantons or Dithmarschen in Holstein). The overwhelming majority of European agriculturalists in the fourteenth century, however, did not own their properties in the modern sense of ownership. They worked land for which

---

[5] Le Roy Ladurie (1976); Fossier (1973).   [6] Raftis (1974), pp. 241–64; DeWindt (1972), pp. 206–41.
[7] Raftis (1974), pp. 129–82.   [8] Razi (1981).   [9] Ruiz (1987), pp. 423–52.   [10] Blickle (1992).

they had to pay a substantial rent to a lord. This rent took three fundamental forms that could be combined: monetary amounts, service in the form of labour and a portion of what the peasant tenant harvested. By the fourteenth century, payment in money was much more common than had been the case when the economy was too primitive to support any very extensive coinage system. Labour service could take various forms, from taking messages to carting provisions to working on construction projects but the most important aspect of peasant work obligations from the lord's point of view was performed on those parts of the estate he kept as a seigneurial reserve (the demesne) rather than renting out. Portions of the harvest varied but could amount to as much as half.

Lords collected revenues from their tenants on the basis of more than a merely economic relationship. They held jurisdictional power in many cases that allowed them to act as judges and tax collectors. They might impose monopolies so that villagers would, for example, be forced to have their grain ground for a fee in the mill belonging to the lord. Such constraints existed even when the peasants were formally free although they were clearest when the peasants were serfs. While France by 1300 had very few serfs, servitude was common in much of England where about one third of all households consisted of unfree persons in the thirteenth and early fourteenth centuries.[11] Serfdom was weak in Languedoc, rare in Castile, increasingly common in Catalonia (affecting one quarter of the rural population).[12] In Catalonia it was uncommon in the south (New Catalonia) and all but universal among the peasantry of the regions around Girona in the north of the Principality.

Such regional and even local variation makes it hard to generalise about serfdom. While it was thought to be a grave indignity, depriving peasants of the ability to appear before public courts or enter the priesthood, its legal disabilities did not always translate into economic inferiority. It has been argued, especially for England, that villeins were often economically better off and more effectively sheltered by custom than the free but marginal labourers.[13] Servitude created a bond but also a degree of certainty over permanent and hereditarily transmissible occupation of land.

What servile status effectively symbolised was a degree of arbitrary control by the lord. It was the emblem of his extra-economic power, but this could extend to both free and unfree. The peasant rebellions of the late Middle Ages centred on arbitrary power, including servitude, but also such things as use of the forest or seigneurial encroachments on common lands, rights and customs that affected free as well as unfree tenants. Servitude not only created formal

---

[11] Hatcher (1981), pp. 6–7.   [12] Vicens Vives (1978), pp. 18–19.
[13] Dyer (1980), pp. 103–6; Hatcher (1981), pp. 22–6.

liability to arbitrary and coercive power, it epitomised what was increasingly resented in the years after the Black Death: the perpetuation and intensification of seigneurial power, including but not limited to attempts to impose serfdom.

For parts of northern Europe, notably England, the thirteenth century had been the heyday of demesne farming. Motivated by high agricultural prices and the ready availability of labour, lords directly exploited their demesne. Peasants worked these lands as part of their obligations or lords hired landless labourers or those who had sub-standard holdings. In the densely populated environment of the thirteenth and early fourteenth centuries, the majority of peasants had inadequate holdings for their self-sufficiency. There was a tremendous difference between those who held land to support a family (a minority), and those who either held no land at all or too little to avoid desperation unless they were able to find work as day-labourers or could acquire income from a craft, brewing or other activity. High prices and the existence of a conveniently large impoverished group of potential labourers encouraged lords to exploit their demesne lands, relying on customary services supplemented by hired labour.

Elsewhere, as in Germany, the fourteenth century witnessed the continuation of an earlier tendency to replace a system of exploitation based on the seigneurial demesne (*Villikation* or *Fronhof* system) by leasing out the manor entirely to tenants in return for rent. In the Mediterranean lands, agricultural exploitations had always been more dispersed and lords never had large reserves exploited by tenants' labour services. Even major landowners, such as the great Cistercian monasteries of the Iberian peninsula, held lands for which they received substantial rents and services but not for the purpose of directly cultivating a demesne. In much of the Mediterranean, payments in kind remained far more important than labour or a purely monetary rent.

The overall effect of the dislocations brought about by the demographic and economic collapse of the fourteenth century would be to remove lords further from direct administration of their estates. At the same time, however, they could no longer maintain themselves in the style they required by means of the relatively benign supervision exerted in the era of labour surplus. With pressure on wages to rise (as a result of the shortage of labour) and falling agricultural prices (the result of a radical decline in demand), lords attempted to recoup their losses by using their coercive power to squeeze more from their tenants. This could take the form of a renewed attention to servile status and an extension and deepening of serfdom, both intended to assert a more arbitrary seigneurial control and to enforce regulations against movement away from tenements that had not been worth bothering about when the supply of labourers exceeded demand. There were other possible strategies for landlords coping with radically shifting conditions (such as converting

lands from arable to pasturage or from wheat to less labour-intensive crops),
but the contradiction between seigneurial power and peasant expectations was
clearly the background to one of the most striking phenomena of the late
Middle Ages: the frequency and violence of peasant uprisings. No longer
capable of profiting from their demesnes and experiencing only limited
success in degrading the condition of their tenants, lords would be forced to
become absentee rentiers, but even in regions where there had never been
extensive demesnes this withdrawal from direct exploitation coincided with
a desperate attempt to wrest as much as possible from peasant tenants,
an attempt whose success varied considerably depending on geography and
circumstance.

In general, the preferences and obligations of the aristocracy and the
method of organising their exploitation of agriculture required lords to allow
peasants a high degree of self-administration. A substantial class of bailiffs,
stewards and other functionaries was charged with enforcing the lords' rights
and assuring the extraction of revenues. The complexity and diversity of these
revenues, however, and the built-in imperfections of a system of indirect
exploitation afforded peasants a certain space for resistance or at least petty
subversion of what were often in theory a crushing set of obligations.

Although the tenants exerted considerable effective control over their properties, it is important not to lose sight of the fact that this was a seigneurial
regime, one in which lords managed to extract a considerable amount of what
their peasants produced and exerted an extra-economic power over them. This
power might be more potential than actual in good times. Many serfs, technically prohibited from moving off the land, migrated to nearby towns, but
during the late fourteenth century, such unauthorised circulation was less likely
to be tolerated and from Hungary to Germany to England lords put into effect
what had previously been regarded as theoretical rights of coercion. Moreover,
where bonds between lord and peasant were loosened, this could work to the
advantage of the former, as when fixed rent with security of tenure was
replaced by limited-term leases that permitted the lord to eject tenants or
renegotiate their obligations.[14]

BEFORE THE BLACK DEATH

The first part of the fourteenth century witnessed a number of man-made as
well as natural disasters that adversely affected the rural economy. The most
shocking and severe of these was the Great Famine that affected almost all of
northern Europe beginning in 1315. It lasted for at least two years and persisted

[14] Genicot (1990), pp. 76–7.

as late as 1322. The immediate cause was a series of extremely rainy summers and unusually cold winters that caused harvest failures whose cumulative effect was catastrophic. The damage inflicted by the weather was exacerbated in many regions by warfare (notably in Flanders and the British Isles) and by epidemics of livestock diseases.

Laments about the disastrous rains and prolonged freezes appear in chronicles written in all parts of northern Europe and this literary evidence is confirmed by tree-ring measurements (dendrochronology). There is some possibility that these conditions reflected a long-term change in the European meteorological conditions and it is conceptually appealing to regard the end of medieval agricultural and demographic expansion as caused by a fundamental change towards a wetter, colder climate. There is little solid evidence for this, however, and more likely that the rain and cold were more random and anomalous fluctuations.

The Mediterranean regions escaped this particular terrible event, but they were not permanently spared. In Catalonia, for example, the year 1333 would be referred to in later sources as 'the first bad year', ushering in a series of poor harvests. Densely populated rural areas were more severely affected than thinly settled ones, but this is a rule with many exceptions. In England, as many as 10 or even 15 per cent of the population may have perished in the south, although in even more densely populated East Anglia, there was relatively little mortality.[15]

Recovery from the famine was quick, but the event serves both as an early indication of the 'calamitous fourteenth century' and provokes questions about how much was due to an external event that could not be avoided or planned for as opposed to an indication of over-population, of having reached beyond the demographic limits of what the land, technology and economy could support.

After centuries of strong growth, the population of Europe seems to have levelled off in the late thirteenth century and may have declined substantially in the fourteenth century even before the staggering losses inflicted by the Black Death. It was the accomplishment of M. M. Postan to have devised a theory of this demographic change based on the internal shortcomings of the medieval agrarian economy. Rather than blaming the population loss on purely external factors such as poor harvests or climate change, Postan approached the relationship between agricultural production and population as an essentially Malthusian problem. In the absence of technological improvement or investment in agriculture, the countryside could not support continued population growth. Postan, in collaboration with J.Z. Titow, assembled indirect evidence for an increase in mortality rates after 1300 based on death duties

[15] Jordan (1996), pp. 118–19.

paid by tenants of the bishop of Winchester.[16] This increase took place not merely because of shocks and catastrophes but was a long-term demographic shift. Having reached extraordinarily high levels of population after several centuries of virtually uninterrupted growth, England surpassed the point of maximum density that its agricultural system could sustain. Expansion of arable land reached the point of diminishing returns. As clearances moved from fertile lands to less favourable soils and climates, the population could no longer expand on the basis of simply increasing the amount of territory being cultivated. Settlements and farms were already being abandoned before the Black Death caused, according to Postan, something in the nature of an ecological crisis of overpopulation, soil depletion and impractical cultivation of marginal land. The population losses of the early fourteenth century were thus 'Malthusian checks', a rising death rate that brutally but necessarily tended to re-establish an equilibrium between population and production.[17]

Recently more direct means of measuring population change have in large measure confirmed the Postan thesis of a structural decline of population for England although with more sudden than gradual changes. England numbered at least 5 million inhabitants at the beginning of the fourteenth century, a figure that would not be reached again until well into the seventeenth century.[18] Similarly high figures have been posited for France, Germany and Scandinavia.[19]

Some of the reduction antedates the Black Death. In his study of the countryside around Pistoia, for example, David Herlihy found that population began to decline as early as the mid-thirteenth century.[20] In rural Essex, on the other hand, there was little change in population until the Great Famine which resulted in a 15 per cent loss. From 1317 to 1347, however, the population appears to have been reduced by a further 30 per cent.[21] Studies of manors in Huntingdonshire, Northamptonshire and Buckinghamshire confirm a significant decline of population over the first half of the fourteenth century, although the manor of Halesowen in Worcestershire presents a somewhat different picture.[22] There a decline in the rate of growth took place between 1300 and 1348, but there was an overall modest increase of 4 per cent in actual population despite a 15 per cent loss due to the Great Famine.[23]

Some parts of Europe experienced only minor setbacks during the early fourteenth century. In central Silesia, for example, after some relatively small difficulties, the agricultural economy renewed its expansion until well after 1350

---

[16] Postan and Titow (1958–9), pp. 392–417.   [17] Postan (1972) and (1973).

[18] Smith (1991), pp. 49–50.   [19] Abel (1980), pp. 21–2; Gissel (1976), pp. 43–54.

[20] Herlihy (1967), pp. 56–7.   [21] Poos (1985), pp. 515–30.

[22] Britton (1977), pp. 132–43; DeWindt (1972), pp. 166–70; Bennett (1987), pp. 13–14, 224–9.

[23] Razi (1980), pp. 27–32.

(the region also managed to escape the Black Death).[24] In many areas, however (Provence, Normandy, Tuscany, for example), there was a reduction of rural population similar to what took place in England.[25] In Brunswick, on the estates of the cathedral chapter of Sankt Blasien, a substantial number of farms were abandoned after 1320, but this was due more to a succession of bad harvests and war than to the agrarian economy's internal tensions or ecological limits.[26]

The case of Brunswick points to a central problem of the Postan approach: the tenuous evidence for a Malthusian crisis despite a widespread (but not universal) population loss. There is little support for his largely inferential positing of an increasingly unproductive expansion into marginal lands. The fact that areas went out of cultivation does not prove the exhaustion of the soil but rather a more dynamic landscape *throughout* the medieval period. The clearest example is Spain, more particularly Old Castile, where population loss began in the mid-thirteenth century without any indication that density limits had been previously approached.[27] In this instance we can point to migration of cultivators to the newly opened lands of Andalusia, the result of the rapid Christian expansion after 1212, but in Germany as well, if not as dramatically, the desertion of villages was due to factors other than Malthusian checks. For England, examination of the history of the landscape and patterns of settlement calls into question the crucial role of marginal land as supposed by Postan.[28]

It is hard to deny the overwhelming significance of demography, but its radical fluctuations interact with the society in which they take place rather than supplanting, overriding or rendering irrelevant social forces.[29] The seigneurial regime was already under stress before the Black Death and it is likely that an agrarian 'crisis' would have existed without the epidemic. Nevertheless, the epidemic, by virtue of destroying an immense number of lives without touching the fields (thus unlike war), created new stresses and a number of new opportunities.

The death of perhaps as much as 40 per cent of the population of Europe between 1348 and 1350 had immediate effects on the structure of agrarian society. Everywhere, with the exception of a few regions that the Black Death for some reason missed (such as Béarn and parts of Silesia and Poland), the sudden demographic decline affected prices and wages and thus the value of land and relations between lords and peasants. On the other hand, the effects

[24] Hoffmann (1989), pp. 114–47.
[25] Klapisch-Zuber and Herlihy (1985), pp. 62–3; Baratier (1961), pp. 80–1; Bois (1984), pp. 50–3.
[26] Hoffmann (1989), pp. 197–207.   [27] Ruiz (1994), pp. 291–313.   [28] Dyer (1989), pp. 48–57.
[29] Bois (1984).

of the Black Death and economic or social reactions to it differed among
Europe's various regions, implying that conditions before the epidemic were
not uniform and that regional legal and institutional structures affected the fortunes of labourers and landowners as much as impersonal demographic
facts.[30]

The Black Death may have accentuated an already existing crisis manifested
by famine and a stagnating or declining population, or it may be regarded as a
brutal but not completely surprising Malthusian check to restore equilibrium
to an overpopulated and economically overextended society. A certain
historiographic consensus, especially but not exclusively in Britain, has tended
to minimise the effects of the Black Death in part because of a reluctance to
credit randomly generated external events with staggering historical effects.
One minimalising approach is, as stated, to focus on antecedent trends that
anticipated what would happen in the second half of the century. The other is
to emphasise how quickly things returned to normal. These are related to the
extent that if a reordering of the demographic equilibrium was already underway before 1348, the shock of rapid population loss would confirm rather than
abruptly reverse existing trends.

Where there is widespread agreement is that rural population loss continued after 1348 and created long-term radical economic and social dislocation.
By 1400 there had been a continuing loss of population, worse in rural areas
than in cities. In 1377, the population of England amounted to little more than
it had at the time of Domesday Book, much of that loss due to the Black Death
but also to the successive plagues of 1360–2, 1369 and 1375.[31] In the rural surroundings of Pistoia there were only about 9,000 inhabitants in 1401, compared with a population of 31,000 in 1244, an astonishing loss of over 70 per
cent. The number of rural communes was reduced to 44 from 124 over the
same period.[32] It has been estimated that over 3,000 villages have at various
times been abandoned in England. Later enclosures for pasturage and creation
of parkland were certainly most important and the largest number of English
villages were voluntarily or forcibly abandoned between 1450 and 1550, but the
Black Death itself constitutes 'the pre-history of enclosure' because the
conversion of land to pasturage was motivated by the plunging demand and
prices for cereal crops due ultimately to the series of epidemics begun so
dramatically in the mid-fourteenth century.[33]

In Germany regions such as Thuringia, the mountainous areas of Swabia
along the Danube and the northern Mark of Brandenburg saw a rate of village

[30] Brenner in Aston and Philpin (1985), p. 21.
[31] Miller in *Agrarian History of England and Wales*, III (1991), pp. 1–8.   [32] Herlihy (1967), pp. 68–72.
[33] Beresford and Hurst (1971).

abandonment of over 40 per cent. The Rhineland, on the other hand, equally hard hit by the Black Death, experienced scarcely any loss in the number of inhabited places. Overall Germany lost 25 per cent of its villages between 1300 and 1500. As Werner Rösener points out, however, it is important to distinguish between places that were entirely abandoned, fields and all, and those where cultivation continued even if the residents had moved nearby.[34]

Despite the desertion of villages and migration to the cities, the overall fall of population did not mean a proportionate abandonment of fields. To the extent that the early fourteenth century had been characterised by a Malthusian saturation, the demographic decline relieved pressure on less fertile terrain while the reduction of density of settlement did not effect a proportionate loss in the productivity of the land. Agricultural prices and the value of land contracted due to reduced demand while wages were under upward pressure due to reduced supply. The aftermath of the Black Death would seem to have benefited those members of the lower orders with the good fortune to survive, and in many cases previously landless labourers now found themselves in unwonted demand and could significantly improve their conditions.

In the long term (that is, by the end of the century), the agrarian economy had collapsed into a depression that affected other sectors as well. The changes in prices and wages as well as the later sharpening of economic crisis are sometimes related to the Black Death specifically (as long- versus short-term effects), but more often to the series of successive epidemics that continued to afflict Europe. Thus for the lands of Sankt Blasien in Brunswick there was a significant reduction in the number of farms being cultivated between 1320 and 1340. The population declined with the Black Death and by the departure of many of the surviving tenants lured by better opportunities elsewhere. The immediate impact on the agrarian economy, however, was not so severe, perhaps because despite the early fourteenth-century decline, the region was still overpopulated in relation to its agricultural possibilities of exploitation before the plague struck. By 1400, however, the rural economy hence the monastery's revenues had collapsed. One fourth of the farms were deserted and the monastery could no longer cultivate its demesne except by expensive casual labour. These conditions were due more to the cumulative effects of epidemics after 1350 than to the Black Death itself.[35]

In a study of late-medieval Normandy, Guy Bois identified several stages of crisis affected by the demographic catastrophe of 1348 (amounting to a 50 per cent mortality) but also by the intrinsic problems of the feudal economy. After an initial period of stagnation between 1314 and 1347, the Black Death brought about a demographic collapse but not an immediate radical reduction in prices

---

[34] Rösener (1992), pp. 255–6.   [35] Hoffmann (1989), pp. 212–24.

or dramatic increase in wages. The period between 1380 and 1413 witnessed a 25 per cent decline in agricultural prices but also a significant recuperation of at least part of the population. The real economic disaster took place between 1415 and 1450 but implicated in this was not only disease but other external factors such as war and the internal tensions of an economy based on small-scale production and seigneurial extraction.[36]

The absence of an immediate radical effect of the Black Death is confirmed by Postan's findings for England.[37] In the area of Brignole in southern France, where most tenants held lands on favourable terms (emphyteutic leases), there seems to have been little change after 1348. Few properties were abandoned, the price of good land remained high and the payment of the annual *census* remained stable both in absolute terms and as a ratio of the price of the land being cultivated.[38]

There are, however, other indications that show that the Black Death did have a direct impact on wages and the attitudes of peasants. While prices did not begin their rapid decline in England until the late 1370s, tenants and labourers demanded improvement in their leases and wages. The earlier Ordinance of Labourers of 1349, confirmed by parliament as the Statute of Labourers in 1351, responded to upward pressure on wages and was vigorously enforced. Manorial records suggest that wages were stable after the Black Death, but they may disguise evasion of the wage control legislation by means of cash payments and other off the record inducements.[39]

The English wage legislation is the clearest evidence of the short-term economic influence of the Black Death, but there is considerable variation of opinion as to how effective it was. R. H. Hilton has found that it was initially successful in restraining agricultural wages until 1360 and that the upward trend accelerated after 1380.[40] The punitive wage legislation was part of a seigneurial reaction that attempted to preserve or even strengthen the lords' position after the Black Death. Labour services and fines were increased and prohibitions on movement became more strictly enforced.[41] Even before the English Rising of 1381, however, and certainly by the end of the century, such efforts had failed. The bishops of Durham, who held unusual political and jurisdictional power in their palatinate, were forced to abandon attempts to collect labour services.[42] The gradual decline of English villeinage was greatly encouraged, if not caused, by the untenable position of the lords with regard to enforcing the bondage of their tenants in the demographic aftermath of the repeated plagues.

---

[36] Bois (1984). [37] Postan (1973), pp. 186–213. [38] Leclerq (1985), pp. 115–28.
[39] Hatcher (1994), pp. 1–35. [40] Hilton (1983), pp. 39–41.
[41] Raftis (1964), pp. 144–52; Brenner in Aston and Philpin (1985), p. 35. [42] Britnell (1990).

The seigneurial reaction was not everywhere unsuccessful, and even in England was not resisted simply by invoking demographic inevitability as the Rising of 1381 indicates. In Catalonia lords would enforce an even harsher form of servitude than what had obtained before the epidemic and it would require a full-scale peasant war in the late fifteenth century to procure the abolition of servitude.[43] In much of eastern Europe, the aftermath of the Black Death marks the beginning of a process of degradation of a once-free peasantry into servile status that would endure well into the modern era.[44]

PEASANT REVOLTS

There had been many local uprisings in European rural communities before the thirteenth century, but the scale and nature of peasant movements changed after 1300 and especially after the Black Death. Unrest spread across a wide area and was no longer provoked by disagreements over particular village or manorial customs but by social demands and expectations.[45] The most dramatic of these conflicts were the French Jacquerie of 1358 and the English Rising of 1381 which convulsed the two kingdoms and had a short-lived but (from the point of view of the upper orders of society) frightening success. The revolts are to be understood as at least substantially related to the social and economic crisis that characterised the fourteenth century. In some cases (notably the Jacquerie) they reflect the desperate conditions of violence, disorder and oppression. They are also in certain respects the outgrowth of a more favourable situation in which peasants felt more powerfully situated to put forward their demands. The English Rising of 1381 is often seen as an example of that favourite historical notion, the 'revolution of rising expectations' in which the failure to secure anticipated improvements in wages, tenurial conditions and status leads to more strident demands than in circumstances of greater oppression with less perceived opportunity.

There are various typologies of peasant revolts that try to account for the difference between small isolated manifestations of discontent and larger movements of the sort that developed in the late Middle Ages. The Russian historian B. F. Porchnev identified three forms of peasant resistance: flight, partial resistance and open revolt.[46] Recent studies of both modern and earlier peasant societies have shown the importance of indirect, everyday forms of resistance that could undermine the claims of the dominant elite without open confrontation.

Günther Franz, the historian of the German Peasants' War of 1525, distinguished between 'Old Law' rebellions that invoked custom and were

---

[43] Vicens Vives (1978); Freedman (1991), pp. 179–202. [44] Brenner (1996), pp. 272–5.
[45] Köhn (1991). [46] Cf. Rösener (1992), pp. 238–40.

prompted by a lord violating local practices and 'Godly Law' uprisings based on principles of general application. For Franz the former were by nature specific to one lordship or jurisdiction while the scope of the 1525 war is explained by the arguments over freedom and Christian equality made possible by the teachings of Martin Luther.[47] Similarly Peter Burke posited a dichotomy between traditionalist movements seeking a restoration of an earlier just order, and radical rebellions that envisioned a transformation of society without reference to an idealised past.[48] Here the radical visions are not as tied to religious discourse as in Franz.

Another taxonomy is one that distinguishes Messianic rebellions motivated by a fervid climate of religious expectation (as in early fifteenth-century Bohemia) from more practical uprisings motivated by a desire for social mobility. Guy Fourquin adds a third category in which an exceptional political or fiscal crisis precipitated uprisings (as with both the Jacquerie and the English Rising).[49]

These and other classification schemes have in common a desire to distinguish between 'serious' movements that encompassed a large geographical area or that seem to represent a radical alternative and the normal discontents characteristic of peasant society which has usually been regarded as conservative and resistant to change. While there is clearly a difference between an uprising limited to one or two manors and a widespread revolt on the scale of England in 1381, the typologies based on putative motivation tend to disguise the degree to which local issues could be framed in radical ideological terms and linked to questions that transcended parish boundaries. In the large-scale revolts of the fourteenth century political matters provoked long-standing social and economic grievances. The impact of famine, war and maladministration in Flanders brought about a rebellion between 1323 and 1328 that was provoked by onerous taxes but joined to an attack against exploitative lordship. The Jacquerie was, as Fourquin argued, the result of a crisis in the French state provoked by the battle of Poitiers, the tightened fiscal demands of the crown and the depredations of lawless troops. The English Rising was precipitated by the infamous poll tax and the unpopularity of John of Gaunt and the royal ministers.

The involvement of peasants in protesting against taxation or corrupt administration is surprising only if it is assumed that they were normally helpless or unaware of anything beyond their localities. Certainly one of the characteristics of peasant revolts after 1300 is that they were framed in terms larger than local grievances. The fiscal demands of the French and English monarchs should not be regarded as the sole cause of these revolts which had

[47] Franz (1984), pp. 1–91.   [48] Burke (1978), pp. 173–8.   [49] Fourquin (1978), pp. 129–60.

as their target the conditions of tenure, the arbitrary exercise of seigneurial power and other local matters.

The first large-scale medieval peasant revolt took place in maritime Flanders against a corrupt comital administration and its pro-French policies. From 1323 until they were crushed at the battle of Cassel by a French army in the summer of 1328, peasants burned castles, drove out the count's officials, administered their own territories and established an army.[50] The districts of Bruges, Ypres and Courtrai formed the centre of a virtual peasant republic stretching along the coast from Bourbourg to the Scheldt river.

At issue in the Flemish Revolt were political and fiscal questions concerning the administration of Flanders as a whole. It was not exclusively a peasant revolt as elements of the population of Bruges and Ypres also participated. In its last two years the Flemish uprising became more radical and tended more forcefully to present itself as directed against the richer landowners and the Church rather than against the corrupt fiscality of the comital government. This rebellion thus combined an articulate political programme and the stimulus of what might seem traditional grievances.

The French Jacquerie of 1358 was relatively short-lived but made a greater impression on contemporaries than the Flemish Revolt, in part because it took place in the centre of France but also because it was perceived from the start as essentially a revolt against the nobility. The Jacquerie began in response to the depredations of French as well as English and Navarrese troops who pillaged the countryside in the aftermath of the defeat at Poitiers (1356). The royal government was ineffective except in attempting to squeeze money for the ransom of King John II and the nobility failed to protect tenants and was discredited by its poor showing in battle with the English.

The peasants began to resist marauding knights in the Beauvaisis late in May 1358 but this turned very quickly into a general uprising against the nobility and spread quickly to the region around Paris, Picardy and had a certain echo in Champagne and Normandy. The contemporary chronicler Jean le Bel believed that the peasants were led by 'Jacques Bonhomme' and the name 'Jacquerie' was soon given to the revolt (the name occurs in the later histories of Froissart and the *Chronique Normande*). A certain Guillaume Calle was identified as the leader of the insurgents but the peasants also elected local captains and the revolt was in large measure spontaneous. It was suppressed quickly by the nobility aided by Charles II the Bad, king of Navarre. In a sanguinary counter-Jacquerie, the town of Meaux which had allied with the peasants was burned and Guillaume Calle was captured and executed by a mock coronation in which he was placed in a red-hot iron 'throne' and 'crowned' with a heated iron circlet.

[50] TeBrake (1993).

The motives for the Jacquerie remain the subject of considerable disagreement. The nineteenth-century historian Siméon Luce attributed the revolt to an excess of misery due to the combination of plague, war, taxation and seigneurial oppression.[51] Guy Fourquin minimised its social basis, seeing the uprising as the result of a specific short-term crisis of the legitimacy of royal and noble authority. The peasants who were active in the uprising, according to Fourquin, were well-off, formed a small minority and were encouraged by outside forces, particularly the urban elites opposed to the rapacity of the royal government and angered by the prevailing disorder inflicted by the unemployed men-at-arms.[52] In her discussion of contemporary accounts of the Jacquerie, Marie-Thérèse de Medeiros also doubts that the Jacquerie was essentially an anti-noble uprising, but acknowledges that the nobles had failed to protect their tenants and had lost the aura of legitimacy. Her work demonstrates the unanimity of the chroniclers in believing that the target was indeed the noble class.[53] The Jacquerie, despite the fact that it lasted only a matter of weeks, would endure as a symbol of peasant rage and of the vulnerability of the upper classes.

The English Rising of 1381 would also be long remembered as an explosion of rustic fury against the landed classes. A secular clerk in early fifteenth-century Oxford wrote a poem in the margins of a cartulary:

> 'Man beware and be no fool
> think upon the ax and of the stool.
> The stool was hard, the ax was sharp
> the fourth year of King Richard'.[54]

Certainly the appearance of the peasant armies in London and their intimidation of the young king was recalled as a horrendous instance of the world turned upside down. John Gower depicted the events in a nightmare vision in which previously useful animals escaped their bonds to bring ruin and disorder to the land.

Here too, however, the rebellion can be seen clearly to emanate from something more than spasmodic anger or Messianic egalitarianism. The revolt began in response to government efforts to collect the third poll tax in four years voted by parliament in 1380. Insurrection spread from south-west Essex where it began in late May or early June until it included Kent, all of East Anglia, Hertfordshire, Cambridgeshire and at least partially Sussex, Surrey and Middlesex. Two peasant armies converged on London, the men of Kent led by Wat Tyler and the Essex rebels. The Kentish forces arrived across the

---

[51] Luce (1894), p. 9.   [52] Fourquin (1978), pp. 134–9.   [53] De Medeiros (1979), pp. 11–23.
[54] Justice (1994), p. 251.

Thames in Blackheath, Southwark and Lambeth by 12 June and burned the palace of the bishop of London. The men of Essex, coming from the north, were allowed into London and now joined by the Kentish army they burned the palace of John of Gaunt and sacked the Temple whose prior was the royal treasurer, Robert Hales. The king and his entourage sought refuge in the Tower of London. A parley at Mile End on 14 June represents the high tide of the rebels' fortunes. They forced the fourteen-year-old king to agree to the abolition of serfdom and to have charters recognising the liberty of specific tenants drawn up. They also won royal consent to a uniform rate of rental payment linked to acreage, the removal of restrictions on trade and a general amnesty. Whether the rebels had more radical plans, such as monarchy depending not on parliament but a 'true commons' of ordinary people, remains debatable. Wat Tyler and his followers did take the matter sufficiently into their own hands as to leave Mile End and enter the Tower where they summarily beheaded Archbishop Simon Sudbury and Hales.

The next day, 15 June, saw another meeting between the king and the insurgents at Smithfield where Wat Tyler is reported by the *Anonimalle Chronicle* to have presented new demands, including the end of all lordship except the king's, the distribution of Church property and the abolition of all bishops except one. Tyler may not have wanted to reach an agreement with the king and is reported to have behaved in an aggressively familiar manner, shaking the king's hand and drinking beer in his presence. The mayor of London, William Walworth, attacked Tyler and killed him while the king managed to calm the peasants by claiming to lead them. The rebels were dispersed relatively peacefully. Later the machinery of judgement was brought to bear against individual rebels, but the rising and its suppression proved to be considerably less bloody than its French counterpart.

To what extent the demands presented in London represent the grievances of the countryside at large is uncertain. Wat Tyler's demands and the sermon preached at Blackheath by John Ball (which cited the couplet 'When Adam delved and Eve span, who was then the gentleman?') put forward a theory of equality and an attack on lordship. Rather than emphasising the radical demands presented at Smithfield, historians examining particular localities have shown connections between earlier disturbances and the events of 1381. Peasants attempted to use legal means against what they regarded as arbitrary treatment by their lords rather than attacking lordship as such. Many of the regions that participated most enthusiastically in the Rising of 1381 had a history of suits over servile status and attendant obligations. Tenants at Elmham in Suffolk and Leighs in Essex had attempted to prove their free status. Forty villages in the south of England in 1377 were swept by a movement called the 'Great Rumour' in which seigneurial demands for labour services were opposed by claims of free tenancy based on Domesday Book.[55] At the monastery of St Albans, rebels in 1381 dug up from the cloister the pieces of hand-mills that had been confiscated and used for paving stones in an earlier confrontation between peasants and the monastery over the seigneurial monopoly on mills. St Albans forbade its tenants to grind their own grain and the memory of the forcible suppression was alive in 1381 so that at the festive occasion when the peasants broke into the cloister, they dug up the stones and divided them into pieces giving some to each other in a ceremony resembling the distribution of communion bread.[56]

Events at St Albans also demonstrate the respect for what was believed to be old custom rather than a remaking of society according to the programme presented at Smithfield. The tenants of St Albans burned documents recording their obligations but at the same time insisted that the abbot present a charter, supposedly issued by King Offa, 'with capital letters, one of gold, one of azure', that contained the fundamental provisions of their free status. The abbot protested that he knew of no such document, promised he would look for it, and eventually was compelled to write another charter granting the rather limited concessions that the peasants claimed.[57]

Given the variety of local demands and the difficulty of reconstructing a peasant programme out of the hostile accounts of the chroniclers, one cannot ascribe a single or principal cause to the English Rising. Most clearly among fourteenth-century revolts, however, the English example must be seen in relation to the conditions arising as a consequence of the Black Death and subsequent epidemics. Earlier local conflicts over tenurial obligations were joined together by common grievances over arbitrary seigneurial and governmental levies, themselves the result of a crisis in land values and royal financing. The desire of the lords to resist increasing wages and to take advantage of the unfree status of many of their tenants to increase their failing revenues ran into peasant expectations of improved conditions, and resentment against serfdom and its indignities.

Suppression of the revolt in 1381 did not mean an end to peasant resistance in England. There would be five regional revolts between 1381 and 1405, especially in Kent, Cheshire and Yorkshire.[58] More importantly, the last decade of the fourteenth century saw an acceleration in the leasing out of seigneurial lands and the consequent abandonment of demesne farming. Peasants in this period were able to use the threat to leave their tenements in order to negotiate better terms for themselves in spite of the renewal of punitive legislation regarding mobility and agricultural wages. The era saw an unusual degree of

---

[55] Faith (1984).   [56] Walsingham, *Gesta Abbatum Monasterii Sancti Albani*, III, p. 309.
[57] Faith (1984), pp. 63–5.   [58] *Agrarian History of England and Wales* (1988), III, p. 797.

movement and it is a reasonable conjecture that what the peasants had not been able to win by direct means in 1381, they were at least partially successful in obtaining by taking advantage of what remained their greatest weapon: the decline in the labour force. While it is impossible to set a date for the end of serfdom in England, there is little doubt that 1381 marked the critical moment in its fading away, a process that the fifteenth century would complete.

CHAPTER 6

URBAN LIFE

Jean-Pierre Leguay

IT is impossible to deny that fourteenth-century towns were profoundly affected by the economic contraction that followed previous expansion, however much historians wish to avoid generalisation and make proper allowance for the very considerable variations between regions. The situation was aggravated by the poor harvests of 1314–17 and the resulting shortages, as well as by the Black Death (1347–50) and subsequent outbreaks of plague. The result was a sharp drop in population levels, barely compensated for by the influx of refugees from the countryside. These factors, combined with high rates of taxation and manipulation of the coinage in some states, hampered commercial and manufacturing activity and exacerbated social tensions.

OUTLINE OF URBAN EUROPE, C. 1300

European towns at the beginning of the fourteenth century were the result of many centuries of expansion; they were denser in the southern, Mediterranean regions (Italy, Catalonia, Aquitaine, Provence) and in certain areas of northern and north-western Europe (Flanders, the Rhineland, the valleys of the Seine, Rhône and Loire, the Channel and Atlantic coastlands).

Urban networks were established in most areas. Economic, demographic and cultural expansion had reactivated the great majority of episcopal cities, dating from late antiquity or the early medieval period. Many substantial villages that had grown up near castles, abbeys and priories succeeded in raising themselves to the rank of true towns, while settlement and clearing, as well as the need to defend vulnerable border areas, were responsible for more recent foundations, the deliberate creations of princes, secular or ecclesiastical lords and the pioneering activities of rural immigrants.

The last years of the thirteenth century and the course of the fourteenth saw the building of the last of Aquitaine's 300 *bastides*, the last 'planted towns' on the Welsh and Scottish borders (Caernarfon, Conway, or Berwick upon

Tweed resurrected from its ruins). In central and eastern Europe there were the recent and continuing settlements of the Teutonic knights, besides those that were the fruit of German and Slav colonisation (Brandenburg, Danzig, Rostock, Stettin). Half of the towns in Mecklenburg date from between 1250 and 1350.

Nevertheless, it would be difficult to draw up a list of towns in each kingdom or great lordship. Contemporary administrators virtually never recorded settlements of any size; when political, military or fiscal considerations happened to make them do so, their conclusions varied from one estimate to the next. So in France, for example, there are extraordinary discrepancies in the gatherings of citizens at provincial assemblies, the estates of the Languedoc and the Languedoïl: 91 towns were listed in 1302, 259 in 1308, 227 in 1316, 96 in 1318! According to the American historian C. H. Taylor, 570 places in all were called to play a part in these representative assemblies, but by no means all of them can be called towns in the full sense.[1] They fail to meet the necessary criteria, whether economic, demographic, institutional, architectural or religious (supporting convents of friars).

Despite the quickening pace of urbanisation in the thirteenth century, Europe remained deeply rural; in some areas as much as 95 per cent of the population lived in the countryside. Entire countries (Ireland, Scandinavia, Portugal), as well as provinces such as the Auvergne or Brittany, or imperial Savoy, were still content with miserable little towns scarcely differentiated from neighbouring villages.

The rise in urban population was more the result of immigration from the rural hinterland (French *plat pays*, Italian *contado*) than of natural growth. People from all levels of society – noble, lawyer and peasant – were attracted by offers of work, opportunities for business, security or tax advantages: they all came crowding into districts within the town walls, or lived outside in the densely populated suburbs. There has been fruitful research on both the geographical and socio-political origins of these immigrant movements in Florence, Genoa, Barcelona and Lyon. In the absence of any real population returns, lists of heads of households (*chefs d'ostels*) liable for direct taxation, lists of rent-payers with feudal obligations, rolls of adults liable for military service or married women (Annecy) enable the historian to make 'accurate approximations' (to use A. Croix's phrase), despite the uncertainties surrounding both the concept of the fiscal hearth and exemption from taxation.[2] This evidence leaves no doubt that most centres of population were small; in fact, the majority of fourteenth-century towns barely reached or exceeded 1,500 to 2,000 inhabitants.

[1] Taylor (1954).　　[2] Croix (1974), p. 43.

The population of Chambéry, the favourite residence of the dukes of Savoy, was undoubtedly less than 4,000 in the fourteenth century; Annecy, capital of the counts of Geneva, scarcely 1,500; the majority of the towns in the Forez (with the exception of Montbrison), of the county of Comminges, the duchy of Brittany (excluding Nantes, Rennes and Vannes) and Portugal were of this order of magnitude. Against this background, towns with 10,000 to 20,000 inhabitants were in a different class: York, Norwich, Bristol (the most important English towns after London) fall within this range. Any urban centre with over 20,000 citizens already had a great range of diverse activities and exceptional influence in the surrounding region. Population levels were highest before the catastrophes of the fourteenth century: Paris, it has been argued, had more than 200,000 inhabitants, followed by Florence, Genoa, Milan, Naples, Palermo, Rome and Venice (all with populations of *c.* 100,000); London may have had 80,000, Ghent, between 50,000 and 60,000 inhabitants, and Bruges around 50,000; others (Rouen, Lyon, Cologne, etc) with levels between 20,000 and 40,000. Of the recently founded towns of central and eastern Europe Lübeck probably had a population of 15,000 in 1300; Danzig, Magdeburg, Nuremberg, Vienna and Prague nearly 20,000. These are hypothetical figures, and those relating to Paris and London in particular have frequently been debated. Nevertheless, even these approximations demonstrate both the expansion of urban populations and their limits. It is questionable whether there were between eighty and one hundred towns with more than 10,000 inhabitants in the whole of Europe.

The urban landscape had been modelled for generations to come in the preceding centuries, above all in the thirteenth. Full topographical reconstruction of town plans reveals either 'double towns' (the association of an episcopal city founded in the classical period and a dynamic, mercantile and artisanal *bourg*, which had developed near an abbey at a later date, such as Périgueux, Toulouse or Narbonne), or complex, multicellular settlements stemming from the combination of an ancient centre with *bourgs* on its periphery, which were the result of major phases of urban expansion (Paris, Reims, Leiden). But the majority of reconstructed town plans have a less elaborate structure. To oversimplify wildly – for every plan is in fact an individual case – sometimes they were no more than a main road, with a lane inside the walls and a few secondary roads joining the two; sometimes they copied some new towns and employed a more or less regular grid layout, which resulted from more considered town planning (Aigues-Mortes, Montauban); sometimes a radial-concentric plan was adopted, with the oval or circular extent of the town walls defining its outer limits and the subordination of the most important roads to a centre, occupied by church (Brive), castle or market hall (Bruges).

Although the available space was seldom measured, except in Mediterranean towns (Venice, Palermo, Naples) and cultivated land was still to be found within the ramparts, circulation within the town remained extremely difficult. Only one or two major roads joining the main fortified gates (the High Street, la Rue, la Grande Charrière) were capable of carrying carts and other heavy traffic. The other ways, the maze of tiny streets, alleys and passageways, further divided into *quartiers*, or districts (Tarascon, Cahors) were no more than steep and twisting passages or *boyaux* (Chartres), darkened by overhanging houses, blocked by tools, materials and filth. At the outset of the fourteenth century there were very few lords or communities with any concern for the maintenance of roads, the alignment of façades, or for public health (Saint-Omer, Aurillac and the Italian towns).

The town walls undoubtedly impeded circulation. They protected most large towns and the extension of walls to encompass settlements on the edge of the town is also an indicator of urban expansion. The surface area of fortified Paris grew from a dozen hectares under the first Capetians to 275 hectares under Philip Augustus, before reaching 400 hectares in the reigns of Charles V and Charles VI, with the extension of the town walls on the right bank. This was a considerable area, but in no way exceptional: Ghent and Cologne, for example, both covered more than 500 hectares. But the majority of middle-sized and unimportant towns made do with a fortress and a fortified church (Saint-Malo) and the walls were very far from being complete along their entire length, let alone harmonious and effective – despite the picture of Epinal familiar from numerous chronicle miniatures.

Over the years – and often at great expense, jeopardising their fragile budgetary equilibrium – European towns had been endowed with the wonders of Gothic architecture which were the focus of their worship, commerce and fellowship. The beginning of the fourteenth century saw the further elaboration of this monumental heritage. Building yards were busy at many cathedrals: the choir of Evreux Cathedral, the nave at York, the cathedrals of Utrecht, Siena, Florence and Lucca all date from this period. The numbers of parish churches, chapels and hospitals increased everywhere in response to the larger areas covered by towns and the changing structures of traditional religious life. The mendicant orders – Dominicans, Franciscans, Carmelites, Poor Clares – established themselves with the support of both the people and the town authorities: 423 convents were founded between 1210 and 1275; 215 between 1275 and 1350.[3] The presence of such convents, as well as their numbers, provide an additional means of identifying and classifying towns, since the gifts of the faithful could lodge and support three or four convents. The church of St Dominic at Perugia (founded in 1305) was a source of inspiration, with its

---

[3] Emery (1962), p. 3.

three naves of equal height dramatically increasing the interior space. The northern communes, the consulates of Italy and Aquitaine and other advanced municipal regimes in England and Germany were all concerned about their official buildings, the places of government and commerce which constituted 'public palaces': the Palazzo Vecchio at Florence (built between 1299 and 1315); the belfries sited at the very heart of northern and Flemish towns (Ypres finished in 1285, Ghent finished in 1337); the squares for public assembly in Italy (the 'piazza del Campo' in Siena or the Florentine 'piazza del Duomo'); the guildhalls of England and Flanders, French *maisons communes* or German *Rathäuser*, such as that at Breslau – to say nothing of covered markets, bridges and so on.

The towns of *c.* 1300 certainly do not present a picture of decline, although there had been ominous portents on the horizon for at least two generations. The bankruptcy of the patrician class (the merchant oligarchy whose dominance was based on money and marriage alliances) was already evident in many centres, where their corruption and inefficient management of public finance had already been denounced and attacked. The rift between rich and poor, the *popolo grosso* and the exploited and humiliated *popolo minuto*, grew wider every day. The first urban problems sprang from this gulf, provoked by countless injustices and the exploitation of the misery of the poor: strikes (Douai), riots (at Ypres and Bruges *c.* 1280, at Paris in 1306–7), lasting revolts in Italy and Flanders.

A CENTURY OF SUFFERING

Chapter headings such as 'Era of the Apocalypse' or 'The epoch of tragedies', 'Century of affliction' or 'Century of the Hundred Years War' underline the profound fracture in the west during the fourteenth century: catastrophe was piled upon catastrophe; no town or generation was spared. The murderous triple procession of famines, plagues and war were branded on the memory, even when all the other factors which helped put an end to earlier expansion were forgotten.

The vicious circle that had started in the second half of the thirteenth century grew steadily worse. At an early date whole regions and complete towns experienced difficulties with food supplies: Castile from 1301, Languedoc the following year, Paris in 1305. Particularly disadvantaged areas suffered regularly from malnutrition, shortages and famines caused by poor harvests, difficulties of supply and the shameless speculation of merchants and tax farmers, together with grossly inflated prices and inadequate arrangements for the storage of grain. People weakened by malnutrition were especially vulnerable to epidemics (Orvieto). The great famines produced wholesale slaughter in a world that was already overcrowded, especially in the towns, which were natural outlets for rural overpopulation. Northern Europe was affected in 1315–16; Languedoc in 1332 and 1375; Catalonia and Barcelona in 1333. In that 'first bad year' 10,000 died in Barcelona, 20 per cent of the population. In the few weeks between 1 May and November 1316, the population of Ypres was reduced by 2,974 inhabitants, or 10 per cent. An eye-witness described how every day the bodies of those who had collapsed from starvation had to be collected from the streets and hastily buried in ditches dug for the purpose in new cemeteries. Moreover, fear of food shortages remained a major concern of municipal administrations throughout the fourteenth century. It partly explains their tight hold over the hinterland (*plat pays, contado*) which was in any case often incapable of feeding the citizens for a whole year (Genoa, Venice), implementing authoritarian price controls and similar measures.

Illnesses termed 'plagues', often of uncertain origin, had already struck the towns of the west more than once. At the beginning of the century Seville (1311) and Valencia (1326, 1335) had been severely affected. But these were a mere prelude to the Black Death, which heralded universal pandemonium. Carried in Genoese ships from Caffa in the Crimea, it reached Messina in September 1347. The 'plague' – bubonic plague, characterised by buboes (inflamed glandular swellings) and often accompanied by pulmonary complications and septicaemia – struck western Europe in 1347–52. The spread of this scourge can be traced from town to town: Marseille was affected in November 1347, Avignon in March 1348, Lyon and Toulouse in April, Rouen in July, Paris in August. It had reached London by the end of 1348, Copenhagen and Bergen in 1349, Lübeck in June 1350. The disease slackened its grip in severe winters, but was reactivated by heat and humidity. It disappeared for a while, to return with a vengeance every ten or fifteen years: these crises occurred in 1360–3, 1373–5, 1382–3, 1389–90 and at the very end of the century. A combination of circumstances made the towns particularly vulnerable: districts with high population densities, the presence of garrisons and refugees in times of war, the insanitariness of poor housing, as well as the promiscuity that prevailed there; then there were the rivers of semi-liquid waste, that accumulated in the streets and contemporary opinion condemned as an undoubted source of infection, and the proliferation of rodents and fleas which carried the disease. There are no precise mortality statistics, for the numbers cited by contemporaries (60,000 deaths at Avignon according to the papal doctor Guy de Chauliac) are sheer fantasy. Nevertheless, the severity of the outbreak can be gauged by the wave of panic which seized those in important positions (such as the rich men, *richs homens,* of Valencia) in their frantic flight to isolated locations; by the attitude and resigned comments of others, and by the violent or emotive reactions of specific individuals. Higher levels of purchase of mortuary cloths (Lyon, Florence), an appreciable increase in the number of wills in notarial writing-offices (Besançon) or bequests to churches and mendicant convents are all significant factors. At the same time there was a sharp drop in the number of taxpayers and apprenticeship contracts, as well as in the revenue from municipal levies. It has been possible to assess the impact of the epidemic upon population level from tax records. Two registers from Albi, the tax lists (*compoix*) of 1343 and 1357, show a fall in the number of taxable hearths in the town from 1,550 to 685. It has been estimated that the population of Toulouse fell from 50,000 to 19,000 between 1335 and 1405, a decline of 58 per cent over seventy years. Most assessments confirm the impression of demographic collapse given by the contemporary chronicler, Jean Froissart, who wrote that 'a third of the world died'.[4]

Individuals in positions of responsibility at local level were well aware of the gravity of the plague, the speed with which it took hold and the dangers of contagion, although they were unable to understand the origin or causes of this implacable calamity, traumatising in its very selectivity – sometimes affecting mainly adults, on other occasions striking primarily at children (the *mortaldad dels infants* at Valencia in 1362), the poor rather than the rich. They were reduced to isolating the dying in their homes, or in hospitals which became little more than places to wait for death; renting rough-and-ready premises, including old wine presses (Nantes) or huts (Annecy); introducing controls and restrictions on travelling, expelling foreigners – such as soldiers or merchants – who came from regions already affected; sometimes they even had to dispose of the sick before they were dead (Uzerche). Doctors and barber-surgeons were recruited everywhere, together with nursing personnel – but so were gravediggers. Every cloud has a silver lining; the plague at least provided a (rare) opportunity to clean roads and adopt public health measures, suppressing liquid sewage and night soil dumps (*bouillons et dépotoirs*) and organising new drains and conduits.

It is still more difficult to assess the impact of wars on urban history – 'wars' in the plural because the Hundred Years War, interrupted by treaties, over-shadowed other shorter and more localised conflicts. We need only mention here the civil war in Castile between Peter the Cruel and Henry of Trastámara in 1366–9 and its continuations, the bloody struggles between various towns, rivalry between seafaring powers in the Baltic, the ravages of brigands in France or of mercenaries in the pay of communes or tyrants in Italy, the conflicts in Florence of 1303, factional struggles (the Blacks and the Whites at Pistoia), vendettas and even urban manifestations of peasant uprisings, such as the revolt of English workers in 1381. Each period of tension was accompanied by

---

[4] Froissart, *Chroniques*, ed. Luce, IV, p. 100.

sieges, pillage and massacres. The onset of peace might sometimes prove still more dangerous, with the demobilisation of mercenaries, deprived of the pay, ransom and booty to which they had grown accustomed. These dangers were of course unequally spread. Properly fortified, the great urban centres were better protected than large villages and – unless there was some untoward incident, such as treason or a revolt – they escaped the destruction of siege and *chevauchée*. It was only the unprotected suburbs that were at the mercy of the smallest band. The *chevauchées* of the Black Prince across Languedoc in 1355, then in northern Aquitaine before the battle of Poitiers in 1356, were campaigns of systematic pillage and destruction in which the suburbs of Narbonne and Carcassonne, and churches and monasteries on the edge of towns (Castelnaudry), together with leather and textile workshops (Limoux), paid a high price. The worst excesses were committed by bands of brigands (*routiers*) operating around Paris and in the Ile-de-France in 1356–60; in September 1358 the Navarrese employed by Charles the Bad, who had just failed to take the town of Amiens, took vengeance by firing the suburbs: according to Froissart, over 3,000 houses were destroyed in the blaze. Even making allowance for exaggerations, there is no doubt that sixty years later there were still traces of ruins and charred walls. The presence of a garrison was just as dangerous for the area in which they lodged as for the hinterland which they systematically ravaged, molested and attacked (*travailliet, herriet et guerriet*). English troops quartered at Lusignan in Poitou were responsible for ravages that discredited the occupying forces in the eyes of the indigenous population. Finally, there was one other form of destruction in time of war: the deliberate burning of houses both to free a clear line of fire and so that they could not offer cover to any assailant. Even when it was justified, this decision had catastrophic effects (Tours, Poitiers).

Yet the trilogy of war, plague and famine, however catastrophic, cannot in themselves entirely explain the difficulties experienced by most of the towns of western Europe in the fourteenth century. There were also individual dramas in the general crisis. A freak flood at Narbonne in 1316 caused 300 dwellings to disappear in the course of a single night. Fires were also frequent, since the majority of homes were still built of wood or cob and roofed with thatch: 355 houses were destroyed in Strasburg in 1298, while an unidentified epidemic accounted for 15,000 deaths in 1313–15, according to a Basle chronicle; fire ravaged Montbrison in 1359 and an earthquake destroyed Montpellier in 1373.

The problems associated with the emergent modern state, the demands of kings and princes confronted with urgent demands for money to establish their administrations and diplomacy, levy armies and sustain their lifestyle must also bear some responsibility for crisis in the towns. The citizens constantly denounced unjust taxes (*maltôtes*) and exactions, complaining about forced loans, the ever-increasing rate of indirect taxation (*aides*), hearth taxes (*fouages*), direct taxation (*tailles*) and the salt tax (*gabelle*). They frequently had to support three levels of taxation: old feudal taxes levied by local lords, new taxes imposed by the king or prince, as well as municipal levies to maintain town walls and garrisons. Like the peasants they had, in some kingdoms, to bear the consequences of repeated devaluation and manipulation of the coinage: eighty-five in France between 1337 and 1360, more under Charles VI after 1385. These measures seemed justified by the shortage of bullion and the hope of wiping out debts while at the same time increasing surpluses, but they discouraged investment by people of independent means, investors and merchants, while creating a climate of uncertainty that was damaging to the economy and trade. Return to monetary stability was one of the principal demands of Etienne Marcel and of the delegates of the estates general of the Languedoïl, meeting at Paris in 1355–8. The scorn, hatred and aggravation felt or suffered by strangers (the English at Paris in 1358), pawnbrokers, Lombard bankers, Jewish communities persecuted during the Black Death and living under the permanent threat of expulsion did nothing whatsoever to encourage investment or the resumption of business.

The city paid a high price whenever disaster struck or there was political conflict. Civic life was disrupted or even paralysed for several years, and the consequences can be measured in terms of economic activity, social unrest and insecurity. Whole districts lay in ruins or were abandoned by their inhabitants. Fiscal records document case after case of desertions, habitually describing places as *frostes, desbastives, dekeues et awasties* (Flanders); here and there, well-maintained houses had been replaced by ruined and deserted buildings (*masures ruineuses, desherbregées*). In 1375 town officials in Reims recorded falls in the rental value of houses of the order of 30 to 50 per cent. At the same time, royal commissioners visiting Troyes gave evidence in their report of the departure of the majority of overtaxed inhabitants: '[they] have left and are leaving the town because of the charge with which they are burdened, and only 300 taxable hearths remain'.[5] The fall of property values in supposedly wealthy areas confirmed the scale of the disaster. Calculations based on the inventories of the townspeople of the Toulousain made for tax purposes (*livres d'estimes*) reveal that the overall estimate of urban wealth in the area, estimated at 1,750,000 *livres tournois* in 1335, fell to 460,000 *livres* in 1384 and to below 300,000 *livres* in 1391.

The situation was repeated at a local level from building yards to workshops, markets to tax farmers. However, we must refrain from generalisation. Towns

[5] Bibolet (1975), II, p. 14.

less acutely affected, or those which enjoyed an extended period of tranquillity, recovered quickly, even from the plague. Lisbon was on the way to becoming a great Atlantic port in the fourteenth century; Barcelona only showed signs of decline at the end of the century; Avignon continued to exploit the presence of the pope, and – at a completely different level – with the return of peace and end of the War of Succession, small towns in Brittany were already turning the modest resources of their hinterland to profit and joining the great trade routes.

The difficulties encountered in daily life were also responsible for the climate of insecurity that prevailed everywhere. Signs of discontent, uprisings prompted by misery and the exasperation of the lowest orders of society became increasingly frequent, culminating with a paroxysm in the period 1378–82, which was marked by disturbances at Florence (1378), Ghent (1379–82), in towns in France and in the great French fiefs (Nîmes, Le Puy in 1378, Montpellier in 1379), in Germany (at Danzig, Brunswick, Lübeck). These revolts did not usually last long, but their violence took people unawares: the inhabitants hurled themselves on to the streets – tradespeople, members of guilds and their servants, building labourers, hired agricultural workers who lived in semi-rural suburbs (Béziers in 1381). The prospect of pillage lured many from the fringes of society; they were joined by agitators with political motives from areas favourable to radical change. Most chroniclers were unsympathetic and speak of *effrois*, *commotions* and *communes*, or use local names, such as the *rebeynes* at Lyon, the *Harelle* (from the rioters' cry of *Haro*) at Rouen (1382), the revolt of the *maillotins* (carriers of mallets) at Paris (1382), the rising of the Ciompi at Florence (1378) and so on. Historical and sociological research has endeavoured to uncover cycles of violence, as at Lyon[6] or in the Languedoc,[7] tracing the increasing level of discontent to its final explosion, and emphasising the xenophobic, anti-clerical and anti-Semitic sentiments that resulted (at Paris in 1382). Efforts have also been made to identify revolts prompted by taxes and uprisings triggered by poverty, as well as those kindled by political movements and dominated by strong personalities, such as Pierre Coninc at Bruges at the beginning of the century, James and Philip van Artevelde at Ghent (1334–45 and 1375–82) and Etienne Marcel at Paris (1355–8).

It is more difficult to document the chronic insecurity experienced by those who had come down in the world, by the maladjusted and delinquents of every description, and by the endlessly scrounging gallows birds – to be found on the streets, beneath porches, in graveyards and at every fair and market. In normal conditions every social unit has a disruptive fringe; in the fourteenth century

[6] Fedou (1964).　　[7] Wolff (1954).

this element was swollen by the influx of refugees, with rural poverty aggravating the situation in the town, and exacerbated by increased destitution and the presence of mercenaries. The town then became a magnet for fringe elements of every kind, a pack of violent men, beggars or *caymans*, vagabonds, ribald men and trollops in 'goliardic' bands, besides professional criminals. The richest judicial sources to date, the registers of the Paris *parlement* or the *châtelet*, which incorporate thousands of trial records or letters of pardon, enable us to reconstruct a disturbing subsection of society whose exploits were the talk of the neighbourhood.[8] Eventually, the towns became concerned and imposed constraints; in 1354 John II of France instructed one of his legal officers, Pierre Lieuvillier, to use all possible means to purge the kingdom of criminals who disrupted public order, citing 'coin clippers, highwaymen, thieves male and female, abductors of women, muggers, swindlers, those who give false witness'. The ordinance proved ineffectual and the situation deteriorated to such an extent that, in 1395, the citizens of Paris were afraid of going out after nightfall, in case they were attacked by 'people of low degree'. Legislation was much concerned with vagabonds and layabouts (particularly shocking at such a time of population decrease and labour shortages), prostitutes and the pimps and ruffians who protected them, whose presence was an affront to honest citizens. An ordinance of John II the Good of 1351 gave beggars three days in which to choose between work and expulsion, with heavy penalties – including branding with a red-hot iron – for those unwilling to work.

But urban violence was by no means the exclusive preserve of down-and-outs. The citizen had every opportunity to have a drink and 'warm himself' in one of the many taverns (sixty-six in Avignon). Behaviour was remarkably impulsive: 54 per cent of the cases heard before the Avignon law courts related more or less directly to physical and verbal violence and brawls alone represented more than 40 per cent of the total, abuse (*injure*) 7 per cent, while theft accounted for a mere 3.5 per cent of the total.[9] There are similar figures for Paris, Reims, Rennes and the towns of the Touraine.

A CENTURY OF CHANGE

The picture of misery habitually presented by contemporary chronicles and by seigneurial and municipal archives should not blind us to the changes which were taking place in towns in the fourteenth century.

Architectural expansion was checked neither by war nor by plague. The general climate of insecurity even encouraged military building. All over Europe authorities took the initiative in improving or extending their town

---

[8] Geremek (1976).   [9] Chiffoleau (1980), pp. 342-3.

walls, so that new areas were protected. Work was in progress at Hamburg and Pisa in about 1300, at Genoa and Regensburg from 1320, at Louvain, Brussels and Barcelona in the middle of the century, at Augsburg *c.* 1380. With the resumption of the Hundred Years War, sleepy French masons' yards that had seen little work during the years of peace and demobilisation were reinvigorated. And so the fortifications were improved in a number of French towns: Reims after 1337, Toulouse (1345–80), Paris at the time of Etienne Marcel (when the city was terrorised by both mercenaries and Jacques), Poitiers under the rule of John, duke of Berry (1372–1416). Everyone – the king himself, castle governors, local lords – encouraged municipal initiative. An edict of Charles V, dated 19 July 1367, ordered the French towns that enjoyed especial royal favour (*bonnes villes*) to put their defences in order with a minimum of delay. Although many town walls were improved and towers, gateways and curtain walls better adapted to changes in siegecraft, nevertheless the results were by no means universally satisfactory, nor do they stand comparison with what remains of the fortifications at Avignon and York, or at Obidos or Guimares in Portugal. By no means everyone was convinced of the long-term importance of good defensive fortifications. Individualism and dogmatism combined to obstruct participation in the requisite collective financial effort (Poitiers). Bishops and canons were accused of culpable negligence; the incensed townspeople of Reims invaded the archbishop's palace, claiming that he had failed to discharge his responsibilities as their protector! Some badly managed and hastily executed works were notoriously inadequate. Lack of funds resulted in sections of curtain wall remaining unfinished, replaced once the opening had been made with a simple fence (Troyes) or by the back of houses (the so-called *murenches* at Annecy).

Improvements in fortification were accompanied by re-enforced garrisons, militias and other defensive forces. When Florence was threatened by Henry VII of Luxemburg in 1312, the city was in a position to mobilise 12,000 citizens, both *contadini* and mercenaries, foot-soldiers and cavalrymen. From 1317 the townspeople of many French towns entreated Philip V to appoint vigorous captains to defend them. As a result, the office of town captain was widespread and it became one of the hubs of local administration, the private preserve of impoverished nobles who were tempted by the wages and material advantages which it offered. Mobilising the militia was one of the duties of the captain-governor. Theoretically, it was the duty of every 'head of household' between sixteen and sixty to present himself, armed, at every muster. These individuals were then dispersed along the walls in units of twelve or of fifty men, known as *dizaines*, or *cinquantaines*. The town guard had three main functions: to keep watch at the gates of the town (a prestigious task, reserved for leading citizens), sentry duty on the towers and the night-watch (or *arrière-guet*) in the streets of the towns. We should not harbour any illusions about the military calibre of the citizens: they were badly trained and equipped, with little motivation. The sorties made by the citizens of Paris in the years 1356–8 and their clashes with mercenaries during the same period were far from successful!

There was a gradual general improvement in the level of equipment in all garrisons. The information supplied by the earliest accounts and inventories is very disparate. The word 'artillery', taken in the very broadest sense, refers to bladed weapons, catapults and other siege engines. The first canons (called *bastons* or *engins*) gradually made their appearance on the ramparts: heavy bombards at first (at Lille or Tournai from the early 1340s), gradually complemented by other, more suitable calibres – serpentines, tapered *veuglaires* and mortars with a vertical trajectory. They required specialists to handle them, under the command of a 'master of canons' – gunners rather than merely blacksmiths. Some towns became famous for the manufacture of arms: Liège had gunsmiths, besides manufacturers and finishers of swords; from the fourteenth century onwards there was a sizeable iron and bronze fire-arms industry at Dinant and Namur, while huge orders for armour and equipment were vital for the economies of Milan, Brescia and other Lombard cities.

Whenever towns had a respite from warfare – or if they were simply lucky enough to escape it – they continued to expand and increase their massive resources. The landscape underwent a process of continual expansion both inside the walls and beyond them, sometimes changed out of all recognition. After the papal move to Avignon, complete with cardinals and all the departments of the papal curia (1309–78) and accompanied by a great wave of immigrants, the town of Avignon was completely remodelled. Continued growth within the town saw the building of a fortified papal palace, individual mansions and other buildings to house a population that quickly doubled to more than 30,000. The Italian towns continued to expand and an increasing number of private and public palaces were built: the mid-century Bargello (or Palazzo del Podestà) at Florence, the Palazzo Pubblico at Siena and the Palazzo Ducale at Venice. These were public palaces on the grand scale, with splendid façades decorated with painting or sculpture, such as the Platea Communis at Parma, or the Sienese Campo. Then there were the fountains, often copying the masterpieces of Niccolo Pisano of Perugia, and the bridges lined with shops, such as the Ponte Vecchio at Florence or the Ponte Nuovo at Pisa. The same vitality was reflected in the new belfries of northern European towns with their clocks and bells (Béthune, Bruges, Douai, Ghent, Termonde), as well as in the town halls (*Rathäuser, Bürgerhäuser*) of German towns (Aachen, Cologne). The commercial facilities which promoted trading activities also developed: they ranged from simple arrangements for bakers and fishmongers, from merchants' booths and covered galleries (such as those documented at Geneva or Chambéry), to purpose-built market halls the size of cathedrals (Florence), the first bourses, or money markets (Bruges, Barcelona) or the monopolistic arsenals of Venice and Barcelona. Even in a country ravaged by war, the presence of a royal or princely court stimulated a revival. The arrival of John, duke of Berry, at Poitiers at the end of the century brought relief to a settlement laid waste by constant warfare, as well as the deliberate fire of 1346. It provided the stimulus for a fresh division of the land into individual plots, construction of a great clock tower (the *Gros Horloge*), restoration of the comital palace, cathedral and town walls. Despite the disruption of the events of 1346–60, Paris and the Ile-de-France experienced renewed urban growth in the reigns of Charles V and Charles VI, with the extension of the Louvre and new town houses for the higher nobility (which stimulated complex land and property transactions); college buildings for students also transformed entire neighbourhoods, such as the university quarter in Paris. There were similar revivals at Mantes, Meaux and Tours, as well as at Rouen, with building works for both the cathedral and the church of St Ouen.

For ecclesiastical building continued in the fourteenth century – witness, for instance, the cathedrals at Florence ('the most noble church in Tuscany'), Orvieto and Siena.[10] English builders produced masterpieces of the Decorated and Perpendicular architectural styles, such as the choir and cloister at Gloucester (after 1340), Exeter Cathedral and the naves of Canterbury and Winchester. This period also saw the construction of the unique church of St Mary-of-the-sea at Barcelona and the cathedrals of Malines and Huy.

Pressure on existing urban layouts is reflected in the further subdivision of plots (along the Strand in London, for example), alterations in the plan of existing neighbourhoods (as in the Rive quarter at Geneva) and the building of more new suburbs. (According to J. Heers, seventy examples of settlements outside town walls are documented for the period 1320–48.[11]) The fourteenth century saw the development of a concept of urban political theory, backed by coercive legislation. From 1309 the city councillors (*aediles*) of Siena required formal permission for building beside a road; elsewhere municipal authorities forbade extensions, projecting towers, galleries or balconies which broke the unity of the existing street façade, as well as impeding the circulation of traffic and cutting off the light. There was also demonstrable progress in sanitary arrangements: at Pavia and Vannes, for example, drains were laid to complete the Roman system that was still in use; elsewhere, priority was given to paving the more important streets; the distribution of drinking water was improved by the construction of wells, aqueducts, underground conduits and fountains.

---

[10] Bargellini (1977), pp. 60–1.   [11] Heers (1961).

Even underground drains, however, could not hide the shortcomings of the system, or the appalling pollution in areas inhabited by butchers, dyers and tanners.

It is difficult to say whether these public works played any part in increasing the responsibility of the individual citizen at a local level, for such municipal progress was by no means universal. A town might lose its right to self-government if it had no charter, or simply in the natural course of political evolution. Even so, it is important to realise that, in the so-called emancipated towns, the common people did not always want to preserve the existing communal or consular privileges which had brought them nothing, preferring to replace corrupt oligarchical government by a royal officer, who could offer them effective protection. The issue was expressed in these terms at Sens, Compiègne and Senlis at the beginning of the fourteenth century. Tournai, virtually on the border with the county of Flanders, had a highly advantageous communal charter that gave it a substantial degree of autonomy; these liberties were suspended by Charles V in the fourteenth century, and a royal *bailli* appointed. Saint-Quentin was similarly unfortunate: the charter was suspended in 1311, for an attempt to 'deceive' the king about the nature of its privileges! There were heavy penalties for the crime of *lèse-majesté*. The king's fury (*ira regis*) struck Meaux, accused of collusion with the supporters of Etienne Marcel and the Jacques; there were executions, followed by the abolition of municipal privileges; henceforth the town was governed by the *prévôt* of Paris. Rebellions incited by extreme poverty and excessive taxation met equally harsh punishments in Rouen and Paris in 1382–3.

Towns that had not yet received the right to self-government remained subject to seigneurial authority (in Brittany). Others (above all in Lombardy) that were embroiled in endless conflicts chose to renounce their unequal and sclerotic pseudo-democracies and put themselves under the tutelage of a *signore* – a tyrant kept in power by the proletariat and mercenaries, who established a dynasty through the transfer of his dictatorial powers to his children. Matteo Visconti (who died in 1322), captain of the people for life, imposed his law and descendants upon Milan, capital of a principality that was elevated to the status of dukedom in 1395. The Visconti were emulated at Ferrara by the marquises of Este, at Genoa by Simone Boccanegra ('lord and doge for life'), as well as at Bologna and Verona. Venice believed this fate had been averted by the execution on 15 April 1355 of the ambitious doge, Marino Falier, a product of the new men or *homines novi*, but the city fell instead into the vice-like grip of the aristocratic ruling Council of Ten.

Setting aside these reservations, it is undoubtedly true that isolation in times of war, the difficulties experienced by governments attempting to control any crisis, the politics of 'continual haggling' between the ruling power and the various collective interests generally favoured the urban privileges enjoyed by the *bonnes villes*.[12] This expression was increasingly used to denote supposedly rich and prosperous urban settlements, enclosed with town walls (thirteen in Forez, twelve in the Lyonnais, eleven in the Bourbonnais), endowed with a minimum of institutions, but enjoying special relations with the king and his court. These took the form of letters exchanged with 'cunning cordiality' (Tours), despatch of delegations to the royal court and to representative assemblies of the nation and displays of loyalty each time the king made a formal entry into the town. Improved relations with the French crown were most evident in the least-developed areas. Chronicle evidence indicates that citizens were most frequently called upon to negotiate directly with princes and their captains, and with the leaders of armies, to discuss matters and to give 'fealty and homage'.

Generally, the apprenticeship of municipal government began with the collection of local taxes (*deniers communs*). This had previously been the duty of the princely and seigneurial authorities, but they accepted a transfer of responsibility and authorised the citizens to levy the taxes necessary for public works themselves. Rebuilding the town walls, purchase of new arms, payment of the garrison and militia, the costs of representation and general improvements all justified the establishment of a budget. Thus we can estimate that about 80,000 *livres* (in money of account) would be required to build an average town wall, two kilometres long, or to construct four gates and some thirty towers. Rebuilding the walls at Cahors required 67,000 *livres* in 1342, repairs at Reims came to nearly 150,000 *livres*, i.e. the cost of 2,000 houses. In the late Middle Ages many towns spent most of their resources – as much as 70 or 80 per cent in some cases – on their ramparts! Financial problems soon loomed large. The usual sources of income of small places – city tolls, rents from fisheries in the town moat and from meadows, income from the operation of quarries or of tile works (Annecy), the sale of salvage, judicial fines – could be no more than a stopgap. It was not long before urban taxation, both direct and indirect, became standard throughout Europe. Municipal administrations everywhere – under the periodically renewed authority of their sovereign – had recourse to exceptional levies. Their level was calculated in relation either to the sum required (Périgueux, Saint-Flour), or (in Italy) on the basis of the *allibramentum*, which was assessed on the *estimo*, or inventory of goods. Elsewhere these taxes might take the form of more-or-less enforced loans (Dijon in 1358–69, Siena, Pisa), subsidies from kings, bishops or popes (Périgueux, Rouen, Avignon). Taxes appeared everywhere on finished and

---

[12] Chevalier (1982).

marketed goods, as well as on foodstuffs. The only differences were the names by which they were called: *leydes* or *leuda*, *barrages* or *cloisons*. Taxes on the sale of drinks, especially wine, guaranteed the best level of return: they were called *souquet* in Aquitaine, *courte pinte* in Burgundy, *billot* or *apétissement* in Brittany. Since the town walls protected the entire community – including the peasants in the surrounding countryside – the taxation that paid for them was theoretically levied on the entire community, but in reality a whole range of exemptions operated for the benefit of clergy, nobles and officials.

The administration of taxation and expenditure meant that registers or rolls of accounts became commonplace from the second half of the fourteenth century. The existence of series of accounts – in some instances complete over long periods (Chambéry, Saint-Flour), in others only fragmentary (Dijon, Poitiers) – make it possible to follow the development of the towns' annual revenues, in money payments or kind, and to determine the principal heads of expenditure: public works, the upkeep of the town walls (*l'hobra dels murs*, as it was called at Rodez), payments for expropriations, weapons, official functions and embassies, salaries of town employees, lawsuits and the repayment of loans. Keeping these accounts, recording minutes, drawing up regulations and estimates – all these functions presupposed a qualified personnel of scribes and notaries (town clerks in England), subject to rigorous control and sometimes including officers of the king of France, the *bailli* of Rouen and members of the *chambre des comptes* (French royal accounting office) elsewhere.

In this way town administrations gradually took shape. The spectacular – but episodic – general assemblies of citizens to discuss 'the common good', the *arengo* of the Italian communes, were soon replaced by oligarchic councils of *élus* or *prud'hommes*, and by their officials, whose role was temporary at first, but then became permanent. Procurators representing each community appeared, together with variously named communal representatives – syndics, consuls and *échevins*. The practice also spread of appointing accounting officers and other officials responsible for public works, artillery, fountains and bridges (Avignon, Dijon).

The difficulties of the century accentuated the differences between rich and poor, between an affluent towndwelling minority, influential business associates or rivals, and a world of toil where there was a great gulf between master and workers and – at the very bottom of the social scale – the underworld of those who had no place at all, a strange mixture of rejects from a society that they themselves had scarcely glimpsed.

Our sources indicate that the range of eminent citizens, those referred to in documentary sources as *riches hommes*, *héritables* or *héréditaires* (in Flanders and Germany), *viri de plate* or *placiers* (Narbonne) expanded. They came to include representatives of the ordinary people (the *popolo grasso*) in addition to the traditional members – merchants of historic towns, often hit by crisis; their equivalents on the new trade routes to the north and east between Europe and the Atlantic, epitomised by the German Hanseatic League; the heads of the great Italian banking companies, still family based. There were also more lawyers, notaries, proctors and advocates, all university educated or trained in the writing-offices of their future colleagues (Lyon); there are records of increasing numbers of high-ranking magistrates, state officials, members of representative assemblies, exchequer or accounting departments, followed by fitters-out of ships, galleys and smaller vessels, then tax farmers, courtiers and (in Florence) masters of the major guilds. It is particularly difficult to understand – let alone classify – this motley world of wages and salaries, commissions and honoraria, pensions or even 'pots of wine'. Some accounts, wills and, above all, tax registers (*estimes, vaillants* and *compoix*) provide the basis for a quantitative assessment of their wealth and social position. Each town had the elite it deserved, and there is no comparison between small shopkeepers in the Forez (such as the Lardier of Montbrison, who could scarcely raise the pitiful figure of 200 to 300 *livres* required to diversify their investments) and the Le Visite, a family of rich lawyers at Lyon; the Rouen merchant family of Le Lieur, or the London wine and wool merchants who enjoyed such influence in the reign of Edward III; let alone the Venetian shipowners along the Grand Canal and the Rialto, or the Bardi of Florence who possessed the huge capital sum of 2 million florins at the zenith of their success.

Nevertheless, these very different individuals have points in common which had a profound effect on urban life and on society as a whole. Their success was often remarkably transitory. Who in Florence in 1300 could possibly have foretold the crash, forty years later, of those same Bardi, who (with the Perruzzi and the Acciaiuoli) became embroiled in risky banking operations, with royal creditors failing to make repayments; nor could anyone have foreseen their replacement by a second generation of financiers – the families of Alberti, Ricci, Strozzi and Medici. Aware of the danger and prompted by their instinct for self-preservation, the rich tended to diversify their activities and seek out fall-back positions which would offer them relative security. Whatever the level or age of their wealth, all these parvenus displayed the same concern with property investment; they also exploited the outward signs of honour and the opening of the ranks of the nobility. No one could become a member of the Council of One Hundred at La Rochelle unless he lived and owned property within the town walls. As the writer Nicholas de Villers of Verdun said, '[Rich] men acquire houses, vineyards, meadows and fields.'[13] The formula

---

[13] Schneider (1956), p. 526.

underlined the minority capacity for acquiring land, property, rights and rents. The family house was the investment *par excellence*, renovated and extended by successive acquisitions, variously called the *ostel, hostel* (Arles), *tènement* (Rouen), *manoir, torre* (Italy) and ideally located in the main street (*grande rue, magna carriera*), near the cathedral or market halls and the hub of the enclosed city. Nevertheless, we should not ignore the citizens' interest in letting property, their speculative activity in the poorest quarters, garrets let out to students, inns (Toulouse), gardens and other areas where building was not permitted (*non aedificandi*) (Geneva, Ghent). Very few of the substantial town houses whose lights in the fourteenth century dazzled the town at night with their magnificence have survived the passage of centuries. The Italian merchant cities of Florence, Venice and Siena were most splendid in this respect. In the absence of surviving examples, there is evidence from classifications according to price of houses valued at 1,000 and 2,000 *livres* and over (Reims, Saint-Flour), references to building materials, to stone 'shining like Parian marble' at Caen, evidence of sculpted panels, wall-paintings and metalwork, in short all the outward signs of wealth: vaulted cellars (Ghent, Geneva), loggias and galleries, monumental staircases, wells, lavatories, fine furniture, windows, works of art. The purchase of plots of land in the suburbs and elsewhere, of farms and smallholdings with sharecropping agreements – more rarely a lordship – constituted another step towards the ultimate and crowning success, the grant of nobility which signified a total change of status. Texts and miniatures also reveal that well-to-do citizens were interested in their wardrobe, as well as in jewels and precious objects, valuable plate, the pleasures of the table and in games of chance to such an extent that sumptuary laws and moralists at times exhorted them to greater moderation, urging them to curb the desires of both themselves and their wives! Their interest in manuscripts is an indication that eminent citizens were far from uneducated at this period. Townspeople played an important role in the development of secular culture, both through the spread of 'communal' schools which are to be found even in the smallest towns of Savoy, Poland and the Armorican peninsula, and by sending their own children to university. The citizen's pride, his concern with being seen to do well and a highly developed fear of an after-life, rather than profound personal devotion, inspired him to sacrifices that no doubt came hard to members of a class that was not by nature generous, and who were criticised for their greed. In fact, their patronage was translated into a sprinkling of gifts to churches, convents and hospitals, by payments to colleges of students, religious guilds, chambers of rhetoric (the *puys* of Flanders, also to be found at Rouen), the commissioning of works of art and, finally, the chapels which would contain their tombs.

Facing this elite was the working world of yards and workshops, which made its mark on the fourteenth century with its numbers and presence, as well as by its demands. In large towns, masters of corporate associations variously termed 'guilds', 'trades' and 'arts' (*confréries, métiers, arti*), with responsibility for their members and apprentices, artisans and labour, were a social force to be reckoned with. Parisian tax registers list at least 5,000 artisans in about 1300. There were thousands of female spinners, weavers, carders, finishers of cloth, fullers and dyers at Bruges, Ghent, Florence, Reims, Rouen and Toulouse and so on, at the mercy of their employers, the merchant-drapers who distributed raw materials and exported the finished goods. Guild members and their servants had miserable wages and deplorable working conditions; in Flanders they had to face the threat of unemployment, as a result of Edward III's embargo on exports of English wool at the beginning of the Hundred Years War; and they had to face the scorn of the more affluent members of society, who called them names such as 'blue nails' (*ongles bleus*) at Ghent, Ciompi at Florence, or even simply 'scum' (*merdaille*). Wages fluctuated for part of the century, increasing after epidemics until they were frozen by ordinances of Kings Edward III and John II (1349, 1351, 1354). They just covered food and the rent of a garret – a room of twenty square metres in the university quarter at Paris, for instance. There was never sufficient to cover price increases or pay off debts. The 15 *deniers* daily wage of a Poitevin worker, for example, bought 3 kg 200 of bread in 1362, but only 1 kg 600 in 1372, when there was a famine! Contracted markets, a reduction in the number of customers as a result of successive epidemics, increased competition from rural industries producing goods at a lower price, or simply a change of fashion – any of these factors could prove disastrous for traditional industries. Leather workers were among the first to suffer (Pisa); because of their dependence upon urban prosperity, drapers and weavers were similarly affected. The effects of economic stagnation soon made themselves felt in the old textile centres of northern Europe, at Arras, Douai, Saint-Omer, Ypres and Ghent. These difficulties explain protectionist measures, both internal and external: strangers were forbidden to sell finished goods in local markets; there was a ban on peasant weaving within a certain radius of the town (five kilometres at Ghent in 1314). Access to the higher echelons of the trade became virtually restricted to the wealthy and privileged sons of existing masters. In the course of the fourteenth century corporate statues, known in France as *la chose du roi*, became standard, as did practices such as the long and costly preparation of a 'masterpiece', the distribution of gifts and banquets for future guild members. This conservatism effectively blocked the social advancement of anyone from the lower classes, aggravating existing inequalities. Together with the pressure of taxes and

price increases, they contributed to a state of discontent, which proved a
favourable breeding ground for illicit 'alliances' and the earliest social movements, such as the Flemish *takehan* or the Italian *ristopio*, as well as the outbreaks of urban violence already mentioned. Many towns were also the scene
of conflict between 'patricians' and guild masters for control of the magis-
trature. A town like Augsburg (which solved its problems with a division of
power and the establishment of a two-chamber system in 1368) was fortunate. Force won the day in most instances (Nuremberg in 1348, Cologne in
1396) and eventually authoritarian regimes were established. Italian despots
were quick to exploit situations of this kind.

Nevertheless, a pessimistic view of economic and social conditions in
the towns at the end of the fourteenth century runs the risk of obscuring
other developments that were taking place. Imperceptibly, work in the
towns underwent a gradual metamorphosis; techniques improved with the
more widespread use of the wheel, more efficient looms and industrial
mills, which sometimes clustered on river banks in such numbers that they
endangered traffic on the water (Annecy). There was a higher level of professional expertise, and occupations became more specialised; new
branches of existing trades were developed in response to both the
demands of less easily satisfied clients and to the increasing complexity of
the job in hand. Cannoneers, who had been no more than blacksmiths in a
different area of work, became entirely distinct specialist craftsmen.
Although crisis in the textile industry had an adverse effect in many cities,
high quality production continued, with an unabated demand for
Florentine brocade and silk from Lucca. This was also a period in which
new centres developed in small towns that were able to adapt to the
demands of a popular clientele, producing lightweight materials that were
competitively priced. This was the case in Malines, Hondschoote,
Herenthals in Brabant, Bergen-op-Zoom and many small cloth towns in
England and Brittany. There was progress in other artisan activities, such as
armoury, the manufacture of paper and parchment, shipbuilding (the naval
dockyard of the French kings at Rouen).

Although the vitality of a city finds expression in its work, it is also
reflected in its entertainments. There are better records from the fourteenth century than from previous periods of the secular festivities which
enabled the townsfolk to forget their daily cares and cast off habitual constraints, as well as of the numerous religious festivals, coronation and
Corpus Christi processions (the latter became common from the
pontificate of Clement V, venerating the real presence of Christ in the
Eucharist), receptions of princes and embassies and the 'joyful entries of
the king' (*joyeuses entrées du roi*) in France, soon imitated by other princes,

when the town received its ruler with a sequence of scenes following a carefully determined route.

The contradictions of urban history at this period make it difficult to draw any general conclusions. I shall end with a quotation from a recent work by R. Fossier: 'difficulties and progress were so finely balanced that contemporaries were uncertain of the direction History was taking'.[14]

[14] Fossier (1983), p. 95.

CHAPTER 7

PLAGUE AND FAMILY LIFE

Christiane Klapisch-Zuber

AROUND 1300, it seemed that the population, to some degree everywhere in Europe, had attained its maximum and reached a ceiling. There were still few signs allowing one to foretell the slowing-down of the expansion begun almost three centuries before; these signs were to multiply in the first half of the fourteenth century. It was then, in the very middle of the century, that the terrible knell of the Black Death sounded. Thus a period opened characterised by the deadly and repeated attacks of what contemporaries interpreted as a sign of divine anger provoked by human depravity. The century closed, in fact, with another major epidemic of the terrible illness and the fifteenth, begun in an atmosphere of mourning, was to bear its ineradicable stigmata. The plague henceforth accompanied medieval man as ineluctably as, to use the words of Alain Chartier, 'the abominable sum of infinitely wicked evils': hunger, war, death.

No historian doubts that the brutal irruption of a scourge which was to become a pandemic and affect the European population for centuries stimulated profound upheavals in modes of production, living and feeling. An evaluation of the precise effects of the epidemic, of its place in the period's procession of evils, is more difficult. Did the plague, falling upon Europe, operate autonomously to subvert or renew the structures of feudal society? Was the terrifying skeleton which led an entire society in the Dance of Death the model on which historians should base their analyses? Did an increased death rate play a providential and decisive role in the human disturbances?

Research undertaken before 1965 attempted to evaluate the blows delivered by the plague; economic historians plotted the graph – or, rather, the graphs, as numerous and diverse as the towns or country villages studied – of the movement of the population at the end of the Middle Ages. For a whole generation who rubbed shoulders with Marxism to a greater or lesser extent, comparison of population graphs with those of prices and wages constituted a promising horizon. Establishing knowledge of the medieval period on solid, quantified foundations, by annexing the methods of 'serial history' which had renewed understanding of the modern period, constituted the most noble of objectives, despite the difficulties scattered in the medievalist's path.

Did historians question more recently the whole numerical range of disasters and modes of evaluation? We should rather speak of a shift of emphasis in research rather than the abandoning of approaches previously followed. One of the most fruitful ways in which the historical writing of recent decades has tackled these questions has been to examine the overall demographic reactions and the behaviour of individuals at the point where they meet – the family. Research undertaken after 1970 has been inspired by the success of works of historical demography on the modern period and reflects the concern to characterise the demographic patterns of the Middle Ages. The study of the life-cycle of the individual and of the evolution of the demographic variables in a population has taken priority over population estimates of a particular town or region. For their part, the sociology and the anthropology of the family have given rise to a shift in interest. Their critical contribution has made clearer to historians the reasons for their dissatisfaction with their own tools: for example, average family size or the estimated number of individuals in a household ('hearth'), which was the eternal stumbling-block of so many medieval estimates, recovered its meaning if it was now considered as the product of complex relationships, a sort of crossroads of demographic and economic constraints, juridical norms and family strategies. Not only the composition of the 'household' and the roles attributed to each of its members, but the articulation with the wider world of kinship, neighbourhood and the community could become central objects of historical analysis. Family structures, relations between spouses, relatives and generations, the functioning of the domestic cell as a unit of production and reproduction thus became a primary preoccupation.

In this historiographical context, the problem of changes possibly prompted by the outbreak of the plague and rise in the death rate required a new approach. It was henceforth a question of reflecting less on an environment and more on the mechanisms and the individual or collective reactions to the challenges of illness, death, numerical reduction, economic annihilation or social decline. It was, moreover, a question of defining the medieval demographic system. Was it possible to talk of continuity between the European demographic system of the Middle Ages and that of the modern periods? Between the high and the late Middle Ages? Did a complete rupture affect the variables of the demographic system and of family organisation sufficiently deeply for one to talk of different systems? If there was a break, what role did the outbreaks of plague play? Medievalists have thus been called upon to assess the place of the death rate and evaluate the other demographic statistics to compare them with those of the modern period.

Alas, their sources did not have the unity, coherence and continuity of the parish registers and fiscal or religious censuses of the *ancien régime*. How, then, were the methods of analysis devised in the use of early modern registers of births and deaths to be applied, when the medieval evidence which could be used remained desperately fragmentary and incoherent, almost always concerned a social elite and was therefore little representative of the population as a whole? The problem of sources was all the more acute as the historian's appetite grew.

Historians of the Middle Ages are used to turning everything to good account; but, in order to make their data reveal something about the death rate, the marriage rate and fertility of these periods, they undertake high-risk operations. Criticisms of such efforts are easily made and often justified. Wills, it is said, can at most be used to calculate a replacement rate, not a death rate, still less to determine fertility. Even censuses, for a long while the only resource of medieval historical demography, are rarely exhaustive and for the most part covered a limited population in such an incomplete way that all generalisation is questionable. Moreover, only exceptionally do we have data at this period about the local population in aggregate and about demographic variables – the number of deaths, for example, over a given period and in a place whose population at the same date is known. Finally, what about seigneurial taxes on marriage, illegitimate children, deaths and succession, which must take account of a degree of evasion which is difficult to assess? Will they ever present anything other than questionable values, obtained at the price of repeated manipulation of evidence?[1]

Does this mean we should stop trying to give the epidemics of times past their rightful place and penetrate the secrets of the medieval demographic system? Certainly not. The work of the last two or three decades has at least enabled us to adjust the working hypotheses. It is this above all which this chapter will attempt to take into account: lines of enquiry much more than the mass of multiple, partial and undoubtedly provisional results which research on population and the family has multiplied in the last twenty or thirty years.

POPULATION DECLINE

A prime necessity retains its urgency; as I have said, to meet this comes down to establishing oneself within an old and fertile historiographical tradition. The

[1] For criticisms of the use made of data drawn from English manorial court rolls, see Hatcher (1986), esp. pp. 20–2. For hearth registers and books of land taxes enabling the calculation of the number of houses and the density of the urban population, see Heers (1968). For surveys of hearths in Burgundy, see Leguai and Dubois in *La démographie médiévale* (1972); Carpentier and Glénisson (1962).

description of the evolution of the population development and its stages, in the various countries of Europe, and the assessment of the extent of its decline, from before the Black Death then in relation to the recurrent outbreaks of the epidemic, has continued to sustain the interest of recent works.[2] Traditionally, the picture which resulted from this was broadly based on narrative sources. These sources were often deceptive and sometimes actually misleading:[3] thus, the silence of more than one contemporary chronicler in the face of the Black Death of 1347–9 has been observed, as if terror and stupefaction had stopped his speech.[4] Worse, when his successors took heart and advanced figures for the losses caused by recurrent outbreaks of the scourge, it is generally impossible to credit them, other than as a gauge of their fear. However, population counts – from cadastres and hearth counts, registers of hearth taxes and assessments of wealth, of salt consumption, of those individuals liable to tax, books of citizenship and so on – have been exhumed or rediscovered, published or utilised in considerable numbers since 1960.[5] While not yet as diverse and abundant as those of the following century, the archives of administrations – royal, manorial or communal – became richer in the fourteenth century. Drawn up for various purposes, all these sources can reveal specific correspondences in the movement of the population and permit calculation of common reasons for it. They shed light not only on the properly numerical effects of the epidemics but also on the vigour of the authorities' reactions and the forms they took.

Deceleration of demographic growth

This is documented throughout Europe, to some extent, in the first half of the fourteenth century; likewise the stabilisation of the population at what was admittedly still a very high level. Uniformity was undoubtedly not the rule; here and there, areas or communities maintained their population level, when others were already falling.

Thus, in the first half of the fourteenth century, contrasting situations seem to have characterised England, whose total population, reaching between 4 million and 6 million (even 7 million) inhabitants after 1300, would have trebled or quadrupled in two-and-a-half centuries.[6] Difficult though an assessment of the evolution of the population between 1300 and 1348 may appear, the stagnation or demographic decline of villages and towns at the local level are scarcely more accessible. Following close on the heels of the debate opened by the

---

[2] The classic picture remains that of Mols (1954–6).   [3] Bulst (1987).

[4] On this silence, see Dubois (1988a), esp. p. 318.

[5] For a detailed list of those works which appeared before 1979, see Fossier (1979).

[6] Russell (1966); Postan (1972); and, for the higher figure, Hallam (1981); Titow (1961).

Neo-Malthusian theses of M. Postan from the 1950s,[7] English and Canadian historians have increased their research on demography and access to the land and the means of production in medieval manors and villages. Without bringing direct proof of continued rise or of an early decline, they have at least produced many examples of rural discrepancies.[8] On the manor of Halesowen in Worcestershire, for example, the population seems to have declined by 15 per cent in the famine years of 1316–17, while the population of that of Coltishall in Norfolk – the country's most densely populated region – seemed to have held up until the Black Death.[9] According to its recent historian, Bury St Edmunds, in western Suffolk, came blithely through the dark years of the fourteenth and fifteenth centuries, although the town may have lost 40 per cent of its population between 1347 and 1377;[10] but Coventry, at the very heart of the country, reached the sixteenth century in a state of total desolation.[11] Throughout northern Europe, recession often had a violent effect upon towns, while mysteriously sparing some of them.[12]

Discontinuity is no less striking between one region of France and another. When the population was at its highest point – marked by the great hearth census (*grand état des feux*) of 1328[13] – the country could have reckoned with some 15 million inhabitants within its borders at that period, but the movement to found new towns (*villeneuves*) and bastides had died out and a good number of recent creations had already disappeared.[14] Stagnation, and even some decline, also characterised the towns during the second, and above all after the third, decade of the fourteenth century, the numerical high point occurring for most of them *c.* 1320–30.[15] This can be observed in Normandy, in Reims after 1320, at Périgueux after 1330, in upper Provence and at Marseille.[16] But this trend was not uniform: the Biterrois, for example, which was no great distance from Provence, and even lower Provence, show no signs of a falling-off before the plague.[17]

Finally, to take only the example of Italy from the Mediterranean countries,[18] the population there seems to have reached its peak *c.* 1290, with perhaps 11 million inhabitants.[19] From Piedmont to the towns of Emilia and Romagna, to Tuscany and even the southern regions and the islands of the Mediterranean,

---

[7] Postan (1950a) and (1950b).   [8] Raftis (1957); DeWindt (1972); Britton (1977); Smith (1984).
[9] Razi (1980); Campbell (1984).   [10] Gottfried (1982), esp. p. 52.
[11] Phythian-Adams (1978) and (1979); Dobson (1977).
[12] For the Low Countries, see Prevenier (1983). For Germany, Dollinger (1972).
[13] Published in Lot (1929).   [14] Pesez and Le Roy Ladurie (1965); Higounet (1965).
[15] Higounet-Nadal (1980), esp. pp. 194–6, and (1988), esp. p. 301; Dubois (1988a) and (1988b).
[16] Bois (1976); Higounet-Nadal (1978), ch. 2; Lorcin (1973); Baratier (1961), pp. 80–1; Desportes
(1979).   [17] Gramain (1972); Bourin-Derruau (1987).
[18] *Les Espagnes médiévales* (1983); Berthe (1984); Guilleré (1984).
[19] Beloch (1937–61); Bellettini (1974); Del Panta *et al.* (1996).

the drop in population did not wait for the Black Death.[20] For Tuscany, the studies of E. Fiumi and D. Herlihy in particular have demonstrated that, at the end of a period of sustained growth, the population stabilised and remained at a very high level between 1290 and 1320; but in the second quarter of the fourteenth century, from before the Black Death, it declined very markedly.[21]

This fall in population did not occur in an orderly fashion by abandoning in a calculated way lands that had been quickly colonised but had proved unprofitable in the longer term, or by leaving sites that were too exposed and indefensible, and by transferring efforts to other more productive locations. It was in the angry rumbling of people made furious by dearth and speculators in foodstuffs, the desolation of devastating crises of mortality, that the great retreat of the population started. Cruel famines ran through the first half of the fourteenth century, sometimes followed by murderous epidemics, heralds of the notorious Black Death. In Italy, shortages became frequent; that of 1328–9 hit much the greater part of the peninsula,[22] and in 1339–40, then 1346–7,[23] the whole of Italy experienced the horrors of famine.[24] A terrible famine, preceded by bad weather, ravaged northern Europe after 1315[25] – Germany and the Low Countries, England and half of France;[26] in Essex three of the rural communities studied by L. R. Poos lost as much as 15 per cent of their population during these gloomy, dark years, and at Bruges and Ypres about 10 per cent of the population died of hunger in 1316.[27] On the other hand, this 'great pestilence of famine and mortality' – to use the words of Giovanni Villani – affected Italy little, only lightly touching Tuscany.[28]

The terms of the Florentine chronicler placed responsibility for 'mortality' from famine directly at the door of the 'plague'. Well before 1347 the infernal pair returned, obsessively, to the prose of annalists of the period, an association more striking because we know with hindsight that a far more formidable 'plague' was to loom on the horizon of the mid-century. The two words then are ambiguous: they associate death and disease without distinguishing the substance of either. What link should be established between deaths and subsistence crises? Did periods of high prices and dearth bring epidemics in their wake, or did the latter, disrupting economic life, prepare the way for the former?[29] The

---

[20] For an overall view, see Mazzi (1982). On particular regions: Comba (1977); Pini (1969) and (1976); Herlihy (1973); Trasselli (1964); Day (1975).

[21] Fiumi (1962); Herlihy (1967); Ginatempo and Sandri (1990). See for Tuscan details in Herlihy and Klapisch-Zuber (1978), pp. 166–71, 177–9. The fall at San Gimignano was more perceptible in rural regions than in the town.

[22] Grundmann (1970). Tuscany suffered acute shortages in 1302–3, 1310–11 and 1322–3.

[23] Cherubini (1970); Pinto (1972).   [24] Mazzi (1982), p. 37.   [25] Lucas (1930) remains fundamental.

[26] Kershaw (1973).   [27] Poos (1991), p. 106, fig. 5.2a, p. 96; Van Werveke (1959).

[28] 'Nel detto anno MCCCXVI grande pestilenzia di fame e mortalità avenne nelle parti di Germania . . . ': Villani, *Nuova Cronica*, (IX. 80), ed. Porta (1990) (X. 80), II, p. 285.   [29] Neveux (1968).

first of these relationships is simpler to grasp, but it is not confirmed in all the mortality crises before 1348. Epidemics of all kinds, diseases resulting from dearth and malnutrition surged in the wake of food shortages.[30] Typhus, tuberculosis, malaria, smallpox, influenza and broncho-pulmonary complications all found easy prey in the poor of the towns, all crammed into unwholesome accommodation, and in the starving crowds driven away from the countryside by war, poor harvests, insecurity and famine.[31] Malnutrition, and the physical weakening which resulted from it, opened the way to bacterial and viral attacks, whatever agents they had; accelerated urbanisation, crowding into insalubrious parts of the city, encouraged contagious disease. Poverty deprived the poor, confronted with disease, of the responses available to the rich cut off in their residences, or fleeing to a locality spared by the plague, resorting to doctors and surgeons, and adopting an adequate diet.

Although it is therefore difficult to identify each of the 'plagues' which decimated some towns and regions of Europe before 1347,[32] it is clear, in any case, that the poor of the towns and country paid a particularly high price. The link which contemporaries established almost automatically between the epidemic and shortages bluntly poses the problem of the equilibrium between a population greatly increased until the first decades of the fourteenth century and the resources at its disposal. In the eyes of numerous historians, the superfluous population of the early fourteenth century would have harboured the means of destruction, famines and epidemics, necessary to maintain its equilibrium with limited resources. If there were 'corrective reactions', in the Malthusian sense, they were, in this analytical framework, undoubtedly inadequate, since in the autumn of 1347 the plague returned to the European scene.

The plague

To evaluate the role and the adequacy of these supposed checks as having contained the population rise before the outbreak of the plague is difficult enough. Determining the place of this plague among the arsenal of Malthusian reactions is still more debateable.

More than a century ago, Yersin recognised the agent responsible for the

---

[30] Carpentier (1962b); McNeill (1976); Del Panta (1980).   [31] Mazzi (1978), pp. 44–65; Biraben (1988).

[32] What, for example, was the nature of the two cruellest plagues (1340 and 1347), which in Tuscany followed periods of high prices and scarcity, and of which the second, as a prelude to the pandemic of the following year, especially attacked women and children and the Florentine poor? Mazzi (1982), p. 31; Villani, *Nuova Cronica*, ed. Porta, III, pp. 225–8, 483–6. On the characteristics not pertaining to the plague of the Florentine epidemic of 1340, which according to Villani carried off 15,000 persons, and which can be measured by the register of deaths of S. Maria Novella, see Carmichael (1986), pp. 63–5. On the epidemics preceding the Black Death in France, Higounet-Nadal (1980), pp. 196–7. On the concept of pathocenosis, that is the interdependence of different illnesses, Bulst (1989).

cataclysm in the bacillus *Yersinia pestis*. Four years later, in 1898, the carrier of the bacillus, the flea *Xenopsylla cheopis*, taking refuge on man when it could not find its preferred rat, was also identified in Bombay. The role of this flea, infecting man and propagating the bubonic plague, was long the object of debate, but today no longer needs to be demonstrated.[33] Light has been progressively shed on the actual ecology of the plague, on the milieux and conditions favourable to its preservation and propagation, as well as on the variations in its symptomatology and the secondary character of pulmonary plague, contaminating directly – without the intermediate stage of a flea-bite – an individual exposed to the spit of a sick person.

This is not the place to describe the course taken by this scourge across Europe from the time when it hit Messina in September 1347: reference need only be made to the great synthesis of J.-N. Biraben, based on the totality of local researches and earlier scholarly works.[34] A rapid glance at the demographic effects of the great pandemic remains necessary, none the less. We should observe, however, that historians are still unable to specify its exact numerical impact everywhere in a satisfactory manner. Global estimates vary between one fifth and one half of the European population. Measurements remain uncertain, for it is rare to have available either detailed accounts of deaths which occurred during the actual period of the plague, or censuses shortly before and after the epidemic. One is reduced to extrapolating from very narrowly localised data, or calculating the size of the death rate by relying on indirect figures.

A first observation is essential. The extent of the epidemic is documented by the number of localities affected annually throughout Europe.[35] Beyond such statements, based above all on narrative sources and inevitably incomplete, it emerges from almost all the statistics from France based on the series of local or regional burials that the Black Death, between the end of 1347 and 1350, or even 1351, stands out as the most murderous of the mortality crises until then listed and quantifiable.[36] In England, work on manorial courts has

---

[33] Bulst (1985), esp. p. 253; Biraben (1975), 1, pp. 7–21. However, another flea, common to several species of rats, transmitted the bacillus from one to the other, while a third (*Pulex irritans*), peculiar to man, could very well have transmitted the plague: ibid., p. 13.

[34] For a chronology of the Black Death, see Biraben (1975), 1, pp. 74–81. For England, Ziegler (1969), pp. 120–201. For Scandinavia, see Benedictow (1992a) and (1992b).

[35] Biraben (1975), 1, p. 124, graph 5.

[36] See the curves of graph 3, based on the obituary list of the diocese of Sens, the deaths of the bishops of France, wills of the Lyonnais and the register of burials at Givry in Burgundy (below, n. 79). Biraben (1975), 1, p. 427, makes the graph of the landholders in the area around Lille an exception. See also observations on the registering of burials at Givry in Burgundy, Saint-Nizier (a parish of Lyon), the wills at Saint-Germain-l'Auxerrois in Paris, and on vacancies of benefices, summarised ibid., 1, pp. 156–84.

made it possible to increase estimates of its effects. The death rate among the clergy, as on many manors, averaged around 45 per cent, with higher localised points.[37] Halesowen, for example, contradicts low estimates with a death rate close to this level.[38]

It was perhaps in Italy that the heavy losses in the heart of the urban and rural populations are most dramatically attested. Bocaccio was largely responsible for the fact that the Black Death was called 'the plague of Florence'. It is true that this town, affected from March 1348 until September, suffered very severely from the attack: the epidemic succeeded in carrying away up to half the population.[39] From the islands and southern Italy, the great ports were quickly attacked,[40] and the plague reached a large part of the interior while sparing some regions like the Milan area.[41] The relatively minor impact of the plague on some localities was to recur throughout Europe in the three years that followed.

From 1349 onwards, while the plague reached Portugal from Spain, and followed its course in northern and eastern France, the Rhineland, the southern Low Countries,[42] Switzerland, Austria, Hungary, a large part of southern England, then between 1350 and 1352, reached Poland, Russia, northern Germany, the Baltic and Scandinavia, the authorities of regions already devastated assessed the damage and adjusted their administrative routine to the new situation created by the disaster. This was not actually because they sought to know the exact number of total losses, either because many people had not yet returned or because, on the other hand, the influx of new immigrants in localities denuded of their population was already apparent, but because they had to record the taxpayers or tenants who had disappeared. To take the example of Halesowen, the court of the English manor was still enquiring into deaths and registering resumptions of holdings in the six months following the end of the epidemic.[43] Florence soon decided to bring

---

[37] Based on *inquisitiones post mortem* of the propertied classes, Russell (1948), pp. 214–17, placed the average around 25 per cent, while admitting a higher death rate among monastic communities. Still lower, Shrewsbury (1970), pp. 122–4, proposed an estimated population loss of 5 per cent, seeing the Black Death as a mixture of typhus and bubonic plague, an estimate and opinion which have been robustly disputed.   [38] Razi (1980), pp. 99–107.

[39] Matteo Villani speaks of three deaths in five among the inhabitants: Villani, *Cronica* (1. 2), 9. The losses were possibly not always as heavy as the chroniclers maintained; for Bologna, where the number of men who could bear arms was reduced by 35 per cent between 1348 and 1349: Pini and Greci (1976), table x, p. 417.

[40] Biraben (1975), I, pp. 73–82; Del Panta (1980). For Venice, see Mueller (1979), esp. pp. 71–6. Carpentier (1962a) remains the fullest account of the invasion of the Black Death.

[41] Albini (1982), pp. 14–16.

[42] See Biraben (1975), I, pp. 72–111, on the spread of the pandemic. Corrections have been made to the theory (summarised in Biraben (1975) and McNeill (1976)) according to which the Low Countries were spared by the Black Death of 1348: Blockmans (1980).   [43] Razi (1980), pp. 101–3.

up to date the list of its taxpayers and undertook a new hearth register.[44] Everywhere, people tried to make good the lack of manpower and the depopulation of parishes by calling on immigration from outside: they attempted to halt runaway prices and wages, to reopen the channels of trade, to fill in the gaps in administrative, notarial and medical personnel. At Orvieto, where the archives examined in depth by E. Carpentier unfortunately do not give exact information about the purely demographic impact of the plague, the authorities increased measures in all these areas after 1348: they decided, among other things, to revise the *Lira* of the countryside, to establish a hearth tax – making a case for those headed by a widow or orphans – to strengthen family councils to protect very young and naïve heirs better from swindlers of all kinds.[45]

The epidemic lurked underground in the 1350s, reappearing suddenly here and there.[46] After 1357, from Germany, where its revisitations were many, it spread to the west and the south. Between 1361 and 1363, and perhaps also from another Venetian starting-point, a large part of the west and the Mediterranean regions were once more its prey, and this time communities which had escaped the first wave of the plague were to lose up to one third of their inhabitants.[47] This 'second plague' was to be followed by other outbreaks, separated by an average interval of eleven or twelve years,[48] until there was a new great plague, at the turn of the century, which, between 1399 and 1401, affected above all Italy, France and the Low Countries. In Tuscany, where registers of death or burial are sometimes preserved from this period onwards, the annual death rate soared, increasing sevenfold at Arezzo, seventeenfold at Florence: here the burials of more than 11,000 individuals were recorded, but contemporaries spoke of 20,000 deaths, and the town would thus have lost, at the lowest estimate, one fifth of its population, and more probably one third. At the height of the epidemic, in July 1400, the daily number of deaths in ordinary years was multiplied by forty or fifty.[49]

The first half of the fifteenth century was characterised by the staggering of epidemics and their frequent recurrence, as well as by the confusion with other forms of morbidity which makes the identification of outbreaks of plague more difficult than in the fourteenth century. After 1450, at least where registers of deaths, as at Florence or in some religious communities, make it

---

[44] Barbadoro (1933).   [45] Carpentier (1962a), pp. 178, 181, 191. See also Bowsky (1964).

[46] Biraben (1975), I, pp. 103–5.   [47] Thus Milan: Albini (1982), p. 18.

[48] Biraben (1975), I, p. 133, refutes the theory that the incursions of the plague can be related to the cycle of sun-spots but does not (p. 154) exclude an indirect influence as a result of the influence of sun-spots on the proliferation of rodents.

[49] On Florence and the *libri dei morti*: Mazzi (1984); Carmichael (1986), pp. 63–6. On Arezzo: Del Panta (1977), esp. p. 304.

possible to calculate death rates, these often once again reach high levels, with some acute periods of crisis occasionally evident from tables of annual numbers of deaths.[50] The association of the plague with shortages seems stronger and more frequent in the fifteenth century, but it is difficult to qualify the direction of this relationship.[51]

The diseases attributed to *Yersinia pestis* or infections giving rise to closely allied symptoms make contemporary diagnoses confused and questionable. It is hardly to be doubted, for example, that a smallpox epidemic had a very considerable impact on the child population from Germany to England, and from France to Italy, between 1359 and 1364 when the second, unquestionably bubonic, plague was developing, perhaps rightly called 'the children's plague' because it was difficult to distinguish deaths resulting from smallpox from those for which the plague was responsible. Moreover, recurrences of the plague in the years 1385–93 were combined with various epidemics; and thus, in 1387, the effects of influenza were mixed with those of the plague in Tuscany and Germany. In the course of the fifteenth century, supposed 'signs' of the plague on the bodies of victims probably stemmed from mistakes and uncertainties in diagnosis; today they are readily viewed as symptoms of exanthematous typhus.[52]

Contemporaries accepted the appearance of axillary or inguinal buboes as an irrefutable indication of plague. When they report them, we can trust their diagnosis and consider the presence of plague as certain (which does not exclude the possibility that it hid other, related epidemics). Another indication put contemporary observers on the alert. The alarm was sounded among those responsible for health and the authorities when they noted that deaths were increasing in a street or a house.[53] In fact, it was perhaps the lightning spread of the plague in the narrow circle of a family, decimated or wiped out in a few days, which struck contemporaries most tragically after 1348. To annihilate even the innocents for the sins of the parents was surely the sign of divine wrath. This second indication was not without importance for the perspective which will soon concern us, the family. It was because it threw into confusion inheritances and the traditional distribution of social roles that the plague most threatened the legitimate order, old solidarities and the family ties which expressed them.

---

[50] See e.g. Hatcher (1986), p. 26, fig. 1.

[51] Dubois (1988a), pp. 327–8; for an opposing view: Biraben (1975), I, pp. 147–54, suggests that, since the epidemic might – or might not – equally precede, follow or accompany famine, it is impossible to draw a conclusion.

[52] An illness caused by a rickettsia and transmitted by lice, it induced internal haemorrhages and covered the body of its victims with dark or blackish-blue marks like the so-called 'Black Death'. Carmichael (1986), pp. 10–26.   [53] Ibid., pp. 21, 24–5.

THE LIFE-CYCLE

The recording of specific signs by which the imminence or presence of the sickness was recognised is a good way of grasping political reactions to the cataclysm of 1348 and its later recurrences and the changes which affected mentalities. It teaches us little, however, about profound demographic trends which challenged the rhythms of life and death and bring us back to individual conduct.

The second half of the fourteenth century opened on a universal cataclysm and, in the course of further outbreaks of the plague, saw its hopes of demographic recovery crumble away. Where the figures are sufficiently exact for the reactions of the population in the post-epidemic period to be analysed, one notes initially the premises of a prompt recovery. Let us take the hearths (households) of one district of the Florentine *contado*, the *piviere* of Sant'Appiano. Using an index of 100 in 1350, in the immediate aftermath of the plague, they recovered in a modest but significant fashion to 107 in 1357, but an inexorable decline and the plague of 1400 made them fall back to 78; in 1427 the lowest point was reached, at index 62.[54] A second case demonstrates the place of the wholesale slaughter of 1348 in the string of different epidemics of the second half of the century and the possibilities for recovery which appeared over a long period. In the Caux region in Normandy, if the index 100 is given to the number of hearths of 1314, then this index was reduced to 97 in 1347, then fell to around 45 in about 1374–80 (of this nearly 50 per cent shrinkage in the population, 30 per cent is attributable to the Black Death, and 20 per cent to the period 1357–74). The following decades saw a very clear demographic recovery: the index had climbed back to 65 in *c.* 1410.[55]

These examples of renewed growth, very quickly reversed by returns of the plague, could be multiplied at local level. The patterns of decline and recovery are different, and the variety of reactions is evidence that the violence of the plague, in 1348, was not an irremediable event, providentially offering historians the sole explanation for the crises of the later medieval period.

In fact, if one were to end the fourteenth century at *c.* 1385, it would be the dynamism of the recovery which would be most striking; the Black Death, thus dismissed from its exceptional position, would not be sufficient to give this truncated fourteenth century its sombre tonality. But if we envisage an extended fourteenth century, lengthened to *c.* 1420, the population, eroded by the demographic fall, would have to acknowledge its defeat. The continued decline from the 1330s would then appear in all its fullness and the dramatic fall in population brought about by the Black Death would be found to be only

---

[54] Muzzi (1984), esp. p. 137.   [55] Bois (1976), pp. 51–7, 249, 277.

partially compensated for by the recoveries of the two following decades, the decline in population appearing finally confirmed by the great attack at the very end of the century and still continuing, at a slower pace, until *c.* 1420–30.

In sum, the extremely low level reached in the first decades of the fifteenth century – a level at which the population was to remain for a long while – put a stop to long-term decline and a process of demographic contraction of which the Black Death, in 1348, was the most spectacular moment. But the phases of recovery surely show that the resources of the population were not completely drained by the epidemics. Understanding the mechanisms of this long-drawn-out recession therefore presupposes analysis of the different constituents of the demographic profile, although, as we know, it is extremely difficult to assemble the necessary data for a medieval population.

The death rate

Let us start with the death rate, to which many writers allocate the prime role in regulating the equilibrium between population and resources. Indeed, it seems the best fitted to this role. However, even when deaths are accurately recorded in a closed population, such as a religious community, or any other professional group, only exceptionally is its composition by age, and thus the distribution of deaths by age, known;[56] and it is still more unusual to follow a specific group from birth, to observe the mortality quotients by age and calculate life expectancy.

Many calculations concerning the characteristics of the medieval death rate are therefore based on the estimated or probable allocation of ages to deaths in these groups of adults. Analyses have been directed towards groups of dignitaries, ruling families or religious communities; advances in prosopographical method will undoubtedly enrich the materials necessary for such an approach.[57] These enquiries have brought to light the shortened lifespan, at the end of the fourteenth century, for which a survivor of the infantile mortality toll could still hope. In the last quarter of the fourteenth century, a young English prince would thus have lost eight years in relation to the average portion his equivalent could reckon with at the end of the thirteenth century.[58]

---

[56] Thus the analysis conducted by Biraben on the death rate of 127 French bishops occupying their sees in 1355 until the total extinction of their cohort in 1391, i.e. in thirty-six years, takes no account of their age when they took office: Biraben (1975), I, pp. 177–84 and table at p. 185.

[57] We should note, however, that they are generally distorted by the uncertainty concerning the point of entry into the group and their age at that time, which makes the construction of cohorts risky: Rosenthal (1973).

[58] Ibid., p. 293, tables 1A, 1B. See also the earlier studies on the English dukes: Hollingsworth (1957); and on the longevity of English princes: Russell (1948), p. 180.

From this reduction in life expectancy, there resulted a shift towards lower ages in the distribution of deaths. Among English peers, for instance, the ages for half of the deceased were below fifty during the entire period 1350–1500, but for almost three-quarters if observation is confined to the generation born between 1350 and 1375.

Using model life-tables, the life expectancy of these adults has been estimated and compared between one period and another: it is usually around thirty years for men who had reached the age of twenty.[59] In some communities or religious orders, where the ages of entry into an institution, and exit on death, are known – or can be estimated – portions of mortality-tables have been constructed. Among the Benedictine monks of the priory of Christ Church, Canterbury, whose age of recruitment is assumed to be constant, the life expectancy, twenty or twenty-five years, was clearly lower in the generation of monks born in the second quarter of the fifteenth century who entered between 1445 and 1480 than among those who entered after 1395.[60] We should also note that, compared to the congregation of Saint-Maur in the seventeenth and eighteenth centuries, death had a much higher impact on the young Benedictines of the late fourteenth and fifteenth centuries than on the young *mauristes* three centuries later.[61]

The distribution of ages, in a close and protected community, can sometimes be observed. The convent of Longchamp, near Paris, had 46 per cent adult women (twenty to sixty years) and 24 per cent older religious in 1325, but one third in both these groups in 1402.[62] We should remember that the age structure reflects the events that had affected the different generations better than the level of general mortality. Here the greater youth of nuns recruited in the first period and the ageing population at the end of the fourteenth century probably stem from changes which affected recruitment.

Was it the same with the global population and its reactions to the stress of the epidemics? The rare age-pyramids available to us between the fourteenth and the beginning of the fifteenth century also bear witness to an ageing population. The population of the little town of Prato, near Florence, displayed some dynamism in 1371, shortly after the plague of 1363 had made drastic inroads; the comparison of this pyramid with that of 1427, almost two generations later,

---

[59] Hollingsworth (1957), pp. 10–11, and cf. Hollingsworth (1977).   [60] Hatcher (1986), pp. 28–9.

[61] Ibid., pp. 36–7; the 8,000 *mauristes* have been examined in Le Bras and Dinet (1980). However, the English peers of the late sixteenth and the seventeenth centuries had a life expectancy that was scarcely better and often worse than that which has been postulated for the peers of the fourteenth and the fifteenth centuries; see Rosenthal (1973); Hollingsworth (1964), p. 56. See also Vandenbroucke (1985); the author notes a perceptible fall in life expectancy among the Knights of the Golden Fleece born after 1500 in relation to their fifteenth-century predecessors.

[62] Dubois (1988a), p. 363.

shows that the recovery recorded then did not hinder, in the medium term, the shift of equilibrium in favour of the top of the pyramid, to the detriment of groups of the youngest ages.[63] In the first quarter of the fifteenth century, the population stabilised at the lowest level, and to some extent everywhere the youngest age categories were eroded in relation to the oldest. At Reims, in 1422, in the parish of St Peter's, those under fifteen years (domestic servants and apprentices were, it is true, not counted in this group, although there were many in the town) constituted scarcely a quarter of the population, and those sixty years and more, 7 per cent, while at Verona, in 1425, the first counted for 29 per cent but the second for 15 per cent.[64] At Florence, in 1427, the same groups of ages counted for 39 and 12 per cent respectively of the population, still very far from the proportions in a population in a growth phase.

We should not be misled by the apparent longevity of adult males frequently from privileged groups, and the real influence undeniably exerted by the old. From the demographic viewpoint, in the fourteenth century, the increased weight of the old conceals a reduction in life expectancy, even though, at twenty, it has been estimated at some thirty years and survivors of that age could still reach a very old age.[65] Moreover, life expectancy at birth remains highly conjectural, since it is almost always impossible for us to construct a mortality-table based on cohorts. The experiment may be attempted where there is – as in family records – exact evidence about births, marriages and deaths, permitting the reconstruction of families; but enquiries of this kind generally deal with very small numbers of individuals. With an infant mortality rate of 28 per cent for some families in the Limousin and using mortality-tables, we can infer that life expectancy at birth did not exceed thirty years; this was scarcely higher in Florentine families who have left us their records, and its lowest point, here too, was reached in the first quarter of the fifteenth century.[66] But we are far from being able to examine exactly its variations between the end of the thirteenth century and the beginning of the fifteenth. The differences in the death rate dependent on age and gender, in particular in the groups of ages of children, remain equally little known.

Birth rate and fertility

The same lacunae characterise our knowledge of other constituents of the demographic profile. The birth rate suffers from an absence of data on the

---

[63] Herlihy and Klapisch-Zuber (1978), pp. 374–8 and figs. 21A, 21B. On the *estimo* of 1371–2, see Fiumi (1968), pp. 88–101; the statements date from the last months of 1371, the drawing up from January 1372.   [64] Desportes (1966), p. 497; Herlihy (1973), p. 101.

[65] Guenée (1986) has recently raised the problem. See also Vandenbroucke (1985), table 2, p. 1011.

[66] Biget and Tricard (1981); Klapisch-Zuber (1995) and (1998).

total population, and nuptiality has additionally to reckon with a considerable ignorance concerning the age of spouses. As for fertility, it is virtually unapproachable, other than by indulging in a series of hypotheses; the female part of the population is in fact much less well documented and recorded than the male, with the exception of a slim upper strata of society, and even in those milieux the registration of births was partial and irregular. However, some results may be advanced.

Age-pyramids and graphs of the movements in births and deaths suggest interaction between a crisis of mortality and the birth rate. Age-pyramids reveal the outline not only of these crises, but of upsurges of births once they had passed. The age-pyramids of Prato and the surrounding countryside in 1371 present a very clear trough at the levels of the young generations hit, eight years earlier, by the 'children's plague' mentioned above. But following this drop, at a lower level of the age-pyramid, which also corresponds to the fall in births resulting from the diminished generations of the Black Death of 1348, there were several years of abundant births and, still lower in the pyramid, three years of moderate births, probably representing the return to normal. It thus appears likely that, after the epidemic of 1363–4, the birth rate experienced a heightened impulse for two or three years. Perhaps, on a lesser scale, the very abundant generations born shortly before the drawing-up of the *catasto* of 1427 are also evidence for the age-pyramid of Tuscany of a jump in the birth rate, after the 'minor' plague of 1424.[67]

The link between short-term movements in mortality and natality is also evident from a comparison of graphs of baptisms and burials. This has been demonstrated for the modern period.[68] During a crisis of mortality, the graph for baptisms drops markedly; it picks up again, after some time-lag, when the crisis has passed.[69] At the end of the fifteenth century, in each epidemic baptisms at Florence and Bologna demonstrate drops of 12 to 30 per cent in relation to normal periods, then peaks two, or sometime three, years after the departure of the plague.[70] At Siena, where there are registers of burials from 1381, peaks mark the years 1388–9, 1393 and then the two years following 1401, after the drops in death rate of the preceding years.[71]

To what should we attribute the fall in the number of baptisms during the crisis? Undoubtedly we must take account of the flight out of town of a

---

[67] Herlihy and Klapisch-Zuber (1978), pp. 376–7, fig. 21 and 382–3, fig. 23.   [68] Livi Bacci (1978a).

[69] See the examples cited and the graphs analysed at Auriol before, during and after the plague of 1720–1 by Biraben (1975), I, pp. 310–31.

[70] Herlihy and Klapisch-Zuber (1978), pp. 182–7, figs. 2–3, and p. 197, table 20; Bellettini (1961), pp. 87–90; Livi Bacci (1978b), pp. 63–91.

[71] Following the figures published by Ottolenghi (1903). A critical study of these data has yet to be made.

considerable proportion of couples and the baptism of their new-born children in other parishes. But were falls in the year which followed, rather than the result of amenorrhoea comparable to that produced by famine, the consequence of fear on the behaviour of spouses during the plague, a fear which would express itself through the interruption of conjugal relations in these times of penitence and dread?[72]

A twofold observation, often made by contemporaries, refers to the extreme fecundity of women after an outbreak of the plague and to the nuptial frenzy which seized the survivors. This appears, moreover, to be borne out by a comparison of the fertility and ultimate descendants of couples made just before and just after the epidemic.[73] Can this be substantiated at the end of the Middle Ages?

The families of the fourteenth century were prolific. Assertions of this kind are generally based on examples drawn from royal or princely genealogies; generalisation to the entire population of results obtained from such a very small number and such an extremely unrepresentative social group clearly does not win support any more than conclusions based on the counting of surviving descendants known through their parents' wills. On the other hand, with family records, we come close to the characteristics of fertility in town-dwelling milieux of lower rank.[74] Between 1350 and 1500, the six couples from Limoges studied by J.-L. Biget and J. Tricard begot an average of 9.8 children each; but at least 54 per cent of these 59 children did not reach adulthood. Furthermore, the average for all families (including both families living until the end of the wife's fecundity – *completed families* – and families prematurely interrupted by the death of one of the spouses – *familles achevées*) was only 6.9.[75] At Arras, four families constituted between 1389 and 1470 engendered an average of 9.75 children.[76] The figures are comparable at Florence, between 1290 and 1530: if, in the *completed families* studied, an average of 11 children were born, compared with only 6.4 in the *familles achevées*, it can be calculated that for all families, 113 in number, where the mother was married before she was twenty years old, the theoretical descent after thirty years of marriage would be 9.3 children.[77]

A very high fertility level, therefore, but not at all 'natural'. Does this indicate that it still had some reserves, to which the population could appeal to

---

[72] These reactions are discussed in detail by Biraben in the case of Auriol: Biraben (1975), I, pp. 323–31.

[73] Ibid., p. 330.

[74] Separate pieces of information are often put forward to demonstrate the prolific character of particular families, but the selection of these isolated cases runs the risk of being precisely made out of the number of their children: see the families of eighteen children in twenty-five years of marriage and of fourteen children in a union of thirty-one years cited by Chevalier (1975), II, pp. 318–19 n. 51.   [75] Biget and Tricard (1981), p. 343.   [76] Delmaire (1983).   [77] Klapisch-Zuber (1988).

counterbalance the inroads of epidemics? Recent studies in historical demography have clarified the mechanisms by which the populations of pre-modern Europe responded to variations in the death rate.[78] They tend to highlight the role of nuptiality, more perceptible than fertility, and more immediately modified in its two constituent parts, the frequency of marriage and the age at which it is established.

Nuptiality

If we superimpose, where we are fortunate enough to possess simultaneously statistics of them, such as at Givry in Burgundy, the graph of marriages on that of burials, one can see that the former are interrupted during an epidemic, but peak immediately afterwards and still remain firm at a higher level than normal in the second year following the plague.[79] Of these new unions, deferred while death reigned, many were between widows and widowers who, once the epidemic had passed, hastened to remarry as quickly as possible; but marriage was also open to young people who had delayed their plans or who, becoming free to marry because they had come into an inheritance, a landholding or a business, endeavoured to establish themselves as soon as possible.[80] The higher fertility level of these new couples would in its turn explain the jump in the birth rate in the second year after an outbreak of the plague.

The more numerous births in the town of Prato and the surrounding countryside appearing in 1371, on the age-pyramid at the level of the years 1365–7, probably conceal a trend of this kind, a rush for marriage in the aftermath of the plague of 1363. Two aspects attract attention here: the proportion of those married was very high in 1371, and the average age of first marriage (calculated from the proportions of married people at each age) very low. Two generations later, in 1427, the *catasto* was to show that the matrimonial behaviour of the grandchildren, both town- and country-dwellers, was no longer that of their grandparents: the marriage of girls, in this region of Tuscany, was deferred by one or two years, that of boys for two to three years.[81] It thus seems likely that at the end of the fourteenth century the age and frequency of marriage in Tuscany was adjusted to boost the birth rate.

---

[78] Wrigley (1969); Wrigley and Schofield (1981), p. 425; Dupâquier (1972); Bideau (1983); Klapisch-Zuber (1993).   [79] Gras (1939) and analysis by Biraben (1975), I, pp. 157–62.

[80] Biraben (1975), I, pp. 318–21, for the example of Auriol between 1701 and 1740, where the proportion of those remarried in the total of marriages celebrated was almost 15 per cent before the plague, fell – as first marriages did – during it and climbed to 64 per cent immediately afterwards.

[81] Calculated by Hajnal's method from the proportion of married individuals of every age, it went from 16.3 to 17.6 years for girls in the towns and from 15.3 to 17.3 for those in thirteen surrounding villages, and for men from 23.8 to 26.9 in towns and from 22.3 to 24 in the same villages: Herlihy and Klapisch-Zuber (1978), p. 207, table 24.

But we know that adolescent fertility below the age of twenty is low, and that it is to remain lower, during the lifetime of their spouses, than that of women married between twenty and twenty-five years: the example of Florence confirms this, where fertility appears the same as that of their contemporaries at Limoges or Arras. In regions where girls were married very young, pressures therefore operated upon the male age of marriage. Without this directly affecting fertility – and here again the Florentine evidence corroborates it – these effects were of enormous social importance, for opening and closing access to marriage to men of twenty, or on the other hand postponing until their thirties the weddings of a high proportion of young people, was to ensure the more or less rapid replacement of the generations, and perhaps also to change what was regarded as desirable relations between spouses. When girls marry later, on the other hand, the resulting increase in births has directly tangible effects on fertility, since women between twenty and twenty-five years old then attain their maximum fertility.

Some qualification should be made, however. Like the death rate, the nuptiality of the late Middle Ages is highly variable in the short term, much more 'rigid' and 'glacial' in the long term, to use the terms of L. R. Poos.[82] Let us therefore distinguish between the effects which, from this dual perspective, the first had upon the second. In the immediate future, a plague tended to concentrate in the following year first marriages, simply deferred during the epidemic, and thus to give a strong impetus to the recovery of the birth-rate, since these unions of young people were particularly fertile. If the prescribed delay for the remarriage of widows was respected, their new unions would raise fertility a little later. They would tend therefore to prolong the recovery of the birth rate into the second, or even the third, year after the plague. In the longer term, however, the adjustment would take place slowly. This has been established from statistics over long periods in pre-modern times, where nuptiality moved to a different level within the space of a generation after the crises.[83] To produce perceptible and lasting effects, there had in fact to be profound changes in custom and mentality. For if the demographic world was not subject to biological constraints alone, matrimonial relations and beyond that the entire sphere of the family, did not submit to their rule without resistance.

Two systems and a breakdown?

The characteristics of Tuscan nuptiality remained relatively stable despite their many ups and downs. From the rare figures available for the beginning of the fourteenth century, as from the statistics about nuptiality available from the end of the

---

[82] Poos (1989), p. 801.   [83] Bideau and Perrenoud (1981).

fifteenth and the sixteenth centuries, a relatively coherent picture emerges: the age of marriage of women was under twenty years, much lower before 1400, less so *c.* 1500, and more in the town than the countryside. That of men varied between wider limits, but was always over twenty-two years, generally remained around twenty-six years and touched thirty in towns and among the rich. It is difficult to estimate the exact proportion of confirmed bachelors; that of spinsters, on the other hand, was trifling, and the state of marriage or widowhood included more than 95 per cent of adult women after 1350. Such characteristics are not peculiar to Tuscany. There is a very high proportion of married or widowed women in the medieval towns of central and northern Italy, and in south-east and still more so in south-west France. In the towns of the Rhône valley and Provence, such as Toulouse and Périgueux, or in the village of Montaillou, women were married before twenty-one, men rather around twenty-seven years.[84] For the pre-modern period, this has also been demonstrated in Spain, and the medieval features persisted in the regions of France and Italy already cited.[85]

These characteristics undoubtedly amount to a model very different from that which, thirty years ago, J. Hajnal designated as the 'European' model of marriage.[86] As is well known, the societies of traditional Europe were distinguished in relation to other human societies by the exceptionally high age of marriage of women and men (twenty-five years or more), by a small gap between the ages of spouses and by a high proportion of permanently celibate among both sexes. The fact that today this entirety is called rather the model 'of north-west Europe' shows that important regional corrections have restricted the field of its application. Moreover, since 1965, Hajnal has suggested that it does not perhaps take account of the situation in England in the late fourteenth century, and that in other respects Mediterranean regions possessed several of the features which he identified as belonging to a model 'of eastern Europe'.[87]

The theory of the 'non-European' character of English marriage had been suggested to Hajnal by the work of J. C. Russell using the English poll tax returns of 1377 to estimate nuptiality in the fourteenth century. His conclusions have been challenged and his use of documentary evidence criticised (while the hypotheses required to correct the data do not make interpretation in the contrary sense entirely convincing).[88] Studies of different English

---

[84] It was 20–1 years in the fifteenth century for women, 24–5 for men, for the inhabitants of the Rhône valley between 1440 and 1500: Rossiaud (1976). It was 16–17 years for the women of Toulouse, 25–8 for the men: Laribière (1967); Higounet-Nadal (1978), pp. 282, 291–2. It was 17–18 years for the girls of Montaillou: Le Roy Ladurie (1975), pp. 275–9.   [85] Smith (1981), summarised in Smith (1983).

[86] Hajnal (1965).   [87] Ibid., pp. 119, 103, 120 respectively.

[88] Hatcher (1986), pp. 21–2, discussing criticisms of Russell's analysis in Smith (1981), pp. 114–15, and (1983), p. 111.

regions do not provide a convincing conclusion because their results are contradictory. At Halesowen, girls of sixteen to nineteen years married youths of twenty-one years before the Black Death; the abundance of land after it lowered this 'non-European' age still further.[89] But in the Lincolnshire Fenland research arrived at the opposite conclusion: the 'European' model of marriage was in place before the end of the thirteenth century and became stronger with the plague. Should we therefore push back in time the problem of the medieval origins of the west European model in England? The historian of the Fenland, H. E. Hallam, did not rule out the possibility that, if it was pushed back chronologically, one would be able to discern there a 'Mediterranean' or an 'east European' model of marriage.[90]

This is also the conclusion which emerges from studies of other regions of England and northern France. Less richly served than the demographers of southern Europe, historians there are forced to deduce from the proportions of married and celibate the chances of late marriage, or of a delayed marriage, in the northern regions. The tendency today seems to be to come round to a vision of a 'prudential' marriage, for both young men and women. The same applies to Normandy after 1460,[91] at Reims in 1422,[92] and Bury St Edmunds in the fifteenth century;[93] but proof is too often lacking. Where there is documentary evidence of the real age of marriage, these data are too few, their results remain in half-tones: at Arras and Limoges between the end of the fourteenth and the fifteenth centuries, towns where young men from the *bourgeoisie* married in their twenties or thirties girls whose age was around twenty years,[94] the age of female marriage remains open to speculation: was it still medieval? Already verging on the modern 'European' model? The debate remains open. To bring it to an end, one would need patiently to accumulate data clarifying matrimonial behaviour, not only in the century of biological and familial upheavals, but in the earlier period.

In conclusion, although nuptiality functioned as the principal demographic self-regulator, this role operated between limits that were not only biological

---

[89] Razi (1980), pp. 60–4, 136–7. It should be noted that Herlihy (1985), pp. 103–11, has collected evidence on the age of first marriage throughout Europe for the whole of the Middle Ages. The author concludes that the female age of marriage was very low everywhere until the thirteenth century and that the male age of marriage began to rise from the twelfth century onwards.

[90] Hallam (1985). Using the seigneurial tax upon marriage, the merchet, Hallam estimates a female age of first marriage of 21.4 and a male age of 26.1 years before the Black Death; the female age of marriage was to rise to 24.6 and the male to 25.5 years after the Black Death. For his part, Smith (1983), pp. 120–4, using the same documents concerning the serfs on two of these manors, calculates proportions of married and single entirely compatible with the model of north-west Europe.

[91] Bois (1976), pp. 317 and 331, for the beginning of the sixteenth century.

[92] Desportes (1966), p. 489.   [93] Gottfried (1982), p. 61 n. 34.

[94] Biget and Tricard (1981), pp. 327–30; Delmaire (1983), pp. 305–6.

but cultural. In a demographic system based on a 'Mediterranean' model of marriage, there could be no real increase in fertility by lowering still further the age of female marriage and it appears to have been above all on the male age of marriage that the pressure of the death rate had direct consequences. The effects of such a demographic strategy remained moderate and perhaps accounted for the fairly slow pattern of growth in the Mediterranean population during the Renaissance. On the other hand, in a system including a model of marriage 'of north-western Europe', manipulating the age of female marriage by a few years ensured a rapid revival of fertility and permitted more flexible responses in the very long term.

FAMILY EQUILIBRIUM

At the meeting-point of many social constraints, marriage, the formation of a couple and the place of the domestic group among a vaster totality of social bonds have become central objects for the understanding of past populations. Nuptiality, this regulator of demographic and social life, fitted into the broader domestic and familial pattern: marriage fell within the province of the family well before being controlled by the state or even the Church. What one understands by 'family structures' thus imposed their requirements on demographic trends; in return these structures experienced the effects of the population movement and modifications to the demographic system. The interaction between family and demography demands that we forget neither of these perspectives.

The models

Limited by the available sources, medievalists have long approached the problem of the characteristics and changes in family structures by according a perhaps undue significance to one of their features, the dimension of the family group. This 'hearth' (household), domestic and property-based, in the best-documented cases, but too often fiscal and notional for administrative purposes, can sometimes be measured. But what can be done with this? What is to be made of the assertion that at San Gimignano, in Tuscany, while the inhabitants were reduced in number by approximately 33 per cent in the town and 15 per cent in the country between 1350 and 1427, the households, falling more steeply in number, included a wider range of members?[95] To explore the reasons for such a disjuncture between the statistics for hearths and those for

[95] Households in towns lost 55 per cent of their total in 1350, and those in the countryside 47 per cent, and their average size went from 3.5 to 4, and from 4 to 7.5, respectively: Fiumi (1962), p. 150.

people we must know the structure of households. Now there are few exact population counts, household by household, in the fourteenth century: what the formulae of average dimension actually represent is almost always unknown.

More than one observer has been struck by the fact that the dimension of the family group is virtually the same from one society to another or in the long term, while at the local level it could experience important fluctuations. This view loses sight of the essential dynamic. Let us take the example of Prato and its *contado*, whose very rich archives provide exceptional information from the end of the thirteenth century. The hearths then numbered an average 5.6 persons in the *contado*; they had only 4.3 in 1339, 4.7 in 1371 and 5 in 1427; evolution in the town was not completely synchronised, where the hearth contained 4.1 persons in 1298, 3.9 in 1339, 4.2 in 1371 but fell back to 3.7 in 1427.[96] What we know about population movement in the fourteenth century leads us to believe that different reasons lay behind the drops observed in 1339 and then in 1427. But we cannot deduce from this series of family indices that family organisation was related to one model rather than another, or was carried along in a coherent historical process. The numerical index says nothing clear about the nature of the bonds cementing the domestic group. It clarifies nothing about the accommodations with demographic constraints except in an indirect and obscure manner.

Frequently, however, one sees the small size of the medieval household stressed and deductions made from this concerning its conjugal character. This has been still more apparent since a model of the family in the Europe of the past, constructed by observation of modern populations and articulated with the model of marriage discussed above, has come to provide a theoretical framework in which to arrange the meagre medieval evidence. According to this model the western couple came into being when it could set itself up, that is to say, when it could attain economic autonomy. At this time, the new household chose a 'neo-local' residence, different from that of the parents; in the expectation of marriage young people accumulated the means necessary for their establishment by entering service with families that were already established.[97] The model thus convincingly integrated late nuptiality into the mechanisms of social reproduction, which presupposes the movement of young bachelors – a reserve of extra manpower and a 'reproductive reservoir' – between the family units of production.

From this there stemmed, not only a high proportion of young servants in the households of strangers, but very simple family structures, stripped of

---

[96] Fiumi (1968), pp. 47–8, 72–3, 89–90, 109–11; Herlihy and Klapisch-Zuber (1978), pp. 211–12.

[97] The characteristics of this family have been sketched by Laslett (1973) and Hajnal (1982).

genealogical depth and reduced to parent–children bonds within nucleated units; the dimensions of such units founded on a single conjugal union showed the effects of every peak in the death rate and of its raised level. In a 'European' population, it would therefore be normal to find a largely dominant proportion of households organised on a conjugal basis, a tiny proportion of households where several couples co-existed, and a very small proportion of families containing a widowed parent or relatives of marriageable age; finally, there were a large number of households keeping servants.

Did such a model characterise the whole of Europe, and as early as the Middle Ages? We should not exaggerate the model. Regional studies have long underscored long-term phenomena, very widespread in various regions of Europe, which seem to contradict this dominant model. In the south of France, in Languedoc for example, juridical forms of association between relatives or strangers, already revealed by legal historians, have been brought out at the level of family practices: the tendency to 'lineal regrouping' (*remembrement lignager,* as E. Le Roy Ladurie called it) and the establishment of *frérèches* at the turn of the fourteenth and fifteenth centuries, resting on a solid contractual framework, permanently stamped the life of family communities, which increased in internal complexity, and sometimes in size, at the end of the Middle Ages.[98] Studies on southern Europe, which grew in number in the 1970s,[99] sanction the integration of these local forms in a 'Mediterranean' model contrasting with that of the family in north-western Europe. It was characterised by patrivirilocal marriage, genealogical depth and the co-existence of several couples from different generations, frequent associations of couples of the same generation – *frérèches* and others – and the tendency to prefer relations to servants from elsewhere.[100]

The notion of a cycle of domestic development[101] has, moreover, brought the means of more sophisticated analysis of the assembled observations. One of its lessons, and by no means the least important, has been to demonstrate that a system characterised by a cycle of development extended over successive generations and by the structural complexity of the domestic group, adapted to a smaller size of household, close to that of nuclear families. Such a system implies, in fact, the possibility of several couples living together, but the complexity resulting from such cohabitation is not realised at all stages of a cyclical development. Periodically, and for a short time, the domestic group became smaller, passing through a simple form, before it began again to expand in a later phase.[102] A high death rate, which increased the breakup of

---

[98] Le Roy Ladurie (1972), pp. 162–8.
[99] See the data analysed for our period by Dondarini (1984); Leverotti (1984).
[100] Smith (1981), p. 125. [101] Berkner (1972). [102] Berkner (1975).

unions, further weakened the chances of an observer hitting upon a point in the cycle when couples constituted a complex and numerous household. A 'Mediterranean' model is therefore not always discernible at any one moment in time. That is certainly the case at the end of the Middle Ages, when the plague struck hard.

The forms of the household

The high death rate at the end of the Middle Ages shook, and perhaps modified, domestic structures in different ways. Admittedly, the misfortunes of the period disrupted families and depleted them, blurring internal hierarchies. However, it is important to distinguish between the consequences of death rates linked to subsistence crises and those of crises caused by the plague. The first provoked flight to the towns, the start of a wandering which could prove permanent and break definitively the bonds with land and family. High prices and famine, with the epidemics that all too often followed in their wake, prompted country-dwellers to abandon their lands, when the survivors of the family which cultivated them could not sow or harvest there. The poor of the cities and refugees from the hinterland crowded into charitable institutions. Here and there the hard-pressed authorities chased outside their walls desperate beggars, who went to swell the numbers of armed bands, devastating the countryside and besieging fortified towns, doubling confusion and misfortune.[103] The historians of the fourteenth century, and above all those of the fifteenth century, return tirelessly to these movements of population, this wandering, this marginalisation of people who had usually broken with their family, and whose family was shattered.[104] Many works have been devoted to attempts at rural recolonisation, and one suspects that reconstituting the family with fugitives from other devastated regions tended to establish family structures which were not very complex.[105]

The plague did not have the same effects. It was to the rich in the towns rather than the poor that it suggested flight, and that just for the period of the epidemic. Once the danger had passed, it indirectly stimulated a less unreasoned influx towards the towns, draining off immigrants who were attracted by privileges and professional monopolies and who were soon to be enrolled on

---

[103] See the introduction to *Il libro del Biadaiolo*, ed. Pinto; La Roncière (1974). On the effects of war and insecurity and their links with the plague, see Dubois (1988a), pp. 337–46; Biraben (1975), 1, pp. 139–46.

[104] See the fine picture drawn by Comba (1984), with a full bibliography of older and recent works. For numerous examples drawn from judicial sources: Gauvard (1991).

[105] Pinto (1984); de Moxó (1979).

the registers of the *bourgeoisie*.[106] There, too, we imagine that the families founded by these new arrivals would have been neither very substantial nor complex. The immigration which renewed the population of the cities decimated by the plague involved the settlement of individuals and of nuclear families.[107] They thus reinforced the effects of the pressures of nuptiality evident after a peak in the death rate; all these developments increased the proportion of young couples succeeding in setting up housekeeping.

To return to the example of Prato after the first two plagues, the predominance of households consisting of a simple conjugal cell (65 per cent) is very striking in 1371. But their share fell once more to 58 per cent after 1427 and 55 per cent in 1470; the difference was even greater in the *contado*.[108] This example shows that the forms taken by families in response to the pressure of the death rate still had no definitive character. This would be still better established by observing the proportions of 'multiple' households. With the rest of Tuscany, at the end of the fourteenth century, the town of Prato undoubtedly fell within the 'Mediterranean' model of the family, as is revealed by the proportion of households in which several conjugal families joined forces (14 per cent) – not an enormous proportion but one which remains incompatible with the 'north-European' model. Later on, at the *catasto* of 1427, this proportion was to double (28 per cent), and a century afterwards it would almost have tripled (36 per cent).

Thus, when the population stabilised, from the 1420s onwards, the standard family model recovered its rights and was once more visibly expressed. The hasty formation of new unions between 1364 and 1371, the rushed setting-up of young couples and immigrants only temporarily displaced the proportions of the different types of households; they did not, in fact, lead to profound change.

Did the plagues of the fourteenth century set up, merely accentuate or, rather, contradict the tendency, so apparent in the Mediterranean towns and rural areas, to express patrilineal interdependence? In southern and central France, as pointed out above, *frérèches* between outsiders and contractual associations between relatives of different generations increased. Were these phenomena similar? Did they respond to the same appeals? Did the *frérèches* of southern France not seek above all to overcome insecurity, breaks in continuity in the occupation of a property or the cultivation of land? The desired forms of association thus exerted pressure for the invention of new juridical theory and practices. In Italy, vigorous patrilineal structures were rooted in an old legal soil,

---

[106] For Germany, Mols (1954–6), I, p. 74; Dollinger (1972), pp. 113–20; Comba (1984), p. 52. For Italy, Pinto (1984), pp. 33–9.   [107] For example Montanari (1966).

[108] Their share was 65, 58 and 55 per cent, respectively: Herlihy and Klapisch-Zuber (1978), pp. 518–19.

fertilised since well before the plagues by the renewal of Roman law and of the law relating to dowries in particular. In the hope of shedding light on other trends and other types of familial organisation one must perhaps go back to before the twelfth century, before the principles of patrilineal succession reorganised the sphere of the family on solid foundations.

Widows and single individuals

Breaking the bonds which united spouses, parents and children under the same roof in the societies of the north, brothers and cousins or uncles and nephews in the south, the plagues left behind them loose aggregates of related individuals, where no conjugal structure was to be discernible for a long while. They increased the vestigial households, composed of single individuals, orphaned co-heirs, surviving spouses remaining in the marital home. Their proportion is striking even in urban societies where the dominant system of organisation would hardly make them expected. It did not fall to below 20 per cent of total households in Prato between 1371 and 1470 and climbed to 25 per cent in Florence in 1427. Rural regions made a fairly striking contrast, for Tuscan sharecropping (*mezzadria*) adapted poorly to very small family units; here, single individuals could only offer a marginal workforce, their presence was cut down to 6 per cent of the total of households (hearths) around Prato in 1371. By contrast, the late medieval town offered the means of survival to the uprooted and to all those who were the casualties of marriage and the family.

The situation of widows is highly instructive. We generally see only those women who achieved autonomy in the eyes of lord or financial administration; the majority were widows. In the first half of the fourteenth century, the chances they had of appearing as such at the head of a family or of a holding varied according to whether they lived in the town or countryside and from region to region; they were dependent on the juridical conditions and the relations of production which controlled access to rural estates locally. In the towns of Tuscany, their proportion in the population as a whole was high: at Prato, 19 per cent of hearths in 1325, 24 per cent in 1339.[109] The fact that in 1339 a quarter of the households of the town were headed by widows reveals the difficulties encountered by those who wished to remarry in a period when the population, which had stabilised at a very high level, began imperceptibly to decline: the town made new openings for the weakest at the moment of demographic upturn. In 1371, the proportion of widows who were the heads of families had fallen again at Prato to 16 per cent, and to 15 per cent in 1427.[110] In the

---

[109] Fiumi (1968), pp. 70, 80, 92.

[110] Ibid., pp. 92, 111; in the rural areas they constituted 6.7 per cent of the total households in 1427.

surrounding rural areas, their presence was much more restricted throughout the entire period. Here the *mezzadria* governed relationships between landowners and farmers, contracts required male workers and a complete family.[111] It is likely that rural widows who did not remarry on the spot had no alternative other than to emigrate into the town or to remain on the farm taken over by an adult son. It is there, in fact, that we find them in the *catasto* of 1427: many scraping a living alone in the city, still more frequently living in the house of a child. Like sharecropping, the laws relating to dowries and inheritances and their application in Italian customary law did not encourage economic autonomy among women; on the contrary, they prompted them to become integrated within the household of an adult male – father, husband or son, even son-in-law – who would administer their dowry. Such a situation fits easily into the more general framework of southern Europe at the beginning of the fifteenth century, that led to a tightening of bonds between relatives: they were encouraged to stand fast together rather than scatter their forces.

Things were different in north-western Europe. On English estates, for instance, landowners directly controlled the marriage of female serfs in their lordship, taxing their marriage to outsiders and resumptions of landholdings, at the same time maintaining control over access to the land.[112] The proportion of female tenants at the end of the thirteenth and the beginning of the fourteenth centuries was much higher than in the sharecropping farms of Tuscany; the great majority were widows, who kept all or part of the goods of their deceased husbands.[113] The other distinctive characteristic of this period was the frequency of remarriage of a widow with land at her disposal: the union agreed by the lord permitted the new husband to enter into possession of a holding in exchange for hard cash. Now it has been demonstrated that, in the first half of the fourteenth century, the remarriage of widows occupied a more important place in the totality of marriages than after the Black Death. There was no lack of claimants at a period when free tenures were rare. Around 1300, half the marriages of serfs at Cottenham, in Cambridgeshire, were remarriages, a proportion which reduced very sharply afterwards when demographic pressure and land hunger eased.[114]

---

[111] Witness the tiny number (1.6 per cent) of sharecropping farms *(mezzadria)* in Florentine Tuscany held by households without family in 1427: Herlihy and Klapisch-Zuber (1978), p. 486, table 78.

[112] Searle (1979); Goldberg (1992).

[113] Independent women constituted between 10 and 18 per cent of heads of household: see Franklin (1986), esp. pp. 188–9.

[114] Smith (1983), pp. 124–7; also Ravensdale (1984). There are comparable observations at Halesowen: of widows known from the manorial court rolls before 1349, 63 per cent remarried, but only 25 per cent after that date: Razi (1980), pp. 63, 138. The proportions, although smaller, remained high elsewhere: as many as 33 per cent of marriages at Taunton included a widow, 26 per cent at Witney (Oxfordshire), 14 per cent at Thornbury, where the figure comparable to Halesowen's 63 per cent would be 33–7 per cent: Franklin (1986), p. 199.

The elevated death rate set in motion a quicker redistribution of the land, and the beneficiaries were the young, younger sons without inheritances who would henceforth choose for their marriage partner an heiress of their own generation in preference to a widow.[115] Widows were to be the 'victims' of this process, in so far as fewer of their number would henceforth achieve control of a landholding.[116] The faster replacement of the old by the young, the greater frequency of marriage and perhaps the lowering of the age of first marriage which contributed to boosting fertility can thus be interpreted as the result of a complex process changing the forms of access to land and the nature of its beneficiaries.[117] Once again, it must be stated that forms of social behaviour not rooted in the strictly demographic sphere played a decisive role in the reactions of the population to the impact of the plagues.

Economic strategies and cultural inheritances

Cultural choices and inheritances also exerted a strong influence on family structures and, through them, on demography. First of all, juridical norms. A principle of equality restricted to male heirs (such as was applied in the later medieval communes of central-northern Italy) did not inevitably produce division and co-residence among male heirs; however, it made them desirable when the inherited goods lent themselves to it. Too small a piece of land would not sustain their daily interdependence, but a sharecropping farm adequate for a family had every chance of keeping a certain number of sons until they married and even afterwards, thus avoiding recourse to waged labour. A commercial business, on the other hand, could be divided without compelling the heirs to live together: when they reached adulthood, they would prefer to separate at the time when they divided the inheritance. Social aspirations and professional commitments moderated the underlying familial model, revealing or concealing it.

Tuscany around 1400 is a good field for observation. Here, small landowners in marginal areas displayed the same persistent co-residence as the sharecropping farmers of the central *contado*, expressed in the high proportion of

---

[115] This phenomenon can be observed at Coltishall, Norfolk, between 1349 and 1359, where the number of women holding a farm slumped at the same time as the replacement ratio of deceased tenants by their surviving sons: Campbell (1984), pp. 96–9, tables 2.1, 2.2, 2.3.

[116] See, however, the more optimistic vision defended by Franklin (1986), who believes that the opportunities for remaining at the head of a household without remarrying, extended in the demographic drop between 1350 and 1450, increased their autonomy, their initiatives and their happiness.

[117] However, even this is disputed; recent works insist on the high fertility of couples consisting of a young husband and an older widow (Schofield and Wrigley (1981), pp. 222–4); and on that of a middle-aged widower marrying a young girl. They challenge the more traditional view of a lower fertility among couples which included one remarried spouse.

households that included several families. Families which did not live solely or directly from the land, on the other hand, did not conform to the implicit norms of the system: surplus sons found work elsewhere and the proportion of complex households fell considerably. In the towns, it was the presence or absence of a patrimony which determined the structure of the household. As between the wealth and size of a household, there was a positive correlation between wealth and internal complexity of the domestic group; the higher the social status, the more chance the family had of realising the implicit family model, which is regarded as characteristic of it.[118] Finally, at the two extremes of the socio-professional spectrum, there are two emblematic figures of the medieval family in all their purity. Among the poorest of poor people – who were in Florence, textile workers, the Ciompi – the conjugal family prevailed (83 per cent) with a size close to the average of the city (3.9) and this social group included a few single individuals as 'multiple family households'.[119] Among the rich, their patrons in the wool- and silk-weaving guilds, single individuals did not live alone and remained an integral part of the family from which they came; as for widows, who did not always recover their dowry without difficulty, they also remained in the family into which they had married. Thus, the domestic group was not principally cemented by conjugality; almost one quarter of households, like those of peasants living on a farm, combined several families bound by their patrilineal relationship.

In the absence of analogous sources, precise comparison with other regions of medieval Europe is demonstrably hazardous. In Limoges, a town of southern culture, the house of the Benoist accommodated a 'polynuclear' unit, where, at some periods, married sons and nephews lived with their descendants side by side with those of the patriarch.[120] But in northern France, we see father and wife succeeded by the inheriting son and his wife, rather than cohabiting under the same roof. Therefore, at Arras, family size appears to have been determined by the number of surviving children rather than by cohesion between generations or between heirs.[121]

Conversely, we know more about the presence of servants in the families of north-west Europe than in the Mediterranean south. Here, undoubtedly, the main sources of information – *estimes* or censuses of fiscal origin – took little account of them.[122] A man-servant living on the farm was not the rule; and a family had to be very wretched to agree to expose the sexual honour of its daughters to the dangers of a place in service. Except perhaps among the

---

[118] Herlihy and Klapisch-Zuber (1978), pp. 469–522.   [119] Stella (1990); La Roncière (1974).
[120] Biget and Tricard (1981), pp. 357–8.   [121] Delmaire (1983).
[122] Herlihy seems to me rashly to conclude that the larger or smaller proportion of children or young people in different income brackets reveals a real circulation of the young at Florence between rich and poor: Herlihy (1985), pp. 155–6.

merchant class, which willingly had its sons, still at a tender age, start their professional experience in a distant house, and except among aristocratic milieux where feudal culture dictated court service, education was not based on the systematic circulation of the young, as was practised in England or other regions of northern Europe.[123]

Socio-economic determinants, cultural factors and value systems therefore had direct repercussions on family organisation. They also indirectly affected behaviour and ultimately demographic variables. Take breast-feeding, for instance. Although decisions made in this sphere by Florentine parents in the fourteenth and fifteenth centuries were not lacking in self-interest, their primary justification rested on an appreciation of the positions and respective roles of men and women in the world-order.[124] Plainly expressed in the daily ethic and permissible forms of behaviour, the values and knowledge which impinged on the female 'nature', for example, were here called upon for aid, and made a contribution by ultimately raising fertility in some social groups. Similarly, the well-established hierarchy between both sexes served to justify, reinforced and implanted the Mediterranean preference for a very young wife: as a result the husband gained in authority – and undoubtedly also in increased progeny, but the latter consequence was not the first to be cited. The 'preventive' or 'corrective' reactions which set nuptiality against biological disasters could only be built upon a foundation of cultural inheritances, all the more telling because they were inert and implicit.

There are two models, therefore, whose implications begin to be evident. But the questions raised above return, still more insistently. From what date can this distinction be found? Do Prato in 1371 and the poll tax of 1377 signal the beginning of a very long-term movement, a breaking-point initiating in some places a process of familial concentration and in others an evolution towards the European specificity of pre-modern periods? Or were these only regressive episodes, expressing, through a small oscillation at the heart of a system that was stable elsewhere, a disturbance provoked by external traumas? In sum, are we dealing here with epiphenomena giving a misleading picture of the development as a whole, or with decisive stages in a process by which earlier tendencies were reversed? It is too soon to say. New pathways of research will have to be opened up, earlier than the fourteenth century, to restore their full meaning to the familial responses aroused by the irruption of the plague.

---

[123] Kussmaul (1981); Smith (1981), pp. 118–19; Desportes (1966), p. 489. Few studies have examined service in Italian peasant families in the Middle Ages, while more is known, if not of their numbers, at least about the servants in citizens' households and the conditions in which they worked: Guarducci and Ottanelli (1982); Romano (1991).   [124] Klapisch-Zuber (1983).

CHAPTER 8

TRADE IN FOURTEENTH-CENTURY EUROPE

Peter Spufford

FOR the purposes of discussing European commerce, the fourteenth century is a very difficult unit. Most of the first half of the century had much in common with the thirteenth century, and in many ways trading patterns in these years are the fruition and culmination of the so-called 'commercial revolution' of the long thirteenth century. In the same way trading patterns in the second half of the century exhibited the beginnings of many of the changes which accelerated in the fifteenth century. I will therefore treat the century in two halves, at the risk of some overlap with the chapters in the previous and succeeding volumes.

Throughout the first half of the century the patterns of short-distance trade remained much as they were around 1300. The extensive network of markets and market towns already established in many parts of Europe remained virtually unchanged. Few attempts were made to create additional markets, and those few that were chartered were generally unsuccessful. Nevertheless, the medieval market economy already generally established in most parts of rural western Europe remained unimpaired and was consolidated.[1] Most rural producers continued to be able to sell at least a part of their produce for money without difficulty, to meet such money obligations as rents and taxes. The overall European money supply probably reached its medieval maximum towards the middle of the century.[2]

As well as the network of markets, where goods could be sold locally on a weekly basis, the long thirteenth century had also seen the establishment of numerous annual fairs, at which local produce could be sold to more distant customers, and more distant products purchased. This encouraged the development of considerable regional specialisation in agriculture, for example the extension of vineyards at the expense of grain in the hinterland of Bordeaux, or the concentration on grain production along the rivers

---

[1] Day (1987); Britnell (1993).   [2] Spufford (1988), pp. 240–63.

flowing northwards into the Baltic. At most of these fairs a single local product was of dominant importance, as with the cheese fairs of Apulia, and it was through such fairs that the specialised produce of an area entered into long-distance commerce. Although most of this chapter will be concerned with long-distance trade, which was primarily consumption rather than production led, it must always be borne in mind that long-distance trade was normally tied to the ultimate producers through this network of local markets, and particularly of specialised annual fairs.

There were, however, a small number of fairs of much more than regional importance. From the twelfth century the sequence of six two-monthly fairs at the four fair towns of Champagne had a supra-regional importance, and acted as contact points between merchants from the southern Netherlands, northern Italy, Paris, the Rhineland and from at least as far into the German parts of the empire as Meissen. These fairs were in decline by 1300. They lingered on into the fourteenth century, but were then largely places for settling accounts.[3] By then Champagne was no longer the right area for such international fairs, since merchants from northern Italy and Tuscany had established permanent agents in Bruges, Paris and London, who were able to transact the business that had been carried on at these fairs more efficiently. However this did not provide for the interests of merchants from the German parts of the empire.

A handful of other fairs of international importance not only continued to flourish, but grew in importance through the fourteenth century into the fifteenth. Some are described as 'successor fairs' to those of Champagne, and like them, they were generally held beside navigable rivers and so were accessible by both road and water. The most important of these were those at Frankfurt-on-Main, where 'German' merchants purchased the products of the Low Countries, principally woollen cloth; at Antwerp and at Bergen-op-Zoom on the Scheldt, where Hanseatic, Rhineland and south German merchants met not only Netherlanders, but also men from many other nations; at Saint-Denis, on the Seine below Paris, where the old Lendit fair achieved a new lease of life in turn; and also those at Chalon on the Saône, and at Geneva on the Rhône.[4]

Unlike modern producer-led economies, that of fourteenth-century Europe was predominantly a network of consumer-led economies. Trade in bulky necessities was heavily determined by levels of population, particularly of urban populations, whilst trade in high-value commodities depended on the demands of a relatively narrow group of wealthy people, whose ability to

[3] Bautier (1953), pp. 97–147; Chapin (1937).
[4] Verlinden (1963), pp. 126–53; Dubois (1976); Blockmans (1991), pp. 37–50, and (1993), pp. 21–6.

purchase luxuries depended primarily on their receipt of landed incomes in money.

There is general agreement that the overall *levels* of population in the early part of the century were very high by pre-industrial standards, indeed were at their highest point for the whole of the Middle Ages. However, there is much debate about the *trends* in population at this time, and that, apart from differences between regions, urban and rural trends may have been different in some parts of Europe. It was more the high levels of population rather than trends that determined the volume of trade, particularly that of urban populations. Most of Europe's principal urban centres were already concentrated by 1300 in a belt that stretched from Perugia in the south to London in the north, taking in the cities of Tuscany and Lombardy, curving through those of south Germany into the Rhineland and the middle Meuse to those of Brabant and Flanders, and ending in those of south-east England. The cities of the Rhône valley formed a western edge to this belt. However, some major cities lay outside it, of which Paris was by far the most important. A subsidiary belt of urban concentration stretched out to the west, from Lombardy and Liguria, through Provence and Languedoc to Catalonia and Valencia. Around 1300, the cities of northern Italy formed the most important group within the 'banana', followed in importance by those of the southern Netherlands.[5]

All these cities needed feeding and most consumed food far beyond the resources of their own immediate hinterlands. Before the 1340s when urban populations were at an extraordinarily high level in relation to agricultural productivity, prices of foodstuffs were high, whilst wages were low, so that for the bulk of city-dwellers there was a heavy emphasis on grain-based foods, such as bread or pasta, and particularly on those foods that used barley and rye, which were cheaper than wheat.

A few cities could rely on their hinterlands, and generated a trade in foodstuffs that, although very large, was not long distance. The 200,000 inhabitants of Paris could rely on grain produced in the vast basin of the Seine and its tributaries, brought to the city by river, whilst Londoners could live on the resources of all southern and eastern England.[6] The governments of the states of northern Italy, however, had to ensure an adequate food supply, sometimes from a great distance and at great expense.[7] Much Mediterranean trade was concerned simply with the movement of grain to northern Italy, and some of the greatest trading companies, like the Peruzzi of Florence, were heavily

---

[5] See Leguay and Klapisch-Zuber above pp. 102–6, 127–30; for a discussion with maps of the evolution of the urban 'blue banana' Davids and Lucassen (1995), pp. 11–19.

[6] Cazelles (1972); Keene (1989), pp. 99–111.

[7] Cf. *Il libro del Biadaiolo*, ed. Pinto, pp. 107–30, and Pinto (1972), pp. 3–84, for 1329 and 1346.

involved in it.[8] The evolution of bulk carriers, like the great round ships of Venice and Genoa, took place to meet this demand. They brought grain to northern Italy, not only from Apulia and Sicily, but also from Greece and the Black Sea, North Africa and Andalusia. The cities of the southern Netherlands, in a dense belt stretching from Calais to Cologne, could only partially be fed from the rich grain lands of northern and eastern France. They depended on the long-distance shipping of grain from the Baltic in the cogs of Hanseatic merchants.

The northern and southern ends of the European urban belt therefore normally relied on quite different areas for their food. There was effectively one partially unified grain market stretching from southern France to the eastern Baltic, and another from southern Castille to the northern shores of the Black Sea, with little interconnection between the two zones except when harvests failed for two or more years in succession. In 1316, for example, during the great north European famine, which resulted from harvest failures from Ireland to Poland, the cities of the southern Netherlands suffered the worst, relying as they did on grain imported from a great distance rather than local resources. One in every ten of the inhabitants of Ypres, then a major manufacturing city for luxury woollen cloth for international markets, died, pauperised to starvation, and had to be buried at public expense in only four months in 1317. Giovanni Villani, the prominent Florentine businessman-chronicler, commented that 'the cost of all foods became so high that everyone would have died of starvation, had not merchants, to their great profit, arranged for food to be transported by sea from Sicily and Apulia'.[9] Such trading in bulky necessities, even carried as cheaply as the largest round ships allowed, was only profitable when prices were high enough to counteract the huge expense of transport.

The grain trade may have been the dominant trade both in local and in long-distance trade in the fourteenth century, but it was by no means the only bulk trade. Amongst 'foodstuffs', wine was second only to grain. Because of its bulk (and frequently its low value), wine, like grain, was generally only worth carrying, except for very short distances, by water, either by sea or river. The four principal wine-exporting ports were Bordeaux, Seville, Naples and Candia in Crete. As with grain, the bulk trade in wine in the Mediterranean was far more important than that elsewhere. Although wine was extensively produced there, the countryside of northern Italy does not seem to have been able to supply its great cities with adequate supplies of wine, any more than they could with

[8] Hunt (1994).
[9] Lucas (1930); van Werveke (1959) reprinted (1968), pp. 326–38; Giovanni Villani, *Cronica*, ed. Porta, Bk x, ch. 80.

grain. Liguria was the sole exception, and produced more than enough wine for Genoese consumption. The Genoese, besides exporting their own wine, also supplied wine in bulk from overseas for the cities of Tuscany, whilst the Venetians brought in wine for Lombardy.[10]

Salt was a necessity for everyone. Furthermore it was used as the prime means of preserving food and no long-distance transport of fish could be managed without salt or oil. Unlike the market for food and drink, that for salt was universal, since country-dwellers had to buy it as much as townsmen. The trade in salt, though large, was not as considerable as that in grain and wine.

Many of the coastlands of Europe, from Norfolk to Cyprus, had salt marshes, which, when properly managed, could be turned into salt pans. In the north, slow natural evaporation was accelerated by the use of fuel, peat, for example, on Walcheren, but in the south the sun provided enough heat by itself. Although salt pans were to be found in many places, only a few were so productive that they could supply more than an immediate local market. The most important of these were those around the Bay of Bourgneuf just south of the Loire; those controlled by Catalans on Ibiza in the Balearics and in Sardinia; those along the coasts of Languedoc and Provence; and those controlled by Venice, particularly in and around their own lagoon. The Venetians also sought to buy up all the other salt produced along the Adriatic coasts, and their barges carried it up the Po and its tributaries, for sale to Milan, Verona, Bologna and all the cities between the Appenines and the Alps.[11] Their attempts to create a salt monopoly in Lombardy were partially frustrated by the Genoese, who, although they had no significant pans of their own, bought large quantities of salt from Provence, Languedoc and Sardinia and above all from Ibiza, the 'island of salt'. The Genoese were then able to act as suppliers of salt to others, just as with grain, and tried to create a monopoly on the Tyrrhenian side of Italy like that of the Venetians in the Adriatic. Tuscany bought its salt from Genoese, as did the Papal States, and the kingdom of Naples, Furthermore, they challenged the Venetian monopoly in Lombardy itself. Salt was the product most often found in the passes behind Genoa, and many thousands of mule loads were carried over the mountains to Piedmont.

Sea salt was not the only salt of medieval Europe. Brine wells and salt mines existed in many places, though most, like so many of the coastal salt pans, had only a local or regional importance. The salt from the brine wells of Cheshire, for example, essentially supplied the needs of midland and northern England and did not enter into long-distance commerce. Some mineral salt, however, supplied a wider market. Lüneburg in north Germany and Hallein, which produced the *Salz* of Salzburg, probably possessed the two largest inland sources

[10] Craeybeckx (1958); James (1971); Lloyd (1982), pp. 83–93.   [11] Hocquet (1978–9).

of salt, and were followed in scale by brine wells and salt mines at Salins in Franche Comté and Halle on the Saale in eastern Germany.[12] While salt from coastal pans generally began its journey by water, and often ended it by road, that from brine wells and salt mines generally began its journey by road, sometimes ending it by water. Salt thus provides an excellent example of the interdependence of road and water transport. Water transport, when available, was generally preferred, since salt was a commodity for which speed was not essential, yet it was so much a necessity that the generally higher costs of road transport could normally be absorbed by eventual purchasers, along with considerable taxation and the profits of middlemen.[13]

Although the amount of olive oil carried about Europe and the Mediterranean was less bulky than that of grain, or of wine and beer, or possibly of salt, the quantities involved were still considerable. Olive oil was a commodity with a multitude of uses. The best oil was used for cooking and eating, and as an alternative preservative for food. The barrels of tuna in oil exported from Tunis and Seville were the southern European equivalent of the barrels of salted Scania herring in northern Europe. It was also important as one of the key ingredients in making hard white soap,[14] and old oil was used for other industrial purposes, as the preferred alternative to rancid butter or pig fat, in tawing leather, or in oiling washed wool in the manufacture of cloth. The greatest production of oil was in southern Italy and southern Spain. In Lombardy, where much was used, none was produced, whilst in Tuscany some was produced, but not enough. The plentiful oil of southern Italy was therefore hugely exported to northern Italy, from Naples and the ports of Apulia. Spanish oil was carried north to Flanders and England. The Genoese began this trade by picking up Andalusian oil on their way north, but by the 1320s Spaniards were sailing north with their own oil, and by the 1360s Englishmen were coming south to look for olive oil, which soon ranked second only to iron in volume among the commodities carried to Bristol from Spain. Apulian and Andalusian oil was also shipped by Genoese and Catalan merchants to the Levant, Alexandria, Syria and to Asia Minor.

The heaviest of all commodities to be carried were building materials. Stone and bricks were only worth carrying, even by water, for limited distances, except for the most luxurious, like marble from the Carrara quarries. Timber, however, was carried a very long way by sea and river. An early fourteenth-century list of commodities coming to Bruges therefore included not only great wooden beams from Liège, floated down the Meuse, and wood for building from Germany, floated down the Rhine, but also wood for building brought by sea from Norway. Timber was needed for building ships as well as houses. The reliance of western shipbuilders on timber from the Baltic lands, particularly

---

[12] Mollat (1968).   [13] Hocquet (1985).   [14] See below p. 174.

masts and spars, can be traced back to the later Middle Ages. As well as building houses and ships, wood was also needed for the innumerable barrels used for transporting grain and salt, furs and fish, besides wine and beer.

The principal use of wood was as fuel, for domestic heating and cooking, in commercial bakeries, and for industries such as making bricks and tiles, smelting minerals, firing pottery, brewing ale and evaporating brine. The armourers of Milan and Brescia, for example, had an insatiable appetite for charcoal, but the amount of fuel that they consumed paled into insignificance beside the glass makers of Murano. The glass industry was responsible not only for the deforestation in the hinterland, which worried Venetians, because it affected the supply of suitable timber for shipbuilding at the Arsenal, but also for rapid and destructive deforestation in Dalmatia. They drew charcoal from greater and greater distances, eventually even from Crete. Mineral coal was available in north-western Europe. Most English coalfields were being worked in a small way from the thirteenth century onwards. Because of transport costs, pit coal was only worth using in the immediate vicinity, except for the coal from the Northumberland coalfield, which lay sufficiently near the coast to be sent by sea as far as London and Bruges. The production of the Northumberland coalfield was surpassed by that around Liège. Outside north-western Europe even travelled people were so unaware of the existence of pit coal that when Marco Polo encountered it in Asia, he reported it as a novelty unknown in Europe! In addition to timber, charcoal and, in a limited number of places, mineral coal, later medieval Europe also used peat as a source of heat, both for domestic and industrial purposes. However, like mineral coal, it was expensive to transport and only used in large quantities close to where it was dug out.

Iron was needed everywhere for making such things as agricultural tools like ploughshares. These things were generally made locally where they were needed, and the trade in iron was mostly one in bar iron for smiths, rather than in goods that had been made up. Iron deposits were scattered irregularly over Europe and mostly served a limited area. Beyond a certain point the high costs of land transport pushed up the cost of iron to a prohibitive price. It was therefore common only to use iron to put metal edges on essentially wooden tools like spades. The lower costs of transport meant that some iron, like that from Elba or the Basque provinces of north-western Spain, where the smelting works lay in or near the ports, could be transported for greater distances. However, most large-scale manufactures of iron objects were situated not very far from the sources of ore. The ore of Lombardy for example was used for the extensive manufacture of armour in Milan and Brescia, or that of Thuringia for making locks in Nuremberg.[15]

[15] Sprandel (1968).

The most complex bulk trade was that in textiles and in the raw materials that were used in their manufacture, wool, alum and cotton. Much of the clothing for the majority of the population was made of the cheaper sorts of woollens, but many clothes were not made from new cloth, but from old clothes, which were often made and remade many times. In large cities there were frequently guilds of *rigattieri*, clothes cobblers, remakers of clothes. Woollen cloth of various qualities was made in many parts of Europe, but even at the cheaper end of the market there were some areas that produced large quantities of cheap cloths. Many Parisians could be clothed with cheap cloth made on the spot, and so could the inhabitants of the southern Netherlands. It was not only the most expensive qualities of woollen cloth that entered into international trade, for much of the lower qualities also had a wide distribution, particularly the cloth made in Artois, Flanders, Hainault and Brabant. In the early fourteenth century the production of woollens in Ghent and Ypres reached its highest point. In several years between 1310 and 1320 over 90,000 rolls of cloth were officially registered annually at Ypres.[16] It is known that Ghent had a higher production, and it is probable that at this stage cheap cloths exceeded luxury woollens not only in volume, but even in value. The production of cloth in Ghent, and particularly in Ypres, declined quite suddenly around 1320. What was mainly lost was the export of cheap woollens to Italy.[17] Some cheaper woollens continued to be exported, alongside much more expensive fabrics, by sea into the Baltic as far as Novgorod, both by sea by Hanseatic merchants and by land into Germany by the men of Cologne. Much was sold at the Frankfurt fairs.

The other great woollen-cloth-producing area was northern Italy, although around 1300 the cities here were not yet self-sufficient in cheap cloth and still imported considerable quantities from the north. Woollen cloth nevertheless already dominated the economies of Tuscan cities like Prato, Pistoia and Siena, and even Arezzo and Volterra, but the key manufacturing city was Florence. Giovanni Villani described its main streets as having the form of a cross, and delighted to emphasise that at the centre point of the cross was the Arte della Lana, the guild headquarters of the woollen cloth manufacturers. This most properly symbolised the way that the manufacture of woollen cloth lay at the heart of all the city's concerns. According to him no less than 30,000 people depended on the cloth industry, and that at a time, the late 1330s, when the total population of the city was in the range of 100,000–120,000, which placed Florence in the topmost league of European cities. If Villani is to be believed, a quarter to a third of the population lived by this single activity, and some

---

[16] Van Werveke (1947) correcting Laurent (1935).
[17] Chorley (1987), pp. 349–79, Munro (1991), pp. 110–48.

80,000 rolls of woollen cloth were produced each year. He was possibly right in believing that earlier in the century Florence had actually produced more cloth, but of considerably less value, since it had all then been cheaper, coarser, cloth.[18] Whilst cheaper cloth production was shrinking slightly in Florence and considerably in Flanders, it seems to have been growing in Lombard cities like Como, Milan, Cremona, Parma, Verona, Padua and Vicenza, where, although important, woollen cloth manufacture was only one activity amongst many. It was also growing in Languedoc and Catalonia.

This vast production of cheap cloths used enormous quantities of cheap wool and alum, so generating bulk trades in wool and alum. Sheep from all the lands bordering on the western Mediterranean, particularly those on its southern shore, contributed their wools to the cheap Tuscan woollen industry,[19] whilst cheap, coarse wools from Flanders itself, France, Germany, Ireland, Scotland and northern England were used for the low-price cloths of Flanders and northern France.[20] Alum was needed as a mordant and removed grease and oil from wool and cloth. That used in fourteenth-century Europe came almost exclusively from Asia Minor, and a Genoese consortium, the *mahona* of Chios, developed a near monopoly in its import. Genoese bulk carriers took it in large quantities to Porto Pisano and Bruges for the cloth manufacturers of Tuscany and of Flanders and Brabant.

Like woollen cloth, linen was made in many places and in many qualities, depending on the skill of the workforce and the quality of the flax used. At the bottom end of the range there were very cheap and coarse fabrics, *grosses toiles*, and even some of these entered into international trade. Not all fabrics were for wear or domestic use. Hemp was made up into tough canvas, often used, for example, for wrapping rolls of superior fabrics. Up to the early fourteenth century the rough hempen fabrics made in the Rhône–Saône valley were carried to Italy across the Mont Cenis pass. Later, they were taken down the Rhône and shipped to Italy from Aigues-Mortes. Hemp was used too, mixed with cotton for sailcloth, as an alternative to linen.

There was also increasing use of relatively cheap cotton fabrics, the manufacture of which in the earlier part of the century was focused on Lombardy. This rapidly growing Lombard cotton industry depended on increasing quantities of cotton imported through Venice and Genoa from Asia Minor, and particularly from Syria where the best cotton was grown. Cotton cultivation was also taken up in Sicily and Calabria, but unlike silk, cotton could not be grown in northern Italy itself, and had to be imported. It was a very bulky commodity, best carried by sea. The cotton fabrics of Lombardy were

---

[18] Giovanni Villani, *Cronica*, ed. Porta, Bk x, ch. 257 and Bk xii, ch. 94.
[19] Melis (1990), pp. 233-50.   [20] Munro (1991), p. 111.

exported throughout Europe and the Mediterranean, including some, bizarrely, sent back to Syria itself. The centres for the manufacture of cotton in the Po Basin were in many cases identical with those for the making of linens and of cheaper woollens, from Piedmont down through Lombardy proper to Emilia, the Romagna and the Veneto.[21]

Demands generated by the high levels of populations, particularly urban populations, in the first half of the century determined the size of bulk trades, but high populations also formed the essential background to the large and growing scale of trade in luxury goods, since they not only enabled employers to pay low wages, but also permitted landlords, both rural and urban, to take high rents. This produced extremely polarised societies, in which an exceptionally high proportion of wealth passed through the hands of the most prosperous. The increase in the demand for luxury goods had thus been backed up by newly liberated quantities of ready cash, arising from a revolution in rents. By 1300 landlords essentially collected their rents in money, in place of an earlier mixture of goods, services and coin, amongst which coin had held the least important part.

Their high, and largely money, rent rolls enabled landlords to live where they chose, and they frequently chose, and were sometimes compelled, to live, for at least part of the year, in capital cities. The growth of these had been another phenomenon of the thirteenth century. The possibilities of large-scale taxation in money had also underpinned the processes of state formation, which had begun in earnest in the thirteenth century, but continued to be elaborated in the fourteenth. The demand for high-value luxuries therefore tended to be concentrated in capital cities and the long-distance trade in such products consequently also tended to be focused on them. Although most 'capital cities', like Paris, Ghent, London, Venice or Milan had had their greatest period of growth in the thirteenth century, some, like Avignon, only became capitals, or like Prague and Buda had their maximum period of growth in the fourteenth. Many of the great cities combined the role of government with other roles, as Ghent with manufacture, or Genoa and London with trade, or Milan, Venice and Florence with both manufacture and trade. Long-distance trade in high-value products, as in the late thirteenth century, therefore continued to be focused on those places where rents and taxes, and the profits of manufacture and trade, were primarily spent.

What did luxury consumption consist of? To be housed, furnished, served and dressed better and even to drink and eat better. In many cases better just meant more. Particularly in diet greater wealth often meant a great deal more meat and fish and less bread and fewer vegetables. But it was not the larger

[21] Mazzaoui (1981).

quantities of beef, pork and mutton, or even game, that made for long-distance trade; it was the ancillary foodstuffs, the spices and flavourings that came huge distances, for even if any individual noble household only consumed small quantities of pepper, cloves, cinnamon and nutmeg,[22] they added together to bring very considerable quantities of these commodities to western Europe from India and Indonesia. And the medieval definition of spices, small goods, included some considerable products like cane sugar, imported for use by the wealthy instead of honey, but it also included drugs, like Chinese rhubarb, used by apothecaries, and dyestuffs used for cloth.

Some of the trade in luxury goods ran in parallel with bulk trade. The superior wines drunk by the kings in England, and by the popes at Avignon, came from the best vineyards in Gascony and Burgundy respectively, but these were areas which also produced cheaper wines in bulk. The largest group of luxury products to be carried for long distances were luxury textiles of various sorts, but clothes for the rich involved not only textiles, but also furs. The furs used so extensively in western Europe for trimming garments, and, more luxuriously, for lining them, very largely came from the forests of Russia. The trappers who hunted down the beasts in the wild largely passed their skins on to their lords, who, in turn, sold them to local merchants who carried them to places where they could be bought by west Europeans. Many of the cheaper furs, particularly squirrel, came out through Novgorod and the Baltic, whilst many of the dearer furs, like ermine and sable, came out through Tana and the Black Sea, where they were bought by Venetians and Genoese merchants. In both areas another forest product, wax, was acquired in large quantities by western merchants, to provide the superior beeswax candles of the rich, with their wicks of cotton. We have scattered statistics for the scale of the northern fur trade. In the winter of 1336–7 there were 160 fur-buying merchants at the Peterhof, the Hanseatic 'factory' or *kontor* in Novgorod, principally men of Lübeck. The unprepared skins were packed in large barrels for the journey. One ship sailing to Lübeck in 1368 carried seventeen such barrels, containing between 75,000 and 100,000 furs in all.[23] Italian purchasers of furs, like their Hanseatic counterparts, preferred to buy skins unprepared so that a greater value could be added to the purchase price of the raw material by their own furriers.

Although the forests of northern and eastern Europe were the prime sources of furs, they were not the only ones. Marten skins from Ireland, for example, were imported into west European commerce through Liverpool, whilst cheap rabbit fur was widely available. The skin of new-born black lambs

[22] For the smallness of the quantities consumed in England see Dyer (1989), pp. 49–85.
[23] Dollinger (1970), pp. 210–19; Veale (1966) for the next paragraph.

was also treated as fur, and known to English buyers as 'budge'. It reputedly owed its name to Bougie in North Africa, one of the places from which it was exported to Italy. The best was that acquired on the Black Sea, later known as 'Astrakhan'. The late medieval European fur trades, whether of bulk furs, carried by Hanseatics, or of both bulk and luxury furs, carried by Italians, converged on Bruges. Furs were then distributed from there. They were shipped into England, for example, by merchants from Cologne and the Low Countries as well as by Englishmen. It is not surprising that the late medieval English gentry were able to have their clothes trimmed with various sorts of Russian squirrel fur, calaber, miniver, grey or, most expensive of all, vair, with its grey back and white belly, whilst its aristocracy went up-market for marten, sable and budge.

The luxury fabric *par excellence* was silk, of which the finest still came from China itself, and some was being brought back to Europe from China by Italian merchants. Before 1340, Francesco Pegolotti, possibly when running the Bardi branch at Famagusta, with its sub-branch in Armenia, put into his notebook what he could gather about the possibilities of trading with China. The whole point of engaging in the incredibly expensive exercise of crossing Asia by land was to bring back the finest silks, the mark up on which would far more than cover the enormous costs.[24] The letters back to Italy from the Franciscan bishops in China also allude in passing to the presence of Genoese merchants there, for example in 1326 in southern China at Zaytun,[25] the city which gave its name to satin. As well as silk fabrics from China, Italians were also importing silks made in Persia, Asia Minor and Syria. However, an increasing quantity of the silks worn in Europe were produced in north Italy itself. By 1300 Lucca had already been long established as the dominant silk-weaving city of western Europe. The raw silk used in the Lucchese industry was partly imported from Sicily and Calabria, but much came from further afield, for example that brought by the Genoese from Asia Minor. A very little raw silk was provided locally for the Lucchese from the Lunigiana, which was the first area to produce silk in Tuscany. The silk fabrics woven in Lucca were carried to all parts of Europe by Lucchese and other Tuscan merchants, who sold them along with the fine silk stuffs made in the Levant and the even finer ones that had come from China. The Lucchese fabrics began as substitutes for middle-eastern fabrics, themselves originally substitutes for Chinese fabrics. Cendal, a light fabric, was the commonest type of silk cloth, which was extensively used for garments and their linings, for furnishings and even for banners.

---

[24] Pegolotti, *La Pratica della Mercatura*, pp. 21–3.
[25] Letter of Andrew of Perugia, bishop of Zaytun in Dawson (ed.), *The Mongol Mission* (repr. 1980), pp. 235–7.

It was available in many plain colours and was woven in all the silk-weaving areas of Asia as well as in Italy. Sactant and taffeta were related to cendal. Both were of eastern origin (taffeta takes its name from the Persian *tafta*), but they were also woven in Europe. Samite was a heavier, stronger, more lustrous plain silk, mostly used for dress and furnishings, particularly favoured for embroidery. Its Greek name, which refers to its twill weave, suggests that it was originally a Byzantine fabric, although much imitated in Italy. Satin was glossier still, and was made in imitation of the fabric imported originally from Zaytun. The heaviest and most luxurious of the plain silk fabrics were the velvets, with their short but dense pile, which were possibly developed in Italy. Most of the richer silks were not of single colours. Patterned versions of samites and velvets were woven. Other patterned fourteenth-century silks were baudekins and camacas, the latter also originally of Asiatic origin with bird, animal, vine and other plant motifs. In 'damasks', Damascus-style fabrics, the pattern was distinguished from the background not by its colour but by its texture.[26] The extraordinary complexity and depth of the patterns involved in many fabrics meant that silk weaving was much more complicated and expensive than woollen weaving. Brocades and brocaded velvets could be yet further enriched by the use of 'silver' or 'gold' thread, which was actually silver or silver-gilt wire wound spirally on a silk thread. All this meant that the eventual customers for such fabrics were limited. They could only be afforded by emperors, kings, popes and their courtiers, by bishops and princes and by the very richest of the *magnati* of the great cities.

Although most, if not all, of these fabrics were oriental in origin, they were refined upon by the Lucchese and other Italians. In the course of the century the silk industry declined in Lucca, but many Lucchese craftsmen carried their skills to Venice, as they had previously to Bologna in the thirteenth century. Venice, already one of the principal ports for the import of raw silk, then replaced Lucca as the most important city for producing silk fabrics. During the century silk industries were also established in Florence and other Tuscan cities.

Around 1300 there was still a large aristocratic market for heavy woollen cloth. However, the most luxurious cloths, which, like silks, were only sold to rulers and their families, and the richest of magnates, were only produced in a very limited number of places. At the beginning of the century the dominant area in which luxury cloth was produced was the southern Netherlands. When the production of cheap woollens largely collapsed there, that of luxury cloth continued.[27] In the 1390s the Lombard illuminator of the *Tacuinum Sanitatis*

---

[26] King (1993), pp. 457–64.
[27] Munro (1991); van der Wee (1975), pp. 203–21, reprinted (1993), pp. 201–22.

illustrated 'woollen clothing' by a tailor giving a customer a fitting, with the legend 'the best is this kind from Flanders'. The crisis that afflicted the Flemish cloth industry did not affect the already well-established cloth industry in neighbouring Mechelen (Malines) and in the Brabant towns like Brussels and Leuven (Louvain). On the contrary, the quantity produced there increased rapidly in the 1320s. Even cloths from a medium-sized Brabant town like Tirlemont (Tienen) were for a time bought as far away as Hungary and Prussia.[28] Later in the century the production of luxury woollens for export began again in England, protected by the heavy duties on the export of English wool, imposed from the opening of the Hundred Years War onwards. The cloth manufacturers of Brabant and England drew on the skills developed in Flanders and encouraged the migration of skilled men.

In the 1330s Giovanni Villani pointed out that a significant part of the cloth production in Florence was the highest quality of luxury cloth designed for the aristocratic market. He wrote that the total production, cheap and dear together, was worth no less than 1,200,000 gold florins, approximately equal to the combined annual incomes of the kings of England and France. This production of luxury cloth was a new development in his own lifetime. In the 1320s enterprising Florentine firms began importing the most expensive English wools directly to Florence. It was initially used to produce imitations of the luxury quality Low Countries cloth, which were generically known as *panni alla francesca*. The most expensive of them was described as *a moda di Doagio*, just as the most expensive imported cloth had been that of Douai, in Flanders. It was followed in price by that *a modo di Mellino* and that *a modo di Borsella* or *a Borsella*, in imitation of the cloths of Malines and Brussels respectively. Indeed skilled workmen from Brabant were lured to Florence to help make these imitative cloths. Thereafter Florence produced two distinct qualities of woollen cloth. On the one hand there was that manufactured with fine-quality English wool for the luxury markets of the Mediterranean world, like the aristocracy at the Neapolitan court. It soon ceased to be thought of as an imitation, but was regarded as a luxury fabric in its own right, and was sold for even higher prices than the woollens from Flanders and Brabant. It was increasingly known as *panna di San Martino*, from the neighbourhood where its manufacture was concentrated. On the other hand, there was still *panna di garbo*, the traditional cheaper mass-market fabric made from poorer Mediterranean wools.[29]

As well as long-distance trade in the luxury silks and woollen cloths themselves, there was also long-distance trade in the dyestuffs used in preparing them for the market. The costs of dyeing varied enormously according to the

---

[28] Peeters (1988), pp. 165–70.   [29] Hoshino (1980) and (1983).

colours used. It could be an extravagant and luxurious operation, and for the finest woollens represented at least a quarter, and sometimes as much as half, of the total production costs. The use of different colours or at least different shades of the same colour in patterned silks meant that they had to be dyed as thread, not as a finished product. Dyeing was probably the most skilled of all the cloth-making processes, and as well as skill, required very considerable capital. This was not only fixed capital in terms of buildings and vats, but above all working capital, for many, although not all, the dyestuffs were very costly. Woad, the source of common blue dye was grown in large quantities in Picardy, around Toulouse and in Lombardy. Madder, the most commonly used red dyestuff, although a plant of Persian origin, was extensively grown in France and the Low Countries. Other dyes, however, came from much farther afield. Brazil wood, from Ceylon and Java was surprisingly widely used to give a rich reddish-brown colour. The most expensive of all dyestuffs was 'grain' or 'kermes'. At one time it cost up to twenty-nine times as much as madder in Flanders. It came from two species of shield-lice, parasitic on evergreen oak trees, which were found in various parts of the Mediterranean from Portugal and Morocco to Armenia and Crete. The females were collected in May and June before their eggs were laid, killed and dried in the sun. When dried they resembled seeds or small worms, hence the names *kermes*, or *vermiculus* (from the Arabic and Latin respectively for small worm). Crushed and mixed with water, they produced a *vermilion* dyestuff. It was used alone for the most brilliant and expensive red fabrics, but because of its expense it was often used in combination with other dyestuffs. All woollen fabrics dyed with 'grain', even partially, were known as scarlets. In this way it was possible to have not only *vermeille* scarlet but also various *sanguine* scarlets, *violete* scarlet, *murrey* (mulberry) scarlet, brown 'scarlet', even black and dark perse-blue scarlet, and most surprising of all was green scarlet. 'White scarlet' seems generally to have been scarlet-quality cloth that had not yet been dyed.[30] It was only worth using so expensive a dye on the most expensive fabrics, made from the finest quality English wool from the Welsh Marches or the Cotswolds. They were often also the largest fabrics which were sheared several times. All this made them yet more expensive. In Cracow at the end of the century, scarlets imported from Brussels and bought by the Polish royal court cost sixteen times as much per ell as the common cloth brought into the city which had been woven in the surrounding villages.

The finest linen, used not only for clothing, but also for bedding and table-coverings, was carried vast distances. At the very beginning of the century, the compiler of the *codex Cumanicus*, probably a Genoese, put into his

---

[30] Munro (1983), pp. 13–70.

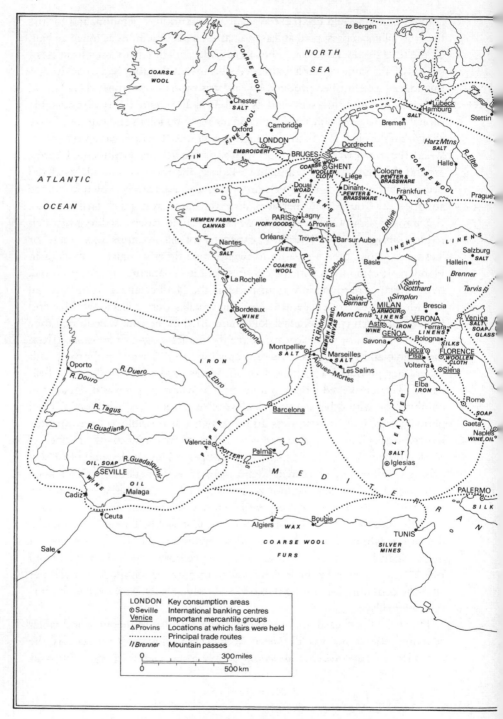

Map 4   Europe's trade, *c.* 1300

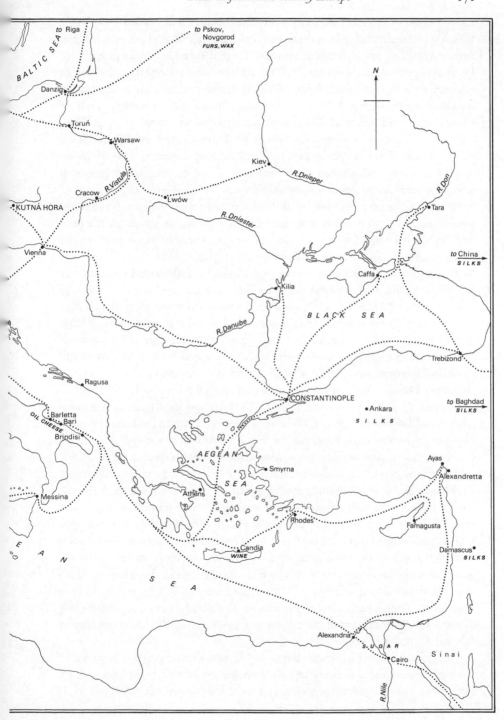

Latin–Persian–Cumanic dictionary words and phrases that would be useful for Italian merchants trading into Persia and central Asia, where Cumanic was the *lingua franca*. The only European commodity that Italians took in quantity to Persia and central Asia was linen. The compiler of this trilingual book thought it worthwhile to distinguish some of the different places from which export quality linen came. Some of his categories, 'linen of Lombardy', 'linen of Champagne' and 'linen of Germany' covered whole manufacturing areas, others like 'linen of Orléans' or 'linens of Fabriano' related to individual places. Some of his particular places, like Reims or Bergamo, fall within his general areas. He pinpointed most, but not all, of the important places in which export quality linen was manufactured by 1300. He was, of course, writing from the point of view of an Italian exporting to the east. A different, north European, point of view is given by the customs accounts for the port of London for 1390. Of something over 12,000 pieces of linen, each 50 ells long, imported into London, around 5,500 pieces had come from the Netherlands, mainly from the county of Flanders, and around 6,000 pieces from Westphalia. This indicates the two principal areas producing high-quality linen in northern Europe, a 'Flemish' area which stretched from Artois into Brabant, and the area around Osnabrück. The latter was not the source of the 'German' linen sent to Asia, which came from the large flax-growing region of Swabia, centring on Lake Constance, which stretched for 250 km, from the Lech on the east, to Basle in the west, and from the Alps northwards to beyond the upper Danube. Linen from this area was carried through the Alps, and so became available for Genoese exporters. In these specialising areas, the manufacture of linens fit to export, like that of woollens, was in the hands of merchant entrepreneurs, who oversaw the various processes involved, and saw to it that the linens produced conformed to fixed standards of size and quality.

As well as producing large quantities of linens, mostly rather expensive, Lombardy also engaged in the manufacture of cotton fabrics, which like woollens varied enormously in quality. Some were very luxurious, like the fine cotton fabrics from Milan and Cremona which were noted for their design, texture and colours, but most were not. There were also many cross-fibre fabrics, like silk–cotton and linen–wool, of which the most important by far were fustians, the linen–cotton mix, which combined the durability of linen with the fineness and softness of cotton, and was, of course, much cheaper than linen. The manufacture of fustians in 'Lombardy' grew particularly fast in the fourteenth century at the expense of both pure linens and pure cotton fabrics.

Closely allied with the production of linens was that of paper. The demand for writing material was rising rapidly with the growth of record keeping of every sort. Central governments led, but were followed at every level of local government in Church and state, and by landowners in records of estate management. The keeping of accounts became a regular feature at every level from that of the *recette générale* of a kingdom to the humblest hospital. In addition there was an explosive use of the written word in business. The supply of parchment could not keep pace with the fast-growing demand, and paper was increasingly used instead, and generally took over for everyday use. Initially all the paper used in Christian Europe had been imported from the Muslim world. However Valencia and Sicily continued to make paper when reconquered by Christians, and in the thirteenth century paper began to be made in northern and central Italy, particularly in the areas of linen manufacture. In the fourteenth century the market in paper was dominated by that made from linen rags in the small town of Fabriano in the Marches, already famous for its high-quality linens. In due course master paper makers from Fabriano moved to set up paper mills elsewhere, carrying their skills with them like Lucchese silk manufacturers, and before the end of the century the manufacture of paper had crossed the Alps, like that of fustian. The first paper made in Germany came from a mill on the Pegnitz just outside the walls of Nuremberg which was converted for this purpose in 1390 by Ulman Stromer, at the time managing director of an old-established import–export house, which had, of course, been importing paper, with many other commodities, from Italy, and therefore had a market ready for it in southern Germany.

The weaving of carpets, for covering tables and walls as well as floors, was yet another replacement for a hitherto imported oriental luxury, as was tapestry weaving. At the end of the century a few 'Turkish' and 'Saracen' tapestries were still being imported from the Levant. However, by 1350 tapestry weaving was well established in Paris, where the court provided a large home market, and the French royal family were prodigious purchasers. John II bought at least 235 tapestries between 1350 and 1364, and his sons continued the tradition. Philip the Bold of Burgundy is said to have owned the finest collection of tapestries existing in Europe in 1400. In the southern Netherlands, Arras was for long the centre of the industry and gave its name to the product – 'arras', 'arras cloths', 'arazzi' – but by 1400 Tournai was almost as important a producer.

Tapestries were naturally sold through Bruges and distributed throughout Europe. The less expensive sort, called *verdure*, greenery, had repetitive foliage patterns, and could safely be sold speculatively, but the most expensive tapestries were made with particular stories, *a personnages* for particular clients to hang in particular rooms, and had to be ordered specially. John of Gaunt, duke of Lancaster, had Arras tapestries woven for hanging in his palatial 'inn' on the Strand between London and Westminster.

On a rather different scale from tapestry weaving was *opus anglicanum*, embroidery in silks and gold thread on various fabrics, but usually on linen. Most of the surviving examples are ecclesiastical, elaborate copes and chasubles embroidered with religious subjects, like the copes at S. Giovanni in Laterano, Rome, and in the Museo Civico at Bologna, which once belonged respectively to Popes Boniface VIII (1294–1303) and Benedict XI (1303–4). Documentary evidence, however, indicates that there was a considerable secular market as well, although little survives. We know that Henry III of England purchased it, and English royal accounts for the next two centuries continue to show the kings of England and members of their families as customers of the London 'broderers'. Embroidered robes once existed in quantity, and were worn, for example, by Edward III, his queen and his son, Edward the Black Prince. Of these only an embroidered surcoat of the Black Prince survives, in Canterbury Cathedral. Matching sets of bed furnishings – coverlet, tester, cushions and hangings – were also embroidered.

Just as the broderers in the English capital developed something of a monopoly in supplying the highest quality embroidery to rulers, nobles and greater prelates throughout Europe, the ivory carvers of Paris did much the same. There was a large home market to support them, but they also found markets throughout Europe. Of over 2,000 examples of medieval European carved ivory in museums throughout the world the overwhelming majority are from Paris. Only a handful were carved in other places, at most sixty in England, and rather more in Italy. Almost all the surviving ivory objects can be dated between the 1270s and 1400. It is not clear whether this chronology was mainly determined by changes in fashion, or in trading conditions outside Europe. Elephant tusks were bought in Acre, Alexandria and Lajazzo by Italian merchants, who shipped them to Marseille, Aigues-Mortes or Bruges for transmission to Paris, where several guilds were involved in a veritable ivory carvers' quarter, where they formed a close group, living and working in a particular area just as the broderers did in London. As with *opus anglicanum*, most of the surviving ivories are religious, small devotional carvings, pyxes for the host, and heads to pastoral staffs. However, documentary evidence again reveals that secular boxes of ivory, combs, mirrors and cups, chess men, dice and counters for draughts and backgammon once existed in considerable numbers, as did knife handles and writing tablets.

White, olive-oil based soap was yet another product originating in the Muslim world. When the Castilians took over Andalusia, they continued to make it, and their soap, exported by sea, became the luxury soap *par excellence* for the nobility of northern Europe in the fourteenth century. The superiority of Castilian soap depended not only on abundant supplies of local oil, but also on the availability of alkali-rich plants to burn to produce ash suitable for making hard white soap. Similar soap was made in Syria, which had superior 'soda ash' and in olive-growing southern Italy at Naples and, above all, at Gaeta. Once Venetians, Genoese and Provençal merchants started importing suitable 'soda ash' from Egypt and Syria, soap making could be transformed in northern Italy and Provence as well. South Italian olive oil was their other key ingredient. Apulian olive oil was shipped across and up the Adriatic to supply the soap makers of Ragusa, Ancona and above all Venice, whilst on the west coast soap was made at Savona and Genoa. The Venetians and Genoese competed directly with the Castilians for the north European market. They also exported soap to the near east, to Frankish Greece, Constantinople, Turkish Asia Minor, Rhodes, Cyprus and in very considerable quantities, back to Syria and Egypt. All this trade was carried by sea, but with the much higher costs of land transport, it was problematic how far it was worth carrying such a heavy product by road. In practice in the late fourteenth century Venetian luxury white soap was about the cheapest commodity that it was profitable to take across the Alps.

Pottery, like cloth, was made everywhere, but just as luxury textiles made in a limited number of places entered into international trade, so did high-class pottery. The most favoured pottery was tin-glazed earthenware of Muslim, eventually Persian, origin. In the early fourteenth century Majorca was key to the distribution of the glazed wares of Valencia and Andalusia, hence its name majolica. This lustrous Hispano-Moresque tin-glazed earthenware was yet another commodity imitated by north Italians. Derivative majolica was produced at Faenza in the Romagna for use as tableware, spice jars, apothecary's pots, tiles and decorative pieces.

As well as majolica there was also brass and pewter tableware for those who wanted something better than treen or coarse pottery, but could not rise to silver plate. Dinant, on the Meuse, was the most important centre for the production of such brass tableware, consequently known as 'dinanderie', which was exported throughout Europe. The customs accounts for Hull, not one of England's most important ports, show that seven shiploads of brass 'pots' were sent there in 1310–11, one of which consisted of 11,400 items. Particularly popular amongst the well-to-do were brass water containers, used for pouring water for hand-washing after meals, in conjunction with broad deep dishes. As well as tableware, brass candlesticks were exported extensively for domestic, as well as church, lighting, whether made to be attached to the wall, or stand on tables.

Majolica, dinanderie and pewter were not the only prestigious tableware manufactured in Europe. There was also the luxury glass of Venice. Because of fire hazards the glass makers' furnaces had been banished across the lagoon to the islands of Murano in 1291. The glass-making skills of Venetian artisans ultimately derived from Syria, and it was from Syria that the special alkaline ash, rich in sodium, had to be imported, which was one of the key ingredients of the superiority of Venetian glass as of its white soap. Ordinary cups and bottles, clear window glass and mirrors were sent out in enormous quantities, as well as spectacles and the prestigious and expensive polychrome bowls and vases, sometimes exotically enamelled, which are so much better known. As well as exporting Murano glass northwards and westwards, Venetians also exported it eastwards, to Egypt by the 1310s, and to Greece, Constantinople, Rhodes and the Black Sea coasts by the 1340s.

It is no wonder that this demand for distant luxuries had brought about an enormous quantitative change in the volume of international trade. Moreover, as the amount of business focused on a limited number of particular places, or rather along a limited number of routes between those places, a critical mass was reached, so that qualitative changes in the nature of commerce had begun to take place as well as merely quantitative ones. Such qualitative changes in the ways of doing business have been dignified with the title 'commercial revolution' on the analogy of the title 'industrial revolution' for changes in the organisation of manufacture. This vital transformation could only take place when the concentrated supply of money, and consequently of trade, rose beyond a certain critical point.

Since much of the long-distance trade in high-value commodities of the earlier part of the century was in the hands of north Italians, it was they who, between *c.* 1250 and 1350, had elaborated most of the interlocking trading techniques which have been bundled together as this 'commercial revolution'. None of these new methods of doing business was abandoned in the fourteenth century. Some indeed, like company structure, local banking and insurance, were elaborated further. Catalan merchants also adopted these 'Italian' methods of doing business, and so, by the end of the century, did some south German merchants.

Until a certain critical scale of operations was reached on any particular route, all that occurred was an increase in the volume of trade within the traditional framework. However, once the critical volume had been reached, the scale of enterprises allowed for a division of labour. Some businesses became large enough and continuous enough to maintain three separate parties: the sedentary merchants remaining full time in northern Italy, who specialised in the financing and organisation of import–export trade; the specialist carriers, whether shipowners by sea, or *vectuarii* by land, who took the goods from the principals to their agents; and the full-time agents themselves, resident overseas or beyond the Alps, who devoted their energies to sales or purchases according to the instructions sent to them.

Such a threefold division of labour had naturally taken place first on the routes along which demand was most concentrated at an early date, those from the ports of northern Italy to the Levant. Only a little later, northern Italian colonies had begun to be found in Rome, Naples, Palermo and Tunis, and at the fairs of Champagne and, at the same time, colonies of agents from other cities had come to settle within cities in northern Italy. Later, but still before 1300, they were to be found in the northern capitals, at Paris and London, and also at some of the greater ports with wealthy hinterlands like Bruges, Seville, Barcelona and Montpellier. It was therefore perfectly reasonable to expect early fourteenth-century firms like the Bardi or the Peruzzi of Florence to have branches in such cities as London or Paris or Tunis with which a great deal of trade was carried out. By the mid-century there were colonies of merchants from Genoa, Pisa and Florence not only in Tunis and Bougie, the wax from which gave the French their word for candle, but in all the major North African ports on the Barbary coast as far as Safi, in modern Morocco. There were also colonies of Catalan merchants from Barcelona in at least some North African ports. Italian trade with even the largest cities east of the Rhine never reached this critical scale. Even on the routes on which large businesses operated through factors resident abroad, merchants trading on a smaller scale continued to travel with their goods. In the 1320s over 150 Catalan merchants still made an annual trip from Barcelona to Barbary, even though there had been communities of resident Catalans in some cities of the Maghreb, the North African littoral, for a century or more.

The host cities made varied provision for these resident aliens. Sometimes they were given a privileged trading place, to which they were more or less confined, like the Hanseatic Steelyard on the London waterfront, the *fondaco dei tedeschi* for transalpine merchants in Venice, or the *funduks* for Italian and Catalan merchants in Tunis. At other times they were less confined, like the merchants from the Italian states resident in Bruges, who could rent rooms in inns, or even houses, wherever they liked in the city, provided they had a citizen as guarantor, often the keeper of the inn where they lodged. However, even if scattered about, merchants from the same state had some sort of common organisation, focused on a consular house. The merchants of Venice, Genoa, Lucca and Florence had such consular houses in Bruges.

A frequent limitation on foreign merchants was that they could only trade with natives and not with other foreigners, or at least had to offer their goods first to natives and, when permitted to deal with others, had to use natives as brokers. In all trading cities, brokers were enormously important for putting together buyers and sellers. Innkeepers frequently acted as brokers. The focus of business was the exchange at which specialised brokers of various sorts were to be found, at fixed hours of the day, ready to introduce to each other buyers and sellers of particular commodities, borrowers and lenders, shippers and underwriters and to put deals together between them. The first exchange building in Europe seems to have been the Lottja, or Lonja, in Barcelona, completed as early as 1392. Before buildings were put up for them, brokers had congregated in particular squares which were gradually set aside for their use, like the Piazza dei Banchi in Genoa, the Piazza of the Rialto in Venice, or the square in Bruges on which the Florentines had their consular house, named after a wealthy family of innkeeper-brokers, the van der Beurse, or de la Bourse.

The by-products of this revolutionary commercial division of labour included the beginnings of international banking and the evolution of the bill of exchange, the creation of international trading companies which lasted for several years rather than for a single voyage, regular courier services to carry commercial correspondence (and bills of exchange), low rates of interest, the beginnings of local banking, and of insurance, the use of double entry book-keeping, and the development of commercial education.[31]

No longer did every prospective purchaser or returning vendor need to carry with him large and stealable quantities of precious metals, whether in coin, or in mark bars of silver or ounce bags of gold dust, depending on the trading area. Instead the static manager could send and receive remittances from his factors and agents by bills of exchange, which had evolved into their definitive form by 1300 and had become normal for commercial payments within the international banking network focused on the great trading cities of Tuscany. This network extended outwards from northern Italy to the papal curia at Avignon, Montpellier, Barcelona, Valencia, Seville and sometimes Lisbon, and northwards to Paris, Bruges and London, and southwards to Naples and Palermo. Even between these cities, although the majority of trans-actions could be carried out by bill of exchange, any eventual imbalances had ultimately to be settled up in gold or silver. When an imbalance between two banking places became too great, the rate of exchange rose (or fell) to such an extent that it passed one of the specie points. In other words, it temporarily became cheaper to transport bullion, in one direction or the other, with all its attendant costs and risks, than to buy a bill of exchange. The net quantity of silver transported from Bruges to London or Paris to Florence, or of gold from Seville to Genoa did not diminish as a result of the development of bills of exchange, but the amount of business that it represented was increased out of all proportion. The bill of exchange enormously multiplied the supply of money available for international transactions between these cities.[32]

Although bills of exchange were developed by merchants for merchants,

---

[31] De Roover (1942), pp. 34–9, republished in Lane and Riemersma (1953), pp. 80–5; see also de Roover (1963), pp. 42–118, and (1974).

[32] De Roover (1953); Spufford (1986), modified in Mueller (1995), pp. 121–9.

they had very quickly come to be used by non-merchants as well. The papacy was the most considerable non-commercial user of bills of exchange; its collectors used them to transmit the money they had collected to the apostolic *camera* at Avignon.[33] Bishops travelling to the curia no longer needed to ensure that their chamberlains were loaded down with an adequate quantity of mark bars of silver. Noblemen, whether on pilgrimage or representing their princes on embassies, could also avail themselves of bills of exchange. There were, however, limits. Certain international political payments, such as wages for armies, subsidies for expensive allies, royal dowries or ransoms like that of John II of France, could easily prove too large for the normal commercial system to handle, and so had to be transmitted largely, or wholly, in silver or gold. For example, when John XXII needed to pay 60,000 florins to the papal army in Lombardy in 1328, he had to send it all in coin. That episode provides an excellent example of the risks involved in carrying coin, for, despite a guard of 150 cavalry, the convoy was ambushed and over half the money lost on the way. Nevertheless a very large proportion of normal payments within this network of cities was made by bill of exchange by the early fourteenth century.

Outside this range of banking places, even ordinary international payments had still to be made primarily in bullion. Where there was a large and continuous imbalance of trade, as there was between the mining centres of Europe and the commercially advanced areas, a bill-of-exchange system had little chance of developing. In the fourteenth century, papal collectors in Poland, Hungary or Austria still had to take bullion to Bruges or Venice before they could make use of the western European banking system, despite the earnest but unavailing request of Benedict XII that Florentine firms should open branches in Cracow. At the very end of the century bills of exchange began to be occasionally used by south German merchants, but throughout the century even the most prominent trading cities elsewhere in Germany, such as Lübeck, basically remained outside this network of exchanges. Similarly bills were of little use for payments from Italy eastwards, although occasionally from the Levant to Italy.

The early fourteenth century witnessed the heyday of the giant Tuscan trading companies with numerous employees scattered about branches in many different cities, but their organisation went back to mid-thirteenth-century companies like the Bonsignori in Siena, Riccardi in Lucca and Cerchi in Florence. Florence and Lucca were at their peak early in the century but Siena, although still important, was already beginning to decline as a trading city. Although this form of multi-branched international trading company was typical of the largest enterprises in Tuscany, parallel but slightly different forms

<hr />

[33] Renouard (1941) and Favier (1966).

were growing up elsewhere in northern Italy in Venice, Genoa and Milan.[34] The Bardi of Florence, probably the largest medieval company, when renewed in 1318, had a capital of 875,000 gold florins, considerably greater than the annual income of any ruler in Europe, even the king of France. At the previous restructuring in 1310, its capital had been divided into as many as fifty-six shares.[35] Such shares were transmissible within the lifetime of a company without breaking up the partnership. They were held not only by members of the founding families of a company, and by its principal employees, who were encouraged to put their savings into their own company, but also by other rich men. These were investors not at all concerned with the actual running of the company.

Many Tuscan companies from the thirteenth century onwards used short-term borrowing at low fixed interest, beyond the shareholders' subscribed capital, to increase their resources. The ready availability of loans for business purposes at a much lower rate of interest than elsewhere was a key factor in commercial success. At the beginning of the century annual commercial interest rates in northern Italy were generally well below 10 per cent. Even in Flanders rates were not lower than 16 per cent, which gave Italians a tremendous competitive edge.[36]

Some of this cheap money was made available through local banks. Whereas international banking grew up in parallel with import–export operations, local deposit banking was grafted on to the work of money-changers, in many cities around the western Mediterranean and in the southern Netherlands, from Bruges to Liège.[37] They offered their current account customers the safety of their vaults and the convenience of being able to make book payments to other account holders. Deposit account holders, often religious houses or orphans, received interest on their deposits which the banker then invested, along with a proportion of the money of the current account holders. International Italian trading companies were also prepared to accept deposits at any of their branches. In the first half of the fourteenth century great English noblemen placed appreciable funds with the London branches of Florentine companies. The earl of Lincoln had money with the Frescobaldi, the earl of Hereford with the Pulci, and the younger Despenser with the Bardi and Peruzzi.[38]

Another key to commercial success was the acquisition of economic information faster than one's rivals. Agents and factors therefore reported often to their principals, and received a constant stream of instructions; their firms paid for frequent couriers to carry commercial correspondence, and bills of exchange, between business centres. Furthermore the risks involved in

---

[34] Renouard (1968), pp. 107–247.   [35] Sapori (1926).   [36] P. Spufford (1995), pp. 303–37.
[37] De Roover (1954), pp. 38–76, reprinted in (1974).   [38] Fryde (1951), pp. 344–62.

sending unaccompanied goods were spread by the development of embryonic forms of maritime insurance, in which the Venetians took the lead.

The sedentary merchant at home was no longer a simple individual capitalist. As head of a company he was also a manager responsible to his shareholders and depositors, and in complex business relationships with factors, agents, carriers, innkeepers, insurers, sub-contractors, suppliers and customers scattered over much of western Europe and the Mediterranean. Those who ran such firms had consequently to keep an enormous number of account books, which began to use new systems of double entry book-keeping.[39] Such businesses assumed the literacy and numeracy of all those with whom they had to deal, and depended on an extensive educational infrastructure which could ensure not merely reading and writing skills, but also commercial arithmetic.

Secular, vernacular, education was already well established in Italy and the southern Netherlands. In the new flood of surviving documentation after 1300, there appears also a flood of school teachers, in Liguria, Lombardy, the Veneto and Tuscany. In the commercial and industrial city of Lucca, the commune paid in 1345 for an *abbachista*, a teacher of commercial arithmetic, who also taught book-keeping and served as an accountant to the commune, with a rent-free house. The rationale for the commune's expenditure was that the citizens of Lucca were 'much engaged in business, which can hardly be carried on if one is ignorant in arithmetic and abacus'. The commune's provision of part of the appropriate educational infrastructure no doubt helped to keep Lucchese businessmen prominent in international trade.[40]

It is no wonder that, in this world of commercial paper, Tuscan, particularly Florentine, businessmen seem to have had an addiction to making memoranda. Very many *libri di ricordanze* survive. Most are primarily concerned with personal and family affairs; some combine personal and business affairs, yet others, like that kept by Francesco Pegolotti, an employee of the Bardi company, are just filled with useful notes for business purposes.[41]

As well as a transformation in the methods of trading, there was also a considerable change both in the routes of trade and the means of transport. The key land trade routes of thirteenth-century Europe may be represented as a triangle. On the west lay the combination of road and river routes running from Flanders to Tuscany, passing through Champagne, where they connected with Paris, which was then the greatest single consumption centre in Europe, and across Alpine passes, the Great Saint-Bernard, the Simplon and the Mont Cenis, to become the via Francigena in Italy. On the east lay the routes from

[39] De Roover (1956), pp. 114–74.   [40] M. Spufford (1995), pp. 229–83.
[41] Spufford (1991), pp. 103–20.

Tuscany to the mining areas of central Europe, which left Italy by the Tarvis pass and went on through Vienna. Flanders was similarly linked to the mining areas by the road running 'from England to Hungary, from the sea coast across the plains of Flanders, and then from Tongres through [Maas]Tricht into Cologne'.[42] The replacement of the triangle of key thirteenth-century land routes by a web of fifteenth-century routes radiating outwards from south Germany was not a direct succession. Although so many goods were carried overland in both the mid-thirteenth century and the late fifteenth century, in the fourteenth century much trade was carried by sea.[43]

From the corners of the thirteenth-century triangle of great land routes, further routes extended outwards; many were sea routes. Trade by road and river and trade by sea were in most cases complementary. The sea routes of the Mediterranean, the North Sea and the Baltic joined the overland routes across Europe. From Bruges, there were not only the short Channel crossings to England, but also the Hanseatic routes through the North Sea and the Baltic. From Genoa, Pisa and Venice, there were sea routes to the Maghreb and the Levant. From the mines of Meissen, Bohemia and Slovakia a route led eastwards, north of the chain of mountains, to Cracow, Kiev and beyond.

Improvements in navigation and the corresponding extension of maritime activity, particularly by Italians, meant that the triangular land routes were partially circumvented by much longer, but still cheaper, sea routes. It became easier to reach Cracow from Italy by travelling to the Black Sea in a Genoese carrack and thence up the Dniester through Lwów, rather than going the whole distance overland. It became easier to reach Cracow from Flanders by travelling to Danzig or Toruń in a Hanseatic cog and thence up the Vistula, rather than going along the 'road from England to Hungary'. Above all, it became easier to go directly by carrack or galley from Genoa or Venice to Bruges itself, rather than travelling overland across the Alps and the Jura, Burgundy and Champagne.

The Atlantic route between north-west Europe and Italy could thus be regarded as an alternative, and a rival, to the land and river routes across Europe. Travel by sea from the north to the Mediterranean had had an intermittent history since Viking times. However, it was only late in the thirteenth century that the sea route came to be much used for commercial purposes. The successes of the Christian 'reconquest' of the Iberian peninsula provided suitable stopping places to make the journey commercially viable. A Genoese community was known in Seville from the year of its capture in 1248. Seville

---

[42] So called by Hendrik van Veldeke, one of the earliest writers of love songs in the German vernacular.

[43] See the chapters in the thirteenth- and fifteenth-century volumes for more detail of these land routes.

became not only a gateway for Italian, particularly Genoese, exploitation of the commercial opportunities provided by its Andalusian hinterland, but also an excellent staging point for journeying onwards into the Atlantic. It was, of course, not the only such staging point. In the fourteenth century the Genoese community in Seville was rivalled in size by that in Cadiz, which had itself been reconquered in 1265. Cadiz possessed a better harbour, but not such a rich hinterland. The Genoese community in Seville was possibly also rivalled by that at Malaga, which had an even better harbour, but lay in the unreconquered kingdom of Granada. There was yet another, smaller, Genoese community in Lisbon. Genoese ships were next to be found rounding Spain and trading as far as La Rochelle. The earliest Genoese galleys known to have gone all the way to Flanders did so in 1277, and may have been preceded by Catalan ships. Such trading voyages were initially sporadic, but became more common as time went on, but it was only in the fourteenth century that regular voyages began.

Political circumstances also brought about a severe disruption of the land route across Champagne to Flanders. Wars between Philip IV and Flanders and in northern Italy itself caused trade to move away from the traditional route across eastern France. This was reflected in falling returns from the tolls at the passes in the Jura and the western Alps. As well as a shift by overland carriers to a Rhineland route, some merchants took advantage of the opportunity of sending goods by the new sea route.

As long as this was only a galley route, it was an expensive alternative to carriage by road and river, for galleys with their huge complement of men were very costly to operate. The earliest Venetian 'great galleys', enlarged mercantile versions of the traditional Mediterranean many oared men-of-war, which were introduced around 1290, required nearly 200 crew, predominantly rowers, for only fifty tons of cargo. In 1314 the Venetian government ordered special galleys to be built for the voyage to Flanders. They were of a slightly larger size than those used exclusively in the Mediterranean, 'alla misure di Romania'. In 1318 those which were to face the Atlantic, 'alla misura di Fiandra' were 40 metres long, 5 metres wide amidships and 2½ metres high. In the course of the next quarter century the Venetians built their 'great galleys' larger and larger until they were threefold their original size. In 1344 they could carry around 300 *milliaria* (150 tons) of cargo. By 1400 they were being built slightly larger still, had a second mast and had become rather more sailing than rowing vessels, although they continued to carry a large complement of rowers. Regulations of 1412 stipulated that there should be 170 properly paid oarsmen, all free Venetians, not convicts or slaves, among a total crew of around 250. Such manning levels meant that, although they were appreciably less costly to operate than in the 1290s, they were still prodigiously dear to run, and still had much less capacity than the round ships, which were themselves being built bigger. Although the Venetians kept them on, the Genoese soon abandoned the commercial use of galleys because they were so expensive. For most of the century the only Genoese galleys were state-owned war galleys kept for military purposes.

After 1300 the Venetian state increasingly intervened in the operation of merchant galleys. Alongside privately owned galleys, which were increasingly regulated and had to be licensed, there also began to be state-owned and -operated galleys. In 1329 the senate opted for state-owned galleys, that were chartered to private operators. Charter contracts were auctioned every year and it is possible to see the development of a number of regular Venetian galley services.[44]

The first known 'Flanders' galleys were sent out from Venice in 1315, although it is possible that some of the private galleys that went to the 'west', i.e. west of the Adriatic, may have gone further than North Africa, the Balearics and the Iberian peninsula, and reached the North Sea. Licensed fleets of galleys were sent to Flanders nearly every year from 1317 to 1336, but became very irregular in the middle years of the century, when there was, for a generation, a revival of road and river routes from northern Italy across south Germany to the Rhineland and the southern Netherlands. The Flanders galleys became more or less annual again from 1384. As well as Iberian ports they also called at English ones, sometimes Southampton, sometimes Sandwich and, in the 1390s, London itself, before arriving at Bruges, or, occasionally at Antwerp in Brabant.

In the east the galleys to 'Romania', i.e. Constantinople and Greece, began intermittently, after peace was made in 1303 between Venice and the Byzantine empire and were regular from the 1320s. They went on into the Black Sea after a treaty was made with Trebizond in 1319. Successful negotiations with the khan of the Golden Horde meant that Venice could also send its galleys to Tana. In 1383 the Black Sea galleys went first to Tana and then to Trebizond.

Galleys to 'Oltramare', originally the Levantine lands captured by western crusaders, continued after the fall of Acre, going instead to Lajazzo in Armenia, by way of Crete and Cyprus. They often only went as far as Cyprus in the first half of the century, but regularly went on to Beirut in Syria from 1366. Around 1300 the galleys to Alexandria went in convoy with those for Oltramare as far as the Venetian base at Modon (Methoni, at the south-west tip of the Peloponnese) and then separated. However trading with Mamluk Egypt was banned by the pope from 1324 and the Alexandrian galleys did not

[44] Lane (1963) reprinted (1966), pp. 193–226; Tenenti and Vivanti (1961), pp. 83–6 and map; Lane (1973), pp. 126–34.

resume until 1345. By 1400 the Venetian galleys to Alexandria were by far the most valuable single convoy of European shipping.

However, even in Venice, 'great galleys' were only a minor, if the most prestigious, part of the merchant fleet. The larger part of this fleet, and almost the whole of those of Genoa, and Barcelona, was made up of sailing ships which grew increasingly larger, more efficient and cheaper to run as time went by. The trading galleys from Venice to Flanders and England may have taken spices and other very highly priced commodities off the trans-European trade routes, but the real competition for much land trade was provided by the development of bulk carriers that could take other merchandise between north and south more cheaply. The development of bulk carriers in both the Baltic and the Mediterranean was, of course, related to the grain trade. Carriage of grain by road for any distance added prohibitively to its price, and yet the cities of the southern Netherlands and northern Italy had to be fed with grain grown at a great distance.

In the thirteenth century the Italians used a rather ungainly sailing ship known as the *bucius* or *buss* in the Mediterranean, and the Hanseatics much smaller, but rather more efficient cogs in the Baltic. Both had a greater capacity than even the largest of the great galleys, with crews tiny by comparison. The largest Hanseatic cogs could carry around 200 tons, the largest *bucius* around 500 tons. From 1300 the smaller Hanseatic cog began to be imitated in the Mediterranean, where it was known as the *cocca*. In the course of the century the carrack was developed in the Mediterranean, which combined the scale of the *bucius* with many of the advantages of the cog. Compared with the old *bucius*, a carrack of the same size needed half the number of crew, and a carrack could be built bigger still. The number and size of such ships developed particularly fast in the last years of the century, particularly in Genoa, where carracks of a thousand tons were built. As well as grain, and the salt of Ibiza, the Genoese used them for carrying alum from Asia Minor and woad from Lombardy, or Toulouse, which they took to Southampton or Bruges. Unlike galleys, which needed to put in at very frequent intervals to revictual for their enormous crews, carracks could sail for huge distances without coming into port. Genoese alum boats frequently stopped only once, even on such a long journey as that from Phocaea to Southampton or Bruges. It is little wonder that freight rates for bulk cargoes dropped in the course of the century, despite a sharp rise in seamen's wages. Early in the century Pegolotti recorded in his notebook that carriage to the north added some 24 per cent to the purchase cost of alum, and 30 per cent to the cost of woad, whilst, at its end, Francesco Datini, the best-documented businessman of the Middle Ages,[45] only paid 8 per cent of the cost of either for carriage.

[45] See below pp. 196–7.

Around 1350 the Venetians extended their regulation of galleys to round ships as well, which they also organised into regulated convoys, those to Alexandria in 1346 and those to Beirut in 1366. Unlike the galleys, however, the control of *cocche* did not progress from official regulation to state-ownership. The regulated convoys of *cocche* that they sent annually to Crete and twice yearly to Syria were known from the principal commodities that they brought back, wine and cotton, as the 'muda vendemian' and the 'muda gotonorum'.[46] The 'Syrian' ships could also, of course, pick up other goods, like sugar in Cyprus, on the way back. The carriage of Jerusalem-bound pilgrims to Jaffa, which the Venetians had earlier shared with the Pisans and Genoese, also became a Venetian monopoly at the end of the century. At least two, and sometimes many more, specially appointed pilgrim ships set out each year from Venice. In 1384, seven galleys and one *cocca* transported 600 pilgrims to the Holy Land.[47]

Of the three great maritime powers of thirteenth-century Italy, Pisa had been eliminated by Genoa at the battle off La Meloria in 1284 at which Genoa had utterly defeated its arch-rival in the western Mediterranean. The harbour chains of Pisa had been carried off to Genoa as a symbol of victory. In practical terms, it enabled Genoa to take over Pisa's role as the principal shipper for the rapidly growing economies of Tuscany. Pisans remained active as traders, but not as shippers. Pisan merchants were most active at Constantinople and in Tunis, and in the first half of the century could still rival the Genoese and Venetians in Cyprus and Lesser Armenia. They principally used Genoese shipping, although they also sent goods in Venetian and Catalan boats as well. The Florentines, although so important as a trading nation in the fourteenth century had no shipping of their own beyond river boats on the Arno. Their goods were normally carried in Genoese ships.[48]

The Genoese repeatedly tried to eliminate the Venetians as they had done the Pisans, and a sequence of major wars between the two great maritime powers brought Mediterranean trade to a standstill for years on end. No Venetian galley fleets were sent out during the third war with Genoa from 1350 to 1355, and in the fourth war, from 1378 to 1381, only to Alexandria. In this war the Genoese very nearly succeeded in destroying the Venetians as they had done the Pisans, and it was only at the last minute that the tables were turned, and the Venetians snatched victory from their aggressive rivals at Chioggia, at the entry to the Venetian lagoon itself. Far from sacking Venice, the Genoese found themselves severely restricted in their own trade instead. Between 1379 and 1401 the customs accounts for seaborne trade from Genoa suggest that it dropped in value from around 2 million gold florins to below 800,000 florins.[49]

---

[46] Doumerc (1991), pp. 357–95.   [47] Ibid., p. 385.   [48] Balard (1991), pp. 1–16.
[49] Felloni (1984), pp. 153–77; Day (1963).

The general indications are that Venetian trade correspondingly gained. After the battle of Chioggia, the Venetian state was in a strong position to insist that certain of the most valuable commodities, such as spices, be only carried in its armed 'great galleys', a necessary provision to keep the service running. By then the import of spices into Europe was very largely restricted to Venetian purchasers in Alexandria.

Although there were numerous other trading ports in the Mediterranean the only one remotely in the same league as Genoa and Venice was Barcclona, the principal city of Catalonia. Catalan shipping, including that of Majorca (Mallorca) and Valencia, was not only enormously important in the western Mediterranean, but also outside it.[50] Professor Melis found that the combined merchant fleets that he could discover for Barcelona, Valencia and Majorca were only exceeded in numbers by the combined merchant fleets of Genoa, Savona and other Ligurian ports, for although Genoa had lost its share of the spice trade after Chioggia, it still maintained the largest merchant fleet. He discovered records of 921 Ligurian boats and 875 Catalan boats in the period 1383–1411. However, the Catalan boats were markedly smaller, mostly less than half the size of their Genoese counterparts. The most common size was only 300 *botti* (around 200 tons). He found none of the new large thousand-ton carracks in Catalan service. Catalan shipping was certainly not confined to the Mediterranean, for he found nearly fifty Catalan boats that had sailed to the North Sea in this period. He also found rather more northern Spanish boats that had done so. These were the boats of the Biscay coast that were carriers of Castilian wool, iron and soap, and of Gascon wine to the Low Countries and to England. These northern Spanish boats were built on the same sort of scale as those from Catalonia and did nothing to rival the Genoese bulk carriers.[51]

The century opened towards the end of a period of enormous investment in the infrastructure of overland trade, the needs of river and road transport often being catered for at the same time, since they were used so much in conjunction, with frequent changes between the two. Rivers were dredged and canalised; new canals constructed; new bridges were built in enormous numbers to replace ferries, frequently at the same time as navigation on the river beneath was improved and new quays constructed. Roads, too, were widened and improved and new passes through mountains were opened, with new roads constructed to lead to them. The first half of the century saw the continuation of these improvements, but at a slower pace.

The county of Flanders and its cities were in the forefront of canal building, but even more than roads, canals demanded continuous and expensive

---

[50] Carrère (1967) and Abulafia (1994). [51] Melis (1984a).

maintenance, particularly dredging and the upkeep of retaining dikes. The costs generally greatly exceeded the revenues from tolls, and even cities of the stature of Bruges and Ghent felt the strain of keeping up their canals. The canal cut from the Elbe to Lübeck was even larger than any of the Flemish waterways, and the arrival of the first boats in Lübeck in 1398, after eight years of work, was greeted with great public rejoicing and festivity.

The overall impression is that between the great commercial revival of the thirteenth century and the end of the Middle Ages the transport of goods became both quicker and cheaper and, with flagrant exceptions, even safer. The ubiquitous trains of pack horses and mules, often still accompanied by the owners of the goods that they were carrying, gave place at varying dates in many parts of Europe, including even some of the mountainous areas, to two-wheeled and then four-wheeled wagons run by professional carriers organised from a network of inns that provided warehousing and packing facilities. Underlying this change was a revolutionary improvement in the width and surface of roads and the building of countless bridges. As the 'road revolution' gathered momentum, the provision of good roads, fit for primitive coaches as well as wagons, became more and more an object of public policy, particularly in places with commercial interests. Expenditure on the improvement and maintenance of roads could, at least in part, be defrayed by the tolls paid by users who could, because of the improvements, carry more goods, more cheaply. As costs dropped, by volume and weight, the range of goods worth carrying over any specified distance increased. Cheaper textiles, as well as the dearer luxury fabrics, became worth carrying over long distances. The ability to carry goods economically over longer distances in its turn encouraged greater specialisation, as well as increasing the volume of trade in many areas of Europe.

In northern and central Italy innumerable bridges were built across rivers and streams, embankments carrying new roads were thrown up in low-lying lands, main roads were widened and either gravelled or paved. The area in which wheeled transport could operate was vastly enlarged, even in a region so broken up by hills, and the speed and ease of transport by pack animals was also greatly increased. All the city states of northern and central Italy picked out for special attention a limited number of routes which were important to them. Even the small commune of Tivoli had a via Maior which it paved, or rather re-paved, for their *via silicata et lapidea* had been the Roman via Tiburtina.

At Florence two additional *strade maestre* were added to the ten main roads for which the state had already taken responsibility by 1300. Along the *strade maestre* large bridges, mostly in stone, crossed the major tributaries of the Arno, like the Elsa, Pesa, Sieve and Bisenzio. They were supplemented by numerous *ponticelli* over tiny streams, perhaps half of them built of wood. Some seventy bridges of various sizes were built for the commune between 1280 and 1380. By 1380 many of the wooden bridges from the beginning of the century had been replaced by stone ones.[52] Pack animals could certainly travel much faster on the improved roads, but only a minority of the new Florentine roads could be improved enough to be fit for wheeled vehicles, like the new road from Florence to Pisa along the south bank of the Arno. When the new stone bridge across the Elsa was finally finished in 1347, it became possible at last to take goods by cart all the way to Pisa.

With a different sort of terrain the Pisans were able to create roads fit for carts. They threw up embankments to carry their main roads in low-lying areas, which they widened up to fifteen feet (4.6m), to allow two of the new large carts to pass, and then paved for enormous distances. By 1308 the new paving of the via Romea, the 'coastal' road southward to Rome, had already advanced twenty-five miles from Pisa and was continuing, having already been widened for eighty-five miles. It was astonishing to consider paving such an enormous distance when the paving of the main streets inside cities was relatively novel and many city streets were as yet unpaved.

Many roads leading to Alpine passes were themselves improved quite considerably. That on the south side of the Brenner pass for example was improved in 1314 by a private citizen of Bolzano who paid for improvements that enabled the old ridge road north of the city to be brought down into the valley of the Isarco. These improvements were partially competitive. After the opening of the Saint-Gotthard in the thirteenth century, a great deal of traffic left the Septimer pass route, which had earlier been the principal pass through the central Alps, connecting Milan and the Rhineland. The route on the north side of the Septimer pass came down into the upper Rhine valley at Chur, which suffered from the loss of traffic, so its bishop had the very top of the pass paved in an unsuccessful attempt to lure some of the lost traffic back.

When a group of merchants had an interest in a particular route they were not merely content to let the local authorities get on with its maintenance, or not, as the case might be. They took positive measures to see that something was done. This was relatively easy if the relevant authority was their own government. Effective pressure for maintenance or improvement was more problematic and demanded patient negotiation when another government was involved. The merchants of Milan had a strong interest in the upkeep of the Simplon pass road. They sent syndics at intervals to negotiate with the bishop of Sion who was overlord of the Valais, the upper Rhône valley, from below Martigny to Simplon. The earliest negotiations, for which records survive, had been in 1271–3 and 1291. Further negotiations took place in 1321, 1336 and

<hr />

[52] La Roncière (1976); compressed and slightly revised (1982).

1351 at least. What the syndicates could offer the bishop and his steward was money, both lump sum payments and consent to increased dues of various sorts.

At its most dramatic and remote the trade of west Europeans with the rest of the world was at its widest extent in the early fourteenth century, when there were regular groups of Genoese and Venetian merchants, together with some Catalans, Provençals, Pisans and Florentines, not only in the cities of the Maghreb from Morocco to Tunis, in the ports of Egypt, Syria and Armenia, in the Byzantine empire and the lands of its Turkish opponents, and in ports all round the Black Sea from the mouth of the Danube to Caffa in the Crimea, from Tana on the sea of Azov to Trebizond, and even inland in Tabriz in the dominions of the Mongol Ilkhans of Persia. Although west Europeans had never managed to penetrate beyond the ports of the Maghreb, sporadic adventurers-cum-merchants did take the roads across Asia to China in search of silks, and to Samarkand and India in search of precious stones, and even very occasionally to the spice islands of the Indonesian archipelago. Some Europeans went to the Persian Gulf to the pearl fisheries there and on by sea to those of Sri Lanka and to the pepper-growing coast of south India. These most distant contacts were a consequence of the Mongol unification of much of Asia in the mid-thirteenth century. So long as Mongol rule remained essentially undisturbed and tolerant, it was possible for western merchants to enter and cross the Mongol khanates to reach China and India. Although Asian trade was important to some Europeans, and some Asian commodities were widely diffused in Europe, it is sobering to realise that Europe was only of minor importance in the whole pattern of Eurasian trade.[53] Europe after all had not much to offer to the rest of the world, apart from fine linen, and some woollens. In the first half of the fourteenth century the balance was made up by vast shipments of silver.

THE SECOND HALF OF THE CENTURY

The Mongol 'peace', however, came to an end in the 1330s and 1340s. There was a successful Chinese rising against their Mongol overlords, and those Europeans who were in China were massacred on account of their association with the Mongols. The other khanates broke up in disorder, and the rulers of the fragments of the Persian khanate also became Muslim and intolerant of Christians.[54] The Venetian and Genoese enclaves in Tabriz were deserted and

---

[53] Abu-Lughod (1989).

[54] The rulers of Genoa vainly attempted to bargain and put pressure on them by forbidding their merchants to go to India across Persia!

fell into ruin. Furthermore the Mamluk rulers of Egypt and Syria conquered Armenia and closed that doorway to Asia.

Breaking direct trading links did not mean a total break in trade, although it was diminished. In the second half of the century western merchants still went on trading to Caffa and Tana, Trebizond and Brusa, Beirut and Alexandria, but they were no longer able to penetrate beyond these points. What Venetians were able to obtain in Beirut were essentially Syrian goods, cotton, and soda ash for the manufacture of glass and soap. It did not substitute for Lajazzo, since it was not a port for long-distance trade. The loss of the Armenian gateway and the Italian merchant settlements in Tabriz meant that a very high proportion of trade in Indian, Indonesian and Chinese goods passed through Alexandria, where, around 1400, Venetian merchants could only buy spices, precious stones, pearls and silks from Egyptians, who bought them from Arab and Gujerati traders, who in turn bought them from various places in the western Indian Ocean, or acquired them from Chinese shippers who had bought them yet farther afield. Increasing the number of links in the commercial chain did not necessarily greatly increase prices, but it gave more opportunities for prices to be increased, and not only by merchants. When the Mamluk rulers of Egypt succumbed to the temptation to increase taxes, the western response was to accelerate the existing process of substitution wherever possible. Silks, tapestries and carpets could all be made in Europe, and animal-bone substitutes for ivory were even produced at the end of the century. Mulberry trees and sugar cane could be cultivated in Europe or on European-controlled islands like Cyprus, so that less raw silk and sugar need be imported from Asia Minor or Egypt. However, Syrian cotton and soda ash were still needed, and there were no substitutes for the culinary and medicinal spices of India, China and Indonesia, and no alternative to paying the prices demanded at Alexandria. In the second half of the century Europeans were consequently still sending out large shipments of precious metal, but, from the 1350s onwards, more often of gold than silver.[55]

Trade with Asia, as within Europe, also shrank because of the decline in demand for luxuries from wealthy customers in Europe, among the principal causes of which were the great increase in war and disorder, with the consequent debasements and expenditure on arms, taxation and forced loans, and the reduction in population which caused a drop in rents, whilst the consequent rise in wages provoked increases in prices for manufactures.

From the late 1330s onwards prolonged wars broke out in a number of places. The ambitions of Philip VI of France, the della Scala of Verona and the Visconti of Milan, all provoked protracted conflict, as did attempts by

[55] Spufford (1988), pp. 283–6, 353–4.

popes to fight their way back to Rome, and civil wars in southern Italy and Castile. War had a number of deleterious effects on trade. Some were direct, but many indirect. War itself was very harmful in a limited number of areas, such as Gascony and the surrounding areas of south-western France, where the deliberately destructive *chevauchées* of the Anglo-Gascon armies and the French responses devastated the region's extensive vineyards. Wine exports from Bordeaux plummeted in consequence.[56] Merchants, and growers elsewhere, adapted flexibly. French consumers were offered more Loire wines, 'Flemish' consumers were offered more Rhine wines and more beer in place of claret, English consumers were offered Andalusian and Portuguese wines instead.

An immediate by-product of wars waged with indentured companies was the disorder that resulted from peace and the cessation of payments to those previously paid under such indentures or *condotte*. They naturally preyed on goods in transit. The ravages of unemployed *condottiere* became one of the preoccupations of governments in many parts of Europe, which took various measures to ensure the safety of goods in transit. The provision of guards, for example, was a concern of a number of German states, but all such escorts had to be paid for, and increased the costs of land transport appreciably. The Florentine state went further and founded a number of fortified settlements on its principal roads, notably on the important route from Bologna along which the grain came which was so necessary for feeding the city. A great deal of attention was given to the protection of this route through the wild heart of the Appenines, for its users were constantly threatened with violence. A new road was constructed across the Giogo pass, with fortified townships at Scarperia and Firenzuola. By 1400 this road had become the principal alternative to the Cisa route as the means of getting from any of the Alpine passes to Rome. The advantage of the new road was not speed, since the terrain was much the same as the old Futa pass road, but comparative safety, for the garrisons were expected to provide some measure of protection to merchants on the road, as did the knights of Altopascio, where the old via Francigena passed through the depths of the forest of the Cerbaia.

Merchants took their own means of spreading risk. Insurance evolved and became much more common. Much insurance was maritime insurance, directed against storm and natural hazards, but there was also an element of insurance against piracy. As a consequence goods transported in the heavily armed galleys of Venice attracted much lower insurance premiums. Francesco Datini insisted that all his companies insure all goods in transit. In addition, his Pisan company participated in syndicates insuring goods setting out from

---

[56] Boutruche (1947); Craeybeckx (1958); James (1971).

Porto Pisano, the outport of Pisa. Insurance could also be obtained for goods being transported by land, where the principal risk was brigandage.

The main indirect effect of war was through taxation. The method of taxation varied from place to place, and so did the consequent effects on trade. In England one of the principal means of funding the Hundred Years War was to increase customs duties on wool exports, and the increased rates, levied per sack rather than *ad valorem*, were maintained for a sufficiently long period that they priced the cheaper English wools out of the international market. Direct taxation, when the nobility and upper clergy were not exempted from it, affected their ability to consume luxuries quite considerably.

The same effect was produced in Italian city-states by ever-repeated forced loans. Well-to-do Florentines not only complained bitterly of their impoverishment from such loans, which could be exacted every month in times of emergency, but also rejoiced in the first years of the fifteenth century at their recovery of prosperity after so long a time. It is easy to discount such complaints, but not the rejoicing. In the first half of the fourteenth century forced loans for less frequent wars were generally repaid in a few years, when peace returned, and interest was scrupulously paid. In the second half of the century one war loan was heaped upon another before there was any chance of repayment, and even the payment of interest became erratic. When this happened the resale value of shares in the communal debt fell to such low levels that the compulsory contributors felt that they had effectively been taxed. After the 'War of Chioggia', interest payments were suspended and a hundred ducats of forced loan to the Venetian state could only be resold for eighteen ducats.[57]

A similar or even more violent effect on the disposable incomes of the wealthy was achieved when governments debased the coinage rather than imposing taxation.[58] This happened in France in the 1340s and 1350s. The effect was dramatically to reduce the purchasing power of all those who lived on incomes fixed in money of account, such as nearly all rent-receiving landowners. In 1360 the nobility insisted on a return to sound money, even if it meant the imposition of large direct taxes which they too had to pay.[59] In Castile after similar debasements in the civil war of the 1350s and 1360s, the return to sound money in 1371 lasted only to the next wave of debasements during the wars of the 1380s. This was ruinous for Castilian landowners, and for the ordinary revenues of the crown itself, as the principal landowner in the country. The consequent changes in exchange rates made imports more expensive, to the disadvantage of landowning consumers of imported luxuries, but they also made exports cheaper. Since Castile was the other great

---

[57] Lane (1973), p. 196.   [58] Spufford (1988), pp. 289–318.   [59] Cazelles (1976), pp. 293–311.

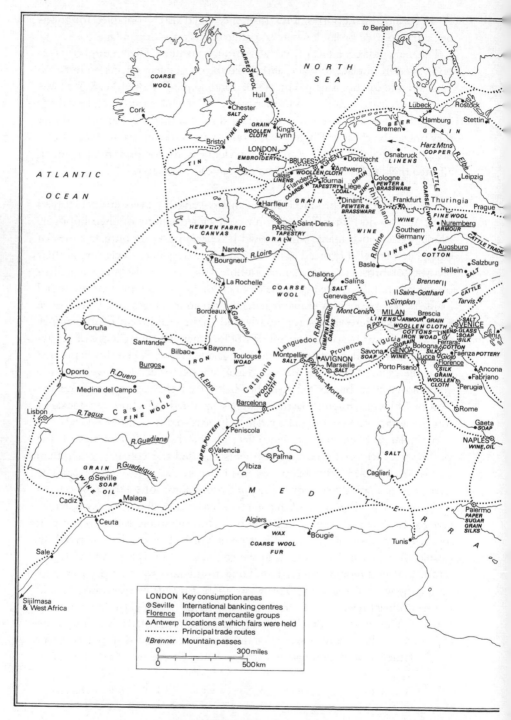

Map 5 Europe's trade, *c.* 1400

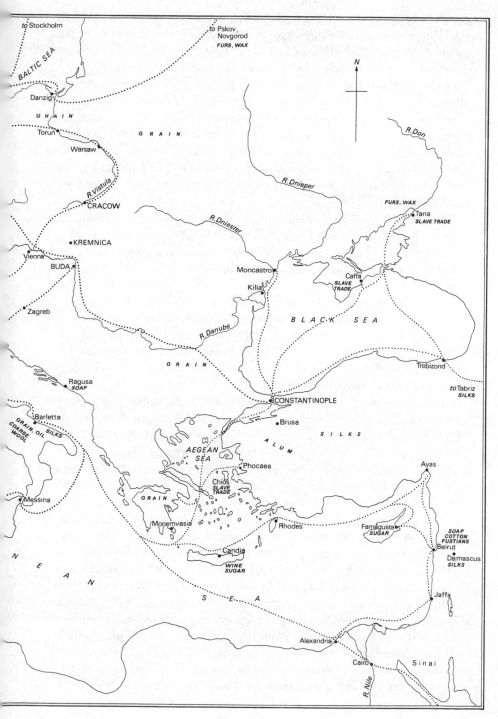

exporter of high-grade wools in medieval Europe, debasement made Castilian wool cheaper just when customs were making English wool dearer, so by the end of the century Castilian wool had begun to replace English in significant quantities in the woollen cloth industries of the southern Netherlands.

Landowners also had to divert expenditure into arms. The armourers of Milan and Brescia did particularly well out of periods of disorder. They could provide everything from mass-produced ready-made armour by the thousand pieces for armies of foot-soldiers, to the most expensive hand-engraved, made-to-measure suits for princes and great noblemen. At the end of the century, when the earl of Derby, later Henry IV of England, ordered armour from Milan, four armourers came with it to give him a fitting, before finishing it and hardening it.

The costs of wars also affected the international financial community. Import–export houses were often forced to lend to the governments of states where they had branches. They were generally offered good rates of interest and the loans were frequently secured on particular sources of revenue. If all went well the merchant houses concerned made a handsome profit and became more entrenched in business dealings within the host country. Unfortunately wars generally lasted longer and were more expensive than anticipated, so that it became impossible to repay the lenders as arranged. From time to time even some of the largest Italian business houses collapsed. In 1326, for example, the Scali of Florence collapsed, after 120 years of existence, and Villani commented that it was a worse blow to the city than the defeat at Altopascio at the hands of the Lucchese. These earlier bankruptcies were as nothing compared with those of the 1340s that carried away the four largest firms in Europe, all Florentine, who suffered from both exceedingly high rates of forced loans levied at home, and over-lending to rulers abroad. These four major bankruptcies triggered others, for these large companies had raised much of the money they lent to rulers by borrowing from others on the strength of their reputations. Over 350 firms failed in Florence by 1346.

The 1340s wave of bankruptcies made for an immense, if temporary, shrinkage in ordinary commercial credit. No Tuscan firm was left of an adequate size to handle the business of transmitting money to and from Avignon for the papacy. The pope, for the first time in a century, used a non-Tuscan firm of bankers, the Lombard firm of Malabayla from Asti. The lesson of 'not lending to rulers' was not easy to learn, for rulers could make it very difficult not to lend to them, by threats of preventing trading activities. A different lesson, however, could be learned: 'not to operate as one single international company'. Instead, post-crash-multinationals like the Alberti took the form of groups of companies, so that trouble in one country only affected the trading company in that country and did not bring down the whole group. The Datini group of companies at the end of the century therefore consisted of separate import–export houses in Avignon, Florence, Genoa, Pisa and Barcelona (with branches in Valencia and Majorca), two woollen-cloth manufacturing businesses in Datini's home town of Prato, a dyeworks in Prato and an independent banking business in Florence. Datini began his business career in Avignon, returned to Prato and ended up running his group of companies from a holding company in Florence. His commercial activities were primarily concerned with western Mediterranean trade, and focused on the manufacture and sale of cloth woven from Spanish wool, but his activities stretched to wool purchases in the English Cotswolds in one direction and to Tana and Egypt in the other. His group of companies, as well as banking and insurance, dealt in virtually every sort of commodity, from armour to cheap paintings. Although the unitary form of the single giant company had given way to a group structure he managed to keep an exceptionally firm grip on all the enterprises by sending out a hail of instructions to each of them, and demanding frequent reports from them. Several letters a week survive from some of the men who ran the individual companies.[60] This group structure, evolved in the second half of the fourteenth century, remained one of the key models for large international enterprises for centuries, from the Medici to the Warburgs.

The 1340s bankruptcies of these great firms caused the collapse of the international courier services that they seem to have been large enough to run for themselves. Seventeen of the surviving Florentine firms banded together for the running of regular common courier services. Couriers thereafter rode out weekly from Florence and Pisa to and from Barcelona, and on two routes to and from Bruges, by way of Paris and by way of Milan and Cologne, and carried correspondence for all business houses. The Lucchese ran a similar service to Bruges, and the Genoese ran services to both Bruges and Barcelona, the latter sometimes going on to Seville. The Catalans ran couriers from Barcelona to Bruges and to Pisa and Florence, whilst the Lombard cities also had a service to Barcelona. Besides these common courier services, private couriers linked in Venice, Avignon, Rome, Naples and London. The amount of business post that they carried was prodigious. On some routes it was possible to send letters by different couriers several times a week. Of the letters sent between different companies of the Datini group, no fewer than 320,000 survive.[61]

Another effect of these bankruptcies was to limit the domination of international business by Italians. Italians had partially been enabled to break into the markets of northern Europe in the thirteenth century by the abundance of cheap credit available to them which permitted them to extend credit from buyer

---

[60] Melis (1962); Origo (1957).   [61] Melis (1973).

to seller by laying out money in advance, for such things as wool that had not yet been grown. Such advance purchases had overturned the traditional extension of credit from seller to buyer and had cut out rival merchants with less extensive access to more highly priced credit. After the bankruptcies of the 1340s, the shrinkage in Italian credit meant a revival in the tradition of credit from seller to buyer and gave rival merchants a fresh opportunity to enter international trade. A much higher proportion of the wool exported from England was dealt with by native English merchants in the last quarter of the century than the first. The merchants of the Staple came to be the dominant group in England's wool exports, rather than Italians. London and Bristol merchants were the most noticeable amongst those Englishmen who traded overseas. The English crown now pressed them, rather than Italians, to provide it with loans. Native Englishmen like William de la Pole of Hull led consortia of merchants lending money to the king.[62] Some, like de la Pole, added to their fortunes from royal finance. Others failed as catastrophically as their Italian predecessors. In a similar way there was a growth in other groups of local traders in international trade in the Atlantic. Portuguese, northern Castilian merchants, who formed colonies in Bruges and Southampton, Bretons and Normans, all joined the English in taking back trade from Italians, as did men from the ports near Bruges like Middelburg.[63] In the interior of Europe the principal gainers were the merchants of south German cities who by 1400 were building on a long-established tradition of trading across the Alps to develop multi-branched groups of companies on Italian models, and, with interest rates beginning to drop there, to accumulate capital that could be invested in mining or in the manufacture of import substitutes, just as north Italians themselves had earlier done.[64]

The shrinkage of international credit was only one aspect of an overall decline in the money supply. There was a general contraction in the availability of local banking services, despite the simplification of methods of payment by the replacement of personal oral requests to transfer funds from one account to another by written cheques. The number of money-changer bankers simply began to decline. However the decline had not proceeded very far by the end of the century. It could be reckoned that one in ten of adult males still had bank accounts in Bruges in 1400.[65] Nevertheless some cities, like Bois-le-Duc and Louvain in Brabant were already taking action to provide municipal money-changing, although not other banking services, because of the decline in numbers of money-changers.[66]

There was also a decline in the quantity of metallic currency itself, which

[62] Carus-Wilson and Coleman (1963); Lloyd (1977); Fryde (1988), pp. 53–86, 181–200.

[63] Childs (1978); Touchard (1967); Mollat (1952); Nicholas (1992).   [64] Von Stromer (1970).

[65] Lopez (1973), pp. 335–41, extrapolating from de Roover (1948).

[66] Van der Wee (1963), II, pp. 358–60.

exacerbated, if it did not necessarily cause, the decline in credit. The whole of European trade with Asia had been expanded on the basis that Europeans had abundant supplies of silver to send to balance out the excess value of the goods brought in from the Levant and beyond over those sent out.[67] When new and larger deposits of silver were being discovered within Europe at intervals, to replace those that had been worked out, there was no problem. However, there was no major new discovery of silver for over a century after that at Kutná Hora (Küttenberg) in 1300. Production was at its greatest in the first half of the fourteenth century. Enough ore was then mined to produce perhaps as much as twenty tons of coinable silver a year, of which over six tons was actually minted. However, production from the mines there gradually sank throughout the second half of the century, although it did not cease until early in the next. The other major European source of silver around 1300 had been the mines in Sardinia at Iglesias (Villa di Chiesa), but production there dwindled abruptly in the 1340s. Early fourteenth-century merchants' notebooks, like that of Pegolotti, give glimpses of both Kutná Hora and Iglesias silver on its way out of Europe. As less and less silver was mined the effect of the continued export of silver to the Levant and beyond was to diminish the supply of silver available for circulation within Europe itself. By the 1390s a lack of silver coin afflicted Europe,[68] the first wave of the late medieval 'bullion famine'. Even in a country like England, which had a strongly favourable commercial balance because of its wool exports, the quantity of silver coin circulating by 1400 was around a tenth of that available a century earlier. However, silver coin did not make up the whole currency in either 1300 or in 1400. In 1300 silver ingots, bars weighing a mark, were still being used for large payments in northern Europe, and particularly for international transactions, whilst in 1400 there was a considerable currency of gold coins (as there already had been in parts of southern Europe in 1300). The discovery, mining and minting of gold at Kremnica in Slovakia in the 1320s made gold currency available on a scale very different from the quantities previously available in southern Europe from West African sources. Large payments for war purposes to north-western Europe from the late 1330s spearheaded the use of gold as currency outside the Mediterranean littoral. The use of gold coins to a certain extent mitigated the increasing dearth of silver, and it replaced silver in payments to the east, so that gold mining came to bear the burden of the imbalance of payments with the Levant. Gold not only replaced the use of bars of silver, and barrels of silver coins, for international payments, but was increasingly used for much smaller payments also. In some parts of Europe, peasants were paid in gold for their produce, and they in turn sometimes paid their rent

[67] Ashtor (1971) and (1983).   [68] Spufford (1988), ch. 15, and Day (1978), pp. 1–54, reprinted (1987).

in gold. Some craftsmen, like weavers, were paid in gold for their work by the end of the century.[69] All these were relatively 'lumpy' payments. What gold coins could not be used for were day wages, and the ordinary daily expenditures of urban life.

The most evident difference between the second and the first half of the century was the recrudescence of bubonic plague in 1348 after several centuries. The effects of repeated waves of plague in reducing populations from the high levels of the earlier part of the century are well known. Although so many of the deaths from plague took place in towns and cities, the overall effect was to reduce the population in the countryside, for cities, particularly capital cities, drew in quantities of immigrants from the country to take the places of those who had died. The immediate economic effects of plague were first felt in the cities. Urban rents fell soonest and furthest, whilst urban wages rose soonest and most. In Florence and Paris the purchasing power of wages more or less tripled within a year of the very first wave of plague, and even in the small towns of southern England the day wages of building craftsmen doubled. The economic effects of population changes were very uneven. In the English or Flemish countrysides, landlords could find fresh tenants for vacated holdings until the 1370s, after the third wave of plague, and there was little abandonment of land even in the last quarter of the century.[70]

Demographic factors in the diminution in agricultural production were compounded by climatic ones. It appears that European climate was gradually becoming colder, and perhaps wetter, in the course of the century. This not only had the effect of producing more 'bad harvests', but of driving down yields in general, and changing what it was suitable to grow in particular places. The beer/wine line, for example, moved southwards. The growing of vines, for making cheap local wines, came to an end in southern England and what is now Belgium, and this helped the process whereby the inhabitants of the densely populated southern Netherlands increasingly became beer rather than wine drinkers.

Demographic effects were also compounded by disorder. In Gascony or Tuscany, rural holdings were deserted much sooner than in England and Flanders, because war and disorder made the safety of town walls even more appealing, and agricultural production dropped much faster. As a consequence urban populations, even when they were greatly reduced, as in the case of Florence, still had to rely heavily on grain imported over long distances, and were still vulnerable to famines.[71] However, an immediate effect of rising real

---

[69] La Roncière (1976).

[70] The first arrival of the plague along routes of trade from Asia is graphically described by Matteo Villani, *Cronica*, ed. Porta, Bk 1, ch. 2; cf. above pp. 131–3.

[71] La Roncière (1976); Hunt (1994) suggests that it was not so.

wages in cities and of falling urban rents was to remove a large body of people, including skilled craftsmen, from near starvation. Instead such men could, from the 1350s, afford more than a basic minimum diet. This meant the possibility of buying what had been semi-luxuries, particularly meat, but also dairy products, and at the same time there was a corresponding drop in the demand for grains, more especially the cheaper grains like rye, for part of the general improvement in living standards was the possibility to exercise a preference for wheaten bread.

Even slight changes in urban population and diet could have a dispropor-tionate effect at long distances. The overall decline in town populations in the Calais–Cologne urban belt was translated into a much larger drop in the demand for grain, particularly of rye, from the Baltic area, Brandenburg, Pomerania, Poland and Prussia. The figures for the minimum value of goods going in and out of the harbour in Lübeck, by general agreement the most important Hanseatic trading city, do not start until 1368, and there are then only three further figures available for the fourteenth century, from the period 1379–84.[72] With such limited evidence it is necessary to look at each figure very carefully to determine whether it may have been typical or atypical. There was a remarkable consistency of the value of trade from 1379 to 1384 (between 62,000 and 66,000 marks weight of fine silver). However, in 1368 the value of trade had been nearly two and a half times as much as it was a decade later (over 150,000 marks weight of fine silver). It does not seem that 1368 was a freak year.[73] These years span the third visitation of bubonic plague, and also the aftermath of it, in which the cumulative depopulating effects of three waves of plague began to bite. It would therefore be reasonable to anticipate a very considerable real shrinkage in Lübeck's seaborne trade between 1368 and 1379. Not only did Hanseatic trade suffer, but mammoth depopulation also took place in these grain-growing areas. Previously cultivated land returned to scrub, and the local market structure was disrupted.[74] It was the first step in the retreat from the large number of markets existing at the beginning of the century. Although the reduction in rural populations was well advanced by 1400, land-lords somehow managed to keep something going in most places, and the ulti-mate effect of depopulation, the total disappearance of settlements, was largely delayed until the fifteenth century.

[72] Dollinger (1964), pp. 431–2; Sprandel (1975), pp. 97–123; Hammel-Kiesow (1993), pp. 77–94. Hammel gives his figures in Lübeck marks, as in the sources themselves, and then converts them into marks weight of fine silver to make comparisons over time.

[73] Hammel has disproved the suggestion that the larger figures only reflect the reopening of the Sound after a closure, and no other proposed explanation has yet been put forward why Lübeck's sea-borne trade should have been specially inflated in that year.

[74] In the Ucker Mark half the peasant farms were already deserted in 1375: Carsten (1954), p. 100.

The other side of the change in diet was the increasing demand for meat. Some areas of Europe took up the opportunity of stock raising on a large scale. Meat, unlike grain, was cheap to transport, since beasts were driven to their destinations before being killed. Some of the growing herds of cattle on the Hungarian plains were driven round the eastern Alps to be refattened after their journey on north-east Italian marshlands, and only then driven into north Italian cities for butchering. Other Hungarian cattle were driven along the south bank of the Danube into south Germany to be eaten in the cities there. Danish cattle, many sold onwards at Hamburg, where they were taken across the Elbe, were driven to the wetlands along the lower Rhine, where they were refattened for the cities immediately to the south. Over slightly shorter distances, cattle rearing increased in the west midlands of England to meet London's growing appetite for meat, and in western France for Paris. The grain trade diminished, but the meat trade began a hundred years of growth.

Improved living standards of large numbers of people were also reflected in clothing. There was a greater demand for the cheaper, lighter woollen cloths, which naturally resulted in the expansion in the production of cheaper cloths. Lombardy increased its production of them, as did many of the small towns of eastern Flanders and northern Brabant. The manufacturers' needs for raw materials consequently increased the demand for imported Castilian and Apulian wool, which in its turn promoted the growth of transhumant sheep flocks on both the central Castilian plateau and the mountains of Apulia.

The demand for cheap cottons also grew considerably, initially for those made in Lombardy from Syrian cotton imported through Venice. The demand for linen, from Lombardy and Flanders, also increased, but since pure linen was rather expensive, the greatest growth was in the demand for fustian, the mixed linen-cotton fabric, and in the last years of the fourteenth century the production of fustian took off in south Germany. By the 1370s merchants from Ulm, Augsburg and Nuremberg, who had been carrying back north Italian cottons and fustians, were buying raw Syrian cotton in Milan and Venice instead. Fustians were soon manufactured more cheaply in south Germany itself, undercutting Lombard fustians north of the Alps. The principal centres for the production of fustians were Ulm and Augsburg and the small towns between, although some fustian was produced elsewhere as at Zurich or throughout the broad Swabian flax-growing region. Much of this fustian was either bleached white or dyed black. By 1400, Augsburg and Nuremberg merchants were taking Ulm fustians to the Frankfurt fairs and Cologne.[75]

Falling rents, urban from the 1350s and rural from the 1370s, benefited the tenants, but they were equally bad for landlords. Empty houses and vacant

[75] Von Stromer (1978); Mazzaoui (1981), esp. pp. 137–44.

lands were even worse, since they produced no income at all. The poorest of urban houses were allowed to collapse and the poorest of rural holdings reverted to waste.[76] Some measure of the effects of this on landlords may be seen from great ecclesiastical estates, which remained much the same over long periods of time. The landed income of the abbey of Saint-Denis in the Paris basin, for example, dropped to under half between 1340 and 1403.[77] Changes in the incomes of individual lay families are virtually impossible to work out, because lay estates rarely stayed the same for long, because of straightforward sales and purchases of lands, marriages of heiresses, dower and partible inheritance, where it still survived. Nevertheless it is clear that the total rental income of lay landlords as a whole dropped like that of ecclesiastical estates in the same region. That of the earls of Stafford dropped from around £3,000 sterling in 1372 to just under £2,000 sterling in 1400.[78]

Just as falling rents benefited tenants but hurt landlords, so rising real wages were as bad for employers as they were good for employees. Since most employment was in arable agriculture or in service, the increased cost of wages could not be passed on. Only the increased wages of that small percentage engaged in manufacture could be passed on, and manufactures increased in price. Luxury goods increased most in price since they used proportionately more labour; for example, luxury woollens had a higher labour component in their price than cheaper cloths. The yarn for them was spun with a drop spindle rather than a spinning wheel, they were fulled by foot rather than in a fulling mill, and they went through more laborious finishing processes, they were burled more assiduously, and their nap was teazled and sheared more frequently.[79]

Between reduced landed incomes, increased war-related commitments and the higher prices of manufactured luxuries, the ability of the rich to purchase luxuries was eroded, although it is not possible to put precise figures to the consequent drop in demand that affected long-distance trade. As a consequence of the decline in demand, the cloth industry in Florence was patently in a bad way from the 1370s, and so was that in the great cities of the southern Netherlands where large quantities of heavy luxury woollen cloths had also been woven from expensive English wool. Brussels, Malines and Louvain, which had become increasingly important as textile towns in the first half of the century, now went into decline.[80] On the other hand, manufacture of high-quality woollen cloths grew in England, using native wools and 'Flemish' skills.

[76] See Herlihy (1958) and (1967); and Dyer (1989), for Italian and English examples.
[77] Fourquin (1964).
[78] Rawcliffe (1978), quoted by Dyer (1989), pp. 27–48, in his discussion of the evolution of English aristocratic incomes.
[79] For a convenient summary of processes see Munro (1988), pp. 693–715. [80] Van der Wee (1975).

English exports of cloths of various sizes and qualities grew from virtually none in the middle of the century to the equivalent of 40,000 standard customs paying rolls at the end of the century,[81] but this growth by no means compensated for the shrinkage in production elsewhere, neither did the increased production of silk fabrics. Historians have postulated a shift in fashion to favour silks over woollens. More silk was being woven in north Italian cities outside Lucca. However, it is by no means clear if this was to substitute for woollens, or for the declining quantities of imported Levantine and oriental silks, or even for those hitherto woven in Lucca. Even the customs records from England, the fullest surviving in Europe, do not enable us to produce figures for the, possibly growing, demand there for imported silk, although specific batches of Italian silks can be found in the accounts at the end of the century.

It seems, and is, a long leap from expensive textiles to slaves, but human beings were also a very important luxury 'commodity' and were bought and sold as such. The trade in slaves was possibly as important as that in silk. It was certainly a trade that grew in the second half of the century. The use of domestic women slaves, although illegal in Latin Christian Europe, had possibly never entirely ceased, when agricultural, predominantly male, slavery had died out.[82] Outside western Europe domestic slavery had continued unabated and was encountered by those who traded there, as well as in the Iberian peninsula and Crete and Cyprus. Legalised domestic slavery returned to southern Europe in the second half of the century. In Florence, for example, it was made legal in 1363. The rise in wages that accompanied the drop in population may or may not have made it cheaper to buy a slave girl rather than hire a free maid-servant, but the former was certainly more flexible, and possibly more prestigious. Whether from motives of economy and utility, or as articles of luxury, slave girls were increasingly 'consumed' in wealthy households, and the slave trade consequently grew in scale. Since the children that these slave girls frequently bore their owners were baptised and free, there was no hereditary group of slaves, and fresh ones needed to be bought all the time. The new slave girls bought in expensive quantities for south European households were mostly Asiatic in origin. At Tana Venetian round ships, as well as grain, loaded up with considerable numbers of Asian slave girls for European use, and the Genoese similarly found their carracks useful for carrying slaves, along with grain or alum from Caffa or Chios. Although it was against the rules to keep fellow Christians as slaves, Genoese and Venetians also loaded up on occasion with Orthodox Greek and Slav girls. The reduction of Asian children to slavery was in part a consequence of the internecine wars which broke out in the steppes,

---

[81] Carus-Wilson and Coleman (1963), pp. 14–16, 75–87, 138–54.   [82] Stuard (1995), pp. 3–28.

although west Europeans salved their consciences with the myth that their parents had deliberately sold them so that they should have a better life in the west! The male children captured in the same Asiatic wars hardly ever ended up in Europe at all. Instead the boys were purchased by Egyptians for service in the Mamluk army.[83] In the same way African children became available for purchase on account of wars in West Africa. There is a long history of women and girls being marched northwards across the Sahara. Those that survived the journey mostly found their way into North African households, and only occasionally reached Europe.

Slaves were unique as a 'commodity', and, so long as their children were born legally free, no substitute for their import existed. In the second half of the century they went on being imported along with precious stones, pearls and oriental spices, for which there were likewise no substitutes. Other imports from outside Europe diminished or ceased, as internal European production of silks, cottons, majolica, glass, paper, tapestry, carpets and white soap took over. Since late medieval trade depended so much on consumers' needs and demands, it was the merchant suppliers of consumers' needs who sponsored and frequently controlled the internal European manufacture of goods that they had been previously supplying from outside Europe. It is no wonder that so many of these import-substituting manufactures were concentrated in northern Italy as the principal area of commercial leadership.

It is possible to make some limited comparisons between the scale of trade, in the second half of the century, in two of the three principal areas of commercial development in Europe. Any comparisons between trade in the Baltic and in the Mediterranean must start from the figures for the minimum value of goods going in and out of the harbour in Lübeck, by general agreement the most important Hanseatic trading city, and similar evidence for the port of Genoa. The Genoese evidence is much fuller. From the fourteenth century there are customs figures for 1334, and then for forty-six years between 1341 and 1406. With these figures we have material for a fair north–south comparison. In the 1350s, 1360s and 1380s, the value of trade going in and out of the harbour of Genoa generally oscillated around 1,400,000 florins. At the end of the 1360s it rose quite sharply, and in 1371 it exceeded 2 million gold florins. In 1376–7 the value of Genoese seaborne trade was still at this level, but in the early 1380s it was below 1,700,000 gold florins and had soon resumed the level of the 1350s and 1360s. To make valid comparisons with these Genoese figures I have converted the Lübeck figures into Italian terms.[84] The figures for 1379–84 show that the shrunken Lübeck trade in those years was in the region of 350,000 gold florins, at a time when Genoese trade was dropping from

---

[83] Verlinden (1955–77); Origo (1955), pp. 321–66; Lane (1973), pp. 132–3.   [84] Above p. 201.

2 million florins to 1,700,000 florins. In other words, the trade through the
harbour at Genoa was, at this point, shrinking from six times as much as at
Lübeck to five times as much. For the short period for which it is fair to make
comparisons, between 1379 and 1384, there is no doubt that trade at Genoa
was many times greater than that at Lübeck. Before the War of Chioggia,[85] the
general, non-statistical impression is that trade at Venice was of the same order
of magnitude as that at Genoa, although possibly slightly smaller. If so, its
trade too might have been around five times as great as Lübeck's. For the
Mediterranean, there were no other ports as important as Genoa, Venice and
Barcelona, although Porto Pisano, Marseille, Ragusa and even Ancona and
Aigues-Mortes were not without importance. For the Baltic, there was no other
port to rival Lübeck, although places like Danzig, Rostock and Toruń cannot
be ignored. It would probably be an exaggeration, but not a very great one, to
triple the evidence for Genoa to take account of Venice and Barcelona, and
then suppose that other ports in each region ranked in proportion, and therefore to suggest that in the 1370s, Mediterranean trade was perhaps fifteen times
greater than that in the Baltic. This is a very wild and risky extrapolation, but
probably in the right order of magnitude.

As well as being so much smaller in scale, the techniques of trading were still
much less developed in the north. While catering for many fewer consumers
and using much less money and less credit, there was still generally a lack of
international exchange facilities or local giro banking in northern Europe, of
insurance syndicates or the possibilities of developing international trading
and industrial groups. Nevertheless, it must not be thought that the centres of
business were ever static. Change was as perpetual as individual initiative could
make it. 'The ongoing shifting of the locus of economic leadership'[86] was particularly noticeable in the fourteenth century, within the central banana-shaped
urban belt of Europe.[87] At its southern end the preponderant weight of commercial and manufacturing development was shifting northwards from
Tuscany to Lombardy. The cheap woollen manufacture of Florence and other
Tuscan cities was declining, that of Lombard cities was increasing. Silk cloth
production in Lucca was diminishing, that in Venice and Bologna was increasing. The manufactures of fustians, majolica, paper, soap and glass were all
developing north of the Appenines, and the production of armour there was
growing prodigiously too. It fits that the trade of Venice, as the principal
seaport for the area, was flourishing, whilst that of Genoa, the principal carrier
of Tuscan goods, was in crisis. It is not surprising that cities like Milan and

---

[85] Above pp. 186–7.
[86] The phrase was used in the Festschrift offered to Herman van der Wee to sum up one of the principal themes of his work on the Netherlands: Blockmans in Aerts *et al.* (1993), pp. 41–58.
[87] Above p. 157.

Venice attracted enough immigrants to maintain, or possibly even slightly increase, their populations, despite the waves of plague. Genoa and Florence were not able to do so. Despite immigration the population of Florence more than halved between 1340 and 1400. At the extreme southern end of the urban belt, cities like Siena and Perugia suffered most of all. A long process of deindustrialisation was beginning from the south.

Whilst Tuscany, particularly southern Tuscany, was losing, southern Germany, the next area northwards from Lombardy in the urban belt, was gaining. By the end of the century the cities of southern Germany were already beginning that growth that was to be so significant in the following two centuries. It was south German merchants, not north German ones, that were taking up 'Italian' commercial methods, accumulating cheap capital and developing their own international commercial-mining-manufacturing enterprises.[88] They were moving on, from simply importing goods from Italy for distribution, to manufacturing substitutes for some of them, like fustians, paper and armour. Significantly, none of these products any longer appear among the range of goods sent over the Alps in 1392, by one of the most important firms of fourteenth-century Nuremberg, the Kress. A vivid impression of these is given by the accounts of Hilpolt Kress, who was responsible for the firm's business in Venice. Rolls of cloth formed the most important group of goods sent from Venice. In one year 101 rolls of cloth, mainly silk, appeared in his accounts, ranging in value from the rolls of cheap 'Pasthart' which were worth only 3½ florins the roll, up to a single roll of rich blue velvet valued at no less than 40 florins – nearly two years' wages for an ordinary Florentine labourer at this date. Most of the cloth fell into a middle range like brocades at 10 or 14 florins a roll, or taffetas at 7¼ florins each. These were still luxury cloths, but not so luxurious as the velvet. By now most were already woven in northern Italy, but others still came from much farther afield, from Damascus or Baghdad, whilst the taffetas even came from Samarkand. Altogether these 101 rolls of cloth were valued at 1,075 florins. Next in value came nearly 880 ducats worth of spices, nearly half of which (by value) was Indian pepper. The third important commodity imported by Kress from Venice was pearls. There were no less than 257¼ ounces of these at seven different prices from 5s 6d to 17s the ounce. No total value for these appears in the accounts, but it cannot have been much less than the total value of spices, and may even have quite considerably exceeded the total value of cloth, depending on how many ounces of each quality were in the total. Far behind silk, spices and pearls in value were a number of other commodities; loaves of sugar for example from plantations in Sicily, or in Crete and elsewhere in the

[88] Von Stromer (1970).

eastern Mediterranean which had been refined in Venice, and bales of raw Syrian cotton, and barrels of soap. Soap must have been near the bottom limit of value of commodities which it was worth transporting the difficult 650 kilometres (400 miles) through the Brenner to Nuremberg. It was only put down in the accounts at 2 ducats per 100 pounds, and the whole half ton that Kress imported was worth far less than the single roll of blue velvet. In the opposite direction the Kress sent over 3,600 florins worth of silver, about two-thirds in ingot form and one third worked up by Nuremberg silversmiths. The value put on skilled craftsmanship seems surprisingly small to modern eyes, for the silver plate was only valued at a rate some 8 per cent higher than bar silver. By contrast with silver, the value of gold sent to Venice by this route seems small. There was only just over 500 florins worth, and since nearly 140 florins worth of gold was sent in the opposite direction, the net value of gold was not very great. Of the four other commodities that Kress sent to Venice, only Baltic amber is possibly even worth mentioning, but this was barely worth more than the sugar sent in the opposite direction.

In essence, then, Kress's trade with Venice consisted almost exclusively of silver and silver plate in one direction, and primarily of silks, spices and pearls in the reverse direction. South Germans were beginning to be able to produce so many other luxury goods themselves. This was just part of an 'ongoing shifting of the locus of economic leadership' which was in the following centuries to move all the way up the urban belt from Lombardy to south Germany, to Antwerp and its hinterland, to the United Provinces, and to England, before starting to move back south-eastwards in the twentieth century. But those histories make up several other stories.

CHAPTER 9

CHIVALRY AND THE ARISTOCRACY

Maurice Keen

AT a date which cannot be pinpointed in the year 1325, King Charles-Robert of Hungary founded the Society of St George, an elite band of fifty knights who were to be entitled to wear a special habit, were to meet three times a year for the 'chapter' of their society (on St George's day, on the feast of the nativity of the Virgin and at Epiphany) and who were sworn to observe a series of religious knightly obligations laid down in the founder's statutes.[1] This, as far as we know, was the first instituted of the princely secular orders of chivalry, whose appearance was one of the most striking novel features of the history of knighthood in the fourteenth century. The foundation of the Society of St George was followed by that of the Order of the Band in Castile (1330), of the Garter in England (1349), the Star in France (1351), the Golden Buckle in the empire (1355), the Collar in Savoy (1364) and the Ermine in Brittany (1381); there were others too. The statutes of all these societies bear a family resemblance to one another. They detail the obligations of the companions to the sovereign or 'master' of the order and to one another, provide for regular chapter meetings (usually on the feast of the patron saint of the order, to be followed by High Mass in its chapel and a lavish banquet) and set out rules about the cut and wearing of the robes and insignia of the company.

Membership was limited to those who were of noble birth and 'without reproach' in reputation. Their founders clearly intended that they should reflect what was in contemporary eyes best and most prized in the aristocratic knightly ethos.

Given that the foundation of the first of these new orders follows a bare dozen years after the dramatic dissolution of the old crusading order of the Templars, their rise inevitably seems to suggest that a growing secular and princely orientation was a significant feature of the fourteenth-century

---

[1] Boulton (1987), pp. 30ff.

development of the chivalric ideal. The circumstances surrounding individual foundations certainly seems to confirm that suggestion.

The Society of St George was founded by King Charles-Robert in the aftermath of his triumph over a great revolt of the older native barons of Hungary, and the principal purpose behind the foundation seems to have been to honour and to cement the fidelity of the new nobility that he had gathered around him during the civil wars of the first fifteen years of his reign. Its primary object, so the prologue to its statutes declared, was to protect the king from his enemies.[2] The *Chronicle of Alfonso XI* speaks very similarly of the early history of the Castilian Order of the Band, the next princely foundation of which we know: 'thus it happened that knights and squires who had done some good deed of arms against the enemies of the King . . . were given the band by the King, in such a way that each one of the others wanted to do well in chivalry to gain that honour and the good will of the King'.[3] The timing of its foundation, again comparably with that of the Hungarian order, fits into the context of the series of remarkable occasions through which Alfonso XI, in 1330, celebrated his victories over his enemies domestic and Moorish, which culminated in his extraordinary reception of knighthood from the image of St James at Compostela and his enthronement at Burgos.[4] The foundation of the two Neapolitan orders of the Knot (1352) and the Ship (1381) were clearly connected to the turns of fortune in the succession struggles in that kingdom, the one being aimed to consolidate the supporters of Louis of the house of Taranto, the other to buttress the cause of the rival house of Durazzo, after its victory over Louis's widow, Queen Joanna, and the coronation of Charles of Durazzo as king of Naples.[5]

The story of the founding of the two most famous princely orders of this period fits into the history of another succession war, the great Hundred Years War of France and England. Edward III founded the Order of the Garter in the aftermath of his great victories at Crécy and Calais, at once to commemorate those feats of English chivalry (most of the founder members had been armed in the field at Crécy), and to assert defiantly the justice of the cause in which he had fought, 'retorting shame and defiance upon him that should dare to think ill of so just an enterprise as he had undertaken for the recovery of that (the French) crown' – honi soit qui mal y pense.[6] John the Good's foundation of the Order of the Star in 1351 was clearly, in some measure at least, a riposte to Edward's institution and the clause in its statutes obliging its companions to seek the sovereign's permission before joining any other order

---

[2] Ibid., p. 36. [3] Ibid., p. 53, quoting *CRC*, 1, pp. 178–9.
[4] Ibid., pp. 52–4; and see Linehan (1987), pp. 229–43. [5] Boulton (1987), pp. 216ff, 291ff.
[6] Ashmole (1672), p. 184, quoted by Vale (1983), p. 76. This latter, pp. 76–91, offers the best modern account of the foundation of the Garter.

was no doubt intended to discourage French noblemen from being lured away towards Plantagenet allegiance by Edward's chivalrous propaganda (he can only have had the Garter in mind).[7]

A clear common theme in these stories of the origins of the secular orders of knighthood is the desire of princes, through the companionships of their orders, to bind to their service individual and distinguished members of their aristocracies, and in doing so to enhance their own worship and repute in the eyes of their aristocratic subjects generally. In this way a comparison is invited between the founding of orders of knighthood and other means by which princes sought to bind men to their service, by grants of pensions, fees, household or military office, often accompanied by gifts of robes and livery collars or badges (often described in terms very similar to the insignia of chivalric orders),[8] and through which they hoped to reinforce, or substitute for, ties of territorial vassallage and allegiance. Viewed in this light, the institution of secular orders of chivalry appears as a kind of special variant of the practice which in England is termed retaining, their companionships as elite bands of retainers bound by special and personal supra-feudal ties and vows to the service of a prince. Thus they seem once again to re-emphasise a growing princely orientation in the ideology of chivalry of the time.

It seems clear that there is much in this way of looking at the new knightly orders of the fourteenth century. The oath that the companions of the Knot, for instance, were to swear, to give 'to all their power and knowledge' loyal aid and counsel to their prince 'whether in arms or in other matters',[9] has distinct echoes of the phraseology of English indentures (and of the French equivalent, contracts of *alliance*), which retained knights or esquires for service in peace and war. The chronicler's description of how Alfonso XI ordered 'that certain knights and squires of his household should wear a band on their clothing, and he himself did the same . . . and from that time on he gave those knights each year similar vestments with a band',[10] reads precisely like a distribution of liveries. It is equally clear, however, that this is not the whole story. There are significant contrasts between membership of a retinue and membership of an order of chivalry as well as significant similarities.

A retainer could expect to be feed for his service: membership of an order was more likely to put a companion to expense than to bring financial reward (of course he might reasonably expect generous patronage from its

---

[7] Boulton (1987), pp. 194–5; Renouard (1949), pp. 281, 300.

[8] De La Marche, *Mémoires*, IV, pp. 161–2, for an attempt to distinguish juridically between the grant of an order and of a livery collar or *devise*, a distinction which he felt, significantly, to be insufficiently understood.

[9] Boulton (1987), pp. 229–30; the quotations are from the statutes of the Order of the Knot of Naples.   [10] *CRC*, I, p. 178; quoted by Boulton (1987), p. 53.

sovereign, but this was in no way constitutionally intrinsic to their relationship). The statutes of every chivalrous order imposed on the companions (including the sovereign or master) very specific obligations of religious observance such as one would never expect to find in a secular contract of retainer. A bond between a lord and a retainer contracted for service from the one party in return for the promise of protection and good lordship from the other, and this relationship might be expressed in language with chivalrous overtones. Such a bond would not find room, however, for those more high-sounding and general purposes which every founder of an order of knighthood took care to emphasise, declaring that he acted 'to honour chivalry and exalt loyalty' (the Band), 'for the honour of God and Our Lady, and the exaltation of Knighthood and the increase of honour' (the Star), 'in order to praise good Knights, and to increase their name, and to exalt Knighthood' (the Ship).[11]

The comparison between the companions of a chivalrous order and an elite group of retainers thus proves inadequate; not misleading, certainly, but nevertheless incomplete. From a lord's point of view, the object of a retaining indenture or of a feed and sworn alliance was to secure good and loyal service, martial or otherwise. The object of the institution of an order of knighthood was not simply to secure service to a lord or prince, but also at the same time to glamorise it in aristocratic eyes, by associating his following with ideas and ideals only tangentially relevant thereto, or even sometimes wholly irrelevant. The founders of such orders sought to do this by avowing the ends and values of the traditional aristocratic culture of chivalry, the service of God in arms (accepting the crusade as the highest expression of this), the maintenance of the good name of knighthood for loyalty and martial prowess, the upholding of the honour of women and womankind. Here the most important debt that their statutes reveal is to the great romantic literature that had grown up in the thirteenth century and had done so much to shape a knightly ethos common in its principles to every region of Christendom: and which was deeply individualistic in tone in the sense that its most powerful recurrent theme was the testing in quality of honour of the individual knight. The debt is often explicit and intentionally patent. The arrangement of the shields of the companions of the Star in their House of Our Lady at St Ouen was directly modelled on the description of the hall of the Free Palace in the romance of Perceforest.[12] All contemporary commentators knew and saw that Edward III, in founding the Order of the Garter, was seeking to revive the glories of Arthur's Round Table.[13] Viewed from this angle, the contrast between the spirit of chivalry reflected in the new secular orders of the fourteenth century and that of the

---

[11] Boulton (1987), pp. 70, 178, 296.   [12] Keen (1984), p. 191.   [13] Boulton (1987), pp. 101–17.

preceding age begins to look less sharp, its growing princely and secular orientation, though still significant, less marked.

A comparison has been suggested between an order of knighthood and a band of retainers: an alternative, overlapping and equally illuminating analogue would be the aristocratic household of a prince or nobleman, an institution through which princes and noblemen likewise sought both to recruit service and to glamorise it. For these purposes it could extend the web of princely influence much further into the aristocratic world than an order could, because the numbers of people involved were so much greater (though it should be remembered here that some princely orders were quite large: the Star was envisaged as a company of 300 knights).

The household was of course an ancient institution. Because it had had, from its earliest days, to double as both the prince's bodyguard and his social entourage (and still could be mobilised as a military unit), a strong chivalrous and aristocratic tone infused its ethos and many of its rituals. As D'Arcy Boulton has put it, the household 'had long served the function of impressing the world at large with the wealth, importance and noble qualities of the prince it served, both by overwhelming visitors with rare foods and costly entertainments, and by enveloping the prince and his family in an elaborate daily ritual, enhanced by magnificent costumes and settings'.[14] The household ordinances that regulated this ritual are eminently comparable with those clauses in the statutes of chivalrous orders that regulated, at ample length, the cut and wearing of robes and insignia, the order of precedence in the procession to High Mass on the occasion of the patronal feast and the seating arrangement for the banquet that would follow. The difference is not in tone or style, but in that the statutes of orders regulate for a single, annual event, the household ordinances for the daily routine of a much larger body of people.

Princely households were growing in size in the fourteenth century, and in the elaborateness of their organisation. The standing personnel of the French royal household already numbered 400 at the beginning of John the Good's reign: by the end of his grandson Charles VI's reign that number had doubled, and of course the queen and any royal children had their own households as well. A major princely household was subdivided into separate departments, each concerned with a specialised service, the chamber (the innermost sanctum), the *bouteillerie*, the *echançonnerie* and so on. Each department had its own hierarchy of salaried officials and servants, the higher ranks being usually confined to those of noble birth (just as membership of orders of chivalry was confined to the nobly born, and often to those who had besides been dubbed to knighthood). The pensioned noble servants of a household usually spent

---

[14] Ibid., p. 2.

periods at court, in rotation, and while they were in attendance they and their
servants (and indeed their horses) would be fed in the household and at the
prince's expense, just as a retainer and his servants would be in his lord's household. The cost of maintaining this aristocratic entourage in a suitably sumptuous manner could be enormous, a steady drain on the princely purse with
serious fiscal implications. That is why the expenditure on the royal household
became a bitter bone of contention in France in the 1350s and again in the time
of Charles VI, as it did also in England in the reign of Richard II. Nevertheless,
princes seem usually to have thought the money well spent, in terms of the
honourable reputation and the assurance of service that it bought: every time
that personnel and allowances were, under pressure, reduced, they quickly
began to climb up again.

The most conspicuously lavish element in princely household expenditure
was upon entertainment, upon feasts, jousting and pageantry, and here we re-
encounter the same brand of ambiguity that raised questions earlier about
the validity of comparing companionship in an order with the bond of a lord
with his retainer. The core functions of the household were to maintain the
prince's lifestyle and to ensure him loyal service, but these ends could not be
served, apparently, without going further than that. In order to impress
effectively visitors and aspirants to his service the prince needed to associate
his household and lifestyle with purposes independent of the current priorities of policy and governance, but which were cherished in the traditions of
aristocratic culture: and princely efforts to do so very naturally served to
strengthen even further the hold of those values and purposes on the aristocratic mentality. Thus throughout the history of the court pageantry and
entertainment of the age there runs the same strand of endeavour to evoke
the aura of past chivalry as recorded in semi-historical romantic literature,
that the statutes of the orders of chivalry likewise strove to evoke. The court
feast that Edward I held to celebrate the knighting of his eldest son in 1306
sought an echo of the story of the Swan Knight, the legendary ancestor of
Godfrey the conqueror of Jerusalem.[15] Godfrey's own feats provided the
theme for the *tableaux* and pageantry of the feast at which Charles V of
France in 1378 entertained as his guest the Holy Roman Emperor Charles
IV.[16] *Tableaux* of the mythical story of how Richard Lion Heart had defended
a pass against Saladin and his Saracen host greeted Queen Isabella at her
entry into Paris in 1389.[17] Twelve years later, courtiers of her household and
the king's sought to while away winter hours by founding a Court of Love
and competing in the composition of amorous poems that would hint that

---

[15] Denholm Young (1961), pp. 251–62.   [16] *CJII*, III, pp. 235–42; Bullough (1974), pp. 97–122.
[17] Froissart, *Œuvres*, ed. Lettenhove, XIV, p. 9.

they could love as well and in as courtly a fashion as ever did Lancelot or Tristram.[18]

Among court entertainments, jousts and tournaments offered special opportunities to evoke a chivalrous aura of magnificence, through lavish spectacle. They also, incidentally, tended to underscore and promote the individualistic tendencies of chivalry, since in the lists the combatants competed on equal terms for the prizes for prowess; and they offered the ideal opportunity to the fashionable young nobleman to impress aristocratic female spectators. He might even be bearing, on his lance or in his helm, a token from a beloved mistress. In the tourney, the history of the chivalric ethos at the princely court and of princely orders interweave directly. Juliet Vale has argued trenchantly that, in selecting the founder members of the Garter, Edward III was guided by the idea of selecting two well-balanced tournament teams (hence the twelve stalls on the king's side in St George's chapel, and twelve on the prince's): the foundation was thus in a way 'an extension of the tournament activities of the chamber and household'.[19] The manner in which an aspirant knight might seek admission to the Order of the Band makes a similar point. He must seek out at least two knights of the order and challenge them to tourney (they were bound to accept), and if he sustained his challenges successfully he would then be sent to the king's court. There is a strong echo here of the stories of Arthur's day, in which 'Knights of the Round Table were constantly challenging (or being challenged by) strangers and constantly sending them back to Arthur's court to be admitted (if deemed worthy) to their company.'[20]

Court tournaments could be, and often were, so staged as to evoke directly a literary reference. In 1334 at Dunstable Edward III tourneyed armed as Sir Lionel (Lancelot's cousin).[21] It was after another tournament, in January 1344 at Windsor, that he announced his intention to found a Round Table 'of the same manner and standing as that in which the Lord Arthur, formerly King of England, had relinquished it',[22] which would be opened at a still more magnificent tourney at Pentecost (which it seems never took place: but the construction of the Round Table was certainly commenced and paid for). At the jousts held in 1401 at Westminster Hall to celebrate the marriage of Princess Blanche, knights participating adopted allegorical titles, reminiscent of the *Roman de la Rose* — *Ardent desireux*, *Voulente d'apprendre*, *Le povoir perdu* — and composed highly literary letters of challenge in a style fitting thereto (but not failing to mention that they came to Henry IV's court because it was a 'true mirror and examplar of all honour, courtesy and *gentillesse*').[23] At the most

---

[18] Green (1983), pp. 87–108.   [19] Vale (1983), p. 88.   [20] Boulton (1987), p. 76.
[21] Vale (1983), pp. 68–9.   [22] *Chronica Adae Murimuth*, ed. Thompson, p. 232.
[23] Barker (1986), pp. 97–8.

famous of all the festivities of this kind in this period, the jousts of Saint-Inglevert in 1390, there was no such mimetic element, but the rituals of the occasion, such as the procedures for the touching of the challenger's targets outside the pavilions to indicate what courses would be run, were particularly ornate and intricate, anticipating the extravagant gestures of the Burgundian *pas d'armes* of the next century.

The extravagance of the display and gesture of the court tournament scene presses the question on the historical commentator: are we here watching chivalry being drawn into the ambit of princely power by generous patronage, or are we rather watching the prince and his court becoming enmeshed in the aristocratic preoccupations of chivalry, with its cult of honour and its romanticisation of individual prowess? It is not easy to give an unambiguous answer.

The staging of court pageants, feasts and tournaments, as the last two examples quoted above help to remind us, was becoming in the fourteenth century progressively more and more elaborate. In the supervision and direction of this side of court entertainments and ceremonies the heralds played an important role. The steady rise of their 'order', in prominence and status, was very marked in the period. When we first encounter heralds, in the twelfth and early thirteenth centuries, they are hardly distinguishable from vagabond minstrels and *jongleurs*: we hear of them wandering from tourney to tourney, seeking *largesse* and a measure of patronage from the participants, but they do not seem to have any settled attachment to particular lords. By the time of Edward I, however, in England at least, royal heralds received regular payments in the household, along with minstrels,[24] and by the end of the fourteenth century their services had acquired such value as to make them indispensable to any princely household. Anjou King of Arms gives a graphic account of the 'coronation' of one Charlot as King of Arms of France by Charles V, and his late fourteenth-century tract also describes detailed rituals for the creation of pursuivants and heralds, who should be dressed in tabards of their lord's arms for the occasion and take a solemn oath to conduct themselves loyally in their office.[25] The men who had once wandered with the minstrels have grown into respected, uniformed officials.

The duties of the heralds' office had become wide-ranging, dignified and important in the chivalrous world of aristocratic ceremony and precedence. They were expected to know the blazons and lineage of the nobles and gentlemen of their march (and of others too), to inspect and verify the arms and helmcrests of those proposing to take part in tourneying and to carry messages

---

[24] Denholm Young (1965), pp. 54–60.
[25] Oxford, Bodleian Library, Rawlinson MS C 399, fos. 77–8; and Keen (1984), p. 137.

between hostile parties in war. They were bound to act too as 'confessors in arms',[26] that is to say to be able to advise on delicate points of honour and to be expert in the nice scales of achievement in knightly prowess. No wonder that Froissart looked to Kings of Arms and heralds for information for his chronicle about feats of chivalry, for as he put it 'such people are of right the just inquisitors into such matters and true reporters of them'.[27] In order to discharge this side of their function heralds needed to be literate men, versed in the romance history that set the standard of knightly values and achievement. By the end of the fourteenth century they were well on their way to becoming a kind of secular priesthood of chivalry.

Blazon, the heralds' special expertise, was vital to chivalric ceremony and to aristocratic culture generally. It was by their coats and crests that knights and squires identified themselves at joust and tournament, and on the battlefield. The coats of arms of companions of orders of chivalry were painted above their stalls and seats, in the chapel of St George at Windsor for the Garter, in the hall of St Ouen for the Star's knights. In the glass and wall painting of church or castle blazon could recall knightly companionship and chivalrous achievement: thus the glass in the east window of Gloucester Cathedral, commissioned by Thomas Lord Bradeston, constituted almost a roll of arms of those alongside whom he had fought at Crécy in 1346.[28] The splendid armorial paintings in Königsberg Cathedral commemorated the adventures in the company of the Teutonic Knights of nobles who had come to Prussia from abroad, to take arms against the heathen.[29] 'Gelre, I have business for you', a certain lady told Claes Haynen, Guelders Herald, according to the prologue of his *Lobdichte* (poems of praise): 'I am going to make a new chamber, and to decorate it with blazoned shields. You shall seek out the knights who are worthy that I should paint their arms in my chamber, those who are without reproach.'[30] Heralds indeed had a vital role to play in the aristocratic world of the fourteenth century, because they could translate its aspirations and its achievements into vivid pictorial and symbolic language, as Gelre was here asked to do. They could also interpret back its significance for the benefit of the noble world at large that they were sworn to serve: '*item*, ye shall be serviceable and secret in all points to all knights and *gentillesse*, to lords and ladies and gentlewomen and cause and counsel them to all truth and virtue that in you is, so help you God'.[31]

Here the ambiguity that has now become familiar occurs once more. The herald is the servant of the prince, whose arms he bears on his tabard and

[26] *BBA*, I, p. 297. [27] Froissart, *Œuvres*, ed. Lettenhove, II, p. 2, 11.
[28] Denholm Young (1969), p. 9. [29] Paravicini (1990), pp. 67–167.
[30] *Wapenboek ou Armorial de 1334 à 1372 . . . par Gelre Héraut*, ed. Bouton, I, p. 67; Keen (1984), pp. 139–41.
[31] *BBA*, I, p. 297.

whose purse sustains him, and at the same time he is the servitor of nobility at large, registrar of prowess and individual honour. To this second role, though, there was a further dimension, which in this instance softens the ambiguity. In the examples quoted so far, heraldry has been used to symbolise aristocratic commitment to certain well-established values, prowess, loyalty, zeal for holy war – the same sort of values as those to which the statutes of orders of knighthood proclaimed commitment. But more often, and much more often, blazon was used to convey a more mundane kind of message, to record noble ancestry and noble inter-family connection, that is to say noble genealogy and social exclusivity. Princes and aristocrats alike had interests that could be promoted by encouraging and exploiting that kind of exclusivity.

The growing eagerness in the fourteenth century of families even of the less exalted nobility to claim for themselves arms and crests of their own was in part no doubt just a matter of fashion, but it was also a symptom of the noble estate's sense of its own insecurity. Seigneurial incomes from land, the traditional mainstay of noble living were coming under pressure, especially after the Black Death, when depopulation tilted the balance of economic bargaining power as between lord and tenants (whose rent was often in the form either of labour dues, or produce, or both) in the latter's favour. The devastation of the countryside in the century's great wars had a parallel effect, in many regions even sharper, because more sustained. The nobility's taste for extravagance and pride in its style of life and traditions were, on the other hand, no whit abated; that style and those traditions were, after all, the outward and visible signs of its dignity, its *apartheid* from the common herd. Aristocracy needed reassurance that its dignity and privileges and exclusivity were recognised, respected and valued in this newly difficult world. The right to blazon, confirmed or authorised by the prince or his herald, offered just such reassurance. So did other rights and privileges which the prince might confirm to the noble (and armigerous), such as exemption from fiscal exaction on the ground that the noble served by the sword (a privilege that spread rapidly and widely in the fourteenth century),[32] or the principle of *dérogeance* (that certain occupations, notably retail trading, were incompatible with nobility), which made its first appearance in jurisprudence in this period.[33] At the same time competition for the favours that princely service could secure was sharpened, as was appreciation of the reservation of offices of dignity in the princely household to those of noble birth. Noble incomes needed the buttressing that fees, pensions and office could bring even more keenly than in the past.

Princes conversely needed the support, service and loyalty of their lay aristocratic subjects quite as much as the nobles needed them. This had always

---

[32] Dupont-Ferrier (1930–2), II, pp. 175 ff.   [33] Dravasa (1965), pp. 135–93 and (1966), pp. 23–129.

been so, of course, but in the fourteenth century the need, from the princes' point of view, had become, in important ways, more imperative than ever before. The web of princely jurisdiction now spread much further than it had done in earlier days, and princely right was intruding in the courts into a far greater multiplicity of cases. The *parlement* of Paris of the time of Philip the Fair was the lineal descendant of the feudal *curia regis* of earlier French kings, but by his day it was no longer concerned just with the affairs of royal vassals and rear-vassals, but in those of a great range of people who, even if thcy held noble fiefs, were tenurially remote from the crown. Wars had become more large scale, and a prince needed to be able to mobilise a wider sector of his noble subjects, regardless once again of their position in the ladder of tenurial vassalage (and so might have to pay for their service). Wars had also become much more costly; a prince therefore needed to be able in a military emergency to tap the whole resources of his lordships or kingdom by assented taxation. Governance, in short, had become a more complicated, large-scale, professional business. The Church was no longer the independent force it had once been. The secular nobility, consequently, in kingdoms such as France and England and Naples and in the Iberian realms, was effectively the only group with the resources, political awareness and organisational capacity to count for an independent force in the games of governance, diplomacy and war in which princes, because of their standing, could not avoid being the leading players, and by their good management in which they prospered or fell. They needed the support of their nobilities, in consequence, more than ever before, and in a more unitary sense. Generous exercise of princely patronage offered only a partial solution here. If carried too far it became financially self-defeating, and in any case the problem had become too large scale. Princes needed to reach more noble hearts and minds than their purses could ever stretch out toward, including, perhaps especially, those of the lesser nobility of the regions in the territories that they ruled. The troubles generated in France in the last year of Philip IV's reign and in the time of his sons Louis X and Philip V by the provincial leagues of noblemen, who felt their privileges and position threatened by royal taxation and over-government, offered an ugly example of what could happen if a prince did not succeed in doing so.

If the situation was shrewdly appreciated, however, noble insecurity could be princely opportunity: that really is the moral of the themes traced here. Nobles cherished their privileges, their rights of jurisdiction, the right to carry arms, to crenellate their houses, to dress differently from others. They also cherished a style of living which they identified as noble and a value system which set a high price on martial service and virtues, on generosity, on loyalty and on courtly manners. The key note of this aristocratic value system was honour. Honourable living, in war and at court, in danger and at dalliance, was the theme round which the authors of the romantic literature of the twelfth and thirteenth centuries had woven their didactic fictions: and those fictions, reaching out to an aristocratic audience of the widest extent, to the urban patriciates as well as to the landed nobility, nurtured what we call chivalry and courtliness into a framework embracing virtually every facet of noble existence. Thus, if the prince wished to win the hearts and minds of nobles, it was in his interest to project himself as one who had taken the heroes of romance as his exemplar, and to present his court as the temple of honour and himself as its fount.

That was the message that princely orders conveyed eloquently on the princely behalf. Here were societies whose membership was limited to those who were of noble birth and were *sans reproche*, men who had sworn to abide by the highest demands of chivalry, never to flee in battle, to stand always by their companions, to uphold the honour of God and of womankind – and of their prince. It was the message to which, likewise, court pageantry and entertainment, *tableaux* of the feats of Godfrey of Jerusalem and Richard Lion Heart, tournies and jousts after the Arthurian fashion, gave expression. The growing practice of granting nobility (and sometimes blazons too) by letters patent, and of bestowing new titles (or newly interpreted titles) of dignity, such as duke, marquis and viscount, fed the same aspirations and restressed the role of the prince as the 'fount of honour'. The heralds, as servitors at once of the prince and of nobility and chivalry at large, worked to systematise this side of princely propaganda into a science.

There were dangers in this way of proceeding, naturally. In the process of wooing the aristocracy by the flattery and espousal of its values, princely patronage breathed vigour into forces which by no means necessarily or always worked to princely interest. The cultivation of martial chivalry's glamour easily leant encouragement to those who, like the leaders of the Free Companies, hoped to hack their way to power and honour independently, living precariously on the spoils of war and aping the manners of knighthood on their brutally gotten gains. Some of them succeeded so well for a time as to render large areas of southern and central France ungovernable and to ruin their prosperity. Princely example could also offer a model for which those very great seigneurs who were his most independent and potentially dangerous vassals could apply in order to make themselves more independent of him, and to erode his authority within their lordships. That was what the Montfort dukes sought to do in Brittany, through their cultivation of semi-mythical Breton history, through the pageantry of their ducal coronations, and the foundation of their own order of knighthood, the Ermine.[34] It was not easy to drive home

---

[34] Boulton (1987), pp. 274–8; Jones (1991), pp. 141–73.

to the aristocracy the distinction, essential from the princely point of view, between honour won by the naked sword of the individual adventurer and honour won in the service of the common weal, or that there was a difference in kind between the loyalty that a great territorial seigneur might command and that due to a sovereign prince who was 'emperor in his realm'. Those were the sort of lessons that the encomiasts of royal authority, like the author of the *Songe du vergier* (writing at the court of Charles V of France) were already trying to articulate, however.[35] Significantly, in the dialogue through which the argument of the *Songe* is developed, the figure who takes up the cue as the spokesman for princely power and its personating of the common weal is 'the Knight': it is a sign of the way the wind was blowing.

In the long run, the strength of the kingdoms that at the end of the Middle Ages came to dominate the European political stage was built on the successful marriage of the interests of princes and their aristocracies, assuring authority to the one side, dignity, privilege and honour to the other. In the fourteenth century we are still a long way from that consummation, back in the time of courtship between the parties. Jean Froissart, the great chronicler of chivalry, caught the tempo of the time and of the story I have been trying to tell, nicely. His apprenticeship in letters had been as a poet, living on the fringe of the great courts, and the formative influence on him as an historian had been his reading in Arthurian romance, which inspired his epic *Meliador*. That is why his chronicle so often reads like a romance, cavalier to the point of naïvety in analysis of *realpolitik* but presenting through its interlaced narrative of war and adventure a splendid array of examples of chivalrous and courtly values in action. He was clearly not much interested in princely power as a principle, but the princes in whose names the wars that he described were fought naturally loom large in his book. Significantly, those to whom his admiration went out most instinctively were those who were also the most skilled at posturing in the chivalrous mode, Edward III, the Black Prince in his prime, Gaston Fébus of Foix. It is no accident that they were among the most successful and influential rulers and commanders of their time, and the best served.

---

[35] The *Songe du vergier* is perhaps most readily consulted in the *Revue du moyen âge latin* 12 (1957); but see also *Le songe du vergier*, ed. Schnerb-Lièvre.

CHAPTER 10

COURT PATRONAGE AND INTERNATIONAL GOTHIC

Paul Binski

NEW REGIMES OF PATRONAGE: AVIGNON AND ITALY

By one reading, the hallmark of the development of Gothic art in the later Middle Ages is not internationalism – the major pan-European styles, whether Romanesque, Byzantine or Gothic of the previous centuries all had an international dimension – but rather extraordinary diversity. The major factor behind this diversification was the emergence of new regimes of patronage, for while the courts of western Europe continued their signal role in commissioning major works of art and architecture, the role of patronage in the newly powerful cities was growing inexorably. Though we can point to significant urban centres in the thirteenth century, for example Paris, London and Rome, the plethora of urban patronage in such cities as Cologne, Prague, Siena and Bruges in the next century entailed both more vigorous art production and a wider range of stylistic possibilities. Ecclesiastical patronage also retained much of its vitality throughout the century. At Cologne, the archbishops presided over the completion of their new French-inspired cathedral with stained glass and Franco-Italian panel paintings, creating a distinctive urban idiom of Gothic art quite comparable to the achievements of civic Italy. In England the incomparably wealthy dioceses continued to see significant building activity in the new showy Decorated Style, itself summarised most splendidly by the Benedictines at Ely (plate 1). Throughout western Europe too, the impact of mendicant architecture as developed in the spacious churches of southern France, notably Toulouse, was now sensed further afield, as for example in Germany.

It is especially characteristic of the new climate of experiment and exchange that the century witnessed the rise of centres whose importance was ephemeral. One such was Avignon in southern France, to which Clement V moved during his pontificate (1305–14). This upheaval signalled the triumph of French hegemony over the papacy and, in effect, the end of significant art patronage in Rome for nearly two centuries. Avignon, the papal palace and cathedral of which were decorated by artists of Italian background and training, attests to the rising European importance of art nurtured in Italian centres whose importance was waxing at Rome's expense, principally Siena, Florence and Naples. With the diaspora of talent from Rome, each of these cities played host to Italian fresco and panel painters of the calibre of Cavallini, Giotto and Simone Martini who did so much to create the new aesthetic outlook of fourteenth-century western European art. Simone, drawn from Siena towards the end of his life, in fact died in Avignon in 1344.

Avignon found itself in the position of those earlier political centres, notably Constantinople and Aachen, which had borne the burden of Rome's mythology. The establishment of the papal curia at Avignon reflected the trend towards fixed centres of government already apparent in the thirteenth century in Paris and London. But its real importance as more than a provincial city was short-lived. Avignon never emerged as an especially formative centre of patronage, so much as a short-lived foyer for the meeting of international idioms of English, French or, more usually, central Italian extraction. For the first time we find popes like John XXII (1316–34) commissioning English painters and masons for papal commissions, notably his tomb at Avignon, similar to that of Edward II (d. 1327) at Gloucester. But only one pope, Clement VI (1342–52), consolidated the permanent presence of the popes at Avignon by completing the construction and decoration of the papal palace. Like so many fourteenth-century patrons, his contribution was idiosyncratic. His bedroom in the new and spectacular Palais des Papes, the so-called Chambre du Cerf, is painted with a dazzlingly profane encyclopaedia of methods of hunting and fishing, set in lush woodland, and dotted with barebottomed putti (plate 2). The subject-matter, at once an allusion to the antique garden painting of *vetusta Roma* and to the seigneurial culture of the *Roman de la Rose*, was echoed in the interiors of the contemporary royal residence in Paris, the Hôtel de Saint-Pol, under Charles V (1364–80), but its scenic presentation already owes much to Italian fresco decoration. It stands as a fine if whimsical introduction to the artistic eclecticism, both modern and consciously conservative, of the period.[1]

Avignon, though only indirectly influential elsewhere, symbolises the emergence of unexpected centres of patronage which benefited from the movement of artists and ideas. Of these, Prague was to be the most exotic, and we shall examine it in the context of dynastic art. Naples under the Angevins had also earlier benefited from the Roman diaspora. Cavallini, Giotto and Simone

---

[1] For John XXII see Bony (1979), p. 65; for Avignon, Enaud (1971); Laclotte and Thiébaut (1983); see also Paris (1981), no. 325. In addition see Gardner (1992).

Martini were all employed there after 1310, and seem to have carried with them
their Roman, Florentine and Sienese idioms. In this sense Naples was the true
heir to Roman clerical and Tuscan commercial patronage. But Giotto (d. 1337),
who was court painter to Robert II of Naples by 1330 and also a Guelf sympathiser, is also known while in Naples to have painted a subject called the
'Nine Heroes', based upon a text composed by a bishop of Liège earlier in
the century, and an example of the type of Franco-Flemish romance culture
of the heroic now fashionable in northern aristocratic circles. His later work
for the Visconti in Milan had much the same heroic yet international and vernacular character.

Giotto's workshop remained immensely influential within Italy, not so much
because of the impact of the Arena Chapel which he decorated for the
Scrovegni family *c.* 1305 (for this was closed for part of the century with the
exile of that family from Padua) but rather because Giotto's team worked at
San Francesco at Assisi, the single most important foyer of Italian fresco painting of the period (plate 3). Here Simone worked too, and it is to him especially
that we must look for a more comprehensive understanding of what international art looked like at this time, and for what it was to develop into.[2] Echoes
of Simone's brilliant artifice, exemplified by his murals in the Palazzo Pubblico
in Siena and at San Francesco at Assisi, are to be sensed as far afield as
Norwich, Barcelona and Prague as well as at Avignon, far further afield than
any work of Giotto or his busy circle. Aside from its influence, Simone's work
seems especially important for two reasons. First, his style indicates to an
extent unusual in trecento Italian painting his understanding and assimilation
of ideas already worked out by French Gothic art, apparent in his earliest surviving work, the 'Maestà' executed *c.* 1315 in the Palazzo Pubblico in Siena. His
work represented a synthesis of northern and Italian elements that anticipated,
and probably informed, the later so-called International Gothic Style of the
period around 1400. If Duccio moulded Sienese painting, Simone advertised
it. Second, Simone's range of commissions and material was unusually extensive (plate 4), and his contribution to innovative royal and civic iconography
impressive. Towards 1320 he painted an altar panel commissioned for Robert
II of Naples depicting Robert being crowned by his canonised Franciscan
brother, St Louis of Toulouse, an explicitly dynastic work;[3] and he also completed the decoration of the Palazzo Pubblico at Siena by confronting his
'Maestà' with the splendid armed and mounted figure of Guidoriccio da
Fogliano (early 1330s), a Sienese military hero and an iconographic combination reflecting fully the self-identity of civic Siena. To him can be attributed the
first portrait painted on panel, an image made around 1336 of Petrarch's lover

---

[2] In general, White (1966); Martindale (1988).   [3] See frontispiece above.

Laura, to which the poet referred in his sonnets. Simone's acquaintance with intellectuals of this stature also points to the new status of artists.

Simone's near-contemporary Giotto alone could have matched his visual humour, versatility and intelligence, and Giotto himself is known to have executed Florentine civic commissions which expressed allegorically the political state of the commune. Such political and allegorical works were not entirely new, though once again their domain had been predominantly the royal art of northern Europe, which explored in manuscript illuminations and wall paintings the ethical basis of monarchy. Until the trecento, Italian wall painting had innovated predominantly in the field of narrative religious art, where its new expressive pathos had immediately found an appropriate outlet. Fourteenth-century Italian secular civic patronage, however, refreshed the theme of allegorical depiction; and the persuasive techniques, the rhetoric, of monumental religious painting were now turned to more frankly political ends.[4] The learned Ambrogio Lorenzetti's allegorical frescos of 'Good and Bad Government', executed in the Palazzo Pubblico in Siena in 1337–9, are the characteristic instance of the new genre (plate 5). They co-ordinate keenly observed and morally characterised landscapes with quasi-allegorical personifications of various types. The most convincing analysis of these pictures sees them as illustrations not of Aristotelian ideas but rather of pre-humanist, Senecan and Ciceronian, political thought.[5] They exemplify notions familiar in Brunetto Latini's *Trésor* composed in the 1260s and, incidentally, studied in monarchical circles in France and England well into the fourteenth century. Perhaps most importantly, in view of the burgeoning capacity of the pictorial arts to convey and initiate substantive speculation on ideas of this type, their relationship to prior written texts is also informal.

DYNASTIC ART AND THE INTERNATIONAL GOTHIC STYLE

Along with the rise of cities as significant locations of patronage increasingly marked by their own aesthetic identity and by the employment of thinking artists, western Europe's royal dynasties retained a decisive importance. If the thirteenth century had seen the emergence of Court Styles in France and England, the fourteenth century saw those styles diversify yet further under the mounting influence of Italian art, which might be described as the one great common factor of the time. However, though the impact of Italy was felt widely it was felt only partially, and often superficially. Stylistic exchanges remained rare until the last quarter of the century, and far-reaching only at upper levels of patronage.

[4] Belting (1985).   [5] Skinner (1986); Starn and Partridge (1992).

At present, art-historical discussion of the highest aristocratic art is still dominated by the ideas of Erwin Panofsky and Millard Meiss, who argued that courtly manuscript illumination of the type developed in thirteenth-century Paris was radically transformed by contact with Italian painting, a transformation which pointed towards the formation of the International Gothic Style, and ultimately towards Netherlandish art in the next century.[6] As a result it became possible to argue that manuscript illumination was actually the leading and so the most representative pictorial medium north of the Alps after 1300. Though more recent scholars have questioned this primacy of the illuminated manuscript, there is no doubt that the *locus classicus* of this metamorphosis is usually held to be the work associated with the courtly Parisian illuminator Jean Pucelle (d. 1334).[7] By the early 1300s there is clear evidence that the French court had begun to patronise Italian artists close to Cavallini and Giotto, and that by the 1320s a more open acknowledgement had appeared that Italian painters were doing something remarkable and potentially relevant to French aristocratic culture. The principal means of transmission of ideas were two: movement of artists and movement of works of art. Jean Pucelle's tiny Book of Hours illuminated in the 1320s for Queen Jeanne d'Evreux of France (plate 6) could exemplify either or both, since its compositions reveal study of something remarkably similar to Duccio's 'Maestà' finished in 1311 and placed on Siena Cathedral's high altar. The growing number of documentary references to Italian panel paintings circulating in northern Europe from now on, notably in French and English royal circles, exemplifies a fluidity of ideas at the level of the art market itself. Access was growing, and the theme of exchange of this type, though socially exclusive, was to predominate in the century between Pucelle and the patronage of John, duke of Berry, and his Burgundian relatives. What it was that French patrons found attractive in Italian art is demonstrable only from the ways in which northern artists copied southern exemplars: clearly the representation of pictorial space, and what has (somewhat ungenerously) been described as the 'pantomime' of Sienese painting were especially compelling.[8] But changes in demand for certain styles in this period were undoubtedly producer- and innovation-led, and may have been influenced by Italian rhetoric of the period, exemplified by Dante (*Purgatorio* XI), which lauded the fashionable competitiveness of painters like Giotto and Cimabue, albeit as a mark of their pride.

By the fourteenth century the role of France in lending momentum to developments in architecture had slackened. To an extent, the assumption of artistic initiative by France's neighbours, England in the field of architecture

---

[6] Panofsky (1953), pp. 21–50; Meiss (1967).   [7] Panofsky (1953), pp. 24–34; Morand (1962).
[8] Meiss (1967), pp. 3–29.

and Italy in that of painting, may indicate the broader realignments in the artistic geography of western Europe already noted, and certainly a decline in French hegemony.[9] By the end of the century Burgundy and Flanders were to assert themselves as well, challenging the dominance of Paris in the one field in which it remained supreme in northern Europe, the figurative arts. If the rise of Gothic art and architecture had been closely linked to the French monarchy, the diversification of its late-medieval development may reflect too the 'crisis' of monarchies of the fifteenth century. The gradual dwindling of French power before and after the reign of Charles V, and especially after its dismal military defeats at the hands of the English in the 1340s and 1350s, may also be related to the increasing cultural conservatism of French royal patronage: this was a period in which the notion of the golden ages of Charlemagne and Louis IX gained concrete expression in architecture (imitations of the thirteenth-century Sainte-Chapelle erected by Charles V's family) and the royal regalia (the figure of Charlemagne was placed upon the French royal sceptre made *c.* 1365). These were efforts to link the Valois dynasty visually to an imperial past.[10]

Yet in their substance they were not unique. Western Europe had still not shed the imperial ideal, and though the power of the empire had waned after the death of Frederick II in 1250, imperial art was now to be galvanized in another new centre, Prague. Here Emperor Charles IV, that eccentric member of the Luxemburg dynasty, was fashioning an imperial governmental centre focused on St Vitus's Cathedral and Karlstein Castle. The former was erected in a variant of the French *Rayonnant* Style developed in the previous century; the latter, which acted as the imperial treasury, was shaped by Charles as the most staggering fabulation of the idea of the medieval castle ever attempted. Its interior decorations executed *c.* 1360, smothered with semi-precious stones, gilt gesso and wall-mounted panel paintings by Bohemian and Italian painters, drew upon decorative methods long superseded in the Latin west (plate 7).[11] Bohemian imperial painting is a central instance of the role of Romanesque, Byzantine and Italian art in contributing to the bricolage of symbolic and aesthetic effects sought generally by northern court patrons, especially those, like Charles, who represented relatively new dynasties occupying the imperial throne at a time of its dwindling authority. Prague in this sense resembles Avignon. Charles was a natural *bricoleur*, with an enthusiasm for apocalyptic ideas like the imagery of the Heavenly Jerusalem's precious stones later celebrated in sermons preached in his memory by the bishop of Prague. But in this respect Charles's aesthetic regime was not exceptional: on the contrary, it

---

[9] Bony (1979).   [10] Meiss (1967), pp. 36–40; Paris (1981), nos. 202, 204; see also ch. 11.
[11] Munich (1978); Gibbs (1989), pp. 176–202.

precisely symbolises the eclecticism, fertility and experimentation of much leading art patronage of the time, though in peculiarly concentrated and archaising form.

In comparison with Charles IV's apocalyptic enthusiasm and compulsive relic-hunting, Charles V's French court was tempered by humanism, by that scholarly *sagesse* attributed to him in Christine de Pisan's retrospective eulogy *Le livre des faits et bonnes meurs du sage roy Charles V* (1404). Charles built up an immense library of 900 volumes, including illuminated manuscripts from the shop of Pucelle, Aristotelian treatises on princely ethics and no less than eight coronation *ordines*.[12] The impression is that of a court placing more emphasis on the scientific formulation of the ethics of princely governance than upon the heroic mode of contemporary romantic culture. Charles was not the only monarch to possess Aristotelian literature – Edward III of England had also been provided with similar texts – but his interest was more comprehensive, and stands as the single most important royal counterpart to the exploration of the notional basis of government of contemporary city-states like Siena. For the first time under Charles V, the French coronation *ordo* employed at Reims received thorough and ritualistically precise illustrations (plate 8). Illustrations of this type indicate the relative rarity of the ritual itself, and perhaps the contribution of illustration to liturgical *memoria*; but much more probably they mark the definitive formulation of the *ordines* themselves and a desire to stabilise the symbolism of power. The English *ordines* too were illustrated formally at exactly the same time, in the so-called *Liber Regalis* (1390s), embodying the final formulation of the English medieval coronation service first used in 1308. Again, as in France, the later fourteenth century in England is a period of striking conservatism, notwithstanding the generally greater strength of the English crown. French and Italian artistic ideas had entered England through the agency of the royal family, notably Queen Isabella, who owned Italian panel paintings, and Queen Philippa of Hainault, who employed a Flemish sculptor for her tomb in Westminster Abbey; and Edward III's murals in St Stephen's Chapel at Westminster executed in the 1350s point to knowledge of the Avignonese and Italian milieux (plate 9). But the reign of Richard II, though producing an entirely international work like the Wilton Diptych (*c.* 1395) (plate 10), is marked in its physical gestures of patronage – the erection of the nave of Westminster Abbey in thirteenth-century style and the execution of a full-length portrait of Richard in the 1390s of strikingly authoritarian type – by a more deep-rooted conservatism.[13] The most widespread consolidation of older trends was the final development of dynastic or royal mausolea which first emerged in the twelfth century,

---

[12] Sherman (1969); Hedeman (1991); Sherman (1995).   [13] Binski (1995).

and which continued to develop at Saint-Denis, Westminster and eventually Santes-Creus.

The image of an increasingly conservative monarchy reminds us that the fourteenth century is often regarded as being one of crisis, of rapid social change, of rising vernacular cultures and of famine and demographic disaster. For Johan Huizinga, it was the century which inaugurated the 'waning' of medieval culture and which brought about a decisive shift towards the pessimism and morbidity of northern Europe in the fifteenth century. In much thought on the period, the phenomena of crisis and conservatism are of course linked. The most celebrated essay in this vein remains that of Millard Meiss, who proposed that the occurrence of plague in Florence and Siena provoked an artistic and spiritual reaction against the humanism and naturalism of earlier trecento art, best represented by the theological austerity and sense of distance from, rather than proximity to, God, of the work of the Florentine painter Orcagna (e.g. the Strozzi altarpiece in Santa Maria Novella) and his circle (plate 11).[14] The obvious strength of Meiss's proposal was that it commanded a certain intuitive assent in the post-war period in which it was written (1951). The analogy between the holocausts of the 1340s and the 1940s, and the artistic abstraction which followed both was apparent. More recently, Meiss's proposals have been reviewed as excessively monocausal and dependent upon a particular understanding of the chronology of the art with which he was concerned. Certain works once attributed to the post-Black Death period have been shifted back before the plague, indicating continuity and not rupture. Precisely because of the high poetic order of the Italian response to the plague (e.g. Boccaccio's *Decameron*), no evidence has been brought forward for corresponding adjustments in northern European figurative art and literature, despite the universality of the plague. Again, the structure of the art market and its patronage in the 1350s and 1360s remains comparatively neglected, despite the likelihood that profound changes were occurring in the distribution and outlay of wealth, as well as the make-up of the artistic community.

Such changes have commonly been linked to the genesis of the so-called International Gothic Style in western Europe in the period around 1400. A succinct definition of this idiom is rendered possible less by reference to a distinct set of stylistic qualities – though at heart the style was the culmination of that mingling of French and Italian practices which had begun shortly after 1300 in the work of Pucelle and Simone – than to specific works of art of canonical importance. The obvious example is the unusually magnificent Book of Hours partially illuminated by the Limburg brothers for John, duke of

---

[14] Meiss (1951); Huizinga (1955); see however Van Os (1981).

Berry, brother of Charles V, and left incomplete in 1416: the *Très Riches Heures* (plate 12). Erwin Panofsky offered a succinct analysis of the style as a 'scintillating interlude' between late fourteenth-century French painting and that of fifteenth-century Flanders in his seminal study of the art of the period, *Early Netherlandish Painting* (1953).[15] To Panofsky the style had two prevalent characteristics, aside from its hybrid nature. It was, first, a style of display, a demonstration of conspicuous consumption as a means of reasserting an atavistic social hierarchy and control in a period of rapid social mobility. By this account the calendar pictures in the *Très Riches Heures* are a document not of harmonious and fertile social order, of *belle ordonnance*, but rather of managed social difference. Second, through the style's social insecurities may be glimpsed the 'nocturnal aspect' of late medieval culture, that aspect emphasising disillusionment, morbidity and nostalgia in the pathological sense of the word.

Panofsky's account still owes much to the broad but dichotomous vision of nineteenth-century Burckhardtian cultural history, which brought about the reduction of International Gothic (a style associated in Italy with Pisanello and Gentile da Fabriano) to little more than the conservative, retrospective and somewhat meretricious brother of the progressive revolution in Italian painting inaugurated by Masaccio (d. 1428).[16] Meiss observed that the International Gothic Style as first defined in the 1890s (by Louis Courajod) was collective not only in its hybrid form but also, as it were, in that its history was not defined by one country or one personality – precisely the opposite of the play of chauvinism and artistic individualism in the Italian quattrocento in mainstream cultural history. But the remedy offered by Panofsky and Meiss – to stress instead the decisively creative roles of individual northern masters like the Limburgs, the Boucicaut Master and the sculptor Claus Sluter (plate 13), was in turn attacked for transferring to the study of Gothic art the critical and explanatory paradigms of Renaissance art and rhetoric, for viewing it in heroic and excessively aristocratic terms.[17] Finally, the emphasis has shifted decisively away from the morass of difficulties presented by such grand narratives, towards the study of the local, of the regions and the cities; in short, to a more democratic but less glamorous and in many ways less courageous vision.

If significant change is occurring in our understanding of the art of this period – the post-war paradigm of connoisseurship remains for the most part unchallenged – it is to be found in the field of art's signification, and not its style. The study of what Julius von Schlosser called courtly art has continued to underline the period's indebtedness to the romanticisation of feudal culture

[15] Panofsky (1953), pp. 51–74; Baltimore (1962).   [16] Christiansen (1982).
[17] For Sluter, Morand (1991).

inaugurated in the twelfth and thirteenth centuries. The salient features of this culture, its stress on chivalric ideals and heroic subject-matter, had attained their character well before 1400, frequently in the sphere of illustrated texts and not monumental decorations. With the establishment of the secular orders of chivalry, notably the English Order of the Garter (1349), the French Order of the Star (1351) and the Burgundian Order of the Golden Fleece (1431), the process was one of final institutionalisation of chivalric ideals. At this level the period was in a very real sense retrospective and conventional.[18] Almost every important monumental picture cycle of the fourteenth century, whether of the 'Nine Worthies', the Arthurian canon, biblical and classical romances, or the 'Apocalypse' (plate 14), and whether in wall painting or tapestry, had been formulated textually and pictorially in northern Europe before 1350, and commonly (in the case of the Arthurian cycle and Apocalypse) before 1300. From the fourteenth century the quantity of surviving secular decoration increases markedly, and the links with smaller-scale works remain apparent, as for example in the case of the calendar images in the *Très Riches Heures* and the paintings in the Torre dell'Aquila at Trento (1390–1407) which, as under Clement VI, depict secular occupations and aristocratic forms of dalliance or leisure.[19]

RELIGIOUS ART AND SUBJECTIVITY

But if the development of dynastic or seigneurial art in this period is marked by a form of routinisation, the relatively neglected field of religious imagery was proving more dynamic. The thirteenth century, with the birth of the Gothic Style in the figurative arts, had seen the emergence of a new 'naturalistic' pictorial rhetoric, the product of the universalising of earlier devotional practices and a renewed but essentially metaphysical attention to the surface appearance of the represented world. This rhetoric, by which the humanity and intimacy of religious subject-matter was projected afresh to the spectator, was associated with new themes, commonly concerned with the Virgin Mary and the Passion of Christ. The fourteenth century continued to develop this rhetorical and thematic world, but concentrated it into new types of image serving the more introspective devotional climate of contemporary religious sentiment. To decide whether or not such themes were essentially 'popular' or not is unhelpful given that they occur at virtually all levels of patronage in late-medieval art. Especially typical was a progressive change in the relationship between devotional religious art and the spectator, developed in both Gothic and Italian art. The century witnessed the growing popularity, especially in

---

[18] Keen (1984) and above pp. 209–13.   [19] Martindale (1981).

northern Europe but in Italy too, of the *andachtsbild*, the devotional image: subjects such as the 'Veronica', the 'Man of Sorrows' and the 'Pietà' now served to concentrate devotional attention upon non-narrative iconic representations typically concerning the Passion of Christ, suited to contemplative immersion.[20] It may not be coincidental that the century which produced the first small-scale portraits painted on panel, usually in profile (e.g. that of John II of France in the Louvre, of *c.* 1350) (plate 15) also witnessed the burgeoning popularity of small devotional panel paintings of a peculiarly claustrophobic form. Images of this type presuppose a mode of individual attention requiring unmediated, face-to-face religious experience of the Godhead, and in them we may legitimately see a form of attention appropriate to contemporary mysticism.

Such contemplative images, related in use to highly ordered devotional practices among laity and religious alike (especially the *devotio moderna*) and occurring widely in devotional manuscripts such as Books of Hours as well as in panel paintings, possess a penitential and confessional dimension relatively unexplored in earlier centuries. This dimension was itself fully international, because the new devotional art and literature was now typical of most of western Europe. The devotional experiences and exercises of lay people were governed by an increasingly similar regime. In shaping them, the influence of forms of spirituality cultivated by the religious orders, and the widespread impact of the doctrine of Purgatory first formally promulgated at the Council of Lyon in 1274, was considerable.[21] The doctrine of Purgatory was to have widespread implications, both in the fields of commemorative art, where the private funerary chapel or chantry was now developing rapidly, and in the field of images, since the essentially individualistic and subjective character of judgement at death and cleansing thereafter, implicit in the doctrine, were to undermine the formal and collective eschatology of those key moments in the drama of Christian salvation which had so dominated the art of previous centuries, notably the Last Judgement. Devotional art was now implicated in an increasingly sophisticated regime of instrumentality driven by the logic of Purgatorial indulgence.

In the new subjectivism of the fourteenth century lies something more fundamentally modern, for it was here, in the sphere of religious imagining, that new notions of individuality were now being explored. Italian art, fresco painting especially, had offered means – the exploration of pictorial space and the direct engagement of images with the spectator's gaze and emotions – whereby the relationship between art and the spectator could be renegotiated. For the first time in western art, images cater specifically to the consciousness

[20] Ringbom (1965); Belting (1981), pp. 301–2.   [21] Le Goff (1984); Hamburger (1990); Van Os (1994).

of the individual spectator, acting as it were as mirrors of individual salvation. What is commonly described as the morbidity of late-medieval religious and funereal art reflects no more than the sophisticated means – primarily a form of Gothic terror little known in Italy – by which the notion of individual or particular salvation was now given concrete expression. Themes such as the Three Living and the Three Dead, the Dance of Death and, most horrific of all, the *transi* tomb (the effigial representation of the deceased as a decomposed corpse), though often taken as exemplifications of cultural pessimism and anxiety, can be understood as consummate instances of the representation of the spectator to himself, and thus of a new self-consciousness. Coincidentally, in an essay which began with the Avignonese papacy, one of the earliest known *transi* tombs commemorated Cardinal Jean de Lagrange (d. 1402) in Avignon Cathedral (plate 16), a monument at once to *vanitas* and *humilitas*.[22]

[22] Cohen (1973).

CHAPTER 11

ARCHITECTURE

Paul Crossley

THE fourteenth century saw the triumphant expansion of Gothic architecture from a largely French into a wholly European phenomenon. Gothic became the dominant visual language of Christendom, and in the process underwent a transformation of almost everything that it had meant in the first century of its life. Conceived as the theological and liturgical handmaiden of a small and homogeneous circle of European higher clergy, it now emerged, revitalised but fragmented, as the architecture of a socially diverse patronage, much of it lay rather than ecclesiastical. In the hands of kings, princes, the higher nobility, a prosperous bourgeoisie and the 'popular' orders of the friars, Gothic proliferated into new, more secular, genres, promoted in part by the expectations of this new clientèle. If the 'great church' – the basilican cathedral and monastic church – dominated the first one hundred years of Gothic, the chapel, the castle-palace, the city and its public buildings were now, for the first time, recognised as the principal architectural challenges of the later Middle Ages. In turn, these new classes of patron altered the geography of medieval art. The architectural hegemony enjoyed by Paris and northern France in the twelfth and thirteenth centuries came to be disputed by centres of patronage hitherto on the fringes of the Gothic world – Naples, Florence, Cologne, London, Barcelona, Prague and Marienburg – many of them new capitals of lay government. Such shifts in the balance of artistic power had profound consequences for the history of architectural style. The uniform, at times rigid, language of thirteenth-century Gothic, the so-called *Rayonnant* Style, had to be rapidly transformed into a looser, more eclectic and more flexible system, sensitive to an almost infinite variety of local needs and local tastes. From a style limited in distribution but relatively consistent in form, Gothic emerged as an international language of extraordinary formal diversity; as it proliferated to the edges of the Christian world, so it splintered into inventive regional and national dialects.[1]

---

[1] Gross (1948); Frankl (1962); Wilson (1990).

It is no coincidence that the vocabulary of much fourteenth-century architecture – indeed of the language of late Gothic as a whole – found its first articulate manifestation not in a great church but in a chapel: Edward I's St Stephen's in Westminster Palace, begun in 1292 (plate 17). Uniting the new, often far-flung, centres of European government was a shared 'court' culture that elevated the aristocratic values of *largesse*, chivalry and dynastic display into a religion of the secular, and found in the chapel and the castle-palace the most eloquent platforms for its sacral-political ideologies.

Like Clement VI's oratory high up in the Tour des Anges in the Palais des Papes at Avignon (*c.* 1343) – his *capella sua secreta* – the traditionally private character of chapels was easily adapted to the introverted piety of the *devotio moderna*. But fourteenth-century chapels also acquired new quasi-secular resonances, as family mausolea (John, duke of Berry's chapel at Bourges, *c.* 1390), as treasuries for relics (Charles IV's castle chapel at Prague, begun *c.* 1370 to house a fragment of the Crown of Thorns), and, where those relics were royal, as public theatres for the cult of rulership. Louis IX's Sainte-Chapelle in Paris (1242–8), as the shrine of the Crown of Thorns, and the *imprimatur* of the God-given kingship of the Capetians, cast its shadow over most of the chapels of the later Middle Ages. It was copied, with a self-consciously faithful conservatism, by a long line of exclusive fourteenth-century French *capellae regis* (Bourges, Dijon, Riom, Vincennes) and it served as the model for freer variations, from St Stephen's in Westminster to St Mary's in Marienburg. In particular, it provided the archetype for the two greatest royal shrines of the century: Edward III's chapel-choir of Gloucester Cathedral, built from *c.* 1337 as the mausoluem of his 'martyred' father, Edward II (plate 18), and Charles IV's glass-house choir at Aachen Minster, founded in 1355 as the resplendent setting for the body of Charlemagne and the coronation of the German kings.[2]

The dramatic and simultaneous appearance of a series of great castle-palaces in the middle third of the century – Edward III's Windsor (1348), David II's reconstruction of Edinburgh (after 1356), the grand master's palace at Marienburg (begun *c.* 1330) (figure 1), Clement VI's extensions to the Palais des Papes at Avignon (begun in 1342), Charles IV's Karlstein Castle (begun 1348) (figure 2), Casimir the Great's Wawel Castle in Cracow (begun *c.* 1350) and Charles V's revival of the keep (*donjon*) at Vincennes (1361–9) (figure 3) – is the single most telling symptom of the new shift in the balance of power from ecclesiastical to secular architecture. Almost all of them were larger and more lavish than any local contemporary church construction (at £51,000 Windsor amounted to the most expensive building in the history of English medieval architecture), and many took over the functions of the old cathedrals

---

[2] Branner (1965), pp. 56ff; *Die Parler* (1978), 1, pp. 121–39; Wilson (1990), pp. 204–8.

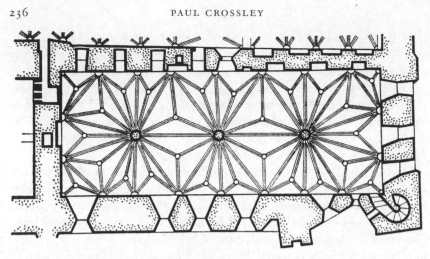

Figure 1   Plan of Chapter House, Marienburg (Malbork), castle of the
Teutonic Knights, *c.* 1330

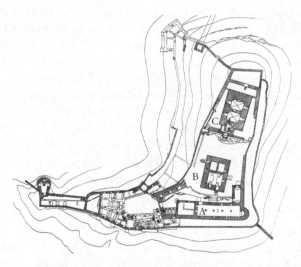

Figure 2   Karlstein (Karlštejn) Castle, begun 1348, complete by 1367
A Imperial Palace
B Church Tower with chapel of St Mary and St Katherine
C High Tower with chapel of Holy Cross

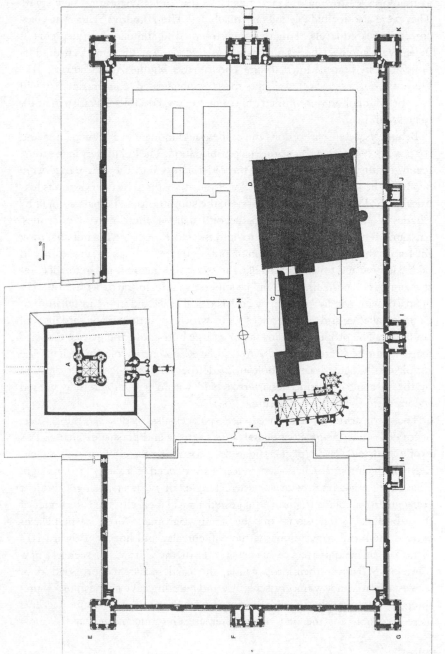

Figure 3   Plan of Vincennes, begun in 1361: A Keep; B Sainte-Chapelle; C, D Previous castle (not surviving)

as training sites for masons, and foyers for the dissemination of new styles. They were also formidable military machines. The Hundred Years War guaranteed increased levels of martial investment, and stimulated refinements in defensive planning. Charles V's revival of the *donjon* at Vincennes ensured its popularity in France down to the end of the Middle Ages. Edward III's Queenborough (1361–5) was the most sophisticated concentric castle in Europe. Marienburg succumbed only once to a medieval siege, Karlstein never (plates 7 and 19).[3]

Behind its defensive cordons the castle could indulge in a growing demand for privacy, comfort and spacious accommodation. The key players in the fourteenth-century transformation of the old fortress into the new palace were probably the kings and dukes of Valois France. Inspired by the notorious luxuries of the Palais des Papes at Avignon, the sumptuous castle-palaces built by Charles V and his brothers in the second half of the century (Vincennes, Saumur, Mehun-sur-Yèvre (plate 30) and the Hôtel de Saint-Pol in Paris) took the lead in the ingenious separation of public and private spaces, in the growth of meditative and private rooms like the *estude* and the oratoire, in the decorative emphasis on the fireplace and its superstructure, in the provision of well-lit spaces with window tracery of ecclesiastical scale and in the installation of delicate galleries and roof terraces from which to contemplate gardens and landscape. The proper maintenance of a large household and guests, that ultimate symbol of late-medieval *largesse*, played a central role in design. The simple quadrangular plan of Bolton Castle (begun 1387) was largely dictated by the vast and diversified quarters it held within it – all carefully stacked according to the rank of the retinue.

These comfortable, introverted castle-palaces also displayed a public face, decorated – like the great cathedrals – to impress and persuade. Charles IV's exotic Karlstein Castle (plate 7, figure 2) – fortress, sacred precinct and sanctuary of the imperial relics – was indeed experienced as a sacred progression. Charles V's Vincennes, with its vast rectangles of walls enclosing a resident court and royal militia (figure 3), suggested a small ideal city, the forerunner of the absolutist pretensions of the High Baroque. Most castle-palaces evoked the more conventional virtues of chivalry and lineage. Edward III's Windsor, the headquarters of his new Order of the Garter, was seen as a new Camelot. Whatever their propaganda, the castle-palace's appropriation of 'ecclesiastical' window tracery, sculpture and painting gave its meanings something of the authority of church imagery. In France these 'church' accents were, probably for the first time, systematically concentrated at the most

---

[3] Platt (1982); Górski (1973); Skibiński (1982); Crossley (1985); Albrecht (1986). For Karlstein, see Gibbs (1989) and Stejskal (1978).

important stations of entrance and audience: at the gatehouse, the staircase and the great hall. Charles V's staircase of the Louvre (1360–*c.* 1370), the masterpiece of his architectural patronage, established the traceried and sculpted stairway as the dominant accent of the main courtyard of French domestic and palace architecture right down to the middle of the sixteenth century. And in the vast audience halls constructed by Philip the Fair in the Palais de la Cité in Paris (*c.* 1300), and by Richard II at Westminster (1394–1401) (plate 20), with their sculpted genealogies of ancient kings and their roofs that count among the greatest masterpieces of timber construction, state ideology was translated into a reality as theatrical and overwhelming as the great imperial throne rooms of antiquity.[4]

The fourteenth century saw the heyday of European municipalities. Independent, wealthy and ambitious, towns mounted an equally creative challenge to the ecclesiastical monopoly of Gothic. The medieval city formed a new genre of architecture: an ordered entity far more complex than the *Gesamtkunstwerk* of the cathedral which it absorbed and, in a sense, replaced. At Cordes, San Gimignano and Nördlingen, some still survive virtually intact. But most come down to us – often in the guise of the Celestial City – only in the backgrounds of panel paintings, their close-packed houses and high steeples girt tightly by a ring of walls. In that single, realistic ideogram the churches dominate, for the city's status depended on their size and number.[5] In central Italy the upkeep and construction of the cathedral had, by 1300, passed from the bishop to the commune.[6] In the north, particularly in highly urbanised Brabant, in the coastal cities of Holland and in the Hanseatic ports of the southern Baltic, a wealthy urban patriciate founded a series of vast brick collegiate and parish churches (e.g. St Mary in Lübeck (plate 21); St Bavo in Haarlem) which rival in scale, if not in decoration, the Franco-Flemish High Gothic cathedral.[7] The commune's most visible symbol of sacred-civic identity was, however, the steeple. In south-west Germany the cities of Reutlingen, Rottweil, Esslingen, Strasbourg and Ulm (figure 4) proclaimed their self-governing status as Free Imperial cities (*Reichstädte*), by colossal single needles (Ulm, if finished, would have been the tallest in the medieval world), pointedly alluding to the old imperial westworks of Romanesque and pre-Romanesque Germany.[8] In Florence the demolition of the numerous private towers of the local aristocracy at the end of the thirteenth century by the new commune (the *primo popolo*) paved the way for Giotto's cathedral campanile (begun in 1334) (plate 24), decorated with the arms of Florence and the *popolo*, and channelling

---

[4] Colvin (1963), pp. 527–33, and Binski (1995), pp. 202–5, for Westminster.   [5] Frugoni (1991).
[6] Braunfels (1953).   [7] Nussbaum (1994), pp. 102–9.
[8] Ibid., pp. 192–204; Braunfels (1981), pp. 138–46.

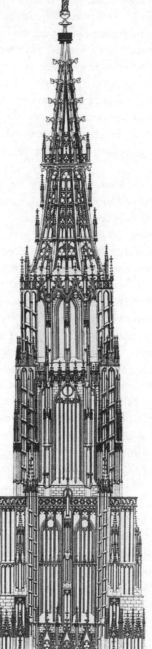

Figure 4   Ulm Minster, Plan A for the west tower by Ulrich von Ensingen, *c.* 1392

into a single central form the city's old identification of towers with political potency.[9]

Within the walls, communal governments found themselves responsible for new types of urban architecture. Guildhalls assumed a new extravagance (Coventry's, begun in 1394, was pretentious enough to model itself on both John of Gaunt's great hall at Kenilworth Castle and Richard II's at Westminster). The market and customs halls of the Catalan-Aragonese trading empire, the so-called *lonja*, were planned to be *molt bella, magnifica y sumptuosa* (as a fifteenth-century source described the *lonja* at Valencia). The great Flemish cloth halls of Bruges (begun *c.* 1239, completed 1482–6) and Ypres (finished 1304) neatly organised their internal spaces according to trade and function, but turned their façades into the most monumental civic accents of the Middle Ages.[10] Above all, the town hall, symbol of the city's sovereignty and, with the cathedral, the main assembly point of town life, assumed a new eminence in the urban hierarchy. In the highly urbanised Netherlands the creative dependency of municipal architecture on church decoration was actually reversed, and the town hall façades at Bruges (*c.* 1377–87) (plate 22) and its fifteenth-century successor in Brussels anticipated and inspired the flamboyant details (and even the whole steeple design) of Brabantine great church architecture in the later fifteenth century.[11] In Italy the greater monumentality of town hall design left it even freer from the constraints of ecclesiastical décor; Florence's town hall, the Palazzo Vecchio (plate 23), combines the severity of a fortress with quotations from church architecture (tracery biforia windows) and domestic building (passageways above the balcony); and in its crenellated walls and its colossal watchtower-like belfry, it acts as the visual microcosm of the whole city.[12]

Nowhere is the control which the commune exercised over the shape and disposition of this new range of urban architecture more spectacularly evident than in the republican cities of central Italy. For the cities of trecento Tuscany, who paraded themselves as Roman in origin or inspiration, building was another branch of government, a public manifestation of a sense of order which translated mere *urbs* (town buildings) into the Aristotelian and Ciceronian ideal of *civitas* (a civic community). In Pisa, Siena and Florence the commune assumed responsibility not just for the enforcement of their detailed building regulations, but also for the provision of new amenities – fountains, loggias, street paving and widening – and, where opportunities presented themselves, for the reshaping of the whole urban structure. Trecento Florence, with an estimated population of 90,000, is an heroic instance of planning on

[9] Trachtenberg (1971).   [10] Nagel (1971) for cloth halls and *lonja*.   [11] Białostocki (1972), p. 345.
[12] Trachtenberg (1971), (1988) and (1989); Rubinstein (1995).

a gigantic scale. The years between 1284 and 1299 saw the layout of an 8½-kilometre-long circuit of walls, of a vast new cathedral and equally impressive Franciscan church (S. Croce), and of the Palazzo Vecchio – all probably by Arnolfo di Cambio. As in most Tuscan cities, Florentine urban planning centred around the bipolar accents of city life, the cathedral and town hall. In the course of the fourteenth century the square around the Palazzo Vecchio gradually assumed its present form, including that ultimate foil to the town hall's closed massiveness, the spacious arcades of the Loggia dei Lanzi (1376– c. 1381) (plate 23). The cathedral square was paved, enlarged and even lowered to enhance the visibility of cathedral and baptistery. And the new Via Calzaiuoli connected the two centres – a street dominated at its halfway point by the third focus of Florentine public life, the church-cum-corn exchange of Orsanmichele (begun 1336), and dramatised at its entrance into the cathedral square by Giotto's campanile (plate 24). This was civic architecture at its most generous and most theatrical; *publicum decus* as the mirror of good government.[13]

Essential components of this urban texture, usually on its poorer edges and built into its walls, were the monasteries of the friars, whose churches added a new stylistic genre to the ecclesiastical architecture of the later Middle Ages. Despite their variety and their (at times) cathedral scale, all friars' churches share an unmistakable simplicity – a lack of transepts, high towers and rich architectural decoration consistent with their espousal of poverty and the heretics' critique of great church building as extravagant hubris. Distinctive too is their often hybrid appearance, suggesting the double character of the mendicant vocation. Their high and luminous single-aisled choirs, recalling the format of *Rayonnant* chapels, proclaimed their status as *ordines studentes*: the favourites of Louis IX, the theologians who shaped and absorbed the intellectual and artistic culture of later thirteenth-century Paris.[14] Indeed, the mendicant 'long choirs' (*Langchöre*) of Germany and central Europe – a form especially favoured by the Habsburgs in Austria and the upper Rhine – seem consciously to recall the Sainte-Chapelle (Königsfelden; the Ludwigschor of the Franciscan church in Vienna, both of the 1320s). But as *ordines mendicantium* the friars built the naves of their churches as preaching halls for an urban proletariat. The contrasts with the choirs (emphasised by screens) could not have been blunter. Frequently unvaulted, divided into open aisles by spacious (often capital-less) arcades, these vast and simple halls resemble barns or – when divided down the middle by a single row of columns – refectories, hospitals, or chapter houses (the Dominican church in Toulouse (plate 25)). To promote semi-profane forms into a new sacred context may help to explain the

---

[13] Braunfels (1952); Larner (1971); Frugoni (1991).   [14] Schenkluhn (1985).

profound influence of mendicant architecture on a thriving genre of later medieval building, the spacious parish and town church; for however 'unmagical' these naves may seem, they sheltered a sacred iconography, either in the form of extensive cycles of wall painting (the visual equivalent of the *exempla* of the friars' sermons), or in the more haphazard clutter of altars, screens, tombs and cult images – small-scale devotional foci articulating the 'neutral' spaces which sheltered them.

For the later Middle Ages, the holy resided as much in innumerable small heavens as in the architecture of the cosmos. Medieval churches were experienced as a spiritually graded progression of discrete spaces, approached through real and symbolic thresholds, and demarcated by arches or niches. To conjure up heaven's 'many mansions' (John 14:2) it was necessary simply to apply to these key barriers and spaces what has been dubbed 'microarchitecture' – toy buildings (usually variants of the niche) decorated with tracery and crowned by arches, miniature steeples or pinnacles.[15] In the fourteenth century these complex canopy structures proved as versatile as they were prolific. They decorated west façades (Strasbourg, Exeter, Rouen) and their small-scale interior equivalents, choirscreens (Lincoln). They were used in miniature for reliquaries (Three Towers Shrine, Aachen) or for their larger variants, the superstructures of tombs (Edward II, Gloucester; Pope John XXII, Avignon). They formed baldachines for miraculous images (Orsanmichele tabernacle, Florence), and not suprisingly monopolised choir furniture – whether stalls (Lincoln) or bishops' thrones (Exeter), high altars (Oberwesel) or altar screens (Neville screen, Durham). Much of the later medieval masons' energies went into the making of these virtuoso confections; and since their forms and geometrical design procedures were identical to full-scale architecture they established a kind of magical kinship between the infinitely large and the infinitessimally small. Practically, they could be treated as testing grounds for novelties which only later were constructed full scale (the earliest pendant fan vaults appear in miniature in a late fourteenth-century tomb canopy at Tewkesbury). Aesthetically, they contributed to a universal order, since their application to all media – to carpentry screens, metalwork shrines, stone niches and the architectural canopies of figures in stained glass – united the whole church in the same language of precise but miraculous geometry. Hence the liberating interchanges between media which opened up the later medieval masons' lodge to a much wider range of decorative effects. The ingenuity of English fourteenth-century carpentry, for example, made its mark on the more eccentric solutions of contemporary church architecture (choir side aisle vaults, St Augustine's Bristol); the transmission of German architectural forms

[15] Boucher (1976).

from Strasbourg to Siena in the second quarter of the fourteenth century has been closely connected to the goldsmith Ugolino di Viero's architectural reliquaries in Orvieto. A century later Filarete was to condemn northern Gothic because it was developed by goldsmiths (*orefici*) and 'carried over to architecture'. His instinct, at least, was right, for in the last resort micro-architecture's symbolic resonances far outweighed its practical and aesthetic advantages. Much of fourteenth-century architecture, from giant spires to reliquary ciboria, is about evoking the sacred by enclosing it in traceried compartments.

The decline in the architectural authority of Paris after 1300 was clearly evident in the European rejection of its most sophisticated product, the *Rayonnant* Style. Since its formulation in the new choir of Saint-Denis (begun 1231), *Rayonnant* had rapidly become the *lingua franca* of great church architecture in Europe. Attenuated, elegant, its thin surfaces dominated by ubiquitous grids of tracery, the style continued to fascinate retrospective French patrons well into the second half of the fourteenth century.[16] But elsewhere in Europe, in the two decades either side of 1300, it found itself seriously challenged. In Italy, Catalonia and parts of southern France it was virtually ignored; in England and Germany it underwent a fundamental and individual transformation.

   Both the vocabulary and the syntax of much Late Gothic building in northern Europe was created in the 1290s in England, whose kings were to have a more decisive impact on their country's church architecture than any monarchy in the later Middle Ages. Despite its general debt to the Sainte-Chapelle, Michael of Canterbury's St Stephen's Chapel in Westminster Palace (begun for Edward I in 1292) subverted the cardinal principles of French *Rayonnant* with a freedom and ingenuity unprecedented in Europe (plate 17). Most obviously, the transformation involved the 'softening' and quickening of French rigidities by the introduction of double-curved, 'ogee' arches into window tracery, by the blurring of bay divisions though a new kind of decorative vault (the lierne), and by breaking the vertical continuity of the *Rayonnant* elevation through a lavishly decorated crenellated cornice, which ran above the main windows of the chapel and emphatically severed vault from vault shaft. But the chapel also posed a challenge to the *Rayonnant* dominance of window tracery by giving pride of place to a new leitmotif: the miniature arched canopy over a niche, a form borrowed from *Rayonnant* portals, but now released from their architectonic framework, and used here as the major component of the interior elevation. Unframed by many grids of *Rayonnant* tracery, these niches, and other elaborate decorative details, took on a singular and idiosyncratic life of their own. Having dissolved all *Rayonnant* rigidities, the way was open to conceive

---

[16] Schürenberg (1934); Branner (1965), pp. 112–37; Freigang (1992).

the chapel as a loose mixture of distinct modes of design: an austere and massive undercroft; an exterior of wiry tracery grids, and a niche-encrusted interior.[17] Michael of Canterbury's method of composition by contrasting modalities was not new, and it was developed independently by a number of continental architects; but it had a profound influence on the buildings of the English 'Decorated Style' (*c.* 1290–1350), many of them directly indebted to St Stephen's and to Edward I's other contemporary enterprises.

The new and exuberant vision of Gothic propounded by Edward's so-called 'Court Style'[18] triggered outbursts of decorative inventiveness through much of early fourteenth-century England, from the flickering curvilinear tracery of Yorkshire and Lincolnshire, to the Muslim-like lierne and net vaults of the West Country, where the *Rayonnant* conception of the vault as a bay-defining canopy is replaced by the idea of a continuous ceiling, embossed and densely patterned (Tewkesbury Abbey and Wells Cathedral choir (figure 5), both 1330s). This new-found freedom entailed not only the prodigious enlargement of a decorative vocabulary, but also the use of Michael of Canterbury's 'modal' composition to distinguish liturgical function or emphasise symbolic meaning. Thus the rebuilt east end of Wells Cathedral (begun in the 1320s) presents a heterogeneous sequence of octagonal lady chapel, low crypt-like retrochoir and a tall chapel-like sanctuary and choir, each evoking their respective liturgical purposes.[19] Over the vast centralised crossing of Ely Cathedral (plate 26), above an extensive sculptural and painted programme celebrating the cult of its Anglo-Saxon patron saint, St Etheldreda, floats a unique wooden vault and lantern (begun 1322), one of the wonders of medieval carpentry, conceived – in sharp contrast to the conventionalities of the adjoining contemporary choir – as a martyrium-like octagon, a Gothic version of the classical *heroa*, literally directing a spectacular *coup de théâtre* on the venerable status of the cathedral priory.[20]

The so-called Perpendicular Style, which began with Edward III's remodelling of the south transept and choir of Gloucester cathedral (1331–67), and which dominated English architecture for the next two hundred years, reinstated the *Rayonnant* notion of tracery as the organising principle of the interior elevation.[21] Gloucester (plate 18), and its great church followers, the naves of Canterbury (1378–1405) and Winchester Cathedrals (begun in 1394), rejected the lavish particularity of Decorated in favour of a comprehensive visual unity based on the principle of extending similar and repetitive panels of tracery over almost all interior surfaces. But the clearest affinities with the *Rayonnant* are found, paradoxically, in Perpendicular's most original creation, the fan vault (the earliest extant example is the east walk of the Gloucester

---

[17] Wilson (1990), pp. 191–6.   [18] Bony (1979).   [19] Wilson (1990), pp. 199–203.
[20] Lindley (1986).   [21] Wilson (1990), pp. 204–23; Harvey (1978).

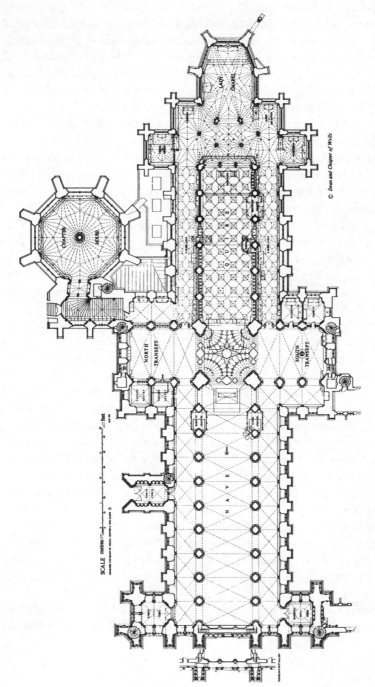
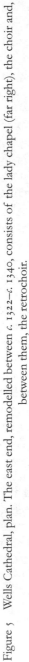

Figure 5 Wells Cathedral, plan. The east end, remodelled between *c.* 1322–*c.* 1340, consists of the lady chapel (far right), the choir and, between them, the retrochoir.

Cathedral cloister of *c.* 1351–64), a form unique to England, whose bifurcating panels of tracery exactly resemble, in plan, half a *Rayonnant* rose window.[22] Perpendicular's simple and reproducible vocabulary was easily adapted to the changing demands of a diversified building market. Like the Decorated, it was in origin and early diffusion a royal, or royal-connected style, and rapidly found favour in the great castle-palaces of Windsor, Westminster (plate 20) and John of Gaunt's Kenilworth. But it was equally effective in giving a new dignity and order to university architecture (New College, Oxford) (plate 28); in creating the restrained splendours of the parish churches of East Anglia and the Cotswolds (structurally modelled on the great London friars' churches); and in providing these 'wool churches', and the crossings of cathedrals, with noble flat-topped towers. As symbols of 'the many-towered city of Sion', they transformed much of late-medieval England into a sacred landscape.

In France, the impoverishments of the Hundred Years War, and the reluctance of its kings to carry out their officially acknowledged duties as patrons of church architecture, ruled out any monarchy-led reform of ecclesiastical *Rayonnant*. It was, significantly, in the 'freer' genre of royal and ducal palaces rather than in a nostalgically retrospective church architecture that we can glimpse the first signs of that transformation of *Rayonnant* into the final phase of French Late Gothic, the *Flamboyant* Style. The flowing tracery that gave the style its name appeared (almost certainly under English inspiration) in Guy de Dammartin's Sainte-Chapelle at John of Berry's castle at Riom, and his fireplace of the same duke's hall at Poitiers, both of the 1390s. The *Flamboyant's* elisions between forms – omitting capitals, and allowing mouldings to interweave, or 'die' into walls or pillars – and its tendency to juxtapose bare wall surfaces with passages of intricate tracery, are variously anticipated in the undercroft of Philip the Fair's *Grand Salle* in the Palais de la Cité (1299–1323), in the ground floor of the *Tour Maubergeon* of the ducal palace in Poitiers (*c.* 1390), and, most dramatically, in Berry's Mehun-sur-Yèvre (begun 1367) (plate 30), where Guy de Dammartin perched an ethereally delicate *Rayonnant* roofscape on a substructure of military austerity.[23]

In church architecture, however, the most adventurous developments of the *Rayonnant* system took place in Germany, where they mingled with a stimulating infusion of local traditions and short-lived but decisive influences from England. German architects took full advantage of a patchwork of wealthy and fiercely competitive patrons: small courts, influential elector-archbishops, semi-autonomous *Reichstädte*, and the increasingly powerful rulers of the more homogeneous eastern territories of Habsburg Austria, Luxemburg Bohemia, and the Prussia of the Teutonic Knights. Together they promoted a stylistic

---

[22] Leedy (1980).   [23] Albrecht (1986) and (1995).

diversity without parallel in northern Europe, a diversity compounded by the sharp division between the brick architecture of the Baltic coast and the north German plain, and the stone-building regions to the south and west.[24]

In the Rhineland, the façade designs for Strasbourg (Plan B, *c.* 1275) (figure 6) and Cologne Cathedrals (Plan F, *c.* 1300) (plate 31), the basis for the present west front) mark the moment of German emancipation from half a century of French tutelage. The French conception of the harmonic west front, where façade and towers are given more or less equal emphasis (Notre-Dame Paris, Laon, Reims) gives way to a sublime vision of steeple-dominated verticality unprecedented in Gothic architecture. The whole vast composition is crystallised into a gigantic screen of tracery, some of it twisted into eccentric and dynamic patterns, much of it miraculously freestanding in front of the core of the façade, like colossal harp-strings. In Cologne, unglazed tracery panels actually dissolve the faces of the spire into filigree openwork. Nothing in contemporary France equals this virtuoso application of *Rayonnant* tracery to a giant version of the German Romanesque westwork; still less did French *Rayonnant* façades anticipate the cumulative power of these myriad tracery motifs – especially the repetitive, cornice-breaking gables – to generate and enhance an overwhelming vertical *élan*. Having subsumed façades into steeples it was inevitable that Germany should revert to its Romanesque formula of replacing façades altogether by single western towers. The tracery-encased western steeple of Freiburg Minster (begun *c.* 1300) became the archetype of the giant single steeples of the later Middle Ages (Ulm, Vienna, Esslingen, Strasbourg, Frankfurt).

Elsewhere, the elaborate traceries of the Rhineland were rapidly absorbed into more 'local' forms, particularly the traditional German hall church, where the high side aisle walls could be dissolved into diaphanous skins of tracery, dominating the exterior as lateral façades (Minden Cathedral, *c.* 1280), and wrapping the spacious interior in tall envelopes of light (Heiligenkruz Cistercian church, finished 1295; Wiesenkirche in Soest, begun 1313). Hall structures, whose interior spaces are defined entirely by pillars and vaults (there are no clerestories), were bound eventually to concentrate their architects' attention on vaulting as much as tracery. Not suprisingly, some of the earliest instances of decorative vaults in Germany appeared in the first third of the century in the context of double-aisled halls: in a group of Cistercian monastic buildings in south-west Germany (Bebenhausen refectory and Maulbronn chapter house), and – clearly under the influence of the palm-like 'umbrella' vaults of English chapter houses – in the Hanseatic north – in the Briefkapelle in Lübeck (*c.* 1320) and the chapter house and refectory of the Teutonic Knights' headquarters at Marienburg Castle in West Prussia (*c.*1320–40) (plate

[24] Nussbaum (1994).

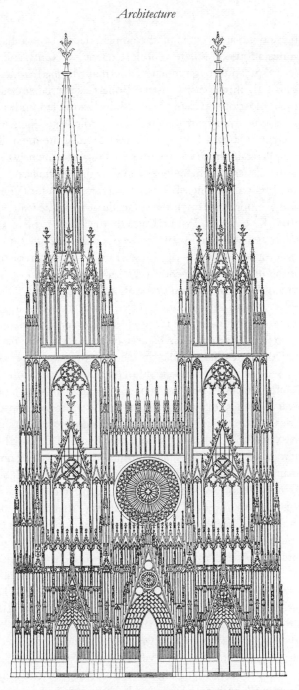

Figure 6   Strasbourg Cathedral, Plan B, 1275–7; redrawing of the original plan
by Dehio-Bezold

19). From these opposite corners of the empire, decorative vaults, one of the clearest manifestations of a Late Gothic tendency to unify and complicate interior space,[25] spread through much of Germany in the second half of the century, particularly in the east (Austria, Bohemia, Silesia, southern Poland) where, by 1400, most of the leading workshops had fallen under the spell of the greatest masonic dynasty of the German Middle Ages, the Parler family.[26]

The partnership between Emperor Charles IV and the most illustrious of the Parler clan, Peter, in the reconstruction of Prague as the new capital of the empire, was the closest Germany ever came to the centralised patronage of contemporary French and English 'Court' architecture. Peter Parler had probably worked as an apprentice on the west façade of Cologne Cathedral, and his completion of the choir of Prague Cathedral (1356–85) (plate 32, figure 7) amounts to a transformation of conventional *Rayonnant* in the same exploratory spirit as Michael of Canterbury's at St Stephen's Chapel. Everywhere the interior of the choir of Cologne Cathedral – the canon of Franco-German *Rayonnant* – is quoted only to be subverted. The geometric tracery is replaced by an idiosyncratic (and very early) curvilinear. The typically French flatness and verticality is undermined by powerful horizontal accents, all conceived in depth: the triforium balustrade, the zig-zagging recessions and projections of the clerestory and the bay-denying tunnel vault encrusted with a net of ribs, the last and perhaps most ingenious of a virtuoso sequence of decorative vaults – triridials, pendant bosses, skeletal ribs – which mark out the most significant liturgical or symbolic areas of the choir and transept.

Whether this bravura assault on *Rayonnant* orthodoxy owed its inspiration to the decorative vaults and set-back clerestories of English Decorated architecture (plate 29), or to more local forms, Prague Cathedral became the fountainhead of much German Late Gothic well into the fifteenth century. The 'baroque' dynamism of its exterior decoration, particularly the tracery- and niche-based vocabulary of its south tower and adjoining transept façade, was enthusiastically developed in the giant steeples of southern Germany – notably St Stephen's in Vienna (properly underway after *c.* 1400), Frankfurt (begun 1415) and Ulrich von Ensingen's prodigious steeples of Ulm (designed in 1392) (figure 4) and Strasbourg (begun 1399). Peter Parler's ingenious decorative vaults triggered a German delight in elaborate rib-patterning which, for sheer inventiveness and complexity, left its English prefigurations far behind. And even before Peter had arrived in Prague, in his (and/or his father Heinrich's?) design for the choir of the Holy Cross church at Schwäbisch Gmünd (begun 1351) (plate 33), he had effectively created the archetype of the numerous hall choirs of fifteenth-century Germany. Using the principle of contrasting 'modal' composition, he combined the bare columns of upper Rhenish mendicant architecture with a smooth exterior ring

[25] Clasen (1958).   [26] *Die Parler* (1978); Stejskal (1978).

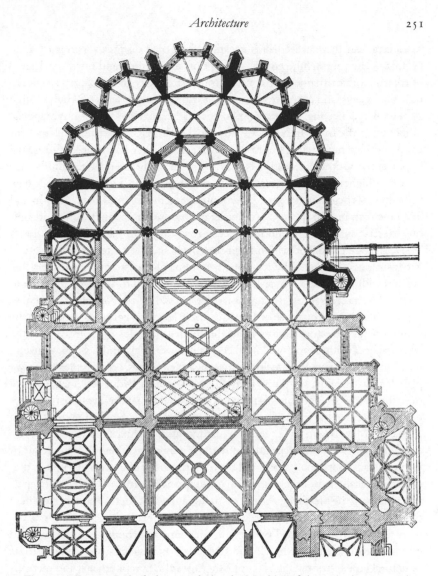

Figure 7   Prague Cathedral, ground plan, by Matthias of Arras (active 1344–52) (black sections) and Peter Parler (active 1356–99) (grey sections)

of chapels modelled on the newly refurbished apse of Notre-Dame in Paris. Neither in decorative detail nor in the composition of interior space did any of the outstanding German architects of the later fourteenth century (Ulrich von Ensingen in Swabia, Hinrich Brunsberg in Brandenburg, Hans von Burghausen in Bavaria) remain untouched by Peter's disruptive novelties.

South of the Alps, the *Rayonnant* system and ornament suffered not so much a transformation as an almost total rejection. In the two areas of the

Mediterranean that succeeded in creating their own distinct versions of Late Gothic in the fourteenth century – Catalonia and central and northern Italy – northern Gothic ornament gave way to mural simplicity and a colossal spaciousness that recalls, and even surpasses, the greatest achievements of High Gothic structural engineering. These simplicities had much to do with the special influence of the friars. In northern Europe their impact was confined largely to town and parish churches, but in the south, where they had been the principal importers of Gothic for nearly a century, they naturally extended their influence over the 'higher' genre of great church architecture. In 1298 Barcelona's new cathedral was begun under the joint encouragement of James II of Aragon and its Franciscan bishop (plate 34). Once again, we are confronted with an ingenious exercise in 'modal' composition, where two systems, a 'mendicant' and a '*Rayonnant*' are combined within an impressively spacious interior whose lateral expansiveness, produced by a stepped, pyramidal cross-section and very tall arcades with prominent side aisles, is certainly indebted to Bourges and Toledo Cathedrals. Its central vessel contains largely 'cathedral' and *Rayonnant* references (the bundle pillars echo those of Limoges and Clermont-Ferrand Cathedrals, the stunted oculi clerestory derives from the inner side aisles of Toledo). But the lateral spaces with simple wall surfaces, cellular chapels and lack of transept, recall a long tradition of Barcelonan mendicant churches, on a simpler *nef unique* plan (Santa Catalina, of the mid-thirteenth century; Pedralbes, 1326). It is a measure of the strength of this mendicant aesthetic that the two most spectacular followers of Barcelona Cathedral – the Barcelonan parish church of Santa Maria del Mar (begun 1324), and the cathedral of Palma de Mallorca (begun 1306) (plate 35) – should reject the cathedral's *Rayonnant* inheritance in favour of its mendicant simplicities. Both rival the dimensions of the largest Gothic cathedrals, and recall the Bourges 'family' in the stepped volumes of their side chapels and aisles and the prodigious height of their vaults. But there is no question here of a servile pastiche. These vast, weightless spaces, with their wafer-thin walls, their impossibly attentuated pillars, and their uncompromising austerity, seem intent on reconstructing the Gothic system all over again – stretching it to its structural limits, stripping it of its prickly *Rayonnant* paraphernalia, and recovering its pristine luminosity and spaciousness.[27]

In trecento Italy the friars cut into a much more fragmented political and artistic culture. We cannot expect the history of Italian Gothic to develop in any clear linear direction when Byzantine, Romanesque, Gothic, classical and even Muslim traditions were variously available to the tyrannical governments of the north, the maritime republics of Genoa and Venice, the republican city-states of Tuscany and Umbria, and the Angevin kings of Apulia and Sicily.[28] One

[27] Lavedan (1935); Durliat (1962).   [28] White (1966); Trachtenberg (1991).

common theme in this mêlée (though the Angevin south will always remain the exception) is the Italian distrust of modernity. Filarete's humanist dismissal of Gothic as *lavori moderni* ('modern work') had its roots in the historicist prejudices of trecento Tuscany, confident of its special position as the guardian of a rich classical and Romanesque inheritance (the two were still inseparable and sometimes confused). For most Italian patrons northern Gothic seemed suspiciously alien and *parvenu*, tolerated only after radical adaptations to local custom. Another common factor in the Italian situation, which springs from its advanced urban culture, was the proliferation and relative poverty of its bishoprics, and the consequent transfer of the upkeep and construction of their cathedrals to civic governments. Particularly in central Italy, the cathedral was revered as the mirror of the city's religious and communal life. This shift in architectural power, almost universal in Italy by the end of the fourteenth century, both extended and restricted the freedoms of the professional architect. As resident city architects, elite *capomaestri* (like Lorenzo Maitani in Orvieto) (plate 37), extended their responsibilities to all urban works, but were also required to conform to stringent building regulations, and in the case of special communal projects, such as cathedrals, to submit their plans regularly to committees of non-expert citizens – painters, goldsmiths, and ordinary laymen – who could solicit rival designs. In this atmosphere of competition and public persuasion the Italians evolved more 'popular' ways of presenting their designs, not by means of the precise projection drawings favoured in the north, but in the immediately understandable forms of architectural models and perspectively drawn parchment plans.[29] Since the architects' skill came to be identified primarily with *disegno* and drawing, it was logical to entrust the design and construction of major buildings to painters (Giotto) (plate 24), sculptors (Arnolfo di Cambio) and goldsmiths (Lando di Pietro). To allow amateurs to direct great churches (unthinkable in the north) is a measure of the enormous prestige enjoyed by the Italian figural arts in the fourteenth century. It also helps to explain the apparent austerity of an architecture often designed as a mere framework for fresco and throws light on the many structural difficulties that beset Italian projects as well as on the obsessive concern for stability revealed in Italian masons' conferences.

Milan Cathedral is the *cause célèbre* of this Italian insecurity (plate 36). Begun in 1386 on a scale designed to rival – even surpass – the largest French cathedrals, it had to import a series of French and German architects to lay a fancy dress of the most modern northern Gothic details over its essentially Lombardic structure.[30] In the process the northerners were confronted with Milanese notions of structural stability sharply opposed to their own, equally unscientific, practices.

[29] Middeldorf-Kosegarten (1984), pp. 147–58.
[30] White (1966), pp. 336–50; Ackermann (1949); Romanini (1973); Welch (1995).

The initiative behind the cathedral's eccentric but sublime north–south compromise came partly from Milan's bourgeois patriciate, eager to emulate the architectural splendours of the German *Reichstädte*, and partly from the duke, Giangaleazzo Visconti, for whom a large *Königskatedral* was calculated to strengthen his claim to the crown of Italy. His premature death in 1402 made that dream as anachronistic as the cathedral which embodied it.

Only in the cities of Tuscany and Umbria was *Rayonnant* properly integrated into Italian tradition, and then principally in those exterior elements of the church most likely to display communal self-importance: towers and façades. The west façade of Orvieto Cathedral (begun in 1310) (plate 37), and its preparatory drawings, show experimental adjustments of traditionally Tuscan elements – polychromatic marble cladding and mosaic decoration – to the linear and geometric disciplines of French *Rayonnant* façade design.[31] The problems inherent in combining such opposites are evident in (?)Giotto's drawing for the campanile of Florence Cathedral (begun in 1334) (plate 24), where a typically Florentine cubic body is incongruously crowned by a pure German *Rayonnant* steeple (never built) modelled directly on that of Freiburg Minster.[32] Tuscan trecento architects continued to employ a licentiously rich *Rayonnant* vocabulary for reliquaries, tabernacles (Orsanmichele in Florence), portals (Talenti's for the nave of Florence Cathedral) and façades, sometimes betraying an intimate knowledge of their (largely German) models (Siena Cathedral, choir and baptistery façade, begun in 1317).[33] But for the main body of the church Romanesque and Early Christian traditions reasserted their authority. The new cathedral begun in 1290 in the papal city of Orvieto was conceived as a loose copy of S. Maria Maggiore in Rome, and the papal banqueting hall in the Lateran (plate 37). The Early Christian pretensions of Florence, praised by Dante as 'the most beautiful and famous daughter of Rome', were given a new authority with the arrival, directly from Rome, of Arnolfo di Cambio, whose Franciscan church of S. Croce (begun in *c.* 1292) rivals the scale of the largest Roman Early Christian basilicas (plate 38). Not suprisingly, Arnolfo's unrealised project for the new nave of the cathedral of Florence (begun in 1294), with wide-spaced octagonal piers and a wooden roof, had a Roman *gravitas* that was closely modelled on the austere spaciousness of S. Croce, and reflected the power of mendicant architecture to shape the highest rank of Italian church building.[34] In the event, Arnolfo's projected nave was superseded by Francesco Talenti's present version (begun in 1357), but without any diminution of mendicant influence, for the design is a congratulatory amalgam of the masterpieces of Florentine church architecture: the piers from Orsanmichele, the balustrade from S. Croce, the square-vaulted bays from the Dominican church of S. Maria Novella.

Arnolfo's project for the eastern parts of the Duomo (figure 8) was nothing

---

[31] Middeldorf-Kosegarten (1984), pp. 148–53.   [32] Trachtenberg (1971).   [33] Klotz (1966).
[34] Toker (1978) and (1983).

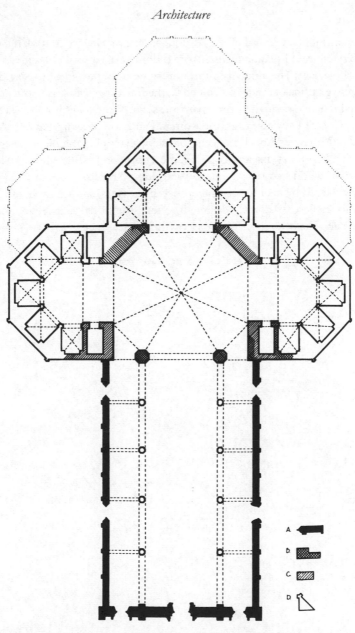

Figure 8   Plan of Florence Cathedral, begun 1294, present nave 1357–78,
walls of octagon 1377–1421
A Rising masonry over foundations still in service today
B Rising masonry over abandoned foundations excavated 1965–80
C Rising masonry reconstructed by probable completion of A and B
D Rising masonry reconstructed as possible extension of A, B and C through
pictorial and documentary evidence (after Toker)

less than a grandiose revival of the Antique Dome of Heaven. It took the form of a colossal trefoil-plan, radiating from a domed octagonal crossing as wide as the whole nave. The immediate stimulus came from the older crossing dome of Florence's principal civic rival, Siena Cathedral, especially since both domes sheltered high altars of their city's patroness, the Virgin, and both evoked the archetype of all Lady churches, the Roman Pantheon, rededicated as S. Maria Rotunda. (Moreover Arnolfo's dome consciously copied the older octagonal Florentine baptistery, itself a copy of the Pantheon.)[35] But whereas Siena's awkward hexagonal crossing remained an oddity, Arnolfo's visionary east end, slightly enlarged by his fourteenth-century successors, and triumphantly real-ised in Brunelleschi's dome, became, in effect, the bridge between Christian antiquity and the centralised churches of the Renaissance.

[35] Middeldorf-Kosegarten (1970).

CHAPTER 12

LITERATURE IN ITALIAN, FRENCH AND ENGLISH: USES AND MUSES OF THE VERNACULAR

Nick Havely

Since the Muses began to walk naked in the sight of men some writers have employed them in high style for moral discourse, while others have enlisted them in the service of love. But you, my book, are the first to make them sing of trials endured in war, for these have never yet been treated in the Italian mother tongue.[1]

THIS is how Boccaccio, at the end of the *Teseida* (later 1330s), describes the subject of his poem. Like Dante before him, he frequently invoked and referred to the Muses, particularly at points of departure and closure. This passage, however, also shows an acute awareness of the uses of the vernacular, the identity of the author and the status of poetry – three of the issues with which this chapter will be concerned.[2]

The *Teseida* passage also alludes to Dante's views on the uses of the vernacular. In the first decade of the century Dante's *De Vulgari Eloquentia* had identified the three subjects for 'illustrious' vernacular writers as: 'prowess in arms, the flames of love, and the direction of the will'.[3] Dante had also anticipated Boccaccio's 'naked Muses' to some extent by referring to his vernacular prose commentary on the poems in his *Convivio* as being like a woman in a state of *natural bellezza* (*Conv.* I, x, 13). Boccaccio's identification of Latin with clothing, however, is interesting as a reflection of the complicated relationship – the *rapprochement*, to use Auerbach's term – between Latin and the vernacular in Italy during the two centuries after Dante.[4]

---

[1] Boccaccio, *Teseida* XII.84 (my trans.).

[2] Although a few references are made here to Spanish and German literature, it has not been possible to do justice to either. For guidance in English to the Spanish literature of the period, see Deyermond (1971) and (on Catalan) Terry (1972) – also Auerbach (1965), pp. 320–4, and Chaytor (1966), pp. 89–90. On Juan Ruiz, see the parallel text of the *Libro de buen amor*; also Zahareas (1965) and Smith (1983). For German likewise, see Garland and Garland (1986), esp. the entries for 'Ackermann aus Böhmen', 'Eckhart', 'Hadamar von Laber', 'Heinrich Frauenlob', 'Heinzelin von Konstanz', 'Konrad von Megenberg', 'Oswald von Wolkenstein', 'Seuse (Heinrich)', 'Tauler (Johannes)' and 'Wittenweiler (Heinrich)'; also Auerbach (1965), pp. 327–32. For concise guidance in German, see Bahr (1987). On Eckhart, in English, Clark (1957) and Borgstädt and McGinn (1986).

[3] Trans. Haller (1973), p. 35 (*DVE* II.ii.8).   [4] Auerbach (1965), p. 318.

LATIN AND THE VERNACULARS

All of the three 'crowns of Florence' (Dante, Petrarch and Boccaccio) wrote in both Latin and the vernacular. But their attitudes to the relationship between these languages were complex and shifting. Dante addressed the issue theoretically (in *DVE* and *Conv.* 1), polemically (in his *Eclogue* to Giovanni del Virgilio) and practically (in the *Commedia*). He also spoke passionately of the vernacular as having 'a share in my begetting', since it was 'what brought my parents together . . . just as the fire prepares the iron for a smith when he is making a knife' (*Conv.* 1, xiii, 4). Yet his attitude to the 'nobility' of the *vulgaris* in relation to Latin led to critical debate in the fourteenth century, as it has in the twentieth.[5] And Boccaccio – whose career reflects even more sharply the complex interactions between Latin and the vernacular – finds himself at the end of that career (in 1373) ruefully admitting the charge that by lecturing on Dante's *Commedia* in the language Dante wrote he was prostituting the Muses.[6] Thus, although (as the imagery of the quoted passages shows) the vernacular was for these two writers quite literally a sexy subject, Latin still remained for both of them a medium to be used and a power to be reckoned with.[7]

The book collections of this period also reflect the increasing interest in vernacular literature along with the continuing prominence of Latin. A survey of fourteenth- and fifteenth-century libraries concludes that 'princely collections revealed a strong leaning towards the vernaculars of which French and Tuscan were the most favoured'.[8] But it is also clear that most collections were still preponderantly Latin in their composition; for example, one of the major fourteenth-century libraries, that of Charles V of France (1364–80), contained a very full range of Latin authors, from those of the classical period (Ovid, Livy) through late antiquity (Augustine, Boethius) and scholasticism (John of Salisbury) to contemporary humanism (Petrarch's *Dialogues*).[9]

Translations, mostly from Latin into the vernacular, however, came to be a significant feature of such collections. The inventories of the library of Charles d'Orléans in 1417 and 1427 list a considerable number of such translations – including several of the most popular items of this period: Boethius's *Consolation of Philosophy* and Bartholomaeus Anglicus's thirteenth-century encyclopaedia, *On the Properties of Things*.[10] The 'translation movement' had been gathering force during the thirteenth century,[11] and it contributed more substantially to the

---

[5] E.g. Grayson (1965), pp. 54–76, and Cremona in Limentani (1965), pp. 138–62. See also Mazzocco (1993).   [6] Sonnet cxxii in *Opere minori in volgare*, ed. Marti, p. 134.

[7] Haller (1973), pp. xxviii–xxxviii, and Grayson (1965), p. 73.

[8] Kibre (1946), pp. 269 and 297.   [9] Ibid., p. 270.

[10] Ibid., pp. 271, 279 and 284–5. On translations of Boethius, see Gibson (1981), Minnis (1987) and Copeland (1991), ch. 5.   [11] Minnis and Scott (1991), p. 374.

development of the vernaculars in France, England, Italy and the Iberian peninsula during the fourteenth.[12]

Translations, of parts of the Bible, for instance, or of saints' lives (e.g. Jacobus de Voragine's *Golden Legend*), also formed a substantial element in the more widely diffused religious literature of this period. The question of whether 'Hooli Wryt schulde not or may not be drawen into Engliche' is clearly a political issue that was to surface again in the debates between Tyndale and More in the sixteenth century, and it is addressed as such in a Lollard tract on Bible translation of around 1407.[13] Yet as the tract in part acknowledges, biblical narrative and (elsewhere in Europe) versions of the Bible had been available well before the English Wyclifite Bible of the 1380s.[14] There were more orthodox religious, such as the Dominicans who provided an Old Testament for John I of France around 1355[15] – or their fictional co-religious and contemporaries who dispensed 'the paternoster in the vernacular, the hymn of St Alexis, the lament of St Bernard . . . and other such nonsenses' to the devout Florentine cloth worker in Boccaccio's *Decameron* (VII, 1). These too, in their various ways, had a vested interest in the vernacular.

Preaching in the vernacular is, as the English translator John of Trevisa asserted, a form of translation.[16] Once again, Trevisa's late fourteenth-century contemporaries, the Lollards, were following in the tradition of the mendicants – particularly the Dominicans.[17] The Dominicans and the Franciscans had been active in this field since their foundation in the early thirteenth century, and since the latter half of that century they had been the main pioneers and producers of the handbooks of material for preachers (the *artes praedicandi*).[18] The prominence of the Dominicans continued during the fourteenth century: the Tuscan vernacular preachers and popularisers Giordano da Rivalto, Domenico Cavalca and Iacopo Passavanti (contemporaries of Dante and Boccaccio) were of this Order – so also were the major exponents of the vernacular sermon in fourteenth-century Germany (Eckehart von Hochheim and Johann Tauler) and Spain (Vincent Ferrer).[19]

---

[12] On translation and the vernacular in France, Kukenheim and Roussel (1963), p. 115; in England, Coleman (1981), pp. 41–2, 184–8, 313–14 and 319–22 (n. 204); Italy, Antonelli *et al.* (1987), pp. 449–50, 463–5; Spain, Deyermond (1971), p. 149, and Terry (1972), pp. 33 and 36. On translation and medieval prose in general, Chaytor (1966), ch. 5, and more recently Copeland (1991).

[13] Bühler (1938), pp. 167–83.   [14] Coleman (1981), p. 186.

[15] Deanesly (1920), p. 20 (with n. 2); on Bible translation see also Fowler (1977).

[16] The best text is in Burrow and Turville-Petre (1992), pp. 213–20.

[17] On 'the social and political significance of Lollardy', see Coleman (1981), pp. 209–31.

[18] Owst (1926), chs. 6–8; Coleman (1981), pp. 172–84; and cf. ch. 3 above, pp. 58–60.

[19] For preaching in Italy, see Rusconi (1981), esp. pp. 114–99, and Lesnick (1989); France, Lecoy de la Marche (1886) and Levy (1981); England, Owst (1926), Wenzel (1986); and Spencer (1993); Germany, Clark (1957), Zeller and Jaspert (1988) and Haug, Jackson and Janota (1983), pp. 76–114; Spain, Deyermond (1971), pp. 140 and 143, and Terry (1972), p. 32.

The Catalan Dominican, Ferrer (1350–1419), has been described as 'a sophisticated theologian who deliberately creates a popular idiom in order to communicate with an uneducated public'.[20] The mendicants were also throughout the century very much involved in the education of that public.[21] Backhanded compliments to such activities are paid by some of the major lay authors of the period – from Dante (attacking the vanity of preachers to the *vulgo* in *Paradiso* XXIX, 85–126) through Boccaccio (in the *Decameron*, esp. VI, 10 and the 'Conclusione dell'autore', as well as parts of the *Corbaccio*) to Chaucer (in the *Summoner's* and *Pardoner's Tales*). Satire from such sources seems itself to acknowledge the strength of the appetites for which the mendicants and their allies catered. One of the chief impulses of the period was the laity's desire for involvement within the Church – hence the increase in lay orders from the late thirteenth century on and the expanding audience for vernacular preaching and devotional writing.[22] It is not surprising, therefore, that Boccaccio in the middle of the century should make so much of the myth of the friar as seducer of the bourgeoisie[23] – particularly when we remember that the inscribed audience of the *Decameron* are urban women and that the author adopts a fraternal and even confessorial role in relation to them. He and other authors of this period (such as Chaucer) may have seen the verbally adept friar as a kind of alter ego, or even as a rival for the attentions of the literate laity.[24]

LITERACY, ORALITY AND AURALITY

The increasing literacy of the laity during this period derived its impetus from other sources as well. For example, the importance of anti-clericalism, from the beginning of the century, as part of the challenge to 'the supremacy of Latin, and the privileges of the *clerici* and *litterati* who upheld it', should not be underestimated.[25] Moreover, as Clanchy points out, during the period with which he deals (1066–1307) the extension of literacy did not mean that the *clerici* were simply able to 'impose their culture on ignorant and passive *laici*. Rather, clerical skills were gradually absorbed, insofar as they were useful.'[26] Practical literacy, the literacy of 'the pragmatic reader . . . who has to read or write in the course of transacting any kind of business', continued to expand during this period – indeed, it has been suggested that its extent during the fourteenth and fifteenth centuries may have been underestimated.[27]

---

[20] Terry (1972), p. 32. Ferrer's sermons have been edited by Sanchis y Sivera (1932–4).
[21] Smalley (1960) and Pratt (1966).
[22] Pullan (1973), p. 62. On devotional literature, see Trinkaus and Oberman (1974).
[23] E.g. in *Decameron*, ed. Branca, III.iv, IV.ii, VII.iii and the *conclusione dell'autore*; see also *Corbaccio*, trans. Cassell, pp. 59–61 and 140 n. 266.   [24] Havely (1983), pp. 264–5.   [25] Clanchy (1979), p. 185.
[26] Ibid., p. 199.   [27] Ibid., p. 265; Parkes (1973), pp. 555 and 564–5.

It was also during this period that the more ambitious lay reader started to come into his and her own. By the end of the century in England, France and Italy it could be said that the conditions for literacy to become 'something more positive for non-churchmen' had indeed begun to be met – for by then 'writing recorded a substantial part of their own heritage in vernacular languages'.[28] Evidence about lay education, book collections, bequests and book production generally confirms this,[29] and a 'literacy of recreation' could be said to have become a significant feature of lay activity (especially if within that category 'devotion' is also included).

The notion of 'the cultivated reader' (Parkes's term) would however be too circumscribed and modern a concept to apply at all widely to the lay literacy of this period – if by it we meant to denote just solitary and silent reading. As Burrow says of the situation of writers, audiences and readers from around 1100–1500, 'the normal thing to do with a written literary text . . . was to perform it . . . Reading was a kind of performance. Even the solitary reader most often read aloud . . . and most reading was not solitary.'[30] And as Clanchy conjectures, by around 1300 'private reading must still have been a luxury, largely confined to retiring ladies and scholars. Books were scarce and it was ordinary good manners to share their contents among a group by reading aloud.'[31] The practice of solitary, silent reading was continuing to extend during the fourteenth century,[32] and Chartier may be justified in his claim that it was more important than the printing press as a means towards new intellectual horizons and 'previously unthinkable audacities'.[33] But the experience of reading, except for a certain elite of the laity, was still substantially oral/aural: writing 'served largely to recycle knowledge back into the oral world'.[34]

Oral performance and communication also continued to be a distinctive feature of the consciousness and procedures of vernacular writers. Thus, late in the fourteenth century, Chaucer's dream-poem, *The House of Fame*, can indeed speak of its narrator as a reader sitting in front of his book, oblivious to the world outside his doors and 'dumb as any stone'. Yet the section of the

---

[28] Clanchy (1979), p. 201.

[29] On education, Graff (1987), esp. pp. 75–106; Orme (1973); and Grendler (1989); also McFarlane (1973), pp. 228–47; Davis (1984), pp. 137–65; and Boyce (1949). On book collections and bequests, Kibre (1946); McFarlane (1973); Clanchy (1979), pp. 125–32; and Coulter (1944). On book production and distribution, Graff (1987), esp. pp. 88–92; Clanchy (1979), ch. 4; Griffiths and Pearsall (1989); and Marichal (1964).   [30] Burrow (1982), p. 47.

[31] Clanchy (1979), p. 198; see also Crosby (1936); Chaytor (1966), pp. 10–19 and 144–7; and Walker (1971), p. 17.

[32] Saenger (1982), pp. 367–414; Burrow (1982), pp. 53–4; and Chartier (1989), p. 125. On public reading in England and France in this period, see Coleman (1996).   [33] Chartier (1989), pp. 125–6.

[34] Ong (1982), p. 119.

poem in which this scene is evoked begins with the traditional oral performer's appeal to his audience:

> Now herkeneth every maner man
> That Englissh understonde kan

and two more verbs denote hearing (*listeth* – i.e. 'listen' – and *here*, 'hear') within the next two lines of this address.[35] Chaucer can also, during a later address to his public (*Canterbury Tales* 1, 3171–86), playfully refer in the same breath to the *private* (and possibly prurient) *reader* of *The Miller's Tale* and to its *public* (and potentially embarrassable) *hearers*. His contemporary, Froissart, whilst constantly asserting the importance of the written word,[36] uses, it seems, verbs that 'designate oral gesture' (*parler*, *oïr*, etc.) for his personal authorial interventions in the text – and the evidence suggests that he 'reserved the verb *écrire* to designate the already redacted text on the sheet in opposition to the present, continuous transformation that constitutes oral composition by dictation'.[37] The process of vernacular writing does not in most cases seem to have been envisaged simply as silent interaction between author and reader – nor as 'peace and quiet', to quote a slightly later (and Latin) writer, *in angulo cum libro*, 'in the corner with a book'.[38]

To recognise these aspects of authorial consciousness as a feature of the interaction between orality and literacy is in no way to deny the importance of such writers' claims to status, name and fame. Froissart, for example, in the latest version of the Prologue to his *Chroniques* exalts the role of the writer,[39] and late in his career he voiced the hope that when he was 'dead and rotten' he would live on in his 'high and noble history'.[40]

AUTHORSHIP

The concept of the *auctor* had already undergone significant changes at the hands of thirteenth-century scholasticism, when scriptural authors had come to be seen as 'divinely inspired yet supremely human beings who possessed their own literary and moral purposes and problems, their sins and their styles'[41] – and St Bonaventure's often-quoted categorisation of writers as 'scribes', 'compilers', 'commentators' or 'authors' gives prominence to the concept of words as personal property (*sua* as opposed to *aliena*).[42] A further

---

[35] *HF*, lines 509–12 and 652–8. All quotations from Chaucer's works are from *The Riverside Chaucer*, ed. Benson *et al.*   [36] For examples, Diller (1982), p. 182 n. 6.

[37] Ibid., p. 151. See also, however, Walker (1971), p. 39.

[38] Thomas à Kempis, quoted in Eco (1983), p. 5.   [39] Boitani (1984), pp. 125–6.

[40] Palmer (1981), p. 1. See also *FC*, XII, p. 2.   [41] Minnis and Scott (1991), p. 197.

[42] Bonaventura, *Opera Omnia*, I, pp. 14–15.

stage in this process is signalled by the development of 'self-commentary' as a means of conferring status upon vernacular writing.[43] Dante provided vernacular prose commentaries for his own poems in the *Vita Nuova* and the *Convivio* (and, if the 'Epistle to Can Grande' is authentic, a Latin introduction to the *Commedia*).[44] Boccaccio wrote extensive *chiose* (glosses) on his *Teseida* which at some points develop into mythographic essays – and Petrarch commented on his own first *Eclogue* in a letter.[45] Later in the century a French commentary accompanies *Les échecs amoureux* (The Chess of Love), a long poem in the tradition of the *Roman de la Rose*[46] – and Chaucer's friend and contemporary John Gower (c. 1330–1408) resorted to Latin for his self-commentary on his major vernacular poem, the *Confessio Amantis*.[47]

Dante's *Commedia* itself rapidly became material for commentary (both Latin and vernacular) during the course of the fourteenth century.[48] He became a model for Boccaccio and a cause for 'anxiety of influence' in Petrarch.[49] By the end of the century his fame had become widespread in Europe. Chaucer refers to him in the *Monk's Tale* (line 2460) as 'the grete poete of Ytaille' and in the *Wife of Bath's Tale* (line 1125) as 'the wise poete of Florence'. Christine de Pisan in her *Livre de la mutacion de fortune* (written between 1400 and 1403) calls him 'le vaillant / Poete', and in her *Chemin de long estude* (1402–3) she pays tribute to 'Dant de Flourence' and his 'moult biau stile'.[50] By 1429 the first complete vernacular translations of the *Commedia* (into Castilian prose and Catalan verse) had appeared in Spain, and by 1417 the poem had twice been translated into Latin.[51] The epitaph that Giovanni del Virgilio composed (in Latin) for Dante in 1321 does not therefore seem to be exaggerating much in saying that 'the glory of the Muses, the most loved vernacular author lies here and his fame strikes from pole to pole'.[52]

---

[43] Minnis and Scott (1991), esp. pp. 375–80 and 382–7; also Minnis (1990), pp. 25–42, and Weiss (1990), pp. 118–29.

[44] For translations of the 'Epistle', Haller (1973), pp. 95–111, and Minnis and Scott (1991), pp. 458–69 (excerpt). Its authenticity is still very much in dispute; see Kelly (1989), Paolazzi (1989) and Hollander (1993). [45] *Familiari*, ed. Rossi and Bosco (1933–42), x, p. 4. [46] Minnis (1990), p. 33 and n. 26.

[47] On Gower's Latin glosses on the *Confessio Amantis*, see Pearsall (1988), pp. 12–26.

[48] Kelly (1989), chs. 3, 4 and 6, and Minnis and Scott (1991), pp. 439–58 (esp. p. 442 and n. 13).

[49] On Boccaccio's view and use of Dante, see Havely (1980), pp. 8–9 with nn. 117–29, and Minnis and Scott (1991), pp. 453–8 and 492–519. For Petrarch's fear of becoming an 'unwilling or unconscious (*vel invitus ac nesciens*) imitator' of Dante, see his *Familiari*, xxi.xv.1 1 (p. 96).

[50] Christine de Pisan, *Le livre de la mutacion de fortune*, II, p. 15, lines 4645–6; and *Le livre du chemin de long estude*, p. 49, lines 1141, 1128–30 and 1136–7.

[51] Friederich (1950), pp. 16–18 (Ferrer's Catalan verse translation of 1429), 27–8 (Villena's Castilian prose version of 1428), 78 (Matteo Ronto's translation ('probably before the end of the fourteenth century') and Giovanni da Serravalle's, of 1416–17). Serravalle's translation appears to have been initiated at the Council of Constance in 1415 (ibid., p. 190).

[52] My trans. of lines 3–4. For the Latin text of the epitaph, see Wicksteed and Gardner (1902), p. 174.

Widespread fame and contemporary recognition were also accorded to some vernacular writers in France and England – even if their work was not translated into Latin or subject, as yet, to the attentions of a thoroughgoing critical industry. Guillaume de Machaut is the dominant figure in French poetry of the period – at the head of a tradition that includes Othon de Granson and Eustache Deschamps and, in the following century, Christine de Pisan, Alain Chartier, Charles d'Orléans and François Villon.[53] After his death in 1377 Machaut was commemorated as 'flower of all flowers, noble poet and famous maker' in two *ballades* by Deschamps,[54] and his work is a major influence on Chaucer's poetry of the 1370s and 1380s, although the English poet does not cite him (unlike Dante) by name.[55] Chaucer's own reputation also appears to have been recognised in his own time, both in his own country (for instance, by his friend Gower)[56] and abroad, in (once again) a *ballade* by Deschamps.[57]

A sense of their own identity is articulated by such writers in a variety of ways. For instance, some recent studies of Machaut see the poet 'self-consciously' forging such an identity 'by conjoining the clerkly narrator figure of Old French . . . hagiography and romance, the first person lyric voice of the *grand chant courtois*, and a new conception of the professional artist'.[58] They also emphasise Machaut's consciousness of writing as 'a specialized, quasi-professional activity', of his 'supervision of the publication of his works and of his concern for their arrangement'.[59] Such supervision and concern is not (for whatever reason) apparent in Chaucer's treatment of his own text – indeed, tidy-minded textual critics have commented on the untidy state in which his papers must have been left.[60]

In Chaucer's case, though, there are other ways in which a sense of poetic identity is mediated. For instance, like his major Italian models – Dante and Boccaccio – he invokes the Muses at certain significant points of new departure in his poetry, from *The House of Fame* to *Troilus and Criseyde*.[61] Such invocations were a well-worn convention in classical and medieval Latin, but they seem in this period to have become, for the status-seeking vernacular poet, an exciting

---

[53] Poirion (1965), pp. 192–3 and 203–5.

[54] Deschamps, *Œuvres complètes*, I, pp. 245–6 and III, pp. 259–60.

[55] Wimsatt (1968); see also Windeatt (1982) and Machaut, *Le judgement*, ed. Wimsatt *et al.*

[56] Gower, *Confessio Amantis*, VIII, p. 2941*. Here, in the 'first recension' of Gower's conclusion to the poem, Venus speaks of Chaucer as 'mi disciple and mi poete'. Gower's own fame abroad was not negligible: his *Confessio* was translated into Portuguese (a version now lost) and then Castilian prose during the first half of the fifteenth century; see Russell (1961) and Moreno (1991).

[57] Deschamps *Œuvres complètes*, II, pp. 138–9. A translation is in Brewer (1978), I, pp. 39–42. Deschamps addresses Chaucer here as 'great translator' (*grand translateur*) and 'noble poet' (*poète hault*) in lines 20 and 31.   [58] Brownlee (1984), p. 3. On poetic identity, see also Miller (1986).

[59] Williams (1969), pp. 434 and 445–6.   [60] E.g. Blake (1985).

[61] *HF*, lines 520–2: *Anelida & Arcite*, lines 15–20; *Troilus* II, 8–10.

means of mobilising imaginative resources and articulating a purpose. Mention of the Muses often has a rhetorical effect similar to that of the author's 'address to the reader' and sometimes even accompanies it – as in canto 11 of Dante's *Paradiso* (1–18), where reference to 'new' and/or 'nine' Muses (*nove Muse*) occurs at the mid point of such an address – and in Book 11 of Chaucer's *Troilus* (1–49), where the invocation of Clio, Muse of history, accompanies an address to lovers, as well as a rich and strange mixture of allusions to Dante and others.

It seems probable that Dante and Chaucer were the first poets in their respective vernaculars to invoke the Muses.[62] Dante follows and develops classical practice by doing this at or near the beginning of each *cantica* of the *Commedia* (*Inf.* 11, *Purg.* 1, and *Par.* 11).[63] Chaucer alludes to Dante's invocations and invocatory language on a number of occasions, from *The House of Fame* to the *Troilus*, and through such 'translations' he effects a powerful response to the *Commedia*'s sense of new beginnings. Several of the Dantean invocations that are reworked in *The House of Fame* and the *Troilus* represent fresh departures,[64] and *The House of Fame* itself, it could be argued, is all about beginnings – including the appeal for Apollo's guidance in the Invocation to its 'lytel laste bok' (1091–1109), which achieves the odd effect of being both Dantean and self-deprecatory in its approach to literary 'craft' and 'art poetical'.

POETS, FABLES AND FICTION

Another sign of the status of the vernacular 'art poetical' is the use in this period of the very words *poeta, poète* and *poet*. In Italian before Dante *poeta* usually referred to classical writers – hence Brunetto Latini in his *Rettorica* alludes to 'the noble *poeta* Lucan' and the Aristotelean notion of *poete* as mediators of praise and blame.[65] Likewise, *poeta* and *poeti* in Dante's *Inferno* and *Purgatorio* nearly always refer to Virgil and Statius – and even in the cantos of *Purgatorio* which explicitly celebrate the traditions of Provençal and Italian verse (*Purg.* xxiv and xxvi) less exalted terms, like *dittator, detti* and *fabbro* are used to describe the activities of the vernacular poet.[66] Only in the *Commedia*'s final use of the word *poeta* does it apply to Dante as a title that he aspires to, when he envisages returning to Florence to receive the laurel crown (*Par.* xxv, 8).

---

[62] *Grande dizionario della lingua italiana*, XI (1981), *s.v. Musa*,[1] senses 1, 3 and 4. For Chaucer, see the *MED*, 'M' (1975) *s.v Muse*, senses a–d. Earliest actual uses of the word in English are probably in Chaucer's *HF* (late 1370s), line 1399, and his translation of Boethius of *c.* 1380 (e.g., I. m. 1.4, pr. 1.78 and pr. 5.72). On Chaucer and the Muses, see Taylor and Bordier (1992).   [63] Curtius (1953), pp. 228–46.

[64] E.g. the re-working of *Inf.* 11, lines 7–9 in *HF*, lines 523–8; of *Par.* 1, lines 1–27 in *HF*, lines 1091–109; and of *Purg.* 1, lines 1–12 in *TC* 11, lines 1–11.   [65] *La Rettorica*, pp. 10 and 65.

[66] *Purg.* xxiv, 59, and xxvi, 112 and 117. All quotations from Dante's *Commedia* are from Scartazzini-Vaindelli (1932).

A similar situation obtains with the use of *poeta* in Dante's other works. In the *Convivio* it usually denotes classical poets, and the *poeta* frequently mentioned in Book II of the *Monarchia* is Virgil. Significant exceptions are, however, to be found in one vernacular work – the *Vita Nuova*, where the emergence of *poeti vulgari* in Provençal and Italian is said to be a relatively recent phenomenon (ch. xxv) – and one Latin treatise – the *De Vulgari Eloquentia*, where the status and precedent of those *poeti vulgares* and 'illustrious teachers who have written poetry [*poetati sunt*] in the vernacular' is the central issue.[67]

The uses of *poète* in French and *poet* in English appear to have undergone a similar process of development later in the century. French authors before Deschamps (in the 1370s) had, like Dante in most of the *Convivio*, *Inferno* and *Purgatorio*, 'used the term only with reference to the classical *auctores*'.[68] Deschamps appears to have been the first to extend the term to a vernacular writer in his two *ballades* commemorating Machaut. In the first of these, where Machaut is given the status of 'Noble poète et faiseur renommé', the earlier term (*faiseur*) is used as a gloss – and, in the second, *poètes* describes a pantheon within which the contemporary author is to be placed – in much the same optative way as Dante had implied in *Paradiso* I, 29. Deschamps's use of *poète* thus 'seems to be deliberate and to involve an intentional expansion of its field of meaning'.[69]

In England too it is not until the late fourteenth century that the word *poet* applies to any vernacular authors, and even then it is reserved for the most illustrious. Langland in the 1360s and 1370s still uses it in the old way, to apply to classical *auctores* (Plato and Aristotle) who were not 'poets' in the modern sense.[70] Chaucer continues to give himself, at the end of the *Troilus* and the *Canterbury Tales*, the modest name of *makere* (equivalent to Dante's *fabbro* and Deschamps's *faiseur*) – and he reserves only for Dante and Petrarch (amongst vernacular authors) the title of *poète*.[71] However, Deschamps (*c.* 1385), Gower (*c.* 1390) and Lydgate (frequently, *c.* 1410 to *c.* 1439) all conferred on Chaucer the title he had withheld from himself.[72] Chaucer, for his part, used the words *poesye* and *poetrie* arguably with a view to his own possible place among the 'illustrious teachers' of whom Dante had spoken. At the end of his *Troilus*, where he enjoins his 'little book' to be subject 'to alle poesye' (V, 1790), he

---

[67] *DVE* I.x.3, xii.2, xv.2 and 6 and xix.2; also II.ii.9, iii.2 and viii.7. See also the *Enciclopedia dantesca*, IV (1973), *s.v. poema, poesia, poeta, poetare, poetica and poetria* (pp. 563ª–571ª).   [68] Brownlee (1984), p. 7.

[69] Ibid., pp. 7–8, and the useful discussion of the term on pp. 220–1 in n. 11. On 'making' and 'poetry' in this period, see also Olson (1979).

[70] Langland, *PP, C-text*, XI, pp. 121 and 306, and XII, pp. 172–4.   [71] *CT*, IV, p. 31, and VII, p. 2460.

[72] Deschamps uses the phrase *poète hault* in the first line of the 'envoy' to his *ballade* (above, n. 57); and for Gower, above, n. 56. For Lydgate's praise of Chaucer as 'cheeff poete' or 'Floure of poetes' in Britain, see Brewer (1978), pp. 46–58.

seems also to be, at least tentatively, envisaging a place for it within the august tradition represented by Virgil, Ovid, Homer, Lucan and Statius, whom he then invokes (1792).

A little later in this conclusion to *Troilus* Chaucer also uses the word *poetrie* in a rather different sense, and in a way that opens up some significant and controversial issues. A passage that scathingly dismisses pagan worship and worldliness ends by seeming to dismiss also the spirit (or perhaps 'style') of the learned pagan writers 'in poetrie' (1854–5). Elsewhere in Chaucer's usage and that of his contemporaries (like Trevisa) *poetrie* gathers a range of associations – from classical myth, fable and fiction to (more discreditably) superstition, deception and error.[73]

The debate about the status of poetry and the value of fable and fiction goes back to Plato's *Republic* and beyond – and the issues involved had been well worked over by the fathers and the schoolmen long before the fourteenth century. For instance, Boethius's Lady Philosophy had vigorously denied her patient the consolations of the poetic Muses[74] – Hugh of St Victor had been generally contemptuous of the 'songs of the poets'[75] – and Aquinas, ranking poetry in relation to other disciplines (a favourite game, it seems, in the commentary tradition) had shown certain distaste for its *defectum veritatis* (lack of truthfulness).[76] On the other hand Augustine had distinguished between lying and fiction with a truthful purpose. John of Salisbury allowed that poetry might be at least 'the cradle of philosophy', whilst in the later thirteenth century Aristotle's *Metaphysics* was being cited as authority for the idea that the earliest poets were also theologians. Some schoolmen, including Aquinas's adversary Siger of Brabant, were prepared to entertain the dangerous possibility that 'the modes of theology were in some sense poetic'.[77]

The debate appears to have intensified during the fourteenth century, particularly in Italy. This was partly the result of the expansion of vernacular literacy and of vernacular authors' attempts to define identity and achieve status. But it also had a considerable amount to do with the advance of Latin humanism. Hence we find enlisted among the fourteenth-century Italian 'defenders of poetry' several humanists whose primary commitment was to Latin (such as Mussato at the beginning of the century and Salutati at the end) – as well as

---

[73] *Poetrie* in Chaucer's *HF*, line 1001, refers to classical myth. The sense of 'myth' or 'fable' seems to be used more sceptically in *The Squire's Tale*, line 206, where 'thise olde poetries' are aligned with 'fantasies' (line 205) and 'olde geestes' (line 211). Trevisa equates *poetrie* with *feyninge* and *mawmetrie* ('idolatry') in his translation of the *Polychronicon*, 11, p. 279 – and it is associated with popular 'errour' in his version of Bartholomaeus (BL, MS Add. 27944, fo. 180a/b, cited in the *MED*).

[74] *De Consolatione* i. pr. 1.   [75] Minnis and Scott (1991), p. 122.

[76] Aquinas, *Scriptum super libros Sententiarum* 1 prol. a.5, ad 3 – quoted in Witt (1977), p. 540 ii. 7.

[77] Minnis and Scott (1991), pp. 209 and n. 39, 122 and n. 29, 210–11 and nn. 43–5.

authors like Petrarch and Boccaccio whose work was in both Latin and the vernacular.

The contribution of several Italian Dominicans to the debate about the status of poetry is a feature of the period that deserves some attention.[78] Amongst these were Giovannino of Mantua who exchanged letters with Mussato on this subject in 1316 and Giovanni Dominici who in 1405 addressed his attack on classical humanism to Salutati.[79] The Dominicans were probably drawn into the debate through their inheritance of Aquinas's brand of Aristotelianism and a concern to defend the supremacy of theology as a discipline. They also, perhaps, had an eye to their own considerable investment in the expansion of lay literacy – an investment which, as we have seen, was noted by one of the most vocal 'defenders of poetry', Boccaccio (in *Decameron* VII, 1).

A crucial text that was often cited in the course of this argument is the passage at the beginning of Boethius's *De Consolatione*, where Lady Philosophy denounces the Muses as *scenicas meretriculas* – 'tragical harlots' (in the seventeenth-century translation). Thus, around 1330, the earliest hostile critic of Dante, the Dominican Guido Vernani, begins his attack (which is primarily against the *Monarchia*) by characterising the poet of the *Commedia* as a deceptively poisonous vessel whose attractive and eloquent exterior was likely to lead studious souls away from the truth by means of 'sweet siren songs' – songs which Vernani explicitly associates with the kind of 'poetic fantasies and fictions' that Boethius's Philosophy had denounced as *scenicas meretriculas.*[80] The Boethian passage was considered important enough for Petrarch to reinterpret it more favourably to poetry in the *Invective contra Medicum*[81] and for Boccaccio to return to it several times. In Book XIV, chapter 20 of his *Genealogie Deorum Gentilium*, Boccaccio is concerned to distinguish at some length between the solitary, contemplative Muse who 'dwells in laurel groves near the Castalian spring' and, on the other hand, the kind of performing *artiste* 'who is seduced by disreputable comic poets to mount the stage, where for a fee she calmly exhibits herself to loungers in low compositions'. He concludes that when Boethius called the Muses 'harlots of the stage' (*scenicas meretriculas* again), he was speaking only of 'theatrical muses'.[82]

This last distinction seems to have mattered so much to Boccaccio that he

---

[78] Curtius (1953), pp. 217–18 and 226–7.

[79] On the exchanges between Giovannino and Mussato, see Dazzi (1964), pp. 110–15 and 191–5. The text of Dominici's treatise is *Lucula Noctis* and the best account of his controversy with Salutati is in Witt (1977).

[80] For the relevant part of the *De Reprobatione Monarchiae* see Matteini (1958), p. 93, lines 7–23. The 'probable' date of composition is between 1327 and 1334 (ibid., p. 33 n. 5).

[81] Petrarch, *Prose*, ed. Martellotti, pp. 658–61.   [82] Translated (irresistibly) by Osgood (1956), pp. 95–6.

reproduced it in his last major work, the vernacular commentary on Dante (1373–4), at a point where he is also engaging in an extensive humanistic defence of poetry.[83] In itself it was nothing particularly new: Mussato had employed it in a letter some time before 1309, where he was concerned generally to make high claims for the 'fictions of poets' whilst condemning their theatrical equivalent (*fictiones scenice*), as, he acknowledges, Augustine had done.[84] The distinction, in Mussato's case, may seem a little odd, coming from the author of a Senecan tragedy (*Ecineris*) but he probably intended his play to be declaimed from a pulpit rather than acted on a stage. There was, it seems, only a certain class of lounger before whom Mussato's Muse would exhibit herself.[85]

The jettisoning of theatre by the humanistic defenders of poetry is an interesting manoeuvre – yet theatre itself (ironically, at this time still substantially religious and moral in its subject-matter) appears to have survived.[86] So also did an interest in performance (however 'disreputable' or 'low'), on the part of some of the period's authors – as is evident, for example, in Boccaccio's own Frate Cipolla (the village Cicero of *Decameron* VI, 10) or Chaucer's Miller, who follows the illustrious Knight with the voice of a villain from the stage.[87]

The capacity of performance and orality to complicate the terms of this elevated literary debate can be demonstrated by the contrasting appearances of Orpheus, the poet *par excellence*, in two texts by these two closely related writers: Book XIV of Boccaccio's *Genealogie* (of the 1360s) and Chaucer's *House of Fame* (of the late 1370s). For when, in the latter poem, Orpheus appears on the façade of the Castle of Fame, he does not do so as the 'earliest of the theologians, prompted by the Divine mind' or one of the 'holy men who have sung divine mysteries in exalted notes', as is the case in Boccaccio's *Genealogie* (XIV, 8 and 16).[88] Instead, Chaucer's Orpheus is, here at least, a performer, heading a line of musicians, minstrels, entertainers and illusionists, and linked to them by the poem's use of the words *craft* and *craftely*, which in this passage cover a wide semantic field from high skill to low cunning.[89] His portrayal could even be an oblique tribute to the English *Orfeo*, and hence to the persistence of romance – another 'low' genre which somehow outlived the disapproval of the humanists.[90]

Such complications may act as a reminder that although the debate about the status of poetry, fiction and performance involved serious issues, it could at times be conducted in a playful way. The Dominican 'enemies of poetry'

---

[83] See Boccaccio, *Esposizioni*, ed. Padoan, I. Litt. III. 108–11 (pp. 42–3).

[84] In *Ep*. VII, to Giovanni da Vigonza, in Dazzi (1964), esp. p. 182 (Italian trans.).   [85] Ibid., pp. 84–5.

[86] Vince (1989) and Simon (1991).   [87] *CT*, I, line 3124.   [88] Osgood (1956), pp. 44–6 and 76.

[89] *HF*, lines 1203, 1213, 1220 and 1267.

[90] Stevens (1973), Ramsay (1983) and Bennett (1986), ch. 5, for romances.

allowed themselves on occasion some flourishes of wit – for instance, when Giovannino of Mantua allegorises the poet's crown (and by implication his adversary Mussato's own laurels) as 'circling around the variety of things and concerning itself solely with them, whilst remaining as far as possible from the truth'.[91] They also on occasion appear genially to subvert their case in the process of presenting it – as Dominici does by quoting classical authors to support his argument for ignoring them, or by playing upon his adversary's name (*Coluccio*) in the title of his otherwise not very brilliant *Lucula Noctis*.[92] Thus Dante's address to his audience, which introduces a very different comic conflict might perhaps also serve to describe the argument about poetry, literature and the uses of the vernacular in the century that followed him:

> O tu che leggi, udirai nuovo ludo
> (Reader, here's a strange new game)[93]

---

[91] Dazzi (1964), p. 113 (my trans.).   [92] The pun is pointed out by Hay and Law (1989), p. 295.
[93] *Inf.* xxii, line 118 (my trans.).

PART II

THE STATES OF THE WEST

ENGLAND: EDWARD II AND EDWARD III

W. Mark Ormrod

THE period of English history between 1307 and 1377 was one of striking and often violent contrasts. The great famines of 1315–22 and the Black Death of 1348–9 brought to an end the demographic and economic expansion of the twelfth and thirteenth centuries and precipitated enormous changes in the structure of society. The advent of long-term warfare with Scotland and France created virtually unprecedented military, administrative and fiscal burdens which brought the English state and its subjects into more regular contact and more frequent political conflict. The increasing complexities of government were reflected in the development of a more refined judicial system and the emergence of parliament as a taxative and legislative assembly. Above all, these changes focused attention on the person of the king and required of him a greater sensitivity, subtlety and flexibility than ever before.

Much of the political agenda of the fourteenth century had been set during the reign of Edward I. In the 1290s Edward had been drawn into war on three fronts: in Wales, where his earlier conquests continued to arouse resentment and rebellion; in Scotland, where his attempts to resolve the succession dispute culminated in a full-scale war; and in France, where his refusal to accept Philip IV's claims to feudal suzerainty over the duchy of Aquitaine produced an inconclusive round of hostilities between 1294 and 1298. The cost of these wars had been immense, and on two occasions the king had been forced to reissue Magna Carta and the Charter of the Forests as a means of placating political opposition to his fiscal and military policies. Even before this, however, Edward had acknowledged the necessity of abandoning some of the more controversial aspects of royal policy. On the eve of the French war in 1294 he had called off the general eyre, a special judicial commission sent out periodically to tour the shires, hearing pleas and making more general enquiries into the state of local administration. The eyre had always been seen as a major threat to provincial rights of self-government, and although it was abandoned principally on administrative grounds, the political implications of the move were obvious enough. If Edward's successors chose to continue his wars, they too would have to offer concessions in return for their subjects' continued moral and material support. Herein lay the greatest political challenge of the fourteenth century.

Edward II was not the man to deal effectively with such a challenge. Although he had the physical presence and athletic qualities that were often seen as attributes of a successful king, his pursuit of personal gratification over and above political stability proved disastrous. Undoubtedly his greatest problem lay in his choice of friends. Having 'favourites' was a common fault of medieval kings, but having homosexual relationships with them was quite another. At the coronation in 1308, the king's closest associate, Piers Gaveston, was actually given formal precedence over the new queen, Isabella of France. Nor did Edward show any real sign of reform after Gaveston's violent death in 1312: by 1317 another group of favourites emerged, led by Hugh Audley, Roger Amory and William Montague; and in the early 1320s the king lavished titles, estates and honours on perhaps the most controversial of all his friends, Hugh Despenser the younger. This obsessive favouritism threatened the political process by restricting access to the court and excluding the king's natural counsellors, the high nobility, from their influence over military, diplomatic and administrative policy. It may be that Edward had an ideological as well as a personal animosity towards his barons: certainly, his interest in the legend of the Holy Oil of St Thomas was a striking foretaste of royalist ideas more usually associated with Richard II.[1] Whatever his motives, however, Edward's personal judgements fundamentally upset the political equilibrium, producing civil war and finally precipitating his fall from power.

Edward III, who succeeded prematurely to his father's throne in 1327, was a very different king. In many ways, indeed, his character and style of monarchy can be seen as conscious reactions to those of his predecessor. Edward fitted perfectly into the contemporary image of kingship. He was a conventional Christian, an enthusiastic supporter of the cult of chivalry and a dutiful patron of the arts. In fact, Edward seems consciously to have used his castles, his court ceremonies and even his clothing as a means of enhancing the mystique and majesty of his office: the new palace that he created at Windsor in the mid-fourteenth century has rightly been called the Versailles of its age.[2] Above all, Edward excelled at the arts of war. During his Scottish campaigns in the 1330s he rapidly discovered that he had a taste and a talent for military leadership, developing skills that he was to exploit to the full during the early stages of the Hundred Years War. Edward's ambitions extended a good deal

---

[1] Phillips (1986), pp. 196–201.   [2] Brown (1963), p. 163.

further than the battlefield, and he may also be credited with a remarkably successful domestic policy that considerably enhanced the authority of the crown.[3] But such ambitions were carefully tailored to accommodate the interests and enthusiasms of the political community and were therefore carried through with a high degree of support. During the middle decades of the fourteenth century, the king's honour became a byword among his subjects and his enemies alike: Edward III was a man who could be trusted.[4]

Of all the themes running through the reigns of Edward II and Edward III, the most significant is probably that of war. Although military campaigns were only sporadic, the Anglo-Scottish and Anglo-French hostilities of this period can be said to have affected almost every aspect of political life. The principal area of activity until the 1330s was Scotland. By 1305, there was every indication that Edward I had carried through a successful conquest of the northern kingdom, and that Scotland would become a mere adjunct of the realm of England. But that expectation was already dashed before Edward's death by the decision of Robert Bruce, earl of Carrick, to lay claim to the Scottish throne and lead an armed uprising against the occupying English forces. Edward I died on his way north to put down this insurrection, leaving to his son the daunting task of countering the Scottish resurgence. The political debate surrounding the patronage of Gaveston and the parlous state of royal finances put a stop to military activity for some years. Consequently, Bruce's forces were able to recover control north of the Forth and make serious inroads into Lothian and the Borders. In the summer of 1314 Edward II marched north with one of the largest English armies ever seen in Scotland, only to suffer a deeply humiliating defeat at Bannockburn on 24 June.

Bruce now posed a major threat to English security. In 1315 his brother, Edward, invaded the north of Ireland and attempted to capitalise on the tensions between Irish chieftains and English administrators in this important outpost of the Plantagenet empire. There was even a plan for a great Celtic confederation drawing support from Wales, Ireland and Scotland. Although this came to nothing, the Scottish raids into the north of England continued to cause considerable hardship. Without adequate military protection, the inhabitants of this region were driven to make private agreements with the enemy: between 1311 and 1327, for example, the people of County Durham paid out between £4,000 and £5,500 in indemnities to Bruce and his supporters.[5] After another disastrous campaign in 1322, the earl of Carlisle, Andrew Harclay, actually defected to the Scottish side. Harclay's subsequent conviction

---

[3] Ormrod (1987b).   [4] See in particular the comments of le Bel, *Chronique*, ii, pp. 65–7.
[5] Scammell (1958), pp. 393, 401.

and execution for treason ironically deprived Edward of the last vestiges of effective leadership in the north. Although he continued to deny the claims of Robert Bruce to the throne of an independent Scotland, the English king was now forced to play for time and concluded a thirteen-year truce in 1323.

The deposition of Edward II and the assumption of power by Queen Isabella in 1327 brought a distinct, though temporary, change in English policy towards Scotland. The truce technically lapsed on the fall of Edward II, and Bruce immediately resumed his cross-border raids. A campaign led by the queen's lover, Roger Mortimer, proved a strategic and financial fiasco and the English were forced to sue for peace. By the treaty of 1328, the government of Edward III recognised both the independence of Scotland and the monarchy of Robert I. The peace was to be secured by the marriage of Robert's heir, David, with the English Princess Joan. Isabella and Mortimer gained some satisfaction from Bruce's promise to pay £20,000 as compensation for the damage inflicted on northern England. Otherwise, the treaty was an unmitigated disaster for the Plantagenet regime, the diplomatic equivalent of the earlier military defeat at Bannockburn.

When Edward III ousted his mother and Mortimer and assumed direct control of the realm in 1330, it was natural to suppose that he would rescind the treaty of 1328 and revert to the policies of his grandfather and father, particularly since the death of Robert Bruce in 1329 had left the Scottish throne occupied by a child. Edward had to tread somewhat warily, for few of the English aristocracy showed any great interest in another northern war. But the determination of a small group of northern barons to recover the land they had once held in the Scottish Lowlands, and the emergence of one of their number, Edward Balliol, as a new pretender to the Scottish throne, allowed the English king the opportunity he had probably been seeking to reopen hostilities. In 1333 the government offices were moved to York in order to co-ordinate the new offensive, and between that year and 1336 the king led no fewer than five separate campaigns into Scotland. Edward agreed to recognise Balliol as king of Scotland, but required him to perform liege homage and to cede eight of the Lowland shires into English hands. To secure the new English regime north of the Tweed, however, required a strong and permanent military presence. From 1336 Edward was increasingly distracted by affairs in France, and after 1337 the remaining English garrisons in the Borders were gradually ousted by the Bruce party. Once more, the war declined into a series of border raids from which neither side derived any great strategic or diplomatic advantage.

This stalemate was broken only by an unexpected event in 1346, when David II was defeated and captured at the battle of Neville's Cross. The English negotiators naturally attempted to use their strong position to secure additional diplomatic concessions, and for a time it seemed that the childless David II was actually prepared to adopt one of Edward III's sons as heir to the Scottish throne.[6] The treaty eventually concluded at Berwick in 1357, however, did little more than set out the terms of David's ransom, and had nothing to say about the deeper issues of English suzerainty over Scotland. Desultory negotiations continued towards a more final peace, and the idea of a Plantagenet succession was still being mooted in the 1360s. But the treaty of Berwick marked the effective end of Edward III's ambitions in Scotland. As so often before, the king's attention had been diverted by the greater issues facing him in France.

The story of the Anglo-French wars follows a very different course, though one that often interconnects with the Anglo-Scottish struggle. In 1307 Edward II succeeded not only to the kingdom of England and the lordship of Ireland but also to the duchy of Aquitaine and the county of Ponthieu. Aquitaine was the last remaining element of the once enormous continental empire controlled by Henry II and his sons, and it therefore had great symbolic and strategic significance. By the Treaty of Paris of 1259, Henry III had been required to renounce his claims to other continental lands and to acknowledge that he owed liege homage to the king of France for Aquitaine itself. Edward I had disliked this idea, but had found no successful alternative to it: the treaty of 1303, which concluded the Anglo-French war of 1294–8, had simply restored the *status quo ante bellum*. Rather more important for the future had been the decision to bind the two dynasties in closer accord by arranging the marriage of the prince of Wales with Princess Isabella, daughter of Philip IV.

When this marriage eventually took place in 1308, Prince Edward had become king of England. Edward took advantage of his wedding trip to Boulogne to pay homage for Aquitaine to his new father-in-law. But the dynastic amity proved superficial and fleeting. The insults suffered by the young Queen Isabella at the hands of Gaveston, coupled with the collapse of the Anglo-French commission set up to resolve territorial disputes on the borders of Aquitaine, produced some sharp exchanges between Paris and Westminster. When Edward II travelled to Amiens in 1320 to be received as duke of Aquitaine by his brother-in-law, Philip V, the French councillors began to raise awkward questions about points of feudal status. Edward impatiently announced to the waiting king that he was prepared to do homage but not to perform the special oath of fealty that would have made him the liege man of the Capetian monarch.[7] Had Edward's position in England and Gascony been more secure, such an aggressive approach might have been successful. But when Charles IV precipitated military conflict by seizing the duchy of

---

[6] Duncan (1988). [7] Pole-Stewart (1926), pp. 414–15.

Aquitaine in 1324, the weaknesses in Edward's position became plain. The insensitive nature of the English administration in Aquitaine had created many underlying tensions, and one of the most powerful of the Gascon lords, Amanieu of Albret, defected to the French side during the ensuing war of Saint-Sardos.[8] For this and other reasons, the fighting proved short-lived, and a form of peace was quickly arranged in the summer of 1325.

At first, the 1325 compromise seemed encouraging. Edward II agreed to hand over Aquitaine to his eldest son, who promptly travelled to France to pay homage to his Capetian uncle. This arrangement helped avoid the humiliating spectacle of a king of England performing obeisance to a king of France. Unfortunately, its permanent application depended on the availability of a Plantagenet heir-apparent. When Edward III succeeded to the throne of England in January 1327, he had no son on whom to devolve his French lands. Consequently, when Charles IV died in 1328, Edward had little choice but to perform homage in person to the new king, Philip VI. In fact, such a submission was probably regarded as a sound diplomatic move. The main preoccupation of the English negotiators in the late 1320s was to restore the boundaries of the duchy of Aquitaine as defined in the Treaty of Paris. The best way to win back the disputed territories, according to received opinion in the 1320s, was to perform homage for them and begin diplomatic proceedings for their formal transfer. It was in this spirit that Edward III finally agreed in 1331 to acknowledge that the oath given in 1329 should be considered as full liege homage.[9] Clearly, there were few people in England in the early 1330s who contemplated, let alone relished, the prospect of a 'Hundred Years War'.

It is now widely accepted that the origins of Edward III's war with Philip VI lay in the failure of diplomatic talks over the contested territories, the growing realisation that they would only be won through force of arms, and the conviction that the future security of Aquitaine could be guaranteed only if it were released from feudal subjection to the French monarchy and declared a sovereign state under the sole control of its king-duke.[10] It is undoubtedly in this context that we can best explain Edward III's decision to lay claim to the throne of France. When the male line of the Capetian dynasty had failed in 1328, Edward's government had formally asserted his right to the throne by descent through his mother, the sister of the deceased Charles IV. But the claim had not been pressed, and nothing more was heard on the subject until the new Valois king, Philip VI, announced his intention to seize the duchy of Aquitaine in 1337. Even then, it took nearly three years before Edward permanently assumed the title of king of France early in 1340. In the intervening

---

[8] Vale (1990), pp. 164–74, 240.   [9] Ibid., p. 50 n. 12.
[10] Jones (1989), pp. 238–43, 245–6, provides a brief summary of the historiography.

period Edward had tried to follow the policies of his grandfather and build up an anti-French confederation of states in Germany and the Low Countries. When he sought to add Flanders to that network, he had to recognise the awkward fact that the county was a vassal state of France. By assuming the French royal title himself, Edward offered the inhabitants a convenient means of avoiding this conflict of interests. At first, then, there was little or no indication that Edward intended to use his new title as anything more than a diplomatic weapon. The Anglo-French conflict of 1337–40 was a territorial, not a dynastic, dispute.

After 1341, however, the position changed dramatically. Edward was able to intervene in the succession dispute in the duchy of Brittany by asserting his French royal title and taking the homage of one of the rival candidates, John de Montfort. The range of his influence within France was thus considerably extended. At the same time, plans were set in hand for the relief of Gascony, which had been left to fend for itself since the French seizure of 1337. Finally, a direct attack on Philip VI was planned as retaliation for a series of hostile French raids on the south coast of England. These various initiatives culminated in the English triumph at Crécy in 1346 and the capture of the town of Calais in 1347. Such victories considerably strengthened Edward's hand and encouraged him to extend the range of his diplomatic demands. By the early 1350s, he was claiming jurisdiction not only over Aquitaine but also over Poitou, Anjou, Maine and Touraine; and in 1356 he took the title of duke of Normandy, dropped by his predecessors since 1259. Some of this diplomatic posturing may have been intended as a personal insult to the Valois royal family, whose members held titles in those regions. But the lands in question were also part of the old Angevin territories that had been lost and renounced under King John and Henry III. Encouraged by his successes and by the need to provide for his fast-growing family of sons, Edward III now seems to have embarked on a project to rebuild the lost continental empire of his ancestors.[11] When John II of France was captured during the Black Prince's great victory at Poitiers in 1356, that dream looked set to become reality.

As in the case of David II of Scotland, however, the negotiations for the release of John II proved rather more difficult than the English had calculated. The weakness of the French state encouraged Edward to press for highly advantageous terms: in 1359 he demanded a huge ransom of nearly £700,000 and complete sovereign control over a great swathe of territory running uninterrupted from Calais to the Pyrenees. When these proposals were refused, Edward launched a further campaign ostensibly for the complete conquest of France. It was only when this also proved unsuccessful that the English were

[11] Le Patourel (1958); Ormrod (1987a).

induced to make a compromise, worked out in the Treaty of Brétigny of 1360. John II was to be released for a ransom of £500,000, while Edward would give up his claim to the French throne and have sovereign control over a much-enlarged duchy of Aquitaine. Interpretations of this agreement vary, but there are strong grounds for thinking that Edward regarded it only as an interim measure.[12] Although he ceased to use the title of king of France, he refused to make a formal statement of renunciation until all the promised lands were delivered into English control. His continued interventions in the affairs of Brittany and Flanders also suggest that he had little intention of honouring all the terms of the treaty. The death of John II and the succession of the more aggressive Charles V in 1364 further increased the likelihood of war. Ironically, however, neither side can have envisaged the dramatic shift of fortunes that was to occur after 1369.

In 1362 Edward III had invested his eldest son with the title of prince of Aquitaine and set him up as the head of an independent administration at Bordeaux. A resident ruler was an unfamiliar phenomenon in south-west France, and the prince's policies were not calculated to endear him to his new subjects. In the late 1360s a number of lords tried to challenge his right to raise taxes by appealing to the *parlement* of Paris. When the prince refused Charles V's summons to attend that tribunal, the Valois regime reasserted its feudal claims over Aquitaine and declared the duchy forfeit. The English state was not slow to take up the challenge, and major military preparations were put in hand from 1369. But the ensuing war proved a disaster for the English. Allies inside and outside France fell away with alarming alacrity, and within a few years the Black Prince's regime was driven out of greater Aquitaine and confined to a narrow coastal strip between Bordeaux and Bayonne. John of Gaunt's French campaign of 1373 brought no strategic advantage and simply ran up further debts for the already exhausted exchequer. In 1375 the English were forced into a temporary truce at Bruges, and the reign of Edward III ended in bitter internal wranglings over the collapse of the war and more general public concern about an imminent French invasion.

The English experience of war in the fourteenth century varied considerably across time and space. Some parts of the country suffered great hardships as a result of enemy depredations. In 1322 a Scottish army penetrated as far as Lancaster and Preston in the west and Beverley in the east, laying waste the countryside as it went. Even the presence of soldiers sent in to defend the region could be a mixed blessing: Easby Abbey in Yorkshire claimed £200 in damages committed by troops billeted there after the victory at Neville's

---

[12] Le Patourel (1960).

Cross.[13] From time to time the south coast was subject to dramatic and destructive French raids: the attack on Southampton late in 1338 left many inhabitants destitute and put a stop to trade in the port for a whole year. However, the naval victory at Sluys in 1340, reinforced by the defeat of a Castilian fleet off Winchelsea in 1350, went a long way to establishing English primacy in the Channel, and despite occasional rumours – some of them deliberately encouraged by the crown – there were few further threats to national security before the 1370s. While Scottish raids were never entirely eliminated, the southern and midland regions of England therefore had no direct knowledge of the hardships of occupation or devastation. The immunity of the most fertile and populous parts of England from foreign attack undoubtedly helps to explain why the crown was able to mobilise its resources so effectively and fight a continental war for so long.

English armies in the fourteenth century were small-scale affairs: even the 32,000 men assembled for the siege of Calais in 1346–7 represented a fraction of 1 per cent of the total population. However, such bald statistics under-rate the true extent of involvement in warfare: not only was there simultaneous campaigning on different fronts, but there were also considerable numbers involved in the shipping and general servicing of armies. In fact, at peak periods it is possible that as many as 10 per cent of all adult males were employed on some form of military service.[14] To raise such forces was a major administrative exercise. From the time of Edward I the state rapidly discovered that traditional military obligations were inadequate for filling up the ranks of royal armies, and a period of sometimes controversial experimentation set in. For most of the first half of the fourteenth century the crown continued to use feudal summonses as a means of providing a proportion of the cavalry forces needed in its Scottish armies.[15] Service in France, however, was a different matter, and by the 1340s the various ranks of the cavalry were being raised through voluntary contracts in which the crown promised to pay daily wages and various other expenses and liabilities incurred during active service. In order to secure infantry forces, the crown initially depended on a system of conscription.[16] In the mid-1320s, indeed, it seemed that the obligation set upon all adult males to arm themselves and defend the locality might be extended so that arrayed troops could fight outside their native regions at the expense of their own communities. This scheme was abandoned after 1327 partly under public pressure brought to bear in parliament and partly because of a change in the methods of warfare which reduced the importance of infantry forces

---

[13] Thompson (1933), pp. 329–32.

[14] Postan (1964), pp. 35–6 (where the estimate is based on the post-plague population).

[15] Prestwich (1984).   [16] Powicke (1962), pp. 118–212.

and increased that of light cavalry and mounted archers. A short-lived attempt in the 1340s to introduce a system for the local provision of such forces also collapsed, and thereafter there was a general agreement that all troops serving on offensive campaigns should be recruited by voluntary contract and paid directly by the crown.

The main consequence of these changes in the organisation of English armies was a huge increase in the financial burden on the state. Edward I's French war of 1294–8 has been calculated to have cost some £750,000. The bill for the war of Saint-Sardos was considerably smaller, at somewhere over £65,000; but during the first stage of the Hundred Years War in 1337–41, Edward III ran up expenditure and debts of at least £800,000, and perhaps as much as £1 million. Although the costs of war declined again in the 1350s, they rose to at least £635,000 in the period 1369–75.[17] It was only in the mid-1320s, when Edward II was enjoying the spoils of victory against his aristocratic opponents, that the crown could afford to pay most of its military expenses out of ordinary income. Otherwise, it depended heavily on the loans offered at first by Italian banking companies and later by groups of English merchants. And to provide security for these loans, it was forced to raise large amounts of extraordinary taxation. The levies on which Edward II and Edward III drew to support their wars fell into three principal categories: compulsory seizures of foodstuffs, wool and other goods; direct taxes negotiated with the laity and clergy; and indirect taxes on overseas trade.

Purveyance had begun as a means of supplying victuals to the royal household but had developed under Edward I into a form of national tax intended to feed – and sometimes also to equip – royal armies. Purveyors were supposed to pay for the goods that they took, but were frequently accused of offering sums well below the market price and of paying not in cash but in credit notes, usually in the form of notched wooden sticks called tallies. Purveyance was a regional rather than a national phenomenon, usually confined to the grain-producing areas of the south and the east midlands. It is for this reason, perhaps, that the occasional rumours of armed uprising reported in official and unofficial sources ultimately proved unfounded: frustration about the inequalities of purveyance could be vented more easily on one's own neighbours than on the state.[18] Nevertheless, there were times – as in the mid-1310s and the late 1330s – when the burden of purveyance, coupled with poor harvests and (in the latter case) an acute shortage of coin, produced widespread and intense economic hardship among the peasantry. Between 1337 and 1347 Edward III also attempted – with varying degrees of success – to make compulsory seizures of

---

[17] Prestwich (1972), p. 175; Fryde (1979), p. 94; Waugh (1991), p. 213; Harriss (1975), pp. 327–40; Sherborne (1977), p. 140.   [18] Maddicott (1987), pp. 299–308, 337–51.

wool in an attempt to provide security for the loans contracted with the merchant community. Complaints about purveyance of victuals and wool became a regular feature of parliamentary business, and in 1351 the Commons were able to secure a major reduction in the quotas of grain, pulses and meat charged on the shire communities to support the new English garrison at Calais.[19] However, it was only in 1362, after the conclusion of peace, that the crown was prepared to compromise its prerogative and restrict the practice of purveyance; until that point, the purveyors were probably the most detested and feared of all the royal agents operating in the village communities of England.

Purveyance is almost impossible to quantify in money terms; the income from direct taxation, by contrast, can be calculated with some precision. Between 1307 and 1377 a remarkable total of £2,070,000 was raised by direct subsidies charged on the laity and clergy, with approximately £1,500,000 of this being collected between the start of Edward III's hostilities with Philip VI in 1337 and the truce of Bruges of 1375.[20] The exact distribution of this burden is not easy to judge. Large numbers of the lower clergy were exempt from ecclesiastical tenths levied on income, and those who were liable to taxation were often treated sympathetically if they had problems meeting their charges. Lay subsidies were assessed not on income but on the value of moveable property, and until 1334 many households – perhaps even a majority – fell below the minimum assessment fixed for liability. In theory, then, the system of direct taxation was not unduly regressive. On the other hand, the sheer frequency of such levies and the corruption of the system by local administrators made it both controversial and economically disruptive. The tax base, which ought to have remained more or less constant, fluctuated wildly; and the overall decline in valuations between the 1290s and the 1330s strongly suggests either real hardship or deliberate deception – or perhaps both. In 1334 the government attempted to arrest this downward trend by abandoning individual assessments of households and negotiating block payments with local communities; the resulting system proved sufficiently popular with parliament that the quotas for this 'fifteenth and tenth' were used regularly for the rest of the fourteenth century and beyond. At the same time, however, the idea of minimum level of liability was dropped and a considerable number of poorer peasant families were apparently drawn into the taxation system. After the Black Death, when the population of England fell dramatically, the proportion of people paying taxes probably rose still further. Under these circumstances, it is not wholly surprising that the experimental poll tax launched in 1377 should

---

[19] Burley (1958), p. 52.
[20] All figures for tax revenues are taken from Ormrod (1990b), pp. 204–7, and Ormrod (1991), pp. 151–75.

have chosen heads of population rather than households as the basis for
taxation. When Edward III lay dying, direct taxation seemed set to become a
universal obligation in English society.

Indirect taxation also developed considerably during this period. In 1307 the
crown had two permanent sources of revenue from overseas trade: the
'ancient custom' on wool exports, first imposed in 1275, and the 'new custom'
of 1303, payable by alien merchants only, and assessed on exports of wool,
imports of wine and imports and exports of cloth and other forms of merchandise. Edward II was forced to drop the new custom between 1311 and
1322, and the revenue from overseas trade, which had averaged £15,500 in the
first five years of his reign, shrank to just £7,000 in the financial year 1315–16.
From 1317, however, the crown began to experiment with forced loans and
extraordinary subsidies on the export of wool. At first, the effects were fairly
modest, and between 1316 and 1336 the profits of indirect taxation averaged
only £13,500 a year. But the situation changed dramatically after the opening
of the Hundred Years War. In 1336 Edward III negotiated an additional levy
of £1 on every sack of wool exported from England. By 1342 the subsidy had
risen to £2 per sack and was successively renewed in a series of interlocking
grants that continued for the rest of Edward's reign and beyond. The result
was a phenomenal increase in revenue: between the start of the Hundred Years
War and the truce of Bruges, the English crown raised nearly £2,275,000 from
the duties on overseas trade, some 50 per cent more than the income from
direct taxation over the same period. It was indeed in the customs houses of
England that Edward III's military fortunes were ultimately shaped.

Not surprisingly, this new emphasis on indirect taxation had major political
and economic consequences. As early as 1297 it had been realised that the cost
of exporting wool was passed back by the merchants to the producers in the
form of lower market prices. When the wool subsidy became a permanent
feature of the tax system, it became a matter of major concern that it should
be negotiated not simply with the merchants but also with the wool growers,
whose natural representative forum was parliament. The native cloth industry
also responded quickly to the new trade conditions, by consuming more and
more raw wool and taking advantage of the much lower duties on the export
of cloth to send an increasingly large number of its products to the markets of
continental Europe. In this sense, indirect taxation affected just as wide a range
of the English population as did direct taxation. And it is certainly no
exaggeration to suggest that the transformation of the tax system in the mid-
fourteenth century was one of the most important and far-reaching innovations in the institutional history of medieval England.

The crown's ability to tap the economic and financial resources of its subjects
depended to a large extent on their co-operation. The fourteenth-century

English state had no standing army or police force; and while it had a large and highly organised staff to run the central administration, it had nothing even approaching a professional bureaucracy in the provinces. Consequently, the king depended on the active or passive consent of the political community. More especially, he depended on the aristocracy. The handful of earls and clutch of great barons who made up the high nobility in 1307 may have lacked the jurisdictional independence enjoyed by their counterparts in continental Europe, but they were still the principal force in English politics. Their importance was forcefully demonstrated after the new king recalled Piers Gaveston from the exile imposed by Edward I and bestowed on his friend the title of earl of Cornwall. On at least two occasions in 1308 the magnates, led by the earl of Lincoln, made formal protestations about the disturbed state of the realm, blaming Gaveston for the open conflicts that were breaking out at court and in the country. More ominous still was the formal distinction they drew between the office and the person of the king:

Homage and the oath of allegiance are more in respect of the crown than in respect of the king's person and are more closely related to the crown than to the king's person . . . When the king will not right a wrong and remove that which is hurtful to the people at large and prejudicial to the crown, and is so adjudged by the people, it behoves that the evil must be removed by constraint, for the king is bound by his oath to govern his people, and his lieges are bound to govern with him and in support of him.[21]

This idea was to be significantly absent from the arguments later put forward in defence of Edward II's deposition.[22] Nevertheless, it says much for the sophistication – and the boldness – of the magnates that they were able to articulate such an important point of political theory at such an early stage in English history.

By 1309 the leadership of the baronial opposition had passed to the king's first cousin, Thomas, earl of Lancaster. Lancaster, who had been much favoured by the otherwise parsimonious Edward I, was the most powerful man in England after the king. He came increasingly to identify himself with Simon de Montfort, the leader of the baronial opposition to Henry III and it was for this reason, perhaps, that he extended the basic demand for the exile of Gaveston into a more general call for political and administrative reform. In the parliament of February 1310, the king agreed to the appointment of twenty-one lords ordainers who were given comprehensive powers to enquire into and reform the government of the realm. Their proposals were officially adopted and promulgated in the autumn of 1311 as the 'New Ordinances'. The

---

[21] *SDECH*, p. 5: 'homagium et sacramentum ligiantiae potius sunt et vehementius ligant ratione coronae quam personae regis . . . quando rex errorem corrigere vel amovere non curat, quod coronae dampnosum et populo nocivum est, judicatum est quod error per asperitatem amoveatur, eo quod per sacramentum praestitum se [obligavit] regere populum, et ligii sui populum protegere secundum legem cum regis auxilio sunt astricti'.   [22] Dunbabin (1988), pp. 496, 501, for further discussion.

Ordinances are in many ways a remarkable testimony to the strong tradition of baronial counsel and the highly technical nature of early fourteenth-century government. They placed some major restrictions on the king, insisting that important business such as the making of war, as well as certain royal prerogatives such as the disposition of patronage and the alteration of the currency, should be undertaken only 'by the common assent of the baronage, and that in parliament'.[23] But the essence of the Ordinances lay in the long, detailed and colourful charges against Gaveston, who was now to be 'completely exiled as well from the kingdom of England, Scotland, Ireland and Wales as from the whole lordship of our lord the king overseas . . . forever [and] without ever returning'.[24] When the king refused to implement this clause, certain of the ordainers took matters into their own hands and had Gaveston executed for treason in the summer of 1312. With their enemy thus removed, most of the earls and barons rapidly lost interest in the implementation of the Ordinances, and for two years the main political debate revolved around the dubious legality of what Edward clearly regarded as Gaveston's murder.

It was only in the aftermath of Bannockburn that Lancaster was able to revive interest in the Ordinances and force the king to accept and implement the various clauses concerning administration and patronage. For some years the government seems to have been reasonably scrupulous in observing the new restrictions, and although Lancaster remained obdurately hostile to the court, a number of other leading figures, including the earls of Pembroke and Hereford, were encouraged back into the royal circle through grants of favour and a natural disposition to remain loyal to the king. In 1318 a compromise was worked out in the so-called Treaty of Leake, which satisfied Lancaster's demands for the continuation of the Ordinances but limited his influence on the council. Whether this arrangement could have provided a lasting settlement remains uncertain, for the king and his cousin were now divided as much on personal as on political issues. Within a few years, another dispute over the patronage of favourites was to provoke not just political friction but outright civil war.

The Despensers were an old family long in royal service, and Hugh Despenser the elder was a courtier for much of Edward II's reign. The family really came to prominence after the death of Gilbert de Clare, earl of Gloucester, at the battle of Bannockburn. The Clare inheritance was divided between the earl's three sisters, the eldest of whom was the wife of Hugh Despenser the younger. In the years that followed, Despenser tried, through a

---

[23] *SDECH*, pp. 12, 13, 16: 'par commun assent de son baronage, et ceo en parlement'.

[24] Ibid., p. 15; 'de tout exilez, auxibien hors du roiaume Dengleterre, Descose, Dirlaunde, et de Gales, come de tote la seignurie nostre seignur le roi auxibien dela la mere . . . a touz jours saunz james retourner'.

mixture of judicial proceedings, harassment and plain brute force, to establish complete control over the Clare estates in the Welsh Marches. By 1320 it was apparent that the king had become infatuated with Despenser, and the threat of another Gaveston loomed. Attempts to banish the elder and younger Hugh failed, and by the end of 1321 Lancaster had emerged at the head of a coalition of Marcher lords prepared to add military force to their political demands. Sieges were set up and skirmishes broke out both in the Marches and in northern England. In March 1322, however, the king defeated Lancaster's army at Boroughbridge. The earl of Hereford died in the battle and Lancaster himself was executed shortly afterwards at Pontefract. There followed an extraordinary spectacle as Edward hounded, imprisoned and executed his enemies, seizing their estates and sharing the considerable spoils of war with the Despensers. Hugh Despenser the younger was now established as the richest magnate in England, with an income of approximately £7,000 a year. Meanwhile, the Statute of York of 1322 finally annulled the Ordinances and restored Edward to the plenitude of power. With his military, political and financial supremacy thus restored, the king was largely free to do as he wished. In the mid-1320s England was apparently moving towards a despotism.

In the end, however, the regime of Edward II and the Despensers was bound to be destroyed by aristocratic opposition. In 1325 Queen Isabella was sent to France as escort to the young Prince Edward. It was probably in France that Isabella began her affair with Roger Mortimer of Wigmore, one of the Marcher rebels who had narrowly escaped death in the aftermath of Boroughbridge. They were joined by a number of lords and bishops, previously loyal to Edward II, but by now alienated from the increasingly threatening Despenser regime. Among these was the king's own half-brother, Edmund, earl of Kent. Encouraged by the support of the king of France and the count of Hainault, Isabella and Mortimer began plotting an invasion of England. When they landed at Orwell in Suffolk in September 1326 they found little or no effective opposition: the rapid defection of figures such as the king's other half-brother, the earl of Norfolk, and Edward's own flight into South Wales, enabled the queen to take over the governance of the realm with hardly a fight. The punishments that followed drew comparisons with Edward's own policies after Boroughbridge. The Despensers and their ally the earl of Arundel were hunted down and killed, and the king himself was imprisoned first at Kenilworth and then at Berkeley Castle, where he died in mysterious circumstances in September 1327.[25]

The abdication of Edward II (as it was formally termed) and the accession

---

[25] For the unlikely story of Edward II's escape to the continent see Cuttino and Lyman (1978); Fryde (1979), pp. 200–6.

of Edward III were officially proclaimed throughout England in January 1327.[26] Most members of political society probably acknowledged that the deposition (for such it was) had been a necessity and were disinclined to question too deeply the constitutional validity of their actions. The succession had been maintained, even if it had been unexpectedly speeded up. Furthermore, the new regime went out of its way to pander to public opinion. Petitions were despatched to the pope requesting the canonisation of the political martyr, Thomas of Lancaster, and the latter's brother, Henry, was restored to his title and estates and appointed head of a regency council for the new boy-king. For a time, such measures helped to disguise the fact that Isabella and Mortimer had ambitions not unlike those of the discredited Despensers. Mortimer's assumption of the title of earl of March in September 1328 provoked much hostility, and precipitated a brief and unsuccessful armed rising led by Henry of Lancaster and the royal uncles of Norfolk and Kent. The arrest and execution of Edmund of Kent early in 1330 made it clear that the minority regime was every bit as arbitrary and threatening as that of the Despensers.

In October 1330, the young Edward III made the first in the series of decisive personal interventions that were to punctuate his active political career. Secretly entering Nottingham Castle by night, he took his mother and her lover by surprise and promptly ordered the arrest and trial of the earl of March. Mortimer was taken off to London, where he was arraigned before the lords in parliament and condemned to death and the forfeiture of all his titles and estates. Edward then set about rebuilding an aristocracy much depleted in numbers and morale. Richard Fitzalan was restored to the earldom of Arundel in 1330, and the lapsed earldoms of Devon and Pembroke were revived in 1335 and 1339. In the parliament of March 1337 the king created his infant son duke of Cornwall and appointed no fewer than six new earls, with the specified intention of replenishing the ranks of the high aristocracy in advance of the impending war with the French. Hopes of a lasting settlement between crown and nobility ran high.

The real success of such measures is difficult to judge. As a young man, Edward III tended to devote most of his time and much of his patronage to a small group of household knights led by the son of one of Edward II's own favourites, William Montague. This group was reasonably acceptable to the existing nobility because it included at least two men drawn from prominent aristocratic families: Henry of Grosmont, son of the earl of Lancaster, and William Bohun, brother of the earl of Hereford. Where Edward failed, ironically, was in his expressed aim of uniting the whole of the baronage in pursuit of foreign war. Aristocratic involvement in the Scottish campaigns of the

---

[26] *SDECH*, p. 38.

1330s was largely confined to those northern magnates who had hopes of regaining lands beyond the northern border. The French war theoretically appealed to a wider group. But the need to provide strong defensive measures in England, coupled with the lack of military action on the continent before 1340, meant that relatively few of the earls and barons were actively involved in the first phase of the Hundred Years War. The resulting breakdown in communications between the domestic administration and the war party on the continent undoubtedly explains the political rupture in the parliament of April 1341, when the earls of Surrey, Arundel and Huntingdon chose to support the leader of the regency council, Archbishop John Stratford, in his appeal against a series of arbitrary charges heaped on him by the increasingly frustrated king. In the negotiations that followed, Edward was forced to concede a statute guaranteeing that the nobility of the realm should be tried only before their peers and that the great officers of the realm should be appointed and dismissed in parliament. Once again, the failure of foreign policy and the growth of baronial opposition had combined to thwart the ambitions of the crown.

It would be a mistake, however, to exaggerate the rift between the king and the magnates in 1341. It had taken Edward II eleven years to defeat his aristocratic opponents and bring down the Ordinances. It took Edward III only six months to effect a working compromise with the aristocracy and secure their consent to the revocation of the statute of 1341. Once the king abandoned the ruinously expensive diplomatic policy of the late 1330s and showed that he was prepared to accept the advice of the magnates on military strategy, personal quarrels and even clashes of principle could easily be forgotten. The upturn in military fortunes during the 1340s removed most misgivings over the wisdom of the French and Scottish wars, and linked the aristocracy's fortunes inextricably with the king's foreign adventures. The widespread adoption of contracts for military service in the 1340s offered the nobility the opportunity for real financial gain by guaranteeing them wages and offering them a share in the ransoms and plunder that were such an important feature of medieval warfare. Above all, the king's wars offered the magnates a chance to demonstrate their duty to the realm and their loyalty to the throne by pursuing the natural activity of their class, the profession of arms. In 1348 the king institutionalised the martial ethos of his court by founding the Order of the Garter, one of the earliest monarchical orders of chivalry. In 1352 he offered another very powerful signal of reconciliation in the Statute of Treasons, which defined and limited the charges of high and petty treason and guaranteed that the nobility would not be subject to the dubious charges and summary justice suffered by so many of their number during the 1320s. Thus was the English aristocracy united in enthusiastic and energetic support of the crown.

The happy conditions of the mid-fourteenth century did not, and probably could not, last for ever. By the time the French war resumed in 1369, many of Edward III's closest friends and ablest commanders were dead, and the new group of aristocratic generals that emerged in the 1370s lacked the powerful *esprit de corps* that had characterised their fathers' generation. From the later 1350s the range of royal patronage had also declined, as Edward had become more and more preoccupied with the needs of his own sons.[27] Unfortunately, the attempt to use the royal family as a kind of court party collapsed with the deaths of Princes Lionel and Edward in 1368 and 1376 and the emergence of the unpopular John of Gaunt as the king's principal spokesman. The real centre of politics in the mid-1370s lay not in baronial great councils but in a narrow clique of courtiers led by the steward, Lord Neville, the chamberlain, Lord Latimer, and the king's mistress, Alice Perrers. They controlled access to the elderly king, and were suspected of dubious financial dealings as well as the more usual offence of manipulating royal patronage. Although they benefited far less from their position than had Gaveston, the Despensers or even William Montague, they proved convenient targets for the increasingly disaffected political community, and in the Good Parliament of 1376 they, along with a number of their contacts from the world of commerce, were impeached, dismissed from office and banished from the household.

For the high aristocracy, the reign of Edward III therefore ended in uncertainty and disillusionment. The Good Parliament exposed rifts even within the royal family, as the Princes Edmund and Thomas deserted their brother John of Gaunt and sided with the opposition. Nevertheless, the picture of disunity can be too sharply drawn. The aristocratic groupings of the 1370s were still a great deal more fluid than they had been at almost any time in Edward III's reign, and the baronage was to show much greater cohesion in the regency administration of Richard II than it had during the minority of Edward III. The most striking fact of all is the complete absence of armed rebellion against the crown between 1330 and 1377. Edward II had lived almost permanently under the threat of military opposition, and within little more than a decade of Edward III's death the magnates would again be in active revolt against the monarchy of Richard II. The intervening years marked probably the longest period of political harmony between crown and aristocracy in the whole of the Middle Ages, an achievement that surely deserves to rank high among Edward III's many political accomplishments.

The aristocracy may have been the main influence on the fortunes of the English crown in the fourteenth century, but they were by no means the only

[27] Ormrod (1987a), pp. 408–16.

group to participate in the political process. Indeed, the reigns of Edward II and Edward III were marked by a distinct broadening of the political community, best illustrated by the development of parliament. Meetings called parliaments had been regular events since the time of Henry III. They were attended by the king, the principal officers of state and a group of secular and ecclesiastical tenants-in-chief, and were intended for the discussion of important matters of policy or controversial judicial cases. From the 1290s, however, the composition of parliaments had changed, as the king more and more frequently summoned elected representatives of the shires and the towns to attend such assemblies. The intention, made specific in Edward I's famous summonses of 1295, was to have every one of the king's subjects symbolically present in parliament; by this means, matters of general import could be publicised and discussed and the decisions reached could be considered binding on the whole realm.[28] In reality, the principal function of the so-called knights of the shires and burgesses was to judge the king's request for money and to sanction direct taxes. But they were also empowered to bring written requests from their constituents and to use parliament as a great clearing-house for judicial and administrative business. From these two functions were to spring most of the political influence of later medieval parliaments.

In 1307 the English parliament had yet to harden into an established institution. Under Edward II there were still numerous assemblies called parliaments which were little more than baronial councils. Even when representatives were summoned, parliament was a very different sort of assembly from its later, more developed, form. The anonymous *Modus Tenendi Parliamentum* of *c.* 1321–2 identified six 'grades' within parliament: the king, the spiritual peers, the proctors or the lower clergy, the secular peers, the knights of the shires and the representatives of towns.[29] The distinction between the last two grades is particularly significant: although Edward III summoned knights and burgesses to every parliament held after 1327, it was not until the later 1330s that the official records began to refer to them as a single group called the Commons. At about the same time the clergy largely abandoned parliament, preferring to meet in their own convocations. Those few bishops and abbots who continued to attend parliament in person were now linked more closely with the earls and barons as one estate referred to as the *grantz* or great men.[30] By the start of the Hundred Years War parliament can definitely be said to have emerged as a bicameral assembly.

It was the theory and practice of taxation that undoubtedly moulded parliament into this final and enduring form. In 1339, for the first time, the Lords

---

[28] Stubbs, *Select Charters*, pp. 480–1.   [29] Pronay and Taylor, *Parliamentary Texts*, pp. 78–9, 91.
[30] Brown (1989), pp. 209–11.

and Commons made different responses to the king's request for an especially
heavy subsidy: while the peers offered a tenth of the agricultural produce of
their estates, the knights and burgesses insisted that they should be allowed to
refer the demand back to their constituents before a decision was taken.[31] Out
of this arose a clear demonstration that the baronage could vote taxes only on
its own members: the Commons alone had the power to grant taxes binding
on the whole realm. Furthermore, in April 1340 the Commons for the first
time authorised a levy of the wool subsidy, thus taking over from earlier merchant assemblies control of the tax that would become the single most important element in the fiscal machinery of the state. It took some time before the
Commons established exclusive control over indirect taxation, but in 1362 they
finally won a statutory guarantee that all such levies would be discussed and
authorised solely in parliament. By the end of Edward III's reign, the king's
parliament, and more specifically the Commons in parliament, had become the
only body with recognised power to impose direct and indirect taxation on the
generality of the king's subjects.

The other principal function of the Commons in early parliaments – that of
communicating petitions from their constituents – was also subject to important changes and developments during the reigns of Edward II and Edward
III. By 1307 the officials of central government were keenly aware that the
mass of private business brought to parliament was threatening to submerge
them and to hold up business of more general import. Consequently, attempts
were made to divert private petitions away from parliament and have them
dealt with by the chancery and the law courts. Far from putting a stop to the
petitioning process, however, this rationalisation actually allowed more attention to be given to those requests labelled by the clerks of parliament as
'common petitions'. The earliest such documents were simply requests from
private individuals or local communities which happened to raise more general
issues and which were therefore deemed worthy of discussion before the king
and council in parliament. Until the 1320s, the knights and burgesses had little
active or creative role to play in the selection of common petitions. Indeed, it
was the barons who continued to speak for the community of the realm,
drawing up lists of general grievances such as those presented in the parliaments of Stamford in 1309 and Westminster in 1310.[32] The vital change seems
to have occurred in the 1320s, when the knights and burgesses took over this
responsibility and began to frame requests which were recognised in themselves as common petitions. The change is probably to be explained by the collapse of baronial opposition after the battle of Boroughbridge and the
reluctance of any remaining Lancastrian sympathisers to declare their hostility

---

[31] Harriss (1975), p. 255.   [32] Tuck (1985), pp. 57–9, 63; but cf. Harriss (1975), p. 120.

to the Despenser regime. That such timidity did not apparently extend to the knights and burgesses is a remarkable testimony to their political and social independence: indeed, some of the harshest criticisms in the extant common petitions of 1324–5 were reserved not for the crown but for the aristocracy.[33]

The Commons' success in persuading the crown to accept their criticisms depended to a large degree on their willingness to grant taxes: the king was much more likely to be generous with political concessions if parliament offered him financial assistance. The notable failure of most of the extant common petitions of 1324–5 can be explained not just by the insensitivity of the Despenser regime but also by the fact that Edward II's pleas for money were twice rejected in parliament during these years.[34] Under Edward III, the Commons were a good deal more forthcoming: indeed, it was not until 1376 that requests for direct taxation were again turned down. The Commons were notably reluctant to make a formal link between taxation and redress of grievances. As early as 1309, however, parliament had warned the king that his tax collectors would face active resistance in the shires unless he heard the complaints of his subjects. In reality, then, the discussions of taxation and the framing and audience of common petitions were often closely linked.[35] From 1327, and more particularly after 1340, came another important change in the way the crown communicated its responses to common petitions. The requests accepted by the crown and the remedies proposed by the council were now formally embodied in statutes and proclaimed in the shires as part of the law of the land. Out of their taxative authority and their new role as spokesmen of the wider political community, the knights and burgesses had therefore won a role in the making of legislation.

The Commons' control over the legislative process should not be exaggerated. It was the members of the king's council, not the knights and burgesses, who still composed the statutes and made provision for their implementation. Moreover, statute law, though theoretically binding, was often ignored and sometimes openly flouted by the crown. In the coronation of 1308, Edward II had been required to swear a new oath that he would 'hold and preserve the righteous laws and customs which the community of the realm shall have chosen'.[36] In practice, however, the king remained free to judge between good and bad laws and to annul those which he held to be contrary to the common law of the land or injurious to the royal prerogative. It was on these grounds that Edward II cancelled the Ordinances in 1322 and Edward III rescinded the statute of 1341. The legislative process therefore remained under the general supervision of the crown. On sensitive issues involving the limitation of royal

---

[33] Ormrod (1990a), pp. 19–20.   [34] Buck (1983), pp. 252–4.

[35] Harriss (1975), pp. 98–127, provides a full discussion.

[36] *SDECH*, pp. 4–5: 'tenir et garder les leys et les custumes droitureles les quiels la communaute de vostre roiaume aura esleu'.

prerogatives, indeed, the crown was particularly careful to stress its freedom of action. The Statute of Purveyors of 1362 was offered by the king 'of his own will, without motion of the great men or commons'.[37] Justifications of this kind, however, tell their own story: in reality, we know that the parliament of 1362 saw some hard bargaining over the proposed extension of the wool subsidy and some vociferous complaints about the practices of royal purveyors.[38] Procedural niceties remained, but the reality of politics had moved on.

The ability of parliament to influence the policies of the crown is perhaps best demonstrated by the changes effected in the administration of justice. The abandonment of the eyre after 1294 had created a large gap in the judicial system only partly filled by the erratic series of extraordinary commissions, nicknamed 'trailbastons', launched by Edward I in 1304–5. The result, according to many, was a serious breakdown in public order. Far from rising to the challenge, the crown and the aristocracy were believed to be taking personal advantage of the situation. In 1317 Sir Gilbert Middleton, a prominent Northumberland knight, was able to raise a force of over 900 northerners, including several members of landed society, in armed rebellion against the crown.[39] In the mid-1320s the Despensers appear to have masterminded a campaign of corruption, intimidation and legalised robbery that left many of their victims in helpless despair. Even after Edward III's impassioned appeal to the magnates in 1331 to behave with greater integrity, the king continued to harbour a number of notorious law breakers, such as Sir John Moleyns and Sir Thomas Breadstone, in his own household. The disruptive activities of criminal gangs also spread from the north into the midlands, where the Folville and Coterel families rampaged unchecked for most of the 1330s.

Under these circumstances, it is not surprising that the parliamentary Commons became increasingly critical of the structure and operation of royal justice. Crown and Commons broadly agreed that the obvious remedy lay in the establishment of a more permanent judicial presence in the localities. The obvious candidates for such a job were the keepers of the peace, members of the minor landed classes who, since the later thirteenth century, had been responsible for receiving indictments and holding suspected criminals until the king's justices arrived in the shire to judge the cases and make convictions. The first extant demand for the promotion of the keepers of the peace into justices dates from 1327, and it became a regular feature of the Commons' political programme by the 1340s.[40] But it was only the challenge raised by the Black Death that finally persuaded the government of the wisdom and necessity of

[37] Ibid., pp. 83–4: 'de sa propre volente, sanz mocion des grauntz ou communes'.
[38] Harriss (1975), pp. 505–6.   [39] Middleton (1918); Prestwich (1992).
[40] Putnam (1929), pp. 24–5, 42–3.

such a move. In 1349 and 1351 the crown issued the Ordinance and Statute of Labourers to halt the steep rise in wages demanded after the plague. The responsibility for enforcing this legislation was handed over to special county tribunals made up of local gentry. The experiment was sufficiently successful that in 1361–2 the commissioners of the peace were given power not only to judge cases brought under the labour laws but also to determine all manner of trespasses and felonies committed within their area of jurisdiction. Although the power of these new 'justices of the peace' was to fluctuate somewhat over the next three decades, the broad policy of delegating judicial power to the localities was now more or less fixed. The persistence of the parliamentary Commons had therefore triumphed and the emergence of the justices of the peace could be counted one of their most signal political successes.

The transformation of parliament into a major political institution under Edward II and Edward III therefore represented both an opportunity and a threat to the crown. The representative nature of the assembly allowed the king to justify and exploit hitherto untapped sources of wealth through direct and indirect taxation and to create a remarkably sophisticated and productive system of public finance. In the process, however, the king's subjects were given the chance to articulate criticisms and precipitate reforms with an effectiveness that had rarely been secured by earlier baronial oppositions. The consequences of this new political dialogue were demonstrated forcefully by events in the Good Parliament of 1376.[41] For the first time in over fifty years, the Commons refused to grant the king a direct tax. Instead, they put forward the longest series of Commons petitions yet drawn up, representing a comprehensive indictment of the crown's military and domestic policies. Through their spokesman, Sir Peter de la Mare, they made a series of formal accusations against the inner circle of courtiers and financiers, forcing John of Gaunt, as the king's representative, to carry through a series of state trials and convictions before the Lords in parliament. The Good Parliament was a highly exceptional event, and too much attention to its proceedings can dangerously distort our picture of late medieval politics. But in a real and significant sense, the assembly of 1376 marked the emergence of the Commons as a mature and independent force. The knights and burgesses were certainly aware of sympathy for their cause among the Lords, but the confident and professional way in which they went about their campaign demonstrates the remarkable developments that had occurred since the time of Edward II. The English political community had come of age.

The first three-quarters of the fourteenth century therefore witnessed some of the most radical changes ever wrought in the political and administrative

---

[41] Holmes (1975) for full details.

structures of the English state. To a large extent, the political mood was still dictated by the personality of the king. The chronicler Ranulph Higden believed that Edward II's misfortunes arose directly out of his devotion to actors and singers, ditchers and dykers, sailors and swimmers, and most especially to his first and greatest love, Piers Gaveston.[42] Equally, Thomas Walsingham later blamed the military and political reversals of the 1370s on the depravity of the aged Edward III and the sinister influence of Alice Perrers.[43] But the chroniclers' emphasis on moral issues tends to disguise the very important institutional developments that had come about during the reigns of these two kings. The involvement of the political community in the authorisation of taxes from the time of Edward I had given it a valuable opportunity to influence the general direction of much of the crown's domestic and foreign policy. Edward II neglected the wider implications of this development; indeed, by the 1320s his regime was wilfully ignoring even the basic principles of political dialogue and ruling in a manner that threatened to disrupt the lives of many of his subjects. The real novelty of Edward III's regime lay in its decision to extend the traditions of counsel and consent and accommodate not only the aristocracy but also the minor landholders and merchants represented by the Commons in parliament. Through this process of political negotiation, the king's subjects probably became better informed of public affairs than ever before.[44] They also developed higher expectations of public service and greater confidence in the crown's ability to defend their rights and interests. Out of this attitude sprang both the hope, and the disillusionment, of late-medieval English politics.

[42] Higden, *Polychronicon*, VIII, p. 298.   [43] Walsingham, *Historia Anglicana*, I, p. 328.
[44] Maddicott (1978), pp. 27–43.

THE REIGN OF RICHARD II

Caroline M. Barron

INTRODUCTION

RICHARD II slipped quietly into his kingship although his reign was to end much more decisively. Richard became obsessed, in a way that Edward III had not been, with the fate of his great-grandfather who had been deposed and murdered in 1327. In his attempts to prevent history from repeating itself, Richard provoked his great magnates into taking exactly that course which he most feared. Yet, in spite of their comparable ends, the reigns of Edward II and Richard II were very different. Unlike his great-grandfather, Richard had a strong character which included some attractive attributes such as bravery and loyalty. Moreover he developed and pursued policies which had long-term objectives and made sense nationally as well as personally. But Richard also lacked certain qualities which were essential for medieval kings: he did not enjoy real war and he got on badly with the English nobility as a group, although he was able to develop individual friendships with some of them. He was not 'one of the lads' in a way that Edward I or Edward III had been, nor as Henry IV and Henry V were to be later, and he had a suspicious and secretive nature which bred unease and insecurity in those around him. Medieval monarchy depended for its success upon the abilities of individual kings: the institution of kingship was not yet sufficiently developed to carry incompetent kings. Richard II had the wrong abilities for his inherited task. But he was not a cipher and his undoubted qualities, even if inappropriate to medieval kingship, lend a distinctive character to the last quarter of the fourteenth century in England.

In looking at a particular reign, the historian is simply holding a frame over a section of the microfilm of English history. The frame helps to focus attention. How is the section between 1377 and 1399 different from other sections? The series of confrontations between the king and his nobility were not novel although they took new forms. But these are not the only conflicts that crowd into the Ricardian frame: the great popular rising in 1381; the attacks of John Wyclif and his 'Lollard' followers on the practices and doctrines of the Church in England; the rise of a wealthy and intensely competitive merchant class in London and other English towns; the development of the Commons in parliament as the voice of the financial (and other) interests of the urban and gentry 'middle classes' and the meteoric expansion in the use of written English, not only as the language of entertainment and enlightenment but also as the language of business and politics. Endemic plague since 1348 had kept the population within its means of subsistence and a rise in real wages ensured a higher standard of living for a considerable proportion of the shrunken population. Men and women had more money and more leisure to develop new skills, to move around the country and to challenge the accepted orders. Churches, guildhalls and great houses were built in the quintessentially English Perpendicular Style and webs of tracery were woven across the stone walls of medieval England. These walls sometimes supported the exuberant intricacies of fan vaults, found, for example, in the new cloister at Gloucester Abbey (1351–77). The reign of Richard II coincided in England with a period of opportunity, competition and experiment.

THE SOURCES

The reign of Richard II is particularly well documented. As for earlier reigns, there are the great runs of the records of the exchequer, chancery and judiciary. A novelty is the journal of the royal council kept by John Prophet, the king's secretary, in the 1390s.[1] To complement the records of central government, local institutions were beginning to keep their own records more systematically: not only the ubiquitous manorial court and account rolls, but the administrative records of towns. In London the earliest consecutive series of the accounts of guilds begin in the 1390s (Mercers, Taylors, Grocers and Goldsmiths) and wills survive in much greater numbers from the last quarter of the fourteenth century.

The reign is also well served by its chroniclers.[2] Monastic chroniclers were particularly busy. Apart from Thomas Walsingham who wrote from the well-established scriptorium of St Albans Abbey, Henry Knighton took up his pen in the abbey of St Mary in the Fields, Leicester, and a monk at Westminster, perhaps Richard Exeter, wrote an account of the years to 1394 which is especially informative about events at the centre. There are also a number of shorter chronicles of particular interest such as the *Anonimalle Chronicle* written in Anglo-Norman and providing distinctive, if not necessarily first-hand, accounts of the Good

---

[1] Printed in Baldwin (1913), pp. 489–504.   [2] See Martin (1997a).

Parliament of 1376 and the revolt of 1381. At the end of the reign Adam Usk wrote a vivid account of Henry Bolingbroke's usurpation and of the fall of Richard II. The last years of the reign are also covered, albeit fitfully, by a small cluster of chronicles from northern Cistercian houses, Whalley, Dieulacres and Kirkstall. Events in England moreover attracted the attention of writers across the Channel. Jean Froissart was well informed about some aspects of the rising of 1381 from talking with foreign lords who were in Richard's entourage, and he himself visited England in 1395.[3] Other Frenchmen who were in England in the late 1390s wrote dramatic accounts of the betrayal and death of Richard.[4] Moreover in Richard's reign a new kind of chronicle makes its appearance, the 'London chronicle' distinguished by the division of events by mayoral, rather than regnal, years and by the use of English.[5]

Literary sources are abundant, some written in Latin, others in Anglo-Norman but many, and increasingly, in English. The writings of Geoffrey Chaucer, William Langland, John Gower, the author of *Sir Gawain and the Green Knight* and even of the convoluted Thomas Usk can all add to our perceptions and understandings of the priorities of men and women in the late fourteenth century. A new audience was emerging comprised of the gentry, the merchants, the artisans and the professional classes of lawyers and doctors. Few documents survive from the personal archives of men and women of these classes: some household accounts, a single merchant's account book and a few letters.[6] Exiguous as these records are they help to throw light on lives which were lived out of the public eye. The impact of events at the centre can sometimes be assessed, and women who were not queens or princesses begin to find a place within the frame and to speak.

THE INHERITANCE: ROYAL GOVERNMENT IN COMMISSION, 1376–1380

Richard of Bordeaux was not born to be king: he was third in the line of succession. At his birth in 1367, his father, the famous warrior, Edward, the Black Prince, was alive and well, and Richard had an elder brother, also Edward, who was four years older than he was. But in 1371 everything changed: his brother died, his father became ill and the family left Bordeaux for England. Now Richard was to be groomed for kingship.

In England the great days of Edward III's reign were past. The Treaty of Brétigny in 1360 had marked the highwater point of English success in the war

---

[3] See Stow (1985).   [4] See Palmer (1978–9).

[5] E.g. *The Great Chronicle of London,* ed. Thomas and Thornley; *Chronicles of London,* ed. Kingsford.

[6] *Household Accounts,* ed. Woolgar; James (1956); Rickert (1926–7); Walker (1991).

with France. Now the newly conquered French lands were slipping out of English control in spite of the great *chevauchées* of John of Gaunt and his brothers. Worse still, the French were beginning to make retaliatory raids on the English south coast, attacking Rye and destroying a large part of Winchelsea. Following the death of his wife, Philippa of Hainault, in 1369, Edward sought solace in the arms of Alice Perrers, the wife of Sir William Windsor. Edward, now in his late fifties, seems to have become senile or, at any rate, uninterested in matters of state to which he had been devoting his attention for over forty years. Since the Black Prince was incapacitated by illness, the task of running the business of the realm fell largely, if not entirely, to Edward's third son, John of Gaunt. The bedchamber style of government is graphically portrayed by the evidence given in Richard's first parliament by a number of the late king's courtiers. It is clear that Edward, confined to his bed, was inappropriately influenced by Alice Perrers who became a powerful force behind the throne.[7]

The Commons in the parliament of 1376 (known as the 'Good Parliament'), led by Peter de la Mare, a shire knight from Herefordshire, mounted a sustained attack on those whom they considered to be lining their own pockets at the national expense. De la Mare was the steward of Edmund, third earl of March, the king's lieutenant in Ireland and the husband of Philippa, the only child of Edward III's second son, Lionel, duke of Clarence. Their two sons, Roger (b. 1374) and Edmund (b. 1376), were the presumptive heirs to the English throne after Richard became king (see p. 886).[8] Those impeached in the Good Parliament included Lord Latimer, the royal chamberlain, a cluster of *nouveaux riches* London merchants and a couple of captains left over from the great days in France who were accused of selling English garrison castles to the French. John of Gaunt did his best to defend Latimer from attack and to uphold the integrity of royal policy. Those who were found guilty were either imprisoned or fined, but they were not accused of treason and they were not executed. All were released within months. By comparison with the parliamentary trials later in Richard's reign, the Good Parliament was a very gentlemanly affair. The attacks, however, served to check the self-interested behaviour of the royal courtiers, and they demonstrated the potential of parliament as a forum for political debate. The 1376 parliament witnessed the development of the judicial process of impeachment which, while it could not fashion royal policy, could be used to criticise that policy, and it was in this parliament that the Commons chose one man to act as their spokesman for the entire parliament who became known as the Speaker.[9] The disgrace of the

[7] *Rot. Parl.*, III, pp. 12–14.

[8] But see the recently discovered document drawn up in 1376 in which Edward III appears to have excluded from the succession his heirs through the female line in favour of the male children of his surviving sons, Bennett (1998), p. 591.   [9] Roskell (1965).

London merchants, Adam Bury, John Pecche and Richard Lyons, led to their ejection from office as aldermen of London and this, in turn, provoked a full-scale revision of the way in which the city of London was governed.[10] These changes, which included the annual election of all aldermen, introduced a period of extreme instability into London's government. Factions fought, not in the courts but on the streets, and the 'smale people' began to have their say.[11]

Although John of Gaunt had managed to reverse most of the acts of the Good Parliament, yet there remained a vacuum at the centre of government where the commanding figure of the monarch should have held sway. The Black Prince died at Kennington in June 1376 and Edward III finally abandoned his life on 22 June 1377. Richard, a willowy, attractive boy of eleven became king on the eve of the vigil of the birthday of St John the Baptist. Since he had been born at the feast of the Epiphany, which was celebrated as the day when John had baptised Christ, Richard throughout his life considered himself to have a special relationship with the saint, to whom he was particularly devoted and whom he considered to be his special protector.[12]

It was extremely important that the young king should be crowned and that the ceremony should be impressive. It is not clear who master-minded this event: perhaps it was Richard's tutor, Guichard d'Angle who had been chosen for his son by the Black Prince, or, more probably, Sir Simon Burley, who succeeded d'Angle as Richard's tutor. Not only was the ceremonial for Richard's coronation different from that of earlier coronations, but the event was carefully recorded. In fact Richard's coronation is the first to be fully described by a contemporary chronicler.[13] It has been suggested that 'The most significant changes in the pageant were the absence of the forms of secular election prior to the procession to the cathedral (*sic*), a probable alteration of the wording of the oath itself, and the emphasis on obedience to the king as lay lord.'[14] In the course of the long ceremonies Richard himself seems to have fallen asleep and had to be carried back to the Palace by Sir Simon Burley who did not stop long enough in the Abbey to remove the precious royal regalia, as a result of which one of the consecrated coronation shoes, said to have been worn by King Alfred, fell off in the crowds and was lost.[15] In spite of his fatigue, the coronation seems to have made a great impression on the young king: he believed that he had been set apart from other men and placed under the direct and special protection of St Edward the Confessor.[16] Later in his reign, Richard would on occasion take visitors, such as the king of Armenia in 1386, to see the royal insignia 'quibus olim fuerat coronatus'.[17]

---

[10] Barron (1981).

[11] The phrase 'smale people' is used by Thomas Usk in his 1388 appeal, *A Book of London English*, ed. Chambers and Daunt, p. 25.   [12] Gordon (1993), pp. 55–7.

[13] *Munimenta Gildhallae*, ed. Riley, II, pp. 456–82.   [14] Jones (1968), p. 15.

[15] *West. Chron.*, pp. 415–17.   [16] Gordon (1993), pp. 54–5.   [17] *West. Chron.*, pp. 156–7.

Once the king had been crowned, it was necessary for the kingdom to be governed, but Richard seems to have been slow to take on the tasks of kingship.[18] At Christmas, following his coronation, the citizens of London entertained him with a pageant of mummers who included esquires, an emperor, a pope and cardinals. They played games with him using dice loaded in his favour so that he 'did alwayes winne when hee cast them'. In this way he 'won' a gold bowl, cup and ring.[19] The festivities may have been fun, but they provided an unrealistic introduction to the business of kingship. It may have been the influence of his mother which led to Richard's childhood being unusually protracted. He was twenty-two before he formally took up the reins of government.

Meanwhile, how was the kingdom to be governed during the minority of the king? There is no evidence that Edward III had made any provision for this, certainly not in his will, although he may have discussed the matter with his councillors. The solution arrived at, by whatever means, was to appoint a series of governing councils on which a selection of great magnates, bishops and working knights and clerks would sit. Obvious interest groups were represented: John of Gaunt and his brothers Edmund of Langley, earl of Cambridge (later duke of York), and Thomas of Woodstock, earl of Buckingham (later duke of Gloucester); some of the household knights of the Black Prince representing the interests of Princess Joan, and the 'radicals' who had challenged the court party in 1376 and maintained a tradition of detached criticism.[20]

There were serious problems facing the councils: in particular the defence of the kingdom. The English presence in France was dependent upon maintaining garrisons in the 'barbican' towns of Calais and Cherbourg, and Brest, which lay within the duchy of John, duke of Brittany, whose loyalty to England was volatile and unreliable, and Bordeaux at the heart of the duchy of Aquitaine.[21] It was expensive to maintain these garrisons and humiliating to lose them. The French king Charles V (1364–80) was more astute than his predecessors at keeping the English armies at bay, and he was well served by his captains Bertrand du Guesclin, Olivier de Clisson and Jean de Vienne. These men carried the war on to English soil, and the *chevauchées* mounted by the English in the early years of Richard's reign (e.g. the earl of Arundel's attack on Harfleur in 1378 and the earl of Buckingham's fruitless siege of Nantes in 1380) were unimpressive and largely unsuccessful. The Scots, in alliance with the French, kept up the pressure on the northern border and thereby allowed the Percies, traditional wardens of the East March, to maintain their retinues in a state of war (largely at the king's

---

[18] Richard was formally presented to parliament in October 1377, *Rot. Parl.*, III, p. 3.
[19] Stow, *Survey of London*, I, pp. 96–7.   [20] Lewis (1926).   [21] Palmer (1972); Jones (1970).

expense) and to challenge all authority, even that of the duke of Lancaster.[22] The policy of the minority councils was to put pressure on the French by mounting *chevauchées* and to make a peace, or at least a truce, with the Scots. But the war had broadened out beyond these two theatres. Flanders was closely linked in its economy with England: it was the major market for English wool, just as England was an important market for Flemish cloth (and other manufactured products). The Flemish weaving towns of Ghent, Ypres and Bruges were inhibited from a full alliance with England by their Francophile count, Louis de Male, who confirmed his preference by marrying his only daughter and heir, Margaret, to Philip of Burgundy, the powerful brother of Charles V, who succeeded to the county of Flanders in 1384. The Anglo-French war had also expanded to include Castile where rival claimants to the crown sought support from the two protagonists. Henry of Trastámara, illegitimate but certainly king (1369–79), allied with the French and took the powerful Castilian navy into the war on the French side. John of Gaunt's marriage in 1371 to Constanza, the legitimate claimant to the throne, provided a potential, rather than an actual, threat to Henry and his son Juan. But John rejoiced in the title of king of Castile while living off the revenues of his substantial English estates. Twice in Richard's reign, in 1381 and again in 1386–9, the English mounted extensive military campaigns to fight in the Iberian peninsula and, when war failed, marriage alliances carried forward the English interests.[23] These campaigns, however, offered no solutions for ending the French war.

Another important task facing the minority councils was to find a suitable wife for the young king. Clearly this would be an alliance of the greatest importance, and a card which, in all probability, could only be played once. For reasons which are not now very clear, the council sought the hand of Anne, daughter of the Emperor Charles IV of Bohemia (d. 1378) and the sister of Wenceslas IV (1378–1400) king of Bohemia and of the Romans. The political purpose of the marriage was to secure a powerful ally against the French, together with a substantial dowry and a fecund queen. Anne provided none of these things, yet she seems to have been a faithful and sensitive wife who made her husband happy, and caused no faction or discord at court. Although the Westminster chronicler probably echoed a widely held view when he commented on the large sum which had been paid out to secure 'this tiny scrap of humanity', and Thomas Walsingham wrote wistfully of the large dowry which would have accompanied a Visconti bride for Richard, yet by the time of her death the chroniclers had come to appreciate her gentle and unobtrusive qualities.[24] The foreign policy of the period 1377–80 could hardly have been

---

[22] Storey (1957); Tuck (1968); Walker (1991).   [23] Russell (1955).

[24] *West. Chron.*, pp. 23–5; *Annales Ricardi Secundi*, p. 169; see Saul (1997a), pp. 455–7.

considered as a triumph either of war or diplomacy: short-term truces with Scotland, a useless marriage alliance, the loss of English influence and markets in Flanders, the expensive maintenance of English toe-holds in France and two unsuccessful, if not indeed disastrous, raids into northern France. It was a bad hand, badly played.

But the minority councils had other concerns. They had to maintain a balance between the rival interests of the magnates, for ultimately the well-being of the realm depended upon such a balance. How was patronage to be dispensed in the absence of an individual royal will? The wealth and influence of John of Gaunt were widely resented and suspected. What role was to be played by Joan of Kent and the household of knights whom she had inherited from the Black Prince: men of ability and influence such as Sir Richard Stury, Sir Simon Burley or Sir John Wroth? But as the magnates jostled around the edges of the vacuum, another much more serious threat to royal authority was gathering in the villages and manors of England.

1381: SEDITION AND LOLLARDY

The sharp decline in the overall population of England following the Black Death of 1348–9 had dislocated the English economy. The great lay and eccle-siastical landlords had not been impoverished by these changes, but the sharp decline in population had certainly shifted the economic advantage to the labourer. In spite of legislation which aimed to restore the *status quo ante*, there was an inexorable rise in the cost of labour and a rather less marked rise in prices. In consequence, the wage labourer, both male and female, was more prosperous than ever before. The unfree labourer chafed now at constraints which in a period of overpopulation might have provided some security, but now served only to constrain economic opportunity. The great landlords had to use ingenuity, and sometimes force, to maintain their customary levels of income from their estates. In towns skilled labour was at a premium, there was plenty of work and more money to spend. The 'small people' could, and did, make their voices heard.

The revolt of 1381 was the culmination of a series of local protests and conflicts between workers and their landlords.[25] The activities of the local JPs in enforcing the labour legislation obviously aggravated hostility to central, as well as local, government policies. It used to be thought that the revolt was the spontaneous and angry response not only to smouldering resentment against villeinage but also to the heavy taxation of the 1370s and in particular, to the novel poll taxes of 1377, 1379 and 1380 which aimed to tax the newly rich wage

----

[25] Hilton (1962); Faith (1984).

labourers and to spread the burden of taxation more evenly, if not more fairly, among the population at large. Taxation may have triggered the rising, but recent research has shown that the revolt was highly organised and well co-ordinated.[26] It was not a spontaneous rising of an angry peasantry. It was, moreover, led by men of standing in their local communities: jurymen, bailiffs and stewards.[27] The frightened monastic chroniclers portrayed the rebels as little better than animals, braying and inarticulate. But, in fact, in the villages of south-east England, where the revolt was fed and nurtured, literacy was much more widespread and access to writing more common than the chroniclers were willing to recognise.[28] The newly rich were also, often, the newly literate. Old Clement Paston (d. 1419), a bondman of the manor of Paston in Norfolk, sent his son William, born three years before the rising, to school.[29] Letters circulated among the rural labourers and some of these fell into 'government' hands and were, miraculously, preserved by the horrified chroniclers.[30] It seems likely that when the rebels met the king at Mile End on Friday, 14 June, and next day at Smithfield, they presented him with written lists of demands in response to which the king promised charters, patents and letters of protection 'written out and sealed'. The rebels knew not to be satisfied with less, although they reckoned without the bare-faced duplicity of the government.[31]

The revolt happened because a newly powerful class of 'peasant leaders' had emerged who could lead and articulate economic and social grievances which grinding poverty had previously kept suppressed. The demands of the rebels were not, however, confined to the injustices of rural life: they were concerned also about national politics and they were aware of the inadequacies of the policies and practices of central government.[32] The unsuccessful war in France, the raids on the south coast, the heavy taxation and the labour legislation were all resented and were perceived to be the work of traitors around the king who stood between him and his 'true commons'. If Richard, who was now fifteen, would rule as well as reign, then all would be well. It was clear that conciliar government lacked force and direction, but was strong monarchical rule really the preferred alternative?

At Blackheath on 13 June, the feast of Corpus Christi, the rebels presented a petition to the king which named eight men as traitors: heading the list were Simon Sudbury, archbishop of Canterbury and chancellor of England and Robert Hales, commander of the English Priory of the Knights Hospitallers and, since February, treasurer of England. When Richard went to meet the rebels at Mile End on 14 June, a posse broke into the weakly defended Tower

[26] Brooks (1985). [27] Dyer (1984). [28] Strohm (1992); Justice (1994).
[29] Richmond (1990), pp. 12–14. [30] Printed in *The Peasants' Revolt of 1381*, ed. Dobson, pp. 380–3.
[31] *Anonimalle Chronicle* printed in ibid., pp. 160–6, esp. 164. [32] Ormrod (1990).

and dragged the two men to execution on Tower Hill. Not surprisingly, Richard chose not to return to the Tower, but spent the night in the Great Wardrobe in the city near Blackfriars. The next morning Richard rode out again to meet another band of rebels at Smithfield, where Wat Tyler, their leader, was killed. Richard, with instinctive courage, spurred his horse forward and claimed the leadership of the rebels for himself and they, in search of a leader, followed him. The men broke up into small bands and returned to their towns and villages. Then the retaliations began. Neighbours accused each other of taking part in the revolt; the royal justices acquitted many and executed quite a number, and the memory of the 'hurling days' of 1381 frightened the government into considering the needs and aspirations of a wider swathe of English people. The political nation had expanded, not by suffrage but by direct action, and the rulers learnt a lesson they never forgot.

How is the comparative success of the rebels to be explained? It is true that they had the advantage of surprise. No one suspected, until June 1381, that local protests could, or would, escalate into such a coherent and well-organised mass protest. The government had seriously underestimated the sophistication of the opposition. But the government was also in disarray. Those who ruled in the king's name were not necessarily traitors in the sense of betraying the best interests of their country, but they were mostly incompetent and self-interested. This was not true of John of Gaunt who was certainly able and loyal, but he was concerned to pursue his dynastic interests in Europe (he was already married to Constanza, the legitimate Castilian heiress). The rebels (and others) distrusted him and shouted that they would have 'no king named John'.[33] It was more than likely that if John had not been in the north negotiating a truce with the Scots, he would have suffered a fate similar to that of Sudbury and Hales.[34] It has been argued that the events of June 1381 exposed the minority government for what it really was, 'an insecure, hesitant and mediocre regime'.[35] The ease with which the rebels entered London was attributed by contemporaries to treachery, that is, they had been let in by fellow-travellers among the aldermen. What seems in fact to have been the case is that the government of the city, like the national government, was in disarray. The 'democratic' reforms of 1376 ensured that the city was governed by men who were new to the job, since new aldermen had to be elected every year.[36] The city, as the monk of Westminster observed, was divided against itself and unable to formulate, let alone implement, a coherent policy in the face of unexpected assault.[37] The centre could not hold.

When the shocked and frightened monks came to reflect on the causes of

---

[33] For attacks on John of Gaunt's property during the revolt see Crook (1987); Walker (1983).
[34] Walker (1991).   [35] Ormrod (1990), p. 90.   [36] Barron (1981).   [37] *West. Chron.*, p. 9.

the rising in June 1381, they apportioned blame in a variety of ways. Only the author of the *Anonimalle Chronicle* could see any justification for the rebels' actions.[38] Thomas Walsingham, a Benedictine monk, took the opportunity to blame the friars, but he also linked the overturning of his world with the heretical ideas of John Wyclif and his followers, known as Lollards.[39]

Wyclif had been teaching at Oxford since the 1360s, but his unorthodox ideas only gradually penetrated the world outside the university. His undoubted abilities brought him to the attention of men of influence and power: John of Gaunt used him on an embassy to Bruges to argue against the validity of papal taxation and in 1378 he was brought to the parliament at Gloucester to oppose the claims of the Church to provide sanctuary for debtors. Wyclif's friends at court included Princess Joan and some of the knights of her household (e.g. Sir Richard Stury and Sir Lewis Clifford), but to be a friend did not necessarily imply full acceptance of Wyclif's ideas. The radicalism of his thinking was not at first fully understood.

Wyclif attacked the churchmen for the misuse of endowments which had been given to them to facilitate their spiritual functions and not for their material comfort. The true authority of the Church lay with its true believers who were destined for salvation. The worldliness of monks and friars, the scandal of the papal schism (1378–1417) and the corruption of the parish clergy and bishops, all inhibited the salvation of Christians.

To these criticisms of the visible Church, Wyclif added an attack upon the doctrine of transubstantiation: how could the real body of Christ appear deceptively as bread and wine?[40] Many of Wyclif's views were essentially negative, undermining the practices of popular religion such as the cult of images, pilgrimages, devotion to saints and confession to priests. In place of these communal activities, he put the individual, his conscience and the Bible containing the wisdom of God. To make the Bible accessible to ordinary men and women, it had to be translated into English and this was the work of a small group of serious and like-minded men, who gathered around Wyclif, some of them Oxford-trained clerics and others who were educated members of the gentry.[41] Much of this work of evangelisation lay in the future, but by 1381 Wyclif's ideas had been publicly condemned by the pope and he had been summoned to answer charges at councils held at Lambeth (1378) and at the Blackfriars' house in London (1382). In spite of these public condemnations, Wyclif was allowed to die peacefully at his parish of Lutterworth. His attack

---

[38] *Anonimalle Chronicle* in *The Peasants' Revolt of 1381*, ed. Dobson, pp. 123–4.

[39] Walsingham, in ibid., pp. 367–9.

[40] Wyclif wrote in *De Eucharistia* that 'the sacrament figures the body of Christ and it is consecrated, worshipped and eaten with the intention of remembering and imitating Christ', cited in Aston (1987), p. 320.   [41] Aston (1987); Catto (1981); Thomson (1997).

on the possessions of the Church was not novel, but it was threatening and found a popular response. The monk of Westminster wrote that Wyclif's aim was 'to please men rather than God and sinfully to spread a number of heretical and wrong-headed doctrines in God's church'.[42] For the first time in England heretical ideas had moved out of the confines of the universities and into the world of lay men and women. Thomas Walsingham was right to see a connection between an unprecedented popular rising and the advent of popular heresy, for both owed much to the increase in prosperity. It was prosperity that nurtured literacy and literacy in its turn encouraged informed protest and the rejection of authoritative pronouncements. Even those who could not read had time to listen to new ideas, to discuss them and to act upon them. A written vernacular culture underpinned the attacks upon the established order in Church and in state. It was not surprising that the monastic communities were frightened, for their control both of labour and of learning had been challenged.

ADOLESCENT GOVERNMENT, 1381–1387

The events of June 1381 drew Richard into the limelight, but he seems to have been remarkably disinclined to take up the reins of kingship. Perhaps he was discouraged from doing so by those around him. The continual councils had been discontinued in 1380 and from then on Richard was in nominal charge of the government. His attention to business appears to have been fitful. In the autumn of 1381 he brought about a reconciliation between John of Gaunt and Henry Percy, earl of Northumberland who had been less than supportive to Gaunt in his troubles during the rising the previous summer. In January 1382 Richard married Anne, newly arrived from Bohemia, and John of Gaunt continued to be the dominant presence at court. In February 1382 the Londoners asked 'that they might have only one king ... they wished to be the subjects of one man alone'.[43] Richard's response to this pointed request is not known, but Gaunt left London hurriedly.

It is not easy to discern patterns or policies in the middle years of Richard's reign, but there is one consistent aim: the king and his councillors began to search for a means of achieving an honourable peace with France. To change a policy which was more than forty years old and associated with national success was not easy and was made more difficult by the fact that the theatres of war included not only France, but also Flanders, Castile, Portugal and Scotland. But fighting had to continue until peace could be secured. Bishop Despenser of Norwich led a disastrous 'crusade' to Flanders in 1383, and John

---

[42] *West. Chron.*, p. 107.   [43] Ibid., p. 25.

of Gaunt headed another political crusade against Castile in 1386–9. Meanwhile Richard himself led an army into Scotland in 1385 in response to the incursion into England by the French captain Jean de Vienne in the previous year. But Richard seems not to have developed a real taste for war and he preferred to watch tournaments rather than to participate in them. His image of his kingship was not a militaristic one: moreover he may well have perceived that wars were costly and involved the king in close encounters with parliament. The Westminster chronicler shrewdly perceived that the king, in order 'to maintain a ceaseless state of war against the king of the French, would inevitably be compelled to be forever burdening his people with new imposts, with damaging results for himself'.[44]

The alliance between Edward III and his people against the French had been remarkably successful, but it had also made the king dependent upon taxation granted by the Commons in parliament (see ch. 13(a) in this volume) if he wished to pursue such wars successfully. Richard II was unable to raise either direct or indirect taxation without first seeking the support of the Commons. It seems likely that Richard found the negotiation and consultation necessary to 'run' a meeting of parliament uncongenial. In the course of the 1380s the Commons became increasingly critical of royal policy. They were concerned about a number of issues: the heavy burden of taxation, the corruption of local officials, the distribution of badges by lords (leading to local gangsterism and the intimidation of juries) and the misuse of the resources of the crown.[45] Not only were the foreign wars largely unsuccessful, but the king appeared to be personally extravagant and, at the same time, capricious.[46] In 1385 the Commons, supported by the Lords, produced a major reform programme: the king was to put a stop to grants from royal revenues for the next year and to agree to an annual review of the royal household by three officers of state; and there were to be reforms in the way that local officers were chosen. Richard gave a prevaricating assent to most of the proposals and the Commons made a generous grant of taxation.[47]

Although Richard could not raise taxation without the consent of parliament, his exercise of patronage remained untrammelled. Richard chose to reward his friends generously: he did not use patronage to build up a wide body of support for the crown. Sir Simon Burley, a man of obscure origins, had risen through service to the Black Prince and served as Richard's tutor. He deserved well of Richard, but his rewards were excessive. He was granted the Leybourne inheritance in Kent and then, in 1385 on the expedition to Scotland, he was

---

[44] Ibid., p. 205.
[45] For the failure of the Commons' attempts at the reform of the government in 1381–2, see Ormrod (1990).   [46] Saul (1997a), pp. 81–2, 146–7.   [47] Palmer (1971b).

made an earl, although this promotion was soon retracted.[48] At the same time, Michael de la Pole, the son of a successful Hull merchant, who had been granted the Ufford lands, was created earl of Suffolk. Robert de Vere inherited the impoverished earldom of Oxford, but was raised by Richard first to be marquis of Dublin (a hitherto unknown rank) and then, in October 1386, created duke of Ireland. Such novel creations alienated the established peerage (e.g. the king's uncles Edmund, who was made duke of York in 1385; and Thomas, who became duke of Gloucester) and the necessary endowment also cost money. In the view of the Commons, inheritances which fell to the crown should be used to support the costs of royal government and should not be capriciously disposed of to greedy and self-serving friends around the king. The skilful exercise of patronage was probably the single most difficult and important task facing a medieval king: the adolescent Richard was obstinate and inept.

There was another area of government in which Richard attempted to intervene in the 1380s, namely the rule of London. Since the Good Parliament of 1376, the government of the city had been characterised by turbulence and brawling.[49] Richard decided to try to build up a 'party' in the city and chose to support the radical John of Northampton, urging the Londoners to re-elect him as mayor in 1382. But Richard seems then to have grown tired of Northampton and, perhaps, of the instability of his control of the city, and switched his support to Northampton's great rival, the grocer Nicholas Brembre. There is evidence that Brembre lent money to the king's chamber and, in return, the king supported his 'conservative' policies which favoured the wholesalers and the wealthier overseas traders. In 1384 Richard even went to the length of sending three of his household knights to act as observers at the mayoral election to ensure that Brembre was chosen.[50] In his interventions in London politics in the 1380s Richard displayed a characteristic tendency to engage in faction politics rather than to stand above them.

It seems clear that in the 1380s Richard had difficulty in establishing his own authority independent of the daunting reputation of his dead father and the overbearing presence of his uncle, John of Gaunt. When the deposed mayor of London was on trial in 1384 he urged Richard not 'to proceed to judgment or to exercise jurisdiction in the absence of your uncle the duke of Lancaster'. Understandably Richard flared up and asserted that he was competent to sit in judgement not only on Northampton, but on the duke of Lancaster as well.[51] Early in 1385, Richard may even have connived at a plot to kill his uncle which

---

[48] Saul (1997a), pp. 114–17.   [49] Bird (1949); Nightingale (1989).
[50] *Calendar of Select Plea and Memoranda Rolls of the City of London, 1381–1412*, ed. Thomas, pp. 62–3.
[51] *West. Chron.*, p. 93.

provoked Gaunt into reminding the king that, since he had the power of life and death over his subjects he, above all, should not countenance private murder. He should find good and loyal councillors and refrain from lawless action. On this occasion Richard responded to Gaunt calmly and his mother, Princess Joan, rushed in to heal the rifts in the royal family.[52] Doubtless Richard received more good advice than he found welcome, but it is clear that he had a very short temper. When William Courtenay, archbishop of Canterbury, criticised Richard's choice of councillors and his plot to murder Gaunt, he was first assaulted by a volley of threats and then the king attempted to run the archbishop through with his sword, only being prevented from doing so by the intervention of three courtiers. Courtenay was later forced to kneel and ask the king's pardon for his offensive words.[53] When the earl of Arundel claimed in parliament that the country lacked good governance and would soon be completely destroyed, Richard told him that he was lying and could go to the Devil.[54] Medieval kings were expected to take counsel with the magnates of the realm, and such counsel was likely to involve both advice and criticism. Richard's inability to listen to advice seriously undermined the authority he sought to establish. He behaved like a wayward teenager and was treated as such.

THE FORMATIVE CRISIS FOR ROYAL AUTHORITY, 1386–1389

These years mark a watershed in the reign, between Richard's adolescence and his mature kingship. He was nineteen when the crisis began and twenty-two when, in May 1389, he formally declared himself to be of full age and ready to assume sole responsibility for his kingdom. Much had happened in the intervening three years.

It seems clear that Richard largely ignored the advice which had been given to him in the parliament of 1385. He made no serious attempts to curb either his spending or his distribution of the lands and offices which fell to the disposal of the crown. When parliament met in October 1386 (the 'Wonderful Parliament') the Commons, in alliance with the Lords, decided to impeach the chancellor, Michael de le Pole. Richard refused to dismiss him and took himself off to Eltham, declaring that he would not dismiss a scullion from his kitchen at the request of the Commons. The leadership of the opposition in the Lords seems to have fallen to Richard's uncle, Thomas, duke of Gloucester, and Thomas Arundel, bishop of Ely. It is unlikely that the situation would have developed in the way it did if John of Gaunt had not left the country on 9 July

---

[52] Ibid., pp. 111–15.   [53] Walsingham, *Historia Anglicana,* II, p. 128; *West. Chron.,* p. 139.
[54] *West. Chron.,* p. 69.

to campaign for his rights as king of Castile and to promote English interests against the French. Gloucester and Arundel visited the king at Eltham and, apparently, asserted the right of parliament to enquire into the spending of grants they had made and also reminded the king of the fate of Edward II. Chastened, Richard returned to parliament, dismissed de la Pole and allowed his impeachment to go ahead. The charges against him focused on his corrupt acquisition of lands and offices and his failure to spend parliamentary taxes appropriately, so that no help had been provided for Ghent in its struggle to resist the duke of Burgundy, and the country had been undefended in the face of a serious invasion scare.[55] The policy of peace with France had simply resulted in humiliation.

But the impeachment of de la Pole was not the main objective of the coalition of Lords and Commons: rather it was to impose upon the king a great council of twelve men who, together with the newly chosen great officers of state (Thomas Arundel had succeeded de la Pole as chancellor), would supervise all the financial and patronage aspects of royal government. These men were to act as a committee of enquiry and were empowered to enter the royal household and to demand to see all 'rolls, records and other muniments' and then to amend all wastage, failures and excesses to be found in any branch of government or in the household itself. They were empowered to discuss and determine all issues 'for the rights and profits of our said Crown, the better governance of the peace and laws of our land and the relief of our said people'.[56] Although this reforming council was presented as having been set up 'by our own accord and free will', it clearly was not, and Richard intended to have as little to do with it as possible. Not all members of the council were opposed to Richard, and Nicholas Morice, abbot of Waltham, seems to have been his friend.[57]

To evade the council's attentions Richard left London. Accompanied by Anne, he spent Christmas at Windsor, where de la Pole joined the court for the festivities, thence to Nottingham and Lincoln and back to Windsor for St George's day. In August 1387 he held two important meetings, the first early in the month at Shrewsbury and the second, later in the same month, at Nottingham. These were meetings not of the members of the parliamentary council but, rather, of a group whom Richard chose to advise him: his friends. These were Robert Wickford, archbishop of Dublin, John Fordham, bishop of Durham, Thomas Rushook, bishop of Chichester and the king's confessor, John Swaffham, bishop of Bangor, Robert de Vere, Michael de la Pole, John Ripon, a useful royal clerk closely associated with de Vere, John Blake an

[55] Palmer (1969); Roskell (1984).   [56] Letters Patent translated in full, *West. Chron.*, pp. 173–5.
[57] Ibid., p. 169; Saul (1997a), pp. 162–3.

apprentice at law and Alexander Neville, archbishop of York, who had been appointed a member of the parliamentary council but seems to have been won over to the 'king's party'.[58] The purpose of these meetings was to seek and to record (the work of John Blake) the opinions of a group of judges including Robert Tresilian CJKB and Robert Belknap CJCP and four others about the legal validity of the acts of the last parliament. The judges declared that the imposition of a council on the king, as in the last parliament, had no force in law and, moreover, it was for the king to determine the order and content of parliamentary business and to dissolve parliament when he wished. The king's ministers could only be legally impeached with his consent. It was also declared to be illegal to have sought for parliamentary precedents from the reign of Edward II. All those who promoted such illegal acts should be punished as traitors.[59] It was not unreasonable that Richard, under pressure from the Lords and Commons, should seek a clarification of the rights of the monarchy. The recently developed legal profession gave him, probably quite willingly, the answer he wanted: parliament was his creature and must act in accordance with his will. The answers provided by the judges, probably led by Tresilian, comprised 'the most remarkable statement of the royal prerogative ever made in England in the middle ages' and they marked an important step in the evolution of the Ricardian interpretation of kingship.[60]

The difficulty for Richard was, however, that political crises are not always susceptible of legal solutions. For the moment Richard decided to keep the answers to himself while he decided how to move against his opponents, the leaders of the 1386 parliament. The Londoners, encouraged probably by Nicholas Brembre, assured the king of their support 'in everything as his royal majesty required and demanded of them'.[61] On 10 November the mayor and citizens welcomed Richard into the city and the abbot and convent of Westminster also received him ceremoniously.[62] But news of the judges' opinions had leaked out to the duke of Gloucester and the earl of Arundel who prudently declined to respond to the king's demand for their attendance and, forewarned, summoned their retinues to meet at Harringay where they launched an appeal against Neville, de Vere, de la Pole, Tresilian and Brembre, accusing them of treason. They realised they must attack before they were attacked. At a formal meeting in Westminster Hall on 17 November, Richard accepted the appeal against his five advisers and supporters and agreed that it should be heard in parliament, summoned to meet on 3 February. Appeals would normally have been heard in the court of the constable (Gloucester himself) where matters would not have gone well for Richard's friends.

---

[58] Davies (1975a).   [59] Chrimes (1956); Clementi (1971).   [60] Saul (1997a), p. 174.
[61] *West. Chron.*, p. 207.   [62] Ibid., pp. 208–9.

Richard's response therefore, to accept the appeal but to have it heard in parliament, was a shrewd one.

But in spite of having been able to choose the forum for hearing the appeal, Richard had lost the initiative: his opponents had moved first. Angry at being out-manoeuvred, Richard allowed Neville and de Vere to escape and the latter was encouraged to ride north to raise the king's retinue in the north-west. It was a wild scheme and ended in disaster. At Radcot Bridge on the Thames west of Oxford, his forces were routed by the combined retinues of the five Appellants, Gloucester, Arundel, Warwick, Henry Bolingbroke, earl of Derby and Mowbray, earl of Nottingham.[63] On hearing of de Vere's defeat, Richard left Windsor for the greater security of the Tower of London. The mayor and aldermen of London struggled to maintain their neutrality while negotiations between Richard and the Appellants continued.[64] It may well be that, for two or three days at the end of December, Richard was actually deposed. At this critical juncture it may have been the rivalry between Gloucester and his nephew Henry of Derby that saved Richard. But there is no doubt that his dignity and royal authority were assaulted.[65] Most of the members of his household, his chamber knights, the dean and clerks of his chapel, his secretary and many of the wives and ladies of the court were expelled and their places taken by people whom the Appellants could trust.[66] In effect, Richard was placed under house arrest. He was angry and unhappy: his effective power was virtually eroded and de Vere's well-intentioned but ineffective efforts had simply served to reveal Richard's vacillation and duplicity. His position was considerably weaker than it had been a month earlier.

The parliament, soon known by the epithet 'Merciless',[67] assembled on 3 February 1388 and continued in session, with a break of three weeks, until 3 June. Neville, de Vere, de la Pole, Brembre and Tresilian were all convicted as traitors although only Brembre and Tresilian were present to suffer their fate. They were not the only victims: others were also tried and executed: Thomas Usk, the undersheriff of London, author and informer on John of Northampton, John Blake the apprentice at law, who had drafted the judges' questions and answers, Sir Simon Burley and three of the other chamber knights, Sir John Beauchamp, Sir James Berners and Sir John Salisbury. Thomas Rushook, a Dominican friar, bishop of Chichester and Richard's confessor, would have suffered a similar fate had he not been saved by his cloth. The offending judges were banished to exile in Ireland, the remaining clerks and knights who had been close to Richard remained in the Tower awaiting

[63] Myers (1927); R. G. Davies (1971).   [64] *West. Chron.*, p. 225.
[65] Clarke (1932); Knighton, pp. 426–7.   [66] *West. Chron.*, pp. 230–3.
[67] 'parliamentum sine misericordia', *Knighton's Chronicle*, ed. Martin, p. 414.

trial but were finally released on the last day of the parliament.[68] It was a ruth-less and wholesale elimination of Richard's household which he had been pow-erless to prevent. The Appellant lords saw these men as those who had

done their utmost to maintain a state of dispute, opposition and division between our lord the king and the good lords and peers of the realm and the good commonalty of the same; to the undoing of the king and of the realm; and supported evil government about the person of our lord the king and caused the king's good and royal heart to be withdrawn from the lords and peers of the realm and the commons of the same.[69]

Like the rebels of 1381, the Appellant lords struck at those who, as they saw it, stood between the king and his true and loyal people. Some of their anger was directed at the failure of patronage to flow in their direction (there were com-plaints about the appointment of Burley as constable of Dover and about the grant to him, by de Vere, of the manor of Lyonshall in Herefordshire)[70] but the Appellants were striking out at a style of government which was secretive, exclusive, partisan and unpredictable. Did the fault lie with the king or with his advisers? Only time would tell.

On 1 June Richard entertained all the Lords to a banquet and, two days later, before the high altar in Westminster Abbey the king renewed his coronation oath and the lords renewed their oaths of fealty.[71] If Richard had, indeed, been deposed for a few days at the end of 1387, it is possible to understand why such a renewal ceremony was considered necessary. A small committee was appointed together with the great officers of state, to oversee the king's actions. Meanwhile Richard spent most of the summer hunting while he left the Appellant lords to get on with the business of government.

The rule of the Appellants was not noticeably successful. In August, the Scots defeated an English army at Otterburn and captured Henry 'Hotspur', son of the earl of Northumberland. At the beginning of September the earl of Arundel returned from an expedition to Poitou in which he had raided successfully and burned towns and shipping, but had failed to meet up with John, duke of Brittany and invade France as had been planned. At the parlia-ment held at Barnwell Priory near Cambridge (9 September to 17 October) Richard seems to have been able to begin to re-establish his authority by sup-porting the Commons in their demand for the abolition of the badges given by lords to their retainers (and others).[72] The king offered to begin the process by giving up his own badges which embarrassed the Lords as it was probably intended to do. Richard also supported the Commons in their desire to have

---

[68] *West. Chron.*, p. 269.
[69] Clause 13 of the articles of accusation against Burley, Beauchamp, Berners and Salisbury, *Rot. Parl.*, III, pp. 241–3; *West. Chron.*, p. 269.   [70] *West. Chron.*, pp. 273, 277.   [71] Ibid., p. 343.
[72] Saul (1990).

the wool staple moved back to Calais from Middelburg. The main business of the parliament seems to have been the drafting of detailed legislation restricting the mobility of labour and attempting to control wages. At Cambridge the interests of the Commons, which had received scant attention in the Merciless Parliament, were addressed.[73] Richard, distrustful of his 'natural advisers', the Lords, was willing to make common cause with the knights from the shires and the town burgesses. It was not a natural alliance, but it demonstrated that the king was turning his mind to the business of government.

THE PERSONAL RULE OF RICHARD II, 1389–1397

On 3 May 1389 Richard summoned a great council of his lords to Westminster and there formally announced his intention, now that he had reached his majority (he was twenty-two) of shouldering the burden of ruling his kingdom himself. For the first twelve years of his kingship he had been under the control of others and now he planned to conduct business himself for the greater peace and prosperity of the kingdom. A proclamation dated 8 May announced the king's intentions to a wider world.[74] To mark the change he dismissed the three great officers of state who had been chosen by the Appellants and appointed William of Wykeham as chancellor, Thomas Brantingham, bishop of Exeter, as treasurer (both elderly men who had been bishops for twenty years), and Edmund Stafford, a younger cleric, the son of one of the most faithful knights of the Black Prince and on his way to becoming a bishop and chancellor, was made keeper of the privy seal. These were safe, rather than controversial, appointments.

Richard's approach to government was measured: he needed to build up his authority among the nobility and to recreate an efficient and loyal household and secretariat. He had to learn to live with the Appellants and, also, to live without the close friends of his youth. Michael de la Pole died in Paris in September 1389 and Alexander Neville and Robert de Vere died in exile at Louvain in 1392. It is clear that Richard grieved at his inability to help his exiled friends. When Gaunt urged him to allow the banished mayor, John of Northampton, back into London, Richard responded by pointing out that if he could do that for Northampton then he knew of others who had suffered hardship, now overseas, for whom he would like to be able to do as much.[75] To allow de Vere to return would have been political suicide and Richard chose not to take the path followed by Edward II. The Appellants, pricked perhaps

---

[73] There is no surviving parliament roll for the Cambridge parliament, see Tuck (1969).

[74] Rymer, *Foedera*, VII, pp. 618–19; *West. Chron.*, p. 393. Charles VI of France had taken over the personal control of his government 3 November 1388. He was a little younger than Richard II.

[75] *West. Chron.*, p. 441.

by conscience, turned their thoughts towards crusading abroad and Richard was probably not sorry to see them go. Arundel's plans to go to the Holy Land came to nothing, but in 1391 Gloucester departed on a crusade to Prussia and Derby also went to Lithuania in 1390 and again in 1392. In the following year both Derby and Thomas Beauchamp, earl of Warwick, visited the Holy Land as pilgrims: only Mowbray, earl of Nottingham (from 1397 duke of Norfolk), appears to have preferred to stay at home in England.[76] In December 1389 John of Gaunt returned from Castile having successfully married his daughter Catalina to Henry, son and heir of King Juan, and sold his own claim for a sizeable sum. He now provided a stable element in the new aristocratic party which Richard was forming. The new recruits included the duke of York and his son Edward, Mowbray, the king's half-brothers Thomas, earl of Kent, and John, earl of Huntingdon, Sir Thomas Percy, created earl of Worcester in 1397, Sir William Scrope, created earl of Wiltshire, and the young John Beaufort, son of John of Gaunt and Katherine Swynford, who became earl of Somerset in 1397 (see p. 886). Richard used the patronage at his disposal to secure the allegiance of the old nobility and to build up the new; by grants of office and land he broadened the base of his aristocratic support and, on occasion, fostered aristocratic faction. Ralph Neville (the brother of the archbishop and royal supporter, Alexander Neville) in 1397 was created earl of Westmorland in part to challenge the overweening power of the Percies on the northern border.[77] In 1393 the earl of Arundel and the duke of Lancaster came into conflict over their adjacent lordships in the north-western midlands.[78] A certain amount of inter-aristocratic rivalry could work to the king's advantage, but it was a dangerous game to play, and the conflict between Thomas Mowbray and Bolingbroke was to prove fatal to Richard's kingship.

But while Richard cultivated magnate support he remained mindful of his need to woo the Commons. In 1391 the council promulgated an ordinance limiting 'livery and maintenance' but it did not forbid the distribution of badges as the Commons in 1388 had asked.[79] There were few prosecutions although Edward Courtenay, earl of Devon, was brought before the council charged with maintenance. Astutely, Richard did not allow the council to reach a decision but at least he had allowed some kind of warning shot to be fired.[80] Moreover, whereas Richard may have been willing to limit the granting of liveries and to curtail the blatant use of intimidation (the dark side of maintenance) he seems to have intended himself, at least from 1390, to build up his own retinue of men in the shires and in his household badged with his sign of the white hart.[81] These men were to serve as his agents in the localities and

[76] Tyerman (1988), ch. 10.   [77] Storey (1957); Tuck (1968).   [78] Bellamy (1964–5).
[79] Saul (1990).   [80] *Select Cases*, ed. Baldwin, pp. 77–81.   [81] Gordon (1993), pp. 49–50.

could be summoned to the centre to defend and 'enhance' the king's person, should that be necessary.

Throughout this period of his personal rule Richard consistently pursued the search for peace with France. From 1389 a series of truces maintained the *status quo* while the continual embassies toiled over the formulae for a perpetual peace. In March 1390 Richard created John of Gaunt duke of Aquitaine, thus opening the way to a solution of the vexed problem posed by the French demand that the English king, as duke of Aquitaine, should do homage for the duchy. This was an ingenious solution but it was not universally popular: in particular the men of Aquitaine were not happy to have their duchy separated from the English crown. They may not have relished the prospect of a resident duke, especially one with as strong a personality as John of Gaunt.[82] The death of Queen Anne in June 1394 opened the way to new solutions. Two years later it was agreed that Richard should marry Isabella, the seven-year-old daughter of Charles VI, and receive a dowry of £130,000. A twenty-eight-year truce was agreed and future negotiations to secure a permanent peace were planned (but did not materialise). The two kings agreed to act jointly to end the Schism and a joint crusade was also planned.[83] In November Richard crossed the Channel and, in the midst of elaborate ceremonies, married his young bride in the church of St Nicholas at Calais. There is no doubt that the Ricardian 'Field of the Cloth of Gold' was extremely expensive (costing perhaps £10,000–15,000) but this outlay was offset by the rich dowry and by the immense savings to be made by ending the posturings of war.[84] The two barbican towns of Cherbourg and Brest which had been leased from the king of Navarre and the duke of Brittany were given up: they had cost the English more than £5,000 a year to maintain and garrison. The problem of Aquitaine remained unresolved, but the 1396 truce was a tribute to the international standing of the English king and to his distinctive vision of a Europe united under one pope and in pursuit of a common cause against the infidel. It seems likely that Richard had a genuine distaste for shedding Christian blood. Gaunt, and others close to Richard, may well have shared his pacifist concerns but the country as a whole may have found it hard to abandon attitudes and expectations which had developed over two generations: England had been at war with France since 1337. For Richard to have turned this policy around was a considerable diplomatic achievement.

In place of a real war against France Richard could offer his more bellicose subjects a series of spectacular tournaments, particularly notable in the late 1380s and 1390s.[85] There was also the possibility of crusades into northern

[82] Palmer (1966a), (1966b) and (1971a); Philpotts (1990); Goodman (1992).

[83] Palmer (1971a); Keen (1998).   [84] Meyer (1881).

[85] *West. Chron.*, pp. 432–3, 437, 451; Barker (1986); Lindenbaum (1990); Gillespie (1997b), esp. pp. 122–5.

Europe and excursions to fight the infidel in the Mediterranean. Gaunt's son, John Beaufort, and a group of English knights, joined in the French attack on Tunis in 1390 and he led another group who were present at Nicopolis in Hungary where a crusading army was annihilated by the Turks in 1396. Richard's half-brother, John Holland, later duke of Exeter, became a patron of the new Order of the Passion of Jesus Christ founded by Philippe de Mézières and he was joined in the Order by other nobles and men of 'middling rank'.[86] Moreover, Richard himself led two military expeditions to Ireland in 1394–5 and again in 1399. He was the first English king for nearly two hundred years to visit Ireland and he brought a new initiative to that troubled part of his realm. His purpose was less to fight than to reconcile and to bring both the 'wild Irish' and the 'rebel Irish' into allegiance to the English crown.[87] Roger Mortimer, earl of March, was appointed as the king's lieutenant in Ireland; this was a logical choice since he held large estates there. Roger was not only popular, but he was also the heir-presumptive to the English throne (see p. 886) and in 1389 Richard replaced him with his nephew Thomas Holland, duke of Surrey. It is doubtful whether Richard's Irish policy had any long-term effects (although the presence of the English king certainly brought peace in the short term). In the 1390s Richard attempted to provide for his nobility and knights an alternative military lifestyle. There were to be no more *chevauchées* into France, but there were to be bloodless tournaments, crusading ventures and royal expeditions, military in style but pacifist in intention, led by the king himself into the further parts of his realm. In Richard's view such armies were not so much instruments of war as agents of diplomacy.

It was Richard's intention to make himself the effective ruler of all his kingdom and not simply of the south-east; indeed he may well have developed a positive dislike of the south-east (and London in particular) for the support given to the Appellants in 1387–8. But his policy was not simply a negative one: he wanted to rule throughout his kingdom. In the south-west he created his half-brother John Holland duke of Exeter to challenge the control exercised by the Courtenay earls of Devon. In 1397 he elevated the county of Chester into a principality and retained many men from the north-west in his retinue.[88] The king spent a great deal of time travelling around his kingdom and, in particular in the midlands and along the Marches of Wales. But he was concerned also with the north. The peace with France brought with it a truce with Scotland and a chance, therefore, for the king to challenge the power of the Percy earls of Northumberland whose great influence had derived, in part,

[86] De Mézières, *Letter to King Richard II*; for a list of the Englishmen who joined the Order of the Passion, see Clarke (1932).
[87] Curtis (1927a) and (1927b); Tuck (1970); Johnston (1980) and (1981).
[88] R. R. Davies (1971); Morgan (1987).

from their role as the guardians of the northern border against the Scots. In the first place the salary of £3,000 p.a. which the Percies received for keeping the East March could be reduced. Richard then thwarted the Percy desire to have also the keeping of the West March by granting it to his half-brother John Holland, earl of Huntingdon, and then to his cousin Edward, son of the duke of York. But as a check to the pretensions of both the Percies of Alnwick and the Nevilles of Raby, Richard in 1398 appointed Gaunt as lieutenant over the wardens of both Marches.[89] In 1392 Richard travelled north to York, in part to emphasise his displeasure with London but also to assert the reality of royal authority in the northern counties.[90]

Richard's desire to rule throughout his kingdom embraced also 'middle England', the knights and gentry from the shires and the merchants and craftsmen of the towns. Between 1389 and his deposition ten years later, Richard recruited eighty-two knights and 125 esquires, all of them for life: others were probably recruited on short-term contracts. Some of these men had formerly been retained by the Appellants. Their purpose was not primarily military but, rather, they were 'to act as an informal network linking the household and court to the outlying regions of the realm'.[91] Some men served as sheriffs, e.g. Thomas Clanvow in Herefordshire and Sir John Golafre in Berkshire. Others, like Andrew Newport, might be appointed collectors of the customs.[92] Many were elected to parliament, and Sir John Bushy who had first been elected to the Commons in 1383 and was a retainer of the house of Lancaster was skilfully recruited by Richard into the royal affinity. He was elected Speaker in the parliaments of 1394, 1395 and twice in 1397 and effectively controlled the business of the Commons in the king's interest.[93] Sir Edward Dalyngridge from Sussex, once a retainer of the earl of Arundel, and Sir Richard Stury, both king's knights, were among the most active members of the royal council in the 1390s.

In the 1390s Richard took trouble both to influence and to control the council and parliament. Although he had resented and ignored the council that had been imposed upon him in 1386, later in the 1390s he was willing to co-operate with the council where the major influence was not so much that of the nobility, whose attendance was infrequent, but rather the group of hard-working professional men, like Dalyngridge and Stury, who dealt with the humdrum business of government but remained mindful of the royal will. Moreover the council began, as in the summons to Courtenay, to answer accusations of maintenance, to act in a semi-judicial capacity. The concern of parliaments in Henry IV's reign to control the composition of the king's

---

[89] Tuck (1968).   [90] Harvey (1971), but see Saul (1997b).   [91] Saul (1997a), pp. 265–9.
[92] Coleman (1969).   [93] Roskell *et al.* (1992), II, pp. 449–54.

council provides a telling index of the success of Richard in developing the royal council into an effective agent of the royal will. Also by careful management the business of parliament was brought under the king's control, as the judges had declared in 1387 that it should be. In January 1397, the Commons reverted to their old habit of the mid-1380s and presented a four-point petition criticising royal government. Only one of their complaints was novel: they were unhappy at the 'great and excessive' cost of the royal household and the multitude of bishops and ladies who were maintained there. Richard reacted sharply to this charge and claimed that it was not for subjects to criticise the royal household and that by doing so the Commons had offended against his majesty. The unfortunate drafter of the petition, an obscure clerk named Thomas Haxey, was handed over by the contrite Commons. The Lords obligingly declared that those who criticised the king's household were guilty of treason and Haxey was duly sentenced, and then pardoned because of his cloth.[94] It has been suggested that Haxey's petition was a 'put up' job, and that he was used to elicit exactly the declaration that Richard wanted from the Lords, but this is probably unlikely.[95] The affair was, however, skilfully managed to Richard's advantage by Sir John Bushy, the Speaker. Again later in the year, Bushy was able to manoeuvre the Commons into accepting the trial and condemnation of Gloucester, Arundel and Warwick and, almost as important, the grant of the subsidy on wool to the king for life. This grant, together with the setting up of a parliamentary committee to transact unfinished business, suggests that Richard intended, now that he was free from expensive foreign wars, to rule without summoning parliament. There is every likelihood that his subjects would have seen this as a lightening of their burdens.

Richard's policy towards the merchants and artisans of his realm is harder to assess: their role in the Commons seems always to have been subordinate to that of the knights. But it is worth remembering that Richard's constant travelling around his kingdom inevitably led to royal spending on a considerable scale in the provinces. A study of Richard's energetic itinerary in the 1390s reveals the extent to which his frequent visits, often more than once a year, must have boosted the economies of towns like Canterbury, Rochester, Gloucester, Worcester, Nottingham, Northampton, Pontefract and York. At least fifty English towns played host to the king in this decade; the royal household itself would have spent money lavishly and even the most peripheral members needed board and lodging.[96] It seems likely that Richard was probably better known to the townsmen of England than any of his predecessors and they may have found the appearance and cost of his royal estate to their

94 *Rot. Parl.*, III, p. 339. 95 McHardy (1997).
96 For Richard's itinerary, see Saul (1997a), pp. 468–74.

liking. York received particular marks of his favour and Shrewsbury was granted a new charter, apparently at the instigation of Queen Anne.[97] Richard's relations with the city of London are best documented and most contentious. With the backing of his uncles, the magnates and the council, Richard decided in 1392 to bring the city of London to heel. He may well have wanted money, but he was also wearied by the endemic instability and factiousness of London government. The mayor and aldermen were taken into custody, tried and the city fined a total of £30,000, no mean sum albeit lower than that originally proposed. The city was taken into the king's hand and ruled through a royal warden, first Sir Edward Dalyngridge and then another king's knight, Sir Baldwin Raddington. In August the king and queen were received in a magnificent ceremony modelled on that recently offered by Paris to the French queen. The cost of royal displeasure was high, but the blow may well have been softened by Richard's extravagant purchases for the royal household in the years 1392–5. The sum of £12,000 was spent, almost all passing into the pockets of London craftsmen and suppliers, such as the draper John Hende and the mercer, Richard Whittington.[98] In this way, Richard wove economic ties between himself, his household and the 'commercial' classes of England. The ties were not, however, only commercial. The career of Nicholas Brembre, the London grocer who was dazzled by court life and suffered in 1388 for his loyalty to Richard, indicates that late fourteenth-century society may not have felt the hostility to trade of later generations. Brembre's widow Idonia, the daughter of a London vintner, married Sir Baldwin Raddington; John Montagu, earl of Salisbury and one of Richard's close associates at the end of his reign, was married to Maud, daughter of the London mayor and mercer, Adam Fraunceys, and Richard Whittington himself married Alice, the daughter of Sir Ivo Fitzwaryn, one of the knights retained by the king.[99] In these diverse ways royal policy was diffused not only in the shires of England but also in the towns and among the artisans and merchants. Richard did not ignore the wider political nation.

Richard's attempts to develop royal power depended upon an alliance with the Church, both at home and abroad. The death of Pope Urban VI in 1389 failed to end the Schism and his supporters elected Boniface IX as his successor. Boniface needed Richard's support and the English king tried to exploit this need in order to secure the canonisation of Edward II. But in spite of considerable expenditure on Richard's part, gifts, embassies and the construction of a book of Edward's miracles, the pope remained unimpressed.[100] He

[97] Harvey (1971); Saul (1997b); the Shrewsbury charter was granted in 1389, illustrated in Gordon (1993), p. 22.   [98] Barron (1969) and (1971); Kipling (1986); Strohm (1992).

[99] *West. Chron.*, p. 407; Rawcliffe (1994), p. 93; *Calendar of the Cartularies*, ed. O'Connor, pp. 21–2; Barron (1971).   [100] Perroy (1933); Palmer (1968).

may have been less willing to fall in with the wishes of the English king because of the parliamentary statute of 1390 which imposed penalties on those who sought English benefices by papal provision. In fact the king was allowed to use his discretion in the implementation of the act, which thus left him with considerable freedom of action, but from the papal point of view it was less than satisfactory. In the 1390s Boniface blocked a number of appointments to the episcopal bench and a clarification of the rights of king and pope was necessary. In November 1398 a concordat was reached between Richard and Boniface which seemed, to some observers, to have conceded more to the pope than was desirable. It may be that the canonisation of Edward II was Richard's main objective.[101]

There seems to be little doubt that Richard was a man of intense, albeit conventional, piety. He was devoted to the saints and in particular to John the Baptist and to his revered predecessor Edward the Confessor.[102] At times of crisis he visited the Confessor's tomb, and constantly attended the Abbey for the feast day of the saint, accompanied by his queen and dressed in full regalia.[103] Although it is possible that in the 1380s Richard may have been influenced by some of the advanced religious ideas associated with the Lollard knights who were influential in his household, men like Sir Richard Stury, Sir John Clanvow and Sir John Montagu, it seems clear that by the 1390s he saw his role as the champion of orthodoxy against the attacks of heretics.[104] In his epitaph he claimed to have trampled on the enemies of the Church.[105] There was little in the teaching of Wyclif or his Lollard followers that would have appealed to Richard. The saints and the ceremonies of the Church were important to him and, just as he had a role to play in defending the Church, so too the Church provided the setting and style for Richard's vision of his kingship. There seem to have been clerics who shared Richard's vision and, just as the judges had provided the legal justification for royal autocracy, so too the Church in the 1390s supplied the spiritual authentication and setting for that vision. Richard had not got on well with the aristocratic bishops of his youth like William Courtenay who became archbishop of Canterbury in 1381, or Thomas Arundel who succeeded him in 1396. Richard preferred more clerkly bishops such as Edmund Stafford whom he raised to the see of Exeter in 1391 or Thomas Merks, once a monk at Westminster who was made bishop of Carlisle. The courtly bishops, who were criticised in Haxey's petition, included also Richard Mitford, bishop of Salisbury, Robert Tideman of Worcester and Guy Mone of St David's.[106] In the same way that he built up a new aristocratic

---

[101] Theilmann (1990); Walker (1995).   [102] Wood (1988), ch. 10; Saul (1997a), ch. 13.
[103] Saul (1996).   [104] McFarlane (1972); Thomson (1997).
[105] For the text of Richard's epitaph, see *Royal Commission on Historical Monuments . . . Westminster Abbey* (1924), p. 31; for a translation and discussion, see Lindley (1998).   [106] Saul (1997a), p. 370.

party, so too Richard was beginning to construct a bench of bishops whom he found congenial. Many of them remained loyal to him after his deposition. Richard also successfully sought the support of the friars: most of his confessors were Dominicans, and it was among the Franciscans that Henry IV was to encounter the most serious and reasoned attack on the legality of his kingship.[107]

Richard saw the Church as a source of power and authority but it also provided the mysterious and magnificent setting for his kingship. It might be expected that Richard's tomb would be replete with religious imagery, but it is also notable that both the surviving painted portraits of Richard place him within a religious context. The Westminster portrait was painted for the Abbey and clearly suggests a parallel between Christ enthroned and Richard in majesty.[108] Likewise in the Wilton Diptych Richard is shown supported by the saints while on earth, and welcomed by the Virgin and Christ child into the heavenly kingdom.[109] Richard's religion did not lead to self-doubt but, rather, to a confirmation of what he already knew, namely that he was specially chosen and destined for kingship and that to challenge that kingship was to challenge the will of God. Just as the saints were to be treated magnificently on earth, so too the king was to be revered and resplendent. When Richard was offered a reconciliation ceremony by the Londoners in 1392 the theme chosen was the second coming of Christ to the new Jerusalem and four pageants emphasised the spiritual aspects of royal kingship, supported by saints, angels, the Almighty and the gifts of the Eucharist.[110] Magnificence was essential to the personal rule of Richard II, but magnificence was expensive, albeit not as expensive as foreign wars.

There is no doubt that Richard's court was splendid: his tomb and the Wilton Diptych (which, we may presume, was commissioned by the king) indicate his delicacy of taste; Westminster Hall which he remodelled from 1394 reveals the scale of his vision of monarchy and the forty-page inventory of the contents of his treasury catalogues his outstanding wealth.[111] The French truce relieved the king of the need to equip armies, but it also provided Richard with a dowry of £133,333 of which £83,000 was probably received before 1399. Some of this may well have been paid in plate and precious objects which are listed in the inventory; some seems to have been paid in cash directly into the royal chamber. But Richard developed other ways of raising money

---

[107] Ibid., pp. 320–1; Roger Dymmok, the son of the royal champion, Sir John Dymmok, was a Dominican who wrote a defence of Orthodoxy in response to the twelve Lollard propositions of 1395, see Eberle (1985). Dymmok was professed at King's Langley, regent of the London convent in 1396, and preached before Richard on Whitsunday 1391, Emden (1957–9), I, p. 617; for illustration of his book, see Gordon (1993), plate 11; for the Franciscans' defence of Richard II, see *An English Chronicle*, ed. Davies, pp. 23–4; Barron (1990), p. 144 and n. 92.   [108] Alexander (1998).
[109] Gordon (1993).   [110] Kipling (1986).   [111] Eberle (1985); Wilson (1998); Ilg (1994).

independently of a parliamentary grant. In January 1398 the Commons were persuaded to grant him the revenue from the customs for life. London had been fined £30,000 as the price of only a partial restoration of its liberties in 1392. In the summer of 1397 commissioners toured the country to raise loans for the king: 220 lenders were noted in the receipt rolls of the exchequer as lending a total of £22,000; but many refused, so the loans cannot have been forced. Very few had been repaid by the time of Richard's deposition. From 1397 onwards Richard also began to sell charters of pardon to those who had been associated with the Appellants in 1387–8. In all, these sales may have raised as much as £30,000.[112] Richard well understood what Sir John Fortescue was later to analyse, namely that it is crucial for kings to be very much wealthier than their great nobles. When Richard departed for Ireland in 1399 he left nearly £50,000 stored in the castle at Holt in his principality of Chester. The English monarchy in the 1390s was financially strong and visually impressive. Richard might be forgiven for thinking that he was invulnerable. What went wrong?

TRIUMPH AND DEFEAT, 1397–1399

Until the summer of 1397 Richard had been able to strengthen the crown without provoking much dissent. With the help of Sir John Bushy, elected as Speaker for the Commons in the January parliament of 1397 and again in September, he had been able to choke off the Commons' criticism of his household and expenditure. The truce with France had been secured in spite of the grumbling hostility of the duke of Gloucester. Many of the retainers of the Appellants of 1387–8 had been recruited into the royal retinue. The king had surrounded himself with a new aristocracy of his own choosing.[113] But in spite of all this apparent security he decided to make a pre-emptive strike against the Appellants: Gloucester, Arundel and Warwick were all arrested and, in the parliament of September 1397, Arundel and Warwick were both appealed of treason and condemned; Arundel was executed in London and Warwick was sentenced to life imprisonment. Gloucester was bundled out of England to Calais where he conveniently died, or, more likely, was murdered on Richard's orders and with the connivance of Thomas Mowbray, earl of Nottingham, who had been wooed away from the other Appellants and was captain of Calais. It has been suggested that, in taking action against the old Appellants, Richard was motivated simply by revenge: to punish these men for the humiliations that he had suffered at their hands a decade earlier.[114] It is true

---

[112] Barron (1968).   [113] Mott (1991), esp. pp. 168–9.

[114] In a letter written to the emperor Manuel Palaeologus in 1398, Richard refers to traitorous noblemen who while he was of a tender age had attacked the prerogative and royal rights, *English Historical Documents*, ed. Myers, pp. 174–5.

that Richard had a long memory, but it seems likely that his main motive was fear. The author of the *Traison* writes that there was a new plot against Richard in the summer of 1397.[115] In fact this seems unlikely, but it may well be that Richard believed that there was such a plot and decided to take pre-emptive action. The fact that Gloucester's brothers, the dukes of Lancaster and York, concurred in Richard's action may suggest that they also believed that Gloucester's loyalty was not certain. When parliament met the scene had been well prepared for Richard's triumph.[116] Edmund Stafford, bishop of Exeter and chancellor, preached on the duties of obedience and his words struck home. The act which established the council of 1386 was repealed as were the pardons to the Appellants. Archbishop Arundel was impeached by the Commons for his part in the events of 1387–8 and was deprived of his office and exiled. When the parliament assembled again in January at Shrewsbury the acts of the Merciless Parliament were repealed. In an attempt to secure the permanence of these new acts it was decided that the main heirs of the condemned Appellants should never be able to sit either in parliament or on the council: a curious attempt to emasculate the political role of some of the leading members of the aristocracy. Since their lands and estates had, in any case, been forfeited to the crown their heirs would have been unable to play a significant political role. New titles were granted to Richard's new aristocratic supporters (the 'duketti' of Walsingham's contemptuous phrase)[117] and estates were carved out of the forfeited lands to support the titles. All those present in the autumn parliament swore on St Edward's shrine to maintain all the acts of that parliament in perpetuity. On the final day of the parliament at Shrewsbury a committee was set up to deal with any outstanding business. With his enemies destroyed, and assured sources of revenue from the French dowry and the customs, Richard may well have thought that was the last parliament with which he would have to deal. He was right, but not for the reasons he supposed.

The two sessions of the parliament of 1397–8 represent a remarkable working out of the principles formulated in the judges' answers of 1387. This was parliament as Richard envisaged it, where the king controlled the course of the business and the Lords and Commons acted in obedience to the royal will. The compliance of parliament in this remarkable transformation of the political scene is not hard to understand: Richard had deprived the Lords of

---

[115] Printed in *Chronicles of the Revolution*, ed. Given-Wilson, pp. 99–102.

[116] Substantial extracts from the accounts of the parliament to be found in the chronicles of Thomas Walsingham, the monk of Evesham, the anonymous author of the *Eulogium Historiarum,* and in the rolls of parliament, are printed in *Chronicles of the Revolution*, ed. Given-Wilson, pp. 55–89; see also the account in *Chronicon Adae de Usk*, ed. Thompson, pp. 22–35; Given-Wilson (1993a).

[117] *Annales Ricardi Secundi*, p. 223.

leadership and provided his own ring-leaders; 42 per cent of the Commons were newcomers and the king had ensured that the Speaker should be his servant, Sir John Bushy.[118] The king had taken considerable trouble to control what took place in parliament and he had been successful.

The policy of seeking oaths to secure the permanence of what had taken place in parliament was extended to the wider community: mayors and bailiffs, sheriffs, clerics and bishops were all required to swear to uphold the acts of these two parliamentary sessions. Men were persuaded to purchase charters of pardon without thereby securing any real security.[119] In this suspicious and uncertain atmosphere two people felt particularly threatened: Henry Bolingbroke, recently raised to the dukedom of Hereford, and Thomas Mowbray, made duke of Norfolk. Both had been Appellants in 1387–8. Mowbray was probably the most insecure for Henry was protected by the great Lancastrian estates and by the pre-eminent position of his father. Norfolk was more isolated: moreover, he was, in some way, complicit in the death of the duke of Gloucester. Mowbray attempted to draw Bolingbroke into partnership with him against Richard but the plan, if such it was, misfired and Hereford instead revealed Mowbray's concerns to Richard.[120] The king was unable to stem the tide of charge and counter-charge and the two men were ordered, by the parliamentary committee which met in March, to submit their dispute to trial by battle. At Coventry on 16 September they met in the lists only to be deprived by the king of the chance to do battle. He could not afford for either man to win and so they were banished, Norfolk for life and Bolingbroke for ten years. Here again Richard appears to have been able to master a difficult situation and to turn it to his advantage. Mowbray was, clearly, an erratic and insecure man and, if he was going to talk a great deal, it was better that he should do so abroad. Bolingbroke could be sent away to cool his heels and to look for a new wife now that Mary Bohun had died in July 1394. With the passage of time his presence in England would become less threatening to the king. The duke of Lancaster had agreed to the sentence and there was no one else to object. But the situation was more dangerous for the king than it appeared for he had eliminated all those from his circle who might have criticised or tempered his views: his finger was on too few pulses.

For the moment, however, all seemed secure. New oaths were elicited from Richard's subjects which now included a promise to uphold the judgements and ordinances made at Coventry.[121] This same concern for the maintenance of the parliamentary acts of 1397–8 and the judgements at Coventry is to be found also in Richard's will (drawn up in April 1399) where the residue of the

---

[118] Roskell *et al.* (1992), I, pp. 197–208.   [119] Barron (1968).
[120] For a recent interpretation of these obscure events, Given-Wilson (1994).   [121] Barron (1968).

considerable royal treasure is to pass to Richard's successor only if he firmly observed and ratified the acts and judgements.[122] That the king placed so much faith in oaths often unwillingly given, suggests that he was losing touch with reality.

The banishment of Bolingbroke was intended as a holding device to keep him out of the way until the gossip had died down. But the success of this delaying tactic depended upon John of Gaunt living long enough for his son and his sovereign to be reconciled. Richard's gamble did not pay off for Gaunt died on 3 February 1399, and Richard was faced with the problem of the succession to the great Lancastrian estates. Could he take the risk and allow Bolingbroke to succeed as duke of Lancaster? Gaunt, whatever his personal failings, had never threatened Richard politically: he had always been conspicuously loyal to his nephew (while offering plenty of unwelcome advice) and it is noticeable that the most serious threats to Richard's rule occurred while Gaunt was out of the kingdom. The comparative success and stability of royal rule in the 1390s may have owed as much to Gaunt's support as to Richard's authority. Richard decided to play safe and on 18 March revoked the letters of attorney which would have enabled Bolingbroke, in his absence, to take possession of his title and his lands. Little was done to make royal power effective within the Lancastrian palatinate and it may well be that Richard intended to hand over the estates, if not to Bolingbroke, then to his son.[123] The Lancastrian inheritance was not treated in the same way as the forfeited lands of the disgraced Appellants, that is they were not divided up and used to augment the royal estates or to reward loyal servants. The revocation of the powers of attorney was simply another holding action on Richard's part.

It is possible that Richard failed fully to appreciate the risks that he took in revoking the letters of attorney. To deny Bolingbroke the inheritance that he had every right to expect and then to leave his kingdom virtually undefended while he sailed off on another expedition to Ireland was political folly. Richard left for Waterford on 1 June and by the end of June Bolingbroke, having slipped the inattentive eye of the duke of Orléans, was sailing along the east coast of England looking for a suitable landing place. On 4 July the keeper of the realm, the ineffective duke of York, sent Richard a message to tell him of Bolingbroke's landing at Ravenspur. The king delayed in Ireland, perhaps because he was treacherously advised, but more probably, because he had dismissed the ships that had brought him to Ireland and it took time for a new fleet to be assembled.[124] Although Richard sent the earl of Salisbury ahead to raise troops in North Wales, the king himself did not arrive in South Wales

---

[122] Richard's will is translated in Harvey (1967), pp. 156–9, App. vi.   [123] Mott (1991).
[124] Johnston (1983b); Sherborne (1975).

until 24–7 July.[125] But at about the same time as Richard arrived, the duke of York capitulated to Henry at Berkeley Castle and, two days later, Bristol fell on 27 July. At Carmarthen Richard decided to abandon his household and to make his way northwards through Wales to join up with Salisbury. While he was making this difficult journey Henry was consolidating his successes: on 5 August Chester, the heartland of Richard's kingdom, submitted to Bolingbroke. By the time that Richard reached the security of Conway Castle he had few cards left to play, except escape by sea. On 12 August Northumberland arrived as Henry's envoy and persuaded Richard to leave Conway for Flint Castle where Bolingbroke was waiting to discuss terms with him. Northumberland, who had received the coveted grant of the wardenship of the West March from Henry under the seal of the duchy of Lancaster, probably intended to make Henry king.[126] Henry himself, however, may well have been undecided at this point, but he knew that he wanted to be confirmed as duke of Lancaster and that a parliament should be held to settle the outstanding matters between him and the king. But even if Henry was undecided at Flint, by the time he and Richard had reached Chester his mind must have been made up for him by the arrival of the mayor of London and a deputation of the citizens who renounced their fealty to Richard under the city's common seal.[127] On 19 August writs were issued, in Richard's name, but by authority of the duke, for a parliament to meet at Westminster at the end of September. From this point it must have been clear that Richard was a prisoner and that Henry was to become king of England. The only remaining question was how that transfer of authority was to be achieved and made legitimate.

While Richard was kept securely in the Tower of London, Henry and his advisers sought desperately for legal formulae and historical precedents to justify what they were about to do. The rightful heir was young Edmund Mortimer, earl of March, who was descended from the second son of Edward III through the female line: Henry was descended from the third son but in the male line (see p. 886). It had not been customary in England to exclude descent through the female line and, indeed, the English claim to the French crown lay through the female line. Henry could not, therefore, seek legitimation through that route. In the end, on 29 September, Richard was persuaded to resign, probably under duress, although it is not clear whether he resigned the crown to Henry or simply resigned it back whence it had come, namely to God. A list of Richard's crimes (thirty-three of them, one for each year of his life?) was compiled and this, together with Richard's resignation, was read out to a

---

[125] It is difficult to establish when Richard left Ireland, and when he arrived in Wales; Sayles (1979) believed he left Ireland on 17 July.   [126] Bean (1959), p. 220; see also Sherborne (1988).
[127] Barron (1990), p. 142.

meeting of parliament on 30 September. Henry then read out, in English, his own claim to the crown which was a blurred amalgam of several possible justifications: by descent from Henry III, by divine grace, and from the need of the kingdom for good government.[128] In spite of the enthusiastic response of the Lords and Commons to Henry's claim, and in spite of his coronation on St Edward's day when oil given by the Virgin herself to Thomas Becket was used for the anointing, Henry was king only *de facto* and not *de jure*.[129] Richard remained the anointed king and, even after his death, he continued to haunt his Lancastrian successors.[130] The Lancastrian propaganda machine produced an official account of Richard's deposition, *The Record and Process*, which has long been discredited as a truthful record of what happened.[131] This Lancastrian view of events deeply influenced almost all the English chroniclers' accounts not only of what happened in 1399, but also of the last years of Richard's reign. The French chronicles written by courtiers close to Richard in the last months present a more favourable view of the king, but fail to analyse the nature of his rule: they explain the catastrophe that overwhelmed him largely in terms of personal malice and treachery.[132] It was convenient for the Lancastrians to represent the rapid collapse of support for Richard in terms of his general unpopularity, thus bolstering Henry's claim that the kingdom was 'on the point of being undone for lack of governance'. But it is possible that it was the vacillating leadership of the keeper of the realm, and the absence of Richard himself in Ireland, which explained the apparent lack of support. There was no effective leader for the Ricardian cause and so his potential support withered away. Had Richard been able, or willing, to return much more quickly from Ireland the whole situation might have turned out very differently. As it was, a number of men in Cheshire and elsewhere, including the redoubtable Henry Despenser, bishop of Norwich, attempted to fight for Richard. Moreover at Christmas, following Richard's deposition, a group of men who had been close to Richard formed a plot to restore him. These included the two Hollands, his half-brother and nephew, Thomas Despenser, earl of Gloucester, and John Montagu, earl of Salisbury. These men had been spared by Henry; they had lost their most recent titles but had retained most of their lands: there was no reason for them to rise against Henry unless prompted by loyalty to Richard. They were supported by a number of knights and clerics. But, just as de Vere's gallant but ill-fated sortie in December 1387

---

[128] *Rot. Parl.*, III, pp. 422–3; Strohm (1992), ch. 4.

[129] *Annales Ricardi Secundi*, pp. 299–300; Wilson (1990).

[130] McNiven (1994); Morgan (1995); Strohm (1996).

[131] Printed and discussed in *Chronicles of the Revolution*, ed. Given-Wilson, pp. 168–89; Stow (1984); Barron (1990).

[132] See the account of Jean Creton in *Chronicles of the Revolution*, ed. Given-Wilson, pp. 137–62.

had proved fatal to Richard, so now, exactly twelve years later, another attempt at a military enterprise on Richard's behalf was easily foiled and proved equally disastrous.[133] Within a month Richard was dead: the rising had revealed the dangers in living predecessors. But it had also revealed that Richard had been capable of inspiring loyalty and that his rule had its supporters as well as its detractors.

It would help to understand Richard's view of his kingship if we knew something of what he read, or of the ideas that influenced him. His tutors appear to have brought him up on a diet of French romances but it is likely that he was able to read Latin. More than his Lancastrian supplanters, he encouraged poets at court: Froissart, Chaucer, Sir John Clanvow and Sir John Montagu; Gower wrote the *Confessio Amantis* at Richard's request.[134] In 1390 Richard paid the clerks of London £10 to perform a play of the Passion of Our Lord and the Creation of the World at Skinners' well.[135] Manuscripts were dedicated to the king, but it is hard to know whether their contents reflect the known tastes of the recipient or simply the preoccupations of the writer. The French knight, Philippe de Mézières addressed his *Epistre* to Richard in 1395/6 in which he urged him to become a patron of the new order of the Passion of Christ dedicated to winning back the Holy Land.[136] At about the same time Roger Dymmok, a Dominican Doctor of Theology presented Richard with a treatise challenging various Lollard heresies: he praised Richard's wisdom and defended the sumptuous lifestyle of the royal court which taught the people to know their place and to respect their superiors.[137] A beautifully crafted manuscript in the Bodleian Library was written for Richard, if not necessarily at his behest, by an unknown author. The king is told how to understand men by following the rules of geomancy, by reading dreams and by assessing physical attributes. In the effusive introduction Richard is praised, not for his military prowess, nor for his justice, but for his intellect and insight. By using the book the king's wisdom will become yet more apparent, his subjects will bless his rule and they will become obedient in all things.[138] These authors were aware of the messages that would be acceptable to the king and their works fit well with the image of Richard's kingship to be derived from his own letters and the wording of his charters.

Richard's rule has been characterised as 'empty'.[139] Perhaps it was not so much empty as unrealistic. It is true that Richard frequently mistook outward

---

[133] Ibid., pp. 224–39; McNiven (1969–70); Crook (1991).   [134] Green (1980).

[135] Lancashire (1984), no. 543.   [136] De Mézières, *Letter to King Richard II.*

[137] *Rogeri Dymmok Liber*, see n. 108 above.

[138] Oxford, Bodleian Library MS 581; Taylor (1971); Carey (1992).   [139] Saul (1997a), p. 467.

show for the reality of power. By his choice of imperial titles, and by his style and dress, he deliberately distanced himself from his people.[140] He might have been well advised to read Bracton, or treatises on the art of war, or of instructions for a prince, but he chose instead to focus on the religious and imperial aspects of his kingship. His vision of a strong, unchallenged, monarchy was rooted in his sense of the past and in the traditions of English kingship as he understood them, but it looked forward also to the centralised kingship of the Yorkists and Tudors.[141]

The reign of Richard II witnessed some remarkable changes, many of them nurtured by a declining population and rising prosperity; new attitudes to religious practice and belief; widespread use of written English by all classes of society (ranging from the 'Peasant' letters of 1381 to Henry Bolingbroke's claim to the English throne in parliament). A wider swathe of the population was making its voice heard: the rural workers of Kent and Essex and the small men in towns like London and York. In parliament the Commons were able to define and defend their procedures, to act independently of the Lords and to take the initiative in forming and criticising policy. In the face of so much change and challenges to the customary ways of doing things Richard, aided by his legal and clerical advisers, developed a theory of royal autocracy. The crown was to control parliament but, preferably, to be able to live 'of its own' without summoning it. This independence was to be secured by the cessation of foreign wars and by building up the financial resources of the crown. Under a magnificent and impressive ruler, subjects would learn the true value of obedience and peace: they would also be unified in their observance of the one Catholic faith.[142] This vision of a united and loyal kingdom encompassed the 'wild' Irish, the Welsh, the Marcher lords and the great magnates like the Percies, Nevilles and Courtenays who lived in the more distant parts of the realm. This harmonious enterprise was to be serviced by an efficient and loyal group of household knights and clerks of the royal chapel who would be guided and ordered by the king supported, in his turn, by his peerage and his bishops. But if the peaceable kingdom could not be secured through willing consent then force might be necessary. There was a ruthless streak in Richard's great plan, as Gloucester, Arundel and Warwick discovered. The king could not accept either opposition or criticism and so his vision became an essentially private one, shared only with a few like-minded courtiers. Even among those close to the king an atmosphere of mistrust and fear grew up which was hard to eliminate. By the end of the reign it had overwhelmed the king himself.

The monarchy in twentieth-century Britain has moved a long way from the

---

[140] Saul (1995).   [141] Barron (1985); Saul (1997a), p. 440.   [142] Eberle (1985).

Ricardian vision: parliament and the 'small people' now occupy the centre stage. It is hard, therefore, to set his vision in its own political context. Richard lacked, indeed he would have despised, the negotiating skills which might have enabled him to sell his vision to his subjects. The social and political tensions in Richard's reign were acute and the king failed to resolve them.

WALES

A. D. Carr

WITH the death of Llywelyn ap Gruffydd, prince of Wales, on 11 December 1282 and the execution of his brother Dafydd the following October Welsh independence came to an end. The Principality recognised by the English crown in the Treaty of Montgomery of 1267 came into the hands of Edward I. Under the Statute of Wales of March 1284 counties and sheriffs were grafted on to the existing Welsh administrative structures and new courts were established. English criminal law and procedure were introduced, although Welsh law remained in civil and personal actions; in the south-west and in parts of the March it survived until the sixteenth century. Edward's hold on the Principality was secured by the construction of a series of castles. Several had been built after the Treaty of Aberconwy in 1277, but the later ones, at Caernarfon, Conway, Harlech and Beaumaris, are among the outstanding monuments of medieval military architecture. Attached to each of these castles was a borough; the terms of their foundation charters were generous and they were intended as centres of English settlement which could reinforce the castle garrisons if necessary and where trade could be concentrated. The changes brought about in 1284 are usually described as the Edwardian Settlement of North Wales; a similar pattern prevailed in the southern counties of the Principality but it had evolved over a longer period.

The fundamental division between the March, comprising those autonomous lordships which were the result of Anglo-Norman penetration since the eleventh century, and native Wales, now the Principality, continued. Edward could not have legislated for the whole of Wales, even if he had wished to; there was no reason for him to interfere in the March and many of the lordships were by now held by English magnates. What he did do, however, was to take advantage of any problems in particular lordships by using his prerogative, as he did when two lords went to war over a boundary dispute in 1291; the royal administration was sometimes able to bring pressure to bear on other lords as well.

Apart from its military and economic aspects, the settlement was generally conservative. At the local level power remained in the hands of the traditional leaders; the only difference was that authority was now exercised in the name of the crown. These men, some of whom had served both prince and king at different times in the past, continued to hold office; indeed, the royal government could not have functioned without their co-operation. On the whole they accepted the new order as long as they were left undisturbed and their local dominance was not threatened; in some ways they may have felt more comfortable under Edward since Llywelyn's financial exactions and his heavy hand during the last years of his rule had been a severe strain on his people's loyalty. Marcher lords had long since realised that Welshmen were best ruled through Welshmen; the lesson had not been lost on Edward.

Between the Statute of 1284 and the end of the thirteenth century there were two revolts in Wales, but neither of them can be seen as an attempt to recover a lost independence. The first, in 1287, was a protest by a disillusioned southern lord; his revolt was soon suppressed and he was captured and executed. The second rebellion, in 1294–5, was far more serious. Led by members of native royal houses, the rebels had some success at the beginning and Edward was obliged to call off a planned campaign in France to deal with them. The rising was eventually put down, but, although the cost was to contribute to a major financial and constitutional crisis in England, there were no reprisals; the king seems to have handled the whole business with tact and sensitivity and the key to this may lie in the part played in the rising by the leaders of the native Welsh community. It was the participation of these men that made Edward realise that something was amiss. There were several reasons for their dissatisfaction; a new royal tax was very much resented, as was the levying of troops in 1294 for Edward's abortive campaign in France. But the main grievance in the Principality came from the demands of royal tax collectors, especially in the north. These demands had been based on the abnormal circumstances of Llywelyn's last years; by 1294 the leaders of the community were impelled to protest and there is some evidence to suggest that the revolt was premeditated. What these men wanted was fair dealing rather than the restoration of the native dynasty and Edward took the point. The whole episode is symbolic of the relationship of crown and community in the years after the conquest; there was collaboration, but there could also be conflict.

In 1301 Edward had made his son, Edward of Caernarfon, prince of Wales. He became king as Edward II in 1307 and it was during his reign that Wales played its most significant part in medieval English politics. This was due to that tension between the king and the baronial leaders that eventually erupted in civil war in 1322. Many of the key figures were themselves Marcher lords and the result was that both Principality and March were inevitably sucked into the troubles of the reign. The division of the lordship of Glamorgan, following the death of the earl of Gloucester in 1314 without a direct heir, threatened the whole Marcher balance of power and alarmed the other lords; the consequence was war, involving much of the southern March, in 1321–2. This outbreak in turn shattered the delicate balance of forces in England, which had depended a great deal on Marcher magnates; the result was civil war and a royal victory. What had begun as a Marcher dispute in Wales brought about the destruction of the baronial leaders and a realignment of forces.

Wales also played its part in the fall of Edward II, especially with the involvement of the leading Marcher magnate, Roger Mortimer of Wigmore, who became the lover of Queen Isabella. After the couple's return to England from France in 1326, the fugitive king was captured near Neath, to be imprisoned and then murdered. The deposition had its impact on Wales; in a sense it marked the end of the political honeymoon which the leaders of the Welsh political nation in the Principality and the crown had enjoyed since 1284. The Welsh in the royal lands seem to have been loyal to Edward II and there appears to have been at least one plot hatched in North Wales to rescue Edward from captivity; it was subsequently claimed that it was a warning from Mortimer's representative there of another plot that led to the decision to eliminate the deposed king. But Welsh attitudes were, in fact, rather more complex than may at first appear. In much of the March the situation was different; Welsh leaders might well take the same side as their lord. And there was always a danger that the native leaders would be led into temptation. The Bruce invasion of Ireland in 1315 seems to have been followed by approaches by Robert and Edward Bruce to some leading Welshmen and these approaches met with a response. Edward II handled the leaders of the community in the Principality with care, although one of them does appear to have undergone a term of imprisonment. But there was no special loyalty to Edward's son and successor Edward III. Royal favour was now shown in North Wales to the English burgesses in the castle boroughs; the result was an increasing disillusion among the leaders of the native community, especially since Edward III, once he had seized personal power, looked on his lands in Wales as nothing more than a source of men and money for his military campaigns.

In 1343 the Principality was granted to the king's eldest son Edward, better known as the Black Prince and the new prince's officials continued to exploit the resources of the lordship. It may have been the enquiries carried out by the prince's administration, coupled with the resentment that had been building up among leading Welshmen, that led to several violent episodes in 1344 and 1345. The result was a climate of hysteria among the English in North Wales and threats that they would leave unless something were done. The prince's administration also tried to extend its authority over the March, going further here than any native prince had ever ventured. But every such attempt was countered by protest and the independence of the March from the Principality was confirmed by a statute of 1354 which reiterated that Marcher lords were tenants-in-chief of the crown.

The impact on Wales of the French wars which began in 1337 was profound. Both Principality and March were sources of men for royal campaigns and some Welshmen distinguished themselves; the typical Welsh fighting-man, however, was the ordinary archer or infantryman, a brave if somewhat undisciplined soldier. Welshmen served in most of the main theatres of the war, although no fortunes seem to have been made with the colours; with the temporary ending of hostilities in 1360 some found their way into free companies. At home in Wales military service may have siphoned off some of the more disorderly elements in the community; on the other hand there was some concern that service in France could leave parts of Wales without adequate defence and there were several reports from officials in the Principality of suspicious ships being sighted off the coast, along with fears of French or Castilian landings.

Like most fourteenth-century economies, that of Wales was predominantly agricultural. Industry was on a small scale, being mainly the mining of coal and metals; many industrial workers and craftsmen were also farmers or smallholders and few were without any connection with the land. The main exports were wool, cloth, cattle, leather and timber; wine, salt and luxury goods were imported and contemporary poetry shows that wine from France or Spain or sugar from Cyprus or India could reach the tables of squires in Cardiganshire or Anglesey. There were no large towns; most were market and service centres, serving local communities and many were little more than villages. The most prosperous towns in Wales were probably the ports of the south-west, Carmarthen, Haverfordwest and Tenby, all of them with an extensive foreign trade; other ports were Chepstow, Cardiff, Swansea and Cardigan in the south and Beaumaris and Conway in the north, while local centres included Brecon, Oswestry, Ruthin and Wrexham. Many of these had originally been intended as English settlements, but by the beginning of the fourteenth century a number included a strong Welsh element and there were some which had always been Welsh. It was not uncommon for burgesses to marry the daughters of Welsh squires and for their descendants to be completely absorbed by the native community; the son of the Caernarfon burgess Walter de Hampton was known as Gwilym ap Wat and he joined the Glyn Dŵr revolt.

At the head of the social order stood the traditional leaders of the native community. Their position was based on the offices they held before and after the conquest, on their power and influence in their own localities and on their land, some of it hereditary and some of it the result of princely generosity. The leading lineage was that of Ednyfed Fychan; in 1485 one of his descendants was to become king of England and during the fourteenth century members of this lineage were the undisputed leaders of the native community, particularly in North Wales. But there were many other families which played a similar part, if not on the same scale; in both Principality and March they held most of the offices at the local level and they formed a close-knit network. They have been described as a squirearchy, but the Welsh term *uchelwyr* is probably more appropriate. In the absence of a native ruler and court after 1282 they also assumed cultural leadership, becoming the patrons of the native poetic tradition. This was the age of Dafydd ap Gwilym, one of the greatest of all medieval European poets, who established a new pattern of lyric poetry composed within a strict metrical system. The poets, professional craftsmen who had served a rigorous apprenticeship, came from the ranks of the *uchelwyr* and some of them held local offices. They expressed the values and attitudes of their kinsmen and patrons and they also gave voice to their political awareness; they formed a key part of the Welsh political nation.

Some families were more successful than others and the fourteenth century saw the beginnings of landed estates as the Welsh pattern of free tenure, under which most land was vested in a kindred group and was therefore inalienable, was being diluted; at the same time, hereditary land was being bought and sold. To facilitate the transfer of land it was possible to use a Welsh legal device called *prid*; this was a kind of gage or pledge in which land was pledged for a term of years in return for a sum of money. Many conveyances in *tir prid* survive in collections of family papers, showing that the device played a part in the growth of estates, but there are even more conveyances by English law, notwithstanding the prohibition, which suggests that it was increasingly a dead letter. Hundreds of deeds testify to the emergence of a flourishing land market in fourteenth-century Wales and this period saw the beginning of the rise of some of the great landowning families. Many of these *uchelwyr* were men of substantial wealth in land, livestock, cash and goods; Cynwrig Sais of Northop in Flintshire, who died in 1311, had £120 in ready money, while Llywelyn Bren, the leader of the 1315 revolt in Glamorgan, had eight books, three of them being in Welsh.

The fundamental division in this society was the universal one between free and unfree, but there was another. In many parts of Wales an Englishman was a rare sight, but some regions, like south Pembrokeshire, were almost completely Anglicised as a result of immigration and settlement going back to the twelfth century. In the north, and especially in the new Marcher lordships of the north-east, it was a recent development; this had sometimes led to the removal of Welsh tenants to inferior land to make way for the new settlers, which caused a long-standing resentment. The two peoples lived under different laws and customs and each was suspicious of the other's way of life and culture. The consequence was a tension which from time to time erupted in violence. To the Englishman in Denbigh or Dyffryn Clwyd the Welshman might appear to be shifty, immoral and dishonest; to his Welsh neighbour the Englishman was often a convenient scapegoat for all his problems.

As in the rest of Europe, the fourteenth century was a period of crisis. In the first half of the century came climatic change, famine, livestock epidemics and natural disasters. Then, in 1349, came the great pandemic of bubonic plague known as the Black Death. By the spring of 1349 it had reached Gwent. It then moved along the border to sweep through North Wales, while in the south-west it seems to have come to the town of Carmarthen by sea and then to have spread from there. Surviving records bear witness to its devastating impact; one contemporary chronicler estimated that it killed one third of the population of Wales and a contemporary poet described its effects. In the short term land was left untenanted and crops unharvested and the effects of the plague are shown in the records; rents could not be collected and more and more land came into the hands of royal and Marcher escheators. The fact that so many victims were bondmen meant a shortage of labour to work seigneurial demesnes and the general dislocation of the times made it easy for many to move away in search of better prospects. Whole communities were decimated and many were never to recover; although evidence does not survive from every region, there is enough to reveal the impact of the pestilence. And the plague of 1349 was only the first and worst visitation; it was to return time and again and parts of South Wales suffered particularly badly in 1361–2 and 1369.

But the long-term consequences of the plague were not universally disastrous. It solved the population problem and played a significant part in the dissolution of the traditional pattern of free tenure, which was further weakened by the operation of partible succession. The result of this was that many who found their shares of the patrimony too small after several generations of partition sold out to more successful neighbours. Most of the untenanted land had found tenants within a few years; so anxious had the authorities been to dispose of this land that few questions were asked and this meant that incomers were able to take up leases and thus take the first steps on the road to prosperity. Another consequence was the abandonment in the March of direct seigneurial exploitation of demesne farming. This process had begun before the outbreak, as some lords found the working of the demesne to be increasingly uneconomic and it was accelerated after 1349. Lordship now became increasingly a matter of collecting rents and dues. And rural depopulation continued; by the early fifteenth century many bond communities had disappeared, their arable lands being let for grazing.

As in the rest of Europe the result of all this was a climate of restlessness and disorientation. There appears to have been a burgeoning disillusion with the crown and the house of Plantagenet among the leaders of Welsh society. In times of trouble and tension it was easy to blame the authorities and if they happened to be the representatives of an alien ruler they were an even more convenient scapegoat. There may always have been an undercurrent of old loyalties, even among the hardheaded realists and men of affairs who made up the Welsh political nation and this may have contributed to the cause of the last heir of the house of Gwynedd who, in the 1370s, was involved in more than one bid to recover his patrimony.

Owain ap Thomas ap Rhodri was the great-nephew of Llywelyn ap Gruffydd. His grandfather, Llywelyn's youngest brother, had retired to England, where he died in 1315. In 1369 his grandson Owain went over to the French. He became one of the leading mercenary captains in French service, being known as Yvain de Galles. In 1369 and again in 1372 he tried, with French support, to recover his inheritance but both expeditions were aborted. Another expedition was planned but nothing came of it; eventually, in 1378, Owain was assassinated by an English agent while besieging Mortagne-sur-Gironde. Owain was a great deal more than an ambitious pretender and many Welsh soldiers in English service joined him, forming a Welsh company; some of these men were still in the service of France in the 1390s. The fact that they joined his cause indicates that there were those in Wales who were well aware of who he was and what he represented; there is some poetry addressed to him and there is also some other evidence which indicates that his claim evoked a response among leading Welshmen. This may explain why the decision was taken to eliminate him in 1378. The whole episode may reflect the restlessness of the leaders of the native community; the restoration of the native dynasty may have been seen as a practical possibility, especially when the claimant was a distinguished soldier, able to draw on French support. Owain was not forgotten in Wales; he was remembered by his nickname Owain Lawgoch (Owain of the Red Hand) and he joined the ranks of the Sleeping Heroes, asleep in a cave awaiting the call to rise and save his people.

The social, political and economic problems of the time affected the whole of Wales and the Church did not escape them. After about 1350 more and more preferment went to royal clerks and chaplains and there was an increasing tendency for the clerical members of *uchelwyr* families to be ignored. This was yet another cause of resentment, as educated Welsh clerics saw themselves deprived of the promotion which they regarded as their right. The lesser clergy were faced with the problems of inflation and falling agricultural prices and the monasteries shared the problems which faced all large landowners. Another problem in the second half of the century was that of law and order. By the end of the century every man with any pretensions to importance had his *plaid* or retinue, made up of kinsmen, dependants and tenants, which he would use to get his own way when necessary. The return of experienced and unemployed fighting men from the French wars meant that a pool of recruits for these retinues was available and surviving judicial records show how far *uchelwyr* could flout the law when it suited them. Nor was the lack of resident lords in most Marcher lordships conducive to the maintenance of good order, even though there were arrangements between many lordships for the extradition and even the trial and punishment of offenders from elsewhere. The political problems in England during the latter part of the reign of Richard II did not have much direct impact although on his return from his last Irish campaign in 1399 the king landed in South Wales and moved north to Flint, where he was taken into custody by Henry Bolingbroke, who, as Henry IV, was to take his place as king.

The central episode in the history of late-medieval Wales began a year after Richard's deposition. In September 1400 a Welsh lord, Owain ap Gruffydd Fychan or Owain Glyn Dŵr, lord of Glyndyfrdwy and Cynllaith Owain, was proclaimed prince of Wales in the presence of some of the leading men of the north-east; this was followed by an attack on the town of Ruthin. Owain was descended from the royal houses of Powys and Deheubarth; indeed, in him these two dynasties met, his father being descended from the former and his mother from the latter. He had seen some military service, having served in Richard II's Scottish campaign of 1385 and against the French in 1387, and he was the wealthiest native Welsh landowner, with an annual income of about £200. In other words he could be described as a member of the contemporary establishment. Yet in 1400, he put himself beyond the pale by being proclaimed prince and beginning a revolt which lasted for ten years. The attack on Ruthin was followed by attacks on other towns in north-east Wales and by a rising in Anglesey; Henry IV's response was to lead an army into North Wales and most of the rebels submitted. Early in the following year parliament enacted a series of penal statutes imposing a number of disabilities on the Welsh; this legislation must have caused outrage among the Welsh leaders and on Good Friday 1401 Conway Castle was seized while the garrison was in church. The following autumn the king led an army into South Wales but this campaign was fruitless, since Owain refused to give battle. For the next few years he enjoyed uninterrupted success and successive royal campaigns achieved nothing. The response of parliament was a further body of penal statutes, imposing yet more restrictions on the Welsh and on Englishmen married to Welsh wives.

In 1403 Henry Percy or Hotspur, the justice of North Wales rose in revolt against Henry IV; the rebels were defeated and Hotspur killed in the battle of Shrewsbury but this had no effect on Owain's fortunes. The following year he captured the castles of Harlech and Aberystwyth and made the former his headquarters; he also summoned a parliament to Machynlleth, attended by representatives from France and Castile. He had now been joined by some of the leading Welsh clerics; these experienced canonists and administrators provided him with the political and diplomatic expertise he needed and the fruit of their advice was soon to be seen. What he needed above all was outside support and the obvious source of this was France; the French could offer him military and diplomatic support and he could offer them the opportunity of a second front. On 14 July 1404 a Franco-Welsh treaty was signed. Another ambitious step was taken early in 1405 when the Tripartite Indenture was drawn up between Owain, Edmund Mortimer and Hotspur's father, the earl of Northumberland. Owain was to have a much larger Wales; his two allies would divide the rest of England between them, with Mortimer's nephew as king. But nothing came of this and in 1405 the tide began to turn.

In this year Owain suffered two defeats, in one of which one of his sons was captured and his brother killed. But in the summer a French force joined him and the allies invaded England, reaching Woodbury Hill near Worcester. This could have been the decisive stroke, but Owain now withdrew to Wales, possibly realising that his lines of communication had been overextended; in a sense Woodbury Hill marked the beginning of the end. But this did not mean the end of the alliance; in 1406 Owain set out his terms for the transfer of Welsh ecclesiastical allegiance from the pope at Rome to his French-backed rival at Avignon. The terms were particularly interesting and they show the readiness of Owain's advisers to take advantage of the papal schism. The terms included an independent Welsh province, to include several English dioceses and with an archbishop at St David's, the restriction of benefices in Wales to Welsh-speaking clerics and the establishment of two universities, one in the north and one in the south. But it was too late. Whole communities were now submitting to the king and paying fines for pardon. Henry IV's position in England was becoming stronger and there was no hope of further support from France. In 1408 Owain's main strongholds at Harlech and Aberystwyth fell. More and more communities made their peace and the last raid on the border was defeated in 1410. He himself was never captured and he may have died in 1415.

The revolt had many causes. It was part of a European pattern; between 1350 and 1450 most countries experienced at least one major rebellion. In part these were a consequence of the general climate of discontent and disorientation engendered by the plague; most of them were social or economic protests but in Wales the rising became a national movement. In England the grievances of the unfree exploded in the Peasants' Revolt of 1381; there must have been similar grievances in Wales but they seem to have been subsumed in the discontent of the leaders of the native community who were the mainspring of the revolt.

After the assassination of Owain ap Thomas ap Rhodri and the death in Ireland in 1398 of Roger Mortimer, earl of March, who had a tenuous descent from the Gwynedd dynasty, Owain, with his descent from the two other ancient royal houses, was the obvious candidate as a national leader and the leaders of the native community knew very well who he was and for what he stood. The revolt was probably planned well in advance of that fateful gathering in 1400 and this may be borne out by some of the poetry addressed to Owain, which suggests that he was being called upon to assume his responsibilities.

There was also a messianic dimension. There was in Wales a long tradition of vaticinatory poetry which called upon the heroes of the past to return and restore the honour of the Britons; this poetry, often very obscure, foretold the coming of the *mab darogan* or son of prophecy and by the fourteenth century its practitioners had absorbed some of the apocalyptic ideas of Joachim of Fiore. Some of it can be associated with the cause of Owain ap Thomas ap Rhodri; other such poems must certainly refer to Owain Glyn Dŵr. And these were not the only causes of the revolt. Churchmen were drawn to his banner; at the very beginning Welsh clerks at Oxford were accused of plotting on his behalf. Educated clerics, embittered by their exclusion from preferment, and the lower clergy, under intolerable economic pressure, were involved. The poorer sections of society, suffering from the increased demands of royal and Marcher tax collectors in a period of extreme hardship were drawn in; the causes of the English revolt of 1381 were also among the causes of the Welsh revolt of 1400. And Owain and his lieutenants were able to take advantage of a fund of military experience accumulated in France and Scotland.

The revolt ultimately failed because the country had fought itself to a standstill; in the end the superior power and resources of the crown were decisive and French support proved a broken reed. But the revolt of Owain Glyn Dŵr was more than a simple rebellion against the English crown. It has been described as the 'massive protest of a conquered people' but it also offered a vision of a united and independent Welsh national consciousness.[1] It was the result of the tensions and problems of the fourteenth century, coupled with the disillusion and resentments of the Welsh political nation and it was, too, in some ways, a civil war. There were gainers and losers but, on the whole, the

---

[1] Davies (1987), p. 462.

uchelwyr emerged still in control of their communities. The revolt caused great damage but there was soon a measure of recovery; the problems reflected in subsequent periods were the result of the crises of the fourteenth century. And in the long term it was the revolt that brought Wales on to a wider political stage. In the words of one historian 'Modern Wales . . . begins in 1410.'[2]

[2] Williams (1959), p. 183.

CHAPTER 13(d)

FOURTEENTH-CENTURY SCOTLAND

Alexander Grant

DURING the twelfth and thirteenth centuries, Scotland's history is a striking success.[1] Five themes stand out. The first is general economic growth: developing agriculture sustained a population rise to around the million mark, while flourishing wool and leather exports through the east-coast burghs boosted the money supply to over 40 million silver pennies (some £180,000), circulating interchangeably with England's in a medieval 'sterling area'. The second is political expansion: from its eastern heartland between the Forth and the Grampians, the kingdom spread north, south and west, reaching virtually its modern boundaries when the Western Isles were annexed from Norway in 1266. The third is the consolidation of political authority behind a clearly defined royal line, which established the principle of succession by primogeniture, and introduced 'modern' governmental and religious institutions,[2] like those of France and England (if less bureaucratised). The fourth is the establishment of a simple but effective system of local power, in which a network of sheriffdoms added a layer of crown authority to an older landowning structure consisting of large 'provincial' earldoms and lordships (see map 6) interspersed with smaller baronies (mostly held by 'Norman' families brought in from England by twelfth-century kings). And the fifth is the maintenance, none the less, of a 'balance of New and Old': Gaelic families and practices survived even at the highest levels, so that, although Scotland had become a fairly typical European kingdom, it was ethnically hybrid, defined simply by its people's allegiance to their king.

These themes are also fundamental to understanding fourteenth-century Scotland, but what went on then was very different. Scotland's 'fourteenth century' begins early, with the extinction of the direct royal line in 1290. Edward I of England exploited the ensuing succession dispute, and in 1296

---

[1] Best described in Barrow (1981) and Duncan (1975).

[2] But Scotland had no archbishops; instead, the Scottish Church (called the 'special daughter' of the pope) was run by provincial councils of its bishops. See Watt (1993).

the kingdom was plunged into a bitter war for national survival – complicated after 1306 by an equally bitter civil war. This ended Scotland's political expansion, and seriously dislocated its government and society. Then plague struck in 1349, devastating the population and fundamentally affecting the economy. And the century's later years saw new disputes within the royal family, together with the emergence of the 'Highland problem'. In Scotland, as elsewhere, the age of expansion and consolidation was succeeded by an age of contraction and upheaval.

THE PEOPLE OF SCOTLAND

Scotland suffered open war in two-thirds of the fifty years between 1296 and 1346 – the most protracted period of warfare in British history. At the outset Berwick, the major town, was captured, and its inhabitants massacred. Subsequently, thousands of Scottish foot-soldiers died in half a dozen major defeats; total casualties were probably, proportionally, at least a third of those suffered by Scots in World War I, and worse than at any other time. And although battles were exceptional, 'normal' campaigns caused huge economic damage. Across the war zone – extending well beyond the Tay – crops were destroyed or neglected, livestock were killed or driven off, money was stolen or lost, and farms, villages and towns were burned. Admittedly, the armies' departures were followed by fairly quick recovery. But in the short term the war brought destruction and disaster (not to mention death) to the people of southern, central and at times northern Scotland.

Moreover, even without the war Scotland's economy was probably in difficulties (though that cannot be proved).[3] Economic expansion could not continue indefinitely; the fact that grain was being grown over 1,000 feet up in the border hills, which is impossible nowadays, indicates that agriculture was reaching the margins. And since northern England and Ireland both suffered the Great European Famine of 1315–17, presumably Scotland experienced that as well. The 1330s also brought famine, while in the 1340s Edward III's fiscal policies drained money out of Scotland as well as England. In general, since the Scottish economy was essentially similar, and closely tied, to the English, there is no reason to suppose that it was not experiencing the same complex downturn. In the first half of the fourteenth century, times must have been much harder for the people of Scotland than they had been during the two preceding centuries.

[3] There is a chronic lack of economic evidence for fourteenth-century Scotland, apart from the customs records. The best analysis of the data that has survived is in Gemmill and Mayhew (1995); see also the briefer discussion in Grant (1984), ch. 3.

The worst years, however, were yet to come. In 1349, wrote the chronicler John of Fordun,

there was so great a pestilence and mortality . . . as had nowhere been heard of or written about in books . . . Such was the severity of that plague that nearly one-third of the whole human race was obliged to pay the debt of nature . . . Once the swollen inflammation of the flesh had taken hold, life in this world hardly lasted for a further two days.[4]

And, as elsewhere, plague returned, in 1361–2, 1379–80, 1392 and 1401–3. Because of Scotland's cold wet climate and low settlement density, the bubonic plague described by Fordun may not have been so severe (the court escaped in 1362 by going north to Aberdeen); conversely, pneumonic plague may have been worse. Fordun's estimate of the death rate could be scaled down, but it would be unwise to do so by much; and by the end of the century the population had probably been halved, to about 500,000. Just as in most parts of Europe, the plagues from 1349 onwards constituted by far the greatest disaster ever suffered by the people of Scotland.

The economic consequences were more complex. More land and food were available for the survivors: the normal size of husbandmen's holdings seems to have doubled, and towards the end of the century there was 'an abundance of provisions'.[5] Meanwhile there was a rapid slump in rents (which in Scotland were mostly set annually): a national valuation of lay estates in 1366 showed a 48 per cent fall by comparison with the thirteenth-century 'time of peace'; one individual estate, Tannadice near Dundee, was worth £60 in 1263 but only £30 in 1361.[6] Landowners' incomes must have been badly affected – but rent-paying husbandmen would have been better off. As for foodstuffs, prices of wheat and malt seem to have risen, those of oats and meal to have stayed roughly the same, and those of livestock to have fallen significantly: this presumably reflects contraction in the most labour-intensive cereal production and a shift towards pastoral farming, which would have led to an increase in the consumption of meat and other animal products. Unfortunately, there is no usable information about wages, but landowners abandoned demesne farming, which must surely be attributed to higher labour costs (since cereal prices did not fall). At the same time, serfdom disappeared. These points (together with the easing of the war with England) indicate that in the post-plague era economic conditions must have improved for the ordinary people of Scotland – so long, that is, as they avoided plague.

A brief export boom is also evident, especially in wool (Scotland was probably Europe's second wool exporter, after England). High demand for

[4] Fordun, *Chron. Gent. Scot.*, i, pp. 368–9; trans. from Bower, *Scotichronicon*, vii, p. 273.
[5] Bower, *Scotichronicon*, viii, p. 63.   [6] *Act. Parl. Scot.*, i, pp. 500–1; *Exch. Rolls Scot.*, i, p. 9, ii, p. 153.

cheap cloth in post-plague Europe meant that in the 1360s annual Scottish wool exports maintained their 1320s average of around 5,500 sacks a year (well over 800 tons, and the clip of about a million sheep; roughly a sixth of English exports). They were even more buoyant in the 1370s, peaking at over 9,000 sacks in 1372. But that was not sustained. Between 1385 and 1390 (after war disrupted the Flemish cloth industry) annual exports slumped to just over 3,000 sacks, and in the early 1400s they were below 2,000.

A sack of Scottish wool usually sold abroad for roughly £4–£5. Thus 'normal' annual exports of over 5,000 sacks would earn around £25,000 for the Scottish economy – apparently more than enough to pay for imports in the pre-plague era. But in post-plague Europe, the manufactured goods which were Scotland's main imports cost more – and in the years 1357–77 over £50,000 went to England for David II's ransom.[7] Consequently by 1367, although wool exports were still healthy, Scotland was suffering a currency shortage, and the coinage had to be lightened by 15 per cent. This broke the old parity with England, and by 1373 the English crown had imposed a 4:3 exchange rate. Then, after 1385, the wool export slump caused worse problems. Between 1385 and 1390 at least 12,000 fewer sacks of wool were sold abroad, which meant a loss to the Scottish economy of well over £50,000 sterling – at a time when its money supply had probably fallen to around £100,000 sterling. Therefore fresh devaluations were needed in 1393 and c.1400: the coins were reduced first to 64 per cent and then to only 38 per cent of their original weights, while the exchange rate with England fell to 2:1.

By the end of the century Scottish money was only worth half what it had been. The result was that 'all things are dearer than in times past', as the abbot of Dunfermline complained in 1409.[8] Although the price rises were in nominal, not real, money values, the inflation (or 'stagflation', like that suffered in modern Britain) probably neutralised any wage rises resulting from labour shortages. Hence late fourteenth-century Scotland did not see such a great rise in living standards as England did: there appears to have been no Scottish 'price scissors'. In European terms, however, England was probably exceptional (thanks to the strength of its currency); the experience of Scotland, where the economic gains of the population fall were rather more limited, seems closer to what happened in much of continental Europe.

WARS OF INDEPENDENCE

In the fourteenth century Scotland's political history is dominated by the war with England.[9] When the succession crisis of the early 1290s brought Scotland

---

[7] See pp. 352–3 below.   [8] Quoted in Nicholson (1974), p. 268.
[9] The best accounts of the first stage (to 1328) are Barrow (1988) and McNamee (1997).

to the brink of civil war, the guardians (appointed by parliament to run the country in the absence of a king) asked Edward I to adjudicate between the rival claimants, John Balliol and Robert Bruce. Edward did so, finding for Balliol in 1292,[10] but at the same time made the Scots accept his own overlordship of Scotland, and interpreted that so rigorously (especially with demands for military service against France) that they rebelled in 1295. A magnate council was imposed on King John; it made an alliance with France, and launched an attack on England in 1296. The short-term result was defeat and conquest by the English; in the long term, Anglo-Scottish warfare lasted in hot or cold forms until the middle of the sixteenth century.

With hindsight, the war seems inevitable since, while Scotland's political expansion had paralleled England's, both countries could not expand indefinitely without clashing. In the 1290s, English expansionism was in full flow after the conquest of Wales, and it is no surprise that Edward should have tried to repeat that in Scotland. He led massive invasions, crushed Scottish armies at Dunbar (1296) and Falkirk (1298), removed King John in 1296, gained mass submissions from all important Scots in 1296 and 1304, and imposed English-dominated administrations. But whenever Scotland seemed defeated, fresh resistance broke out, and Edward had to begin again; he died heading yet another invasion in 1307.

The sustained Scottish resistance is difficult to explain. A strong sense of national identity had developed, but the submissions make explanations in terms of patriotism seem over-simple. It is easier to look for vested interests: churchmen resisted the superiority of York; wealthy peasants and townsmen suffered when Scottish wool was seized; landowners disliked Edward's harsh royal authority; individuals were swayed by personal factors. But to stress Scottish inconsistency is to put things the wrong way round. Edward I found it difficult to campaign effectively north of the Forth, expensive to maintain large garrisons in Scotland, and impractical to replace the entire Scottish landowning class; so to conquer Scotland he had to make most Scots renounce their loyalty to the Scottish crown and accept English rule permanently. That, however, could be achieved only through persuasion, not through the threat of military might. Yet while Edward demanded Scottish loyalty, he would not buy it with worthwhile patronage.[11] Therefore, so long as there was the alternative of loyalty to a Scottish king (or guardians), lasting Scottish acceptance of English conquest was unlikely.

That alternative remained because Scotland – like other 'developed' European kingdoms – had a system of government capable of continuing

---

[10] See Duncan (1995), and, for the vast documentation, Stones and Simpson (1978).

[11] These points are based on Prestwich (1972), pp. 111–12, and (1987); Duncan (1992), pp. 143–4; Barrow (1978), pp. 118–19, and (1988), pp. 132–6.

even after military disaster. Thus Scottish leaders such as William Wallace (most famously), Andrew Murray and John Comyn maintained an administration in King John's name, and raised forces through the normal call-up mechanisms, with which they whittled away at English bases, and defeated English armies at Stirling Bridge (1297) and Roslin (1303). It was essentially a 'people's war', fought especially by the wealthier peasantry.[12] Its leadership, however, was aristocratic. Because of intermarriage, most Scottish nobles had 'Norman' descent, just like the Anglo-Welsh and Anglo-Irish. But while the latter were subjects of the English crown and worked for it, in Scotland the 'Normans' and their descendants were subjects of the Scottish crown – and provided essential if erratic leadership for the independence cause.

The most successful leader was Robert Bruce, earl of Carrick (grandson of the 1290 claimant); in 1306, with Scotland apparently conquered, he raised the rebellion that ended English rule. It began inauspiciously, however, when he killed his rival, John Comyn of Badenoch (John Balliol's nephew), and then rebelled in self-defence. Bruce legitimised his actions by having himself made king, as Robert I.[13] But in Scottish terms he was a usurper, who had deposed King John, and his initial support was limited. Meanwhile the powerful Comyn/Balliol faction became his implacable enemies – and sided with the English to destroy him.

They nearly succeeded: Robert was soon a beaten fugitive, vainly seeking Irish help. But after Edward I's death, English pressure relaxed, and in a remarkable series of campaigns Robert isolated and defeated his Comyn/Balliol enemies in northern Scotland. By 1310 he controlled most of the north, and was able to turn to southern Scotland and even raid across the Border; by mid-1314 only a few strongholds were held against him, notably Stirling Castle. And when, in June 1314, Edward II attempted to relieve the siege of Stirling, Robert's army of spearmen destroyed the English host at Bannockburn – a battle which ranks with Courtrai (1302) and Morgarten (1315) in military history, and is probably even more significant, for it taught English commanders the value of defensively sited infantry.

Bannockburn ended the English occupation of southern Scotland (though Berwick was not regained until 1318). But Edward II would not recognise Scottish independence, and so Robert intensified the border raids, while his brother Edward invaded Ireland in 1315. The Scots could not reach southern England, however, and the 'Bruce invasion' of Ireland ended disastrously with Edward Bruce's defeat and death in 1318. Conversely, English invasions of 1319 and 1322 were starved into retreat by Robert's scorched-earth strategy.

[12] Barrow (1976), pp. 155–7; Duncan (1970), pp. 14–17; Grant (1994), pp. 85–8.
[13] See now Duncan (1992), pp. 135–6.

The war had reached stalemate – and Edward II grudgingly agreed a long truce in 1323. But that lapsed with Edward's deposition in 1327. Major Scottish raids followed, which forced the insecure government of Isabella and Mortimer to agree a peace confirming Scotland's independence (in return for £20,000!) by the Treaty of Edinburgh in 1328.

Robert I, however, died within a year, leaving a five-year-old son to succeed as David II[14] – and the deaths of Robert's main lieutenants, James Douglas (often known as 'the good Sir James') and Thomas Randolph, earl of Moray, soon followed. The weakened Bruce regime was attacked in 1332 by exiled Balliol/Comyn supporters led by Edward Balliol (son of King John) and encouraged by Edward III of England – who repudiated the Treaty of Edinburgh in 1333 and reopened the Anglo-Scottish war. Twice the Scots were routed by defensively positioned English archers and men-at-arms, at Dupplin (near Perth) in 1332 and at Halidon Hill (near Berwick) in 1333. These battles devastated the Bruce establishment. The young David II was sent for safety to France, while Scotland was partitioned between Edward III (who annexed most of the south) and Edward Balliol.

Again, however, the conquest of Scotland was not consolidated. Guerrilla resistance broke out, led in particular by Andrew Murray (son of Wallace's colleague, and brother-in-law of Robert I), who defeated a Balliol force at Culblean on Deeside in 1335. Massive invasions by Edward III in 1335 and 1336 achieved only temporary submissions; and after 1337 his main attention shifted to war against France (caused partly by the French help for the Scots, under the 'auld alliance').[15] From then on, English efforts slackened, and (despite Murray's death in 1338) the Bruce supporters, with the heir-presumptive Robert Stewart now guardian,[16] steadily regained control of the kingdom. The teenage David II was brought back from France in June 1341, and by mid-1342 only Berwick was held by the English.

The warfare of the 1330s is not simply a postscript to that of 1296–1314. Edward Balliol was a better leader than his father; while deaths in battle almost destroyed the Scottish (or Bruce) leadership. Edward III learned from his predecessors' failures: instead of trying to exercise feudal or direct rule over the whole country, he annexed southern Scotland outright, and gave Balliol the

---

[14] The main account of the war under David II is in Nicholson (1974), chs. 6–7, supplemented by Nicholson (1965), Webster (1993) and Boardman (1996a), ch. 1.

[15] Campbell (1965), pp. 189–91; Curry (1993) pp. 140–4, 150.

[16] Robert I's grandson by his eldest daughter. He is commonly known as 'Robert the Steward', which denotes that he was the 'Steward of Scotland', an honorary office held (until 1371) by the head of the family of Stewart (the surname derives from the office). For clarity, I simply use the surname here; but note that the title 'Steward' carried with it lands in the south-west which were as extensive as most earldoms or great lordships.

rest under nominal lordship. This 'non-feudal' approach parallels his new battle tactics, and foreshadows his later policy towards France;[17] for Scotland, it solved the problem of the north by assigning it to Balliol. And the military strategy was harsher: to terrorise local opposition into submission, and if necessary to expel and replace the local freeholders.

Edward III was thus as great a threat as Edward I; it is tempting to see his diversion into France as providential. Yet in 1337 Scotland was far from conquered. Scottish support for Balliol was never strong; he was too dependent on Edward III to be widely accepted as the rightful king. Also, restoring the 'disinherited' to lands which had been given to Bruce followers strengthened the latter's commitment to David II. And Edward III's new approach was flawed. Annexing the south stimulated southern Scottish opposition. In the north, Balliol's lieutenant had insufficient backing (there were no archers at Culblean). In general, the policy of devastation and forfeiture was counterproductive. Meanwhile, those who accepted Edward III or Balliol were attacked by pro-Bruce guerrillas; for many, allegiance was a matter of the lesser of two evils.[18] Local power therefore fluctuated depending on circumstances. But when Edward went to war with France, Scotland obviously became a lower priority for him. That is when the pendulum finally swung in favour of the Bruce – and independence – cause.

The war did not end in 1342, however. Instead, David led raids into England, no doubt hoping to emulate his father's military prowess. The opposite happened. In autumn 1346 a full-scale Scottish invasion crossed the Border, in response to French pleas for help after Crécy and in the mistaken belief that Edward III's siege of Calais had stripped the north of England of men. At Neville's Cross (near Durham) it was surprised and defeated by a northern English army. Many Scottish magnates were killed or captured; among the latter was David II himself. The following year southern Scotland was overrun once more by English troops under Edward Balliol.

Ironically, Balliol was soon jettisoned by Edward III, who realised that the best way to profit from Neville's Cross was to treat the captive David II as king.[19] He therefore tried to force the Scots – again under Robert Stewart, who had fled from Neville's Cross – to buy their king back on his terms. Initially Edward wanted full superiority over Scotland; and when that was rejected, he demanded that his son John of Gaunt should be treated as heir-presumptive, and become king of Scots should David die childless. David favoured that, but not surprisingly Stewart refused – and, with French encouragement, also blocked a ransom agreement. But after Edward ravaged Lothian in 1356 (and following the French defeat at Poitiers), a settlement was made. David was

[17] Keen (1973), p. 110.   [18] See Webster (1993) and Brown (1997a).
[19] For the negotiations, see Duncan (1988) and Campbell (1965), pp. 196–203.

released in 1357, in return for a ransom of 100,000 marks (£66,667), payable over ten years during which there would be a truce, and guaranteed by twenty-three hostages; the issues of superiority and the succession were shelved, but Edward III kept a buffer zone of Scottish territory along the Border.

By 1357 Edward had clearly accepted that he could not conquer Scotland, and the treaty probably gave him what he realistically wanted: prestige, cash and a quiet frontier. In Scotland, however, David found that despite special taxes he could not pay the ransom and finance his household, and so in 1360 he stopped the payments. Fraught negotiations followed, in which Edward offered to cancel the ransom in return for becoming heir-presumptive himself, David wanted to go back to the John of Gaunt proposal, and the Scottish parliament of 1364 (to which the 'pros and cons' were presented) rejected both ideas.[20] The eventual outcome was a higher ransom at more manageable instalments. Then in 1369, after new Anglo-French warfare broke out, the total was reduced to the original amount, the instalments fell to £2,667 a year, and a new fourteen-year 'long truce' was agreed.

Edward III's diplomacy had been backed by the implicit threat of another invasion, but that was largely a bluff, as the Scots came to realise. Nevertheless, they were careful not to provoke him too far, and paid the reduced ransom instalments regularly – even after David II's death in 1371 and the accession of Robert Stewart as Robert II.[21] Only when Edward died in 1377 were the payments stopped. Much of the buffer-zone, however, remained in English hands, and there was a natural desire to regain it. Thus the long truce's final years saw Scottish magnates whittling away at the English-held territory, and on its expiry in early 1384 the remnant was quickly overrun (except for the strongholds of Jedburgh, Roxburgh and Berwick).

Robert II hoped to follow this with a new truce. But there was strong pressure for war: from a younger, 'hawkish', generation of nobles (headed by the heir to the throne, the earl of Carrick, and by the second earl of Douglas) who sidelined the king;[22] from the French, who wanted a second front for their war against England, and sent troops to Scotland in 1385; and from Richard II of England, who naturally retaliated. The result was a sequence of attacks in both directions, culminating in 1388 with a two-pronged Scottish invasion, in which the eastern army heavily defeated its English pursuers in the twilight battle at Otterburn. The Scots' intention was probably to exploit the Appellants crisis in England to force a satisfactory peace treaty, as in 1328. And although that was not achieved, war weariness eventually led to a series of truces after 1389, by which the earlier gains were consolidated. Thus the century ended with relative peace between Scotland and England.

[20] Duncan (1994).
[21] For the rest of the warfare, see Boardman (1996a), chs. 4–8, and Grant (1992).
[22] See pp. 360–1 below.

Unfortunately that did not last: further warfare broke out after Richard II's deposition, and a Scottish invasion ended in disaster at Humbleton Hill (Northumberland) in 1402. But Humbleton was not followed by the English occupation of southern Scotland: the English crown had come to recognise the futility of waging war north of the Border. Although no formal peace was concluded, the basis of Anglo-Scottish relations had changed. It no longer involved conquest and liberation; now it was essentially a matter of border friction between two separate countries. Despite the efforts of Edward I and Edward III, Scotland's independence had been successfully maintained.

The war had been fought to preserve the thirteenth-century *status quo*, but it profoundly affected Scotland's nationhood. Although a Scottish state and identity already existed, both were greatly strengthened. Individual vested interests were increasingly identified with the national state, while the cross-border landownership of previous centuries was no longer possible. Also, a national ideology redefining the crown–people relationship was developed. In the 1290s, 'descending' ideas had been followed: if the king accepted subjection, the people had to do so too.[23] But the Scots' defiance of Edward I rejected that, and an ideology following 'ascending' ideas was eventually articulated – especially in the 'Declaration of Arbroath' sent to the pope in 1320, 'the most eloquent statement of regnal solidarity . . . of the middle ages'.[24] This stated that Robert I was king because he defended the independence of the Scottish community, and if ever he submitted to the English he would be deposed. It was, admittedly, Bruce propaganda, and hardly fitted the political realities.[25] Yet, as the war continued, so (consciously or not) the Declaration's ideology was upheld, against Edward Balliol, Edward III and (implicitly) David II. Moreover, in the later fourteenth century John of Fordun's *Chronicle of the Scottish Nation* and John Barbour's vernacular poem *The Bruce* provided nationalist accounts of the distant and recent Scottish past; and at a popular level, ballads about William Wallace also spread the message of national freedom. These all reflect ways in which the principle of national independence was consolidated – making it axiomatic for centuries.

POLITICS AND PRIMOGENITURE

Fourteenth-century Scotland had its domestic politics, too, though they are hard to disentangle from the war.[26] In all states at all times, of course, domestic

---

[23] For 'descending' and 'ascending' theories, see, e.g., Ullmann (1978), esp. pp. 19–26.

[24] Reynolds (1984), pp. 273–6, at 274. For the text, *Act. Parl. Scot.,* I, pp. 474–5; best trans. in Duncan (1970), pp. 34–7; cf. Bower, *Scotichronicon,* VII, pp. 5–9. Discussions include Barrow (1988), pp. 302–11, Simpson (1977), Reid (1993) and Grant (1994).   [25] See p. 357 below.

[26] Nicholson (1974) gives a detailed account of domestic politics; but the discussion here derives more from Grant (1984), ch. 7, modified in the light of Boardman (1996a).

0 ————— 50 miles
0 ————— 100 km

E ORKNEY and SHETLAND
(Norwegian to 1468–9)

E CAITHNESS

E SUTHERLAND

E ROSS

Inverness S

E MORAY

L BADENOCH

S STRATHBOGIE

E BUCHAN

S GARIOCH

X 1411

Aberdeen

E MAR

S

E ATHOLL

S Montrose

E ANGUS

Dundee

Perth S

E STRATHEARN

X 1332

E FIFE

S

E MENTEITH S

Stirling

X 1314

Edinburgh

C Haddington

Linlithgow S

L LENNOX

(S)

L RENFREW

L CUNNINGHAM

E MARCH

Berwick

(S) (S)

X 1333

Roxburgh

S

L ANNANDALE

S

L SELKIRK

S

X 1402

L JEDWORTH

Ayr S

L KYLE

L CARRICK

L NITHSDALE

L LIDDESDALE

X 1388

L GALLOWAY

E WIGTOWN (S)
(Cr. 1341)

SKYE

THE

L ARGYLL

ISLES

- - - Inter-regnal boundary (to
      1468, and excluding Berwick)
E   Earldom   L Lordship
•   Important burgh, either admin-
      istratively or commercially
S   Seat of a sheriff (except in
      sheriffdom of Argyll)
(S) Seat of a sheriff for part of the
      period, or of a sheriffdom incor-
      porated into an earldom or lordship
C   Constabulary within sheriffdom
      of Edinburgh

X Battles
1314 Bannockburn   1388 Otterburn
1332 Dupplin   1402 Homildon
1333 Halidon   1411 Harlaw

Map 6   Scotland in the fourteenth century

politics focus essentially on the control of government. Nowadays that is mostly determined by elections; the medieval equivalents were rebellions and succession conflicts. From the twelfth century, however, succession disputes were greatly reduced in 'developed' kingdoms (including Scotland) through the introduction of primogeniture: a king's death would be followed by the succession of his eldest son rather than by partition among sons or by conflict among his main adult kinsmen. As a result, sequences of 'rightful' kings could establish fundamental long-term loyalties. But primogeniture had its problems – which bedevilled fourteenth-century Scotland. They focused on the royal family. Who would rule if the king was under age, or incapacitated? What was the role of the royal kindred's major cadets? And, worst of all, what would happen if a king died without leaving an obvious heir (which brought the disasters after 1290)?

In the great succession dispute of 1290–2, John Balliol had the stronger claim and backing, but the elder Robert Bruce did have a case.[27] Unfortunately Bruce resorted to violence, and also looked to England, offering to accept Edward I's overlordship (which meant Balliol had to accept it too).[28] And though, before he died, Bruce recognised Balliol as king, his family would not fight for Balliol in 1296. Similarly, although after Balliol's removal the younger Robert Bruce (the future king) did join the independence cause in 1297, he submitted to Edward in 1301 when a Balliol restoration seemed possible. At that time – not surprisingly – Scottish ambassadors to the pope were implicitly blaming their country's calamities on the Bruces.[29]

Scotland's politics were transformed, however, by the Bruce *coup d'état* in 1306. Civil war merged with international war, as Balliol's powerful Comyn kinsmen, erstwhile leaders of the independence cause, fought beside the English against Robert I – producing an indelible image of Scottish internecine quarrelling and collaboration. Yet Bruce's political opponents could never have accepted his seizure of the throne. Less partisan Scots, meanwhile, faced an agonising dilemma: should they support independence and the Bruce usurpation, or the rightful Balliol kingship and English overlordship?[30] Most of them probably waited to see what would happen – which was Robert I's eventual victory, sealed at Bannockburn.

After 1314, Robert I's triumphant kingship was accepted by all but a few irreconcilables, who suffered forfeiture. His staunch supporters – including Hays, Keiths, Campbells, Flemings, Lindsays, Setons and Hamiltons – were well rewarded from the forfeited estates, and their descendants headed the

---

[27] For the period 1290–1306 and of Robert I's reign, see Barrow (1988).

[28] Duncan (1995), pp. 214–21; Stones and Simpson (1978), II, p. 187.

[29] Duncan (1995), p. 212; Bower, *Scotichronicon*, VI, pp. 159, 177.   [30] Duncan (1992), pp. 125–35.

Scottish nobility for centuries. Three were especially prominent: his nephew Thomas Randolph, earl of Moray; 'the good Sir James' Douglas; and his son-in-law Walter Stewart. All received huge amounts of land from the king, and the later interplay between their descendants is a major political theme.

Yet the regime's base appears narrow. Robert had won the crown by force, and did not enjoy long-established general loyalty. His patronage excluded many magnates, and (despite the Declaration of Arbroath's hyperbole) it is hard to see positive commitment to him across the entire elite; half the earls, for instance, seem distinctly lukewarm.[31] There were also potential succession problems. In 1315 his adult brother, Edward, was made heir to the throne, because his only child was a daughter, Marjorie, who was considered unsuitable. But by late 1318 both Edward (who was probably jealous of Robert, and sought his own kingdom in Ireland) and Marjorie were dead, leaving Marjorie's baby son, Robert Stewart, as the king's sole descendant. The Bruce regime did not offer long-term stability. Moreover, since 1314 the war had gone less well (and disastrously in Ireland); and Robert was also under intense papal pressure to agree a truce. These circumstances probably explain legislation of December 1318 against conspiracies and seditious talk, which can perhaps be glimpsed in the survival of the untrue 'smear' that in 1298 Bruce had fought for Edward I against Wallace.[32]

Matters came to a head in 1320. While the Declaration of Arbroath stated the whole nobility's support for the king, it was followed by the discovery of a plot to kill him and, probably, enthrone John Balliol's son Edward.[33] The conspirators were mostly former Balliol/Comyn supporters, who had had no crown patronage; and there was a significant element from Strathearn, which Robert had harried in 1306. In the event, the conspiracy was easily crushed, and Robert's domestic political position was greatly strengthened; yet it indicates residual tensions, and points forward to the 1330s.

That decade's warfare, too, was brought on by a royal family problem: although Robert I did have a son in 1324, he succeeded as a minor.[34] The obvious regent, the earl of Moray, died in 1332; while 'the good Sir James' Douglas, his son and his brother all perished between 1330 and 1333. Thereafter, the Bruce cause suffered from rivalry between Robert Stewart, the heir-presumptive, and John Randolph, the new earl of Moray, who was probably a better military leader and resented Stewart's precedence. Their quarrels polarised antagonisms among other resistance leaders; although David II's

---

[31] This is my impression from, e.g., Robert I's *acta*, in *Regesta Regum Scottorum*, v.

[32] *Act. Parl. Scot.*, I, p. 472; Fordun, *Chron. Gent. Scot.*, I, p. 330; Bower, *Scotichronicon*, VI, p. 95. The smear's most dramatic expression is in the recent Mel Gibson film, *Braveheart*.   [33] Duncan (1992), p. 129.

[34] For David II's reign, see Nicholson (1974), chs. 6, 7, Webster (1966) and especially Boardman (1996a), ch. 1.

supporters were eventually victorious, they were by no means united. Nor did David's return from France bring unity, because he favoured Randolph and disliked Stewart, who, although David's nephew, was eight years older. This tension within the royal family lasted for the entire reign.

It was exacerbated by Robert Stewart's flight from Neville's Cross in 1346, and by his refusal to agree a quick release for David II. That raised in a new form the issue of who ruled Scotland, focusing not on the succession but on the guardianship. Stewart's position was strengthened by the earl of Moray's childless death at Neville's Cross; Moray's nearest kinsman, his brother-in-law Patrick Dunbar, earl of March, also fled from the battle, and subsequently co-operated with Robert Stewart. So too, when he came of age in 1348, did William, lord of Douglas (nephew of 'the good Sir James'). Stewart rewarded them well: March received most of the earldom of Moray, despite its restriction to heirs-male; Douglas extended his estates and got vice-regal powers over them. Stewart himself added Badenoch (which had been Randolph's) and the vacant earldom of Strathearn to his lands of Atholl, creating a huge territorial block across the central Highlands. The Stewart–Dunbar–Douglas triumvirate had done nicely for itself. But the political situation was not the same as that of Balliol *versus* Bruce, for they all upheld the Bruce kingship – so David II was bound to return sooner or later.

When he did, in 1357, the situation changed again. Although initially David ratified Stewart's grants and raised both him and Douglas to the rank of earl, by 1360 he was asserting his own kingship and pressurising the magnates. Local lairds were recruited to his affinity, and used (especially as sheriffs) to hold regular courts and audits; in the 1360s, royal government appears aggressive. There was also the ransom issue. The 1360 default left most of the hostages in England, where several died; and it meant (under the treaty) that either David had to return to captivity, or some top magnates had to go instead. Fear of the second alternative helped to provoke a rebellion in 1363 by Douglas, March and Robert Stewart.[35] They condemned David's governance and mishandling of the ransom, and threatened to exile him – that is, send him to England, and so cancel the ransom, redeem the surviving hostages and relieve the governmental pressure.

The rebels overestimated their strength; prompt action by David and his supporters made them submit. But there were no executions, nor other obvious punishments. David did, however, target Robert Stewart, who had to promise loyalty to the king and his officers on pain of being barred from the royal succession. Actually, in David's eyes, that was as good as lost, for he had recently remarried; the new queen, Margaret Logie (*née* Drummond), was a widow who had a son. In 1363 David was confident of fathering an heir – and

---

[35] Cf. Duncan (1993), pp. 264–5.

took that confidence into the negotiations with Edward III,[36] when he proposed Stewart's replacement as heir-presumptive by John of Gaunt.

In this Bruce–Stewart antagonism the wires seem crossed. Robert Stewart took the post-1306 Bruce stance of absolute independence, whereas David II 'greatly favoured the cause of the king of England'; one argument for Gaunt's succession was that Gaunt's wife had Comyn blood![37] The new queen's connections (from Strathearn) had an anti-Bruce background, including executions for treason in 1320 and 1332. The rest of David's affinity (drawn mainly from Lothian and eastern Scotland) was based on different families to those in Robert I's – while the heirs of Robert I's affinity seem closer to Robert Stewart. Thus Stewart could have been called the real successor to Robert I – as parliament perhaps recognised in 1364. One important result was a propaganda effort by David's court circle to discredit Stewart's actions, guardianships and 'tyranny' before 1357; it even includes Fordun's chronicle, which consistently denigrates Robert Stewart.[38]

After 1363, however, there was no more open conflict, because Stewart would not react against David's pressure. Instead, the main political theme is the dramatic promotion of the queen's kinsmen and clients, to create a powerful 'Drummond faction'. This was significantly broadened when her nephew Malcolm married Douglas's daughter and her niece Anabella married Stewart's eldest son, John. Then, in 1368, John was granted the Bruce family earldom of Carrick, showing that he, not his father, was seen as heir-presumptive – or as heir-apparent, by those who reckoned David would be childless. Robert Stewart had been by-passed (and indeed was temporarily imprisoned in 1368), and his eldest son drawn into the royal circle.

The initiative possibly came from the queen, who must have realised that David was infertile. But David thought differently – and divorced her in 1369. He now planned to marry Agnes Dunbar, sister of George, earl of March,[39] who came to the fore politically along with his brother John, to whom David diverted the earldom of Fife. They were backed by Robert Erskine, a Renfrew baron who had been a leading administrator since the 1350s. The new regime signalled an end to the aggressive government of the 1360s (which may have been blamed on the former queen) by legislation in 1370 forbidding local officials to obey illegal royal commands. But pressure was maintained on Robert Stewart, who lost Strathearn for a time. On the other hand, John Dunbar married one of Stewart's daughters – suggesting that the Dunbars actually anticipated a Stewart succession, and were establishing ties with the expected future king, John Stewart, earl of Carrick.

---

[36] See p. 353 above.   [37] Duncan (1994), pp. 55–7.   [38] Boardman (1997).
[39] Another descendant of Thomas Randolph, he succeeded his cousin Patrick in 1368.

The manoeuvrings of 1369–70 were, however, upset early in 1371, when David II suddenly died, and the fifty-four-year-old Robert Stewart finally became king.[40] The earl of Douglas at once made an armed demonstration, probably against Erskine and the Dunbars;[41] but they strongly upheld Robert II's authority, and the earl backed down. The outcome is illuminating. Douglas's son married another of the new king's daughters, and received a large annuity, while Douglas replaced Erskine as justiciar (chief justice) of southern Scotland. Erskine kept his prominence at court, but Edinburgh and Stirling Castles, which he had controlled, went to the king's two eldest sons. John Dunbar lost Fife, the premier earldom, to the king's second son, but in compensation was made earl of Moray, like his ancestor Thomas Randolph, while his brother, the earl of March, got Randolph's lordship of Annandale; but Badenoch (part of Randolph's Moray) was given to the king's third son.

This typifies the first decade of Stewart kingship. Good patronage kept the magnates happy – but Robert II's sons topped the political tree. The eldest, John, had Carrick, Atholl, the Stewart lands and Edinburgh Castle; the second, Robert, was earl of Fife and Menteith and custodian of Stirling; the third, Alexander, was lord of Badenoch, royal lieutenant north of the Moray Firth, and (from 1382) earl of Buchan and lord of Ross; the fourth, David, was earl of Strathearn and Caithness. Previously domestic politics had been determined by the narrowness of the immediate royal family; now (as elsewhere in Europe, coincidentally) they would revolve around a large royal family and a *Hausmacht* policy which 'stewartised' the earldoms.

But large royal families were rarely united. In the 1380s the house of Stewart split. One problem was that Carrick was still connected with the Drummonds, and with other David II supporters who had seen him as the future king before 1371; they were becoming increasingly impatient. Those with northern interests, moreover, objected to the great power given to Alexander Stewart, earl of Buchan;[42] while Buchan's abuse of that power undermined the king's general support. Also, Robert's wish to end the 1384 warfare was opposed by most of Carrick's affinity, and especially by the new earl of Douglas, who succeeded his father that summer. The upshot was political upheaval in November 1384, when a council-general[43] gave the king's executive powers to Carrick, making him king's lieutenant. Robert's age – sixty-eight – was the ostensible reason, but

---

[40] For Robert II's reign, Boardman (1996a), chs. 2–6, is now the standard account.

[41] It is generally said that Douglas wanted the crown: e.g. Boardman (1996a), pp. 39–43. But the best chronicle account, in Wyntoun, *Original Chronicle*, VI, p. 264, appears to me to state that Erskine was Douglas's target; that would make much more sense.

[42] Subsequently generally known as 'the Wolf of Badenoch'; see pp. 372–3 below.

[43] A slightly less formal version of a parliament.

a *coup d'état* had taken place, and the guardianship (or its equivalent) became a major political issue again.

As lieutenant, however, Carrick (whose interests were in the south) did not deal with the earl of Buchan. That disappointed his supporters, but they welcomed Carrick's and Douglas's active war policy, which led to the 1388 invasion of England. Unfortunately, Douglas died childless at Otterburn. Carrick tried to ensure that the vast Douglas estates went to his brother-in-law Malcolm Drummond, husband of the dead earl's sister; but they were entailed on Archibald Douglas lord of Galloway (illegitimate son of 'the good Sir James'). Archibald allied with the king's second son, the earl of Fife – who was supported against Carrick by Robert II's followers, and also gained wider backing by undertaking to tackle his brother, Buchan. Carrick's power melted away, and at a council-general in December 1388 Fife replaced him as lieutenant; while Archibald Douglas became the third earl of Douglas.

The effects of this counter *coup* lasted beyond Robert II's death in 1390, for although Carrick succeeded to the throne as Robert III,[44] Fife's lieutenancy continued (probably because he did manage to curb Buchan, despite the latter's infamous reaction).[45] It ceased in 1393, however, when the king's eldest son, David, earl of Carrick, was deemed old enough (at fifteen) to assist his father. But Carrick acted increasingly independently: Robert III had to contend with an ambitious son as well as ambitious brothers. He could not cope with this unprecedented situation. Fife's power in central Scotland stayed undiminished; Carrick took over the 'Drummond faction' and the Stewart territory in the south-west; while the king's efforts to rebuild his position in the south-east antagonised the earl of Douglas.

In the later 1390s, in fact, Robert III steadily lost control of his kingdom; Carrick and Fife (made dukes of Rothesay and Albany respectively in 1398) really ran it, together with Douglas. And a council-general formalised this in January 1399 by appointing Rothesay (now aged twenty) lieutenant – though initially for only three years, and under an Albany/Douglas-dominated council. The political deal was cemented by Rothesay's marriage to Douglas's daughter. But that had required the annulment of an earlier marriage by Rothesay to the daughter of the earl of March (who as in 1370 wanted close ties with the heir to the throne). March was furious, and in 1400 defected to England – where he played a major role in the border warfare of 1400–2.[46]

In Scotland, the earldom of March was taken over by the fourth earl of

---

[44] He changed his name from John to Robert, probably to avoid the issue of whether to count John Balliol among his predecessors; instead, 'Robert III' stressed continuity with Robert I. Boardman (1996a), chs. 7–10, is now the standard account of this reign.

[45] Shortly after Robert II's death, Buchan burned Elgin Cathedral; see p. 373 below.

[46] March was mainly responsible for the English victory at Humbleton.

Douglas (who had succeeded his father at Christmas 1399); but Rothesay apparently had designs on it too, which soured their relationship. Also, by 1401 Rothesay was challenging Albany's interests in central Scotland – in association with his other uncle, the notorious earl of Buchan.[47] And he ignored the supervisory council, increasingly behaving as if he was actually king. His uncle's response was dramatic: when Rothesay's three-year term expired early in 1402, Albany had him seized and (with Douglas's backing), imprisoned him in Falkland Castle (Fife), where he died. A council-general exonerated Albany and Douglas, and made Albany lieutenant; shortly after, Malcolm Drummond died in the same way as Rothesay. In the early fifteenth century, politics had become much more violent. That is, no doubt, because Rothesay would never have let himself be overshadowed like Robert III, while Albany and Douglas would have viewed the prospect of Rothesay's becoming king with the utmost alarm – and so executed a pre-emptive strike. Future, rather than current, kingship was the issue.

Rothesay's death created a blood-feud in the royal family between Robert III's surviving son James (eventually King James I) and the house of Albany: it led to the execution of the second duke of Albany and his kin in 1424, and (partly) to James I's assassination in 1437.[48] All were horrific acts of violence. Yet in the years in between, Scottish high politics were mostly relatively calm: the early fifteenth century did not see constant political strife. That is even truer of the fourteenth century; after all, the tensions which led to Rothesay's death can be traced back to the 1340s – and the main point is surely that they did not erupt into violence sooner. One likely reason is memories of the consequences of the earlier Balliol–Bruce dispute. Another is that the lieutenancy provided a means of sidelining a king without having to depose and kill him. But the main explanation is probably that – despite the rivalries and quarrels inherent in all politics – Scotland's elites simply did not want widespread violence to erupt, and generally achieved peaceful settlements to political crises which accepted the *faits accomplis*. While the narrative will tend to highlight confrontation, compromise was more the norm. Once the Bruce–Balliol civil war had ended, it was only in the exceptional circumstances of Rothesay's lieutenancy that high politics became a matter of life and death; before then, they were not.[49]

CROWN, GOVERNMENT AND COMMUNITY

In the political narrative, the theme of dialogue and confrontation between crown and wider community – so prominent in English constitutional history –

---

[47] Boardman (1992), pp. 7–8.   [48] See Brown (1994a), chs. 2, 8.

[49] For a less sanguine view see Brown (1994b). But, despite the stress on political conflict in Dr Brown's and Dr Boardman's admirable books, my abiding impression from both is of a vast amount of compromising which greatly outweighed the acts of violence.

is conspicuous by its absence. Yet that does not mean that fourteenth-century Scotland has no constitutional history.[50] There is, for example, the fundamental issue of national independence which dominated the century. There is the redefinition of the crown–community relationship, legitimising removal of the king's executive power if he did not uphold the kingdom's interests (as happened in 1295). And, when that merged with the use of guardians during royal minorities or absences, there is the practice of sidelining the king through the office of lieutenant.

The guardians and lieutenants were parliamentary appointments. The Scottish parliament had developed in the later thirteenth century,[51] and in the fourteenth century parliaments and councils-general were held frequently. They were the institutional embodiment of 'the community of the realm', or (in terminology used from the 1350s) 'the three estates': the supreme forum for doing whatever the national interest required, such as enacting statute law, ratifying treaties, supervising defence, justice and finance, authorising taxation, or hearing petitions and appeals. In other words, they had exactly the same functions and powers as English parliaments, including standing up to the king when necessary. But that was rarely necessary; the parliamentary history of fourteenth-century Scotland was generally non-confrontational.

That was largely due to the system of government. As elsewhere, the king had his council to help him rule, his chancellor and secretariat to transmit his commands and 'brieves' (writs), his household to maintain him, and his exchequer to oversee his finances. But central bureaucracy was limited. There were no separate administrative departments beyond the secretariat (called the 'chapel', reflecting its origins in the royal household priests). The head of the household, the chamberlain, was in charge of royal finance, while the exchequer was merely a roughly annual meeting of *ad hoc* auditors. Under the chamberlain, the permanent household contained only a steward, some clerks and ushers, and various minor servants;[52] it was supplemented by members of the royal affinity, some of whom had retaining fees, but there was no formal structure of knights or esquires of the body. As for royal revenue, it was rarely above £10,000 a year, and often less than half of that.

In the localities, the network of sheriffdoms was run by sheriffs, 'crownars' and some subordinate officers; while supervisory links with the centre were provided by peripatetic justiciars (chief justices) and by the parliaments and councils-general. But although the sheriffdoms technically included the earldoms,

---

[50] It has yet to receive a modern study, though Mackinnon (1924) and Rait (1924) are still quite useful. The best introductions to medieval Scottish government are in Duncan (1975) and Webster (1975). The account of parliament and government given here derives from Grant (1984), ch. 6, which is mostly based on material in *Act. Parl. Scot.*, *Exch. Rolls Scot.*, and the *Regesta Regum Scottorum* volumes for Robert I and David II.   [51] See Duncan (1966).   [52] See Duncan (1993), pp. 244–50.

provincial lordships and ecclesiastical estates, these were effectively separate units, where the earls, lords and prelates exercised the same powers as the sheriffs, and in some cases also had palatinate or 'regality' rights. And within the sheriffdoms' core areas the lords of baronies (of which there were some 300–400, roughly like parishes) also had the same powers as the sheriffs, albeit under the latter's supervision.[53] Thus, in practice, local government was mostly in the hands of the earls, lords, prelates and barons, and the scope for action by royal office holders was limited – as is illustrated by the fact that there were only two justiciars.

It does not follow, however, that government was necessarily inadequate. Consider its main functions, defence and justice. In the long run, fourteenth-century Scotland was defended successfully, by means of the age-old obligation on all able-bodied men to fight to protect the homeland; they served, without pay, in forces recruited either by earls (each earldom had its 'army') or by sheriffs and local barons. The result varied from large coherent armies to collections of guerrilla bands; but the call-up was always on the king's behalf – as were the punishments for failure to serve.[54] As for justice, the main way of settling violence was, again, age-old, through arbitration and compensation agreed by heads of kins; but where that could not be achieved, the seigneurial and sheriff courts were used. These also heard land disputes and dealt with theft, but the major offences of murder, rape, arson and armed robbery were reserved to the justiciars and lords of regality. In most cases the initiative came from below, but it was the kingdom's laws that were invoked, be they the 'old laws' about inter-personal violence, the laws codified in the fourteenth-century treatises *Regiam Majestatem* and *Quoniam Attachiamenta*, or the new laws enacted by statute. And the seigneurial courts were supervised through appeals or complaints to the sheriffs, justiciars and parliament.[55] The actual machinery may not have been complex, but there is no reason to believe that justice was upheld less well than anywhere else.

Be that as it may, the level of local initiative means that the phrase often used of medieval England, 'self-government at the king's command', is inapplicable. Instead, Scotland had 'self-government in the king's name'. Local lords were mostly responsible for governing their own estates, under crown authority. The concept was maintained in the tenurial structure: everyone holding land of the king had to give him homage and fealty, and could not transfer their property without his permission. Refusal to recognise crown authority was a breach of fealty, for which the offender's lands could be seized; continued

---

[53] For maps of sheriffdoms, baronies and regalities, see McNeill and MacQueen (1997), pp. 192–4, 201–7. [54] Barrow (1990); Duncan (1975), pp. 378–85; Grant (1984), pp. 154–6.
[55] Wormald (1980); MacQueen (1993), esp. ch. 2.

offence implied rebellion, which could be treated as treason. Even the least impressive kings invoked that: John Balliol against the Bruces in 1293,[56] and Robert III against the earl of March in 1400. But in such cases, the king had to deal only with individuals or small groups, and was normally supported by the bulk of the political community. Usually recalcitrant nobles either backed down voluntarily or were forced to do so, and (as with the Stewart–Douglas–March rebellion of 1363) submissions and fresh promises of fealty to the king would bring the matter to a close.

The system's roots went back to the long-distant past, but the interlocking of sheriff and seigneurial courts was a product of the twelfth and thirteenth centuries. In that era, the kings had used loyal local lords (natives and incomers) as their main instruments for asserting crown authority throughout the kingdom, and there had been no serious clash of jurisdiction between royal and seigneurial justice. Also, the earldoms, lordships and baronies had covered coherent areas, within which seigneurial courts had operated effectively; so royal courts had not flourished at the expense of the lords'. Nor had the kings waged costly overseas wars, which is what made their English counterparts put such fiscal pressure on local administration and justice. As a result, the Scottish crown's attitude to government never became 'predatory',[57] and its relations with local lords were usually good.

That continued to be the case after 1296. Despite the devastations and upheavals, the structure of land tenure and government was maintained; indeed the kings widened seigneurial jurisdiction by creating new baronies and erecting regalities. And the new warfare, while intense, was essentially defensive – for which royal wages were not required. The war, in fact, only led to heavy taxation twice: in 1328–30, for the £20,000 paid to England under the Treaty of Edinburgh, and in 1358–60, for the initial instalments of David II's ransom; the amounts were around £6,000 a year, which is proportional to English taxation, but they were levied in no more than six years. Otherwise, the crown's fiscal needs were relatively light: roughly some £5,000–7,000 a year, mostly to sustain the fairly small royal household.[58]

The fiscal basis did change, however. Originally Scottish kings had lived off their estates, and that still happened in the thirteenth century, though by the 1280s there were also customs on exports (especially 6s 8d per sack on wool); at a rough guess, the crown lands then produced some £5,000 a year, and the customs another £2,000. But Robert I and David II made such generous grants to their supporters that in the 1360s the crown lands were probably worth less

---

[56] *Act. Parl. Scot.*, 1, p. 449.

[57] The term strikingly used of Henry I's government in Southern (1970), p. 231.

[58] For taxation and finance, see Grant (1984), pp. 162–6; also Nicholson (1974), at index.

than £500 a year. Instead – as a *quid pro quo* for his grants – parliament agreed in 1326 that Robert I should have about £2,000 a year for life from direct taxation. That lapsed when he died three years later, however, and the guardians who ran Scotland for David II had their own households, financed from their own income. Crown finance was not a major issue again until the crisis caused by David II's ransom after 1357. Initially the ransom was paid from heavy direct taxation; but the eventual solution agreed by parliament was to pay the ransom out of quadrupled customs (to £1 6s 8d per sack on wool), while direct taxes were occasionally authorised to keep the royal household solvent. And when, in the late 1360s, the customs receipts rose to over £10,000 a year while the ransom payments were reduced, direct taxation became unnecessary; it was last collected in 1373 by Robert II. Crown finance had thus come to be based almost entirely on the customs. While wool exports boomed, the crown was very well off by Scottish standards. But that did not last; by the 1390s wool exports had fallen sharply, and that led to acute fiscal problems in the fifteenth century.

Before then, however, crown finance was only a contentious political issue in the 1360s, and did not cause continuous disputes, as in England. That has obvious implications for Scottish parliamentary history. A related point is that a separate 'house of Commons' did not develop in the Scottish parliament, which remained a unicameral assembly of clergy, nobles and burgesses.[59] Burgesses were chosen from each burgh, but rural society was treated differently, on a tenurial basis. Everyone holding land directly of the crown was entitled to attend – so, in a sense, the whole kingdom was covered. But the lairds or gentry who turned up sat with the magnates, in the noble estate; there was no concept of separate 'shire' and hence 'community' representation. Instead, in the late 1360s parliaments began to elect special committees (subsequently called 'Lords of the Articles'), to deal with the bulk of parliamentary business. In function, they were like the English Commons; but they consisted largely of members of the royal council and affinity, and so were hardly a forum for pursuing grievances against royal government on behalf of the wider community. Given the way Scottish government worked, however, 'popular' grievances were more likely to have been local, against individual lords, and parliament did provide a supreme forum for organising collective action to deal with those – in the king's name, of course.

The Scottish parliament, therefore, was very much an institution which worked on the crown's behalf. Yet it was not a king-dominated rubber stamp. None of the kings had the practical power to impose their wishes on a reluctant

---

[59] Burgh representatives were first summoned under Robert I, and by the 1360s their presence was automatic.

community, in or out of parliament, or to defy the law; even David II could not get his own way completely in the 1360s. Instead, in practice, the kings were dependent on the community's general support. The parliaments and general councils were where that was formally expressed – or where, occasionally, it was withdrawn, as happened in 1384 and 1398.

There was nothing new about that: no Scottish king could have governed without widespread community support. In terms of direct practical power, however, the fourteenth-century kings may have been somewhat weaker than their predecessors. In the thirteenth century, the kings clearly enjoyed the positive backing of virtually the entire political community, but that could not be said of Robert I, David II, Robert II and Robert III. Each, in effect, was the head of a faction, and although after 1314 outright active opposition was rare (except in 1332–42), it is unlikely that any of them received more than lukewarm acceptance from quite broad sections of the nobility.

That raises the issue of patronage: as faction leaders, the kings had to reward their followers and buy the support of others. Crown patronage in fourteenth-century Scotland consisted chiefly of grants of land, cash annuities,[60] and privileges, particularly baronial and regality powers. As with all patronage, such grants had an essential political role. But the effect was double-edged. Grants of land and cash, for instance, diminished royal resources. Also, when the crown lands were alienated, the kings lost numerous estates which their predecessors had visited regularly in order to maintain an active royal presence across the localities.[61] And grants of regality reduced the area under 'normal' administration; by *c.*1400 regalities covered roughly a tenth of the kingdom.[62] One effect of crown patronage, therefore, was further to reduce the kings' own practical power.

So long as the local nobles were loyal and reliable, that was not a problem. Naturally, however, no king (or guardian or lieutenant) would take that entirely for granted. Each in turn promoted members of his affinity and kindred to be leading figures throughout the localities: patronage was not just for reward. That is why so many of the old crown lands were granted away, along with the forfeited Balliol–Comyn estates. Also, because (as elsewhere) about a quarter of fourteenth-century Scotland's magnate families died out in the male line every generation, escheated property was available for granting out. And, more significantly, a vast amount of territory, including most of the earldoms and lordships, was inherited by females – whose marriages commonly went to supporters of whoever was in power.[63] Not surprisingly, therefore, the

---

[60] When royal resources were chiefly on the customs, patronage in cash increased.

[61] Grant (1993a), esp. pp. 48–9, 63–70.

[62] An estimate from my map in McNeill and MacQueen (1997), p. 207.

[63] Extinction of magnate families and female inheritance are discussed in Grant (1985).

advantageous transferring of property was a particularly important consideration in domestic politics during the century.

Since the acquisition of land by either grant or marriage to an heiress was usually in perpetuity, however, those who had done well under one regime normally retained their possessions under its successor – at least after the end of the civil war. Thus while the various factions had plenty of incentive to gain political power and so enjoy crown patronage, from the 1340s onwards previous grants and property transfers were generally not reversed by a new regime. The consequence was that, while there was considerable competition for power, there was also considerable continuity of landownership. So long as supporters of the previous regime co-operated with the new one, they would be able to keep their estates and local positions. Moreover, the Scottish system (unlike the English) did not enable royal favourites to victimise others and to take over their lands through corrupt manipulation of the law.[64] In later fourteenth-century Scotland, therefore, a change of central regime generally had fairly limited repercussions. Even those who were out of sympathy with whichever king, guardian or lieutenant was in power at the centre generally had nothing to lose by accepting his authority – and so the system of 'self-government in the king's name' could be maintained.

THE FRONTIERS OF THE REALM

Although in the long run the war with England caused relatively little change to the Scottish system of government, it did have an obvious effect on the area that was governed: the expansion of the twelfth and thirteenth centuries ceased, and was replaced by contraction. The Isle of Man, annexed after 1266, was lost permanently to England in 1333. On the mainland, the losses were less permanent, but substantial parts of the south remained in English hands for over half the century.[65] And even after the last part of Edward III's buffer zone was regained in 1384, Jedburgh, Roxburgh and Berwick continued to be English-held outposts until well into the fifteenth century.

It was not just a matter of shifting political boundaries. As with so many fourteenth-century wars, a fluid frontier region emerged in which local conflict became endemic.[66] This stemmed partly from the Scottish policy of not letting the inhabitants of the occupied areas live in peace; that caused English retaliation against Scottish territory, and counter-retaliation into England proper. More generally, the opportunity for booty, especially in the highly mobile form

---

[64] A point discussed in Grant (1987), pp. 40–51.
[65] Before 1314, in 1333–41, after 1346, in 1356–77 and during much of 1377–84.
[66] For the Anglo-Scottish frontier, see Goodman (1987) and (1992).

of cattle, was a most powerful incentive. Much activity, of course, was simple lawlessness – with criminals in one country evading justice by fleeing to the other. In times of open war, the result was a virtual free-for-all. In times of truce, the problem of the occupied areas meant that the situation was often little better, despite the efforts of both governments to maintain order by appointing March wardens and truce 'conservators' who administered special border laws at joint 'March days'.

In those circumstances powerful regional magnates were needed to lead the reconquest, resist attacks and generally keep control. But the circumstances also encouraged the rise of local warlords. One example is the violent Douglas cadet, William Douglas of Kingscavil, who was prominent in the Scottish recovery of 1335–41.[67] An attempt was made to distance him from the Borders by giving him the earldom of Atholl, but he exchanged that (with Robert Stewart) for the border lordship of Liddesdale. Then in 1342, when a local rival, Alexander Ramsay, was made sheriff of Roxburgh, Douglas had him killed. Because of his military significance, however, he escaped punishment, and was himself made sheriff of Roxburgh. In 1346 he had a leading role at Neville's Cross, but was captured. While a prisoner, he agreed to support Edward III's claims in return for restoration to Liddesdale. But when he returned to Scotland to do so in 1353, he was killed by his young namesake, the head of the main Douglas family, whom he had largely eclipsed and who also claimed Liddesdale. Clearly the older William Douglas was dangerously concerned with personal aggrandisement on the Borders – but was so important that he could get away with murder. In this case, the system of 'self-government in the king's name' had broken down.

How typical the lord of Liddesdale was, however, is hard to say. Had the war gone differently, problems might have been caused by William Wallace, who in 1296 led a band of thieves;[68] as it was, he became a hero. Similarly, in the 1290s the lord of Douglas was a notorious troublemaker, whose son, James, might have followed suit had personal conflict with the English not led him to join Robert I.[69] 'The good Sir James' was the most successful of the warlords. His rewards were vast lands and privileges in the Borders, where Robert I probably used him as a military governor. But he was not in sole command, for others, including Thomas Randolph, also had major lordships there; Robert's policy was to share out the regional power. Later, however, accidents of inheritance, exacerbated by deaths in battle, resulted in Sir James's successors, the earls of Douglas, becoming increasingly dominant – especially when the third earl added his own lordships of Galloway and Bothwell to the main Douglas

---

[67] Brown (1997a) contains an excellent analysis of William Douglas's career.
[68] *Cal. Doc. Scot.*, II, p. 191. [69] Barrow (1988), p. 83; Duncan (1992), pp. 139–40.

estates in 1389. And the earl of March's defection to England in 1400 removed the final counterweight to the fourth earl, who duly received March's lordships of Dunbar and Annandale.

The fourteenth century, therefore, saw the house of Douglas come to control the Scottish Borders. All the earls seem distinctly 'overmighty', especially the fourth, who was probably the greatest Scottish magnate ever. Douglas propaganda justified their might as the reward for continuously defending the nation against England, and the earldom is typical of the overmighty lordships based on military leadership which were springing up in frontier zones throughout fourteenth-century Europe.[70] But while the corollary to the rise of Douglas dominance on Scotland's southern frontier must have been a shrinkage in the crown's power there, that was not absolute. All the earls were good politicians, constantly active at the centre of royal government – and so can be seen as, in a sense, upholding the basic system. Their influence, of course, was immense, especially over foreign policy – but they do not appear to have abused their regional might. There is an instructive contrast with the mid-fifteenth-century eighth earl (1445–52), who flagrantly disregarded the crown: it led to his death at the king's hands, and to the earldom's destruction.[71] The fourteenth-century earls of Douglas, conversely, wielded their power within the system, and never risked that fate.

There is also a significant contrast with the Highlands, which contained Scotland's other, internal, frontier.[72] It was not geographical or linguistic, but a division within the Highland Gaelic world itself, between areas where lords accepted the crown's authority and national laws, and those where they gave the crown token allegiance and followed the principles of traditional Gaelic lordship. These gave succession rights to any adult male member of a chief's kinship group, but did not permit female inheritance, which meant that territory could not be acquired by marriage. Conflict was endemic, either in succession disputes or to take over the lands of weaker kindreds.[73] Gaelic society was highly militarised, and chiefs acquired and held territory by extracting tribute and by billeting their warriors on the subjected peasantry – as was common practice in Gaelic Ireland.[74] Might, in other words, was right.

By the mid-thirteenth century, this frontier had been pushed back to the west Highlands and Islands, and even those began to be assimilated after 1266. The process was spearheaded by east-Highland magnates, in particular the Comyns of Badenoch and the earls of Ross, but it also involved the greatest west-coast Gaelic lords, the MacDougalls of Argyll. It was rudely interrupted,

---

[70] Brown (1997a) and (1997b).

[71] Grant (1984), pp. 191–5; for details, see McGladdery (1990), ch. 4.

[72] For the Highlands, see Barrow (1973), Bannerman (1977) and Grant (1984), ch. 7.

[73] Bannerman (1977), p. 213.   [74] Boardman (1996a), pp. 83–8; cf. Simms (1987), pp. 116–28.

however, by the outbreak of war – especially the civil war, in which the MacDougalls, like the Comyns, opposed Robert Bruce, were defeated, and lost their lands. There was no MacDougall-led integration of the west; instead, their rivals the MacDonalds of Islay rose to dominance, creating the quasi-independent, traditional Gaelic 'Lordship of the Isles'.[75]

The MacDonalds had supported Robert I because of their feud with the MacDougalls, and in the 1330s they played Balliol off against Bruce.[76] In both cases, they received grants of territory – which they had no doubt overrun already. But their main advance came in 1346. The then earl of Ross, whose west-coast land had been attacked by another major kindred, the MacRuairis of Garmoran, had the MacRuairi chief assassinated. That enabled John MacDonald of Islay, husband of MacRuairi's sister, to take possession of Garmoran – perhaps as his wife's inheritance, more probably by force. John had called himself 'Lord of the Isles' in 1337, but it is his acquisition of Garmoran that marks the real emergence of the MacDonald Lordship. Also in 1346, the last Randolph earl of Moray died at Neville's Cross. When Robert I created that earldom (which included Badenoch), he intended the Randolphs to replace the Comyns in dominating the central Highlands and penetrating towards the west. But that was difficult in the 1330s, and impossible after 1346 (when the earldom went to the earl of March). Just when the Lordship of the Isles came into being, one of the main counterweights to it disappeared. The Highland power structure was transformed.

This was appreciated by the guardian, Robert Stewart, whose eldest daughter married John MacDonald.[77] As for Stewart himself, he married the sister of the other main Highland magnate, the earl of Ross – who was the husband of a sister of the Lord of the Isles. A new family network had come to dominate the Highlands – especially when Stewart (who already possessed Atholl) took over the lordship of Badenoch.[78] But this did not integrate the Lord of the Isles into the national community. John MacDonald regarded the guardian as an equal; and after David II's return in 1357, he defied the crown by refusing to let the Lordship be taxed. The earl of Ross supported him against the king; both were 'contumaciously absent' from parliaments in the 1360s.[79] Moreover, in 1366 parliament condemned rebels in Atholl, Argyll, Badenoch, Lochaber and Ross; since Atholl and Badenoch were in Stewart's hands, he seems to have been associated with MacDonald and Ross. Perhaps, since Stewart was no doubt an absentee, he had let local kindreds get out of control. But it also

---

[75] McDonald (1997), chs. 4–6; Bannerman (1977).
[76] For the MacDonalds, see, e.g., Munro and Munro (1986), and Grant (1988).
[77] It used to be said that MacDonald divorced his first wife; but she probably simply died.
[78] His wife was the widow of the earl of Moray, and Badenoch may have been her terce.
[79] Nicholson (1974), pp. 178–9.

appears that he was employing Highland warriors, like a traditional Gaelic lord.[80] If so, then by the later 1360s Scotland's internal frontier was moving significantly to the east.

There are broader factors to consider, too. First, as in the Borders, accidents of war and inheritance disrupted earlier structures and caused much absentee lordship (not only Stewart's) – a situation in which traditional Gaelic lordship was bound to flourish. Secondly, the power exercised by John MacDonald within his Lordship meant that the best opportunities for militaristic activity now lay outside it. Thirdly, it is likely that the Highlands and Western Isles were not hit so badly by plague as the rest of Scotland, and hence that the population balance altered. The extension of Lowland settlement into the Highlands ceased (as did the extension of the Scots language at the expense of Gaelic), and population movement may now have come from the western Highlands, often in a lawless form. In general, therefore, northern Scottish society was experiencing fundamental change.

One response was to meet force with force, as David II did in 1369 when he led an expedition north which made the Lord of the Isles and the earl of Ross submit. That was the normal crown reaction to magnate defiance, but in the new Highland circumstances it did not offer a long-term solution. An alternative was to install a full-time military governor – as Robert Stewart did after he became king in 1371. He gave Badenoch to his fourth son Alexander,[81] appointed him lieutenant over most of the country beyond the Great Glen, and in 1382 put him in control of Ross through marriage to the late earl's heiress. That made Alexander (who took the title earl of Buchan) the greatest lord ever seen in the Highlands, at least on parchment.[82]

The policy would have been excellent, had Buchan's lordship been effective. But it was disastrous. The countess of Ross had previously been married to a relative of the important Lindsay family, and, on behalf of his young son, they strongly opposed Buchan's position in Ross. So did the kindred of the previous earl. Also, Buchan quarrelled bitterly with both the earl and the bishop of Moray. More generally, he adopted the methods of traditional Gaelic lordship, recruiting a force of Highland fighting men whom he billeted locally, and demanding protection money. To make matters worse, he was unable to maintain public order.

Not surprisingly there was a storm of protest, which helped to discredit Robert II's kingship.[83] Finally, after the earl of Fife became lieutenant of the kingdom in 1389, Buchan was removed from office as 'useless to the community'.[84] He reacted furiously: in 1390, soon after Robert II's death, he and his

---

[80] Boardman (1996a), pp. 31–2 (n. 66); from *Act. Parl. Scot.*, I, pp. 497–8.

[81] Badenoch was detached from John Dunbar's earldom of Moray: above, p. 360.

[82] Alexander's career is examined in Grant (1993b), Boardman (1996a), at index, and (1996b).

[83] See above, p. 360.   [84] *Act. Parl. Scot.*, I, p. 556.

band of 'wyld, wikkit heland men'[85] burned the cathedral of Moray at Elgin – an outrage justifying his later nickname 'the Wolf of Badenoch'. He had united the political community against himself, however, and was soon made to submit and pay reparations; he lost Ross when his wife divorced him for desertion, and although his illegitimate sons took part in a great raid southwards in 1392; they were caught and imprisoned. The system of government did, eventually, manage to deal with the Wolf of Badenoch.

His career, however, seriously exacerbated the situation in the central Highlands. At the same time, he left them open to penetration from the west coast, via the Great Glen; in the 1390s, various MacDonalds appeared there, asserting their own brand of military power. Also, his enemies in Ross reacted by looking for help to the Lord of the Isles. Thus while at the beginning of the fourteenth century the west-coast Gaelic lords had been confined to the periphery, by its end the tentacles of the Lordship of the Isles were spreading right across the Highlands. The Wolf of Badenoch had helped to bring about the opposite of what was intended of him. To make matters worse, whereas John MacDonald had maintained fairly good relations with his father-in-law Robert II, after his death in 1387 his widow did not get the lands to which she was entitled under Scots law. She appealed to parliament, and action in her favour was ordered on her behalf. This caused a major confrontation with the new Lord of the Isles, which necessitated more armed expeditions by government forces.

Thus the century was ending with an apparently constant state of emergency in the north. And now the trouble was not confined to the western periphery: the whole of the Highlands seemed to be in crisis. The result was that, in the Lowlands, the whole of the Gaelic Highland world came to be perceived as troublesome and dangerous, and thus the consciousness of a clear-cut Highland–Lowland division, which is not to be found in the early fourteenth century but which was so important in later centuries, had taken root. Instead of Scotland's internal frontier being on the west, all of the Highlands had come to be a frontier zone – which represents an even greater contraction for the kingdom than that on the Borders.

It would be wrong to end this account of Scotland's fourteenth century on quite such a note of crisis, however. For instance, the kingdom never contracted to a narrow 'Pale' round Edinburgh. In other words, although there are extremely close parallels between what was going on in the Highlands and what was going on in Ireland, the problems caused by the resurgence of the Gaelic world were actually much less in Scotland; while the perceptions of Highland–Lowland differences, though hardening, were not institutionalised

---

[85] Wyntoun, *Original Chronicle*, VI, p. 368.

into a form of apartheid. And, more generally, whatever troubles affected the kingdom of Scotland at the end of the fourteenth century, they were far less serious than those faced at its beginning; around the year 1300, after all, the entire kingdom seemed to be on the verge of extinction. Thus, while domestic problems appear to have increased as the century went on, that is more than balanced by the fact that the external threat slackened off. Indeed 'survival through adversities' is probably the best way of summing up the history of fourteenth-century Scotland.

IRELAND

Robin Frame

WHEN in 1394 Richard II led an army to Ireland, he was the first ruler of England to visit the lordship since John in 1210. Richard's expedition did, however, have recent precedents, most notably that of his uncle, Lionel, earl of Ulster and duke of Clarence, who had been Edward III's lieutenant there from 1361 to 1366. In a great council held at Kilkenny in 1360 the English of Ireland had told Edward of the perilous state of the country, portraying themselves as assailed on all sides by the Irish, and the justiciar as hampered by shrinking revenues and faced by attacks on so many marches that he could no longer cope.[1] The despatch of Lionel with a large retinue paid mostly from English sources was in part an answer to this plea for assistance. Likewise in 1385, the prelates, lords and commons of Ireland had predicted an imminent conquest of the land and had asked Richard II to 'prepare in his own person to survey and visit his said lordship for its rescue and salvation'.[2] A not dissimilar message was sent by the citizens of Dublin in 1392.

Such appeals, and the English responses to them, would have amazed Edward I, who had taken his authority in Ireland largely for granted. In his day the Dublin government had been financially self-sufficient; it had regularly sent cash to England, raised supplies for the Welsh and Scottish wars and recruited expeditionary forces for royal campaigns in Flanders and Scotland. They might have surprised Edward II, in whose time the English of Ireland had fought back against a Scottish invasion, in 1318 defeating Robert Bruce's brother, Edward, who had occupied the earldom of Ulster and taken the title 'king of Ireland'. Even allowing for a degree of special pleading by the settler elites, who wished to open English purses and by doing so limit demands for taxation within Ireland, much had clearly altered over the century; the note of

---

[1] Richardson and Sayles (1947), pp. 19–22.

[2] Berry, *Statutes*, pp. 484–7: 'qil soi vodra tailler en sa propre persone de surveer et visiter sa dit seigneurie en rescous et salvation dycelle et en resistance del conquist semblable en hast affaire et en salvation de sez povres lieges en celles parties'.

gloom and panic struck in many official documents betrayed real anxieties. Changes within Ireland had made the country less amenable to English law and government and to conventional forms of aristocratic management. They had also produced an acute sense of vulnerability in the population of the heartlands of the colony.

In the early fourteenth century power in Ireland was shared between Gaelic lords, resident magnates of Anglo-French descent, communities of lesser landholders in the counties and of burgesses in the towns, and English lords who, like the king, exercised their authority and took their profit from a distance. The distribution of influence between these groups differed from area to area, reflecting among other things the physical geography of the island. The Dublin region shows how the local configuration of arable lowland, upland, forest and bog could create sharp contrasts. Dublin itself, home of the exchequer and the court of common pleas, and seat of an archbishop who was usually closely associated with royal government, was one of the chief cities of northern Europe. Its elite was English-speaking and maintained close trading contacts with England. From Dublin north to Drogheda and Dundalk lay lowlands controlled by an Anglophone gentry whose memory is preserved in a multitude of placenames made up of the family name with the suffix 'town'.[3] Even within this heavily settled part of Ireland the native population probably formed the majority; yet the dominant culture was English. Things were very different south of the city, where the land rises into the Wicklow hills. A ring of manors belonging to the crown and to the archbishop of Dublin contained within their notional southern borders a landscape of glen and hillside where settler kins vied with each other and with their equally competitive Irish counterparts for stock and pasture. In this milieu feuds and cattle raids were normal; the habitual violence invaded the manorial cores, where crops were often stolen, and could lead to military mobilisation in the city of Dublin itself. In Wicklow and north Wexford native lords were conscious of the past, and harnessed it to validate their role as local masters of men and cattle, and arbiters of what the royal records described as 'peace' and 'war'. The grandest example of this is provided by the old royal dynasty of MacMurrough, which from 1327 periodically revived the title 'king of Leinster'.[4]

Such contrasts were present throughout Ireland. Their local variations render the social and political make-up of the country hard to describe; but it is possible to make a broad distinction between the zones lying on either side of a line running roughly from Dundalk on the Ulster border to Limerick and

---

[3] Otway-Ruthven (1968b), plate LXII at p. 455; Smith (1993).
[4] Simms (1987), pp. 16–17; Frame (1995), pp. 162–75.

Cork. South and east of the line, English rule was dominant. The region contained the major seaports and royal centres of Drogheda, Dublin, Waterford, Cork and Limerick, and also trading towns such as Kilkenny, New Ross and Youghal which were under magnate lordship. Within it lay a network of shires and great liberties where English law was administered. Office holding in these districts was limited to men of English status: each community had its landed families who supplied sheriffs, keepers of the peace, coroners and sergeants, and provided knights to attend the parliaments that usually met at Dublin or Kilkenny. The wealth and status of such families arose in part from their lordship over a population which contained, in the fertile river valleys, large elements whose ancestors had originally come from England and Wales.

Yet many parts of the south and east besides Wicklow were not much settled or within the ambit of English law; indeed even before 1300 there appears to have been a retreat from marginal districts in Offaly, Leix, west Meath or north Tipperary which had seen attempts at settlement.[5] The colonised parts of every county and liberty lay close to march areas, which in turn shaded off into the 'land of war'. In these border regions kins whose leading members remained aware of their English status intermarried with the Irish, and inhabited a hybrid legal world where Gaelic custom – especially in the form of pledge- and hostage-taking and the violent pursuit of compensation for injuries – was influential.[6] By the fifteenth century the cattle raids of marcher lords were celebrated in verse commissioned from the Irish bardic class.[7] A chief preoccupation of royal authority was defending the English areas, or 'land of peace', against intrusion from the marches. The legislation of parliaments and great councils imposed duties on individuals (to keep horses and arms according to their means, to rise to the hue and cry, not to traffick with those outside the peace) and on communities (to aid one another, to avoid the temptation to make separate truces, to muster at the order of the sheriff or keepers of the peace).[8] The government also intervened directly, every year mustering small armies to punish raiders.

The military activities of the king's ministers in eastern and southern Ireland amounted not so much to war against an enemy as to the exercise of lordship. Rather like Gaelic overlords, justiciars backed candidates for rule in the Irish districts, exacted hostages, and (under the name of 'fines') imposed cattle tributes. Government in Ireland was in some contexts English and bureaucratic; in others it amounted to force and diplomacy along Irish lines. Royal rule in

[5] Nicholls (1982), pp. 372–4. [6] Mac Niocaill (1976), pp. 39–40, and (1984), pp. 110–17.
[7] O'Sullivan, *Poems on Marcher Lords*; Simms (1989), pp. 180–2.
[8] E.g. Berry, *Statutes*, pp. 194–213 (1297), 374–97 (1351).

the south and east depended on co-operation with the resident magnates, especially the Geraldine lords of Offaly, who became earls of Kildare in 1316, and the Butlers, whose power lay chiefly in Kilkenny and Tipperary, and who were made earls of Ormond in 1328. The earls also operated in two modes. They drew revenues and services from manors that lay in the land of peace and had attracted heavy settlement;[9] they were in addition warriors and skilled diplomats among the kins of the marches and lands of war that lay within the orbit of their influence. Surviving written contracts reveal the flavour of this marcher world: in 1350 two Gaelic leaders from the Kildare–Meath border undertook, in return for aid and maintenance in their disputes with other Irish, to serve the earl of Kildare at their own costs in war within their own districts and, at his wages, 'to follow and attend [his] banners, expeditions and wars throughout all Ireland'.[10] While English power was strong in most of southern and eastern Ireland, it was not synonymous with English custom; the ability to devise mechanisms of control and influence outside the scope of regular administration – to rule, that is, with rather than against the local grain – was central to royal and aristocratic authority.

North and west of the imaginary line, patterns were different. This zone was not wholly without towns and stretches of manorialised lowland. Galway, for example, was a rich port with a well-settled immediate hinterland. Twescard, the area around Coleraine in northern Ulster, contained a prosperous, though isolated, group of manors; as late as the 1350s, Elizabeth de Burgh, lady of Clare, drew significant income from her property there.[11] But despite pockets of settlement and close exploitation, the terrain of the north and west had not been favourable to colonising enterprises. The magnates and their military followers who entered these regions from around 1177 had created fluctuating overlordships which left Gaelic society largely intact. Native lords (of whom the chief were the O'Donnells and O'Neills of modern Ulster, the O'Connors of Connacht, O'Briens of Thomond and MacCarthys of Desmond) kept control of large parts of their ancestral territories. They might find themselves tributary to magnates who now acted as provincial rulers; but should the power of the latter falter, they were well placed to rebuild their primacy over a wider area.

On the eve of the Scottish invasion in 1315 the south-west was tied to Dublin and England by the Geraldine lords of Desmond and Kerry and the de Clare lord of Thomond, who between them provided a counterpoise to the MacCarthys and O'Briens. But their power in the outer zone of the lordship

[9] Empey (1986).

[10] *Red Book of Kildare*, no. 168: 'vexilla viagia et guerras per totam Hiberniam sequentes et respondentes sumptibus dicti domini Mauricii filii Thome [the earl]'.

[11] McNeill (1980), pp. 136–47; Frame (1982), pp. 63–4.

of Ireland was dwarfed by that of Richard de Burgh, earl of Ulster and lord of Connacht from 1280 to 1326, who presided over settler communities, feudal sub-lords and Gaelic chiefs alike, ruling with little interference from Dublin. The earl was no backwoodsman. He had property in England and arranged marriages into the English and Scottish aristocracy for members of his family: Elizabeth de Clare, wife of his son and heir, was a sister of the earl of Gloucester; Gloucester himself married one of his daughters, as did Robert Bruce, the future king of Scots. The remoter parts of Ireland were not beyond royal influence; but whereas in the south and east the king's authority was exercised through detailed administration backed by multiple links with families and communities, further afield it depended on ties with a small number of powerful magnates.

Despite the shrill complaints that reached England from the 1350s onwards, the story of the fourteenth century is not one of total collapse. But the period undoubtedly saw the balance of advantage tip in favour of local as against central authority, and of marcher custom as against English law. The process of change is still imperfectly understood. One difficulty is that the sources available from the late thirteenth century are richer and more varied than those for earlier times. Financial records of the Dublin government reveal expenditure on war; Latin annals from Dublin and Kilkenny recount Irish raids; court rolls provide ready evidence of criminality and disorder; records of private lordships disclose the intimate ties between magnates and native Irish lords. Such material makes it easy to paint a picture of decline from a more orderly world – which itself may be in part a creation of the formal charters and distant English records from which those concerned with earlier periods have to work. Nevertheless, though the contrast between the thirteenth and fourteenth centuries has sometimes been presented in unduly stark terms, it is not an illusion.

Change can most easily be pinpointed in the outer areas, where royal and aristocratic control was in any case vulnerable. There the years of the Scottish invasion were critical. The presence of the Scots destabilised Gaelic Ireland and altered the balance between Irish and English from Ulster to west Munster. In 1318 Richard de Clare was killed by the O'Briens; after the death of his son in 1321, the lordship of Thomond was partitioned between absentee coheiresses, and English influence west of Limerick proved irrecoverable. The fate of the de Burgh lordships was more serious for crown authority in Ireland. When Edward Bruce landed in Ulster in May 1315, Earl Richard was still expanding his influence, as his acquisition of lands around Derry and building of a castle on the Inishowen peninsula shows.[12] By the end of the year, Bruce and his ally Donal O'Neill had shut him out of Ulster and had fomented a

---

[12] Sayles, *Documents*, no. 86; Otway-Ruthven (1968a), pp. 214–15.

rising in Connacht. Despite the eventual defeat of the Scots, the coherence of the vast de Burgh empire was lost. After the murder in 1333 of Earl Richard's grandson and heir (who paid with his life for his abrasive attempts to restore it), the effective earldom of Ulster was progressively reduced to a few coastal enclaves; the O'Neills moved eastwards, while the Glens of Antrim played host to a branch of the MacDonalds of the Isles. In Connacht cadets of the de Burgh family consolidated their lordships, competing for power with each other and with the O'Connors. Although Edward III arranged the marriage of Lionel to the Ulster heiress as early as 1342, influence over the inheritance was hard to maintain. Neither Lionel nor his Mortimer heirs had much impact in Connacht, and the assertiveness of the Mortimers in the north was vitiated by their early deaths and by O'Neill power.

These events meant that Ulster and Connacht contained lordships of varying size, in the hands of Irish and hibernicized English dynasties. Major figures might have occasional dealings with central authority, but their position was, in English eyes, *de facto* rather than *de iure*. The changed circumstances are visible in the heightened importance of the archbishops of Armagh, who from the time of Richard Fitzralph (1348–60) were invariably of English birth or descent. The archbishops were normally resident among the settler population of Louth and Meath. From there they conducted an intensive diplomacy among the native lords and higher clergy of Ulster, by turns cajoling, excommunicating and balancing one interest against another. Archbishop John Colton (1383–1404) was to be instrumental in bringing the O'Neills and other northern lords to submit to Richard II in 1395.[13] In the south-west the Geraldines, who had become earls of Desmond in 1329, could bridge the gap between central authority and local society. Both the first earl (1329–56) and the third earl (1358–98) had brief spells as justiciar of Ireland. But because of their remoteness from Dublin and close links with Irish dynasties they attracted official suspicion and posed problems of political management. While nobody seems to have doubted that all Ireland was in theory within the king's lordship – the title to some of its remotest parts after all belonged to members of the royal family – regular and effective channels of obedience were in short supply.

Changes in the south and east were more subtle. At the end of the four-teenth century the framework of major towns, counties and liberties was intact; sheriffs and keepers of the peace were still appointed; the earls of Kildare and Ormond remained powerful and usually biddable. None the less there was a retreat of English law and culture. Sources from within the lordship paint a picture of reconquest of English areas by the Irish. What took

13 Simms (1974); Watt (1981), pp. 200–13.

place might be better described as a deepening intrusion of the social patterns of the marches into former lands of peace. This may be associated with a retreat of arable farming and an extension of pastoral activity, with its concomitant cattle raids and competition for grazing.[14] The effect was to enlarge the regions that had to be managed through punitive expeditions, parleys and *ad hoc* deals rather than through the routines of administration. This bred a sense of crisis in official circles and also, of course, in the communities of the shrinking lands of peace on whom the burdens of defence fell. Their fears lay behind the legislation of the mid-fourteenth century, most fully developed in the 1366 Statute of Kilkenny which sought to limit and monitor the contacts between English and Irish, and prevent further erosion of English social patterns.[15]

The impact of these changes is visible in various ways. The revenue collected by the Dublin government declined dramatically between the time of Edward I, when it came to £5,000 a year or more, and that of Edward III, when it rarely rose much above £2,000 – just enough to pay official salaries and for occasional brief punitive expeditions.[16] From the 1360s onwards, when greater pressure began to be placed on English lords to defend their lands in Ireland, many absentees reacted by liquidating their Irish interests. The decline in security can be traced in key areas. The valley of the river Barrow in south Leinster, running between the Gaelic redoubts of Wicklow and Leix, was the artery of communication between Dublin and the cities and counties of the south. From the 1320s onwards there are instances of southern mayors and sheriffs being excused attendance at the exchequer because of the hazards of the journey. By mid-century, towns such as Castledermot and Carlow in the Barrow region were frontier-posts, and the government at times had to devote scanty resources to maintaining garrisons along the route. In 1359 for the first time MacMurrough to the east of the Barrow and O'More to the west were able to join forces: though the justiciar, the earl of Ormond, defeated them in Leix, the ominous alliance may explain the statement in the 1360 appeal to Edward III that 'the Irish, your enemies, are collectively rising to war by general agreement and conspiracy'.[17] By the time of Richard II 'black rent' (protection money) from the communities of the Barrow valley was swelling the income of Art MacMurrough, who is said to have had a seal that described him as 'by the grace of God, king of Leinster'.[18] The decline of security in the area served progressively to sever the south-coast region (where the considerable wealth

---

[14] Simms (1986), pp. 379–90; Nicholls (1987), pp. 413–16; Down (1987), pp. 480, 490.

[15] Berry, *Statutes*, pp. 430–69.   [16] Richardson and Sayles (1962), pp. 93–5, 99–100.

[17] Richardson and Sayles (1947), p. 20: 'les Irrois vos enemys par tote la terre d'un assent et covyn sount communcment levetz de gerre, ardauntz, destruyantz et praiauntes de jour en altre vos liges celes parties'.   [18] Graves, *Roll*, pp. 128–30; Curtis, 'Unpublished Letters', p. 286.

of the ports fell increasingly under the control of local magnates) from the governmental core of the lordship in the eastern counties, which was in the early Tudor period to be described as the English Pale.[19]

The reasons for the shrinkage of the colonial heartlands remain to be fully analysed by historians. Royal policies and changes in lordship did not help. Ireland had always contributed to the military activities of the king; but from the outbreak of the Scottish war in 1296 Edward I squeezed it particularly hard through taxation, the siphoning off of 'surplus' revenue, and scouring the hinterlands of the ports for supplies. As work on England has shown, we should not underestimate the ability of a rapacious medieval administration to affect the economy adversely. Though Edward II and Edward III continued to take supplies from Ireland for their Scottish wars, Dublin had virtually ceased to make cash payments to England by 1307.[20] Royal demands naturally fell heaviest on the areas where central government was most effective. These were suffering at the same period from tenurial instability. Kilkenny was partitioned after the death of the earl of Gloucester in 1314, and Wexford upon that of the earl of Pembroke in 1324. The large holdings of the de Verdon family in Meath and Louth were shared among heiresses after 1316. Carlow and Kildare passed in and out of royal hands, being run sometimes as counties and sometimes as liberties. Trim in Meath was inherited by Roger Mortimer and his wife in 1307, but more than once forfeited because of the storms that attended Roger's career. The central government thus found its tasks growing at the same time as the king was calling its attention and resources elsewhere. These difficulties were compounded by the troubles of 1315–18. Edward Bruce led damaging *chevauchées* from Ulster, penetrating into Louth in 1315, crossing Meath and north Leinster in the winter of 1315–16, and, with King Robert himself in tow, reaching the outskirts of Dublin and then ravaging his way to Limerick early in 1317. These raids coincided with the European famine, so that the people of the lordship were tormented both by natural disasters and by the demands of starving soldiery.

Together these developments produced dislocation and a marked fall in royal revenue. They did not, however, create a sense that the lordship of Ireland was irretrievably damaged. After all, the Scots were beaten in the end; and their presence in Ireland, like the famine, had borne heavily on their allies as well as their opponents. The arrival of the Black Death and later outbreaks of plague were another matter. English and Irish sources claim that the pestilence fell unevenly in Ireland, damaging the inhabitants of the land of peace, who lived in towns and manorial villages, more than it injured the pastoralists of the marches and beyond. Such contemporary judgements were probably

[19] O'Brien (1988), pp. 14–26.   [20] Lydon (1964), p. 57.

oversimplified, but there is no reason to doubt their broad accuracy. Royal records from the later fourteenth century often refer to the depopulation of the English areas, coupling the effects of plague with those of war.[21] It seems too that rising wage rates in England drew people from Ireland. When Richard II proclaimed that all those born in Ireland should return there at the time of his 1394 expedition, more than 500 exemptions were recorded, revealing considerable emigration from the lordship at this time.[22] In 1398 when the duke of Surrey assumed the lieutenancy of Ireland, among the conditions he tried to lay down was that the English government should organise a recolonisation programme, involving the movement of a man and his wife from every parish, or every second parish, in England 'to inhabit the land where it is destroyed along the marches'.[23]

It was against this background that English policy towards Ireland unfolded. The trouble, from the viewpoint of those trying to run the country for the king, was that royal actions were not, and could not be, governed only or even primarily by conditions in the lordship. English politics, and the state of the Scottish and French wars, shaped kings' attitudes. Yet if Ireland came low on the list of royal priorities, changing perceptions of the lordship did influence what was attempted, as Edward III's reign shows. Edward planned an Irish expedition in 1331–2, and was within weeks of crossing the sea when events in Scotland offered opportunities for intervention that he could not resist. He had been moved to go to Ireland primarily by worries about the influence Roger Mortimer had wielded there during his minority and doubts about the loyalty of magnates whom Mortimer had favoured (the Mortimer regime had created the earldoms of Ormond and Desmond). His decision to marry Lionel, his second surviving son, to the Ulster heiress suggests that he saw Ireland as a place where a member of his family could make a career. In 1344 the chief tasks of the new justiciar Ralph Ufford, a banneret of the royal household who had married Lionel's mother-in-law, Maud of Lancaster, the widowed countess of Ulster, were to show the flag in the north and check the ambitions of the earl of Desmond in the south-west; shoring up the frontiers in south-east Ireland against the MacMurroughs and others was a secondary matter.

Gradually, as the chorus of complaint from Ireland swelled, Edward began to think that his lordship was not merely troubled but threatened with decomposition. It may be no coincidence that in July 1349 – when the effects

---

[21] E.g. Richardson and Sayles (1947), p. 20; Dublin, National Archives, RC 8/27, pp. 679–81.
[22] Lydon (1963), p. 137.
[23] Gilbert (1865), p. 561: 'pur la dite terre enhabiter la ou ele est destruyte sur les marches'.

of the plague were well established – he accompanied the appointment of a new justiciar, Thomas Rokeby, with dark remarks about the disturbed state of Ireland. By the time he crossed to France in 1359 he felt it necessary to apologise to his Irish ministers for his inability to send them help.[24] Those in Ireland who drew up the appeal at Kilkenny in July 1360, a few weeks after the sealing of the Treaty of Brétigny, must have known that the moment was right.

While Edward's response to the petition was shaped by wider events, it is significant that the diagnosis of Ireland's ills made at Kilkenny passed almost verbatim into documents accompanying Lionel's appointment as lieutenant in 1361. The episode reveals the skill with which the English of Ireland played the political game. Their ability to do so, ironically, owed much to the pressures royal government had placed upon them. During the 1350s, for instance, grants of taxation, whether by individual counties in their courts, by clusters of counties in regional great councils, or by the lordship as a whole in parliament, had grown in frequency. Discussion of fiscal matters had been accompanied by the emergence, over a longer period, of a set of issues – the military and cultural threat from the Irish, the failure of absentees to do enough towards defence, the ineptitude of ministers from England – that made up a distinctive political programme.[25] As the secure areas shrank, so the sense of identity and solidarity within them grew, as did the habit of dialogue with royal representatives and with the king himself.

Lionel's arrival marked an upward movement of Ireland on the royal agenda that was difficult thereafter to reverse. The experience of having been ruled by a king's son, and having seen Edward pay almost £38,000 (a vast amount in Irish terms) towards Lionel's military expenditure between 1361 and 1366, sharply altered the expectations of the English of Ireland.[26] The next English governor was William of Windsor, a household knight not so different from many of his fourteenth-century predecessors; calls for the appointment of the earl of March, or some other magnate (who would find it easier to gain the king's ear and extract English funds) soon reached court. When in 1375 William failed, largely because of the war in France, to obtain the money that had been promised him, the Irish commons obstructed his efforts to raise taxation, pleading poverty and telling him that it was his affair and that of the council to find wages for his English soldiers – they really meant it was the king's.

On the English side the assumption by the 1370s seems to have been that the inflow of money and troops should soon repair the condition of Ireland.

---

[24] Otway-Ruthven (1967), pp. 47, 58; Frame (1996b), pp. 280–1.
[25] Richardson and Sayles (1964), pp. 111–18; Frame (1982), pp. 315–17; Frame (1998), pp. 28–30.
[26] Connolly (1981), p. 117.

When Windsor was appointed in 1369, his funds from England were scheduled to reduce year by year, and the king clearly hoped that Ireland would soon be profitable again. When Richard II granted the lordship to his favourite, Robert de Vere, in 1385 the deal was that de Vere would eventually pay 5,000 marks a year for it. (In the event the English political crisis of 1386–7 prevented him from setting foot in Ireland.) Such aspirations suggest a failure to grasp the situation in the lordship. Official rhetoric in Ireland constantly asked the king to believe that there was an enemy that could be definitively vanquished; in reality there was only a complex marcher society that required constant monitoring and management. The presence of a well-funded lieutenant with a few hundred English troops, to form the core of armies and be scattered here and there in garrisons, could increase confidence among the settlers, make leading marchers more responsive to authority, create links with some native Irish lords and increase the revenues by perhaps £1,000 a year.[27] When the lieutenant was withdrawn, it soon became apparent that little had changed. To keep even quite small forces on a permanent footing in Ireland cost sums that the crown, with all its other commitments, was reluctant to bear for long.

Richard II's arrival was in certain ways the culmination of the approach to Ireland that had developed since 1360. He came at the head of an army, campaigned against the Irish in the south-east, took submissions and told the council in England that he had 'conquered' Leinster.[28] But by 1398 little remained of the achievement in which he had invested his reputation; it was to rescue it that he went back to Ireland in 1399, so facilitating Henry Bolingbroke's invasion. To the sceptical eye it looks as though Richard was the main victim of the notion that short-term military and political measures could refashion a lordship whose condition sprang from the interplay of economic, social and cultural (as well as political and military) changes. There was, however, more to his policies than this suggests. He not only came in person, but brought more than 5,000 troops (Lionel had had fewer than 1,000).[29] He was accompanied by members of the English nobility whom he sought to involve in Ireland through the grant of vacant and forfeited lands in Leinster and Munster. At least he had drawn the conclusion that greater commitment and more radical action were needed than had been attempted in the past.

More important, while Richard was in Ireland between September 1394 and May 1395 his approach changed. He became aware of the inadequacy of the

---

[27] Richardson and Sayles (1962), p. 100; Frame (1973), pp. 37–8; Connolly (1981), pp. 109–10.

[28] Curtis, 'Unpublished Letters': 'nous semble estre conquis et d'estre vraisemblablement en paix toute la terre de Leinstre'. The prelates of the English Parliament responded by saying 'il est vraisemblable que vous avez conquis le greindre partie de mesme vostre terre' (Curtis, *Richard II in Ireland*, p. 138).

[29] Lydon (1963), pp. 142–3.

picture of the Irish polity that had shaped English actions in the past. His predecessors had dealt almost entirely with royal ministers, absentee landholders, colonial councils and parliaments, communities of the major towns and the greater of the resident lords – in other words with the establishment of the English lordship. By this time such relationships, which had been sufficient for the crown's purposes 100 years earlier, were a wholly inadequate reflection of the distribution of authority within Ireland. As Gaelic lords, together with some of the heads of unruly English marcher kins, came in to submit to him, Richard had to decide what attitude to take to powerful figures who lay outside the legal structure of the lordship.

His answer was to receive 'rebel English' into his peace, and, more significantly, to create (or restore) a direct link between the crown and the major Gaelic lords. Irish leaders did homage and were accepted as liegemen, a procedure which may well have been accompanied by formal grants of English legal status;[30] they promised to come to councils and parliaments (from which they had normally been excluded) when required; some of them were knighted, reflecting Richard's wish, according to Froissart, to draw them into polite society.[31] The king on his part would act as protector and arbitrator, not least in the territorial disputes many Gaelic lords had with resident or absentee magnates. Richard's actions amounted to a belated attempt to grapple with some of the realities of an Ireland where patterns of power had shifted markedly. Those realities proved, however, more complex and less tractable than he may have hoped. His appearance in Ireland raised contradictory expectations. Resident lords, such as the earl of Ormond, who had claims in Wicklow and Connacht, hoped to recover lands and rights long occupied by the Irish. So too did absentees who had come to Ireland with the king, among them Roger Mortimer, earl of March and Ulster, and Thomas Mowbray, earl of Nottingham, to whom the lordship of Carlow had descended. Native Irish lords for their part claimed that they wished to hold only what was rightfully theirs. But how was legality to be defined? One man's justice, as the disputes between Mortimer and O'Neill over land and the military service of northern Irish sub-lords showed, was another's dispossession.

Though Richard after his departure did what he could to forward the settlement sketched out in the optimistic early months of 1395, he found no way of reconciling the incompatible claims that his presence had evoked. A king based in Ireland and backed by English resources for several years might have made more headway – or might merely have sharpened the points of possible conflict. But steady focus on a peripheral dominion was never likely. Under Henry IV there was return to levels of intervention, and of financial difficulty,

---

[30] Otway-Ruthven (1980), pp. 92–4.   [31] Johnston (1980), pp. 1–2.

similar to those in the generation before 1394. Henry V, with his eyes on France, reduced English support sharply; interestingly, in view of the predictions of disaster that had emanated from the English of Ireland since 1360, there were no catastrophic results.[32] From the standpoint of the Irish historian, the main interest of Richard's visit may be in exposing the gulf between the theoretical framework of the English lordship and the map of actual authority within the island of Ireland. That gulf had always been present, but it had widened greatly during the fourteenth century; a few months of concentrated attention from a ruler not noted for his political acumen was insufficient to bridge it.

[32] Matthew (1984), pp. 97–108.

THE LAST CAPETIANS AND EARLY
VALOIS KINGS, 1314–1364

Michael Jones

THE premature death of Philip IV on 29 November 1314 proved to be a major turning-point in the fortunes of Capetian France. It coincided with clear signs of an economic crisis, European in scale, that provides a backdrop to the political events which are the main concern of this chapter. Poor harvests, dearth and disease, following several wet summers, caused widespread misery as 'the Great Famine' of 1315–17 took its toll of men and animals. Ypres in Flanders lost 10 per cent of its population in these years; losses elsewhere in northern France approached this magnitude. In many regions (Normandy, Forez, Haute Provence) the medieval population peak was passed. Paris, the greatest city and intellectual capital of the west, topped 200,000 inhabitants before disease, war and political troubles reduced it by two-thirds in the next hundred years. Its hinterland, the Ile-de-France, the ancient heart of the royal domain, which was amongst the most densely settled and richest parts of the kingdom around 1300, was within fifty years devastated by plague and war. In May 1358, partly consequent upon the general economic crisis, partly on short-run political and military factors, the Jacquerie, a violent revolt of rural artisans and craftsmen, broke out in the Beauvaisis and quickly affected an area from Picardy in the north to Orléans in the south. The particular target of the Jacques was the nobility, blamed for dereliction of duty and recent military defeat. Many rural manors, castles and estates were sacked whilst any nobles unfortunate enough to fall into rebel hands were killed with extreme cruelty. Though other factors must be considered in this violent and bloody revolt, it symbolises the dire effects that combined natural disasters and human error had on royal France in this period, destroying social harmony and placing government under the greatest strain.

When Petrarch, who had known France before the wars with Edward III of England and his allies began to take their toll, returned in 1363, he contrasted in a famous lament the devastation he witnessed with the bountiful riches he had known in his youth.[1] If, around 1300, France was the greatest Christian power and its cultural influence widely acknowledged, it now presented a very different image; its territory was truncated, its administration divided, its countryside ruined, its king humiliated. Reasons for this startling transformation form a main theme of what follows; but that is complemented by attention to changes that even in the kingdom's darkest days provided a base for later constructive developments. As Françoise Autrand later demonstrates, this was partially achieved in the latter half of the century before further disasters struck and the task of reshaping Valois France had to recommence with Charles VII.

POLITICAL SOCIETY: THE LEGACY OF PHILIP IV

The period from 1314 to 1364 is fascinating from many points of view, not least because for the first time in France 'politics', the formulation of policy and the everyday conduct of business, can be followed in some detail, while the history of the royal household, council, chancery, treasury and *parlement* of Paris, departments of state and institutions that decisively shaped the *ancien régime*, can be investigated at a formative stage. Not only can particular programmes pursued by successive governments be followed but an attempt made to associate specific policies with their probable proponents in the king's council or among the growing circle of politically articulate. Patronage and clientage networks, the essence of politics in this as in later centuries, may be examined as public issues were discussed and private interests served. For in addition to the crown and its servants, there were many others with ideas on how the kingdom should be governed. Princes ruling the great principalities which ringed the kingdom (Flanders, Brittany, Burgundy, Gascony), the holders of royal apanages (Anjou, Valois, Poitou, Evreux, La Marche, Bourbon) or counties (Alençon, Blois, Forez), turbulent southern French lords (Foix, Armagnac, Albret, Comminges), the *bonnes villes*, and so on, all had their own administrations, customs and privileges determining relationships with the crown. The concept of 'the nation' was embryonic: there were no national institutions apart from the monarchy itself. Under Philip IV fissures in the body politic had been disguised by authoritarian government; internal divisions, a change of dynasty (1328) and foreign war exposed them again. 'The reign of Philip the Fair marks the culmination of the medieval French monarchy':[2] it would be many generations and in very different circumstances that a king of France enjoyed again a similar degree of control.

---

[1] Petrarch, *Letters of Old Age* (*Rerum Senilium* x.2), II, pp. 366–7; Delachenal (1909–31), II, p. 21. Jordan (1996) for the Great Famine.   [2] Strayer (1980), p. xii.

Although misjudgement over the resources needed for the Flemish wars and an autocratic streak in his later years clearly contributed to the crisis of the leagues in 1314–15, when royal authority was challenged and the crown conceded formally many charters setting out provincial privileges, to contemporaries Philip IV was an austere, enigmatic and awesomely powerful ruler whom it was dangerous to thwart. 'Whatever he wants, he will do', commented two Aragonese envoys in 1305; 'He is our lord, and we cannot force him or his counsel' remarked the king's favoured brother Charles of Valois to other ambassadors in 1308.[3] By ruthless expropriation of the Jews, Templars and Lombards, Philip demonstrated the growing administrative competence of his government as well as his own inflexible will. To accommodate his policies, significant institutional and governmental developments were also set in train. The search for the origins of the 'modern French state' – a state within which a sovereign power exercised its authority over a given territory, its resources, goods and people, and came to control the latter's destiny socially, economically and culturally as well as politically, through a monopoly of justice, the power to wage war, make peace, impose taxes, control coinage and so on – has been pushed back in recent work to the twelfth century.[4] There is little argument but that Philip IV imparted a decisive momentum to its growth. The politics of succeeding reigns in many senses represented a reaction to this development.

Perhaps as important as the practical ends pursued by Philip IV, were the ideological changes that his reign witnessed. These promoted the crown's image and interests at the expense of those with whom it had previously shared power, especially nobles and barons, provincial princes and the Church. This was of special significance because an earlier model of Christian kingship that much influenced Philip himself, that of St Louis, with his policies of sound money, low taxes, equitable justice and the protection of the Church and nobles, was adopted in 1314–15 by the crown's opponents as a programme for reform that influenced much thinking down to 1360. It limited the extent to which the last Capetians and early Valois kings could exploit their sainted ancestor to justify their own rule.[5]

To set against the model of St Louis, among many other writings, both the *Quaestio in Utramque Partem* (1303) and John of Paris's *De Potestate Regia et Papali* emphasised the prescriptive rights of the crown. These were buttressed by careful reading of Roman law and the application of its maxims, especially on *lèse-majesté,* to justify enhanced royal powers. Though the last Capetians were hesitant to prosecute treason and rebellion as severely as civil law allowed,

---

[3] Brown (1988), p. 238.   [4] Duby (1991), pp. 129, 298; Balard (1991), pp. 101–25.
[5] Beaune (1985), pp. 140–1 = Beaune (1991), pp. 104–5.

Charles IV's pursuit of the Gascon troublemaker Jourdain de l'Isle-Jourdain, which ended with his exemplary execution in 1323, showed what could be done. 'Never since the days of Ganelon had such a very great and gentle man died in such a fashion', wrote the continuator of Guillaume de Nangis's chronicle of a noble who had defied royal authority, murdered officials and cynically exploited the delays of the law since a private feud had first brought him to notice over a decade earlier.[6]

The early Valois kings quickly learnt the lesson. Philip VI (1328–50) used increasingly arbitrary procedures even against powerful figures (sometimes with unforeseen and damaging political consequences). The concept of *cas royaux*, serious crimes only justiciable in the king's court and which, in the final resort, the king alone could define, was one that allowed infinite and flexible extension in the hands of adroit lawyers. French kings were well supplied with these: it is no accident that the growth of the *parlement* of Paris is a major feature of the period nor that litigation was extensively used by the crown in pursuit of both domestic and foreign policies. The war with England after 1337 inevitably pushed Philip VI and John II into exacting exemplary punishment from those accused of delivering towns and castles or holding 'treasonable' communications with the enemy in an attempt to maintain loyalty. Significantly, however, there are many instances where proper legal procedures were instituted only after fugitives had escaped the crown's clutches and were being tried *in absentia*.[7]

Like Philip IV, the Valois kings could thus display cruelty and impulsiveness in dealing with their subjects. The most spectacular instances were Philip VI's treatment of Breton and Norman rebels in 1343–4, the judicial murder of Raoul de Brienne, count of Eu, in 1350 by John II, and his seizure and execution of the dauphin's supporters at Rouen in 1356. But throughout, politics were marked by many savage acts of revenge. The murder of the constable, Charles de la Cerda, in 1354 by Charles II, king of Navarre, a leading French landholder, is a good example; it prompted John II's reaction two years later. Much factional fighting was encouraged by frequent changes of regime consequent upon a succession of brief reigns. Each change created an opportunity to turn the tables on former opponents as scapegoats were found for unpopular policies.

The fate of the leading financial advisers of Philip IV (Enguerran de Marigny), Philip V (Gerard Gaite) and Charles IV (Pierre Rémi), each executed by their successors, is perhaps the best illustration of this instability. Indeed, some have seen in the changes in personnel that followed each accession two

---

[6] Ducoudray (1902), I, pp. 489–93; Cuttler (1981), pp. 144–5; Vale (1990), pp. 132–9.
[7] Perrot (1910); Cuttler (1981).

loose groups of counsellors, labelled for convenience a *chambre des comptes* party and a *parlement* party, alternating in royal favour. Henry de Sully (d. 1336) and Mile de Noyers (bearer of the Oriflamme in 1304, d. 1347) have been identified as typical of those advocating the aggressive fiscal policies of Philip IV, favoured also by Philip V, which seem to characterise the *chambre des comptes* viewpoint. Etienne de Mornay, counsellor of Charles of Valois (d. 1325), chancellor to Louis X (1314–16) and a leading adviser of Charles IV (1322–8) typically represents the *parlement* party. At the start of Philip VI's reign, with a king hesitant to offend those who had recently helped him to power, Guillaume de Sainte-Maure (chancellor 1330–5), played a key role. However, after his death, Mile de Noyers once again assumed a leading part and from 1335 to 1346 the *chambre des comptes* faction enjoyed high favour.[8]

Less controversially, the policies pursued by Louis X and Charles IV in broad terms marked a reaction to their father's, while Philip V and then Philip VI reverted to personnel who had experience of government under Philip IV. In the case of Louis X, often judged a weak and ineffectual king because he sacrificed Marigny and delivered the charters, the need to conciliate the opposition roused by his father sufficiently explains his actions and he deserves credit for quelling criticism in a statesmanlike fashion. In response to the demands of the leagues of nobles, clerics and townsmen that had formed in many provinces in the autumn of 1314, he conceded the *Charte aux Normands* on 19 March 1315. Further charters followed for Languedoc (1 April 1315, January 1316), Burgundy (April and 17 May 1315), Artois, Champagne (May 1315, March 1316), Auvergne (September 1315, confirmed again in 1324), Picardy, Poitou, Touraine, Anjou, Maine, Saintonge and the Angoumois (September 1315), Berry (March 1316) and Nevers (May 1316). Though there was no French 'community of the realm' and the leagues, unlike the barons of Magna Carta, did not seek to establish lasting controls over the monarchy, many charters did raise general issues in addition to particularist ones. They thus placed a formal limit on many practices that had enabled the Capetians to extend their power so dramatically in recent decades and formed a point of reference for future negotiations between the crown and its leading subjects.[9]

Along with 'parties' and 'leagues' the interests of royal princes like Charles and Philip of Valois, the future Philip V and Charles IV when still *apanagistes*, or great lords like Eudes IV, duke of Burgundy (1315–47), Robert of Artois (d. 1342) or, latterly, Charles II of Navarre (1349–87), need to be considered in a full discussion of political society in this period. Familial and patrimonial concepts still strongly shaped royal ideas about the state. The princes and nobles closely related to the king played a leading role in his council, formulating and

---

[8] Lehugeur (1897–1931) and (1929); Cazelles (1958).   [9] Brown (1981); Contamine (1994).

executing policy (especially military policy). They could make or break ministers as Marigny discovered in 1315 and Béraud de Mercoeur, constable of France, in 1319. Most retained counsel permanently in Paris to conduct business during inevitable absences in their own lordships. The link between Etienne de Mornay and Charles of Valois has been mentioned; he also employed Jean de Cherchemont and Jean Billouart whose main careers were later made in crown service. The notoriously unscrupulous lawyer Guillaume de Breuil, author of the *Stilus Curie Parliamenti* (1332), had Edward III, the count of Comminges and Robert of Artois among his clients, Comminges partially paying debts by ensuring Guillaume's ennoblement.[10] The princes also had clientèles to satisfy.

Such ties created a dense network of links between the centre and the periphery, governed by subtle rules and conventions. Different regional groupings have been discerned as dominating at Paris for varying periods in these years – Burgundians, Champenois, Normans. On occasion, as in the 1350s with the Navarrese 'party', this led to bitter in-fighting. To gain access to the royal presence, forward a case or gain a favour, it became imperative either to have friends already in high places, or to use intermediaries, 'fixers', who could smooth a path increasingly strewn with red tape.[11] Minor players also expected rewards: Hélie de Papassol, notary of Périgueux, on a legitimate mission for his town council in 1337, slipped Ferri de Picquigny, master of the royal household, 5lb of lemons and 5lb of sugar so he could approach the king; in 1330 some Lombards offered the countess of Alençon a box of oranges to oil bureaucratic wheels. For many this, rather than high matters of state, represented the reality of politics.

THE SUCCESSION AND THE KING'S IMAGE

Ceremonial had long been exploited by the Capetians to supplement their material resources. Although personally remote and ascetic (an enthusiasm for hunting apart), Philip IV knew well the importance of presenting an impressive regal appearance. Pointers to his ideas on the symbolic and visual imagery of kingship can be detected in an emphasis on his Carolingian ancestry, in the reordering of royal tombs at the abbey of Saint-Denis to suggest that France had been ruled from its origins by a single dynasty, and in the fashioning of the 'Life and Works' of St Denis by Yves, a monk of that abbey (1317), to emphasise the unity and Christian inheritance of the kingdom. Contemporary views on France as a 'Holy Land', its inhabitants a 'Chosen People' and its ruler 'The

---

[10] Ducoudray (1902), I, pp. 221–2; Lewis (1981), pp. 179–92; Rogozinski (1976), p. 284.
[11] Lewis (1985), pp. 151–65, and cf. Higounet-Nadal, 'Le journal des dépenses'.

Most Christian King', were very much the creation of Philip IV and his advisers.[12] Like Louis IX, he dignified kingship.

In 1314 that dignity was in question. A scandal rocked the royal family, when all three of Philip IV's daughters-in-law were accused of adultery, placed in custody and their alleged lovers, Philippe and Gautier d'Aunay, executed (*NCMH*, vol. V, p. 313). This event certainly cast a shadow over the last Capetians, though it is difficult to decide the long-term significance of this domestic crisis. It assuredly came as a severe shock to Philip IV; it may have contributed to his final illness but it was the king himself who revealed the affairs and had the lovers publicly tried. He had cultivated a reputation for Christian kingship and displayed few evident weaknesses of the flesh. Of greater importance, it probably reinforced prejudices against female succession, thus unwittingly ensuring the extinction of the direct Capetian line within a few years. Among other disqualifications, enough doubts were expressed about the legitimacy of Louis X's daughter, Jeanne (born in 1311), for her ambitious uncle, Philip of Poitiers, to prevent her succeeding her short-lived half-brother, John I (1316), Louis's posthumous son by a second wife. But though his wife, Jeanne of Burgundy had eventually been exonerated, Philip V also only left infant daughters, set aside in favour of Charles IV in 1322, whom the scandal also closely affected.

Following the annulment of his first marriage, Charles remarried three times but still failed to father a son. By his death in 1328, leaving a posthumous daughter, prejudice and precedent had hardened to such a degree that the idea of a woman succeeding to the French throne (or of transmitting a claim) was sufficiently improbable for Philip of Valois, a grandson of Philip III in a cadet male line, to defeat Edward III of England, a grandson of Philip IV by Isabella, the late king's sister, in the competition for the vacant throne. Though it was not called 'Salic law' at the time, François de Meyronnes had already written a treatise on the *lex voconia*, which excluded women from succession, enshrining the fundamental principles adopted later in the century to justify royal practice in France.[13] Others entertained doubts over the legitimacy of the Valois succession, a scepticism reinforced by later misfortunes. In 1337 Edward III, who had engraved fleur-de-lis on his great seal in 1328, made a formal bid for the French throne, whilst another with a good claim derived from a female was Charles of Navarre, born in 1332. His frequent changes of allegiance and political ambitions in the 1350s defy simple analysis but his proximity to the succession is relevant in any discussion of them.

Philip IV's sons, whatever their personal views on the adultery scandal or the

---

[12] Strayer (1971), pp. 300–14; Beaune (1985), pp. 91–3, 120, 209 = Beaune (1991), pp. 30–2, 63–4, 175.

[13] Beaune (1985), p. 266 = Beaune (1991), p. 247; Lewis (1981).

larger issue of female succession, understood the importance of the rituals and regalia of kingship for enhancing the 'religion of royalty' in this period. Whilst coronations had for long been used to demonstrate the mysteries of kingship, they placed increasing emphasis on funerary ceremonial and, in cases where queens had not received unction or been crowned at their husbands' coronations, on arranging suitably impressive crownings in the Sainte-Chapelle (as happened to Marie of Luxemburg and Jeanne of Evreux, second and third wives of Charles IV, and Blanche of Navarre, second wife of Philip VI). Such occasions propagated certitudes about royal power and its continuity; at the very least, particularly in the case of funerals, it made the best of adverse circumstances in which five kings swiftly followed one another to the grave between 1314 and 1328. Efforts were made to encourage a larger participation on these occasions (that of the infant John I apart) and to publicise them. Written descriptions were prepared for a learned audience; the rites became more fixed; the symbolism of the transfer of power more explicit.

There was much stress on the Christian and royal attributes of the dead kings manifested by exemplary deathbed scenes. That of Philip IV contains all the classic elements: he is described confessing, asking pardon of all, taking communion and the last rites, kissing relics, stretching out his arms in the form of a cross or signing himself with a cross when addressing his confessor and responding to litanies until the last moment. It was in such solemn final moments that Philip was reported to have passed on the secrets of his thaumaturgic powers for curing the king's evil (scrofula) as well as offering other advice to his son. Philip VI, conscious of questions about his right to succeed the Capetians, ostentatiously demonstrated that he shared with them similar attributes by taking communion in two kinds and making considerable display of his curative powers (thirty-five people from places as distant as Brabant, Brittany and the Vivarais were touched in one short period between 1 January and 30 June 1337 for which accounts survive).[14] He also allegedly rehearsed the main points of his case against the English to his son while on his deathbed.

Other dying monarchs handed over tokens of kingship like crowns or rings to signal continuity and legitimacy. Famous relics might also be used like the crown of thorns present at the bedside when Philip V died. He, like his father, cancelled taxes at his death, as Charles V did later in 1380, another sign that the change of dynasty in 1328 did little to alter essential patterns of rule, hedged about by ancient symbols and ritual. Embodied in evocative emblems like the sword *Joyeuse*, the sceptre and *main de justice*, the two major royal crowns (attributed to Louis IX and Charlemagne, the latter called the *grande couronne impériale*

---

[14] Fawtier, 'Un compte de menues dépenses', p. 187 (= Fawtier (1987), ch. xiv, p. 4); for funerary ceremonial see also Brown (1978) and (1980); Beaune (1985) = Beaune (1991).

in a decree of Philip VI in 1340), the Oriflamme and the ubiquitous heraldic motif of golden fleur-de-lis on a blue ground, all those who ruled from 1314 to 1364 actively promoted visual signs to inspire loyalty to their idea of France. The necessity for doing so became more urgent as domestic difficulties and external quarrels gradually combined to bring war on several fronts in the late 1330s.

RELATIONS WITH OTHER POWERS

In his day Philip IV was dominant in international affairs, thanks to victory over Pope Boniface VIII, the Flemings and the English. Leadership of the crusading movement and support for Valois and Angevin schemes in Italy and the empire allowed France to act on a larger stage. The king's brother, Charles of Valois was a candidate in the imperial election of 1308 and in 1313 it was the turn of Philip's son, Philip of Poitiers. Of future significance was the way in which many imperial vassals along France's long eastern frontier from the Netherlands to Savoy and Provence were gravitating into the orbit of the French crown. Other important alliances, some sealed by marriage, linked France with its closest neighbours in the British Isles or Iberian peninsula and presented opportunities for diplomatic manoeuvre. Thanks especially to surviving reports from Aragonese ambassadors and memoranda, financial and other records relating to the work of professional envoys like Elias Johnston, 'keeper of the processes' (i.e. the records of Anglo-French negotiations), this complex diplomacy, involving all major western powers including the papacy, can often be followed in daily detail.[15]

The last Capetians and early Valois built on this framework. Though further campaigns were necessary in Flanders (1315, 1319), by 1322 French influence was uppermost with the accession of Louis I, a son-in-law of Philip V, who succeeded Robert de Béthune (cf. below pp. 574–5). He gratefully accepted French aid to put down an uprising that broke out in maritime Flanders in 1323 but which had much urban support. Brought briefly to heel in the Treaty of Arques in April 1326, the Flemish towns led by Bruges and Ghent resumed the struggle shortly afterwards until Philip VI inflicted a resounding defeat on the rebels at Cassel (July 1328). Brutal repression followed, including the exemplary execution of William Deken, burgomaster of Bruges. The feud between the count of Flanders and his urban subjects resumed after 1337, as the French continued to support the count (he was killed fighting for them at Crécy, 1346) and Edward III supported the towns, the consumers of England's essential wool exports.

---

[15] Finke, *Acta Aragonensia*; Cuttino (1971); Hillgarth (1971); Cheyette (1973); Strayer (1980).

In the bishoprics of Cambrai, Tournai and Verdun, royal control was extended beyond the traditional frontier between the kingdom and empire. In 1324 Pope John XXII, struggling to topple Emperor Lewis of Bavaria, with Austrian prompting, offered Charles IV the imperial throne. One of Lewis's main rivals, John of Luxemburg, king of Bohemia, spent as much or more of his time at the French court or in Italy than he did in his distant kingdom. At the beginning of the Anglo-French war he became royal lieutenant in the Midi and he also died heroically in the Valois cause at Crécy. But the alliance of Valois and Luxemburg endured; his daughter, Bonne, married John, duke of Normandy, in 1349; his son and successor, Emperor Charles IV, lent critical support to the dauphin Charles in the mid 1350s. Earlier, Philip VI recruited heavily amongst the princes and nobility in the Rhineland, Low Countries and east of the Rhône. To counter any diplomatic advantages Edward III had gained by marriage to Philippa of Hainault, Philip VI also established links with her father, Count William of Hainault, with Duke John of Brabant and with other Netherlandish princes in the 1330s, as England and France vied to resurrect the alliances that had formerly served Edward I and Philip IV. In 1342 Lewis of Bavaria, who had made Edward III his vicar-general in 1338, deserted him by sealing a pact with Philip VI.[16]

Another sphere where patterns established in an earlier period continued to influence affairs during the early phases of the Anglo-French war concerned Scotland. The first formal agreement of what was later termed the 'Auld Alliance' between France and Scotland dated from 1295. After its renewal by Robert the Bruce and Charles IV at Corbeil in 1327, it remained a constant factor in the ensuing Anglo-French war. The renunciation by Edward III of 'any right in the realm of Scotland which we or our ancestors have sought in past times', formally agreed at Northampton (May 1328), was merely a breathing space, since Edward refused to recognise Bruce's infant successor, David, and supported Edward Balliol and the 'Disinherited', those deprived of their lands by the 1328 treaty. English invasions of Scotland every year between 1332 and 1336 followed; David Bruce was driven into exile in France (1334–41), but Philip VI rallied to his cause and provided just enough essential military as well as diplomatic aid for his supporters to weather the storm.[17]

Events after 1337 reinforced this alignment of forces. Returning to Scotland in 1341, Bruce re-established himself and repulsed the latest English attacks only to be defeated and captured at Neville's Cross (1346), while invading England to help his French ally as Edward attacked Calais. During David's captivity (he was finally released in 1357 for a huge ransom), French diplomatic

---

[16] Lucas (1929); Lyon (1957); Trautz (1961); Nicholas (1971); Vale (1991).
[17] Prestwich (1989), p. 187; Campbell (1965); Nicholson (1965); Webster, *The Acts*, nos. 20–1, 23–4.

and military help once more prevented Edward III pressing home his advantage to the full. French troops were despatched to Scotland in 1356 and, despite John II's capture at Poitiers (19 September 1356), protection of its Scots ally remained an aim of French diplomacy through the arduous Anglo-French negotiations that finally led to the Treaty of Brétigny–Calais (1360). There they traded off for a time the Franco-Scottish alliance against Edward III's promise to forsake an alliance with the Flemings. By then the English had learnt the hard way that the pursuit of continental ambitions usually invited trouble on their northern frontier (cf. above, pp. 352–3).

Before the Anglo-French war became a predominating concern, affecting the posture of all western powers, much early fourteenth-century diplomacy centred on the issue of the crusade. Here the papacy traditionally expected France to take a lead, until events in the early 1330s allowed the initiative to pass to those Mediterranean powers who had more direct links with the east. If Charles IV was lukewarm in his response to papal appeals, Philip V and Philip VI, especially, reacted more favourably as the plans they laid and the resources they committed to smaller, preliminary, expeditions to the east indicates (cf. below, p. 868).[18] Between 1328 and 1331 Philip VI was also, along with his cousin Philip of Evreux, king of Navarre, John of Luxemburg, and leading southern nobles like Gaston of Foix and the lords of Albret, in close communication with Alfonso XI of Castile over plans for a crusade against the Moors of Granada. This was first timed to begin in the spring of 1330 and then postponed to 1331.[19] In the end Philip withdrew, alleging growing difficulties with the English, the same reasons that undermined later plans for a crusade in the Mediterranean in 1336. Nevertheless, relations with Castile remained generally good. They were exploited after 1337 especially for naval assistance; a Castilian fleet raiding England in 1350, for instance, was defeated by Edward III off Winchelsea.

The main reasons for worsening Anglo-French relations are well understood; they centred on the problem of Aquitaine (Guyenne). The Treaty of Paris (1259) had re-established the king of England, hereditary ruler of this duchy, as a vassal of the king of France. Subsequent treaties (Amiens, 1279; Paris, 1303) confirmed his vassal status. But the simultaneous development of clearer views on what constituted 'sovereignty' in the late thirteenth century under the influence of Roman law, had led Capetian lawyers since 1259 to define the services homage entailed very precisely and to insist that the English king-duke and his administration should comply fully. Attempts to implement royal *ordonnances* in Guyenne limited local autonomy, as did the encouragement

---

[18] Viard (1936); Housley (1980) and (1986); Tyerman (1984a), (1984b) and (1985).
[19] Miret y Sans, 'Lettres closes'; Mahn-Lot (1939); Cazelles, *Lettres closes*.

of appeals from Gascon courts to the *parlement* of Paris. The turbulence of Gascon politics helped to embitter relations by offering many further opportunities for officious intervention by the French.[20]

Anglo-Gascons naturally found this irksome when it went against their interests but were prepared to encourage it when it suited them; Amanieu VII of Albret, for one, had exploited the appeal system, so too had competing urban factions at Bordeaux or abbeys in dispute with the ducal administration. Nobles and others thus played off the king-duke's officers against the Capetians. This gave rise to a swelling stream of complaints from the ducal side after 1314 and there was much litigation. In England there was also a growing feeling that the only means of escape from this dilemma would be to obtain recognition of Guyenne as sovereign in its own right, a position first argued around 1300. It became a principal, perhaps the main, aim of Edward III and his government after 1337.

The generation between the Treaty of Paris (1303) and Philip VI's confiscation of Guyenne on 24 May 1337 saw both sides expend considerable effort to resolve their differences peacefully but with a growing sense of mutual frustration. Charges of bad faith and mounting hostility had already turned briefly to war in 1323. Its cause was a typical imbroglio of rights and jurisdictions in an area where Anglo-Gascon and French interests had frequently clashed since 1259. Wishing to turn a priory at Saint-Sardos in the Agenais into a *bastide* to be held in *pariage* with the French crown, the abbot of Sarlat had provoked a neighbour, the lord of Montpezat. When the *parlement* of Paris gave a verdict in favour of the abbot and Montpezat murdered a royal official sent to implement the decision and then appealed for assistance to Ralph Basset, seneschal of Guyenne for Edward II, the interest of the two crowns directly clashed.

Initially Edward II disavowed his seneschal, but it was difficult to control forces in the field and the dispute escalated. On 1 July 1324 Charles IV declared Guyenne confiscated. Troops had already been despatched from England. Charles of Valois riposted by leading an army deep into Guyenne, laying siege to La Réole on the Gironde, which capitulated on 23 September. A truce was arranged but within weeks further troop movements were planned and much expenditure incurred as the protagonists manoeuvred for position. Eventually the overthrow of Edward II, in the *coup* led by Queen Isabella, allowed peace to be concluded in March 1327. In return for most of the land captured by the French, the Anglo-Gascons agreed to pay heavy reparations.

The peace of 1327 left festering grievances, however, not least among those who suffered confiscation and exile as boundaries were redrawn, though the

[20] Gavrilovitch (1899); Chaplais, *The War of Saint-Sardos*, and (1981); Vale (1990).

accession of Philip VI delayed the renewal of war.[21] In 1331 Edward III paid
a short visit to the French court (previous royal meetings had seen Edward II
at Paris in 1313 and Amiens in 1320), and he acknowledged that the homage he
owed for Guyenne was liege. Another diplomatic 'process' similar to those
held at Montreuil-sur-Mer (1306) and Périgueux (1311) to resolve issues outstanding from the 1294–8 war was held at Agen in 1332–3 and many previous
arguments resurfaced. The tendency of the French to conduct all these meetings 'as if they were part of a lawsuit between unequals rather than between
two sovereigns' and the way in which over the years the French crown acted as
'both accuser and judge in the matter of Aquitaine' had by now thoroughly
undermined English confidence.[22] As often as not formal diplomatic meetings
exacerbated rather than solved problems. Other issues in dispute between the
two kings by the mid 1330s – French intervention in Scotland, economic as
well as diplomatic rivalry in the Low Countries, Edward's fears over Philip VI's
crusading intentions and the use to which he might put his formidable fleet,
the flight of Robert of Artois to Edward's court after condemnation for lèse-
majesté in his battle for his apanage – brought relations to breaking point.[23]

WAR AND POLITICS, 1337–1360

The war which flickered slowly into life after 24 May 1337 did not begin for
Philip VI with the easy successes that had marked the 1294 and 1324
confiscations of Guyenne when French armies rapidly overran the duchy.
Directed by the English seneschal, Oliver de Ingham, local Gascon forces displayed from the start a greater willingness to resist. Numerous sieges gave the
conflict an attritional character it seldom lost in later years, though it is the
spectacular campaigns and battles of this and later periods which have usually
attracted most attention. Apart from the surrender to the French of Penne
d'Agenais by treason in December 1338 and the loss of Bourg in April 1339,
Ingham resisted the early onslaught in Guyenne with much credit.[24] In the
1340s more help was despatched from England to Bordeaux to stiffen resistance and military activity in the Midi spread. Henry, earl of Derby, successfully took Bergerac and inflicted another defeat on French forces at Auberoche
(1345). John, duke of Normandy, failed to retake Aiguillon (1346) and Derby
was able to launch destructive raids deep into Poitou, relieving pressure on
Guyenne.

In the north negotiations for peace, encouraged by Benedict XII, had at first

---

[21] Dossat (1978); Vale (1990). [22] Vale (1990), p. 228, cf. also Cuttino (1944) and (1971).
[23] Cuttino (1956); Allmand (1988); Vale (1989, 1990).
[24] Vale (1990); Sumption (1990) for a detailed narrative account of the war to 1347.

continued alongside preparations for war. But eventually Edward III launched his first major continental campaign in mid summer 1338, landing in the Low Countries. Here he had constructed elaborate and costly alliances in a tradition of trying to encircle France that can be traced back to Richard I's reign. After desultory manoeuvres, warfare was more seriously conducted in 1339–40 with raids and counter raids along France's northern frontier. Edward III, who had tentatively used the title 'king of France' in October 1337, openly adopted it in his style from February 1340 at the prompting of his Flemish allies. He sent a letter of defiance to 'lord Philip of Valois who calls himself king' and offered to restore the customs of St Louis in the kingdom, thereby placing himself at the head of internal opposition to the Valois as well as of his grand foreign alliance.[25]

After these preliminaries, war began in earnest. The first major Anglo-French battle for a hundred years was fought at sea off Sluys (24 June 1340) when English ships, bringing troops to Flanders, trapped a large French force under Admirals Quiéret and Béhuchet in the confined approaches to the harbour and inflicted enormous losses. On land Saint-Omer was attacked by Robert of Artois and Tournai besieged. Huge forces were mobilised: in 1339 the French planned to raise 10,000 cavalry and 40,000 infantry; in September 1340 Philip VI had 28,000 men-at-arms and 16,700 infantrymen in his pay whilst Edward III and his allies may have commanded a closely comparable number.[26] A decisive encounter seemed imminent but neither king was yet prepared to risk fortune. A truce was arranged at Esplechin (25 September 1340) leaving a sense of anti-climax and disillusion. Philip VI retreated to lick his wounds as discontent with his rule openly surfaced. In England, too, the enormous expenditure incurred for so little apparent return provoked a severe political and economic crisis for Edward III in the winter of 1340 (cf. above, p. 289); it was clear that if he were to continue fighting on the continent he would have to adopt a strategy consonant with his resources.

A disputed succession in Brittany in 1341 presented Edward with a chance to subvert Valois rule more cheaply as well as to protect English lines of communication with Guyenne; for a hostile Brittany could disrupt the wine trade on which the economy of the Anglo-Gascon administration depended as well as the passage of men and supplies to Bordeaux. Seizing the initiative, Edward offered support to John de Montfort, half-brother of the late duke John III (1312–41), in a bid for the ducal throne against Jeanne de Penthièvre, the late duke's niece, wife of Charles de Blois, nephew of Philip VI. The case was heard before a special commission of *parlement*. By the time Philip VI

[25] Froissart, *Oeuvres*, ed. Lettenhove, XVIII, pp. 170–2; Déprez (1902); Le Patourel (1984); Jones, (1989).
[26] Contamine (1972), pp. 65–74; Sumption (1990).

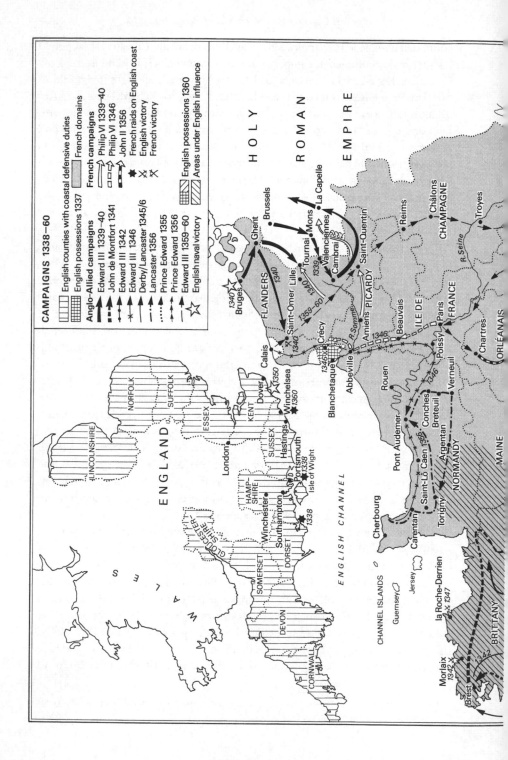

CAMPAIGNS 1338–60

English counties with coastal defensive duties
English possessions 1337

French domains

Anglo-Allied campaigns
Edward III 1339–40
John de Montfort 1341
Edward III 1342
Edward III 1346
Derby/Lancaster 1345/6
Lancaster 1356
Prince Edward 1355
Prince Edward 1356
Edward III 1359–60
English naval victory

French campaigns
Philip VI 1339–40
Philip VI 1346
John II 1356
French raids on English coast
English victory
French victory

English possessions 1360
Areas under English influence

HOLY ROMAN EMPIRE

Brussels
Ghent
La Capelle
Mons
Valenciennes 1339
Tournai
Cambrai
Saint-Quentin
Reims
Châlons
CHAMPAGNE
Troyes
R. Seine
FLANDERS
Bruges 1340
Saint-Omer
Lille 1359–60 1340
Crécy
R. Somme
Amiens
PICARDY
Beauvais
ILE DE FRANCE
Paris
Poissy
Chartres
ORLÉANAIS
Calais 1350
Dover
Winchelsea 1360
Hastings
Abbeville
Blanchetaque
1346
Rouen
Verneuil
MAINE
NORFOLK
SUFFOLK
LINCOLNSHIRE
ESSEX
KENT
SUSSEX
London
ENGLAND
Portsmouth 1338
Isle of Wight
HAMP-SHIRE
Winchester
Southampton
DORSET
SOMERSET
GLOUCESTER-SHIRE
DEVON
CORNWALL
WALES
ENGLISH CHANNEL
CHANNEL ISLANDS
Guernsey
Jersey
Cherbourg
Carentan
Saint-Lô Caen 1356
Torigny
Argentan
Conches
Breteuil
Pont Audemer
NORMANDY
la Roche-Derrien 1347
Morlaix 1342
Brest
BRITTANY

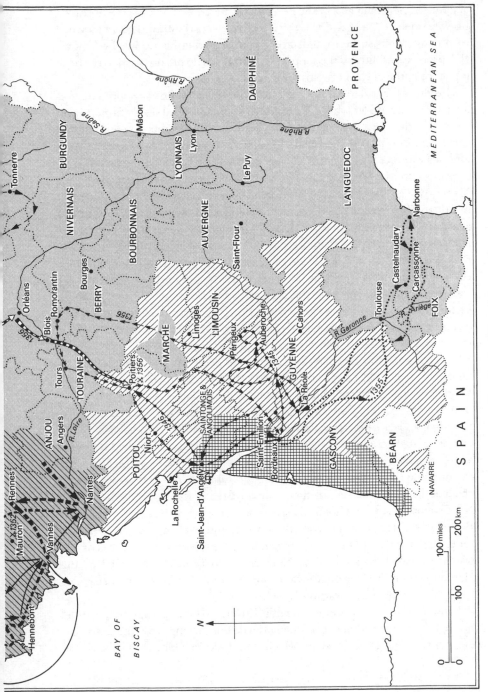

Map 7   The Hundred Years War to 1360

announced he would accept the homage proffered by Blois for the duchy on his wife's behalf (*Arrêt de Conflans*, 7 September 1341), Montfort had returned to Brittany to resist the royal decree, strengthened in his resolve by Edward III's promises of aid and the support of Bretons who did not wish to see royal influence in the duchy grow any stronger.[27]

Hostilities that led to a bitter civil war which raged in Brittany until 1364 followed. An army under John, duke of Normandy, advanced slowly from Angers to enforce the *Arrêt de Conflans*, seizing Nantes in November where Montfort was taken. But his wife, Jeanne de Flandre, continued to oppose royal forces after his capture. She urgently requested Edward III to send the help he had promised. In 1342 three English forces of increasing size under Sir Walter Manny, William Bohun, earl of Northampton and Edward III himself arrived in Brittany. Key coastal positions, most notably Brest, were seized. Edward led a fast-moving mounted attack (*chevauchée*) through the duchy, besieging Vannes in December, and sent captains to attack Nantes, Rennes and Dinan and ravage the countryside. Some Breton lords, including Olivier III de Clisson, a former companion in arms of Philip VI, rallied to the Anglo-Bretons. Philip VI responded by raising his own forces in strength. But moving slowly towards the duchy, he repeated his 1340 tactics. After confronting each other at a safe distance, a truce was again arranged (Malestroit, 19 January 1343), during which the two kings agreed to hold further negotiations at Avignon where Clement VI acted in a personal capacity as mediator. In the interim the Anglo-Bretons tightened their hold on the Breton coast and set up their headquarters at Vannes, delivered to them shortly after the truce began.

When peace talks eventually took place in October 1344, though the pope protested his lack of bias, the English viewed his mediation suspiciously. In the end none of the long-standing issues that divided the two kings was resolved. The Breton truce was ill-kept; in 1344 Charles de Blois besieged Guérande, at the mouth of the Loire, and took Quimper. Other towns and castles rapidly changed hands, some several times. Anglo-Breton forces under the earl of Northampton and Sir Thomas Dagworth were especially active in northern Brittany from 1344 to 1347, when Blois was captured at La Roche Derrien (20 June 1347) and taken prisoner to England. By then, however, the focus of the war in the north had shifted to Normandy where local nobles led by the Harcourt family welcomed Edward's intervention. In 1346 the first major English *chevauchée* of the war was launched.

Landing at La Hogue in the Cotentin Edward III cut a devastating swathe through Normandy, generally avoiding towns but sacking Caen and despatching booty to England in ships which had followed him along the coast.

---

[27] Jones, 'Some Documents', (1987) and (1988a); *Recueil des actes de Charles de Blois*.

Discovering old plans for a French invasion of England, Edward used them as propaganda to raise support for the war which entered its most productive phase for the English. Turning up the Seine valley Edward approached to within sight of Paris before heading north to Picardy as French forces finally gathered to counter-attack. On 26 August 1346 at Crécy in Ponthieu the two armies at last came to grips. Having skilfully chosen and prepared their ground,[28] the smaller English force of around 13,000 men, using tactics developed since the Scottish wars of the early 1330s, displayed first on a grand scale the awesome power of massed archers. A superior French force of cavalry rode down auxiliary Genoese crossbowmen in their eagerness to reach the enemy lines but, although more than twice as numerous as the English, they were completely routed. The earls of Northampton and Warwick played a conspicuous part in the battle but the day was most notable on the English side for the way in which at sixteen Edward, prince of Wales, gained his spurs. Philip VI fled from the field on which John of Bohemia, Louis, count of Flanders, and many other great nobles as well as thousands of other ranks lay dead. Whilst few questioned the king's bravery a storm of criticism against his government, already brewing before the battle, now broke. The *états* demanded reform; the gabelle was suspended; changes were made in personnel (cf. p. 419). Worse followed: making his way in leisurely fashion to the coast, Edward proceeded to invest Calais.

Although Philip VI made serious efforts to lift the siege, not surprisingly he reverted to his policy of avoiding direct military confrontation. Eventually after holding out for almost a year Calais capitulated on 4 August 1347. Although it later cost enormous sums to maintain the town and its Pale, the English now had a bridgehead conveniently close to London and the south coast from which to launch *chevauchées*. On the French side, the winter of 1347–8 witnessed renewed negotiations for supplies. Following the 'joyous accession' of Duke John, who after Crécy played a more important role in government, the *états* of Normandy alone agreed to contribute 450,000 *livres tournois*, more than the total raised from a war subsidy on the whole country twenty years previously.[29] By March 1348, using the Norman model of a sales tax of 8d in the pound and calculating the sum required in terms of the salary of mounted men-at-arms, agreement was reached to raise around 3,000,000 *livres tournois* nation-wide for the war effort. But the outbreak of plague prevented full collection of the tax: the Black Death reached Marseilles around 1 November 1347, Avignon in March 1348, Lyon by May and, having probably gone by sea from Bordeaux to Rouen, Paris about 20 August. There was no alternative to a truce with England and her allies agreed on 1 September 1348,

[28] Sumption (1990); Fowler (1991), p. 79.   [29] Henneman (1971), pp. 228ff.

and several times renewed in the next few years. Like previous ones it was poorly observed.

The war had begun to develop a momentum and character that differentiated it from previous Anglo-French wars, accounting for the particularly severe impact it had on France. In many regions ambitious captains and footloose soldiery (*routiers*), last seen in the days of Philip Augustus, proved difficult to control as the war spread and gave cover for the pursuit of noble feuds like that between Armagnac and Foix, a good example of the private wars the 1315–16 charters authorised. A remarkable memorandum from Sir Walter Bentley, newly appointed as lieutenant in Brittany by Edward III in 1352, sought urgent advice from Westminster on how to deal with a lawless soldiery fighting a dirty war (*guerre guerroyante*).[30] The scourge was extremely damaging in all kinds of ways. Country-dwellers were forced to pay protection money (*rançons* and *patis*) or goods in kind to the holders of local strongholds who acknowledged only the loosest allegiance to their nominal sovereigns. In Brittany these exactions were the first regular taxation its inhabitants had known.

In neighbouring marcher districts towards Anjou, Normandy and Poitou or between zones of English and French allegiance along Gascony's long frontier, the indigenous population was often forced to pay garrisons on both sides. But no region was safe. Remote ones like the Auvergne provided refuges for the *routiers* just as rich and populous ones close to Paris attracted their attentions. There was enormous destruction by looting and burning; seigneurial incomes rapidly declined. Nor were townsmen safe behind hastily constructed or refurbished defences as chronic fear and insecurity seized the population.[31] The boldest *routier* captains might launch their own ambitious *chevauchées* like Robert Knolles's raid on Auxerre and the Auvergne in 1358 and James Pipe's ravaging of Normandy and the Ile-de-France in 1358–9. Their actions culminated in the movements of the Great Companies between 1360 and 1368, when hardened professional warriors, attracted to France by the lure of booty and adventure but temporarily released from their contracts when the Treaty of Brétigny was agreed, wreaked havoc as far afield as Alsace, Provence and Languedoc. Alongside English, French, Breton or Gascon troops, men from Germany, Spain, Italy and even Hungary could be found for whom the Anglo-French wars provided a way of life.

A complicated pattern of diplomatic manoeuvre, campaigns and truces, interrupted briefly by the Black Death, resumed after 1349. Edward III allied with the young and ambitious Louis de Male, count of Flanders, then with

---

[30] Froissart, *Œuvres*, ed. Lettenhove, XVIII, pp. 339–43.
[31] Contamine (1978); Desportes (1979), pp. 539ff, for a case study.

Charles II of Navarre with whom plans to partition France were drawn up. In 1353 draft terms were agreed for the release of Charles de Blois when Edward momentarily appeared willing to sacrifice the Montfortists in Brittany. To combat these moves, John II of France was also active, though he was hampered by serious disagreements among his own councillors. A particularly obscure sequence of events followed the murder of Charles de la Cerda in January 1354 at Charles of Navarre's instigation. Learning of Navarre's dealings with the English, John hid his true feelings and on 22 February 1354 came to terms with him at Mantes, fearing that Edward III would use Navarre's Norman possessions to gain entry into the kingdom as he had used Brittany and Calais. New negotiations with the English themselves opened at Guines in April 1354. Draft terms were prepared for ratification at a conference to be held later at Avignon though in the end hopes of peace collapsed since neither side would ratify the treaty.[32] When they next came to the table the English were in an infinitely stronger position thanks to military success.

Fighting was widespread in northern France for much of the 1350s; at Mauron (August 1352) Sir Walter Bentley defeated a strong French force under Guy de Nesle. In Normandy Henry of Derby, now duke of Lancaster, extended English control then spent a period as lieutenant in Brittany (1355–8), failing only to take Rennes after a nine-month siege. In the south, the arrival of Edward, prince of Wales, at Bordeaux in 1355 signalled a resumption of hostilities with a highly lucrative raid as far as Narbonne and the Mediterranean in October. Next year he marched east and north from Bordeaux, sweeping up towards the Loire, a campaign planned to coincide with similar thrusts from Calais and Normandy. When John II chose to march against the prince, he turned for Guyenne but, weighed down by booty, was overtaken just outside Poitiers where on 19 September 1356 he inflicted another crushing defeat on the French army, crowned by the capture of the king himself. Taken to Bordeaux and eventually to England, John II was paid every respect by his captors but the political and military consequences of his defeat were disastrous as the English eventually exacted a huge ransom and John was forced to agree to renounce sovereignty over a third of his kingdom (map 8). If this defeat forced the crown to devise a new and effective means of taxing its subjects, reform its currency and overhaul its administration, John himself had little control over these developments; they were largely accomplished by the dauphin Charles and advisers (cf. below, p. 417).[33]

[32] Bock, 'Some New Documents'; Fowler (1969); Cazelles (1982); Jugie (1987).
[33] Delachenal (1909–31); Hewitt (1958); Cazelles (1982).

Map 8   France in 1360

ADMINISTRATION, JUSTICE AND FINANCE

Philip IV's reign was marked by many important administrative advances as the royal demesne and the judicial and financial activities of the crown expanded. The accessions of Philip V, Charles IV and Philip VI brought back under direct control several apanages, including Poitou, La Marche, Anjou, Maine, Touraine and Valois. The royal demesne reached its greatest medieval extent; whereas in 1302 there were twenty-eight *sénéchaussées* and *bailliages*, by 1328 there were thirty-six.[34] Until John II began to make provision for his younger sons in the 1350s there were few changes. The duchy of Bourbon was created in 1327 mainly from lands already in the new duke's hands. In 1332 Philip VI conferred Normandy on his son John, but its administration (and critically its revenues) essentially remained in royal hands until the duke was finally given some autonomy after Crécy.[35] In 1345 Philip gave his younger son, Philip, the duchy of Orléans to compensate him for the Dauphiné, which he had been promised when negotiations to purchase this imperial fief from Humbert II were complete. In 1349 the Dauphiné was conferred on John of Normandy's eldest son, Charles, to be held separately from the demesne as the royal heir's special apanage. When the duchy of Burgundy reverted to the crown in 1361, John II had already established his sons Louis in Anjou and John in Berry; in 1363 a newly constituted Burgundy was conferred on Philip.

The policy of moving seneschals and *baillis*, the key figures in local civil and military administration, to prevent them striking deep roots in any one region, already practised in Louis IX's time, continued. Although some changes coincided with accessions, there is little evidence that general changes were implemented then. Many were recruited among northern noble or knightly families even if they served in the Midi. But Philip VI broadened the pattern of recruitment by employing men from beyond the traditional borders of the kingdom like Agout des Baux from Provence and Pierre de la Palud from Savoy as seneschals. Two or three years was a usual term of service. At Meaux between 1319 and 1342 there were thirteen changes. Those who held office for longer periods included Hugues Quiéret, who was seneschal of Beaucaire and Nîmes for seven years between 1325 and 1332, and Godemar du Fay, *bailli* of Vitry-en-Perthois from 1328 to 1335. He was succeeded between 1337/8 and 1345 by Erard de Lignol who, with his son, Thomas, then held Meaux between 1343 and 1352. No one after 1328 could match, however, the record of Pierre de Hangest, a burgess from Montdidier, who was *bailli* of Rouen from 1303 to 1320 and again from 1322 to 1326. In addition, Hangest had also served terms as *bailli* of Verneuil

---

[34] Dupont-Ferrier (1902), p. 14.   [35] Tricard (1979), *contra* Cazelles (1974).

(1300–2) and of the Cotentin (1320–2) in a long and distinguished career. A son was Philip VI's chief notary in 1334.[36]

Dupont-Ferrier called such men 'indefatigable levellers', preparing for the day when 'there would no longer be anyone between the king and his subjects except the king's officers'.[37] More recent investigators have modified this picture of fanatical servants of the crown, more royalist than the king himself. For the Midi, at least, it has been argued, that while the seneschals did work to extend royal authority at the expense of the Church and nobles, they did so with considerable help and counsel from local ruling elites, especially townsmen and university-trained lawyers, who were well rewarded for their labours.[38] Such men provided the permanent staff of the small councils which advised seneschals and provided that element of administrative continuity and local knowledge which frequent changes at the top threatened. The widespread use of regional and urban assemblies in the Midi also encouraged the employment of legal experts. Like seneschals and *baillis* who proved their talents in the provinces, for the most successful lawyers these minor posts often paved the way to a brilliant career in central government service. Many members of the *parlement* of Paris under Philip VI and John II were descended from 'legists' who had first made their mark under the last Capetians.[39]

Growth of central institutions was a marked feature of this period. Although the king and his household remained itinerant, albeit within a fairly traditional circuit in easy range of Paris (Charles IV has been dubbed 'le roi voyageur' and in 1332–3 alone Philip VI changed residence seventy-eight times),[40] the tendency was for leading officers and departments to go 'out of court' and take up permanent residence in the capital. The movement was initiated as early as the reign of Philip Augustus, but it gathered momentum in the early fourteenth century. From Louis X's reign the chancellor (now slowly assuming again an authority in royal counsels lost as long ago as 1185) was normally to be found away from the royal entourage, usually in Paris. Here from 1318 he had an office near to the Sainte-Chapelle, between the *trésor* and the *parcheminerie*, for use as an *audience* (court). By John II's day the Palais de la Cité housed all the principal departments of state. Its transformation into a medieval *cité administrative* was consummated when the dauphin Charles moved permanently to the Louvre and the Hôtel de Saint-Pol.[41]

The growing complexity of government and with it the accumulation of bulky archives encouraged these developments. Philip V, 'un prince centralisateur et épris de réglementation', 'the most inventive and imaginative of Philip

---

[36] Delisle (1904) and Dupont-Ferrier, *Gallia Regia*, for changes of personnel; Rogozinski (1969).

[37] Dupont-Ferrier (1902), p. 873.   [38] Cazelles (1958); Rogozinski (1969).

[39] Pegues (1962); Autrand (1981).   [40] Bautier (1964), pp. 92, 110.

[41] Cazelles (1982); Guenée (1985), p. 132.

IV's sons', overhauled the royal household, councils, chancery and the *chambre des comptes* in a welter of reforming activity and carried out investigations into royal rights.[42] Philip VI also expanded both the judicial and financial organs of government: the *requêtes de l'hôtel, requêtes du palais* and *chambre des enquêtes* as well as the *chambre des comptes* and *parlement* all burgeoned. Philip's reign also began with a series of investigations into royal rights. A novel concern with statistics and the way in which government departments worked can be attributed to the king and his close advisers. Tools for improving administrative competence, like inventories of chancery records, were compiled. A famous enquiry into the number of *feux* or tax units in the kingdom was completed in 1328; the survival of several 'budgets' and 'war-plans' are further evidence of how Philip's administrators attempted to quantify, a necessity in time of war and limited resources.[43] Seeking economies, a report presented to the king in 1343 showed that since 1314 there had been a fivefold increase in the number of officials employed in certain key departments.[44] Specialised services, like the royal secretaries and notaries, began to develop collegiality, for while the crown attempted to restrict their growing numbers between 1343 and 1361, it also confirmed conditions of employment, a graduated hierarchy of posts and the collective privileges of the notariate on more than one occasion.[45]

Bureaucratic development is well illustrated by the chancery itself. It was as recently as 1307 that it began to register documents with any frequency; many still escaped registration, an important matter when assessing whether government could conduct even routine business efficiently. However, by refining earlier practices through copying the more advanced Aragonese or English chanceries and subjecting personnel to more rigorous training and selection procedures, significant progress was achieved as the rapidly growing bulk of surviving registers attests. From Charles IV's reign, adequate financial rewards and the prospect of stable long-term employment beckoned for clerks in royal employment. Not only the chancellor but many lesser officials served in successive reigns with an obvious gain in proficiency. Some royal clerks, in addition to their professional duties, also revealed interests in history and literature, following an older tradition. Jean Maillart wrote the *Roman du comte d'Anjou* (1316) and his colleague Gervais du Bus, whose notarial career lasted from 1313 to 1338, completed a bitter satire, the *Roman de Fauvel* (1314). It was a tradition that the pre-humanists continued later in the century.[46]

There remained weaknesses which highlight the limitations of medieval bureaucracy and were a constant source of political debate. For example, not

[42] Lehugeur (1897–1931); Brown (1971a), p. 399.
[43] Jassemin, 'Les papiers de Mile de Noyers'; Lot (1929).   [44] Moranvillé (1887).
[45] Bautier in Lapeyre and Scheurer (1978).   [46] Bautier (1964) and (1986).

all chancellors displayed the highest standards of conduct. Jean de
Cherchemont, who served Philip V, and then, with only one short interruption, Charles IV and Philip VI as well, was severely censured by his successor,
Macé Ferrant, for exacting unduly high fees, a charge modern investigation
substantiates. A close associate of Ferrant, Guillaume de Sainte-Maure, dean
of Tours and chancellor (1330–5), not only took four and a half years to register as many documents as his conscientious and hard-working predecessor
had in a year, but when he died there were so many unregistered charters in his
house that his heirs paid 4,000 *livres* to be free of legal process. To official
incompetence were added character defects: Sainte-Maure is alleged to have
intimidated an Italian farmer of the Châtelet seal by saying that he would only
pay assignations due if he could sleep with his wife! It is thus hardly surprising
that complaints about the corruption and greed of royal officials at all levels
were perennial and that reformers from 1314–15 to the 1350s were so anxious
to improve ethical standards. St Louis had already issued a major *ordonnance* on
this subject in 1254. In 1303, as part of his own reforming efforts, Philip IV
promulgated another great *ordonnance* which was frequently reissued, most
recently by John II in 1351, providing a comprehensive programme for rooting
out corruption, but it was never more than partially implemented.[47] By
expanding their civil service and creating sovereign courts – *chambre des comptes*,
trésor and, above all, *parlement* – the kings of this period gave bureaucratic
institutions a life of their own that survived as long as the *ancien régime*.

The *parlement* of Paris was by far the most sensitive central institution.
Already by 1314 it had developed many of the specialised functions that it performed as the supreme royal court of law until 1789. The hearing of appeals
from lower courts was an increasingly important element in its business
though it still dealt with many matters of first instance. Evidence for the
growing sophistication of justice in this period is revealed by many new series
of documents recording *parlement's* business – separate criminal registers are
found from 1312, compilations of judgements and sentences from 1320. It also
put together its own collection of royal ordinances (from 1337) and letters
(1342).[48] But at the start of Louis X's reign, there were still some resemblances
to the English parliament.

Like that body under Edward I, *parlement* was still more of an occasion than
an institution. It had a political as well as judicial role. Membership was extremely
fluid, with many participants making only irregular appearances, dependent on
royal favour or the pressure of other business. Until an important decree in 1345
defined personnel, fixed salaries and conditions of employment, *parlement*

---

[47] *Ordonnances*, I, pp. 354–68, 560–1, 694–700, II, pp. 450–64.
[48] Ducoudray (1902), I, pp. 272–3; Lot and Fawtier (1957–62), II, pp. 332–67.

continued to represent a wide cross-section rather than the exclusive caste of legal officers it came to be. For royal princes, leading courtiers, officers holding high honorific posts (constable, butler), bishops and other clerics, nobles and burgesses drawn from a wide geographical circle, including many civil lawyers from the Midi, could all be found at its sessions as well as the first dynasts who dominated it as the century progressed: Flote, Bucy, Presles, Dormans, d'Orgemont.[49] Nor was it yet as eager to attract business as it later became. With regard to the great lordships (Burgundy, Brittany, Gascony before 1337), for example, conventions developed by which *parlement* sent back to their courts many cases that did not meet the criteria for appeals of denial of justice or false judgement. Much of the pressure for expanding *parlement*'s appellate jurisdiction in this period was not self-engendered but welled up from below – from individuals or collectivities dissatisfied with the justice offered by their own local courts – if evidence from Artois is typical.[50]

What *parlement* lacked in contrast to the English parliament, with its developing system of petitions for redress of grievance, was any serious elected element. This was to be found in the various national or regional assemblies of notables that Philip IV had first called together. Under Philip V, in particular, extensive use was made of assemblies of barons, clergy and townsmen in a bewildering combination of forms to obtain counsel, support, even money, above all to get political backing and to explain royal policies.[51] The Flemish wars, crusade, coinage and administrative reform were frequently on the agenda. In 1318 and 1321 the crown tried to negotiate a subsidy through assemblies. Some meetings comprised a single estate (the term 'the three estates' was first used in connection with an assembly in the Auvergne in 1355). Between January and March 1316 at least 227 towns were represented in three separate assemblies at Rouen, Meaux and Bourges and 45 towns met at Paris in March 1317, whilst around 275 nobles were present in December 1315 and no fewer than 431 in April 1318. A 'core' list of around 300 noble names, possibly dating from Philip IV's day, appears to have formed the nucleus for these sessions; in the case of the towns, representation was much more haphazard and irregular. The best-attended meeting was in May 1317 when over 500 prelates, nobles and barons were certainly present and possibly 'several hundred more',[52] a figure not approached again until 1346.

Other meetings brought together a wide cross-section of the political community for sessions that might only last a couple of days but more usually lasted a week or two. It became usual, because of practical difficulties in bringing together a single assembly in a kingdom the size of France, to hold several

---

[49] Autrand (1981).   [50] Small (1979).
[51] Taylor (1938), (1939), (1954) and (1968); Brown (1971b); Russell Major (1980).
[52] Taylor (1954), p. 436.

almost simultaneous regional assemblies rather than one single central meeting. Toulouse, Bourges and Poitiers were favoured venues for meetings of representatives from Languedoc; Paris, Orléans or one of the smaller towns of the royal demesne usually acted as host to those from Languedoil. But after a reign in every year of which there had been at least one major assembly, there followed twenty years (1322–43) when the crown largely avoided 'national' meetings. Disappointment with the results of Philip V's many and varied assemblies was probably the main cause of disenchantment; assemblies failed to furnish binding commitments and the continuing need to consult at a local level vitiated royal efforts, prolonged the time taken to reach urgently needed decisions and sapped enthusiasm.

Philip VI, for instance, clearly felt little need for assemblies in the early years of his reign; *états* held in 1329 and 1333 have left little trace in the record and it was not until financial needs drove him to summon an assembly in 1343 that there was a return to large meetings. From 1345 to 1346 it became usual for administrative convenience to summon two separate meetings for Languedoil and Languedoc. Further important general assemblies were thus held in 1346 and 1347. At the latter a major programme of reform was accepted, probably at the prompting of the king's son, John.

He proved to be more sympathetic to representative assemblies than his father. He had already presided over the *états* of Languedoc when acting as royal lieutenant in 1346 and over those of his apanage of Normandy. His reign began with general sessions in 1351 at Paris and Montpellier (recently purchased from the king of Majorca). But the most intensive period of consultation occurred between December 1355 and May 1358. The twists and turns of that tumultuous period cannot be related in detail: what began as a co-operative venture to meet the crown's urgent requirement of men and money for the war turned sour after the king's defeat and capture at Poitiers, when the crown lost the initiative and the *états* sought to control policy.[53]

In 1357–8 those of Languedoil were in session every few months, falling progressively under the revolutionary zeal of Etienne Marcel, provost of the merchants of Paris, Robert le Coq, bishop of Laon, and their allies calling for root and branch reform of the administration. In February 1357 they carried out a purge of the government and a year later executed two of their bitterest opponents in the dauphin's presence, before internal disputes and the assassination of Marcel (31 July 1358) delivered the regency council from thraldom. It is scarcely surprising that the future Charles V was no friend of assemblies. After 1359 (apart from short meetings at Amiens in 1363 and Compiègne in 1367), as the crown painfully pieced together a kingdom

---

[53] Delachenal (1900) and (1909–31); Funk (1944); Cazelles (1982); Cazelles (1984).

shattered by military defeat and social revolution, general *états* were not summoned again before 1420.

The period 1314–64 demonstrated that a single assembly as a regular solution to the imperative needs which faced successive French kings was impractical. It determined that most formal consultation would remain local. For while a single *états* failed to take root, regional assemblies, especially the *états de Languedoil*, together with several provincial assemblies, did establish themselves as regular features of the political landscape.[54] Such *états* were actively encouraged by the crown in Normandy from 1339, in Burgundy after 1352 and existed in the Auvergne by 1355, Dauphiné (1357) and Artois (1361), whilst those of Brittany first met in 1352 to consider Edward III's demands over the ransom of Charles de Blois.[55] These and later assemblies in what became known as the *pays d'états*, exercising varying degrees of authority and influence, giving counsel and consent, especially in financial matters, could never be entirely dismissed from the government's calculations. They required constant wooing or coercion thereafter; many survived to 1789.

Wars with Aragon, England and Flanders stimulated financial institutions and more elaborate taxation in Philip IV's reign, though he generalised older taxes rather than invented entirely new ones.[56] This set a pattern that determined developments for the next half-century; the legal principle of 'evident (or urgent) necessity' was used to justify raising taxes. There was broad agreement that military service was owed in time of war but after summoning the feudal host (*arrière-ban*) men were now often asked to pay taxes rather than serve in the royal army. This 'age of war subsidies' (Henneman) lasted until 1356. The precedent of 1313, when Philip IV agreed to return money that had been collected once the emergency that justified it had passed (*cessante causa, cessante effecta*), also governed the expenditure of taxes for much of the period after 1314.[57] Money could only be raised by subsidies for, and spent on, specific campaigns. In most minds, direct taxation remained an extraordinary occurrence. The political risks of imposing general levies prevented successive governments from grasping that nettle before 1356.

As a result the crown was often forced to use traditional methods to raise extra resources, or to experiment with indirect taxation. The principles of this were simple: *impôts* were levied on the sale of basic domestic commodities, foodstuffs, drink and manufactured goods whilst customs dues like the *maltôte* were placed on goods destined for export. The initial rates were extremely low, a penny in the pound, and imposed for limited periods. But sales taxes proved to be one of the most reliable ways of raising steady revenues and they became a permanent

[54] Russell Major (1980); Lewis (1968), pp. 328–74.   [55] Pocquet du Haut-Jussé (1925).
[56] Henneman (1971), p. 27.   [57] Brown (1972).

feature of local and national taxation. It was by this means, for example, that most urban fortifications were financed from the 1330s. One destined for a long future was that on salt: the *gabelle* was first imposed in 1341, dropped in 1346, but raised again between 1356 and 1380 and permanently from 1383.

The first two Valois, like Philip IV's sons, followed his example by exploiting to the full their prerogatives in taking customary aids for knighting an eldest son, marrying a daughter, going on crusade or raising a ransom. Attempts to raise simultaneously aids for knighting John of Normandy and marrying his sister Marie to the heir of Brabant in 1332 provoked so much resistance that in the end Philip VI renounced his rights. He even repaid some money after his daughter died and John fell so ill that his life was despaired of in 1335. It was the desperate necessity of ransoming the king himself in 1356 that forced the development of a radically new taxation system. The ransom was levied as a *fouage*, a hearth tax, widely used in the Midi since Philip IV's day but now generalised. *Aides*, sales taxes, were also extended. To collect them royal France was divided into districts (usually following diocesan boundaries) known as *élections* because the first collectors were nominated (*élus*) in the *états*. But the crown speedily took over control, forming *recettes générales*, supervised later in the century by general councillors answerable to the *chambre des comptes* and the *cour des aides*. From 1360 it nominated and paid the *élus* and their subordinates.[58]

Another traditional means of raising money, issuing and manipulating the coinage, habits which marked Philip IV's rule, also remained a central plank of royal financial policy till 1360. Records relating to the total revenues of French kings in this period are very sparse (they probably averaged between 500,000 and 1,000,000 *livres* most years). But in 1349 (admittedly an exceptional year because of plague) two-thirds of royal income for Christmas term (over 520,000 *livres* out of 781,000 *livres*) came from the king's seigniorage profits, his right to call in and remint the coinage.[59] A more reasonable sum appears to have been taken by Charles IV in 1324–5 when about 20 per cent of his income derived from this source. More risky was altering rates of exchange and devaluing currency in order to derive short-term cash benefits, one of the most over-exploited and unpopular royal policies. By 1330 royal coinage had lost 30 per cent of its intrinsic value since the 1290s; in the next thirty years it lost a further 50 per cent. Between 1 January 1337 and 5 December 1360 there were no fewer than eighty-five *mutations* or changes in value, silver content or type of coin issued by the crown (fifty-one alone between 1354 and 1360). Such *mutations* usually followed a cyclical pattern of revaluation, followed by a brief period in which there was an attempt to return to sound money, only to be followed by a further and more exaggerated round of debasement. Cazelles identified five cycles between 1346 and 1355.[60]

---

[58] Henneman (1976); Cazelles (1982), pp. 389–401.
[59] Fawtier, *Comptes de Trésor*; Henneman (1971), pp. 44–5.
[60] Cazelles (1962b) and (1966b); Fournial (1970), pp. 97–125.

The policy was justified in traditional terms. As Philip VI announced in the preamble to an order sent to the seneschal of Beaucaire on 16 January 1347, 'We cannot believe that anyone can be in any doubt but that to us and our royal majesty alone belongs, in so far as it concerns our kingdom, the art, practice, provision and all regulations for the making of money.' Reasons for pursuing this stratagem were also bluntly put in letters of 18 March 1348: 'we have to do it because of our wars and for the defence of the realm'.[61]

Advice was taken from expert Parisian merchants on what level of devaluation the market might stand to minimise the worst effects; excess was avoided. But the frequent changes brought mounting pressure not only from urban oligarchs who did not enjoy the government's ear but also from the lay nobility and higher clergy whose rents declined with every devaluation. Return to the good money of Louis IX had been a war-cry in 1314–15; the 'astonishing anarchy'[62] of the mid 1350s, when the government even occasionally instructed its own officials not to prosecute those infringing a mass of contradictory regulations and Gresham's law worked with a vengeance, finally provoked a reaction.

Against the view that coinage was the exclusive preserve of the crown, under the influence of Nicolas d'Oresme, a group of reformers led by Guillaume de Melun, archbishop of Sens, advocated a return to 'strong money'. This was adopted as royal policy in an *ordonnance* issued by John II on 5 December 1360 shortly after returning from captivity. A sound gold currency, based on the newly minted *franc*, restoration of the quality of the silver mark and reunion of the silver currencies of Languedoc and Languedoil (which from 1356 had been struck at different rates), marked the start of twenty-five years of monetary stability.[63]

Financial necessity, allied to a growing sense of moral and religious purity, the belief that France was a special land beloved of God and that it ought to mirror the kingdom of God by its faith and devotion, sometimes prompted moves against unpopular minority groups. The expulsion of the Jews in 1306 was a model for the attack on the Templars in 1307, whilst longer-term milking of Lombard financiers was interspersed with fierce bouts of hostility, another policy with a long future. It was under financial pressure that Louis X in 1315 agreed to readmit the Jews to France for twelve years. Preaching of the crusade in 1319, a resurgent Pastoreaux movement and the extraordinary affair of the Lepers' plot in 1321 (when it was alleged that the Muslims of Granada planned to enlist Jews and lepers to poison wells to avenge the Christian *Reconquista*) marked another bout of persecution, especially violent in the Midi. Philip V once again arrested Jews and confiscated their goods. Charles IV continued to harry them by exacting fines, some initially levied in his father's reign, until the

---

[61] *Ordonnances*, ii, p. 254; Fournial (1970), p. 145.   [62] Fournial (1970), p. 103.
[63] Cazelles (1966b); Spufford (1988), pp. 295–306.

twelve years elapsed in 1327, by when there were virtually no Jews left in the kingdom.[64] The last Cathars, including the well-publicised heretics of Montaillou, were also persecuted to extinction; royal officials at Toulouse were still disposing of Cathar properties in the 1330s.[65]

The Lombards, who played an even more important role at the Champagne fairs and in the provision of loans and other banking services to crown, nobility and urban communities, were regularly harassed by the crown seizing debts owed to them, arbitrarily ordering their reduction, prohibiting payment of interest or exacting excessive sums for protection. Periods of war saw them under even greater pressure. Philip V was particularly active against them but Charles IV (1324) and Philip VI (1331, 1337, 1340, 1347) also issued decrees which restricted their freedom in the kingdom and it was not until 1363 that the crown finally annulled debts seized from them many years earlier.[66]

As far as the commercial consequences of this policy are concerned, they were partially offset as the first half of the fourteenth century saw an increasing presence of merchants from the Iberian peninsula in northern France. Philip IV's permission in 1310 for Portuguese merchants to trade at Harfleur, for example, was renewed in 1341; two years earlier similar licence had been granted to Aragonese and Majorcan traders to use that port, whilst the important diplomatic alliance between France and Castile after 1336 also brought commercial contacts.[67] The same was true for some favoured Italian city-states like Genoa and Venice, whose citizens escaped the fate reserved for the Lombards, because they had troops and naval resources essential to the war effort. Many Genoese and Monagesques were employed at the royal naval arsenal of the Clos des Galées at Rouen, one of few instances where the French rivalled English war organisation.[68]

CROWN AND CHURCH

As a result of the titanic struggle between Philip IV and Boniface VIII, royal control over the Church in France tightened. The removal of the curia to Avignon by Clement V (1308) placed the papacy physically closer to Paris and encouraged frequent exchanges. The future Philip V was at Avignon in June 1316 when Louis X died; John XXII bombarded him with advice on foreign and domestic policy once he succeeded. Philip VI in 1335 and John II on more than one occasion also visited the curia. All the popes from Clement V to Urban V were either former royal servants or French clerics; several felt a close

[64] Barber (1981); Beriac (1987); Jordan (1989); Brown (1991c).

[65] HL, x, Preuves, pp. 793, 813–15; Le Roy Ladurie (1975).

[66] Lot and Fawtier (1957–62), II, p. 204; Henneman (1971), pp. 82–3, 127, 227, 240, 254, 310.

[67] RPV, nos. 4070 and 4406, cf. also nos. 3342, 3830, 4407; Daumet (1898).

[68] Merlin-Chazelas, Documents relatifs.

allegiance to the French king, proffering advice (like John XXII and Clement VI) or material aid by providing royal candidates to benefices, bulls, dispensations and other privileges. They allowed the king to tax the French Church for crusading ventures as well as more secular ends. In the case of Clement VI there were also extensive financial loans gratefully received by Philip VI for the war against Edward III.[69]

From Philip IV's reign onwards clerical tenths (*décimes*) were levied in France as royal or national rather than ecclesiastical taxes.[70] Philip V was granted *décimes* for four consecutive years by John XXII; Charles IV enjoyed a biennial grant as did Philip VI in 1328. In 1333 a sextennial one was authorised, though it was reclaimed by Benedict XII when Philip VI did not depart on crusade. In 1344 all outstanding repayments owing from this (more than 2.8m florins) were remitted by Clement VI and Philip again enjoyed biennial grants. There was an interruption between 1355 and 1360, but later kings continued to levy *décimes* until the sixteenth century, their frequency and national character contributing to the idea that they were truly 'kings of France'.

This view was also encouraged by Philip IV and his sons actively promoting their clerical counsellors to bishoprics and other major benefices throughout the kingdom, since they often put them forward for dioceses distant from Paris as a means of extending royal influence into remote regions. This is especially apparent in the case of Brittany and south-western France in the early fourteenth century, though in Brittany's case there was a reaction later as John III and his successors had their own nominees to promote.[71] Other trusted ecclesiastics like Jean de Marigny, bishop of Beauvais (younger brother of the man executed in 1315), were despatched as royal lieutenants to the Midi at the beginning of the Anglo-French war or served in the central administration as presidents of the *chambre des comptes* or clerical counsellors in *parlement*. In 1347 a commission of three leading abbots was appointed to oversee financial reform, signalling the eclipse of the '*chambre des comptes* party'. A bishopric became the usual reward for a clerical chancellor.

After the battering received at Philip IV's hands, there was something of a reaction over ecclesiastical jurisdiction. At the time of the leagues, charters of privileges were issued in which the crown promised to maintain bishops in their rights and many individual confirmations were issued to abbeys and chapters as they were to lay nobles.[72] Complaints from provincial synods show, however, that pressure was still brought to bear by lay authorities. The hoary issue of Church–state relations was given a thorough airing when shortly after his accession Philip VI summoned an assembly at Vincennes in December

---

[69] Faucon (1879); Henneman (1971), p. 197.
[70] Lot and Fawtier (1957–62), II, pp. 207–8; Henneman (1971), pp. 348–50.
[71] Pocquet du Haut-Jussé (1928), I, pp. 225 ff.   [72] *Ordonnances*, I, pp. 615, 647.

1329. What his motive was remains obscure; it may simply have been another sign of his wish to inform himself fully of his rights (cf. above p. 411). Whatever the case, Pierre de Cugnières, an extremely able *avocat* in *parlement*, acting as the king's main spokesman, declared to the prelates, lawyers and other assembled dignitaries on 15 December that the king intended to 'reintegrate their temporalities'.[73] He elaborated reasons for doing so by listing sixty-six specific complaints arising from the administration of ecclesiastical justice which, he argued, trespassed on the rights of temporal lords.

Although many present were veterans who could remember the great disputes between Philip IV and Boniface VIII and had certainly absorbed the enormous literature those arguments produced, they were clearly taken aback by the comprehensive and bitter tone of the royal attack and asked for time to consider their reply. In subsequent sessions those charged with responding on behalf of the Church, Pierre Roger, archbishop-elect of Sens (the future Pope Clement VI) and Pierre Bertrand, bishop of Autun, president of the *chambre des comptes* (and from 1331 cardinal), put up a stout defence that even elicited a conciliatory response from Pierre de Cugnières. On 5 January 1330 he preached on the theme 'Pax vobis, nolite timere, ego sum.'[74] Further exchanges followed but the whole affair ended inconsequentially with the king apparently admitting that he would not further erode ecclesiastical privileges whilst warning the bishops to put their house in order unless they wished to invite further royal attention. There matters largely rested until the Schism later in the century rekindled the debate, summarised in the *Songe du vergier*.[75]

Forty years ago Raymond Cazelles wrote about 'la crise de la royauté sous Philippe de Valois'.[76] The period 1314–64 was one of prolonged crisis as social, economic and military difficulties increased. The adultery scandal of 1314 and the failure of the last direct Capetians to father sons, leading to the extinction of the Capetian dynasty in the direct male line in 1328, raised for the first time since the tenth century serious and controversial issues about the succession. Domestically Philip IV's policies left a legacy of discontent that boiled over in the leagues of 1314–15 and forced a reconsideration of the crown's relations with the politically articulate throughout the kingdom. Reform was on the agenda but views on how to achieve it differed. So, too, did ideas on how the crown should finance its ever-expanding requirements. By the end of his reign Philip V, like his father, was making demands which many considered excessive. His successor sensibly retreated, though warfare continued to eat inexorably into the crown's resources.

After a honeymoon period, doubts about the Valois succession in 1328 and

---

[73] Durand de Maillane (1771), III, p. 445; Olivier-Martin (1909).
[74] Durand de Maillane (1771), III, p. 501.   [75] *Le songe du vergier*, ed. Schnerb-Lièvre.
[76] Cazelles (1958).

mounting internal opposition were skilfully exploited by Edward III of England in the pursuit of his ambitions, a sovereign Guyenne certainly, the crown of France perhaps. The Anglo-French war which followed was a civil war as well as one of external aggression: military defeats undermined the Valois. After Crécy, the *états* of 1346–7 again called for reform and, after the Black Death and the accession of John II, from 1355 these demands in a time of great social dislocation became imperative. The king's capture at Poitiers and the partition of the kingdom in the Treaty of Brétigny marked the nadir of Valois fortunes while, taking advantage of the crown's weakness, new forces were rising to threaten the fragile unity of Valois France.

In 1347 Gaston III of Foix asserted that he recognised no superior for his *vicomté* of Béarn but God; the same idea, culled from Roman law texts and earlier used to justify the king's assumption of sovereign powers, also emanated from Brittany in 1336 and 1341 when lawyers argued that the dukes were 'princes who recognised no superior'.[77] If kings could claim sovereignty, why not princes? France was entering an 'age of principalities' in which the power of the crown, so apparently dominant around 1300, was to be seriously challenged by provincial rivals, none strong enough on their own to defeat the king, but capable (especially in alliance with Edward III) of exploiting the crown's difficulties for their own advantage during the Anglo-French war.[78] There were other ominous signs of royal impotence where there had once been strength: Philip IV levied taxes in Brittany and nominated to Breton benefices; his successors could not. Royal efforts to establish a monopoly of coinage in the kingdom since Louis IX's days faltered after an important *ordonnance* in 1315.[79] The most powerful princes had their coinage rights recognised; their burgeoning administrations were increasingly capable of functioning without royal intervention. In provinces like Guyenne, Brittany and Flanders crown influence had in any event rapidly evaporated after 1337.

Exaggeration should be avoided, of course: even the weakest French kings enjoyed certain innate advantages and considerable resources in a society where power was otherwise widely distributed and that of the princes, in particular, as yet lacked advanced administrative support or well-articulated political programmes. The Capetian idea of 'France' under one monarch retained a strong appeal. Some steps taken during this period would ultimately allow the kings to tap these resources effectively and to rebuild the monarchy. In the short term, however, the crown had suffered serious reverses: time would show whether the dauphin Charles, who with an able group of advisers had effectively governed France during his father's captivity in England, could restore its image after his accession on 8 April 1364.

---

[77] Tucoo-Chala (1960), p. 62, and (1961), pp. 160–1, 'Iaquoau tee de Diu e no de nulh homi deu mont'; Jones, 'Some Documents', p. 5.   [78] Le Patourel (1984).   [79] Dieudonné (1932).

FRANCE UNDER CHARLES V AND CHARLES VI

Françoise Autrand

IS it possible to write history centred on the reigns of individual kings sixty years after the first criticism by French historians of the factual and biographical methodology of political history? The answer must undoubtedly be, 'yes'. Broadened by anthropological and sociological approaches, political narrative has been transformed into the history of power structures and of the developing state. And the figure of the king lies at the very centre of all these new fields of historical enquiry investigating the centres of power, its symbols and insignia, as well as the ceremonial and ritual of the state. As a result, the state itself is now viewed in a fresh perspective, but the king remains the primary focus.

Historical narrative, complete with dates and battles, has won back its place in this history of power structures, ever since the study of attitudes demonstrated that such historical facts provided a framework for corporate memories. In the 1420s and 1430s an advocate in the Paris *parlement* did not need to specify that he was talking of the battle of Agincourt in 1415 when he dated a fact to 'the year of the battle'. The narrative approach has regained its place in historical studies, but its emphasis has changed dramatically since the days of Ernest Lavisse and the positivist historians of the nineteenth century.

The cardinal importance of structures is now recognised: the social foundations of power, as well as its intellectual basis (that is, the concepts that determined political action) and ideology. At the same time, traditional research has greatly improved our knowledge of the mechanisms of the state: the army, taxation and administration.

France was a kingdom: the state was monarchic. The king was a distinct figure at the apex of the political system. We need to identify any distinctive features that figure takes during the years 1356 to 1422, the period covered by the regency and reign of Charles V and by the reign of Charles VI.

The power of the consecrated king was bestowed on him by God. The author of *Le songe du vergier* wrote that he was 'the vicar of Christ in his temporality'.[1] On special occasions (coronations, royal entries and even, in the reign of Charles V, when he moved from one place to another), the king provided the crowd with a tangible display of his majesty. The 'honours of the court' – established rules relating to precedence and niceties of behaviour – were more precisely and logically defined, becoming a backdrop for kingly sovereignty when Charles V made two of his closest companions responsible for protocol. (They were his cousin Louis, count of Etampes, and his friend and first chamberlain, Bureau de la Rivière.) When the emperor Charles IV visited the king in 1378, they were careful to ensure that he entered Paris on a black horse, leaving the white horse (a 'sign of domination' according to imperial custom) to the king of France, according to the narrative in the *Grandes chroniques*. The sovereign king was the mainspring of political action.

But he was also the fount of grace; and he was a human being. The state at this period had not yet become cold and inhuman. The affective bond between king and subjects was what constituted the national monarchy. For these were the subjects whom the king invariably addressed in letters as 'his dear and well beloved'. They in turn learnt of the capture of King John at Poitiers 'with the greatest sadness in their hearts'; at a later date they processed barefoot in the streets of Paris in response to Charles VI's illness, beseeching God to cure their much-loved king; they could not commit treason or rebel without 'shaming' the kingdom. Love and hate played a primary role in the language of contemporary politics.

During this period, the throne was initially occupied by the prisoner-king John II, who had been captured on the battlefield at Poitiers (1356), ransomed and held in captivity in London. Although he had been forced to delegate power to his son Charles, the king still imposed his own counsellors from a distance and they followed a particular set of policies. Then came Charles V 'the Wise'.

Even in his own lifetime Charles V was considered a model king, and his reign as a time of reconstruction after the disasters of the first Valois kings of France. Recent history has dulled this dazzling image. Some have questioned the originality and the efficacy of his policies; others have viewed the historical fact of the king's reputation as the product of royal propaganda, the work of the king's scholarly entourage, who were dedicated to the fabrication of the image of the wise king. It is more constructive to examine the image itself in greater detail. According to Christine de Pisan, the king's wisdom lay in 'his great love of study and knowledge'.[2] It was reflected in the king's taste for

---

[1] *Le songe du vergier*, ed. Schnerb, i, p. 51.   [2] Christine de Pisan, *Le livre des fais*, ii, p. 42.

books and intellectual activity, his readiness to refer diplomatic issues to civil
lawyers (which infuriated the Black Prince) and his friendship with intellectuals. It was seen, too, in the management of his time and work, as well as his
calm and cool demeanour and the even temper, which had been so lacking in
John II, whom Froissart described as 'hot-tempered and unpredictable'.[3] In
short, Charles V's approach to government was intellectual and rational, with
efficacy as a main aim.

Charles V surrounded himself with a circle of intellectuals. The most
famous of these was the Norman clerk Nicolas d'Oresme, universal scholar of
his time. As master of the College of Navarre, in opposition to John II, he had
written a treatise on the coinage, *De Moneta*, in which the prince's right to
manipulate ('remuer') the coinage was challenged. A supporter of Charles V,
he translated the works of Aristotle for the king and 'for the common good'.
Other scholars were invited to translate into French St Augustine's *City of God*,
John of Salisbury's *Policraticus*, the works of Vegetius and so on. At the beginning of his translation of Aristotle's *Politics* Nicolas d'Oresme placed a glossary of new words that he had invented to represent 'those which were not in
common speech'. French vocabulary was thus enriched with words such as
'economy', 'legislation', 'anarchy' and 'democracy'. It was in the reign of
Charles V that France was equipped with the essential concepts of political
thought.

Charles V was also the founder of the library in the Louvre, where a thousand books were meticulously kept and inventoried, but also – and above all –
put at the disposal of readers. Besides books of history and romances, they
found a remarkable range of political science. This was a working library and
by the end of the reign it had also acquired *Le songe du vergier*, a political encyclopaedia, written on the king's own orders, besides collections of texts assembled as working tools for the king and his council: a revised *bullarium* or register
of the most important letters from the popes to the kings of France, a
compilation of treaties concluded with the king of England and a 'Book of
Alliances', containing diplomatic documents.

The king set an important example in the manuscripts where he decided
upon the illuminations personally, choosing to have himself portrayed in academic dress, enthroned before a revolving bookcase. The king's wisdom,
together with his success, meant many aspects of his reign – including taxation
– were either accepted or forgotten. People were already speaking of 'the good
time of wise King Charles', when he was scarcely dead.

Charles VI was not yet twelve years old when he succeeded his father. He
was under twenty-four when he suffered his first bout of madness in the forest

---

[3] Froissart, *Œuvres*, ed. Lettenhove, IV, p. 202.

of Le Mans, after eight years of minority (in practice, if not in strict legal terms, since he was crowned on 4 November 1380) and four years of personal government. It is impossible to identify his illness precisely five centuries later, but the king suffered a series of crises and remissions. Between crises Charles was sufficiently lucid to take up the burden of the crown once more. At least that was the case until 1415, for after Agincourt his reason became permanently dulled. The king's 'absences' gave free rein to the rivalries of the princes of the blood, Charles VI's uncles (the dukes of Berry and Burgundy) and his brother (the duke of Orléans).

The royal image had not been entirely obliterated, however, and it would be a complete misunderstanding of contemporary attitudes to think that the figure of the wise king had simply been replaced by that of the mad king. Athletic, excelling at joust and tournament, bathed in the reflected glory of his victory over the militias of the Flemish towns at Roosebeke in 1382 and dreaming of crusade, Charles VI was first and foremost a chivalric prince. Later, when there was nothing but war and disaster, the French saw their own image reflected in their suffering king. In his unhappy face they also saw the features of Christ of the Passion. They called him Charles 'the Well Beloved'.

Charles V was only the third Valois king of France. In the middle of the fourteenth century the monarchy was still experiencing the after-effects of the dynastic change of 1328. This explains the considerable efforts devoted to stressing royal legitimacy, and the lineage and blood of the French kings. The most important act was the ordinance of 1374 which simultaneously fixed the royal age of majority at fourteen and set out the law of succession that applied to the crown, that is, the exclusion of daughters, primogeniture and inheritance by the male blood relation closest to the dead king. Other acts established the principle of the inalienability of the royal domain (1361) and introduced this into the coronation oath. They also promulgated the notion that the kingdom (truncated by the Treaty of Brétigny) was indivisible and that royal sovereignty could not be surrendered in any way whatsoever. This concept was to dominate diplomatic negotiations with England until the Treaty of Troyes.

In the reign of Charles V principles that were identical (unity, indivisibility) or very similar (succession only through the direct male line) were also applied to the duchies that had been created as apanages for the sons of John II in 1360, and then to the duchies of Orléans and even Burgundy, in spite of ancient custom. Set apart from the barons of France by the special status of their lordships, the king's closest relatives enjoyed a privileged position in the kingdom. Close to the sources of power and endowed with substantial resources, thanks to the money they received from royal taxation, they were placed at the summit of the feudal hierarchy by the king's express command

and dominated or absorbed the *comtés* which were struggling to survive on annual incomes of between 10,000 and 12,000 *livres*.

Charles V's scholarly entourage constructed a body of doctrine from the various legends which had always surrounded the king, his coronation and his thaumaturgical power (which enabled him to cure those afflicted with scrofula); focusing on the Holy Ampulla, the oriflamme and the fleurs-de-lis on the king's arms, while also exalting the kingdom of France as the new promised land with its chosen people. The charisma of the king also extended to his close relatives; in the decisive years of the mid-fourteenth century they were known as the 'lords of the blood of France', then 'lords of the fleurs-de-lis' (first mentioned in an official document in 1355) because of their coats of arms, which were decorated with three fleurs-de-lis like those of the king. It was the lineage of France which first Charles V and then Charles VI honoured in the cult of St Louis, when they built further Saintes-Chapelles (at Vincennes, or Le Vivier-en-Brie) on the model of the one in the royal palace at Paris, or when Charles V gave 'holy thorns' (from Christ's crown of thorns) to the princely members of his family, who then built Saintes-Chapelles in their turn (for instance, at Riom and Bourges).

The crown was the royal insignia to which Charles V attached greatest importance. In fact, both as jewel and concept, the crown symbolised royal office, at a time when a distinction was beginning to be made between the person and the office of the king. Documents dating from the years 1360–80 eulogise the crown in the most lofty terms. This was the period which saw Charles V abandon the Palais de la Cité to administrative departments (*parlement, chambre des comptes* and so on) and establish a royal residence at the Hôtel de Saint-Pol and largely remodel the Louvre. Then, too, the assembled body of the councillors-general on the *fait des aides* instituted a strict distinction in royal finance between what was destined for 'the king's estate' and what was earmarked for public expenses.

The concept of the two bodies of the king found concrete expression for the first time at the funeral ceremony of Charles VI in 1422. The coffin containing his mortal remains was topped by an effigy which was identical to the king and carried the insignia of royalty, until Charles's body had been laid in the ground and the heralds had proclaimed his successor. The king was mortal, but he also possessed a mystical and imperishable body, which symbolised the continuity of the monarchy over and above the lives of individual sovereigns.

When the history of medieval France was essentially the history of pre-revolutionary times, scholars tried to establish the contours of state centralisation, national unity and French territorial expansion. The story of the years 1356–1422 begins with the disastrous defeat of the French at Poitiers and the capture of John II on the battlefield. The dauphin Charles, duke of Normandy, returned to Paris without either troops or money and summoned the estates general. He beat off the attacks of the opposition in which the figure of Etienne Marcel, provost of Paris, featured prominently. The activity of John II's son-in-law and enemy Charles the Bad (king of Navarre and grandson of Louis X through his mother), together with the Jacquerie (or peasant revolt) until the assassination of Etienne Marcel (31 July 1358) further contributed to the disarray. The Treaty of Brétigny (1360) brought the first part of the Hundred Years War to a close, and the king was forced to cede to the English king full sovereignty over the south-western third of the kingdom. John II was freed for a ransom of 3 million *écus* (only part of which was ever paid, but which was responsible for the imposition of direct taxation). On his return to France, one of his first acts was the creation of the *franc*, the strong coinage demanded by the landholding lords. Shrunken, ruined and depopulated, France at this time was ravaged by companies of freebooting mercenaries making war for their own ends, while the king of Navarre had taken up arms against the king over the Burgundian succession. The dark days of Charles V's accession were brightened by Bertrand du Guesclin's victory over the Navarrese at Cocherel (May 1364). There was, however, another setback a few months later when John de Montfort (supported by Edward III of England) defeated his rival Charles de Blois, assisted by du Guesclin, at the battle of Auray (29 September 1364), though it effectually brought an end to a civil war in Brittany of more than twenty years.

The appeals brought before the French king and the *parlement* of Paris by some Gascon lords against the prince of Wales, duke of Guyenne, and his taxes in 1368, provided Charles V with an opportunity to resume sovereignty in the provinces yielded under the terms of the Treaty of Brétigny. As a result, hostilities recommenced. A combination of logic and necessity forced the French king to adopt a new and essentially defensive strategy, employing a small permanent standing army. In 1375 (when papal intervention led to the truce of Bruges) almost all the lost provinces had been reconquered and England held only Guyenne, the March of Calais, Cherbourg and a few Breton strongholds. But the French had paid dearly for the reconquest in high levels of taxation. Together with the Great Schism and the Breton uprising, the revolts of the southern French towns that were ruthlessly suppressed in 1378–9 by the king's lieutenant, the duke of Anjou, cast a shadow over the end of Charles V's restorative reign.

The death of Charles V left power in the hands of the young Charles VI's three uncles, each of whom was motivated by the interests of his own principality, as well as the kingdom as a whole. Louis, duke of Anjou and heir to Queen Joanna of Naples, needed the king's money to conquer his Italian

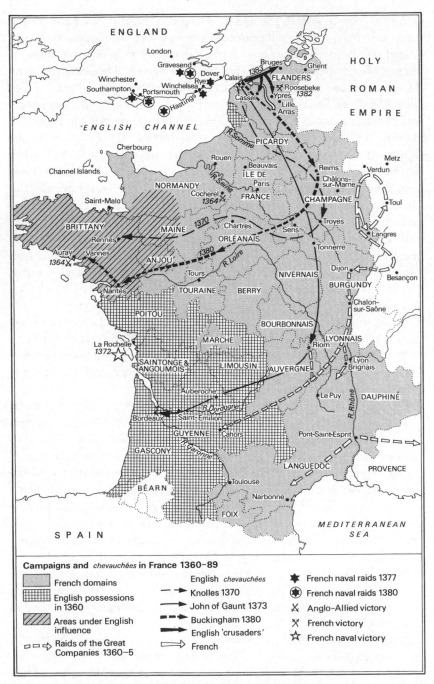

Map 9   The Hundred Years War, 1360–96

kingdom. Philip, duke of Burgundy (who was soon to inherit Flanders through right of his wife), needed the king's army to put an end to the revolt of the Flemish towns. John, duke of Berry, was appointed lieutenant-general of Languedoc. He thus obtained the revenues from this province close to his own lordships, whose taxes had been amongst the most lucrative in the kingdom in the reign of John II.

Meanwhile direct taxation, which had been clumsily abolished in 1380 and reintroduced the following year, provoked a wave of violent revolts. The Midi experienced the Tuchins, but the northern towns also rose up, with disturbances at Reims, Laon, Orléans and, most seriously, the 'Harelle' at Rouen and the 'Maillotins' or 'Maillets' at Paris. For two years Paris lay outside royal authority and only yielded after the crushing defeat inflicted on the Flemings at Roosebeke by the royal army (27 November 1382).

The return of the Marmosets when the king was twenty provided some continuity with the reign of Charles V. But in 1392 the king's madness brought the dukes of Berry and Burgundy to power, henceforth in competition with the king's brother, Louis, duke of Orléans. They very quickly split into two camps, one led by the duke of Burgundy, the other by the duke of Orléans. At stake was not only control of royal finances, but also government of the country and, above all, influence in foreign affairs; for the duke of Burgundy sought to extend his influence in the Low Countries, while the duke of Orléans favoured a warmongering policy towards England. The Church was another source of disagreement. Louis of Orléans remained a staunch adherent of the Avignon pope, while the duke of Burgundy supported attempts to bring the Schism to an end. The absence of the king's personal will which let princely rivalries flourish unchecked also strengthened the principalities, since – thanks to royal finance – they were able to provide themselves with an administration, capitals and courts, patterned on the royal model.

The assassination of Louis of Orléans on the order of John the Fearless, duke of Burgundy (1407), the movement of the Cabochiens (Burgundian supporters who wanted to impose their reforms by force) in Paris (1413), as well as civil war between Armagnacs and Burgundians, all contributed to the destabilisation of royal power, despite the efforts, supported by royal officials, of the aged duke of Berry and then, in 1414–15, the dauphin Louis, duke of Guyenne, who died in December 1415.

Weakened by these divisions, France was in no position to repulse attacks by the English. After the first bellicose years of the reign of Charles VI, the Marmosets embarked upon a long series of peace negotiations. But the French refused to cede any sovereignty, and the English had nothing to lose by allowing this 'cold war' to continue. Since they were unable to make peace, the diplomats concluded a twenty-eight-year truce, sealed by the marriage of Richard II and Charles VI's daughter, Isabella of France (1396). The wedding provided an opportunity for another summit meeting, followed by a personal alliance between the two kings. But this did nothing to establish a final peace between their two kingdoms, nor did it impinge on frontier questions in Guyenne and the March of Calais, where there were constant hostilities and a daily war of attrition, which was so damaging to the inhabitants of these areas.

Hostilities were resumed with the fall of Richard II and the accession of Henry IV of Lancaster. There were campaigns in Guyenne, much naval activity and in 1411–12 a confused series of military and diplomatic manoeuvres as the English exploited internal political divisions in France. In 1415 Henry V landed in Normandy. The French army was annihilated at Agincourt (25 October), and the English advanced into Normandy. The conflict between Armagnacs and Burgundians continued. On 29 May 1418 the Burgundians succeeded in capturing Paris, massacring the constable, Bernard d'Armagnac, and any of his supporters whom they could find. The others fled, taking with them the young dauphin Charles. They withdrew to the provinces of Berry and Poitou (the dauphin's apanage), where, within the space of two months, they were able to establish a government led by the dauphin, who proclaimed himself regent of France.

The following year France was torn apart by the murder of John the Fearless, duke of Burgundy: a crime witnessed by the dauphin and plotted in his council, when he was present. The new duke of Burgundy, Philip the Good, and Queen Isabella concluded the Treaty of Troyes (21 May 1420) with Henry V, in the name of the king (who was more 'absent' than ever). The dauphin Charles was disinherited because of his 'crimes', in other words because of the murder of the duke of Burgundy. On the death of Charles VI, Henry V was to inherit the crown of France and, by marrying the French king's youngest daughter, Catherine of France, he would become the 'son' of the king and queen and would henceforth govern the kingdom. The 'double monarchy' of France and England was thus established, with each of the two kingdoms preserving 'its rights, liberties and customs, practices and laws'.

Far from bringing peace, the Treaty of Troyes gave fresh impetus to the war in a kingdom now divided into three alliances: Normandy, the Ile-de-France, Guyenne and the March of Calais were occupied by the English; Champagne and Picardy, in addition to Burgundy and Flanders, were under the authority of the duke of Burgundy; the provinces of central and southern France remained loyal to the dauphin, together with Anjou, Maine and – of course – the Dauphiné. Ravaged by soldiers and parcelled out like this, there was a real threat that the kingdom of France might disappear altogether. However, when Charles VI died on 22 October 1422 two months after Henry V, and was succeeded by Henry VI, king of France and England, in his little kingdom of Bourges the dauphin Charles proclaimed himself king of France. Some people – at Joan of Arc's village of Domrémy and elsewhere – thought he was right to do so.

In the three-quarters of a century spanned by the reigns of Charles V and Charles VI the historian can detect two main currents, sometimes working together, sometimes in opposition. On the one hand, there was the rise of the modern state, with its accompanying bureaucracy, taxation, the abstract and sovereign power of the crown and the imperious and overriding primacy accorded to the public good. On the other hand, there was also the traditional structure of kingship: feudal, personal, respectful of privilege, established custom and personal ties, an ideal model for the basis of reform.

The roots of both these elements lay in the past. The origins of the modern state must be sought in the changes that took place in the late twelfth century. The impetus in particular of the reign of Philip Augustus (1180–1223) continued in the reign of Philip the Fair and his successors, in the years 1280–1348. As for the reforming ideal, it looked back nostalgically to the 'good old days of our lord St Louis', when moderation and worthiness had brought the monarchy incomparable moral and sacral prestige.

By 1360 the onward march of the modern state was broken by defeat, revolts and the resulting civil wars and gradually lost some of its initial momentum. When John II returned to France, a 'new regime' was installed which acknowledged the dominant socio-political role of the nobility.[4] The establishment of regular taxation and the gradual formation of an organised body of officials provided a framework for the development of the state; based on clearly defined principles, genuine decentralisation was also set in hand. The establishment of this new political and social order in France in the years following the Treaty of Brétigny, its maintenance under Charles V and subsequent evolution, the resulting tensions and its eventual breakdown is an important strand in the history of France under Charles V and Charles VI.

POLITICAL SOCIETY: THE NOBILITY IN POWER

When Robert de Lorris was attacked in his castle of Ermenonville by the Jacques in 1358, 'because he was so frightened, he renounced his noble status and swore that he loved the *bourgeois* and the commune of Paris more than the nobles, and because of this he was saved, together with his wife and children'.[5] Son of a Paris innkeeper, since 1348 this influential politician had had letters

---

[4] Cazelles (1982). [5] *Chronographia Regum Francorum*, ed. Moranvillé, II, p. 273.

of ennoblement that would admit him to the ranks of the nobility. This was essential for political and social success. His renunciation, ten years later, did not last long. Once the crisis was past, Robert de Lorris resumed his title of knight, arranged a distinguished marriage for his son Jean (known as Lancelot), went hunting, and made full use of the judicial system to persecute his country neighbours – in short, he adopted all the attitudes and modes of behaviour characteristic of the noble lifestyle. Once the upheavals had passed, the nobles were once again the undisputed governing class in France, and nobility remained the focus of all social aspiration.

The critical years 1356–60 in fact saw the reputation of the nobility sink to its lowest, then quickly recover its political and military importance. Defeat, and especially the 'discomfiture' at Poitiers, provoked a violent, anti-noble reaction, which all fourteenth-century sources simply call the 'tumult of the non-nobles against the nobility'. This did not prevent a very typical group of the nobility under the energetic leadership of Archbishop Guillaume de Melun of Sens (1345–76) – the Cardinal Richelieu of the fourteenth century, as R. Cazelles called him – from playing a leading part in the council of John II and establishing a system of government which, whilst restructuring the kingdom, also restored the nobility to their pre-eminent political position.[6]

But was it the same position? Was it even the same nobility? The claims of the nobility to constitute an unalterable body, in which their unique social quality and political role were transmitted by blood, should not conceal the profound transformations which they were experiencing. Some of these were long-term changes which affected all of western Christendom. Falling revenues, the relative decline of vassalage in political terms and even the creation of orders of chivalry fall into this category, but others can be attributed to political decisions of the reigns of Charles V and Charles VI.

To appreciate the significance of these changes we must evaluate the place occupied by the nobles in French society in the middle of the fourteenth century. They comprised 1.5 to 2 per cent of the population, perhaps some 40,000 to 50,000 families, or between 200,000 and 250,000 individuals.[7] There was a strict internal hierarchy: a list of 1350 starts with the names of 350 *barons*, two dukes, twenty-seven counts, sixteen *vicomtes*, with the remainder simply classified as *sires*. The hierarchy thus distinguished a comital level and a baronial level below the princes of the blood, but there were other discriminatory factors: some *barons* had lands that formed a coherent territorial whole, while the holdings of others were scattered. This in turn affected their political role and decisions.

[6] Cazelles (1982).   [7] Contamine (1997), pp. 48–56.

Beneath them was the great mass of knights and squires, the petty nobility whose revenues and powers were both reduced in relation to earlier feudal levels. However, poverty was a spur to the ambitions of their sons and they formed a pool of service in Church and state, with a network of castles that criss-crossed the entire kingdom. As a social group, the nobility was more accessible than is generally believed. If an individual was no longer in a position to 'live nobly', he left the group; while newcomers continued to be admitted, in so far as the nobility remained the only social model for those who aspired to upward mobility.

Whatever its composition, in 1360 the nobility remained the framework within which the nation's military, political and social affairs were still conducted. It was this framework, shaken by military defeats, political crisis and, indeed, the brutal rise of the state, that had to be strengthened in the reigns of Charles V and Charles VI.

Crucial measures were taken in 1360 when John II returned from captivity, and the money for his ransom had to be found. Taken together, they formed a package with three main elements. First, there was the introduction of the *franc*, a strong gold coinage, which blighted the money markets but guaranteed high revenues and stable yields to those (notably lay and ecclesiastical lords), who received payments established in money of account. Monetary stability lasted until 1385, when a small devaluation aided recovery. The currency continued to deteriorate slowly until 1417, when crisis forced the king to return to the policy of currency debasement that provided most of his income between 1417 and 1422.

Secondly, direct taxation was established, with a fiscal system that remained essentially unaltered until 1380, and then survived with various alterations and controversies. Here, the most important aspect was the nobility's exemption from taxation. Despite both the precedent of the feudal aids, levied in four different contexts (one of which was the ransom of a lord) and the specific instructions for the collection of taxes in 1360 ('all of the king's subjects are bound to pay by the general custom of the kingdom'), the nobility paid nothing. Exemption was formally granted in 1363. And thirdly, there was a restriction in the number of officials in the royal administration, which symbolically halted the progress of the state.

In the reign of Charles V the military reconstruction of the kingdom, both defensive and with the army of reconquest, offered the nobility new opportunities, whilst giving them back their military vocation. There were nobles who held salaried positions as captains of towns and castellans of royal castles. Others were paid to guard their own castles. The nobles also had a place in the army of reconquest. They dominated the college of twelve councillors-general on the *fait des aides* which managed war finances. The noble's duty was henceforth, 'To serve the king in his wars', and soon afterwards simply, 'To serve the king' in any capacity whatsoever – at his court, in his councils or as one of his officials.

Thus noble status was refurbished with salaries, wages and, sometimes, by pensions that were granted to help nobles 'maintain their estate', so that they might continue to participate in the war, as well as by individual gifts rewarding specific services or acts of loyalty. 'To live off his own', that is solely from the income derived from his lands and lordships, was rare amongst Charles V's noble subjects, although poets might declare that 'service at court is no inheritance', 'I wish for nothing more than to live off my own', sighed Eustache Deschamps though he knew perfectly well that, far from the service of the king, he would be able to do no more than go and kick his heels (*manger ses poreaux*).[8]

The example of Guy de la Trémoille sums it all up. He died on crusade at Nicopolis in 1396. Dino Rapondi, the Italian merchant responsible for his financial affairs, estimated that the revenue from his lands and lordships amounted annually to 11,225 *francs*, but in addition, the pensions, wages and gifts that Guy received from the king, the pope and the duke of Burgundy guaranteed him an income of 29,060 *francs* a year.

Royal policy did not only put the nobility on a secure financial footing. It also had a moral dimension, to which each of the three kings of the period made his own distinctive contribution, sketched in the following examples. In 1352 John II founded the Order of the Star. This was not to last (it disappeared in the aftermath of the disastrous defeat at Poitiers), but the king had intended it to be both a response to the English creation of the Order of the Garter (1348) and as a means of rallying the knights of the kingdom around the king and the crown.

Charles V, however, was concerned with improving the political education of the nobility and providing them with a theoretical knowledge of political theory. Why else did he have so many translations made from Latin to French? And why did he establish his famous library in the Louvre, if not for the use of his family, court, household and council? As for Charles VI, from the outset of his personal reign, he exalted noble values, adopting devices and liveries, selecting colours and a symbolic badge that was worn by everyone at his court. There could be nothing more noble than the emblem of the crowned winged hart (*cerf volant*) which he chose on 17 September 1381, the first anniversary of his accession.

The nobility were in power from the time of Charles V, with the king's help, but also in his service. And this same service necessitated changes to the

---

[8] Eustache Deschamps, *Œuvres complètes*, I, p. 148.

political structure of society, which made themselves acutely felt in the reign
of Charles VI.

SERVANTS OF THE KING: TOWARDS A BUREAUCRATIC STATE

Like that of the nobility, the history of state officials must be viewed in a long
perspective. Nevertheless, the reigns of Charles V and Charles VI constitute a
crucial phase in the construction of a 'bureaucratic state', with some stages that
can be specifically dated.

Thus in 1360 the ordinance 'restricting the number of officials' checked the
progressive bureaucracy of the state. It fixed the numbers of the central
administration. The idea of an excessively large number of officials was so well
entrenched that, with the help of reforming ordinances, it proved possible to
adhere to this minimum for a century, but it meant employing auxiliaries and
watching as the Paris *parlement* (which had been overtaken by its own success)
became incapable of judging the stream of cases which poured into it within
a reasonable period. More could not have been expected from the scant
hundred or so councillors of the *parlement*, who gave between 100 and 150
judgements, year in, year out; besides seeing to a multitude of other tasks. The
sum total of officials in the central administration was less than 250 (excluding
the taxation system, which had always been considered an exception, with its
own administration).

The concept of election, or choice, was new in the reign of Charles V, and
it no doubt originated with the king himself. Practised by the Church, extolled
by the learned readers and translators of Aristotle and Cicero, election was
believed to reveal to the king the best candidate, the one who would be 'good
and most fitting', 'suitable and appropriate'. Moreover, it reinforced the stability of the team in power under Charles V, and acknowledged the existence of
a class of royal servants under Charles VI. In 1372 Charles V had the chancellor of France chosen by a plenary assembly of the council, just as he had had
Bertrand du Guesclin elected constable. But the Paris *parlement* had been electing its presidents since 1366, whilst from 1391 it also regularly elected its councillors. *Parlement* was the undisputed model for the whole bureaucratic world,
and thus official elections became standard practice. The ordinance of the
Cabochiens which prescribed it in 1413 was in no sense innovatory. The enthusiasm for elections lasted from 1370 until 1420 because public opinion, which
now demanded higher standards of public service, expected the council to
make an enlightened choice – a safer means of appointment than the king's
favour, which was always open to 'those making importunate demands'.

The work of the 'Marmosets' during Charles VI's few years of personal
government was a significant period for the machinery of the state. Each

institution was provided with precise regulations designed to improve its efficiency. Above all, a collection of measures established the real status of public office. Two persons were distinguished in the royal official, the private and the public persona, the latter henceforth given royal protection when he was engaged 'in the exercise of his duties', absolved of responsibility for his deeds when he acted on behalf of the king. No official could be removed from office (which began to be irrevocable) 'without having been given a hearing', unless he had committed a crime.[9]

Re-enforcement of the administrative hierarchy went hand in hand with a concern for efficiency and a sense of group identity and common purpose. This served to bind together men whose unity was built only on their devotion to public service. The Marmosets and their followers turned public service into an almost mystical ideal, witness the masses they stipulated in their wills, not only for the king and his lineage, but also for the government, the king's council, for *parlement* and for the state.

'You are the royal clergy', the papal legate told the lawyers of the *parlement* in 1416.[10] A clergy, in the sense of a group of people with a ministry to exercise, was certainly an apt description of the king's officials. It has already been observed that their evolution into a social group was – like that of the nobility – a long and gradual process. But the years 1380 to 1420 were an important period, when the king's officials could be said to constitute a social group, but did not yet constitute a social 'estate'.

The king's officials were not in themselves sufficiently numerous to constitute one themselves. But they were the kernel around which others gathered – the personnel of urban and seigneurial administrations (lay or ecclesiastical), and all those involved in the administration of justice, advocates, proctors and notaries, as well as the clerks who worked for them. Administrators, lawyers and financial officials shared a common culture (dominated by canon and civil law), activities and sources of income, besides their language – or rather their Franco-Latin bilingualism (and what Latin! 'Plain Latin . . . for a secular friend' – *Latinum grossum . . . pro laïcis amicum* – an old councillor recommended to the *parlement*).[11]

This group was characterised above all by dynamism in the reign of Charles VI. Intellectual dynamism, because the turn of the fourteenth century saw the first appearance of humanism in Paris, emerging in those departments of the chancery which were in close contact with the Italian towns and the papal chancery. Then there was the economic dynamism of a group which did not lack money, since their income (in the form of salaries, wages, pensions and gifts) took the form of cash payments. There was too evident social

[9] Autrand (1969), pp. 314–19.   [10] Ibid., pp. 324–31.   [11] Guilhiermoz, *Enquêtes et procès*, p. 198.

dynamism, as these families climbed higher. In short, there was nothing static about this world, accessible through study, work and professional efficiency and offering great opportunities for social advancement. Too great, some thought. For many viewed these new arrivals with a baleful eye. There was criticism throughout this period of these 'Marmosets' or 'Mahomets', favourites who had risen as a result of the king's approval. Such individuals could only have climbed so high at the expense of the old noble families, who had been ruined by war and political crises. The political crisis caused fortune's wheel to turn once more, so that those who had incurred most criticism for their social rise fell fatally: Jean de Bétizac, Jean de Montaigue and Pierre des Essars among others.

According to the ordinance of 1345, there were about a hundred officials, presidents, councillors, clerks, notaries and ushers in the *parlement* of Paris. Their history reflects the rhythm and the process of the creation of a *parlement*-centred social grouping. Before the end of the century the length and stability of their careers transformed the *parlement* into a body of professional administrators of royal justice.

An increasingly tight network of alliances and relationships stretched across the court. In 1345 one councillor in three was related to another member of the court (past, present or future). In 1418 the proportion had risen to 70 per cent. The Cabochien reformers of 1413 thundered that the first president, Henri de Marle, had relatives in the *parlement*. However, it was not only a question of sharing the advantages of high position in a family. Family ties and alliances strengthened by marriage helped them to resist external pressure, made up for inadequately defined hierarchical ties and, in short, contributed to the better functioning of the court. In the time of Charles VI each president was surrounded by a nucleus of loyal followers. Nevertheless, there was always space for new men. For accessibility is a prime characteristic of a milieu founded upon talent.

Finally, there was a group identity. In order to ensure itself and to ensure that the requirements of public service were met, *parlement* had to break old alliances. Local loyalties were most resistant, when there was rivalry between princes. But the court countered the pressure exerted by territorial princes with its uncompromising dignity and unity. And thus it formed the first great body within the state.

It was as a body that the lawyers of the *parlement* embarked on the conquest of privileges that had hitherto belonged only to the nobility: noble inheritance customs, priority of access to ecclesiastical benefices and fiscal exemption, which were acquired gradually between 1398 and 1411. This was all demanded – and obtained – in the name of the king's service. As a result the lawyers of the *parlement* enjoyed a status very close to nobility. Can we legitimately talk of an 'official' or 'robe' nobility at this period? Did the king's officers constitute a new estate within society as a whole?

It is impossible to make a clear-cut distinction between office and nobility, since so many nobles were employed in the king's service. Financial positions were generally held by *bourgeois*, business men with the money to advance loans. But military positions and the posts of *bailli* and *sénéchal* generally had a majority who were members of the nobility, and there were very substantial numbers in the legal departments. The composition of the *parlement* included 60 per cent noble in 1345, 43 per cent in 1384, but 55 per cent once more in 1398, and this level was maintained until the crisis of 1418.

Some were more noble than others, however. Some councillors of the *parlement* came from the old nobility. Towards the end of the fourteenth century, contemporary texts began to distinguish such men, who were called 'of military descent' (*de militari genere*) or 'of noble descent through both parents' (*ex utroque parente de nobili genere procreati*), from the great majority of those who had been ennobled and their sons. The origin of this nobility lay far in the past, but it was obscure. They belonged to knightly families, now almost all impoverished, which at this same period also supplied most of the bishops of Paris, the Avignon popes and a fair number of their cardinals.

Beside the petty nobility, from the reign of Charles VI there was another pool of talent for the service of the state, as there was for that of the Church: the sons of parvenus, nephews of bishops or canons, descendants of those who had reached high positions and been ennobled because of their talent, in short those whom we call the new nobility, born in the service of the king. This was the sector that dominated the *parlement* at the end of the fourteenth century.

The rise of this new nobility did not pass unnoticed. At the beginning of the fifteenth century there was a heightened awareness of the old, chivalric nobility, together with a noble reaction against the non-noble and, above all, against the recently ennobled. But in the service of the king these tensions did not cause a rift in the ancient cohesion of the nobility. The old framework cracked but held firm, and the official (or 'robe') nobility was not yet recognised as such.

Despite all these changes, despite the overwhelming role of the state in the definition, privileges, functions and resources of the nobility, French society in the time of Charles V and Charles VI had not yet seen the dawn of a new ruling class.

KINGDOM AND PRINCIPALITIES

One aspect of the system of government established in the 1360s demands particular scrutiny, and that is the decentralising tendency reflected in the creation of three apanages for the sons of John II: Louis, duke of Anjou; John, duke of Berry; then Philip, duke of Burgundy. They were the origin of the territorial principalities that were to be such a heavy liability in the course of the fifteenth century and such a drain upon French social and political structures for very much longer.

Their origin lay in the development of the great lordships that had started at the end of the thirteenth century, at least of those which constituted coherent geographical entities as territorial principalities. This was the case with the duchy of Brittany and the county of Flanders and, at a lower level, of the county of Forez. These principalities had a good number of the attributes of the state. One, however, was always lacking: the unquestionable right to levy direct taxes though it was usurped by the duke of Brittany. Admittedly, the princes with apanages had a share of the money raised by royal taxation. In this way royal policy speeded up the evolution of the territorial principalities during the reigns of Charles V and Charles VI to such an extent that the old feudal order was completely overturned. With the exception of Burgundy, the apanages were based on gathering together some old lordships, given the status of duchies held by peers in liege homage from the sovereign. They differed from old feudal custom in that, like the kingdom of France, they were indivisible, and they could not be inherited by women or collaterals.

Since John II's policy was not only maintained under Charles V and Charles VI but extended to the duchy of Orléans and even of Bourbon, the feudal geography of the kingdom was completely changed. From Brittany to Burgundy large and strongly consolidated principalities were inserted between the two large blocks of the royal domain, from Champagne to Normandy in the north, and the Languedoc in the south.

The princes were the king's natural counsellors, but also represented their subjects in the central administration. They thus wielded considerable influence on the direction of the kingdom. But at the same time they either introduced the apparatus of the modern state into their own territories (or speeded up its introduction), with an efficient administration and a fair legal system that included the possibility of appeal. Their capitals and courts brought new life to towns in these provinces. Many members of the petty nobility were attracted to their service – as they were to that of the king – where they found wages, pensions, gifts and profit.

This was undoubtedly a type of decentralisation, strongly promoted by the monarch. Since the reign of Charles V, the princes of the blood – thanks to the king – enjoyed much higher levels of income than other dukes or counts. In the years 1375–80 the dukes of Berry and Burgundy spent around 80,000 *livres* a year, while the richest of the counts had no more than 20,000 to 25,000 *livres*.

In the reign of Charles VI, between 1390 and 1410 (years of relative prosperity and heavy taxation), the princes made even greater inroads. For the single year 1404–5 Louis of Orléans received 400,000 *livres*, 90 per cent of his revenues, from the king. The previous year the duke of Burgundy received 185,300 *livres*. It was thus in no way surprising that the apanagist principalities absorbed so many *comtés* because of the financial difficulties that plagued them and which caused so many ancient feudal houses to disappear to the profit of the duke of Orléans or the prolific house of Burgundy.

The case of the duke of Berry demonstrates the way in which the system worked. When he left for London as a hostage in 1360, he received Berry and the Auvergne as an apanage. Charles V added Poitou in 1369. But in 1369 Berry and the Auvergne were pillaged by companies of freebooters, and Poitou was devastated by the English in the same year. The prince was thus initially fully occupied with the pacification of his lands and with reconquest. Charles VI's minority and, later, his illness placed the duke of Berry, with the other princes, at the head of the government. John of Berry was an active supporter of the progress of the state, inclined more towards efficient administration than dialogue with his subjects. He played a role in the imposition of permanent taxation, while the royal administration was full of his men. In his apanage he set up a modern administration and established a court (the *grands jours*) for appeal court hearings, as well as a *chambre des comptes* at Bourges (1370). Bourges, Poitiers and Riom, with their palaces and Saintes-Chapelles, their courts, merchants, artists and clerics, acquired the status of regional capitals.

The cost of these policies was borne by royal finances, and this, combined with disagreements over the government of the kingdom, dragged the old duke into the turmoil of inter-princely rivalry and civil war. But when Berry died without a son in 1416, his apanage reverted to the dauphin, the future Charles VII. In 1418 Charles found the institutional structures and human resources there that enabled him to constitute a government and an administration in the kingdom of Bourges within the space of two months.

The constitution of the 'Burgundian states' and their expansion outside the frontier of the French kingdom was the result of action by the French king. In 1361, John II declared himself rightful heir to the Burgundian inheritance. It was Charles V, on his accession, however, who ignored the principle of the inalienability of the royal domain and invested his brother Philip with the duchy. Philip's marriage in 1369 to Margaret of Flanders (heiress to the county of Flanders, to Artois and to the county of Burgundy) was a great diplomatic coup. There was an exchange of personnel between king and prince, *chambres des comptes* were established at Dijon and at Ghent (1386), legal cases were sent from the duchy of Burgundy to the *parlement* of Paris, all evidence of the close relations between sovereign and prince.

When the duke of Burgundy made heavy inroads into royal finances or John the Fearless played a leading part in reform, they had no thought of destroying the monarchy. When the county of Flanders continued along the path which had detached it inexorably from the kingdom of France for the last century, it was no fault of the duke. Nor was he to blame if the territorial expansion towards the Low Countries and around the duchy and county of Burgundy, that started with John the Fearless and was completed largely under Philip the Good, ended by making the 'Burgundian' lordships into something very like an independent state.

The expression 'from lordship to state' is particularly appropriate for the duchy of Brittany. With a duke who supported the English and with strongly marked national features, it scarcely seemed possible when Charles V became king that Brittany could still be part of the kingdom. 'My nation and my country', declared of Brittany the Breton-born constable of France and enemy of the Montfort duke, Bertrand du Guesclin. Breton national feeling, based on historical tradition and with distinctive religious characteristics, was an indisputable reality. When Charles V confiscated the duchy from John IV in 1378 and attempted to annex it to the royal domain, the move was opposed by all Bretons, even the Penthièvre family (previously rivals for the ducal throne) and their supporters.

The death of Charles de Blois, killed at the battle of Auray in 1364, and the second Treaty of Guérande of 1381, assured the duchy conclusively for the Montforts. Brittany then pursued a policy of neutrality towards England and France, as well as autonomy within the duchy, which was more rigorously independent of the French king in its finances, legal system and religious policy than any other. Nevertheless, the royal model was adopted in Brittany as elsewhere. Was it not John V who went so far as to style himself duke 'by the grace of God' in 1417? And throughout the period Bretons themselves remained strongly attracted by the French king and his court, army and official appointments.

The history of the principalities had not yet been brought to a close in 1422. Could any one then have imagined that, less than a century later, they would have disappeared and been absorbed without trace into the royal domain? Towns and social structures, institutions and associations, palaces and the churches founded within their confines – all the foundations of active provincial life – would survive. The reigns of Charles V and Charles VI saw their establishment.

The history of the kingdom did not come to an end in 1422, despite the contemporaries who abandoned all hope and foretold its imminent destruction. We are in a position to appreciate, as they could not, that – despite the political and economic disasters – there was continual, if imperceptible, progress in social and institutional structures.

THE ITALIAN NORTH

John Law

THE EXPEDITION OF HENRY VII

ON 23 October 1310, the emperor-elect, Henry of Luxemburg, completed his crossing of the Alps.[1] A principal reason for his expedition was to receive an imperial coronation in Rome; he was also determined to recover his rights within the kingdom of Italy, a constituent part of the western empire whose frontiers encompassed much of the north of the peninsula. Connected to both aims was a desire to achieve a general pacification of his Italian lands. But that task was formidable. The area had no recent tradition of centralised let alone imperial rule. It was composed of a mosaic of lordships (*signorie*) and communes, protective of their autonomy while generally jealous of their neighbours. Rivalries had economic roots: the control of land and the trade routes within the region which connected it with the rest of Europe and the Mediterranean. They also had a political dimension polarised around allegiances which made up in ferocity and tenacity what they lacked in consistent ideological content. The Ghibellines looked to the empire and its Italian allies for support and justification. The Guelfs allied themselves with the papacy whose leading protagonists in Italy were the commune of Florence and the Angevins, who as well as being counts of Provence and kings of Naples, had lands in Piedmont. And not only did these allegiances express divisions within the region and Italy as a whole; they were also linked to factions struggling for ascendancy within individual cities.

Henry had no experience of Italy, and the impression given by some contemporary sources and later historians is of a rather naive and anachronistic idealist. Yet the empire north of the Alps was hardly untroubled and the contemporary evidence, and most obviously the records of the imperial chancery, reveals a man of conscientiousness, energy and determination. In the spring of 1310 he had despatched an embassy to announce his expedition, seek

---

[1] Bowsky (1960); Tosti Croce (1993).

support, urge reconciliation and gauge reactions. He carried out protracted negotiations to gain the blessing of Clement V; the pope's support was expressed in an encyclical of 1 September 1310. Finally, Henry did not come as a usurper, invader or conqueror, but as a legitimate ruler who evidently believed in his role as a peacemaker.

Initially Henry's expedition appeared remarkably successful. His ambassadors had nowhere been rebuffed. If some Guelf regimes – notably in Milan – had been cautious, elsewhere their response had appeared co-operative. Henry himself was welcomed en route, and his programme to return exiles and effect public reconciliation between enemies was generally implemented. In some cities – Asti and Milan – he initiated sweeping reforms involving the revision of statutes, and more generally he despatched imperial vicars to preside over communal governments. His coronation in San Ambrogio, Milan, at Epiphany 1311 – the royal cult of the Magi was strong in the city – was well attended. On 14 January 1311 he appointed his cousin, Count Amedeo of Savoy, as vicar-general of Lombardy and a massive levy of 300,000 florins was distributed between the northern cities. A series of rebellions beginning in Milan on 12 February and spreading to other cities was led by Guelf leaders alarmed at the implications of such policies; in general these revolts were stilled by reconciliation.

But Henry's successes were superficial. Chroniclers close to events admitted to the fickle nature of Italian politics and underlined the hostility of many lords. Guido della Torre, the leader of the Guelf faction in Milan – and of the Guelf cause in Lombardy – had made friendly overtures to Henry before he had crossed the Alps; he then showed himself to be a more reluctant subject. Exiled for his involvement in the revolt of 12 February, he refused to be reconciled to the emperor-elect. Even the Ghibelline della Scala of Verona, though fulsome in their expressions of loyalty and ready to provide political and military support, pursued their own interests: they refused to allow their own Guelf exiles to return to Verona. More generally Henry's anxiety to secure the return of exiles appeared to favour the Ghibelline cause: on his arrival in Italy most of the northern regimes had been Guelf in alignment. Again, some of his policies were unrealistic: shares in the levy of 300,000 florins were assigned to cities like Venice which had no intention of paying them. The appointment of outsiders as imperial vicars could be ill-judged especially when they appeared partisan and politically tactless.

In the face of opposition, Henry found it increasingly difficult to maintain the role of 'king of peace' asked of him by Clement V, and which he had set himself. When the rebel city of Cremona surrendered on 26 April 1311 he did not forgive the citizens but razed their gates and walls, revoked their privileges, assigned the *contado* (the city's rural jurisdiction) to direct imperial administration and imposed a massive penalty. The need for allies and for military and financial assistance forced him to look increasingly to local lords, selling the title of imperial vicar to such Ghibellines as Matteo Visconti of Milan (July 1311) and opportunistic Guelfs like Riccardo da Cammino of Treviso (May 1311).

The more overtly partisan nature of Henry's actions, combined with the threat he posed to communal autonomy and the position of Guelf lords, roused the Guelf cause in the north as well as the alarm of Florence, convincing that city of the need to thwart Henry's progress and to win allies in Italy and abroad. The siege of Brescia (May to September 1311) was a trial of strength between Henry and the growing Guelf opposition, and its successful outcome for the emperor-elect proved a pyrrhic victory in terms of loss of life and political momentum. It also revealed Henry's military and financial precariousness; when he moved to Pavia to hold an imperial diet in October, it was feared that he would be held captive by that city's barely loyal Guelf lord, Count Filippo Langusco.

However, at Pavia Henry was urged to extend his efforts at pacification to Genoa. The politics of that commune were dominated by powerful aristocratic clans. Their clash of interests may have prevented the seizure of signorial power by any one dynasty, but it also prompted the *popolani* – families of newer wealth and political influence – to demand a share in government, as well as encouraging foreign powers to seek allies and clients in the city. The opening years of the century had seen an uneasy truce between Bernabo Doria and Opizzano Spinola, related respectively to the Visconti of Milan and the marquis of Montferrat. However in 1309 Opizzano had sought to rule as rector and captain-general for life. This provoked a coalition which had driven him into exile, but he returned in the entourage of the emperor-elect on 21 October 1311.

As had happened on Henry's arrival in Italy, the prestige of his office, the yearning for peace and political patronage – the Doria hosted Henry and were allowed the privilege of adding the imperial eagle to their arms – brought him early success. After discussions with leading nobles and guildsmen Henry received the homage of Genoa and its lordship for twenty years on 14 November. However, the disintegrating situation in the north, the mounting hostility of the Guelfs led by Florence and the need to press on to Rome ensured that his impact on Genoese government would be brief. He left the city on 16 February 1312, and although he did achieve a Roman coronation his death quickly confirmed the collapse of his work in the north.

FOREIGN INTERVENTION

In most respects Henry's intervention in Italy must be judged a failure: the revival of the Ghibelline cause – notably with the victory of the Visconti over their della Torre rivals in Milan – led to an intensification of faction.[2] However, the hopes and fears aroused by his expedition inspired a generation of chroniclers and political thinkers, most notably the Florentine Dante Alighieri (1265–1321). And for the historian, the events of 1310–13 illustrate many of the themes that characterise northern Italy in the fourteenth century.

Perhaps the most obvious is that of foreign intervention. In general terms, this can be explained by the region's wealth, its strategic position and its internal political divisions. However, more specific political reasons can also be identified. The region's status as part of an imperial kingdom and the fact that it controlled the routes necessary for a Roman coronation help to account for the intervention of imperial claimants, their supporters and their opponents. In the century following the expedition of Henry VII, five imperial candidates entered the peninsula in person: Lewis IV (1314–47); his rival Frederick of Habsburg (1314–30); his successor Charles IV (1347–78); Robert of Bavaria count of the Palatinate (1400–10); Sigismund (1410–36).

There were also other interested powers. Pope John XXII (1316–34) refused to recognise the claims of Lewis IV, and in 1317 he assigned himself the kingdom of Italy *vacatio imperii*. To make good this claim, he used spiritual weapons; he was also prepared to intervene militarily and to enlist the support of others, notably Robert of Anjou (1278–1343). If the Habsburgs failed in their imperial aspirations, in this century, they did make territorial and jurisdictional gains in the peninsula. On 26 January 1363 Rudolf IV secured the succession to the Tyrol and with it the hereditary advocacy of the sees of Bressanone and Trent. The appointment of his chancellor to Trent in the same year led to the dynasty acquiring most of the bishop's temporal jurisdiction in the Trentino.[3]

Again foreign powers entered the peninsula as the protectors and allies of Italian communes and rulers. In 1319 Treviso and Padua recognised the overlordship of Frederick of Habsburg to thwart the territorial ambitions of Cangrande I della Scala, lord of Verona.[4] When John, king of Bohemia, entered Italy in December 1330 – initially as an ally of Lewis IV – a large number of Lombard cities accepted his lordship. In 1396 Genoa surrendered to Charles VI of France, seeking protection from Giangaleazzo Visconti, duke of Milan. Earlier, Giangaleazzo had allied with France. The marriage agreed on 8 April 1387 between Louis, duke of Orléans, and Valentina, Giangaleazzo's daughter – and at that point his heir – brought with it the city of Asti as part of the dowry, but also the prospect of the Visconti inheritance.

---

[2] Cipolla (1881); Valeri (1949), pp. 1–326; Simeoni (1950), I, pp. 1–223; Valeri (1959); Fondazione Treccani degli Alfieri (1954–5); Partner (1972), pp. 266–383.
[3] Stella (1979a), pp. 512–3.   [4] Varanini (1991), pp. 181–3; Riedmann (1991), pp. 243–67.

Lastly, some north Italian states were powers on the European stage and attracted the hostility of foreign powers. Venetian ambitions to dominate the Adriatic brought the city into conflict with Hungary over Dalmatia. In 1357 Hungarian armies overran the region, forcing the republic to surrender its territories, including the city of Zara (Zadar), and the doge to renounce his ancient title of duke of Dalmatia (1358).[5] Later Hungary joined a coalition that briefly blockaded Venice in the War of Chioggia (1378–81), forcing the republic to cede territory in Istria and mainland Italy. In 1391, in an attempt to check the lord of Milan, Florence enlisted John III, count of Armagnac, though his expedition ended in defeat at Alessandria (25 July). In 1401 Robert of Bavaria entered Italy in Florentine pay to face defeat by the Visconti at Brescia (24 October).

Although both the count of Armagnac and Robert of Bavaria justified their actions by representing Giangaleazzo as a usurper, both could also be regarded as titled mercenary leaders, as *condottieri*, and another consequence of the wealthy but divided state of northern Italy was an influx of foreign soldiers.[6] Some came with the expeditions referred to above. Others were invited to fight in the peninsula. Some came looking for employment after the Peace of Brétigny brought a temporary halt to the Hundred Years War (1360). Thus in 1361 the marquis of Montferrat hired the White Company of Albert Sterz made up of various nationalities, veterans of the wars in France. Undoubtedly the impact of these battle-hardened professionals with few local loyalties could be considerable. Leagues were periodically formed against them. Chroniclers routinely lamented their activities, and those of the far more numerous Italian *condottieri*.[7] A few military leaders attained fame and fortune, notably the Englishman Sir John Hawkwood (d. 1394). But their numbers, discipline and political support were never strong enough to make a lasting impact, and the same could be said for most of the foreign powers that entered the region: few had the resources or the political will to establish permanent rule.

This was also true of crowned and aspiring emperors. Lewis IV has been characterised as a mercenary in the pay of the Ghibelline cause and before leaving Italy – never to return – in 1329, he was virtually bereft of political support. Charles IV was much more skilful and pragmatic, using his office to sell privileges and shrewdly exploiting political divisions to make territorial gains, though again only in the short term: before ascending the throne his support of an alliance against the della Scala had brought him Belluno and Feltre (1337–58).

Papal ambitions to exercise temporal dominion were never realised despite

---

[5] Lazzarini (1969), pp. 217–20.　　[6] Mallett (1974), pp. 25–50.
[7] Bueno da Mesquita (1941), pp. 187–205.

the expenditure of much effort and money, especially under John XXII. Grandiose ideas, encouraged by Giangaleazzo (1391–2) to end the Schism by establishing a French kingdom in the Papal States came to nothing, as did an alliance between Florence and France in 1396 to divide up the Visconti dominions. Unrest in Genoa brought French rule to an end in 1409, while Hungarian gains at the expense of Venice were reversed by 1420.[8]

INTERNAL DIVISIONS

Political division was another issue exposed, and intensified, by the expedition of Henry VII.[9] It was an issue that deeply concerned contemporaries, and partly for that reason apologists for Visconti expansion readily identified unity and concord as among the dynasty's aims and achievements. On a more religious and emotional level a wish for peace explains the enthusiastic response given to the penitential movement of the *Bianchi* in 1399. But the problem preoccupied contemporaries because it had no easy solution. Visconti attempts to ban party slogans other than those in support of the regime were tantamount to admissions of failure. The *Bianchi* had no lasting influence.

Faction could be intensely local, a struggle for power between rival families and their adherents, or *consorterie*, as was the case in Milan between the Visconti and the della Torre or in Asti between the Salario and da Castello. Faction could also acquire a regional character. This is not surprising. For all its diversity, northern Italy did not contain ethnic, linguistic, cultural and geographical entities of such divergence that internal 'natural' frontiers were created. Hence families and their followers driven into exile readily found allies and protectors elsewhere; the court of Cangrande I della Scala (1291–1329) was a magnet for Ghibelline exiles and a base from where they could plan their return to power. Furthermore, in the struggle for ascendancy within a city, external powers could become involved as they contrived to exploit the situation, or as their local allies sought their intervention, as was the case with the Visconti and the marquis of Montferrat in Vercelli in 1335. The ramifications of local confrontations can also be seen in the way parties tried to associate themselves with broader issues of principle – allegedly – to gather support and justify their partisan actions. Hence the ascendant families of late thirteenth-century Vicenza could brand their political opponents as heretics.[10] But much more common, notorious and long-lasting were groupings under the standards of Guelf and Ghibelline.

For many contemporary and near-contemporary observers these parties were themselves the cause of faction: hence the chronicler Pietro Azario

---

[8] Cusin (1937), I, pp. 251–315. [9] Above n. 2; Hyde (1993), pp. 58–86. [10] Carlotto (1993), pp. 24–5.

(1312–66) traced the origins of the terms to two devils, Gualef and Gibel. However, shrewd observers tended to see them as flags of convenience without any real ideological content or consistency. For example, in Book Ten of his *Chronicles* the Florentine Giovanni Villani drew his readers' attention to the fact that in 1332 Guelfs in Brescia allied with the traditionally Ghibelline della Scala to oust John of Bohemia from power, and with him his Ghibelline supporters. Villani went on to remark on how the principal Guelf powers of Italy – Robert of Anjou and Florence – were prepared to ally with the Ghibelline Visconti and della Scala to drive the Luxemburg ruler from his Italian lordships in that year. Among modern historians, the consensus sees the parties as representing patterns of political, military and even economic alliance, operating on both local and regional levels; it also sees these patterns as lacking any core ideological content.

However, if the battle cries of Guelf and Ghibelline were the symptoms rather than the original or fundamental cause of local faction and regional division, and if a narrative history of northern Italy is hard to construct, the situation was not so anarchic as to defy explanation. Foreign intervention was undoubtedly influential. In part related to this is the fact that the region lacked a sense of political unity.[11] It is true that the concept of the kingdom of Italy survived. It is also true that a sense of Italy existed as too did a sense of northern Italy as expressed in the term 'Lombardy'. But these ideas were largely the preserve of a few men of letters, and political leaders and their advisers, and they lacked sharp, consistent, definition: for some 'Lombardy' could embrace most of the north; for others it was a region among several.[12] Moreover, the concepts of Italy and Lombardy rarely shaped political action. The occasional leagues formed among north Italian states – to combat John of Bohemia or mercenary companies, for example – were never all-embracing or long-lasting.

Local loyalties were much more intensely felt and they can be seen to find expression in a number of ways. Rural communities, singly or in association, could seek to retain or extend their administrative, fiscal and juridical liberties. In some cases their autonomy was based on their strategic importance, as with the Val d'Aosta in the lands of the counts of Savoy. In others it was because of their economic significance; for example, the charcoal-producing region of the Montagna dei Tedeschi in the mountains north of Verona won privileges from the della Scala.[13] Sometimes the demand for privileges stemmed from

---

[11] Hay (1988), pp. 375–88.

[12] *Anonymi Ticinensis, RIS,* XI/1 (1903), p. 64; *Chronicon Veronense, RIS,* VIII (1726), p. 642; Dati, *Istoria di Firenze,* pp. 84–5; Azario, *RIS,* XVI/4 (1938), pp. 10–11; Cortusi, *RIS,* XII/5 (1941), pp. 78, 80; Lunig, *Codex Italiae Diplomaticus,* I, pp. 1365–72; Cipolla and Pellegrini, eds., 'Poesie minori', 75; Dante, *Paradiso,* IX, lines 25–7, 43–4.   [13] Law (1974), pp. 152–63, and (1981a), p. 7.

political and military circumstances. Savona hoped to detach itself from the lordship of Genoa by submitting to Louis of Orléans (1394).

Aspirations for greater autonomy form a major theme in the history of Trieste.[14] The city was wary of the commercial and political designs of Venice, and the republic's efforts to reinforce a direct lordship with the construction of a citadel (1371–7) provoked a rebellion and submission first to the patriarch of Aquileia (1380) and then, in 1382, to Leopold III of Austria. Habsburg rule in Italy was later criticised by irredentist historians, but in the late fourteenth century it allowed Trieste wide autonomy: it was not incorporated into the duchy; the dukes' powers of taxation were restricted; the city continued to be governed by its own statutes and officials.

Finally, if the search for autonomy was normally couched in the relatively formulaic language of petitions – when it did not become a matter for direct action – the desire for liberty could inspire poets, orators and preachers. For example, the Paduan lawyer, poet and historian Albertino Mussato (1261–1329) composed his *Ecerinide* (1311) to warn his fellow-citizens of the dangers of tyranny. In his epic poem, the contemporary threat posed by Cangrande I della Scala was thinly disguised in the person of Ezzelino III da Romano (1194–1259), an earlier expansionist tyrant in the March of Treviso. Such was the impact and relevance of the work that Padua rewarded Mussato with a laurel crown and ordered public readings of his poem.[15]

A still more engaged defence of communal liberty is provided by Pavia. For much of the first half of the century the commune was dominated by the Beccaria family, often as clients of the Visconti from neighbouring Milan. On 3 June 1355 Emperor Charles IV granted the vicariate of Pavia to Giovanni Palaeologus II, marquis of Montferrat as part of a grand strategy to weaken Visconti influence, but internally the city's fight for independence was led by an Augustinian friar, Jacopo Bussolari.[16] His passionate association of the issues of liberty with reform and his organisation of the city's defences won him the support of the marquis and the citizenry. It also earned him a rebuke from Petrarch – at that stage making his eloquence available to the Visconti – and the hostility of the Beccaria; in 1357 the clan was driven from the city, accused of corruption, treason and undermining Pavian liberty. However, as the Visconti came to terms with their adversaries, Pavia was left to fight alone. After a determined resistance it surrendered to Galeazzo II Visconti on 13 November 1359.

The fall of Pavia marked an important stage in the growth of Visconti

[14] Lazzarini (1910), pp. 229–36; Stella (1979a), pp. 500–9.
[15] Gianola (1984), pp. 201–36; Avesani (1988), p. 507; Berrigan (1990), pp. 67–80.
[16] Novati (1904), pp. 59–61; *DBI*, xv, pp. 580–2; Ceriotti (1972–3), pp. 3–34.

power, and it serves to introduce a final major reason for the instability of northern Italian history: the urge to expand. There are several explanations for this. As mentioned, the region was not clearly divided by natural frontiers; rather, its rivers, lakes and passes encouraged communications. Secondly, exiles could encourage a ruler's ambitions: Paduan exiles joined the campaigns of Cangrande I which eventually led to the fall of that city in 1328. Again, rural communities and cities could opt for the lordship of one foreign ruler in preference to another: in 1387 Vicenza surrendered to Giangaleazzo Visconti rather than to the Carrara of neighbouring Padua. But more fundamentally expansion is to be explained in terms of strategic and economic interests. A classic case here is provided by Venice, which had trade routes vital to its prosperity – indeed to its survival – to defend. The republic was not always successful. A war initiated in 1308 to dominate Ferrara near the mouth of the Po ended in costly and humiliating defeat (1313). However, from 1388 the republic embarked on a series of campaigns which led to considerable territorial gains, in Italy, Istria and Dalmatia.[17]

FORMS OF GOVERNMENT: THE *SIGNORIE*

A final characteristic of northern Italy revealed by Henry VII's expedition is the number of regimes in place, and their variety in terms not only of size and wealth but also of forms of government. Three types can be identified: ecclesiastical and lay principalities, feudal in origin; communes ruled by republican forms of government affording participation to privileged citizens; lordships or *signorie*. The last have often been represented as the antithesis of the second where a 'despot' abruptly and violently deprives a commune of its liberty. But this view obscures the fact that most communal regimes were dominated by a few families vying for ascendancy, that forms of lordship can be found well before this period and that in the fourteenth century *signorie* represented the most prevalent form of government in northern Italy.[18]

Among the *signorie* it is possible to discern two principal forms. Some lordships remained predominantly rural in character; others came to dominate the major cities of the region. Of the former, some had ancient origins; such were the Pallavicini with castles, lands and jurisdictions in the territories of Parma, Piacenza and Cremona. The division of the family inheritance was a weakening factor, and they never achieved the political prominence in Lombardy of the Visconti; yet alliance with that family, charters from their

---

[17] Cozzi and Knapton (1986), pp. 3–48.

[18] Jones (1965), pp. 71–96; Waley (1978), pp. 133–40; Law (1981b). Philip Jones's latest (1997), major, contribution to this subject appeared after this chapter was written.

immediate overlord Charles IV and the ability of some family members – Manfredino 'the Pious' (1254–1328) and Uberto (1302–78) – helped to preserve a *stato Pallavicino* into the fifteenth century.[19]

Other rural lordships date from the period itself. The dal Verme rose to prominence as soldiers and administrators of the della Scala of Verona, receiving lands, offices and privileges from Cangrande I and his immediate successors. A branch of the family was exiled in 1354, only to be rewarded by the Visconti with lordships in the territories of Piacenza and Parma, the basis of the *stato Vermesco* of the following century. Back in della Scala favour from 1377, the able *condottiere* Giacomo was confirmed in his Veronese holdings, which were later sanctioned by imperial diplomas (1387) and added to by subsequent governors of Verona, Giangaleazzo Visconti (1387–1402) and the republic of Venice (from 1405).[20]

The city-orientated *signori* also drew much strength from estates and retainers in the *contado*. Their rise to prominence in general took place in the late thirteenth and early fourteenth centuries and represented the victory of a party or faction leaders. To hostile contemporaries, and through them to later historians prepared to exaggerate the democratic credentials of communal regimes, these figures often appear as tyrants.[21] There are many reasons for this; generally they were usurpers, seizing power without the immediate sanction of their rightful overlord, empire or papacy, and at the expense of the communal governments they came to dominate. Their rise was often violent and accompanied by the exile of opponents. Their policies were frequently expansionist, further challenging imperial and papal interests as well as other Italian regimes. Internally, their government could be shaped by party interest and a disregard for the common good. Finally, as individuals some of the *signori* appeared as wilful, unstable and dangerous figures.

Many of these features appear to characterise the Visconti who came to power in 1311 after a prolonged struggle with the della Torre. These aggressively Ghibelline *tiranelli* attracted the hostility of John XXII. Tried *in absentia* and excommunicated in 1322, the long list of charges brought against Matteo and Galeazzo Visconti included heresy and seeking the services of the necromancer Dante Alighieri to kill the pope. Later in the century, the expansionism of Giangaleazzo caused alarm in Florence and elsewhere, resulting in a propaganda war against him and charges that ranged from seeking the lordship of all Italy, to betraying the crusade of 1397, to poisoning his enemies.[22]

[19] Litta (1819–99), v, tavola xvi; Nasalli Rocca (1968), pp. 65–113; Chittolini (1981), pp. 591–676.

[20] *DBI* (1986), pp. 279–81; Varanini (1988a), pp. 198–203, and (1988b), pp. 65–81.

[21] Ercole (1929); *Enciclopedia Italiana* (1949), XXXI, pp. 754–60; Simeoni (1946), pp. 413–54; Baron (1955); Sestan (1961), pp. 41–69; Lanza (1991).

[22] Biscaro (1920), pp. 446–81; Romano (1894), pp. 309–60; Besozzi (1981), pp. 235–45.

But perhaps the member of the dynasty who appeared the most controversial was his uncle Bernabò. His apparently savage and unbalanced understanding of justice classed him as a tyrant. His occasional humiliation and brutal treatment of members of the clergy made him an enemy of the Church. His elevated vision of his own authority – seen most dramatically in his commission *c.* 1364 of an equestrian statue of himself to be placed above and behind the high altar of S. Giovanni in Conca near his palace in Milan – earned him the charge of idolatory.[23] The picture of tyranny he presented to hostile contemporaries seemed confirmed when he was dramatically arrested by his nephew on 6 May 1385; Giangaleazzo sought to justify his action by listing Bernabò's evil deeds.[24]

However as Giangaleazzo's exercise in propaganda suggests there is another side to the *signori* which balances the hostile picture created by their eloquent enemies in Avignon, Florence and elsewhere. Some ascendant families had no title to rule like the Beccaria of Pavia in the early fourteenth century, but many signorial dynasties sought a title to legitimise their government. They turned first to the communes over which they ruled, and although it would be a mistake to see their election as genuine and spontaneous, the acceptance of communal authority as a source of legitimacy, linked to the survival of communal institutions, encouraged historians like Ercole to describe this type of government as a diarchy, with traditional forms and ideas existing with the new.[25] Thereafter, the *signori* sought vicariates from their overlords, generally from the empire but also from the papacy; hence Matteo Visconti acquired the vicariate of Lombardy in 1294 and that of Milan in 1311. Thirdly, as their power became more entrenched so they sought to acquire a princely or courtly style.[26] And at the same time, growing numbers of political thinkers and historians began to accommodate the *signori* into accepted categories of government no longer seeing them as aberrations.[27] Related to this is the fact that established dynasties began to employ their own propagandists to sing their praises and justify their actions.[28]

In the eyes of such writers Giangaleazzo is a peacemaker in his own grateful dominions and in Italy as a whole. He is a deliverer, a Messiah-like figure, or a new Caesar saving Italy from barbarian foreign armies.[29] Indeed, even his uncle could be presented in a positive light. The Florentine poet and novelist Francesco Sacchetti, who certainly saw Bernabò as a cruel and warmongering tyrant, could also represent him as a generous accessible ruler, concerned for

---

[23] Cognasso (1922), pp. 121–3.   [24] *Annales Mediolanenses, RIS*, XVI (1730), pp. 784–801.

[25] Ercole (1910); De Vergottini (1941), pp. 41–64; Cognasso (1955), pp. 78–89.

[26] Green (1990), pp. 98–113; Kirsch (1991); Varanini (1994), pp. 311–43.

[27] Canning (1987), pp. 209, 221–3; Green (1993), pp. 335–51.

[28] Cipolla and Pellegrini, 'Poesie minori', pp. 5–206; Lanza (1991).   [29] Romano (1915), pp. 138–47.

the poor and guided by a sense of justice. The anonymous Laments written after his abrupt fall, could represent him in sympathetic terms: once a great ruler, feared and respected in Italy and Europe, he had been brought low by the deceit of his nephew and the caprice of Fate.[30]

THE ECCLESIASTICAL PRINCIPALITIES OF TRENT AND AQUILEIA[31]

The bishop of Trent owed his secular authority, in an area of great strategic importance, to imperial grants. However, by the fourteenth century this authority had been severely compromised, by his own subjects and in particular by vassal dynasties like the Castelbarco. Their castles and lordships lay south of Trent in the valley of the Adige, and though members of the family held their fiefs from the bishop, they tended to pursue independent strategies as the allies, clients and *condottieri* of their neighbours further south: the della Scala of Verona; the Gonzaga of Mantua; the Visconti of Milan. But the clan was much fragmented and the bishop's authority was even more seriously compromised by the hereditary advocates of his see, the counts of the Tyrol. When George of Lichtenstein (1390–1419) tried to reduce comital influence, Frederick IV of Habsburg exploited unrest in Trent and the Trentino (1407–9) – itself another attempt to curtail episcopal authority – to intervene. Despite the protests of the papacy, the Council of Constance and Sigismund king of the Romans, the bishop was effectively stripped of all secular power.

In certain respects the situation was similar in the other ecclesiastical principality of northern Italy, the patriarchate of Aquileia.[32] Here too the prince-bishop owed his temporal authority to imperial investiture, but by the fourteenth century its extent had been reduced virtually to the region of Friuli in the face of aspirations for autonomy, as in the case of Trieste, and the territorial ambitions of other powers, for example of Venice in Istria. Even within Friuli the patriarchs had been compromised by their subjects: communes, principally Udine and Cividale; great feudal dynasties like the Savorgnan or the counts of Gorizia, the latter being advocates of the Church of Aquileia for most of the century. Finally, and again as in the case of Trent, the strategic importance of the patriarchate attracted the intervention of neighbouring and more distant powers, anxious to secure sympathetic appointments to the see. For example, three patriarchs were closely linked to the imperial house of Luxemburg: Nicola (1350–8) was half-brother of Charles IV; Marquardo di Randek (1365–81) had been imperial chancellor; Giovanni di Moravia

---

[30] Medin, 'La letteratura', pp. 568–81, and (1891), pp. 753–95; Conti, *Novella inedite*; Musatti, *Lamento*.

[31] Costa (1977), pp. 108–15; Stella (1979a), pp. 510–16.

[32] Joppi (1888); Cogo (1898), pp. 223–320; Cessi (1914), pp. 414–73; Cusin (1937), I, pp. 27–316; Seneca (1952); Leicht (1955), pp. 3–40; Paschini (1975), pp. 421–746; Corbanese (1984), pp. 217–40.

(1387–94) was Charles's nephew. On Giovanni's assassination – the consequence of a vendetta with the Savorgnan – the empire, Venice, the Carrara of Padua, the Visconti of Milan, as well as the communes and feudatories of Friuli, presented candidates to the papacy.

However, the picture is not entirely one of political decline and disintegration. For example, the patriarch Marquardo was able, as well as being in office for sixteen years. He sought to defend the rights of his Church; joining the coalition against Venice in the War of Chioggia (1378–81), he was able to recover – if only temporarily – authority over Trieste and Istria. Secondly, for all its divisions the patriarchate preserved a remarkable sense of unity, perhaps stronger than can be found in the other regions of northern Italy. This was expressed in – and encouraged by – its parliament which had acquired powers over matters ranging from defence to taxation, from legislation to foreign relations. So great was its role that a sixteenth-century observer described fourteenth-century Friuli as a republic rather than a principality.[33]

But however remarkable, the parliament was itself not cohesive enough to control the situation after 1381. Urban VI's unwise appointment of Cardinal Filippo d'Alençon as patriarch *in commendam* provoked a polarisation of loyalties and the aggressive intervention of foreign powers, above all Venice and the Carrara. The Venetians initially presented themselves as peacemakers or as champions of the liberties of Aquileia, but they rapidly took sides as allies of the Savorgnan and opponents of the Carrara. The commercial and strategic importance of the region led to the republic's increasing involvement and finally, by 1420, the conquest of Friuli and the virtual elimination of the patriarch's temporal authority.[34]

THE PRINCIPALITIES OF PIEDMONT

Political hegemony in early fourteenth-century Piedmont was contested between five principalities.[35] The Angevins, counts of Provence and kings of Naples, ruled a county based on Cuneo. There were two marquisates, Saluzzo and Montferrat; the latter was ruled by a branch of the Palaeologus dynasty which had inherited it through marriage in 1305. Most of the lands of the principal Savoyard line lay north of the Alps, but the counts of Savoy ruled the Val de Susa and the Val d'Aosta. A cadet branch held the 'barony' of Piedmont based on the cities of Pinerolo and Turin; the cadet branch is referred to as Savoy-Achaia after Filippo I married the heiress to that Latin principality in Greece in 1301.

---

[33] Koenigsberger (1978), pp. 40–2; Hay and Law (1989), pp. 231–6.

[34] Law (1988a) and (1996); Ortalli (1996); Girgensohn (1996).

[35] Gabotto (1894), (1895), pp. 75–324, (1896), pp. 81–95, and (1897); Marie-José (1956); Ruggiero (1979); Cognasso (1971); Nada Patrone (1986), pp. 61–86.

The line of Savoy-Achaia and the marquises of Saluzzo were the vassals – often reluctantly – of the house of Savoy; both the county of Savoy and the marquisate of Montferrat were held directly from the empire. In 1355, for example, Giacomo of Savoy-Achaia sought a direct feudal relationship with Charles IV. Among the privileges he was able to secure was the right to impose tolls; this brought him into conflict with his immediate superior, Amedeo VI of Savoy: Giacomo was eventually forced to surrender his fiefs and to purchase their recovery for 160,000 florins (1360–3). By contrast, the Angevin county of Piedmont was created by Charles II for his son in 1304 without imperial sanction. It was only in 1355 that Joanna I, countess of Provence and queen of Naples, sought a mandate from Charles IV.

The history of the region is a bewildering catalogue of short-term dynastic and diplomatic alliances designed to protect and extend the territory and authority of the participants, a catalogue further complicated by the fact that Piedmont was a frontier zone of strategic importance, and also by the fact that the participants had international interests, most notably the Angevins and the house of Savoy, both closely involved in French affairs. However, in the course of the century several trends can be discerned.

The authority of the Angevins gradually decreased until by the end of the period they had lost all their lordships in Piedmont; in 1381 Louis of Anjou ceded the last territories to secure the support of the house of Savoy for his bid to inherit the kingdom of Naples. By contrast, the involvement of the house of Savoy increased. This was matched by an accumulation of Visconti lordships; following the acquisition of Vercelli in 1335, the Milanese dynasty gradually became one of the major powers in the region. At times, the house of Savoy and the Visconti seemed intent on dividing Piedmont between them; for example, following a marriage alliance of 1350 between Galeazzo II Visconti and Bianca, the sister of Amedeo VI, or again in 1386 when the count assigned some Angevin cities to the Visconti. That they were not able to do so was in part due to the smaller principalities seeking to preserve and extend their autonomy, and bargaining with the major players and the French crown to do so.

Behind these general developments lay an ever-changing geo-political situation. Cuneo changed hands ten times before being ceded to Savoy in 1381. Asti assigned by Henry VII, Charles IV and Wenceslas IV to the house of Savoy was held by it only briefly (1305–6 and 1327); otherwise it was passed between the Angevins, the marquises of Montferrat and, eventually, the Visconti, only to be assigned by Giangaleazzo as part of the dowry for his daughter Valentina when she married Louis of Orléans (1387). Various reasons can be suggested for this agitated situation. First, as elsewhere, much depended on the ruler; when Robert of Anjou died in 1343 his inheritance passed to

Joanna I who had neither the sex nor the ability for the task. By contrast, Amedeo VI, the 'Green Count' (1343–83) was a ruler of style, energy and ability who advanced the cause and prestige of his dynasty during his relatively long reign.[36]

Secondly, Piedmont contained no major city to dominate, or to allow others to dominate, the region; Ivrea had a pre-plague population of *c.* 5,000 while Turin and Pinerolo had *c.* 4,000 inhabitants. As elsewhere in Italy, the relatively small scale of the cities did not lessen local loyalty, which – paradoxically perhaps – facilitated superficial changes in allegiance to distant lords, a process further encouraged by internal factions that looked beyond their walls for foreign protectors: the struggle between the Guelf Solari and the Ghibelline da Castello of Asti is a good example here.

Finally, Piedmont was not of course isolated from broader developments. For example, a general alliance of Italian powers against the Visconti in 1356 allowed the Angevins to recover some of their territory. The ascendant powers at the end of the century could draw on resources from outside. Both dynasties had embarked on policies of expansion: the Visconti in northern and central Italy; the house of Savoy had lands in what are now France and Switzerland, and like other members of the French 'provincial' nobility were able to exploit the difficulties of France in the Hundred Years War and during the unstable monarchy of Charles VI. In addition, of course, the house of Savoy controlled key Alpine passes.

The efforts of later historians to disentangle the dynastic and diplomatic history of the region and to chart the rise of the house of Savoy has rather distracted them from analysing the nature of the various states of Piedmont. The political history of the region might suggest that subject lords and communes enjoyed considerable autonomy and that the authority of the ruler was often nominal. This was the case with the Angevin county even before the death of Robert of Anjou. More generally, the history of parliamentary assemblies with a voice in such matters as defence, taxation and the succession points towards the same conclusion.[37] Again, the house of Savoy was itinerant; Chambéry was one of their principal residences but not the site of a stable court. The dynasty also faced the seasonal barrier of the Alps and was forced to acknowledge wide immunities for some of its subjects, like those in the Val d'Aosta.

On the other hand, the dynasty did seek to advance its authority, for example by exploiting its relations with the empire and its feudal position. In 1356 Amedeo VI secured valuable jurisdictional privileges from Charles IV; his was declared the final court of appeal in cases from ecclesiastical as well as lay tribunals. In 1365 his feudal authority was increased with the grant of a

[36] Cox (1967).   [37] Koenigsberger (1978), pp. 42–6.

hereditary imperial vicariate. Amedeo also exploited his feudal superiority over Saluzzo and the house of Savoy-Achaia. For example in 1362 he encouraged the contrite Giacomo of Savoy-Achaia to marry Margherita of Beaujeu, sister of one of his principal adherents. This led to the disinheritance of Filippo, the son by a previous marriage. Filippo's subsequent defeat – and possibly his death – were master-minded by the count who subsequently became regent to Giacomo's designated heir, revealingly also called Amedeo (1368–77). These moves anticipated the integration of all the lands of Savoy under Amedeo VIII in 1418, following the extinction of the cadet branch.

A further insight into the way the house of Savoy was able to increase its authority by inventiveness and opportunism is provided by the revolt of the *Tuchini* (1386–91) in the Canavese and other regions of Piedmont. The term probably derives from 'tutti uniti', and the revolt bears a resemblance to rural anti-feudal rebellions in England and France. However, this rebellion was exploited by the marquis of Montferrat, jealous of Savoyard power in the Canavese, and by some of the count's vassals. The revolt was eventually suppressed by force, fines, confiscations and exile, but Amedeo VII also made concessions to contrite rural communities, bringing them under his direct lordship. He also compelled his vassals in the region to renew their homage, seizing the opportunity to trim some of their traditional feudal privileges.

THE REPUBLICS OF VENICE AND GENOA

Venice was unusual:[38] not only did it preserve its political independence, but unlike the majority of the communes of northern Italy it also maintained its republican constitution. Moreover, it appeared relatively free of faction: the slogans of Guelf and Ghibelline scarcely appear in the city's annals. Admiring contemporaries, early contributors to the 'myth of Venice', attributed these achievements in great measure to its constitution and institutions, and to a considerable extent more modern historians would agree. Much of the focus of the latter's attention has been on the so-called *serrata*, or 'locking in' of the Greater Council, effectively the sovereign body of the constitution. The *serrata* was a process, a series of measures taken between 1297 and 1323 which created a defined, hereditary nobility whose membership became synonymous with membership of the Council. These measures were once thought to be revolutionary in character, representing the triumph of an aristocracy over the people and completing the emasculation of the powers of the doge as head of state.

---

[38] Brown (1895); Lane (1973); Cozzi and Knapton (1986), pp. 3–21.

More recently, however, the *serrata* has been seen in a rather different light, stemming from the realisation that following 1297 the Council grew dramatically in size, from 210 in 1296 to 1,017 in 1311 and to 1,212 in 1340, when work began on a new council hall in the ducal palace to accommodate the larger numbers. Frederic Lane and others[39] have seen these events in the context of military and commercial disasters for Venice in the eastern Mediterranean and Adriatic, and understand the enlargement of the Greater Council as an attempt to assure prominent families that they had a place in government irrespective of short-term reversals. Moreover, while it was once thought that rigorous vetting procedures were put in place, it may be that in practice membership remained open for longer. In 1381, thirty non-noble families were granted hereditary membership as a reward for their financial help in the War of Chioggia. More significant, perhaps, is the fact that the mechanisms for screening membership birth and marriage registers were not instituted until the next century.[40] In other words, the reason the constitution had a part to play in securing the relative peace and stability of Venice was not because it fulfilled an ideal balance of elements – as some contemporaries argued – nor because it was rigid and defined, but because it remained flexible and able to accommodate enough of the actual and aspiring members of the political class.

However, by itself the city's constitution cannot provide the entire explanation for its relative stability and the survival of its republican government. In the first place, there were two serious attempts to overthrow the government. The first, of 1310, was led by three prominent members of the nobility – Baiamonte Tiepolo, Marco Querini and Badoer Badoer – angered by the republic's involvement in a disastrous war to dominate Ferrara and anxious for more influence in government. Their following was small and poorly organised, and the revolt was quickly put down. However, the rebellion was taken sufficiently seriously to warrant the setting-up of a magistracy to oversee security, the Council of Ten. The second threat came in 1355, and was an attempt by the doge, Marino Falier, to seize power.[41] His motives are not entirely clear. After a long and prominent career – remarkably for a Venetian noble he had been made a count and was knighted by Charles IV – he may have reacted against the constraints placed on the office of doge. Coming from a relatively small, but ancient, noble family and taking office at the age of seventy-six, he may have felt jealous or fearful of more prolific noble clans and their younger members. He may also have been responding to a general climate of unrest in the aftermath of the Black Death and an unsuccessful war against Genoa (1350–5). He may even have been influenced by the example of

---

[39] Lane (1966), pp. 288–308, and (1971), pp. 237–74; Chojnacki (1973), pp. 47–90; Rösch (1989).
[40] Chojnacki (1994), pp. 1–18.   [41] Lazzarini (1963).

the proliferating signorial regimes on the mainland. Whatever, his conspiracy was discovered and crushed with ease.

Nevertheless, as in 1310, the government viewed the events of 1355 with sufficient gravity to order annual processions of thanksgiving. This suggests a lack of complacency which compels historians to look further for explanations for the city's relative stability. Why were there not further instances of rebellion? Why did the revolts of 1310 and 1355 attract so little support?

Explanations can be drawn again from the influential myth of Venice. This claimed that there was a sense of cohesion in Venice both within and between classes. Noble families trimmed their ambitions for the common good and acquired a sense of responsibility towards the state and their subjects, the majority of the population. However, once again it is easy to question such suggestions. In society as a whole there was a growing awareness of social status in the years following the *serrata*.[42] Within the nobility there were considerable variations in family size, wealth and political prominence, hardly a recipe for harmony. Nobles can be found exploiting their privileged status to gain preferential treatment in the courts.[43] Individuals can be identified conspiring with the republic's enemies, notably the Carrara of Padua.[44] Corruption in government can be readily identified.[45] The conventions of the constitution were flouted to such an extent that from 1396 measures against *broglio* – improper constitutional practices – began to be passed. Doges other than Falier challenged the confines of their office. The able and ambitious Andrea Dandolo (1343–54) had such an exalted view of his office that he had become intensely unpopular with his fellow-nobles by the end of his life.

But if Venetian society and government were more restless and flawed than admiring commentators would admit, the fact remains that its history was not punctuated by changes in regime, mass exile or explosions of social discontent. Could it be that the city's unusual site made an important contribution? As commentators noticed, the city's isolation from the mainland made it less vulnerable to attack, frequently a destabilising factor elsewhere. Its mercantile aristocracy did acquire estates on the mainland, but the fact that the republic had no large mainland state in the period possibly prevented these estates from becoming the base for political and military power, as could happen in the *contadi* of the *terraferma* cities.

Moreover, as Lane has suggested, the example of faction on the mainland may have taught the Venetians a lesson. This may have contributed to a sense of uniqueness and solidarity noticed by contemporaries and finding expression in the republic's celebration of its history and institutions.[46] Finally, the

---

[42] Mueller (1992), pp. 53–62.   [43] Ruggiero (1980).   [44] Kohl (1988), pp. 707–9.
[45] Queller (1986).
[46] Robey and Law (1975), pp. 3–59; Fortuni Brown (1988), pp. 31–45; Crouzet-Pavan (1992), pp. 527–66, and (1994), pp. 416–27; Lane (1973).

unusual site may have contributed to the stability of Venice, despite its large, cosmopolitan and mobile population. The effort in terms of planning, finance and labour required to preserve the fabric of the city, to maintain its essential waterways and to keep its population supplied with the necessities as well as the luxuries of life may have encouraged a greater sense of unity and respect for the common good, and the need for government, than can be found elsewhere.

Certainly Genoa, its principal commercial rival, was frequently associated with faction.[47] In 1396, for example, an anonymous tract urged the Genoese to surrender to the Visconti to restore the city to its former greatness and to bring an end to 'infernal and diabolical faction'.[48] This reputation was not undeserved, and the explanation for the city's agitated history is largely of a socioeconomic nature. Genoese politics were much influenced by a nobility which drew strength from lordships on the Riviera, and on the islands of Sardinia and Corsica, as well as from commerce: families like the Grimaldi, Lomellini and Doria. Also important were popular 'clans' like the Adorno and Fregoso; it is hard to distinguish them clearly from the nobility other than in length of pedigree, but their more recent rise to prominence was also fuelled by land, lordships and trade. Lastly there was the *popolo minuto* of the city itself, not at all a homogeneous group but embracing a wide range of wealth and occupation, from notaries to sailors.

Social tensions undoubtedly contributed to the troubled history of Genoa, but it would be a mistake to interpret that history too exclusively in class terms. Noble houses could themselves form rival branches, like the Spinola. Rivalry rather than class solidarity produced decades of feuding, as between the Adorno and the Fregoso and their adoption of the Ghibelline and Guelf causes. Moreover, families like the Adorno would draw on allies and clients from a wide social spectrum in the city and its *contado*. This phenomenon, common enough elsewhere, was taken further in Genoa and led to the creation of *alberghi*, clans which adopted a common surname and occupied fortified enclosures in distinct areas of the city.

Impatience with this situation led to the popular acclamation of Simone Boccanegra as doge in 1339.[49] The office was new to the constitution, but Simone's family had long been prominent citizens. He instituted a more popular regime; noble families were banned from the office of doge and membership of the council of elders, the *anziani*. He set about restoring Genoese authority on the Riviera and defending the city's commercial and colonial interests in the Mediterranean. But these policies not only offended the nobility;

---

[47] Vitale (1955); De Negri (1968); Benvenuti (1977); Petti Balbi (1991).   [48] Novati (1886), pp. 3–15.
[49] *DBI*, xi, pp. 37–40.

high levels of taxation and an exalted view of his own office lost him popular support. Failing to rally the people or to find allies among the nobility, Boccanegra went into self-imposed exile in 1344.

A further period of internal instability and defeat abroad led Genoa to accept the *signoria* of the Visconti in 1353. It was under their auspices that Boccanegra returned, soon to lead a revolt against foreign rule and to recover the office of doge (1356). Once more he pursued anti-noble policies at home while trying to defend Genoese interests abroad, particularly on Corsica. However, again he lost support due to the cost of his policies, the advancement of his family and his lofty understanding of the dogeship: in 1358 Charles IV made him vicar and admiral of the empire. Conspiracies were planned against him, and when he died in 1363 poison was suspected.

However, the office of doge survived, if few of its occupants were able to stamp their authority on the city for long. The first time Antoniotto Adorno was in office (1378) it was only for a matter of hours. During his fourth attempt (1394–6), rival noble families – the Lomellini, Spinola and Fieschi – turned to France for support.[50] Their candidate was Louis of Orléans, brother of Charles VI and son-in-law of Giangaleazzo Visconti, and with other territorial ambitions in the peninsula. To outflank his rivals, the doge surrendered the city to the king. He even served as royal governor (1396–7) until Charles became dissatisfied with the voted office of 'defender of the commune' and instituted a more direct rule, especially after the appointment of Jean le Meingre, Marshal Boucicaut, as governor in 1401. He saw Genoa as a base for crusading expeditions and extending French influence in Italy, but his government – by Genoese standards – was purposeful and authoritarian. He strengthened fortifications and enlarged the garrison. He reduced the power of the guilds and presided over legal and financial reforms. In 1402 his Genoese supporters asked Charles to appoint him governor for life, but by 1409 his rule had become so demanding and unpopular that the Genoese rebelled. If the French king charged them with treason, they condemned Boucicaut for tyranny.

The internal weakness of Genoa influenced events outside its walls. Its authority over its own dominion in the Riviera was spasmodic. *Maone*, consortia of entrepreneurs, were set up to defend and exploit its colonies, Chios (1347) and Corsica (1378). Noble families like the Doria pursued policies – for example in Sardinia – often independently of the commune.[51] But it would be wrong to exaggerate the weakness of Genoa or to give too negative a picture of its consequences. Looked at closely the factionalism of Genoese politics can reveal a remarkable continuity; none of its leading participants were

[50] Jarry (1896); Puncuh (1978), pp. 657–87.
[51] Assereto (1900), pp. 119–60; Petti Balbi (1981), pp. 147–70.

destroyed or suffered perpetual exile. The commune survived and with it an intense feeling of loyalty to the city which could not tolerate foreign rule for long. Measures credited to Boucicaut – to reform the statutes in 1403 and the institution of the Bank of St George to administer the public debt – were in reality Genoese creations. And the 'diaspora', in part created by internal faction, gave the Genoese an international role as merchants, bankers, mercenaries on land and sea and explorers.

A SIGNORIAL REGIME: THE DELLA SCALA OF VERONA

From the early thirteenth century, the della Scala dominated the *contrada* of Sta Maria Antica, one of the central districts of Verona.[52] They owed their prominence to wealth derived from land, urban properties and commerce rather than to ancient noble titles and feudal lordships in the countryside. Their rise to power in their native city and the March of Treviso was probably also a consequence of their support for Ezzelino III da Romano (1194–1259), the Ghibelline warlord who had dominated the politics of north-east Italy in the mid-thirteenth century.

Like most other *signori*, the della Scala secured their position by defeating and driving into exile their opponents, but they were again typical in that they were party leaders who depended heavily on the co-operation and support of other leading families in Verona and neighbouring cities. For example, in the 1270s they were allied to the Bonacolsi of Mantua who were establishing a *signoria* of their own. Again typically, the della Scala sought to strengthen and legitimise their authority by acquiring offices and titles from the commune. In 1259 Mastino I was elected *podestà* and in 1262 captain of the people. On his assassination in 1277, his brother and successor Alberto I was made captain of the people for life, an event which has come to be seen as marking the formal start to the della Scala *signoria*.

However, such offices, and the ceremonies that went with them, should not be understood in terms of genuine election but rather as stage-managed acclaim. Moreover, like other *signori* the della Scala were not content to let their mandate depend on popular sovereignty alone: they also tried to acquire an imperial vicariate. Cangrande I and Alboino were the first to do so, purchasing the title from Henry VII on 7 March 1311.[53] But the acclaim that legitimised the power and succession of members of the family – jointly or singly – was not dispensed with even when the hereditary principle was acknowledged, in the case of the della Scala from 1359.

---

[52] Carrara (1966); Istituto per gli Studi Storici Veronesi (1975); Varanini (1988b); *DBI*, xxxvii, pp. 366–462; Varanini (1995).   [53] Sandri (1969), pp. 195–250.

A principal reason why the della Scala, and other *signori*, continued to value such procedures was the fact that the legal, political and economic powers conferred were extremely wide. As a consequence, the government of the della Scala might be expected to have had a considerable impact, and in certain respects it had. The communal statutes were revised (1276 and 1328). The institutions of the commune were manipulated. The *podestà*, or chief magistrate, became a client of the dynasty while the larger consultative assemblies fell into disuse. A financial office – the *fattoria* – was set up; initially created to administer the family's assets, it eventually dominated communal finance.

As was the case with other *signori*, the della Scala had a considerable impact on the Church. From the late thirteenth century they were styled as its 'defenders' and from 1331 as its 'advocates'. Behind such titles lay the allocation of benefices to members of the family and its allies. For example, from 1268 to 1275, as the dynasty was establishing itself, Guido della Scala, brother of Mastino I, was bishop. In 1361 a canonry was assigned to the two-year-old son of Cansignorio. From 1361 to 1375 the *fattoria* administered the revenues of the dioceses of Verona and Vicenza and assigned their clergy stipends. More generally, the della Scala and their allies were invested with Church lands and rights to tenths. But the relationship was not always exploitative. As with other signorial dynasties, a blend of personal piety and a concern for their reputation led members of the family to enter the Church and to endow churches, the religious orders and charities. Cangrande I, despite being excommunicated, established the Servites in Verona in 1324 and founded the church of Sta Maria della Scala.

As that suggests, the della Scala had an impact on the physical appearance of the city. Public works were undertaken under their direction, from the building of fortifications to the construction of bridges and aqueducts. The ascendancy of the family was expressed in stone in other ways, by building palaces and magnificent tomb monuments close to the city's administrative centre. And the dynasty's taste for magnificence and concern for its reputation attracted men of letters to its court; indeed in the course of the period 'courts' ceased to be splendid but occasional events held to mark diplomatic marriages and knighting ceremonies and became 'the court', a permanent aspect of their rule.

One such man of letters – though never a courtier – was Dante who possibly visited Verona in 1304 and who lived there from 1312 to 1320. For the poet, Cangrande I was seen as fulfilling the mission of Henry VII; to the dynasty's enemies, like the Paduan lawyer Albertino Mussato, he was heir to the tyranny of Ezzelino. Behind these contrasting views lay the fact that the della Scala, like many other *signori*, pursued an expansionist policy, and in their case with initial success. They came to dominate the March of Treviso, beginning with the acquisition of Vicenza in 1311 and encompassing important cities outside the region – Brescia (1332–7), Parma (1335–41), Lucca (1335–41) – encouraging the rumour that Mastino II aspired to the crown of Lombardy.

These policies can partly be explained in terms of prestige: the nickname adopted by two members of the dynasty (Cangrande) was chosen to evoke the achievements of the Great Khans, while court poets and eventually his tomb monument celebrated the conquests of Cangrande I. Expansion also had economic motives, to acquire further sources of revenue to enrich the dynasty and its supporters and to increase the size and professionalism of its armies. There were also political motives. The della Scala felt the need to sustain clients in cities other than Verona. Lastly, expansion had a strategic aim, to deny cities and trade routes to rival powers.

These points might suggest that the della Scala had a profound impact on the cities they ruled; however – and as is the case with many other signorial regimes – the scope and success of their policies should not be exaggerated. The image created for the rulers themselves – chivalry, piety, magnificence, care for their subjects – was hardly new. The structure of the communes over which they ruled remained substantially intact, while in general city and guild statutes were allowed to evolve rather than being subjected to radical revision. As mentioned, the dynasty did not remain aloof from its subjects; like other *signori* the della Scala depended on the support of other leading families to govern. Credit and military and political support were rewarded with marriage alliances, offices in Church and state, ecclesiastical lands and rights, property confiscated from exiles, fiefs and lordships. Hence the ascendancy of the della Scala furthered the interests of other families from Verona (the Bevilacqua), from subject cities (the Serego of Vicenza) and from other regions of Italy (the Alighieri of Florence).

Finally, their political success was fragile. The large 'state' built up by Cangrande I and his nephews Mastino II and Alberto II, displayed little profound loyalty to the dynasty and fell apart when a coalition led by Florence and Venice turned against it (1337–9), eventually reducing the della Scala lordships to Verona and Vicenza. Marriage alliances did not guarantee support. The marriage of Regina della Scala to Bernabò Visconti in 1350 later encouraged them to aspire to the lordship of Verona once the succession had passed from the legitimate line, claims that had to be bought off for 440,000 florins in 1379. And as this suggests, the ruling dynasty itself did not remain cohesive, and fissures within it could create a fragile hold on power. A revolt in February 1354 against Cangrande II, led by his half-brother Fregnano, persuaded the lord of Verona to place large investments for security in Venice and to build a fortified palace or citadel in the city, measures that increased his unpopularity and contributed to his murder by his own brother on 14 December 1359.

Other instances of fratricide are thought to have contributed to discrediting the dynasty further as well as to its fall from power.[54] In 1381 Antonio murdered his elder brother to secure the *signoria,* and his subsequent actions alienated some leading Veronese families. But what really brought him down were failures in foreign policy and military defeat. Antonio joined Venice against the Carrara of Padua in 1385. Losing heavily in battle, he was then turned on by the lord of Milan. An attack on Verona in October 1387 revealed few ready to stand by their beleaguered ruler, and Antonio fled to Venice. Subsequent efforts by members of the family to recover the *signoria* could never muster sufficient internal and external support to succeed.

TOWARDS A NEW STATE?

It is on the Visconti in general, and Giangaleazzo in particular, that historians of northern Italy have focused most attention;[55] especially following Italian Unification and during the Fascist era, the dynasty could be seen as a powerful new force in Italian politics and as the architects of a new, more unified, state. There are many arguments in favour of such a view. At its greatest extent in the late fourteenth century, Visconti rule embraced a vast area stretching from Belluno in the north-east to Siena in the south-west. The records and chroniclers of other states, both friend and foe, reflect the fact that the Visconti were a major influence in peninsular politics. Moreover, their dominions included some of the most densely populated and economically active areas of the country, providing the dynasty with the resources to employ powerful mercenary armies.

Related is the fact that surviving archives, both in Milan and in such 'provincial' centres as Reggio and Voghera, show an active and ambitious government at work.[56] The new state many historians have constructed from these records was increasingly centralised and authoritarian. Communal consultative bodies like the Council of Nine Hundred of Milan were supervised. The immunities and privileges of noble families, the Church, subject communes and rural communities were placed under growing scrutiny. The *podestà* of the subject cities, and other local officials, became the appointees of the central government, while communal governments themselves had their powers reduced leaving them as little more than reluctant tax gatherers. Local statutes were revised and vetted centrally, and they could be by-passed by signorial decree. Nor was the Church exempt from the process; exploiting the Schism, in 1382 Giangaleazzo

[54] De Marco (1938), pp. 107–206, and (1939), pp. 1–20; Law (1988b), pp. 83–98.

[55] Above n. 2; Cognasso (1922), pp. 121–84, and (1923), pp. 23–169; Valeri (1935b), pp. 101–32; Ilardi (1978), pp. 331–42; Chittolini (1980); Soldi-Rondinini (1984), pp. 9–37.

[56] Comani (1900a), pp. 385–412, and (1900b), pp. 221–29; Cau (1969–70), pp. 45–98.

decreed that benefice holders had to be approved by his government.[57] Corruption was attacked and steps taken to strengthen public order.

Closely related to such developments was a growing self-esteem on the part of the dynasty itself. Increasingly, its dynastic, diplomatic and military successes became matters for celebration. It attracted a growing number of propagandists. It associated itself with the cults of local saints, like those of St Ambrose or the Magi at Milan.[58] It embarked on an increasingly ambitious policy of dynastic marriage with other princely and royal houses, in Cyprus, Germany, France and England. Such alliances became the occasion for courtly magnificence. And the Visconti's exalted sense of status can be seen in other ways: from 1363 threats to Galeazzo II were defined as *lèse-majesté*; Bernabò claimed that he was pope and emperor in his own dominions; Giangaleazzo purchased the hereditary titles of duke of Milan and count of Pavia in 1395 and 1396. Rumours circulated that he coveted a royal crown. His standing as a ruler on a par with other European princes can be measured from the elaborate and well-attended funeral that followed his death in 1402.[59]

However, this was quickly followed by the breakup of the Visconti state. Some cities reverted to communal independence while others fell prey to onceloyal *condottieri* and neighbouring powers. These developments suggest that the Visconti state was not as different nor as solid a creation as historians once believed. Its unity under Giangaleazzo was rather exceptional: his father Galeazzo II and his uncle Bernabò had divided its territories, while the latter delegated authority to his wife Regina and later to his sons. Giangaleazzo himself envisaged the division of his dominions among his heirs.[60]

Moreover, if immunities and privileges could be attacked, they could also be created for supporters of the dynasty and for the Visconti themselves, in some cases – as in the Lodigiano – at the expense of the Church and local property owners.[61] If Visconti influence and intervention appear marked in some areas – in general those that were more accessible, closer to Milan and with a tradition of strong government – in others it appears marginal and spasmodic. The Bergamasco, for example, was in a state of almost constant civil war, and Visconti rule scarcely developed beyond occasional attempts at reconciliation, more frequent punitive expeditions and, by necessity, support of the Ghibelline faction. A similar, if less anarchic, situation can be traced elsewhere, in Belluno for example.[62]

The considerable archival legacy of Visconti rule is not evidence for their

[57] Prosdocimi (1973), p. 60.   [58] Kirsch (1991), p. 9.

[59] *Ordo Funeris Joannis Galeatii Vicecomitis, RIS,* xvi (1730), pp. 1023–50.

[60] Comani (1902), pp. 211–48; Valeri (1935a), pp. 461–73, and (1938).

[61] Agnelli (1901), pp. 260–306; Black (1994), pp. 1150–73.

[62] *Chronicon Bergomense, RIS,* xvi/2 (1926); Miari, *Cronaca Bellunese.*

influence and authority alone. It also reveals the great difficulty they had at establishing peace, licensing castle building, raising revenue and controlling a tide of petitions for special treatment from individuals, noble families, urban and rural communities and the Church. Lastly, it should be noted that there is little evidence that a radically new understanding of the state emerged. Advice given in 1408 by Carlo Malatesta to Filippo Maria, one of Giangaleazzo's heirs, is characterised by standard, mirror of princes, material which stressed such themes as the need to respect God and justice, to earn the trust of his subjects, to value good counsel and to eschew partiality.[63]

CONCLUSION

Northern Italy in the fourteenth century has often been characterised by the arrival of signorial regimes and the graduation of a few of them to the status of principalities. Lordship was the most common form of government, but the *signorie* varied considerably in terms of date of origin, extent, juridical character and durability. Moreover, republics survived. This was most obviously the case with Venice and Genoa, but republicanism continued to shape the government of subject cities, like Trieste, and survived as a potential alternative form of government, in Pavia and Trent for example.

The period has also been associated with the rise of larger, stronger Italian states. The Visconti managed to recover their authority in the early fifteenth century, though never to the frontiers reached by Giangaleazzo. This, together with the growth of the Savoyard dominions and the emergence of Venice as a major power in Italy, can suggest that the period saw a shift from an agitated plethora of lordships and communes to a more stable situation shaped by a few territorial states, a process linked to a decline in the influence of foreign powers. This view has still much to commend it: the employment of larger more professional mercenary armies provided a new incentive and means for some states to expand. However, smaller powers like the marquisate of Montferrat and the Gonzaga lordship of Mantua survived, if often as the clients of their larger neighbours. Moreover, Habsburg power was established south of the Alps, while at the end of the period the influence and territorial ambitions of France and the empire – and even of the papacy – were only in abeyance.

Finally, the structure of the new territorial states remained fragile. They were not the end product of some inexorable historical process, but depended on the skill and resources of their governors to survive. The challenges they had to meet came, as ever, from the wider geo-political situation. They also came

[63] Valeri (1934), pp. 452–87.

from subject lordships, cities and urban and rural communities. Loyalty to the newer forms of government was rarely conditioned by more than self-interest: the search for protection and patronage in the form of offices, honours, privileges and immunities. Local loyalties and ambitions retained their importance throughout the period, and well beyond.

FLORENCE AND THE REPUBLICAN TRADITION

Louis Green

BY the first decade of the fourteenth century, Florence had become a great trading city, had evolved a political system which allowed its leading merchant families to enjoy power without provoking the destructive feuds that had marred its earlier history and was on the threshold of an outburst of creative vitality in literature and art that produced the great works of Dante, Giotto and their contemporaries. A hundred years later, it stood on the verge of the most brilliant age of its culture, that of the Renaissance. In between, it passed through a crisis that led to ideological and intellectual readjustments, enabling some of the inheritance of the past to be preserved in a modified form and some to be transformed to suit new circumstances. Between about 1301 and 1342, the city drew on the capital of its previous achievements, enjoying a period of commercial expansion, of comparative internal stability and of successful, if ultimately wasteful, military conflicts with its neighbours. Then, between 1342 and 1382, came a time of economic and demographic contraction and crisis, and of tension between elements in the Florentine community which had previously either been reconciled to each other or held in check by dominant political forces. This was a stage in the city's history when there was a break with the lines of development of the past without a clear sense of new directions emerging to replace them. Finally, between 1382 and about 1402, the authority of its political elite came to be reasserted and the foundations laid for a new culture.

Despite the appearance of discontinuity over this period, there was a sense in which the changes that occurred during it brought to fulfilment developments already in progress, but the direction of which was altered because of new circumstances. The tendency towards the assertion of the authority of a mercantile elite was present already in the thirteenth century, as was a strong intellectual tradition. But it was to be some time before the tensions that had divided Florentine society at that period could be reconciled or overcome. The constitutional settlement effected by the creation of the Priorate in 1282 and

469

by the enactment of the Ordinances of Justice of 1293 represented a first step towards the achievement of this result. But the feud between the 'White' and 'Black' Guelfs which had ended with the condemnation and exile of the former at the end of 1301 had demonstrated the fragility of the attempts since 1280 to bring peace to the city. However, from this time on, a degree of stability was attained, even though the early years of the 'Black' Guelf regime were to be fraught with difficulty for those who had established it.

Brought into power with the support of Boniface VIII and (at his behest) through the military intervention of Charles of Valois, they found themselves in a vulnerable position when that pontiff died in 1303 after his humiliating clash with the French monarchy. Boniface's successor, Benedict XI, instead of supporting the ruling party in Florence, sought a reconciliation between it and the exiled 'Whites'. Sending Nicholas, cardinal of Prato, to Tuscany as papal legate, he tried to effect a pacification between its factions and, when the more intransigent 'Black' Guelfs frustrated his efforts to achieve this, placed the city under an interdict. But his death in July 1304 once again allowed the dominant party in the commune to resume with vigour its campaign against its enemies.[1] In May 1305, the combined armies of Florence and Lucca, under the command of Robert, heir to the throne of Naples, laid siege to Pistoia on which the banished 'Whites' had (in 1301) imposed the rule of their faction and to which many of them had since fled. The ensuing military operation which, as the chroniclers testify,[2] was conducted with great ferocity, reanimated the alliance between the prevailing regime in Florence and its traditional Guelf allies, the Angevin monarchy and the commune of Lucca. The Church, under a new pope, the French Clement V, elected in 1305, attempted once again to mediate, ordering the besieging troops to withdraw from Pistoia, under threat of a reimposition of the interdict. The response to this of the Florentine authorities was to allow their commander, Robert of Naples, to negotiate with the pope, while maintaining their investment of the encircled town. It surrendered in April 1306. The terms imposed by the victors on the defeated city were harsh. The Florentines and Lucchese were each to occupy half of its *contado* and the walls of Pistoia were to be razed, while its *podestà* was henceforth to be appointed by the government of Florence and its captain by that of Lucca.[3]

The defiance of the papacy in the closing stage of the siege of Pistoia and of its new legate, the so-called 'Ghibelline' cardinal, Napoleone Orsini, caused the city once again to be placed under an interdict till September 1309. This, however, does not appear to have undermined its regime which, perhaps

[1] On the feud between the 'Whites' and the 'Blacks' and its aftermath, see Davidsohn (1956–68), IV, pp. 238–360; Del Lungo (1921), pp. 110–360; Holmes (1986), pp. 168–82.

[2] Compagni, *Cronica*, III, chs. 13–15; G. Villani, *Cronica*, bk VIII, ch. 82.

[3] Davidsohn (1956–68), IV, pp. 410–42; Del Lungo (1921), pp. 367–71.

because of its recent military success, consolidated its position from this time onwards. Earlier, in 1304, dissension had broken out between the closest associates of Corso Donati, the original leader of the 'Black' faction, and others of his party. This rift had seemed to signal a parting of the ways between those prepared to compromise with the cardinal of Prato on his visit to Florence and those unwilling to make any concession to him. By December 1306, however, the regime was sufficiently secure to allow the reconstitution of the *gonfaloni*, or armed companies of the *popolo*, originally authorised in 1250 and now reduced in number from twenty to nineteen. In March 1307, a new office, that of the executor of the Ordinances of Justice was created. These measures indicated not only an acceptance by those in power of legislation which had once been anathema to the 'magnates' at the head of the 'Black' faction, but also the willingness to use it and an enlarged militia of guildsmen to buttress its own authority. These apparent concessions to the popular cause do not, however, seem to have led to any broadening of participation in government, for real authority still remained in the hands of a restricted circle of families.[4]

But the aristocratic figures who had originally dominated the 'Black' Guelf party lost their leading role in it from 1308 onwards. In that year, Corso Donati fell out with his former allies, was condemned by the commune and killed by Catalan mercenaries while attempting to flee from the city. Of the other previous heads of the faction, Rosso della Tosa died in an accident in 1309, while Betto Brunelleschi and Pazzino dei Pazzi were assassinated in 1311 and 1312 respectively. The departure of these men from the political stage left their former supporters among the *popolani grassi* in control of the government, with families such as the Soderini, Valori, Albizzi, Strozzi, Altoviti, Buonaccorsi, Acciaiuoli, Ricci, Peruzzi and Medici playing an increasingly important part between 1310 and 1313.[5]

The consolidation of the 'Black' Guelf ascendancy was favoured not only by the shedding of its earlier, unruly leaders and by its ability to exploit to its advantage the institutions of the Florentine state. It was also helped by external military threats which enabled what had originally been a factional regime to assume the role of a defender of the city's freedom. Apart from two short intervals between 1317 and 1320 and 1339 and 1341, Florence was to be at war for the three decades from 1312 to 1342, first with the emperor and then with Ghibelline tyrants or neighbouring communes. It was, in particular, during the expedition to Italy by Henry VII that its rulers developed a justification of their resistance to him in terms of a Guelfism defined not just as support of the

[4] Najemy (1982), pp. 79–81.
[5] On internal developments in Florence between 1302 and 1313, see Compagni, *Cronica*, iii, chs. 2–3, 8–9, 19–21, 28–41; Davidsohn (1956–68), iv, pp. 361–9, 460–7, 485–94, 544–52.

cause of the Church but also of their city's independence from imperial authority.[6] The enthusiastic support of the exiled 'Whites' for the emperor from the time of his election in 1308 and even more after his entry into Italy in 1310 made it easy for their enemies to adopt the role of the champions of their city against the threat they believed he posed to it. Even though Henry VII had, to begin with, the approval of Clement V for his journey to Rome where he was to receive the imperial crown, those in power in Florence did all they could to hinder his progress through the Italian peninsula, secretly encouraging rebellions in Cremona and Brescia and intriguing against him with Robert who had succeeded his father, Charles II, as king of Naples in 1309. Eventually, in 1312, they managed to win over even Clement V, when Henry VII, after having passed through Genoa and Pisa, was on his way to Rome. Despite this, the emperor was able to proceed with his coronation and then return to Tuscany where, in September 1312, he besieged Florence. But without enough troops even to encircle the city, he was compelled to withdraw in November. The threat he posed continued, nevertheless, to alarm the Florentines sufficiently for them to concede lordship over their commune to King Robert of Naples, for five years, in May 1313. Henry VII's death, in the following August, at Buonconvento, soon delivered them, however, from their fear of him.[7]

In the ensuing period, the ideological foundations laid by the justification of the struggle against the emperor were to form the basis for political attitudes developed during the conflict with the Ghibelline despots, Uguccione della Faggiuola and Castruccio Castracani, when the preservation of constitutional government against the threat of tyranny displaced opposition to the empire as the essential element of the Guelf cause espoused by the Florentines. Following Henry VII's death, they had taken it for granted that they would soon be able to re-establish their city's hegemony over Tuscany. But the engagement by the Pisans of 800 of the late emperor's mercenary cavalry and their appointment of his former vicar-general in Genoa, Uguccione della Faggiuola, as their captain was to frustrate these expectations. With the troops under his command, Uguccione succeeded not only in seizing power in Pisa but also in forcing on neighbouring Lucca a peace requiring it to readmit its exiles. When these betrayed that city to him in 1314, he found himself master of a sizeable territory in western Tuscany over which he was to consolidate his hold as a result of his crushing defeat of the Florentines and their allies at Montecatini in the following year.[8]

[6] Bowsky (1958).
[7] On Henry VII and Florence, see Davidsohn (1956–68), IV, pp. 524–43, 552–752; Del Lungo (1921), pp. 398–435; Bowsky (1960), pp. 153–205.
[8] Davidsohn (1956–68), IV, pp. 762–810; Vigo (1879), pp. 6–84; Green (1986), pp. 30–8, 51–71.

The overthrow of Uguccione through simultaneous risings in Pisa and Lucca temporarily eased the situation in 1316. A *rapprochement* between Robert of Naples and the new emperor, Frederick III, created a diplomatic climate within which peace could be made in 1317 between the Guelf and Ghibelline Tuscan states. But this produced no more than a lull in hostilities. Pisa and Lucca, under their new captains who soon became in effect rulers, Gaddo della Gherardesca and Castruccio Castracani, retained their pro-imperial political allegiance and remained outside the Florentine zone of influence. Also, Robert of Naples's intervention in Genoa in 1318 in support of its Guelfs set off a conflict between him and his party on the one hand and that city's Ghibellines and the Visconti of Milan and their allies on the other. Into this were drawn first the Florentines when they sent troops to Lombardy, then John XXII, the pro-Angevin pope elected in 1316[9] and finally Castruccio Castracani (by this time lord of Lucca), and the Pisans who launched a diversionary attack on the Guelfs in Tuscany in 1320 to relieve the military pressure on the Visconti. As a result, Florence found itself once again at war in its own immediate region. The cession to Castruccio Castracani of Pistoia by its dominant family, the Tedici, in 1325 and the rout of the Florentines at Altopascio later in the same year brought these hostilities to the very walls of their city. As in 1313, the presence of a marauding enemy army at their gates drove them to seek the protection of the Angevin monarchy; and, in 1326, they appointed Charles of Calabria, son of King Robert of Naples, as their lord. The Ghibellines then responded to this prince's presence in Tuscany by inviting to Italy Lewis of Bavaria who had displaced Frederick III as emperor after the battle of Mühldorf in 1322. Thanks to his intervention, Castruccio Castracani was able to secure not only a dukedom but, in 1328, also a vicarate over Pisa, thus enlarging his dominions to an extent which made of them a serious threat to Florence. Fortunately for it, after losing and regaining Pistoia, Castruccio died later that year and his state disintegrated when he was no longer there to hold it together. After Lewis of Bavaria returned to Germany in 1329, Pisa regained its independence, Pistoia came to terms with Florence on conditions which brought it under that city's virtual suzerainty and Lucca was left weak and vulnerable to conquest under the control of a detachment of the emperor's unpaid and mutinous knights.[10]

The years of war and those of the brief truce between 1317 and 1320 had not only stimulated a fear of tyranny and made of the struggle against despots in Tuscany in Lombardy the focus of Florentine foreign policy. They had also

[9] Tabacco (1953), pp. 39, 153–5, 179–88.
[10] Ibid. pp. 152–92; Davidsohn (1956–68), IV, pp. 874–1162; Caggese (1922–30), II, pp. 10–130; Azzi (1908).

helped to consolidate and legitimise the 'Black' Guelf predominance in the city. From 1313 to the end of 1321, it had been under the nominal overlordship of Robert of Naples (whose period in authority had been extended beyond its original five-year term) and between 1326 and 1328 under that of his son. The oligarchic character of the regime had been reinforced by the practice, common between 1310 and 1323, by which the *signoria* or Priorate was empowered by the councils to elect its successors. After the death in 1328 of Charles of Calabria, who had appointed many of the communal officials himself, a new procedure was, however, devised for the choice of those in the main executive bodies of the Florentine state. This gave the appearance of allowing wide participation in government to members of the political class while, at the same time, favouring dominance over it by an elite of leading families. By the major reform enacted in December 1328, those eligible for office were to be voted on in what came to be known as a 'scrutiny' by a large committee, made up of the *signoria*, the nineteen Gonfalonieri of companies, two consuls or rectors from each of the twelve most prominent guilds, the five members of the *mercanzia*, or board of trade, and specially chosen representatives from the city's six wards. All who received a two-thirds majority were then to have their names placed in bags allocated to those posts for which such a vote qualified them, from which these were to be extracted when these offices needed to be filled, until a new 'scrutiny' was compiled two years later. Various exclusions (*divieti*) were to apply to prevent individuals or members of the same families from occupying more than one position within a specified period of time and to debar those who were guilty of certain offences or had failed by pay their taxes from taking up the posts for which they had been drawn.

The rapid rotation of office bearing, due to its short duration (two months for the Priorate and four months for the so-called 'colleges' of the Gonfalonieri of companies and of the Twelve Good Men) did allow this system to distribute available positions fairly widely, but only among those who had been approved by a 'scrutiny'. Analysis of the composition of the Priorate between 1328 and 1342 reveals that there was a heavy concentration of members of leading families in this council over this period with ninety-seven of the most prominent of these holding as many as 74 per cent of the places on it.[11] There were, furthermore, over the same years, frequent *balie* or concessions of authority, to the *signoria* or to special committees which, particularly during wars, such as those against Verona in 1336–9 and against Pisa in 1341–2, came to control what were, in effect, financial fiefdoms that enabled them not only to spend money but also to dispose of the yield of certain taxes or *gabelle*

---

[11] Najemy (1982), pp. 117–18, and, on the government of Florence 1310–28 and the electoral reform of the latter year, pp. 79–116, and Guidi (1972).

or to raise forced loans to meet their needs.[12] Despite the apparently democratic character of the Florentine electoral system, the actual conduct of
government remained largely in the hands of a restricted group of mercantile
families. The influence of these was increased at this time by the growing
dependence of the commune on loans from wealthier citizens, owing to the
ever-escalating costs of war. At this period, the Bardi, Peruzzi and Acciaiuoli
companies had acquired a dominant position as financiers to the kingdoms of
Naples and England and, through their banking and general trading activity,
had accumulated an enormous capital.[13] It was the ability to draw on the credit
provided by these and other similar enterprises that had enabled the Florentine
state to neutralise the reverses it had suffered at the hands of Uguccione della
Faggiuola and Castruccio Castracani and ultimately to triumph over the
ephemeral tyrannies these rulers had established.

Unfortunately, however, the increasing reliance on wealth to make up for the
deficiencies of policy carried risks which became more serious in the 1330s as
a result of the changes which occurred over that decade in the balance of
power in northern Italy. Until about 1329, Florence had benefited not only
from its extensive financial resources but also from its alliance with the papacy
and the kingdom of Naples. Led by men inured to the Guelf tradition and
accustomed to being able to overcome difficulties by spending their way out of
them, its government was, however, ill-adapted to respond to a situation in
which diplomatic alignments were not fixed by factional loyalties but, subject
to considerations of temporary expedience, were liable to alter with bewildering speed. Involved in the shifting sands of Italian politics of this period
through its efforts to gain control of Lucca, it ran itself deeper into debt and,
by overstraining the resources of its commercial economy, aggravated the
impact on it of the overextension of the commitments made by its merchant
companies to their foreign clients, thereby helping to precipitate a financial
crisis.

The Florentines had moved against Lucca in 1329 when the Genoese
Ghibelline, Gherardo Spinola, had bought it from the German knights who
had earlier seized the city. When he found himself unable to defend it, he ceded
it, in 1331, to King John of Bohemia who had just entered Italy and been
acclaimed as overlord by a group of Lombard communes which were threatened with conquest by their more powerful neighbours. The latter, together
with Florence, responded to his coming by combining against him with the
intention of partitioning the dominions which had placed themselves under
his rule. The league Florence concluded in 1332 with Milan, Verona, Ferrara,

---

[12] Barbadoro (1929), pp. 572–603, 614–22.
[13] Sapori (1926), pp. 5–92, and (1955–67), II, pp. 653–763, 1037–70.

Mantua and Como failed, however, to yield it Lucca which, after John of Bohemia's withdrawal from Italy in 1333,[14] passed first into the hands of the Rossi of Parma and then, in 1335, into those of Mastino della Scala of Verona. Outraged by the failure of the latter to abide by his previous undertaking to cede them Lucca when he had acquired it, the Florentines then made an alliance against him with the Venetians and later also with Milan, Mantua and Ferrara. The ensuing war, between 1336 and 1339, was to cost them more than half a million florins,[15] but once again failed to deliver Lucca, when Venice, in the latter year, made a separate peace with Verona. By this, Florence was to be granted only the province of the Val di Nievole which its troops had already occupied. Indirectly, however, it had benefited from the recent hostilities by acquiring Arezzo in 1337 by purchase from its lords, the Tarlati, who had imprudently cast in their lot with Mastino della Scala and then been unable to withstand a combined assault by the Florentines and their Perugian allies on their city which they had consequently been forced to sell.[16]

These minor gains, made at disproportionate expense, did not compensate for the efforts devoted to achieving them and left Florence in a diplomatically weakened position. Not only was it now inferior as a territorial power to Milan, the main beneficiary of the wars of the 1330s, but it could no longer count, as it had been able to do up to 1329, on the support of the Church and the kingdom of Naples. The replacement of John XXII as pope by Benedict XII and the expulsion of his legate, Bertrand de Poujet, from Bologna in 1334 had ended the close collaboration between Florence and the papacy that had already been undermined before this by the Church's alliance with John of Bohemia.[17] The preoccupation of Robert of Naples, towards the end of his reign, with his attempt to reconquer Sicily[18] and his disengagement from north Italian politics after the restoration of the Ghibelline regime in Genoa in 1335 also contributed to the breakdown of what had, until then, been fundamental supports of Florentine foreign policy. The city's government, however, failed to take sufficient account of these changes, as it did of the implications of the new diplomatic equilibrium which had evolved in Lombardy and Tuscany over the previous decade.

In 1341, together with Luchino Visconti, the pope, Robert of Naples and some other rulers it encouraged the Correggio to seize Parma from Mastino della Scala, being prompted by the hope that, with this commune lost to him, he would no longer be able to hold Lucca. It then negotiated to buy the latter city from him for the enormous price of 250,000 florins. But the plan thus to

---

[14] On John of Bohemia's intervention in Italy, see Dumontel (1952), pp. 12–124.
[15] ASF, Capitoli 17 fol. 47.   [16] On these wars, see Perrens (1877–83), IV, pp. 144–258.
[17] Dumontel (1952), pp. 31, 69–71, 108–14; Tabacco (1953), pp. 316–25.
[18] Caggese (1922–30), II, pp. 241–50.

acquire this town and its territory, possession of which had so long eluded it, was to be thwarted. The Pisans, apprehensive at the possibility that their own independence would be threatened if Lucca passed under Florentine control, immediately besieged it with the support of the Castracani faction which found the prospect of a restoration of a Guelf regime there unacceptable to it. More serious still for its recent purchasers was the decision of Milan, Mantua, Parma and later also Padua to align themselves with Pisa to prevent Florence from making good its acquisition of Lucca.[19] These enemies of Mastino della Scala, distrustful of what was now, in effect, an alliance between him and the Florentines, acted to preserve what they saw as the *status quo* and the existing balance of power. Taken by surprise by this development and defeated in their first attempt to break through the encirclement of Lucca in October 1341, the communal authorities tried to fall back on the time-honoured device of seeking help from the papacy and the Angevin monarchy, by granting lordship over Lucca to Robert of Naples in January 1342, in the hope that this would induce him and the pope to force the Pisans to abandon the siege of that city. This expectation was not, however, realised, both Robert and the Avignon papacy urging the Florentines to make peace rather than to persist with the campaign to secure Lucca. When another attempt to relieve it failed in May 1342, the civic government appointed as its new captain and as 'conservator' of the commune Walter of Brienne, duke of Athens, a close associate of the Angevin and French royal families who had, in 1326, acted as vicar in Florence for Charles of Calabria. Far, however, from bringing the Lucchese enterprise to a successful conclusion, this military commander stood idly by while Lucca negotiated its own surrender in July 1342 and then, in the following September, used the forces entrusted to him to seize power and have himself declared lord for life over Florence, Pistoia and Arezzo.[20]

The 'tyranny' of the duke of Athens which began in this way has been variously interpreted. The Italian economic historian, Armando Sapori, explained its acceptance by the Florentine ruling class by the need of the city's merchant companies to secure a moratorium on the repayment of debts to avert the bankruptcy they faced because of the failure of Edward III of England to restore the vast sums he owed them.[21] The contemporary chronicler, Giovanni Villani, however, considered support for him came in the main from the *grandi* and the *popolo minuto*, the former favouring him because he was prepared to suspend the Ordinances of Justice and the latter because it wished to break the

---

[19] Ibid., II, pp. 260–9.   [20] Ibid., II, pp. 271–9; Paoli (1862), pp. 7–17.

[21] Sapori (1926), pp. 145–9. He argues (pp. 149–54) that, when the duke also suspended repayment of the forced loans these companies had made to the commune, those involved in these enterprises, who had formerly given him their support, turned against him.

dominance of the *popolani grassi*.[22] The initial adherence of families such as the Bardi, Frescobaldi and Rossi to his cause can perhaps be more plausibly accounted for by the fact that they had been in exile since plotting unsuccessfully against the commune in November 1340, had been fighting against their city with the Pisan army at the siege of Lucca[23] and had been closely associated with the Tarlati, Ubertini, Ubaldini, Pazzi of Val d'Arno who had tried to seize Arezzo in July 1342 and had since raised a revolt on the Florentine *contado*. When he made peace with Pisa in October, the duke of Athens also did so with those rebel houses, whose condemnation he cancelled and to whom he restored their former property, rights and privileges.

His harmonious relations with them and with other leading Florentine families did not last long. In part, this was because his attempts to court the favour of the *popolo minuto*, by conceding the dyers who had been subject to the Arte della Lana a separate guild and by allowing six *brigate* from the lower classes to parade in festivities he held in 1343, horrified the city's merchants who felt such concessions undermined a social order and economic system based on the subordination of workers to entrepreneurs. A more significant cause of the rapid disillusionment of the Florentine elite with the duke's rule was, however, the series of prosecutions launched by his government against the members of the *balìa* of twenty which had been responsible for conducting the war to retain Lucca. Accusing them of misappropriation of public funds it imposed heavy fines on them and executed other patricians such as Giovanni dei Medici, castellan of the Augusta or citadel of Lucca, Naddo Rucellai, a treasurer there, and Guglielmo Altoviti, captain of Arezzo, on charges of treachery and peculation. Although Walter of Brienne's assumption of the lordship of the city was not, despite the later representation of it as a 'tyranny', an altogether unusual development in Florence, anticipated as it had been by the granting of a similar authority to Robert of Naples in 1313 and Charles of Calabria in 1326 (as well as, in effect, to Charles of Anjou in 1267), what distinguished his rule from that of these predecessors was that, while they had been content to act as the instruments of its ruling class or dominant faction, he had chosen to try to cow it into submission through punitive measures. After the death of Robert of Naples in January 1343 had removed the strongest external support of his regime, it was not long before even the 'magnates' and bankers he had originally favoured began to intrigue against him with the most prominent *popolani grassi*. No fewer than three conspiracies were hatched which coalesced into a single armed rising on 26 July of that year. This cut off some

---

[22] G. Villani, *Cronica*, bk XII, ch. 3. On the duke's government of Florence and his overthrow, see also ibid., bk XII, chs. 8, 16–17.

[23] See ibid., bk XI, chs. 118, 134, and ASP, Comune A 31 fols. 9ᵛ–12ᵛ.

of his troops before they could reach the Piazza della Signoria. The rest which had mustered in that square were eventually trapped, together with the duke, in the Palace of the Priors. After being besieged for eight days, during which Florence's subject cities also rebelled against him, he came to terms with the insurgents, agreeing to renounce his authority on condition he and his men were allowed safe passage out of the town and its territory.[24]

In the meantime, the patricians who had led the revolt against him had, with the blessing of the city's bishop, established a new government under a council of fourteen, made up of seven *grandi* and seven *popolani*, drawn from the Bardi, Rossi, Ricci, Peruzzi, Magalotti, Cavalcanti, Gianfigliazzi, Altoviti, Tornaquinci, Strozzi, Medici, della Tosa, Adimari and Biliotti families. But the attempt by this committee to draw up a constitution which would have created a Priorate of twelve, of whom four were to be 'magnates', provoked a popular rising on 22 September, as a result of which the Ordinances of Justice were revived and a relatively broadly based regime installed in power. The division of the city into four quarters by the previous aristocratic administration was retained but the number of priors (including the Gonfaloniere of Justice) reduced to nine, all of whom were to be *popolani*.[25]

The expulsion of Walter of Brienne had led to the loss to Florence of most of its dominions: of its subject cities, Prato was recovered in 1351, Pistoia in 1353 and Arezzo not until 1384. The bankruptcies of its leading merchant companies followed his fall, that of the Peruzzi coming in 1343, the Acciaiuoli in 1345 and the Bardi in 1346.[26] The outbreak of the Black Death in 1348, a mere eight years after a less devastating epidemic of the plague in 1340, drastically reduced the city's population from over 90,000 to no more than half that number.[27] These disasters severely depressed the level of economic activity. Though it revived later in the fourteenth century, Florentine bankers never regained the position of pre-eminence they had enjoyed in western Europe in the period up to 1340.[28] Within the city, the standing of the prominent families dominant in political life before the seizure of power by the duke of Athens was undermined by the collapse of their business enterprises and by the liberal nature of the 'scrutiny' carried out in 1343 under the influence of the anti-aristocratic forces which had prevailed in the street-battles of

---

[24] On the duke's rule, see Paoli (1862), pp. 18–45, 64–145; Becker (1967–8), I, pp. 150–72.

[25] Becker (1967–8), I, pp. 173–6; G. Villani, *Cronica*, bk XII, chs. 18–23; Najemy (1982), pp. 129–38.

[26] Sapori (1926), pp. 158–82.

[27] La Roncière (1982), pp. 673–4, suggests it fell from 95,000 in late 1347 to 41,000 in 1349, and Pardi (1916), p. 58, from 93,000 to 40,000 over the same period. On the effects of the Black Death on Florence, see also Falsini (1971).

[28] Sapori (1955–67), II, pp. 1067–70, III, pp. 127–33; Hoshino (1980), pp. 194–206; Brucker (1962), pp. 11–27.

September of that year. In contrast to the situation up to 1342, only a third of the positions in the Priorate between 1343 and 1348 were occupied by those Brucker has described as patricians and of the remainder about half were held by members of the fourteen lesser and middle guilds (as many as 140 out of 265 going to men from families new to political office).[29]

The combined effects of the changes of the 1330s and 1340s was not only shattering to Florence and its ruling class but also called into question many of the values and attitudes built upon practices that had brought the city singular success and prosperity between 1267 and 1329. The alliance with the papacy and the kingdom of Naples and the prominence in civic politics of families linked ideologically and financially with the Church and the Angevin monarchy, as well as enriched by trade and banking in countries the markets of which were opened up by loans to their governments, had both been decisive in shaping the outlook of those guiding the commune's destinies. The diplomatic revolution of the 1330s and the ultimate inability of an economy of the scale of Florence's to generate enough credit to sustain the military expenditure of large kingdoms had, however, undermined the viability of policies grounded on circumstances which had now altered, with the result that political failure, financial collapse and the resurgence of popular resistance to oligarchic power had weakened the position of those formerly unchallenged in their authority. As a consequence, two opposing tendencies manifested themselves in the ensuing period. On the one hand, some sections of the governing elite became willing, in order to retain a leading role in civic politics, to work with the new elements which had entered it since 1343 and respond to their demands. Others in the ruling group, however, sought, with the support of the *grandi*, to restrict power to the city's leading families and to preserve the commune's traditional adherence to the Guelf cause.

The more conservative forces were able to take advantage of the absence of many citizens from Florence during the plague of 1348 to secure the enactment of provisions limiting the number of priors from the lesser guilds to two and reducing from fourteen to seven the total of such guilds conferring eligibility for office.[30] Then, in 1358, they won an even greater victory by achieving the passage of a measure which allowed the Parte Guelfa, at that time dominated by the 'magnates' and *popolani grassi*, to prevent those it declared to be suspect Ghibellines to take up positions in government for which they had been drawn, by 'admonishing' them that they fell within this category.[31] Despite these successes, however, the ability of the more intransigent elements

---

[29] Brucker (1962), pp. 105–7; Becker (1962), and (1967–8), 1, pp. 178–230; Becker and Brucker (1956), p. 96; Najemy (1982), pp. 145–52.   [30] Najemy (1982), pp. 158–62; Brucker (1962), pp. 120–2.

[31] Brucker (1962), pp. 165–72.

in the old ruling group to dominate civic politics was limited because of a split in the city's patriciate, round about 1350, between two factions, one led by the Albizzi, the other by the Ricci. The latter, by aligning itself with the popular party, was generally able to prevail in the deliberations of the councils, managing for instance, in 1350, to have them reverse the earlier decision to restrict to seven the number of lesser guilds qualifying their members for office.[32] Only in the Parte Guelfa did the Albizzi and their allies have a decisive advantage, exploiting it to 'admonish' and thereby debar from positions in the government those of whom they most disapproved. But even this device had to be used with caution, lest overexploitation of it should provoke a reaction against its employment. When, in 1366, an attempt was made to rely on it to proscribe the chancellor of the commune, Ser Niccolò Monachi, the Ricci and their supporters responded by using their influence in the councils to have a provision enacted that two lesser guildsmen be added to the six aristocratic captains of the Parte Guelfa. Recognising the risk to its control of this body of the overuse of 'admonition', the Albizzi faction desisted from frequent recourse to it between 1367 and 1371.[33]

As a result, an uneasy balance of forces came to prevail in the political life of the city, with neither the oligarchic nor the popular tendency gaining a decisive advantage. Despite the use of various devices to try to restrict their participation in office, 'new men' continued to be much better represented in it than had been the case before 1342.[34] In 1371, however, the position of the Albizzi party was enhanced when it succeeded in winning over Uguccione dei Ricci, till then leader of those opposed to it, who was rescued from financial embarrassment by having his debts paid by Piero degli Albizzi and Carlo degli Strozzi, two of the heads of the 'oligarchic' faction.[35] Encouraged by this development, it soon began, once again, to play a more aggressive role in civic politics, provoked to some extent by the disagreement of those who adhered to it with the foreign policy pursued by the commune.

Since 1343 there had been a widening divergence between those in Florence who had retained their traditional attachment to the cause of the Church and those who, recognising the differences between the political interests of the city and the papacy, came increasingly to repudiate it. Tension had arisen with Clement VI because of his continued support of the duke of Athens after the latter's expulsion and because of the decision in 1345 to subject the local clergy to secular jurisdiction. Then, in the 1350s, the adoption by the Church of a policy aimed at the reconquest of the papal state, under the direction of its

---

[32] Ibid., pp. 123–8.   [33] Ibid., pp. 202–21.

[34] Ibid., p. 160; Najemy (1982), pp. 195–216; Becker (1967–8), II, pp. 95–133. Their proportion was, however, lower than between 1343 and 1348 (Witt (1976), p. 248).

[35] Brucker (1962), pp. 249–50; Becker (1967–8), II, pp. 134–5.

legate, Cardinal Albornoz, had created friction with Florence which considered its interests threatened by the consolidation of a strong power in central Italy. At the same time, disagreement with the pope as to how to deal with marauding 'free' companies and the incursions into Tuscany of the Milanese despot, Archbishop Giovanni Visconti, sharpened the sense of alienation between a papacy intent only on promoting its own interests and a commune consequently left to its own devices when it came to protecting itself.[36] The suspicions aroused at this early period were to resurface in the 1370s when Gregory XI resumed his predecessor's efforts to impose control over the papal state. The forced submission of Perugia to him in 1371 particularly alarmed the Florentine government which saw it as the first step in a systematic campaign to undermine communal institutions in central Italy, thus taking seriously rumours which spread the following year concerning purported papal designs against Siena.

This perception of the threat posed by the Church to the cause of civic liberty was not, however, shared by all sections of the city's political elite. Those of the Albizzi faction who still dominated the Parte Guelfa retained their previous loyalty to the pope and increasingly distanced themselves from the positions adopted by the commune. Unfortunately, this served only to heighten the apprehension felt by its enemies at the supposed secret intentions of the Church. In 1373 and 1374, reports of contacts between Gerard du Puy, the pope's nephew, and the Albizzi aroused fears of collusion between them and the papacy. The climate of suspicion was further intensified by the discovery of a plot in Prato in 1375 in which Guillaume Noellet, the papal vicar-general in Bologna, was believed to be implicated. Alarmed by what they saw as indications of the hostility of the Church, the communal authorities resolved to act. Entrusting the conduct of military operations to a committee, the members of which, ironically known as the 'Eight Saints', were to give their name to the ensuing war, the civic government offered assistance to the subject cities of the Papal State, successfully urging them to rebel against Gregory XI. When Bologna, Perugia, Città di Castello, Viterbo, Orvieto promptly did so, the pope reacted by imposing an interdict on Florence which had disastrous effects on its trade. The impact of this and the cost of hostilities soon provoked opposition to a continuation of the conflict. In 1378, the Parte Guelfa took the lead in this and the number of those it 'admonished' increased rapidly, even Giovanni Dini, one of the 'Eight Saints' being included among those proscribed.[37] This, in turn, led its opponents to seek to curb what they saw as its

<hr />

[36] Becker (1967–8), II, pp. 119–23; Becker (1959); Panella (1913); Baldasseroni (1906); Brucker (1962), pp. 131–43, 172–83.

[37] On the war of the 'Eight Saints' and its origins, see Brucker (1962), pp. 265–357; Gherardi (1867–8); Trexler (1974), pp. 133–62.

excesses. In May of that year, Salvestro dei Medici who had replaced Uguccione dei Ricci as the patrician leader of the popular or more moderate party became Gonfaloniere of Justice. When he acquired the power to initiate legislation, he tried unsuccessfully to persuade the colleges and councils to approve a decree requiring the Ordinances of Justice to be enforced with greater rigour. His failure was followed, on 22 June, by a rising, led by members of the guild community, but involving also the disenfranchised wool workers outside it.

Thus began what came to be known as the Tumult of the Ciompi, from the nickname of these labourers, subject to the authority of the Arte della Lana, but without power either in it or in the commune. Some of them had enjoyed transient recognition under the duke of Athens, but after his expulsion when the dyers, whom he had allowed to form a corporation of their own, had had this privilege withdrawn, the right of association had been denied them and one of their numbers, Ciuto Brandini, executed in 1345 for attempting to obtain it.[38] Following this, there was little indication of working-class militancy in Florence for more than three decades, perhaps because of the rise in living standards due to a shortage of labour after the Black Death. By the mid 1370s, however, this improvement in the condition of wage-earners was halted, a circumstance which may explain the outbreak of popular violence in 1378.[39] But, in the main, it would appear to have been an unintended effect of conflict among guild members with political rights, some of whom were prepared to allow the disenfranchised workers to rally with them to swell their numbers, in order to put pressure on the councils to pass measures against the 'magnates' and the Parte Guelfa. This immediate aim was, indeed, realised; for, after the rioting crowd had burnt down the houses of the leaders of the Albizzi faction, the appointment of a *balìa* of eighty-one citizens was approved, which resolved that all who had been 'admonished' should have their cases reviewed by the incoming *signoria* and that several of their aristocratic enemies should be excluded from office.

These concessions to popular feeling did not, however, succeed in appeasing it. On 20 July, the Ciompi rose to attempt to enforce a set of demands of their own. After they had killed Ser Nuto da Città di Castello, a hated police official, they forced the priors to abandon their palace and elected one of their number, Michele di Lando, Gonfaloniere of Justice by acclamation. This seizure of power was followed by the creation of three new guilds, one for the Ciompi or workers in the wool industry, one for the dyers and one for the doublet makers and related trades. New constitutional provisions were enacted, requiring a third of the offices to be allocated to these three corporations, a third to members of the lesser guilds and a third to those of the major

[38] Brucker (1962), pp. 110–11.   [39] La Roncière (1981).

ones. The heads of the Albizzi party were then exiled and a militia of Ciompi established to protect the regime.

The more radical elements among those who had brought about this revolution were not, however, completely satisfied with these reforms and proposed to carry them further. Meeting first outside the convent of San Marco and then at that of Santa Maria Novella, they elected eight representatives whom they instructed to negotiate with the priors to secure the acceptance of other decrees, prohibiting the arrest of debtors and granting delegates of the Ciompi direct participation in executive government. But these demands produced a split between this more extreme proletarian group and its previous allies. Michele di Lando, making common cause with the greater and lesser guilds and with those of the dyers and doublet makers, crushed his former supporters among the *popolo minuto* in an armed confrontation with them on 31 August. As a result of this, the guild of the Ciompi was dissolved at the beginning of September and the leaders of those who had gathered at Santa Maria Novella executed or banished. A further change in the constitution added the remaining two new guilds to the fourteen lesser ones and divided offices equally between the now sixteen *arti minori* and the seven *arti maggiori*.

The resulting regime which survived till 1382 drew on the support of the artisans and *mezzani* or middling sorts of men, in the major guilds, as well as of some renegade patricians. Salvestro dei Medici had ceased to play a prominent part in the city's politics after the rising in July 1378, but Giorgio Scali, Tommaso Strozzi and Benedetto degli Alberti remained influential figures. When the first two of these were condemned, in January 1382, for bringing unfounded accusations against the innocent and respected Giovanni Cambi, their disgrace precipitated its fall.[40] The wool merchants, taking advantage of the political isolation of those in power, rose against them and succeeded in securing their defeat in the ensuing *parlamento* or meeting of the citizens. This then elected a *balìa* which readmitted those exiled in 1378, restoring them their property, rights and status as *popolani*. It also dissolved the dyers' and doublet makers' guilds. Even so, the change in government effected by these measures did not restore a truly oligarchic predominance. At first four and, after the following month, three of the positions in the Priorate were still reserved for the lesser guilds. The power to 'admonish' citizens as Ghibellines which had lapsed since 1378 was revived, but accorded to the *signoria* and the 'colleges', rather than to the Parte Guelfa. Those previously proscribed in this way were, however, to be excluded from office for the next four years.

---

[40] On the Ciompi revolt, its causes and aftermath, see Brucker (1968); Rodolico (1899) and (1945); Rutenburg (1971), pp. 96–110, 157–354; Najemy (1981). On the financial demands of the Ciompi, see Barducci (1981); Bernocchi (1979), pp. 23–36; and Cipolla (1982), pp. 96–102.

At this stage, the two men with the strongest political influence in the city, Donato Acciaiuoli and Rinaldo Gianfigliazzi, adopted a fairly moderate position. Their standing was enhanced in 1384 by the leading role they played in the recovery of Arezzo, bought in that year from the soldier of fortune, Enguerrand de Coucy, who had seized it shortly before. However, in 1387, following further civic disturbances, the faction led by Maso degli Albizzi succeeded in having a new *balìa* constituted to effect additional reforms. As a result, the lesser guilds were restricted to only two positions in the *signoria* and provision was made for a more select purse or *borsellino*, from which the names of two of the major guild priors were to be drawn, a number that was increased in 1393 to three. From this point onwards, two tendencies became increasingly evident in Florentine politics – first, a consolidation of the position of the governing elite and, secondly, the exclusion from office of those prominent citizens who might challenge the ruling group or become the focus of popular opposition to it. Maso degli Albizzi, who acquired a prominent position in the regime, already in 1387 managed to secure the exile of Benedetto degli Alberti whom he blamed for the death of his uncle Piero, executed in 1379 for conspiring against the government of that time. Then, in 1393, when Maso was Gonfaloniere of Justice, further proscriptions of other members of the Alberti family followed, with Cipriano, Alberto, Giovanni, Piero and Nerozzo being banished for alleged complicity in a plot and several of their kinsmen condemned or declared to be 'magnates'. In the same year, the most influential of the aristocratic houses, till then designated as *grandi*, including the Bardi, Frescobaldi, Rossi, Tornaquinci, Adimari and Ricasoli, were made *popolani*. The drawing up of a new 'scrutiny' at this time also reinforced the tendency towards the exclusion of certain elements from government, while permitting quite wide participation in it of the broad body of supporters of the regime. The exile of Filippo Bastari in 1394 and that of Donato Acciaiuoli in 1396 subsequently removed from positions of power two more of its potential opponents.[41]

These political changes had the effect of making the Florentine upper class more homogeneous and less prone to division. Whereas in the late thirteenth century, many leading merchants had been prepared to ally themselves with the artisan guilds against the more turbulent of the old nobility, by the end of the fourteenth, their descendants, perhaps as a result of what they saw as the excesses of the Tumult of the Ciompi, preferred to collaborate with the former *grandi* against any resurgence of the popular cause. Another motive

---

[41] On the political history of Florence 1382–96, see Perrens (1877–83), VI, pp. 1–50; Rado (1926), pp. 58–222; Molho (1968a) and (1968b); Herde (1973); Witt (1976); Brucker (1977), pp. 46–101; Rubinstein (1981); Najemy (1982), pp. 263–300.

prompting the need for greater unity and cohesion among the ruling group at this time was the threat of external aggression. While Florence had been spared formidable enemies between the death of Archbishop Giovanni Visconti in 1354 and the end of its internal crisis in 1382, it was to face, from 1385 onwards, a dangerous opponent in Giangaleazzo Visconti, a ruler determined to use the extensive territories built up by his forebears around Milan as a base for the creation of a state that would dominate northern Italy. After he had gained control of Verona and Padua, Florence became involved, between 1390 and 1392, in a war against him intended to halt the rapid growth of his power. This was followed by a more serious confrontation, between 1397 and 1402, in which the commune found itself at a disadvantage, partly because its territory was so much smaller than Milan's and partly, paradoxically, because efforts to make up for this, notably through the acquisition of Arezzo in 1384, had led its neighbours to be so apprehensive of Florentine expansionism that they sought Giangaleazzo's protection. Thus, in 1399, Pisa passed in to his hands, while Milanese troops were admitted, later in the same year, to Siena and, in the following one, to Perugia. The fall of Bologna to him in 1402 enabled his state to half-encircle that of Florence which was delivered, shortly afterwards, from the danger he posed only by his death by plague.[42]

The ensuing disintegration of his dominions, as well as the subsequent Venetian conquest of Verona and Padua and the Florentine acquisition of Pisa in 1406, had the effect of blocking the possibility of a revival of Milanese hegemony in northern Italy and of creating a balance of power between the three main states of that region. These developments enhanced the prestige of the prevailing regime in Florence and made it easier for it to consolidate the authority it had acquired through the constitutional changes of 1387 and 1393. They also provided the background for the emergence in the city of what Hans Baron has described as 'Civic Humanism'.

The key figure in developing and promoting this in its early stages was Coluccio Salutati, chancellor of the commune from 1375 to 1406. Once seen by earlier scholars, such as Alfred von Martin and Hans Baron,[43] as a conservative and inward-looking thinker, he has been shown, through the more recent work of Peter Herde, Armando Petrucci, Ronald Witt and Daniela De Rosa,[44] to have been a writer and publicist who linked the Roman heritage to the political causes espoused by the city he served. From his letter to Francesco Guinigi in 1374, composed before he came to Florence, to his polemic with Antonio Loschi, dating from 1403, he identified liberty as the essential value

---

[42] On the wars with Giangaleazzo Visconti and their sequel, see Landogna (1929), pp. 56–91; Mesquita (1941), pp. 69–172, 187–292; Brucker (1977), pp. 125–208.

[43] Martin (1916); Baron (1966), pp. 96–166.

[44] Herde (1965); Petrucci (1972); De Rosa (1980); Witt (1983), pp. 146–77, 247–52.

shared by the Florentines of his day with the ancient Romans, transforming the traditional Guelf defence of republican freedom[45] and opposition to tyranny into a belief in the persistence from classical times of the ideals of constitutional government, the rule of law and the equality of citizens before it. Although, unlike his more radical disciples, Bruni, Poggio and Niccoli, he did not allow his admiration for antiquity to cloud his reverence for the great Florentine authors of the recent past, Dante, Petrarch and Boccaccio, he nevertheless shaped the character of the 'Civic Humanism' his younger followers were to extend and elaborate. By divesting his adopted city's previous Guelf ideology of its religious overtones, he laid the foundations for an intellectual validation of a political order which, like his ideas, had its roots in early fourteenth-century antecedents, but which had been modified as a result of developments that had occurred in Florence between 1342 and 1382. Through the changes issuing from these, a society based on an alliance between merchants and artisans, wedded to the cause of the Church and that of communal freedom, had given way to one exalting the ideal of a cultivated elite, inspired by a classical conception of republican liberty.

[45] On the changing connotations of Guelfism in late fourteenth-century Florence, see Witt (1969).

THE ITALIAN SOUTH

David Abulafia

IN the fourteenth century two kingdoms of Sicily vied for influence in Italian affairs, and one, that based on the mainland, also sought again and again to reabsorb its island rival. Such conflicts were a severe drain on the resources of the combatants; they also necessitated increasing reliance on powerful regional nobles and on foreign banking houses. The dissolution of political power was accompanied, as a result, by economic dislocation, particularly in the countryside. The fourteenth century saw, therefore, a significant change in the character of the southern realms; the open question is how permanent the damage was, the more so since the calamity of war was compounded by the mortality of plague. In Sicily, recovery was stimulated by the arrival at the end of the century of the royal house of Aragon-Catalonia, which took advantage of the extinction of the cadet Aragonese dynasty of Sicily to reimpose its authority, with growing success and with beneficial effects on the island's economy. On the mainland, recovery was hindered by the persistence of weak government, characterised by serious internal strife within the ruling Angevin dynasty itself.

This discussion lays emphasis on the role of the Angevin kings of Naples and the Aragonese kings of Sicily in the wider political conflicts within Italy and the Mediterranean. Particular attention has to be attached to Robert of Naples, whose reign marks the culmination of Angevin attempts to act as the arbiters of Italian politics.

The accession of Robert of Anjou, 'the Wise', in 1309 coincided with developments which were greatly to influence the Angevin kingdom of Naples. At the end of 1308 Henry, count of Luxemburg was elected king of the Romans by the German princes. During the same decade the residence of the popes became fixed not in Italy but at Avignon in the Angevin county of Provence. The proximity of the popes to the Angevin court in Provence and the popes' absence from Italy elevated Robert to the status of prime defender of Guelf interests in Rome, Tuscany and Lombardy. Robert could confer with the pope on his frequent visits to Provence. Equally, the papacy had to take care not to allow the Angevins to consolidate their hold over the whole of Italy. Thus there were tensions pulling several ways – towards the policies of the French or Angevin courts; towards a possible mediator who could create a non-Angevin peace in Italy. The papacy never ceased to hope that the Angevins would lead a crusade, and the priority given to the recovery of Jerusalem naturally attracted them still more to the self-styled 'kings of Jerusalem and Sicily'.

Clement V rapidly came to conceive of Henry VII as a balance to Robert of Anjou. Indeed, he tried to encourage Robert to show grace to Henry. Henry sent to the north Italian towns to ask for promises of fealty, but he aroused Robert's suspicions still further when his ambassador instructed the citizens of Asti, in Angevin Piedmont, not to pay homage to King Robert just yet. They promised their loyalty to Henry VII meanwhile (1310). Robert was, of course, technically an imperial vassal, since the county of Piedmont was held from the emperor; but there had not for a long time been any German king so anxious to enforce his claim to the imperial lands and title in Italy.

Henry did not, however, originally seek to dispossess Robert. He fell in with a papal plan to arrange a marriage alliance with his Angevin rival, with the imperial kingdom of Arles as dowry for Henry's daughter. It was a generous offer which tempted Robert, for the kingdom of Arles included the county of Provence, another of Robert's technically imperial fiefs. Yet on the other hand he had allies in Florence who urged him to stand firm against the emperor-elect, as they intended to do. Robert visited Florence in 1310, and was lavishly entertained by his bankers, the Peruzzi, with whom he stayed. Increasingly, he stood to gain from Clement's alarm at Henry's progress. Clement appointed Robert his vicar in Romagna despite his reluctance, in common with earlier popes, to let the Angevin king hold office in papal lands in northern Italy (1310). Bowsky has argued that the reason Clement made him vicar was not that he wished to strengthen Robert in case a struggle with Henry developed, but that Clement wished to use Angevin troops to contain uprisings in the towns of Romagna, for instance, Ghibelline rebellions in favour of Henry VII.[1] No doubt this consideration pushed Clement even further towards Robert, but the pope's main fear was probably that Henry would not respect the territorial integrity of papal Romagna. It was headache enough to have to allow Henry into Rome for the traditional imperial coronation.

Henry VII did in 1310 and 1311 begin to heal some of the wounds of faction-fighting in the Lombard towns, but major foci of opposition remained in Guelf Tuscany. Florence was determined to resist Henry, who avoided Florence. He went to Rome, but the city was partly occupied by Angevin

---

[1] Bowsky (1960), pp. 122–4.

troops. He was crowned amid street-battles (June 1311). The presence of an Angevin army, hostile to his own forces, only helped Henry swing more towards the Ghibelline groups who had his ear; he reacted decisively against Robert. His daughter would now be sent in marriage to the Aragonese court in Sicily, that established focus of Ghibelline interests. King Frederick III of Sicily became an 'admiral of the empire'. Papal attempts at mediation were rapidly set aside. Henry had no difficulty in choosing the ideal targets for a war in defence of imperial interests: Florence, which he besieged (1312–13) and the kingdom of Naples, whose king he stripped of all imperial honours and even of the throne of Sicily over which his suzerainty was, to say the least, controversial. He planned an invasion of Naples in order to put into effect these proclamations; and Clement, now fully roused, riposted with a threat to excommunicate anyone who attacked his vassal Robert. Italy was saved from a papal crusade against Henry and from new havoc in southern Italy only by the death of Henry, from fever, in August 1313.

Robert of Anjou emerges much less clearly from these episodes than Clement or Henry. He was genuinely perturbed at the danger of loss of authority in Piedmont, since he himself had helped his father Charles II re-establish Angevin rule there. He seems also to reflect his father's outlook in his initial willingness to discuss – though without any commitment – a marriage alliance with the house of Luxemburg. He did explore the possibility of peace, but he feared an anti-Guelf movement in Lombardy and Tuscany, and he was greatly guided by what he had seen and heard in Florence. He was led towards an attempt at military intervention against Henry which he had not at first planned to put into effect. Yet these final moves towards all-out war reflect more accurately the tone of his reign than his initial *pourparlers* with Henry VII. Imperial adventurers continued to come into Italy, but Robert of Anjou had survived the most serious threat he would face to the tenure of his throne.

Robert of Anjou's initiation into Italian politics was marked also by another papal conflict: the crusade launched against Venice in 1309, and the struggle between Clement V and the Venetians for suzerainty over Ferrara. This city had been bequeathed by its ruler Azzo VII d'Este to an illegitimate son, Fresco, rather than to his legitimate heirs. Since Azzo VII had been married to Robert's sister Beatrice past Angevin alliances were affected. Fresco invited the Venetians to accept suzerainty over Ferrara, which they had long coveted, if they would maintain him as its lord. This brought the Venetians into association with Fresco's other allies, Ghibelline exiles and petty lords. The pope maintained Ferrara was an unredeemed part of Romagna, of the lands of the Holy See. He preached a 'crusade' against the Venetians, and he tried to interest Charles II in his claim, to little effect, but he managed to arouse the wrath of King Robert against the Venetians. Their goods were confiscated from them in the trading cities of Apulia. This was all the greater blow since Charles I had maintained good relations with Venice (especially against Michael Palaeologus) and Charles II had also favoured the Venetians. Robert accepted the post of papal 'vicar' in Ferrara after the crusade against the Venetians had won its way, but he also surrendered the office once the papal representatives were ready to integrate the city into the papal patrimony. Robert's involvement can be attributed partly to his family link to the Este, partly to the fact that the pope actually talked with him in Provence about the affair. Above all, Robert was keen to establish harmony with the papacy over common objectives in northern Italy. He was ready to do Clement considerable favours in return for support in vigorous new 'crusades' against Sicily and other objectives. In the process of supporting this crusade he threw away the friendship of the Venetians. He was confident that, with the support of other allies, Venetian political assistance was superfluous. With the pope a close ally, with his nephew Carobert pursuing grand aims in Hungary, with Florence (not Venice) his closest business partner, with Henry VII soon dead, Robert could pursue aggressive ends of his own.

The first experiences of Robert as king seemed to urge him into more decisive action against the Ghibellines and their allies in Sicily. He realised that southern Italy was in danger of being trapped between two anti-Angevin forces: the resurgent Ghibellines who had drawn encouragement from Henry VII's brief career; and Frederick of Trinacria, who now for his part dropped his fancy title to resume that of king of Sicily, and thereby revived direct competition with the house of Anjou. Robert's first assault on Sicily, in 1314, achieved nothing, except to confirm Robert in his strongly held desire to destroy his Aragonese rivals. In the north of Italy he did acquire titles: the death of the emperor Henry left Pope Clement free to dispose of imperial offices in northern Italy, according to the debatable position that, *vacante imperio*, during an imperial vacancy, the pope assumed temporary authority over the empire. Robert became imperial vicar in Italy at papal behest (1314), and was encouraged to turn against the most powerful Ghibelline family in Italy, the Visconti of Milan. The restoration of the Visconti in Milan had itself been made possible by Henry's reconciliation between them and the rival della Torre family. Thus the Visconti were the most potent remaining symbol of Henry VII's expedition. But Robert's attention was also needed outside the Lombard plain: another anti-papal champion, Castruccio Castracani degli Antelminelli, gained power at Lucca in 1314. So too Piedmont demanded Angevin attention, after its partial abandonment of Charles II for Henry of Luxemburg. (Asti was recovered for the house of Anjou as early as March 1314.) Robert's slow advances in northern Italy were not easily shaken even by the defeat of

Angevin and Guelf forces at Montecatini (August 1315), when the Tuscan Ghibellines aided by Matteo Visconti left members of the house of Anjou dead on the battlefield. This defeat could not be a total calamity while the Angevins still possessed important bases in northern Italy, including middle-range towns such as the Angevin seigniory at Prato, and eventually the major city of Genoa.

The creation of an Angevin seigniory in Genoa was perhaps the most ambitious attempt at resistance to Matteo Visconti and the Ghibelline revival. It signalled, also, the inception of a close but uneasy relationship between Robert and Pope John XXII (1316–34), an ambitious pontiff whose fulminations against the Ghibellines came to echo in ferocity the statements of Innocent III or Boniface VIII. Like them, he was keen to use the crusade as a weapon for the defence of papal interests in Italy, preaching holy war against Matteo Visconti and Frederick of Sicily. This determination to use the full force of papal armaments made him a useful ally for Robert; but John's insistence on rigorous respect for papal rights could also lead to tension between the allies; John's remarks that, *vacante imperio,* he could dispose of the imperial county of Piedmont and could not see by what right Robert assumed it was without doubt his own, only left the Angevin king irritated. Essentially, it was Robert who made the important military decisions in Italy.

In Genoa the conflicts between noble factions were expressed with an extreme bitterness and an extraordinary persistence which threatened to undermine the city's trading position; some Genoese, such as the Grimaldi of Monaco, saw salvation in the rise of the house of Anjou. It was in 1317 that the Ghibellines of Genoa overreached themselves. At the end of that year the Guelf families (Fieschi, Grimaldi) gained power at home and their rivals, the Doria and Spinola clans, appealed to Matteo Visconti for armed help. The Guelfs in reply appealed to Robert to send men, money and ships to defend their besieged city. They recognised him as lord of Genoa, jointly with Pope John; Robert even transferred a small crusading flotilla, waiting at Marseille, from campaigns in the east to the relief of Genoa. Robert's lordship was renewed until 1335, when a government of reconciliation ejected the Angevins; before then the king stayed for some months in Genoa and perhaps saw the city as a lever for the extension of Angevin authority eastwards from Provence along the coasts of north-western Italy.

The papal-Angevin crusade against the Visconti almost but never quite broke their power. By 1324 Robert of Anjou's diplomatic intervention secured from Matteo's son and successor Galeazzo Visconti a promise to resist any future imperial adventures in Italy. This success in diplomacy was all the greater because by 1324 the claimant to the throne of the Holy Roman Empire, Lewis of Bavaria, had begun to interfere directly in north Italian politics. Robert of

Anjou showed few signs of being greatly scared by Lewis, even when the emperor was crowned by the Colonna in Rome in 1328. He seems to have reasoned that wars in Tuscany above all would distract Lewis from interference in Neapolitan affairs; Frederick of Sicily raided the coasts of southern Italy when his fleet was sent north to aid Lewis, but it was only after Lewis's coronation that Robert slowly fell in with papal plans. After a few months he allowed a crusade to be preached against Lewis. He began to raise an army. But it is not clear he wished to attack the emperor. He may, for instance, have hoped to benefit from the levy of crusade taxes, that is, those tithes which the pope would allow him to keep in his own hands to cover war expenses. Another dimension to Robert's attitude was probably his irritation at John XXII. Whether its source lay in the excessively vigorous attempts of this aggressive pope to guide Angevin policy, or whether it lay in Robert's apparent affection for the Spiritual Franciscans whom John persecuted, the late 1320s saw the path of Robert and John diverge.

This is not to say that the Angevins failed to recognise the danger of a Ghibelline revival in Tuscany. The brilliant soldier Castruccio Castracani frequently, though not constantly, gained the upper hand in battles with the Guelfs. The Angevin vicar at Pistoia was sent packing (March 1324), and a hard-won victory over the Florentine Guelfs, under an Angevin captain-general, was achieved by the Ghibellines at Altopascio (May 1325). Similarly, the Angevin vicars of a line of towns in Romagna – Faenza, Imola, Forlì – had lost power as early as 1314–15; and Ghibelline influence in the region was consolidated by a victory at Zappolino (November 1325) in which the great Ghibelline tyrants, Castruccio and Cangrande della Scala, invested many troops of their own. The Guelfs were increasingly on the defensive; even the Florentines thought they could only guarantee their liberties by accepting an Angevin governor. Robert had tried to foist Nicholas de Joinville on them as long ago as 1317, but the Florentines insisted that a royal vicar would be incompatible with their traditions of freedom. But in 1325 they offered the seigniory of the city to Robert's heir, Charles, duke of Calabria. He was to bring with him several hundred knights, and he was to receive 100,000 florins per annum from the city to cover his expenses. Other Guelf communes such as Prato and San Gimignano also accepted him as seignior. And he was indeed able to make a contribution to the security of the Guelfs: in 1328 his forces seized Pistoia from the Ghibellines. But the same year Charles of Calabria died unexpectedly and the Florentines did not seek a replacement until 1342, when Duke Walter of Brienne arrived at Robert's renewed bidding. There were advances in Romagna too, despite Zappolino: the papal legate Bertrand de Poujet brought a number of towns back under papal control, and at Bologna the citizens displayed Robert's coat of arms alongside that of Pope John, a sign that in some eyes at least the old union of forces was still worth defending (1327). It was in the last years of John XXII's pontificate, until 1334, that irrefutable signs of a breach between the Avignon papacy and the Angevin king emerged.

The arrival in Italy in 1330 of King John of Bohemia opened the way to unexpected co-operation between Guelfs and Ghibellines, and the Angevins too, against eccentric papal policies. John was the son of Henry VII, but he did not seek to become emperor, nor to displace Lewis of Bavaria whose Italian links were by now very attenuated; it was rather that the Italian towns, beginning with Brescia, began to see in him a herald of peace reminiscent of his father Henry. The search for an imperial protector was particularly urgent in Brescia during 1330, since the city was threatened by Mastino della Scala, Ghibelline lord of Verona. Its former protector, Robert of Anjou, seems to have made no effort to help. With the appeal of the Brescians to the king of Bohemia, John of Luxemburg became more conscious than ever of his father Henry's dreams of pacifying northern Italy. When the Milanese, led by Azzo Visconti, submitted to John, the Bohemian king's plans took more concrete form: his allies were appointed as his 'vicars' in Lombardy; his army intervened in a joint Angevin–Florentine siege at Lucca, and occupied peacefully a town the Guelfs had been struggling to take by force (1331). Even Bertrand de Poujet made haste to face new realities, by making an alliance with King John and conferring on him the lordship of Parma and other Lombard towns.

The Ghibellines as a whole – even the Visconti, who were soon disenchanted – looked with distaste at Pope John's new alliance. And Robert of Anjou felt that his place also lay with the opponents of Bohemian intervention, which he apparently identified with earlier imperial intervention. Giovanni Villani, the Florentine chronicler, observed that the motive of King Robert in supporting Ghibellines, of all people, lay in his resentment at the papal–Bohemian alliance and his fear of Lewis of Bavaria and John of Bohemia. It was with French armies behind him that John re-entered Italy in 1333, only to be defeated three months later at Ferrara, by the Lombard League of Guelfs, Ghibellines and Angevins. By 1334 Robert of Anjou and Lewis of Bavaria were actually making peaceful noises to one another. After all, each was a patron of the poverty movements; it was John XXII who was in that respect the odd man out. So too in politics. John had had specific aims: to re-establish papal rights in central Italy, to return to Rome, to maintain the Guelfs. But he was better at deciding on his ultimate intention than on working out how to achieve that goal. Throughout John's pontificate, Robert the Wise had managed to remain master of himself.

To understand Robert's lack of enthusiasm for some of John XXII's north Italian schemes it is necessary to consider the king's other preoccupations.

Sicily, above all, demanded attention, for King Frederick had allied himself to Lewis and the Ghibellines; moreover, Frederick broke the terms of the Treaty of Caltabellotta in 1320 by naming his son Peter as his heir, when the island was supposed to go after his death to the Angevin king. In addition, the successors of James II of Aragon gave open support to Frederick of Sicily from the 1330s onwards. Thus the years of the Bohemian entry into Italy saw an intensification of Robert's struggle for dominion over Sicily; between 1330 and 1343 six Angevin expeditions were launched against Frederick and his heirs. There were striking successes in the short term, such as the capture of a castle at Palermo and of Milazzo, near the straits of Messina; in 1346, three years after Robert's death, Milazzo was in fact permanently occupied, but during his lifetime none of the conquests lasted long and they could not even be used to force the Aragonese into negotiation. The failure of the expeditions is all the more surprising since the Sicilian nobility was deeply divided between two factions, the 'Catalans' and the 'Latins', there were even defections to the court of Naples, such as that of Giovanni Chiaramonte, a very illustrious nobleman who acquired from Robert what proved to be an empty title: vicar-general for Sicily. Even the accession of a child-king in Sicily, Lodovico, in 1342 and the rebellion of the 'Latins' against the new regent brought no permanent Angevin success.

The Sicilian war was, as has been seen, presented as a 'crusade'. The Angevins continued to take seriously their duties in the east. There were a few Neapolitan ships in the expedition to Smyrna, on the coast of what is now Turkey, in 1337; this region had become an important theatre of war since the Knights of St John of Jerusalem occupied Rhodes in 1310. In the former Byzantine lands claimed by the Angevins there was more progress. The 'kingdom of Albania' seemed to acquire again some reality, with the co-operation of the native Thopia family. The Albanian nobility was loyal to the house of Anjou in the 1320s and 1330s; probably it saw the Angevins as generous defenders of their own domains against the Serbs. In 1336–7 an Angevin prince, Louis of Durazzo, gained successes against the Serbs, fighting in central Albania. It was his family that received Durazzo and the hinterland as a fief from Robert of Anjou. So too in Achaia the Angevins enforced their authority (1338–42), or rather the authority of Charles of Valois's daughter Catherine de Courtenay, who had married into the Angevin dynasty and had brought the imperial title of Constantinople with her, as it were in her dowry.

More importantly, she brought to high office and royal attention a remarkable man who was greatly to help shape the kingdom of Naples in future years: the Florentine Niccolò Acciaiuoli, the son of a prominent banker. For his help in holding Achaia he was awarded his first fiefs, in the western Peloponnese, and on his return to Naples he won office as justiciar of the Terra di Lavoro, the province around Naples.

The links between the court of Naples and the Hungarian court were intensified. A series of projects for a marriage alliance between the two Angevin dynasties reached fruition in the betrothal of Joanna, granddaughter of Robert, and Andrew, younger son of the Hungarian ruler Carobert. Joanna had become heiress after her father Charles of Calabria died in 1328, and a responsible prince was needed to help her rule her future kingdom. Andrew was in fact a questionable choice as royal consort, and he aroused sufficiently intense hatred to be murdered in 1345, to no great regret of Queen Joanna. But the murder of Andrew meant also that Robert's good intention in bonding Naples and Hungary led rather to conflict. Andrew's elder brother Lajos, or Louis, the Great led two devastating expeditions into southern Italy to avenge his death. These unforeseen results of Robert's Hungarian alliance, after that king's death, should not be allowed to detract from his real achievement: after careful negotiation the king of Naples secured an arrangement which was intended neither to lead to the union of the two Angevin kingdoms nor to the automatic acquisition of a crown by Andrew. In addition, Robert took care to set aside papal claims to assume authority in the vassal kingdom of Naples should he die before his granddaughter came of age.

In his will King Robert passed Provence, southern Italy and funds for the reconquest of Sicily to Joanna (December 1342). The lands which he had kept intact were not to be divided. Apart from the loss once again of Asti (August 1342), even Robert's power in Piedmont had survived the enormous pressures of bitter wars and intensive diplomacy carried on without cease. The influence of Robert the Wise was always present in the policy of Florence and in that of many Guelf towns. Even when, as briefly in 1342, the Florentines departed from Angevin diplomacy they were conscious of the possible risks they ran – in this case, as will be seen, financial risks also. Robert entered equally into the calculations of his enemies. They knew he was watching them, but they could not always deduce his intentions. Robert, despite his commitment to the Guelf cause and his link to the pope, was a flexible, agile politician, a point shown clearly by his reaction to Lewis of Bavaria and John of Bohemia. He seems to have been the main policy maker himself; it was only under Joanna that a virtual prime minister, Niccolò Acciaiuoli, began to shape royal policy on the ruler's behalf. Robert's policies in northern Italy earn him some right to his sobriquet 'the Wise'.

The lengthy, bitter wars of the Angevins had somehow to be funded. The resources of the house of Anjou shrank at once with the loss of Sicily, whose grain had produced tax revenue, military supplies and valuable political leverage over centres of consumption in northern Italy. A sophisticated redistribution system under Charles I ensured that mainland provinces, especially the area of Naples, that were habitually short of grain could be fed from the generally abundant spare resources of the island. Expenditure on the recovery of Sicily was thus seen as investment in the restoration of state finances. It is not, then, surprising that the monarchy was content to rely on loans from foreign bankers to finance its wars and its other needs; moreover, the existence of good wheat lands in Apulia and other corners of southern Italy meant that the crown could still to some degree capitalise on the great tradition of grain production. The relationship with foreign merchants can be seen in its most extreme form in the instance of Angevin favours to the great Florentine banks. In 1284 members of the Bardi, Acciaiuoli and Mozzi houses made Charles II a loan of 1,000 ounces of gold, and in return were permitted to export 2,250 tons of wheat from Apulia. Further loans enabled them also to export barley and beans the same year. Charles de la Roncière has counted over forty grants of export rights to these and lesser Florentine banks, in the thirty years 1290–1329, all of them secured by handsome loans to the crown.[2] In 1311 alone the quantity of recorded grain exports was about 45,000 tons, enough for a very large fleet of ships; and the steady rise in the volume of these exports was aptly matched by massive amounts of gold advanced to Charles II and Robert the Wise, such as a sum of over 18,000 ounces in 1305. Nor, indeed, could the crown any longer express its gratitude solely through payments of interest and renunciation of the right to charge for licences to export grain. The Florentines were allowed exemption from all customs dues on these exports; but an important feature of these privileges was that they were granted to the banks singly, in return for a specific favour, and they were not conferred on the whole commune of Florence nor on all Florentines trading in southern Italy. Repayment took many forms, such as permitting the banks control over the collection of revenue from royal assets. The fishing port of Castellamare was conferred first on bankers from Lucca who had supported the crown; in 1300 it was transferred by royal fiat to the Bardi of Florence: in the 1350s it was actually a fief of the illustrious Florentine courtier in Naples, Niccolò Acciaiuoli. Florentines gained control of the mint, too, for a time; they acquired the right to tax grain exports, first in the Abruzzi, on the Adriatic coast, then further south along the same coast, in Apulia. At another level, access to south Italian markets gave the Peruzzi the chance to sell considerable quantities of Florentine cloth in the Regno.

Such activities planted in the minds of the rulers of Naples schemes to develop internationally successful textile industries of their own. Native assets appeared to make such plans viable: the existence of a local wool supply, in which Charles I expressed interest as early as 1279, in an attempt to increase

[2] La Roncière (1976), II, pp. 565, 571–3, 625.

the quality of domestic cloth production; the existence of a dyeing industry in such centres as Salerno, where the Jews had a special role; this industry was given further impetus by Charles II in 1299 when he tried to set up new dyeing workshops in southern Italy. Later Charles II paid two brothers from Florence the sum of 48 ounces of gold, to encourage them to set up a textile factory in Naples, and in 1308 the Florentine merchant Giovanni da Milano agreed to remain ten years in Naples, to help create a woollen cloth industry on the basis of English, French and North African fibres, which suggests that the wool of southern Italy was not really considered sufficient in quality to rival that used by the main Tuscan textile towns for their prestige exports. These efforts, which have ample contemporary parallels in neighbouring lands such as Majorca, were repeated under Robert the Wise; but success was limited, and even the monarchy's attitude cooled when it became apparent that there were heretics among the north Italian textile workers who came to Naples.

The great banks, the Bardi, Peruzzi and Acciaiuoli, whose size was not even rivalled by the Medici and Strozzi in the fifteenth and sixteenth centuries, were deeply involved with the Angevins not merely in their rise to prosperity, but also in their cataclysmic fall in the 1340s. The peak of Florentine involvement in Naples was reached before 1330. Thereafter a number of cracks appear in this neat façade. Internal squabbles undoubtedly reduced the effectiveness of the Florentine government in influencing papal and Angevin affairs, though at first this may not have affected the big banks very seriously. External quarrels brought Florence into expensive wars, such as the Lombard League of 1332 in which such improbable allies as the della Scala and Visconti joined Florence and King Robert in an attempt to rebuff King John of Bohemia. Florence had to contribute to an expensive force of 600 knights; it had also to hold back local allies of King John, above all Castruccio Castracani, lord of Lucca. Even after John's defeat in 1333, adherents of Lewis of Bavaria remained active, and Florence worked hard to resist the Ghibellines in Tuscany and Lombardy. The result was that by 1341 Florence had to ask its allies for help with its war expenses; the commune turned, in desperation, to King Robert of Naples: 'we are spending an uncountable amount of money nowadays on Lombard affairs, so that all our existing and future revenues have already been taken up'. The Florentine banks were either reluctant to help or incapable of helping. Armando Sapori suggested that the Peruzzi at least were being drained of funds: in 1331 the firm reorganised, with £60,000 capital, but by 1335 £59,228 1s 2d had already gone.[3]

The collapse of the Bardi and Peruzzi in 1343–5 marks the end of an era of great commercial adventurousness, and the beginning of a dramatic decline in

[3] Sapori (1926).

the fortunes of the Neapolitan crown. The bankers' support for Edward III's invasion of Flanders was a financial disaster, while Florentine attempts to extricate the republic from its traditional Guelf alliance against Lewis of Bavaria excited serious alarm in Naples, on political and financial grounds. The Florentine chronicler Villani writes:

many of his barons and prelates and other rich men of his kingdom, who had deposited their money with the Companies and the merchants of Florence, became so suspicious at this turn of events that each wanted to be repaid, and confidence collapsed in Florence, and everywhere else where the Florentines did business, in such a way that not long afterwards many Florentine Companies failed.

The traditional view that breach of faith on the part of Robert and Edward destroyed the banks must be corrected; calculated risks in Flanders and a wobble away from a pro-Angevin government policy were the really ruinous factors. Sapori is right to remark that it was not 'a badly based suspicion by the King of Naples that provoked the crisis. It was the official policy of the Commune of Florence.'[4] Subsequently, the companies asked Robert and his heiress Joanna to repay the accumulated debts of decades; but they must have realised that there was no hope of immediate repayment. The demand was a formal process; its rejection by Queen Joanna only confirmed that the banks were doomed. For Joanna this was not a light matter: she had inherited Robert's debts, which she could renounce; but it was not clear where the Angevin rulers could henceforth turn in their search for funds. For the Florentine banks which survived the 1340s were smaller and more cautious than those which had financed Robert of Anjou. Yet there were still wars to be fought, in Sicily and against the Hungarians, and there was still a magnificent court demanding its upkeep.

This negative picture of Angevin finance must not be exaggerated. John H. Pryor has discussed Angevin attempts to stimulate the economy:[5] the careful protection of merchants travelling within the kingdom; improvements in port facilities at such centres as Manfredonia (under Charles I); the establishment of more than a dozen new fairs; the provision of ships from the royal fleet to merchants, when not needed in war; the opening of new silver mines in Calabria, whose exploitation was farmed out at a charge of one third of the proceeds. Few of these measures were entirely new. The crown stockpiled salt, as it had done under Frederick; profits could reach 1,300 per cent once the mineral was released to buyers. Export taxes were maintained and, when reformed, were sometimes increased: Charles II introduced a light tax which was actually to be levied on goods exempt from all tax (the *jus tari*); under

---

[4] Sapori (1926).   [5] Pryor (1980), p. 46.

Robert it developed into a tax on all goods irrespective of whether they were otherwise exempt.

Pryor places these measures before the war loans of the Tuscan banks in seeking to explain the stagnation of the Angevin economy. The Angevin kings were not impoverished by comparison with their contemporaries:

Annual revenue of certain European rulers (in florins p.a.)

Charles I (before 1282)	1,100,000
Robert of Anjou	600,000
Louis IX of France (1226–70)	500,000
Philip VI of France (1329)	786,000
Despots of Milan in 1338	700,000
Edward III of England (1327–77)	550,000–700,000
Pope Boniface VIII (1294–1303)	250,000
Pope John XXII (1316–34)	240,000

The difference is that the Angevin figures declined over time; the French increased, up to the Hundred Years War. Partly this is simply attributable to the loss of Sicily, which was a source of great wealth: but in the later years of Robert and during the reign of Joanna I there was increasingly dramatic erosion. Moreover, Charles I maintained his court and armies by failing on occasion to pay the tribute due to the pope; 93,340 ounces of gold – approaching half a million florins – were due at the time of his death in 1285, though after the loss of Sicily the tribute was reduced to only 5,000 ounces a year. Yet Robert of Anjou, in diligent agreement with the pope, paid off his predecessors' debts by 1340. This was also the time of Robert's Sicilian campaigns; it is thus impressive that even then Robert's war needs did not absorb all this revenue: 'when military success began to wane and the Angevin domains contracted, and when revenue itself contracted, the crown became able to hold its deficit, to reduce it gradually, and finally to extinguish it'. On the other hand, Robert's abilities were not matched by those of his successors, under whom the Regno became the battle ground of mercenary companies.

The effects of these difficulties on the population at large are hard to estimate; the picture is distorted by the ravages of plague, which first reached Sicily in 1347. The loss of millions of records in the destruction of the Naples archive (1943) means that the social history of the Regno in the fourteenth century cannot now be written. Romolo Caggese alone made use of the Angevin registers to illustrate the violent tenor of rural life: royal protection of merchants and pilgrims often worked better in theory than in practice.[6] Tough landlords, such as the Teutonic Knights, found their pastures invaded by the

---

[6] Caggese (1922–30).

peasantry of the Barletta region (1313). The lord of Castroprignano complained that his peasants not merely refused to pay their rents and perform their services, but that he and his family had been attacked, and his bailiff killed. But the peasant case was precisely that many of the labour services were a novelty; he imposed on his peasants the duty to help repair his castle and his mills: he was himself guilty of grabbing royal demesne land. It is difficult to know how typical these cases were of Robert's Regno, or of Europe as a whole.[7] Certainly, it was the baronage that exploited weaknesses in royal power to enhance its regional authority; the monarchy's own liberality to favoured subjects, such as Niccolò Acciaiuoli, further eroded royal control of the provinces. The tendency persisted to dream of the reconquest of Sicily as the panacea to the kingdom's ills.

King Robert's 'wisdom' was most evident to his contemporaries in his patronage of letters and the fine arts. These activities were turned to the political advantage of the Angevin royal house and, quite apart from Robert's genuine devotion to the arts, his willingness to use his artists also as propagandists sheds light on his policies. Robert's father and grandfather had maintained the cultural patronage of the court of Sicily, inherited from the Hohenstaufen and Normans and by them from distant Lombard and other predecessors. It was, rather, the scale and fame of Robert's court which excited special admiration. The king sought to display his affluence, an extension of his power. The Angevins were known for their interest in rich silks and damasks, expressive of their special royal dignity and wealth. Robert sought to display the legitimacy of his dynasty amid the counter-claims of his Aragonese rivals. The most eloquent document of their political interest in the fine arts is a painting by the eminent Sienese, Simone Martini, dating to about 1317 (see frontispiece) Robert's eldest brother, the saintly Louis of Toulouse is shown conferring his crown on Robert after his renunciation of the throne in favour of life in the Franciscan order. Not merely Robert's own claim to the throne of Sicily but that of the Angevin dynasty to rule in southern Italy is enhanced by the presence of a saint in the royal family. Can the Angevins be mere usurpers if the body of St Louis of Toulouse works miracles? Giotto, the unrivalled Florentine painter of the time, came to the Angevin court too, and received a pension from Robert. Around 1330 he was at work on a series of paintings now sadly lost, showing the great classical and biblical heroes with their wives or lovers: Paris and Helen of Troy, Aeneas and Dido, Samson and Delilah.

---

[7] Hilton (1973), pp. 110–12, certainly assumes that he can generalise to the rest of Europe from these cases.

Here were classical themes, with romantic overtones: the subject of Giotto's work reflects the combination of French 'Gothic' cultural traditions brought by Charles of Anjou to Naples, with innovatory Italian styles and motifs. Many of the great buildings of the Angevins in Naples are heavily influenced by French Gothic architecture: the church of Santa Chiara, for instance, where Robert and other Angevins are buried in lavish marble tombs which recall French and Provençal styles. Nor is this surprising in a dynasty which took a keen interest in the county of Provence, and proudly displayed in decorations the fleur-de-lis of Charles I's royal French ancestors. Provençal poets, blending with south Italian lyricists whose work had been fostered by the Hohenstaufen, remained active around the Angevin court, and Charles I fancied himself as a composer of verses. The Norman and Hohenstaufen courts were no more eclectic in taste than that of the Angevins; the close attention of the Angevins to French and Provençal courtly models simply added to the diversity at court. Like many fourteenth-century courts, that of Naples patronised chivalric orders, imitated from the Order of the Star in France and of the Garter in England; ten years after Robert's death Niccolò Acciaiuoli organised the 'Order of the Holy Spirit' for the flower of the Neapolitan nobility. Attention to the ideals of chivalry, at a time of growing misconduct in war, shows further responsiveness to the influence of north European courts.

More disinterested was the Angevin patronage of letters, though even there King Robert acquired glory in his own day by his friendship for Petrarch, who came to Naples in 1341 so that Robert could examine whether he was worthy to receive the Laurel Crown, not awarded since antiquity, for his knowledge of poetry. Giovanni Boccaccio, active also in the study of classical literature, was present at Petrarch's examination in Naples. Although less lucky in his attempts to gain lavish patronage from the Angevins, Boccaccio had spent his youth in Naples, apprenticed to the Bardi bank. He was then a close friend of Niccolò Acciaiuoli, though later they quarrelled. The young Boccaccio spent more time at the picnics and revels of the Neapolitan nobility, less at the royal court itself; but his admiration for Robert the Wise and the influence of his Neapolitan education upon his writing were both substantial. Among lesser figures more permanently at court must be mentioned Barlaam, a Greek-speaking Calabrian, from whom Boccaccio learned some Greek; the Angevin court was the only European court where steadily sustained study of Greek texts could be found. Scientific and medical study was also active, with the help of Jewish translators whom the Angevins protected, more it seems for their knowledge than out of tolerance: Robert's wife Sancha of Majorca was hostile to the Jews generally. In 1308 loans from Florentine bankers were used to pay a fee for the translation of Arabic books into Latin and a stipend for the distinguished

Roman painter Cavallini. The parallels to the rather more tolerant Norman and Hohenstaufen court are, in the scientific field, rather striking.

There was a further area of intellectual activity which helped the Angevin dynasty politically. The king's lawyers willingly demonstrated the independence of the kings of Naples from all superior control. The jurists Marinus de Caramanico and Andrea of Isernia, under Charles II and Robert, used the historic legatine status of the rulers of southern Italy the *monarchia sicula,* as evidence for the freedom of kings from day-to-day interference in their affairs. They stressed that the king was not subject to imperial or other authority: he was emperor in his own kingdom. In his commentary on Frederick II's lawbook of 1231, Andrea of Isernia insisted that the king's decrees must be accepted as law and that his power consisted in determining the law; he was not bound by the law. This gloss on a lawbook which itself stressed that the ruler's word was law helped the Angevin dynasty to claim the exalted authority of their Hohenstaufen predecessors. Though Robert was more scrupulous than Charles I and II in paying the tribute due to the pope, in other respects he was a prolific legislator, insistent on the supreme authority which his legal advisers instructed him to employ. Emile Léonard has provided a list of the vivid and varied preambles to royal decrees, rich in the insistence on the need for careful exercise of justice and in warnings against human tendencies to pervert the course of justice.[8] Easier to ascribe to Robert are many sermons and treatises; his views on the Beatific Vision even contradicted those of Pope John XXII. He drew his texts for the sermons from biblical passages which could not but arrest the attention of a warrior king: 'My soul hath long dwelt with him that hateth peace. I am for peace: but when I speak, they are for war' (Psalm 120:6–7). In fact, it was theology and jurisprudence that attracted him most, intellectually; just as it had been poetry and other courtly literature which engaged the prime interest of his grandfather Charles I.

King Robert's attempts to present himself as a sincere advocate of peace and justice impressed many north Italian citizens. The Venetians, it is true, received from him little but rough justice, but the veneration of the citizens of Prato for their seigneur the Neapolitan king was expressed with more devotion than literary skill in a lengthy verse celebration of Robert's justice and wisdom. Of the three surviving manuscripts of the Prato eulogy one, now in the British Library, shows King Robert in a majestic profile, against a backcloth of fleur-de-lis: perhaps a reliable portrait, with its long Angevin nose and face. The message is clear: Robert did in his own lifetime impress and win the loyalty of those whose support he sought. Charles I had been an intruder in Italian politics, a strong man who could provide much-needed help to the

---

[8] Léonard (1967), pp. 340–3.

Guelfs; Robert for his part showed great political adroitness and a highly
developed sense of how to care for his subjects' interests. He could indeed
pursue his policies obstinately – as his wars to recover Sicily indicate – but the
more grandiose dreams of his ancestor were abandoned for more limited,
more practical objectives within Italy itself.

Both Robert the Wise and Frederick III of Sicily were deeply pious men,
willing to show favour to the Spiritual Franciscans. Frederick went further than
Robert in demanding (to little immediate effect) the removal of Palermo's Jews
into a separate ghetto. It is thus a paradox that so Christian a monarch should
have spent so much of his career as king bitterly engaged in conflict with the
papacy. Such was his respect for the Holy See that, when excommunicate, he
dutifully avoided attending mass, unlike his flamboyant ally Matteo Visconti of
Milan, whose Christian devotions were employed to discredit papal accusations against himself. Indeed, one important element of his programme of
reforms after 1302 was the restoration and rebuilding of churches and monasteries, and the establishment of schools for the teaching of religion.[9] Frederick
emerges as a pious evangelist, aware of the need to promote recovery, and
similar to his Angevin rivals in his insistence that moral reform would generate lasting peace and welfare. His interest in the abstruse edges of Christian
belief culminated in his patronage of the missionary mystics Ramon Lull and
Arnau de Vilanova.

Frederick became king of Sicily because he was to all intents a Sicilian. In
1295–6 the Sicilian barons were fearful of being betrayed into Angevin hands,
as part of a global peace which would assign Sardinia and Corsica to Aragon in
return for the renunciation of Sicily. Since Peter the Great's arrival in 1282 it had
been clear that the Sicilian rebels saw their aim as the reconstitution of a
'national' monarchy, not the creation of a Catalan-Aragonese dependency. For
his part, James II of Aragon made cynical use of his own agreement with the
papacy; he provided some troops to help the Angevins fight his brother, but
also maintained a cordial correspondence with Frederick. The best outcome
would be the maintenance of Frederick in power, and the maintenance of peace
between Aragon, France, Naples and the curia. This was achieved at the Treaty
of Caltabellotta (1302), when Frederick was granted control of Sicily for his lifetime, under the title king of 'Trinacria', and subject to papal overlordship. There
followed a series of attempts to reinvigorate religious life in an island which had
long been deprived of the adequate service of priests, during long years of
interdict; moral reform involved not merely the seclusion of the Jews of
Palermo so long as they refused to undergo conversion, but also legislation to

---

[9] Backman (1995).

ensure that slaves were given the chance to enter the Latin Church, and were treated humanely. Measures were also taken, more successfully in the short than in the long term, to stimulate the economy, notably reform of weights and measures and of commercial taxation, both of which had suffered from lack of uniformity; a large number of edicts confirmed the right of the principal towns to exemption from internal tolls. High intentions were, however, increasingly frustrated by the internal strife that developed between the Chiaramonte clan and its rivals in Sicily.

Frederick's own failure to observe the conditions of Caltabellotta (as interpreted by the house of Anjou) provided the main excuse for repeated Angevin invasions from 1312 onwards; conflict also continued, by proxy, within southern Greece, where pro-Angevin and pro-Sicilian factions emerged, notably the Catalan duchy of Athens, which was nominally under Sicilian obedience. As early as 1322 Frederick elevated his son Peter to the throne as co-king, thereby trampling on the stipulation that the island would revert to Naples after his death; Angevin expeditions to Sicily followed in 1325–7. The elevation of Peter II did not prevent rebellion the moment Frederick III died, and Peter II ruled alone only for five years (during which the Palizzi were thrown out of Sicily), before the child-king Lodovico came to the throne, a plaything in the hands of the rival factions. In 1355 another minor, Frederick IV, succeeded in the midst of Angevin raids on Milazzo and Messina. The Angevin invasions of Sicily would have achieved even less than they did without the support that existed within Sicily for an Angevin restoration. Rivalries between towns, notably Messina and Palermo, were one factor; Messina constantly sought to keep open supply lines to Calabria, to which its economy was in some respects traditionally more closely tied than to the island of Sicily. But still more powerful was the impact of great barons who, under Frederick III and his successors, were able to carve out great dominions in the island: the Ventimiglia in the north and west, the Palizzi in the east, the Chiaramonti in the south, where the county of Modica offered them every opportunity to extend their power over their subjects. Royal rights such as control over capital crimes and the minting of coin were granted to, or usurped by, noble princes who were becoming more important power brokers than the king himself. The fourteenth century in Sicily (as also in Naples) was the great age of the baronage, who acquired rights over the alienation of fiefs (in some respects eased under Frederick III's law *Volentes* of 1296, a law which stood in direct contrast to the policies of Roger II and Frederick II). On the other hand, the monarchy had little choice; despite the handsome revenues to be obtained from grain sales, the Aragonese kings were desperately short of resources with which to fight their Angevin enemies, or with which to exert influence on Ghibelline factions in northern Italy. Loans from the Bardi, Peruzzi and Acciaiuoli were available to the kings of 'Trinacria' no less than to the kings of Naples, but they could not solve the monarchy's financial difficulties. Increasingly, the great barons came to dominate even the export of grain. The monarchy tolerated the expansion of noble power in the hope of creating a strong baronial buffer against the Angevins; but the price, in the alienation of crown demesne land, was very high. As Epstein remarks, the civil wars that raged from the 1330s to the 1360s had 'effects on institutional and economic life far more serious and long-lasting than the War of the Vespers itself'.[10]

Masters of themselves, the Chiaramonti and their rivals, known by the factional labels 'Latin' and 'Catalan', allowed private disputes to mushroom into civil wars; while the former built ties to the Angevin court in the confidence that the island kingdom could not withstand the force of a large-scale invasion. In the mid-fourteenth century, at a time when Sicily, first of all in western Europe, was afflicted by bubonic plague, conflict carried on regardless. The barons took several decades to understand that there were no winners in a conflict that undermined their own power through devastation and unlimited expenditure on war. Seventy years after the Treaty of Caltabellotta the young Frederick IV made peace with the papacy and the Angevins on terms which were barely different from those agreed by Frederick III. But it was not a peace that could be usefully enjoyed: baronial power had not been challenged, Frederick IV himself remarked bitterly in a letter of 1363 to Francesco Ventimiglia:

What use is the barons' peace to us, if we lack our royal justice and dignity, if our great cities and towns are usurped, if our name is invoked but others enjoy the demesne's fruits, and we live in need and are ashamed of our majesty? This seems a hard life to us, all the more so now we are adult and know how things stand: yet, if everyone knew their limits, they would render to Caesar that which is Caesar's and be content with their baronies and benefices.[11]

Finally, the death of Frederick IV without a male heir, in 1377, reopened internal rivalries. Artale d'Aragona, in charge of the 'Catalan' faction, took charge in his power base of Catania of Frederick's daughter Maria, in the hope of arranging a Milanese marriage, as much to serve his interests as to solve the island's problems; he and his rivals, Manfredi Chiaramonte of Modica, Guglielmo Peralta around Sciacca, and Francesco Ventimiglia in the area of Geraci, carved Sicily into four vicariates where they exercised virtually sovereign authority, perpetuating officially the broad divisions that had been achieved unofficially by the 1360s.

The sharing of power among potential rivals also involved the exclusion from any share of other great barons; and it was Guglielmo Raimondo

[10] Epstein (1992), p. 317.   [11] Cited by Epstein (1992), p. 320.

Moncada, a non-vicar, who spirited Maria away from Catania to Barcelona, and marriage with Prince Martin of Aragon. The implications of this move were clear at once; towards the end of his long reign (1337–87) Pedro IV of Aragon had been contemplating the restoration of Aragonese rule in Sicily, and the Catalan duchy of Athens had already broken its formal, and weak, links to the crown of Sicily, taking the king of Aragon as its nominal overlord. It was especially obvious after 1377 that Sicily lay open to conquest, the more so once the Great Schism and internal rivalries within the house of Anjou diverted the rulers of Naples from reactivation of their own now ancient claim to the island.

The invasion of Sicily by Aragonese armies in 1392 was less readily welcomed by the island's nobles than the earlier Aragonese invasion of 1282: Manfredi Chiaramonte resisted in Palermo, and paid the price of execution. His lands passed to the leader of the invading army, Bernat de Cabrera. Martin I was not himself king of Aragon, but heir to Aragon's throne, and it was only on his premature death in 1409 that the island was reunited to the Catalan-Aragonese complex of territories, when he was succeeded by his own father, confusingly, in the circumstances, known as King Martin II. The death of Martin II a year later reopened, not just for Sicily, the question who would control the five kingdoms and one principality that made up the crown of Aragon, and threatened yet again to open up Sicily to predatory invaders such as the king of Portugal; attempts to re-establish an Aragonese cadet dynasty did not succeed.

It has been seen that Bernat de Cabrera was endowed with extensive lands in Sicily. Another major beneficiary was Guglielmo Raimondo Moncada, who acquired what has been called 'un enorme concentrazione territoriale sotto la propria signoria';[12] the age of great lordships was not at an end, but what would change would be their relationship to a more effective monarchy. The personnel of the nobility underwent rapid change, as great estates, such as those of the Alagoni, were torn to shreds, and a new elite emerged, in which Catalan supporters of the crown were heavily represented.[13]

Yet what did succeed, as studies by Pietro Corrao and Stephan Epstein have made clear, was a gradual revitalisation of the economy and a gradual reassertion of royal control over the baronage.[14] In part this may reflect a degree of exhaustion which took its toll in reduced revenues for great princes whose lands were suffering from the effects of depopulation through plague and devastation through war. Initiatives included the establishment of fairs; local industries revived, and inter-regional trade became lively. At the same time the monarchy sought to recreate an effective administration, recovering control of

---

[12] Léonard (1967), pp. 339–66.   [13] Corrao (1991), pp. 203–60.   [14] Corrao (1991); Epstein (1992).

the coastline (and thereby asserting control over revenues from exported grain), drawing up a register of landholdings, recovering control of serious criminal cases. The monarchy tried to find a balance between the need to recover its authority over the royal demesne and its need to placate the baronage. An important bonus was the declining revenue of the baronage in the post-Black Death era, which increased noble dependence on the crown in Sicily as elsewhere in Europe; in the long term, the towns became an important alternative source of support for the monarchy, though under Martin I the relationship of crown and town remained delicate. Efforts were made to create urban militias which would reduce dependence on feudal levies, and hence on baronial interests; urban elites were emerging which were a potential source of strength to a revived monarchy. But it would also be wrong to exaggerate the immediate success of the monarchy, which still stood a long way from 'proto-absolutism' in its ability to command its subjects; there was stiff opposition until 1398, and the concessions to Catalan and Valencian landholders risked replacing the old great families with a multiplicity of bountifully franchised settlers. Martin's own parliaments in 1397 and 1398 made exactly this point: there were too many Catalans being granted lands, and the monarchy must make more effort to live of its own, which would mean an end to the disbursement of royal rights and lands. Readjustment was therefore slow, painful and compromised by conflicting interests. Often initiatives came from below; this is perhaps especially true of the foundation of new fairs.[15] Even Martin I was distracted from his own kingdom into his father's service, sailing at the end of his reign to Sardinia, a permanent trouble spot, and dying there for Aragon, not for Sicily. Yet this was also part of his achievement: the reintegration of Sicily into the lands of the crown of Aragon resulted in reopening its markets to Catalan businessmen scared away by internal strife; and the issue of the reincorporation of Sicily into the Angevin realm disappeared from view.

The disorder which characterised Sicily in the fourteenth century began also to characterise southern Italy after the death of King Robert. The premature death of Duke Charles of Calabria left Robert's granddaughter, Joanna, as heiress to the kingdom; the existing cadet male lines, those of Anjou-Durazzo and Anjou-Taranto were passed over, and Joanna was married to the younger brother of Louis the Great, the Angevin king of Hungary. The result was that rivalries were established within the house of Anjou; and they were accentuated when the objectionable husband of Joanna, Andrew, suffered defenestration in 1345. It is still unclear whether Joanna was a conspirator in his murder. There were many possible beneficiaries, not least Joanna, who by all accounts

---

[15] Epstein (1992), pp. 113–15.

detested her overbearing husband. Andrew's own expectations of a royal title were the subject of controversy. On the other hand, the cadet line of Anjou-Taranto was well placed to confirm its ascendancy over a young queen uncertain of her aims. They brought with them as adviser to the crown Niccolò Acciaiuoli, Florentine man of affairs and of letters turned Neapolitan nobleman, who had been a devoted servant of Catherine de Courtenay in her Achaian lands.

The struggle among branches of the house of Anjou began, however, with the fierce response of the Hungarian king to his brother's murder. Ruler of a vast complex of lands that very nearly stretched from the Baltic (or at least the borders of pagan Lithuania, against which he crusaded) to the Adriatic, where he ruled the kingdom of Croatia, Louis the Great demanded of the pope, as Joanna's overlord, the cession of the entire south Italian kingdom into Hungarian hands. Louis did not win over the pope; but he convinced some south Italian barons, such as Lalle Camponeschi, master of L'Aquila, that he was a viable prospect, entering the city in May 1347; an even more dangerous ally was the Roman dictator Cola di Rienzo, who saw in Hungarian support the means to consolidate his own hold on Rome. Late 1347 and early 1348 saw what appeared to be a smooth take over by Louis of Hungary of the northern provinces of the Regno, culminating in a troublesome occupation of Naples itself just as the plague bacillus also began to occupy the Italian peninsula. What seems to have gone wrong is that Louis failed to win the confidence of the Neapolitan baronage, executing Charles, duke of Durazzo, and acting ruthlessly against those suspected of complicity in Andrew's murder. Niccolò Acciaiuoli's son organised a spirited defence of the key inland town of Melfi, which his father was to acquire as a county.

These were not the only difficulties that piled upon Joanna I's shoulders. Continuing disputes with Genoa over the lordship of Ventimiglia were not settled until 1350; only deft papal diplomacy prevented a Genoese–Hungarian military alliance being created. The arrival of bubonic plague coincided with Joanna's own decision to travel to Provence and supplicate the help of Pope Clement VI at Avignon, early in 1348. The price for favour was an agreement to sell Avignon to the pope, lord already of the neighbouring Comtat Venaissin; no longer would the papacy have to be an honoured guest on the soil of Angevin Provence, but to the Provençaux this was a *venditio maledicta*, an 'accursed sell-out'. Joanna sought public exculpation for the murder of her first husband, as well as papal approval for her second marriage which had been contracted with Louis of Taranto, leader of a powerful Angevin faction that had been restive while Andrew was alive (she was in fact pregnant when she arrived at the curia). Her absence from the Regno while it was being torn apart by Hungarian invaders, as well as predatory mercenary bands such as the soldiers of Fra Morriale (Montréal de Grasse), had little effect on the outcome of Louis the Great's invasion: as well as the ravages of plague, Venetian agitation in his rear threatened to prejudice his survival, for on control of Dalmatia depended Louis's ability to create a vast Angevin domain stretching from the borders of Lithuania to the Straits of Messina. The struggle for the Adriatic, which was to culminate in the loss of Venetian Dalmatia in 1352, now preoccupied him. The pope opposed his expedition. The south Italians themselves were restive. It was time for Louis of Hungary to go home.

This did not mean that the Hungarians evacuated the Regno. Louis of Taranto was active in the suppression of Hungarian units. He also purged the court of Joanna's own supporters, elevating to high office the Acciaiuoli. Predictably, Louis of Taranto's marriage to Joanna had been an attempt to secure the kingdom for Louis more than an attempt at compromise between the opposing factions in the house of Anjou. A second Hungarian invasion, with Genoese support, in 1350 resulted by 1352 in a narrow victory for Louis of Taranto; but Louis's real victory lay within the Regno, where he was crowned king in May 1352, with papal approval, subject to the proviso that he held the throne in right of Joanna, none of whose children survived very long. The same year, with the death of Clement VI, the house of Anjou lost a powerful, if qualified, supporter.

There was another victor: Niccolò Acciaiuoli, the cultured Florentine businessman who had acquired lands and favour in the Morea and who now rose to be grand seneschal of the Regno and count of Melfi. His devotion to noble values, mocked by Florentine contemporaries, led him to establish a chivalric order, the Order of the Knot or of the Holy Spirit, which would celebrate knightly prowess and promote the standing of the 'King of Jerusalem and Sicily' both at home and as patron of crusades to his titular kingdom in the east. Writing in 1354, Niccolò spoke of the need 'to recover the kingdom of Jerusalem after having recovered Sicily', an idea which was rooted in the past policy of Angevin kings. As the Hungarian menace evaporated, Naples turned its war machine towards that other territory from which the kings of Naples took their official title. The death of Robert the Wise had been followed by Angevin successes at Milazzo and in the Lipari islands; the 1350s saw a change in approach, with appeals from the Chiaramonte faction to the court of Naples, and the formulation of elaborate plans to ensure that the island would retain a degree of autonomy within a reunited kingdom. Without such internal support, Acciaiuoli's small fleet and army could not possibly have achieved, in April 1354, the submission of much of Sicily, including Palermo but excluding the power bases of the Catalan faction in Messina and Catania. To hold down his gains, Niccolò Acciaiuoli needed further resources, but Louis of Taranto failed to provide them, and his success evaporated, though fortunes later revived to the point where the king and queen of Naples could make their triumphant entry into Messina (24 December 1356). Other concerns dominated the king's thinking in 1354–5: there was trouble in the Abruzzi, where Lalle Camponeschi, ally of the Durazzo faction, was murdered at the behest of the Taranto faction, and where the mercenary companies continued to wreak havoc. There was trouble with the pope, Innocent VI, who taught Louis and Joanna a lesson, excommunicating them for failing to pay their annual tribute to the Holy See; a visit to Avignon by Acciaiuoli would be required (in 1360) before this issue could be laid to rest. There was trouble in Provence, where the Durazzo faction had powerful allies; in 1361–2 Louis of Durazzo became the focus of opposition to Louis of Taranto in Apulia, while, with Durazzo encouragement, German and Hungarian mercenary companies were unleashed on the Regno. A final attempt to overwhelm Sicily became enmeshed in the rivalries of Ventimiglia and Chiaramonte, as well as making ever plainer the interests of a dangerous outside party, Peter IV of Aragon, who saw himself as a possible heir to Frederick IV. The Neapolitans had continually underestimated the degree to which internal rivalries within Sicily, rather than their own intervention, were the controlling factor in the island's intricate politics.

In 1362 Louis of Taranto died, perhaps of plague; two years later Niccolò Acciaiuoli was buried in the vault of the magnificent Charterhouse he had built outside his native Florence. 'The death of Louis of Taranto caused great corruption in all the kingdom', a chronicler wrote.[16] Louis had lacked the broad vision of Robert the Wise, but he had also had little time for political initiatives of his own, caught as he was amid the scheming of Durazzeschi, Hungarians and other rivals. Yet by appointing Acciaiuoli to high office, he had provided the Regno with a capable administrator who was also competent on the battlefield; Acciaiuoli's fault was perhaps a desperate wish to be recognised as a true grandee, count of Melfi and of Malta, an attitude which fellow-Florentines such as his boyhood friend Boccaccio tended to mock. Joanna, alone again, sought the support of a new husband, rapidly choosing James IV, son of the last king of Majorca, a figure of no political weight who was also mentally unstable, aptly described by a papal legate as *argumentosus*. Before long he wandered off and found himself once again in a Spanish prison, to no great regret of Joanna. Yet he injected further instability into the government of a kingdom which was already severely fractured.

The history of the last years of Queen Joanna I is a constant record of court intrigues, lightened to some degree by the final end to the Sicilian war, now that

[16] Léonard (1967), pp. 495–8, for contemporary judgements on his reign.

all sides accepted the treaty of 1373. The papacy sought to draw Naples into an alliance which would help clear Italy of the scourge of the mercenary bands (1371), yet this soon became transformed into a crusade against Visconti Milan. Even so far north, the Neapolitans still had interests on the ground, and a positive result of the war against Milan was the recovery of several territories in Piedmont occupied by the Visconti; James IV of Majorca was involved in these campaigns until 1375, when he died of fever, to be succeeded in the queen's bed by Otto of Brunswick, a soldier who knew the Regno from past conflicts, and who was explicitly barred from taking the crown.

Changes within Italy precipitated further crises in the Regno. Increasing hostility on the part of Florence towards a papal restoration in Italy reached the point where Gregory XI hurled an interdict at the papacy's ancient ally (1377). At the same time definitive plans for a permanent return of the Holy See to Italy culminated in the arrival of the pope in Rome, where he died a few months later (March 1378). The turbulent conclave that followed elected the disagreeable Urban VI, formerly archbishop of Bari in the Regno, whose high-handed actions prompted the cardinals to attempt his removal and replacement by Clement VII, from Geneva. Although at first sympathetic to Urban's claims, Joanna carefully sounded out expert opinion, and concluded, like the French king, that Clement VII was worthy of her support. Her approval went so far that she remitted to him 64,000 florins due from the census imposed on the Regno, an obligation she could easily have avoided; she also welcomed him into her domains. Her new problem was that opinion in Naples resolutely supported Urban, if only because he was a *regnicolo* himself; under threat of an uprising, Joanna capitulated, but Urban was not satisfied with her retraction, citing her for heresy and schism (1379). Of course he could see that her power was now exceedingly frail. The question was who might replace her, and the obvious candidate was Charles, duke of Durazzo, who had also benefited from the patronage of Louis of Hungary, another supporter of Pope Urban. Against him, Joanna was inclined to favour Clement VII's adherent Louis I, duke of Anjou, a very distant relation whose line harked back to Charles II of Naples's renunciation of Anjou in favour of Charles of Valois. Already active in setting Languedoc in order, Louis was, like his Valois ancestor, something of a collector of royal titles: Majorca was one aspiration, Sardinia too perhaps; but his most lasting legacy as a pretender was as would-be 'king of Jerusalem and Sicily'. In 1380 Joanna agreed to name him as her heir, in view of the fact that, even after four husbands, she had no surviving heir from her womb.

No doubt Louis would have shown more enthusiasm had his brother, Charles V of France, not died in September of that year; needed in Paris, until 1382 he ignored the threat of Charles of Durazzo, who made determined progress marching southwards to dispossess Joanna, with an army well stocked with Hungarian mercenaries. In a sense, the plans of Louis the Great were now paying off, thirty years later, and with the added benefit of papal support, for Urban VI crowned Charles III king of Sicily in Rome in June 1381. The capture of Joanna's consort Otto meant that the gates of Naples fell open, and Queen Joanna was carried off into imprisonment. By the summer of 1382 she had been killed by suffocation; her body was displayed in the church of Santa Chiara as a token that, after a reign of nearly forty years, her kingdom had now passed to her nearest male relative, Charles of Durazzo. There is little doubt that Charles III wanted her out of the way before Louis I of Anjou, recently nominated duke of Calabria by Clement VII, could cross the borders of the Regno with his own motley army.

Louis of Anjou did achieve some remarkable successes in his south Italian campaign: by 1383 he had penetrated far down the eastern side of the Regno, and on 30 August he publicly took the royal crown. Until his death in 1384 he managed to hold his position in Apulia with a certain amount of French aid. His son Louis II took the crown in his place, but failed to hold together his father's army. The menace from the dukes of Anjou then receded; Charles III could congratulate himself that he was safe on the throne of Naples. And so he might have been had not the unpredictable Urban VI hurled anathema against him, calling a crusade against Charles and excommunicating not merely him but his heirs to the fourth generation, all this apparently because Charles had not been vociferous enough in the defence of papal interests. Charles sent Urban packing, and prepared for an even greater conquest, that of Hungary, which was also open to claimants after the death in September 1382 of Louis the Great without a male heir. Although he briefly established himself as master of Croatia and of the Hungarian heartlands, Charles made powerful enemies, with the result that he was struck down in his palace in Buda in February 1386, dying not long after. In Naples as in Hungary, it had been a short reign; and, though he had shown ability and ruthlessness in winning two crowns in quick succession, he had underestimated the sheer persistence of opposition among the barons of both Naples and Hungary. Other claimants still existed, and the assumption that he could rule both Hungary and southern Italy at a time of extreme disorder in Italy, of schism in the papacy and of uncertainty in the central European monarchies indicates a lack of practical political wisdom.

Against the brief gain of dominion in Hungary, with all the vast material resources that the central European kingdoms could offer, must be set the loss of Provence, which remained in the hands of the dukes of Anjou, providing them with a power base from which to plan further invasions of the Regno. Urban VI died soon after trying to launch his own much vaunted invasion of the Regno, but in 1390 the new pope, Boniface IX, accepted the claims of

Charles III's son Ladislas to the Neapolitan throne. For nine years Louis II and Ladislas effectively divided the Regno between them; and, as in fourteenth-century Sicily, the arbiters of power were the barons, notably the house of Sanseverino, which led the pro-Provençal faction finally into the Durazzo camp in July 1399. A true heir of Charles II, Ladislas continued to aim for the Hungarian throne, though without success, while the pope dangled in front of him the throne of Cyprus, the sister of whose king Ladislas married in 1402.

Ladislas's major achievement was that he at last addressed the problem of baronial power in the Regno, turning on those such as the Sanseverino and the Ruffo (in Calabria) who had shown sympathy for the claims of Louis II of Anjou. His brutal methods, including the mass arrest of the Marzano at a wedding feast, are reminiscent of the more famous machinations of Ferrante I of Naples nearly a century later. Even so, the threat from the duke of Anjou remained constant, punctuated by startling victories that assured him briefly of ascendancy in the Papal States and posed a severe threat to Florence. His death in 1414 thus marked the end of a period of high adventurism in which the house of Anjou-Provence had again and again failed to displace the Durazzeschi, even though they frequently occupied large portions of the Regno and won the support of a fickle baronage, which had worked out that its best interest lay in a weakening of royal authority.

FROM ADOLF OF NASSAU TO LEWIS
OF BAVARIA, 1292–1347

Peter Herde

ADOLF OF NASSAU, 1292–1298

RUDOLF of Habsburg died on 15 July 1291. Long before his death he had tried to win over the electors (who had been responsible for the election of the German king – that is the king of the Romans – since 1257) to the succession of his eldest son, Albert. After the failure of Henry VI's plans to make the empire a hereditary monarchy on the pattern of France and England, Rudolf could only follow the old practice of having one of his sons crowned king in his own lifetime and thereby secure his succession. Although Pope Honorius IV had supported these plans, they were not to be realised because the death of Honorius postponed Rudolf's coronation as emperor indefinitely once more and because they were opposed in the electoral college. The situation in itself was not unfavourable for Rudolf in the last years of his reign: the highest ecclesiastical prince in the empire, Archbishop Henry of Mainz, was a confidant of the king's, Trier was vacant, and the lay electors – the Palatinate, Saxony, Brandenburg and Bohemia – were related to him by marriage. The archbishop of Cologne, Siegfried II of Westerburg, however, saw a threat to free election by the electors in these plans for controlling the succession, and he found an ally in King Wenceslas II of Bohemia who, despite Rudolf's ultimate recognition of his electoral vote, refused to support Albert, since the latter refused to cede Carinthia to him. Albert had none of his father's likeable characteristics; he was described as ugly and his behaviour ignoble. Immediately after the death of his father, noble opposition sprang up in the core Habsburg lands in Swabia, as well as in the newly gained Austrian lands, which won support by Wenceslas. The Bohemian king was resolved to prevent Albert's election as king, and he found sufficient allies for this purpose, such as Duke Otto III of Lower Bavaria, who continued his father's policy of enmity to the Habsburgs. Duke Lewis II of Upper Bavaria, elector as count-palatine of the Rhine, thus remained the only Habsburg supporter, since

Wenceslas was endorsed by an electoral pact with Saxony and Brandenburg giving their consent to his future decision, the new archbishop of Mainz, Gerard I of Eppenstein, went over to the anti-Habsburg camp and also drew to his side the newly elected archbishop, Bohemund of Trier. The candidate was of course presented by Archbishop Siegfried of Cologne.

Election and foreign policy

Following the death of Count Waléran IV of Limburg (1280), Archbishop Siegfried of Cologne had become entangled in territorial wars as the ally of Reginald of Guelders against Brabant, the count of Berg, and the town of Cologne which at this period always sided with the archbishop's enemies. In June 1288 he had been decisively defeated at the bloody battle of Worringen. The election of the king presented him with the opportunity to make good at least a part of these losses. His candidate was his faithful comrade in arms, the insignificant Count Adolf of Nassau, with lands south of the Lahn between Weilburg and Wiesbaden. In Andernach on 27 April 1292, he had to agree to the archbishop's demands for aid to the Church in Cologne and help against the townspeople. In the event of a disputed election, he was not to renounce his claim; if he broke his agreement, he would lose his right to the throne. The Treaty of Andernach was specifically designed to win the Bohemian king's vote for Adolf as well. Among other things, therefore, a betrothal was agreed between Adolf's son Rupert and Wenceslas's daughter Agnes. By this means – and by Adolf's agreement to pass judgement favourable to Bohemia on Austria, Styria and Carinthia (occupied by Ottokar) – Wenceslas was won over, and with him Brandenburg and Saxony. Archbishop Gerard of Mainz joined this group, likewise Bohemund of Trier and finally Lewis of Bavaria. Thus, after authentication of the electoral treaty (*Wahlkapitulationen*), the archbishop of Mainz, in the name of all the rest, elected Adolf on 5 May 1292 in Frankfurt (*electio per unum*). The archbishop of Cologne crowned him in Aachen on 1 July.

As a result of these events, Rudolf of Habsburg's policy of consolidating the empire on the foundations of a strong dynastic power was destroyed, and the electors believed that in Adolf they had created a tool for their own interests. In this they were certainly soon disappointed. Albert of Habsburg, who was to have been driven out of his lands in favour of Wenceslas, was able to escape this danger by means of a clever policy. In a skilful move, he recognised Adolf's election. The latter was already beginning to slip out of his electors' grasp, and when he accepted Albert's homage Wenceslas was cheated of all his hopes. The archbishop of Cologne was bitterly disappointed when Adolf came to an understanding with the duke of Brabant; the archbishop of Mainz saw all his hopes betrayed when in January 1294 Adolf negotiated a marriage between his daughter, Mechthild, and Rudolf, the son and heir of Ludwig II, count-palatine of the Rhine and duke of Upper Bavaria and the archbishop's keenest rival in territorial politics. Since Adolf also took the remaining Wittelsbach princes under special imperial protection, he had thus created a counter-weight against the remaining electors. To their disadvantage, the Wittelsbach remained closely tied to Adolf until his death. Adolf's foreign policy followed the old policy based on the interests of Cologne, concluding an agreement in August 1294 with Edward I of England, who with the aid of substantial subsidies secured the German king as an ally against Philip the Fair of France.

The alliance also satisfied German interests, as in the preceding period (since the reign of Philip III) the French kings had seized every opportunity to expand towards the imperial border and to annex portions of the empire to the French kingdom by exploiting local grievances, for instance in Lyon, around Verdun, and in Hainault. Similarly, Count Henry of Luxemburg, the future emperor Henry VII, became a French vassal, while the further case of the county of Burgundy was particularly aggravating, since it belonged to the empire, but was on the verge of French allegiance. On 31 August 1294, Adolf sent a declaration of war to the French king because of the seizure of rights and possessions of the empire, to which Philip IV replied contemptuously on 9 March 1295. Admittedly, it did not come to open war, for Edward I was prevented from participating in a campaign against France, first because he was occupied until mid 1295 with a rebellion in Wales, then until mid 1296 with his campaigns against Philip IV's Scottish ally, John Balliol, by the resistance of his barons because of the expenses his policy entailed, and by the papal prohibition on clerical taxation. When he finally landed at Sluys with his relatively small number of troops in August 1297, the German king did not come to his aid against Philip IV who was advancing into Flanders. On the one hand, Adolf of Nassau was experiencing difficulties with the prince-electors, on the other, there are some indications (although no certainty) that French money held him back from active intervention at the side of his English ally, who then also agreed a truce with the French in October 1297, until Boniface VIII finally negotiated peace by arbitration in June 1298. This signalled the end of Adolf's attempts to intervene in the west by means of an Anglo-German alliance, and Albert of Austria immediately resumed relations with Philip the Fair, drawing policies back into the old Hohenstaufen mould, which was not to be broken again until the reign of the emperor Lewis of Bavaria.

Dynastic policy and overthrow

The legal and ideological foundations of the German kingdom were insufficient for a successful dynastic policy; the ruler also required a strong territorial basis. The tiny Nassau estate was totally inadequate for this. Adolf therefore attempted to extend his dynastic power, following the example of the Hohenstaufen and the Habsburgs. An opportunity presented itself in Thuringia, where the succession had been disputed since the death of Landgrave Henry Raspe (1247). Most of his possessions had fallen to the Wettin margraves of Meissen; a small portion, Hessen, was separated and granted to Landgrave Henry I, whom Adolf raised to the rank of prince of the empire in May 1292 in one of his first acts of government. After the cadet Meissen line died out in 1291, Adolf seized Meissen as a vacant imperial fief and appointed a cousin as his representative there. He then also bought the landgraviate of Thuringia from the licentious Landgrave Albert at the beginning of 1294. This legally disputed purchase provoked the opposition of the archbishop of Mainz, since a large part of the landgraviate of Thuringia consisted of ecclesiastical fiefs owing homage to Mainz and the purchase should have required the consent of the archbishop. Since, additionally, Wenceslas of Bohemia (whose southwards expansion into the Habsburg lands had been halted by the king's enfeoffment of Albert and who now saw his remaining opportunity for expansion to the north also obstructed by Adolf's encroachment upon Thuringia and Meissen) became alienated from the king, the situation became threatening for Adolf. Nevertheless, it took until Whitsun 1297 for a coalition against Adolf to come into existence.

At that time, most of the prince-electors met at Prague for Wenceslas's long-delayed coronation by the archbishop of Mainz. On the advice of his chancellor, Peter von Aspelt, Wenceslas had drawn close to Albert of Habsburg. Now the plan to depose Adolf was hatched in Prague, a project that was continued in later meetings, lastly at Vienna in February 1298, where Albert made Wenceslas some territorial concessions, in the event of his election as king. Albert began the war against Adolf; on 1 May 1298 Archbishop Gerard of Mainz summoned the king and electors to Mainz on 15 June, to advise on ending the lawlessness and lack of peace in the empire. He maintained that in this emergency he was authorised to do this as imperial archchancellor for Germany, according to old legal principle. On 23 June 1298 Gerard of Mainz announced the deposition of the king, who was absent, in his own name and on behalf of the archbishop of Cologne and the king of Bohemia, together with Count Albrecht of Saxony-Wittenberg and the margrave of Brandenburg; in the process he quoted, sometimes literally, the wording of Innocent IV's bull of 1245, announcing the deposition of Emperor Frederick II, on the grounds of numerous breaches of the law. The prince-electors Archbishop Bohemund of Trier and Rudolf I of the Palatinate were not party to this act; the latter was still loyal to his father-in-law Adolf; his twelve-year-old brother, on the other hand, had given full powers of proxy to Duke

Albrecht of Saxony. Immediately afterwards, Albert of Austria was elected king. The prince-electors had thereby, in a questionable extension of their electoral rights, deposed a king whom they themselves had elected; it was the first time such a deposition had occurred without previous papal ban and deposition. This was indicative of the growing importance of the electoral college. Albert of Habsburg returned to his army, then near Alzey, and marched against Adolf, who sought to decide the issue by battle. This was joined on 2 July 1298 at Göllheim, west of Worms, where Adolf of Nassau was defeated and fatally wounded. His corpse was first of all laid to rest in the Cistercian monastery of Rosenthal, then in 1309 placed beside that of his victorious conqueror in the vault of Speyer Cathedral. Thus ended the reign of a not unattractive king (a contemporary paints the picture of a friendly man of average height, well educated for a layman; he knew French and Latin, as well as German): elected as the tool of the prince-electors, he had then blazed his own trail and was ultimately deposed by his own electors. His rule was no more than a fleeting chapter in German history.

ALBERT I

Conflict with the Rhenish electors and the alliance with France

To establish the legality of his rule beyond all doubt, after the death of Adolf of Nassau Albert had his election repeated at Frankfurt on 27 July 1298; a month later, on 24 August, he was crowned in Aachen by Archbishop Wikbold. Unlike his predecessor, his kingship was founded on the extensive Habsburg possessions in their original home in the upper Rhine area and Switzerland, together with the substantial addition of Austria, through his father Rudolf. Albert was able to assuage the enmity of the king of Bohemia with substantial compensation: Wenceslas II received the imperial vicariate over Meissen, Osterland and Pleissenland; the king invested him with the imperial territory of Cheb (Eger) previously organised by the Hohenstaufen and recognised Bohemian claims to Cracow and Sandomir; Bohemian expansion was to be steered in a north-easterly direction. He was able to calm the remaining prince-electors, on the one hand, with considerable financial inducements and the handing over of possessions and, on the other, by the fact that he undertook additions to the imperial general peaces (*Reichslandfrieden*) which were hostile to the towns and favoured the princes, and in carrying out his dynastic policy tried to avoid the impression of establishing a centrally governed Habsburg territory; he therefore invested his sons with Austria, Styria and Carniola (the territories won by Rudolf) as if he, as king of the Romans, did not want to expand from this power base to the disadvantage of the prince-electors. This initial adjustment was admittedly only of short duration and turned to intense enmity when Albert began to follow an independent policy after he had consolidated his position in Germany.

Albert's policy towards France furnished opportunity for the first clashes among the princes. In previous years King Philip the Fair had not, it is true, had any systematic plan of expansion to the east, but he had seized every opportunity to extend French influence; above all around Lyon and in Lorraine on the Meuse he had succeeded in making significant inroads into imperial territory (here the old boundary of the empire ran far to the west of the linguistic Germanic–Romance border). It was an old tradition dating back to the time of Frederick Barbarossa for the emperor and the French king to meet near Vaucouleurs. When the German king was invited there at this time, it had a symbolic significance: he was to recognise the latest French gains. Already before his coronation Albert had had dealings with the French king over a marriage treaty: Albert's oldest son Rudolf was to marry Philip's sister Blanche and give as her dowry the Habsburg dynastic lands in Upper Alsace and Üchtland (near Freiburg). Albert thus followed in the footsteps of the pro-French policy pursued by the Hohenstaufen. However, this provoked the opposition of the Rhenish electors. Archbishop Gerard of Mainz wanted to weaken the Habsburgs; Bohemund of Trier had been directly affected by French expansion; and Wikbold of Cologne pursued a pro-English policy from old political and economic interests. In this situation, Albert initially attempted to support France's enemy, Gui de Dampierre, in Flanders against Philip's ally, Jean II d'Avesnes of Hainault. The German king also enjoyed good relations with Brabant, Holland and Lorraine. In the Franche-Comté and Savoy, Albert also opposed Philip's allies. Yet there were further negotiations with the French king. In the little village of Quatrevaux between Toul and Vaucouleurs, at the beginning of December 1299, a secret treaty was agreed.

What Philip and Albert agreed, with the help of interpreters, has nowhere been recorded and soon gave rise to the wildest rumours, which were evidence of the strength of anti-French feeling in the western regions of the empire. It was, for instance, asserted that both monarchs had planned a new European order, in which the borders of both the Meuse and the Rhine, the kingdom of Arles and northern Italy were conceded to France; in return, the German empire was to become a dynastic Habsburg monarchy. This was all undoubtedly more propaganda on the part of the Rhenish electors, who saw their own electoral rights threatened by too close an alliance between France and the Habsburgs. In reality, Albert seems only to have confirmed Philip the Fair's acquisitions in the region of Verdun and allowed him a free hand in the Franche-Comté. On the French side, the renowned propagandist Pierre

Dubois sketched the picture of a French-influenced Habsburg dynasty in Germany in the future. Because Rudolf had already been treated as the successor to the throne in the marriage negotiations, the electors of Mainz and Cologne (concerned about their rights) refused their consent, since they deemed it a squandering and alienation of the imperial domain. The marriage took place in Paris at Whitsun 1300; as settlement the bride did not, contrary to rumour, receive the kingdom of Arles, but much more modest lands in Upper Alsace, around Freiburg and Waldshut.

The complete break between Albert and the Rhenish electors came when the emperor attempted to extend his dynastic holdings in the region of the Rhine estuary. After the counts of Holland, Zeeland and Friesland had died out in 1299, Jean II d'Avesnes, count of Hainault, was to succeed, according to an agreement made in the reign of Rudolf of Habsburg. However, the German king seized the county as a vacant imperial fief, in order to give it to one of his own sons. Certainly he then shrank from advancing in alliance with the bishop of Liège and the count of Flanders against Hainault allied to Guelders and Brabant, especially because Philip the Fair was disinclined to support Habsburg expansion in the Rhine estuary. His brother, Charles of Valois, occupied Flanders. The French were of course driven out of Flanders in 1302 because of the 'Matins' of Bruges and the victory at Courtrai (Kortrijk), but Albert was then no longer in a position to carry out his plans relating to Holland. A decisive factor in their failure was the enmity of the electors, now openly manifest. Wikbold of Cologne in particular saw himself threatened by Albert's policy, but Gerard of Mainz too, who then is said to have declared he had another king or two in his quiver, again seized the opportunity to move against the Habsburg king. Since Dieter, a brother of Adolf of Nassau whom Albert had defeated, had succeeded Bohemund to the archiepiscopal see, the anti-Habsburg coalition among the electors was complete. The count-palatine of the Rhine, Rudolf of Wittelsbach, was won over to them. On 14 October 1300, an alliance was concluded at Niederrheinbach, near Bingen, between the archbishops of Mainz, Cologne and Trier and the count-palatine, which, while naming no opponent, was nevertheless clearly directed against Albert. His deposition was planned, whereby the count-palatine of the Rhine would assume the function of judge, according to contemporary views. One further vote was won for the planned election of a new king. The Saxon vote was disputed between Saxony-Lauenburg and Saxony-Wittenberg. Albert had supported the Wittenberg claimant, which is why the electors recognised his Lauenburg rival as one of their number thus securing his support.

In contrast to his predecessor Albert did not allow himself to be outmanoeuvred. He sought alliances among the opponents of the electors and found them in one section of the Rhineland nobility and the towns, whose demands for the lifting of the tolls established since the death of Frederick II he supported. He then activated the imperial domain, administered by *Landvögte*, where he had appointed loyal supporters in, for instance, the Wetterau (northeast of Frankfurt) and in Speiergau. Other armed forces arrived from Austria and the Steiermark. By mortgaging the imperial domain, and with financial support from the towns, he succeeded in making available sufficient funds for the planned campaign. The electors' preparations, by contrast, were uncoordinated. Albert thus had little trouble in defeating them one by one. First of all there was the attack on the possessions of the count-palatine. In June 1301 Albert besieged Heidelberg and laid waste the surrounding area. Rudolf was forced to make peace. He had to recognise his brother Ludwig as co-regent and provide military service against the men who had until recently been his allies. Gerard of Mainz gave up all resistance when his principal fortification, Bingen, fell on 25 September 1301 and the Rheingau was devastated by imperial troops. On 21 March 1302 peace was agreed between Albert and Mainz which destroyed Gerard's power. On 24 October the archbishop of Cologne also had to condescend to make peace. At the beginning of November the archbishop of Trier also made peace; linked to this was Albert's reconciliation with the house of Nassau.

In this way Albert crushed the opposition of the Rhenish electors within two years; they did not, in the words of a chronicler, 'dare to low against him' ('ut de cetero contra eum mugire non auderent').[1] Unlike Adolf of Nassau, Albert of Habsburg had proved that he was both politically and militarily superior to his rivals. Ageing and one-eyed, he seemed reserved, but had proved himself an adroit political tactician, who had succeeded in drawing the towns to his side by exploiting the economic rivalry between them and the electors. Despite the defeats of his German opponents, Albert did not resume his ambitions in the Low Countries, when Boniface VIII recognised Jean II d'Avesnes as count of Hainault, Holland and Zeeland and simultaneously prepared the way for closer ties with the imperial court. This resulted in Albert's involvement in the dispute between the papacy and the French crown.

Relations with Boniface VIII

The German empire was linked to the papacy like no other European power; it was after all the German kings alone who had been crowned emperors by the pope since the revival of Charlemagne's empire by Otto I in 962. The popes from Innocent III (1200/1) had derived particular rights from this special relationship. According to the curial translation theory, the pope had transferred the

---

[1] *Chronicon Ecclesiae Wimpinensis*, p. 673.

empire from the Greeks to the Franks on the coronation of Charlemagne as emperor; since then, the empire was by its origins and destination (*principaliter et finaliter*) the concern of the pope, who had conferred on the German princes the right to elect the German king as the future emperor, whom the pope would crown emperor, from which the pope derived the right to scrutinise the German king's aptitude and approve his election. The majority of the German kings in the previous period had rejected this papal claim to approbation. The claims of the papacy to exercise the imperial vicariate during a vacancy in the empire like-wise went back to Innocent III. With the advent of the electoral college, which did not want to see its rights to elect the king reduced, papal claims of this kind were also refused by this body. The election of Adolf of Nassau occurred at the beginning of the vacancy of the papal throne following the death of Nicholas IV on 4 April 1292, which lasted more than two years. With the election, on 24 December 1294, of Boniface VIII, who always laid the greatest stress on papal power, the question of papal approbation became particularly acute. He did not at first condemn the deposition of Adolf, whom he had severely rebuked; since then the empire had been vacant in his eyes. The electors communicated the election of Albert to Boniface VIII and obsequiously requested his imperial cor-onation, while adroitly avoiding asking for approbation of the election. Boniface was outraged by this, declared the electoral process illegal, Albert totally unsuit-able, since he had rebelled against his predecessor and killed him, and refused to carry out the imperial coronation.

It did not, however, come to a serious quarrel because Boniface was totally absorbed in his conflict with France. The alliance between Albert of Habsburg and France provoked great distrust in the papal curia. Still the pope negotiated further with Albert, as duke of Austria, not as king, and in the spring of 1300 a German embassy proceeded to the papal curia, together with a French dele-gation led by Guillaume de Nogaret to secure confirmation of Albert's elec-tion and make preparations for the imperial coronation. The embassy was received by the pope during the jubilee year which strengthened his power remarkably. His reaction was correspondingly brusque. Referring to the trans-lation theory, he depicted the empire as entirely dependent on the papacy and emphasised the possibility of deposing unworthy rulers. Then he went still further and demanded the cession by Albert of Tuscany (which, as part of the kingdom of Italy, *regnum Italie*, was part of the empire), whose incorporation within the Papal States Boniface was then plotting. This earned him the oppo-sition of Dante, who had to go into exile in the feud which broke out over this issue between the Black Guelfs and the White in Florence at the beginning of 1303. Albert had apparently refused the pope's demands, and Boniface VIII obviously found no support for his claims among the electors. In April 1301, the pope declared Albert a usurper of the throne and ordered the electors and all subjects to withdraw their allegiance. However, the king did not accept the challenge and refused to be drawn into any discussion of papal claims. Only after the defeat of the electors did he politely express his legal standpoint in a letter to Boniface in March 1302, emphasising the legality of the deposition of Adolf of Nassau and his own election by the electors, and asking the pope to uphold him as a true son of the church. His envoys offered full support for the Church, in so far as the interests of the empire were not damaged. They found the pope at the height of his struggle with Philip the Fair. In this difficult situation Boniface altered his stance towards the German king, since he had urgent need of him as an ally against France and in order to enforce the claims of the Angevins in Naples to the Hungarian throne after the extinction of the Árpáds in 1301. As early as November 1302 Boniface sent a sharp protest over the French occupation of Lyon, which belonged to the empire.

At the end of April 1303 (when the final blow against Boniface had been prepared and Guillaume de Nogaret was already on the road to Italy, to take the pope prisoner, drag him back to France and be judged by a council), negotiations took place at which Albert was represented by his chancellor John of Zurich. On 30 April, at a solemn session in the Lateran Palace Boniface VIII first made a speech such as no pope had ever made about the emperor. While he took up the old comparison with the sun and the moon, he interpreted it to the emperor's advantage: it was the monarch who illuminated everything like the sun. The text from Jeremiah, 'I have set you over peoples and kingdoms', which the popes usually quoted to depict their own power, Boniface used in relation to Albert: with the aid of pope and Church he was to stand over all peoples and kingdoms. Here it was the pope who attempted to confer a new gloss on the empire at a period when its star had long faded and every claim, even the merely theoretical, by the emperor to supreme sovereignty was rejected by the European monarchies. Admittedly this papal rhetoric in part pursued an obvious short-term goal: to humiliate the French king by emphasising the universality of imperial dominion, and Boniface had expressed this clearly: 'French pride, which claims that it does not recognise higher authority, is not to be raised against it. That is a lie, for by law they [the French] are and have to be subject to the Roman emperor and king.'[2] But behind this apparently paradoxical emphasis (which seemed to fly in the face of reality) on the absolute sovereignty of the emperor, by a pope who otherwise summoned all theories of ecclesiastical scholarship for the promotion of papal supremacy, there stood a specific dialectic necessity.

While the empire had been subordinated to the pope by the theoreticians of papal hierarchical structures since the mid-thirteenth century, its universality

[2] *MGH, Legum Sectio IV: Constitutions . . . Tom. IV*, ed. Schwalm, p. 139.

had increased as a result, since its structure was assimilated to the hierarchic principles of the papacy. Admittedly, Boniface did not miss this opportunity to underline the dependence of the emperor on the pope. Albert had to tolerate the fact that the pope continued to consider his election as illegal, but subsequently pronounced it valid by virtue of papal power. His chancellor joined in the paeon of praise for universal papal power. Albert, through him, swore an oath of obedience, not an oath of allegiance, which was much closer to the oaths of subjection common in the Papal States rather than those sworn by previous emperors. In a *promissio* he became the pope's subject, confirmed all the donations and rights conferred by his predecessors and undertook not to appoint an imperial vicar in Lombardy or Tuscany for five years and after that only to nominate imperial vicars there agreeable to the pope. However, there was no question of any separation of Tuscany from the empire and annexation to the Papal States. If Boniface had thereby induced the German king to accept the theoretical viewpoint of the papacy concerning its relation to the empire, Albert – for whom these theories evidently had little interest – had achieved political success by this submission, in that he won the pope as an ally against the German opposition. The alliance with France was admittedly void; Boniface annulled all alliances of the German king, including the Treaty of Quatrevaux. When this news reached Paris, Philip the Fair and his councillors took it as a declaration of war. The charges against the pope which had until then been secret were now openly stated in Paris on 13 January 1303. On 7 September Boniface VIII was taken prisoner at Anagni by Guillaume de Nogaret and Sciarra Colonna. After his release two days later and his return to Rome, he was defeated and powerless. On 12 October 1303 he died. With his death, the agreement with Albert was no more than a passing episode. The latter certainly remained passive in relation to France in the years that followed.

Final years and death

Strengthened by his victory over the opposing electors and his agreement with the pope, Albert could tackle the problems on the eastern border of the empire. First, the dispute over Hungary after the extinction of the Arpád line (1301) flared up. Already in 1290, after the murder of Ladislas IV, Rudolf of Habsburg had confiscated Hungary as a vacant imperial fief, since Béla IV had recognised the feudal overlordship of the emperor during the Mongol attack of 1241. Admittedly, the Church of Rome had long advanced claims to suzerainty over Hungary, and Nicholas IV and Boniface VIII thus supported the inheritance claims of the son of Ladislas's sister, Mary of Hungary, and of her husband, Charles II of Anjou, Charles Martel (d. 1295) and of his son, Charles-Robert, by his marriage to Clementia of Habsburg. However, the Hungarians decided on a nephew of Béla IV, Andrew III, whom Albert recognised and to whom he married his daughter, Agnes. Their daughter Elizabeth then married Wenceslas II of Bohemia's son, the future Wenceslas III, whom the Hungarian opposition recognised as king after the death of Andrew III (1301), thus ignoring the claims of the Angevin candidate, Charles-Robert. The Přemysls thereby encroached on Hungary, which was not in the least in Albert's interests. All the less so, when Wenceslas II exploited the confusion and had himself crowned king of Greater Poland, for which he received the permission of the German king. In the face of the great consolidation of Přemysl power, Albert now supported the Angevin candidate promoted by Pope Benedict XI, who was additionally his nephew. From Bohemia he demanded not only the renunciation of Hungary and Poland but also the return of Meissen and other lands.

After lengthy preparations on both sides it came to war in Hungary (where Charles-Robert was successful in 1304) and in Bohemia and Moravia. Before the outcome was decided, however, Wenceslas II died on 21 June 1305; his son Wenceslas III renounced Hungary and in return had his claims to Poland sanctioned. As he set out for Poland, he was the victim of a private feud in Olmütz. Since Wenceslas III had no male heirs, Albert claimed Bohemia as a vacant imperial fief for his son Rudolf. Rudolf, whose French wife Blanche had died, married the Polish widow of Wenceslas II and was invested with Bohemia with the agreement of the estates on 18 January 1307; in the event of his dying childless, his brothers were to succeed him. With this the Habsburgs seemed to have taken another big step towards the expansion of their power. Their claims now stretched from the powerful kingdom of Bohemia far into Poland; the great area that Ottokar of Bohemia had once dominated now appeared to have been resurrected under their lordship. This huge complex in the east was united with the Habsburg possessions in the upper Rhine area by the reorganised imperial domain which lay between them. No German ruler had ever before united such a powerful block of possessions in his control. After their defeat, the Rhenish electors had been eliminated as an opposition force; the king ignored them in his important decisions. It also seemed as if the German king was completing what the French monarch had succeeded in doing a century before, laying the foundations of a strong, central, national monarchy through the expansion of dynastic power. But this endeavour quickly disintegrated because of chance, which so often plays an important role in history. On 3 July 1307 Rudolf died, aged only twenty-six, and with his death Habsburg rule in Bohemia immediately crumbled. The barons and towns passed over Rudolf's brothers, called Henry of Carinthia into the country and elected him king on 15 August. Albert's enemies flocked round him, and the imperial campaign against Bohemia came to nothing in the autumn of 1307. In 1308 Albert assembled new allies and forces in southern Germany and his home area. At the end of April, the king stayed in his hereditary possessions near the castle of Habsburg. His nephew John was there, son of his younger brother Rudolf and Agnes, sister of Wenceslas II of Bohemia. Evidently John advanced claims to Bohemia which Albert did not recognise. He therefore conspired, with some young nobles from the Swiss region, to kill his uncle. As they crossed the Reuss at Windisch, John – henceforth called 'the parricide' – stabbed the king with the assistance of his accomplices on 1 May 1308.

This ended a reign characterised by dynastic policies. Albert had only half-heartedly pursued imperial coronation, the goal of all German rulers since the Ottonians. This played a subordinate role in his negotiations with Boniface VIII and his second successor, Clement V; Albert clearly intended, as emperor, to have his son crowned king of the Romans during his own lifetime. Greatly to Dante's indignation, Albert made no serious plans for an expedition to Rome and these were also impeded by the fact that Clement V took up residence in southern France and finally settled in papal Avignon. As far as the internal structure of the empire was concerned, Albert continued the imperial policy of his father. In the regulation of general peaces, he strengthened the element hostile to the towns, prohibition of the *Pfahlbürger* (1298), peasants who tried to settle in towns, additionally leaving the execution of the general peace to local rulers. He tightened the administration of the imperial domain by means of *Landvogteien*, by nominating *Landvögte* and, like his father, keenly pursued the recovery of the alienated imperial domain. Particular weight was attached to the newly established *Landvogtei* of Nuremberg, in which the imperial domain in Franconia was organised. The emperor had encouraged the accelerated demographic and economic growth of the imperial towns, which in part served the purposes of military security, here too continuing his father's policy. However, there could be no question of a systematically planned expansion of the imperial towns as the basis for strengthening imperial power. For equally, the king supported the foundation of towns by secular and ecclesiastical princes. He had encouraged supra-regional trade, above all to Italy (also in his own interests), but he certainly did not follow any general policy of lifting customs duties, which impeded trade; this only occurred from time to time to obstruct the electors. Venetian merchants, Florentine bankers and trading houses were repeatedly supported in the empire.

There was just as little formal financial administration then as at earlier and later dates. The towns had to bear the lion's share of imperial taxation; there were no mechanisms dedicated to the administration of taxes, levels were negotiated from case to case. Although Albert was no burghers' king, the towns did not oppose him, since they needed the protection of imperial power against the territorial princes. A further important source of income was taxation of the Jews. They had long been treated as servants of the imperial chamber in the kingdom of Germany. Albert's government coincided with a period when demonstrations against the Jews on grounds of alleged desecration of the host and the ritual killing of Christians finally poisoned relations with Christians. The king had stood up energetically for their protection, a stance in which financial motive played a considerable role; but great damage was inflicted on imperial finances by excessive pledging of resources.

The only central administration was the imperial chancery, which also had superintendence of income and expenditure. The purely formal role of the archchancellor for the three kingdoms which constituted the empire (Germany, Burgundy – kingdom of Arles – and Italy) was undertaken by the archbishops of Mainz, Cologne and Trier. The first had, at the start of Albert's reign, wrung from him the right to nominate the royal chancellor. His candidate, Eberhard von Stein, canon of Mainz, held office only until 1300, when the conflict with the Rhenish electors broke out. His successor, first as protonotary, then as vice-chancellor and, finally, chancellor, was a priest's son trained in law and theology, John of Zurich, who led the difficult negotiations with Boniface VIII and Benedict XI, later becoming bishop of Eichstätt and finally bishop of Strasburg. The high court of justice established under Frederick II was under the direction of a judge of the royal court; under Albert too counts were active in this office. The king attempted to evade discussion with the electors in the government of the empire; thus only one parliament (*Reichshoftag*) took place in Nuremberg (1298). Instead, the role of imperial councillors (*familiares, conciliarii, secretarii*) was strengthened. This group included officials of the imperial chancery, court chaplains, a few bishops (especially Henry of Constance) and counts, mostly from Swabia. The king's wife, Elizabeth of Görz, wielded especial influence over the emperor. Moreover, he had a very personal style of government, making use of changing personnel. The Habsburg domain was administered separately. In Nuremberg in 1298 Albert had invested his sons jointly with the Habsburg dukedoms; however, the eldest, Rudolf, was responsible for the administration and *c.* 1300 the younger brothers renounced the Danubian lands. When Rudolf became king of Bohemia in 1306, the next-oldest, Frederick, took over the lordship of the hereditary lands. Here too the towns were substantially drawn upon for the regional lordship. We are well informed only about the organisation of the *Oberen Lande*, the old Habsburg possessions on the upper Rhine, through the land register (*Urbar*) drawn up by the notary, Burchard von Fricke.

The Swiss Confederation

These decades witnessed the origin of the Swiss Confederation, the federation in 1291 of the Forest Cantons (*Waldstätten*) of Uri, Schwyz and Unterwalden.

The remote areas on the *Vierwaldstättersee* had become important because of the opening of the Saint-Gotthard pass, as the shortest line of communication between the upper Rhine and Italy. Their legal positions varied. Uri had been part of the empire since 1231, when the young Henry (VII), son of Frederick II, bought it from the Habsburgs. Schwyz received imperial freedom (*Reichsfreiheit*) in 1240 from Frederick II, but the Habsburgs nevertheless had seigneurial rights here. Unterwalden was Habsburg. At this period there were any number of alliances for war and peace (*Schwertbünde* and *Landfriedensbünde*). Here was a number of peasant communities, regional nobles and, in the future, also towns swearing not to tolerate any alien judge. In 1291 the Confederation wanted the concession made by King Rudolf to the people of Schwyz, that they should only be judged by freemen of their own valley, to be extended to all three Forest Cantons. This was directed in the first place against the Habsburg *Vögte* and officials. That it came to an anti-Habsburg revolt on the death of Albert in 1308 is a tradition first documented in 1471/2; the figures of William Tell and the *Landvogt* Gessler are not historically proven. Moreover, there was no such revolt in 1291. The original Confederation was thus a union for the preservation of rights; it did not imply opposition to Habsburg lordship for the foundation of a state of their own. In 1297 Adolf of Nassau had granted imperial freedom to Uri and Schwyz; Henry VII extended this in 1300 to Unterwalden. Only the double election after his death resulted in conflict with the Habsburgs, since the Forest Cantons supported Lewis of Bavaria and were banned by Frederick the Fair. When his brother Leopold of Habsburg attacked them, he was crushingly defeated by the peasants at the Morgarten pass on 15 November 1311. On 9 December the Confederates renewed their 'eternal union' in Brunnen. They had won their freedom by fighting not the empire but the Habsburgs. The non-Habsburg kings looked favourably on their independence; the union grew in the fourteenth century through the addition of Lucerne, Zurich, Glarus, Zug and Berne. When the Habsburgs occupied the imperial throne continuously from 1438 onwards, the Confederates – who stood in the way of joining the Habsburg territories in the east with those on the upper Rhine – slowly disengaged themselves from the empire and became an individual state, although one which was, admittedly, only finally recognised in the Peace of Westphalia in 1648.

HENRY VII

Election and conquest of Bohemia

After Albert's unexpected death, Philip the Fair of France promoted the candidature of his brother Charles of Valois, who had already been at his disposal for special duties in Italy and as claimant to the throne of Aragon. His aim was the German kingdom, thereby transmitting the empire to the Capetians, as the French king's propagandist Pierre Dubois asserted in his treatise on the recovery of the Holy Land, even calling on Philip to stand as a candidate himself. This time the plan seemed to have good prospects, since Pope Clement V (who was under the influence of Philip the Fair) had filled the three important Rhenish archbishoprics with French supporters during Albert's lifetime. In 1305 the son of a minor Rhineland count, Heinrich von Virneburg, became archbishop of Cologne and made an alliance with the French king. The archbishop of Mainz was Peter of Aspelt, formerly personal physician of Rudolf of Habsburg, who had become an opponent of the Habsburgs and implemented Wenceslas II of Bohemia's policy of alliances with France against Albert. Finally, the French king and Count Henry of Luxemburg had secured the archbishopric of Trier for the latter's younger brother Baldwin, who had spent a long time studying in Paris; he too swore Philip an oath of allegiance. In May 1308 the French king started his campaign for the election of his brother as king of the Romans, for which French money flowed freely. Clement V undoubtedly displayed the greatest tactical skill in his dealings with the French king and above all postponed the threatened trial of Boniface VIII; he behaved circumspectly and avoided open support for Charles. He had apparently decided not to let Capetian power expand still further. In the first instance only Archbishop Henry of Cologne then seriously supported the candidacy of Charles of Valois, whose chances were not improved by the fact that the count-palatine Rudolf and others were also striving for the crown and Henry of Carinthia-Bohemia was undecided.

In this situation, Count Henry of Luxemburg cleverly exploited his opportunities. Although he was a vassal of Philip the Fair he succeeded in damaging the French king's plans. His brother Archbishop Baldwin of Trier won the archbishop of Mainz over to the Luxemburg candidature. To what extent fear of French expansion already played a role, as later became evident, is difficult to decide. The two Rhenish electors succeeded in drawing the secular electors to their side, with the exception of the king of Bohemia, and finally also the archbishop of Cologne, in return for substantial concessions, was won over to Count Henry of Luxemburg. He was elected by six votes at Frankfurt on 27 November 1308 and crowned at Aachen on 6 January 1309.

The new king was about thirty years old and son of Count Henry VI of Luxemburg and La Roche. Thrown back on his little territory between the Moselle and the Meuse, Henry was a minor count who sought the protection of the French king. He spent part of his youth at the French court, which marked him strongly. French was his mother-tongue; French courtly life had left its imprint on him and his political ideas were also strongly influenced by

Paris. The German kingdom had migrated for a short while to the west. Clement V endorsed his election, without being asked to do so by the electors.

Unexpected developments in Bohemia then caused the interests of the new king to turn eastwards. Henry of Carinthia was unpopular there, and the fact that he kept his distance during the imperial election had isolated him further. Consequently, influential ecclesiastics, especially Cistercians, and a part of the Bohemian nobility, approached the new king offering his only son John marriage with Elizabeth, younger daughter of Wenceslas II, to legitimate claims to the Bohemian crown. In July, Henry of Carinthia was deprived of Bohemia, and John of Luxemburg invested with it shortly afterwards. Henry VII did not wait for the final settlement of matters in Bohemia but set out for Italy before John and Elizabeth were crowned by the archbishop of Mainz in Prague on 7 February 1311.

Thus, virtually without doing anything themselves, the Luxemburgs amassed a great dynastic power which was to last over a century; a powerful dynasty grew from an insignificant comital family in the German–French border area and one which could also assert Bohemia's claim to Poland. Henry VII soon reached agreement with the remaining German opponents. Already in September and October 1309 the king altered his policy towards the Habsburgs, which had initially been hostile, finally confirming Frederick and his brothers their imperial fiefs including those of the regicide John, with Moravia handed over as a five-year pledge. Leopold of Habsburg agreed to participate in the king's Italian expedition with his own body of troops.

The Italian expedition

In contrast to his two predecessors, who had kept their eyes firmly on the political situation in Germany, Henry VII was vigilant over Italy and the imperial coronation. For almost a century, no German ruler had received the imperial crown at the hands of the pope. There were several factors determining Henry's resumption of the Italian policy of earlier periods. In the first place he undoubtedly wanted to avoid a disagreement with the Rhineland electors to whom he owed his election. He had not really given his full attention to the perspectives that had opened in the east at any rate, leaving policy there to his son John. In contrast, his interests in Italy were founded on the one hand on German imperial tradition, on the other on the fact that, while he had been at the French court, he had become familiar with French imperial plans. The dignity of emperor was to secure him lordship of the other two kingdoms of the empire, Arles and Italy; it was also intended to strengthen Henry's position against Philip the Fair. In this respect his interests coincided with those of Clement V. A royal delegation, which negotiated with the pope in June and July

1309 at Avignon, secured ratification of Henry VII's election and a declaration that he was fitted for the imperial dignity and thus the pope would crown him.

In return Henry VII swore an oath of protection; this corresponded to earlier obligations of German rulers to the pope: it was not an oath of obedience such as Albert had given Boniface VIII. Clement V stipulated Rome, where he then still planned to return, at Candlemas 1312 for the imperial coronation. This date was too late for Henry; already in August 1309 he announced his expedition to Rome and sent ambassadors to Italy. The success of his Italian plans largely depended on the attitude of the Angevin ruler of Naples, King Robert, who in 1309 succeeded his father Charles II to the throne of the kingdom of Sicily, reduced in size and limited to the south Italian mainland since the Sicilian Vespers in 1282. In order to promote Henry VII's Italian expedition and the return of the pope to Rome, Italian cardinals – above all Jacopo Gaetani Stefaneschi and Niccolò da Prato who wanted to remove the papacy from the influence of Philip the Fair – suggested an alliance between Henry and Robert of Naples. The latter's only son Charles of Calabria was, according to these plans, to marry Henry's daughter Beatrice and hold as an imperial fief the kingdom of Arles, where the Angevins had long been securely established as counts of Provence. Such a plan also promised to soften the Italian conflict between Guelfs and Ghibellines. In the summer of 1310 the relevant negotiations took place at the papal curia, which, however, were greatly hampered by Robert's excessive demands for money and by the French king, who did not want the kingdom of Arles to fall into Robert's hands. At the same time negotiations for a treaty continued until 1311 between Henry VII and Philip the Fair, who at this time took permanent possession of Lyon, but these came to no conclusion because the German king did not want to let Philip have the Franche-Comté and Lyon.

Before these issues had been clarified, Henry VII set out on his Italian expedition in October 1310, heralded by enthusiastic manifestos by the pope, who commended peace to the towns of Lombardy and Tuscany. Henry's son John remained in Prague as imperial vicar. The king's army was small and comprised around 5,000 soldiers; there could be no talk of a general feudal levy. Most knights came from the king's dynastic lands on the western border of the empire, from Luxemburg, the Low Countries, Lorraine, Alsace, Switzerland, Burgundy, Savoy and the Dauphiné, many of them endeavouring through their support of the German king to withdraw themselves from the powerful French king. Of the electors, only Henry's brother Baldwin of Trier accompanied him; the count-palatine Rudolf followed later. Among other high-ranking princes, Leopold of Habsburg was only in the army until October 1311 and then fled from the epidemic which broke out at Brescia. From the Lake of Geneva the little army crossed Mont Cenis to Susa. Dante heralded the approaching king as the saviour of Italy: 'Rejoice, O Italy! Though now to be pitied even by the Saracens, soon you will be envied throughout the world! For your bridegroom, the solace of the world and the glory of your people, the most clement Henry ... is hastening to the nuptials.'[3] For the country was torn apart by internal conflict, the outcome of social developments, which were admittedly often superseded by irrational factionalism.

The inhabitants of the dominant towns consisted of a powerful oligarchy at the top (in which the old ruling classes, the feudal nobility and the upper strata of the merchants and artisans had coalesced), and the *popolo,* that is the great majority of artisans, who for a century had pressed, largely successfully, for participation in civic government. Social conflicts between the *popolo* and the ruling oligarchy should be differentiated from struggles within the ruling class which had a great number of motives, rational and irrational, and in which the parties mostly sought the support of the great powers of the period, empire and papacy, only as a secondary consideration. In Florence, since the middle of the thirteenth century, the Guelfs had been the pro-papal and pro-Angevin party, the Ghibellines pro-imperial. The names of these parties were soon widely disseminated by means of Florentine exiles in Tuscany, only later in Lombardy as well. Around 1300 the tendency of the communal constitution to change from government by a great number of citizens to rule by a single lord (*signore*) had burst forth almost everywhere (Florence and Venice being exceptions). The reasons varied from place to place. The majority of the *signori* were members of the feudal nobility; usually, their assumption of power in the towns was the consequence of the economic domination by the regional aristocracy of the town, and their territory, the *contado*. In this desperate situation Dante (himself a victim of the split of the victorious Guelfs in Florence into 'Whites' and 'Blacks') saw a glimmer of hope in Henry of Luxemburg.

Henry had every intention of establishing peace between the parties, and between rulers and exiles. He tried to remain neutral, avoided taking sides and using the names of the factions. But already in Milan he came to grief. Here, following ancient tradition, on 6 January 1311, he received from the archbishop, the crown of the Lombard kingdom, symbol of the inclusion of the *regnum Italie* (kingdom of Italy) within the imperial union. In Milan in the preceding period, the Torriani had, with the aid of the *popolo*, been elevated to the status of *signori* and had banned their opponents in the oligarchy, the Visconti. When Henry called the latter back from exile, in accordance with his policy of reconciliation, Guido della Torre, assisted by the inhabitants of the city (who did not want to raise the taxes demanded to cover the costs of the army)

---

[3] Dante, *Epistola V* (to the kings, princes, etc., of Italy, *c.* September–October 1310), most widely used critical edition in England: *Le Opere di Dante Alighieri*, p. 406.

organised a revolt which was put down by the king. Henry banned Guido and appointed Matteo Visconti imperial vicar. This was the signal for Guelf propaganda; from then on he was branded a Ghibelline; all attempts at mediation failed. He severely punished Cremona, where the rebels had found refuge. By contrast, Reggio, Parma, Crema and Lodi accepted his rule; in Verona the Scaligers received the dignity of the imperial vicariate and Padua also submitted; here the chronicler Albertino Mussato was among Henry's supporters. The centre of anti-imperial forces was Brescia, which Henry besieged in the middle of May with the help of the Italian Ghibellines, and whose captain Theobald Brusati he had horribly executed. After a four-month-long siege, during which an epidemic claimed many – even Henry fell ill – the town surrendered in September and was treated relatively leniently; the fortifications were, however, destroyed.

Henry's principal opponent was Florence, which had united the Guelf communes of Lucca, Siena and Bologna in an alliance directed against him and since April 1311 conducted an increasingly articulate propaganda war against him in Lombardy, at the papal curia and at the royal court at Naples. Florence contested his role in Italy and called to fight for 'freedom' against the foreign 'tyrant', the lord of the Ghibelline *signoria*. Clement V soon felt the pressure of Philip the Fair as well as that of the Italian Guelfs, and in the spring of 1311 slowly retreated from his friendly stance towards Henry and gave increasingly clear support to the Guelf opposition – also out of consideration for the Papal State. Robert of Naples, the ideological head of the Guelfs, held himself back at first because of the prospect of acquiring the kingdom of Arles which he had been offered. Thus, despite his appointment as papal rector in the Romagna in 1310, he remained aloof from the conflicts in Lombardy, particularly since danger threatened from the south, from Frederick, the Aragonese ruler of the island of Sicily (Trinacria). For all that, in August 1311, the cardinal-legate Niccolò da Prato, an ally of the Ghibellines and the 'White Guelfs', and Luca Fieschi, who were to perform Henry's imperial coronation in Rome, arrived in his camp.

When Henry marched on Rome in October and proceeded first to Genoa, the situation in Lombardy was only outwardly peaceful. In Genoa an epidemic broke out once more, and Queen Margaret, who had thus far exerted a moderating influence upon Henry, died. Henry attempted to mediate in the quarrel between the hostile families of Genoa and, by means of reform of the communal constitution, to content the *popolani*. At this point, he entered once more into negotiations with Robert of Anjou concerning a marriage alliance; however, this came to nothing. Since he was simultaneously engaged in negotiations with Frederick of Trinacria, Robert became increasingly distant, especially as Henry required him to appear in person at Rome for the imperial coronation and swear an oath of allegiance for his imperial fiefs in Piedmont, Provence and Forcalquier. However, Henry of Luxemburg did not, above all, want to drive Robert of Anjou into the arms of Florence and make relations with Clement V still more difficult. Florence now adopted an ever more hostile attitude to Henry and also mobilised his opponents in northern Italy, where there were uprisings at Parma, Reggio, Brescia and Cremona in December 1311 and January 1312. Already in November 1311 Henry, following Dante's advice exactly, started legal proceedings against Florence on the grounds of *lèse-majesté* and a month later placed her under imperial ban. Equally, he proceeded against the Lombard rebels, sustained his supporters, among them Matteo Visconti in Milan and Cangrande della Scala in Verona, and appointed Count Werner of Homburg as captain-general in place of the general vicar for Lombardy, so that he could lead the military action against the rebels. Henry himself went by ship in February 1312 from Genoa to Pisa, which he entered on 6 March. Large numbers of Ghibellines and White Guelfs from Tuscany and the Marches now assembled in this town, traditionally hostile to Florence and loyal to the empire; Count-Palatine Rudolf also brought reinforcements. Henry resumed talks once more with Robert of Anjou, encouraged by the pope. But he also renewed negotiations with Frederick of Trinacria; a possible marriage alliance troubled the papacy again with the threat of encirclement of the Papal State. At the end of April Henry's army marched along the Via Francigena in the direction of Rome, where on 7 May fighting broke out with Angevin soldiers on the Milvian Bridge. Of the great noble dynasties, the Colonna who controlled the areas of the city around the Lateran and S. Maria Maggiore sided with the king of the Romans, while St Peter's, scene of imperial coronations, was in the hands of his enemies. Since Henry's troops did not succeed in opening a way to St Peter's and since negotiations with the Angevins failed, the king aimed at coronation in the Lateran.

Robert of Anjou had meanwhile greatly increased his demands under the influence of Florence: he claimed a decisive role throughout Italy and naval support against Frederick of Trinacria, denied Henry effective rule in Tuscany, demanded the appointment of his son as imperial vicar in Tuscany and the emperor's departure from Rome within four days of his coronation; but made no further mention of the kingdom of Arles. On 29 June 1312, in the Lateran, Henry of Luxemburg was crowned emperor by the two cardinals deputed to do so. The pope, who in response to French pressure had not sent bulls already prepared demanding the departure of John of Gravina, Robert's brother, from Rome, left Henry to his problems. On the very day he was crowned emperor, in a constitution against heretics, Henry stressed, in the old tradition of the Hohenstaufen, the direct dependence of the empire on God, thereby passing over papal rights, and declared that all peoples and kingdoms were subject to the emperor, which Philip the Fair at once rejected. Shortly before the coronation, Clement V had demanded that Henry should make a one-year truce with Robert and forbade him any attack on the kingdom of Sicily. When the emperor refused an oath to this effect and, supported by legal opinion and emphasising his unique claim to temporal power, represented the planned advance against Robert of Anjou not as war but as a punitive expedition against a rebel, the relationship between emperor, pope and the king of Naples was finally destroyed. Henry concluded a marriage alliance and a treaty of mutual support with Frederick of Trinacria and then on 20 August withdrew from Rome to the north, to begin a campaign against Florence and her allies.

Not from Rome but, following the advice of his jurists, from Arezzo, which was in imperial territory, the emperor commenced legal proceedings against King Robert of Naples in September 1312; he based this on grounds of universal imperial law, and not solely on feudal law. After besieging Florence in vain, at the end of 1312 Henry conquered a large part of the *contado* and in the campaign treated his opponents with striking leniency. The Guelfs, however, won notable successes against him in Lombardy. Pisa, where Henry withdrew in March 1313, continued to remain the centre of imperial supporters. Here he decided to attack with all force Robert of Naples who had meanwhile, after long hesitation, accepted the office of captain of the Guelf League; a series of Lombard towns also yielded to him. At Pisa the proceedings against the Tuscan rebels and Robert were brought to a close. The former were deprived of all rights and possessions, although the judgement could not be carried out. Then on 26 April 1313 Robert of Naples, who meanwhile basked in boundless papal favour, was declared guilty of high treason, *lèse-majesté* and rebellion and sentenced to death. A propaganda war followed, in which Philip the Fair intervened on Robert's behalf. Numerous legal and political treatises composed at this period defended the current imperial, papal or Angevin viewpoint; Dante's *Monarchia* was admittedly not among them, for it was only produced some years after the death of the emperor and shortly before that of the poet himself. The emperor prepared for war from the financially drained town of Pisa, for the attack on Naples. But his Italian allies were very reluctant to support him. Thus Henry left Pisa on 8 August 1313 in the direction of Rome with a relatively small army of some 4,000 knights; a fleet was to attack the kingdom of Sicily at the same time. At the siege of Siena the emperor fell seriously ill; already he had succumbed to numerous infections. Presumably this time it was a strain of falciparum malaria, usually raging since August, which together with other infections led to rapid death: on 22 August he moved along the Via Francigena into the little town of Buonconvento, south of Siena, where he died on 24 August, not yet forty years old. His body was brought to Pisa where he found his final resting-place in the cathedral; the remains of his monumental tomb, by Tino da Camaino, frequently moved, are today to be found in the south transept. After his death the Italian campaign quickly fell apart; his army scattered and the country was more divided than before.

LEWIS OF BAVARIA

Election and beginnings

After the death of Henry VII, Philip the Fair again, and once more in vain, attempted to have one of his sons (the future Philip V) elected king of the Romans. Since both the French king and the pope were close to death, the electors could proceed to the election relatively uninfluenced. Henry's son, John of Bohemia, was passed over for fear of establishing a hereditary monarchy. There was a double election, however, Rudolf, the Wittelsbach count-palatine of the Rhine, who had fallen out with his brother Lewis of Upper Bavaria, and Duke Rudolf of Saxony-Wittenberg, together with Archbishop Henry of Cologne, elected Frederick of Habsburg (later known as 'the Fair') on 19 October 1314 at Sachsenhausen (on the south bank of the river Main near Frankfurt); on the following day, before the gates of Frankfurt, Archbishops Peter of Mainz and Baldwin of Trier, King John of Bohemia, Margrave Waldemar of Brandenburg and Duke John of Saxony-Lauenburg (the Saxon vote had been contested between Wittenberg and Lauenburg since 1295–6) elected the Wittelsbach Duke Lewis of Upper Bavaria as king. The coronation was equally disputed: Frederick was crowned by the duly qualified archbishop of Cologne with the true insignia but in the wrong place (Bonn), Lewis in the right place (Aachen) but by the archbishop of Mainz (who had no authority to do so) and without the lawful insignia. He was given the more authoritative votes, and the majority of the electors were on his side, but the majority vote had not yet prevailed: the issue had to be decided by force.

Lewis had been brought up at the Habsburg court, but little is known about his sojourn there. In serious disputes over the Wittelsbach inheritance in Upper and Lower Bavaria he had been able to prevail over his brother, the count-palatine Rudolf, and the Habsburgs. After his election as king, he had the strategic advantage of having the Bohemian–Bavarian region behind him, as a buffer between the Habsburg possessions in the east and in anterior Austria (*Vorderösterreich*). For financial reasons an intensive military campaign was virtually impossible for both sides; the dispute thus turned into a kind of noble feud. Battle was only joined on 28 September 1322 at Mühldorf on the Inn (east of Munich); before the two sections of the Habsburg army advancing from Swabia in the west and Austria in the east could unite to launch a double attack, Lewis inflicted an annihilating defeat on the force advancing from Austria; Frederick was taken prisoner. The victory undoubtedly consolidated Lewis's position, but the struggle was continued by Frederick's brother, Leopold. It was therefore a great achievement for Lewis when, after the Ascanians of Brandenburg had died out, he was able in 1323 to invest his son, another Lewis ('the Brandenburger'), with the Margravate of Brandenburg. Although he had to make significant concessions to the Ascanians and the Wettin dynasty in the process, and alienated himself from the Luxemburgs, the acquisition of an electoral voice and a landed base in the north-east of the kingdom was an advantage for him, and Wittelsbach rule of the March of Brandenburg continued until 1373. Later, after a long period of transition, the Hohenzollern dynasty that originated in Swabia and had extended its rule to Nuremberg, was enfeoffed with it in 1417, and from then on began to play its important role in German history.

In the same way – although it could certainly not have been anticipated at the time – Lewis's second marriage in 1324 with Margaret, daughter of Count William III of Hainault, Holland and Zeeland offered him the prospect of lands in the north-west of the empire. The king attempted to end the division of the old Wittelsbach territories in Bavaria and the Palatinate on the Italian campaign of 1329 by means of the Treaty of Pavia, which granted Upper Bavaria to Lewis and his heirs, and the Palatinate to Rudolf. The areas north of the Danube were divided between both lineages, those which were added to the Palatinate (around Amberg) were henceforth called the 'Upper Palatinate'; they only returned to Bavaria in 1628. Electoral rights were to alternate between the Palatine and Bavarian lineages; however, this was not observed and the vote remained with the Palatinate. Thus until 1623 the oldest and most united territory in Germany was denied participation in the royal election.

The dispute with Pope John XXII

John XXII, who had been elected on 7 August 1316 after a vacancy of more than two years, did not at first intervene in the dispute over the German crown. On the basis of a decretal of Innocent III, issued in an insignificant lawsuit in the Papal State, the popes considered themselves vicars of the empire during imperial vacancies, a right they claimed and tried to make good in Italy above all, in view of the almost total breakdown of imperial power there. In Italy, Frederick the Fair, who had married a daughter of James II of Aragon, established contact with her brother Frederick III of Sicily (Trinacria), but he had also entered a marriage alliance with the latter's enemy, Robert of Naples, and appointed him imperial vicar for the areas ruled by the Guelfs. John XXII pursued his own policy there, vigorously proclaimed the theory of the papal vicariate of the empire and declared that all vicars and other officials appointed by Emperor Henry VII were to be removed from office unless their appointments were confirmed by the pope. In particular he took measures against the Ghibelline rulers, Matteo Visconti in Milan, Cangrande della Scala in Verona and the Este in Ferrara who were to be outlawed on grounds of heresy. Robert of Naples, whose appointment as imperial vicar by Clement V was renewed by John XXII in 1317, only hesitatingly, however, allowed himself to become party to papal policy. After his victory at Mühldorf, Lewis of Bavaria (who had not taken up the pope's offer of mediation in the dispute over the dual election) intervened in Italy in the spring of 1323 and sent an imperial vicar appointed by himself, Count Berthold of Marstetten, to aid the Visconti and the Este.

This laid him open to the charge of supporting heretics in October 1323. The pope accused him of unlawfully exercising the rule of king without papal approbation after the disputed election: within three months Lewis was to renounce rule in Germany and the other parts of the empire and to rescind all his acts. Although his legal case was weak, Lewis let himself be dragged into litigation. On 18 December 1323 at Nuremberg he lodged an appeal to the Holy See (as if that were a different institution from the pope); accepting the conciliar theory already announced by Frederick II, he promised to appear before a council, emphasised his orthodoxy and, taking up complaints by the secular clergy against the Franciscans, maintained that they disregarded the confidentiality of confession and imperilled the Church and yet enjoyed full support by the pope who was therefore suspect of heresy himself. Lewis's election by the majority of the electors was rightful and did not require papal confirmation. However, the king did not publish this version, but one formulated at Frankfurt on 7 January 1324, in which charges of heresy against John XXII were left out, the pope rejected as a judge, and appeal made to a council. John refused to take any notice of these statements of defence and on 23 March 1324 passed sentence of excommunication on Lewis, which was to bind him the rest of his life. In Sachsenhausen on 22 May 1324 the king made his appeal to a council in still stronger terms. Once more he stressed that his election had been valid and did not require papal approbation. In addition, however – and in total contrast to the Nuremberg appeal – the pope was accused of heresy because he had entered into conflict with the Franciscans, condemning their conception of the total poverty of Christ and the Apostles. As Franciscans were not yet to be found at the imperial court, Lewis's ambassadors from Avignon seem to have brought information about this dogmatic controversy; moreover, a treatise was utilised that probably originated in Franciscan circles in Italy hostile to the pope, and which the imperial protonotary Ulrich Wild inserted into the document without the king's knowledge.

Lewis was later to distance himself from it, emphasising that he had only been concerned with imperial law. The Sachsenhausen appeal was circulated in Latin and in German translation in the imperial towns; the dispute that followed was widely disseminated among all sections of the population; above all, towns-people were drawn actively into politics, which were thus no longer the concern of a small governing class. The appeal was not officially communi-cated to the curia. The pope continued legal proceedings and on 17 July 1324 deprived Lewis of all right to rule, pronounced excommunication and inter-dict on his supporters and threatened to deprive them of their imperial fiefs; he had no intention of summoning a council.

The situation in the empire was hazardous for Lewis, since after the death of Peter of Aspelt (1320), the Habsburg supporter Matthew of Bucheck became archbishop of Mainz. John of Bohemia deserted the Wittelsbach cause because of Brandenburg and Meissen, and a marriage alliance brought him closer to France; his son Wenceslas, the future Emperor Charles IV, grew up at the French royal court. Schemes to confer the German crown on John of Bohemia or Charles IV of France found no support at Paris; John XXII's attempts to promote a Capetian candidate were also unsuccessful. Lewis antic-ipated such plans when he made an alliance with Frederick the Fair (who was imprisoned in the castle of Trausnitz) and recognised him as joint king (*Mitkönig*) in September 1325 – but this was opposed by the electors. Early in 1326 Lewis declared himself even ready to abdicate, provided that the pope recognised Frederick as king within six months. John XXII refused, if only on the grounds that Frederick had incurred ecclesiastical penalties through his dealings with the excommunicated king. This clever policy branded the pope as implacable and weakened his position in Germany. Frederick virtually ignored his joint kingship and soon died on 13 January 1330; his brother Leopold had already predeceased him in 1326, and his younger brother Albert II devoted himself wholeheartedly to territorial expansion. The Habsburgs were thus eliminated as contenders for the German throne.

The Italian campaign and the imperial coronation

Stabilisation of the situation in Germany made it possible for Lewis to yield to urgent requests from the Italian Ghibellines and go to Italy to be crowned as emperor. This coronation had to take place without – indeed, in opposition to – the pope. The fact that Lewis was prepared to do so was the result in no small part of the arrival of Marsilius of Padua and his friend John of Jandun at his court in 1326. In June 1324 Marsilius, a supporter of the Ghibellines in his native city, then master and rector at Paris university, finished the *Defensor Pacis* (Defender of Peace) which laid him and his assumed co-author, John of

Jandun, open to the accusation of heresy and forced them to flee. Although the radical nature of this abstract Aristotelian work, undoubtedly permeated with the experiences of politics in the northern Italian communes, did not correspond to the socio-political reality of Church and empire, it did to some extent influence Lewis's policy, if only for a short while. Marsilius's uncompromising teaching on the sovereignty of the people, the *legislator humanus,* whose relationship to the abstract emperor is certainly not at all times clear, the total subjection of the clergy and the Church to the rule of the people was a Utopia and could not be translated into practical politics. But Lewis was nevertheless able to use this teaching on the sovereignty of the people to have himself elected emperor by the Romans.

The friendly reception granted to Marsilius and John at Lewis's court offered John XXII the opportunity to institute further legal proceedings against the king on the grounds of heresy in April 1327; this time he also deprived him of his Bavarian dukedom and the fiefs of the empire and referred to him contemptuously as 'Lewis of Bavaria', or just 'the Bavarian', an epithet which has stuck to the present day. Lewis wanted to encircle Robert of Naples by means of his alliance with Frederick III of Sicily. The Italian campaign ran its course without any major battles except the siege and occupation of Pisa. Lewis was crowned at Milan in customary fashion as king of the *regnum Italicum* with the old crown of the Lombards at Whitsun 1327. The Ghibelline rulers of Verona, Ferrara and Mantua were appointed imperial vicars, and Lewis's most active supporter, Castruccio Castracani declared hereditary duke of Lucca. On 7 January 1328 the king entered Rome, amid popular rejoicing. The supporters of Robert of Naples had been driven out before and a government set up of fifty-two representatives of the *popolo,* presided over by Sciarra Colonna, the assailant of Boniface VIII at Anagni in 1303. On the Capitol Lewis announced his intention of ruling, supporting and elevating the Roman people. The coronation took place in St Peter's on 17 January 1328. It seems to have been a compromise (although the sources are not quite clear with regard to what actually happened): two bishops carried out the anointing; Sciarra Colonna either placed the imperial crowns on the heads of Lewis and his wife or assisted one of the bishops in doing so. Four days later, still unaware of these events, John XXII ordered a crusade to be preached against Lewis. On 31 March the pope had the coronation declared null and void. Under the influence of Marsilius, on 18 April the emperor declared John XXII deposed, on the conventional grounds that the pope had carried war into the Margravate of Brandenburg and into Italy and was guilty of heresy; according to canon law this last was the only legal basis for deposition of a pope.

On 12 May, Ascension Day, once more in harmony with the teachings of Marsilius, the Franciscan Peter of Corvaro was elected pope by the people of

Rome; he took the name of Nicholas V. As if he had doubts about his first coronation, Lewis had himself crowned emperor by the new pope in traditional fashion at Whitsun. However, this last imperial anti-pope was doomed to failure: without cardinals and curia, and with no financial base, in August 1328 he was forced, by the Romans, who were embittered as a result of the exorbitant financial demands, to leave Rome together with the emperor. His city soon returned to the obedience of John XXII. The attack on Robert of Naples, in alliance with Frederick of Sicily, did not materialise, since funds were lacking. On the return journey northwards Franciscans fleeing from Avignon – the general of the order, Michael of Cesena, the procurator, Bonagratia of Bergamo, and the Oxford theologian William of Ockham – joined up with the emperor, who, under their influence, renewed his charges of heresy against John XXII. In Munich the Franciscans continued the attacks with Marsilius; they proved an evident liability for the emperor, who soon sought new advisers. Nicholas V submitted to John XXII, and the Ghibellines of northern Italy also sought a reconciliation with him; moreover, Cangrande della Scala and Castruccio Castracani died. When Lewis returned to Germany in February 1330, the Italian campaign had proved a failure.

German and international politics, 1330–1338

The concept of a form of imperial authority based on popular sovereignty had thus evidently failed. Like his predecessors, Lewis was thrown back on to the real power basis of the German kingdom. Here, however, despite the renewed efforts of John XXII to see an anti-king in the person of Philip VI of Valois, the situation developed to the emperor's advantage. In Mainz, Archbishop Baldwin of Trier, elected once more after the death of Archbishop Matthew of Bucheck, for the most part established himself against the papal appointee, Heinrich von Virneburg; he increasingly favoured Lewis's party, which John of Bohemia also joined. Papal influence on the electoral college dwindled as a result. In addition, the towns, whose political influence was growing all the time, were on the side of the excommunicated emperor, and worried very little about ban or interdict. The taxes paid by the towns made a substantial contribution to the financing of imperial policy. The bishops' support for John XXII was either lukewarm or non-existent; in addition, in many dioceses there were struggles between papal candidates and those elected by the cathedral chapter. The Swabian League of imperial towns from 1331, and associations of general peace (*Landfriedensbünde*), helped calm the situation in the south-west of the empire and elsewhere. One can justly see these events – the alienation from the papacy of substantial sections of the German people – as the beginning of the great shift of opinion against the papal curia which would later result in the

Reformation. A considerable number of the secular and regular clergy adhered to Lewis, for example, the majority of the Franciscans (supporting their superiors who had been deposed by the pope), while the Dominicans sided with the pope. The interdict was frequently ignored; clerics who refused to hold services and administer the sacraments were often driven out by the townspeople. After the death of Frederick of Austria, the emperor made a final agreement by the Treaty of Hagenau with the Habsburgs, in August 1330, recognising their rights and possessions.

On the other hand, the double game initiated by John of Bohemia at the end of 1330 was dangerous for the Wittelsbach for some while. He started an unsanctioned Italian campaign, which had originally been planned with the emperor and was at first successful, since most of the Ghibelline towns of Lombardy transferred lordship to him. As a result Lewis had to concede these Italian acquisitions to John as an imperial pledge and make a 'pact of eternal friendship' with him in August 1332. Already at the beginning of 1332, John had, however, made an agreement with Philip VI of France, strengthened by the marriage of their children, in which should he or one of his sons become German king and emperor he pledged the French king full support and recognition of his possessions. John of Luxemburg also came to an understanding in Avignon in November 1332 with John XXII, who had at first opposed his Italian plans, agreeing to hold Parma, Modena and Reggio, which the pope considered part of the Pontifical State, as papal fiefs, to forgo Lucca and not to attack Florence or Naples. In addition he promised to withdraw his support from the emperor. In this way John hoped to obtain sanction for his Italian acquisitions from all sides. This was all the more urgent, since John of Luxemburg's plans were being opposed both in Germany, where a coalition was formed of the counts-palatine, the margraves of Brandenburg and Meissen, as well as the Habsburgs, and in Italy, with a great league led by Robert of Naples and Florence. It was in this context that the king of Bohemia suggested to the pope that he should grant the emperor absolution, provided that Lewis declared himself ready to renounce the throne in favour of John's son-in-law, Henry XIV, duke of Lower Bavaria, from whom he anticipated strong support for his Italian policies.

Lewis, who had also attempted to treat with the pope in 1331–2, at first responded to this plan, gave his assent to Henry of Lower Bavaria, who in return promised that, in the event of his election, he would, with the consent of the electors, pawn the kingdom of Arles and the bishopric of Cambrai to France. John XXII, however, did not want to meet Lewis's conditions, lift the ecclesiastical penalties and thereby indirectly acknowledge the legitimacy of his kingship. Therefore the emperor also withdrew his agreement in the summer of 1334, especially since the other motive – to neutralise John of Bohemia – disappeared, when the king of Bohemia was driven from Italy by the Guelf coalition. John XXII had also manoeuvred himself into a dangerous corner, with a doctrinal blunder concerning the Beatific Vision, when he advocated the view, strongly opposed by the Paris theologians, that the souls of the blessed in Heaven would only see the Divine Being at the Last Judgement, and not immediately after death. The scheming Cardinal Napoleone Orsini, who wanted to restore the papacy to Rome, seized the opportunity and urged Lewis to appeal to a general council, which he did.

Since Franciscans and Dominicans also rejected the pope's doctrine, and it was unanimously condemned as heresy by a council convened by the French king in December 1333, the pope was isolated, and the emperor had the upper hand again, without doing anything himself. However, on 4 December 1334, John XXII died. His successor, the Cistercian Jacques Fournier, who took the name of Benedict XII, was already elected on 20 December. He was a good theologian and a more balanced personality than his litigiously fanatical predecessor. The chances of an agreement with the emperor seemed favourable initially, since Lewis raised no objection to the process of reconciliation and instructed his proctors to meet the new pope half-way concerning the illegality of his imperial dignity, his appeals and the claims to papal approbation. However, he was not prepared to admit that he had associated himself with the heresy of Marsilius and the Franciscans. That no agreement resulted, despite goodwill on both sides, was because Benedict's demand that the emperor should be reconciled with Philip VI and Robert of Naples was unrealisable; the French king hesitated because of the kingdom of Arles and fear of an Anglo-German agreement. In this situation the pope gave way to French wishes and let the negotiations founder. The old fulminations against the emperor were renewed. Lewis now permitted himself to be drawn, to the disadvantage of the empire, into the beginning of the Hundred Years War between England and France.

On 23 July 1337 he concluded an alliance with ambassadors of Edward III of England in Frankfurt in which, in exchange for substantial sums of money (of which, however, he only received one quarter), he promised to assist the English king with 2,000 men in France. The emperor may then have planned an expedition against Avignon, but he did not succeed in winning the dauphin Humbert II of Vienne to his side. Moreover, the alliance with England did not take effect, since Edward III did not start the war in the autumn of 1337 and had to delay it for two years.

The imperial reform of 1338

The English alliance had strengthened the emperor's position in Germany and the uncompromising nature of the pope had influenced public opinion further in favour of Lewis who made use of the opportunity to decide the urgent constitutional problems, by obtaining the aid of the German estates, undoubtedly on the pattern of Edward III, who availed himself of the English parliament to support his policy against France. It was important for the emperor to make peace with Heinrich von Virneburg, who succeeded to the archbishopric of Mainz after the retreat of Baldwin of Trier. Henry, who had fallen from papal favour, sought to mediate, but the envoys of the German bishops in Avignon were bluntly sent away by Benedict XII. The episcopate was under pressure from the anti-papal mood of the people which burst out in the assembly of the estates which the emperor had summoned to Frankfurt in May 1338. In thirty-six identical letters of the imperial towns addressed to the pope, Lewis's kingdom and empire were decreed legitimate and the pope criticised sharply; early national notes sounded there, when it was asserted that the behaviour of the pope was directed against the empire and 'our German Fatherland'. Lewis made a fresh confession of his orthodoxy (*Fidem catholicam profitentes*), which betrayed the authorship of his Franciscan advisers; the opinion that the pope should be subordinated to the council points to the future, and the fact that the emperor made observance of the papal sentences of interdict and excommunication a punishable offence was proof that he was sure of the support of the majority of the electors, the bishops and the population. The electors then gathered on the Rhine, south of Koblenz. Four of the seven were definitely on Lewis's side: Archbishop Henry of Mainz; Archbishop Walram of Cologne, who was interested in an alliance with England; Lewis's son, the margrave of Brandenburg, and his cousins, who exercised the Palatinate vote jointly. The two Luxemburgs, Archbishop Baldwin of Trier and King John of Bohemia, were not unequivocally on the side of the emperor, and the Saxon vote was disputed.

On 15 July 1338 the electors present met with Lewis in Lahnstein; on the next day, in the absence of the emperor, they issued two documents at Rhens on the opposite bank of the Rhine. In the first, composed in German, they announced their intention of protecting the threatened imperial laws. In the second, a notarial instrument in Latin, essential laws were laid down in the form of a precedent (*Weistum*) after consultation with other clerics and laymen: a king chosen by the electors, or the majority of them, did not require the nomination, approbation, confirmation, agreement or authorisation of the Holy See to assume the administration of the goods and rights of the empire and the royal title; this had been imperial law since time immemorial. The remaining controversial issues, above all the imperial coronation and papal lawsuits, were not mentioned. By these means the precedent assimilated only a part of Lewis's views. The electors, probably under the influence of Baldwin of Trier, confined themselves to clear imperial and electoral rights, which they defended in their own interest against the pope, but they did not assume responsibility for Lewis's disputed imperial coronation; they thereby kept the way open for agreement with the pope. This corresponded to the views of Lupold of Bebenburg, given theoretical foundation in the tract *De Iuribus Regni et Imperii* (Of the Laws of Kingdom and Empire) of 1340, which he dedicated to Baldwin.

When these limits had been established, Baldwin – in contrast to his nephew, John of Bohemia, who continued to support France – went over to the imperial camp, but did also for his part conclude an alliance with England in September 1338. The archbishop of Mainz seems even to have advocated Lewis's viewpoint on the imperial coronation and papal litigation. Encouraged by these developments, at an imperial diet (*Reichstag*) at Frankfurt on 6 August 1338, Lewis issued a law about the election of the king (*Licet iuris*), in which, going beyond the precedent of Rhens, it was decreed that the emperor was elevated through the vote of the electors alone and required no approval; he was to be regarded as 'true king and Emperor' and had full power to administer the possessions and rights of the empire, and all the subjects of the empire owed him obedience; offenders were guilty of the crime of *lèse-majesté*. It did not become clear whether Lewis thereby also laid claim to use of the imperial title before coronation by the pope. At the beginning of September 1338, in the presence of Edward III at Koblenz, he summarised and renewed the decisions of Rhens and Frankfurt and issued further decrees against private war and violation by vassals of their obligation to military service in the imperial army (*Heerfolgepflicht*). The claims of the English king to the French throne were supported in return for renewed subsidies over seven years, and Edward was appointed vicar-general of the empire to the west of the Rhine. War against France was to begin in the spring of 1339; popular opinion was behind Lewis to such an extent that Baldwin of Trier meanwhile recognised Lewis's imperial dignity. A last attempt at agreement with Benedict XII failed in March 1339. Since John of Bohemia had also finally paid homage to the emperor, Lewis's position in Germany had become virtually unassailable.

Lewis's rapprochement *with France; negotiations with Clement VI*

Despite his strong position, the emperor seems to have been disinclined to take full advantage of the alliance with England. Rather, he apparently continued to hope for an agreement with France; his lethargic behaviour in the following months cannot be explained in any other way. When Edward III invaded northern France in the autumn of 1339, while the emperor's son, Lewis of Brandenburg, stood with the other princes in the English camp, the emperor in contrast used the non-payment of English subsidies as an excuse for avoiding his commitments under the terms of the alliance. When Philip VI offered negotiations after the destruction of the French fleet at Sluys in June 1340, the emperor publicly went over to the French camp, in the hope of French mediation at Avignon, called off the alliance with the disappointed Edward III and, in January 1341, concluded an agreement with France. However, this changing sides damaged Lewis; satirical songs about the emperor demonstrate that public opinion was turning against him. Benedict XII did not make any attempts at reconciliation, but died on 25 April 1342. His successor was the southern French Pierre Roger, who took the name Clement VI. Although a *bon vivant*, he was not a particularly conciliatory personality. He championed, and indeed sharpened, the demands of his predecessor from Lewis. The young son of John of Bohemia (the future king and emperor Charles IV) had been his pupil, and the pope seems to have grasped at an early stage the idea of a Luxemburg candidate in opposition to Lewis. All attempts to reach agreement failed in 1342; at the beginning of 1343 the situation intensified. Charles had already been crowned king of Bohemia, with papal approval in 1341, by the bishop of Prague (instead of by the appropriate metropolitan, the archbishop of Mainz); then, in 1344, Clement VI raised Prague to the status of archbishopric and thereby strengthened Bohemia's autonomy.

The final breach between Lewis and the Luxemburgs came over the succession to the duchy of Carinthia. The Meinharding family who ruled there faced extinction in the male line with Duke Henry. The hand of his daughter and heir, Margaret Maultausch, was sought by the Habsburgs, as well as by the Bohemian Luxemburgs and the Wittelsbach emperor, for whom the acquisition of the Tyrol inevitably had the greatest strategic importance, since it gave access to Italy. Margaret in fact married in the first instance John of Bohemia's son, John-Henry (1330), who ceded Carinthia to the Habsburgs after Duke Henry's death (1335), keeping only Tyrol. Nevertheless, at the end of 1341 she drove her husband from Tyrol and gave her formal consent to marriage with the emperor's widowed son, Lewis of Brandenburg. The emperor – who in 1340 had reunited the entire duchy of Bavaria after the extinction of a cadet collateral Wittelsbach line in Lower Bavaria – immediately seized the opportunity and declared the marriage between John-Henry of Carinthia and Margaret invalid, married her to his own son without obtaining papal dispensation for their union within the forbidden degrees of consanguinity and invested them both with Tyrol. Here Marsilius of Padua and William of Ockham, languishing in oblivion in Munich, came to the fore once more.

At the emperor's demand they composed expert opinions on the marriage business. Marsilius's opinion (*De Iure Imperatoris in Causis Matrimonialibus* – Concerning the Right of the Emperor in Matrimonial Cases) entirely followed the lines of the *Defensor Pacis*: he saw all matrimonial law, including dispensations from impediments to marriage and declarations of invalidity, as a secular affair and placed it under imperial jurisdiction. William of Ockham came to similar conclusions *(Consultatio de Causa Matrimoniali* – Consultation on the Matter of Matrimony), admittedly based on less radical premises. He adjudged Lewis jurisdiction in matrimonial affairs as successor to the Roman emperor, or alternatively on the grounds of emergency law and the public interest; moreover, in this case the pope would be a partisan judge. Lewis seems to have followed the substance of Ockham's opinion. However, the fragility of the legal arguments inflicted further public damage on the emperor. The success was only short-lived, too. After the death of the son of Lewis of Brandenburg and Margaret, Tyrol finally passed to the Habsburgs in 1363. Wittelsbach rule in the lower Rhine lasted somewhat longer, until 1425. Here the emperor had seized the lordship without scruple on the death of the last of the Avesnes, William IV of Hainault-Holland (1345). Of William's three sisters, Margaret was married to the emperor, Philippa to Edward III of England, the third to the margrave of Jülich. Without consideration of any other claims to the inheritance, Lewis confiscated the counties as vacated imperial fiefs and invested his wife Margaret with them, which must have alienated him still further from the English king.

The anti-kingdom of Charles IV and the death of Lewis

The emperor bought his territorial successes of 1338–45 with a further loss of public reputation. As a result, the idea of the anti-kingdom of Charles of Luxemburg, margrave of Moravia, who had been brought up in Paris, now finally emerged. This well-educated young man (he wrote an autobiography of his youth after 1348) had become Lewis's decided opponent after activities in northern Italy, Moravia and Tyrol; after his father, John, went blind around 1340 he had been the real ruler of Bohemia. In 1344 the emperor thought he could still turn the situation to his advantage. However, although at a meeting of the electors at Cologne in August and at an assembly of towns and princes at Frankfurt in September, the pope's claims to approve the election of the German king, to exercise the imperial vicariate, to enjoy feudal supremacy over the emperor and the right to depose him were again rejected, the misdeeds that Lewis had committed against the Church were not denied. It became clear that the defence of electoral rights and the rights of the empire were beginning to part company with Lewis himself. The Luxemburgs pressed for a fresh election; the emperor rejected the compromise of joint rule with Charles of Moravia, since his aim was to see the succession of his eldest son as king. Baldwin of Trier had gone over to the emperor's opponents, who now had a majority in the electoral college. The fact that there was no new election already in the autumn of 1344 was essentially because Heinrich von Virneburg who, as archbishop of Mainz, played a prominent role in the election of the king, was still on Lewis's side. In April 1346 Clement VI deposed him. At the same time Luxemburg envoys to Avignon complied in Charles's name with most of the papal demands, refusing only to endorse the right of papal approbation of the king's election, which was opposed by the electors. This tractability gave Charles the reputation of being an 'Emperor by the grace of parsons' (*Pfaffenkaiser*).

After the preliminaries, Charles's election as German king took place at Rhens on 11 July 1346; he had the votes of the three ecclesiastical electors, the king of Bohemia and the duke of Saxony; the two Wittelsbachs – the count-palatine and the margrave of Brandenburg were absent. The pope was asked to acknowledge Charles as king and crown him emperor, not, however, for confirmation of the election; none the less, the prudent Charles only used the title of king after Clement VI had bestowed the unsought approbation in November. On 26 November Archbishop Walram of Cologne performed the coronation at his palace in Bonn, since Cologne continued to support Lewis. Yet Charles's reign had opened with a catastrophe. As at Bouvines in 1214, a dispute over the German throne was once again decided in battle between the English and the French. In contrast with Lewis, who had never come to the aid of his English ally, John of Bohemia and Charles IV joined the army of Philip VI advancing towards the English who had landed in France on 12 July 1346. At Crécy, the French army suffered an annihilating defeat on 26 August 1346, at the hands of the English archers and dismounted men-at-arms, leaving the road open to the vital port of Calais, which fell to the English in the following year. Blind John of Bohemia met his death on the field at Crécy, Charles was wounded and, after his coronation in Bonn, fled in disguise to Prague, then to the Tyrol, which he vainly attempted to incite to rebellion against the Wittelsbachs. Certainly the emperor was unable to profit long from this favourable situation: on 11 October 1347 he died following a heart attack he suffered on a bear hunt near the monastery of Fürstenfeld (west of Munich). The extent to which the repeated excommunications and interdicts had worn themselves out is demonstrated by the fact that, although excommunicated, he was buried next to his first wife, Beatrice, in Our Lady's church at Munich. He was not posthumously absolved by the pope; about 1490 Duke Albert IV had an elaborate tomb built with a magnificent tomb-top of red marble in the south chapel of the tower of the recently completed new church. Elector Maximilian I, the pillar of the Counter-Reformation, commissioned a magnificent funerary monument from Hans Krumper in 1619–22.

For thirty-three years Lewis had fought a tough fight with the papacy over imperial rights. In this he was ultimately successful: as a result of the precise definition of the kingship, which alone guaranteed its holders concrete imperial rights, the coronation of the emperor by the pope was debased and later became superfluous; with this, the end of the potential for intervention by the pope in the history of the empire was near. In the population at large papal authority also began to decline. Despite tenaciously pursuing his goals, there was something inconstant about Lewis. At the beginning of his reign he made the mistake of relying too much on Marsilius of Padua, William of Ockham and the Franciscans; he was successful only when he abandoned these intolerable positions and concentrated on the defence of the old imperial rights. But he also lacked decisiveness and a longer perspective after 1338. His sudden desertion of the English alliance and his unskilful handling of the Tyrolean inheritance lost him much prestige. As long as his opponent was a ruler as devoid of resolution as John of Bohemia, such political mistakes did not have serious consequences. It is difficult to say what the outcome of the struggle between Lewis and the circumspect Charles would have been, had he lived longer.

THE LUXEMBURGS AND RUPERT OF THE PALATINATE, 1347–1410

Ivan Hlaváček

POLITICAL DEVELOPMENT UNDER CHARLES IV (1346–1378)

IN view of the complex political situation that prevailed in the empire (on both an international and a domestic level) towards the end of the reign of Lewis IV of Bavaria, it seemed likely that the transfer of power from the Wittelsbachs to the Luxemburgs would be a very turbulent process, if indeed it took place at all. The young Charles, son of the Bohemian King John of Luxemburg and grandson of Henry VII, was elected king of the Romans at the direct instigation of the papal curia, which was implacably opposed to the ageing Wittelsbach. Matters having been brought to a head by the intrigues of the Luxemburg side at Avignon, the election of Charles represented an attempt to resolve the situation. During negotiations, the Bohemian delegation made a whole series of far-reaching promises (of a political and military nature) to the pope. These were mainly concerned with concessions to France, as well as various prerogatives of the papacy with regard to its involvement in imperial affairs. The participants thus had every reason to denounce Charles as a papal stooge (*Pfaffenkaiser*).

Yet although it was not possible to establish an inherited right to the Roman throne, it was still considered desirable for power to be concentrated in the hands of a few leading dynasties, at the same time as that power was being inexorably fragmented between the territorial states then coming into existence. The election of Charles IV, who until then was only margrave of Moravia and heir to the Bohemian throne, took place on 11 July 1346 at Rhens, and was carried by four genuine votes and one of doubtful validity. The king of Bohemia, the archbishops of Cologne and Trier and the duke of Saxony cast four legal votes, whilst the archbishop of Mainz, to whom was reserved the right to summon the council of electors and to be its chairman, also voted for Charles. His position had, however, originally been held by Heinrich von Virneburg, a staunch supporter of Lewis, and Clement VI had stripped him of his office and appointed Gerlach of Nassau in his place. Henry naturally refused to accept this, and so the shadow of schism fell over the archbishopric; however, the Luxemburg side was able to achieve its fundamental objectives, even if the long-term realisation of its ambitions was from the start in some doubt. This was evident from Charles's coronation, which was not held in the ancient coronation city of Aachen, for this (along with most imperial cities) remained loyal to Lewis of Bavaria. Charles thus had to make do with Bonn, where the archbishop of Cologne resided.

Charles's election was followed by a period of taking stock, both politically and militarily; this period was in fact the calm before the storm, during which Charles attempted to consolidate his position both at home and abroad. In August 1346 he was to be found accompanying his blind father on the French side at Crécy. The death of John meant that Charles (who was only slightly wounded) was now free to ascend the Bohemian throne. Of even greater import was the death of Emperor Lewis, which occurred as a result of his fall from a horse while out hunting not far from Munich (11 October 1347), substantially simplifying the situation in Charles's favour. In the same way, he benefited increasingly from the deaths of his rivals in the years that followed. Not one of his opponents was able to gain an advantage over him. Charles first decided to strike a blow at the Wittelsbachs in Brandenburg by acknowledging the claims of the so-called False Waldemar (a mentally disturbed usurper pretending to be the last margrave of Brandenburg of the Ascanian family, who had died in 1319) in order to embarrass the sons of the dead emperor. The opposing side was of course not idle, and after several unsuccessful attempts the minority of electors under Wittelsbach control chose the insignificant Thuringian count Günther of Schwarzburg as anti-king on 30 January 1349. By then Charles IV had already (by means of various concessions) adroitly persuaded Edward III of England to decline the honours offered to him by the Wittelsbach princes.

Charles's counter-attack was waged on two fronts. His political success was crowned with the breakup of the Wittelsbach coalition, when after the death of his first wife he married Anne, the daughter of Rudolf of the Palatinate, a member of the Wittelsbach camp. Charles's extensive military action against Günther at the siege of Eltville was also brought to a successful conclusion. Having been offered a number of inducements, Günther surrendered his royal prerogatives. Charles also made peace with the sons of Lewis by acknowledging their territorial rights, including rights to the Tyrol and to Brandenburg. Thus Charles IV became the undisputed ruler of the empire, recognised by all, including most of the imperial cities which had hitherto opposed him. This consolidation of central power was further strengthened by his coronation in Aachen (July 1349). The situation was, however, complicated by various other circumstances. Charles's independent conduct in political matters did not endear him to the papal curia. Moreover, Europe was at this time in the throes of the plague, which was especially severe in Germany and led directly to serious anti-Jewish pogroms (of which the new ruler was not entirely innocent) in the imperial cities.

Charles's policy at this time, and even more markedly later on, developed along two interconnected paths. His point of departure was his native domain – the Bohemian state – which provided an important economic, political and (when necessary) military base for the wide-ranging international policies he began to develop from the outset. These were soon orientated towards consolidating his position within the empire. The outward expression of this was to be his coronation journey to Rome. Of course, Charles's Italian policy was no longer prompted by the imperial ambitions of his predecessors. Ever the political pragmatist, he was especially reluctant to be influenced by those Italians who advocated the renewal of the old Roman empire, although he retained great admiration and respect for Petrarch. Yet when the Roman tribune Cola di Rienzo came to Prague, he had him thrown into prison and then handed him over to the pope. The conflict raging between the Visconti of Milan and the central powers of the Tuscan and Florentine *signorie*, and the representations of the papal legate Cardinal Albornoz finally persuaded him to make the journey. In 1355 Charles IV arrived in Rome with a relatively small escort (including his third wife Anne of Schweidnitz (Świdnica)), and without any claims to real power in Italy, to be crowned Roman emperor in the Lateran basilica on Easter Sunday (5 April). He set off immediately on the return journey without spending even so much as a night in the city – something which those urging the renewal of imperial Rome considered to be an undignified rout. Politically speaking Charles was too much of a realist not to be aware of where his true interests lay, and he devoted all his energies to tending and advancing his transalpine empire. Besides, during this period the *imperium Romanum* was undergoing some important changes; its western and southern borders in particular were not firmly fixed, and were liable to change at any moment as a result of shifting feudal loyalties.

Although Charles was quickly dubbed 'stepfather of the empire' by those in favour of a strong centralised monarchy, and was accused of always favouring his own native domain, a reassessment of his reign leads to more even-handed conclusions. For it was not possible to wield influence in the empire, without the sovereign having a solid base in his own domain, which would command respect and guarantee the balance of power. In addition to a whole series of integrational measures in the economic sphere, where he established the prerequisites for the development of trade, Charles also enacted legislation and worked hard to extend a network of family connections on all sides, in which activity he automatically tended to act as the king of Bohemia.

Of Charles's legislative initiatives, a significant position in imperial law is occupied by the so-called Golden Bull, promulgated in Nuremberg shortly after his return from Italy, with amendments added a year later in Metz: clauses 1–23 were published in Nuremberg, clauses 24–31 in Metz. This was to be the basic law of the empire for several centuries. Its central theme was the election of the king of the Romans and the consolidation of the status of the hereditary lay electors, who were now *de jure* accorded full sovereign rights. Three cities were confirmed in their leading positions: Frankfurt-on-Main as the seat of elections, Aachen as the place of coronation and last but not least Nuremberg as the venue of the first imperial diet. Apart from this, however, the terms of the Bull militated against the towns and any leagues formed by them, although it could not prevent this from happening or put a stop to their activities. There have been many different assessments of the value of the Golden Bull. Today its provisions are regarded as a compromise between the central power and the electors, while the remaining estates were relegated to the sidelines.

Especially worthy of note among Charles's economic activities are his numerous attempts to intensify and safeguard long-distance trading links, as well as his support for the economic development of the imperial cities. This interest in commerce is reflected in the large number of documents pertaining to trade issued by the imperial chancery. This was gradually transformed (especially after the reforms instituted by chancellor John of Středa (Neumarkt in Silesia) in the mid 1350s) into an efficient and relatively flexible organ of central government, regularly accompanying the sovereign on his frequent travels throughout the empire (as well as occasionally travelling independently of him). The *Reichshofgericht* tended to function as the mouthpiece of the sovereign; it also fulfilled the role of an imperial court of law. In addition to this, there were a number of local imperial courts of law, in particular one at Rottweil.

Charles's tireless political activity led him to make extensive journeys to all parts of the empire, but the greater part of his attention was reserved for the east, especially for Poland and Hungary. This was partly because of the possibility that both these thrones might be won for the Luxemburg dynasty. A further important consideration was the fact that these two states, together with the Austrian Habsburgs, never ceased to represent a potential threat to Charles and his Bohemian dynasty – or rather to his Luxemburg policy. However, although Charles devoted considerable time to these 'eastern-central European' ties and connections, he certainly did not neglect to consolidate the central power of the empire within a pan-European context. In this he was assisted especially by his resumption of various traditions, and the winning of two further royal crowns was intended to have the effect of consolidating his authority.

The first of these coronations, as the king of Lombardy (in early January 1355), preceded Charles's coronation as emperor. His coronation as the king of Burgundy in Arles on 4 June 1365 took place in connection with an imperial journey to Avignon, where he attempted to persuade Pope Urban V to return to Rome, hoping at the same time to restrict French influence on the supreme spiritual authority. Although Charles's exceptional mobility (testifying to his unflagging political energy) means that it is impossible to give an adequate account of even his most important journeys, mention must be made of a further visit to Italy prompted by his imperial policy. He began this journey during the second half of 1368 and remained in Italy for a substantial part of the following year, spending more than fifteen months in the country. Charles spent a good two months in Rome itself, where his last wife, Elizabeth of Pomerania, was crowned empress. Here he fulfilled the main purpose of his visit by installing the pope in the Eternal City; the latter, however, did not remain there for long, returning once more to Avignon.

In other respects, the entire Italian journey (and especially the time spent in the north Italian *signorie*) was literally crammed full of meetings with local powers, some of them quite important – such as the Visconti of Milan, formerly vehement opponents of the emperor. But the emergence in central Europe of a new anti-Luxemburg coalition, made up of the kings of Hungary and Poland as well as the Wittelsbachs of Bavaria and others, persuaded Charles to return home quickly and launch a vigorous military and diplomatic counter-attack. By means of this, he was able to split the coalition and eventually to bring about its downfall. The many individual journeys made by Charles within central Europe, were the simultaneous expression of his imperial and his Bohemian ambitions.

Returning to the question of the Church, it should be pointed out that this occupied Charles to the very end of his reign. He was concerned with the most far-reaching aspects of Church reform, with the fight against heresy and above all with applying constant pressure on the pope to return to Rome. When therefore on the eve of the emperor's death there arose the insoluble question of the Great Schism, Charles was prompted by this to set off on a long journey to Paris accompanied by his son Wenceslas, who had already been crowned king of the Romans. In fact, Charles's efforts to establish a line of succession to the Roman throne had for many years cost him much time and energy, for conditions in the empire were unfavourable. After 1373 he was himself entitled to two electoral votes, for in this year he secured the succession to the margraviate of Brandenburg. But his efforts to win over the Rhenish electors cost him dear, both in financial terms and also because of a whole range of concessions he was forced to make, especially in the form of new privileges. If understandable on the grounds of political expediency, the effects of this ill-advised policy were to leave their mark on the entire reign of Charles's son, who for various reasons proved to be unequal to the role assigned to him.

Yet after all the horse-trading had been done and financially draining incentives offered, after political concessions had been made to both lay and ecclesiastical representatives of the empire, Charles still had to seek the pope's approval (although there had been nothing in the Golden Bull about consulting him, and certainly no stipulation that it was necessary to gain the papal imprimatur). Charles's appeal to Gregory XI to agree to the candidature and election of Wenceslas as king of the Romans in the light of his own ill-health has been preserved, dated 6 March 1376 (more than three months before the election), while the papal approval dates from the beginning of May; however, there is evidence to suggest that both documents were in fact drawn up about a year later, but were antedated for reasons of political expediency. This too bears eloquent witness to Charles's relations with the supreme spiritual authority in the west.

When Charles died on 29 November 1378, the reins of central government were transferred without a break into the hands of his son; nevertheless, this was indeed the end of an era. With the death of Charles, Europe lost not only its most cultured medieval monarch (the list of his own writings is impressive, and includes educational and theological as well as historical works), but also a monarch who created a great political and ideological conception, to whose realisation he was completely dedicated.

POLITICAL DEVELOPMENT UNDER WENCESLAS IV (1378–1400)

From the beginning of his reign Wenceslas was deeply involved in political life, and it would be wrong to assume that his efforts in this sphere were entirely in vain. On 29 November 1378, about two and a half years after Wenceslas was crowned king of the Romans, Charles IV died in Prague, bequeathing a turbulent situation to his son (who was then not quite eighteen). Wenceslas had, it is true, from the start been able to rely on his father's own experienced advisers for assistance, although these had always remained in the background during Charles's lifetime. The early years of his reign were marked by two important if short-lived successes in imperial politics, though it is not certain whether the credit for these should go to the young king or to his advisers. The first was the so-called Heidelberg *Stallung* (Settlement) of 26 July 1384; the second was the imperial *Landfriede* (Public Peace) of Cheb (Eger) in 1389, which had been preceded by the so-called Mergentheim *Stallung* in November 1387. Both events have of course a substantially broader historical significance, and so it is necessary to dwell on them and on the background to them a little longer – all the more so, as they came about in response to the chief domestic political conflict of the empire. The roots of this evidently went back a long way; nevertheless, it was only during the reign of Wenceslas that it assumed a greater significance, for his father had always been able to rely on his authority and diplomatic skill to suppress this conflict or at least to defuse it.

The most pronounced conflict in the empire was that between the towns on the one hand and the nobility on the other. The increasing economic importance of the towns led to a growing political awareness. Since it was difficult for individual towns to withstand the combined offensive pressure of the nobility, it was in the interests of their own survival for the towns of a given area to join together in an urban league. The Hanseatic League had already been formed some time before in northern Europe; this mainly linked coastal towns, but its influence also extended to individual towns much further inland. For the first time now the Hansa began to be an organisational force in southern and south-western Germany, as well as in the Rhineland. There were of course other reasons why it was to the advantage of the towns to band together for mutual assistance. Ever since the reign of Charles IV, the monarch had been interested in the towns mainly as a source of revenue. Large sums of money were needed to pave the way for Wenceslas's election as king of the Romans, and this meant that many imperial cities were assigned in pledge to leading noblemen. The cities fought back as best they could; in 1376 the Swabian town league was formed, whose membership grew to forty in less than a decade. Other town leagues were created on the basis of geographical proximity (especially in Alsace, the Rhineland and Saxony), all of them with a defensive political programme, although the tensions of the moment meant that former enemies often found themselves on the same side (as for example when the Swabian towns and the Habsburgs formed an alliance against their common enemy, Eberhard count of Württemberg).

Although Wenceslas was in essence well disposed towards the towns, he took steps to prevent the town leagues from forming strong permanent alliances, favouring instead the creation of regional *Landfrieden* embracing both towns and princes of the empire, as these tended to diminish the political power of the town leagues. This approach proved largely successful, at least with the *Landfriede* of Cheb, 1389, which had been preceded by a number of military conflicts between the towns and princes, as well as confrontations between various other centres of power. Although infantry troops from the Swiss Confederation had won a decisive victory over Habsburg cavalry at the battle of Sempach (9 July 1386), thus laying the foundation for a more lasting peace in this area, the towns in the central part of the empire had suffered one military débâcle after another. The most damaging was the comprehensive defeat inflicted on the Swabian imperial cities by Eberhard II of Württemberg on 23 August 1388 at Döffingen (not far from Stuttgart), followed by the defeat of the Rhenish towns at Worms three months later. These two events proved that it was practically impossible for the towns to gain the upper hand, but at the same time the resources of the princes became depleted. But the common people suffered most, for they had to bear the brunt of a scorched earth policy and pay dues to both sides. Nevertheless, the *Landfriede* of Cheb at least placed limits on this type of confrontation and induced the king to rethink his policies, i.e. to pay more attention to the upper levels of imperial feudal society. However, his gradually declining interest in imperial (and also in Bohemian) affairs, as well as a growing rivalry with the Palatinate of the Rhine, meant that the seeds of future conflict were sown.

The potential for conflict was evident in both the secular and ecclesiastical spheres. The focal point of the first was foreign policy, especially the issue of Wenceslas's coronation journey to Rome, the successful conclusion of which would undoubtedly have enhanced royal prestige. On the other hand, an unsuccessful expedition would certainly contribute towards the disintegration of central power in the empire. Wenceslas's attempts to realise his ambition were obstructed not only by the unequivocally negative attitude of France, which set up all kinds of obstacles, but also by chaotic conditions in Italy itself, not to mention unstable conditions in the king's own domain. These led to increasingly strained relations between Wenceslas and the upper ranks of the Bohemian hierarchy, culminating in the king's two periods of imprisonment at the hands of the chief Bohemian nobles and their allies. Both these events have a bearing on the problem of the empire itself, although the second belongs to the period after Wenceslas's deposition in 1400.

It was in the interests of the upper ranks of the nobility to find a solution to the first of these clashes (when the king was held captive in southern Bohemia in 1394), and the involvement of the leading nobles played a large part in stabilising the situation. This faction was led by the head of the Wittelsbach side, Rupert II of the Palatinate, who, immediately after hearing of the events in Bohemia, had himself elected a vicar of the empire by an imperial diet on 13 July 1394. Rupert II (d. 1398) did not travel in person to Bohemia to negotiate the release of Wenceslas IV, but he did send imperial troops headed by his son Rupert III. Wenceslas was released as a result of these negotiations; however, his position was now weaker than ever, although in the years that followed he attempted to resume his administrative activities. This was not enough, however, to persuade the nobles to revise their increasingly negative opinion of him, while the imperial cities came to regard the king as the only possible counterweight against the ever-growing pressure of electors and princes. Several of them continued to support him even after his deposition from the imperial throne on 20 August 1400. Wenceslas's minimal interest in the fate of the cities after 1400 also led the most persistent of them to seek a *modus vivendi* with the new king, who was chosen by the Rhenish electors without the participation of the three other electors. Rupert III became known as King Rupert I of the Romans, and his reign lasted from 1400 to 1410. But before treating it, we must return to the final years of Wenceslas's reign as king of the Romans in order to investigate the reasons for his deposition and whether or not these were justified – a matter of some debate.

No one would claim that Wenceslas's reign was in general a success, and it is even more difficult to arrive at a positive assessment of his role as ruler. However, it would be unfair to deliver a blanket condemnation, especially as a less interventionist approach to the functioning of the realm could sometimes yield better results than ill-advised interference in the internal affairs of a particular region. If we consider the king's itinerary during the second half of the 1390s immediately preceding his deposition, his marked mobility may be noted and a comparable administrative activity. There must have been literally hundreds of documents addressed to all kinds of recipients, almost without exception all in the empire proper; Bohemia did not figure largely in this correspondence.

Even a cursory glance at the contents and addressees reveals the exceptional breadth of his interests. In an ever-changing kaleidoscope there appear here imperial cities, all kinds of ecclesiastical institutions and prominent prelates, as well as secular representatives of the feudal system, from the upper ranks of the nobility down to the local gentry. The list of subjects covered also reflects an exceptionally wide range of interests – something that was quite unprecedented, with the possible exception of Wenceslas's first years as king of the Romans. This correspondence did not consist merely of the passive conveying of requests for confirmation or the conferring of various privileges, but also contained many of Wenceslas's own administrative decrees (these make up the largest part of the total correspondence) concerned with safe passage or freedom of movement, or reviewing the economic prosperity of the central organs of the empire. On the other hand, it is of course true – and this evidently was especially detrimental to the functioning of the empire as a whole – that all this business was conducted almost entirely through the Bohemian administrative apparatus, whose linchpin was Wenceslas's 'imperial expert', the Bohemian knight Bořivoj of Svinaře. Two other men are frequently mentioned as associates of Wenceslas: the landgrave of Leuchtenberg, who was considered to be closely connected to the Bohemian state, and Bishop Lamprecht of Bamberg, who had been a friend of and assistant to Charles IV and Günther of Schwarzburg. All other representatives of the empire (including the electors) found themselves excluded from Wenceslas's court, with no hope of gaining access to it or of exerting any kind of influence there. This was in stark contrast to Charles IV, who had by various means ensured that the highest-ranking nobles and ecclesiastical dignitaries, at least formally as witnesses to royal acts, were involved in the political activities of the court, with the intention of preventing any build-up of tension between the two main political forces in the empire, as was to happen at an ever-increasing pace once Wenceslas had ascended to the throne, and especially after 1384.

The electors' first official complaint against the king was made in December 1397. In this they voiced their dissatisfaction with his policy of making concessions in the west and in Italy, and criticised a number of his economic measures. They also complained of his excessive reliance on paperwork, and they especially resented the way in which Wenceslas failed to keep them adequately informed. The implementation of policies, and especially the day-to-day business of government, was of course manifestly impossible at this time without some kind of paperwork; however, it seems that there was certainly nothing like as much of this as one might suppose from the electors' complaint and from other indications. At the same time, there again arose the question of how to end the Schism, as well as an issue closely connected with this: the question of a royal journey to Rome – although negotiations on this failed to achieve any concrete results.

The complaints culminated in the promulgation of an imperial *Landfriede* for ten years in January 1398 in Frankfurt. After this, the situation gradually improved. Wenceslas lost interest in imperial matters on his return to Bohemia; he limited his contacts to a narrow circle of officials, relying only on those who were from his native kingdom. It should be pointed out that it was already possible to govern effectively even from a distance; this naturally meant government by proxy but it was not always accepted or recognised. In any case, the days of Wenceslas's direct rule within the empire were already over. As Heinrich Heimpel rightly said (1957), the criticisms levelled against Wenceslas's rule by the electors were the criticisms of the Palatinate camp, and the whole course of action against Wenceslas was a well-planned intrigue. Nevertheless, matters had already gone so far that on 20 August 1400 the four Rhenish electors met at a judicial session at Oberlahnstein, near Koblenz to depose Wenceslas on the basis of a declaration made at the same time by the dean of the electoral college, Archbishop John of Mainz. At Rhens, on the opposite bank of the Rhine, the three ecclesiastical electors and Rupert III chose the latter to be king of the Romans.

POLITICAL DEVELOPMENTS UNDER RUPERT OF THE PALATINATE (1400–1410)

The declaration of deposition of Wenceslas IV reiterated many long-standing grievances, the most serious of these being of a markedly subjective nature with little bearing on the realities of the situation. This can be seen at its clearest with regard to Wenceslas's ennoblement of the Visconti of Milan, former vicars of the empire whom he raised to the level of dukes – by which action he was considered to have abused his imperial authority. It would be unfair, however, to suggest that conferring the title of duke had the effect of setting the Visconti apart from the rest of the empire; to imply this would be to ignore the political realities of northern Italy, where France was beginning to exert a strong influence and where Wenceslas's manoeuvre was in fact intended (among other things) to bring the Visconti into line with the rest of the empire and to discourage them from forming too close an association with France. Wenceslas's position in the empire was also significantly undermined by this action, but it was still not entirely hopeless. Indeed, Aachen refused to open its gates to the new king Rupert, who thus had to be crowned in Cologne instead. Relations with the papacy were likewise complicated, as Boniface IX had not been consulted and was reluctant to sanction the nomination. The pope came round to supporting the Palatinate cause very slowly, for not only did he insist that the election required papal approval, he also felt that his agreement should have been sought on the deposition. In addition to this, the Schism was also important in that it opened up the prospect of a shift of allegiance, or at least made it possible to adopt a relatively neutral position towards Wenceslas IV. Both these factors were potentially capable of bringing about significant changes in the unstable balance of power. And so Rupert had to wait until 1 October 1403 to receive papal approval of his election. From then on he was a firm supporter of obedience to Rome. Meanwhile, France was credited with attempting to promote the *via cessionis*, i.e. the election of a new pope following on from the resignation of both old ones. However, all Rupert's attempts to conduct a foreign policy, especially his efforts to be crowned in Rome, proved futile, and his reign was notable only for its failures.

Rupert's pact with Florence (entered into with the intention of enabling the king to gain the upper hand in Italy against Milan) from September 1401 was largely an agreement on paper only; Germany similarly failed to provide him with adequate financial support. His Italian campaign, despite all the extravagant claims surrounding it, ended in fiasco after 1401 on account of the negative attitude of Venice. Much of the blame also lies with the Roman pope Boniface IX for his insistence on having the final word and only approving Rupert's election after three years of delicate negotiations. This inevitably had an extremely adverse effect on Rupert's domestic situation, for his attempts at consolidating his power base, and especially his strong preference for a *Landfriede* policy, was opposed by the faction which had deposed Wenceslas IV and elected him. This included the archbishop of Mainz, the margrave of

Baden, and the count of Württemberg, as well as a number of cities (the so-called League of Marbach of 14 September 1405) that had begun to hold negotiations with France, Rupert's chief opponent.

Whereas in the question of Schism Rupert held firmly to the principle of obedience to Rome, Wenceslas IV began actively to cultivate ties with France, and after the murder of Louis of Orléans these were strengthened by family connections. This came about by the marriage of Elizabeth, the daughter of Wenceslas's brother John of Görlitz, to Duke Anthony of Brabant, who thus assumed an important role in the country. Gregory XII, who was elected Roman pope on the death of Boniface, after some Italian political wheeling and dealing rejected the *via cessionis* proposed by a majority of the cardinals forming the Council of Pisa, which was strongly backed by France. As Rupert continued to cling to Roman obedience, Wenceslas IV seized his opportunity, forming an alliance with France and seeking representation at the Council as king of the Romans (the Pisan cardinals were prepared to consider this, as Rupert had declined to show any sympathy for their cause). Even when the Frankfurt princes' assembly (January 1409) failed to assure Rupert of its unconditional support (some of its most eminent representatives, including the archbishops of Cologne and Mainz, took the side of the reformist Council), he still refused to reconsider his position. His envoys to the Council were not surprisingly unable to convince the assembled gathering, and not even the association formed by Rupert with several Roman notables in March 1410 in Marburg did much to help him. On the contrary: at one point it seemed that there might be yet another anti-king, this time very much under French influence. Fate put an end to this seemingly intractable situation. On 18 May 1410, King Rupert of the Rhineland-Palatinate died in Oppenheim (he was not yet sixty), once again offering an opportunity to the house of Luxemburg. Not, however, to Wenceslas IV (who retained his title of king of the Romans), but to other members of his family, after an attempt to reach a compromise with the election of an English candidate had fallen through.

Two kings were elected practically simultaneously, in a contest which reflected their attitude towards the resolution of the Schism: Wenceslas's half-brother Sigismund of Luxemburg received two votes (those of the Palatinate and of Trier), along with the support of the burgrave of Nuremberg, while his cousin Jošt (Jobst), margrave of Moravia and Brandenburg, received three (if we count merely the votes of Brandenburg, Mainz and Cologne) or four (Jošt also enjoyed the support of Wenceslas, to which could be added that of the duke of Saxony). When fate (evidently not without some assistance) brought about the sudden death of Jošt, Sigismund was the choice of all the electors at a repeat contest held in June 1411, opening a new and even more complicated chapter in the history of the empire.

1   Ely Cathedral, Lady Chapel, 1321–*c.* 1349, looking east

2 Avignon, Palais des Papes, Chambre du Cerf, executed under Pope Clement VI (1342–52)

3 Assisi, San Francesco, lower church, showing frescos by Cimabue (far left), workshop of Giotto (crossing vault) and Pietro Lorenzetti (opposite transept); Simone worked in chapel off the nave

4   Simone Martini, *The Holy Family*, signed and dated 1342, executed at Avignon; the subject-matter,
Christ's defiance of his earthly parents, is almost unique in western art

5   Palazzo Pubblico, Siena: Ambrogio Lorenzetti, *Allegory of Good Government*

6   The Hours of Queen Jeanne d'Evreux of France, illuminated by Jean Pucelle, *c.* 1325–8, fols.
15v–16r, *The Arrest of Christ and the Annunciation*

7 Karlstein Castle, Prague, interior decorations of Emperor Charles IV's private chapel dedicated
to St Catherine; the painted niche is Italian in style, the altar frontal Bohemian

8   Coronation Book of Charles V of France (1365), the king receives the kiss of his peers

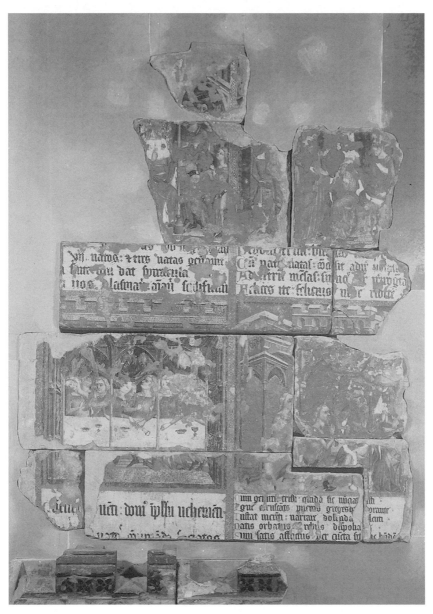

9 Fragments of murals from St Stephen's Chapel, Westminster, 1350–63, showing Old Testament
   stories; the scheme of paintings shows Italian, French and Flemish influence

10 The Wilton Diptych, *c.* 1395

11 Strozzi altarpiece in Santa Maria Novella, Florence, Orcagna workshop,
Triumph of Death (detail), 1350s

12 February, from the *Très Riches Heures* of John, duke of Berry, 1413–16, fol. 2v

13   Prophet from the Moses fountain, Chartreuse de Champmol, Dijon, by Claus Sluter, 1395–1403

14 Angers Apocalypse tapestries, illustration of Revelation 8:10–11, the star wormwood, made in the 1370s for Louis I, duke of Anjou

15　Portrait of King John II of France, *c.* 1350

16   Cadaver effigy, detail from the tomb of Cardinal Jean de Lagrange (d. 1402), Saint-Martial, Avignon

17 St Stephen's Chapel, Westminster Palace, begun 1292, interior elevation of the north side of the eastern bay of the upper chapel (drawing by Richard Dixon, *c.* 1800, Courtauld Institute)

18   Gloucester Cathedral, choir looking east, begun *c.* 1337

19 Marienburg (Malbork), castle of the Teutonic Knights, from the west, the High Castle (begun before 1280) to the right, the grand master's Palace (begun *c.* 1330) to the left

20 Westminster Hall, 1391–1401, interior

21 Lübeck, St Mary, choir begun 1277

22 Bruges, town hall, *c.* 1377–87

24 Florence, Giotto's Campanile, begun c. 1334

23 Florence, Palazzo Vecchio, 1299–1315, view from north-west, with the Loggia dei Lanzi (1376–c. 1381) on the right

25   Toulouse, Dominican (so-called Jacobin) church, begun 1229, completed 1390,
interior looking north-east

26   Ely Cathedral, octagon and lantern, 1322–40

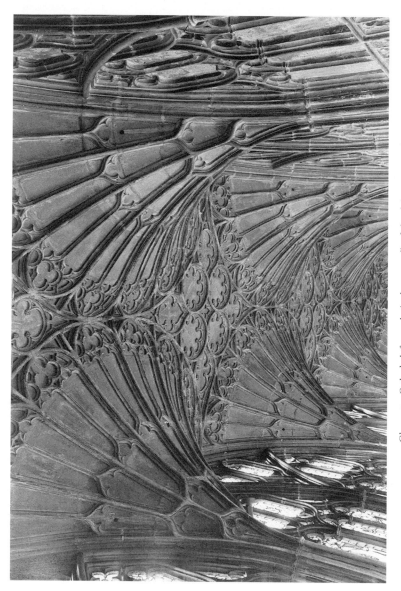

27　Gloucester Cathedral, fan vaults in the east walk of the cloister, *c.* 1351–64

28 Oxford, New College, 1379–86, view from the west

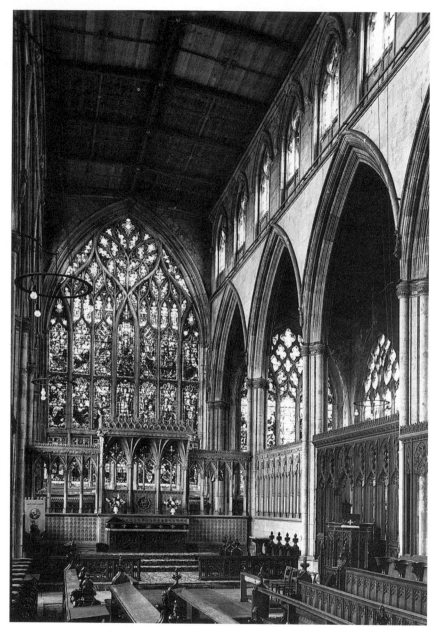

29   Hull, Holy Trinity church, choir interior, looking east, *c.* 1320s and later

30   Mehun-sur-Yèvre Castle, begun 1367, view from the north (from a miniature by the Limburg
     brothers in the *Très Riches Heures* of John, duke of Berry, 1413–16)

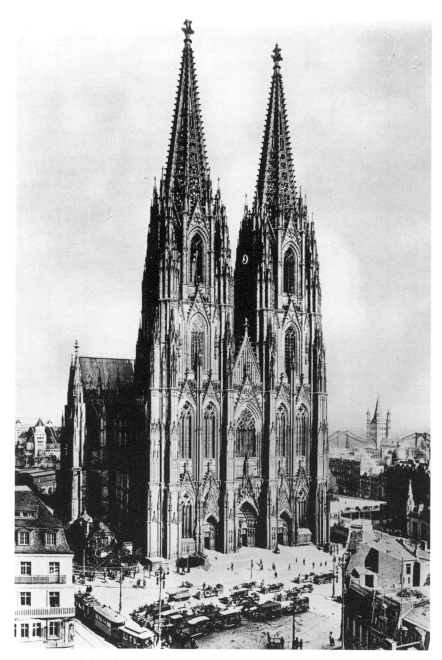

31 Cologne Cathedral, west façade, designed *c.* 1300–10: the two lowest storeys of the south-west
tower *c.* 1310 – early fifteenth century; the lowest parts of the north-west tower fifteenth century; the
remainder constructed 1842–80 according to the surviving medieval Plan F

32 Prague Cathedral, 1344–85, interior of the choir

33　Schwäbisch Gmünd, Holy Cross church, interior of the nave and choir, looking east

34   Barcelona Cathedral, begun 1298, interior looking north-east

35   Palma de Mallorca Cathedral, begun 1306, interior looking east

36 Milan Cathedral, exterior of choir looking west, begun 1386

37 Orvieto Cathedral, nave exterior from north-west, begun 1290, façade begun 1310 by Lorenzo Maitani

38 Florence, S. Croce, interior looking east, begun in c. 1292

CULTURAL, ECONOMIC AND SOCIAL DEVELOPMENT

Universities

Several aspects of the domestic history of the empire and its territories deserve attention. In so far as the system of schools, universities and culture in general was concerned, the territories of the empire definitely lagged behind Italy and France. In order to study the higher branches of knowledge, especially law, it was invariably necessary to turn to foreign universities. These were attended by large numbers of students from the empire (many of whom had an ecclesiastical or at least clerical background). The situation was slightly better in theology, for there were several outstanding centres of learning run by religious orders (chief among these were Cologne and Vienna for Dominican studies; one could also study with the Franciscans and with other orders), but theology was of interest only to a relatively small number and its significance was therefore limited.

Charles IV was the first to realise the importance of establishing and developing a system of higher education. This evidently first dawned on him in Italy, where he issued a whole series of deeds of foundation for universities in the imperial areas of Italy and Burgundy (without taking any interest in their further development). It was a different matter in his own native region, where as king of Bohemia he founded the first university in central Europe in Prague (7 April 1348), for which he had already more than a year previously (26 January 1347) requested papal approval. By the diploma of Eisenach he placed this educational establishment under public protection of the empire (14 January 1349). The university was intended to be more wide-ranging in its scope than any such previous institution. Its students were to be drawn not only from the empire, but from the whole of central Europe and Scandinavia. Its organisation was thus to be quite different from those universities which catered only for individual nations. It was of course some time before it became firmly established, and it soon emerged that it could not fully satisfy growing needs, so that there gradually began to appear other universities, under the protection of all kinds of founders.

The first of these was the university of Vienna, which was founded in 1365 by Rudolf IV of Habsburg after preliminary consultations with the pope in Avignon, though it did not begin functioning until over a decade later (in 1377). Credit is also due to Albert III for this, for it was he who in 1383 managed to attract several distinguished theologians from the university of Paris. A year later he established the faculty of theology, which had until then been the prerogative of Prague. Thereafter the reputation of Vienna continued to grow. For a while around 1400 it was claimed, in exaggerated fashion, that it was

attended by 4,000 students. In fact, there were less than 1,000. The university
of Heidelberg, established in 1385/6 by the elector palatine, also owed its existence to several eminent scholars; with Prague and Vienna, it performed an
important intellectual and clerical function by providing its founder with counsellors, diplomats and leading officials.

Likewise the last of the universities to be founded at this time within the
borders of the empire, Leipzig (which came into being as a result of the secession of German masters and pupils from Prague, when in January 1409 by the
decree of Kutná Hora Wenceslas IV deprived the foreign nations of their
electoral advantage), immediately became the chief supporter of its founder,
the margrave of Meissen. Only two universities, those of Cologne (1388) and
Erfurt (which received papal deeds of foundation in both 1379 and 1389,
although it did not begin functioning until 1392) were founded by cities and
consequently had a quite different outlook. Würzburg, constituted by Bishop
John I of Egloffstein in 1402 with the approval of the Roman pope, had only
a brief existence for a few years.

At individual universities there inevitably evolved various other structures
or substructures of an administrative, economic or cultural nature. Among
these libraries deserve mention. Within a short time they rivalled the long-
established ecclesiastical libraries and soon surpassed them in the range of
subjects covered. Their organisation resembled that of the universities themselves, especially where the libraries were attached to individual colleges. Large
numbers of manuscripts were kept, and the production and sale of manuscripts took on a markedly professional character. The universities worked
together in other ways too, even if they had a more direct influence on the
towns in which they were located thanks to increasing laicisation.

Of course, the universities were merely the highest point of the educational
system, below which (and obviously also preceded by) a lower system of education was developed. This had already begun to disassociate itself from the
narrowly focused viewpoint and organisation of the Church. It is not surprising that the old network of church schools in monasteries or chapter houses
should have retained its privileges, as this was of course predominantly a question of the education of future members of the clergy. Apart from this,
however, the necessity for at least an elementary and secondary education in
the practical requirements of lay life became apparent. This was obviously of
particular relevance in the towns, for in the countryside the rudiments of education were limited to the minimum provided by the parish schools. On the
other hand, in the towns there gradually came about a more differentiated
urban or civic education aimed at equipping students with the practical skills
necessary in order to embark on a trade, although we do not have a great deal
of information on this kind of education.

The towns

Despite adverse economic conditions after the mid century, towns displayed many signs of dynamism in a period of considerable change. With regard to the political aspirations of the imperial cities, which frequently gave rise to military confrontations with varying results, it has already been hinted that their standing was directly in proportion to their economic power. This was distributed somewhat unevenly. Although the network of imperial cities was fairly tightly knit, the economic influence of most individual towns and cities was limited to their immediate locality. Only a small number of towns succeeded in extending their influence to the whole of central Europe and beyond. One need name only a few of them, partly in order to illustrate their diversity, but also their immediate function – not only in the areas hinted at above, but also from the viewpoints of technological progress, the arts and culture in general. For the cities were in the process of becoming bastions of secular authority, which could be held either by members of the nobility or by leading princes of the Church, although the latter often came into conflict with their original places of residence (Passau, Würzburg, Cologne, etc.).

If we leave to one side Prague (which, in addition to forming the centre of the Bohemian state until 1400, also served as the centre of the Holy Roman Empire), one only has to mention cities such as Nuremberg, Frankfurt, Cologne, Lübeck, Augsburg, Vienna, Heidelberg and Meissen for it to be immediately apparent what a wide range was covered here – geographically as much as anything else. This list includes cities situated in the very centre of the empire as well as towns on its periphery, cities which maintained a close contact with the central authorities as well as towns from outside the empire whose links with it were relatively tenuous. This was especially the case with the Hanseatic League under the leadership of Lübeck, which practically built up its own world. Since the preceding century the Hanse had dominated trade. It had also played a major part in the political development of the North and Baltic Sea coasts, although various of its members like Soest and Brunswick were also deeply involved in the affairs of the empire itself. Chief among the cities governing their own virtually independent republics was Cologne (which was orientated more towards western Europe), followed by Frankfurt and Nuremberg – two of the leading supporters of the central power, as defined by the Golden Bull of Charles IV (cf. above p. 554).

The cities like Vienna and Meissen functioned more as the residence of individual feudal lords, and were thus extremely dependent on their respective rulers: Vienna on the Habsburgs, Heidelberg on the Wittelsbachs, Meissen on the Wettins. These cities offered a base from which powerful ruling families could implement their own policies (which often had implications beyond the

borders of the empire). Yet they could only to a limited degree compete with
the town leagues, and this as a rule only to the extent to which their rulers'
impulse towards self-aggrandisement prompted them to enhance the status of
the cities, especially in the cultural sphere (e.g. by founding universities) or by
establishing ecclesiastical institutions. At the same time a number of particularly ancient monastic communities, which had lost sight of their *raison d'être*,
irreversibly declined.

In the economic sphere, not only did the towns develop their own banking
and accountancy systems (which still, however, tended to lag behind the Italian
systems), they were also the scene of considerable technological progress. For
example, the first paper mill in Germany was set up in 1389–90 by the
Nuremberg citizen Ulman Stromer; eight years later, another paper mill was
built at Chemnitz in Saxony by Niclas Buwalde. There were many other technical inventions, which were not confined to the towns, although these provided the most fertile soil for such developments. Eventually, even members
of the ruling dynasties found it advantageous to become involved in these
kinds of activities. Even though Charles IV's plans for the establishment of
new waterways came to nothing, it did result in various innovations, and led to
a more intensive use of water power, the building of a transport system, but
most of all to unceasing (although not always very successful) attempts to safeguard the security of road traffic. This was regularly disrupted on account of
all sorts of feuds (*Fehden*) waged at every level of the nobility, thus condemning whole areas to endure a constant state of turmoil.

In the face of this, central authorities and other stabilising forces were at
times only with great difficulty able to maintain any semblance of control. The
transport of goods was further impeded by a multitude of customs duties,
which together with the right to hold a monopoly of trade (*Stapelrecht*) stood in
the way of a fully developed system of commerce and the greater integration
of individual territories. The progress made in agriculture was not inconsider-
able, especially where the older methods had outlived their usefulness and were
replaced by more effective ones. An important part of public life (which
suffered from many disorders, especially in the social sphere) was public charity
and the official attempts to curb these disorders or at least to control them. In
addition to the various forms of military activity connected with 'affairs of
state', there were also more localised conflicts: 'domestic' confrontations
which left few traces in the records.

Two further scourges of medieval society may be mentioned, which played an
ever greater role as a result of the increasing concentration of the population in
towns. These were the various epidemics and conflagrations, the first of which
in particular decimated the medieval population. The worst example of this was
the Black Death, which affected the whole of Europe in the mid-fourteenth

century, and as a result of which whole areas became practically depopulated. During the first half of the fourteenth century, the population of Germany has been estimated at about 14 million. After the epidemic of 1348 and its recurrences (1357–62, 1370–6 and 1380–3) this was reduced by almost 50 per cent in some places. Recovery was slow: it is estimated that by 1470 the population of the same area was only 10 million. One should also take into account various other demographic changes, which affected the countryside rather more than the cities (as any decline in the urban population tended to be compensated for by a greater influx of people from the country). Although the subjugation of outbreaks of fire in towns that were still built predominantly of wood was virtually a hopeless task, nevertheless various ever more detailed police regulations issued by the town councils attempted at least to reduce the danger a little.

As far as health provision was concerned, this began, in spite of all its deficiencies, to be more systematic and gradually to become independent of the Church, which until now had in fact been the only institution to provide any kind of care for the sick. Hospitals run by the Church were still in the majority, but in addition to these there now appeared more frequently institutions built by city authorities or by individuals, although these could never quite match the demands made upon them.

Literature and art

The growth of education and culture was dependent on the one hand on general tendencies, on the other on outstanding personalities in individual branches of the arts and sciences, although up till this time the artists and writers were still to a large extent anonymous. This artistic anonymity is not due merely to inadequate sources of information; it is also a product of medieval tradition (although a new spirit of individualism was beginning to emerge in places). Both wealthy patrons and leading members of the urban middle classes also had a contribution to make here, for they recognised the importance of public support for works of art and scholarship. The universities have already been mentioned, but it should be added that from the second half of the fourteenth century, significant numbers of students went to study at the old-established universities of the Roman world, bringing back with them new ideas which acquired a new dimension when transplanted to the soil of the empire. This is both directly and indirectly reflected in literary activity, whose scope extended to all the then known genres in both Latin and the vernacular, i.e. in German. This had a whole series of dialectically very disparate forms; nevertheless, certain unifying tendencies were already beginning to be apparent in several of the larger chanceries.

In so far as literature itself is concerned, writings associated with university life (then in a state of reaction against the shortcomings of clerical life) were the most directly relevant to contemporary conditions. Matthias of Cracow (d. 1410), a leading figure at Heidelberg university and chief adviser to King Rupert I, later bishop of Worms and the author of dozens of works, and others turned against the secularisation of the Church. In the Bohemian state this wave of criticism grew into a powerful reform movement led by Master Jan Hus (d. 1415), which naturally had repercussions especially at the universities of Vienna and Heidelberg. This movement was pan-European in scope, and its effects continued to be felt for decades to come.

In addition to the literature written in Latin, which was largely devoted to the subtle exegesis of theological and philosophical questions, a flourishing literature in the vernacular was established, and this concerned itself both with clerical themes and also especially with urban life. Apart from historiographical works (here mention should be made of the auto-biographical *Püchel von meinem geslecht* written by the Nuremberg citizen Ulman Stromer at the end of the fourteenth century, which belonged to the flourishing tradition of urban historiography), *Der Ackermann aus Böhmen* (The Bohemian Ploughman), by Jan of Žatec (Johann von Saaz, also known as Johannes von Tepl) deserves special mention. Cast in the popular dialogue form (between a widower and Death), this is a work rich in ideas – sometimes considered to be already renaissance in character, yet deeply imbued with medieval conventions. A number of authors wrote in both German and Latin on the most varied branches of applied knowledge. One of the most important was Conrad of Megenberg (d. 1374), who specialised in political and economic matters as well as in medicine and natural sciences, about which he wrote in German.

Religious themes were still predominant in painting and sculpture, although after the great upheavals of previous eras the Church was beginning to lose its hold on artists. Architecture was dominated by the outstanding figure of Peter Parler, who founded a whole dynasty of disciples, whose works were to be found in many different parts of the empire in Nuremberg, Schwäbisch Hall, Schwäbisch Gmünd, etc., although their chief 'workshop' was the Bohemian state. In addition to lofty churches in the imperial cities and whole monasteries, secular architecture was also beginning to demand its share of attention. This often took the form of fortified constructions for feudal lords, but there were other contributions to the urban landscape, notably many municipal buildings and large patrician residences. The art of sculpture was closely connected with architecture, with which it often created a unified whole. By the end of the century, the intimate symbiosis with painting of all kinds had resulted in a particular mode of expression, which became known as the 'beautiful style', or International Gothic.

The period surveyed here is important for the way in which firm foundations were laid for the development of territorial states within the structure of the empire. The king of the Romans definitely lost the right to interfere in their internal affairs. Proximity to or distance from the centre of power became all the more clearly evident. The king of the Romans thus became in fact only one of many, even though he was as a rule naturally regarded as *primus inter pares* among the governing classes. His stature was to a large extent determined as much by the economic potential of his native realm and by his military and political base as by his personal qualities; family connections had an important role to play in this sphere, and were thus increasingly cultivated.

CHAPTER 17

THE LOW COUNTRIES, 1290–1415

Walter Prevenier

'THE Netherlands' or 'the Low Countries' is a collective name for a group of provinces which since the early Middle Ages formed a strong socio-economic and cultural unity in which, in these respects, the mutual ties binding them were stronger than those with the outside world. In the politico-institutional field, however, that unity was missing. The various principalities had dynasties of their own, which none the less were not sovereign. Most of these ruling houses (Brabant, Liège, Holland, Zeeland, Guelders, etc.) came under the feudal jurisdiction of the German emperor. Others (e.g. Walloon-Flanders) came under the French king. The Flemish dynasty was subject for the greater part of its territory to the French crown, except for a minor portion east of the river Scheldt (the district of Aalst), which was subject to the German empire. A number of principalities in the Netherlands were intermittently combined by joint rulership, such as Flanders and Namur or Holland, Zeeland and Hainault.

In the ecclesiastical sphere, Flanders came completely under the jurisdiction of bishoprics, the seats of which were all situated outside the county (Cambrai, Tournai and Thérouanne), whereas Brabant and Liège and the north of the Low Countries belonged to Utrecht. The bishop of Liège was simultaneously head of a secular principality of the same name, as was the bishop of Utrecht.

THE BALANCE OF POWER WITHIN THE TERRITORIES AND TOWNS OF THE LOW COUNTRIES: RELATIONS WITH FOREIGN POWERS (*c.* 1290–*c.* 1360)

As compared with preceding and following periods, the Low Countries in the first half of the fourteenth century display a clearly distinct profile with respect to participation in the exercise of power and as regards the political impact and hegemony of various territorial rulers. Internally, within the cities of the Low Countries, a monopoly of power had been held by a closed political elite, the so-called patriciate, who were at this time superseded by a broad range of social groups participating in urban government. In the state government of each of the provinces, in which until then power had likewise resided in a relatively simple combination of the prince and an aristocratic and ecclesiastical upper class, new groups acquired political weight. In certain provinces, provincial estates and other representative bodies started to set down in constitutions their right of participation in and scrutiny of the activities of government. In other provinces, they were able to enforce this participation in practice, especially by using their authority, acquired over time, to vote the taxes of the county.

On the other hand, with regard to the balance of power between the various neighbouring principalities, the first half of the fourteenth century was rather a continuation of the previous century. The principalities of the Low Countries continued their defensive policy aimed at minimising the interference of the great powers (France, the empire and England). Economically and culturally, they maintained good mutual contacts; in the political field, they limited themselves to rather banal neighbours' squabbles on a one-to-one basis (e.g. Flanders versus Holland, Brabant versus Flanders, Brabant versus Liège). There was a lack of overall vision or any active policy through which one of the principalities might have aspired to the domination of the whole or a large part of the Netherlands. This did not become generally the case until the second half of the century.

The county of Flanders (1297–1360)

Until around 1300, a closed caste of well-to-do citizens held a monopoly of power on the benches of the aldermen of the Flemish towns. Since 1252, and especially from 1280, the status of this patriciate had been challenged through strikes and social revolts by a heterogeneous front of manual labourers from the textile sector, 'middle-class' artisans and the new rich, merchant entrepreneurs whose success had come too late for them to be admitted into the closed ranks of the patriciate. In 1297, these groups forced their way on to the benches of the aldermen. The breakdown of authority caused by international conflicts between the Flemish count and the French king, and between France and England (1297–1305) undoubtedly paved the way for this process of change in the *status quo*. The old patricians lost their monopoly. However, there was no take over by the commons (the 'working class') as the interests of the groups involved in this front were too divergent. After 1305, urban policy was a matter for radical as well as moderate representatives of the weavers' and fullers' crafts working in the textile export industry. It was also a matter for the numerous trades that produced for the local market, and for the traditional patrician families, the cleverest of whom also succeeded in politically maintaining themselves after the purges around 1300. This political co-operation was anything but smooth. Every now and then, social conflict flared up, as in 1311, when the Ghent weavers and fullers together opposed the wealthy burghers. After 1319, however, the latter group succeeded for the greater part in regaining its old influence through a coalition with the fullers and the trades, keeping the weavers off the benches of aldermen. Then, in 1336, the interruption of wool imports from England and the ensuing threat of unemployment and starvation gave the weavers the opportunity to take the lead in the social unrest in Ghent and the rest of Flanders and to re-establish themselves politically in 1338 as the driving force of a broad pro-English, anti-French and anti-count front under the leadership of James van Artevelde. However, the weavers' bloody suppression of a wage revolt by the fullers, the political murder of Artevelde in a conspiracy of weavers, both of which took place in 1345, and the arrogance furthermore of the weavers in their monopolisation of government offices, set all the other groups so much against them that in 1349 they were banished from urban government for a decade. Not until 1359–60 were these tensions resolved by a compromise intended to manage future conflicts: the well-to-do citizens, the 'middle class' and the weavers definitively and across the board (until 1540) divided urban government functions among themselves according to fixed quotas, to the exclusion, of course, of the fullers.

With regard to the government of the county as a whole, the centre of gravity equally shifted. In the thirteenth century, the count ruled with a curia of noblemen and clerics which he had carefully selected. To be sure, the burghers had a political voice through the representative organ of the *scabini flandrie*, but they remained the mouthpiece of the patricians of the five main Flemish towns, whose political views and social interests did not differ substantially from those of the ruler. The picture changed fundamentally after the protests around 1297. From thenceforth, the representation of the people – the 'parliament' of members – comprised a whole range of social groups, including craftsmen who had socio-economic interests that strongly differed from those of the previous political elite. Sporadically, representatives of the smaller towns and from the countryside succeeded in getting a say. But above all, the hunger for power of the three Great Towns – Ghent, Bruges and Ypres, also called the Leden – escalated, reaching its peak during the revolutionary years 1338–45, under the impetus of the leading Ghent politician James van Artevelde. This manifested itself in two directions. On the one hand, they split up the county into three spheres of influence (quarters) in which each of the three towns monopolised the political decision-making process. On the other hand, they acquired exclusive control of the government of the county; by virtually eliminating the count, who had fled to France, Artevelde was acting on a razor's edge of legality. The situation became dangerously similar to that of the Italian city-states, although the Leden tried their best to keep to the form of and respect traditional institutions, including the function of the count. In 1345, discord among members of the urban front and among social groups within each of the towns nearly caused everything to revert to the previous legal basis. The new count, Louis de Male (1348–1384), knew how to handle the condominium of the towns. In 1359–60, he let them install a commission that was to suppress effectively any abuses in the count's administration. Parallel with the growing participation of the towns, the counts had since 1300 increased their autonomy in matters of government by replacing those members in their council who, as noblemen, clerics and burghers, had until that time been the mouthpiece of their social groups, with loyal financial and legal technocrats.

The international position of the Flemish counts was essentially determined by two basic facts. One was the continual temptation for the French king, as suzerain of the count, to interfere in the policy and successions of the county (the German emperor could lay similar claims to imperial Flanders – the district of Aalst – but his impact was considerably less). The other was that Flanders was economically dependent on good relations with the Italian and north German towns for trade and on England for the supply of the essential raw material – wool – for its basic industry of textiles. These factors were complicated by a number of cyclical ones such as the comparative strengths of the personalities of successive suzerains and counts and their ambitions – of the former to pursue the greatest possible hegemony over, and even annexation of, Flanders; of the latter to claim the greatest possible autonomy. Moreover, the balance of power between the counts and the domestic political elite – essentially the large towns – was continually tilting.

After his victory at Bouvines (1214), the French king dominated European politics to such an extent that the annexation of Flanders to the crown was within the bounds of possibility. For the remainder of the thirteenth century, however, the suzerain contented himself with placing people whom he considered reliable on the Flemish throne and with weakening their political power by ending the dynastic union of Flanders-Hainault. Until about 1280, the Flemish Dampierre dynasty played the French card in its conflicts with the Avesnes of Hainault and with Holland.

This state of affairs was brought to an end by Gui de Dampierre (count from 1278 to 1305) and his son Robert de Béthune (1305–22) due to a threefold challenge. First, in Philip IV the Fair (1285–1314) they had to face a strong personality on the French throne who, ideologically inspired by his able jurists (*légistes*), outlined a centralist and expansionist policy which left little room for an autonomous Flemish count. In addition, from the Flemish–English political crisis which began in 1270 and which, among other things, led in 1273 to the suspension of English wool imports, it had become clear that bad relations with England were catastrophic for the Flemish economy. Finally, these international problems were linked with domestic affairs. In the social tensions between 1280 and 1305, the old patriciate was clearly seeking the support of the French king. Other sections of the population turned to the count and to England. In contemporary eyes, this polarity was so obvious that the two political groups were labelled 'leliaards' (the lily being the emblem of the French king) and 'klauwaards' (the lion being the Flemish emblem). When in 1294 the great powers of England and France clashed, Gui de Dampierre hesitated about taking action against his French suzerain. However, this position soon turned out to be a blind alley and in 1297 he broke with Philip the Fair by renouncing his feudal loyalty and entering into an alliance with England. In May 1300, the French king occupied Flanders, *manu militari* and annexed it to the royal demesne. Although a Flemish army inflicted a humiliating defeat upon French knighthood at Courtrai on 11 July 1302 (the battle of the Golden Spurs), the king took his revenge two years later and in 1305 the Treaty of Athis was concluded. This on the one hand restored the autonomy of the county but on the other it imposed on the Flemings heavy reparations and territorial losses, namely the annexation of Walloon-Flanders (the districts of Lille, Douai and Orchies). This treaty was confirmed by the further Treaty of Pontoise (1312). Throughout his reign, Robert de Béthune opposed the French interpretation of the financial agreements, as being very disadvantageous to Flanders. He also offered resistance of a military kind in 1314–16 when the pattern of events of 1300–2 was more or less repeated.

Louis de Nevers (1322–48) was a much weaker personality than both his predecessors. In 1323 in coastal Flanders, a rural revolt broke out. This was no act of despair out of hunger but rather the work of well-to-do farmers agitating for a more favourable property statute. Louis lacked the diplomacy and insight to control this situation. He turned to a minority group – that of the old Ghent *leliaard* families – for support and in 1328, like his predecessors of the period before 1280, he had the rebellion put down by the French king. In the ruthless repression that followed, which included the towns, Louis laid the foundation for a build-up of frustration and motives for new revolts. The fact that he slavishly took sides with France, which was strongly resented by the greater part of the population because of the armed interventions and the fiscal burdens of the Treaty of Athis, lost Louis all credit. Most significantly, it induced Edward III of England, at the beginning of his war with France, to strike at Flanders by stopping exports of English wool and grain in August 1336. Louis now found himself in the same predicament as Count Gui in 1294, with the difference that he had too expressly thrown in his lot with France to be able to make any diplomatic approach to England. On top of that, both the urban elites and the commons of several towns, under the leadership of James van Artevelde, had unanimously chosen, for self-preservation, to take a pro-English stance. In December 1339 the count fled to Paris and in January 1340, Artevelde recognised the English king as suzerain. However, internal tensions between arrogant Ghent and the other towns, and the insolence of the radical wing of the weavers towards other social groups, caused the front to fall apart, especially after Artevelde had been murdered in 1345.

Division in the urban alliance gave the new count Louis de Male a unique opportunity to take up a more independent position towards foreign countries. To be sure, social revolts flared up against the count and the urban magistrates who were supported by him in 1359–60. But Louis was astute enough no longer to call in the French king's military power but rather to try and find a diplomatic balance of interests between the various social groups.

The duchy of Brabant (1294–1347)

In thirteenth-century Brabantine towns, as in Flanders, a numerically restricted upper stratum of wealthy merchants and entrepreneurs dominated the labouring classes and craftsmen who were without a political voice. In imitation of Flanders, revolts also broke out in Brabant in 1303 in an attempt to break loose from this monopoly, but with limited success. In Louvain, admission to the benches of aldermen could not be achieved even once. In Brussels it was, but this only lasted until 1306. This quick restoration points to the fact that the Brabant patriciate manifested greater tenacity than their Flemish counterparts. They linked their fate more artfully to that of the duke, succeeded in getting the merchant guilds to function as the arbitrators of wage disputes among the workers and gave newly prosperous merchant-entrepreneurs opportunities to be received into their ranks. Not until 1361 did the commons come up with new political demands.

As far as the government of the duchy was concerned, Brabant in this period developed from a traditional feudal situation, in which the duke, assisted by a handful of clerics and noblemen, sovereignly shaped his policy, into a form of popular sovereignty according to which the duke carried out the will of his subjects through a council and a representative body. The realisation of a share in political power was greatly facilitated by the fact that in three out of five successions between 1248 and 1356 the successor was a minor. It is typical of Brabant that this reshuffling of political power took shape in formal constitutional texts, whereas in Flanders the count's opponents considered themselves so strong that they did not need to commit to writing their share in the exercise of political power. The wills of Henry II (1248) and Henry III (1261), although still drawn up without the towns' intervention, were the forerunners of real constitutions in which the sovereignty of the people was more and more rigidly outlined. A second factor was concern with the notion of 'public interest', for an even-handed treatment for groups which made up the whole population. In reality, it was rather a euphemism for the promotion of typically commercial and industrial demands with which the urban elite hoped to strengthen its position. The essence of these changes in Brabant in the early fourteenth century can in fact be characterised as doing away with a policy in which the interests of an agrarian and aristocratic elite took priority over urban ones. Before 1300, the dynasty had based its authority on a broad following of families from the nobility. It was this coalition which attempted to polish its image by means of an expensive policy of expansion, culminating in the annexation of Limburg in 1288. Military exploits, however, emptied the princely treasury and, worse still, they were the reason why foreign debts could not be redeemed. This in turn led to Brabantine merchants abroad being arrested. As many Brabantine noblemen were acting as financiers to their duke, they too felt duped and were thus inclined to force the duke to change his policy. Just before his death, John II (1234–1312), under pressure from both groups, granted the Kortenberg Charter (27 September 1312), which provided for a supervisory council consisting of ten townsmen and four noblemen. In May 1313, two regents for the duke were appointed, but when they continued the traditional policy, they were both dismissed in an urban coup. The influence of the towns was now total and their control of public finances was secured on 12 July 1314 by a Flemish and Walloon charter. The effectiveness of the Kortenberg council, however, was not established until after the Charter had been confirmed in 1332 and by the *Blijde Inkomst* (Joyous Entry) of 1356.

In matters of foreign policy, the annexation of Limburg (1288) concluded a century of active expansionism. From then on, the stress lay on defence against the claims of the German ruler and of the prince-bishop of Liège. An alliance between John III (1312–55) (who had been educated at the French court and married a French princess) and France lay at hand. During the years 1328–34, the duke was aiming at the support of King Philip VI in his double-edged conflict with Liège: on the one hand there were the pretensions of the Liège law court, the Tribunal de la Paix, in matters of jurisdiction in Brabant; on the other hand, there was John III's ambition to bring the economically and strategically important Liège enclave of Malines under his rule. It was very unfortunate for John III that at exactly that time there was a pro-French bishop on the throne of Liège whose interests, therefore, Philip VI also had to consider. Moreover, to counter the influence of his English rival there, the king then aspired to the role of neutral arbitrator in the Netherlands. This factor played a role when, in 1332, John III's military arrogance in the east brought about a broad anti-Brabant coalition of the counts of Gulik, Namur and Guelders, and the bishops of Liège and Cologne under the leadership of the German king John of Bohemia (also duke of Luxemburg). Malines took the side of Brabant, but during the war it was sold to Flanders and in 1340 it was incorporated by France. Meanwhile, however, suspicions about an overly strong French-dominated political network had grown in the Low Countries and in 1334 Namur, Gulik and Guelders entered into a coalition with Brabant against France. With the outbreak of the Franco–English Hundred Years War, the international cards in the Netherlands were thoroughly shuffled. Edward III succeeded in bringing the whole of the Low Countries, with the exception of Flanders, under his spell. John III, hoping to make use of the situation to steal a march on his inveterate rival Flanders, persuaded England to move the woolstaple to Antwerp. It was a short-lived success.

As early as 1339, the Flemish towns had removed their pro-French count, and under Artevelde taken a pro-English stance, Flemish–English commercial relations were restored and Brabant was no longer a privileged partner. However, England did see to it in 1345 that, at the expense of France, Malines was incorporated into Brabant. Then the intensity of the Hundred Years War abated somewhat and there was therefore space for a new pragmatism which turned away from making connections with the great powers and towards safer alliances within the Low Countries. The marriage in 1347 of the new Flemish count Louis de Male to the Brabantine princess Margaret can be seen in this light. John III even achieved a *rapprochement* with Emperor Charles IV. By means of the Golden Bull of 1347, the latter eliminated the influence of the Liège Tribunal de la Paix, decreeing that in secular matters Brabantines could only be tried in a ducal court. On the other hand, neighbourly relations with Flanders broke down due to disputes over the sovereignty of the river Schelde, the natural boundary between the two provinces, and over Malines. After an armed encounter, Brabant was forced to swallow the humiliating Peace of Ath (1357) and to cede Malines to Flanders.

The counties of Holland, Zeeland and Hainault (1296–1356)

At the start of the period, both Holland-Zeeland and Hainault were principalities which, by virtue of having long-standing native dynasties, had identities of their own. Hainault, it is true, had formed a dynastic union with Flanders between 1195 and 1278, but after this time it reverted to having its own dynasty, the Avesnes. Thirteenth-century Holland-Zeeland was also ruled by a local dynasty, of which Floris V (1256–96) was the strongest representative. But when in 1299 his son, John I, died prematurely and without heir, the Avesnes dynasty took the opportunity to succeed to the throne. As a consequence,

Hainault-Holland-Zeeland formed a dynastic union (which was to last until, between 1427 and 1433, these provinces were added to the duke of Burgundy's territorial complex). It was a most remarkable, paradoxical combination of a classic, somewhat isolated, feudal province (Hainault) and an international mercantile area (Holland) which, owing to its favourable geographical position, was privileged and had developed ahead of its time. During the thirteenth century, prominent aristocratic families had set the tone in both provinces, but in the fourteenth century the dynamism of its towns proved considerably stronger in Holland.

Under Floris V, Holland had expanded greatly, reaching its maximum territorial extent through the annexation of Zeeland and part of Utrecht and the reannexation of West Friesland. Towards the end of his reign, international tension here too brought about a conflict between a pro-French and pro-English faction. The latter was responsible for the murder of Floris (1296) but got the worst of the conflict overall, so that after the death in 1299 of the son of Floris, the count of Hainault was able to succeed to the rulership under the name of John II. As a result Flanders was now hemmed in between France and its ally, Holland-Hainault. The war between Flanders and Holland over Zeeland increased Holland's self-confidence and led to its military success at Zierikzee in 1304. William III (1305–37) seemed to be continuing the French connection, for example in his marriage to Jeanne of Valois. But in reality he went his own way playing games of diplomatic poker, although he clashed with equally opportunistic adversaries. In 1308, for example, it was precisely because he wished to avert a further increase in French power that he supported the election of the Luxemburg count Henry to the throne of Germany. The latter, however, completely betrayed William by subsequently refusing to support his claim to Zeeland and taking the side of Flanders instead.

William was more successful, however, in his support of the next candidate for the kingship of Germany, Lewis of Bavaria. He gave one of his daughters in marriage to the king and another to Edward III. These exercises in power brokerage made William an essential pivot in Anglo-German machinations over France, Avignon and Flanders. The position enabled him to push through the expansionist policies of Floris V by establishing his power in Friesland east of the Vlie (1325–8) and bringing the Nedersticht under Holland's influence through an agreement with Guelders by which the latter was allowed to lay its hands on what remained of Utrecht (1331). At the beginning of the Hundred Years War, William III was the architect of the great coalition of Hainault-Holland, Flanders and Brabant against France (April 1336) and developed his court at Valenciennes into the centre of English propaganda on the continent.

William IV (1337–45) displayed a very different profile. Impulsive and undiplomatic, he left the pro-English alliance but set about it so ineptly that the French king also considered him unreliable. He threw himself into hopeless military adventures in Spain, the near east and Prussia, and could not even maintain Holland's territorial integrity. A campaign against the Frisians ended with William's inglorious death on the battlefield in 1345. As he had died childless, a difficult episode over the succession ensued. In January 1346, the emperor Lewis of Bavaria granted the counties as a fiefdom to his wife Margaret, William III's daughter. Although she bestowed a number of privileges on her subjects to temper their anger at the financial debacle which William IV had caused, she was hardly able to maintain her authority. Neither did she succeed in calming down these emotions when she appointed her son William V as count of Holland-Zeeland (January 1349). A coup was only just avoided. In May 1350, various groups of noblemen, including Egmond, Heemskerk and Borsele, set up an alliance with the aim of preserving the integrity of Holland. Over time, this 'national' party began to call itself the Kabeljauwen (Cods). Against it developed the Hoeken, an opposition party of other noblemen and towns such as Dordrecht. This group was prepared to talk to Margaret. After military intervention, William V had by the end of 1350 got control of Holland, although only by taking the Kabeljauwen under his wing and banishing the Hoeken. Through the mediation of the English king, the Hoeken were soon able to buy an acceptance of their return and Margaret, who in 1354 stepped down as ruler, was given financial compensation. After her death in 1356, the dynastic union with Hainault was re-established under William V. His rule, however, did not last long: by 1358 the first symptons of insanity were becoming apparent, whereupon his wife and his brother Albrecht, who then functioned as regent, put him under lock and key until his death thirty-one years later.

Within the towns of Holland and Zeeland, in contrast to those of Flanders and Brabant, there were no political shifts of power around 1300. There were, to be sure, some disturbances among the guilds in Leiden in 1313, and there was uproar among the weavers against the patriciate of merchants in Middelburg some time before 1319. But it was not until 1371–2 that serious clashes and strikes occurred. This difference in timing, amounting to close on a century, can be ascribed to the relatively late development of commerce and industry and consequently also of expansion in the social sector.

The government of Holland and Hainault in the thirteenth century was run by the count in co-operation with councillors taken from the ranks of the nobility. A strong personality like William III of Hainault (William I of Holland) (1304–37) was not prepared to delegate much authority. In Hainault he held the council under a tight rein. In Holland, where he resided only rarely (and not at all after 1328), the normal practice would have been for him to appoint a *stadholder*. However, he preferred instead to allow his council, after having purged it of political adversaries, a degree of latitude (he thus initiated the rise of a comital clan there). Outside the formal framework of the council, William III also tried to establish a basis for co-operation with the urban patriciate. The count and citizens of fast-developing Dordrecht clearly formed a common interest group as the latter regularly acted as his financiers. And yet, in 1330 he did not hesitate to restrict Dordrecht's staple function as soon as that town's arrogance began to hinder the opportunities for development of other towns in Holland. William III always played a balance-of-power game. His far less diplomatic successor William IV, who was heavily dependent on subsidies from the towns, was obliged to accept their representatives in the councils of Holland and Zeeland and in 1343 to appoint a governor (John of Beaumont). In 1350, under the ever-weakening rule of William V, the towns and the nobility extorted the right to be present when accounts of the county treasury were drawn up. However, the count ordered his clerk Philip of Leiden, who was trained in Roman law, to draw up a monarchical tract which led in 1355 to a general withdrawal of those privileges already granted.

The prince-bishopric of Liège (1295–1364)

Liège was not a province like the others. In 980, it had been elevated to the status of prince-bishopric by the emperor who, by thus extending his system of *Reichskirche*, hoped to curtail the influence of both the feudal system and the Church. Paradoxically, though, as the twelfth and thirteenth centuries unfolded and the emperor's influence waned and the pope's waxed, politics came more and more to the fore at episcopal elections. In practice, the ambiguity of the statute invited both ecclesiastical neighbours (e.g. the archbishop of Cologne) and secular neighbours (e.g the duke of Brabant) to interfere. Several candidates, representing various clientages, regularly stepped forward. Hugo of Chalon (1295–1301), for example, was, like others before him, a pawn of the German king Adolf of Nassau, and the pope refused to enthrone him. With the coming of a strong pope like Boniface VIII, the balance tilted completely. He removed Bishop Hugo to Besançon and replaced him with a protégé of his own, Adolf of Waldeck (1301–2), and afterwards with Thibaut of Bar (1303–12). For the rest of the century, the pope remained the appointing authority but this concealed the real figure of power, the French king, who dominated the papacy after it settled in Avignon in 1305. At the same time, France also showed its ambition to play the role of arbiter in the Netherlands. Adolf of Mark (1313–44), having been recommended to Avignon by France, promised support for the king against England in 1320 and sealed a coalition with France four years later. Engelbert of Mark (1345–64) also remained a loyal vassal of France.

As the bishops of Liège were for the most part puppets of external powers, the emergence of a national consciousness in the principality came about in spite of, and even in opposition to, these bishops. It came from the internal dynamism of the towns, who perceived in their weak sense of identity the danger of annexation and in their clerical label a handicap to their economic prosperity. Moreover, the people of Liège were extremely irritated by the expansionist arrogance of Brabant. They saw the annexation of Limburg in 1288 and of small territories around the periphery of Liège by Duke John III as causing them to be surrounded. Only after Bishop Adolf of Mark had brought his own subjects under control in 1328 was he able to put a firm stop to this Brabantine 'imperialism'. However, the weak internal position of his successor Engelbert afforded the Brabantines the opportunity to indulge their urge for expansion once again.

The fundamental aim of the inhabitants of Liège in the fourteenth century was to turn their prince-bishopric into a principality along the same lines as others in the Low Countries; a 'Land of Liège' with a distinctive, proud identity, the government of which would not be imposed from outside. To put this vision into practice, its subjects had to enforce their participation in politics. Both within the towns and in the government of the area, the balance of power was shifting.

Social stratification in the Liègeois towns was of a specific type, partly on account of their high percentage of clergy and of privileged serfs, the ecclesiastical tributaries (who to some extent enjoyed clerical immunity), but mainly because of the absence of any large or concentrated working proletariat involved in international trade. There were, however, manual workers who provided for local markets, and they had engaged in protests as early as 1253–5 at the instigation of newly enriched citizens who had been excluded from the exercise of political power, the closed patriciate of that time having succeeded in maintaining their monopoly. The Flemish revolts served as the model for more successful insurrections in Huy, Fosses and Liège (1300–3). Subsequently, the urban administration of Liège contained equal representation of patricians and craftsmen. During the episcopal vacancy of 1312, the patricians attempted to regain their former position. However, many of them were forced to retreat to St Martin's Church in Liège, where they were burnt alive (Mal St Martin). This old patriciate remained politically powerless for some time after that, but in the Peace of Vottem (1331), Adolf of Mark turned the clock back by excluding tradesmen's representatives from the executive system.

The play of social forces, however, was more complex than this simple opposition suggests. The prince-bishop Adolf of Mark had distilled from his university education an authoritarian-monarchical model for his bishopric.

Soon after his accession in 1313, he began to implement his ideas, whereupon new patricians, specialised craftsmen and workers alike, as well as aristocratic families and clerics, felt sufficiently alarmed to demand civil liberties and the right to political participation. There followed a series of conflicts between the towns, in coalition with some members of the nobility, and the bishop. The latter was humiliated by his forced flight to Brabant, and the fact that the dean and chapter attempted to mediate caused him further loss of face. He was forced to agree to the Peace of Fexhe (1316), which established the involvement of a representative body (the *sens du pays*) in the administration of the prince-bishopric consisting of nobility, clergy and third estate, and the text of which soon assumed the function of a Liège national constitution. In 1325 the crafts caused this scenario to be repeated and the bishop was again forced to take flight on this occasion to Huy. But this time he mobilised external military support and crushed the Liègeois towns at Hoesselt (1328). Subsequently, he abandoned military power and employed instead the more subtle methods of diplomacy and judicial repression. The Peace of Vottem (1331) turned back the clock by imposing severe restrictions on the crafts and depriving them of a political voice.

TERRITORIAL RULERS WITH EUROPEAN AMBITIONS
(c. 1360–c. 1415)

In this second phase, the political cards in the Netherlands were thoroughly reshuffled by a very unlikely combination of circumstances. In three of the four most important territories, the male line died out – in Hainault-Holland in 1345, in Brabant in 1355, in Flanders in 1384 – and in each case the descendant of a foreign dynasty was introduced. In two cases he belonged to the German royal house and in the third case to that of the French. Their introduction to a new prosperous territory and their familiarity, as a result of their origins, with the exciting political game of chess at European level, enticed these able 'foreigners' to aspire both to playing a role in the politics of their dynasty of origin and also to realising autonomous territorial ambitions. The remarkable thing is that this two-sided approach was not without success because it occurred at a time when the great powers were severely weakened either by the wars they had fought against each other (France and England), or by internal disintegration (Germany) or by lack of any clear direction in policy (the papacy).

The Burgundian-Flemish scene (1360–1415)

Louis de Male was a stronger and more diplomatic exponent of *realpolitik* than his predecessors. He drew the correct conclusion from the failure both of their policies and those of his towns: neither the Flemish economy nor the prestige of the Flemish count was helped by obediently turning on the merry-go-round of the great powers or by blindly following France or England. He began the construction of his aura of power in a classical way – that of military prowess. In 1356 he invaded Brabant with his army precisely when, in a laborious struggle for the succession, Duchess Joan had been forced into making serious political concessions to her self-confident subjects which thoroughly undermined her authority. Without scruple, Louis took the ruler of Hainault into his camp, even though the latter was an ally of Brabant, and through the Peace of Ath (1357) succeeded in annexing the trade centres of Malines and Antwerp, thus upsetting Brabant's economy. In 1367 Louis then deceived Albert of Hainault by compelling the French king, Albert's ally, to come over to the Flemish camp (if he wanted to save certain pending marriage negotiations), and in the Brabant–Flemish border conflict he imposed upon Albert a peace that on the one hand increased the Flemish count's chances of succession in Brabant and on the other still further weakened the count of Hainault's authority over his towns and nobility.

On the international stage, Louis de Male had meanwhile set up a position, which was on the face of it as classic as the other, by securing himself the support of a powerful ally through a matrimonial alliance. The count had only one daughter, Margaret, to succeed to his throne. This fact involved some danger, but in view of Flanders's economic power, it also represented a significant asset. The originality of Louis's tactics lay in his understanding of this. He played off the great powers against one another. In 1351, he entered into negotiations regarding a possible English marriage. But this was just a means of exerting pressure, for in 1355 he agreed on his daughter's marriage to Philip of Rouvres, duke of Burgundy. After the latter's sudden death in 1361, negotiations with England were resumed, again simply to push the price up. England offered him successions in Ponthieu and Holland, but now that Margaret's market value had risen, Louis started talks, again without scruple, with the French king, whom he kept hanging on for a further three years. Finally, in 1369, he accepted the candidature of the new Burgundian duke, Philip (the Bold), brother to the king, but not before the latter had ceded Walloon-Flanders to him. This marriage opened up even more territorial perspectives since on Louis's death in 1384, the counties of Artois, Franche-Comté, Nevers and Rethel, as well as the *seigneuries* of Malines and Antwerp, also fell to the Flemish-Burgundian couple.

Apart from these two, essentially dynastic, policies, Louis played a third game which encompassed an even broader sphere: this was a kind of diplomatic tightrope-walking between the great powers. To safeguard relations with England, which were vital to the Flemish economy, he eschewed adventures like

Artevelde's and opted for an Anglo-Flemish peace treaty (1348), and together with his son-in-law he attempted to mediate a Franco-English *rapprochement* (1375–7). Louis's strategy was perfectly in line with the age-old struggle to protect economic and political identity within the familiar borders of the old county. On his death, however, this policy was superseded. Some time beforehand, his successor Philip the Bold had already embarked on different policies. At his marriage in 1369, he had simultaneously sworn two secret oaths: one to his royal brother in which he promised that on the death of his father-in-law Walloon-Flanders was to go back to France, and another to Louis de Male that it was *not*. This further example of two-faced tightrope-walking perfectly illustrates that Philip the Bold was aiming at different objectives, namely a political role at the French court *and* a role as Flemish-Burgundian territorial ruler.

The great Flemish revolt of 1379–85 against the old count and his son-in-law was an unexpected hiccup in the progress of events, and occurred in spite of the fact that Louis had achieved domestic peace by reintroducing the Ghent weavers into the political decision-making process and by admitting the magistrates of Bruges and Ypres to the ranks of his clientage. In fact, the revolt can be seen as a last reactionary uprising of the towns along the lines of James van Artevelde's adventure, motivated by radical Anglophilia and aiming at a reduction in the count's authority and the dominance of the three great towns as quasi city-states.

The Peace of Tournai of 1385 was moderately repressive. It obviously meant a political rupture between Flanders and England, but this did not prevent the duke from promptly striving for an Anglo-Flemish trade agreement within a politically neutral context. Operating within this flexible framework, Duke Philip (1384–1404), as a French prince, did not find it too hard to sponsor in 1396 a marriage of the English king to the French king's daughter and in so doing to open the door for his son John the Fearless (1404–19) to conclude an Anglo-Flemish trade agreement in 1407.

This policy of non-alignment assisted in replacing a political with a purely commercial Anglophilia. But in fact both dukes also pursued a second line of policy, and in so doing displayed quite remarkable Machiavellian abilities. This second track was that of playing an active role in French national policy. This was, again, a consequence of pure coincidence. From 1380 to 1388, Philip the Bold had, along with other relatives, acted as regent for the minor Charles VI. In 1392, he resumed this role when the king began to show signs of insanity. Philip and his colleagues conducted themselves as defenders of their own dynastic interests, neglecting those of the monarchy and cynically transferring French public funds to their regional princely treasuries. In these fraternal quarrels, John the Fearless was not above eliminating through assassination the leader of the rival clientage, the duke of Orléans, in 1407. Only then did the political strife between Armagnacs and Burgundians really start. They all pretended to be serving the French *bien public*. In fact, John was happy to watch the flower of the Armagnacs lose their lives 'for France' at the battle of Agincourt (1415) while he flirted with the English, giving them the illusion of being willing to live together with them in France. He really had only one dominant motive – that of his own dynastic interests.

It was the same objective that moved Philip the Bold in 1385 to give away two of his children in a double marriage to members of the Bavarian house, which at the time ruled over Holland and Hainault. It is unlikely that at such an early date Philip foresaw that this would later bring about the joining of the two territorial blocks and thus take a significant step towards the unification of the Low Countries under a Burgundian sceptre. The agreement, however, did imply the coming into being of a balance of power, and it is an example of the duke's desire to get the Low Countries under his sway. Along the same lines, Philip managed in 1396 to persuade the childless duchess of Brabant to accept his son Anthony as her successor. This is why Brabant was ruled until 1430 by a branch of the Burgundian dynasty, which in this way had indirect political control there as well.

In domestic affairs, a realistic balance of power was achieved by the Peace of 1385 between the prince and the self-assured Flemish towns. In 1407, after a long period of increasing reconciliation, Duke John the Fearless found the time ripe to impose a number of measures which curbed the autonomy of the towns and their hunger for power. However, between 1411 and 1417 the high cost of his political ambitions in France, for which he had to rely on taxes from his Flemish subjects, forced the sovereign into concessions and a number of measures pertaining to his centralising national policy were withdrawn. Only in the long period of peace under Philip the Good did the growth of the central state prove possible.

Hainault, Holland and Zeeland (1358–1419)

From 1358 to 1389, Albrecht of Bavaria replaced his insane brother William as count of Hainault, Holland and Zeeland. At the same time, he remained duke of Bavaria, with ambitions within the German empire. This dual position was both an advantage and a handicap. It was an advantage in that, like the duke of Burgundy after his marriage to the Flemish heiress, he was able to face his subjects from a position of power and with the glamour of a foreign dynasty around him. Just like the Burgundian, Albrecht must have found it a great challenge to be confronted with a flourishing province whose prosperity essentially depended on the viability of its textile, beer and other industries, and on unimpeded access to international trading connections. This was all the more the

case as he himself came from a traditional agrarian territory. One of the
Bavarian's first initiatives in 1358 was to transfer the staple of the Hanse from
Flanders to Dordrecht. Another of his priorities, as with Philip the Bold in
Flanders, was the pursuit of political neutrality in his provinces in order to safe-
guard their economic prosperity.

However, neutrality was the last thing Albrecht of Bavaria could expect on
his accession either with regard to the great powers, or with regard to his neighbours, as they could only benefit from a weakened rival. Edward III, for
example, challenged him by laying claim to his territories on behalf of his wife
Philippa, Albrecht's aunt. There were also quarrels with the bishop of Liège,
which were not settled until 1360, and conflicts with Brabant, settled only in
1366 (and again, after new clashes, in 1376). His most annoying rival was the
count of Flanders, who claimed the border area between Flanders and
Hainault (the so-called *terres de débat*). In a humiliating agreement in 1368,
Albrecht was obliged to accept holding the area as a fief from Louis de Male.
Internally as well, Albrecht's authority was eroded by the political conflicts
between the Hoeken and Kabeljauwen in Holland. Because of this, and also
because of his many and frequent periods of absence from the Low Countries
demanded by his Bavarian duties, he had to put up with serious loss of power.
In 1362, he had to accept that in each of his three Low Countries provinces a
council controlled by the towns, and also sometimes by clerics and noblemen,
was to take over some decision-making functions. Consequently, it was not
until after the period of crisis in 1366–8 that Albrecht was able to opt resolutely
for a policy of neutrality in the European political arena, resisting temptations
to side with either the English or the French king.

From then, the Bavarian scene was almost identical to that of the
Burgundian-Flemish. Both power blocks, which were also similar from a socio-
economic point of view, had ambitions for political control in the rest of the
Low Countries. However, the logic of *realpolitik* forced them to replace direct
confrontation with a diplomatic alliance in which they neutralised each other.
This took shape in the double marriage at Cambrai in 1385, at which John,
Philip's eldest son (and therefore the dauphin) was married to Margaret of
Bavaria, and Philip's daughter Margaret to William of Bavaria, the later Count
William VI of Holland-Hainault.

Thus a balance of French and German influence was created in the Low
Countries. It enabled the principal actors of the Burgundian and Bavarian
spheres to negotiate with England for good trading contacts with Flanders and
Holland divorced from the large military conflict that was dividing Europe, a
policy of neutrality which also had a beneficial effect on the corn exports
of agrarian Hainault. Within the Low Countries themselves, the
Burgundian–Bavarian agreement of 1385 meant that Albrecht of Bavaria, as a

fully fledged count (1389–1404), was able to strive more freely for expansion into Utrecht and Friesland.

In keeping with this logic, the treaty of friendship between Holland and Flanders was renewed in 1405 and also extended to Brabant, which, under the rule of a parallel Burgundian line, was showing similar interests. Whenever, during the years 1405–8, the Burgundian John the Fearless was obliged to demonstrate his military strength in Paris in order to give credibility to his political ambitions in France, the troops of his coalition partners, William VI of Hainault-Holland and Anthony of Brabant, were a welcome backing for the Burgundian clan. He was also served by the efficient diplomatic assistance which these two gave him in the laborious Burgundian–French negotiations which ended in the Peace of Chartres (1409) and the Peace of Arras (1414). The coalition of the three big blocks also proved its worth in the Low Countries by collectively giving military support to the bishop of Liège and shattering the Liège urban militia at the battle of Othée (1408) and, as a result of this, by more emphatically establishing its political prestige.

The deaths of Anthony of Burgundy (1415) and William VI (1417) signalled the end of a stable balance of power among the three power blocks and the start of a civil war in the Low Countries. In this new tangle of intrigues and rivalries, both Jacqueline of Bavaria, William VI's only daughter and married to the new duke of Brabant, John IV (son of Anthony of Burgundy), and also John of Bavaria, William VI's brother and until that time bishop of Liège, indicated their interest in the Holland-Hainault succession. The arbitrator in this matter, as was to be expected, was John the Fearless, the only survivor of the trio of strong rulers. It was also John who, in February 1419, was able to put an end to the conflict between John of Bavaria, supported by the German king, and John IV (a true 'Burgundian') through the Peace of Woudrichem, according to which the two opponents were to administer the three counties together, with John of Bavaria being allowed to keep the territories he had conquered but having to give up his title of count of Holland-Zeeland.

The duchy of Brabant (1345–1419)

After 1345, at the conclusion of the first intense phase of the Hundred Years War, John III, like his Flemish and Hainault counterparts, opted for a more neutral position. In this context, he sought to move closer to the German emperor and in 1345 he gave his eldest daughter Joan in marriage to the emperor's brother Wenceslas. At the time, the marriage did not appear to be anything more than a symbolic manifestation of the new option. Later, however, it turned out to be more than this since the sons of John III, one after the other, all died prematurely. After John III's death in 1355, only Joan remained, and, together with her German husband, she unexpectedly succeeded to the throne. This succession was not really seen as a German coup in the Low Countries (as it might have been earlier) since by 1355 the prestige of the Holy Roman Empire had already considerably faded. Wenceslas's German background did not impress his new Brabantine subjects much. In 1356, his weak position induced the representative assembly in the duchy to exact from their duke a constitutional text. This document stipulated that the representative body should have a say in every declaration of war or peace, obliged the ruler to recruit his officials exclusively from Brabant and confirmed that the obedience of his subjects was conditional. On top of that, Louis de Male, the Flemish count, promptly took advantage of the weak position of Joan and Wenceslas and invaded Brabant in 1356. The conflict was settled, to the humiliation of Brabant, by the Peace of Ath (1357), which secured the claims to Brabant of Margaret, Louis's spouse and sister to Joan, and which incorporated Antwerp and Malines into Flanders.

All of this, as well as a number of revolts with which Joan was faced subsequently, meant that politically speaking Brabant was a weakened, poor relation when, in 1385, the double marriage at Cambrai started the Burgundian–Bavarian alliance (see above). In 1390, the wily diplomat Philip the Bold persuaded Joan (Wenceslas had meanwhile died) to appoint, albeit secretly, his spouse Margaret as her successor, and to have his son Anthony educated at the Brabantine court. In 1401, the latter was given the right of succession in the event of his mother's and aunt's deaths, and in 1404 he became co-regent. On Joan's death in December 1406, he became full duke.

The introduction of the Burgundians into Brabant did not lead to a straightforward annexation but rather to an indirect Burgundianisation. This came about as a result of the appointment of Flemings to positions within the government apparatus, the setting-up of a chamber of accounts and the reorganisation of the court along Flemish–Burgundian lines. For a few months, following his marriage to Elizabeth of Görlitz, the emperor's niece, in 1409, it seemed just possible that Anthony would allow himself a more independent stance. Nevertheless, in his capacity as a good French vassal, he then fell at the battle of Agincourt (1415). The succession in Brabant went to his son Philip IV, who in 1418, under pressure from the Burgundian John the Fearless, had been married to Jacqueline of Bavaria, the count of Hainault's only daughter, thus demonstrating that by around 1419 Burgundy had gained political hegemony over nearly all of the Low Countries.

The prince-bishopric of Liège (1345–1417)

Engelbert of Mark (1345–64) endured at Vottem (1346) a humiliating military defeat at the hands of the burghers of Liège and Huy. He and his successors,

John of Arkel (1364–78) and Arnold of Hoorn (1378–89) were in a weak position relative to the fast-maturing representative body of the principality of Liège. This 'Common Land' of Liège *(sens du pays)*, rather than the bishop, was the driving force behind an expansion which, in 1366, ended in the incorporation of Loon. Liège's sense of national identity was nourished by dynamic towns, with the city of Liège in the vanguard. Within these towns, after their political setback in 1331, the thirty-two trades regained their right to vote in urban government elections (1343). They even exacted a Commission of XXII in 1373 to curb electoral abuses. In 1384 they succeeded in reserving exclusively for themselves the right to elect the municipal council.

At the level of the principality, the 'Common Land', in 1343, forced through the establishment of a high court *(tribunal des XXII)*, consisting of four clergymen, four noblemen and fourteen burghers. This composition suggests that the intention was to curb episcopal power, and indeed one of its tasks consisted of prosecuting episcopal officials who were breaking the law.

In 1390, as a result of the Western Schism, the vacancy of the see of Liège became an ecclesiastical-political question. Rome, against Avignon, pushed through its own candidate, John of Bavaria (1390–1418). He was the grandson of a Wittelsbach emperor, related to the French, Holland and Burgundian-Flemish dynasties and ambitious to make of Liège a centralised principality according to the Burgundian model. However, this dream was opposed by the self-confident 'Common Land', which was averse to this type of monarchism. Resistance took the form of a party conflict, in which craftsmen, the nobility and even the clergy joined forces as the anti-episcopal clan of the Haydroits. In 1406, they considered the ruler to have been deposed. The duke of Orléans, arch-rival of the Burgundians in French politics, together with the pope in Avignon were ready with their rival candidate. But then John of Bavaria called in the help of John the Fearless and the rulers of Hainault and Namur, and thereby crushed the Liègeois army of craftsmen at the battle of Othée (1408). But it was a pyrrhic victory for the bishop. It was, in fact, John the Fearless who became guardian of Liège and he was the one who, behind the prince-bishop's back, politically dismantled the Liège crafts and turned the prince-bishopric into a Burgundian protectorate.

THE OTHER REGIONS (1280–1418)

The bishopric of Utrecht (1291–1423)

Like Liège, Utrecht was simultaneously a bishopric and a secular principality, and at the same time a plaything of external political forces. Until 1301, the pope played the most dominant role in the appointment of bishops, as a variant of the *Reichskirche*. John of Sierck (1291–6), for example, fitted nicely into a papal scenario of internal Church reform, and William Berthout (1296–1301) was ideal as an English agent and capable financier when Boniface VIII was seriously at odds with the French monarch Philip the Fair. After 1301, Utrecht became more or less a protectorate of Holland, and the Avesnes, having easy access to the pope in Avignon, succeeded in putting their relatives Guy of Avesnes (1301–17), Frederick of Sierck (1317–22) and John of Diest (1322–40) on the throne. Because of their political vulnerability and financial weakness, however, these rulers became easy prey to their neighbours. In 1331, control over the temporal possessions of the bishop of Utrecht was taken, divided between the count of Holland, who took the Nedersticht, and Guelders, which got Oversticht.

It is not clear whether it was the headstrong character of the new bishop John of Arkel (1342–94) (though he too was a protégé of the count of Holland) or whether it was the population itself, exasperated by external provocation, which contributed to Utrecht's growing sense of national identity, after the model of Liège, soon after 1342. At any rate, in 1375, with the capital Utrecht in the van, a representative body of clergymen, noblemen and burghers was formally constituted, and in 1345 the bishop had even had the audacity to take up arms against Holland. In 1423, the burghers of Utrecht were able to get an anti-Burgundian candidate appointed as their bishop, so that Utrecht's integration into the Burgundian Netherlands was postponed.

The county and duchy of Guelders (1280–1418)

The emergence of a dynasty in Guelders in the eleventh century, supported by a council of clergymen and noblemen from around 1200 onwards, had given rise by the thirteenth century to a strong sense of territorial identity in the county. This was stimulated by the realisation of a dynastic union with Limburg in 1280, although it was badly damaged by the conquest of Limburg in 1288 by Guelders's inveterate rival Brabant. This setback, however, became at the same time the stimulus for an even stronger pursuit of independence. In this context, well-developed mercantile towns such as Nymegen and Roermond played a dynamic part by outdoing their commercial competitor Brabant. Reinoud II (1326–43) raised Guelders's prestige so much by his prominent role in the pro-English camp in the Low Countries that the emperor promoted him to duke in 1339. He eliminated the threat from Brabant and was able, in a coalition with Holland, to gain temporal control over the eastern part of Utrecht (Oversticht). Following a period of relative decline, William I of Gulik (1371–1402), who established the union with Gulik, was a ruler of European stature. The extent to which the sense of territorial identity had grown in the meantime became apparent when, in 1418, the four capitals (which each governed a quarter of the duchy) and the nobility of Guelders agreed to stay together as one territorial union even if their ruler died childless. This strong sense of identity also explains why Guelders was not conquered by the Burgundians and was not annexed to the Habsburg empire until 1543.

Peripheral regions

The other areas of the Low Countries had less influence on the general state of affairs because they had remained as traditional feudal-agrarian societies and had fewer urban centres (the pioneers of modernisation and demands for political participation). From an economic point of view, however, they were very important in their role as agrarian reserves. But in international politics they were merely fellow-travellers; one time they sided with the English, another time with the French. Frequently, they were either annexed or governed by neighbours. In between these storms, they led somewhat isolated, marginal, but hence relatively unperturbed, lives, with their own dynasties whose autonomy, therefore, was often of longer duration than that of the central territories.

The northern districts of Friesland, Drenthe and Groningen are worthy of note. As imperial fiefdoms, they came under the emperor, but their supervision was assigned to territorial rulers from outside their borders. In 1165, the bishop of Utrecht and the count of Holland were given joint control over Friesland, but in 1339 supervision was assigned to the duke of Guelders; in 1343, Groningen came under Utrecht. The absence of dynasties of their own, however, did not prevent them from considering themselves as territories as autonomous as any other. They drew this sense of identity in the one case from the traditional love of freedom of the rural Frisian populace and in the other from the dynamism of a town (Groningen) with a central economic function.

The eastern and southern belt, consisting of Namur, Luxemburg and Loon, was agrarian and wooded. In contrast to the northern districts, these had their own dynasties, all of them feudally under the emperor. In the thirteenth century, the county of Namur was first governed by a branch of the Flemish-Hainault dynasty and subsequently by a dynastic union of Flanders and Hainault. In 1298, the count of Flanders ceded it to his son, and it thenceforth remained autonomous until 1429. In 1421, the duke of Burgundy had bought it from the previous count, John III, who was then allowed to enjoy the usufruct for a further eight years. In Luxemburg, the sense of territorial identity was considerably stronger because of the continuity of its own dynasty from the tenth century onwards. This distinctiveness was greatly enhanced by the fact that several counts (and, after 1354, dukes) were called on to be rulers of the German kingdom and empire. These were Henry VII (1308–13), Charles IV (1346–76), Wenceslas (1376–1400) and Sigismund (1410–37). The marriage of Count John the Blind to the king of Bohemia's daughter created a dynastic union of Bohemia and Luxemburg between 1310 and 1439. This union added much lustre to the dynasty and allowed it to play a significant role. Against the will of her own subjects, the last duchess, Elizabeth of Görlitz, sold her rights to her nephew Philip the Good in 1441. Loon had had its own count, vassal to the bishop of Liège, since 1078. In the context of their territorial rivalry with Brabant, the towns of Liège and the chapter considered it wise to annex the region to Liège when Count Louis IV died childless. Loon was definitively incorporated into Liège in 1366. Walloon-Flanders was governed by the count of Flanders, as part of a dynastic union, until around 1300. In 1305 it was annexed to France but returned to Flanders in 1369.

SOCIO-ECONOMIC EVOLUTION (1280–1415)

The Low Countries did not constitute a political unity in this period. At most a few power blocks, which dominated their satellites and competed against each other, had ambitions towards political control. However, at the economic (and also cultural) level, there was a clear collective identity and solidarity. The central areas of Flanders, Brabant, Holland and Liège had some identical features which were paralleled only in northern Italy. These were proximity to the sea, a mild climate and a geography which allowed for a dense network of canals and roads. From the eleventh century, Flanders developed a flourishing textile industry and an accompanying international sales network. In the north, a number of towns in Holland (e.g. Dordrecht) and Guelders (e.g. Kampen) grew relatively early. The Brabant textile and the Liège textile and metal industries profited from their location on the land route between Bruges and Cologne. The more peripheral regions (such as Friesland, Luxemburg and Hainault) were more geared to agriculture and forestry but thus played an extremely useful complementary role in the supply of grain to the maritime zone of Flanders-Holland, which had an urban population of between 36 and 54 per cent. A striking sign of the Low Countries's self-perception as a single economic entity is the initiative taken by Brabant and Flanders to gear their monetary systems to each other (1299–1300), which was followed by fully fledged monetary agreements between these two areas in 1339 and 1384, and also between Brabant and Hainault in 1337.

In this period in the Low Countries it was the textile industry which dominated. The Flemish towns (Ghent and Ypres) at first and later Brabantine (Louvain), Liège (Huy) and Holland (Leiden) towns conquered world markets with their production of luxury textiles. Such a monoculture offered advantages in its qualitative superiority. However, it was also risky both because it aimed at a small elite and also because it depended on trade routes which were vulnerable to outbreaks of war for its sales and, for the supply of quality wool, on English imports which were particularly at risk during the Hundred Years War. In addition, demographic growth in Europe halted after 1300, so that sales decreased. The Flemish industry had already entered a period of recession by the beginning of the fourteenth century and Brabant followed in the 1340s. Production in Ypres halved between 1310 and 1350 and in Malines it decreased by two-thirds between 1332 and 1370. The centres in Holland offered better resistance for a number of reasons. They had started later; they carried less of a burden of tradition; they were flexible enough to introduce cheaper English wool (which they had already done by the end of the fourteenth century); finally, through the use of appropriate sales techniques, they conquered the Baltic market. Holland also had alternatives such as the production of beer. Liège, too, was somewhat better off because, along with textiles, it had developed a range of metal industries. In the older industrial areas of Flanders-Brabant, the reaction to the crisis was at first protectionist, with cheaper textile production in the countryside being eliminated by force. Economic realities proved to be stronger, however, and in the second half of the fourteenth century, the production of cheap textiles started in both the countryside and the smaller towns. Large towns which refused to adapt in this way, such as Ypres, fell into further decline, while others, such as Ghent, were able to stand firm precisely because of a great flexibility which led them to transfer a larger proportion of their market from the elite foreign to the domestic one.

There were also significant chronological differences between the regions concerning the rate and nature of commercial development. Not long after 1300, Flanders changed over to passive trade, while Brabant kept an active model of trade throughout the century. The sedentary model can, however, be reasonably successful: in the fourteenth century, Bruges was the undisputed fulcrum of European trade, where English, Italian, Spanish and Hanseatic merchants came together and where a modern banking system was in operation. At this time in Holland, Dordrecht played a central role in the storage and exchange of almost all goods coming up or down the Meuse, Rhine and Waal. It was also at this time that the shipping industry in Holland began to develop its own dynamism independent of trading functions.

There was also regional variation in the Low Countries regarding social organisation. In the various sections above, it has been shown how, at first in Flanders and later elsewhere, the political monopoly and social domination of a closed patriciate was breached after 1300 by organised merchants and craftsmen, and how the latter, in the course of the fourteenth century, soon lapsed into a conservative corporatism which often functioned as a brake on economic innovation and adaptation.

CULTURAL EVOLUTION (1280–1415)

The sheer density of impressive churches and town halls was the first thing which struck any visitor to the Low Countries at that time. These edifices had, of course, a primarily religious, economic or administrative function. But a secondary function of the high church towers, the proud belfries and the spacious infirmaries was that they were very much symbols of municipal power and wealth. Above all, these works of art manifested a homogeneity of style which characterised the Low Countries as a collective entity. After a Romanesque period with its centre in the Meuse area, the Flemish Scheldt Gothic (in the thirteenth and the first half of the fourteenth centuries) and the Brabantine Gothic (from the middle of the fourteenth century) dominated. These were distinctive variants on the French style and were imitated in Holland-Zeeland and also in Liège when Romanesque buildings were renovated during the fourteenth century.

A remarkable feature of the Low Countries is that the patronage of both cities and rulers flourished simultaneously, and that their involvement functioned as a strengthening force for both. This is especially striking at the end of the fourteenth century, when, in the regions with the strongest urban economies, ambitious external dynasties (the Bavarians in Holland and the Burgundians in Flanders) promoted a prosperous court life which was in perfect harmony with the municipal environment. These cases illustrate to what extent art was a component part of the self-image of these dynasties, as well as being an important international commercial product; whilst at a lower social level, the dynamic spiritual and intellectual life developed in the Low Countries, especially in towns, has already been illustrated in earlier contributions to this volume.

THE CROWN OF ARAGON

Alan Forey

IN the fourteenth century the Crown of Aragon's external policy focused mainly on islands in the western Mediterranean and on the Iberian peninsula itself, and it was in these areas that most of its military activity was centred. At the beginning of his reign James II (1291–1327) ruled not only the kingdoms of Aragon and Valencia and the county of Barcelona, which made up the lands of the Crown of Aragon in the Iberian peninsula, but also the Balearics and Sicily. Mallorca had been conquered from the Muslims in 1229 by James's grandfather, James I (1213–76), although the latter had used it, together with Roussillon, Cerdagne and Montpellier, to constitute a kingdom for his second son. Pedro III of Aragon (1276–85) had, however, asserted overlordship over the Mallorcan kingdom in 1279, and in 1285 his eldest son Alfonso, shortly to become Alfonso III (1285–91), had taken Mallorca by force from his uncle, though not the mainland parts of the Mallorcan kingdom; Alfonso later also asserted direct rule over Minorca, which until then had been a dependent Muslim state. Sicily had been brought under Aragonese rule in 1282, when Pedro III had occupied the island following the rebellion of the Sicilian Vespers against Charles of Anjou. This action led to ecclesiastical censure by the French pope Martin IV and the award of the kingdom of Aragon to Charles of Valois, the younger son of Philip III of France; and this in turn occasioned an unsuccessful French invasion of Aragon in 1285. Despite these international pressures, however, coupled with opposition inside Aragon, Sicily passed on Pedro's death in 1285 to his second son, the future James II of Aragon; but the latter lost the support of his brother Alfonso III, who shortly before his death tried to make peace with the Church and France.

James, as Alfonso's successor, sought to rule Sicily as well as the other Aragonese lands, appointing his younger brother Frederick as his representative on the island. But James was subject to many of the same pressures as his predecessors and in an agreement made at Anagni in 1295, following protracted negotiations, he abandoned his claims to Sicily, and also undertook to restore the lands taken from his uncle James of Mallorca; it was agreed that the Aragonese king should marry Blanche, daughter of the Angevin Charles II of Naples; and in compensation for Sicily, Pope Boniface VIII promised James II the islands of Corsica and Sardinia, although the Aragonese king did not receive investiture of these until 1297. The question of the Balearics was settled in 1298 when they were transferred to the king of Mallorca, although James II reasserted the overlordship which had been imposed by Pedro III. In the meantime the return of Sicily to the Angevins, as envisaged at Anagni, was prevented by the setting-up of James's brother Frederick as king of Sicily. It became necessary to remove him, and the pope expected James II to assist in this task. The Aragonese king did in fact launch expeditions against his brother in 1298 and 1299, but Frederick remained in power and it was not until the treaty of Caltabellotta in 1302 that a settlement was reached, whereby Frederick was to retain Sicily for life, though abandoning claims in Calabria; after his death the island was to revert to the Angevins. In fact Sicily continued to be ruled after Frederick's death by his descendants.

Although James had been awarded Sardinia and Corsica it was not until towards the end of his reign that an expedition was launched to secure the former island, where authority rested mainly in the hands of Pisa, although the Genoese and local families, especially the Judges of Arborea, also had rights there. In the meantime the Aragonese king became involved on other fronts. Although at the beginning of his reign, when he needed support, James had made an alliance with Sancho IV of Castile, relations soon became strained, and James took the opportunity provided by uncertainties concerning the Castilian succession following Sancho's death in 1295 to advance the claims of Alfonso X's grandson Alfonso de la Cerda, in return for the cession of Murcia. In 1296 James occupied much of that district. Yet altered circumstances in Castile and Granada led James to accept a compromise in 1304 which allowed him to retain merely Guardamar, Alicante and certain other lands to the north of the Segura. Changing relations with Castile paved the way for joint action against Granada: it was agreed that the Aragonese king should receive a sixth of the Muslim kingdom. In 1309 James attacked Almería, while Fernando IV of Castile turned against Algeciras. Although Gibraltar fell to the Castilians, nothing was achieved from the siege of Almería, which lasted from August 1309 until January 1310. Further proposals by James II to attack Granada came to nothing, while during the minority of the Castilian king Alfonso XI, who succeeded in 1312, James sought to exercise influence in the neighbouring Christian kingdom merely by diplomacy and family connections: his son John was even made archbishop of Toledo in 1319. It was also by diplomacy that James in 1313 secured recognition of his rights to the Valle de Arán in the Pyrenees, which was of strategic importance and which had been occupied by the French in the 1280s, though in 1298 it had passed under the control of Mallorca.

For much of the opening two decades of the century the Aragonese king was also conducting negotiations about Sardinia, especially with the papacy, the Tuscan Guelfs who were opposed to Pisa and some families based in the island: at one stage Pisa itself even offered to submit to Aragonese lordship. But the island was gained by an expedition led by the infante Alfonso in 1323. Initial conquest took a little over a year, but James II was soon faced by rebellions on the island, occasioned in part by the conduct of the officials imposed by the Aragonese crown; and the Genoese sided with the Pisans. These developments – together with papal intervention – hindered any determined attempt on the part of James II to reclaim Mallorca on the death of its king Sancho, who died without a direct heir in 1324. The throne passed to the late king's nephew, who became James III.

In the first part of his short reign, James II's son Alfonso IV (1327–36), whose health was not strong and who at times displayed indecisiveness, was mainly concerned with Granada. An alliance between the latter and the Marinid ruler of Morocco prompted a pact between the Aragonese king and Alfonso XI of Castile in 1329. But in 1331, when Alfonso IV was still seeking aid from the pope and before he had personally entered the conflict, the Castilian king made peace with Granada. In that and the following year Aragonese lands were in fact subject to raids from Granada. There were also problems in Sardinia, where there was a rebellion in 1329 which had the support of Genoa, and this led to conflict with Genoa in the western Mediterranean.

In 1339, when Morocco was planning an invasion of the peninsula, Alfonso's son Pedro IV (1336–87), of whom it has been said that 'the Battler' would be a more appropriate epithet than the generally accepted 'the Ceremonious',[1] entered into an alliance with Alfonso XI and provided ships against the Marinids; and shipping was similarly provided for the Castilian attack on Algeciras, which fell to the Christians in 1344. But in Pedro's early years there was the further preoccupation of Mallorca. His intention was to bring the island kingdom under his direct control. James III of Mallorca had done homage to the new Aragonese king only belatedly, and had also made a treaty with the Marinids in 1339. James was summoned to Barcelona to answer a manufactured charge of unlawfully minting money in Roussillon, and when he failed to appear sentence of confiscation was pronounced. James was unable to call on French help, and Mallorca, where he was unpopular, quickly came under Aragonese control in 1343. Although stronger resistance was provided on the mainland,

[1] Pere III, *Chron.*, p. 95.

the Mallorcan king surrendered in July 1344. But he was soon seeking to re-establish himself, and was killed in Mallorca in 1349 when trying to reassert his claims. The whole of the Mallorcan kingdom, except Montpellier, was reincorporated into the Aragonese realms. But Sardinia and the Genoese were still causing problems for Pedro. There was a rebellion on the island in 1347, and the situation was made more difficult by the alienation of Mariano IV of Arborea, who came out in open opposition in 1353. The Judges of Arborea had found that they did not enjoy the independence which they had expected under Aragonese rule. To counter the Genoese threat, Pedro allied with the Venetians in 1351, and in the following year an inconclusive victory was gained over the Genoese fleet in the eastern Mediterranean, while in 1353 the Genoese were more decisively defeated off Sardinia. But opposition on the island was still maintained, and although Pedro himself led an expedition in 1354, this did not bring the 'good order' claimed in his *Chronicle*.[2]

In the mid 1350s Pedro had to turn his attention, however, to his western borders. The so-called 'war of the two Pedros', apparently initiated by Castile, broke out in 1356. The incident which immediately occasioned it was a Catalan attack in a Castilian port on ships carrying Genoese goods, but the wider issues at stake included peninsular hegemony and Aragonese rights in Murcia. Despite an alliance between the Aragonese king and Henry of Trastámara, half-brother of Pedro I of Castile, the city of Tarazona fell to the Castilians in March 1357. Subsequent negotiations produced no settlement, and in the following year fighting began again, with both sides conducting offensives on land: early in 1359 the Aragonese advanced as far as Medinaceli. War was also being fought at sea: in June 1359 Barcelona survived an assault by the Castilian fleet. In 1360 Pedro IV recovered Tarazona by offering money to its Castilian *alcalde*, and in the Peace of Terrer (May 1361), it was agreed that conquests were to be restored and that Pedro IV would not allow Henry of Trastámara or the infante Fernando, the Aragonese king's half-brother, to make war against Pedro I from Aragonese lands. But in 1362 the Castilian king recommenced hostilities, supported to a certain extent by Navarre, Portugal and Granada, and made considerable headway. Calatayud fell at the end of August; in 1363 Tarazona was retaken, and Saragossa threatened, and farther south Teruel, Segorbe and Murviedro were among the places conquered. A fresh peace negotiated at Murviedro in July 1363 allowed Castile to keep considerable gains in Aragon, while the acquisitions made by Pedro I in Valencia were to pass to Pedro IV's son Alfonso, who was to marry Isabella of Castile. Yet this agreement did not hold, and Aragon and Valencia were again under threat: Alicante, Elche and a number of other towns and strongholds in the south were taken

---

[2] Ibid., p. 490.

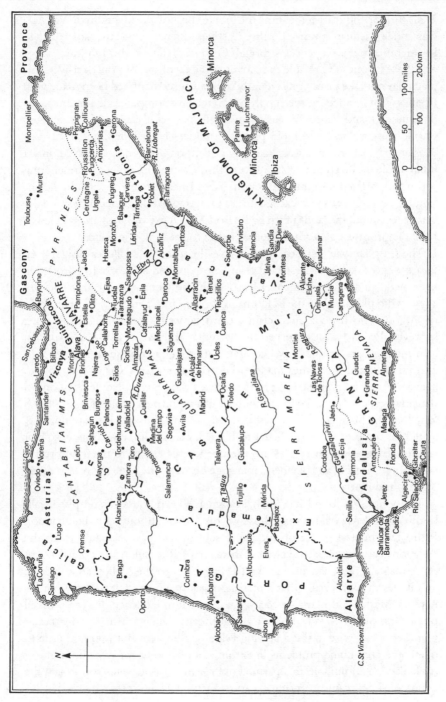

Map 10   The Iberian peninsula

at the turn of the year: at that time the greater part of the kingdom of Valencia was under Castilian control. Further Castilian offensives in 1364 and 1365 had less significant consequences – though Orihuela fell to Pedro I in June 1365 – and the Aragonese were able to recover some territory. But the decisive campaign did not take place until 1366. By then an agreement had been made with Charles V of France for the supply of mercenary companies led by Bertrand du Guesclin, and Pedro IV was again in alliance with Henry of Trastámara. Castile was invaded, and rapid progress made. Pedro I fled, and Henry of Trastámara was crowned Castilian king at Burgos. Aragon later played only a limited role in the continuing conflict within Castile: diplomatic manoeuvring was not translated into military action. Yet a final settlement with the neighbouring kingdom was not reached until 1375. Aragon had gained little from the war: it recovered the lands taken by Pedro I but Henry of Trastámara failed to fulfil the promises of territory he had made to the Aragonese king.

The Castilian war also served to revive the issue of Mallorca, for in 1362 James, son of James III, escaped from captivity and supported Pedro I. He later made an attempt to recover Roussillon and Cerdagne, but this failed in 1375, as did plans to gain the Mallorcan kingdom by Charles V's brother Louis of Anjou, who had acquired claims from James's sister. In his later years, however, Pedro had less success in Sardinia, where the Judge of Arborea remained in opposition. At sea conflict with Genoa continued, and was not altogether halted by treaties made in Pedro's later years. Nor was he able to achieve his ends in Sicily. In 1377 Frederick IV of Sicily died, leaving only a daughter called Maria. Pedro sought to claim the reversion of the Sicilian kingdom and planned to cross to the island; but this proposal came to nothing, as did his attempt to marry Maria to his elder son John: the Aragonese heir refused to have her. In 1380 Pedro then ceded his claims to the island to his second son, Martin, and planned a marriage between the latter's son, also called Martin, and Maria.

The policies of John I (1387–96), known as a keen huntsman despite his ill-health, were less positive than those of his father, although he did abandon Pedro IV's neutral stance on the papal schism and gave his support to the Avignon claimant. He also averted an invasion of Roussillon by Bernard, count of Armagnac, who had advanced a further claim to the Mallorcan kingdom; and it was in John's reign that a marriage was finally contracted between his nephew Martin and Maria of Sicily. An expedition launched in 1392 secured possession of the island, although the authority which Martin and his father managed to exercise in the following years was limited. But John did little to overcome continuing problems in Sardinia: a planned royal expedition never took place. On John's death an armed bid for the throne by his son-in-law, the count of Foix, came to nothing, and Martin I (1396–1410) succeeded his brother. He was more devoted to religion than to fighting, and difficulties continued in Sardinia: a peace with Genoa did not prevent the Italian city from supporting opposition in the island. The affairs of Sardinia did, however, serve to bring Sicily under the direct rule of the Aragonese king, for in 1409 the younger Martin died of malaria in Sardinia, shortly after gaining a victory over rebels there, and he was succeeded in Sicily by his father, although the latter died without a direct heir in the following year.

Although most Aragonese military activity in the fourteenth century took place in the Iberian peninsula and in islands of the western Mediterranean, in this period Aragonese kings also sought to extend their interests in the Muslim states of North Africa. The Treaty of Monteagudo with Castile at the beginning of James II's reign had allotted the districts to the east of the river Moulouya – these were then ruled mainly by the Ziyanids and the Hafsids – as Aragonese spheres of expansion; but in the fourteenth century, as in the thirteenth, North Africa was a zone of influence rather than of conquest. Instead of acquiring land, Aragonese kings sought to profit from tribute, from monies paid in return for the provision of Christian militias and ships to North African rulers, and from a share of the import dues paid in North African ports by Catalan merchants. These benefits were sought from the Marinids as well as from the Hafsids and the Ziyanids. Force was employed to these ends rather than for conquest; and the crusading expeditions launched against North Africa in 1398 and 1399 were merely reprisals for piratical attacks on the Valencian coast. But, partly because of Aragonese preoccupations on other fronts and of rivalry between Christian powers, and also because of political changes within North Africa, the gains made did not match the expectations of the Aragonese rulers.

Links with eastern Mediterranean lands and western Asia were less significant. At the beginning of the century James II was in contact with the Mongol Ilkhan of Persia, who wanted a western alliance against the Mamluks. A background to these exchanges was, of course, provided by the recent loss of the Holy Land. But relations were also maintained by Aragonese rulers with the Egyptian sultans. Before the Anagni settlement in 1295 James II was looking for political support, but after that date the interests of Aragonese rulers were limited to commercial matters and to such issues as the freeing of Christian captives, the security of pilgrims journeying to Jerusalem, reopening Christian churches and guarding of the Holy Sepulchre. In 1315 James II extended his links with the eastern Mediterranean by taking as his second wife Mary of Lusignan, the eldest sister of Henry II of Cyprus. As the latter was unmarried and his brother Amaury was held in prison, there was the prospect that Cyprus might pass in due course under Aragonese rule: the records of the negotiations for the marriage indicate that the Aragonese were certainly looking for that outcome. There would also have been a claim to the kingdom of Jerusalem. But Mary's claims to the succession do not seem to have been countenanced by Henry, who favoured his nephews; and in any case, no children were born of the marriage.

Early in the fourteenth century the Catalan company of mercenaries had, after fighting for and then rebelling against the Byzantine emperor Andronikos II, established itself in parts of Greece. But this district did not come under the formal authority of the Aragonese kings until 1379, when Pedro IV took over Sicilian claims to lordship following the death of Frederick IV. By then these Greek lands were under threat and, although Pedro sought allies and also sent out a small force in 1381, in 1388 Athens fell to the Florentine Nerio Acciaiuoli, lord of Corinth, and John I appears to have renounced his rights in Greece several years before Salona was overrun by the Turks in 1394. Aragonese authority in Greece was very short-lived.

It has often been pointed out that the traditional directions of Aragonese expansion to north and south were blocked in the thirteenth century by the growing power of the French monarchy in southern France, and by the completion of the conquest of Aragon's share of Muslim territories in the peninsula. Aragonese kings therefore looked increasingly to the Mediterranean. But clearly in the fourteenth century they did not wholly turn their backs on peninsular expansion. This has raised the question of the relative importance of peninsular and maritime interests. Some, for example, have argued that in the 1290s peninsular concerns came to take precedence in James II's plans; but it has also been asserted that his activity in the peninsula always served the interests of maritime expansion, in that the latter required a firm territorial base; and the importance of gaining ports in southern Spain has been stressed.[3] Although the conquest of Sardinia was delayed, the repeated diplomatic exchanges on the subject certainly indicate that James had not lost interest. But it would be surprising if a totally coherent and consistent line of policy was pursued over several decades: at the time of the Almería campaign, James was seeking to divert monies which had originally been assigned for Sardinia. He seems in fact to have been taking opportunities wherever they presented themselves, rather than concentrating on one particular area. The same is probably true of Pedro IV. Although much of his activity focused on the western Mediterranean rather than the peninsula, he did not hesitate to seek territorial gains on his western and southern frontiers from the war with Castile and from diplomatic negotiations relating to Castile.

Some gains in the peninsula, as well as in the Mediterranean, however, could be commercially advantageous to Catalonia, and it has been suggested that the

[3] For differing views, see Soldevila (1963), pp. 404–5, and Salavert y Roca (1956), I, pp. 169–70.

furtherance of commercial interests was a dominant factor in determining Aragonese policy: expansion in the Mediterranean was along the spice route.[4] It is certainly true that Mediterranean expansion was supported by Catalan merchants, who hoped for benefits. In the early decades of the fourteenth century, for example, Mallorca was a rival to Barcelona, with its own independent consulates in North Africa, though attempts at tariff discrimination on the island against Barcelona merchants failed. Yet, although Aragonese kings clearly sought to promote the interests of merchants, the extent to which they wanted, or were able, to pursue a policy mainly in the interests of commerce over a number of generations may be questioned. The objectives of expansion were again probably determined by the available opportunities and rights; and not all expansion envisaged by Aragonese rulers in this century carried commercial benefits. The argument that commerce was a major influence on royal policy would also carry more weight if there had been a consistent intention to keep Mediterranean conquests under unified control. But this was not the case for most of the thirteenth century, when dynastic concerns led to separation of conquered territories from the Aragonese crown. It was only from the late thirteenth century onwards that a trend towards maintaining unity becomes apparent: at the beginning of his reign James II repeated the undertaking given by Alfonso III not to separate Mallorca from the other lands of the crown, and in 1296 he made a similar statement about Alicante, while in 1319 he declared the indivisibility of all the lands then under his control. Pedro IV similarly promised on the conquest of Mallorca to keep it under direct Aragonese rule, and it was also to his elder son that he sought to marry the heiress to Sicily. But this change does not, of course, necessitate the conclusion that commercial interests then predominated.

While modern explanations have often stressed the importance of commerce, contemporary sources emphasise the religious motivation behind some expansion. At the time of the Almería expedition James II wrote to Fernando IV that 'you and we have begun these deeds to serve God and to exalt Christianity, and to evict the sect of Muhammad from Spain'.[5] It was also argued that the marriage alliance with Cyprus would have as its greatest benefit the furtherance of the recovery of the Holy Land; and in 1321 the infante Alfonso similarly maintained that the conquest of Sardinia and Corsica would be a preliminary step towards a crusade to the east.[6] Yet, despite such statements and despite the encouragement to crusading given by writers such as Ramon Lull, there was no consistent policy of hostility to Muslim powers in the western Mediterranean. A few years before the Almería campaign, James

---

[4] Vicens Vives, Suárez Fernández and Carrère (1959), pp. 105–6. [5] Chamberlin (1992), p. 18.

[6] Martínez Ferrando (1948), II, p. 77; Goñi Gaztambide (1958), p. 289.

II had been in alliance with Granada against Castile, and before the attack on Granada in 1309 an agreement had been made with Morocco. Relations with Muslim rulers often differed little from those with neighbouring Christian powers. And although Alfonso IV gave priority to Granada over Sardinia, John XXII thought that he was primarily interested in securing money from the papacy. John's successor Benedict XII in turn censured Pedro IV for his over-friendly relations with Muslims. Pedro's alliance with Castile against Muslim powers in 1339 was motivated by political, rather than religious, considerations. Nor did fourteenth-century Aragonese kings show much concern for the recovery of the Holy Land: despite contacts with the Ilkhan of Persia and James II's Cypriot marriage, little was done in practice to further its restoration to Christian rule.

In some contemporary sources, however, the honour of God was linked with the honour of the Aragonese king and his kingdom. In 1312, for example, James II told his envoys to Cyprus that a marriage agreement would be to the 'honour' and 'exaltation' of himself and his kingdom.[7] Honour was certainly not without significance in the minds of fourteenth-century Aragonese kings, as is apparent from coronation ceremonies of the period, and one way of enhancing reputation was by success in deeds of arms and by extending the range of the crown's authority.

But more material benefits for the crown were also to be obtained through conquest. The extinction of the Mallorcan kingdom would prevent it from entering into alliances against Aragon, and the elimination of Granada would make for greater security and stability in Valencia. The resources to be gained included not just the benefits to be derived from the increasing prosperity of Catalan merchants. The profits gained from North Africa have already been mentioned, and Sardinia produced silver and salt as well as grain. Although it is difficult to assess the precise wealth of Sardinia in the early fourteenth century, during negotiations relating to the island the Aragonese envoy Vidal of Villanova wrote of the 'abundance of money' which was to be had from it.[8] By the time of its conquest by Pedro IV, the island of Mallorca had, through its geographical position, become a commercial entrepot in western Mediterranean trade, with links especially with the Maghreb. In the early four-teenth century it was not primarily important for what it produced – a textile industry on the island was only beginning to develop – but in the mainland ter-ritories of the Mallorcan kingdom textiles were already being made in quantity in Perpignan, and the royal patrimony in Roussillon and Cerdagne was consid-erable. If they could be effectively ruled, all conquests could be profitable, and provide patronage which could be dispensed to royal followers.

---

[7] Martínez Ferrando (1948), II, p. 77.   [8] Salavert y Roca (1959), p. 435.

The factors which determined the success or failure of Aragonese foreign ventures were inevitably varied – in the Almería campaign, for example, adverse weather conditions and the stance of some Castilian nobles hampered chances of success – but at all times a major influence was resources. The Aragonese kings did not always have to rely on the kinds of revenue, such as income from the royal patrimony and extraordinary royal taxation, which any ruler in this period could expect. There were occasional windfalls. James II had most of the Templars' extensive Aragonese possessions in his hands for ten years from the end of 1307, and some costs of the Almería campaign were met from Templar revenues, even though not all of this income could be used for the king's own needs. Mary of Lusignan's dowry amounted to 300,000 besants, although difficulties were encountered in securing full payment. Help might also be obtained from the papacy, even for campaigns which were not against Muslims: James II received grants of tenths to be paid by the Aragonese Church for the conquest of Sardinia and Corsica. But the papacy, which had numerous calls on income and which was not altogether convinced of the sincerity of Spanish proposals, did not always satisfy Aragonese demands. In 1329, for example, John XXII was prepared to offer much less than Alfonso IV's envoys were seeking. Apart from such occasional gains, help could also be expected from Mallorca when it was a vassal kingdom. It provided aid both against Granada and against Sardinia, supplying twenty galleys for the conquest of the latter.

Yet, although extra assistance might be obtained in various ways, the Aragonese kings' own resources were limited. By the early fourteenth century Catalonia had, of course, acquired importance commercially and industrially. Barcelona merchants traded across the Mediterranean, with consuls established not only in ports in North Africa but even as far afield as Beirut by the mid-fourteenth century, and later at Damascus. The production and export of Catalan textiles were growing and developing. Yet in 1300 the Crown of Aragon was territorially less than a third of the size of León/Castile, and the population of the latter was probably several times that of Aragonese lands. War placed considerable strains on resources, especially in the reign of Pedro IV, and it was not easy to amass the necessary funds. Demands for taxes provoked lengthy discussions in sessions of the *cortes*: in 1364 Pedro was writing that meetings at Barcelona were 'extraordinarily slow and difficult'.[9] As was apparent in 1358, some Catalans objected to providing aid for the defence of Aragon and Valencia, and there was also opposition to financing campaigns in Sardinia. The sums granted were sometimes considerably less than those requested by the king. In 1368 Pedro sought 425,000 *librae* of the *cortes* of

[9] Pere III, *Chron.*, p. 13.

Barcelona, but was promised only 150,000 *librae*. Those attending the Catalan *cortes* in 1372–3 would agree only to a loan to meet costs in Sardinia. Nor was it easy to obtain the taxes which had been agreed or imposed. In 1341 several Catalan cities and towns resisted the imposition of the subsidy which had been granted at an assembly in the previous year, and there were also various other attempts to avoid payment. Some Jews, whose communities bore a heavy burden of financial demands, saw emigration as a solution to excessive demands. Towns sold pensions in order to help meet their obligations, thus creating long-term burdens, but kings had difficulty in obtaining funds as rapidly as they wished. To raise cash quickly it was necessary for them to resort to loans. Even then the pay of troops was often in arrears. According to Pedro IV's *Chronicle*, in 1364 even church ornaments in Valencia were requisitioned in order to make payment.[10]

The financial strains which were experienced are made obvious by the alienations of royal patrimony which were taking place at various times during the fourteenth century, although at the end of the century Martin I took measures to recover earlier losses, after he had found 'all our revenues and royal rights, through no action or fault of our own, alienated and dissipated'.[11] The problems of resources are further illustrated by the limited size of the fleets which the Aragonese kings could mobilise. Although Aragonese policy in the fourteenth century was frequently focused on the western Mediterranean, and sea power was necessary, the fleets which the Aragonese kings could themselves support in the first half of the century rarely comprised more than thirty galleys: some rival powers could fit out rather larger fleets. Inevitably, the Aragonese were often dependent for success on alliances, whether it was with Hugh, Judge of Arborea, and other elements in Sardinia when the island was initially conquered in 1323–4 or with the French and others when the Castilian threat was overcome in the 1360s.

The problem of resources is to be seen against the broader background of general economic trends. The overpopulation which has been posited for some parts of Europe at the end of the thirteenth century seems not, however, to have been generally characteristic of Aragonese lands. Although holdings in some parts of Catalonia were apparently tending to become smaller, settlement charters were still being issued for new colonisation in the late thirteenth and early fourteenth centuries, although not on the same scale as earlier, while in northern Catalonia some lords were having to make concessions in order to preserve and attract manpower. In 1292 the Templars were even seeking to dispose of their lordship at Puigreig, on the upper Llobregat, because they could not find settlers and it was no longer profitable. Nor did Aragonese lands

---

[10] Ibid., pp. 554–5.   [11] Ferrer i Mallol (1970–1), p. 355.

suffer as severely from harvest failures in the years 1315–17 as other parts of the west. But crop failures did occur in the first half of the century; in the city of Valencia there were grain shortages in 1310–14 and 1324–9. But 1333 was referred to in the statute book of the church of Gerona as 'the first bad year',[12] and was followed towards the end of the next decade by the Black Death. The impact of plague in the mid-fourteenth century varied. On the basis of entries in episcopal registers it has been calculated that about 40 per cent of beneficed clergy in the diocese of Barcelona died between June and September 1348, while in the year from May 1348 to April 1349 the figure was 60 per cent. On the other hand at least fourteen of seventeen Hospitallers who attended a chapter in 1346 were still alive in 1349; and Villarreal in Valencia appears to have escaped altogether. Overall figures are, however, difficult to obtain: tax assessments, commonly employed to estimate population, are infrequent and hard to interpret; calculations vary. One estimate is that ten years after the first onset of plague the population of Catalonia was 20 per cent smaller than before the Black Death.[13] There may have been some recovery in the 1350s, and towns benefited from migration from the countryside, but long-term recovery was hindered by recurrences of plague, as in 1362–3, 1371, 1381, 1384 and later, while in 1358 there was a plague of locusts, and drought in 1374. In some districts the effects of plague were, of course, exacerbated by the consequences of war: at the Aragonese *cortes* of 1365–6 the Hospitaller castellan of Amposta and the master of Calatrava complained of the losses caused by Henry of Trastámara's forces and by the French companies.[14] The population of Catalonia continued in fact to fall in the fifteenth century, although in Aragon and Valencia there was stabilisation and recovery.

The result of plague and other factors was that lands, especially marginal holdings, were left vacant, rents were lost and there was a shortage of labour. Pedro IV claimed that as a result of the plague in Roussillon and Cerdagne 'our revenues have been very greatly reduced',[15] although he seems to have exaggerated the importance of this factor. An immediate response was to enact legislation to control wages and prices; but this was ineffective, and the decrees passed in the *cortes* of Saragossa in 1350 were quashed two years later. Both wages and prices rose for several decades. In the long term there were changes in the nature of production. In some districts sheep rearing increased in importance, and crops such as saffron were developed: from the mid-fourteenth century saffron was exported in quantity from both Catalonia and Aragon. The economy of the latter was becoming more commercialised.

In seeking to ensure a labour supply, lords adopted varying approaches. In

---

[12] Batlle (1988), p. 87.   [13] Nadal i Oller (1983), p. 66.   [14] Laliena Corbera (1987), p. 218.
[15] Küchler (1969), p. 68.

Valencia, declining population brought pressure from lords to restrict movement and emigration of Muslim peasants: the culmination of this trend was
marked by a decree of the Valencian *cortes* in 1403, banning all emigration. It
has been argued that in Aragon, especially the more northerly parts, the Black
Death helped to produce a deterioration in the status of the peasantry: the
right of maltreatment (*ius maletractandi*) became generalised and peasants were
bound to the soil. But detailed studies have not always revealed a situation
which was deteriorating in all respects. On Calatravan estates in Bajo Aragón
there is no evidence of binding to the soil, and the Hospitallers, at least in the
short term, reduced rents in all parts of their Aragonese province in order to
retain labour. They realised that 'it is more to the benefit of us and our order
to lower and reduce rents and tributes than that the said possessions should
revert to the direct control of the order'.[16] In Aragon there was peasant discontent, but this found only sporadic and isolated expression.

On some estates in Catalonia, rents were reduced, but coercion was also
employed: the right of maltreatment was exploited in the more northerly parts
of the principality, and redemption payments for freeing from serfdom were
increased. Peasant discontent was voiced in the later decades of the century.
But it has not always been accepted that the main cause of unrest was harsh
conditions in the period after the Black Death. Some have argued that the chief
issue concerned empty manses (*masos rònecs*) in fertile areas, which well-established peasants were trying to annex on favourable terms. This provoked a
reaction on the part of lords, who wanted them to be separate properties carrying heavy burdens. This was probably an issue in some cases, but it seems
that a more general cause of conflict was provided by large redemption payments and the other *mals usos,* which were the other dues of serfdom.
Discontented Catalan peasants found a supporter in the king. In 1388 John I
sought to bring about the abolition of servile dues, proposing that peasants
should compensate lords for the rights lost by the latter. But it was not until
almost a century later that serfdom was abolished in Catalonia.

These were not the only signs of economic difficulties in the second half of
the fourteenth century. There was also monetary instability. In 1346 Pedro IV
had ordered the minting of a gold florin, but this was rapidly devalued and in
1365 was worth less than three-quarters of its original value. But the silver *croat*
was not devalued, and this led to a flight of silver. Later there were bank failures.
Between 1381 and 1383 a number of firms in Barcelona, including the Descaus,
Pasqual and Esquerit banks, overextended their credit to the crown and became
bankrupt, as did the Gualbes bank in 1406. It has also been argued that capital
was in the later fourteenth century being deflected from commercial enterprises

---

[16] Luttrell (1966), p. 503.

into land and annuities, and attention has further been drawn to riots in Barcelona in 1391 when the rich as well as the Jews were attacked: one factor at this time has been seen to be a decline in industrial wages. A crisis of confidence towards the end of the century has been postulated. The measures taken in response included the establishment of a public bank (*taula de canvi*) in Barcelona in 1401 and protectionist decrees. Some have seen these problems as part of a long-term 'decline of Catalonia' in the later Middle Ages, beginning in the mid-fourteenth century. This question cannot, of course, be discussed without an examination of fifteenth-century developments, but it may be noted that widely diverging views about the chronology, continuity and inevitability of decline have been expressed.

Internal political problems, as well as economic trends, affected – and were in turn affected by – relations with outside powers. Fourteenth-century Aragonese kings at times faced opposition from various individuals and groups, including members of their own family, the Aragonese Union and the Templars. The Aragonese Union, prominent in opposition to the crown in the 1280s, was revived in April 1301, when sixty-six nobles met in Saragossa; among the leaders was James of Jérica, a son of James I. The avowed aim of the movement was to secure the sums which the king owed the nobles for their *caballerías*, although there were probably other causes of discontent, including decrees contrary to their interests, which had been issued in the *cortes* of 1300. But the range of demands was much narrower than in the 1280s, and the movement attracted little support; in 1301, unlike the 1280s, no towns joined the Union. James II was able to overcome the threat by obtaining judgement against his opponents by the justiciar of Aragon in the *cortes* held later in 1301.

Six years later James II was faced by the problem of arresting and detaining the Templars in his realms, who had been accused of apostasy, heresy and immorality. Although the king was able to take over the bulk of the Order's property without difficulty, most of the brothers shut themselves up in their castles, and a series of sieges had to be undertaken, some – such as that at Monzón – lasting as long as a year and a half. Some Templar castles were still holding out when preparations were being made for the Almería campaign. When the Temple was abolished in 1312, the king claimed to see a potential threat from the Hospitallers, for Clement V wanted to assign Templar possessions in Aragonese lands, as in other countries, to the Hospital. Both orders held extensive estates in James II's realms, and the king argued that 'if two sets of castles and strongholds, vassals and rents, such as the said orders have, were brought together in the said kingdoms, the strength would be such that the king, his people and his lands could be in very great danger'.[17] He wanted

---

[17] Finke (1907), II, p. 213.

Templar properties in his realms to be used to create a new magistracy of the Spanish military order of Calatrava. The compromise which was eventually reached with John XXII in 1317 was that both Templar and Hospitaller properties in Valencia were to be used to endow a new order called Montesa, which was to adopt Calatravan observances, but that Templar possessions in Aragon and Catalonia should pass to the Hospital. In fact, the Hospital gained much more than it lost, and came to hold very extensive properties, especially in the more southerly parts of Aragon and Catalonia. Yet James secured certain safeguards from the Hospitallers and any envisaged threat to royal power did not materialise.

It was shortly after the Hospitallers had taken over Templar possessions that James, the heir to the throne, was received briefly into their order, after he had reluctantly married – and immediately abandoned – Eleanor, daughter of Fernando IV of Castile. These events, which took place in late 1319, marked the culmination of a period of difficult relations between James II and his heir, whose conduct did not measure up to his father's expectations, and who later, in 1320, transferred to Montesa and resided at the monastery of Stas. Creus, only to be reported in 1323 to be living a depraved life in Valencia. Yet, although there had been a family crisis, and relations with Castile were further strained, the political consequences were not disastrous. Greater practical problems arose from the later marriage of Eleanor to Alfonso IV in 1329, two years after the death of his first wife, Teresa of Entenza, who was the mother of his heir Pedro. Eleanor sought in due course to further the interests of the sons she had by Alfonso, and he agreed to create a marquisate of Tortosa for Fernando, and also gave lands in Murcia. But proposals for further concessions in Valencia aroused hostility, and were abandoned. At the beginning of his reign, however, Pedro IV sought to deprive Eleanor as well as his half-brothers of their rights; but internal opposition, coupled with difficult relations with Castile at the time, led him to abandon his plans. Fernando continued to be intermittently troublesome up to the time of his murder, at Pedro IV's instigation, in 1363, and played a role in the conflict involving the Aragonese Union in the later 1340s.

This episode, which occurred while the Aragonese king was still being troubled by James III of Mallorca, was prompted by Pedro's provision for the succession, although this was not the sole cause of discontent. The opposition movement has also been seen partly as a protest against the preponderance of Catalan interests in the Crown of Aragon and against attempts to strengthen royal power. There was a demand for the removal of Pedro's advisers from Catalonia and Roussillon, who were seen to favour the more autocratic teachings of Roman law. Pedro's wife Mary of Navarre had only produced daughters, and after taking legal advice in 1346, the king nominated his daughter

Constance as his successor. Mary then produced a son, but both mother and child quickly died, and although Pedro then married Eleanor of Portugal, opposition was voiced on the matter of the succession, and was led by Pedro's brother James of Urgel. The Aragonese Union was revived and was joined on this occasion by many towns as well as nobles, and support was also obtained in Valencia. Pedro was obliged to accept the demands made by the Union at an assembly held in Saragossa, and although James died in November 1347, the leadership of the opposition was assumed by his half-brother Fernando. Pedro was forced to accept him as his heir. A royal victory in Aragon was, however, gained in battle with Catalan support at Epila in July 1348, and opposition in Valencia was similarly overcome by force a few months later.

Later in Pedro's reign further problems were occasioned by another royal marriage. In 1377 the king took as his fourth wife his mistress Sibilla of Fortià, daughter of a minor noble from Ampurias. She sought to promote her friends and followers. Her brother Bernard became king's chamberlain, and posts were given to members of minor families from Ampurias. Not only the king's sons, John and Martin, but also other nobles, including Pedro's son-in-law John, count of Ampurias, expressed their discontent, and resort was made to violence. The seriousness of the crisis was, however, lessened by the heir to the throne's refusal to take up arms against his father, even though relations between them had long been strained: John's own marriage in 1380 to Yolande of Bar had itself added to friction.

Although Aragonese kings encountered opposition from various quarters, the fourteenth century was not characterised by constant and widespread armed resistance by the baronage to the crown, and it has been said of the Catalan nobility that in this period it was undergoing a transition from using force towards an employment of parliamentary procedures to secure its ends.[18] The activities of the *cortes* could therefore be seen as a further expression of ambitions on the part of both nobles and towns. Just as Aragon, Catalonia and Valencia were distinct in law and administration, so each had its own *cortes*, although occasionally joint sessions for all three regions were held, as at Monzón in 1362–3. In the early years of the century these assemblies included clergy, nobles and townsmen, with the upper and lower nobility forming two separate estates in the Aragonese *cortes*. Meetings of the *cortes* certainly provided opportunities for seeking to ensure that rights and privileges were upheld, and the defence of liberties was a constant theme: an example from the very beginning of the century is provided by James II's agreement in the Catalan *cortes* to the establishment of a commission in each vicariate to ensure that the decrees of previous *cortes* were observed by royal officials. But in

---

[18] Sobrequés Vidal (1970–1), p. 522.

assessing the precise significance of the *cortes* in the relations of king and subjects in the fourteenth century it is necessary to consider the frequency of meetings and the extent of the aspirations of those participating. In the 1280s attempts had certainly been made to give the *cortes* a considerable role in government. Both in Aragon and Catalonia promises were extracted from Pedro III to hold annual meetings and he also made concessions about consultation on matters of war and peace and on new legislation, while in 1287 Alfonso III had further been obliged by the Aragonese Union to accept that the *cortes* could nominate members of his council. These concessions made in the 1280s have often been seen as marking a significant stage in the development of the *cortes* in the Crown of Aragon, and contrasts have been drawn between the powers enjoyed by the *cortes* in the Aragonese realms and those possessed by assemblies in León/Castile.

Yet the importance of the concessions made in the 1280s is to be measured by their long-term consequences. James II summoned the Aragonese *cortes* at the beginning of his reign in 1291, but the next meeting was not until 1300; and similarly in Catalonia no *cortes* were summoned for eight years after 1292. In the meantime, of course, decisions on matters such as Sicily and Sardinia had been taken. Although a clause about annual sessions was included in the decrees of the Catalan *cortes* in 1300,[19] in the intervening years there appear to have been no strong protests. The concessions made in the 1280s were mainly of short-term significance. The demands made then can be seen primarily as responses to a particular set of circumstances, when royal policy was arousing opposition, and it was felt that the king needed to be restrained. Once the immediate cause of opposition – in this case the Sicilian involvement – had lost its early importance, there was a readiness to allow the king to resume control. It is difficult to see in the *cortes* as consultative bodies at this stage clear evidence of pactist ideas, to which some historians have attached importance.

The summoning of *cortes* in the early decades of the fourteenth century continued to be irregular. It was apparently on the initiative of James, who was more punctilious in observing obligations than many other rulers, that in 1307 it was agreed that the Aragonese *cortes* should be held once every two years, and a few years earlier it had similarly been decreed that the Catalan and Valencian *cortes* should meet every three years. But sessions at such intervals could not ensure meaningful consultation on major issues; and these rulings were not rigidly observed in practice. Only nine meetings of the Aragonese *cortes* were held in the whole of James II's reign, and although the Catalan *cortes* assembled more frequently, the stipulated sessions did not always take place. In James's

---

[19] *Cortes de los antiguos reinos de Aragón y de Valencia y principado de Cataluña*, I, p. 170.

reign, moreover, by no means all those who were summoned actually attended: attendance was seen by some as a burden rather than an opportunity.

The pattern remained the same in the reign of Alfonso IV, who did not summon a *cortes* in Aragon between 1328 and 1336. Yet the demands made in the 1280s could act as a precedent, and be revived when there were new causes of opposition. When the Aragonese Union was reconstituted in 1347, fresh demands were made for annual meetings, and for the confirmation of the Privilege of the Union, which had given the *cortes* the right to nominate the king's council. In this instance the demands were overcome by force, and at the *cortes* of Saragossa in 1348 the Privilege of the Union, though not the General Privilege of 1283, was destroyed. Yet it is questionable whether the events of 1347–8 signify a changing attitude in the long term on the part of the Aragonese aristocracy and towns towards participation as a group in government. They were again merely reacting to particular circumstances.

In much of Pedro IV's reign, however, meetings of the *cortes* were called frequently, and sessions were often long-lasting. But this was because of financial necessity occasioned by war against Castile and in Sardinia rather than because of pressure from subjects; and some of those summoned absented themselves, especially when sessions were prolonged. Repeated requests for money did, however, provide an opportunity for the *cortes* to exact concessions from the king. Control over the collection and administration of the taxes granted in assemblies was to be exercised mainly by committees of the *cortes*. These responsibilities were being taken out of the crown's hands. A committee or *diputació* of the Catalan *cortes* had already begun to emerge for this purpose around 1300, though it was at first only of a temporary nature; but repeated grants of taxes to Pedro IV, coupled with the establishment of a public debt, served to give it permanence: the year 1359 has often been seen as the time when it became firmly established. Similar committees also began to develop in Aragon and Valencia, but only in the later decades of the fourteenth century. Although the primary functions of these committees were fiscal, this role served to give them a voice in the conduct of war, as was spelt out on various occasions in the second half of the century. In 1352 the Catalan *diputats* were to decide how many galleys and men were required for the war against Genoa and to ensure that they were used only for that purpose, and in 1365 these officials were to appoint the captain of the fleet. In that year it was also demanded that the money assigned to the king should be used only for the defence of Catalonia, and restrictions were similarly placed on the use of the 700 mounted troops for which the Aragonese *cortes* was paying in 1357. The granting of subsidies could, of course, also be made dependent on the redress of general grievances: this condition was imposed when a Catalan subsidy was granted in 1365.

Yet although the king's freedom of action was being restricted, the activities of the *cortes* in Pedro IV's reign may be interpreted mainly as a reaction to excessive demands for taxes: participants were above all seeking to safeguard their financial interests. Restrictions on the king were not always taken as far as possible: grants were not on every occasion made dependent on redress of grievances, and the actions of the *cortes* affected the implementation of policy rather than its formulation. It is true that in 1356 the *cortes* meeting at Perpignan advised the king to make peace with Genoa and proposed that no other war should be begun without the counsel of the *cortes*; but Pedro was not bound by this advice.

In the later part of the century, *cortes* were again summoned less frequently. Complaints about royal misgovernment voiced in Barcelona and Valencia towards the end of John I's reign could not be expressed in the *cortes*, because the king was not then summoning such assemblies. Martin I called only two Aragonese *cortes* in a reign of fourteen years, and no Catalan *cortes* were held between 1388 and 1405. Reality did not altogether coincide with the picture presented at that time by the theorist Eiximenis. Meetings of the *cortes* could, of course, deal with a wide variety of issues, but their powers were still limited, as were the aspirations of those participating. Even if there had been a wish to assert a greater role for the *cortes*, attempts would have been hampered by the practice of summoning separate meetings for each part of the Aragonese realms.

The king not only faced opposition from subjects: he also had to try to maintain peace and order among them. Quarrels and feuds between noble families commonly led to violence and disorder, especially in the later decades of the century. One conflict involving several leading Aragonese families began in 1378 when Brianda of Luna left her husband Lope Jiménez de Urrea, claiming that the marriage had not been consummated, and went through a form of marriage with Louis Cornel, while in the following year, in a vain attempt to halt a long-standing Valencian feud, Pedro IV agreed to act as judge in a duel between Bernard of Vilaragut and Jimeno Pérez de Arenós.

Conflicts also occurred within towns and cities. Many enjoyed a certain degree of self-government, which was usually in the hands of an oligarchy, though none possessed the full independence of an Italian city. Struggles were sometimes between family-led factions which were rivals for power and standing, as in the case of the Tarines and Bernaldinos in Saragossa, or the Sayas and Liñanes in Calatayud. In Huesca early in the century there was, more unusually, conflict between the lesser nobility, who normally had no role in town government, and other inhabitants: by an agreement made in 1322 the *caballeros* and *infanzones* gained a share in office holding in the city. In Barcelona, municipal rights were in the hands of a council (*consell*) of a hundred and an executive of five *consellers*. Although various trades and callings were represented in the council, the patriciate of 'honoured citizens' had the greatest influence: in 1334 they provided sixty-four members of the council, and they also monopolised the office of *conseller*. But in 1386 Pedro IV approved a plan which proposed the appointment of six *consellers*, of whom two were to be patricians, two merchants and two craftsmen, while the *consell* was to be chosen in the same proportions. Yet it has been questioned how far there was class conflict: it has been suggested that there was rivalry between elite factions, which might ally with others who aspired to office in order to obtain their own ends.[20] John I, however, quickly abandoned the new arrangements, and changes introduced in 1391 were similarly short-lived.

Both in towns and in the countryside the effects of banditry and habitual violence were also felt. The problem was probably made worse in the later part of the century by the presence of groups of unemployed mercenaries and by rural discontent. A decree issued by the town authorities in Daroca in 1384 related that 'many persons, covered with masks and disguises, were going along the roads and through the districts of the town and villages of Daroca, seizing, robbing and committing all kinds of excesses'.[21] In frontier regions there was also the problem of cross-border raiding. Parts of Valencia were commonly raided by Muslims from Granada. The geography of the region allowed easy infiltration, and local Muslims sometimes gave assistance.

In the fourteenth century the Crown of Aragon remained a land of three religions, and this was a further source of tension. In Valencia Muslims comprised the majority of the population, although the balance was changing as a result of Muslim emigration and Christian settlement. It has been suggested that Muslims made up about 30 per cent of the inhabitants of Aragon,[22] while in Catalonia they were numerous in the lower Ebro valley, but not in the more northerly districts. Jews were fewer – one estimate is that in Aragon they comprised nearly 5 per cent of the population,[23] although their wealth was in proportion probably greater.

The Muslim population included numerous slaves, although not all slaves in the fourteenth century were Muslims: some Greeks and Mongols from the eastern Mediterranean were then being acquired by slave-owners in Aragonese lands. The total numbers of slaves are not known, but in Mallorca during the later fourteenth century they were numerous enough to be seen as a threat to law and order. In 1374 Pedro IV ordered the expulsion of all those whose services were not needed. Many slaves were Muslim – and occasionally other – captives taken in war or piratical raids in the western Mediterranean, but the

---

[20] Fernández Armesto (1992), p. 28.   [21] Sarasa Sánchez (1981), p. 117.   [22] Boswell (1977), p. 7.
[23] Motis Dolader (1990), p. 10.

status could be inherited, and enslavement was also the penalty for certain offences, while free Muslims in Aragonese lands might find themselves arbitrarily enslaved by Christians. Yet slavery was not necessarily a permanent condition. Muslim slaves who fled could expect aid from their co-religionists, and treaties with Muslim powers, such as those between Aragon and Granada in 1377 and 1382, commonly provided for exchanges of captives. Redemption was also common. By the fourteenth century officials known as *exeas* and *alfaqueques* frequently acted as intermediaries in ransoming captives in both Christian and Muslim lands. Gratuitous emancipation by a slave-owner was also possible, but baptism of a Muslim slave subject to a Christian master did not automatically lead to freedom, though it might facilitate it.

The fourteenth century in some respects saw a tightening of restrictions on non-Christians, although these were not always rigorously enforced in practice. Jewish and free Muslim communities enjoyed a certain degree of autonomy, but the privileges which had been granted to Valencian Muslims at the time of their negotiated surrender in the thirteenth century were not always observed: some officials were imposed rather than elected, and in practice many judicial cases were not decided by Muslim officials or according to Muslim law. In the larger centres of population Muslims and Jews already normally lived in separate quarters, and legislation existed forbidding certain contacts, especially of a sexual nature. To make clear the differences of person, laws on Jewish dress had been enacted in the thirteenth century, but it was apparently not until around 1300 that general legislation of this kind was passed for Muslims; thus in 1301 a distinctive hairstyle for them was decreed in the *cortes* of Aragon and Catalonia. Towards the end of the fourteenth century it was further decreed that Muslims should wear a distinctive badge on their sleeves. It is not altogether clear to what extent regulations about dress and hairstyle were enforced. In Valencia the latter issue is mentioned much more frequently than dress in the surviving documents; but in 1387 the Muslim *aljama* of Huesca stated that the hairstyle known as the *garceta*, which Muslims were expected to display in the second half of the fourteenth century, had not been customary there. Certainly, in practice segregation was by no means absolute. Individuals did not always reside in the districts assigned to their own religion; Christian prostitutes plied their trade in *morerías*; and Christians and Muslims frequented the same gaming houses and taverns. There were inevitably contacts through trade and commerce; Christians, including kings, commonly resorted to Jewish and Muslim doctors; and although Jews no longer occupied the official positions in royal administration which they had often held earlier, Aragonese kings still made use of them at court, and not only for administrative purposes: Pedro IV employed Jewish astronomers and astrologers as well as cartographers.

Religious restrictions were also imposed. In 1311 Clement V banned the

Muslim call to prayer and also pilgrimages to Mecca by Muslims living in Christian territories. In the Crown of Aragon the first of these decrees found support among some prelates and inquisitors, and amongst the populace. James II therefore decreed in 1318 that the public call to prayer should cease. But later repetitions of this decree indicate that it was not altogether effective, and in 1357 – at a time when he needed the loyalty of the Valencian Muslims, as well as money – Pedro IV allowed the call to be made at Játiva in return for payment. There is also evidence to show Muslim pilgrims leaving for Mecca throughout the century from ports such as Barcelona. It was also in the fourteenth century that inquisitors attempted to extend their jurisdiction to Jews, in matters such as violations by Jews of their own religion and the giving of support to individuals reverting to Judaism from Christianity. Both Jews and Muslims were also expected to show respect to Christianity. In 1300 it was decreed that Jews or Muslims who were in a street when a Corpus Christi procession passed should either kneel or hide themselves away, while in Huesca Muslim metal workers were in 1307 forbidden to work on Sundays and festivals when services were being held in the nearby church of San Lorenzo because Christian worshippers were disturbed by the noise.

In placing restrictions on Jews and Muslims, the crown was usually responding to pressures from others. Both Jews and Muslims were the 'royal treasure' and it was in the crown's interest to provide support and protection for them, while at the same time heavily taxing them. Aragonese kings sought to check attacks on Muslim communities and also the growing number of assaults which took place on the Jewish population. Apart from frequent instances of violence against Jews in Holy Week, attacks were made on the Jewish communities at Jaca and Monclús in 1320 when the Pastoreaux moved from southern France into Spain. The arrival of the Black Death prompted further assaults on Jews in Barcelona, Cervera, Tárrega and several other places, and anti-Jewish riots occurred in Mallorca in 1370 and 1374. Most seriously, in 1391 violence against Jews spread from Castile to Valencia, Catalonia and Mallorca. Many Jews were killed – the figure in the city of Mallorca was put at 300 and in Valencia at 250 – and many others converted to Christianity, with some *aljamas* ceasing to exist, although attempts were later made to restore them. It was, of course, not only Jews who were subject to attack on such occasions. In 1320 James II, anticipating that Muslims might also suffer, gave orders for their protection, and in 1391 there was a short-lived attempt to assault the *morería* of Valencia. There was further violence against Muslims in 1398, when a crusade against North Africa was being preached. Muslims in Valencia were widely suspected of sympathising with, and aiding, the rulers of Granada and Muslim raiders from Granada, and suffered assaults, particularly at times of hostility between Aragon and Granada, as in 1331–2, when the Valencia frontier was under attack. Muslims also suffered insults from the Christian populace: in 1363, for example, it was reported that the Christians of Huesca were letting their pigs root in the Muslim cemetery there.

Attacks on Jewish communities are to be explained at least in part by the demonisation of the Jews which was taking place in Aragonese lands by the end of the thirteenth century, just as had happened earlier elsewhere. In 1294 there were rumours in Saragossa that a Christian child had been murdered by Jews, and the discovery of the body of a baby boy in the Jewish *call* of Barcelona in 1301 prompted fears of an accusation of ritual murder; and a claim of this kind was investigated in Mallorca in 1309. There were also assertions that Jews had stolen or acquired the consecrated host – one case occurred in Barcelona in 1367 – and that wells had been poisoned by them, as was claimed at Teruel in 1321, while in 1348 they were thought to have caused the plague. No doubt there were also material reasons for attacks: Christians had an exaggerated view of the numbers of Jews involved in money-lending, and complained of abuses of usury laws. During attacks acknowledgements of debt might be destroyed and wealth seized. In 1391 assaults on Jews in some parts of Catalonia were linked with social protest, while in Mallorca at that time opposition began as rural unrest inspired by economic grievances. In some instances, as at Montalbán in 1391, attacks apparently did not extend beyond robbery and pillage. But, although there were other factors at work, the killing and forced conversion of Jews, reminiscent of earlier popular crusades, is an indication of attitudes towards the Jewish faith and of the desire to eradicate it. *Convivencia*, which in any case had never implied full acceptance of other religions, was under strain, and tension between religious groups was growing. Localised tensions of various kinds were characteristic of the Crown of Aragon in the fourteenth century.

CASTILE, NAVARRE AND PORTUGAL

Peter Linehan

TO fourteenth-century visitors from north of the Pyrenees the Spanish peninsula remained what it had always been, the land that persisted in disregarding western Europe's familiar categories and disappointing its reasonable expectations. In 1341, when Philip of Evreux, king of Navarre, set out from northern France – the usual haunt of fourteenth-century kings of Navarre – to assist Alfonso XI of Castile in wresting Algeciras from the Moors, the authorities at Tudela – *his* authorities – naturally enough made a financial contribution. But they also spent money on ensuring that their Christian king's crusading army should not disturb the peace and quiet of his Moorish subjects there. In the same spirit, in 1357 Philip's son, Carlos II, petitioned Pere III of Aragon on behalf of two of his *mudéjar* subjects en route for Mecca. Although a flagrant breach of the prohibition decreed at the general council of Vienne, his intervention was not exceptional. Twelve years later, even further into Christian Spain, while the 'crusading' Enrique II was hunting down his half-brother Pedro I, the vicar-general of the bishop of Burgos had a group of non-tithe-payers to deal with, which was not exceptional either – except that these defaulters were all reported to be 'Moors of the said city'.[1]

By 1400, when to judge by the fiscal evidence Jews were about ten times as visible as Moors,[2] the emulsion of peninsular *convivencia* was beginning to separate out, precipitating animosities which made Iberia more readily recognisable to visitors from Lincoln and Bremen. Yet as a rule peninsular fights continued to be fights between Christian and Christian, as they had been a hundred years before. In the second of his *Siete Partidas* Alfonso X had described the 'many ills' that tended to befall a kingdom during a royal minority,[3] and in the thirty years that followed the premature death of his son Sancho

---

[1] Harvey (1990), pp. 141–2; Boswell (1977), p. 292; Tanner, ed., *Decrees*, p. 380; Peña Pérez, *Documentación*, p. 262. [2] Suárez Fernández (1977–82), I, p. 359.
[3] *Part*, II.15.3 (ed. II, pp. 133–4).

IV in April 1295 all of them were realised as the fault-lines of the regime upon which Alfonso had sought to construct an empire revealed themselves. At the instigation of the rulers of Portugal and of Aragon, the kingdoms which chance and sentiment as much as dynastic considerations had recombined in 1230 threatened to go their different ways, and the persistently provincial character of peninsular society reasserted itself again.

In April 1295 Fernando IV was a child of six, illegitimate in the eyes of the Church, and, in the estimation of all those both within and beyond the peninsula with reasons of their own for supporting the de la Cerda claim to his throne, a second-generation usurper. Over the next century bastards were to establish new dynasties both in Castile and in Portugal. But in 1295 bastardy was still held to count, and chief amongst those who insisted on its counting were the new king's uncle and great-uncle, the infantes Juan and Enrique. While the former, fresh from the siege of Tarifa where he had made common cause with the Marinid enemies of his brother Sancho IV, claimed the throne, the other – the bane of Alfonso X's early years who, having languished for twenty-six years in an Italian prison, in the summer of 1294 had returned to haunt the Castilian scene again – appropriated the tutorship. They were soon joined by other spectres from the past: Jaume II of Aragon and Dinis of Portugal, and the leaders of the great troublemaking families of the kingdom, all equally intent on exploiting the minority to their own territorial advantage. Diego López de Haro mounted an invasion from Aragon and made common cause with Juan Núñez de Lara.[4]

Against them stood the queen-mother María de Molina, then in her midthirties. In the account provided by the Chronicle of the reign partly compiled from chancery records in the 1340s, Sancho IV's widow emerges as the one fixed point in a turbulent age as well as a paragon of prudence and self-effacement. Indeed, according to the Chronicle, our principal source for the history of these years, Sancho IV's redoubtable widow could do no wrong: a plainly partisan view which has been canonised by María's modern biographer. Still, its account is well informed and circumstantial, and it is doubtless to be trusted in its report of the queen's jealous custody of her only asset, the precious person of the child-king. She would not surrender her son 'to any person in the world'. Not until the spring of 1297, and then only briefly, was he ever out of her keeping.[5]

Fernando IV reaped where his father had sown. By appealing to the kingdom's municipalities (concejos) in 1282 and fostering the creation of a nationwide alliance of them – the Hermandad general – the rebel infante Sancho

---

[4] Gaibrois de Ballesteros (1922–8), II, p. 393; NCMH, V, pp. 712–14; CFIV, p. 94b; González Mínguez (1976), pp. 29–33.   [5] CFIV, pp. 95a, 108b; Gaibrois de Ballesteros (1967).

had unleashed forces that were to dominate political affairs for the next fifty years. In the spring of 1295 the *concejos* were the arbiters of Castile's future, and accordingly D. Enrique – the 'great stirrer': *gran bolliciador* – toured the kingdom touting for their support, reminding them of the golden age which had ended on the death of his sainted father Fernando III, and preaching (the Chronicle's word) that the land was no longer governed as it deserved to be. Only at Avila and Segovia were his blandishments resisted.[6] In harping on the theme of lost innocence – a theme which came equally easily to the infante D. Juan[7] – however, he was preaching to the converted. At the meeting of the *cortes* which the queen summoned at Valladolid in July–August 1295, the *hermandades generales* of all the *concejos* of Castile and of León and Galicia – comprising sixty-four and thirty-three *concejos* respectively – expressed the same view of the recent past. Throughout the reigns of Alfonso X and (even more so) of Sancho IV they had suffered continuous injustice at the hands of their kings. Significantly, however, not only did they date their corporate existence from the moment in 1282 when the latter author of their misfortunes had 'added his voice to the general complaint', they also bound themselves to uphold the rights of Fernando IV, committed themselves to retributive measures against any *rico ome*, *infanzon* or *caballero* who threatened the interests of any one of them, specified what taxes they would pay and how often, and struck corporate seals. Further associations of thirty-three *concejos* of Extremadura and the archbishopric of Toledo, and of nine in the region of Murcia, adopted similar measures.[8]

The queen's fostering of the *concejos* both at the *cortes* of Valladolid and throughout the reign was therefore neither a quixotic gesture on her part nor yet a demonstration of 'democratic tendencies'.[9] It was rather an acknowledgement of the political corollary of the economic strength which the *concejos* had acquired since the beginning of the reign of Alfonso X.[10] Having initially found the gates of Valladolid barred against her, by sheer persistence she eventually had her way there, first securing the agreement of the municipal representatives to her fiscal requirements, and then receiving them one by one and hearing their grievances from early morning until mid-afternoon. The stamina she displayed amidst the August heats 'amazed' them – on account of her sex, presumably, rather than her age. She treated with them as though they were the representatives of sovereign states – which in the spring of 1295 was what they were – and in her dealings with them throughout her son's minority regularly outmanoeuvred the opposition, by means of a superior intelligence network

---

[6] *CFIV*, p. 94a. [7] Ibid., pp. 99ab, 107a.
[8] Benavides (1860), II, pp. 3–12; Suárez Fernández (1951); Moreta (1978), pp. 173–4.
[9] Thus Gaibrois de Ballesteros (1967), pp. 94, 200, 246. [10] Ruiz (1977).

exploiting civic divisions to secure the support of Palencia and other major centres. But what in 1295 was paramount was to have secured agreement to a vote of *moneda*, not only because she needed money (which she did) but also because – as the Chronicle emphasises more than once – the grant of money was an acknowledgement of authority.[11]

Meanwhile there was a high price to be paid. The demands of the Haro–Lara alliance, that the queen cancel the *cortes*, María of course refused to entertain. But to every other proposal she was ready to agree. In 1295 and the years that followed, compromise, concession and the purchase of support were the order of the day. Diego López de Haro recovered the lordship of Vizcaya which his murdered brother, Lope Díaz, had lost in 1288, and D. Enrique was entrusted with the tutorship – though not the person of the king. The price of loyalty was 2,000 *maravedís per diem*. In the first year of the reign 150 times that sum was paid to secure the allegiance of the Haro–Lara condominium.[12] And so it continued.

The *cortes* of Valladolid served notice of the extent to which the old order had collapsed. It was an assembly at which the municipalities were in the ascendant, and their objective was to ensure that the levers of power remained permanently in their hands. Archbishop Gonzalo Pérez of Toledo, the dominant figure of Sancho IV's later years, found himself excluded from its sessions, prelates and clergy were expelled from court, and the royal administration and custody of the seals were transferred to 'good men of the towns'. However, the municipal revolutionaries were neither exclusively nor specifically anti-clerical in character. Their ranks included representatives of the lower clergy as well as laymen, and their fire was directed as much at the secular nobility, the *ricos omes* and *fijosdalgo*, as at the clerical aristocracy. They were visionaries whose vision of the future encompassed, *inter alia*, the prohibition of further grants of royal land (*realengo*) out of the fisc and the entrusting to themselves of custody of the royal castles.[13] It is no accident that the proceedings of the 1295 *cortes* are shorter than those of any other assembly of this period. María de Molina was an accomplished listener.

As the Chronicle relates it, the story of the reign of Fernando IV is one of dizzying inconsequentiality with self-interest and lack of trust its principal features, and with the king's enemies returning to his obedience only in order to secure payments from the depleted treasury sufficient to finance the renewal of rebellion. As the king of Aragon's man reported towards the end of the reign, 'there is neither truth nor faith to be found here, on either side'.[14] Thus, in 1296–7 Fernán Rodríguez de Castro demanded the castle of Monteforte as

---

[11] *CFIV*, pp. 95b–6b, 97b, 102a.   [12] Ibid., pp. 96b, 104a.
[13] *Cortes*, I, pp. 130–3; Linehan (1993a), pp. 526, 543–8.   [14] Giménez Soler (1932), p. 392.

his price for supporting the king and as soon as he had been granted it brazenly defected to D. Juan. The complexity of the political formations that grouped and regrouped during the king's minority beggars all description, and since then students of the fourteenth century have consistently fought shy of providing one. Although over the last century various paraphrases of the Chronicle of the reign, and of that of Alfonso XI, have been published, there exists no adequate modern account of the kingdom of Castile between 1295 and 1348. And there is no adequate secondary literature to be summarised. The present survey, therefore, needs to be treated with more than the usual degree of scepticism.

With the anti-king, Alfonso de la Cerda, installed at Almazán, and Fernando IV remaining close to Valladolid and not venturing south into New Castile until 1303, the rulers of Portugal and Aragon allied themselves with D. Juan and Alfonso de la Cerda respectively and plotted the partition of the kingdom. In 1295–6 the two claimants agreed that León, Galicia and Seville be assigned to D. Juan, the kingdom of Murcia to the king of Aragon, and the city of Cuenca to the latter's brother the infante Pedro. In April 1296 Alfonso de la Cerda and his Aragonese allies invaded from the east and besieged Mayorga, D. Juan was declared king at León, Alfonso was declared king at Sahagún, Muhammad II of Granada recommenced hostilities in Andalusia, and D. Enrique interrupted his demanding programme of feasting and hunting to suggest to María de Molina that she marry the already married Aragonese infante:[15] a proposal which received very short shrift. The kingdom had lapsed into a state of nature. One member of the recently evicted elite, Jofré de Loaisa, wrote of a land empty of livestock, the haunt of hares, bandits and arsonists. Lacking both men and money, María was reduced to sending her children, the youngest a girl of three, to represent the king's cause in Toledo, Palencia and other strategic centres.[16]

In the event, the siege of Mayorga failed and the Aragonese withdrew in disarray – though the true victor here was not the young king but the grim reaper. In a famished land disease was endemic. The deadlier contagion, however, was that carried by the tutor D. Enrique, who at the *cortes* of Cuéllar – a *cortes* of the kingdom of Castile alone (February–March 1297) – proposed the sale of Tarifa, Sancho IV's solitary conquest in the south, back to the king of Granada. But, as before, the municipal representatives were persuaded by the queen to reject the infante's scheme and, in return for the appointment of twelve of their number to serve as a permanent consultative council, to vote a *servicio* for

[15] Moreover, the infante Pedro's wife was Guillerma de Moncada, the once-betrothed of Sancho IV!: Gaibrois de Ballesteros (1967), p. 104.

[16] *CFIV*, pp. 97–108; Jofré de Loaisa, *Crónica*, p. 177; González Mínguez (1976), pp. 31–56.

military purposes. Throughout the late 1290s the *concejos* and the taxes they voted proved María de Molina's mainstay. Although pressure from the west was eased somewhat by the double marriage treaty agreed at Alcañices in September 1297 – a thinly disguised form of hostage-taking involving the betrothal of Fernando IV to Constanza, daughter of Dinis of Portugal, and that of María de Molina's four-year-old daughter Beatriz to Afonso the Portuguese heir – even that degree of relief was only achieved at exorbitant cost. Fernando was effectively to provide his future wife's dowry, and Castile was to meet the expense of securing the (inevitably necessary) papal dispensation – and all for scant return. Because four years elapsed before the dispensation was secured, the treaty's expected benefits proved largely nugatory.

The principal achievements of the period 1297–1301 were, first, the mere survival of the king and thereafter, with the approach of his majority, the diplomatic campaign at the papal curia to secure his legitimisation – the very prospect of which, as well as disconcerting D. Enrique, had the effect of bringing D. Juan back into line. The sometime contender for the crown was now planning a bishop's move, James of Aragon's agent reported home in chess terms.[17] At the *cortes* of Valladolid (May 1300) D. Juan made his peace with his nephew, and collected his compensation: the greater part of the 10,000 marks of silver that Boniface VIII had set as the price of the bull of legitimisation (the pontiff very sensibly did not quote in Castilian currency) and which María de Molina had been husbanding and the *cortes* had voted for the purpose.[18] In September 1301 – by which time D. Juan had returned into opposition – the eagerly awaited bull was published together with others authorising the Portuguese marriage and a triennial grant of ecclesiastical *tercias*. Later that autumn, D. Enrique had it spread about that the bulls were all false. But in December Fernando IV celebrated his sixteenth birthday and achieved his majority.[19]

In his novel of chivalry, *El Libro del Cavallero Zifar*, Ferrán Martínez, archdeacon of Madrid and a member of the old guard which had been ousted in 1295, presented an allegorical account of the events which ensued, and the chronicler of the reign provided chapter and verse.[20] Passing straight from boyhood to playboyhood, the feckless monarch expressed his gratitude to María de Molina by allowing his uncle, D. Juan, to alienate him from her and subjecting her to indignities of every sort – though the requirement that she render accounts served only to reveal that it had been she who had financed the system throughout the minority, not it her. In August 1303 D. Enrique expired at the age of seventy-three, his marriage to the fifteen-year-old sister of Juan Núñez de Lara (as part of the price of the latter's return

---

[17] Gaibrois de Ballesteros (1967), p. 119.   [18] *CFIV*, pp. 117b, 119a.
[19] González Mínguez (1976), pp. 56–121.   [20] Hernández (1978); Linehan (1993a), pp. 537–42.

to the king's obedience in 1299) perhaps having hastened his demise. The role of troublemaker-in-chief to the Castilian court thus vacated soon devolved upon D. Juan Manuel, the son of Alfonso X's youngest brother. While he was in training for the post, however, D. Juan enjoyed ascendancy, and in 1301, as the wherewithal was being amassed for the purchase of the king's legitimisation, according to the Chronicle a quarter of the population perished from famine. As the Portuguese Hospitallers reported back home in 1298, conditions in Castile were 'hopeless, absolutely hopeless'.[21]

At Torrellas in August 1304, a summit attended by the kings of the three peninsular kingdoms, the ruler of Castile accepted the loss to Aragon of a substantial part of the ancient kingdom of Murcia – the coastal region between Valencia and Cartagena including Alicante and Orihuela. The Treaty of Elche (May 1305) attended to details.[22] However, although Alfonso de la Cerda had been deprived of Aragonese support, the de la Cerda threat had still not been eliminated. The legitimisation of Fernando IV had not removed that dynastic challenge to the throne. It would remain until 1331.

Fernando IV's later years – his early years as they appeared at the time – were largely taken up with hunting, sulking in the south and canvassing for funds. In order to pay his Castilian troops, the king had recourse to his Portuguese father-in-law, to his Portuguese wife (who sacrificed her three gold crowns and a brooch), to Edward II of England (without success) and when all else failed to the traditional practice of appropriating Church revenues – for which he was excommunicated on at least two occasions.[23] But at least he now had troops to pay. This was a new departure. The assault on the south in 1309 was the first to have been undertaken in almost twenty years – though after capturing Gibraltar it ended in failure in the following year when D. Juan and D. Juan Manuel abandoned the siege of Algeciras. For this defection the king never forgave D. Juan, and it was only María de Molina's timely intervention that prevented him from having his uncle murdered.[24]

On 7 September 1312 the king who according to the Chronicle ate too much meat expired after an early lunch at the age of twenty-six.[25] If for anything, the reign of Fernando IV was principally memorable for the number of meetings of the *cortes* which it witnessed. In a period of just seventeen years the *cortes* of Castile and León met almost annually, either separately or together.[26] But

---

[21] *CFIV*, p. 119a; Benavides (1860), II, p. 170 ('pravum et pravissimum').

[22] *CFIV*, p. 136a; González Mínguez (1976), pp. 179–201; Costa (1981); Torres Fontes (1990), pp. 483–5.

[23] Gaibrois de Ballesteros (1967), p. 168 (*CFIV*, c.14); Lopes (1970a), pp. 64–72; Benavides (1860) II, pp. 355–6, 820; Linehan (1983), p. 283.

[24] D. Juan departed from court in a hurry on the pretence of going off on a heron-hunt: *CFIV*, p. 166a–b.   [25] Ibid., p. 169b.   [26] González Mínguez (1976), p. 342.

although indicative of Fernando's straitened circumstances, the frequency of these gatherings did nothing to secure the triumph of the principles of democracy, so-called, enunciated in 1295. Indeed, in direct contravention of the Cuéllar legislation of 1297, at Grijota in March 1308 the king specifically repudiated those principles and acceded to the demands of the nobility that they should nominate his counsellors.[27] In 1307 Juan Núñez de Lara had defied Fernando's decree of exile and fortified himself at Tordehumos: an unheard-of act. The enforcement of the decree was regarded as the acid test of Fernando's authority. Fernando failed it. Juan Núñez remained.[28] The capitulation at Grijota confirmed the outcome. Anyway, by then the prescriptions of the first *cortes* of the reign were already a dead letter. By November 1301 at latest there were clerics back in the royal chancery,[29] and despite the Grijota agreement there they remained. In September 1311 an Aragonese agent reported home that D. Juan and his satellites were intent on making a clean sweep of the royal household by murdering certain of its members and restaffing it with creatures of their own who – it was reported – as well as bishops, *ricos homnes* and *cavalleyros*, were to include 'those men of the towns whom they would nominate'.[30]

The strategy of D. Juan and his oligarchical associates, as reported by the king of Aragon's man, greatly complicates the Marxist historian's task of establishing firm foundations in the social rubble of thirteenth-century Castile. The Castilian municipalities and their *concejos* were the playground of competing oligarchies whose divisions invited exploitation, as María de Molina so capably exploited them, and as they would continue to be exploited in meetings of the *cortes* for the rest of the century.[31] Regarding the *cortes* of the reign of Fernando IV, of course, their *cuadernos* do not acknowledge the existence of such divisions – any more than they record evidence of conspiracy to murder. The *cuadernos* are not the repository of such information; they are the record of the king's response to the petitions of the municipal *procuradores*. Nor, by the same token, can any certain inferences be drawn from them as to the king's own attitude with regard to anything at all. In the frequent meetings of the *cortes* during his reign, Fernando IV functioned merely as a conduit of public opinion. To that extent, the received wisdom that the legislation of the *cortes* of Valladolid of 1312 enshrined his 'political testament' appears simplistic.[32] All that distinguishes the measures envisaged on that occasion from what successive

---

[27] *CFIV*, pp. 158b–9b; González Mínguez (1976), pp. 254–61; O'Callaghan, 'Las cortes de Fernando IV', p. 324.   [28] *CFIV*, pp. 152–6; Giménez Soler (1932), p. 352.

[29] Benavides (1860), II, p. 192.

[30] '. . . e homnes de villyas aquellyos que ellyos le dirian': Giménez Soler (1932), p. 399.

[31] Mínguez (1989), p. 554.

[32] Colmeiro, *Cortes de los antiguos reinos*, p. 213; Bueno Domínguez (1991), pp. 128–9; González Mínguez (1976), pp. 317–22.

assemblies since 1295 had proposed for the reform of the judicial system is that they were the last of a reign throughout which the king had remained the creature of the territorial nobility. Had he lived longer he would merely have prevaricated further.

In August 1311 Fernando IV had fathered a son – of that there was no doubt, at least at the time[33] – and before dying he nominated his brother D. Pedro as the one-year-old Alfonso XI's tutor. On Fernando's death the kingdom was under interdict on account of his seizure of ecclesiastical revenues,[34] and a second minority in succession reactivated all the old rivalries within the royal family, with the difference that whereas in 1295 there had been just one mother and one great-uncle in play, because the action had so suddenly moved on one generation in 1312 the political scene was now rather more crowded. D. Juan claimed the tutorship from D. Pedro, and in April–June 1313 the *cortes* at Palencia divided into two factions in whose respective decrees something of the agenda of the rival infantes can be discerned. Thus, while D. Juan's meeting expelled all the late king's *privados* from court and entrusted the royal seals to laymen of the towns, María de Molina and D. Pedro provided for there to be four bishops amongst their permanent counsellors. And whereas the latter committed themselves to convene *cortes generales* of the whole kingdom every other year, the former provided instead for annual meetings of the regional *hermandades*, thereby accelerating the process of national fragmentation which underlay the anti-Jewish measures common to both groups.[35]

On the unexpected death in November 1313 of the youthful – though already scheming – queen-mother, Constanza of Portugal, the contenders consented to share the tutorship with María de Molina (Palazuelos, August 1314). But the process of social and territorial disintegration continued, symbolised by the hybrid *Hermandad general* established at the Burgos *cortes* (September 1315), comprising 109 *cavalleros* and 96 *concejos*, with 6 members of each group appointed as a permanent commission to shadow the tutors.[36] The *cortes* of Carrión (March 1317) received reports of widespread anarchy, the wholesale alienation of royal lands, a bankrupt government and the currency in collapse which the records of the papal collector Raimundus de Serra and his assistants who traversed the kingdom at this time amply confirm.[37] And in June 1319 the pact collapsed completely when after D. Juan had joined

---

[33] In view of Alfonso XI's unusual competence, Grassotti (1987), p. 724, is not so sure.
[34] Linehan (1983), pp. 283–4.
[35] *Cortes*, I, pp. 224 (c. 10), 227–31 (cc. 25–35, 37), 235 (c. 4), 236 (c. 11), 241 (cc. 25, 27–8), 244 (c. 42).
[36] Ibid., pp. 247–72.
[37] Ibid., pp. 303 (c. 6), 311 (c. 28); *CAXI*, pp. 180b–1a; Valdeón Baruque (1969), pp. 6–8, 13; Linehan (1971), pp. 247–9, and (1983), pp. 286–8. Cf. Kershaw (1973), p. 5 n. 7: 'There is no evidence of a famine in southern Europe in 1315–17.'

D. Pedro on campaign near Granada (in order to qualify for a share of the papal grant of Church revenues), the two infantes both perished there – D. Pedro cut down and his uncle expiring of shock at the news. Thereupon the latter's son D. Juan *el Tuerto* (the squint-eyed) and D. Juan Manuel moved into the political vacuum, each claiming the tutorship for himself, with the latter enjoying the support of his Aragonese father-in-law Jaume II. Castile in its weakened state was particularly prone to Aragonese interference during these years. In 1319, at Jaume's request, John XXII appointed the high-handed infante of Aragon, D. Joan, to the archbishopric of Toledo, and later that year there occurred the 'Gandesa scandal', when on his wedding day the unstable D. Jaume, the Aragonese heir-apparent, renounced both the succession and his brand new wife, Leonor of Castile, and fled the wedding breakfast in order to embrace (briefly) the religious life.[38]

In 1295 María de Molina's daughter, Isabel, had been rejected by Jaume II.[39] Now her granddaughter suffered the same fate. Throughout the intervening years María de Molina had remained committed to the *cortes*, and the wisdom of her insistence on holding a meeting in 1295 was adequately demonstrated by the consequences of not doing so between 1319 and 1321 when, instead, the contenders for power exploited local grievances, the *hermandad* of Andalusia conducted its own foreign policy with the kingdom of Granada and specified the terms on which it would accept the tutor or tutors chosen by the *cortes*,[40] and the attempts at pacification of the papal legate Cardinal Guillaume de Pierre Godin proved fruitless.

The legate – the first to visit Castile in almost a century – had come to assist María de Molina and stayed to bury her. The death of this remarkable woman on 1 July 1321 removed the kingdom's one rallying-point. On her deathbed, according to the Chronicle – though its text appears to have been tampered with at this point – she entrusted the ten-year-old king to the custody of the *concejo* of Valladolid, and in the will she made in her last days she elected to be buried in that northern city rather than, as she had specified in 1308, alongside Sancho IV in Toledo Cathedral: a change of mind indicative of the political realities of the summer of 1321 and the extent to which public order had collapsed over the previous thirteen years.[41]

The legislation (to stretch the meaning of the word) of the *cortes* of the *concejos* of Castile, León and 'the Extremaduras' which the king's uncle and new tutor,

---

[38] *CAXI*, pp. 181–5; Giménez Soler (1932), pp. 58–71; García Fernández (1991), pp. 155–60; Avezou (1930); Linehan (1993a), pp. 628–31; Sturcken (1979); Martínez Ferrando (1948), I, pp. 92–100.

[39] *CFIV*, p. 97a.

[40] García Fernández (1985), pp. 370–5; Anasagasti Valderrama and Sanz Fuentes (1985).

[41] *CAXI*, pp. 184–92; Fita (1908); Zunzunegui (1954); García y García (1988); Gaibrois de Ballesteros (1967), pp. 169, 243.

D. Felipe, assembled at Valladolid in June 1322 described a land dominated by the strongholds from which bands of *malfechores* terrorised the countryside and given over to murder, torture, imprisonings, arson, extortion, robbery and dishonour. Under cover of the darkness that covered the land innumerable private scores were settled, with D. Felipe as great a *malfechor* as any. After the infante's challenge to the archbishop of Compostela for control of the city of Santiago had driven that formidable French Dominican into the camp of D. Juan Manuel, in August 1324 the opposing armies met to do battle outside Zamora.[42] At this juncture, however, although (as the chronicler remarks) still 'of small age', Alfonso XI asserted himself, and instructed the warring factions to settle their differences.[43] Manuscripts of the *Partidas*, many of which will have been tampered with to suit political convenience, provided the thirteen-year-old (or those who controlled him) with authority for taking control of his own affairs at the age of fourteen, sixteen or twenty.[44] Fernando IV's father's minority had lasted until his sixteenth birthday. The precocious Alfonso XI moved early, however, though – to judge by the Chronicle's account of his kingdom when in the autumn of 1325 he declared his majority at the *cortes* of Valladolid – only just in time. The kingdom was in a state of shambles. Anarchy prevailed, and there was wholesale emigration to Aragon and Portugal.[45]

The exhaustion of the royal treasury was due to 'the large number of places and towns that the kings had alienated by hereditary grants', the chronicler stated in his account of the *cortes* of Carrión (1317),[46] and the theme of his history of the reign between 1325 and 1344, when his narrative is interrupted, and the underlying purpose of all his master's actions as he portrays them is the halting and reversal of that process and the re-establishment of royal authority and of the royal fisc.

'Henceforth there shall be no *hermandat*', Alfonso decreed at Valladolid in February 1326.[47] That was the first step. The next was to bring the grandees to book. Five months later Castile's churchmen were made to make substantial recompense for their earlier appropriations of royal lands (*realengo*),[48] while before the end of the year the fate of the king's cousin, Juan *el Tuerto*, gave notice to others of the more summary treatment awaiting them. Summoned to court on the safest of safe-conducts provided by the king's *privado*, Alvar Núñez Osorio, the lord of Vizcaya was hacked down on arrival in accordance with the principle of 'sentence first – judgement afterwards'. The presentation

---

[42] *Cortes*, I, pp. 338 (c. 6), 361 (cc. 78–80), 366–7 (c. 100); *CAXI*, pp. 186b, 194b; *Hechos de D. Berenguel de Landoria*, ed. Díaz y Díaz *et al.*, pp. 12–20   [43] *CAXI*, p. 194b.

[44] *Part.*, II.15. 4, 5 (ed. II, pp. 134, 136).

[45] *CAXI*, p. 197a–b: confirmed by the *acta* of the *cortes* (*Cortes*, I, pp. 372–89). Cf. Valdeón Baruque (1969), pp. 14–18; González Mínguez (1983).   [46] *CAXI*, p. 180b; *Cortes*, I, p. 306 (c. 14).

[47] *Cortes*, I, p. 393.   [48] Nieto Soria (1984).

of the case for the prosecution followed execution and Alvar Núñez received the victim's lands. D. Juan Manuel drew the correct conclusion after Alfonso jilted his daughter Constanza in favour of María of Portugal,[49] whereupon D. Juan Manuel 'denatured' himself – that is, formally severed all links with the king, and reverted to his pen and ink.[50]

In 1313, the *cortes* of Palencia had concerned itself with the three-year-old Alfonso's education and decreed that he be exposed to 'good customs'.[51] In 1326 the teenage monarch superintended the murder of his cousin, and D. Juan Manuel was well advised to parley with his king from the other bank of a wide river.[52] By then, however, Alfonso XI was under the tutelage of the *letrados*, that elevated clan to whose allegedly secularist influence historians confidently attribute so many of the achievements of the reign, yet which, when its membership is revealed, proves to contain, as well as the royal chronicler Fernán Sánchez de Valladolid, such pillars of the ecclesiastical establishment as Pedro Gómez de Barroso (bishop of Cartagena, later cardinal), Juan del Campo (bishop successively of Cuenca, Oviedo and León), and Gil de Albornoz, archbishop of Toledo (1338–51) and the papacy's principal warrior thereafter.[53] This suggests that the adolescent ruler's privy council bore at least a superficial resemblance to those of his more conventional predecessors.

But if the distinctive ideological characteristics of the *letrados* remain to be identified, their achievements – if theirs they were – were soon manifest in a land whose catastrophic recent history had scarcely prepared for the consequences of the climatic changes by which the whole of southern Europe was plagued in these years.[54] During the late 1320s the kingdom of Castile experienced royal government with an immediacy unknown since the 1270s. Thus, religious sentiment was manipulated, ostensibly on behalf of the new shrine of Guadalupe, effectively in the interest of the colonisation of those areas of the remote south-west which the 1322 *cortes* of Valladolid had identified as especially exposed to Portuguese influence. At the *cortes* of Madrid in 1329, both Castile's domestic enemies and such foreign intruders as notaries public and papal providees were put to flight.[55] Finally, in 1332, the king, whose heroes

---

[49] *CAXI*, p. 203a (although the grandson of Sancho IV and the son of an infante, Juan *el Tuerto* had adopted the maternal title Juan de Haro); Giménez Soler (1932), pp. 81, 531, 549, 551–2 (Dec. 1327: in this case the fiancée had become a formal hostage, thereby acknowledging the true nature of early fourteenth-century peninsular marriage alliances – though their primary objective appears to have been the devising of the maximum possible number of unions in the shortest possible time involving the smallest conceivable number of closely related infantes and infantas). Alfonso had already rejected an English match. The first extra-peninsular royal marriage of Fernando IV's reign had not occurred until 1310: Gaibrois de Ballesteros (1967), p. 178.

[50] *CAXI*, p. 209b; Giménez Soler (1932), pp. 86–112; Gautier-Dalché (1982).   [51] *Cortes*, I, pp. 234–5.

[52] *CAXI*, p. 220a.   [53] Moxó (1975); Dupré Theseider (1972).   [54] Cf. Rubio Vela (1987), p. 144.

[55] *Cortes*, I, p. 348 (c. 40); Linehan (1985) and (1993), pp. 624–37.

included King Arthur and el Cid and who never passed up the chance of a joust or a round table in order to keep his warriors up to the mark, established the Order of the Band (La Banda) – one the earliest orders of chivalry, thereby reviving chivalric practices which (according to his chronicler) had lain dormant for 'a long time' – was himself knighted by an automated statue of Santiago, and on his twenty-first birthday was first anointed and then crowned himself at Burgos, struck a new seal on which he was portrayed in majestic pose, and incorporated the *señorío* of Alava into his now again confident kingdom.[56] Of all the events of 1332, this incorporation was arguably the most significant – for both parties. Castile's first indication of political robustness since 1295 coincided with Navarre's re-entry into the mainstream of peninsular affairs.

Since 1305 the kings of France had abandoned all pretence of Navarrese independence. On the death of Juana I, the *hombres buenos* of seventeen towns of the kingdom had assembled at Estella (May 1305) and committed themselves to meet at Olite three times a year in defence of their liberties. But to no effect. After Juana's widower, Philip the Fair, had declared himself king of both France and Navarre, their son Louis, on visiting Pamplona in October 1307 and swearing to defend his new subjects' liberties, only remained long enough to install a governor, pack the Navarrese Church with Frenchmen, and round up the usual suspects – in this case Fortuño Almoravid and Martín Ximénez de Aibar – and have them transported to French prisons. His one meritorious act was to beget a daughter, Juana, whom on his death in 1316 the Navarrese acknowledged as one of them, though in 1319 Arnalt of Barbazán – Pamplona's fifth bishop in two years, four of whom had been French appointees of the French pope John XXII – led a deputation to Paris and swore Navarre's allegiance to Philip V. Bishop Arnalt's lengthy pontificate (1318–55) provided the kingdom with a semblance of stability. In 1319 he reached an accord with the Capetian king concerning the Church of Pamplona's long-disputed secular jurisdiction in the city, and secured permission for the reconstruction of the Navarrería, destroyed in 1276. Three years later, however, there was no persuading the political community to accept Charles IV – 'the Handsome' according to French tradition, in Navarrese 'the Bald'.[57]

The end of Capetian rule in February 1328 passed without incident in Navarre. At Pamplona three months later, the *cortes* summoned by the regents unanimously declared Juana their queen. The deputies were cautious about Juana's husband, however – understandably so: Philip of Evreux's French base

---

[56] *CAXI*, pp. 231a–7a, 266b; López-Ibor Aliño (1984); García Díaz (1984); Linehan (1993a), pp. 572–601; Ruiz (1987), p. 224; Linehan (1993b).

[57] Lacarra (1972–3), I, pp. 251–69; Goñi Gaztambide (1979), pp. 19–105.

was even more remote from Navarre than that of his thirteenth-century predecessors had been – and required him to undertake to withdraw in the event that Juana predecease him or die without issue. In the event, their misgivings proved unfounded. Although they were not often there themselves, preferring to rule their kingdom through governors, between them Philip III (1328–43) and Juana II, who survived him until 1349, ruled Navarre better than Navarre had become accustomed to being ruled, updating its laws in 1330 (*amejoramiento de los fueros*), superintending the reform of its administration, establishing generally harmonious relations with both Castile and Aragon, and – above all – producing eight children and marrying their daughter María to the future Pere III of Aragon. Felipe's death at Jérez in September 1343, whither he had gone to assist Alfonso XI at the siege of Algeciras, demonstrated the seriousness of his peninsular commitment.[58] It was no fault of theirs that by mid century that commitment had become unsustainable.

By definition, any Norman succeeding to the throne of the Pyrenean kingdom midway between the battles of Crécy and Poitiers was bound to have a hard time of it. Politically accomplished though he undoubtedly was, however, throughout his long reign (1349–87) Carlos II, the Bad, displayed an intermittent genius for complicating the task of balancing the interests of two inheritances one of which required English assistance and the other Castilian (and therefore French) acquiescence in order to survive. A description of his exploits in France during the 1350s leading to his imprisonment there is provided elsewhere in this volume. By the time he returned south in 1361 all the Spanish kingdoms were being drawn into the Anglo-French conflict.[59] Before we proceed, their various strands had better be gathered together.

On 7 January 1325 King Dinis of Portugal died, after a reign of forty-six years, and was succeeded by his son Afonso IV who lasted for thirty-two. The fortunes of Portugal between 1279 and 1357 prove the rule that the greatest service that any ruler in this period could render was simply to survive. Whereas Sancho IV died at thirty-six, Fernando IV at twenty-six, Pedro I would be struck down at thirty-four, and even Alfonso XI – whose career seems to bestride the history of the fourteenth-century peninsula – expired before he was forty, the history of Portugal in these years gives all the appearances of stability, continuity and growth.

Dinis of Portugal (1279–1325), grandson of Alfonso X of Castile, inherited many of the intellectual qualities of *el rey sabio*, but few of his fatal flaws as a man of affairs. *O rei letrado* had the other's *Partidas* translated into Portuguese but spared his people their prescriptions. He too was a poet of parts. He too

---

[58] Lacarra (1972–3), II, pp. 11–48; Goñi Gaztambide (1979), pp. 129–35; Martín Duque (1970–1).
[59] Lacarra (1972–3), II, pp. 49–66; see also above chs. 14(a), p. 407; 14(b), p. 427.

promoted the use of the vernacular and its adoption in acts of government. In the person of his illegitimate son, Pedro Afonso the count of Barcelos, he placed Portuguese historiography on the same footing as Castile's had been placed by Alfonso X. By 1290 he had established Portugal's first *studium generale* at Lisbon. Throughout the following century its masters and students periodically commuted between that city and Coimbra, in response to the hostility of the one place and the uneventfulness of the other. As at Alfonso X's Salamanca, the teaching of both laws, medicine and arts was licensed, but not that of theology. Its foundation was due to two stated objectives: the promotion of knowledge for the sake of religion and government, and the removal of the need for Portuguese scholars to travel abroad in pursuit of it. The myth that Dinis himself owed his education to French teachers, which lingers on in the literature, was demolished long ago. Then as now, under cover of the principles that give universities their name, the dominant sentiments were those of autarchy and intellectual parsimony.[60]

Closely though King Dinis resembled Alfonso X, however, by the beginning of the fourteenth century there was one quite crucial respect in which Portugal and Castile were fundamentally different. Portugal had no Granada to contend with. Portugal's external reconquest was over. So while in 1317 the infantes of Castile were busy eliminating their brothers and their cousins, the king of Portugal was engaged in recruiting the Genoese Manuel Pessagna as his admiral with right of succession and in pottering round his pine-forest at Leiria planting the trees which would provide the ships for Pessanga's descendants and the conquest of new continents in the age of Henry the Navigator.[61]

On his succession at the age of seventeen, Dinis's right to the throne was challenged by his younger brother Afonso on the patently false grounds that he had been born before the Church had regularised his parents' marriage. Together with the kingdom, he had inherited Afonso III's long-running dispute with the Portuguese Church and its associated sentences of interdict and excommunication, the settlement of which was not reached until 1289 when the king and his bishops reduced their differences to forty items and enshrined them in a concordat.[62] In marked contrast to his father, Dinis was adept at avoiding confrontation. While negotiations with the papacy continued to drag on, he also displayed considerable ingenuity in the art of damage limitation. Thus, although he revived the *inquirições* into title in 1284, and in 1286 introduced mortmain legislation

---

[60] Catalán Menéndez Pidal (1962), pp. 289–312, 409–11; Rashdall (1936), II, pp. 108–11; García y García (1976), pp. 31–4; Serrão (1979), I, pp. 231–2, 371–8; David (1943), pp. 21–3; Coelho and Homem (1996), pp. 651–4.

[61] Almeida (1922), pp. 248–51; Serrão (1979), I, pp. 259–61; Vones (1993), pp. 178–80; Coelho and Homem (1996), pp. 144–63.

[62] *NCMH*, v, pp. 702–4; García y García (1976), pp. 223–5; Almeida (1967), pp. 200–2.

designed to halt and reverse the transfer of royal land (*regalengo*) to ecclesiastical foundations, on neither occasion did he experience the ructions of the previous reign.[63] Equally, in 1319 he succeeded in persuading John XXII to assign the property of the Portuguese Templars to a new national military order, the Order of Christ. In the previous year, after a thirty-year campaign, he had secured the independence of the Portuguese houses of the Order of Santiago. This had been achieved in the teeth of both Castilian and papal opposition. Boniface VIII in particular had been rootedly opposed: secession would encourage other religious orders to secede, and kingdoms to fragment – as Castile was indeed currently fragmenting, to the Portuguese king's significant advantage.[64]

Into Castile's murky political waters D. Dinis plunged with alacrity, by the Treaty of Alcañices securing an advantageous settlement of the long-running frontier dispute.[65] As throughout the reign, so on this occasion Dinis's long-suffering queen, the saintly Isabel – daughter of Pere II of Aragon, and María de Molina's Portuguese counterpart – promoted the cause of conciliation. In return, her husband fathered numerous bastards, and such was his affection for one of them, Afonso Sanches, that in 1314 Dinis promoted him *mordomo-mor*. The effective transfer of the government of the kingdom which this appointment entailed spurred Dinis's heir by the queen – another Afonso, and the other's junior by two years – to rebel against his father in 1320. The end of the old reign was marked by intermittent civil war, Dinis's virtual imprisonment of his wife, and the exile of Afonso Sanches to Alburquerque, from which Castilian stronghold between then and his death in 1329 he conducted a series of assaults into Trás-os-Montes and the Alentejo.[66] So while Alfonso XI was making himself master of Castile, the early years of the reign of Afonso IV of Portugal (1325–57) were overshadowed by a series of events which until recently any observer of the peninsular scheme would have regarded as characteristically Castilian. The peninsular balance seemed to have shifted.

In March 1328 Alfonso XI's betrothal to María of Portugal, Afonso IV's daughter, acknowledged the new order and six months later the knot was tied – though furtively, because the couple were intimately related. However, the new alliance soon soured. Even before John XXII had decided that the couple's incestuous union was in Christendom's best interests after all,[67] Alfonso's attention had been captured by an enchanting young widow of Seville, Leonor de Guzmán, *la Favorita* – who because she was both irresistible and prolific, while María was neither, and because the king could not be in two

---

[63] Almeida (1967), p. 113.

[64] Ibid., pp. 151–6; Serrão (1979), I, pp. 254–8; Benavides (1860), II, p. 15; *As Gavetas da Torre do Tombo*, II, pp. 409–13; Mattoso (1993), pp. 147–61.   [65] Above, p. 624; Serrão (1979), I, pp. 148–50.

[66] Lopes (1970b); Serrão (1979), I, pp. 263–7; Mattoso (1993), pp. 161–3.   [67] Linehan (1985), p. 288.

beds at once – and plainly had no wish to be – determined the course of Castilian history for the remainder of the century and beyond.

In the course of the reign of Alfonso XI a combination of circumstances relieved the kingdom of a number of those ancient lineages which for centuries had governed their patrimonies as though they were kings themselves. Weakened by the cumulative effect of many generations of endogamous unions, after 1350 many families which had been spared the treatment that had accounted for Juan *el Tuerto* and for the lord of Cameros, Juan Alonso de Haro, in 1333, succumbed to the combination of intermittent warfare and endemic plague. However, the potential political advantage of their removal had already been sacrificed to the need to provide for Alfonso's ten children by *la Favorita*, nine of them boys. As D. Juan Manuel complained to Pere III of Aragon in 1345, the king and 'that bad woman' would deny their offspring nothing 'other than the crown itself' – though in the event that too was to be taken from Alfonso's legitimate heir to the throne.[68]

That heir – the future Pedro I, María of Portugal's second and last child – was born in August 1334. But by then the new arrival's outraged grandfather was past assuaging. In alliance with Juan Núñez de Lara III, whom Alfonso XI was currently besieging in his castle at Lerma, and the incorrigible D. Juan Manuel, in 1336–7 Afonso IV invaded Castile. Moxó regards the siege of Lerma and its outcome, the king's conciliatory treatment of the defeated Juan Núñez, as the turning-point of the reign. It certainly contrasts sharply with Fernando IV's failure to dislodge Juan Núñez's uncle from Tordehumos in 1307–8. The Portuguese invasion ended in rout.[69] And three years later, on 30 October 1340, Afonso IV, D. Juan Núñez and D. Juan Manuel, as well as the Aragonese fleet, all participated in Alfonso's famous victory over the combined forces of Yusuf I of Granada (1333–54) and the Marinid sultan of Morocco, Abu'l Hasan, on the river Salado outside Tarifa. Also present were a papal envoy and Genoese galleys, indicating that as well as constituting the Spanish crusade's most spectacular achievement since 1248, the battle of Salado also provided an excellent opportunity for speculative businessmen. Such were the quantities of booty seized that as far afield as Paris gold lost a sixth of its value, the king's chronicler reported – though presumably it was not for that reason that he described the victory as even more 'virtuous' than that of Las Navas de Tolosa.[70] Perhaps what mattered most, however, after more than a half a century of domestic strife,

---

[68] *CAXI*, p. 263a; Moxó (1969), pp. 24–5, 51, 57; del Arco (1954), pp. 283–9; Beceiro Pita (1987), pp. 90–1; Giménez Soler (1932), p. 645.

[69] *CAXI*, pp. 273–83; Almeida (1922), pp. 261–4; Moxó (1990), pp. 312–13; above n. 28.

[70] *CAXI*, pp. 329–30; Goñi Gaztambide (1958), pp. 316–32; Hillgarth (1976), pp. 339–42; Harvey (1990), pp. 190–4.

was the restoration of Castile to a place of honour in the calculations of contemporary Europe.

The victory of 1340 vindicated the policies that Alfonso XI had pursued since 1325. His promotion of chivalry had proved profitable: all those round tables had paid off. He also had ample reason for invoking the Virgin of Guadalupe before battle and for visiting her shrine thereafter: the effect of his *ordenamiento* of the previous year which had rerouted the transhumant flocks through Extremadura had been to reroute humans too into that previously vulnerable corner of his kingdom.[71]

Despite the hostility caused by the grant of Aragonese apanages to his nephews Ferran and Joan, the children of Alfonso IV of Aragon and Leonor of Castile, and his intervention in favour of the Aragonese *unión* in 1347–8,[72] the post-Salado Alfonso XI was the first king of Castile in almost seventy years to enjoy simultaneously amicable relations with Aragon and Portugal, a circumstance which enabled him to consolidate his position at home. Alfonso's urban policy was tailored to particular circumstances. The officials appointed to represent royal authority on the new institution, the *regimiento*, were sometimes noble *caballeros hidalgos* (as at Seville in 1337), sometimes members of the urban oligarchy of non-noble *caballeros villanos* (as at Burgos and León in 1345), sometimes a mixture of the two. Thus, although the establishment of the *regidores* entailed the destruction of the open councils which had flourished since 1282, as a rule these agents of self-government at the king's command were lights of the local community.[73] Alfonso's dealings with the *cortes* and with the papacy were equally pragmatic. Despite the extreme severity of the methods he employed to secure the allegiance of the old military orders, and the deep misgivings of such representatives of traditional values as D. Juan Manuel and – as expressed in his searing critique *Speculum regum* – by Alvarus Pelagius OFM, in practice the absolutist tendencies of the king's Roman law-imbued advisers were tempered by a healthy realism. The *Ordenamiento of Alcalá* promulgated in 1348, with its assertion of the king's power to make, interpret, declare and emend *fueros* and laws, has been described as dealing a 'mortal blow' to municipal self-determination. Yet the function of those precepts of the *Siete Partidas* which were incorporated on that occasion, complementing ordinances issued at Villa Real and Segovia in 1346 and 1347, was not to replace the municipal *fueros* but to supplement them.[74]

---

[71] *Gran Crónica de Alfonso XI*, II, pp. 429–30, 449; Linehan (1993a), p. 620; Díaz Martín (1984), pp. 238–40.   [72] See ch. 18(a) above.

[73] Ruiz (1977), pp. 26–9; Casado Alonso (1987a), pp. 201–6; Rucquoi (1987a), pp. 242–53; Torres Fontes (1953); Alonso Romero (1990), pp. 571–3.

[74] González Alonso (1988), pp. 226–8; Moxó (1990), pp. 349, 355–61, 386; cf. Hillgarth (1976), pp. 345–6; Moxó (1976); Linehan (1993a), pp. 603–13, 639–53, 663; Alonso Romero (1990), p. 542.

With the booty captured in 1340 Alfonso XI was able to hire Genoese galleys and in 1342 undertake the siege of Algeciras. In 1344 – with the assistance of the Catalan fleet and sundry foreigners (including the earls of Derby and Salisbury, 'men of great standing in the kingdom of England' as the Chronicler describes them), and after the Castilians had had their first experience of cannon-balls – the place was taken.[75] Five years later, intent on recovering Gibraltar which the Marinids had taken in 1333, Alfonso returned to the south. The outlook was encouraging: the defenders had no hope of support from war-torn Morocco. In the spring of 1350, however, a deadlier peril than anything from across the Straits intervened. Black Death passed from the besieged city to the Castilian encampment. Amongst its earliest victims, on Good Friday (27 March), was the thirty-eight-year-old king.

Although the plague had already reached Barcelona and Valencia two years earlier, the fatal outcome of Alfonso XI's final confrontation with Spanish Islam was none the less grimly ironical. Castile in 1350 was a country inured to famine: the first petition presented at the *cortes* of Burgos in 1345 had complained of freak weather and sky-high prices, since when the cost of wheat had increased sixfold.[76] From the Pyrenees to Andalusia the weakened population readily succumbed. Navarrese statistics indicate the severity of the epidemic's ravages, with the *merindad* of Estella losing 63 per cent of its inhabitants between 1330 and 1350, further drastic losses attributable to the renewed outbreak in 1362, and the rural population driven to depend on Jewish credit for survival: an ominous development in a community within which the political vacuum of 1328 had already occasioned the peninsula's earliest widespread outbreak of anti-Semitism, with as many as 10,000 deaths reported. In Portugal estimates of mortality as high as two-thirds, even nine-tenths, are recorded. In 1358 the number of those extant from the reign of King Dinis was said to be exiguous, whilst amongst the survivors such had been the devotion bred of terror that at the *cortes* of Lisbon (1352) it was alleged that the Church was on the point of acquiring the whole kingdom. The *cortes* of Valladolid (1351) recorded the same psychological reaction, with consequences capable of frustrating all Alfonso XI's attempts to halt the drift of royal land into mortmain, while its decrees in respect of prices and wages testify to the severity of the epidemic in Castile. Of 420 settlements in the diocese of Palencia north of the Duero, in the eight years after 1345 no fewer than eighty-two disappeared from the map altogether. However, there is no knowing whether that degree of mortality was typical, or whether the rural population

---

[75] *CAXI*, pp. 358–90; Harvey (1990), pp. 199–204.
[76] *Cortes*, I, p. 484; *CAXI*, p. 253b; Valdeón Baruque (1969), pp. 11, 19; Gautier-Dalché (1970–1), pp. 242–9.

had been in a state of absolute decline (rather than of redistribution) in the previous half-century. As elsewhere, the historians disagree. But the variations of the Valladolid legislation according to region (*Ordenamientos de menestrales y posturas*) certainly suggest that the impact of the plague had not been uniform.[77]

The *cortes* of Valladolid (1351) was one of just two such assemblies of which record has survived from the bloody reign of Pedro I, the Cruel (1350–69). Pedro was fifteen on his accession, and bouts of serious illness in his first year immediately raised the question of the succession and the claims of his elder half-brother Enrique, count of Trastámara. The consummation of the latter's marriage to D. Juan Manuel's daughter Juana in Leonor de Guzmán's very chamber sealed *la Favorita*'s fate. Early in 1351 she was murdered at Talavera, on the orders of the queen-mother, María de Portugal, and María's cousin and alleged paramour Juan Alfonso de Alburquerque: an act which set the course of the rest of a reign characterised by López de Ayala, the chronicler who abandoned Pedro's cause, as one of 'much wrong and much war'.[78]

Alburquerque's hold over the young king was soon broken. In pursuit of a French alliance, a marriage was arranged between Pedro and Blanche de Bourbon. As Blanche arrived in Castile in the spring of 1353, however, the king's mistress María de Padilla gave birth to their first child, and when it emerged that Blanche's father lacked the means of paying the dowry of 300,000 gold florins, Pedro asserted himself. Three days after their wedding he ostentatiously repudiated his bride. The fate of the French queen of Castile provided both the king's various domestic enemies – amongst them the two claimants to his throne, Enrique de Trastámara and his cousin the infante Ferran of Aragon, as well as his mother, and now Alburquerque – and also the papacy in the person of the Frenchman Innocent VI, with an ostensibly respectable cause. It was reinforced when Pedro prevailed upon the bishops of Salamanca and Avila to nullify his French marriage, thus enabling him to take Juana de Castro as his wife. By the end of 1354, Pedro was trapped at Toro and forced to a humiliating settlement. At the *vistas* of Tejadillo the king surrendered control of his household, as his grandfather had done in 1308. But unlike Fernando IV, Pedro I showed himself capable of exploiting the divisions within the opposition. In little over a year he recovered the initiative and established complete control over his kingdom.[79]

Secure at home, Pedro now moved against Aragon. Although fomented by

---

[77] Zabalo Zabalegui (1968); Leroy (1984), p. 240; Lacarra (1972–3), II, pp. 29–30, 194–8; Goñi Gaztambide (1979), pp. 104–5; Rau *et al.* (1963), pp. 215–16, 239; Sousa (1993), pp. 340–2; Verlinden (1938), pp. 127–42; *Cortes*, II, pp. 75–124; Cabrillana (1968); Sobrequés Callicó (1970–1), pp. 86–96. Cf. Vaca (1977), p. 392; García de Cortázar (1990), pp. 179–200; Amasuno Sárraga (1996).

[78] *CPI*, pp. 409a, 412b–13a.   [79] Ibid., pp. 455a, 458b; Suárez Fernández (1976), pp. 3–42.

the presence in Aragon of both pretenders to the Castilian throne, this latest struggle for peninsular hegemony was now part of a larger European contest, with Aragon aligned with France and Castile with England. Yet it was an Aragonese attack on Genoese merchantmen in the Castilian port of Sanlúcar de Barrameda in 1356, with Pedro who was there for a day's fishing looking on, that sparked hostilities. The Castilians swept all before them. Despite truces at Tudela (1357), Terrer (1361) and Murviedro (1363), by 1365 more than half of Pere III's lands had been occupied and domestic resistance crushed by the ferocity of Pedro's oppression. In 1358 his half-brother Fadrique was butchered while the Scarpia-like Pedro ate dinner in an adjoining room, and between then and 1361 both his wife and his aunt (Blanche de Bourbon and Leonor of Castile) amongst scores of others were disposed of. In 1362 the Red King – *el Rey Bermejo* Muhammad VI, whose seizure of power from Muhammad V of Granada two years before had interrupted Pedro's sombre progress – was despatched by the king's own hand, and at the *cortes* of Seville his liaison with María de Padilla (d. 1361) was stated to have been a valid marriage – though the death later that year of the Infante Alfonso, the only male of the four children of that union, nullified the advantages of the declaration.[80]

Meanwhile, after his wife had been spirited out of Castile in 1358, Enrique of Trastámara had fathered a son – the future Juan I – and, in the wake of the ignominious failure of his first invasion of Castile (battle of Nájera, April 1360), in July 1362 he purchased the assistance of the Free Companies and by the Treaty of Monzón (March 1363) secured the alliance of Pere III in return for a promise of the cession to Aragon of a sixth part of his Castilian conquests. With Carlos II conniving, in March 1366 Enrique's armies crossed Navarre and entered Castile with the companies under the command of Bertrand du Guesclin. Enrique had himself crowned at Burgos and – maintaining the pretence that this was a crusade – himself crowned du Guesclin king of Granada. Because his own forces were deployed in the kingdom of Valencia, Pedro was taken by surprise. In May Toledo fell to the companies and Pedro was driven from Seville. Refused sanctuary by Pedro of Portugal, he sailed to Galicia and, after arranging for the archbishop and the dean of Santiago to be murdered, reached Bayonne in Gascony in early August, and opened negotiations with the Black Prince and Carlos of Navarre with a view to securing his restoration.

At Libourne (23 September 1366) his allies agreed their price. Pedro was to foot the military bill in full, the county of Vizcaya – the cradle of Castilian sea-power – was to be ceded to the prince, and the provinces of Guipúzcoa and

---

[80] *CPIII*, pp. 492–576 (p. 569); Russell (1955), pp. 13–35; Abadal (1976), pp. cxxxviii–cxlviii; Suárez Fernandez (1976), pp. 43–101; Harvey (1990), pp. 209–14.

Alava to Carlos, thereby recreating the kingdom of Navarre as it had been when it had controlled the fortunes of Christian Spain 300 years before. As became apparent immediately after the allies' victory at Nájera (3 April 1367) and Pedro's restoration, these terms were entirely unrealistic. The military bill in full amounted to some 2.7 million gold florins. The prince's title to Vizcaya was found to be worthless. Relations between the victors were further soured by the English prince's quixotic insistence that prisoners be ransomed rather than butchered, leaving Enrique's supporters to fight another day. By the autumn of 1367 when Enrique and his mercenaries returned, the out-of-pocket prince's preference was for the partition of Castile between Aragon, Navarre, Portugal and himself. Meanwhile, however, the king of France had been active. Intent on securing the services of the Castilian fleet, in November 1368 Charles V ratified the Treaty of Toledo with Enrique, and in the following month sent du Guesclin to Castile. In the spring of 1369, while moving through La Mancha, Pedro found himself trapped in the castle of Montiel. Uncharacteristically (such was the desperateness of his situation) he agreed to conversations with du Guesclin, who handed him over to Enrique. On the night of 22/3 March 1369 Enrique hacked him to death. Pedro I 'slept little and loved many women', López de Ayala noted by way of epitaph. 'And he killed many in his kingdom, whence all the misfortunes he suffered of which you have heard.'[81]

In the case of Portugal it might be – it certainly has been – argued that, just as elsewhere, the country's mounting political crisis was an effect of the 'great mortality',[82] and although other less sophisticated explanations for the train of events that culminated in the 1380s suggest themselves it is certainly true that immediately pre-1348 Portugal had enjoyed a measure of prosperity. In the aftermath of the Salado victory, Afonso IV requested funds from Avignon to enable him to prosecute the struggle against the Marinids. To the considerable detriment of the Portuguese Church, his request was granted, and in July 1341 two ships set out from Lisbon under the command of Genoese and Florentine masters. Their destination was not North Africa however. Five years before, the Genoese mariner Lanzarotto Malocello had visited the island in the Canaries which is named after him, and there they too now went, returning with evidence of the existence of land across the ocean.[83]

But it was another event of these years that made Afonso IV's reign a landmark for Portugal's literature as well as for its history. Inês de Castro had come to Portugal in 1340 in the entourage of Constanza, the daughter of D. Juan

[81] Delachenal (1909–31), III, pp. 419–40, 467–86; Russell (1955), pp. 35–148; Suárez Fernández (1976), pp. 101–29; *CPI*, p. 593.

[82] H. C. Baquero Moreno, M. Caetano *contra*, in Rau *et al.* (1963), pp. 237–9.

[83] Serrão (1979), I, pp. 270–1; Phillips (1988), pp. 158–9.

Manuel whom Alfonso XI had spurned. Constanza was now the wife of Afonso's heir, D. Pedro. By the time she bore him their second child, however, Constanza had her suspicions. Inês was recruited as the child's godmother. The child died. Constanza's suspicions were confirmed. In 1345, after giving birth to the future Fernando I, Constanza also died, and D. Pedro took up openly with Inês. By 1351 the mistress with whom the prince was besotted had given him three sons and a daughter. But she had also raised in Afonso IV's mind the spectre of a duplicate royal family and a Portuguese re-enactment of the miseries currently being experienced in Castile. So in January 1355 Afonso had Inês killed. As soon as he was king himself, in May 1357, Pedro I wreaked vengeance. In June 1360, he declared that he and Inês had married secretly some seven years earlier. This anticipated Pedro of Castile's claim regarding María de Padilla. There was, indeed, not much to choose between the two Pedros. Later, in exchange for three fugitives from his royal namesake, the king of Portugal secured the extradition from Castile of two of his mistress's murderers and, as he watched and ate, had their hearts removed, one through his back and the other through his chest, recalling the precedent of Pedro of Castile's supper-time entertainment – though it was not the psychopathic voyeurism of the two Pedros that dismayed their chroniclers, López de Ayala and Fernão Lopes, so much as the shameful agreement between them that had delivered the victims to their fate.[84]

For Fernão Lopes, what made Pedro I's ten-year reign memorable was the king's inflexibility in administering justice. Portugal had never experienced the like of it, men said.[85] By a series of measures promulgated at the *cortes* of Elvas (May 1361) the respective jurisdictions of secular and ecclesiastical tribunals were defined and the practice of submitting papal letters to royal veto was confirmed.[86] A pragmatic ruler, throughout the early 1360s Pedro contrived to avoid involving his kingdom in the prevailing peninsular turmoil. Accordingly, when Pedro of Castile was driven from his kingdom in 1366, he refused him shelter and cancelled the betrothal of his son and heir Fernando to Pedro's heir and daughter, Beatriz. During his reign Lisbon and Oporto prospered as never before, and on his death in January 1367 – according to the chronicler – he bequeathed a greater fortune than any previous king had ever possessed.

The dynastic ambition and uncontrolled libido of his successor squandered it all. On the death of Pedro of Castile, Fernando I (1367–83) allied himself with Aragon and Granada and declared war on Enrique II, claiming the Castilian throne as the great-grandson of Sancho IV. In this capacity he

[84] *CPI*, p. 506; Macchi and Steunou, *Fernão Lopes*, pp. 160–85; Serrão (1979), I, pp. 275–82.

[85] Macchi and Steunou, *Fernão Lopes*, pp. 13–67, 249.

[86] Barros (1945–54), II, pp. 195, 213, 264, 281; Almeida (1967), pp. 355–7, 381–2.

invaded Galicia in June 1369. The venture was a disaster. Fernando was forced to renounce his claim and promise to marry the infanta Leonor of Castile (Treaty of Alcoutim, March 1371). No sooner had he done so, however, than he threw in his lot with John of Gaunt who on his marriage to Pedro I's eldest surviving daughter Constanza in September 1371 assumed the title of king of Castile. But when the promised English force failed to materialise the campaign of 1372–3 proved a disaster too, and Enrique II's armies entered Portugal and pillaged Lisbon, imposing upon him the humiliating treaty of Santarém (March 1373). Fernando was forced back into the Franco-Castilian camp. Meanwhile, however, nothing daunted, and despite his commitment to the infanta of Castile, in April 1371 Fernando had married Leonor Teles de Meneses. The influence of this unscrupulous and lascivious lady – Portugal's Lucrezia Borgia, Herculano called her – caused widespread resentment. For as well as being married already (to João Lourenço da Cunha), Leonor soon took Gaunt's agent in Portugal, Juan Fernández Andeiro, as her lover. Under Andeiro's influence, Leonor pressed Fernando to enter into the alliance with the English which was concluded at St Paul's (London) in June 1373 – just three months after the treaty of Santarém.

By 1373, therefore, just six years into the reign, Portuguese political society was deeply divided and irreversibly polarised. Further complications ensued when, first, the Schism of the western Church in 1378 resulted in England declaring allegiance to Urban VI and Castile to Clement VII and, then, in 1380, the heiress to the throne, Beatriz, finished up betrothed both to the future Enrique III of Castile and to the son of Gaunt's younger brother, Edmund, earl of Cambridge. In August 1382 the inglorious outcome of Cambridge's comic-opera expedition carried the reign forward in appropriate fashion. While the queen was giving birth to – as was generally assumed – Andeiro's child, the English army at Badajoz learned that their Portuguese allies had made peace with the Castilians, that Beatriz was to marry Enrique of Castile after all and that they were to be ignominiously shipped home courtesy of the Castilian navy.[87]

For all its complications, however, Portuguese policy during the 1370s was positively candid when compared with that of Carlos II of Navarre whose indecision as to which side to back was such that, in order not to have to commit himself to either Castilian claimant, in 1367 he arranged to have himself incarcerated by a cousin of Bertrand du Guesclin until the outcome of the battle of Nájera was known – and had then to part with his wife's jewels

---

[87] Russell (1955), pp. 151–203, 296–344; Suárez Fernández (1960), pp. 3–11, and (1976), pp. 134–70; Lomax and Oakley, *The English in Portugal*, pp. 37–153; Serrão (1979), I, pp. 283–90; Sousa (1993), pp. 488–94.

to purchase his conspirators' silence.[88] Thereafter, he was involved in peninsular alliances of every conceivable complexion, adjusting barometrically to successive shifts in the relationship of Aragon, England and Portugal to Enrique of Castile. In the year after the Castilian galleys had repaid Charles V for his support for the Trastamara cause by destroying the English fleet off La Rochelle (June 1372), he was forced to submit to Castilian demands and to surrender Logroño, Vitoria and the other Alavese towns which he had seized in 1368 on the strength of the Libourne agreements.[89] Nevertheless, he continued to scheme against both Castile and France. In March 1378 his chamberlain, Jacques de Rue, was arrested in France carrying evidence which revealed the extent of Carlos's negotiations with the English, the existence of a conspiracy involving the *adelantado mayor* of Castile, Pedro Manrique, for the recovery of Logroño, and details of plans to assassinate both Enrique of Castile (codename *intrusor*) and his brother-in-law, the king of France. For Carlos II the consequences of the discovery were doubly catastrophic: all his French possessions were confiscated, the assistance promised by Richard II of England in return for the leasing to him of Cherbourg was delayed, his heir the infante Carlos and two of his other children were detained by Charles V, he himself only narrowly escaped capture at Logroño where Pedro Manrique was playing a double game, and the Castilians invaded and overwhelmed Navarre. The Treaty of Briones (March 1379) bound Carlos II hand and foot. He died in January 1387, leaving his kingdom devastated and its treasury empty.[90]

Portugal's circumstances had been hardly better in October 1383 when, weighed down by his thirty-eight years, Fernando I of Portugal had died and the question of the Portuguese succession had become actual. With no fewer than three of his father King Pedro's bastards in play – João and Dinis (by Inês de Castro) and (by another mother) a second João, the Master of Avis (the Portuguese branch of the military Order of Calatrava) – with the king believed to be beyond begetting a child himself but perfectly capable of strangling at birth any other of his wayward queen's offspring, and with Queen Leonor herself in the ascendant and her good friend Andeiro (now count of Ourém) in the offing, the question had been on the peninsular agenda at least since August 1382. Then, in the aftermath of the débâcle of the English expedition, the ten-year-old heiress to the throne – the already extensively betrothed Beatriz – had been promised to a younger son of Juan I. But in the following month Juan I's wife had died in childbed, and in March 1383 Ourém had arranged for Beatriz to marry Juan himself. The kingdom was to be governed

[88] *CPI*, p. 550; Lacarra (1972–3), II, pp. 99, 103.

[89] Delachenal (1909–31), IV, pp. 407–16; Russell (1955), p. 139; Lacarra (1972–3), II, pp. 110–14.

[90] Russell (1955), pp. 249–82; Lacarra (1972-3), II, pp. 121–33, 149–54.

by a regency (of Andeiro and Leonor presumably) until the couple had
produced an heir to the throne. If they failed, or neglected, to do so then the
king of Castile and his heirs would succeed instead. So Juan I, who was twenty-
five at the time, had only to leave his child-bride alone and Portugal would be
his – and in due course Castile's.[91]

Juan I had only to wait therefore, and contain himself. Yet such was his
desire to possess another kingdom that, rather than leaving the regents to
create their own confusion, he proceeded to annex the royal arms of Portugal
to his standard and entered the country in force. Historians who think they
understand the thought-processes of medieval kings consider his actions odd.
There was a degree of method in his madness, however. In 1383 the prospect
of completing an anti-English occupation of the entire coastline from
Flanders to Cape St Vincent made good strategic sense.[92] But considerations
such as these evoked little sympathy in Lisbon where popular opinion was outraged. The Master of Avis (who as yet had no ambitions in the matter, it is
implausibly suggested) murdered Ourém, the capital's Castilian bishop Martín
was thrown to his death from the cathedral tower, and Leonor Teles fled the
city. Lisbon was besieged by the invaders, the crowd acclaimed Avis *regedor e
defensor* of the kingdom (December 1383), and envoys were sent to England to
raise troops. At this point plague intervened, accounting for the best of the
Castilian commanders and forcing Juan I's withdrawal (September 1384).

Peninsular plague and the less dependable English, who arrived in small
numbers in April 1385, together proved effective. They were assisted, fifteenth-
century tradition relates, by the admixture of political thought and legalistic
special pleading to which in March 1385 the *cortes* of Coimbra was subjected by
Avis's *chanceler-mor*, João das Regras. The Bolognese-trained jurist was the
impresario of the *cortes* of Coimbra. In a virtuoso display of learning and
forensic skill which cut a swathe through royal Portugal's recent history of
adultery, cuckoldry and plain carelessness, he made light of all claims to the
throne other than those of his master. A letter of Pope Innocent VI was produced to establish the invalidity of Pedro I's marriage to Inês de Castro,
thereby putting paid to the prospects of their sons João and Dinis. Fernando
I's paternity of Beatriz was brought into question, and Beatriz herself was
ruled out for having married a Castilian supporter of the Avignonese Clement
VII.

For an old Bologna hand, all this would have been plain sailing. The problem
was that the Master of Avis was as much a bastard as his half-brothers and that
as a member of a military order he was technically excluded from exercising
royal power. (Indeed, Urban VI had to be persuaded to dispense him from the

[91] Russell (1955), pp. 362–3.   [92] Suárez Fernández (1955), p. 47.

monastic vows which had not hampered him when it had come to committing murder.) What secured the proclamation of the Master of Avis as King João I was not his legitimacy but his proven success and the strength of his political following.

Equally, what secured both his own survival and that of Portugal's independence was his victory over a numerically superior Castilian force at Aljubarrota on 14 August 1385, a victory which – in Russell's words – 'must rank among the most decisive engagements of medieval warfare'.[93] The 'Crisis of 1383–5' continues to preoccupy Portuguese historians. For Fernão Lopes in the 1430s it ushered in the Augustinian seventh age of History, no less. Today the question is whether to classify it as patriotic uprising or as an episode in the class war.[94]

Now as then, however, Portugal's crisis defies facile categorisation. As well as representing the struggle for mastery in these years as the entry into a 'new world' of a 'new generation of people', Fernão Lopes also recorded the real divisions within real families that it created.[95] And in the immediate aftermath of battle, the first thoughts of the first king of the new dynasty ran along traditional lines and found expression in the strengthening of his alliance with England and his marriage with Philippa, Gaunt's daughter (Treaty of Windsor, May 1386).

The terms in which the Portuguese chronicler sang his hero's praises mark a sharp contrast between João I's Portugal and Castile's seedy discontinuities under its first three Trastamaran kings. Flanked by Pere III of Aragon in his dotage and Fernando I of Portugal at his best, however, Enrique II flourished and, with what a modern Castilian historian describes as the 're-establishment of a peninsular equilibrium',[96] for the time being Castilian predominance was assured. But the price to be paid for the restoration of the old order was not modest. At least in the earliest years of the reign, the lavish scale of the usurper's remuneration of his confederates – members of his family and of the lesser nobility whom he rewarded with titles and offices respectively, as well as the French companies (with du Guesclin receiving a ducal title) and the Church – seriously endangered the royal fisc, as did the creation of entailed estates (*mayorazgos*) and the devaluation of the currency in order to pay off Enrique's French debts. A halt was called by the reactivated *cortes* (Medina del Campo, 1370; Toro, 1371) at which at the insistence of the *concejos* these ruinous measures were abandoned and the judicial system was overhauled by the creation of an *Audiencia* staffed by a permanent cadre of seven *oidores*.[97]

---

[93] Caetano (1951); Brásio (1958); Russell (1955), pp. 357–99.
[94] Caetano (1953); Coelho (1984); Rebelo (1981) and (1983), pp. 57–110; Mattoso (1985).
[95] Serrão (1979) I, pp. 298–313.   [96] Valdeón Baruque (1966), p. 203.
[97] *Cortes*, II, pp. 185–256; Suárez Fernández (1959), pp. 17–27; Valdeón Baruque (1966), pp. 273–363.

If it be legitimate to endow periods of history with human characteristics then it may be suggested that on Enrique II's death in January 1379 the Castilian fourteenth century lost its nerve and that the brooding Juan I (1379–90) was a fitting representative of the new neurasthenic age. Aljubarrota was Juan I's Waterloo. Victory there would have established him and his dynasty on a firm footing. As it was, the *cortes* took advantage of the king's military humiliation and, by claiming the right to control the crown, not least in its financial dealings, sought to 'subvert by revolution the country's constitutional structure'.[98] At Valladolid in 1385, the royal council was reconstituted, comprising four members of each of the three estates of the realm. At Briviesca in 1387 the members of the third estate were replaced by four jurists, reflecting the ascendancy of a group which was also apparent at the Portuguese court, the *audiencia* was reformed and located in specified cities for regular three-monthly periods, and (echoes of Aljubarrota) plans were tabled for the creation of a standing army of 10,000 men – though, because the cost proved prohibitive, at the *cortes* of Guadalajara in 1390 its size was almost halved.[99]

As to the significance of the '*cortes* revolution' in the reign of Juan I, his most recent historian appears uncertain.[100] As to that of the *cortes* of Guadalajara of 1390, however, he inclines to the view that its extensive legislation represented a new deal for Castile, reflecting the new power and influence of the ascendant oligarchy of royal servants who had distinguished themselves in the royal service at and after Aljubarrota at the expense of those members of the old nobility who had either disgraced themselves or had perished there.[101] This appears fanciful. For despite the truces with Gaunt and João I (Bayonne 1388, Leulingham 1389), whereby Gaunt renounced his claim to the Castilian throne in return for 600,000 gold *doblas* and the marriage of his daughter Catalina of Lancaster to the future Enrique III,[102] King Juan's Portuguese obsession remained intact. Indeed, at the Guadalajara *cortes* itself he declared his intention of abdicating in order to pursue his Portuguese claim. But for his council's patient demonstration of the fatal consequences of territorial partition over the previous three centuries, he would have appropriated Andalusia, Murcia, the lordship of Vizcaya and the *tercias* of the kingdom to himself, leaving what was left of Castile to his ten-year-old son and a regency government. It is clear from the terms in which he did so that his acceptance of sane advice to the

---

[98] Pérez-Prendes (1974), pp. 58–9; Suárez Fernández (1977–82), I, pp. 253–4.

[99] Russell (1955), pp. 400–531; Suárez Fernández (1976), pp. 287–303; Serrão (1979), I, p. 309; Suárez Fernández (1977–82), I, pp. 337–50, 373–6.

[100] Thus Suárez Fernández (1977–82), I, p. 318 (*cortes* 'wholly submissive'), 335 (role of *cortes* 'indispensable'). Cf. Burns (1992), pp. 74–5.

[101] Suárez Fernández (1977–82), I, pp. 373–88 ('Las Cortes de Guadalajara . . . constituyeron, sin duda, una puerta a la esperanza', p. 388).   [102] Both were great-grandchildren of Alfonso XI.

contrary was only temporary.[103] Fortunately for Castile, Juan I fell off his horse later that year and died.

There was another sense, dynastic rather than personal, in which Aljubarrota was as much a watershed for Castile as it was for Portugal. After 1385 both countries were ruled by kings of dubious legitimacy. But João had won the battle, which enabled his propagandists to represent him as a messianic figure,[104] whereas Juan had lost it, and with it the kingdom for which he was prepared to sacrifice the kingdom he actually possessed. In his post-Aljubarrota dejection Juan I prohibited the representation of the king of Castile as the king of kings and sought reassurance elsewhere. At the *cortes* of Segovia (1386) he cast around for alternative inspiration, and found it up the family tree. His legitimacy, he now claimed, derived from Alfonso X's eldest son Fernando de la Cerda and had descended not through his father but via his mother Juana Manuel.[105] Alongside this perilous argument he declared a commitment to the cause of ecclesiastical reform and adumbrated the sense of those religious responsibilities of the Christian king with which the extraordinary measures contained in the three tracts promulgated at Briviesca in the following year were imbued. Rooted in the conviction that the implemention of the moral law was the monarch's responsibility – especially perhaps at a time when the Schism had fractured the principle of papal authority – the Briviesca measures included prescriptions for the chaining up of disobedient children and the correction of clerical concubinage as well as for the rigid segregation of Jews and Moors. In the mid-1380s we are light years distant from the Castile of Alfonso XI.[106]

In order to eradicate the abuses that had long plagued Castilian society – and during the reign of Alfonso XI had been immortalised by the archpriest of Hita, Juan Ruiz, in his *Libro de buen amor* – at the same *cortes* of Guadalajara Juan I undertook the reform of the economic basis of the Castilian Church. In this task, which was a tall order, he was assisted by prelates of the stature of Archbishop Pedro Tenorio of Toledo and the bishop of Oviedo, Gutierre Gómez de Toledo – to whose church the county of Noreña was transferred after Alfonso Enríquez, Enrique II's bastard, had eventually exhausted his half-brother's patience. In the same spirit he patronised the Carthusian Order (newcomers to Castile) and the Jeronimites, further promoted the latter's shrine at Guadalupe, and lavishly endowed the Benedictines of Valladolid – conditional upon their strict observance of the rules of claustration.[107]

---

[103] *CJI*, pp. 125–9; Russell (1955), pp. 530–1.   [104] Rebelo (1983), pp. 57–89.

[105] Nieto Soria (1988), pp. 57, 72; *Cortes*, II, pp. 352–3, 363; Russell (1955), pp. 496–8.

[106] *Cortes*, II, pp. 362–78.

[107] Ibid., pp. 449–59; *CJI*, pp. 133–4; Suárez Fernández (1977–82), I, pp. 316, 362–72; García y García (1981–); Fernández Conde (1978), pp. 97–127, (1978), pp. 97–127, and (1980–2), I, pp. 451–61.

Hardly less pronounced than the contrast between Juan I and his father was that between him and his genial contemporary Carlos III of Navarre (1387–1425). And the latter, in turn, was the antithesis of *his* father, the disasters of whose administration Carlos III, 'the Noble', dedicated his own early years to repairing, restoring the royal finances and navarrising the administration. In pursuit of a settlement with the French king regarding the lands confiscated from his father – a settlement finally secured in 1404 by the exchange of the counties of Champagne, Evreux and Avranches for the rents and title of the newly created duchy of Nemours and the sale of Cherbourg for £200,000 – Carlos III was obliged to travel frequently to France on the off-chance of coinciding with one of Charles VI's lucid intervals. He was nevertheless the most peninsularly committed ruler of Navarre since the 1230s, peaceful and straightforward by temperament and a firm adherent of the Castilian alliance, which secured the recovery of Tudela, Estella and San Vicente (August 1387). Yet his melancholic wife, Juan I's sister, Leonor conceived the idea that he was intent on poisoning her, and in 1388 took up residence in Castile, where she remained for all of seven years, contributing by her mischievous presence to the state of imminent anarchy which constantly threatened throughout the minority of Enrique III.[108]

As the young king's aunt, in 1390 Leonor provided the Trastámara old guard with timely reinforcement when, after decades of plague and warfare, and with the *cortes* effervescent, the various elements which Juan I had somehow maintained in uneasy equilibrium threatened Castile with a return to the divisions and tensions of the 1290s and 1310s. With no María de Molina in the offing – Beatriz of Portugal was hardly fitted for the part – on this occasion the *cortes* occupied the political void. It is a measure of the political shift that had occurred over the century, as well as an indication of the growing importance of Madrid in the kingdom's affairs, that in 1390 it was the 123 *procuradores* of the 49 cities represented there that decided the outcome, invoking the scheme of a regency council proposed by Juan I on the occasion of his attempted abdication, and ensuring that members of their estate constituted a majority – fourteen out of twenty-four – on that body. The seizure of the initiative by the *cortes* of Madrid (January–April 1391) revealed the extent of the divisions within the political establishment which undermined the attempts of Archbishop Pedro Tenorio to maintain oligarchical control by appealing both to a long-forgotten will of Juan I and to the provision of the *Sieta Partidas* that there be one, three or five regents. There were not that many men in the kingdom with whom the kingdom would be content, the chronicler Ayala remarked.[109] Talk of tutors

---

[108] Castro (1967); Lacarra (1972–3), II, pp. 161–91, 204–17; Leroy (1988).

[109] *CEIII*, pp. 161–4, 186–94; *Cortes*, II, pp. 485–7; above, n. 3; Suárez Fernández (1955), pp. 609–14.

and regents served as reminder of the bad old days of Alfonso XI's minority, he added. If the self-confidence of the *cortes* represented an advance on the exploratory constitutionalism of the 1310s, as then the towns and cities of the kingdom were divided and liable to social breakdown. The tendency of the provinces to slip the leash of authority is said to have been especially prevalent in the north in these years.[110] But it was in the south that in June 1391 public order collapsed completely and the Jewish *aljamas* were besieged. Popular prejudice had associated the Jews with Pedro I. But Spain's Jews had been at risk since the 630s, and Pedro I's downfall had not exposed them to the venom and vituperation that they encountered in 1391. Incited by the fanatical Ferrán Martínez archdeacon of Ecija, the pogroms of 1391 registered the final disintegration of the last semblance of authority in fourteenth-century Castile. Launched at Seville, where as many as 4,000 deaths were recorded, from there the mania spread throughout Andalusia. The north was less affected. According to Ayala, it was avarice that was the cause, not devotion.[111]

With the ending of the regency (August 1393), the personal reign of Enrique III *el Doliente* (the Doleful, d. 1406) commenced. It was notable for the restoration of a semblance of order in the south and the purposeful pursuit of the seditious old nobility. Thus, the year 1395 witnessed both the re-establishment of the *corregidores* in Seville and the Basque country, and the elimination of that inveterate troublemaker the count of Noreña and the destruction of his stronghold at Gijón. The beneficiaries of this process were members of the newly ennobled families which had occupied the social and political vacuum created at and after Aljubarrota.[112]

On Christmas Day 1384 the use of the Spanish *era* in the dating of Castilian documents had been abandoned in favour of the chronological practices of the nations of Europe with which the peninsular kingdoms had become increasingly enmeshed.[113] It is therefore tempting to regard this adjustment, together with the initiatives taken by Enrique III in the later 1390s, as symbolising the end of an era at an altogether more profound level. Tempting but scarcely justified. True, Enrique III was the first king of Castile since Fernando III to father no bastards. Otherwise not very much had changed over the previous two centuries – as the ordinance enacted in 1396 to discourage the use of mules demonstrated.[114]

The mule law confirmed that Castilian society at the end of the fourteenth century remained what it had always been, a horse-centred society, a society organised for war. But midway between the death of Sancho IV and the

[110] Valdeón Baruque (1975), p. 383.   [111] Wolff (1971), pp. 8–9; *CEIII*, p. 177b.
[112] Suárez Fernández (1976), pp. 328–42; Mitre Fernández (1968), pp. 23–70, and (1969); Bermúdez Aznar (1989), pp. 580–4.   [113] *CJI*, pp. 148–9; García y López (1892–3), II, pp. 261–2.
[114] *Cortes*, II, pp. 532–7.

reconquest of Granada, it also testified to the strength of the various vested
interests upon whose sundry services that society depended which had frustrated Alfonso XI's similar attempt to promote Castilian chivalry in 1331.[115]
Archbishops, royal physicians, masters of theology, falconers and the rest –
all were assigned their hierarchically calculated variation from the norm.
Castilian society remained as honeycombed with exceptions to every rule as
its rulers continued persuaded that they were actually capable of keeping
count of the mounts astride which those archbishops and the rest sat saddled
as they went about their business.

[115] Linehan (1993a), p. 582.

PART III

THE CHURCH AND POLITICS

CHAPTER 19

THE AVIGNON PAPACY

P. N. R. Zutshi

ROME OR AVIGNON?

SEVEN popes in succession resided at Avignon in the years 1309–76.[1] That the pope, the bishop of Rome, did not live in the Eternal City was neither new nor remarkable by the fourteenth century. In the thirteenth century (and earlier) Rome was a dangerous place because of the riots and tumults there, in which the Roman aristocracy took a leading part. Moreover, the city was unhealthy in summer. The popes habitually spent periods away from Rome in one of the towns of the Papal State, notably Viterbo, Anagni, Orvieto, Perugia and Rieti. It has been calculated that in the years 1198–1304 the popes spent about 60 per cent of their time away from Rome. The one pope in this period who spent his entire pontificate in Rome was Celestine IV, and he was pope for only seventeen days. After 1226 no pope spent the whole summer in Rome.[2] Yet it was quite unprecedented for the popes in the fourteenth century to spend seventy years away from Italy.

Benedict XI (1303–4) established himself at Perugia. In 1305, the cardinals elected Bertrand de Got, archbishop of Bordeaux, as his successor (Clement V, 1305–14). Although Clement on various occasions declared that he intended to journey to Rome, he never managed to leave southern France during his pontificate of almost nine years. There were several reasons for this: Clement's love of his native land, Gascony, and of his fellow-countrymen, on whom his patronage was lavished; his close relations with Philip the Fair of France; his desire to negotiate a peace between the kings of England and France; his plan to hold a general council at Vienne, which took place in 1311; his poor health; and the chaotic state of northern and central Italy.

---

[1] Mollat (1965) and Guillemain (1962) are the standard works on the Avignon popes. The main primary sources are the registers of their letters (published in part by the Ecole française de Rome), the accounts of the papal chamber (published in part in the series Vatikanische Quellen) and the contemporary lives (edited by Baluze, new edn by Mollat, 1914–27).

[2] Paravicini Bagliani (1991), pp. 502–3.

Following his election, Clement moved from one place to the next. In 1309 he came to Avignon. He did not intend to make this peaceful town his permanent residence. He lived in the Dominican convent there, and occasionally left Avignon for Groseau, Carpentras or another town in the region. However, the advantages of Avignon for the papacy soon became apparent. It was adjacent to the Comtat-Venaissin, which had been in the possession of the papacy since 1274, and which was the only extensive papal territory outside Italy. However, Avignon itself belonged to the count of Provence, who was also king of Sicily (Naples) and thus a vassal of the Holy See. To complicate matters further, Avignon's ultimate temporal suzerain was the emperor, although his powers there were only nominal. Avignon is on the eastern bank of the Rhône, which was one of the main European trade routes, above all for the traffic between the Netherlands and Italy. The city was more conveniently situated than central Italy for most countries with which the papacy was in frequent contact. This applies to France, England, Germany and, to a certain extent, the Iberian kingdoms; the main exceptions were the Italian states.[3]

Avignon became the stable seat of the papacy under Clement's successor, John XXII (Jacques Duèse, 1316–34). Before he became a cardinal, he had been bishop of Avignon, and even as pope John lived in the episcopal palace, which he altered and extended. These arrangements would have been inconvenient for the then bishop, who was the pope's nephew. John elevated him to the cardinalate and then left the see vacant. In 1330–2 there were plans to move the papal curia to Bologna, as the first stage in returning to Rome. The idea was reiterated at the beginning of the pontificate of Benedict XII (Jacques Fournier, 1334–42) but soon abandoned. The episcopal palace became the basis of the construction of a massive new residence at Avignon, the Palais des Papes. This indicates that there was now no prospect of an early return to Italy. The austere appearance of the palace befitted a pope who was a Cistercian monk and a reformer of both the papal curia and the religious orders. Clement VI (Pierre Roger, 1342–52) was also a monk (a Benedictine), but he extended and decorated the palace in a more lavish style; for instance, a team of painters under the direction of Matteo Giovanetti of Viterbo was employed. Clement bought the town of Avignon from Queen Joanna of Sicily for 80,000 florins in 1348. This strengthened the popes' independence from secular control, at least in theory. Work on the palace continued under Innocent VI (Etienne Aubert, 1352–62) and Urban V (Guillaume Grimoard, 1362–70). These popes and Gregory XI (Pierre Roger de Beaufort, 1370–8) fortified the town when it was threatened by the mercenary companies unleashed by the Hundred Years War. Building activities were not confined to Avignon. John

---

[3] On the advantages of Avignon see Renouard (1954), pp. 13–19, 25–8; Guillemain (1962), pp. 77–88.

XXII, for instance, constructed at least six castles in the region, as well as the summer palace and papal mint at Sorgues. From 1316 to 1322, the building costs at Sorgues were greater than those at Avignon. The mint remained there until it was moved to Avignon in about 1354. At Villeneuve-lès-Avignon, situated on the opposite bank of the Rhône from Avignon and lying within the kingdom of France, several cardinals built summer palaces. Napoleone Orsini's palace was acquired by Pierre Roger. When the latter became Pope Clement VI, the palace was extended and used as a papal residence. In addition the popes promoted the construction of new churches, monasteries and educational foundations. Thus Innocent VI established the vast Charterhouse at Villeneuve-lès-Avignon, and Urban V founded two colleges at Montpellier and reconstructed his old abbey of St Victor, Marseille.

Under Urban V the question of the return of the papacy to Italy was again in the foreground. The Avignon region was now less secure, and the pacification of the Papal State by Cardinal Albornoz made this ambition realisable. In October 1367 Urban entered Rome. Faced with the rebellion of Perugia and other difficulties in Italy, Urban returned to Avignon in 1370. Gregory XI was equally anxious to return to Rome and left Avignon in 1376, undeterred by the war with Florence then raging. Unlike Urban, Gregory succeeded in dying at Rome. The decision of these two popes to abandon Avignon is doubtless associated with the religious sentiments of their age. Rome, rather than Avignon, was still the focus of devotion and the destination of pilgrimages, including those inspired by the successful Jubilee of 1350. From Gregory's words to certain citizens of Avignon in 1375 we can see that to him returning to Rome was a matter of conscience. He said that the previous year he had been seriously ill, and he attributed this illness to his failure to reside in Rome.[4] There was opposition to the wishes of Urban and Gregory from those who had benefited from the papal residence at Avignon, notably the king of France, the cardinals and the inhabitants of the town. In both 1367 and 1376, several cardinals remained behind at Avignon.

The popes' return to Rome was partly dependent on conditions in Italy, especially in the Papal State. The latter was an agglomerate of distinct territories: the Campagna and Marittima (Lazio), the Patrimony of St Peter in Tuscany, the duchy of Spoleto, the March of Ancona and the Romagna. A major preoccupation of the Avignon popes was controlling these now more distant provinces. There were marked differences of approach between the popes. Clement V, Benedict XII and Clement VI were anxious in general to avoid heavy military expenditure. They contented themselves with exercising a lesser degree of power than was acceptable to John XXII and to Innocent

---

[4] Segre, 'I dispacci di Cristoforo da Piacenza', p. 70.

VI and his successors. Clement V, as a sign of favour to the Gascon Amanieu d'Albret, rector of the Patrimony, permitted him to collect taxes without rendering an account of them. It is difficult to conceive of such a concession being made by John XXII, who ordered more elaborate accounting procedures to be adopted in the duchy. John's desire to control Italy closely is evident in his declaration in the constitution *Si fratrum* of 1317 that during a vacancy of the empire the pope exercised imperial jurisdiction, in his consequent appointment of Robert II of Anjou, king of Sicily, as imperial vicar, and in his sending the uncompromising Cardinal Bertrand du Pouget as papal legate to Italy. He was the first of a series of legates in Italy equipped by the popes with extensive, 'viceregal' powers. Despite the vast sums expended (in fourteen years 2,480,000 florins were sent to du Pouget), the papal army was crushed at Ferrara and the papacy lost control of Bologna (1333–4). The task of Benedict XII's legate in Italy, Bertrand de Déaulx, was to reform the Papal State, and he issued constitutions for the various provinces in 1335–6. None the less, papal power in the March and the Romagna was rather limited at about this time. Clement VI again sent Bertrand de Déaulx as legate to Italy, but with greater powers. One of his tasks was to deal with Cola di Rienzo, who took control of Rome for six months in 1347. A new development was the enlisting of a band of foreign mercenaries by Astorge de Durfort, rector of the Romagna, in 1350. Mercenary companies were to be used extensively by Cardinal Gil Albornoz and his successors.

Innocent VI appointed the Castilian Albornoz legate in Italy and vicar-general of the papal territories there in 1353. Albornoz reasserted the authority of the papacy over these territories with remarkable energy and speed. In the Tuscan Patrimony, where the rebel Giovanni di Vico was entrenched, the key towns submitted. In the March, Albornoz came to terms with the Malatesta of Rimini. In the Romagna, Cesena and Forlì were captured from Francesco Ordelaffi and, most spectacularly, Bologna was wrested from the rule of the Visconti (1360). Four years' war with the latter followed. It was only with the conquest of Assisi and other towns and the defeat of Perugia (1367) that papal control of the duchy was effectively exerted.

Albornoz's conquests were followed by the building of fortresses. When he came to terms with an existing tyrant, his practice was to confer the apostolic vicariate on him, which legitimised the tyrant's rule. In return, a census was payable. The Malatesta, for instance, were appointed vicars of Rimini and three other towns for ten years and undertook to pay a census of 6,000 florins per annum and to provide the service of 100 horsemen. In 1357, at a *parlamentum generale* held at Fano, Albornoz published his celebrated law code for the Papal State, the *Constitutiones Egidiane*. It largely re-enacted earlier legislation, including that of Bertrand de Déaulx, but there was some new material, while superseded or redundant laws were excluded. Revised in the sixteenth century, the constitutions remained in force until 1816. They were Albornoz's most durable legacy. He died in 1367, having failed to enjoy the complete confidence of the curia. There were doubts about the cost of his warfare and about his policy of granting away papal rights to vicars. Albornoz sometimes found it necessary to ignore papal instructions. Innocent VI replaced him with the more pacific Androin de la Roche in 1357–8. Although Albornoz was then restored to office, from 1363 his legation was divided with de la Roche, who was appointed legate in Lombardy, to which the Romagna was soon added.

The political legacy of Albornoz was fragile: 'ignis de brevi extinctus faciliter reaccenditur' (fire quickly extinguished is easily reignited), as the vicar-general in the Papal State from 1367 to 1371, Anglic Grimoard, wrote. He was faced with the rebellion of Perugia and a further war with the Visconti. Grimoard was in the tradition of papal governors interested in compiling information about their lands. At his instance, a detailed description of the Romagna was compiled in 1370–1. Grimoard's difficulties in ruling his subjects – *homines . . . passionatissimi* – are vividly depicted in the advice he prepared for his successor in the Romagna and the March, Cardinal Pierre d'Estaing.[5] No sooner had the papacy made peace with the Visconti (1375) than a revolt broke out from a more unexpected quarter – Florence, traditionally a papal ally. It spread to much of the Papal State, including Perugia and Bologna. By the time of Gregory XI's death, many towns had come to terms, and the Florentines were negotiating with the pope.

RELATIONS WITH FRANCE

Few questioned the legitimacy of the Avignon popes prior to the Schism. The pope was not obliged to live in Rome. The adage *ubi est papa, ibi est Roma* acquired a new relevance in the fourteenth century. It is true that, at the time of the struggle between the emperor Lewis of Bavaria and the papacy, there were thorough and radical attacks on the latter (extending far beyond the place of its residence). However, the views of Marsilius of Padua or William of Ockham were not typical. This is not to say that the popes were exempt from criticism. Contemporaries often attacked them virulently for, *inter alia*, their failure to reside in Rome. Such critics were above all Italian, for the Italians felt the economic loss and the loss of prestige occasioned by the absence of the popes. The most famous and, at least as far as later generations are concerned, the most influential critic was Francis Petrarch. He spent long periods in Avignon and its region and was friendly with Clement VI and with cardinals

---

[5] Theiner, *Codex Diplomaticus*, II, pp. 527–39, no. 527 (the quotations are on pp. 537 and 539).

and curialists; but he evidently hated Avignon. He referred to it as 'Babylon' and 'hell'.[6] Even today historians, echoing the language of Petrarch and of Luther, sometimes talk of the 'Babylonish captivity' of the Church in this period. It is no coincidence that the most convincing corrective to such views has come from French historians, notably Etienne Baluze in the seventeenth century and Guillaume Mollat in the twentieth. Indeed, historians have tended to divide on national, rather than confessional, lines in their attitude to the Avignon papacy, the French and Italians typically acting as the protagonists for and against.

A constant question in the historiography has been whether the Avignon popes were subservient to the French monarchy. In the absence of an up-to-date general study of the relations between these two powers, it is a difficult question to answer. It is necessary first to remember that Avignon was situated in the empire, not in the kingdom of France. The Avignon popes all came from southern France, but their connections with the French crown before their elections differed. Clement V had been in the service of both Philip the Fair and Edward I of England. As archbishop of Bordeaux, he was the immediate vassal of the duke of Aquitaine, that is, the king of England. Both kings received valuable financial concessions from him as pope. John XXII had been chancellor of the Angevin kingdom of Sicily. Robert II of Sicily and Philip V of France supported his election as pope. Benedict XII, Urban V and Gregory XI had no particular association with the French crown before their elections. Clement VI and Innocent VI, on the other hand, had both been in the royal service. Clement VI, who made his name as a theologian in the university of Paris, was sent by Philip VI on diplomatic missions, and he was a member of the *chambre des enquêtes* and presided over the *chambre des comptes*.

The Avignon popes were in general conciliatory in their relations with secular powers. They favoured these powers, and the kings of France were undoubtedly favoured the most. Only with the Angevin rulers of Naples were relations at times as close. It is worth noting that almost all the successful processes of canonisation in the period were promoted by these two houses. Clement V was the most pliant of the popes towards the French monarchy, partly because of his own weak character and partly because of the vulnerable position in which the papacy found itself following the struggle between Boniface VIII and Philip the Fair. In 1311 Clement succeeded in taking full control of the posthumous process that Philip had ruthlessly instituted against Boniface on the charge of heresy, and it was then abandoned. In return, Philip was exculpated for the attack on Boniface at Anagni. The destruction of the

---

[6] E.g. Petrarca, *Le Familiari*, XII.8: 'mox enim michi iterum invito babilonicus uncus iniectus est retractusque sum ad inferos'. For other passages see de Sade (1764–7), I, pp. 25–7.

wealthy Templar Order was now a higher priority for Philip, and the pope dissolved the order at the Council of Vienne in 1312. The king of France received generous financial assistance from the papacy, much of it in the form of the proceeds of taxes on ecclesiastical revenues. The taxes were in general intended for the crusade, but the kings of France used them for their wars against the kings of England or against Flanders. Clement VI lent the king of France 620,000 florins, and it was hardly to be expected that this sum would be repaid. The Avignon popes intervened in these wars (the Hundred Years War and its precursors), attempting to establish peace. They emphasised their impartiality, but the English suspected them of favouring the French. It is not difficult to find examples of this bias. In 1338 Benedict XII excommunicated the Flemings after they had formed an alliance with Edward III. Edward thought that he had been so poorly treated by Clement VI that he considered appealing to a general council. Through their authority to grant marriage dispensations, the popes hindered Edward's alliances and assisted those of the kings of France. Thus Urban V refused a dispensation for the marriage between Edward's son Edmund and Margaret, the heiress of the counties of Flanders, Burgundy, Artois, Nevers and Rethel. This marriage would have greatly increased English power in France. Margaret instead married Philip the Bold, duke of Burgundy.

It should not, however, be assumed that the Avignon popes were no more than creatures of the kings of France. The popes often rejected royal demands, and there were major disputes between the two powers, especially over ecclesiastical jurisdiction within the kingdom of France. If the popes in general inclined to the French crown, this did not only reflect their personal preferences and background; it was also a matter of policy. The fate of the papacy was now bound up with that of the French monarchy. The popes looked to the French to support their crusading plans and their Italian policy. The close relations with France had advantages for the papacy. A substantial part of papal income came from France, and a disproportionately large number of provisions concerned benefices in France. Under Benedict XII the figure was about 60 per cent.

CRUSADES AND MISSIONS

If it is desirable to distinguish between the attitudes of different popes in considering Franco-papal relations, this applies even more to their attitudes to the crusade. One may compare the behaviour of Benedict XII with that of his predecessor and his successor. The cautious Benedict cancelled the crusading project of Philip VI of France. John XXII also had reservations about the involvement of the kings of France in crusading, but in other respects he was more enthusiastic. He intervened in the affairs of the Hospitallers, and he sent money to assist the Armenians in their resistance against the Muslims. Clement VI gave high priority to crusading. His objectives were in general limited and realistic. He formed a naval league against the emirates of Anatolia. In 1344 its fleet of twenty galleys, four of which were provided by the pope, captured Smyrna, which remained in Christian hands until 1402. Under Urban V another modest expedition, intended to aid the Byzantine empire and commanded by Amedeo, count of Savoy, was successful. It captured Gallipoli and other towns from the Ottoman Turks in 1366. The expedition doubtless encouraged the emperor John V's submission to the Roman Church in 1369. This did not, however, lead to the reunion with the Greek Church so much desired by the popes. Gregory XI concentrated on making fuller use of the resources of the Hospitallers for crusading expeditions.

In the Avignon period the crusade continued to be a papal monopoly. Even if crusades were not invariably papal initiatives, they required papal approval. Only the pope could grant the indulgences and other special privileges which distinguished a crusade from other military expeditions. The popes had an active role in the promotion, organisation and direction of crusades. Expeditions were sometimes accompanied by a papal legate; for instance, Pierre Thomas was legate on the crusade of Peter I, king of Cyprus, which captured (but failed to retain) Alexandria in 1365. None the less, papal control of the crusading movement was far from complete. The inability of the popes to prevent secular rulers from directing crusading taxes to other purposes is notorious. Great interest in the theory and practice of crusading continued to be shown in the fourteenth century, but the results of that interest were meagre. Most of those involved in launching crusades against the Muslims, including the popes, had more immediately pressing preoccupations. This can be illustrated by the fate of the small fleet assembled on the orders of John XXII for an expedition to be commanded by Louis of Clermont. The pope lent the ten galleys in 1319 to King Robert of Sicily to assist in his war against the Ghibellines in the gulf of Genoa, and no more is heard of them. They may have been destroyed in a storm. The problem is even better illustrated by Urban V's assurance to Albornoz in 1363 that there would be no crusade to the east until Bernabò Visconti had been dealt with.[7]

The papacy declared crusades against the Moors in Spain and the pagans of Lithuania, but crusades were not limited to expeditions against non-Christians. In the eyes of the popes, heretics and schismatics were equally legitimate targets. These terms were defined with latitude and included those who resisted

[7] Housley (1986), pp. 78, 114–15.

the temporal authority of the papacy in Italy. In 1322 the pope condemned the Visconti as heretics and proclaimed a crusade against them. There were later crusades against the Visconti and against mercenary companies. A crusade against Venice in 1308–9 brought the republic to terms.

The Avignon popes devoted less energy and fewer resources to the extension of Christianity by missionaries than to crusades against the infidel. None the less, the missionary work bore some fruit, even if success was confined to territories not under the control of Muslim rulers. The missionaries were mainly Franciscan and Dominican friars. An off-shoot of the Dominican Order, the *societas peregrinantium*, was formed especially for missionary work. The establishment of missionary sees in the Mongol empire was a particular feature of the Avignon period. Clement V created an archbishopric at Khanbaliq (Beijing – Peking) in 1307, and appointed the Franciscan Giovanni da Montecorvino to it. Spectacular successes in converting the population were reported here, but they do not seem to have been durable. In 1318 John XXII created another missionary province, with six suffragan bishops, that of Sultaniyeh, the capital of the Mongol khans of Persia. The province was under Dominican control and the *societas peregrinantium* supplied three of its archbishops. Three metropolitan sees were created in the territory of the Golden Horde (consisting of the area surrounding the Black Sea and of the Caucasus), Vospro (1333), Matrega (1349) and Sarai (1362), but none of them lasted for long. Sarai was carved out of the province of Khanbaliq. In southern India John XXII appointed an experienced Dominican missionary, Jourdain Cathala de Sévérac, as bishop of Quilon. Special circumstances determined the course of missions in Armenia, since the Church here was, at least nominally, subject to the papacy. Complete union with the Latin Church was agreed at the Council of Sis (1307), but its precepts were not observed outside the Cilician kingdom of Armenia (Lesser Armenia). There were concerted efforts to achieve a closer union, especially in the use of Latin rites, in both Lesser and Greater Armenia. These were led by the Armenian bishop Nerses Balientz. The Dominicans in Greater Armenia, who desired strict adherence to Latin rites, formed a new order, the *fratres unitores*, approved by Innocent VI in 1362. They became the principal instruments of the expansion of Latin influence in Armenia.

The papacy furthered missions in various ways. John XXII, for instance, in 1328 asked the Dominican chapter meeting at Toulouse to supply at least fifty friars for missionary work. There was also direct financial support. As we have seen, the popes created and filled missionary sees. They granted special privileges and wide powers to missionaries, permitting missionary archbishops to create new suffragan sees, something which normally only the pope could do.

THE PAPAL COURT: ADMINISTRATIVE ORGANISATION AND
CARDINALS

The papal curia at Avignon differed from the thirteenth-century curia through its stability. It was largely free from the disruption caused in the thirteenth century by the curia's itinerant character. When the pope was absent from Avignon, much of the administration seems to have remained there. Even when Urban V and Gregory XI left for Rome, numerous officials stayed behind. The stability of the curia enabled the organs of government to develop; and this development was also necessary, since the central and accessible location of the town meant an increase in the amount of business at the curia.

The largest administrative department was probably the apostolic chancery. Its head was the vice-chancellor, who was normally a cardinal. It was responsible for producing letters issued in the name of the pope. The majority of these were common letters, that is, responses to petitions. If someone wished to obtain a favour from the pope, he had to submit a petition in the chancery, and the petition was heard by the pope or, in the case of less important business, by the vice-chancellor. The chancery was therefore in contact with petitioners from all over Latin Christendom or with their agents. A petitioner would appoint an agent (or proctor) if he did not wish to travel to the curia himself. It was also advantageous to do so, in so far as proctors tended to have a good knowledge of what Petrarch called the *inextricabile curie labyrinthum*.[8] They were active in various departments of the curia, including the chancery. Towards the end of his pontificate, John XXII introduced reforms, notably in the constitution *Pater familias*, which were probably intended to enable the chancery to cope better with the increase in business. From now on, there was greater differentiation in the treatment of different types of letters. The process of issuing letters of justice, which for the most part only appointed a judge or judges to hear a particular case, continued to be rather simple. This does not apply to letters of grace, which contained definite concessions (for instance, they bestowed ecclesiastical benefices or spiritual favours on their beneficiaries). With these, the controls multiplied. It became normal practice, for example, for such letters to be copied into the papal registers. Under Benedict XII, if not earlier, official registers of petitions for letters of grace were instituted. The reforms of John XXII and Benedict XII had the effect of making the procedure by which common letters were issued more regular.

In addition to papal letters issued in response to petitions, there were those issued on the initiative of the papal curia. These so-called curial letters concerned

---

[8] Petrarca, *Le Familiari*, XIV.4.

mainly political, diplomatic and financial matters and the government of the Papal State. Although they were engrossed by chancery scribes, it was primarily the apostolic chamber, which was the financial department of the curia, not the chancery, that was responsible for them. Under Benedict XII officers with special responsibility for such letters appear, the secretaries. Because their position brought them into close contact with the pope, they were men of considerable influence. It is not surprising that curial letters often had to be prepared with the greatest speed. An instruction to a scribe from the secretary Nicolaus de Auximo, which appears on the draft of a letter in the Vatican Archives, states that the fair copy should be ready the same evening; the scribe was being sent only a portion of the draft (so that he could start work at once).[9]

At the head of the chamber were the chamberlain and the treasurer, assisted by three or four clerks of the chamber. They all enjoyed great powers. At Avignon the chamber grew in sophistication. Gasbert de Laval, treasurer and then chamberlain of John XXII, reformed the accounting procedures, and there were further changes under John's successors, notably those attributable to the successive treasurers of Innocent VI. Except during Benedict XII's pontificate, the income of the chamber increased. Already under Clement V, it was twice that of the chamber of Boniface VIII. The high-point was the pontificate of Gregory XI, with on average an annual income of over 500,000 florins.

In order to raise these large sums, the popes mainly exploited and extended existing sources of revenue, above all various taxes associated with benefices. The service tax (*servitia*) was payable by those appointed by the pope to major benefices (archbishops, bishops, abbots, etc.). Its main constituent, common services, amounted to a third of the benefices' gross annual income. Under Clement V we find some prelates in addition paying 'secret services' to the pope, and the sums were higher than for common services. There is no firm evidence that secret services were exacted by Clement's successors. Annates, a tax comparable to the *servitia*, were paid by clerics provided to minor benefices (benefices not liable to *servitia*). John XXII first levied annates systematically. They normally consisted of the first year's assessed income of the benefice. By the tax known as *fructus intercalares*, the papacy appropriated the revenues of vacant benefices reserved to papal provision. The tax was extended in 1377 to include major benefices. As the number of papal reservations and provisions increased, the number of benefices liable to *servitia*, annates and *fructus intercalares* increased too. Among the other papal revenues were general taxes on clerical income (normally a tenth of the assessed income), levied for the crusade and other needs. 'Charitable subsidies', which in theory were voluntary payments, were also

---

[9] Vatican Archives, Reg. Vat. 244I, fos. 66–7, no. 137.

exacted from the clergy for special needs. Through the *ius spolii*, the chamber laid claim to control of the moveable property of the deceased clergy, typically those who died at the papal court or intestate, or were in debt to the chamber. A more erratic source of income was the census due from the kingdoms that were papal fiefs (the kingdom of Sicily was the most heavily burdened, with 8,000 ounces of gold per annum) and from vicars in the Papal State. Naturally, political circumstances determined whether payment was actually made to the chamber. The clergy paid many of the taxes locally. For this reason western Christendom was divided into regions (*collectorie*), each under a resident collector. The system was only properly established in the time of Clement VI. The collector's responsibility was to gather the sums due and to transmit them to Avignon.

The examination of the expenditure of the popes provides some insight into their priorities, although the categories under which expenditure appears in the accounts of the chamber are not always helpful. One is surprised to find nearly 2,700,000 florins spent by John XXII on 'wax and certain extraordinary matters', until one realises that most of the costs of war were included under this heading.[10] The construction of the Palais des Papes was expensive. Nearly 18 per cent of Benedict XII's expenditure served this purpose. The campaigns in Italy were the greatest burden on the chamber. The costs rose greatly under John XXII and then under Innocent VI and his successors. The military expenditure of Albornoz in the first seven years of his legation (1353–60) amounted to over 1,500,000 florins (although less than half this figure was sent from Avignon, the remainder being raised in Italy).

If one compares the revenue and expenditure of the papal chamber, one finds that the first three Avignon popes seem to have enjoyed an adequate income: each left a surplus for his successor. The position changed with the extravagant Clement VI, and the resources of Innocent VI and his successors, with their more active Italian policy, were increasingly strained. Gregory XI had for the first time to borrow substantial sums from Italian bankers, notably the Alberti Antichi of Florence. Another problem concerning the relation between income and expenditure deserves mention. The popes' income derived mainly from countries north of the Alps, but the money was largely spent in Italy. It was therefore necessary to exchange different currencies and to transport large sums. For these purposes, Italian, and mainly Tuscan, companies were used. They included the Acciaiuoli of Florence, the Nicolucci of Siena and a Piedmontese company, the Malabayla. Papal policy towards the companies was prudent and skilful. Money was not left on deposit with them, and the chamber avoided large losses when companies went bankrupt.

Some transactions by-passed the chamber. Thus, the legates in Italy were

---

[10] Renouard (1941), p. 31: 'pro cera et quibusdam extraordinariis'.

partly financed by sums levied on the spot. There was also the pope's private treasury, the *camera secreta*. There are no accounts of the *camera secreta*, only occasional references to it. These show that large sums which the pope received as presents or in other ways went into it. Under Innocent VI and his successors, transfers between the apostolic chamber and the *camera secreta* are known to have taken place.

The chancery and the chamber – the principal departments of the papal bureaucracy – each had its own court. The *audientia litterarum contradictarum* in the chancery was principally concerned with the issue of letters of justice. When one party in a case objected to an opponent's request for a letter appointing a judge or judges delegate, the *audientia* heard the objection. The auditor of the court of the chamber judged financial cases. Innocent VI greatly strengthened the judicial powers of the chamberlain. The latter now heard appeals from the auditor's court, and he was granted summary jurisdiction in any case involving the rights of the chamber. It is likely that there was an increase in the amount of litigation at the curia in the Avignon period. Important cases, some of which had political implications, might be heard by the pope and cardinals in consistory. Cases were also committed to individual cardinals to judge or to report on to the pope. The *audientia sacri palatii*, also known as the *Rota*, was a court with its own judges (auditors). Its earliest surviving regulations are to be found in the constitution *Ratio iuris* of 1331. The *Rota* mainly dealt with cases concerning ecclesiastical benefices. The auditor hearing a case was required to consult with other auditors before he made his judgement. The auditors' *consilia* were collected into books called *Decisiones Rote*, the earliest known collection dating from 1336–7.

While the petitioners' enthusiasm for litigation was met by the various courts in Avignon, the penitentiary was intended to serve their spiritual needs. It was able to provide absolution from sins and ecclesiastical censures, to grant marriage dispensations, and to commute vows and penances. Its powers were exercised in cases reserved to the pope. Some types of cases were the monopoly of the head of the penitentiary, the cardinal penitentiary, but most were dealt with by the minor penitentiaries. The constitution *In agro dominico* (1338) defined their powers. At any one time there were between twelve and nineteen minor penitentiaries at Avignon, but there were also some at St Peter's, Rome, for Rome was still the destination of penitent pilgrims. Although the majority of curialists were French, this does not apply to the minor penitentiaries, who needed to be able to understand the petitioners' confessions. It was therefore intended that the principal linguistic areas should be represented in the penitentiary. There were, for instance, always one or two English penitentiaries. The penitentiary issued its own documents, and a special body of scribes existed for this purpose.

The papal chapel played a leading part in the liturgy and ceremonies of the papal court. Benedict XII founded a new chapel, the *capella privata*, so that there were now two chapels. The chaplains of the *capella privata* were closely associated with the pope and had purely liturgical functions. The principal ceremonies remained primarily the concern of the old chapel, the *capella magna*, and its members (known as *capellani commensales*). The ceremonies in Avignon resembled those in Rome to only a limited extent. While in Rome in the thirteenth century these took place in public in different parts of the city, in Avignon, after the completion of the Palais des Papes, almost all ceremonies, even processions, were confined to the palace. Here only members of the curia and high-ranking visitors were able to witness them properly.

The richness of the sources, and especially of the records of the papal chamber, enables one to study the chapel and the other institutions and offices of the Avignon popes much more closely than is possible in the case of their predecessors. The names of men detained in the papal prisons or what sums were paid to the poor by the almonry can be discovered. These records illustrate the work of those responsible for the physical well-being of the curia – the chamberlains (*cubicularii*), doctors, cooks, butlers, grooms and porters, the town's garrison, the sergeants-at-arms and squires, the marshal of the papal court (who had jurisdiction over the lay members of the curia) and so forth. The papal library, which was one of the largest libraries in the west, deserves special attention. The archives of the chamber contain two catalogues of books in the papal palace, compiled in 1369 and 1375. The earlier, more complete catalogue contains some 2,000 volumes. As one would expect, biblical, patristic, theological and legal texts predominated. There were few Greek manuscripts, but 116 in Hebrew. Oversight of the library rested with officials who were variously designated. Their duties included supervising scribes who were employed to copy manuscripts for the library. The library also contained books bought by or given to the pope and among the latter were books dedicated to him. Many books came to the chamber through the *ius spolii*, and some of these found a home in the library.

The presence of a great library was appropriate to a city of the cultural importance of papal Avignon. The ethos of the court, dominated as it was by popes, cardinals and curialists who were lawyers, was doubtless conservative. However, the very nature of the papacy made its court a meeting place for men from all over the Christian world and a forum for the transmission of knowledge and ideas. Literary interests were not excluded. Petrarch referred, albeit in a condescending vein, to the enthusiasm for poetry at the curia.[11] Petrarch's own career, with its long but bitter association with Avignon, reminds us that

---

[11] Petrarca, *Le Familiari*, XIII.6–7.

early humanists were attracted there and that he was only the most famous of these. Among the others was the papal secretary Francesco Bruni. Just as Petrarch tried to learn Greek at the curia from Barlaam, Bruni was taught by Simon Atumano, archbishop of Thebes. The latter translated Plutarch's *De Cohibenda Ira* from Greek into Latin at the request of Cardinal Pietro Corsini (1372–3).

Avignon was a university town. Boniface VIII formally established its university in 1303. It was almost exclusively a centre of legal studies. Through the presence of the papal court the university prospered. Students came from a wide area, attracted no doubt by the prospects of patronage in the curia. The residence of the popes brought a second university to Avignon, the university of the Roman curia. It had been founded by Innocent IV, but it has been argued that it only became a fully fledged university (a *studium generale*) in the Avignon period.[12] It was one of five universities directed by the Council of Vienne to appoint professors of Greek and oriental languages. It was primarily a school of theology with a very restricted number of students, although canon and civil law was also taught. Its lecturer in theology, invariably a Dominican, was known from 1343 as the *magister sacri palatii*. In addition to his university duties, he appears to have given more elementary instruction to the members of the curia. The pope consulted him on theological questions. Thus, when Thomas Waleys was incarcerated as a result of his views on the Beatific Vision and related matters, John XXII required Armand of Belvéser to give his response to Waleys's views – to Armand's discomfort, since he disagreed with the pope.

The position of the cardinals mirrored that of the pope. They had their own courts, palaces, administrative arrangements and *familiares*. Chamberlains, secretaries, auditors, confessors, almoners and chaplains, among others, were in their service. Bertrand du Pouget, when he was staying as papal legate in Bologna, was surrounded by at least fifty-two *familiares*. In the first pontifical year of Clement VII (1378–9), the households of the cardinals were larger still. For the six Limousin cardinals there were between fifty-three and seventy-nine *familiares*. The vast majority of cardinals were French. Clement V's promotions transformed a predominantly Italian college of cardinals into a predominantly French one. When Philip VI requested John XXII to raise two Frenchmen to the cardinalate, the pope pointed out that sixteen of the nineteen cardinals were already French, which seemed sufficient.[13] None the less, he then appointed one of the royal candidates (1331). The popes tended to confer the cardinalate on their fellow-countrymen, so that most cardinals were from the Midi. Since there were three Limousin popes, many cardinals came from this

---

[12] Creytens (1942), especially p. 31.   [13] Rinaldi, *Annales*, a. 1331, cap. 33.

region. Clement V appointed so many Gascons that on his death they formed the largest group within the Sacred College; and in the ensuing conclave at Carpentras they were at loggerheads with the Italian cardinals. On the other hand, the conclaves at Avignon, at which the popes from Benedict XII to Gregory XI were elected, were speedy and peaceful.

The cardinals were rich. Some papal revenues, notably the common services, the census due from the vassal kingdoms and the net income from papal territories, were divided equally between the pope and the college of cardinals. An equal share of the college's income went to each cardinal resident at the curia, and so the small number of cardinals enhanced the income of each of them. It became customary for the pope on his election to make a substantial present to the cardinals; even Benedict XII gave 100,000 florins. The cardinals, including those who were friars, were provided to lucrative benefices. In his will Audoin Aubert admitted that in this respect his uncle Innocent VI had been excessively generous to him.[14] The cardinals received pensions and presents from rulers and petitioners. It was, for instance, intended that two cardinals should share 5,000 florins for their assistance in obtaining a papal dispensation for the marriage of Louis, king of the island of Sicily, to Constance of Aragon in 1355. Contemporaries deplored the cardinals' luxury and greed, as did the popes to some extent. John XXII's constitution *Dat vivendi normam* sought to limit the size of their households and the lavishness of their meals, and Innocent VI in *Ad honorem* legislated along similar, if less strict, lines. On his accession Innocent would accept only ten petitions from each cardinal on behalf of the latter's *familiares*.

The cardinals who took part in Innocent VI's election made a pact which each of them undertook to observe if elected pope. This sought to reinforce and extend the existing rights of the cardinals, but was declared invalid by the new pope. He had subscribed to the pact as a cardinal, but he was one of those who had done so with the restrictive clause 'si et in quantum scriptura hujusmodi de jure procederet'.[15] Despite the failure of their electoral pact, the cardinals had important powers. They formed a closely knit group, which reinforced their claim to be the pope's inner counsellors. The pope and cardinals considered weighty questions in the consistory. The most influential cardinals had close links with secular rulers and tended to pursue policies independent of, or even antagonistic to, the pope's. This applies to Napoleone Orsini, cardinal deacon of St Adrian from 1287 to 1342. The most powerful cardinals of their day, Elie Talleyrand de Périgord and Guy de Boulogne, by 1346 were supporting rival factions which sought to control the throne of the Angevin kingdom of Sicily, the houses of Durazzo and Taranto. However, a

[14] Mollat (1951), p. 63.   [15] Ibid., p. 100.

cardinal of the first rank was never elected pope before the Schism. The opposition to such a cardinal would have been too great. Less prominent cardinals or men from outside the Sacred College were preferred. Some historians, perhaps influenced by the role of the cardinals in bringing about the Schism, see the Avignon period as one when the power of the cardinalate vis-à-vis the papacy increased;[16] but it remains very difficult to generalise about this. The cardinals' financial position was consolidated, and the expansion of the administration at Avignon meant that they were given greater responsibilities. However, while it is clear that the cardinals as a group aspired to increase their political power, the evidence does not suggest that they were successful in doing so.

The population of Avignon grew enormously as a result of the popes' presence. It was swelled by papal officials, *familiares*, servants and soldiers, and by the households of the cardinals. Then there were the bankers, merchants, shopkeepers and others who were attracted to Avignon, as well as the temporary population of petitioners who had business at the curia. It has been estimated that towards the end of the Avignon period the inhabitants numbered around 30,000, while before the Black Death the figure was probably higher.[17] Avignon became the largest town in France after Paris. Its inhabitants were predominantly French, but it was a cosmopolitan place and there was a substantial Italian community.

PROVISIONS TO BENEFICES AND COMMUNICATIONS

The Avignon popes established a new degree of control over the western Church. It is symptomatic that the only general council held in this period, at Vienne, was dominated by the pope. One area of the relations of the Avignon papacy with the Church which deserves special attention is appointments to ecclesiastical benefices. Although the popes made such appointments in the twelfth and thirteenth centuries, at Avignon the role of the papacy here was transformed.[18] It is necessary to distinguish between major benefices (bishoprics and monasteries) and minor benefices. The reservation of major benefices to papal provision increased. In addition to reservations of particular sees, there were general reservations of whole classes of sees. Clement V and especially John XXII made such reservations, for instance, of all sees vacated by death at the curia or by the translation, promotion or removal of the existing holder. The climax came in 1363, when Urban V reserved all sees valued at over 200 florins per annum and all monasteries valued at over 100 florins. Occasions

---

[16] Cf., e.g., Ullmann (1972), pp. 6–7, 186–7.   [17] Guillemain (1962), especially pp. 722–3.
[18] See especially Mollat (1921).

for papal intervention became more numerous because it was no longer customary for a bishop to remain in the same see for his entire career: bishops were translated by the pope from one see to another. The chapters and above all secular rulers continued to influence appointments, but even the kings of France did not always prevail. Irrespective of who was appointed, it was the curia which was now the focus of aspirations and intrigue.

While provisions to major benefices were made by the pope in the consistory, provisions to minor benefices resulted from petitions submitted in the papal chancery. A petitioner might request, and be granted, either a particular vacant benefice or the next benefice in a specified category to fall vacant (an expectancy). The scope for making provisions to minor benefices increased greatly as a result of general reservations. John XXII, for instance, in his decretal *Execrabilis* (1317) required the resignation of all benefices with cure of souls held in plurality and reserved such benefices to papal disposition. The Avignon popes issued provisions to minor benefices in huge numbers, but a large proportion of provisions, especially of expectancies, never took effect. Letters of provision merely instituted proceedings which might eventually lead to the petitioner gaining possession of a benefice: the implementation of the letter was left to an executor or executors, who enjoyed considerable discretion; the provisor often faced competition or opposition; and a defect might be found in the letter which invalidated it. None the less, if one considers the proportion of benefices filled by papal provision instead of the proportion of provisions which were successful, a different picture emerges. An examination of two collegiate churches in Zurich, the Grossmünster and Fraumünster, has shown that, in cases when it is known how vacant benefices were filled, the main method was papal provision: in the years 1316–1523 there were 149 instances of benefices filled in this way, while only 119 were filled by ordinary collation.[19]

The proliferation of provisions to minor benefices in the fourteenth century is largely explicable in terms of the wishes of those who petitioned for benefices. Obtaining a benefice through the pope was in general a more impersonal matter than applying to a local patron and must have been attractive to many for this reason. The papal system particularly favoured graduates. The rolls of petitions submitted by universities were given priority over most other petitions, and graduates had other advantages. Some types of graduates, for instance, were exempted from the examination *in litteratura* that provisors normally underwent. The registers of petitions, which reproduce the popes' responses to petitions which were approved, show differences in the attitude of the popes. Clement VI was generous to petitioners and rarely introduced

---

[19] Meyer (1986), especially p. 159.

modifications to their requests. Innocent VI and Urban V, on the other hand, expressed concern about churches already overburdened with provisions, and Urban was anxious to prevent non-residence and pluralism. His reply to one petitioner was 'recede de curia et resideas'.[20]

One type of provision requires separate mention – the expectancy *in forma pauperum*, that is, in favour of clerks without a benefice. These poor clerks flocked to the curia following the election of a new pope to petition for a benefice. The largest number (estimated at 5,500–6,000) came after Clement VI's election.[21] It is unlikely that more than a small proportion of these expectancies took effect, mainly because of the large numbers that were issued and the resulting competition among the poor clerks.

The system of provisions permeated the institutions of papal government. Provisions involved the chancery (which issued letters of provision and other letters concerning benefices), the chamber (to which taxes on benefices were payable) and the *Rota* (where litigation over benefices took place). They are the key to the centralising tendencies of the Avignon papacy and of the greater influence it exercised over the Church. The papacy itself profited greatly from provisions – financially, through the taxes paid by provisors, and politically, through control of the main ecclesiastical offices. Provisions were also a means of rewarding cardinals, curialists and relatives of the pope. It is hardly surprising that the curia was seen by contemporaries as the centre of a trade in benefices. There was opposition to provisions from those who felt that their rights were being infringed by them, above all the ordinary collators and secular rulers. Together with fiscal policy, provisions were probably the main cause of the unpopularity of the Avignon papacy. Within the curia there was concern about various aspects of the system, as is shown by the various attempts at reform, notably under Benedict XII. The criticisms voiced by contemporaries have sometimes been echoed by more recent historians. There is, however, a danger of attaching disproportionate importance to untypical provisions, notably to cardinals and foreigners. The system, as it operated in the majority of cases, included numerous checks. Thus both the moral and educational standing of most provisors was scrutinised before they could obtain a benefice. Regional differences were also taken into account; for instance, under Gregory XI a lower standard in the poor clerks' examination *in litteratura* was expected from Gascons and Spaniards than from others.[22] Moreover, there was a real attack on pluralism, especially from John XXII and Urban V.

One final aspect of the centralisation achieved at Avignon deserves to be

---

[20] Schmidt, in *Aux origines* (1990), p. 363 (with further examples).   [21] Meyer (1990), pp. 8–9.
[22] Ottenthal, ed., *Regulae Cancellariae Apostolicae*, p. 34, nos. 54–54a; cf. Tangl, ed., *Die päpstlichen Kanzleiordnungen*, p. 48.

mentioned – communications, and especially the transmission of information, between the curia and the individuals and institutions with which it was in contact. Secular rulers and major ecclesiastical bodies might retain a resident proctor to represent their interests. The practice was so widespread that Clement VI in 1349 complained about the failure of the king of France to observe it.[23] Proctors also supplied their clients with news from the curia; and where the proctors' reports survive, they are a most valuable source. The finest series are those of the proctors of the king of Aragon.[24] Louis Sanctus, proctor of the chapter of Bruges, sent home an account of the effects of the plague in Avignon in 1348.[25] The popes, for their part, despatched legates and envoys as the need arose, and their financial interests were overseen in the localities by collectors. Papal letters were conveyed to their addressees or beneficiaries in a variety of ways. In general, common letters were handed out in the curia to the beneficiaries or their proctors. A curial letter might be delivered by someone returning home from Avignon. The popes had their own messengers, but they were used to transmit only the most urgent and important letters. It was found cheaper to entrust letters to the postal services operated by the Italian commercial companies. The speed with which letters were transmitted by special couriers is remarkable. The normal time taken by those travelling between Florence or Bologna and Avignon was eight days; and a courier of the Malabayla reached Avignon from Paris in four and a half days. The commercial companies also provided the popes with information. Clement VI specifically asked the Alberti Antichi to supply him with news.[26] It was essential for the pope to be well informed and he could be ruthless in obtaining intelligence. Gregory XI in 1374 intercepted the correspondence of Bernabò and Galeazzo Visconti and of the count of Savoy with their ambassadors at the curia.[27]

CONCLUSIONS

This chapter has sought to describe the principal ways in which the establishment of the papacy at Avignon influenced the character of that institution. The entry of the papacy into the cultural and political orbit of France is already apparent under Clement V. It was, however, only with John XXII that many of the other distinctive features of the Avignon papacy emerged. John enjoyed the longest pontificate among the Avignon popes, and he was the most autocratic of them in temper. He introduced reforms which enabled the bureaucracy to

---

[23] Déprez, Glénisson and Mollat, *Clément VI*, III, p. 18, no. 4231.   [24] Finke, ed., *Acta Aragonensia*.
[25] Welkenhuysen (1983).   [26] Renouard (1941), pp. 389, 397–8.
[27] Segre, 'I dispacci di Cristoforo da Piacenza', p. 64.

deal more effectively with its expanding responsibilities, and Benedict XII continued the work of reform. Under John we also find the papacy playing a more decisive role in the definition of doctrine. Although John's views on the Beatific Vision were decisively rejected after his death, he succeeded in imposing his condemnation of the doctrine of Apostolic Poverty in the face of the opposition of the Franciscan Order. This meant the end of alliance between the popes and the Franciscans which had been one of the great strengths of the thirteenth-century papacy.

The behaviour of the Avignon popes towards the kings of France and other rulers was in general conciliatory. The main exception was the prolonged struggle with Lewis of Bavaria, which even led to the election of an anti-pope, Nicholas V (1328–30). More typical was the atmosphere of compromise and indifference under Emperor Charles IV. The papacy was amply compensated for the concessions made to secular princes by the greater control that it was able to exert over the Church in their territories. In this respect, the Avignon period represents the zenith of papal power. The powers exercised from Avignon depended on the growth of the machinery of government there. However, this governmental system did not withstand the effects of the Schism, when financial and other pressures undermined the curia's administrative practices, and lay princes increased their control over the Church at the expense of the papacy. It was not possible after the end of the Schism for the Renaissance popes to re-establish the old system. Too much had changed in the intervening period.

CHAPTER 20

THE GREAT SCHISM

Howard Kaminsky

1378 AND ITS CONSEQUENCES

THE southern French popes who ruled the universal Church from Avignon during most of the fourteenth century brought papal monarchy and the papalist ecclesiology that justified it to their highest pitch. What drove them chiefly was the need for enormously higher revenues to finance the endless wars that they fought to subdue the Papal States in Italy. For at the core of Avignon's papal monarchy was a rampant 'fiscalism' in which the steady extension of papal rights of provision to benefices steadily generated new or heightened impositions on clerical revenues.[1] But the communes and *signorie* of the Papal States never learned to accept their French overlords and in 1375 they joined Florence in war against them. The seventh Avignon pope, Gregory XI (1370–8), realising that papal domination could not be consolidated from afar, gave ear to pious voices urging a return to Rome and decided to make the move; he left Avignon in 1376 along with seventeen of his twenty-three cardinals and hundreds of officials of the papal curia, mostly French; only six cardinals and a reduced staff were left behind. The papal party entered Rome on 17 January 1377; just over a year later Gregory was dead.

---

[1] Thus *spolia* or 'spoils' were the personal property left by a dead prelate; the papal collectors claimed all of it except for funeral expenses and the prelate's patrimonial heritage. *Annates* were the first year's assessed net revenue of ordinary benefices granted by papal provision or under papal reservation; *servicia* were a third of a year's assessed revenue of major benefices granted by the pope in consistory – they were often also referred to as annates. *Procurations* were moneys that bishops or others were entitled to collect to defray the costs of visitation of subject churches; the Avignon popes claimed these for themselves. 'Caritative' *subsidies* were contributions exacted at the pope's will in various amounts, from various clerics or from various regions. *Tenths* of clerical incomes were exacted by the popes at will, in principle to finance crusades but in fact to meet all sorts of needs; the revenues were normally shared, sometimes entirely assigned, to the secular princes in whose territories they were collected. In addition there were fees paid for papal 'graces' (like provisions to benefices) and, in France, there were 'aids' paid by the clergy, under papal authorisation, directly to the secular rulers. All except the last can be understood as substitutes for the regular direct taxation of clerical property that the papacy did not enjoy.

What the papal party had found was a troublesome commune and a populace that, however glad to have the papacy back, was fearful of losing it, resentful of the French curia, and responsive to Florentine agents inciting them to outright mutiny.[2] The hostile magistrates and people now repeatedly told the eleven French cardinals in the city that unless they elected a Roman or at least an Italian, and did so quickly, their lives would not be safe.[3] Their only allies in the city, the Roman nobility, were made to leave; the Roman populace was afforced by contingents of armed men from the countryside; the cardinals were not allowed to leave the city to make an election in a peaceful place.

Divided among themselves and given no time to compose their differences, the cardinals entered their conclave in the Vatican palace on 7 April, with the Romans massed outside shouting for 'A Roman! A Roman!', 'A Roman or at least an Italian!', some adding 'Or else we'll kill them all!' The palace was full of troops; the conclave rooms were neither quiet nor secure; Roman officials came and went. The circumstances did not encourage deliberation and the cardinals made their election the next morning, going outside the college to choose not a Roman but at least an Italian – the Neapolitan Bartolomeo Prignano, a long-time papal official, now archbishop of Bari and acting papal vice-chancellor, well known to them as a competent bureaucrat who they supposed knew his place – 'my very familiar friend when he was of lesser estate', as the princely Cardinal Robert of Geneva would observe a week later.[4] They even repeated the election that evening when things were calmer. But fresh incursions of the Romans with new cries of 'Romano! Romano!' terrified them into pretending to elect the old, frail, but Roman Cardinal Pietro Tebaldeschi; they dressed him in papal robes, sat him on the papal throne and showed him to the people as their new pope, he all the while protesting that it was not so. This allowed the cardinals to leave the palace and find safe refuge, and even though they came back the next day and confirmed their election of Prignano, the curious incident made the abnormal conclave seem more so.

In the event, Prignano accepted his election and was crowned as Urban VI on Easter Sunday, 18 April 1378. The cardinals, expecting him to carry on the Avignon tradition of a *de facto* condominium with the college and in

---

[2] Trexler (1967), pp. 489–509; cf. Brandmüller (1974), p. 84.

[3] Of the sixteen cardinals in Rome at the time, four were Italian, six were of the southern French or 'Limousin' group that had dominated the papacy since Clement VI (1342–52), five were 'French' opposed to this group, and one, Pedro de Luna, was an Aragonese allied to the 'French'. The 'French' cardinal Jean de La Grange was out of the city.

[4] His letter to Emperor Charles IV of 14 April 1378, reporting Urban's election, in Brandmüller (1974) (= 1990), pp. 33–4, 'Vocatus est Urbanus sextus, mihi, dum erat in minoribus, valde domesticus et amicus, quamvis de gradu infimo nunc sit sublimatus ad supremum.'

due time lead them all back to Avignon, were ready to put their experience of intimidation behind them and make things normal by behaving normally. They treated Urban as a true pope, proclaiming his election to the princes of Europe, attending his consistories, asking for and accepting the usual papal favours, in what many then and since have taken as the 'convalidation' of an admittedly irregular election; they themselves would later claim that they still felt menaced by the Romans.[5] But Urban's abrupt translation to the sublimity of papal omnipotence – 'now raised from the lowest degree to the highest' (again the words of Cardinal Robert) – had made him a different man, a moralist driven by the invidious passions of a servant become master. He at once began a righteous but abusive attack on the cardinals' worldliness, luxury, pluralism, and neglect of their titular Roman Churches. So far from taking up their Avignon vision he clearly intended to end the Avignon system: the existing cardinals would be reduced from princely co-governors of the Church to obedient courtiers; their share of papal revenues would be reserved for the upkeep of their Roman churches; their style of life, even their meals, would be brought down to a more humble level; and they themselves would soon be outnumbered by new Italian appointments. At the same time, Urban's actions and discourse betrayed an unbalanced personality, lacking in self-control, apt to meet personal or political contradiction by explosions of rage and invocations of absolute papal power. Obviously the cardinals had made a mistake. Voting under duress – 'otherwise', Coluccio Salutati would later remark, 'so many French cardinals would hardly have voted for an Italian' – they had also been deprived of their right to take their time in careful deliberation and study of the candidate.[6] In any case Urban had to go. When Cardinal Robert of Geneva realised what a prodigy of repressed resentment had been concealed in his quondam *domesticus et amicus*, he did not shrink from telling Urban the truth: 'Holy Father, you have not treated the cardinals with the honour due to us and that your predecessors used to show us, but you are diminishing our honour. I tell you in all earnest that the cardinals will work to diminish your honour too.'[7]

The cardinals' self-interest marched here with their conception of the

---

[5] Their claim is usually rejected, but cf. Baumer (1977a), pp. 144, 171ff, for acceptance of it by two modern Catholic scholars, K.A. Fink and A. Franzen.

[6] Salutati's letter of 20 August 1397 to Margrave Jobst of Moravia, in Martène and Durand, *Thesaurus*, II, p. 1156. The question of forced haste and its consequence is most clearly laid out by Cardinal Pierre Flandrin in his treatise of 1378/9, in Bliemetzrieder (1909a), pp. 25, 27, 31–2. Cf. Přerovský (1960), pp. 63, 87, 188; Fink (1968), p. 496.

[7] 'In effectu, Pater beatissime, vos non tractastis dominos cardinales cum illo honore, quo debetis, sicut antecessores vestri faciebant, et diminuitis honorem nostrum. Dico vobis in veritate, quod cardinales conabuntur etiam diminuere honorem vestrum.' See Ullmann (1948), pp. 45–8; Souchon (1898–9), I, pp. 5ff.

'Roman Church' as the union of the pope as head with the cardinals as body; a head who destroyed the 'honour' – welfare, rights, *status* – of the body was destroying the Church. And there were canonistic authorities to justify removing a pope who damaged the *status ecclesie,* to say nothing of a pope who gave such clear signs of an abnormally disordered character; such texts were presumably known to the seven or so doctors of canon law among the French cardinals. But the cardinals were ardent papalists themselves and shied away from authorities that pointed so clearly to a limitation of papal omnipotence; they chose instead the more discreet argument from intimidation, which allowed them to nullify the election rather than formally depose a reigning pope, and which rested on proof that only they could supply. So too they rejected judgement by a general council, by this time generally recognised as the ordinary remedy for a defect in the papacy – only a pope, they said, had the right to summon such a council, and there was no pope.

And so they acted on their own authority, the 'French' and 'Limousin' parties putting aside their differences under the leadership, respectively, of Cardinal Jean de La Grange and the Camerary Pierre de Cros. Some of them withdrew to Anagni in the first part of May; others followed and so did Cros with the papal archives and treasure (including the tiara), as well as the papal officials. There was still no open break but on 8 May Cros sent a messenger from Anagni informing the French king Charles V of the true state of affairs. By 21 June all the French cardinals and Pedro de Luna were there together, and on 20 July they requested their four Italian colleagues still with Urban to join them because Urban's election had been vitiated by intimidation: Urban was no pope. Then on 2 August 1378 they published a statement of their case and demanded that Urban step down from the office that he held *de facto.* On his refusal they issued a public 'Declaration' (9 August) anathematising him as a usurper of the papacy, and on 20 September, in Fondi, they elected the French cardinal Robert of Geneva pope, as Clement VII: the three Italian cardinals (Tebaldeschi had died) had joined them but did not vote. Clement was crowned on 31 October. When the two popes anathematised each other and their adherents the Schism in the Church was made; when the political powers of Europe variously stayed with Urban or switched to Clement the Schism became a political fact; when Clement, having failed to establish himself in a secure Italian base, took his cardinals and the 500 or so curial officials back to Avignon, in May 1379, he set the political and geographic parameters of the schismatic years to come. At issue henceforth was not the privileged status of the Avignon cardinals, now secure, but first, whether Clement could end the Schism 'by way of force' *(via facti),* and then, as he failed, how much of the papal monarchy could survive its division into two competing fragments.

Not at issue were the rights and wrongs of 1378, which were impenetrable at the time and have 'escaped the judgement of history'[8] ever since – continuing controversy merely proves the point. That the conflict moved into schism, however, was something else – here the responsibility lay with Charles V of France and his brother Louis of Anjou, who fostered the renewal of an Avignon papacy that would otherwise have aborted. The division of Europe, at any rate, came down to which rulers would accept the French lead (Charles formally recognised Clement on 16 November 1378) and which would not. Queen Joanna of Naples had supported the cardinals all along; other powers in the French orbit followed: Burgundy, Savoy, Scotland, later on Castile (1380); there were Clementists too in both Italy and the empire. Aragon, long uncommitted under King Pedro the Ceremonious, joined the Avignon obedience after his death in 1387; Navarre followed in 1390. The rest of Europe stuck to Urban: England, most of the empire (Charles IV declared for Urban at the end of September 1378), Poland, Scandinavia, Hungary, most of Italy and Sicily. But there were dissident pockets in both 'obediences' as well as fluctuations – Portugal switched four times – and from time to time there were lapses into neutrality. While some princes studied the evidence of 1378, most did not; the decisions were political,[9] as was the more fundamental decision of virtually all to make a choice rather than refrain and work for union.

THE GREAT SCHISM IN HISTORY

The princes' decisions determined those of their subjects – we can no doubt generalise the first-hand observation of Simon de Cramaud, patriarch of Alexandria: 'In the realms of France, Castile, Aragon, and other lands of Clement's obedience, many thought that his election had not been canonical; but their kings' laws and commands compelled them to "put their minds in captivity, in obedience to Christ".'[10] A few intellectuals were less flexible and their writings are often cited to show how much concern the Schism evoked, but in fact the general attitude was rather one of 'indifference' accompanied by a 'remarkable tolerance' on both sides – no persecutions to speak of even though each half of Europe was supposed to regard the other half as schismatic. What

---

[8] Valois (1896–1902), I, p. 82.

[9] Swanson (1984), pp. 377–87, at 382: 'If it was anything, the decision of which pope to recognize was a political decision: Europe divided not as a result of legalistic persuasion, but according to a perception of political realities.' Cf. also Fink (1968), pp. 496ff; Favier (1980), pp. 7–16; Bautier (1980), pp. 459ff.; Hauck (1958), p. 682; Harvey (1983), pp. 7–8.

[10] Kaminsky (1983), p. 27, for the Latin text (written in 1402) and references to sources; the 'put their minds in captivity' passage plays on 2. Cor. 10:5, 'et in captivitatem redigentes omnem intellectum in obsequium Christi'.

one sees in any case is the irrelevance of the conflict to the religious life of the laity in general, the refusal of bankers and merchants to let the Schism in the papacy interfere with banking and commerce, the perception that the 'legal issue concerning a disputed succession to a particular office' came down to two competing individual property rights in the papacy, and the more fundamental perception by prelates and secular powers that as far as their respective territorial churches were concerned, the papacy had become 'little more than an administrative stratum' whose tasks could be discharged by each pope in his own 'obedience'.[11] That is why virtually all clerics, however devout, could so calmly accept their rulers' choice of a pope.

It had indeed been the preceding Avignon papacy's triumphant construction of papal monarchy as governance of the Church in detail that had led to this matter-of-fact attitude, by reifying the ecclesiastical institution into a system of benefices apprehended as property rights, acquisition and preservation of which were the primary objects of clerical interest. And while this interest was ordinarily secured through the working of papal government, it could also be secured by territorial princes working with the clergy as the clerical estate of the polity – as was already the case in France and, to varying degrees, in England and elsewhere. The crisis of the Schism reinforced this line of development. Avignon's hypertrophy of papal monarchy was increasingly perceived to be a burdensome superfluity, while common sense made it obvious in any case that obedience to the pope could hardly be necessary to salvation, as *Unam Sanctam* had claimed, for then half of Europe would go to Hell merely for not knowing who the pope was. There were indeed some who imagined how fine it would be to have even more than two popes – perhaps a dozen, in the fantasy of one Florentine.[12]

This is not to say that the legitimating effect of a united Church under a single pope was not generally appreciated, only that neither a general 'thirst for union' nor its presumed consequences can be postulated without proof. For the rest, talk of union appears most often as a sincere but inconsequential cliché of public discourse or as the specific reaction of university professors to the Schism's disruption of academic universality and its prejudice to the careers of graduates whose homes lay in the other obedience. It is no accident that the university of Paris's most notable advocates of a solution, conciliar or otherwise, in the early years of the Schism were two German professors, Henry of Langenstein and Konrad of Gelnhausen. But their idea of a general council to judge between the two sides was precisely what neither side could

---

[11] Swanson (1984), pp. 377, 386; cf. Kaminsky (1983), pp. 8–11, for Church offices, including the papacy, apprehended as property; Favier (1980), pp. 7–16; Mollat (1980), pp. 295–303; Esch (1966), pp. 277–398. For the contrary view see Rusconi (1979).

[12] Herde (1973), pp. 190, 192; Boockmann (1974), pp. 45–6.

ever accept; the conciliar solution could become practical only later, as we shall see, when its purpose would be not judgement between the papacies but, as in 1409 at the Council of Pisa, the coercive termination of both. Judicial conciliarism abided by papalist doctrine; depositionary conciliarism would proceed from that doctrine's loss of credibility.

For the crisis in the papal monarchy was also a crisis of the papalist ecclesiology that had validated it. The extraordinary extension of papal powers of collation and taxation by the Avignon popes had been based on the postulate that Jesus Christ had founded the Church as an authoritative institution in the Apostle Peter, whose powers were transmitted to his successors the popes; the bishops, heirs of the other Apostles, received their administrative and juridical powers by delegation from the pope, who could therefore take over or abridge their powers as he wished. Hence the popes' endless reservations of benefices to their own provision, overriding the common law of the Church on the basis of papal plenitude of power,[13] and their arrogation of the finances tied to collationary rights. This development of papal monarchy from an idea into a governmental system, in collaboration with the secular powers who shared in its benefits, privileged the papalist ecclesiology as quasi-orthodoxy. But when the papal institution split in two, its papalist ideology could propose only a solution by *via facti,* sharing in the disrepute entailed by that via's evident futility. The more practical 'ways' that eventually succeeded would be justified by alternative ecclesiologies.

The historical import of the Schism, at any rate, lies in this movement of ideas and the experiences that were its matrix, rather than in such historically factitious topics as who was right in 1378, the agonies of the faithful confronted by the rent in Christ's Seamless Garment, or the Catholicity of the Council of Constance's constitutional conciliarism. In a period of general reaction against centralising policies, a reaction of both lay and clerical members of the Church against the high-pitched papal monarchy was to be expected, and it swallowed up the issues of accidence that had triggered it. In any case the solution of the Schism would turn out to come from exactly this reaction. The key to a historical understanding of the Schism lies indeed in the brutal fact that although it began as a contest over the presumably urgent issue of which pope elected in 1378 was the true Vicar of Christ, it could endure unresolved for three decades and then be ended when the leaders of Europe agreed that the original issue *did not matter*: the competing papacies could then be terminated without a judgement between them.

---

[13] There were many complaints about the popes' 'new law'; see e.g. 'Speculum Aureum de Titulis Beneficiorum', ed. Brown, II, p. 63, a condemnation of 'omnes qui a jure communi per exorbitantes gratias, beneficia ecclesiastica sunt adepti, Papae plenitudinem potestatis pertractando'; below n. 17.

AVIGNON AND THE *VIA FACTI*: FAILURE AND NEMESIS

Clement VII differed from his Avignon predecessors only in his questionable title, his sharply reduced obedience and of course his proportionally smaller income – the 300,000 florins a year of papal revenue under Gregory XI had fallen to an average of 180,000 from 1378 to 1398.[14] His dependence on France for these revenues was all but total – if before the Schism the French collectories had provided 44 per cent of the Apostolic Camera's revenue, now they provided almost all of it (the northern ones delivering the lion's share), with Aragon contributing 10 per cent after 1387. Most of this money had to be spent by Clement in financing Italian military campaigns aimed at imposing himself on the other side by conquest of his rival's adherents. The *via facti* was Avignon's only hope, the condition indeed of its support by the Valois princes of France, some of whom hoped to secure Italian kingdoms under papal auspices and with papal financing. Clement would spend a million florins of revenues extracted from the French Church on eight years of the *via facti* pursued by Louis of Anjou, who got the income of four papal collectories in 1379 and all the pope's net income for three years after 1382. These commitments would bring Avignon's nemesis, for with Clement's ordinary revenues so drastically curtailed, he had to intensify the old impositions, invent new ones, and systematically fiscalise his collationary powers by selling benefices and favours. His simony was unprecedented and notorious; his fiscalism was odious to its victims, the clergy of France, already aware of how heavy a fiscal burden had been laid especially upon them by the whole line of Avignon popes. They would soon begin to think of throwing it off.

The first avatar of *via facti* appeared when Clement VII, while still in Naples, 17 April 1379, granted much of the Papal States as a fief to Louis of Anjou – a 'Kingdom of Adria' that he would have to conquer. Then he supported Louis's plan to have himself adopted by Queen Joanna as her heir, which she did on 29 June 1380, with Louis to fight on her behalf after Urban VI had deposed her (Naples was a fief held of the papacy) in favour of her cousin Charles of Durazzo. Joanna was also defended by her husband Otto of Brunswick who could not, however, prevent Charles from taking Naples itself in July 1381 and putting Joanna to death the next year. Louis invaded the realm in September 1382 and fought there until his death in 1384; his claim would later be pursued

---

[14] For the data in this paragraph see Favier (1966), pp. 475, 580, 687–9 (after 1403 the papal revenues would fall even more, to 125,000 florins); Kaminsky (1983), pp. 40–7. Castile had received lavish exemptions as the price of her adherence to Avignon in 1381 and for the rest of the 1380s got control over local Cameral revenues to pay for her participation in the Angevin campaigns in Italy – Favier (1966), p. 235; Kaminsky (1983), p. 28; Suarez Fernandez (1960), pp. 13-14, 21–2.

on behalf of (and later by) his son, Louis II (d. 1417), throughout the Schism with important if spasmodic gains.

It was not the only case in point. There was a time in 1390–1 when Charles VI himself planned to join Clement, Louis II and others in a great expedition to conquer Italy and install Clement in Rome. The preparations were extensive, Clement was joyous, but it fell through, chiefly because the war between the Valois and the Plantagenets did not allow Charles to turn his back to England. Then the 'Kingdom of Adria' was revived in 1393–4 in favour of Louis of Orléans, Charles VI's younger brother and the son-in-law of Giangaleazzo Visconti of Milan; but nothing was done because no one would pay the costs. A more modest *via facti* pursued by Benedict XIII in 1404–5 petered out, also for want of Valois support. All these initiatives can best be appreciated in terms of what might have been: a strong French king might have brought them off, but Charles VI, who succeeded his father as a minor in 1380, would later enjoy only four years of direct royal power before going insane in 1392, after which the government of his uncles of Berry and Burgundy, neither of them interested in Italian acquisitions, would give up the *via facti* and, ineluctably, the Avignon adventure itself.

ROME: FROM PAPAL MONARCHY TO ITALIAN PRINCIPALITY

The Roman papacy was faced with different imperatives. Deprived by the French defection of virtually the whole apparatus of papal government, to say nothing of the French and Spanish Churches, it also lacked Avignon's advantage of a relatively secure site convenient for traffic with the whole of Europe. In the turbulence of Italy's mutually aggressive cities and principalities, both Urban VI and his successor Boniface IX had to become Italian princes themselves, enjoying only such residues of papal monarchy as their adherents would allow – in England, where successive Statutes of Provisors had barred papal provisions in principle, it was not much. Neither in any case could emulate the sophistication of Avignon's governance. Instead of the comprehensive Avignon collectories, with their sub-collectors and dense infrastructure of clerks and officials, the Roman papacy could deploy only a skeleton – one collector for England, one for Poland, one for Portugal, and so on, with very poor communication between them and the curia; bankers funded both payments and collections. Crucial bureaucratic principles were violated: the collectors had other functions as well, they were often doubled for the same collectory, their circumscriptions were incessantly redefined, they rarely rendered either accounts or receipts, and a number of fiscal resources, including tenths, were assigned for collection to local bishops or farmed to *condottieri* or moneylenders. Under such conditions there could be no improvement in professional competence and the Roman popes' income from their obedience outside Italy reflected a drastic regression from the revenues enjoyed by the papal monarchy before the Schism. In Italy they had to rely chiefly on seigneurial revenues from the Papal States (whose net yield was at first negative), revenues from churches under direct papal control, and the sums that could be charged for papal appointments and other graces. Urban himself eschewed such simony (although he did alienate church properties and rights to raise funds for his military enterprises) but others did not; given the lack of an orderly financial system, simony became a normal modality of curial economy.

Urban VI was chiefly interested in implementing papal overlordship of Naples – he stemmed from one of its noble families. While his pontificate figured significantly in political conflicts north of the Alps, especially in the western empire, his role there was limited to offering honours and financial concessions. Even in Italy he let the Papal States lapse into chaos as he turned to Naples both for curial personnel to fill the hole left by the French defection and for the territorial base without which the Italian papacy could not survive. In October 1378 he appointed a new college of twenty-five cardinals; all but four were Italians and about a half-dozen were his relatives; the administration and curia were also filled with relatives and connections. As for the kingdom of Naples, he expected his vassal Charles of Durazzo to hold it in his interest and make part of it an autonomous principality for his nephew Francesco Butillo. But Charles of Durazzo had no desire to do either and the contradiction would push Urban into the aggressive fury that had been so disastrous in 1378, as he broke with Charles and began a war to end only with his own death, 15 October 1389. Meanwhile he deposed his cardinals who favoured Charles and at the end of 1384 created eighteen new cardinals, of whom six were Neapolitan. Informed in January 1385 that six cardinals were conspiring to declare him unfit to rule and put him under tutelage, he had the rebels arrested, eventually tortured and (except for the English Adam Easton) killed – we see him at one point reading his hours outside the torture chambers so that he could hear his victim's screams.[15] One sees what the French cardinals had perceived in 1378; this time however the cardinals who condemned Urban as mentally unbalanced and 'incompetent' *(inutilis)* were all of his own creation, all but one Italian.

Perhaps the only enduring result of his pontificate, besides provoking the Schism, was to deliver the papacy to the Neapolitan nobility, especially after 1387 when Otto of Brunswick's conquest of Naples on behalf of Louis II of Anjou was followed by a massive migration of Neapolitan noble families into the curia. Henceforth, the papacy would be the patria of this closely interrelated group of families, consolidated there after Urban's death when

[15] Erler (1890), p. 94.

the cardinal of Naples, Perrino Tomacelli, was elected pope as Boniface IX (1389–1404).[16] His papacy became a Neapolitan possession with the vast Tomacelli clan at its heart: about fifty of them are known to have flocked to Rome along with the related clans of Brancaccio, Filimarino, Capece, Carbone to receive high papal offices and valuable benefices. These relatives in Rome, including his mother, the formidable Gatrimola Filimarino, routinely sold their influence, directing a heavy flow of papal favours, privileges and graces to those who paid them, with all impediments of age and incapacity removed by dispensations – a six-year-old nephew could become a canon, a seven-year-old a prior. Boniface dealt similarly with the cardinalate: when he died in 1404 the college of ten included eight from the kingdom of Naples, five of them his relatives.

Boniface's fiscalism and simony, like Clement VII's, were initially due to the exigency of the Schism: enormous military expenses but sharply reduced papal revenues. His fiscal expedients were even more exquisite. He began with the residues of Avignon papal monarchy, including the extensive reservations of benefices to papal appointment and the consequent collection of *servicia* and annates, which he demanded with rigour – so, for example, on 24 December 1390 he excommunicated thirty bishops and sixty-five abbots because their *servicia* were in arrears. He also sold 'expectancies' to benefices not yet vacant, often to multiple supplicators for the same one – when the time came the one best poised to win was the one whose provision carried the most formulas of privileged priority, each of which the chancery sold. Offices of the papal government were also sold to the highest bidder, while indulgences remitting the pains of Purgatory to those who made pilgrimages to Rome in the 'Jubilee' year of 1390 or for that matter elsewhere and afterwards were simply sold for cash to those who wanted the indulgence but did not want to make the pilgrimage. On 22 December 1402 Boniface even fiscalised a proposed reform by cancelling all indulgences, provisions and priorities still outstanding – with, however, the proviso that their holders might buy them anew; in any case the same practices were continued afterwards. When we add to all this the intensive taxation of the Church and Papal States under his control, with the collection entrusted to *condottieri*, and when we note that most of the papal revenue was funded by banking houses that collected the money themselves, we can understand why Boniface appeared – at least to his more shockable northern subjects – as corruption incarnate. It was no accident that the two most savage attacks on papal abuses appeared in 1403 and 1404–5 – the *De Praxi Curie Romane,* also known as *Squalores Romane Curie,* and the *Speculum*

---

[16] The following discussion is taken chiefly from Esch (1969); for a summary see *DBI,* xii. For the Neapolitan occupation of the papacy, see Esch (1972).

Aureum de Titulis Beneficiorum – nor that their authors were not Italians but northerners – respectively, two Germans (Matthew of Cracow, bishop of Worms, and the Heidelberg protonotary Job Vener) and a Pole (the canonist Paweł Włodkowic).[17] Nor can the movement of reformist thought among the Czech masters at the university of Prague in these years, culminating in Jan Hus's attack on simony and his associates' inclination to see the pope as an image of Antichrist, be understood without computing the loss of papal prestige due to the fact of the Schism and the manifestation of the pope as an Italian prince.

For that is what Boniface IX became, as he focused his papacy on the reduction of the Papal States to recognition of papal overlordship, of which Urban VI had left him close to nothing: 'a decimated chancery, a dispersed archive, an exhausted treasury, and the Papal States largely remote from direct papal influence', with Clementists in power close to Rome, whose own commune made the city itself insecure for the curia.[18] In Naples Boniface could only remedy Urban VI's inept policy by supporting Charles of Durazzo and, after his death, his son Ladislas, crowned king on 29 May 1390; but Louis II of Anjou arrived soon after and quickly won most of the realm. In the Papal States Boniface had both to fight against virtually independent 'vicars' and to cope with the aggressive drive of Milan under Giangaleazzo Visconti, whose neutrality in the Schism opened the way to French penetration. Boniface could only struggle city by city, battle by battle, raising money by loans, *ad hoc* imposts and other abnormal means, often losing, always threatened by defections to Avignon. His eventual victory was due to this persistence, as his enemies were removed by death or otherwise. The death especially of Giangaleazzo (3 September 1402) changed the whole north Italian picture; the papal lordships that had been lost to him could now be recovered – most notably by Cardinal Baldassare Cossa, who became the papal lord of Bologna – and by the time he died (1 October 1404) Boniface was master of the Papal States – not, to be sure, as the ruler of a centralised group of provinces, but as overlord of the 'apostolic vicars' (there were at least sixty-three of them, including a good number of the pope's brothers and other relatives) who actually exercised power. His work would allow his successors eventually to reduce the vicariates and rule more directly. That they could do so from Rome was also due to their predecessor: 'With Boniface IX the free Roman commune was ended once and for all.' The popes could now become the Renaissance papacy.

---

[17] For a discussion of the texts and authors see Heimpel (1974); he shows *inter alia* that the *De praxi* of Matthew of Cracow was given a canonistic apparatus by Job Vener, an official of the Elector Palatine Ruprecht, then also king of the Romans.

[18] *DBI*, xii, p. 4 (I cite from an independently paged offprint), for this and the quotation at the end of the paragraph.

THE FRENCH SOLUTION

If the story of the Great Schism be given only one peripety, it must come on 5 August 1392 when King Charles VI was first struck by the intermittent insanity that made him unable to rule and brought his uncles, John, duke of Berry, and Philip, duke of Burgundy, back to the seats of power from which Charles VI had removed them in 1388. They once more began to redirect royal policy to the benefit of their purses and apanages, which they wanted above all to enjoy in peace – peace with England and peace in the Church. Ending the Schism was essential on both counts. But for 'France' to end the Schism was to give up the original project of imposing Avignon on Europe and to concede that the papacy would henceforth be Italian and Roman. Both surrenders were acceptable but each had its *sine qua non*. The renewed Avignon papacy could be given up only if everyone would agree that it had not been schismatic in the first place, so that the Clementists would not be branded with the infamy of schism; this meant that both papacies had to be terminated without a judgement between them, and a single papacy would have to be created anew. That this would be an Italian papacy seated in Rome could be accepted only if it did not enjoy the kind of monarchy over the French Church that the Avignon popes had exercised. The dukes' decision to end the Schism meant devising a policy that would meet these conditions.[19]

Already in January 1394 the university of Paris had been asked by the crown to present honourable 'ways' to union and after polling its members and alumni had concluded that there were three such: a general council (*via concilii generalis*), arbitration (*via compromissi*) and a double abdication (*via cessionis*). A public letter of 6 June resumed these ways but put cession first – 'chiefly because it avoided scandal and preserved intact the honour of the princes and realms of each side'. For unlike the other two ways, cession supposed that both papacies would be terminated without judgement and was therefore the *only* way the royal government could seriously consider. As the royal dukes would put it a year later, the king and princes of France 'would not allow their honour to be put in the hands of judges', and as Pedro Tenorio, archbishop of Toledo, would put it in 1397, 'Who would want to be judged to have been schismatic for the past twenty years?' This is the key to what would follow; for if the road to union would after all turn out to be the *via concilii generalis* of Pisa and Constance, these councils did not judge the issues of 1378 – that via's original project – but were rather extensions of the *via cessionis* from abdication to deposition, its coercive equivalent. For conciliarism and the *via cessionis* were based on the same ecclesiological premise, the idea of the Church as the *congregatio*

---

[19] For this and what follows see Kaminsky (1983), chs. 2, 4–8.

fidelium, the whole community of lay and clerical Christians, whose spiritual life derived from Jesus Christ, not from the pope, and whose supreme interest in preserving its *status* demanded an end to the Schism regardless of the papal contenders' respective claims to legitimacy. Whether the *congregatio fidelium* would be represented for purposes of political action by its secular rulers or by a general council was merely a question of opportunity.

The second exigency, the reduction of papal monarchy, would be met by another anti-papalist line of thought, the episcopalism that had come to the fore at the university of Paris in the thirteenth century in opposition to the mendicant orders whose papal privileges exempted them from episcopal authority in the dioceses. Jesus Christ, in this view, had established the episcopate directly in the Apostles, not through St Peter, so that the bishops' jurisdictional and governmental powers were theirs as bishops, not by virtue of a papal grant, and might not be infringed by the pope. In the French territorial context and in relation to the protective function of the crown, this would become the 'Gallicanism' destined for much action in the post-medieval centuries; meanwhile, never forgotten at the university of Paris or by the French prelates who were its alumni, it could emerge as the ideology of an *ecclesia gallicana* whose 'liberties', drastically eroded by Avignon's implementation of papalism, could only be restored by the crown.

We see this pattern becoming a political fact even in the first period of Berry's and Burgundy's control of the royal government, after the death of Louis of Anjou in 1384 and before the assumption of direct rule by Charles VI in 1388. In ordinances of 3 and 6 October 1385 the crown made itself the protector of 'the liberty and franchise' of the Gallican Church against Clement VII's fiscal innovations – his excessively frequent subsidies and levies of tenths, his practice of claiming a year's revenue from all vacant benefices (not just those he himself conferred), his demands for *servicia* and annates on the basis of the full assessed value of churches whose real value had meanwhile been much reduced, and his claim to the integral *spolia* of all prelates.[20] The result, according to Clement's envoy sent to negotiate a relaxation, was 'the annihilation of the rights of the Apostolic Camera', as clerics invoked the ordinances to excuse themselves from paying what they owed. This would be the paradigm for the future; the royal power that had been used to enforce Avignon's exaction of finances from the French clergy would now be used to protect the 'liberties' of the French Church against the papacy.

The dukes' move away from the Avignon project was facilitated by Clement's death on 16 September 1394; the royal council immediately wrote to the cardinals not to elect a successor. They accepted the letter only after they

[20] Léonard (1923), pp. 272–86.

had elected Cardinal Pedro de Luna on 28 September, crowned as Pope Benedict XIII on 11 October. In deference to Paris, however, each cardinal had first sworn an oath that if elected he would do everything to achieve union by whatever means necessary, including abdication if a majority of the cardinals deemed it advisable; Benedict repeated the oath after his election. He had already as cardinal declared himself anxious to end the Schism, by abdication if necessary, and now, announcing his election to the king, he summoned the crown to find appropriate 'ways' and send an embassy to bring them to Avignon. At the same time, however, he instructed his envoys to Paris to explain to the dukes that cession without a determination of rights could lead to something far worse than schism, namely 'to adore an idol on earth' – a pope elected by pseudo-cardinals. Convinced of his own legitimacy and believing as a matter of course in the high-papalist ecclesiology of his Avignon predecessors, he neither then nor ever could accept a *via cessionis* in its obligatory 'Paris form', predicated on ignoring the issue of justice and forcing the popes to give up their respective claims in submission to secular policy.[21]

The dukes' response was worked out with their chief ecclesiastical advisers, Burgundy's chancellor Jean Canart, bishop of Arras, and Berry's client Simon de Cramaud, once a professor of canon law, for a time Berry's chancellor, and now both an archiepiscopal prelate (patriarch of Alexandria) and a member of the royal government. It was to mobilise the French Church behind the government's policy by summoning the French upper clergy to a 'First Paris Council' to 'counsel' the crown and thereby impart ecclesiastical authority to it. The key role here and henceforth was played by Cramaud, who also worked with two luminaries of the university of Paris, the theologian Gilles Deschamps and the canonist Pierre Leroy (the still more distinguished Pierre d'Ailly and Jean Gerson preferred not to join the machine); together they worked out the programme to secure the council's approval of the *via cessionis*. The university's spokesmen were now ready to advocate this via exclusively, as the *only* way to resolve the Schism, hence obligatory, with any discussion of rights precluded as 'absolutely inexpedient'. Simon also indicated the corollary, that a pope refusing to abdicate would have to be coerced. The council met, 2–18 February 1395, under Simon's presidency and tight management; he reported its vote to the crown as favouring obligatory cession, eighty-seven to twenty, with two abstentions.

The crown's decision in this sense would be brought to the pope by an embassy headed by all three royal dukes – Berry, Burgundy and the king's brother Louis of Orléans – with instructions drafted by Simon that allowed no room for negotiation with a pope whose hard intractability he had already

---

[21] Girgensohn (1989), pp. 197–247, offers the best appreciation of Benedict's character and ideas.

come to know and detest.[22] Benedict's insistence on a *via iusticie,* calling for a meeting between the two popes *(via convencionis),* discussion of legitimacy and then abdication of the loser, was not even considered by the dukes and the embassy returned without an agreement. It had, however, bullied the Avignon cardinals into support of the Paris programme – the only recusant was Benedict's fellow Spaniard, Martin de Zalba – and this in effect activated the conclave oath: Benedict was now, in his refusal to adopt the *via cessionis,* a perjuror.

The next three years saw the French government working to draw other polities into support of the *via cessionis:* Castile followed the French lead; Richard II of England was won over in the context of a long-term truce with a French alliance and marriage to a French princess; Emperor Wenceslas IV, king of Bohemia, would go along passively; Florence entered a French alliance, 29 September 1396. While no Urbanist power or indeed Urbanist intellectual agreed to a *coerced* cession, the effect of French diplomatic action was to create a European image that turned public opinion from general acceptance of the Schism to a sense that it had to be ended, with an eventual realisation that this meant terminating both papacies without judgement. A major milestone on this *via* was the joint embassy of France, England and Castile in 1397, to ask both popes to resign; neither would, but the action itself made the new image more real.

Meanwhile, however, French policy had to deal with Benedict's recalcitrance. The *via cessionis* would now be extended to 'subtraction of obedience', with obedience understood primarily in its reified sense as the rights and revenues that the pope enjoyed in the French Church.[23] In its original version, to be known as partial or particular subtraction, it called for action within the context of the *via cessionis* to restore the 'Liberties of the Gallican Church', which meant concretely cutting back papal fiscal and appointive rights over the French Church. The university sought to have this taken up as royal policy at a Second Paris Council meeting from 23 August to 15 September 1396, but the joint embassy being planned made it inappropriate. Meanwhile Benedict was rallying support in Paris for his 'juridical' solution that would preclude the *via cessionis* in what he called its 'non-juridical' Paris form; both d'Ailly and Gerson

---

[22] Kaminsky (1983), p. 105, for testimony by Martin de Alpartil that in 1391 Simon's entry into the cardinalate had been frustrated by Pedro de Luna – one guesses because Pedro did not want yet another Valois client in the college. Cf. the report of Benedict's envoys to Pisa in 1409, referring to their frustration by Simon, 'de quo notum erat a diu et est adhuc quod nomen domini nostri pape Benedicti nedum nominare, immo eciam audire horrebat' (Brandmüller (1975a) (= 1990), pp. 68–9).

[23] The term itself was canonistic: the twelfth-century Decretist Huguccio had written, in his gloss on 'Si duo forte' (79. dist., c. 7), that a pope causing grave scandal could be deposed by a general council, 'et si permittitur depositio, permittitur eius praeambula, scilicet subtractio oboedientiae solitae' (Bliemetzrieder (1904a), p. 153).

were among his supporters. Cramaud took up the challenge, first of all by composing a *questio*, 'De substraccione obediencie', showing that cession was at any rate canonical, also obligatory, and that a pope rejecting it was rejecting the only way by which the Schism could be ended; such a pope was therefore schismatic and, since schism was equivalent to heresy, also heretical, hence *ipso facto* no pope at all, entitled to no obedience. On another tack, a pope who scandalised the Church by refusing the only way it could be united was destroying the *status universalis ecclesie* and the canons justified resisting or even removing such a one. This was the doctrine of 'total' subtraction, leading to the same immediate result as partial subtraction but with the advantage that it nullified in advance any papal reprisals. On the other hand it had the disadvantage, from a Gallican point of view, that it restored Gallican liberty only as a side effect, to vanish automatically with the restoration of a single pope; partial subtraction on the other hand, from a pope still recognised as such, could establish Gallican liberty on a foundation that might endure. Simon, who had no interest in Gallicanism or any other ism, would have somehow to bring the Gallicans, who included his main collaborators Jean Canart, Gilles Deschamps, and Pierre Leroy, into a subtractionist coalition to promote total subtraction without precluding partial as well. Meanwhile he sent copies of his treatise all over Europe.

Its programme would be fulfilled, after the triple embassy to the two popes had run its course, at the Third Paris Council from 22 May to 8 August 1398. The royal dukes and other princely personages presided, with Cramaud giving the initial speech on behalf of the crown, and two teams of debaters arguing for and against the question he put: given the *via cessionis* as royal policy, not to be called into question, how should it be implemented? The answer that everyone knew the government wanted was total subtraction. The subtractionist coalition appeared with Deschamps and Leroy joining Cramaud as chief speakers on that side, and in the university of Paris's corporate opinion which supported total subtraction even while adding partial subtraction to it. The vote, which was taken by having each prelate or other participant come singly into the presence of the dukes to read out his written ballot, was an overwhelming subtractionist victory: in the generally correct official count, 247 voted for immediate subtraction of total obedience until Benedict should have accepted the *via cessionis;* 18–20 voted for subtraction with execution deferred until Benedict should have been summoned once more to accept cession; 16–18 voted for another summons and then, if refused, a council of the Avignon obedience; 17 votes were 'singular'. The results were presented to the crown on 27 July, and this was the date given to the royal ordinance subtracting France's obedience from Benedict XIII.

The Third Paris Council was important in other respects too. It was for one thing an unprecedentedly comprehensive confrontation between papalist and episcopalist ecclesiology, the latter now coming into its own as Gallicanism to validate the French territorial Church that would be constituted without a papal head. This required the royal protection of Gallican Liberty that was in any case implied by the crown's request, at the council, that the clergy vote financial 'aids' to the crown – taxes that the Avignon popes had been granting routinely for the past thirty years but that Benedict had refused to renew after they lapsed on 1 April 1398; now, with total subtraction, the crown could ask directly for a grant by the clerical estate of the realm. At the same time the prelates provided for other functions of papal governance to be supplied either by their own rights that Avignon had overridden or by the royal government with clerical advice. All of which meant that the crown would now exercise lordship over the French Church, protecting the clergy's rights, privileges and estate, in return for 'aid and counsel'. At the Second Paris Council Elie de Lestrange, bishop of Le Puy and a supporter of Benedict XIII, had objected that the so-called 'Gallican Church' was not a juridically viable *corpus* because it had no head within France 'distinct from the common head of all Churches, which is the Roman Church and its pope'; it could not, therefore, act as a corporation. He was now refuted in public law if not canon law by the new Gallican Church headed by its king, with an establishment of Gallican Liberty that a number of prelates intended to make permanent.

Another momentous novelty of the Third Paris Council was the emergence for the first time of the idea of a depositionary general council as the means of implementing the *via cessionis*. It appeared at the point when Simon de Cramaud, realising the inadequacy of his earlier idea of action by a concert of kings, added the *via concilii generalis* to the *practica cessionis* in his ballot during the voting:

I think that to have one pope a certain limited number of princes and prelates, empowered by the rest, should be assembled from each realm, to determine a place to meet with the cardinals of both colleges and with the two contenders, willing or not. Then the whole church thus assembled by representation can make the contenders resign or punish them as schismatics, and go on to make an uncontested legitimate pope.[24]

Its function at first limited to the sphere of public relations, the scheme would ten years later become the programme of the Council of Pisa: the politics of the *via cessionis* were in fact the medium through which the conciliar idea had to pass before it could animate an actual council.

The pursuit of the subtractionist programme in the next few years met with more setbacks than successes. Although virtually all the Avignon cardinals duly

---

[24] The French text in Paris, AN, J 518, fol. 366r; it is printed by Valois (1896–1902), I, p. 163; Kaminsky (1983), p. 223 (q.v. for background); and now by Millet and Poulle (1988), pp. 54–6.

subtracted their obedience from Benedict, the pope was able to hold out in the papal palace with the help of forces from his native Aragon. Richard II of England was deposed in 1399 and a similar step was taken by at least the western electors, against Wenceslas IV of Bohemia and the empire, the other prime hope of French policy in the Urbanist camp. In 1402 the university of Toulouse produced an anti-subtractionist 'Letter', taken up by Louis of Orléans who now secured a restoration of obedience to Benedict, who even promised, insincerely, to accept the Paris *via cessionis*. In any case he regained only a fraction of the rights and revenues that had been subtracted and would not long hold on to those.

FROM PARIS TO PISA

The apparently inconclusive results of the French programme after 1398 conceal a solid success, for it changed the climate of opinion even in the obdurate Roman papacy. So it was that in 1404 when Boniface IX died, his cardinals swore a conclave oath that each if elected would do everything to end the Schism, including abdication if this should be expedient; the new pope, Innocent VII, repeated it. The next year Cardinal Baldassare Cossa, dominant in the college, commissioned the jurist Petrus de Anchorano to write a treatise on union that accepted the French rejection of any discussion of legitimacy. When Innocent died in 1406, the consequent election was preceded by a conclave oath in precisely this sense: each cardinal swore that if elected he would abdicate *pure, libere, ac simpliciter* if the other papal contender would do the same and if the 'anticardinals' would join the Roman ones to make a new election. He would also send letters within a month announcing this to the emperor, the 'antipope', the king of France, and other powers, appointing envoys to agree with the other side on the place of meeting for the double abdication; meanwhile he would create no new cardinals. The Urbanist cardinals had obviously come to realise that the new current of unionist sentiment even in their own obedience could not be ignored and could indeed be turned to account for themselves, for a peaceful reunion of the Church would presumably leave them in possession of what they had, augmented by the revenues and opportunities that the addition of the other obedience would bring. When the Venetian Angelo Correr was elected as Gregory XII on 23 November 1406 by the overwhelmingly Neapolitan college, it was in order for him to resign.[25]

---

[25] 'Fuit . . . assumptus ea condicione tantummodo, ut per citam renunciacionem cupitam et populo necessariam pacem afferret; credatque tua dileccio firmiter ipsum dominos nullatenus aliter assumpsisse' – so Cardinal Antonio Caetani in a letter from Pisa to Carlo Malatesta of Rimini (Gregory's protector after the pope had broken with his cardinals), 26 November 1408 (Girgensohn (1984), pp. 223–4).

He indeed repeated the oath after his election and sent out the letters, which reached Paris during a Fourth Paris Council summoned at the urging of the university in order to validate a new subtraction due to Benedict's failure to keep the promises on which the restitution had been conditioned. The council recommended partial subtraction and two royal ordinances of 18 February 1407 so decreed, with a third decreeing total subtraction as a last resort. All, however, were held in abeyance in order to respond to the new initiative. Meanwhile Gregory had sent his envoys to Benedict, now in Marseille, who agreed to a double abdication, with, however, the stipulation that a discussion of rights – always his *sine qua non* – would come first; on 21 April a meeting between the two was set for October in Savona, at the fringe of the Avignon obedience. A comprehensive embassy sent by 'the realm and Church of France', led by Simon de Cramaud and the Orléans client Pierre Fresnel, to obtain Benedict's final acceptance of unconditional cession perforce accepted the arrangement but still demanded that Benedict commit himself to abdicate without conditions. On 18 May he refused and went on to protest against Simon's previous attacks on him as a schismatic and heretic; Simon's response was not conciliatory. The next day Benedict drew up a bull excommunicating all subtracters of obedience, no matter how high their estate, as a weapon to be kept in reserve. The envoys then went to Genoa, where they hired two galleys to take Gregory to Savona, and in July they went on to Rome.

There they had to deal with Gregory's change of heart: he now made Venetian difficulties about entrusting himself to Genoese galleys and began to talk of a new meeting place in his own obedience, also of the disadvantages of simple cession as against a discussion of rights. While his new attitude was no doubt due to the importunities of his relatives and of Ladislas of Naples (who feared that the reunion of the papacy under French auspices would favour Louis II of Anjou's claim to his kingdom), it also owed something to Benedict XIII's persistent argument that even a continued Schism would be better than a solution in which the papal claimants were coerced into a non-juridical solution by the secular powers. Some of the French envoys, including d'Ailly and Gerson, now gave up and left; Cramaud and Fresnel, however, stayed on in order to put pressure on the pope by dealing directly with his cardinals. In the event Gregory did move but on land: he left Rome on 9 August, arrived in Siena on 4 September and stayed there until 22 January 1408. Benedict, in contrast, sailed into Savona on 24 September, and when Gregory missed his deadline proposed an alternative: Gregory would go to Pietrasanta, Benedict to Portovenere – where he arrived on 3 January and stayed until 15 June; Gregory, however, went only to Lucca, thirty-eight miles away, on 28 January, where he would stay until 19 July. Benedict was clearly ahead on points, but behind his readiness to keep his word there lay the same hopes he had cultivated from the first, and only the capture of Rome by Ladislas on 25 April 1408 prevented him from going there and consummating a *via facti*.

Meanwhile things had changed in Paris. The university of Paris had suspended classes to protest over the government's failure to publish the subtraction ordinances of 18 February 1407 after the unsatisfactory talks at Marseille. With the assassination of Louis of Orléans on 23 November 1407 by agents of John the Fearless of Burgundy, Benedict lost his only Valois sympathiser, and on 12 January 1408 the government decreed that if the two popes had not reunited the Church by Pentecost (24 May) France would move to neutrality. On 4 March the university was given the subtraction ordinances to publish if the deadline were not met. Benedict's response was to send a copy of his unpublished bull of 19 May 1407 as a warning, which was deliberately taken in Paris as an actual insult to the royal majesty: the subtraction ordinances were published on 15 May, Benedict was charged with *lèse-majesté*, and on 25 May 1408 France was proclaimed neutral. Another Paris council of the clergy was summoned for August to set up the constitution of the Gallican Church once again subtracted from papal obedience.

Matters in Italy now came to a head. The French envoys, with Cramaud as the driving force, kept in touch with the two papal courts, moving back and forth several times, in order to mobilise both sets of cardinals to act even without their popes. In early May 1408 Gregory broke off negotiations altogether (he would formally repudiate the *via cessionis* on 12 May), forbidding his cardinals to confer with the French envoys, whom he ordered out of Lucca. They went to Pisa, where most of Gregory's cardinals joined them on 11 May, appealing from Gregory to Christ, a general council, and a future pope. Benedict sent a group of his own cardinals to Livorno to negotiate with them, but Cramaud was also there to frustrate Benedict's effort, and on 15 June Benedict left Portovenere for safety in Perpignan under Aragonese lordship. On 29 June most of both colleges of cardinals finally joined in Livorno, in the presence of the French envoys, to declare their intention of reuniting the Church:

We promise each other . . . by irrevocable oath to pursue the union of the Church . . . by the way of abdication of both papal contenders, . . . and if they refuse or are contumacious we will take other measures by deliberation of a general council; we will then provide the Church with a single, true, and indubitable pastor by a canonical election to be made by both our colleges meeting as one.[26]

They subsequently issued letters convoking a general council to Pisa on 25 March 1409; finance would be provided by France but also by Cardinal

---

[26] Martène and Durand, *Veterum scriptorum*, pp. 798–803.

Baldassare Cossa, who had banked his profits as lord of Bologna with the Medici in Florence and who drew 42,000 florins out of his account three days before the Council of Pisa.

FROM PISA TO CONSTANCE

The Councils of Pisa and Constance have their own interest but need figure here only as the double ending of the Schism. The Council of Pisa, meeting from 25 March to 7 August 1409, with the adherence of France, England and a number of principalities in Italy and the empire, including King Wenceslas of Bohemia, turned out to be a relatively simple instrument for dealing with both papal contenders, who were duly summoned but refused to attend: each celebrated his own council, Benedict at Perpignan (21 November 1408 to 12 February 1409), Gregory at Cividale (6 June to 17 August 1409). At Pisa the charges against both popes were drawn up, read out and acted upon: at the session of 5 June 1409 Simon de Cramaud read out the council's decree deposing the two – an epitome of the doctrine of total subtraction that he had worked out in 1396:

The holy synod representing the universal Church, sitting as a tribunal in the present case against Pedro de Luna and Angelo Correr, formerly known as Benedict XIII and Gregory XII, decrees that all their crimes are notorious, and that they have been and are schismatics, fosterers of schism, notorious heretics deviating from the faith, ensnared in notorious crimes of perjury and violation of their oaths, and notorious scandalisers of the Church: and that they have been notoriously incorrigible, contumacious and stubborn in these respects. For these and other reasons they have rendered themselves unworthy of every honour and dignity, even the papal; and the synod decrees that they are ipso facto deposed *(abjectos)* and deprived of all right to rule or preside, by God and the sacred canons. At the same time the synod, by this definitive sentence, deprives, deposes and cuts off the aforesaid Pedro and Angelo, prohibiting them from acting as supreme pontiff. And the synod decrees that the Roman Church is vacant.[27]

In other respects too the council appears as a French production, with Cramaud as 'the most important personage', presiding at key sessions, controlling access to Pisa itself and managing much of the proceedings, including the decision, unpopular with others of the French delegation, to elect the new pope by a simple fusion of the two colleges, even though the French would be in a minority.

For the rest, the Council of Pisa deferred the work of reform that some desired and proceeded on 26 June to elect a new pope, Peter Philarges, Greek by origin but a cardinal of the Roman obedience, backed by Cardinal

[27] Ibid., pp. 1095–8; Vincke (1938), pp. 295 ff.

Baldassare Cossa; he took the name of Alexander V. When he died soon after, he was succeeded by Cossa himself as John XXIII (17 May 1410). In as much as both Benedict XIII and Gregory XII held on to reduced obediences, the former recognised by Aragon, Castile, Scotland and some principalities in the south of France, the latter recognised by Emperor Rupert and some German principalities, Carlo Malatesta of Rimini, Ladislas of Naples and a few other Italian powers, the Pisan solution was not definitive, although it did accomplish the primary French purpose of joining France to almost all the polities of Europe – the Pisan papacy had or acquired recognition from England and France; Italy except for the cases just noted; all of the empire except Emperor Rupert (who died in 1410), the landgrave of Hesse, the archbishop of Trier and eight other bishops. John XXIII's inability to win the rest and continue the work of reform was due chiefly to his precarious Italian situation under constant pressure from Ladislas of Naples, who was also responsible for the miscarriage of John's Council of Rome (1412–13). In the end John had to turn to the Emperor Sigismund and the two arranged for a new council, to meet not in Italy but in Constance, in order to continue the Pisan programme, take up reform and finally dispose of Benedict and Gregory.

As it turned out the Council of Constance, opening in November 1414, would in due course depose John XXIII as well as Benedict XIII, while Gregory XII avoided a like sentence only by agreeing to abdicate on condition that he first 'summon' the council – a concession *pro forma* that has, however, allowed the Italianised papacy ever since to trace itself back to the Roman line. A single papacy was finally restored with the election of Martin V on 11 November 1417. It was not, however, the *status quo ante*. Martin's revenues were only a third of what the papacy had enjoyed before the Schism; his right to *spolia* was ended; his rights of provision and the consequent finance were drastically curtailed in the concordats that he had to negotiate with the polities of Europe before they would recognise him. Nor could the new papacy regain Hussite Bohemia. The Great Schism indeed marked 'the end of the medieval papacy'.[28]

[28] Holmes (1975), p. 174; Thomson (1980), p. xiii; Wood (1989), pp. 120–1.

PART IV

NORTHERN AND EASTERN EUROPE

CHAPTER 21

BALTIC EUROPE

S. C. Rowell

IF in April Chaucerian man longed to go on pilgrimage, his fellows, as described by the poet's French contemporary Eustache Deschamps, also understood that by August 'fault d'aler en Pruce . . . / ou en Yfflelent, à la rese d'esté'.[1] The crusade (*reysa*) to Lithuania (via Prussia and Livonia), in which the fictional Knight of the Canterbury Tales took part, was established in the chivalric calendar throughout the Catholic world by 1350. In the late Middle Ages west European relations with the Baltic region thrived. The Bridgetine Order leavened religious life throughout northern Europe; the mission to the Baltic provoked questions of moral theology and recruited crusaders across the continent. These pilgrim-soldiers left monuments in Königsberg and at home to mark their achievement. Lithuanian motifs became fashionable in *belles lettres* and to 'raise a pagan prince from the font' was a sign of highest chic. Emperor Charles IV maintained a convert affine, Butautas-Henry, at court in Prague and endowed him with the imperial title of *Herzog von Litauen* as evidence of the breadth of Caroline jurisdiction. By the 1390s Richard II of England was finding it useful to conclude commercial agreements not only with Scandinavians but also with the German Hanse and the Teutonic Order. Prussian and Lübeck merchants trading in war goods with Scotland and France were particularly irksome to the English, just as Rigan supplies of *matériel* and food to the Lithuanians had disturbed the Knights themselves earlier in the century.

The Baltic Sea provided a focus for several northern cultures – Germanic, Slavonic and Baltic, Catholic, Orthodox and pagan – which met and occasionally mixed on its southern shores. The Baltic stretches from Denmark and her western colonies to Russia, from Sweden to Constantinople, or in the tenth-century phrase, from the Varangians to the Greeks. By 1400, Lithuanian rulers governed an empire which connected the Baltic world once more with the

---

[1] *Le miroir de mariage*, lines 2192–4 – composed *c.* 1381/9.

Map 11   Baltic Europe in the fourteenth century

Black Sea. The heart of 'Baltic Europe' is formed by the lands of the Grand Duchy of Lithuania (with the kingdom of Poland) and the Teutonic Order. The Danish *dominium maris baltici* which characterised the thirteenth century slowly gave way to the German-dominated Hanse and the Lithuano-Polish joint monarchy in the fourteenth and fifteenth centuries. To use a Mediterranean metaphor, the Scandinavian peninsula played Carthage to the southern Baltic Rome.

The fourteenth century witnessed the interaction of several pan-European movements in the north: the expansion of mercantile contacts, migration of artisans and other specialists, the flourishing of mendicant orders, the (re)centralisation of kingdoms, the rise of aristocratic power at the expense of kings and the propagation of the chivalric ethic. It is within and largely due to this welter of continental war, trade and mission that Baltic culture thrived. The Baltic community presents a microcosm of European culture and civilisation borrowing heavily from developments to the south and west and contributing to continental life in its turn: the mysticism of St Bridget, the legal thought of Paulus Vladimiri, crusades against the Turks, and on a more materialistic plane, timber, furs and grain for the western market. Here we shall concentrate on the emergent polities of the Grand Duchy of Lithuania and the Teutonic *Ordensstaat* in Prussia and Livonia; their relations with the restored kingdom of Poland and the Scandinavian monarchies. The Norse monarchies themselves, their expansion into Estonia and the White Sea and conflicts with Novgorod will command less attention.

SOURCES

What we know about the Baltic region in the fourteenth century comes from varied sources: chronicles from the Teutonic Order, Denmark, Sweden, Poland and northern Russia. Letters and diplomatic texts survive from Lithuania, Poland, Scandinavia and the Teutonic Order. The endorsements of manuscripts in the Order's Secret Archive (now in Berlin) illustrate neatly how the Order maintained a postal service which only the Tatar *iam* could rival – post horses, letter boys and messengers bore letters which were endorsed as they passed through major points in the commanderies, day and night. Thus we see how a letter could be sent from Königsberg at nine in the morning, reach Brandenburg by noon, leave Balga at six p.m. and arrive at Elbing by 8.00 the following morning, a journey of around seventy kilometres.

From Novgorod we have the birchbark letters, which although runelike (in that they rarely tell us more than we already know) indicate levels of literacy and economic worries of a wide social span. Correspondence also survives from the court of the pagan Grand Duke Gediminas, illustrating his diplomatic intrigues, economic policy and not a little of his character – something we lack for Rus'ian rulers of the same period.

Livonian, Prussian, Polish and Rus'ian chronicles tell us much about the expansion of Lithuania. Lithuanian chronicle records begin in the late fourteenth century with accounts of the political scene after 1342. In the fifteenth century Smolensk became the chief chronicle centre of the Grand Duchy. West Rus'ian was used as the main, but not sole, language of local record although international agreements were concluded also in Latin and Low German. During the reign of Vytautas (1392–1430), the Lithuanian Grand Dukes established their first chancery. The Lithuanian Metrica which preserve official documents from the first half of the fifteenth century to 1795 are a major source for the Grand Duchy's history. Danish sources are much more sparse: the Old Sjelland Chronicle relates events up to 1307; it is continued up to 1363 by the author of the (probably Franciscan) New Sjelland Chronicle.

Rhymed chronicles become fashionable in Prussia and Livonia (Jeroschin's German translation of Peter of Dusburg's Latin prose chronicle, Wigand of Marburg's Prussian Chronicle; *Livländische Reimchronik*) as well as Sweden (the chevaleresque *Erikskrönikan*). The *Erikskrönikan* (composed *c.* 1331–2) aims to describe how lords and princes have lived in Sweden from the time of Eric Ericsson to Magnus Ericsson. The style follows that of Swedish romances and German epic. Elsewhere in the Norse world the fourteenth century also marks a high point in saga writing.

Poetry and *belles lettres* abound, giving an indication of how north Europeans regarded themselves and how they were regarded by others. We see the gradual whittling away of space for the Amazons and dog-headed serfs which classical authors had located in central Europe and the christianised barbarians moved from Germany to Scandinavia and finally to the territories of the Balts. The chivalric literature of the late Middle Ages would not be complete without references to the crusade in the north-east and even imagined marriages between the French and Lithuanian nobility (in Jean d'Outremeuse's *Myreur des histoirs*).

Land registers and lawbooks survive from various parts of the region. Registers from Denmark (*Jordebogel – Århusbogen* (1313–), *Roskildbispens Jordebog* (1370s)) and Sweden (*Registrum Ecclesie Lincopensis* (fourteenth to fifteenth centuries)) not only describe incomes from landed property but also give indications of buildings, landing places, bridges, fisheries and the like. The Reval rentbooks, safe-conduct records and other council documents are of prime importance for Estonian history. Of laws we learn from Danish codices (Thord's Articles from Jutland, *c.* 1300) and Swedish lawbooks (from Södermanland, north and south of Stockholm, Våstmanland (west of Stockholm)) and the *Landaslag* of Magnus Ericsson. We learn of Prussian law from the *Jura Prutenorum* (copied *c.* 1340) which is used by legal scholars to reconstruct pagan legislation. Rigan law as used in Livonia and the cities of Lithuania survives in several manuscripts held by the Order's archive in Berlin. Economic life is revealed by the charters of the officers of the Teutonic Order, the treasury book of the Order and its customs' register, the debt books of Riga and Lübeck, the records of the Hanse collected in published form as the *Hanserecesse* and the *Hansisches Urkundenbuch*.

THE GRAND DUCHY OF LITHUANIA

Lithuania lies to the north-east of the Nemunas (Niemen, Neman, Memel) in the watersheds of the Nevežis and Neris rivers. The land which covers an area roughly two-thirds the size of England was heavily afforested and remains richly endowed with rivers and lakes. Crusade bards sing of 'horses standing saddle-deep in the quagmire' and the branches which slash painfully across the knights' throats as they hacked their way through the dense outback rich in game – wild horses, bears, elk, boar and bison. The human population which, according to the Bohemian historian Dubrawius, was hardly less ferocious than the fauna, was largely agricultural, centred on the farms and castles of a warrior elite, the *bajorai* (or noble servitors whose title is borrowed from Rus' – *boiars*) and dukes (*kunigai, kunigaikščiai*) – cf. king/*könig*). By dint of a series of military conquests in Rus', the Grand Duchy of Lithuania in 1398 had borders close to the Crimea in the south, and to within 100 miles of Moscow in the east, making it the largest polity in central and eastern Europe.

The Lithuanians, who are a Baltic, not a Slavonic, people, share the culture of other Indo-Europeans. Their language, cognate with those of the Latvians and (now extinct) Prussians, retains forms and vocabulary common to other Indo-European tongues. Fifteenth- and sixteenth-century humanists, like the Pole Jan Długosz (d. 1480), the Sienese Pope Pius II (1458–64) and the Lithuanian Michalo Lituanus (fl. 1550), had little difficulty deducing (erroneously) that the Lithuanians are descended from the ancient Romans and speak a Graeco-Latinate tongue where *ugnis* (L: *ignis*: fire), *vanduo* (L: *unda*: water), *dievas* (L: *deus*: god), *vyras* (L: *vir*: man) and other words, like the pagan cult, retain their ancient form.[2] In its peasant and warrior structure, Lithuanian society bears comparison with that of the Merovingians or Anglo-Saxons. Their religion also has much in common with Germanic and Slavonic pagan cults. In the thirteenth and fourteenth centuries the Lithuanians appear to have venerated a particular group of divinities – Perkunas, the Lithuanian equivalent of thundering Thorr and Perun, Andai and the smith-god, Teliavel/Kalevelis.

[2] Hartknoch (1679), pp. 92–3.

Map 12   The Grand Duchy of Lithuania

Sacred spirits filled the cosmos and communicated via sacred animals: pigs, toads and green snakes. As befits a rural society, the sacred places of the cult were rivers, lakes and groves. Sacred groves where the pagans cremated their dead and worshipped feature frequently in the Teutonic Knights' descriptions of campaign routes. The fifteenth-century chronicler, Jean Cabaret d'Orville mentions how the crusaders were willing to respect such holy shrines of pine and oak. Temples, as in Scandinavia, appear to have been a late and largely irrelevant development. Religious celebrations often took place on the farm, ministered by both men and women. This utilitarian cult was open to other gods, including Christ, fearing to offend other divinities by insisting on the jealous uniqueness of God. When the Lithuanian Grand Duke Mindaugas converted in 1251 to Catholicism he still retained a reverence for the old gods.

The Grand Duchy of Lithuania first came to the attention of her neighbours as a serious military and economic organisation, rather than a bolt-hole for bandits or merely a place to pillage, in the early thirteenth century, as a group of five leading clans established themselves as contenders for power in the land. In 1219, twenty princes and dukes and one (dowager) duchess concluded a treaty with the rulers of Galich (south-western Rus'); in the 1250s the Lithuanian dukes, now encouraged by a more or less acknowledged overlord, the Grand Duke, began to expand their dominion into the mercantile principalities of western Rus'. It is probable that the formation of the Lithuanian state was heavily influenced by the economic possibilities and political necessities created by western and eastern expansion in the region in the late twelfth century – itself part of a general European migratory search for a better life in the east as the Flemish song has it.[3] In the competition for supreme office, kinsmen of the Grand Duke turned not only to Rus' for land and support but also to the Teutonic Order in Livonia. As a result of one such manoeuvre Grand Duke Mindaugas (Mindovg, Mendog) (c. 1238–63) was baptised a Catholic in 1251 and crowned king, possibly in his new cathedral in Vilnius two years later by a papal envoy. After King Mindaugas's apostasy (1261) and murder (1263) civil war ensued. By 1290 the political situation had stabilised during the twelve-year reign of Traidenis (Trojden) (c. 1270–82) and there emerged, under the leadership of Pukuveras (Pukuver), the dynasty which ruled Lithuania and later Poland until its extinction in the direct line in 1572: the Gediminids, or Jagiellonians. It is the consolidation of the pagan state in Lithuania and Orthodox western Rus' under Gediminid control in the face of a Catholic mission to convert the heathens by force which marks the single most important chain of events in the Baltic fourteenth century. Lithuania turned from being a third-rank periphery to the dominant power in the region.

---

[3] 'Naer Osstland willen wif rijden / Deer isser en betere stee.'

Grand Duke Vytenis (Viten) (*c.* 1295–*c.* 1315), son of Pukuveras (*c.* 1290–5), established the long-term collaboration with his Rus'ian and Livonian neighbours which marks the emergence of Lithuania as an international agent. In 1298 he concluded a treaty with the citizens of Riga whereby a pagan garrison would defend them, the subjects of the archbishop, from the depredations of the Teutonic Order. The Rigans had already tried (and failed) to enlist the support of the king of Denmark in a similar endeavour. This military contract remained in force until 1313, protecting and strengthening Lithuanian commercial ties with the city. A surviving Rigan register of debts illustrates the importance of Lithuanian trade in the city from the 1280s and the services rendered by Rigans to the pagan Grand Dukes, who used Rigan messengers to communicate with western Europe and employed a city goldsmith. At the same time Vytenis finally annexed the west Rus'ian mercantile city of Polotsk (*c.* 1307) by military force, completing a process which Lithuanian princelings had begun in the 1250s. Lithuanian control of the Dvina trade route was important to the economies not only of the Grand Duchy but also her neighbours in Livonia and Rus'.

Under the guidance of Vytenis's brother and successor, Grand Duke Gediminas (Gedimin, Giedymin) (*c.* 1315–*c.* 1342), Lithuania came much closer to general European life – in diplomacy, commerce and matters of religion. Before 1317 an Orthodox metropolitan (the Byzantine equivalent of an archbishop) was appointed by the emperor of Constantinople, Andronikos II, and Patriarch John Glykys to govern the Church in Lithuanian Rus'. Although the province of the Lithuanians was frequently left without an incumbent, Lithuanian Grand Dukes continued to press for a metropolitan of their own, lest a prelate resident in the principality of Moscow fall under local political control. From now on ecclesiastical politics formed a major if eventually impotent weapon in Lithuanian eastwards expansion, competing with the princes of Moscow for influence over Rus'ian duchies.

The Lithuanian empire in Rus' was strongest in central-western, that is Black and White, Rus'. Grodno (*c.* 1250) was an important trading post on the route from Prussia and Mazovia to Kiev and the Black Sea. Further east lay Novogrudok, the patrimony of Mindaugas's heir and the centre of the Lithuanian Orthodox metropolitanate. It too flourished on Byzantine trade and like Volkhovysk and Slonim lay in the personal gift of the Grand Duke. Polotsk (1250, finally 1307) was the major Dvina (Düna, Dauguva) commercial point and its satellite Vitebsk came into Lithuanian hands when Algirdas (Olgerd, Olgierd) married the local heiress around 1318. Smolensk was under the influence of Vilnius by the 1340s – although not subject to the Grand Duchy of Moscow, the city's princes were fully aware of the Lithuanian grip on the Dvina trade route with Polotsk, Riga and Novgorodia which was essential to Smolensk's prosperity. In Gediminas's day Lithuanian control extended to Podlasie, the westernmost region of Rus' which bordered on Poland – its chief city being the Brest which retains the sobriquet 'Litovsk'. In the south, Lithuanian forces stormed Galich-Volyn' in the 1320s and Gediminas agreed to the establishment of a Mazovian prince there – Bolesław-Yury II, who later married Gediminas's daughter Eufemia (Ofka). Liubartas (Liubart) Gediminaitis[4] took control of Volyn' after Bolesław-Yury II's murder (1340). Kiev, 'mother of Rus'ian cities', may have fallen to Lithuanian control in 1323 but it was certainly in the Grand Duchy after 1362, as a result of Algirdas's victory over the Tatars at Sinie Vody. The Lithuanian presence in south-western Rus' led to vigorous conflict with the Poles (who seized Galich in 1340, establishing a Catholic ecclesiastical province centred on Lvov/Lwów/ Lemberg) and the Hungarians who had been watching developments on their own eastern border with interest since the early fourteenth century.

Alongside their practice of war and careful commercial alliance, the four-teenth-century Grand Dukes pursued a policy of dynastic diplomacy. Gediminas succeeded in marrying a daughter to each of his chief foreign rivals, Casimir, heir to the kingdom of Poland (ruled 1333–70; married to Aldona-Anna, 1325–39), and Semën Ivanovich, prince of Moscow (1340–53; married to Aigusta-Anastasia, 1333–45). These unions settled peace for a while, but not for long, as the Beowulf poet could have warned him. The Gediminids understood this, arranging marriages mainly to bolster the rivals of Lithuania's main com-petitors, the kingdom of Poland and the Grand Duchy of Moscow. Gediminas and later his sons Algirdas and Kestutis (Keistut, Kinstut) established a network of anti-Cracow and anti-Moscow alliances mainly with the ducal houses of Tver' and Mazovia. These unions were successful because they were born of common need. So effective was this arrangement that the last Piast king of Poland, Casimir the Great, had two wives of Lithuanian descent and had to seek papal permission for the marriage of his favoured grandson and likely heir Kaźko to a Lithuanian princess because they were related too closely by blood. Moscow was encircled by Lithuania's allies in Suzdal' and Serpukhov, Novosil' and Karachev, Riazan' and Tver' (see map 14). Semën Ivanovich of Moscow was Algirdas's brother-in-law twice – once through his marriage to Algirdas's sister Aigusta and secondly through his third wife, Maria Aleksandrovna of Tver' who was the sister of Ul'iana, the Lithuanian's second wife.

The spread of the Gediminids around the Rus'ian provinces of the Grand Duchy is well attested. Lithuanian control of Vitebsk increased markedly after Algirdas married the local heiress around 1318 and other Gediminids estab-lished dynasties in Rus': Narimantas's sons who acted as princes of Pinsk and

---

[4] The suffixes -aitis and -aitė / -ovich and -ovna signify son/daughter of; here Liubartas son of Gediminas.

military commanders of Novgorod eventually defected to Moscow, so Rus'ian did they regard their interests; Dmitry Algirdaitis swore not to attack his half-brother Jogaila-Władysław II (Jagiełło) but remained a vassal of Dmitry Ivanovich because that Muscovite ruler offered him greater political authority; Jaunutis's sons settled in the region of Zaslavl'. The Olelkovichi descendants of Vladimir Algirdaitis governed Kiev. By governing far-flung provinces, the junior Gediminids removed the need for the Grand Duke to share the Lithuanian heartlands with them. In this way, ties were strengthened between the Rus'ian acquisitions and the Grand Duke, who relied on military and silver tribute from the provinces to maintain the war effort against the Teutonic Order. The distant kinsmen of the Grand Duke maintained their princely rank but gradually came to act as his *namestniki* in Rus', rather than as regional princes in their own right. Vytautas (Vitovt, Witold) succeeded in taking even their independence away from them and transformed them into grand-ducal servitors. By contrast, Gediminid princesses were married to foreign princes and thus the royal women contributed to the formation of a network of close alliances in Tver' and Mazovia to counter the ambitions of the rulers of Moscow and Poland. Just as importantly, perhaps, these foreign marriages protected the ruling house from any native ducal competitors for supreme power within Lithuania herself. When such a marriage did take place, it was unhappy to say the least. In 1381 Kestutis murdered the noble husband of his niece Maria Algirdaitė in order to prevent Vaidila's becoming too dangerous a player in the Lithuanian civil war (1380–2).

In the wake of almost forty years of war and the famine decade of 1310–20, Gediminas sought to revive his economy through the encouragement of specialist immigration (including clerics to tend the newcomers' souls), gain at least a ceasefire in the conflict with the Order and official recognition of his borders. To facilitate matters, Gediminas joined his voice to Rigan complaints against the Order which had been raised during his brother Vytenis's reign, sending his indictments and hints of a willingness to be baptised to the pope in Avignon. Styling himself 'ruler of the Lithuanians and many Rus'ians', he despatched letters to north German Franciscans, Dominicans (his advertising agents) and merchants in 1323, inviting them to come to settle in Lithuania:

we ask you to announce this to your congregations in the cities, towns and villages where you preach. If there be any knights or noblemen who are willing to come we will give them revenues and as much farmland as they wish; we grant free entry and exit free from all customs and duties and encumbrance to merchants, builders, carpenters, crossbowmen (*balistariis*), cobblers and craftsmen of all types with their wives and children and livestock.[5]

---

[5] Gediminas to the Dominicans of Saxony 26 May 1323: *Gedimino Laiškai*, p. 49.

After securing a peace treaty with the Order (October 1323), confirmed by Pope John XXII (in August 1324), Gediminas declared somewhat theatrically before his courtiers and envoys sent to Vilnius by the papal legates that he had never wished to be baptised and that 'the devil can christen me!'. The tactic of offering baptism for peace and then withdrawing the offer as soon as circumstances allowed became a feature of the Baltic crusade throughout the fourteenth century. Gediminas's sons, Algirdas and Kestutis (d. 1382) negotiated in a similar style with the kings of Hungary and Poland in 1351, with the Order and Charles IV in 1358. One unsolicited outcome of the approach to Avignon may have been the increase in west European crusaders coming to defend the Order against its formidable and astute enemy. The crusades against Lithuania increased sharply from the 1330s onwards.

Algirdas (1345–77) came to power as a result of a palace coup in 1345. His predecessor (and brother) Jaunutis (Evnuty, Jawnuta) (*c.* 1342–5) fled to their sister, Aigusta (or her husband, Grand Duke Semën) in Moscow. There Jaunutis accepted Orthodoxy but failed to gain substantial support from his new co-religionists and brother-in-law. He returned to Lithuania to accept an apanage from his brother, the new Grand Duke. Algirdas rewarded his chief ally, his younger brother, Kestutis, by granting him territories and authority in the southern and western Marches of the Grand Duchy. Kestutis served his lord well establishing a reputation for himself with the Knights and dukes of Poland as a chivalric warrior. He did not rule jointly with Algirdas but in subordination to him. Such use of siblings in positions of power is not uncommon in fourteenth-century Europe: John of Gaunt and Charles of Luxemburg (who governed Moravia for his father, King John, in the 1330s) or Eric and Valdemar of Sweden (below, p. 719) come to mind. Fortunately for Algirdas and Kestutis, their other brothers accepted the situation: Jaunutis was content to accept land from Algirdas's own patrimony in 1347. Manvydas (Montvid) does not appear in the record after 1342 and Narimantas (Narimunt) died in battle in 1348. Liubartas was content with his lands in south-western Rus'. Karijotas (Koriat) likewise was occupied with disputes in his southern duchies. The daughters of Gediminas, Algirdas and Kestutis were sent abroad to marry Polish and Rus'ian dukes, placing considerable pressure on the rulers of Cracow and Moscow, who also had Lithuanian spouses at one time.

Under Algirdas the Grand Duchy continued its relentless march to the east. Algirdas married into the Tverite princely house and assumed pretensions to the throne of All Rus', attacking Moscow three times without success (1368, 1370, 1372). He pressed for the (re)appointment of an Orthodox hierarch to govern the Church in Lithuania (with an eye to spreading further eastwards). His wife's Tverite kinsman Roman was metropolitan during the period 1355–62. Algirdas maintained the religious and diplomatic balance between

Constantinople and the west which had marked his father's reign. Like Gediminas he continued to welcome certain clergy to his lands, maintaining a special approval for the Franciscans, as supplications to the curia make clear. Nevertheless, clergy or lay Christians who flouted his express command were dealt with forcefully. Apparently around 1369–70 as he prepared to attack Moscow at a time of increased Teutonic pressure on his western border, Algirdas put to death three courtiers who refused to obey grand-ducal commands concerning court life (they refused to eat meat during lent or to cut their beards) and executed five Franciscans who had preached publicly against the Lithuanian cult.

After Algirdas's death (1377) the fragile alliance between Gediminid siblings was upset by competition between Algirdas's heir, Jogaila and the latter's uncle (Kestutis) and cousin (Vytautas). In 1381 Kestutis overthrew Jogaila in a *coup d'état* in Vilnius only to be imprisoned and murdered the following year. Vytautas fled to Marienburg and became a Catholic (for the first time) with the support of the grand master. In 1384 Jogaila and his mother considered a Rus'ian wedding for the Grand Duke. Jogaila would marry the daughter of the prince of Moscow. However, in view of the recent razing of Moscow by a Tatar army (1382), a much more useful possibility lay in Poland. In 1385 Jogaila, now reconciled with Vytautas, sent a delegation of his brothers and leading *boyars* to Hungary to negotiate the hand of Jadwiga of Anjou, heiress to the crown of Poland. He promised to pay compensation on behalf of the queen of Hungary to the Austrian father of his bride's jilted fiancé, to make good all Poland's losses by his own labours and at his own expense; to free Polish prisoners of war held captive in Lithuania; to baptise as Catholics all the pagans in his realm and to join those lands of Lithuania and Rus' with the Polish crown forever, a timespan which is remarkably short in practice. The vague, but apparently weighty, phrase *perpetuo applicare* haunts Polono-Lithuanian relations and fear of revanchism still. In return, Jogaila would marry Jadwiga and be adopted as son and heir by Jadwiga's mother, Elizabeth of Hungary. In February 1386 Jogaila was elected king of Poland in Lublin, baptised Władysław (to remind everyone of the restorer of the Polish crown, Władysław Łokietek) in Cracow twelve days later and married to Jadwiga on 18 February. Jogaila was thus thrice king: through election, adoption and marriage. In February 1387 Jogaila took a bishop, his mother-in-law's former confessor, to Vilnius and began the long process of converting his pagan people to Christianity in the Roman rite.

The union of Lithuania and Poland is the high point of fourteenth-century international affairs. Theoretically, it put an end to pan-European crusades led by the Teutonic Order against the Baltic pagans. In fact, the crusades intensified after 1387, as the Order claimed that the conversion was a sham and western princes, including Henry Bolingbroke, continued to make their way to Königsberg. Throughout the 1390s and as late as 1416 western European knights and princes continued to come on *reysa* to Lithuania. In 1399 the Order gained a temporary territorial victory over the Lithuanians when Grand Duke Vytautas surrendered Žemaitija to the grand master. However, the Knights never managed to achieve their long-asserted aim of appropriating Lithuania herself. In 1410 the joint forces of the Grand Duchy of Lithuania and the kingdom of Poland defeated the Order in battle at Tannenberg, the symbolic watershed of Teutonic power. The union created the largest state in Europe, tempering Polish and Lithuanian competition over the carcase of Kievan Rus' to the east. Before the end of the century the Polish king-supreme duke was proposing that the Byzantine and Roman Church fathers meet in council in his realm to effect a healing of the schism within Christendom.

The Lithuano-Polish union flourished in the tension of competing political ambitions. The Polish nobility which had invited Jogaila regarded itself as the upholders of the Polish crown, kingmakers in a literal sense; the Lithuanian boyarate struggled to improve its position in the Grand Duchy, supporting various candidates for the office of Grand Duke – a habit familiar to us from Scandinavia and Poland. The Gediminid dynasty played out a series of moves aimed at ruling Lithuanian territories separately from Poland, or rather from Jogaila. Jogaila showed himself an expert (that is, from hindsight a very lucky) gambler. He recognised his cousin Vytautas's power in Lithuania and granted him title of Grand Duke from 1392, retaining for himself a theoretical political supremacy. After the death of his wife in 1399 Jogaila desired recognition of his rights from the Polish nobility and also from Vytautas, who in 1401 (by the treaty of Vilnius–Radom) was recognised as Grand Duke of Lithuania for his lifetime only, the grand-ducal cap returning to Jogaila after his death. In the early fifteenth century Jogaila played out similar moves with his brother Švitrigaila and Vytautas's son, Žygimantas. By Jogaila's death in 1434 the two realms were securely in the hands of Jogaila's own wife and sons, despite the death-throes of armed dynastic competition in the territories of the Grand Duchy. Thus in many senses the years 1398–1409 mark an important watershed in Baltic history: Jogaila was recognised fully by both his Polish and Lithuanian subjects, as king and supreme duke, and Vytautas, recently defeated by the Tatars at Vorkslai, gained enough to enable him to collaborate with Jogaila. The temporary surrender of Žemaitija to the Order (1398) until the Žemaitijan uprising of 1409 marked the Knights' greatest, albeit unmaintainable, territorial expansion.

The joint monarchy created at Krevo has been compared with other less successful fourteenth-century dynastic states, especially the Scandinavian kingdoms which were united officially in 1397 at Kalmar. The geographical coincidence of the two unions, the southern and eastern Baltic dominated by

Lithuania-Poland, the northern and western reaches by Sweden and Denmark, has caused much superficial comparison. The union of Kalmar was built on inter-Scandinavian noble foundations which lacked a secure dynastic heart. It was largely an anti-German trade and political cartel and it collapsed almost as swiftly as it was formed. The Lithuanian union was far more than a common alliance against the Teutonic Order. It settled important territorial squabbles in eastern Europe, provided a common front against the Order, whose strength was already on the wane by the late 1380s. It was a dynastic solution to various Polish and Lithuanian difficulties and established the strongest regime, but not the strongest monarchy, in central Europe, whose members came in time to rule in Bohemia and Hungary as well as in the joint monarchy. The family connections made by the pagan Gediminids in Polish, Rus'ian and imperial territories eased the entry of the newly converted regime into general European culture.

THE TEUTONIC *ORDENSSTAAT* – PRUSSIA AND LIVONIA

Like the Grand Duchy of Lithuania, the monastic state (*Ordensstaat*) in Prussia rose to prominence on the back of war and trade, colonisation and mission. The Teutonic Order, or to cite its full title the Knights of the Order of the Hospital of the Blessed Virgin Mary of the German House in Jerusalem, which arrived in the southern Baltic in the 1230s at the invitation of a local Polish duke, Konrad of Mazovia, was firmly established in the region by 1300. In 1237 the Knights subsumed the remnants of the Order of Swordbrothers, which had been created by the bishop of Riga in 1202 to protect German merchants in Livonia (and defeated by the Lithuanians at Saule in 1236) – and took over control of large parts of Livonia.

By the 1280s the Knights had secured most of Prussia and (Polish) Pomorze and in 1309 the grand master transferred his residence from Venice to the fortress monastery of Marienburg and the office of master of Prussia ceded place to him. Following the arrival of Grand Master Siegfried von Feuchtwangen in Prussia, Marienburg, which had gained its charter in 1276, served as both an ecclesiastical and political capital, a monastery and a palace, a fortress and a prison on the banks of the Nogat – a clear symbol of the Order's majesty and its intention to stay in Prussia (cf. above, pp. 235–6).

The fourteenth century witnessed a massive programme of colonisation in the north-east. The cycle of inclement weather and famine which affected the whole of Europe in the second decade of the century did not spare the Baltic region. It has been suggested that one of Gediminas's reasons for improving contacts with Catholic Christendom in the early 1320s was economic, a response to a crisis in food production and international trade on which he relied to maintain his nascent empire. A similar predicament faced the Knights in Prussia and Livonia. The Knights concentrated on the settlement of colonists in the Wildnis on the frontier with Lithuania. Westphalian immigration into Prussia, especially to the restored Polish towns of Elbing, Chelmno and Toruń is well attested in the first half of the century. Similar policies were pursued in Poland and south-western Rus'.

In the first sixty years of the *bellum lithuanicum* (calculated by the Order's chronicler, Peter of Dusburg, from 1283) five hundred or so grants of land and legal privileges (Culm and Magdeburg law) were issued to settlers in Prussia by the Knights. The biographies of the grand masters of the Order, in so far as we can piece them together, bear witness to area after area being colonised with new settlers. Master Meinhart von Querfurt (1288–99/1300) actively promoted the colonisation of Graudenz, Christburg, Mewe and Preussisch Holland (the latter, as the name suggests, largely with immigrants from the Low Countries). Werner von Orseln (1324–30) concentrated his efforts on the Vistula territories; his successor, Luder von Braunschweig (1331–5) is noted for his achievements in Pomezania. Military service or the provision of weapons, often specified as Prussian or other Baltic designs (the *brunie*), was required from many of the colonists who came from German duchies, Poland, Rus', Baltic peoples and even Lithuania. In some cases the war against the Lithuanians was stipulated as the reason for these requirements.

It may be helpful to divide this survey of Teutonic settlement into several areas: the former Polish maritime provinces of Pomorze, central Prussia and Livonia. The citizenry of Danzig rose up in arms against the pretender to the Polish throne, Władysław Łokietek in 1308. In response the Polish prince invited the Teutonic Order to restore calm to the town and this was achieved. The Order, however, declined to leave Danzig and incorporated the territory into the *Ordensstaat*. Between 1321 (when Łokietek prosecuted the Order in the curia) and 1410 (Grunwald) the Knights issued 508 settlement privileges (the majority, 258, in the thirty years period 1351–80) for the area of Danzig Pomorze. Danzig grew ten times between 1300 (population: 2,000) and 1416 (20,000 inhabitants) and became significantly Germanised – 22 per cent Low Germans and Westphalians, 25 per cent Prussian, 10 per cent from Holstein and maritime Pomorze, 2.5 per cent Silesian, 3 per cent Slav. By 1340 Danzig had a strong fortress and in 1343 the town was endowed with Chelm law. In 1378 a Gothic council chamber was erected in the Long Market (*Długi Targ*). The Danzig question, opened in 1308, was settled in 1945.

After 1310 colonisation efforts were concentrated on the Elbing commandery, Pomezania and Ermland. Around 1325 attention turned to north-western Prussia between the Vistula and the Vistula Gulf, and the Drwęca and Lyna rivers; the north-eastern commanderies of Brandenburg, Balga and

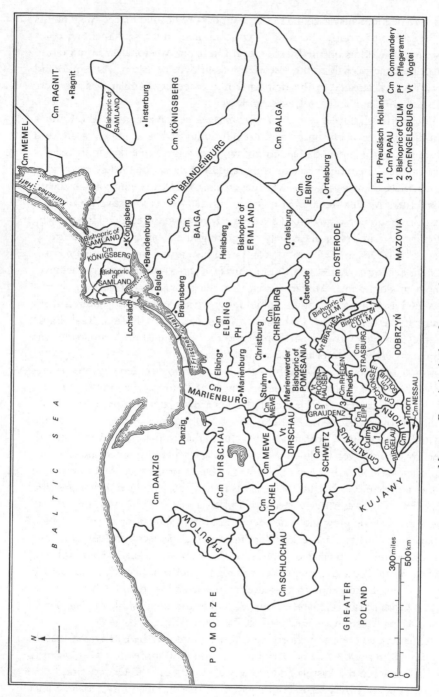

Map 13 Prussia in the late fourteenth century

Königsberg (see map 13). From the mid-fourteenth century a slow down in Prussian colonisation is noticeable. According to ethnicity, Polish settlers can be found near Kujawy, Dobrzyń and Mazovia. Eighty-four (of 436) villages were settled with Polish law (especially in the north-western parts of Danzig Pomorze). Poles moved from Chelmno and the Danzig region to Prussia, especially when colonisation was strong in the diocese of Pomezania. Prussians meanwhile moved from Pomezania to Allenstein (Olsztyn) and the southern parts of the commandery of Elbing. Prussian villages are also to be found near Stargard in the Danzig region and Ermland. In the fourteenth century the old Polish town of Toruń which was refounded on a nearby site by the Knights with German Law had a population which included Germans (13 per cent), Silesians (12 per cent), Slavs and Prussians (23 per cent) and incomers from other areas of the *Ordensstaat* (28 per cent). Twenty new towns were built by the Knights before 1350 and by the time of the Order's defeat at Grunwald (Tannenberg) (1410) ninety-four cities had been founded or expanded on the basis of German Law.

At the turn of the thirteenth and fourteenth centuries the Order's colonisation in Livonia decreased. Between 1300 and 1450 only forty-two enfeoffments were made. Many Baltic peasants took German names and fade away into the record. The Order, profiting from its financial resources, also added to its territorial holdings by accepting land in mortgage from indigent dukes – the so-called *Pfandverträge* or pledge treaties. In this way the Knights consolidated their hold on borderlands, especially in the south and west. Michałowo was mortgaged by the duke of Kujawy in 1304 and sold to the Order outright in 1317. Between 1329 and 1341 the grand masters bought up the Pomeranian town and district of Stolp from the local Piast dukes. The dukes of Mazovia likewise pledged Wisna and even the king of Poland mortgaged Dobrzyń (1352/3 – 1363/4) for 40,000 gulden. Perhaps the most spectacular purchase made by the Order was the 10,000 marks it gave the king of Denmark, Valdemar Atterdag in 1346 in exchange for the Danish colony of Estonia.

The grand masters of the fourteenth century were appointed from German princely families, such as Luder von Braunschweig, the higher nobility (Dietrich von Altenburg, 1335–41), the lower nobility (Werner von Orseln) and urban patriciate such as Karl von Trier (1311–24). The grand master was obliged by the statutes to consult the brethren in all important matters such as those involving property and recruitment and to take counsel with his chapter. The day-to-day government of the monastery – that is, of Prussia – was overseen by a council of five major officers who retained their ancient titles, if not those precise functions: grand commander, marshal (the chief military officer, especially responsible for the Königsberg commandery), master draper (i.e. the commander of Christburg), senior hospitaller (the commander of Elbing) and treasurer (in Marienburg Castle). The commandery of which there were ten in Prussia was the chief administrative unit of the Order's realm. Sometimes it was subdivided into *Waldämter* or *Pflegerämter* which were centred on a fortified place. The advocates (*Vogt*) presided over native courts and militias in the outlying districts.

In Livonia brethren were often of burgher origin and thus ineligible as commanders or masters of a house in Livonia or Prussia but they could be so in Germany. The greymantles were sergeants who wore grey coats and performed subsidiary duties. Priests lived as brothers of the Order and it was not unusual for them to be of burgher origin, although Prussian and Livonian recruits were rarer. In the thirteenth century recruits to the Order came largely from eastern and central Germany (especially Thuringia). However, in the fourteenth century the pool of new members was particularly deep in Rhineland-Westphalia (supplying 64 per cent of known brethren between 1309 and 1410). Of all commanders, marshals and masters, 40 per cent came from these western provinces of the empire. During this later period it became traditional to elect a master for a longer period than previously. If a Low German noble decided to join the Livonian Order he did so now for life rather than as a step to a career in Prussia. The Livonian Order was dominated by the Low German petty nobility – in contrast with the case in Prussia. German-speaking Livonian nobles tended not to join the Order despite their having come originally from Low Germany themselves and retained family ties in the empire.

The Teutonic Order was not the only social organisation in Livonia. The archbishopric of Riga, an institution which predates the military orders, controlled most of the land in Livonia. In the fourteenth century the Order sought to incorporate the archbishopric into its territorial holdings. This caused considerable conflict, as the clergy and citizenry of Riga strove to maintain their independence – especially when the Knights bought up property belonging to other religious, such as the Cistercians of Dünamünde, which gave them effective control of the river access to Riga from the sea. Archbishops tended to be drawn from across the region (John III (1295–1300) was count of Schwerin; the former archbishop of Lund, Jens Grand, in dispute with the Danish king, refused to transfer to Riga in 1304) and occasionally from further afield in the hope of finding a neutral candidate. The Bohemian nobleman Frederick von Pernstein (1304–40) resided in his metropolis for barely two out of his thirty-five years. From his exile in Avignon he sought to place a Bohemian bishop in Prussia (Hermann of Ermland) and prosecute the Order for irregularities. The court cases continued throughout the century – in 1353 Innocent VI sent papal commissioners to Riga to govern the province in the name of the Holy See. In 1375 the pope was still finding it necessary to urge

Map 14 Livonia in the fourteenth century

the Knights not to molest the bishop of Ösel – but the curia was far from Livonia.

Unlike the other people of the southern Baltic the Estonians are neither Slavs nor Balts but a people closely connected by language and culture to the Finns and Hungarians. As a result of Danish and German expansion in the region, in the early thirteenth century Estonian lands were captured by the Sword Brethren, and by the Treaty of Stensby, Harrien (Harjumaa) and Wirland (Virumaa) were handed over to the Danish crown in 1238. The Danes held these territories until 1346. The south-western parts of Estonia formed the bishopric of Dorpat; the western lands and islands were controlled by the bishops of Ösel and Leal.

The duke of Estonia rarely resided in the province itself. In his place government was in the hands of the bishop and lieutenant (*capitaneus*) of Reval (in Estonian Tallinn: city of the Danes). The lieutenant was appointed by the king in council with *potiores nostri*. The number of royal counsellors varied, from a dozen in 1282 to fifteen in 1343 and perhaps seventeen in 1346. The vassals of the king formed their own corporation: *universitas vasallorum*. From cases involving the infrastructure of Reval and mercantile losses it is clear that the local counsellors and vassals worked in consort with the crown in making or confirming decisions.[6] Free transit to Novgorod was safeguarded on royal command by the lieutenant of Reval, the sworn counsellors of the king and the *universitas vasallorum* in 1307. Collaboration between the archbishopric of Riga, the other Livonian bishops, the Order in Prussia and Livonia and the representatives of Estonia and the king of Denmark is a frequent occurrence – in peace negotiations in 1309, 1313, 1323 and in commercial accords. A particularly apposite example is the Treaty of Vilnius (2 October 1323) which made peace in the region for four years between the Livonian Order, the Danes of Estonia, the archbishopric of Riga and the Grand Duchy of Lithuania. Gediminas sent representatives to Denmark to treat with the king, as the Rigan debt register illustrates.

Danish rule in Estonia during the interregnum in Denmark appears to have been so oppressive towards the native population that on St George's Day 1343 the natives of Harrien rose up against the Danish and German colonists. In the diocese of Reval peasants cast off the mantle of Christianity and massacred German colonists, burning homes and churches. The Cistercian monastery at Pades was razed and twenty-eight monks put to the sword. It seems that the rebels contemplated surrendering to the Swedes (sending embassies to the bishops of Åbo and Vyborg). On 24 July the natives of Ösel rose up and attacked the bishop and clergy in Hapsal. The grand master is reported by the

[6] Riis (1977), p. 329.

chronicler Hermann von Wartberge as having despatched 630 troops to settle the war in Harrien and Reval. The following year the grand master sent another army, this time to Ösel. On 17 February 1344 the Order defeated the Öselians and hanged their leader Vesse upside-down *in quadam machina* (a punishment for those who by treason had sought to turn the world upside-down) as an example to his fellows. The Lithuanians used the troubles in Estonia as an excuse to attack the Knights in Livonia (20 February 1345). A local Liv leader attempted to form an anti-Teutonic alliance with the Lithuanian prince but this failed: Algirdas beheaded the Liv for his presumption of royalty.

SWEDEN

Thirteenth-century Sweden saw its last powerful monarch, Magnus Laduslas (d. 1290), who attempted to restrict noble privileges and is remembered chiefly for having introduced the criminal offence of *lèse-majesté* into Swedish law. His reign saw the adoption of continental cultural fashions; the dubbing of knights and the practice of 'chivalry'. However, his attempts at consolidating royal power met with considerable opposition and he found it necessary to create a royal council which clearly delineated the extent of royal and noble privilege. After his death his eldest son, Birger (eleven years old), was elected king and a regency council of magnates was formed. The election of a minor as king was a favourite ploy of the magnates who could then dominate a regency council. In 1302 Birger was crowned but extensive lands were granted to his brothers Dukes Eric and Valdemar. The marshal of the kingdom, Torgil Knutsson invaded western Karelia, taking land from Novgorod and building the border fortress of Vyborg (Viipuri). The dukes and noblemen forced the king to execute Knutsson and then turned on Birger himself. The king arrested his brothers and starved them to death in jail. Birger fled to Denmark to be replaced on the Swedish throne by his nephew, Duke Eric's son Magnus, a three-year-old infant who was already king of Norway. This *coup d'état* strengthened the principle of elective monarchy and united the Scandinavian peninsula under the rule of one king, albeit an infant. According to the 1319 'Freedom Letter', a royal council (*rikis radh*) of between sixteen and thirty-five members, drawn from the aristocracy, episcopate and representatives of the various districts, was supposed to be appointed after the king's coronation. The *radh* was to swear allegiance to the king and the kingdom, giving good counsel and showing no favour to friends or kin. The king in his turn was to love justice, protect the people, maintain royal castles, respect charters given to the Church, nobility and knights. He was not to admit foreigners to his council nor grant them land, castles or crown property.

During King Magnus's minority the eastern border with the Rus'ian

archiepiscopal republic of Novgorod was established at Noteborg
(Orekhov) (1323). Between 1311 and 1320 Swedish and Novgorodian
armies had fought one another five times, according to the Rus'ian chronicle, mainly in Ladoga and Karelia near the Swedish fortress of Vyborg. In
1320 Novgorodian pirates attacked northern Norway. The Novgorodians
aided by the Muscovite Grand Duke, Yury Danilovich, attempted to resist
Swedish pretensions. In 1323 Yury sent an army to ravage Norwegian
Haalgoland and set about establishing control of the Neva. In 1323 he
founded the fortress of Orekhov where the Neva flows into Lake Ladoga.
On 12 August the Swedes and Novgorodians concluded a peace treaty
establishing their common border in Finnish territory. Having settled this
dispute temporarily with the Swedes, the Novgorodians made an alliance
with the Livonian Knights against Lithuania and Novgorod's former
dependency and Lithuania's frequent satellite, Pskov. The anti-Lithuanian
alliance would be overturned only when a new Grand Duke and new archbishop were willing to make peace with Gediminas in 1326. On 3 June 1326
a similar treaty was made with Magnus's other kingdom, Norway. In 1333 a
Lithuanian princeling, Gediminas's son, Narimantas, was christened Gleb
in order to command garrisons in several Novgorodian border forts,
including Orekhov. The interlocking of Teutonic, Scandinavian, Lithuanian
and north-west Rus'ian interests and competition most perfectly summar-
ises the complexity and occasionally apparently self-contradictory nature of
the Baltic world: territorial expansion for economic needs combined with
religious zeal (and pragmatism).

   In 1332 Magnus seized the island of Skåne from the Danes, thereby gaining
control of the major herring market. He held Skåne for nearly thirty years. To
pay for his military adventures in Scandinavia and his 1348 crusade to
Novgorod (below p. 728), Magnus attempted to raise his revenues through taxation, thereby stirring up discontent throughout Swedish society which was
still recovering from the effects of the Black Death. He contravened the conditions of the 1319 charter by granting royal castles to a foreigner, in this case
to his brother-in-law, Albert of Mecklenburg.

   The province of Finland was a pawn in the conflict between the nobility and
the Swedish crown. Magnus Ericsson enjoyed personal influence in the province and strengthened Swedish law there. Finland had traditionally been
granted to nobles of the blood royal. In 1353 Magnus granted the province to
a non-royal noble, a faithful servant. The nobility rebelled and forced the king
to share power with two of his sons. In 1362 Haakon Magnusson was elected
king of Finland and the province sent representatives to the royal council for
the first time. The bishop of Turku represented the voice of the clergy.
Haakon was removed in 1363 and replaced by Albert of Mecklenburg.

DENMARK

Denmark was the most advanced of the Norse kingdoms, which in the thirteenth century had dominated the Baltic sea from Jutland to Estonia. The monarchy was weak and unable to counter the ambitions of nobles and prelates. Archbishop Jens of Lund (1289–1302), whose successor was transferred by Boniface VIII from Riga, preserved ecclesiastical immunities against the interference of the crown. The king, Eric VI Menved (1286–1319), was allowed to collect the *leidang* or tax in lieu of military service in ecclesiastical lands but the clergy maintained control of their peasants. The secular nobility managed to strengthen its position against royal authority. Attempts by Eric to take control of Mecklenburg and Pomerania weakened the crown's financial resources. Eric was forced to recognise the autonomy of his kinsman, the duke of Schleswig, and pawned large domains to the German counts of Holstein. A similar response to a chronic shortage of income was made by the restored kings of Poland who pawned northern territories to the Teutonic Order. Among the noblemen arrayed against the king was his brother Christopher who was elected king in 1320 after Eric died. In order to receive the crown, Christopher (II) was compelled by the *communitas regni* to swear a capitulation according to whose several clauses the king acknowledged his subordination to an annual parliament of nobles, ecclesiastical and secular. He was unable to make laws, conduct wars or levy taxes without consent. Meanwhile the nobles were granted rights to fine their own peasants. In Jutland three royal castles remained and all new castles were destroyed immediately. As elsewhere in the Baltic region the royal council sought to forbid the election of German members. In 1325 Christopher married his daughter, Margaret, to Emperor Lewis IV's son, Lewis, against the wishes of John XXII. The king's inability to pay his daughter's father-in-law the required 10,000 marks dowry led his son Valdemar to pay off the debt by handing over Estonia to the Teutonic Order in 1346 in return for the necessary cash. When Christopher attempted to levy a tax, he caused a civil war as a result of which he was compelled to flee from Denmark, leaving the throne vacant for the election of Valdemar of Schleswig (1326–30) under the regency of the German Gerhard of Holstein. Christopher II returned in 1330 but without further success in the competition with the aristocracy. Eight years of government by Gerhard resulted in his murder in 1340. When Christopher's son Valdemar returned to Denmark as king in 1340, he found the royal demesne in pawn and the treasury empty. Valdemar IV Atterdag enjoyed the support of the Church and established himself in Copenhagen, which had previously belonged to the bishops of Sjelland. He married the sister of the duke of Schleswig, Valdemar, who had ruled Denmark in the late 1320s. He ceded Skåne to Magnus of Sweden (who had already taken the region by force) and sold off his Estonian lands to the Teutonic Order, using the 10,000 marks to purchase Sjelland and Funen from the counts of Holstein three years later. The king succeeded in imposing taxation and gaining the support of his subjects. The parliament of 1360 was not hostile to his interests. He thus embarked on a policy of expansion, recovering Skåne from the Swedes and gaining control of the mercantile island of Gotland.

The weakness of the Danish crown is reflected in the decline in minting in Denmark. We know that Atterdag levied a tax of 6 gros (tournois) per head of cattle in Sjelland in 1355 in order to mint coins, but it is doubtful whether the whole of this revenue was used for its stated purpose. Foreign specie was widely used in Denmark, especially the English sterling, French gros tournois and the Lübeck mark. Bar silver also played an important role in exchange in Denmark as it did elsewhere in the region, including the Grand Duchy of Lithuania and Rus' (known for their *grivny*).

UNION OF KALMAR 1397

Valdemar IV died in 1375 to be succeeded by his grandson Olaf, son of Margaret (the Danish princess) and Haakon VI of Norway, who had lost the Swedish throne to Albert in 1363. During Albert's reign the Swedish nobility had strengthened their political power. The Swedish magnate Bo Jonsson ('the Griffin') is a typical example of one who had gained control of several royal castles. When he died in 1387 he bequeathed his holdings to Margaret. Olaf succeeded to the Norwegian crown in 1380 and pretensions to the throne of Sweden were also made. Discontented with Albert's rule, the Swedes, including the executors of Jonsson's wife, now courted Margaret's favour. Following her son's untimely death in 1387 Margaret, now regent of Denmark and Norway, was recognised as *fuldmaetige frue og rette husbond*, the almighty lady and rightful lord, of Sweden. The king's mother was invited to lead a revolt of Swedish aristocrats against their German king in 1387. In 1389 her army defeated the forces of Albert of Mecklenburg. In 1389 Margaret's nephew, Eric, was elected king of Norway and seven years later he was recognised at Kalmar as having been crowned king of all three Scandinavian kingdoms. On 17 June nobles and prelates from all three realms, including the archbishops of Lund and Uppsala, witnessed his coronation. It was agreed a few days later that Eric's heir should succeed him and if no heir should be born, then all three kingdoms would elect a common monarch. Each kingdom would defend its fellows and the king should control foreign policy with the advice of councillors from the kingdom where he was resident at the time of any negotiations. Eric's seal, like that of Jogaila-Władysław II of Lithuania-Poland, reflects the joint monarchy, displaying the crowns of Sweden and the leopards of

Denmark, the Norwegian lion and the griffin of Pomerania, the lion of Birger Jarl. However, unlike the Jagiellonian federation, the Union established at Kalmar did not survive the fifteenth century.

SOCIAL STRUCTURE

Lithuania can be best summarised as a barbarian kingdom focused in the four-teenth century on the members of one dynasty. The expansion of Lithuania into Rus' provided lands for the superfluous members of the ruling house, thus relieving pressure on the Gediminid Grand Duke to partition the original Lithuanian patrimony. In Rus' the Lithuanian dukes were content to maintain the structures they found there (if they worked). Local boyars and especially the bishops served as respected counsellors to the local ruler. The bishops of Polotsk were so faithful to the Grand Dukes that Vytautas (illegally) granted the ordinary there archiepiscopal status before 1406. The north-western territories of Lithuania proper, Žemaitija, where the family had less influence due to the power of local lords, were open to barter with the Teutonic Order – although only on a temporary basis. The dukes of Lithuania were willing to serve the ruling house; some such as the Alšeniškiai (Holszanscy) learned to co-operate at a relatively early date and reaped the rewards for such service, being the affines of Vytautas, they were the only Lithuanian family to gain an entry to the grand-ducal line, providing in the end the last of the Jagiellonian line. In the fourteenth century boyars were important members of the grand-ducal council and took part alongside the Gediminids in international treaty making, espe-cially where the terms of a given peace involved their own estates. As a result of the conversion, the Lithuanian (Catholic) boyars gained their first written charter of rights from Jogaila in 1387. The majority of the population remained in the villages and on the farms. As in Scandinavia, so in Lithuania slaves (*drelle*) were still part of the local economy. The inhabitants of the towns which formed around ducal castles were German, Rus'ian and Polish immigrants. From 1388 there is a Jewish population in the second city of Trakai, members of the Karaite sect. Tatars lived in villages near important defence posts – Tatar soldiers having been settled, voluntarily or otherwise, by Grand Duke Vytautas at the end of the century. Rabbinic Jews also settled in the Grand Duchy. The various communities lived according to their own privileges and customs. Between 60 per cent and 90 per cent of the Grand Dukes' subjects were not of Baltic origin. By the sixteenth century Vytautas was a mythic figure for most of these groups who remembered (accurately or otherwise), as a sixteenth-century Tatar chronicle shows, a supporter of *their* rights.[7] The down-side of this policy,

---

[7] *Risalei Tatari Leh* (1538) cited in Kričinskis (1993), p. 18.

the failure to establish an integrated political society, would become clear only later. In the fourteenth century, it was nothing out of the ordinary.

The Order established a society where a religious corporation took the place of a king, and as such it came to suffer problems similar to those facing the monarchs of western and northern Europe: the alienation of peasant and urban society. The Order was made up mainly of German noblemen, employing servants of German, Slavonic and Baltic descent. The populations of Prussian towns and villages especially those founded with German law included not only immigrants from Germany but also Slavs (Poles and a few Bohemians and Rus'ians) and Balts (including Lithuanians). Slavonic and Baltic settlers tended to receive much smaller parcels of land, their size being regulated by technology: German settlers using the metal plough (*Hufen*) were, apparently, capable of farming larger areas than the native populations which were disadvantaged by their hook-ploughs or *Haken*. Baltic and Slavonic populations tended not to live in the areas where they had been born – Sambia for example was settled not by Sambians but by other neophytes. If it is anachronistic to accuse the Order of favouring German immigrants over the native population, then perhaps we can note the general apathy of the Knights in exploiting their land to the full. There was little attempt to spread German technology among the Balts and Poles. Prussians were admitted to German towns only in the wake of the ravages of plague in mid century and on condition that they could meet the same payments as the German denizenry.

Scandinavian society was formed by a privileged nobility, by whom the Swedish and Danish monarchs were dominated and to whom they owed election as king. Seventy or so towns had charters in Denmark under the supervision of royal bailiffs, but the majority of the population remained rural. Inheritance, guardianship and property rights were dependent on kinship ties and during trial at the Thing a man depended on the support of his own people. In the Danish countryside villages were abandoned, as elsewhere in Scandinavia, before the Black Death. Swedish society consisted of nobles, freehold and tenant farmers and casual labourers. As elsewhere in Europe the practice of slavery was no rarity. In 1296 the Uppland law forbade trade in Christian slaves; in 1335 the Skara Ordinance prohibited holding Christian slaves in Våstergötland and Vårmland.

THE NORTHERN ECONOMY

The economy of the Baltic is dominated by the Hanse of towns. The Hanse was an association of towns and their merchants who lived and traded around the Baltic and North Seas. The association was united by its Confederation of Cologne (1367) which strengthened opportunities for united commercial and diplomatic action in the north. German and southern wine, notably Rhenish and Istrian Rainfal (below p. 731) was sold in quantity to Scandinavia and Prussia. After the League's members defeated Valdemar Atterdag militarily, the Peace of Stralsund (1370) assured German merchants freedom of passage through the Sound and came to control the Scanian fair. Bergen had one of the four great *Kontore* (the others being in London, Novgorod and Bruges). The fairs in Stockholm and Copenhagen were dominated by German merchants.

In the early fourteenth century the chief products of the region still came from its forests: furs, wax and timber. From the middle of the fourteenth century Polish, Livonian and other Baltic timber dominated western markets. Baltic pine, yew and fir were the major Hanseatic import to England. Russia was the single most important source of medieval pitch and tar. Poland, Lithuania and the Teutonic *Ordensstaat* in Prussia became major exporters of grain, especially rye, well into the seventeenth century. Sweden produced copper (from the Kopparberg at Falun) and high quality iron (from near Lake Mällar), known in the sources as *osmund*. The fishing industry whose year culminated in the Skåne herring fair sold North Sea fish in greater quantities than Baltic fish.

Towards the end of the thirteenth century Lübeck began to import Bay salt from the Atlantic coast of France, from the shallow waters between the mouth of the Gironde and the Ile d'Oléron which was cheaper, albeit of poorer quality, than the traditional product from Lüneburg. A Hanse fleet sailed annually to the Bay of Bourgneuf, just south of the mouth of the Loire, to load up with the salt, filling holds now emptied of Baltic rye – *in unde und ut mit solte und roggen*. The salt was essential to the preservation of herring, whose greatest fisheries were to be found off the Danish-controlled Skåne coast of Sweden.

The eastern Baltic provided canvas and linen for the cloth merchants along with alum and potash (again forest products) for the preparation of woollen garments. The Baltic was a ready market for wool produced in England, Spain and Flanders. In return the beaver, bear and fox furs, the pelts of ermine and sable from Russia, Scandinavia and the Baltic were important symbols of wealth and prestige in western Europe. Prussia sent amber paternosters to the devout of the west.

The trade network of the Baltic which had been active in Viking times was integrated into western European commercial routes and credit networks. The Itinerary of Bruges (*c.* 1380) notes the dry route from Königsberg to Vilnius and the road via Memel to Livonia and north-western Rus'. The German merchants maintained one of their most important *contors* (trading posts) in Novgorod based in the city's German quarter (*Gotskii Dvor*) around the church of St Peter. The community regulated itself (according to its *Schra*) in matters stretching from honest weights and measures, the storage of goods in the church to the imposition of a one mark fine for throwing stones at the church's guard dog. In 1301 the Novgorodians guaranteed access to the city for north German and Livonian merchants and six years later the Danish king granted safe passage for merchants travelling through Estonia. Lithuania's ability to maintain her war effort relied heavily on her ability to tap into the Lübeck–Livonia–Estonia–Novgorod network and her control of the Dvina trade route into the Rus'ian heartlands: to Polotsk, Smolensk and eventually the south and the Tatar–Genoese Black Sea fur trade. Control of the river encouraged co-operation with the Livonian merchants of Riga who appreciated that access to Pskov and Novgorod could depend on good relations with the heathens to their south and east. Both sides perfectly understood the significance of such trade and took steps to safeguard the passage of merchants through their territories – along the *vredeweg* or *vredeland* which were often only a spear's throw wide. Similar agreements were made between various parties in the Iberian peninsula.

International trade depended largely on the Baltic cogs, compact flat-bottomed boats highly suited for heavy cargoes. Inland the extensive river routes were plied by large rafts or *dubassy* which brought timber and other bulky cargoes up the Vistula, Nemunas and Dvina.

The economies of Prussia and Lithuania were fundamentally war economies based on internal settlement and control of international trade routes. The Lithuanian Grand Duke maintained estates, termed *koniges hoff* or *villae regis,* in strategic points, used for the rearing of horses and the production of grain. The Teutonic Order settled German, Slavonic and Baltic farmers in villages in their various commanderies.

The main fixed international market of the region was the Skåne fair. Around 1200, the king of Denmark founded a castle at Skanoer on the sandy island at the south-western tip of Skåne (the southern part of Sweden which was under Danish control until 1658). By the end of the fourteenth century the island abounded in fishing villages. According to its *motbok* (the surviving texts of these statutes are in Danish and Low German), the fair was to take place from Assumption to All Saints (15 August – 1 November) during which time the peace was to be observed 'on land everywhere that nets are dried and wherever at sea they are cast'. From the thirteenth century royal privileges mention a wide regular participation in the fair, with merchants coming from Lynn (eastern England), Kiel and Lübeck in the west and from as far east as Riga and Reval. Hamburg and the Netherlands also sent traders. When the Hanse merchants gained control of the fair in 1368 (until 1385), they excluded Scottish and English merchants and later forbade Flemish and northern French traders. Following the Peace of Stralsund (1370) the Danish king surrendered important rights to the Hanse.

The main merchandise was local herring, salted according to charter by special preservers. Fishermen had to carry a special mark and pay dues to the crown officials. Philippe de Mézières claims that 500 merchant vessels and 40,000 fishing boats (totalling 300,000 fishermen) regularly visited the fair. According to customs reports, 34,000 barrels of herring were registered at Skåne in 1368 and 33,000 in 1369. Fish markets at the end of the fourteenth century were much more important than in 1500.

The impact of the Black Death on the demography, economy and culture of the region is difficult to estimate. The plague reached Norway from England by sea late in 1348 and infection came again in 1349, lasting in the west of the country until 1350. The pestilence spread quickly into Sweden from Skåne in 1349 and from Hanse shipping the following year. The chronicles of Novgorod speak of plague in 1352 – a major outbreak killed the archbishop, Vasily Kaleka. There are no records for Lithuania in this period and the Teutonic Order's chroniclers in Prussia and Livonia give little idea of the impact of the pestilence in the early 1350s. There seems to have been no outbreak of popular religious protest in the aftermath of the plague, as occurred when flagellants from Hungary came to Poland, spreading their message of repentance and hatred.

RELIGIOUS LIFE AND CRUSADE

Catholic life in the fourteenth-century Baltic was much the same as elsewhere in Europe with characteristics induced by distance from the centres (Avignon, Paris, the empire) and proximity to the Orthodox and pagan worlds. The religious movements which sought to bring Christ to the heathens were also active in Catholic countries. The expansion of the Franciscan and Dominican Orders into the newly settled areas of northern Poland, Prussia and Sweden is matched by the special favour enjoyed by those friars in the Grand Duchy. It is hardly coincidental that the Lithuanian state formed when merchants, settlers and their spiritual service industries arrived in the eastern Baltic. The mendicants did not spread widely in Scandinavia where urban life was underdeveloped – Dominicans tended to settle in episcopal centres whilst the Greyfriars sought out trading outposts inland – a policy followed further south and east. The Franciscans of the Saxon and later the Bohemo-Polish provinces followed merchants eastwards to Prussia, Lithuania, Rus' and Tartary. Of seventy new houses erected in the Bohemo-Polish province in the late fourteenth century, twenty-five were founded in the Lithuanian and Rus'ian territories of the Jagiellonian monarchy. Franciscans were particularly favoured in pagan Lithuania and were appointed to missionary sees throughout the region: to Riga, Seret (Moldavia), Lwów and Vilnius (1387). The Franciscans com-

plained most loudly about the tactics of the Teutonic Order. They provided
scribes for the Grand Dukes and served merchants in trade centres such as
Vilnius. It is hardly surprising therefore to find Franciscan texts, whether from
Switzerland and Lübeck or Poland and Spain, among the commonest western
sources for Baltic history.

For the first time in its history Sweden became the birthplace of a European
religious movement, the Order of the Saviour, founded by St Bridget
(1303–73). The foundress was the daughter of the powerful lawman of
Uppland, Birger Persson. She appears to have been a typical noblewoman –
married at thirteen, the mother of eight children. She and her husband went
on the fashionable pilgrimage to Santiago de Compostela in Spain. During the
spiritual crisis which followed her widowhood (1344), Bridget received a vision
of Christ who promised her that 'you shall be my bride and my mouthpiece'.
She settled at Avastra, where her husband was buried in the Cistercian monastery. Magnus Ericsson granted her an estate at Vadstena where she proposed
to build a monastery for men and women under the guidance of an abbess –
similar to the Gilbertine movement which began in England in the twelfth
century. In 1350 she went to Rome, where Clement VI showed himself briefly
for the Holy Year celebrations, to seek papal blessing for her proposed order
and persuade the pope to return permanently to his city. Her revelations stoked
noble opposition to Magnus. Clement VI did not recognise her order but his
successor did grant approval to her house at Vadstena for Austins under
Bridget's own rule. In 1391 her Rule of St Saviour was approved. She died in
Rome but her body was taken back to Sweden where the tomb at Vadstena
became an object of popular pilgrimage. The most renowned Bridgetine
convent in England, Syon Abbey, was founded by Henry V. However, the first
daughter houses of Vadstena outside Sweden were founded at Florence and
Danzig. The latter monastery was inspired by Magnus Peterson who passed
through the city en route to Italy in 1394. The Bridgetines also enjoyed the
support of the Teutonic Order which was influenced in this respect by a local
mystic, (St) Dorothy of Montau (1347–94), the daughter of a peasant colonist
of Dutch origin. Dorothy, who studied theology in Marienwerder after her
husband's death and became renowed for her visions (in the style of St Bridget
or Julian of Norwich) was revered by the grand master for her piety. On the
day the Scandinavian kingdoms were united, Swedish bishops assembled in
Kalmar sent relics of St Bridget to Danzig. The spread of religious cults across
the Baltic, especially those of female mystics, is an aspect of regional ecclesiastical life which should not be overlooked.

One alleged early influence of Bridgetine theology appears in the Swedish
'crusade' led by King Magnus against Novgorodia in 1348. Magnus Ericsson
apparently held Bridgetine intentions to convert the Orthodox by discussion

rather than the sword. Early in 1348 he sent envoys to the archbishop of Novgorod proposing a theological debate: whichever party won, Orthodox or Catholic, would surrender to the other. In the meantime he strengthened his position around Vyborg, close to the Novgorodian frontier. The archbishop suggested that envoys be sent instead to Constantinople and preparations for war continued. On 23 July the Swedes were defeated by the Novgorodians at Toads' Field, but two weeks later on 6 August Magnus seized the Novgorodian Neva fortress of Orekhov, defeating the fort's Lithuanian garrison and capturing the embassy which the Novgorodians had sent earlier to Vyborg. It took six months for the Rus'ians to regain Orekhov and control of the Neva trade route to Karelia. During the Swedish campaign the republic of Pskov asserted its *de facto* independence of action from Novgorod at Bolotovo. However, this did not lead to a substantial increase in Pskovite dependence on Lithuanian military help against its Rus'ian and Livonian enemies. From a theological point of view the campaign is of interest for the dichotomy it reveals in Swedish opinions of the legitimacy of making war on the infidel Orthodox (schismatic Novgorod) and pagans (Karelians). This reflects the debate further south and west about the war against the pagan Balts in Teutonic and counter-Teutonic writings. Franciscan authors already such as Roger Bacon had discussed the Baltic crusade in the context of a debate of pen versus the sword. Such academic contests reflect the competition between the Orders on the ground.

The crusades in the Baltic focused mainly on the Baltic pagan lands, rather than the Orthodox north-east, which the Swedes viewed as an important source of valuable furs. The southern littoral was dominated by international campaigns led by the Teutonic Order to safeguard its acquisitions in Prussia from Lithuanian attack. In Livonia the Order's junior branch maintained war on two fronts; against Lithuania to the south and Lithuanian Rus' to the south-east and against the Orthodox Slavs of Novgorodia to the north. It is no surprise to find the northern Rus'ians making defence contracts with Lithuanian princelings throughout the fourteenth century. The Swedes might well have claimed that their encounters with the Lithuanians in Novgorodia were enough to excuse their absence from the *Preussenreisen*.

The crusades in Prussia concentrated piety and war in a way experienced nowhere else in Europe save perhaps Spain. Knights came on pilgrimage, *reysa* to use Chaucer's adaptation of the German term, from all over Europe, encouraged by the grand master and his agents. The majority of the 'pilgrims' and 'guests' came from the empire, largely from the areas of Germany and the Netherlands which were home to the Order's convents and bailliwicks. It is noticeable that Bohemia played no part in the movement after the accession of Emperor Charles IV who, after two abortive campaigns declared that the *reysen* were a waste of time and money. The crusades took on a more pan-European form after the 1320s, that is after the papally recognised truce between Lithuania and the Order came to an end late in 1328. Whether the Lithuanian approach to the pope in 1322–4 drew wider attention to the crusade in the cast is a moot point. However, the coincidence is clear. English knights came to Prussia for the first time during the winter *reysa* of 1328–9 and continued to campaign as late as 1410, with less activity in the mid 1350s and 1370s. Henry Bolingbroke, the Beauchamps, Bohuns and countless knights and gentlemen made their way north to 'beginne the borde' (Chaucer). The French began later than the English (in 1330s) but continued to campaign until the Council of Constance took away the final official doubts as to the genuineness of the Lithuanian conversion. The knights came largely from the royal territories (Paris and the Ile de France), northern France and Picardy and mid-western France. The Iberian peninsula, region of the competing theatre (the Luxemburger, John of Bohemia, had to choose between fighting with the Knights in Prussia or for the Aragonese against the Moors), provided fewer crusaders, as did the Italian territories. Scandinavian crusaders are not known from written records although the arms of two Swedes were depicted in the Bellenville Roll in the late fourteenth century. The king of Denmark came east in 1345. The Swedes led their own crusade against the Orthodox Novgorodians in an attempt to gain control of the fur sources in Karelia and the White Sea.

The *Reisen* were carefully organised. They took place at times of the year when the climate made the terrain passable and coincided with the major Marian feasts. Campaigns were led in winter when the waterways 'ben yfrore', especially around the feast of the Purification (2 February), and in summer when the marshes were dry and the Lithuanian population was preoccupied with the harvest. Assumptiontide (15 August) and Our Lady's Birthday (8 September) marked the period of the *rese d'esté*. Words for the phenomenon spread into west European languages and even the German-Prussian wordlist written down in Elbing in the early fourteenth century records *karyago-Reise*, *cariawoytis-Heerschaw, cinyangus[caryangus]-Bannir*. Prussian military terminology entered German charters.[8] It is important to note how each side influenced the other – Germany is not the *fons et origo* of all.

The warriors were well provisioned (with fish, meat (pork, mutton), sausage, bread, cheese). Land and river transport was carefully arranged and they even took their doctors with them on campaign. The international gatherings in Marienburg and Königsberg with princes vying for a good place at the grand master's table were for a time a self-perpetuating show, which hides from our eyes the essential weakness of the *Ordensstaat*. The largely imported aristocratic

---

[8] Mažiulis (1981), II, p. 31 for the Elbing wordlist (*c.* 1300) and *PU*.

oligarchy eventually alienated its urban and rural colonists who were established in Prussia. The Order was not capable of maintaining its position in the late fourteenth and early fifteenth centuries in the face of united Polish and Lithuanian opposition.

The Order's strength, while real and dangerous to the Lithuanians, is something of a chimera magnified by our Brandenburgian hindsight. The Order built up a monastic state where the Order took the place of a prince. It succeeded in establishing new towns and villages and reviving old ones in its territories. It was strong enough with the assistance of western volunteers to maintain a punishing cycle of raids into Lithuanian territory, razing major commercial sites such as Grodno, Novgorodok, Kaunas and even Vilnius. However, it is noticeable that the greatest victories were won not in pagan territory but mostly in the Order's own lands, as at Woplauken (1311) and Rudau (1370) deep in eastern Prussia.

BALTIC CULTURE

It is difficult but not impossible to speak of a certain cultural unity within the fourteenth-century Baltic and that common denominator is the warrior ethos. The Austrian poet Peter von Suchenvirt describes the scene in Prussia where:

That noble and virtuous duke gave a banquet at the castle. Trumpets and pipes played between the courses. The dining was lavish. Each course was fourfold: spiced, gilded and decorated, baked and roasted. The table was bedecked with wine from the south and wine from the east and clear Istrian Rainfal. All were served generously in fine vessels . . . silver and gold were brought forth to be given as signs of honour. Two knights and a noble squire, each renowned for his feats of arms and acknowledged as the very best of his land, received the gift . . . Then in keeping with old traditions the grand master gave a banquet at Königsberg in the hall. The feast was lavish you can be sure. When places were allotted at the table of honour Konrad of Krey was seated at the head by unanimous acclaim.[9]

The pagans could be included in this glamorous life, and not only as objects of prey. The grand masters' Chronicle notes how 'Kestutis was a valiant and just man. He would give forewarning of his planned attack and then really carry it out. When he made peace with the Master, he kept to it. If he knew a brother of the Order was brave and daring then he would show him much love and respect.'[10] The prince maintained close relations with his daughter's godfather, Gunther von Hohenstein, commander of Brandenburg, dining with him and benefiting from inside information provided by the Knight

---

[9] Peter von Suchenvirt, 'Duke Albert's Crusade', lines 106–17, 123–9, 148–54 (*SRP*, II, pp. 163–4). Smith and Urban (1985), pp. 13–14. [10] *SRP*, III, pp. 593–4.

concerning the Order's dealings with Kestutis's nephew and rival, Grand Duke Jogaila.

Military technique and equipment was copied by both the Order and the Lithuanians from the enemy. The Order used both *prusche* and *littische schild*, and helmets developed by the Balts. The Lithuanians also adopted certain western tactics and weapons. The appearance of firearms in the Order's armies was soon met by Lithuanian use of the same. However, this military interaction was not restricted to the Knights and the Lithuanians. In the 1380s English courts of arms, as in the celebrated case of Scrope and Grosvenor, could recall the depiction of blazons commemorating the English dead in Prussia and in the fifteenth century Beauchamp family propaganda could claim a *reysa* in Königsberg and the baptism of a Lithuanian princeling as part of their glorious past. Chaucer's Knight provides the classic example of the man who fought in the three major theatres of crusade: the Holy Land, Spain and the Baltic.

The material culture of the Teutonic Order was as high as one would expect of a corporation dominated by western nobility in a rich territory – gold and silver, fine glass, luxury cloth and imposing public architecture were intended to create an impression of corporate majesty. Petrarch recalls seeing a magnificent drinking vessel carved from an auroch's horn. According to a Marienburg inventory of 1394, the cathedral held seven missals, a commentary on papal letters, antiphonals, a gradual, psalter, biblical commentary and lives of the saints (all in Latin); in German they had chronicles, suitably stoic or military Bible stories (Job, Barlaam, Esther, Judith), a passional (especially detailed on the life of Our Lady) and lives of the fathers. The book of Maccabees, a suitable role-model for religious warriors, was especially popular.

The Knights were not only owners but also authors of valuable texts. The Thuringian Knight, Henry von Besler, composed a translation of the apocryphal Gospel of Nicodemus and the Apocalypse and Luder von Braunschweig, the grand master, composed a poem on the life of St Barbara. The Middle Low German cultural sphere spread from Bruges and Friesland in the west to Reval and Novgorod in the east. It functioned as an interregional and international language in the kingdoms of Sweden, Norway and Denmark. Cultural influences may be detected in the opposite direction: *schülting* (Norwegian) is the word used for guildhall in Lübeck, Bremen, Lüneburg and Stralsund. City chronicle traditions grew up in Hanse centres, written in Low German, as the Dietmar Chronicle from Lübeck shows.

The question arises as to who could read such creations. The second half of the fourteenth century saw the foundation of a Latin school in Marienburg. A cathedral school was established in Frauenburg and the Ermland clergy paid for twelve Prussian peasants to be taught in the castle at Heilsberg (Lidzbark).

From Prussia students were sent to study in Bologna (especially those intended as future legal secretaries) and Prague where faculties of canon law were strong; in 1386 Pope Urban VI founded a *studium generale* in Bologna for the Order for students of theology and laws (civil and canon).

Town schools were set up in Denmark and Sweden during the later Middle Ages, often with ecclesiastical approval. Swedish scholars continued to travel to Paris (on whose *pauperes studentes*, a part of the Uppsala tithe was spent in the fourteenth century) but were also attracted to northern and central European universities, including Prague. We have records of several thousand Scandinavian students in the universities of the Empire and eastern Europe in the period 1350–1536, although markedly fewer studied in Paris. The first known school in Lithuania was founded hard by the chapel in the royal castle in Vilnius before 1397. Queen Jadwiga founded a college for Lithuanian students in Prague university (1397) and her husband refounded Casimir the Great's university in Cracow (1400).

We learn from the Knights' treasury book of the musicians in Grand Duchess Anna's court in Trakai in 1398; elsewhere in the Order's treasury records we read of flautists in Vytautas's service (1399) and a gift of a clavicord and portable organ costing six marks which the grand master sent to Anna in 1407–10.

The architecture of Prussia reflects the concerns of the Teutonic Order: to dominate newly settled lands, defend them from Lithuanian attack and to impress the colonists with the magnificence and power of the Knights. After 1309 Marienburg became the political, religious, economic and cultural centre of the *Ordensstaat*. From the late 1320s the grand master's chaplain performed the office of chancellor of the Order. By the second half of the century German eased out Latin as the language of the Order's growing bureaucracy. The chapel of St Anne (mother of the Order's Patroness) in Marienburg Castle became the necropolis of the grand masters from 1341. It was dominated by an eight-metres high statue of the Mother and Child against a Byzantine style mosaic – again indicative of the mix of cultures in the Baltic.

Cathedral chapters and Prussian bishops built castles to defend their centres of power. The bishop of Ermland built himself a castle in Heilsberg in the second half of the century. Gothic cathedrals in defensive style were constructed in the Prussian sees – in Frauenburg the bishops of Ermland constructed a cathedral with walls, gates and defensive towers (1329–88) and decorated the interior in the Flemish manner. The basilica of Marienwerder (Kwidzyn), built in English style, was also defensive in character (1320–40). In the towns Gothic town halls were built – in Danzig and Marienburg. The hall of the Old Town of Toruń also dates from this period (1393).

In fourteenth century Scandinavia we find stone-built castles and city walls with projecting towers, as at Kalmar Castle built between 1275 and 1300. Vordingborg, famous for its Gåsetårn, and Kalundborg are typical Danish castles (c. 1350). The Finnish construction at Raseborg (1380) is similar. The influence of the Teutonic Order was strong in castles rebuilt in the fourteenth century – Åbo in Finland, Visborg in Gotland, Kronborg in Denmark. These are typified by four building ranges built around an open courtyard. Most Scandinavian towns were built of wood until the end of the Middle Ages, although in Denmark from the thirteenth century we find half-timbering.

Lithuanian castles reflect the mixture of cultures in the region, with bricks tending to be of Livonian type whilst the decoration is often eastern. Fourteenth-century Vilnius was a largely wooden city dominated by its double castle complex – the upper and lower castles. It appears likely that a stone temple functioned in the ruins of a thirteenth-century Gothic church built by King Mindaugas after his conversion to Catholicism. The city had two distinct mercantile quarters – one for western merchants, the other for Rus'ians – the so-called *russkii konets* or Rus'ian End. The Franciscan church of St Nicholas (now in its fifteenth-century brick Gothic form) is probably the oldest church in Vilnius alongside the cathedral and the Orthodox church of St Nicholas. It is no surprise to find the patron of merchants so frequently in the city. In Trakai two castles formed the centre of the second grand-ducal seat in a town which by the early fifteenth century consisted of Tatar, Karaite, Catholic and Orthodox enclaves.

CHAPTER 22

THE KINGDOMS OF CENTRAL
EUROPE IN THE FOURTEENTH
CENTURY

Claude Michaud

THE fourteenth century saw the union of the crowns of central Europe. One by one, the last Přemysls, the house of Anjou in Hungary and the Luxemburgs, attempted to construct states whose national identity might have appeared threatened by the collapse of the old indigenous dynasties and the diffusion of foreign influence. These dispositions were based upon a dynastic policy of marriages, which represented a middle way between the right of conquest and the popular sovereignty of the future. In 1301, the son of Wenceslas II of Bohemia was elected king of Hungary; but he was unable to maintain his position and abdicated in 1304: exchanging the Hungarian crown of St Stephen for those of Bohemia and Poland (which his father left him) in the following year. Wenceslas III was assassinated in 1306. He was the first to occupy – admittedly in succession – the three thrones of Hungary, Bohemia and Poland.

The fourteenth century was also a kind of apogee for these states, associated in each instance with the vigorous personality of an exceptional sovereign. People like to recall that Louis of Anjou was the only king of Hungary surnamed 'the Great'; he shared this epithet with his predecessor in Poland, Casimir. As for the Emperor Charles IV, he was the 'father of his country' (*pater patriae*) of a Bohemia in full political and cultural expansion. In each case, after succession difficulties at the beginning of the century, these long and great reigns marked a period of clear equilibrium in all fields, whether in territorial matters, political and social institutions, economic and material life or cultural developments.

HUNGARY FROM 1301 TO 1387

The accession and achievements of Charles-Robert of Anjou

During his reign, Andrew III had failed to break the feudal anarchy of a kingdom virtually divided into rival principalities. On the death of this last

Arpád in 1301, various factions endeavoured to give the crown to their candidate. The first to carry it off was the son of Wenceslas II, king of Bohemia and Poland, and Anne, daughter of Béla IV. Unable to maintain his position, he abdicated in 1304, and his place was taken by the German prince, Otto of Bavaria, another of Béla IV's grandsons. He undoubtedly enjoyed the support of the Transylvanian Saxons. But he failed to win over to his cause the Transylvanian *voiévode*, Ladislas Kán, who preferred an alliance with Uros II of Serbia to that of a prince without support. Otto was even taken prisoner by Ladislas who kept the holy crown of Hungary as security.

The third claimant, Charles-Robert of Anjou, great-grandson of the Arpád king, Stephen V, had the support of the pope (in 1290, Nicholas IV had invested him with Hungary, declared a papal fief) and this won him the support of the Hungarian clergy, who sought protection from the feudal lords. He was also championed by the Slav lords in the southern provinces who were attracted by prospects in the Adriatic. But ecclesiastical censure of his opponents was less effective than Charles-Robert's own patient reconstruction of a new clientele from the ranks of the aristocracy who were threatened by the power of the great barons. Although he ascended the throne in 1309 and was crowned on St Stephen's Day (20 August) 1310 at Székesfehérvár, he had to combat oligarchic factions for a further eleven years, defeating the Aba clan in 1312 and the Borsa clan in 1316. The year 1318 saw him rid of the Transylvanian rebel, Ladislas Kán (whose successors, nominated by the king, slowly brought the province back to crown allegiance after the defeat – thanks to *coumane* troops – of the Saxon revolt in 1324). In 1321, Máté Csák, the last of the great oligarchs, died. From that date onwards, Charles-Robert was able to leave the south of the kingdom to establish his capital at Visegrád, upstream from Buda.

Each victory resulted in the recovery of royal castles: eight after the defeat of the Aba, twelve after that of the Borsa, twenty-eight on the death of Máté Csák. This policy of rebuilding the patrimony of the crown was reinforced after 1327 and Charles-Robert ended by possessing half of all the castles (about 100). In these he placed men loyal to him as *castellani*, whose military functions were henceforth less important than their responsibility for the economy of the domain lands, the collection of taxes and the exercise of justice over their tenants. The domain lands thus became true feudal lordships, since the peasants escaped the administration of the count (*ispán*). The effects of this reconstruction of the royal patrimony (second only to that of Béla IV) were lasting; neither Charles-Robert, nor his son, were unduly extravagant in this area and the crown still possessed 100 castles in 1382. A new aristocracy admittedly took over from those who had been eliminated – the Lackfi, Széchenyi, Drugeth, Kont-Ujlaki – but there was nothing comparable to the chains of castles held by the Borsa or the Csák.

The system of domain lands and castles remained the basis for the distribution of power. Was it also always so for the revenues of the state? The discovery of new gold mines and increased silver production made Hungary the main European supplier of precious metals (a quarter of silver and a ton of gold each year). A clever combination of state monopoly (all raw metals had to be handed over to the Offices of the Mint) and profit sharing among seigneurial landowners encouraged prospecting and provided the kingdom with a strong and plentiful coinage. The gold florin of 1325 facilitated access to international trade. Did it also leave room for modern taxation? Royal towns and mining centres paid subsidies at a level that was henceforth fixed for several years. The Church, poorly served by the Avignon papacy, made occasional contributions to expenditure. Despite lords who claimed that the labour of serfs belonged entirely to their masters and that any taxes paid by serfs to the state was a reduction of their own revenues, Charles-Robert levied extraordinary taxes on the unfree population. But since peasant taxation was collected in the lordships by the lord himself, just as the castellans (*castellani*) did in the royal domain lands, no royal financial administration developed as a result. The wealth of the treasury was thus accompanied by a failure to establish a fiscal state.

The foreign policy of Louis the Great

Charles-Robert died in 1342 leaving his son, Louis (born in 1326), a throne that had been strengthened and was on a sounder financial footing. His father's work of consolidation enabled the new king to follow an energetic foreign policy from the Mediterranean to the Baltic and the Black Sea. Marxist historians view the father's reign in a more favourable light than that of the son. For them, Louis would have been little more than a fourteenth-century Don Quixote, entangled in dynastic quarrels and religious wars, had not the Turkish threat absorbed all his energies. Recently, the trend has been reversed. Without going so far as to adopt once more the uncritical praises heaped upon Louis by his contemporary biographer, Johannes Küküllei, to Bálint Hóman, an official historian of 'Trianon' Hungary, contemporary Hungarian historians like to emphasise the king's education and culture, as well as the authority of his kingdom, preserved from both internal division and threats from outside. The reign of Louis the Great was clearly an important stage for the development of national awareness and of a national language.[1]

It was undoubtedly to his dynamic foreign policy rather than his achievements at home that Louis first owed his reputation. It must again be stressed that his objectives were quite as much those of a new dynasty as a restatement

---

[1] Vardy, Grosschmid and Domonkos (1986), pp. 349–69, 417–25.

of Arpád traditions: union with Croatia had inaugurated an orientation towards the Adriatic and Italy strengthened by the dynastic potential of the house of Anjou; expansion in the Balkans and in Walachia, the christianisation of the eastern territories, the union of the kingdoms of central Europe – all these had been sought in the past. Rivalry with Venice over the Dalmatian coast was also part of this inheritance. And it was against the Venetian government rather than to convert the peoples of the Balkans that Louis's first hostilities were directed, even before the Neapolitan imbroglio drew him further south.

The treaty concluded between the kings of Naples and Hungary in 1332, Robert and his nephew Charles-Robert, had anticipated not only the marriage of their respective granddaughter and son, Joanna, heiress of Naples and Andrew of Hungary, but also their joint coronation. As long as the dispute with Naples was confined to violations of the agreement of 1332, Louis limited himself to diplomatic moves in which Hungarian gold played a major part. The assassination of Andrew in 1345 at the instigation of his wife (queen in 1343) forced Louis to take military action to obtain redress for the death of his brother. Moreover, if Joanna was toppled from the throne, and if descent through the male line secured it, would he – Louis – not be heir to Naples? Peace with the Venetians thus became essential, all the more so since they had just gained the upper hand over him at Zara (1 July 1346). The eight-year truce that was signed, together with Louis's policy towards the Italian towns and his alliance with Lewis of Bavaria, provided optimal circumstances for the expedition of 1348. Louis of Hungary entered Naples (from which Joanna fled), put his brother's murderers on trial and assumed the title of 'king of Sicily and Jerusalem'. This successful invasion was nullified by the Black Death, which forced Louis to return to Hungary. A second campaign in 1350 led to the recapture of Naples, after which the new Alexander made a pilgrimage to Rome. Despite his military successes, Louis realised his plan for a great Adriatic empire was an illusion. In 1352, he made an alliance with the pope, who was frightened of the prospect of an Angevin empire stretching from the Danube to Messina and had always supported Joanna, despite initial condemnation of the murder. Louis renounced his claims to the throne of Naples, without, however, acknowledging Joanna's legitimacy.

Once the idea of the union of the two crowns was no longer a real possibility, Louis had room for negotiation with all those who had been worried by his imperial ambitions. He returned to more traditional objectives, first Dalmatia, then the Balkans, where his political aims were strengthened by desire to eliminate the Bogomil heresy. The Serbian tsar, Stephen Dušan, was killed in 1355; the following year the war with Venice began again, while Louis campaigned in Bosnia, where he founded monastic houses. In 1357, Ragusa, Venice's second-in-command, went over to Louis; at the beginning of 1358, the most important towns and islands fell into the king's hands. In the same year, the peace of Zara confirmed the surrender of Dalmatia to Hungary. Thus, under Louis's authority, ancient Croatia was restored, encompassing Dalmatia north of Kotor and the islands which had previously been under Venetian rule.

During the following decade, Louis fought in the Balkans, not so much to acquire new territories as to obtain tribute, extend Christianity and secure access to the Black Sea. His achievements were slight, as much because of national resistance as a result of growing Ottoman pressure. Promises of conversion to Christianity by indigenous princes proved vain. One by one, Moldavia, Walachia and Serbia became tributary provinces for a while. Suzerainty over Moldavia was lost in 1367.[2] Only the Bulgarian *banat* of Vidin was administered directly by Louis. In 1369, nothing at all remained of this expansion beyond the river Sava and in the regions of the lower Danube. Louis had to restore the prince of Vidin who, like Radul, *voiévode* of Walachia, had paid tribute to the Turks from 1374. Since then, with the exception of a victorious expedition against the Turks and the Bulgars in 1377, Hungary did not play any part in the Balkans in this decisive period, when a stand should have been made against Ottoman invasions. Should Louis (whom Innocent VI had made captain of the Roman Church in 1356) have let slip the great opportunities which his lands offered for a genuine crusade?[3]

Hungarian priorities changed in the 1370s. The son of a politically effective Polish woman and the nephew of Casimir the Great, Louis had always been interested in the future of the kingdom of Poland and had demonstrated kingly and Christian solidarity in joining Polish expeditions against pagan Lithuania. In 1352, he was one of the principal authors of the attempted conversion of the Lithuanian prince, Kieistut. The latter then broke his word, thus prompting two more campaigns, at the end of which Louis left his conquered principalities of Halyč and Lodomeria to the king of Poland, while reserving their right of reversion to the Hungarian crown after the latter's death. Louis used this opportunity to force the Tatar Khan Dschenin-bey to open his lands to religious and trading missions. Since Casimir had no direct male heirs, he acknowledged his nephew as his successor; he died in 1370. Despite some opposition, Louis had himself proclaimed king of Poland and made his mother regent of the kingdom. In 1372, he transferred Halyč and Lodomeria to the Hungarian crown. Louis the Great's kingdom then stretched from Gniezno to Kotor.

King, nobles and peasants

This policy exacted a high price in men and money. The meagre results of the Neapolitan campaigns led to dissatisfaction amongst the nobility who were

[2] Deletant (1986), pp. 189–95.   [3] Housley (1984).

indispensable for military action and who (unlike the great barons) had not enriched themselves either with booty or rewards from the king. In 1351, pressure from the nobility forced Louis to summon the only diet of his reign. The result was the famous decree of 1351, which went well beyond the confirmation of the Golden Bull of 1222. Article 11 declared that all nobles were to enjoy the same privileges that had previously been granted to the barons alone: *sub una et eadem libertate gratulantur.* There was therefore to be one single nobility. The differences between the descendants of the original conquerors and the servants and familiars of the king (*servientes regis et familiares*), on the one hand, and the Hungarian nobility (narrowly defined) and that of the lands between the rivers Sava and Drava, on the other, were abolished. This single nobility had its right to revolt (*insurrectio*) confirmed. Formal unification by law also ended the distinction between landholding since time immemorial (dating from the conquest) and royal gifts to servants of the king attached to a specific office. Henceforth, all patrimonial holdings were governed by the same inheritance law, that is, they were handed down within a clan along the male line of descent until it was extinct. War had emptied Charles-Robert's treasury and impoverished the nobility. The decree of 1351 extended the *nona* (or levy of a ninth on all they produced after payment of the ecclesiastical tithe) to all serfs. Only the inhabitants of enclosed towns (*civitates*) escaped this tax which was levied by the nobles and enabled them to put their financial problems behind them and maintain the *banderia* (groups of armed followers) which were indispensable to the king's campaigns. The strengthening of the economic position of the nobility was accompanied by formal recognition of their full and absolute jurisdiction over their serfs. There was still the question of peasant migration in a period when the Black Death had dramatically reduced the labour force and when the magnates tended to induce (by force or persuasion) the serfs of smaller landholders to work on their lands. While the decree confirmed the freely given consent of a landowner to such forced movement of his serfs, it did not formally restrict their freedom of movement. At a later date laws removed the right to migrate. Nevertheless, the fiscal and judicial provisions of the decree gave the new form of serfdom (*jobbagysag*) constitutional legality, while simultaneously furnishing the lesser nobility with what were to be the ideological bases of its justification as a social order in the future.[4]

Despite these measures, political and social supremacy remained in the hands of the magnates. A new stratum of oligarchs replaced that suppressed by Charles-Robert. They received lands, royal castles and counties which tended to become hereditary fiefs in recompense for their service, or so that

---

[4] Vardy, Grosschmid and Domonkos (1986), pp. 429–83.

they might provide for their *banderia*. Thus the bonds of *familiaritas* which made the lesser nobility dependent on the magnates grew stronger. The magnates turned some villages in their domains into small towns (*oppida*), with relatively autonomous administrations and obtained licences to hold a market. This was how these country towns began to develop, subject to the ninth and to seigneurial jurisdiction: some of them achieved a high level of artisanal and commercial activity. Other towns on the great plain, such as Kecskemét, Cegléd or Nagykőrös, grew rich thanks to rearing beef cattle, already destined for export to southern Germany. Thus, fostered by the economic expansion of the second half of the century, a new patriciate came into being, ready to challenge the ascendancy of the old landowning aristocracy. Their time was to come in the next century. A few great rival lineages rose above the rest, such as the Lackfi, who owned seven castles and 260 localities and who held the office of marshal for forty years and the Transylvanian *voiévodie* for thirty; or the Szécsi with six castles and 170 localities; the southern counties were dominated by the Garai and their clients who at last eliminated the Lackfi in 1397. Nicholas Kont, palatine between 1350 and 1367, was *ispán* of four counties. In the 1370s the reconstruction accomplished by the Angevins seemed threatened by a revival of centrifugal forces.

The end of Louis's reign

The potential dangers were increased by the uncertainty surrounding the succession to the Hungarian crown. By his first wife, the daughter of Emperor Charles IV, Louis had no heirs. After a further seventeen years of marriage to Elizabeth of Bosnia, there was still no heir. Louis therefore summoned to his court his kinsman Philip of Taranto, to whom he had married his niece. But three daughters then made their appearance in rapid succession, Catherine, Mary and Jadwiga, for whom Louis dreamt up the most appropriate marriages, designed to secure all his thrones for them – Hungary, Poland and Naples (to which he had still not yet renounced his claims). Catherine was promised to her distant cousin, Louis of Anjou, second son of John II 'the Good' of France, in the hope of recreating through the rights of the king of Hungary a second Capetian dynasty in Naples; Mary was destined for Sigismund of Luxemburg, the second son of Charles IV, with whom Louis had been reconciled by the peace of Brno of 1364; as for Jadwiga, she was betrothed to the son of the duke of Austria, Leopold III. In 1378, the death of Catherine, and Leopold III's support for the Avignonese pope (while Louis championed the pope in Rome) made it probable that Mary and Sigismund would be Louis's only heirs.

The same year, war broke out once more between Hungary and Venice. Commercial tensions had never really abated, despite the peace of Zara. A coalition of Hungary, Genoa, Padua and Aquila inflicted a crushing defeat on the doge at land and sea. The Hungarian troops were led by Charles of Durazzo, the governor of Croatia-Dalmatia and claimant to the throne of Naples. This offered a good opportunity for final revenge on Queen Joanna who, moreover, supported the Avignonese pope. Charles was crowned king of Sicily and Jerusalem at Rome. From there, he went on to conquer Naples, where he had Queen Joanna strangled in May 1382. Louis died soon afterwards, on 10 September, having had the satisfaction of seeing his brother avenged.

Had Naples been anything more than an extravagant delusion? Some historians would claim that these Italian expeditions brought Hungary a proto-Renaissance, discernible in the style of documents produced in the Hungarian chancery, the historical work of Küküllei and the foundation of the short-lived university of Pécs. This interpretation places great emphasis on a few classical references here and there, and on the brief stay of the civil lawyer Galvano of Bologna in *Quinque Ecclesiae*, that is Pécs. Although Italian influence is apparent in the illustrations of the famous *Illuminated Chronicle* or the Neckcsei-Lipócz Bible, as well as in the sculpture of the brothers Márton and György of Kolozsvár (the Prague St George), in the architecture of the royal palaces at Visegrád, Buda and Diósgyőr, this was less the result of Hungarian soldiers on campaign in Italy than of Hungarian students and artists staying there during the reigns of the Angevin kings.[5]

Would Hungarian policy in the Adriatic have been redeemed by the opening of a new trade route which would have brought the commodities of the Levant to Hungary and thence to Poland, Bohemia and Germany via the port of Zara? This had been Louis the Great's ambition. But reality was quite different. Despite losses in Dalmatia, Venice increased the blockade, and Zara–Zagreb remained a minor route. Hungarian merchants from Pozsony continued to take in supplies at Vienna which the Semmering route joined to Venice. The continental link joining the Genoese trading stations on the Black Sea to Hungary via the passes of Transylvania and the Danube, used by the Saxon merchants of Brassó and the Walachians, was never completely abandoned.[6] From 1408–9 onwards, Venice controlled Dalmatia once more, while the Balkan principalities fell like dominoes under the Turkish yoke. Italy had been no more than a fleeting mirage after all.

Nevertheless, the Italian ideal lived on in the consciousness of the magnates of southern Hungary, the Garai and the Horváti. And it was they who caused problems over Louis's successor. The king had envisaged all his kingdoms passing together to his daughter Mary, who married Sigismund of Luxemburg in 1379. It is possible that Louis anticipated the eventual enlargement of the

---

[5] Ibid., pp. 203–36. [6] Pach (1975), pp. 283–307.

Polno-Hungarian kingdom to encompass Bohemia as well. The magnates of Lesser Poland (who had always supported the Teutonic Knights and were enemies of the Luxemburgs) broke the union with Hungary and had Louis's third daughter, Jadwiga, crowned. Mary was crowned in Hungary: this was the first time a woman had become king of Hungary and was proof of the strength of the monarchy restored by the house of Anjou. But Mary and her mother were mere playthings in the hands of the palatine, Nicholas Garai, who was worried about the central European focus of the new reign. The Horváti clan appealed for help from the new king of Naples who had been the instrument of Louis's revenge upon Joanna. Charles of Durazzo assumed the crown of St Stephen in 1385, but he was assassinated soon afterwards on the order of the palatine, Garai, who feared his power. The expedition undertaken by Mary of Anjou, her mother and the palatine (who had joined their side once more) was a disaster; the vengeance of the Horváti fell upon the queen mother and the palatine, who were murdered. Mary was imprisoned.

All hopes lay with Sigismund, and a large group of magnates rallied to him because they realised that he was the closest embodiment of Louis the Great's final policy. Forcefully supported by his brother, Wenceslas IV of Bohemia and his cousin Jodok of Moravia, assisted by rivalries between the barons, and benefiting from the total autonomy resulting from Mary's imprisonment, Sigismund succeeded in establishing a legitimacy that owed nothing to his dynastic bond with the Anjou. He would not be his wife's co-regent. He bought the support of the nobility, with substantial grants of royal castles and he succeeded in rescuing his wife. On 31 March 1387, he was crowned at Székesfehérvár in his turn, in the presence of a magnate league before whom he undertook formally to respect the privileges of the upper nobility.[7] Restrained for a while within the confines of constitutional law, the oligarchy held up their heads and returned to their ill-fated clan warfare. Their aim was to have a king whom they could keep on a very short rein at the very moment when the Ottoman threat was becoming a mortal danger for the country.

POLAND IN THE FOURTEENTH CENTURY

At the end of the thirteenth century, there were great similarities between Poland, where decentralising forces predominated, and Hungary. The unity of the kingdom was seriously threatened after the death of Boleslas 'Wry Mouth' in 1138 and the division of the country into rival principalities in accordance with the hereditary law of the Piast. The concept of a kingdom of Poland (*regnum Poloniae*) had not disappeared, however, but was nurtured by the

---

[7] Mályusz (1990), pp. 7–26.

Church and its leader, the archbishop of Gniezno, who crowned the Polish kings and whose province encompassed the whole kingdom and beyond. In addition, the threat from the Teutonic Order nurtured the development of a lively sense of national identity.[8] There was a strong current of opinion supporting unification; but there was as yet no agreement as to what should be the unifying centre of the kingdom – Greater Poland, Lesser Poland or even Bohemia.

The kingdom restored

Přemyslas II, crowned in 1295 by the extremely anti-German archbishop of Gniezno, Jakob Svinka, made a short-lived attempt to restore the kingdom. The first attempt of Ladislas the Short, duke of Kuiavia (elected as successor in 1296 after the murder of Přemyslas and deposed in 1300), was equally unsuccessful. The kings of Bohemia, whose southern ambitions had been decisively checked at Marchfeld, took their chance on their north-eastern border. Wenceslas II was crowned in 1300 with the support of the nobles of Greater Poland and the burghers, often German, who looked to the crown for protection against the magnates and promise of a unity that would provide favourable conditions for trade. The Piast Ladislas the Short successfully exploited the antagonism directed against a foreigner who approved the appointment of Germans and Czechs in the state's administration; he also won the support of Boniface VIII, Charles-Robert of Anjou (then struggling for the Hungarian crown) and the princes of Ruthenia and Halyč. After the death of Wenceslas II (1305) and the assassination of Wenceslas III (1306), Ladislas ousted the foreign claimants, John of Luxemburg and Rudolf of Habsburg, and quickly recovered Sandomir and Cracow. But eastern Pomerania was conquered by the Teutonic Knights in 1308, after they had massacred the populations of Danzig and Tezew. In 1311 Ladislas had to suppress a revolt in Cracow that had been provoked by the mayor and the Czech bishop, both supporters of John of Luxemburg, whom they believed would do more to aid the development of the town. Resistance in Greater Poland continued until 1314. In 1320, acknowledged throughout the kingdom, Ladislas was crowned, not at Gniezno, but at Cracow. His kingdom covered 110,000 square kilometres with just over 1 million inhabitants, but it was only half that of the first Piasts. Even so, unity had been restored and, despite the tensions between Greater and Lesser Poland and the ethnic problems between Slavs and Germans, as well as the contemporary confederations, it was not to be challenged until the divisions of the eighteenth century.

[8] Labuda (1970), p. 161.

Ladislas, the restorer of Polish unity, was succeeded in 1333 by his son, Casimir. He was extraordinarily successful in ensuring both the stability and the expansion of the kingdom, and his reign was the apogee of medieval Poland. He gave common institutions and structures to Ladislas the Short's motley assortment of duchies. The competent lawyers with whom he surrounded himself proclaimed the principle: 'one prince, one law and one coinage in the whole kingdom'. A single ruler for all the lands of the crown of the kingdom of Poland presupposed recognition of royal suzerainty by the dukes of the outlying provinces, Silesia, Kuiavia and Mazovia, who were always tempted to pay homage elsewhere. Ladislas the Short had successfully imposed royal authority on the last two; under Casimir, the line of the Piasts of Mazovia and Kuiavia died out, making it possible for these duchies to revert to the crown. This was not sufficient in itself to establish suzerainty, which had to be imposed by the authority of central government. *Starostes*, provincial governors instituted by the Přemysls, were preserved: appointed and rescinded by the king, they represented the administrative and judicial authority of the state over and above privileges and immunities. At the very apex of the state was the royal chancery, which robbed ducal chanceries of their *raison d'être*. Amongst its high-ranking officials were remarkable civil lawyers, such as the great chancellor Jan Suchywilk and the vice-chancellor Janko of Czarnków, author of a famous chronicle. Ladislas convened *conventiones magna* or *generales* four times in his reign. These were constructed on the model of the provincial assemblies (which had a role as local law courts), uniting in a single chamber the great magnates, Church dignitaries and some representatives of the nobility, the towns and ecclesiastical chapters. But there was still no question of formally constituted representation of estates. The council of barons was the principal organ of government, composed of high-ranking state office holders, who came from less distinguished families after 1320 than had earlier been the case. Casimir the Great preferred to govern with a small group of nobles, mostly from Cracow, who owed their rise to the monarchy. They made up the inner council where the most important decisions were taken and the great officers of state were nominated. But even in this context we cannot talk of a truly institutionalised council in any real sense under Casimir or his two successors.[9] On the other hand, the role of the *conventa magna* or *conventa solemna* was strengthened in the reign of Ladislas, when it was convened almost annually and sometimes twice a year.[10]

Providing a uniform legal system was a more difficult task. Polish towns and many villages were governed by the law of Magdeburg, which ensured them some degree of autonomous administration, but did not confer fiscal

---

[9] Russocki (1974), pp. 33–52.   [10] Bardach (1965), pp. 266–7.

exemption, contrary to what has sometimes been asserted.[11] The nobility and the peasantry were bound by Polish customary law, which Casimir had set down in writing. Especially in economic matters, legislation by ordinance tended to be imposed across the country as a whole and upon entire social groups. As for the coinage, Casimir failed to make the *groschen* of Cracow the basis of a Polish system. The kingdom did not have the mineral resources of Hungary or Bohemia. Some silver mines and rare copper deposits were worked in Lesser Poland. There was gold and silver in Silesia, but this province was under Bohemian suzerainty. Foreign coins, especially Hungarian, continued to be used in the kingdom and were still more prevalent in international transactions. Despite this dependence, the system of taxation made huge strides. Urban taxation had been systematised under the last two Piasts.[12] The recovery of lost possessions was pursued so energetically by the crown that it provoked a noble alliance against the *staroste* of Greater Poland by the *voiévode*, Maciej Borkowic, in 1352. This enabled many small towns to be founded by letters of *locatio*.[13] Finally, the administration of the royal domain was completely reorganised on the basis of a continually growing store of documentation, with information on both the extent of lands and the value of revenues. A general tax replaced the old ducal taxes. In a century which saw a great increase in external trade, revenue from customs duties increased. At the end of the century, the principal source of treasury revenue was the salt workings of Bochnia and Wieliczka. These had been brought under government control in 1273–8 and reorganised in 1368 under the authority of the 'great saltmaker'; they produced more than 12,000 *tonnes* of salt annually, a level which made it possible to export salt to Hungary and southern Russia.[14] The central financial administration, directed by the great treasurer of the kingdom, took increasingly systematic charge of the accountability of the treasury. In short, the modern state, which we know above all to be the product of fiscality, made considerable progress.

The new territorial equilibrium

The foundation of the Polish state also rested partly on the consolidation of its territorial base, as well as the defence of its frontiers by lines of towns and fortified castles. There were two threats to the kingdom: the Teutonic Knights to the north and Bohemia in the south-west. In the east and south-east, however, there was the possibility of intervention in the pagan grand duchy of Lithuania and the kingdom of Galicia-Lodomeria, plunged into total anarchy. There were two causes for conflict with Bohemia: on the one hand, John of

---

[11] Ludwig (1984).   [12] Ibid.   [13] Lalik (1976), pp. 97–120.   [14] Wyrozumski (1978b).

Luxemburg claimed the Polish throne as successor to the two last Přemysls; on the other, the seventeen Silesian duchies (where there was an increasingly large German population in rural settlements and mining towns) were drawn into the Bohemian king's sphere of interest; ethnic and political questions were inextricably intertwined. The shift in allegiance of the Silesian Piasts from Cracow to Prague may have been facilitated by the sense of a community of western Slavs among Poles and Czechs – the prologue added in the fourteenth century to the *Chronicle of Greater Poland* of 1295 made the two peoples the descendants of two mythical brothers, Lech and Čech.[15] In February 1327, five principalities were carved out of Oppeln (present-day Opole): Falkenberg, Teschen, Ratibor, Kosel-Beuthen and Auschwitz-Zator (now Niemodlin, Cieszyn, Racibórz, Koźle-Bytom and Oświęcim-Zator); in April the duchies of Oppeln and Breslau (Wrocław) paid homage to John of Luxemburg. In April–May 1329, it was the turn of Steingau, Öls, Sagan, Liegnitz-Brieg and Jauer (Scinawa Nyska, Oleśnica, Żagań, Legnica-Brzeg and Jawor); finally, in 1331, Glogau (Głagów) turned away from Greater Poland. Casimir was threatened by the Teutonic Knights and did not have the resources to fight on two fronts. By the terms of the Treaty of Trencsén (Trenčín) of August 1335, he abandoned suzerainty over the Silesian duchies and paid 20,000 *gros* of Prague to John of Luxemburg, in return for which the latter renounced his claims to the Polish throne. Some local dynasties died out subsequently, with the result that some duchies became fiefs held directly from the Bohemian crown. In 1348 the incorporation of Silesia into the kingdom of Bohemia was solemnly proclaimed.

The Teutonic Knights were more formidable opponents. From 1308 they had occupied Pomerania from Danzig and the Vistula estuary, barring access to the Baltic. In 1309, their grand master set up at Marienburg (now Malbork), the strategic and logistical headquarters of the Teutonic state. Ladislas the Short attempted to secure papal arbitration: the judgement of 1321, which was favourable to Poland, was quashed by John XXII two years later under pressure from the grand master Charles of Trier. The war which then started saw the first alliance between Poland and pagan Lithuania, both equally threatened by the common enemy allied to John of Luxemburg. Ladislas's victory at Płowce (1331) was short-lived, since Kuiavia was lost the following year. In 1335, arbitration by John of Luxemburg and Charles-Robert of Anjou forced the Knights to return this province and the land of Dobrzyń, but it left them Chełmno with Toruń, as well as all of Pomerania from Danzig. The settlement was long drawn-out. A new arbitration by the nuncio, Galhard of Chartres, at Warsaw in 1339, completely favourable to Poland, was not endorsed by

[15] Graus (1980), pp. 133–4.

Benedict XII. Finally, in the peace of Kalisz (1343), Casimir negotiated with the Teutonic Order on the basis of the agreement of 1335 and left eastern Pomerania to the Knights, with Danzig, Chełmno and Michałowo, without, however, ceding his claim to be 'lord and heir of Pomerania'. Throughout this confrontation, Casimir had had the advantage not only of the support of the ethnic Poles but also of the German citizens. They were very influential in the towns which the king's policy had encouraged and were curbed in their Baltic expansion by the monopoly of Toruń. The conflict between Poland and the Teutonic Knights was as much more a war of nations as the classic confrontation of two rival powers.

Eastern expansion, enormously significant, was the result of the Lesser Poland lobby, nobility in the royal entourage, the urban bourgeoisie and the Church. They all cast covetous glances at the Orthodox kingdom of Galicia-Lodomeria, where the male line of the Romanovich dynasty had died out in 1323. Duke Boleslas-Jerzy of Mazovia, related through the female line, had been summoned by the boyars; he was assassinated in 1340, leaving his rights to Casimir. This region in the upper valley of the river Dnestr was crossed by trade routes joining Cracow to the markets of the Black Sea; it also comprised the fertile lands of Podolia. Many therefore cast greedy eyes upon it, including the Hungarians on the other side of the Carpathians, the Lithuanians to the north and the Poles to the west, but also the Mongols who had ravaged Galicia a century earlier. Since 1340 the Lithuanians had held Volhynia with the towns of Łuck, Włodzimierz (Luts'k and Volyn/Volodjmjr) and Chełm. Casimir at once undertook the conquest of Ruthenia from Halyč (Halych), a metropolitan seat in the Orthodox Church. The territory of Přemysl was occupied from 1344 onwards. In 1349, a victorious expedition was launched against Halyč and Włodzimierz. But permanent occupation of Ruthenia presupposed agreement with Hungary, which had acted as arbiter in the disagreements between Casimir and John of Luxemburg; for Casimir and Charles-Robert of Hungary had after all acknowledged their reciprocal rights to Ruthenia at Visegrád in 1338.

Advance to the east was combined with Christian expansion in Lithuania, where it looked as if Prince Kieistut, duke of Troki, and his brothers had been won over to Christianity. In September 1349, Clement VI announced the imminent conversion of the Lithuanian princes. In 1350–1, Casimir and Louis the Great (who had renounced his rights to Ruthenia during Casimir's lifetime) campaigned in Lithuania with a view to the conquest of the province as much as Lithuanian conversion. Casimir left the conduct of operations to his nephew, who made Kieistut renew his promise that he, his family and his people would be baptised into the Christian faith in exchange for a triple alliance between Poland, Hungary and Lithuania against the Teutonic Knights.

But Kieistut did not keep his word and the expedition of 1351 ended in military failure and diplomatic ridicule.[16] The following year, Louis was wounded at the siege of Bełz (Belz). The expedition led by Casimir with the aid of Hungarian troops in 1355 was better prepared and ended in the capture of Włodzimierz. The following years saw new attempts to force the conversion of the Lithuanian prince, Olgierd; they ran aground because of his territorial needs vis-à-vis the Teutonic Knights. Moreover, Lithuanian diplomacy was in no hurry and played Rome off against Constantinople. A final expedition, without Hungarian assistance, against the Lithuanians in 1366 resulted in the complete annexation of the ancient kingdom of Galicia and Lodomeria to the Polish crown. Stretching as far as Podolia, the Polish kingdom now contained many nations; it had increased its surface area by more than one third and its population by at least 40 per cent. An archbishopric was established at Halyč in 1365. In 1414, it was transferred to Lwów, which had superseded Włodzimierz in another sphere, as the centre for the transfer of Levantine goods. It became an important base for the polonisation of Ruthenia and its integration within the Roman Church. Orthodox Christianity additionally undermined by internal rivalries became progressively weaker. In 1401, the metropolitan of Halyč was not replaced.

Situated on the frontiers of the Latin Church and the Christian west, the Poland of Casimir the Great had not only become more strongly unified, but had also consolidated its territorial position. It had already proved itself to be the very bulwark of the Christianity of Rome in the face of both Lithuanian paganism and the Orthodox Church in Ukraine.[17] Poland's privileged position in central eastern Europe gave Casimir such prestige that he was called upon to arbitrate between other rulers: in 1360 his mediation between Louis of Anjou and Rudof IV of Austria was an important step leading to the peace of Brno in 1364 between the two protagonists as well as Charles IV, who married the Polish king's granddaughter, Elizabeth of Pomerania. The same year, the Emperor, as well as his son, the king of Bohemia, the kings of Poland, Hungary, Denmark and Cyprus, the dukes of Silesia and Bavaria met together at Cracow to discuss how they might aid Peter of Lusignan against the Turks, a fair indication of the prestigious position of Poland in contemporary Christendom.

Population, economy and society at the time of Casimir the Great

Poland's position in Europe and these political achievements went hand in hand with economic development. Although the region was still very sparsely

---

[16] Giedroyć (1989), pp. 34–57.   [17] Seibt (1987), p. 1069.

populated (5.5 inhabitants per sq. km *c.* 1300) and demographic expansion had been checked by the Black Death (although it was less deadly than in western Europe), population growth was sufficient to allow agricultural and artisanal production to rise. There was most activity in Lesser Poland, whose most important town and member of the Hanseatic League – Cracow – became the capital of the kingdom. The region had lead mines, iron, copper and, above all, salt workings. It was the crossroads for routes joining Germany and the west to southern Russia and the Black Sea, on the one hand, and the Baltic to Bohemia, Hungary and the Mediterranean on the other. They were travelled by merchants from Italy and Germany but also by traders from the east, Armenians, Jews and Greeks who often settled in Ruthenia. These men did not only deal in goods in transit, such as English cloth in exchange for oriental commodities; they also sold local products – metal, livestock from Ruthenia; wax, skins, furs and, above all, cheap cloth from Poland and Silesia. Alongside these foreign merchants were those of Cracow: protected by Casimir, they made their presence increasingly felt in Pomerania, the Baltic and in Flanders, endeavouring to deny merchants from Toruń access to Russia and Hungary and take control themselves of the trade between these countries and western Europe. Cracow's staple rights were extended in 1354; agreements with Archduke Rudolf IV simplified the route to Italy.[18] From the end of the fourteenth century, Poland was an exporter of wheat and wood to western Europe. Beech and oak from Mazovia, Podlachia and even the foothills of the Carpathians, often chopped into planks for shipbuilding, were sent via the lower and middle Vistula, the Bug and the Narev, and Warsaw played an important role in this trade. But then there was total dependence on Prussian traders and the Teutonic Order, both for capital investment and transport on the lower Vistula and in the Baltic. Economic considerations thus played a part in Polno-Teutonic tensions.

This subordination to foreign interests accounts for the small size of Polish towns. There was admittedly progressive urbanisation from west to east. Casimir granted many charters to settlements on royal lands that had been recovered or which had belonged to the Church or to monasteries, especially in Lesser Poland, where there were fifty grants of urban charters in the fourteenth century, compared with thirty in the thirteenth.[19] Between 1320 and 1396 the number of towns in Greater Poland increased from 76 to 130; new towns were established in the frontier zones of the old dukedoms, along transit trade routes and in the afforested boundary area of Pomerania.[20] There were thirty-six foundations in backward Mazovia, ten in conquered Ruthenia. But the largest towns (such as Danzig or Breslau, with 20,000 inhabitants) lay

[18] Carter (1987), pp. 543–4.   [19] Wyrozumski (1978a), pp. 31–41.   [20] Wiesolowski (1981), p. 5.

outside the kingdom proper. Cracow had a population of only 14,000; Poznań only 4,000. Next in size were Sandomierz and the mining towns of Olkusz, Bochnia and Wieliczka, where a mixed law code operated, the *jus theutonicum magdeburgenses et montanum*.[21] Powers in all these towns were monopolised by rich patrician merchants, often of foreign origin. From the 1360s there were numerous social conflicts with the Polish population. (The participants in the revolt of the bakers' guild in Cracow in 1375 all had German names.) These tensions increased with the overflow of Hussitism from Bohemia, which gained a foothold amongst considerable sections of the ordinary people. For the time being, the patriciate was a source of loyal political and financial support for Casimir, whose policy promoted urban development: by his order more than twenty towns were enclosed with brick ramparts.

Cracow was the incontestable capital of the kingdom: the king lived there and it was henceforth also the venue for his coronation. Destroyed by the Tatars in 1240, the area of the town grew to thirty-two hectares with the emergence of two satellite towns, Kazimierz (which was granted autonomy in 1335) and Kleparz (which received the grant of *locatio* in 1366). Famous Gothic buildings were constructed there, earning it the name of *urbs celeberrima* (most renowned city). Work on the cathedral of the Wavel began in 1320, when the royal castle (destroyed by fire in 1306) was also being built. The town hall and the cloth hall were evidence of municipal splendour. In the 1360s the building yards of the churches of Our Lady and of St Catherine both saw renewed activity. The foundation of the university in 1364 (the second in the Slavonic lands after Prague) gave the kingdom a law faculty capable of providing the state with the lawyers it needed. A faculty of theology was added in 1400. The institution only became successful at the beginning of the fifteenth century when Hussitism brought to Cracow the Polish students who had continued to study in Prague. The reign of Casimir the Great was thus a period of the affirmation of the Polish national state.

Nevertheless, German influence remained significant. Christianisation had come from the west and the Piast princes had often taken brides from the Empire. In the twelfth and thirteenth centuries the German Cistercians had made massive investments in Poland and their dozen monasteries had become centres of colonisation. Before the Tatar invasion – and even more so afterwards – dukes, lords and ecclesiastical institutions had attracted German settlers; letters of *locatio* proliferated above all after 1280 and at the beginning of the fourteenth century in Greater Poland and in Kuiavia. After 1306, in Lesser Poland, it was the turn of the Carpathian foothills and the region to the north of the Vistula to benefit from *locationes* (respectively forty and thirty-three in the

---

[21] Molenda (1976), pp. 165–88.

course of the fourteenth century). German law (which was more favourable to peasants than Polish) was even more victorious and accepted in numerous villages with Polish inhabitants. Even so, not all towns with German law were German towns; equally, if the evidence of personal names is to be trusted, the large Polish towns had mixed populations, and up to 50 per cent of them might be German, as at Olkusz.[22] Moreover, it was the presence of Germans in towns with important responsibilities in secular government and the Church which gave birth to real xenophobia. At the beginning of the fourteenth century an anonymous French Dominican stressed the *naturale odium* (natural antipathy) between the Poles and the Germans. Concealed for a while, first by the rivalry between Greater and Lesser Poland then, after 1370, by anti-Magyar feeling, anti-German xenophobia was to persist in a Poland which was, however, largely open to external influences, and despite the loyalty of the Polish Germans to the monarchy and their specific patriotism.[23]

The Hungarian succession and Polno-Lithuanian union

It might have been feared that Casimir's work of restoration would have been threatened by the problem of his succession, since uncertainty was guaranteed to revive the old demons of intrigue and faction. Even before the death in 1339 of his first wife, who bore him no children, Casimir had contemplated a Hungarian succession. His sister Elizabeth had married Charles-Robert and since 1328 Casimir had paid visits to Hungary and been dazzled by the entirely western splendour of the Visegrád court. For his part, Charles-Robert demonstrated interest in the Polish throne, also claimed by the king of Bohemia. In 1338 the latter gave his support to Charles-Robert should the throne become vacant, in return for Hungarian neutrality should Poland wish to recover Silesia. When he was widowed, Casimir thought in terms of a Hungarian succession, rather than that of a Piast prince whose choice would be contested. In 1339, Elizabeth of Poland was recognised as heir and Charles-Robert undertook to aid Poland in the conquest of her lost territories, to respect her political and fiscal privileges, and not to appoint foreigners to the government. Henceforth the king of Hungary was the constant ally of Poland. The assistance granted him at the time of the Lithuanian wars provided Louis the Great with the means to secure his links with the Polish nobility. Casimir's serious illness at Lublin in 1351 made the question of succession seem imminent. The Polish nobles then demanded that Louis should give them an undertaking on oath not to appoint Germans to offices or castles and not to take more money from the kingdom than he required for the maintenance of

---

[22] Higounet (1986), pp. 200–14.   [23] Zientara (1974), pp. 5–28.

himself and his family during their stays in Poland. In 1355, at Buda, Casimir confirmed the Hungarian succession, while four Polish dignitaries, speaking in the name of the kingdom, obtained specific undertakings from Louis in relation to taxation (no new tax without the agreement of the nobles), expenditure of the future king (he would travel to Poland at his own expense) and military obligations (the Polish would not fight outside their own borders). Additionally, the Angevin succession was limited to Louis and his male heirs. The rights of the king of Hungary were thus firmly established, but at the expense of significant concessions. The future regime of 'gilded liberty' and *pacta conventa* was foreshadowed.

The Hungarian succession seemed threatened for a while by Casimir's remarriages. The king's second marriage was encouraged by Charles IV who had no interest whatsoever in the union of the two crowns. In 1341 Casimir married Adelaide of Hesse, by whom he had no male heirs and whom he soon repudiated. After a sham papal dispensation he forced the bishop of Poznań to officiate at his third marriage in 1365 with Hedwig of Sagan who also failed to provide him with a son. Louis thus remained well and truly heir; but as second in line Casimir named his grandson, Casimir, duke of Słupsk, son of his daughter Elizabeth and Bogisław V of Pomerania, who thus had precedence over any possible female heirs of the king of Hungary. Two days before his death Casimir granted this grandson the entire northern quarter of the kingdom as a fief. Was this last-minute remorse at the thought of disinheriting the Piasts? Grandpaternal solicitude? A desire to balance the tropism of the south and east with a western and Baltic policy? Whatever the case, an apanage on this massive scale could not but jeopardise the whole achievement of the reconstruction of the kingdom.

Casimir died on 8 September 1370 and on 17 November Louis was elected king. A seigneurial faction from Greater Poland, led by Janko of Czarnków, author of a violently anti-Angevin chronicle, sought to lend their support to Casimir of Słupsk. But the latter, although deprived of the greater part of his inheritance, was fairly quickly reconciled with Louis the Great; moreover he died in 1377. Of the Piasts of Kuiavia there remained only Ladislas the White, a monk at Dijon, who returned to take up arms against Louis and ended by joining his supporters in 1377. As for the Piast dukes of Silesia, they owed homage to the king of Bohemia or were in fact Hungarian supporters, such as Ladislas of Opole, whom Louis made governor of Ruthenia before conferring a veritable vice-royalty upon him in 1380. Before him, Louis had entrusted the government of Poland to his mother.

Judgements on Louis as king of Poland are as conflicting as those on his role as king of Hungary. In the tradition of Janko of Czarnków and sources originating in Greater Poland, some continued to denounce Angevin government as domination by foreigners and as the reign of pillage and prevarication. Janko reproached Louis above all for being crowned at Cracow rather than at Gniezno, of being absent from Poland and entrusting the government to a woman. In fact the magnates of the Angevin party were able to avert the triumph of decentralising forces and Louis preserved a strong central government as Casimir had done. The new sovereign's counsellors were defenders of the state and of the unity of the kingdom.[24] If Louis can be accused of anything it is of having made additional concessions to the magnates and granting them most of the royal towns (91 per cent in Lesser and Greater Poland) in order to consolidate his rights. Louis had to go still further to secure the throne for his daughters: in 1374 by the Privilege of Kassa (Košice) the Polish nobility accepted female succession but obtained a substantial reduction in their contribution to public expenditure. The clergy were won over by similar concessions. Thus the realisation of dynastic ends hindered progress towards more equitable taxation. Nevertheless, if Louis had then succeeded in turning the *poradlne*, a peasant tax, from an irregular to a regular levy, fixed at 2 *groschen* per household, he would have taken one step towards a more modern taxation system.[25]

But the dynastic scheme was not to have only disastrous consequences, since it permitted the completion of a plan that had long been cherished, the union of Poland and Lithuania. When Louis died in 1382, a party opposed the accession of a German prince by means of one of Louis's daughters. The oldest of the surviving daughters, Mary, had married Sigismund of Luxemburg, the son of Charles IV; now the Luxemburgs had always supported the Teutonic Knights. The younger, Jadwiga, was betrothed to William of Habsburg. The Piast party raised its head once more. Eventually, the thirteen-year-old princess was crowned king (*rex*) at Cracow in 1384. Power remained in the hands of the magnates. The union of the Hungarian and Polish crowns, which Louis the Great had sought to make permanent, was thus broken.

On the death of Louis, Lithuania had just experienced a serious defeat at the hands of the Teutonic Knights, to whom part of Samogitia had to be ceded. Moreover, the Grand Duchy was weakened by family quarrels between Duke Jogaila and his cousin, Witold. Finally, in the east, Moscow had stated her desire to unite the Russian territories and expand westwards. Conflict between Lithuania and Moscow seemed inevitable and this threat put an end to the age-old balance of the Grand Duchy between Orthodoxy and Latin Christendom. Henceforth nothing would thwart the solidarity uniting Poland and Lithuania against the Teutonic Knights. The agreement was concluded at Krevo in 1385: it proclaimed the personal union of the duchy and the kingdom under the

[24] Vardy, Grosschmid and Domonkos (1986), pp. 129–54.   [25] Matuszewski (1985), pp. 33–50.

sceptre of Jogaila who was baptised on 15 February at Cracow, took the name of Ladislas, married Jadwiga three days later and was crowned king on 4 March. The conversion of the Lithuanian people to Christianity followed. The bishopric of Wilno was established in 1387 and richly endowed. Besides the Franciscans, the Cracow congregation of the Penitential Friars also played a major part in evangelisation.

The act of Krevo concealed a mortal danger for the Teutonic Knights, because it combined the forces of two hostile states and because the renunciation of paganism by the Lithuanians deprived the Knights of all ideological justification. They accordingly did everything in their power to sabotage the union and support the opposition in Lithuania, whose standard-bearer was Vytautas, son of the late Duke Kieistut. Jogaila Ladislas set about disarming the prejudices of the independent faction by allowing the Grand Duchy very considerable autonomy. In 1392 Vytautas was reconciled with Ladislas, who appointed him governor of Lithuania. The defeat he suffered in 1399 at Vorskla against the Tatars destroyed his eastern ambitions – he had dreamt of conquering Pskov, Novgorod and (why not?) Moscow and the shores of the Black Sea – and anchored him firmly in Ladislas's camp. As for the latter, he realised that the incorporation, pure and simple, of Lithuania was an impossibility. By the agreements of Vilna-Radom of 1401, Vytautas became Grand Duke of Lithuania, Ladislas retaining for himself the title of Supreme Grand Duke. Ladislas's widowerhood two years earlier had not compromised his status as king of Poland at all. The personal union of the two states was well and truly sealed.

Conflict with the Teutonic Knights was postponed because of the priority given by the nobility of Lesser Poland and some Lithuanian boyars to expansion in the east. But the nobility of Greater Poland, the merchants who exported wood and corn, and the majority of Lithuanians threatened by incursions of the Teutonic Knights pressed for war, which was precipitated by the election of Grand Master Ulrich von Jungingen in 1407. After a year of preparation, the Polno-Lithuanian armies took the offensive in July 1410 and marched on Marienburg (Malbork). The Teutonic Knights, supplemented by mercenaries and western volunteers, attempted to cut off their march. The decisive clash, which involved more than 100,000 combatants, took place at Grunwald (Tannenberg) on 15 July. The Teutonic Knights were totally crushed, the grand master and numerous officials lay dead on the battlefield. The Teutonic towns and fortresses surrendered one after another. But the Polno-Lithuanian forces failed before Marienburg. Supported on the diplomatic level by Emperor Sigismund and Gregory XII, the Order preserved the critical part of its possessions in the peace signed at Toruń in 1411: it returned Samogitia but not Pomerania or Danzig. The military power of the Order was anything but shattered by these terms, nor were all the hindrances which had weighed down on Poland and Lithuania for more than a century removed. Henceforth the annexation of the Baltic coast became a short- to medium-term objective. Tannenberg also sealed the Polno-Lithuanian union in blood. At Horodło in 1413, forty-three noble Polish families adopted the same number of Lithuanian families and shared their coats of arms. The Lithuanian lords now benefited from the same fiscal and judicial privileges as their Polish counterparts. Lithuanian autonomy was unquestionably formally recognised once more. But the admission to brotherhood demonstrated that Lithuanian institutions and culture were being polonised. The Polno-Lithuanian monarchy was becoming a veritable state.

BOHEMIA IN THE FIRST HALF OF THE FOURTEENTH CENTURY

The accession of John of Luxemburg

The assassination of Wenceslas III in August 1306 precipitated a lengthy succession crisis in Bohemia. The last of the Přemysls had no descendants but many sisters; his mother, Queen Elizabeth of Poland, was still alive. The first conflict pitted Henry of Carinthia, husband of Anne, one of the sisters, against Rudolf of Habsburg, son of the Emperor Albert. The year 1306 saw a double election, Henry in August and Rudolf in October. The latter strengthened his chances by marrying the widowed queen and having his father confirm Bohemia's electoral right in the imperial election. Rudolf was immediately exposed to a coalition of nobles from the south-west of the country, led by Zajec of Waldeck and supported by the Bavarians and the Saxons. He died on 3 July 1307 at the siege of Horaždovice. Twelve days later, the Bohemian lords elected Henry of Carinthia for a second time. The Emperor Albert was defeated before Kutná Hora in the autumn; on 1 May 1308 he was assassinated as he undertook a new campaign to secure the throne for another of his sons. The Habsburg threat was henceforth averted, without Henry of Carinthia's position being consolidated, however.

In November, the election of Henry of Luxemburg to the German throne resulted in the entry of a third candidate into the lists, his son, John. Henry VII, closely connected to the French crown, was supported in his eastern policy by the two abbots of the great Bohemian Cistercian convents, Conrad of Zbraslav and Henry Heidenreich of Sedlec, former diplomats of Wenceslas II, who had suffered from the demands of the higher nobility. On the way back from the general chapter held at Cîteaux in 1309, Conrad met Henry VII at Heilbronn. On his return to Prague, he persuaded the young Princess Elizabeth, daughter of Wenceslas II, to marry John of Luxemburg. During the summer of 1310, Elizabeth fled from Prague to Germany; on 31 August at Speyer, eighteen years old, she married John who was only fourteen, and whom his father invested with the fief of Bohemia. After failing before Kutná Hora and Kolin, John of Luxemburg's little band, led by Peter von Aspelt, archbishop-elector of Mainz and former chancellor of Wenceslas II, appeared before Prague. Reassured by the promise that loans to Henry of Carinthia would be repaid, the townspeople opened the gates of the capital on 3 December 1310. John was crowned in February 1311 by Aspelt and acclaimed by the Bohemian nobility before whom he promised to reserve offices for the inhabitants of the kingdom.

It was not long before this consensus was broken. The German counsellors, among them Aspelt, were dissatisfied. John's candidature for the imperial throne, opened by the death of his father in 1313, took him away from Bohemian affairs, as did the armed support which he eventually offered to Lewis of Bavaria, whom he supported against Frederick the Handsome, a Habsburg, whom he suspected had designs on Bohemia. The old dualism rose up once more in his absence, with, on the one hand, the party for centralisation and the Přemysl tradition around the queen and the Cistercians, some barons and above all towns dominated by a German bourgeois elite and, on the other, the larger part of the upper nobility led by Henry of Lipá and supported by the queen mother. In the spring of 1315, John had to send away the Germans. Henry of Lipá, appointed marshal of the kingdom, replaced Aspelt; supported by a vast clientele, it was not long before he became a formidable force and wanted to control the expenditure of the king, who had him imprisoned in October. Civil war broke out. Recalled, Aspelt succeeded in negotiating a compromise: Lipá was freed but John secured unfettered control of crown revenues, which enabled him to go to the aid of Lewis of Bavaria in the Empire. Aspelt, captain general of the kingdom, did his utmost to stabilise the situation. But he could not prevent anarchy; he left Bohemia in 1317, leaving power in the hands of Queen Elizabeth, who was very hostile towards the nobles who had forced her to leave Prague.

John of Luxemburg returned to Bohemia in December. At the diet of February 1318, the nobility tried to impose very strict conditions on him. A large number of them played the Habsburg card against him. Agreement was only reached thanks to the intervention of Lewis of Bavaria, who feared above all that Bohemia would fall into the hands of his Habsburg enemy. This was the 'reconciliation of Domažlice'. His fingers badly burnt in these first attempts, John of Luxemburg was now concerned only to secure a guarantee of sufficient revenue for himself, thanks to the monopoly of silver and minting at Kutná Hora. As far as everything else was concerned, he renounced the royal tradition of centralisation and reduction of the political power of the nobility.

The barons then had a free hand in the kingdom; the most powerful of them, Henry of Lipá, became its governor. As for John, he concentrated on his ambitions outside the kingdom and spent virtually no time in Bohemia, other than to furnish himself with good silver.[26] There was another twist to this political *volte face* with the break between the king and his wife, in whom the Přemysl tradition still flourished, and who, in 1319, with the support of the Prague bourgeoisie, made a vain attempt to seize power once more. The threat brought the king and the noble party together. John eventually separated his children from their mother: they were mere pawns in his European policy. The oldest, Wenceslas, was sent to France in 1323, to the court of his uncle, Charles IV 'the Fair' – the king who had married John's sister, Marie of Luxemburg, the previous year. Charles IV was his sponsor at confirmation, and it was on this occasion that Wenceslas adopted the Christian name of the French king.

John of Luxemburg and Europe

Henceforth John, absent from his kingdom on a colossal scale, always very attached to his Luxemburg domains, passed most of his time concocting diplomatic schemes. They were not all beneficial to Bohemia. An early association, in which John was allied to Lewis of Bavaria and Charles-Robert of Hungary, to whom he gave his sister Beatrice in marriage, was directed against the Habsburgs (who were thus caught in a pincer movement) and against Poland which John claimed as heir of the Přemysls. These alliances enabled Bohemian sovereignty to be established over the principality of Troppau (present-day Opava) and, profiting from the extinction of the Brandenburg Ascanians, they also permitted the recovery of western Upper Lusatia, with Bautzen, which Wenceslas I had relinquished as dowry for one of his daughters in 1320.

But this system of alliances disintegrated almost at once. Beatrice died and Charles-Robert remarried a sister of Ladislas the Short, king of Poland in 1320 and recognised by the pope. Two years later, the splendid victory of Lewis of Bavaria and John over the Habsburgs at Mühldorf made the Emperor less dependent on the king of Bohemia, who nevertheless received the district of Eger (present-day Cheb) as the prize for his vote and armed support.[27] But it was to his own son that Lewis of Bavaria assigned the electorate of Brandenburg, which John had coveted. From then on a new system of alliances had to be constructed. After some western ventures – the betrothal of his son John-Henry to Margaret of Carinthia, daughter and heir of his old rival for Bohemia, a plan for the reorganisation of the three kingdoms of the Holy Roman Empire in which

---

[26] Janáček (1973), p. 252.   [27] Bosl (1967–74), II, pp. 46ff.

he would hold the crown of Italy himself and Charles of Valois that of Arles – John returned to his Polish ambitions. The intervention of Ladislas the Short against Brandenburg, with the aid of the pagan Lithuanians who made raids on Christians and sold them as slaves, gave legal justification to John's armed intervention against the king of Poland, allied with Charles-Robert and protected by John XXII. Although the king of Bohemia was defeated before Cracow, he was able to secure his position in Silesia. As has already been mentioned, the passing of Silesian fiefs to the Bohemian crown began in 1327.[28] Here John harvested the lasting fruits of a policy that had started under the Přemysls. In the fourteenth century Silesia, already very urbanised, became an important region for the production of iron, thanks to the mines of Beuthen (present-day Bytom). In 1328–9, with the Teutonic Knights, John undertook a new crusade against the Lithuanians whom the Poles vainly attempted to help.

His western policy was not abandoned, however. It was reactivated by the candidature of the bishop-elector of Trier, Baldwin, uncle of King John, for the vacant throne of Mainz, of critical strategic importance in any royal German election. John XXII's opposition to Baldwin in 1330 catapulted John into the anti-pontifical camp, where he rejoined Lewis of Bavaria, who had been excommunicate since 1324 and whose Italian ventures had just failed. John of Luxemburg thus took up the cause and, in the autumn of 1330, busied himself with rallying to his side the Ghibelline towns of northern Italy, from Brescia to Lucca, as his father had attempted to do before him. Initial enthusiasm was soon followed by disillusion as a result of the 'German' occupation and fiscal pressure. John's absence was turned to account by all his enemies, and even by Lewis of Bavaria, who made a secret agreement with the Habsburgs about a scheme to divide the duchies of Henry of Carinthia, which John of Luxemburg hoped would pass to his son John-Henry. After June 1331 John had to return to central Europe, leaving his son Charles at Parma as governor. Two years later, the coalition of Italian powers in the great league of Ferrara was the product of the establishment of the Luxemburgs in Italy.

The conquest of the Empire

Did John of Luxemburg realise that he could not keep two irons in the fire indefinitely? From 1335, the king focused on a single project: obtaining the imperial crown for himself or his son Charles, subordinating everything else to this end and equipping himself with the means to realise this ambition. The most important diplomatic axis was the strengthened alliance with France; in 1332 the heir to the Valois throne, John, had married Bonne, daughter of the

[28] Pustejovsky (1975).

king of Bohemia who, now that the last of the Přemysls had died, married Beatrice of Bourbon, great-granddaughter of St Louis in 1334.[29] John held faithfully to this French mooring until his death. He also had to free himself from encumbrances in the east. Casimir's accession in Poland (1333) facilitated the establishment of a lasting peace, the new king simultaneously renouncing war on the Luxemburgs and the Teutonic Knights. In 1335, the death of Henry of Carinthia provided an opportunity for reconciliation with Charles-Robert, who was worried at the spectacle of the Habsburgs strengthening their presence on Hungary's western borders. Under his auspices, John of Luxemburg and Casimir the Great met at Trencseń, the one renouncing his claims to the throne of Poland, the other to Silesia. The next year, John relinquished Carinthia, Carniola and the March of Windisch to the Habsburgs in return for recognition of Luxemburg sovereignty in the Tirol; he hoped thus to secure the support of the Austrian dukes for his imperial policy. In 1341 Lewis of Bavaria's attack on John-Henry, which deprived him simultaneously of the Tirol and his wife (the Emperor, usurping papal rights, annulled the marriage and married Margaret Maultasch to his own son, the elector of Brandenburg), strengthened the alliance with the Habsburgs, who were also threatened by the Bavarian Emperor. From then on the majority of the electors, with the support of Clement VI, were on the side of Charles, who had in 1340 become regent of Bohemia when his father went completely blind. On 11 July 1346, he was elected king of Germany by the three ecclesiastical electors, Rudolf of Saxony and John of Luxemburg. Since Aachen supported the Wittelsbach, the coronation took place at Bonn, at the hands of the archbishop of Cologne. The death of Lewis of Bavaria on 11 October 1347 allowed the imperial towns to change their policy. John of Luxemburg had then been dead for more than a year, killed at the battle of Crécy (26 August 1346), where he had tried to fight in the French ranks, despite his infirmity. Charles thus harvested the fruits of a policy which had been followed with determination for more than a decade. The impulsive and somewhat disorganised ventures of the beginning of the reign had been succeeded by the fully formed scheme of achieving the imperial throne. Alliances with the Valois, the Habsburgs and the Angevins in Hungary, together with the agreement with Poland, resulted in what was to be a lasting success, for the German crown remained in the dynasty for almost a century.

Bohemia under John of Luxemburg

More than once, the ambitions of John of Luxemburg outside the kingdom severely depleted the treasury of the kingdom of Bohemia. The shortage of

[29] Troubert (1988), pp. 252–80.

money was such in 1336 that they went so far as to search for hoards hidden in the synagogue and in the tomb of St Adalbert. Despite these periodic crises, John of Luxemburg succeeded in extracting the funds for his policy from his possessions. As in Hungary, it was less taxation than mineral wealth that enabled the king to play a part on the European stage. The main taxes were a general subsidy (*berna generalis*) for a specified purpose, paid by all subjects and therefore submitted for the consent of the upper nobility; an extraordinary tax (*berna particularis*), this time levied without the consent of the estates on the possessions of the crown, the royal towns and the possessions of the Church under crown patronage; lastly the tax on the Jews which was the price of crown protection. The *berna generalis*, despite the resistance of the barons who, as early as 1331, secured agreement that it would only be granted on the occasion of the coronation of a prince or the betrothal of a princess, was frequently levied by the Luxemburgs. The *berna particularis* often depleted monastic treasuries rather than towns cushioned by commercial expansion.[30] Regalian rights over the mines were much more significant. Although Bohemia only produced one fifth of Hungarian gold production, it supplied 40 per cent of European silver in around 1300 (between twenty and thirty tonnes per year and a further ten tonnes around 1350).[31] John of Luxemburg received one eighth of all that was extracted; he controlled the monopoly of trade in silver and that of the striking of coin. All monetary administration was concentrated at Kutná Hora, a town of 18,000 inhabitants where silver mines had been discovered around 1280 and which had supplanted Jihlava as the principal centre of mining and coining since the reign of Wenceslas II.

Generally speaking, despite this fiscal pressure, the reign of John of Luxemburg was beneficial for the towns. In the first half of the fourteenth century, peasant mobility was not seriously hampered and it was this, rather than the flow of colonisation from outside (which dried up), that sustained the population of the towns with all those country dwellers who hoped for a better life. The towns expanded, undertook building works and obtained privileges and franchises; the citizen judge, a seigneurial official, was gradually replaced by an elected member of the community of inhabitants, following the example of the German law codes which prevailed in Bohemia (those of southern Germany and that of Magdeburg).[32] This increased municipal autonomy did not yet result in genuine participation in political life. Only the royal towns (thirty-two in Bohemia and seventeen in Moravia), and mainly the Old City of Prague (*Stare Mesto*), sent representatives to the diet of the kingdom, summoned scarcely six times in John's reign. Municipal administration was in the hands of a narrow patriciate, often German, not yet really threatened by the

<hr>

[30] Kejř (1966).   [31] Janáček (1973), pp. 247–52; Šmahel (1987), pp. 511–12.   [32] Kejř (1968).

largely Czech *artifices et operarii*, regrouped into guilds. John of Luxemburg benefited from the support of this influential patriciate which supplied him with several counsellors, including his great financier, Ulrich Pflug. On the other hand, he attempted, without any real success, to tap the transit trade between the Mediterranean and northern Europe (which contributed to the wealth of the neighbouring towns of Vienna, Linz, Ratisbon, Nuremberg, Breslau and Cracow) for the profit of the Bohemian towns and above all Prague, which already numbered 35,000 inhabitants. He had no more success in diverting the Danube trade route to the north. Prague did not become a trading centre.[33]

Another source of support for the king was the Church. We have mentioned the role of the Cistercian convents of Zbraslav and Sedlec at the time of his accession. We should add that of John IV of Dražice, whose long tenure of the bishopric of Prague (1301–43) was a fundamental step in the assertion of episcopal rights against the centralising tendencies of the papacy. Very hostile to the friars and to the Inquisition, he was, on the other hand, responsible for the introduction into Bohemia of the Augustinian canons regular, whose spiritual and pastoral life he admired. In 1333 he founded the first chapter of the Order at Roudnice, on the Elbe; it was a foundation exclusively for Czechs, *nisi sit Bohemus de utroque parente idiomatis bohemice ortum trahens* (unless they could speak the language of Bohemia, learnt from one of their parents),[34] while the Cistercian and Premonstratensian abbeys, established in the twelfth century, daughters of German mother-houses, were centres of settlement and German influence. The same situation prevailed with the mendicant orders. As for John of Luxemburg, he established the Carthusians in his kingdom; their first house – soon to be the head of the north German province – opened near Prague in 1342. Admittedly, the first half of the fourteenth century did not see the same number of foundations as the previous century, which had witnessed an increase in mendicant orders and convents connected to the clearing of land, nor as many as the reign of Charles IV was to witness. But that of John was marked by the development of a Czech monasticism which was to have a fundamental role in national and literary culture in the future. The good relations between John of Luxemburg and the papacy, and the energetic action of his son Charles, were crowned in 1344 by the emancipation of Prague from Mainz: the new archbishopric of Prague encompassed the dioceses of Prague (2,084 parishes) and Olomouc (550), as well as the recently created Litomyšl (153).[35] The new archbishop of Prague, the second person in the kingdom after the king, was at the head of a powerful Church, which owned almost one third of the land of the kingdom, and in which, despite some traces of Waldensianism

---

[33] Graus (1960); Mezník (1969).   [34] Graus (1966), pp. 26–37.   [35] Šmahel (1987), p. 513.

which had arrived with German settlers, there was little hint of the first signs of future crises.

On the other hand, inter-ethnic problems already marked out the lines of a split which would deepen at the time of the Hussite crisis: an elite urban German bourgeoisie eager for recognition, simultaneously opposed to the developing Czech bourgeoisie and, above all, the rural Czech nobility, defender of Bohemian manners and customs; German mendicant clergy against Czech seculars – in short, economic, political, religious and ethno-linguistic tensions fed the demands of one upon the other. In their struggle with a bourgeoisie who were very frequently the natural ally of the king, the nobility, very attached to a political dualism which left all local powers and the control of taxation with the diet, became the self-appointed guardian of 'Czechicity' (Czech national identity). All the resentment and bitterness of the nobility were expressed in a Czech chronicle, supposedly by Dalimil, dating from the early fourteenth century: it praised the good Czechs, the lords of ancient lineage, and made Germany the hereditary enemy. The work promoted two concepts: the *regnum Bohemiae* (kingdom of Bohemia) and membership of the Czech linguistic community. In this respect it was an important stage in the ideologisation of the national conscience. Was there an opposing *deutsch-böhmisch* (German-Bohemian) conscience? The most important work of medieval history after Kosmas, the *Chronicle of Zbraslav*, was written in Latin. Its author, the priest Peter of Zittau, coming from the German ethnic region, boasts of the bravery of the Germans. But that did not prevent him from feeling Bohemian, from identifying with Bohemians – *nostri Bohemi* ('our Bohemians') – or from maintaining an equilibrium by denying the mutual hatred of Germans and Czechs. He preached *Landespatriotismus* (loyalty to country), a sentiment shared by the upper clergy. In this respect, the creation of the archbishopric of Prague was the summit of the aspirations of an elite that belonged to both ethnic groups. But did that provide sufficient social and institutional support for the lasting success of a peaceful compromise between Germans and Czechs, based on *Landespatriotismus*?[36] The constituent parts of the crisis that lay ahead, smoothed over in the reign of Charles IV, were already in place in the middle of the century.

[36] Graus (1966) and (1980), pp. 89–113.

CHAPTER 23

THE PRINCIPALITIES OF RUS' IN
THE FOURTEENTH CENTURY

Nancy Shields Kollmann

THE Rus' principalities in the fourteenth century were not 'Russia', although their history in this century is often subsumed into that rubric. The state centred at Moscow that became Russia emerged from one of the Rus' principalities over the course of the century. During the 1300s political and cultural diversity was the dominant feature of these lands in the eastern reaches of the forested European plain. The territory with which we will be concerned lies east of Poland and Prussia, stretching to the Urals and extending from the Baltic to the steppe north of the Black Sea. Ethnically East Slavs predominated, gradually displacing the Finno-Ugric peoples native to these forests. Finno-Ugric peoples remained the dominant population in Estonia and the lands north of Moscow and Novgorod, reaching to the White Sea. Balts (Letts, Lithuanians) lived on the Baltic littoral south of Estonia and somewhat inland. Indigenous Siberian peoples lived on the far northern shores of the White Sea. By 1300 only the East Slavs were officially Christian, belonging to the Byzantine Orthodox faith. Surrounding this large area were peoples of different religions, ethnicities and historical heritages: polytheistic Tatars and Turks in the steppelands to the south and east, Catholic Poles to the west.

What gives this area its historical cohesion was the shared common political heritage of the Kiev Rus' state, whose Riurikide dynasty had controlled most of these lands (not the Baltic littoral or farthest northern lands) from the tenth to the twelfth centuries. By the beginning of the fourteenth, however, the grand principality had evolved into many different principalities, all descended from the Kievan ruling family. At least five political centres in these lands can be identified, taking as a measuring stick the later development of nations: the heartland of the modern Ukrainian nation in the principalities of Galicia, Volhynia, Kiev, Chernihiv and Pereiaslav; that of the modern Belarus'ians in the principalities of Smolensk, Polotsk, Turov and Pinsk; that of the Great Russians, comprising the numerous principalities of Vladimir-Suzdal', often called (in relation to Kiev) north-east Rus'; not constituting the ancestors of a modern nation, and later subsumed into Russian history, were the city republics of Novgorod and Pskov. Furthermore, the lands of the modern Lithuanians on the Baltic, that had not been part of the Kievan state, constituted a political entity by 1300. None of these lands in 1300 was dominant, because of the overarching political authority of the westernmost outpost of the Mongol empire, the so-called Golden Horde or, more properly, Kipchak khanate. The khanate, centred at Sarai on the lower Volga with a predominantly Tatar steppe nomadic population, exacted taxation, tribute and political submission from most of the lands heir to Kiev Rus'.

The drama of the fourteenth century is the transformation of this political constellation. With hindsight one can identify the Grand Duchy of Lithuania and the grand princes of Moscow as the historical winners in the quest for regional power, but in the fourteenth century their later successes were by no means foreordained, and these two rivals at times seemed equally matched by others – Tver', Suzdal', Novgorod and Pskov. While the power struggles between these areas were resolved finally in the fifteenth century, the fourteenth century established the course of development these lands would follow.

SOURCES

Surviving fourteenth-century sources draw our attention to high politics. Chronicles were compiled throughout the area and in the Livonian and Teutonic Orders on the Baltic;[1] Byzantine sources reveal ecclesiastical politics;[2] diplomatic correspondence between the Grand Dukes of Lithuania and numerous European states survives,[3] as do treaties between Novgorod and Pskov and various trading partners and princes, and among north-east Rus' princes;[4] Hansa records detail the trade of Novgorod and Pskov.[5]

Sources for social and cultural history are less plentiful. Law codes, ecclesiastical and secular, taken from Kiev Rus' or extending its heritage, circulated. These included the *Nomokanon*, or *Kormchaia kniga*, a collection of Byzantine and Rus' Church and civil laws; the Ecclesiastical Charters of Princes Vladimir and Iaroslav of Kiev; the Just Measure, or *Merilo pravednoe*, and Court Law for the People (*Zakon sudnyi liudem*), ecclesiastical law codes of Byzantine provenance that, like the *Nomokanon*, mixed civil and religious issues; the Russian Law, or *Russkaia pravda*. Pskov (1397) generated its own code in this century; the late fifteenth-century Novgorod Judicial Charter is

---

[1] *Polnoe sobranie russkikh letopisei*; on Baltic chronicles, see Rowell (1993) and (1994), ch. 2.
[2] Meyendorff (1980) demonstrates these sources.   [3] Rowell (1993) and (1994), ch. 2.
[4] *DDG*; *Gramoty Velikogo Novgoroda i Pskova*.   [5] Dollinger (1970).

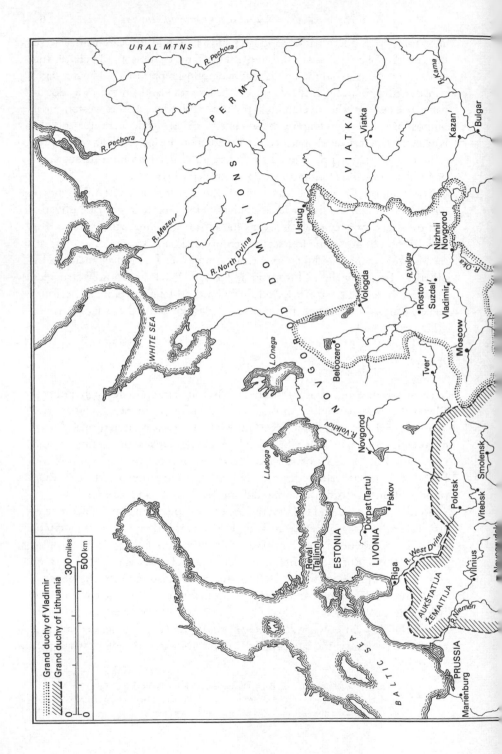

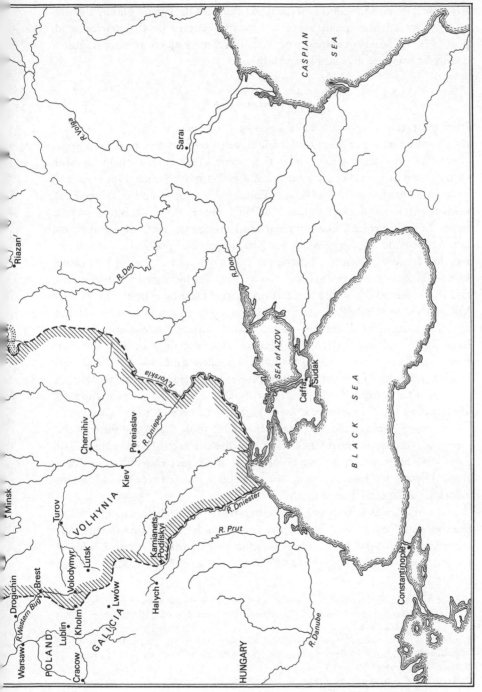

Map 15   Russia, *c.* 1396

based on a fourteenth-century redaction.[6] Both for the Grand Duchy and the
Moscow grand principality some fourteenth-century deeds, charters and
privileges of local government survive.[7] Literary production is represented
mainly by hagiography and historical tales.[8]

POLITICAL EVENTS

Until the 1350s geo-politics was shaped by two modern versions of the *pax
Romanorum*: here a *pax Mongolica* (stable international trade across the steppe
grasslands of Asia maintained by the several khanates of the Chingisid
dynasty) and on a smaller scale a *pax Lithuanica* (a similarly stable trade sphere
from the inland forests to the Baltic).[9] Thus, trade patterns subdivided the Rus'
lands into two interlocked arenas, the Baltic and the Volga–Caspian–steppe
nexus. In the fourteenth century northern Europe's demand for forest products, particularly fur, generated several Baltic-oriented political centres. First
was the Hanseatic League or Hansa, a network of German trading cities with
its headquarters at Lübeck; second, Novgorod, which claimed territory north
and north-east to the White Sea and northern Dvina river basin and east to
Vologda and the Urals. Pskov, another urban republic, also flourished, located
on trade routes linked with the three major towns of Livonia and Estonia:
Riga, Reval (Tallinn) and Dorpat (Tartu), all in the orbit of the Teutonic
Knights. These towns' inland network included Smolensk, Polotsk and
Vitebsk, utilising land routes as well as the western Dvina river (with its mouth
at Riga). The Teutonic Order, with its capital at Marienburg, was comprised
after 1236 of the Teutonic (or Prussian) and the Livonian Orders. These military monastic communities had settled the Baltic shore in the first third of the
thirteenth century as a northern outreach of the crusades. By the beginning of
the fourteenth century the two branches of the Order controlled the coast
from Danzig to Estonia, with the exception of ethnically Lithuanian
Žemaitija, and pressed persistently inland.

The Order's steady pressure, the vulnerability of the Rus' principalities in
the thirteenth century and Baltic trade opportunities, stimulated the political
consolidation of the Lithuanians, a Baltic people whose ethnic heartland
ranged from south of the western Dvina to the basin of the Niemen river,

---

[6] Kaiser (1980), ch. 2; *Drevnerusskaia slavianskaia kormchaia XIV titulov bez tolkovanii*, ed. Beneshevich;
Zakon sudnyi liudem kratkoi redaktsii, ed. Tikhomirov; *Merilo pravednoe*, ed. Tikhomirov and Milov;
Rossiiskoe zakonodatel'stvo, I–II.

[7] *Akty, otn. k istorii Zapadnoi Rossii*, I–II; *Akty, otn. k istorii Iuzhnoi i Zapadnoi Rossii*, I; *Akty sotsial'no-ekonomicheskoi istorii*, I–III; Okinshevich (1953); *Akty istoricheskie*, I; *Akty feodal'nogo zemlevladeniia*, I–III.

[8] *Slovar' knizhnikov* (1987–9), I–II; Kliuchevskii (1871).

[9] Rowell (1994), p. 79, for the *pax Lithuanica*.

comprising the lowlands (Žemaitija) and the high country (Aukštatija).[10] The Lithuanian ruler Mindaugas, attested since at least 1238, accepted Catholicism in 1251 in a vain attempt to avert the Order's violent missionary attacks; he won a king's crown from the pope in 1253, as well as a bishopric for Lithuania. All to no avail; the attacks continued and after Mindaugas's murder in internecine struggles in 1263, the pace of official christianisation slowed. By the end of the century another strong ruler, Vytenis (1295–1315) had emerged from the strife among Lithuanian clans; his brother Gediminas (1316–41) founded a dynasty whose ruling line lasted until 1572 (see also above pp. 703–12).

The Gediminid was a powerful and astute dynasty. It conducted itself in traditional patterns of Scandinavian and Viking bands, such as those who had founded the Kiev Rus' state in the ninth and tenth centuries and with whom the Lithuanians engaged in trade well before the fourteenth century. The clan was the dominant political structure, both for the ruling family and the landed military elites that supported it. Patrimonial political relations based on ties of kinship and personal loyalty shaped politics; the Grand Dukes ruled in close consultation with their kinsmen and the leading clans of the realm.[11] The Gediminids's political ambitions brought them into two spheres, the world of Catholic Poland and the Order to the west, and that of Orthodox Rus' to the east and south. In the fourteenth century they skilfully played these two traditions off against each other – allying with the Order when expedient against a Rus' rival and, even more saliently, supporting Rus' traditions (Orthodoxy, East Slavic language, local Rus' elites and customs) as a bulwark against Polish political and cultural influence.

By the time of Gediminas's death in 1342 his dynasty ruled over vast territories. The core lands of the Grand Duchy already consolidated in the thirteenth century were comprised of ethnic Lithuanian territories (although Žemaitija was generally independent until the early 1400s); the so-called 'Black (*Chernaia*) Rus', south of Kaunas and Vilnius, an area of mixed Baltic and East Slavic settlement with centres at Novogrudok, Grodno and Slonim. In the first third of the fourteenth century contiguous lands were added: the Brest-Drogichin area south-west of Black Rus'; the Turov-Pinsk principality, southeast of Black Rus'; the Minsk principality, north-east of Black Rus', and assorted small principalities. Outside this core acquired territories on vulnerable borders received charters of autonomy guaranteeing that the Grand Dukes 'will not introduce new, nor destroy the old'.[12] Polotsk (1307) and Vitebsk (1318–20) were the earliest to be so incorporated. The dynasty estab-

---

[10] Rowell (1994) and Ochmański (1967) for Lithuania's early history.
[11] Rowell (1994), pp. 59–73, 291–4; Kollmann (1990).
[12] Quoted from a fifteenth-century charter: *Akty, otn. k istori Zapadnoi Rossii*, 1, no. 127, p. 151.

lished a tradition of shared rule whereby a senior prince, who ruled from Vilnius, shared duties and authority with an almost equally important kinsman, one of whom defended the west against the Teutonic Order and the other expanded east and south into the Rus' lands. Gediminas's sons Algirdas (ruled 1345–77; the senior prince, who covered the eastern lands) and Kestutis (ruled 1342–82; western border) in the 1340s–70s represent an excellent example, as does the more stormy relationship of Jogaila (ruled 1377–1434; senior prince) and his cousin Vytautas (ruled 1382–1430) from the 1380s on.

In the 1320s Gediminid expansion turned to the Galician-Volhynian principality, perhaps the most direct heir to the Kiev Rus' legacy. Galicia stretched from the Carpathians to Volhynia, encompassing the headwaters of the Dniester and Prut rivers and east–west trade routes through Halyč and Peremysl. Volhynia stretched from Galicia to the Kiev principality; its major city, Volodymyr, sat near the western Bug river, a tributary of the Vistula leading to the Baltic, and also on an east–west trade route linking Kiev to Polish centres at Lublin, Cracow and points west.

Part of the grand principality of Kiev Rus' from the late tenth century, Galicia and Volhynia by the mid-twelfth century were independent of it, and by 1199 they had been politically united by Prince Roman Mstyslavych of Volhynia (d. 1205). Despite titular Mongol suzerainty and constant struggles with Poland and Hungary, the Romanovychi in the thirteenth century presided over great economic and political achievements. Roman Mstyslavych was offered a king's crown by the pope and his son, Danylo Romanovych (1205–64), actually received one between 1254 and 1256, but did not convert from Orthodoxy to Catholicism in the process. The step reflects both Galicia-Volhynia's immersion in central European political relations and symbolism, and its princes' stubborn independence. Prince Danylo sponsored urban settlement, founding the town of Lwów in 1256, inviting artisans from Germany and Poland and welcoming Armenian and Jewish settlement. Cultural activity continued apace, symbolised by the Galician-Volhynian chronicle, which continues the Kievan Primary Chronicle to 1289. Around 1303 Galicia had won a separate Orthodox metropolitanate in Halyč (which lasted briefly until 1308). With the demise of the Romanovych dynasty in 1323, Gediminas conquered Volhynia but Polish opposition prevented him from consolidating power immediately. With the assassination of the Polish-supported Volhynian ruler, Prince Iurii (Bolesław) of Mazovia in 1340, Galicia-Volhynia unravelled. The Grand Duchy sparred with the kingdom of Poland through the 1340s and when the conflicts were settled by 1352 (and ratified in 1387), Galicia and western parts of Volhynia (Kholm, Belz) were annexed to Poland; the rest of Volhynia was claimed by the Grand Duchy.

Straddling the Baltic and Volga-Caspian trade arenas was north-east Rus', a rich 'mesopotamia' in the upper Volga and Oka river basins, bounded in the north and north-west by Novgorod, on the west by the Grand Duchy, to the south by the steppe and to the east at the Sura and Vetluga rivers by the Volga Bulgars (nomads of the Black Sea steppe who had settled the middle Volga and controlled its trade since at least the tenth century). Furs gathered here as Mongol tribute or shipped by merchants from Moscow, Tver' and other centres joined those shipped by the Bulgars; at Sarai they joined the legendary 'silk road', moving east across the Caspian to Urgench at the foot of the Aral Sea and on to central Asia and India, or south to Iraq, Syria and Egypt, or west across the Black Sea steppe, or over the Black Sea to Caffa (ruled by the Genoese since 1266) or Sudak (Soldaia, Surozh) and on to Europe. The Dnieper, the region's quintessential trade route until late in the eleventh century, remained in recession. The north-east had flourished politically since the twelfth century, when Princes Iurii Dolgorukii (1149–57) and his son Andrei Bogoliubskii (1157–74) declared the area independent of Kiev and Prince Vsevolod Bol'shoe Gnezdo ('Big Nest') (1176–1212) declared it the 'grand principality of Vladimir'. Here too in the fourteenth century a process of sweeping weak principalities into a few dominant centres was taking place. Three or four centres – Moscow, Tver' and Riazan' (joined by Suzdal'-Nizhnii Novgorod in 1341) – styled themselves 'grand principalities' and vied for the symbolic role of 'grand prince of Vladimir', which by then had no indigenous dynasty but boasted lucrative lands.

Ambitious principalities in north-east Rus' concentrated on expanding their territory and maintaining good relations with the Kipchak khanate in the four-teenth century. Moscow was most aggressive, taking over weak principalities on key river routes and junctions by negotiation, inheritance, purchase or con-quest. Its dynasty was founded by Prince Daniil Aleksandrovich (d. 1303), youngest son of Alexander Nevskii (1252–63). He was followed by his sons Iurii (d. 1325) and Ivan I Kalita ('Moneybag') (d. 1340). Historians have argued that Moscow's geographical position, within reach of river routes to the Black, Caspian and Baltic Seas, was fundamental to its historic rise.[13] But Moscow was not endowed with that geographical flexibility by birthright; its grand princes and boyars won it by concerted territorial expansion. Thus, V.O. Kliuchevskii's famous dictum that Moscow's early rulers were nonentities, as alike as 'two drops of water', should be discounted.[14] If the geographical factor played a crucial role in the rise of a north-east Rus' principality to prominence, it should have aided Tver'. This latter's position on the upper Volga was superb: at the intersection of land and water routes to Novgorod and the Grand Duchy and thus to the Baltic, Tver' was dominant in north-east Rus' by the end of the

[13] Kliuchevskii (1956–7), II, lect. 21; Tikhomirov (1952).   [14] Kliuchevskii (1956–7), II, lect. 22, p. 49.

thirteenth century. Ruled from mid century by the dynasty of Prince Iaroslav Iaroslavich (grand prince of Vladimir 1263–71), younger brother of Alexander Nevskii, it quickly grew into a flourishing trade and cultural centre. Prince Iaroslav's sons Sviatoslav (1271–85) and Mikhail (1285–1318) succeeded him in Tver'; Mikhail became grand prince of Vladimir in 1304. From then to 1318 and from 1322 to 1327 Tver' princes held the title. Although it did not expand significantly, Tver' consistently worked to subordinate Novgorod to its authority and curtail Moscow's ambitions.

But the success of Tver' was also its downfall; the Sarai khans, wary of its potential to ally against it with the Teutonic Order or the Grand Duchy, three times executed princes of Tver' at their court in Sarai, in 1318 (Mikhail Iaroslavich), 1325 (his son Dmitrii) and 1339 (Aleksandr Mikhailovich and his son Fedor). The Kipchak khanate eventually shifted its preference towards Moscow, awarding it exclusively the grand prince's title in 1331, after Moscow had aided the Tatars in sacking Tver', hindering but not destroying the ambitious principality's aspirations for regional power. The Moscow Daniilovich dynasty faced persistent challenges for the title not only from Tver' but also from Suzdal'-Nizhnii Novgorod. Under Grand Prince Dmitrii Konstantinovich (ruled 1365–83) and Archbishop Dionisii of Suzdal' (1374–85), this ambitious principality flourished culturally and politically; it won the title of grand prince of Vladimir briefly in the early 1360s, but in the face of internal dissension was forced to yield to Muscovite pressure. Thus, once winning it, Moscow never significantly lost the title of grand prince of Vladimir.

It is often said that ecclesiastical politics aided Moscow's rise,[15] in as much as metropolitans were resident in Moscow by the late 1320s. But as a rule four-teenth-century metropolitans, like the patriarchs of Constantinople who appointed them, were guided by a vision of the Rus' lands as a single united spiritual flock, and tried not to favour one political contender over another in the power struggles of the century.[16] Thus the metropolitans resident in Moscow did not necessarily support Moscow's interests, as later hagiography and chronicles suggest. The see of the metropolitan of 'Kiev and all-Rus'' had moved from Kiev to Vladimir only in 1299; in 1325 Metropolitan Peter (1308–26) took up residence in Moscow where he died in the following year. He did not officially transfer the see to Moscow, because, by Orthodox tradi-tion, sees were located in the political centres of a realm, which in 1325 was either Vladimir or Tver'. But Moscow became the see as it took over the grand-princely status, and in the second half of the century Moscow pro-ceeded to embellish the cult of Peter accordingly. Meanwhile the Grand

---

[15] Ibid., lect. 21.   [16] Meyendorff (1980); Borisov (1986); Rowell (1994), ch. 6.

Duchy actively campaigned throughout the century for its own metropolitan see as a legitimising symbol. Galicia's see in the lands of the Catholic kingdom of Poland was renewed in 1371, while the Grand Duchy received a metropolitanate of Lithuania in Novogrudok in 1317. But with Constantinople endeavouring to restore the unity of the 'Kiev and all-Rus'' see whenever possible, this see waxed and waned, despite repeated, and sometimes briefly successful, requests from the Grand Dukes for its renewal. Not until the mid-fifteenth century did the Grand Duchy receive a permanent see, in response to Moscow's break with the Orthodox Church over the proposed union of Florence–Ferrara (1438–9).

Beginning in 1359 the patterns of trade and geo-politics described above were shaken by bitter struggles for succession in the Kipchak khanate. By the first third of the fifteenth century the struggles had splintered the Kipchak realm into khanates at Kazan', the Crimea, on the lower Volga (called the Great Horde) and in western Siberia. Stepping into the vacuum of power were Novgorod, Moscow, the Grand Duchy, Tver', Riazan', and Suzdal'-Nizhnii Novgorod, as well as ambitious Tatar leaders, some of whom (Mamai, Timur or Tamerlane) lacked the Chingisid legitimacy to become khans. In the 1360s and 1370s Mamai acquired significant power from his base on the right bank of the Volga, even while rival claimants battled in Sarai.

Each of the major contenders turned the Kipchak khanate's disarray to political and territorial advantage. Novgorod was particularly active. Its archbishop won judicial autonomy from the metropolitan despite bitter opposition by the metropolitans and grand princes of Moscow. Novgorod also embarked from the 1360s to 1409 on a campaign of armed raids on upper and middle Volga trading towns. These raids were intended to discourage towns in the upper Volga, Dvina and Kama river basins, such as Kostroma and Viatka, from yielding to Muscovite political pressure.[17] Taking advantage of disarray in the Bulgar as well as in the Kipchak khanates, they also aimed to win for Novgorod the right to trade in Nizhnii Novgorod, Bulgar, Sarai, Astrakhan and other Volga ports. The raids failed in the latter goal but had some success in the former: Moscow was forced to relinquish control in the Dvina lands after an abortive take over in the late 1390s. But Moscow made other territorial gains in the north: it had collected taxes from Ustiug and Vychegda Perm since 1333; by 1367 Moscow had won from Novgorod the right to collect tax in Perm' Velikaia on the upper Kama as well as in the Pechora and Mezen' river areas (although that right remained an object of contention with Novgorod into the fifteenth century).[18] It should be understood that what was at stake was tax-collecting authority, not political incorporation; both the Novgorodian and

[17] Martin (1975).   [18] Martin (1983).

Muscovite presence here remained superficial until the end of the fifteenth century. In 1379 the subsequently venerated St Stefan of Perm' converted the Vychegda Permians to Christianity; monastic colonisation into the Vologda area intensified from the 1390s. Moscow also humbled the Suzdal'-Nizhnii Novgorod grand principality, first forging an alliance in 1367, binding it with the marriage of Grand Prince Dmitrii Donskoi of Moscow (1359–89) to Prince Dmitrii Konstantinovich's daughter Evdokiia, and ultimately subordinating Nizhnii Novgorod in 1392.

Meanwhile, as the Kipchak khanate fell into disarray, the Grand Duchy was also enjoying a spectacular rise to regional power. After a brief era in which the realm was divided among Gediminas's seven sons (1342–45), two of the most forceful seized power to rule jointly: Algirdas (1345–77) taking the east and Kestutis (1345–82) the west. In addition to Volhynia, by 1363 Algirdas won the Kiev and Pereiaslav principalities and Podilia (south of Galicia and Volhynia; it was taken over by Poland by 1430) and in the 1370s several small principalities of the Chernihiv lands (but not the upper Oka area hotly contested with Moscow and Riazan'). To the north-east of Polotsk, Algirdas won Toropets by 1355. From the 1360s to 1380 the Grand Duchy allied with the grand principality of Tver' to counter Moscow's rising strength; this coalition laid siege to Moscow three times – to no avail – from 1368 to 1372. At Algirdas's death in 1377, quarrels over succession set in motion momentous events. Algirdas's son and successor, Jogaila, was initially opposed by his uncle Kestutis (d. 1382) and subsequently by Kestutis's son Vytautas, and also by his own half-brother, Andrei of Polotsk. Andrei turned to Moscow for aid. Jogaila responded by mounting an anti-Moscow coalition including Riazan', the Tatar leader Mamai, Tver' and the Livonian Order; at the time, Mamai regarded Moscow as an obstacle in his designs to re-establish Mongol authority in north-east Rus' (starting in the late fourteenth century, for example, Moscow frequently took advantage of Sarai's disarray to withhold tribute). Moscow, aided by local principalities including Suzdal'-Nizhnii Novgorod, Iaroslavl', Kostroma and Beloozero, defeated Mamai and his coalition at the battle of Kulikovo Field in 1380. In the next year Mamai was crushed by Tokhtamysh, a Chingisid prince patronised by the upstart non-Chingisid ruler of central Asia, Timur. For a decade thereafter Tokhtamysh managed to exert some control over north-east Rus'; he sacked Moscow and Riazan' in 1382, setting back temporarily Moscow's rise to regional power. Meanwhile, Jogaila in the Grand Duchy, politically isolated by the 1380 defeat and beleaguered by domestic opposition, considered a marriage and *rapprochement* with Moscow, but ultimately turned to Poland. In 1385 in the Union of Krevo he accepted the crown of Poland, married Jadwiga, heiress to the throne, and promised to christianise his realm and unite it with Poland dynastically. Although the step definitively set the

Grand Duchy on a path of cultural and political integration with Catholic Poland, the road started out rocky. Jogaila faced the opposition both of Andrei of Polotsk (who was quickly defeated), and of Kestutis and Vytautas, who fought tenaciously and successfully for maximum Lithuanian autonomy in its relationship with Poland.

In 1391 Vytautas neutralised Moscow by marrying his daughter Sofiia to Grand Prince Vasilii I Dmitrievich of Moscow (1389–1425). This gave him breathing space to vie with Jogaila; several times he allied with the Teutonic and Livonian Orders to force concessions, by 1399 winning from Jogaila the concession of the title of 'Grand Duke of Lithuania' (even while Jogaila reserved for himself the senior Grand Duke's dignity).[19] Meanwhile Vytautas tried to take over Timur's role as regional kingmaker. Allying with Tokhtamysh, who had fallen out with Timur, Vytautas mounted a campaign against Tokhtamysh's rivals in the Great Horde on the lower Volga. But, defeated on the Vorskla river in 1399, Vytautas was forced to rein in his ambitions in the east but continued to contest the terms of union with Poland. He nevertheless succeeded in consolidating authority over the principality of Smolensk by 1404, which had been *de facto* subordinate to the Grand Duchy since the early 1340s. Vytautas also made war on Novgorod and Pskov. After he and Jogaila defeated the Orders at Grunwald in 1410, Vytautas negotiated the 1413 Union of Horodło, in which Jogaila and the Polish nobility recognised the Grand Duchy's right to have its own ruler and the necessity of both sides consulting in the selection of new kings and Grand Dukes. This was a clear victory for Vytautas. But the union was also affirmed by provisions that more broadly distributed Polish noble privileges among the Catholic Lithuanian elite. Until his death in 1430 Vytautas was undisputedly the major player in east European politics; he was even offered a king's crown by the Holy Roman Emperor (although was prevented from receiving it by opposition from Poland and the Teutonic Order).

The denouement of the disarray in the Kipchak khanate worked to Moscow's favour as well as that of the Grand Duchy by the turn of the fifteenth century. Tokhtamysh's erstwhile patron, Timur, defeated him after Vytautas's failure to do so in 1399; Timur destroyed Sarai and any possibility of restoring the Kipchak khanate's unity and strength. Timur redirected trade away from the Volga–Caspian nexus to the Black Sea, opening up opportunity for Moscow and the Grand Duchy directly to trade with the Italian colonies (Sudak was in Genoese control from 1365). Although Timur's appointee in the lower Volga, Edigei, claimed authority over the north-east, and even sacked Moscow in 1408, and although in the subsequent century the lower Volga

---

[19] Presniakov (1938–9), II, fasc. 1, ch. 9; Kolankowski (1930).

'Great Horde' frequently claimed authority over north-east Rus', the fiscal and political power of the Mongols in the Rus' lands was broken by the turn of the century. Moscow was poised to take regional authority in the east. A new political equilibrium balanced between Vilnius and Moscow had replaced the nominal sovereignty of the Kipchak khanate.

SOCIETIES HEIR TO KIEV RUS'

Because the harsh climate of the Rus' lands limited productivity and population growth, climate is an important factor in assessing administration, society and economy. Three fundamental features shaped the physical environment. The first is northern latitude. Kiev lies just above 50° north and Moscow close to 56°, farther north than London (at 51° 30') and all major American and Canadian cities save those of Alaska. Among major cities in the British Isles, Edinburgh and Glasgow are marginally more northern than Moscow, but their climates are moderated by ocean currents. Cold Arctic air sweeps down from the north unobstructed by any natural barriers in these essentially flat lands, which are part of the European plain extending to the Urals. The third formative feature is lakes and rivers that, with portages, form an intricate transportation network from the Baltic to the Black and Caspian Seas. Major north or south-flowing rivers are the Dniester, Bug, Dnieper, Don, middle and lower Volga, northern Dvina and Kama rivers; east- or west-flowing waterways include the Niemen and western Dvina, upper Volga and Oka rivers. Soils and vegetation proceed in horizontal bands of increasing fertility from north to south. Novgorod and its lands include some Arctic tundra but by and large lie in the *taiga*, or coniferous forest. Spruce, pine and birch predominate. Soils here are podzolic, rich in humus but leached of their iron and minerals and poorly drained. Peat bogs and marshes are common. In the area of Belarus' and Muscovy and north almost to Novgorod lies the zone of mixed evergreen and deciduous vegetation where white oaks and spruce predominate. South of Moscow starts a narrow belt of broad-leaf deciduous trees. Soils range from podzolic to grey-brown forest earths, more fertile and less acidic than the *taiga*, but still marshy. Farther south, covering the modern Ukrainian lands, begin the wooded steppe and then the steppe, with strips of successively richer black earth soil. Vegetation ranges from deciduous trees to grassland, easily cleared for farming.

Marginal differences in climate and precipitation historically created significant divergences in agricultural potential between the Kievan heartland and north-east Rus'. Moscow's climate is damper, cooler and more cloudy than Kiev's; snow remains on the ground five months here to Kiev's two and a half, yielding boggy and leached-out soil and a brief growing season (five months to Kiev's six or more and to western Europe's eight or nine). While most European grains, vegetables and animals can be cultivated in Kiev, the northeast Rus' lands are limited to hardy crops of rye, barley, oats and flax.

From the mid-nineteenth century scholars and publicists in Russia began to offer an alternate vision to the theory of an unbroken and exclusive historical continuity from Kiev to Moscow espoused by Muscovite ideologues from at least the sixteenth century and adopted by most Russian historians. Pointing to Kiev Rus' active international trade and cultural contacts and to its pluralistic political system of prince, retinue and urban communes, scholars have postulated that these various traditions descended separately to various heirs of Kiev. N. I. Kostomarov postulated that Kiev Rus' bequeathed two heritages – democratic, embodied in the Ukrainian path of development – and autocratic, embodied by Great Russia (Muscovy). Historians and publicists, notably Alexander Herzen, meanwhile depicted Novgorod as heir to Kiev's communal republican tradition.[20] By the modern day a threefold cliché has become current: that from Kiev Rus' descended three traditions – autocracy (Russia), aristocracy (Galicia-Volhynia, Ukraine) and democracy (Novgorod). But one should use such terms warily; in no case did the medieval versions of these traditions replicate their modern embodiments.

GALICIA AND VOLHYNIA

The principalities of Galicia and Volhynia did nurture a strong aristocracy and monarchy, stemming from their frequent interaction with the Polish and Hungarian kingdoms, the papacy and the Holy Roman Empire (as noted above, Prince Roman Mstyslavych was offered a crown and Prince Danylo received one). Galicia's boyars, inspired by their heritage (they were purported to have descended not, as was usual in the Kiev Rus' lands, from the prince's retinue, but from the indigenous elite) and by their wealth from Galicia's salt trade, exercised real power. Numerous times – the 1180s–90s, 1205–38, the 1340s – Galicia's boyars took power into their own hands, even electing one of their own as ruler in 1213 and 1340. But strong Romanovychi by and large maintained political equilibrium in the realm, and the aristocratic element of this part of the Kievan triad did not blossom into full parliamentary government until after Galicia, and later Volhynia, were acculturated into the kingdom of Poland.

In Galicia aristocratic development was accelerated under Polish rule after

---

[20] Kliuchevskii (1956–7), I–II; Solov'ev (1959–62), I–II; Kostomarov (1903–6),I, v; Herzen is cited by Birnbaum (1981), p. 6. Historiography on Novgorod: Ianin (1962), pp. 3–13.

1340, even though Galicia was initially allowed autonomy in Poland as the 'kingdom of Rus''. The first Catholic archdiocese was founded in Lviv in 1375, followed by active monastic colonisation; Polish kings granted land to Catholic noblemen from Poland, the Germanies, the Czech lands and Hungary and welcomed large numbers of German townsmen. Urban privileges (under Magdeburg law) for the Catholic urban populations were introduced in Lviv in 1356, in Kamianets-Podilskyi in 1374, and gradually spread through Galicia. Many Galician boyars adopted Catholicism. By the mid-fifteenth century Galicia was reorganised as a province in the Polish kingdom, and Latin replaced East Slavic as the official language. Galicia developed into a dynamic amalgam of Orthodox culture and European traditions of political pluralism, and later provided intellectual leadership for the emergence of Ukrainian national consciousness from the late sixteenth century onwards.

NOVGOROD AND PSKOV

Modern Russian social and political thought accords Novgorod a special place. It is held up as a bastion of urban democracy, as proof that Russians possess the innate ability to govern themselves and thus as demonstration that autocracy is not inevitable in Russian history.[21] Clearly tendentious, this scheme has inspired historians to look carefully at Novgorod; their work is aided by a remarkable array of extant records. Sources already mentioned are Novgorod's chronicles, treaties with Baltic trading partners and with grand princes of Tver' or Moscow, the Novgorod Judicial Charter and Hansa records. Sources are sparse on the city's vast rural hinterland, but peasant obligations have been extrapolated from Muscovite cadastral books of the late fifteenth century. Most unusual are the findings of archaeology: several hundred birchbark documents that reveal day-to-day activities; seals that trace the evolution of political offices; excavations that expose settlement patterns and the residue of production and consumption.[22]

Socially, Novgorod's populace was divided into four or five distinct groups.[23] The elite was the boyar families – about fifty by the fifteenth century – who were large landholders, financiers and holders of an almost exclusive monopoly on the city's offices. Unlike their eponymous Moscow counterparts, Novgorod's boyars played no military role. Below them in social status, although often equal in wealth, were the *zhit'i liudi*, also wealthy landholders. Below them were the merchants, who probably did not have guild associations

---

[21] Debates on Novgorod as a democracy or oligarchy: Ianin (1962); Birnbaum (1981); Langer (1974).
[22] Thompson (1967); *Novgorodskie gramoty na bereste*, ed. Artsikhovskii; Ianin (1970).
[23] Kliuchevskii (1956–7), II, lects. 23–4; Bernadskii (1961), ch. 5.

like their western counterparts. The rest of the urban populace – artisans and workers – paid taxes; in that role they were paralleled by the peasants of the hinterland.

The principle of assembly structured Novgorodian politics, exemplified not only in the town assembly *(veche)* but in successive layers of lesser assemblies that oversaw daily governance. The Volkhov river divided the town between the Sophia side (home of the archbishop) and the market side (place of wharves and the *veche* meeting house), but its political division was more complex. On the Sophia Cathedral side were three boroughs *(kontsy)*: the Zagorodskii and Liudin, or Goncharskii, and Nerevskii boroughs; on the market side, the Plotnitskii and Slavenskii boroughs. Within a borough, each major street constituted a political entity, with its own assembly of freemen that selected a local boyar as its representative to the *veche*.

By the fourteenth century the town assembly may have been limited to the elite landholding strata and merchants, excluding the commoners. It chose the mayor *(posadnik)* for an annual term. The defeated borough representatives, as well as the thousandman *(tysiatskii)* and past mayors and thousandmen, enjoyed lifetime rights to sit on the council of lords *(sovet gospod)*, thereby assuring that boyar interests dominated the city's administration and the town assembly. This latter met on an irregular basis and had nominal authority to legislate, declare war and settle peace, choose and dismiss the prince who ran the city's military defences, and authorise similar important tasks.

Having rejected direct rule by Kievan grand princes in 1136, Novgorod by the early fourteenth century acknowledged the titular sovereignty of one of the grand princes of north-east Rus', generally favouring Tver' over Moscow. The grand prince was represented only by his lieutenant *(namestnik)*, who collected carefully limited judicial and customs fees and taxes in the city and selected environs and rendered justice in the criminal court, under the oversight of the mayor. By treaty the grand prince could not live in the city, nor acquire Novgorodian land for himself, his family or retinue, nor could he distribute the city's land without the mayor's permission, participate in domestic municipal politics or replace city officials at will. The relationship was less one of sovereign and vassal than one of equal foreign powers.[24] At the same time, the city contracted with hired princes to provide military defence with their retinues and to lead the urban militia. In the fourteenth century the city frequently chose such princes from the Gediminid dynasty to counterbalance Moscow.

With the grand prince held at bay and the hired prince similarly estranged from political life, other institutions took over governing roles. The office of mayor began as a princely appointment, but by the fourteenth century it had

[24] Bernadskii (1961), pp. 15–35.

power to share criminal court with the grand prince's lieutenant and to ride herd over him as well as to oversee the town assembly. The thousandman also grew out of the princely administration; originally the military commander of the city's ten 'hundred' units, by the fourteenth century the thousandman had become the chief judicial authority for the merchants, head of the Merchants' Hundred (*Ivanovskoe sto*) at St John's Church and overseer of trade and police affairs in the town. A third political authority was the archbishop, elected by the town council; his see at Holy Sophia Cathedral stood as the political symbol of the city. He represented the city in foreign affairs; ran a court for church affairs, church people, and property disputes; oversaw the regulation of weights and measures; affirmed all deeds of land transfer and chaired the council of lords. By the fourteenth century the archbishop was becoming the greatest landholder in the Novgorod territories, head of a secular administration of majordomos, bailiffs and retinues of fighting men. As the archbishop's wealth and power grew, the city's boyar families counterbalanced him by cultivating urban monasteries. Each borough had a flagship monastery, from among the five hegumens of which a 'Novgorod archimandrite' was selected, significantly, by the town assembly, not the archbishop.

Novgorod politics in the fourteenth century were as stormy as they had been in previous centuries. The city's geographical divisions tended to channel class tensions into factional strife; streets and boroughs banded together in alliances that cut across class lines. Violent conflicts grew out of rivalries between boyar families or popular protests over high taxes and economic hardship. Quiescent in normal times, in times of conflict the town council became the vehicle for constitutionally sanctioned change. Over the fourteenth century the city government evolved in the direction of oligarchy: at mid century the council of lords instituted a collective mayoralty, with six mayors (two from the Slavenskii borough and one from each of the others, thus balancing representation from each side of the river).[25] But at least in the fourteenth century the city's political system remained sufficiently responsive to popular needs to avoid the extreme of oligarchy and to govern effectively.

Novgorod in the fourteenth century ruled over a hinterland whose basic outlines had been established by the mid-thirteenth century. Most of the region was ruled by the five urban boroughs and thus were called in later Muscovite sources the 'fifths' (*piatiny*). Some of the hinterland was administered directly by the city as 'commune' (*volost'*) lands; these included the Dvina lands, the Ter Littoral of the Kola peninsula, and several key border towns. Novgorod's hinterland was sparsely populated by East Slavs, Finno-Ugrians and Siberian natives; the East Slavs established some farming, but all depended

---

[25] Ianin (1962), chs. 5–6.

primarily on forest exploitation and hunting, or reindeer herding in the very far north. In the fourteenth century peasants paid taxes to the city (*dan'*) and to Novgorod's grand prince (*chernyi bor*) and performed various services for city and princely officials. Landlords also demanded services and taxes, rarely assessed in money or labour, more often in furs, foods or grain, or in natural resources such as iron or wax where available. Much of the land was privately owned, by the archbishop or other religious establishments, by the city itself, or by secular landholders. Generally landlords acted as absentee owners; demesne land was rare, as was slavery. Peasants were free to move, although several categories of debt dependence are cited.

The Baltic trade made Novgorod wealthy: the city exported fur (squirrel, beaver, rabbit, luxury furs), wax, honey, leather and pig iron; it was constrained by the Hansa and Livonian towns from exporting finished goods. It imported textiles, generally Flemish in this century, ranging from the very best quality to cloth affordable to urban artisans; also salt, precious metals, wines, weapons, even salted herring and grain in famine years. While the travelling Novgorodian merchant was the stuff of legends beloved by the city, by the fourteenth century Novgorodian merchants generally did not venture abroad. The Hansa handled foreign trade almost exclusively. Novgorod was one of four *Kontore*, or depot points, in the Hansa;[26] the group of German merchants who constituted the *Kontor* lived in a self-governing neighbourhood called Peterhof on the market side. The volume of trade was large. In 1311, for example, Pskov seized 50,000 furs of German merchants; in 1336–7, 160 merchants were recorded in Novgorod; three ships sailing from Riga in 1405 carried 450,000 pelts, 1,435 pounds of wax and over 1,000 pounds of linen, most from the Novgorod trade. In sum, Novgorod in the fourteenth century was a thriving urban republic similar in political structure and economic activity to its counterparts in northern Europe and Italy. Neither a full-blown oligarchy nor a popular democracy, Novgorod was unprecedented in the Rus' lands for its cultural diversity, active economy and relative personal freedom.

Virtually politically independent of Novgorod by the second half of the thirteenth century, Pskov struggled in the fourteenth and into the fifteenth century to gain ecclesiastical autonomy from Novgorod, and relied heavily on the Grand Duchy for political protection against Novgorod and the Teutonic Order. Its government mirrored Novgorod's: six boroughs, each with an assembly, elected elite men for a council of lords and a collective mayoralty of one or two mayors. Its hired princes came almost exclusively from the Grand Duchy from the late thirteenth century onwards. Pskov differed from Novgorod chiefly in its seeming tranquillity; far fewer urban uprisings are

[26] Dollinger (1970).

recorded for Pskov than for turbulent Novgorod, perhaps because the city's smaller scale made consensus more achievable among the boyar factions. Because of its proximity to the Livonian Order, Pskov gave greater authority to its hired prince, mandating that he live in the city and granting him broader administrative and judicial authority than his Novgorod counterpart enjoyed, although here too he was overseen by the mayor and other city officials. Like Novgorod, Pskov in the fourteenth century developed a thriving cultural life, architectural style and vibrant school of icon painting.

THE GRAND DUCHY OF LITHUANIA

One might argue that the Grand Duchy's political customs were a more faithful continuation of Kiev Rus' traditions, even though it had never been a part of the Rus' state. But the clans of Lithuania demonstrated similar political traditions to those of the rulers of Kiev, as suggested above. These were loosely, centrally ruled patrimonial principalities, based on clan organisation and the integration of landed and urban elites into consultative governance.[27] The Lithuanian Grand Duke ruled with the advice of a council of the leading clans of the realm (*consiliarii*), analogous to Kievan princes' retinues or the Moscow grand prince's boyars. The scale of government was personal and face-to-face; Gediminas had twenty such advisers in 1324, for example.[28] Not until the fifteenth century with growth and Polish influence did the Grand Duke's counsellors become a more formalised institution with constitutional rights (guaranteed by charter from 1492 to 1529). The Grand Dukes also, far more than Muscovite princes, tolerated local elites and local autonomies, much as medieval European kings made their peace with privileged groups, towns and corporations. Territories outside the core lands of the Grand Duchy were virtually independent principalities: generally the dynasty placed one of its members in an occupied principality and allowed him to found a hereditary dynasty. Such local princes were obliged to render taxes and military service and to consult with the Grand Duke, but otherwise they respected local traditions. Local elites were not dispossessed, local officials were appointed from among them and they were included in the prince's councils. The East Slavic language and legal traditions were maintained, as were Kievan-era administrative divisions. Even when, in the 1390s, most princely dynasties were replaced with centrally appointed governors from ethnic Lithuanian families, regional autonomies were not fully abolished. Fifteenth-century political tensions (in the 1430s, 1447, 1492) yielded affirmations of local autonomies and noble privileges.

---

[27] On political traditions and governance, Rowell (1994), p. 294; Kolankowski (1930); Khoroshkevich (1982); Bardach (1970). [28] Rowell (1994), pp. 202, 61–2.

Thus the Grand Duchy featured a balance between ruling dynasty and social interest groups.

Its elite was composed of landholders who rendered service to the Grand Duke, ranging from princes, mainly of the Gediminid dynasty and a few Riurikides, to two landed ranks, the boyars and the *zemiane*, distinguished primarily by degree of landed wealth. Some members of these groups served as vassals of leading princes and other magnates, receiving land for service on conditional tenure. The urban populace, like the landed elites, performed military service, paid taxes and could own land outside their cities; their primary occupations, however, were trade and artisan work. Urban freedoms spread to towns in the Grand Duchy after the Union of Krevo – Vilnius (1387), Brest (1390), Grodno (1391), Drogichin (1429), Bel'sk (1430), Lutsk (1432) and Kiev, Volodymyr in Volhynia, Polotsk and Minsk (second half of the fifteenth century). Rural life continued the structures and occupations of the Kiev Rus' period. Agriculture continued to be the basis of the economy, augmented by apiculture, animal husbandry, hunting, fishing and forest exploitation. By the middle of the fourteenth century, expansion of cultivated land is evident, suggesting economic regeneration and population expansion. Peasants were obliged to pay tax (*dan'*) to the Grand Duke (assessed according to unit of land cultivated, and paid in cash, fur or honey), upkeep for his administrators, and labour services such as cartage and construction. They also paid taxes to landlords but were not subject to labour obligations (*barshchina*). Peasants were not limited in their mobility in the fourteenth century, but judging by the persistence of judicial regulations borrowed from the Russian law in Grand Duchy law codes, slavery continued to be a source of labour for landlords.

NORTH-EAST RUS'

North-east Rus' best preserved the Kievan principle of strong central, dynastic princely rule; its grand princes claimed all power and faced few corporate entities, such as urban or landed elites, which they had to accommodate (in contrast to the Grand Dukes of Lithuania). Thus it is often called an autocracy, and indeed the claim became part of Moscow's official title, in the late sixteenth century. But the term should be used with caution: Muscovite 'autocracy' by no means connoted power as total or absolute as modern usages imply. Muscovite rulers were constrained by many factors: custom, ideology and political realities, the most significant circumstances of the latter being the paucity of population and the exactions of the Kipchak khanate. The majority of the population consisted of free peasants, living in hamlets of two to three households of generally two or three adult males, plus women and children. They farmed with techniques that varied with local conditions:

slash/burn where land was plentiful or newly cleared, enclosed fields where settlement was denser and more established. Peasants sowed winter rye or barley and spring oats, supplementing their diet with fish, some meat (game, pigs, chickens, cattle), honey, berries, nuts, mushrooms, peas, turnips and other root vegetables. Peasants belonged to communes that joined together numerous villages and hamlets. Peasants farmed their fields and household gardens as individual families but yielded to communal authority over such resources as meadows, forest, ponds, rivers and the settling of abandoned land; communal officers also liaised with princely officials. There were very few towns, most of which were small fortified princely encampments; since most artisan work was done in villages, towns' trade significance was limited. The taxpaying residents of towns formed a commune (*posad*) analogous to that of the countryside.

In the realm of governance princes carved out a modest sphere: exploitation of resources, execution of high justice, and military expansion and defence.[29] They accomplished these goals through circuit officials such as *dan'shchiki*, who collected the Mongol tribute (*vykhod*) and the princely tax (*dan'*), or rendered justice. Other men managed monopolies (*puti*) on princely privileges such as forests, horse trading, falconry, trapping, brewing and victualing. Taxpayers were also responsible for other princely exactions, paid in grain or occasionally cash, such as the provision (*korm*) of the resident and circuit officials, their staffs and horses; provision of grain and riders for the postal system (*iam*); provision of men for militia service (*pososhnaia sluzhba*); miscellaneous cartage, field and artisan services; fortifications work and building projects; customs levies on the transport and sale of goods (*myt, tamga*). Communes and private holdings could arrange to pay a lump sum (*obrok*) for all these fees.

In the late fourteenth century, Moscow (evidence is lacking for other principalities) created a settled system of tax collection, plus judiciary and military and civil administration, through vicegerents and district administrators (*namestniki* and *volosteli*), one-year administrative appointees. Vicegerents were resident in towns, while district administrators were subordinate to them in the rural hinterland. At the end of the fourteenth century only fifteen vicegerents and about a hundred district administrators existed; appointees were compensated by upkeep provided by the community (the 'feeding', or *kormlenie*, system). The power of all these officials, and hence of the prince, however, was limited by the parcelling of authority in fourteenth-century north-east Rus'.

---

[29] On governance, landlords and dependent relations, see Howes (1967); Veselovskii (1926), (1936) and (1947); Kashtanov (1982) and (1988); Eck (1933); Pavlov-Sil'vanskii (1988); Gorskii (1982); Blum (1961).

Immunities from princely administration were widely distributed, even in towns. North-east Rus' towns were not of the 'European type' – oases of municipal sovereignty, citizenship and personal freedom. Rather they were 'oriental', proprietary conglomerates of merchant and artisan neighbourhoods that each paid taxes and services to its owner. The countryside was the same. Princes used immunities – decentralisation of sovereignty, in essence – to maintain local stability, maximise the exploitation of resources and, most importantly, to support and attract a landed elite who rendered military service.

As a rule, then, private land was immune from the prince's administration and most taxation. Landlords regarded their property as a form of 'feeding', taking little direct role in its exploitation unless poverty drove them to it.[30] What small demesne they carved out was farmed and administered by slave labour. Landlords let out the rest of their holdings on terms ranging from rental to sharecropping to indentured servitude and slavery. They demanded taxes in cash or kind, labour services and customs tolls analogous to the burden exacted by princes; their peasants did not, however, participate in the militia levy. Landlords' exactions were constrained only by the willingness of the free peasantry to accept their terms – no small constraint, given the scarcity of manpower and the willingness of other landlords (and free communes also) to offer advantageous terms, such as exemptions from payments for several years and loans of equipment, money or seed.

Thus, there was a tension between peasants' freedom of mobility and their likely dependency on a lord. The causes of personal dependence are many: for some, it was advantageous terms; for others, dependency resulted when princes awarded their communes to a landlord; for yet others, a landlord could offer emergency protection if they had suffered natural disaster. The same goes for slaves, clients and indentured servants: some were renters who failed to fulfil their obligations, others were prisoners of war and still others sold themselves voluntarily into slavery in desperate search for economic stability. Bonds of personal dependency also structured society above the landlord–peasant relationship. Landholders faced with the task of administering and working their lands, and often of maintaining military retinues, found the manpower for these needs not only by renting land or bestowing it on slaves, but also by giving it to retainers, sometimes outright in allodial tenure (*votchina*), but often conditionally (as *sluzhnie* lands). Recipients ranged from free men to clients to slaves, and are accordingly referred to variously as a lord's 'people' (*liudi*), servants (*slugi*), clients (*zakladniki*), domestics (*cheliad'*) and so on. Such men served variously as cavalrymen and equerries in the lord's retinue, his counsellors, majordomos and bailiffs, judges and tax collectors on his lands, leaders of

---

[30] Veselovskii (1936), p. 142.

the hunt, blacksmiths and other specialised craftsmen. Often monasteries, receiving land as a gift, returned it to the original owners under conditional tenure. Lay lords who received large grants replicated the process: they rented some out and bestowed some on estate managers, artisans and cavalrymen.

Governance was essentially carried out through such bonds of dependency. The administrative network of vicegerents, district administrators and *putnye* boyars, for example, was structured by personal dependency to the prince. Similarly, the army was an occasional assemblage of the personal retinues of princes and their men. The grand prince mustered a retinue of courtiers (*dvoriane*) and free landed cavalrymen called 'boyars' sons' (*deti boiarskie*); his boyars contributed their own retinues, as did his kinsmen and allies and their boyars. The hierarchs of the Church, metropolitans and bishops also sent their troops. It was primarily a cavalry army, although regional militias mustered from among the taxable peasants and city people provided infantry and siege defence forces.

The relations of princes and their most eminent advisers and servitors, their boyars, sharply illustrate the privatisation of political relations in north-east Rus'. Elites were small: in Moscow about ten boyar clans served at any one time and the number of boyars fluctuated from six to eleven depending on family mortality and political circumstances.[31] They, the grand-princely family, the metropolitan and other Church hierarchs, some merchants, all lived in a Kremlin fortification only two-thirds its present size. Military servitors joined a prince or left his service by free choice; princely treaties specifically protected their mobility: 'And our servitors and boyars have free choice between us.'[32] They were free to acquire land in various principalities, being required only to pay taxes and render emergency military service to the local prince, but not to serve him personally. Similarly, they did not suffer confiscation of lands located in their lord's principality should they transfer loyalty to another prince. Narrative sources describing rulers and their boyars also depict a personalised politics. Such texts drew on the standard *topoi* of Christian rulership from Byzantium and Kiev Rus': rulers were placed on the earth by God, authority was God-given and the proper exercise of authority was governed by God's rules. Rather than imbuing the prince with quasi-divine status, as later Muscovite texts did, chronicles put forward an image of a human, humble and pious ruler. His task was primarily moral: to lead his people to salvation by pious example, to give charity to the poor, beneficence to the Church, loyalty to his men. The 1353 will of Grand Prince Semën Ivanovich of Moscow instructed his heirs as follows: 'and you should not heed evil men and if anyone tries to breed discord among you, you should heed our father, Bishop Aleksii,

---

[31] Kollmann (1987), chs. 1–3 and tables 1–4, 6.   [32] *DDG*, no. 2, p. 13 (1347–54).

as well as the old boyars who wished our father and us well'. Dmitrii Donskoi wrote in 1389: 'And, my sons, those of my boyars who take to serving my princess, care for them as one man.'[33] Politics turned on personal, family and moral relationships.[34]

Within this framework, Moscow's grand princes played out their political strategies. Their treaties with Tver', Moscow and their apanage kinsmen used the language of kinship to characterise political relations: 'we will hold our elder brother in the father's place and respect him as a father'; 'I, the grand prince, will treat you as a brother in all things without insult.'[35] They affirm the right of servitors to depart freely to another lord, but they often stipulate that each party will not accept in service men from the other's retinue. They often impose a similar prohibition against accepting rural and urban workers as clients (*zakladniki*). They demand apanage princes, subordination to them in foreign policy and fiscal affairs. Thus did hierarchy and differentiation of power among the north-east Rus' principalities develop, but they did not undermine the fundamentally patrimonial nature of politics.

Many scholars have exaggerated the power of Moscow's rulers and attributed their 'autocracy' to Mongol influence, but such a claim is by and large untenable, particularly for the fourteenth century when Muscovite central government was so weakly developed.[36] Borrowing from the Mongols in the fourteenth century was strongest in areas of direct contact between the Sarai khans and north-east Rus' princes: fourteenth-century Rus' princes travelled frequently to Sarai; often their sons were left there for years as sureties. Mongol structures and terminology appear in north-east Rus' military organisation, fiscal administration and some political institutions.[37] But to attribute Moscow's later centralised autocracy as a Mongol-based form of 'oriental Despotism' is unwarranted, since politics in the Kipchak khanate was actually quite decentralised. As for cultural life, contact with the Kipchak khanate had little impact, since the East Slavs were Orthodox and the Tatars polytheistic until their conversion to Islam in 1312; similarly for society and economy, since the East Slavs were forest-dwelling farmers and the Tatars nomads of the steppe.

Much ink has also been spilled debating whether the society and politics of personal dependency described here was 'feudal'. From the nineteenth century on, this question has been used to compare Russia with the west, because European political philosophy since the early modern period considered a feudal stage an essential step in the development towards liberal democracy

[33] Ibid., no. 3, p. 14.
[34] Kollmann (1987), ch. 5; Val'denberg (1916); D'iakonov (1889). The themes remain the same in later texts: Rowland (1979).   [35] *DDG*, nos. 2, 5.   [36] Halperin (1985); Vernadsky (1953), ch. 5.
[37] Ostrowski (1990).

(the argument is that the reciprocal obligations between lord and vassal or lord and peasant forged legal precedent and cultural aspirations for political pluralism).[38] Russian historians and publicists tried to make the best of the generally accepted conclusion that Russia had no feudal stage. Some, such as S.M. Solov'ev, depicted 'Slavic', Russian development as separate but parallel to 'Germanic' European development; others, of a Slavophile bent, exalted Russia's non-western 'communal' past; still others, such as B.N. Chicherin, stressed the negative aspects of Russia's non-feudal, patrimonial autocracy. Only N.P. Pavlov-Sil'vanskii, writing from the late 1890s, and a few who accepted his viewpoint, have seen fourteenth- and fifteenth-century north-east Rus' as parallel to western feudalism, while Soviet Marxist historians see Russia as 'feudal' from Kiev Rus' to 1861.[39] But the problem of 'feudalism' is really a discourse about modern Russia's future. Only a loose and non-evolutionary definition of the term – akin to Marc Bloch's dictum that feudal society was based on 'ties of dependence'[40] – applies well to fourteenth-century north-east Rus'. The problem of feudalism is more a historiographical construction than a useful category of analysis.

In assessing the changes we have detailed here, a Great Russian historiographical interpretation has dominated. Based on claims made in Moscow in the fifteenth and sixteenth centuries (in such sources as the tales associated with the 1439 Florence/Ferrara Church union, the *Tale of the Princes of Vladimir* and the *Book of Degrees*) that Moscow was the heir of Kiev,[41] modern scholarship has tended to assume such continuity regardless of the social and political diversity these lands developed from the twelfth century on. To explain the evident discontinuities between Kiev and Moscow in political practice, urban development, economy and social structure, some resort to a *deus ex machina* – the Mongol invaders. Those who prefer indigenous factors as driving forces in history cite geography, national character or other issues.[42] The effect of this presumption has been to obscure the varieties of historical development in the future Ukrainian and Belarus' lands and to cast the Grand Duchy in the role either as passive vehicle for the continued expression of Rus' culture or as spoiler of Moscow's role in 'gathering the Rus' lands'. A few historians have

---

[38] Poe (1993), ch. 9; Brown (1974). Pipes (1974), pp. 48–57, is a good statement of this point of view.

[39] Solov'ev I (1959–62), I; Kireevskii (1966); Pavlov-Sil'vanskii (1988) and Eck (1933). See also modern Soviet and western debates on feudalism in Russian history: Baron (1977); Crummey (1984); Szeftel (1965); Vernadsky (1939).   [40] Bloch (1970).

[41] Zimin (1972); Miller (1979); Pelenski (1977) and (1983); Gol'dberg (1975).

[42] The argument that opposing the Mongols made Russia autocratic: Karamzin (1842–3), bk I, vol. III, pp. 137–42, 166–74; Cherepnin (1960). Indigenous factors: Solov'ev (1959–62), I, ch. I, 7 VII, ch. I; Kliuchevskii (1956–8), I, lects. 16–17, II, lect. 22.

argued that the Grand Duchy played as positive a role as did the grand principality of Moscow in 'rescuing' the Rus' lands from foreign oppressors,[43] but
most have condemned it for inhibiting Moscow's foreordained responsibility
for that task. One can argue less anachronistically that the political expansion
and territorial aggrandisement of Lithuanian and Muscovite fourteenth-
century princes was aimed at capturing lucrative trade routes, trading centres
and natural resources, not at reuniting a putative nation. Indeed, scholars such
as Mykhailo Hrushevsky, A.E. Presniakov and P.N. Miliukov have argued that
Russian history begins only in the fourteenth century with the rise of
Moscow.[44] There has also been a tendency to read back into fourteenth-
century political events and texts nationalist sentiments that were not present
with anything like the fervour and exclusivity of modern nationalism – for
example, the historiography that co-opts the role of the Church in the fourteenth century to serve Moscow's rise. Similarly, if we look at cultural expression and also at the efforts of fourteenth-century ideologues and rulers in the
Grand Duchy, Moscow, Novgorod and elsewhere to create legitimising con-
structs, we see that their visions were generally regional or dynastic in focus,
were expressed in religious idiom and often inchoate and only nascently
'national'. Novgorod in the fourteenth century, for example, developed an
integrated local culture that stood as a symbol of its wealth, energy and political power. Unlike the fifteenth century, when pressures from outside stimulated Novgorod to produce politicised works of art and literature, the
fourteenth century exhibits stability and self-confidence. The city's strong
chronicle tradition continued unabated, producing after the 1330s the oldest
surviving redaction of the Novgorod First Chronicle, which brought the Kiev
Primary Chronicle up to that date with local Novgorodian and some north-
east Rus' items. At the same time, by contrast, the less secure republic of Pskov
was taking steps to bolster its independence; by 1374, Prince Dovmont, a
revered thirteenth-century defender of Pskov, was canonised as a local saint.
Novgorod's fourteenth-century cultural life marks the apogee of its development. Like many European urban republics, Novgorod reflected its cultural
diversity in free thinking. In the late fourteenth century it witnessed the
strigol'nik heresy, supported by cloth cutters and resembling the later Hussites
in its rejection of Church hierarchy and demands for social justice. It is in the
elaboration and glorification of Orthodox belief in icon painting, frescoes and
architecture, however, that the city's greatest achievements lie. Small, square,
single-domed churches with graceful trefoil-gable roofs became the architectural standard: the Church of the Saviour on Il'in Street (1374), for example,
has unusually lavish external decoration and exquisite interior frescoes by

---

[43] Khoroshkevich (1982).   [44] Miliukov (1930–64); Presniakov (1918b); Hrushevsky (1952).

Feofan the Greek (its trefoil roof line is now concealed under a superimposed eight-sloped pitched roof). Having worked in Constantinople and Black Sea littoral cities, Feofan brought to Novgorod the emotionalism and humanity associated with Hesychasm and South Slavic influence then penetrating the Rus' lands. His painting, in a new monochromatic palette with dramatic highlights, was intense, subjective and emotional. Icon painting reached similar heights, exhibiting a serene, almost naive simplicity. Line and silhouette define the subject two-dimensionally; the painting style is straightforward, using a bright palette of reds, yellows, blues and greens. Locally favoured saints – Elijah, Blaise, George, Paraskeva, Florus and Laurus – were frequently depicted, often with small representations of the patrons added.

The Grand Duchy's cultural and ideological activity in the fourteenth century was less cohesive than Novgorod's, befitting its regional diversity and relative youth as a state. The Grand Dukes were nevertheless assiduous in cultivating their political status by skilful use of titles, ceremony and diplomatic language in the idiom of the European powers with which they corresponded. Local chronicles were probably being compiled in Smolensk, Polotsk, Slutsk, Pinsk, Novogrudok, Kiev and other centres in this century, and by the death of Vytautas in 1430 a large chronicle codex of Lithuanian history was being assembled at the bishop's court at Smolensk to legitimise Gediminid power. Thereafter followed numerous chronicle and genealogical compositions to ground the dynasty in ancient heritage and to celebrate its achievements.[45]

Meanwhile cultural endeavours followed Rus' Orthodox traditions in most parts of the Grand Duchy. The local dialect of East Slavic remained the official language of the Grand Duchy until it was displaced by Polish in the seventeenth and eighteenth centuries; legal traditions were maintained, as evidenced by the copying and transmission of Kievan and Byzantine ecclesiastical and civil law codes. Religious cultural expression is represented by an illustrated psalter executed in Kiev for the bishop of Smolensk in 1397 and the copying of homiletic compositions and hagiographical compendia such as the Kievan *Paterikon*. It discounts the achievement of the Lithuanian Grand Dukes to portray this cultural toleration as the passive reception by pagans of a more superior culture. The Gediminids could as easily have patronised a European-based political discourse or cultural idiom, given their international contacts, but chose the strategy of maintaining the Rus' tradition to maintain stability and to counterbalance the lure of Polish and Catholic influences. At the same time the Rus' tradition grew and changed in the rich cultural atmosphere of the Grand Duchy, with Lithuanian and Polish political, social and cultural influences. Separate Belarus' and Ukrainian languages developed by the four-

---

[45] Priselkov (1940a); Khoroshkevich (1982); Ulashchik (1985); Rowell (1994), ch. 2.

teenth or fifteenth century (dates are disputed), reflecting the separate historical experiences of these lands within the Grand Duchy and kingdom of Poland. New political and social structures developed, particularly after the dynastic Union of Krevo with crown Poland (1385).

In the north-east, cultural developments followed patterns similar to those of Novgorod. South Slavic influence penetrated, exemplified by icons, frescoes and literature, especially the works of Epifanii 'the Wise', a widely travelled and cultured Russian monk of the Trinity-St Sergii monastery who lived at the turn of the century. He exemplified an ornate 'word-weaving' style and emotional expressiveness in his *Lives* of Sergii and Stefan of Perm'. Contacts with Byzantium, Bulgaria and Serbia were frequent in the exchange of travellers, artists, icons and especially books. From Serbia and Bulgaria, translated Byzantine works of hagiography, liturgy, homiletics, history – a major missing category was theology – were brought to Novgorod and north-east Rus'. The second half of the century in north-east Rus' was an era of spiritual efflorescence, epitomised by Sergii of Radonezh. Founder of the Trinity monastery in the 1330s or 1340s, Sergii until his death in 1392 inspired followers with an asceticism, mysticism and ethereal spirituality characteristic of Hesychasm. His model was enshrined in the monasteries founded by students or admirers: the Saviour monastery founded by Dmitrii Prilutskii in 1371, those founded by Kirill and Ferapont in the Beloozero area in 1397 and 1398, and numerous others, as Moscow-based monks both followed and led Muscovite expansion to the north and east.

Building projects provided the arena for much cultural activity. New churches were constructed in stone, not to speak of wood, at a blistering pace in the fourteenth century: the Kremlin ensemble saw the construction of over ten stone buildings or fortifications from 1326 to 1397. New monasteries were founded: the Miracles monastery in the Kremlin in 1350s, the Saviour-Andronikov about 1360, the Simonov in 1370, and the Kremlin Ascension convent in 1386. The apanage prince of Galich ornamented his capital at Zvenigorod with a stone Dormition Cathedral in 1399 and a stone Church of the Nativity of the Virgin in the new (1398) Savva-Storozhevskii monastery in 1404. The founding of the Saviour-Evfimii monastery in Suzdal' in 1352 and a stone kremlin in Nizhnii Novgorod in 1372 similarly reflect the ambitions of local princes. In Tver' from the 1390s to 1409, Bishop Arsenii founded monasteries and sponsored book production, commissioning a copy of the Kiev *Paterikon*. In the 1340s Metropolitan Feognost invited a group of Greek painters to Moscow to decorate new churches in the Kremlin and elsewhere, Greeks who in turn spread their ideas to native painters. Feofan the Greek painted in virtually all the Kremlin churches in the 1390s; a brilliant Russian painter, Andrei Rublev, in the early decades of the fifteenth century painted in the

Kremlin churches, in the Vladimir Dormition Cathedral, in Zvenigorod (an exquisite Deesis tier) and at the Saviour-Andronikov monastery. Rublev produced his masterpiece 'Old Testament Trinity' as the patron icon for the cathedral of the Trinity-St Sergii monastery.

Political aspirations were often expressed in the medium of art, architecture and literature. The building projects of the Kremlin, Nizhnii Novgorod and Zvenigorod, cited above, promoted their princes' status, as did the much earlier 1285 construction of a stone cathedral in Tver'. The Tver' princes indeed were active in turning cultural life to political use. Regular compilation of historical materials was started there by 1285, culminating possibly in a codex of 1305 (some attribute this codex to Vladimir and date it 1306/7) and certainly in the codex of 1327. Tver' put hagiography to political use; immediately after the murder (by a Moscow prince in Sarai) of Grand Prince Mikhail Iaroslavich in 1318, he became locally venerated as a saint and his life was eulogised in a tale that was reworked in the fifteenth century into a hagiography. Further grand-princely chronicle codices trace the aspirations of other political centres in north-east Rus'. After the 1327 Tver' codex, Moscow, its successor to the title of grand prince of Vladimir, produced major codices in 1340 and 1354 or 1359. The ambitious grand princes of Suzdal'-Nizhnii Novgorod did likewise in 1383. But these chronicles were still regional in focus; only in Moscow in the 1390s, and even more fully in the Trinity Chronicle (1408), compiled at the metropolitan's court, were assembled annals that aspired to be 'all-Rus' – that is, that included materials from many Rus' lands and thus expressed a broader political self-conception than had been previously displayed.[46]

Pride of place clearly goes to Moscow in wielding the tools of art and literature to enhance political status. As suggested, the cult of Metropolitan Peter is exemplary. Peter held to a broad vision of Orthodoxy in his long career and was justly venerated by many political centres in the north-east after his death. His miracles were recorded and his *Life* was written (most attribute it to Bishop Prokhor of Rostov); he was officially canonised in Constantinople in 1339, a rapid step in the Orthodox tradition which tended not to canonise as formally as did the Catholic Church. In the late fourteenth or early fifteenth century Metropolitan Kiprian rewrote in the new style and expanded Metropolitan Peter's *Life*, turning the events of Peter's life into an *apologia* for his own trials and tribulations in trying to steer a course between Moscow, Tver', the Grand Duchy and the patriarch. Metropolitan Peter was depicted on a sakkos of Metropolitan Fotii (1408–31); churches and icons were dedicated to him in the first half of the fifteenth century in Tver' and Novgorod. But Moscow was

---

[46] Nasonov (1930); Lur'e (1976); Murav'eva (1983).

fast co-opting the cult of Peter for its own purposes. Peter was depicted in icons, his grave was embellished and venerated, and he became revered as a 'Moscow miracle worker',[47] one of a group of four metropolitans closely associated with the Moscow grand-princely dynasty.

The beginnings of efforts to depict Moscow as the symbolic and religious heir to the grand principality of Vladimir began in this century as well. Evidence includes the dedication of Moscow's principal cathedral to the same theme as the Dormition Cathedral in Vladimir, seat of the grand princes and metropolitan in the twelfth and thirteenth centuries; the temporary transfer in 1395 from Vladimir to Moscow of the revered Vladimir Mother of God icon (a twelfth-century Byzantine work brought to Kiev in 1125 and to Vladimir in 1155); the restoration of eleventh- and twelfth-century churches in Vladimir and Pereiaslavl'-Zalesskii, including Rublev's repainting of the frescoes in the Vladimir Dormition Cathedral in 1408. All these efforts were sponsored by the grand princes of Moscow.

More problematic is the issue of Moscow's claim to be heir to the Kiev grand principality. The assertion that Moscow claimed this legacy as self-conscious representative of the Russian people is associated in part with a cycle of tales concerning the 1380 Kulikovo battle, tales which some have dated to the 1390s, others to the mid- and late fifteenth century.[48] Those tales that can most readily be dated to the late fourteenth century indeed make analogies between Muscovite rulers (Dmitrii Donskoi in particular) and counterparts from Kiev Rus', and they do use the term 'the Russian land' *(Russkaia zemlia)* to refer to the Moscow principality (in Kievan sources the term was used for the heartland around Kiev and/or all the territory ruled by the Riurikide dynasty). In addition, since the time of Ivan I Kalita (1325–40) Muscovite grand princes had been adding the phrase 'of all-Rus'' to their titles, emulating the metropolitans.[49] But these were tentative beginnings: the reality of power, and most ideological statements concerning the authenticity of Moscow's power, had to do with the grand principality of Vladimir. Moscow's claim to the Kievan inheritance belongs to the next century, and its significant achievements in establishing regional political power were not merely the predetermined fulfilment of national destiny – *pace* Kliuchevskii, who argued that the Great Russian people rallied around Moscow because they realised they needed a strong ruler[50] – but rather products of specific historical tensions and conjunctures.

In sum, by the end of the fourteenth century the Rus' principalities were

[47] Stökl (1981).
[48] Likhachev (1973), ch. 2; Pelenski (1977) and (1983); Salmina (1966), (1970), (1974) and (1977).
[49] Szeftel (1979).   [50] Kliuchevskii (1956–8), II, pp. 46–7.

being forged into larger and different cultural entities: the empires of Lithuania and Muscovy, the colonial republic of Novgorod, the ambitious Tver'. Rich possibilities for change were nurtured by the dynamic economy and international contacts of the region; for the Grand Duchy and its subordinate lands, interactions with the Teutonic Order, Baltic trading partners and particularly the kingdom of Poland brought potent cultural paradigms to mix with Lithuanian and Rus' traditions. For Muscovy Rus' and Orthodox traditions adapted to a markedly different political, social and economic constellation than Kiev Rus' had faced. The fourteenth century was the era in which the putative unity of the Rus' heritage was destroyed and these lands were set on new and vibrant political and cultural directions.

CHAPTER 24

THE BYZANTINE EMPIRE IN THE FOURTEENTH CENTURY

Angeliki E. Laiou

IN the course of the fourteenth century, Byzantine society underwent a series of major changes, in some ways similar to those in western Europe, in other ways quite different, and complicated by the presence of external threats that progressively led to the dissolution of the state and the conquest of its territory. While economic, social and cultural developments show considerable vitality, the weakness of the state, radically reducing its ability to provide order and security for its subjects, could not but influence the dynamic of other developments. Innovation, in practice more often than in theory, was not lacking; on the contrary, the responses to new conditions often present interesting if contradictory aspects.

For political history, a new era begins not with the start of the century but rather with the recovery of Constantinople from the Latins by a small expeditionary force of Michael VIII Palaeologus, emperor of Nicaea since 1258. This event, which occurred on 25 July 1261, had been long desired by the leaders of the major Greek splinter states, the emperors of Nicaea and the despots of Epirus, and it had certainly been prepared by Michael VIII.[1] The restoration of a Byzantine emperor in the old capital of the empire had certain important consequences. For one thing, it displaced the focus of interest of the rulers from Asia to Europe, as they had to deal with western claims. The papacy, Charles of Anjou, the house of Valois and the Venetians all became engaged in various efforts to retake Constantinople, so that there was hostility between Byzantium and at least one western power at almost any time between 1261 and 1314; in 1281, as in 1308, powerful coalitions were aligned against Byzantium. These were deflected, in Michael's day, by masterful diplomacy as well as by a major concession on his part. This was the acceptance, by the Byzantine emperor, of ecclesiastical union with the Church of Rome. The Union of Lyon (1274) was undertaken in order to

---

[1] Geanakoplos (1959), pp. 75ff, for the recovery of Constantinople.

defuse the imminent danger of an attack by Charles of Anjou and his Balkan allies, and it succeeded, since the papacy forced Charles to abandon his plans for a time. When, in 1281, Martin IV decided that Michael VIII had not really implemented the union and gave full support to Charles of Anjou, Michael's diplomacy again came into play; he negotiated with the king of Aragon and others, contributing significantly to the attack of Aragon on Sicily, occasioned by the Sicilian Vespers. Diplomacy as well as good luck allowed his immediate successors also to survive the western threat. But, even as contacts between Byzantines and westerners became closer, through the marriage alliances of the imperial house, through diplomatic negotiations and because of the presence of Italian merchants, the threat of a western offensive kept the emperor occupied in Europe. So also did the effort to create a compact state by recovering the European territories which had been lost at the time of the Fourth Crusade. The results for Asia Minor were disastrous. The most thoughtful historian of the times, George Pachymeres, had this situation in mind when he reported the words of the *protasekretis* Kakos Senachereim who, upon learning of the reconquest of Constantinople, pulled at his beard in dismay and cried, 'Oh, what things I hear! . . . What sins have we committed, that we should live to see such misfortunes? Let no one harbour any hopes, since the Romans hold the City again.'[2]

This, then, is a first contradiction of the Palaeologan state, from the beginning of the dynasty until about 1314. The recovery of Constantinople, considered a divine gift by Michael VIII,[3] forced the empire into political, diplomatic and ideological positions which were often untenable. Anachronistic voices spoke of the universal emperor, and the first three Palaeologi tried to restore the unity of the geographic space, by restoring at least the European frontiers of the Byzantine empire. But no shadow of universality remained, and geographic integration ran counter to long-term decentralising tendencies, evident in the late twelfth century and exacerbated by the Fourth Crusade. The westerners kept part of their possessions in the principality of Achaia and the islands, while the Greek splinter states of the despotate of Epirus and Thessaly still retained their independence. The empire of Trebizond was the other Greek splinter state, although its geographic remoteness did not involve it in the power struggles for the recovery of the old Byzantine empire. Non-Greek states, Serbia and Bulgaria, had also become independent, and Serbia in particular was to witness a great expansion

---

[2] GP, ed. Failler, p. 205 = Bk. 11, 28–9; cf. ibid., pp. 25 ff = Bk 1, 1–2ff.

[3] Grégoire, 'Imperatoris Michaelis Palaeologi "De Vita Sua"', especially p. 457; cf. GP, ed. Failler, Bk 1, 1.

in the course of the late thirteenth and the first half of the fourteenth century, aided by financial resources which became available through exploitation of the silver mines at Novo Brdo and elsewhere. Michael VIII tried to make reality conform to ideological imperatives. He fought against the principality of Achaia, rather successfully, and against the Venetians in the Aegean, and tried to reduce the independence of the despotate of Epirus. In Bulgaria, he scored successes with the recovery of some of the Greek-speaking cities of the Black Sea coast, important outlets for the grain which was necessary for the provisioning of Constantinople. At the same time, Michael VIII continued the policy of alliance with the Mongols, first begun by the emperors of Nicaea. The alliance with the Ilkhanids of Persia, especially Hulagu, was a defence against the Turks, and was continued by Andronikos II, who tried to seal it with a marriage alliance. Michael VIII also made a marriage alliance with the Mongols of the Golden Horde, in the person of Nogai, as a defence against Bulgaria. This, coupled with an alliance between Michael and the sultan of Egypt (Baybars), opened lines of communication between Egypt and the Crimea, from which the Egyptian sultans got their Cuman slave troops. A remote effect, intended or not, was to facilitate the Egyptian conquest of the last crusader outposts in the Holy Land.[4]

The successes of Michael VIII have given him a rather good press, as a consummate diplomat who was able to retain Constantinople against multiple threats, and to enlarge the possessions of his state. At the same time, the cost was heavy and long term. The policy of union was bitterly contested at home, and was soon repudiated by his successor. Worst of all was the disaffection of Asia Minor. Michael had reached the throne through deposing and blinding young John IV Laskaris, offspring of a dynasty which had been based in Asia Minor, and grandson of John III Vatatzes (1222–54), a much loved emperor, whom the people of Asia Minor considered a saint. The Laskarid dynasty had followers in Asia Minor who were difficult to conciliate; so did the patriarch Arsenios, deposed in 1265 for having excommunicated Michael after the blinding of John Laskaris. The policies of the Laskarids, focused on the defence of Asia Minor, were not continued by Michael VIII; indeed forces were withdrawn from there to fight wars on European soil.[5] The emperor did not even visit the province until the end of his reign. Asia Minor was neglected, heavily taxed and suffered from Turkish attacks. By the end of Michael's reign, the sources speak of depopulation and impoverishment, calling the area beyond the Sangarios river a 'Scythian desert'. The situation was to deteriorate rapidly after 1282.[6]

[4] GP, ed. Failler, Bk III, 3; Bk III, 5; GP, ed. Bekkerus, II, pp. 86–7 = Bk I, 32.
[5] GP, ed. Failler, p. 35, Bk I, 6.   [6] Ibid., Bk III, 22; p. 633 = Bk VI, 29.

SUCCESSES AND CONFLICTS (1282–1341)

Political affairs

Despite these problems, the immediate heirs of Michael VIII had some successes. This is a time of significant contradictions: between the ideology of government and actual government, between a progressive impoverishment of the state and the wealth in some segments of society, in the ambivalent relations between Byzantium and the west. Many of these contradictions exploded in the great civil war of 1341–54, which left Byzantium a greatly altered state in a changed world.

Andronikos II (1282–1328) and his successor, Andronikos III (1328–41), shifted once again the centre of their interest, from western Europe to Asia Minor and the Balkans. Yet they had to retain close diplomatic relations with western Europe, primarily to ward off an attack and secondarily to seek aid against the Turks. On the whole, there is a shrinkage of the areas of interest and involvement in terms of foreign policy. Here the major successes of Byzantine policy were with regard to the splinter states of Greece: Thessaly, which was acquired piecemeal in 1333, and Epirus, where the city of Ioannina accepted Byzantine overlordship in 1318, and the rest of the despotate in 1340. In the Peloponnese, the process of reconquest proceeded throughout this period; after 1349, the Byzantine possessions, organised as the despotate of the Morea, became one of the most vital parts of the state.

Relations with western Europe were successful as far as the first objective is concerned: there was, in fact, no major expedition against the Byzantine empire. The reduced Byantine diplomatic activities centred around efforts to thwart any coalition of forces that might attack the empire; that is, to make alliances with Ghibelline forces. Matrimonial policy served this purpose, as Andronikos II took as his second wife Yolanda/Irene of Montferrat, whose father was allied to Castile, and Andronikos III married Anne of Savoy, daughter of Count Amedeo V. For the rest, Andronikos III had even less close relations with the west than did his grandfather Andronikos II, although the penetration of individual westerners, of western customs and of Venetians and Genoese into the empire continued apace. The second aim, an alliance against the Turks, was not successful, for it hinged upon the union of the Churches, discussions on which took place under Andronikos II, after 1324, Andronikos III and John VI Kantakouzenos (1347–54), but foundered upon the divergent interests of the papacy and the Byzantine emperors.

The situation in Asia Minor became the nemesis of the Byzantines. The area rapidly fell into the hands of the Turks, especially after the Byzantine defeat at the battle of Bapheus, near Nicomedeia (1302). Andronikos II made a number of efforts to remedy the situation, and for a short time, in 1294, the campaigns of the great general Alexios Philanthropenos raised hopes. But he was opposed by powerful landlords in the area, was pushed into an unsuccessful rebellion, and his successes were short-lived. The countryside was rapidly brought under Turkish control, and one by one the cities were starved into submission. The Ottomans took Brusa (Bursa) in 1326, Nicaea in 1331 and Nicomedeia in 1337. Further south, Ephesos, Smyrna, Miletos, Sardeis and Tralleis fell to the Seljuk emirates in the first decade of the century. Philadelphia and its immediate region remained as the sole Byzantine possession, until 1390.[7] Andronikos III waged several campaigns in Asia Minor, to no avail. More importantly, after 1329, Andronikos III and, later, John Kantakouzenos had close relations of friendship and alliance with the emir of Sarukhan and with Umur, emir of Aydın. Directed originally against the Genoese lords of Phocaea and Lesbos, this became a more general alliance, in the course of which the Byzantines recognised the Seljuk conquests in Asia Minor.

The realities of government

Despite ideologically driven claims of an all-powerful emperor, in reality government became increasingly weak, and its authority and prerogatives fragmented. In the fourteenth century, the business of government was primarily connected with the collection of taxes, the army and justice. State finances were being eroded by the high cost of pervasive warfare and dwindling resources. For one thing, imperial territories were much more restricted than during the twelfth century, and Asia Minor was lost during this period, so revenues from the land tax were commensurately reduced. War, invasions and inclement weather sometimes made it impossible to collect taxes. Secondly, this was a state and a society administered by privilege. The privileges granted to the aristocracy further eroded the tax base, while treaties with Italian city-states incorporated commercial privileges to their merchants that considerably reduced the benefits accruing to the state from the very active commercial exchanges in this part of the Mediterranean. Some Byzantine merchants, namely those of Ioannina and Monemvasia were successful in obtaining similar privileges, which, although they worked to their benefit, had a detrimental effect on the state treasury.[8] The government made some effort to overcome these fiscal difficulties: after 1283, a series of new and extraordinary taxes

---

[7] Ahrweiler (1983), pp. 175–97, on Philadelphia.

[8] Miklosich and Müller, *Acta et Diplomata*, v, pp. 77–84, on the privileges of Ioannina issued in 1319; for those of Monemvasia, Schreiner (1978), pp. 203–28, and (1981–2), pp. 160–6; Laiou (1980–1), pp. 206–7; Kalligas (1990), pp. 101–34.

Map 16   The Byzantine empire during the reign of Michael VIII

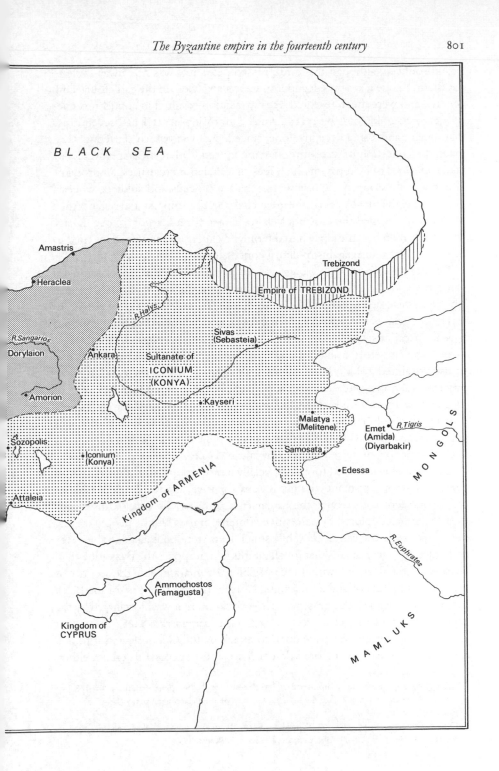

was introduced, although the hard-pressed peasantry was not always able to pay them. Excise taxes on salt and iron were also levied, in the early fourteenth century, and were much resented. Heavy taxation resulted in annual revenues of 1,000,000 gold coins by 1321; a small sum (Michael VIII had seven times that much), and also a deceptive one, since a civil war, which started in 1321, made the collection of taxes problematic indeed. Other measures were also taken: in order to help pay the high fees of Catalan mercenaries, Andronikos II temporarily stopped the payment of palace officials and soldiers, while in 1343, during the first stages of the great civil war, the empress and regent Anne of Savoy mortgaged the crown jewels to Venice for a loan of 30,000 ducats. The jewels then became a pawn in diplomatic games, as the Venetians tried to negotiate their return against political concessions of some magnitude.[9]

The devaluation of the coinage was in part the result of the same fiscal problems, and also a short-term remedy for the emptiness of imperial coffers. The successive deterioration of the gold coin (from 17 carats in 1230–60 to less than 11 carats by the middle of the fourteenth century) has been linked to specific fiscal crises, occasioned in turn by military problems.[10] Sometimes, indeed, the emperors could not meet their military expenses in coin and had to use unminted gold.[11] The issue of gold coins stopped for good at some point between 1354 and 1366, partly, perhaps, because of a general movement of gold toward western Europe, but undoubtedly also because the state could not sustain a gold coinage any more. Venetian ducats as well as silver coins appear frequently in Byzantine documents of the late Palaeologan period; it is likely that people preferred them to Byzantine issues.

The Palaeologan armed forces, especially native troops, were quite small. In 1285, the navy was dismantled, since it was expensive, and the death of Charles of Anjou seemed to reduce the threat from the sea. This was a disastrous measure, much deplored by perceptive contemporaries and by people writing in the middle of the century.[12] While small fleets were built again in the 1330s and 1340s, the fact remains that for all intents and purposes the Byzantines had abandoned the fleet, and with it the possibility of guaranteeing the security of the seas in the Aegean and even around Constantinople itself; as for the Black Sea, for centuries a closed preserve of the Byzantines, it was dominated by the Italians. Their fleets sailed freely in all these waters. By 1348 the city of Constantinople itself was wide open to attack by the Genoese, and it took a special levy to create a fleet for its defence; not a very successful defence either.

---

[9] Laiou (1972), pp. 186–7, on Andronikos II; for the crown jewels, Bertelè (1962), II, pp. 87–188.

[10] Morrisson (1991), II, pp. 308ff, for the monetary system of the Palaeologan period.

[11] E.g. Laiou (1972), p. 189.

[12] GP, ed. Bekkerus, II, pp. 69–71 = Bk I, 26; 322–4 = Bk IV, 23; 530–3 = Bk VI, 26; Gregoras, I, pp. 174–6 = Bk VI, 3; 208–9 = Bk VI, 11; II, pp. 866–7 = Bk XVII, 7.

Piracy also went unchecked. The piratical expeditions of the Seljuk maritime emirates could not be countered by the Byzantines, nor could the detrimental effects on the islands of the Aegean.[13] When, in the 1330s, the Byzantines discussed with western powers a response to these raids in the guise of a crusade, the Byzantines took a good deal of time to arm twenty ships which, however, never participated in the enterprise, for reasons that are not known.[14]

As for the army, native forces were small, while recourse to other expedients was very expensive. The native forces were in part composed of *pronoia*-holders. The *pronoia* is an institution which goes back to the eleventh century, and consists of the grant of land and its revenues in return for service, especially military service since the time of the Komnenoi. Michael VIII, in his efforts to gather support for himself, allowed some *pronoia* lands to become hereditary, and also gave such lands to members of the senate. By the fourteenth century, one can find military *pronoia*-lands in the hands of two quite distinct groups: the aristocracy, who might have some of their holdings in *pronoia*-land, and soldiers of a lower social and economic level, who, at the lowest strata, might even hold these revenues collectively.[15] The civil wars of the 1320s and the 1330s increased the number of *pronoia* grants, since rival emperors were engaged in a competition for supporters; the emperors also increasingly gave these lands, or part of them, in hereditary possession which undermined the military effectiveness of the restitution.

Other troops were paid in cash. These can no longer be considered as constituting a standing army, since they served occasionally, and on particular campaigns. There may have been an unsuccessful effort to create a standing army in 1321, to be composed of 1,000 horse in Bithynia and 2,000 in Macedonia and Thrace; the small numbers are noteworthy.[16] For the rest, the soldiers paid in cash were mostly mercenaries.[17] Occasionally, they were Greek speakers, such as the Cretan mercenaries in Asia Minor in the late thirteenth century. Much more frequently they were foreign troops, sometimes preformed. The use of foreign mercenaries, known since the eleventh century, became more frequent in the Palaeologan period. Italians, Alans, Catalans and others served in the Byzantine army. The dangers inherent in the use of such foreign mercenary troops were realised in Byzantium no less than in fourteenth-century western Europe. What did not frequently occur was an effort on the part of leaders of mercenaries to take over the government, as was to happen in Italian cities. Only once did a comparable situation develop. To deal with the disastrous situation in Asia Minor, Andronikos II called in a group

---

[13] Zachariadou (1989b), pp. 212–25.   [14] Laiou (1970), pp. 374–92.
[15] Oikonomidès (1981), pp. 367–71.   [16] Gregoras, I, pp. 317–8 = Bk VIII, 6; 223 = Bk VII, 3.
[17] Bartusis (1992) and Oikonomidès (1981), pp. 353–71, for the army.

of Catalan mercenaries, under Roger de Flor, to fight against the Turks. Soon, the Catalans developed an interest in acquiring territory, and formed ties with the kings of Sicily and Aragon, and later with Charles of Valois. They were a great threat to the state, but eventually they moved on, conquered Thebes and Athens (in 1311), and set up a Catalan duchy, which lasted until 1388.

When all else failed, and when stakes were high, the emperors had recourse to a much more dangerous expedient: the use not of mercenaries, but of the troops of allied foreign rulers. The first half of the fourteenth century saw two civil wars, which involved a contest for power between two rival emperors: one from 1321 to 1328 and the other from 1341 to 1354. Both sides appealed to foreign troops: Serbs and Bulgarians on the first occasion, Serbs and Turks on the second. The results were catastrophic.

The administration of justice had always been an imperial prerogative in Byzantium. Unlike medieval western Europe, where judicial authority had been fragmented and passed, variously, to the Church, to seigneurial lords or to the towns, in Byzantium until the Fourth Crusade, justice was in the hands of the state, and was administered in imperial courts. The emperor functioned not only as the legislator but also as the ultimate judicial authority, guaranteeing good justice and acting as a judge, both on appeal and sometimes in the first instance. True, Alexios I Komnenos (1081–1118) had given ecclesiastical courts the right to judge all matters involving marriage.[18] True, also, the principles of imperial justice were eroded in the late twelfth century, because of privileges granted to western merchants. Still, the real changes came after the Fourth Crusade, in the despotate of Epirus, and in the Palaeologan period. The emperor retained his legislative role, although occasionally we find synodical or patriarchal decisions being issued as imperial legislation.[19] Justice, however, although ostensibly in imperial hands, became considerably fragmented and decentralised in the course of the fourteenth century. The Italian city-states, primarily Venice and Genoa, sought and received extra-territorial privileges which gave them the right to be judged by their own courts, even in cases involving Byzantine subjects, if the defendants were Italian.[20] In another development, patriarchal courts judged all manner of cases involving laymen, especially before 1330 and after 1394, when imperial tribunals malfunctioned; by the end of the century, it was quite common for the patriarchal tribunal to judge even cases involving commercial law. No wonder that, along with a manual of civil law, compiled by a learned jurist in Thessaloniki in the 1340s (the *Hexabiblos*, of Constantine Harmenopoulos), we also have a compendium of civil and canon law together (the *Syntagma* of Vlastares, compiled in

---

[18] *JG*, I, p. 312.   [19] Ibid., 533ff.
[20] Miklosich and Müller, *Acta et Diplomata*, III, pp. 81, 92; *DVL*, I, Venice, no. 80.

Thessaloniki in 1335). The role of ecclesiastics in the judicial system is indicated also by their participation in the highest tribunal of the Palaeologan period, that of the general judges of the Romans. Established by Andronikos III in 1329, it was an imperial court, originally consisting of three laymen and a bishop, and was invested with its authority in a solemn ceremony in the great church of Haghia Sophia. Characteristically, although originally the tribunal sat in Constantinople and its authority extended throughout the empire, soon there were 'general judges of the Romans' in the provinces; in Thessaloniki as early as the 1340s, perhaps in Lemnos in 1395, certainly in Serres during the Serbian occupation, in the Morea, as well as in the empire of Trebizond.[21]

Developments in finances, justice and the army show a dynamic between the state, in the traditional Byzantine sense of a central government, and regional forces or particular groups which were agents of decentralisation. The central government retained the formal right to levy taxes, to appoint army commanders, to reform justice and appoint judges. At the same time, taxes tended to disappear into the hands of regional governors, while army commanders often acted on their own, easily sliding into open rebellion; the *pronoia*-holders, although they held their privileges from the emperor, were not easy to control, and their very privileges resulted from and fostered a particularisation of finances and of military power. As for justice, that too was in some ways decentralised. If one is to compare the situation to western Europe, it is much closer to the eleventh or twelfth centuries, not to the fourteenth when states were engaged in the process of recovering a control long lost over finances, the army, justice. In important ways, then, the government in the Byzantine empire was undergoing a transformation quite different from that of parts at least of western Europe. It was not necessarily negative, but for the force of external circumstances.

Social groups and social relations

Palaeologan society was more structured than at any other time in the history of the Byzantine empire. The aristocracy emerges as a group with considerable power and a high degree of consciousness of its social position, while at the same time, and continuing until the end of the formal existence of the state, merchants hold an important economic position and, for a moment, lay claim to political power. These groups prospered economically, certainly until the 1340s.[22]

---

[21] Lemerle (1948), (1949), (1950) and (1964) on the judicial institutions of the Palaeologan period.
[22] Laiou (1973) and (1991) on the aristocracy; on Palaeologan society, see also Maksimović (1981) and Matschke (1981) and (1991).

The development of the Byzantine aristocracy has a long history, in some ways continuous since the tenth century. When the throne was captured by two of the most powerful families (the Komnenoi and the Doukai) in 1081, some important features were consolidated, and continued into the fourteenth century. By then, this was an aristocracy dominated by a few families, linked by intermarriage: their numbers were fewer than in the twelfth century, but most of them could claim descent from the twelfth-century aristocracy, and those in the highest ranks could name at least one ancestor of imperial stock. Many aristocrats (and the wealthy generally) had fled Constantinople at the time of its capture in 1204 to go to Nicaea. There, their power and influence had been somewhat challenged by the policies of John III Vatatzes and Theodore II Laskaris (1254–8). The first had initiated a policy which made some of the army independent of imperial (mostly aristocratic) commanders, and even issued sumptuary laws directed against the aristocracy,[23] while the second had appointed as regent for his young son George Mouzalon, who, with his brothers, can appropriately be termed the king's men: men from a relatively humble background, who owed their power and loyalty only to the dynasty.[24] The power of king's men was brought to a bloody end when a conspiracy of aristocrats, led by Michael Palaeologus, murdered them. In the fourteenth century, men who did not initially belong to the highest aristocracy but became powerful through office, civil or military, tended to acquire social prestige by marrying high, and only the most status-conscious person, such as the empress Yolanda/Irene of Montferrat could find fault with their social origins.[25] The most important exception to this statement is Alexios Apokaukos, who progressed from tax collector to *megas doux* (commander of the fleet). A king's man in some respects, he followed a policy which pitted him against the most vocal representative of the aristocratic class, John Kantakouzenos, and was never considered by that class to be anything but a *parvenu*.[26]

One significant difference between this high aristocracy and that of western Europe was that the Byzantines did not have a nobility. There were no official prerogatives, no official rights and derogations, no privileges legally guaranteed to a specific class and passed from one generation to the next. Undoubtedly, there were attitudes which could eventually have led to the creation of a nobility. High

[23] Gregoras, I, pp. 42–4 = Bk II, 6.

[24] It should be noted, however, that George Mouzalon married a Kantakouzene, who, after his death, remarried, and is well known as the *protovestiarissa* Theodora Palaeologina Kantakouzene Raoulaina: Nicol (1968).

[25] Reference is to Nikephoros Choumnos, whose daughter Irene married John Palaeologus, and to Theodore Metochites, whose daughter married a nephew of the reigning emperor, Andronikos II. It was to the marriage of Irene Choumnaina with her son that the empress Yolanda – western-born and not of the highest ancestry herself – objected: GP, ed. Bekkerus, II, pp. 289–90 = Bk IV, 7.

[26] See below p. 813, and IC, *Hist.*, I, pp. 117–18 = Bk I, 23; II, p. 89 = Bk III, 14; II, p. 278 = Bk III, 46.

birth counted for a great deal: in the twelfth century, the Emperor Manuel I Komnenos had legislated against *mésalliance*;[27] and while in the fourteenth century there was no such state control of marriages, nevertheless matrimonial alliances were very carefully arranged. So much was intermarriage regarded as a feature of the aristocracy, that one text dedicated to social reform, the *Dialogue between the Rich and the Poor* of Alexios Makremvolites, proposed marriages between poor and rich as a remedy for the ills and inequalities of society.[28] This suggestion also indicates a certain opposition to the stratification of society and to the place of the high aristocracy in it.

Aristocratic women played an important role in politics and society. They were the medium through which alliances between aristocratic families were made and, since they had property of their own, in the form both of dowry and patrimonial property, they had considerable economic power. Names, lineage, property and family connections were transmitted along the female as well as the male line; and aristocratic women were as acutely conscious and proud of their lineage as their male relatives. As in the twelfth century, the administration of the family property seems to have been in the hands of women; and although literacy may not have reached very low in the social scale, some women of the high aristocracy were learned indeed, and patrons of literary men, scholars, theologians and artists. A number of women, mostly those close to the imperial family, such as Theodora Raoulaina or the sister of Michael VIII, or Theodora and Irene Kantakouzene (respectively, the mother and wife of John Kantakouzenos), or Irene Choumnaina Palaeologina, became actively involved in the political and religious controversies of the period.[29]

The aristocracy, both in its highest echelons and at lower levels, was less of a Constantinopolitan group than it had been in the twelfth century. This was partly the result of the rise of regional aristocratic foci of power. Thus the Komnenoi–Doukai in Epirus and Thessaly had formed independent states, as did the Grand Komnenoi in Trebizond. There were other important regional magnates, such as the Maliasenoi, the Gavrielopouloi, the Raoul in Epiros and Thessaly, and a number of families in the Morea; many frequently opposed the authority of the central government. Furthermore, with the reconquest of the European provinces, the great families of the reconstituted Byzantine empire acquired lands in Macedonia and Thrace. Typically, members of these families might also be appointed governors of one of the areas in which they held their properties, so that regional economic power and political authority were often

---

[27] Laiou (1992b), p. 44.
[28] Ševčenko, 'Alexios Makrembolites', pp. 187–228 (on marriage, pp. 207–8).
[29] Laiou (1981), pp. 255–7, on female literacy. On women as patrons of the arts, Buchtal and Belting (1978), Nelson and Lowden (1991) and Talbot (1992).

concomitant. Thus, for example, in the rich agricultural region of Serres, the Tzamplakon family held estates since the days of the Nicene empire; in 1326, Alexios Tzamplakon was governor of the city, and in charge of its fiscal administration.[30] The family of John Kantakouzenos, later emperor by rebellion and usurpation, had large estates near Serres; his relative, Andronikos Kantakouzenos, became governor of the city, and Andronikos's successor, Angelos Metochites, was also a member of a family with estates in the area.

The aristocracy remained an urban one, preferring residence in the cities to residence on their estates. But, especially in the first half of the century, it was a group whose economic power was based on land. Money was also made from abuse of imperial office and trade in foodstuffs; but land remained both an actual source of wealth and ideologically sanctioned. Despite the fact that the aristocracy was stratified, its members had in common landownership and a degree of privilege, i.e., fiscal privileges granted by the government for all or part of their estates.

The other great landlord in this period was the Church. The monasteries, especially those of Mount Athos, acquired very considerable estates, which were also tax exempt. Urban monasteries also had real estate and revenues, although nothing to approach those of the great monasteries of Mount Athos. The political power of the Church in this period, as well as its moral authority, went hand in hand with economic power.

The countryside was complex and variegated. Proprietors of medium-sized holdings with production that could be marketed are known to have existed. These might hold imperial privileges, and thus qualify for the label 'gentleman-farmer', like Theodosios Skaranos in the late thirteenth century. They could also be city inhabitants with rural holdings but no visible privileges, such as Theodore Karavas, inhabitant of Thessaloniki, who was in all probability also a merchant, marketing his own products along with those of others.[31] Independent peasants, who paid taxes to the state, and cultivated a plot of land primarily to provide for their families, also appear in our sources, but for the most part when they sell or donate their properties to monasteries; they are under economic stress, at least in Macedonia. In Epirus, the small landowner seems to have been more frequent. Nevertheless, the large estate, held by laymen or ecclesiastics, is the dominant aspect of the countryside. It was cultivated in indirect exploitation, by tenants, including dependent peasants.[32]

The Byzantine dependent peasant, the *paroikos,* is a category which proliferates in the course of the thirteenth and fourteenth centuries. The dependence is from a landlord, lay or ecclesiastical, including a *pronoia*-holder, and takes the

[30] Guillou, *Les archives de Saint-Jean-Prodrome,* nos. 19, 20. Cf. Theocharides (1963), esp. pp. 160–4.
[31] Lefort (1986c); *Actes de Chilandar,* ed. Petit, no. 27.   [32] Svoronos (1982), IV, pp. 167ff.

form of payment of taxes and dues to the landlord rather than to the state.[33] There is also cultivation of the demesne lands of the landlord but, with some exceptions, labour services seem to have been rather limited, the usual number being twelve days in a year; but twenty-four days and even, once, fifty-two days are attested.[34] On lands which were not his, but which he rented from the landlord, the peasant either paid a fixed rent (*pakton*) or more commonly shared the crop, so that there was a double, or triple, source of revenues for the landlord: the tax (calculated and expected to be paid in coin),[35] the rent (*morte* or *dekatia*, literally one tenth of the produce, although the normal arrangement would give the landlord one third or half of the produce)[36] and some labour services. The dependence, then, was both fiscal and economic. At the same time, it must be stressed that the peasant did own property, particularly the type of property that can be cultivated without much equipment, such as vineyards, olive trees and gardens. This he could leave to his heirs (in a system of partible inheritance, traditional in Byzantium, which leads to considerable instability in the size of the holdings and is not in the best interest of the landlord, but nevertheless survived), or sell, probably without having to obtain the permission of the landlord.[37] The peasant was free in his person, and had freedom of movement.

The legal and economic position of the dependent peasant, and the existence, alongside the large estates, of medium and small holdings, is linked to a type of exploitation which is based primarily on family cultivation of small plots of land, and less on the direct exploitation of domanial reserves.[38] The peasant household in the fourteenth century was both a fiscal unit (upon which the tax was estimated) and an economic unit, a unit of production. It is noteworthy that households and families could be headed by women as well as men, although male heads of household are typical, and that there was no difference in the fiscal obligations of households headed by women. Peasant women like other women in this period could and did own property, much of it in the form of dowry. Typically, the household consisted of a nuclear family, although it is

---

[33] Laiou-Thomadakis (1977); Lefort (1985), (1991) and (1993) for the peasantry.

[34] Laiou-Thomadakis (1977), pp. 181–2.

[35] But see the case of the peasants of Paphlagonia, during the reign of Michael VIII, who found payment in coin a great burden, since 'they had the necessary products in more than sufficient quantities, for the land was productive, but they had little coin, because each was producing what was necessary' (GP, ed. Failler, p. 293 = Bk III, 22). They were none the less forced to pay their taxes in cash, a source of great unhappiness.

[36] Sathas, Μεσαιωνικὴ Βιβλιοθήκη, VI, pp. 6, 620–2; cf. Laiou-Thomadakis (1977), p. 219 and n.121.

[37] An ambiguous text of the late fourteenth century suggests that the landlord may have a right to a tenth of the value of a piece of land that changed hands; but it is not at all certain that we are dealing with a *paroikos*. For the text, see Fögen (1982), pp. 236–7; but also Laiou-Thomadakis (1977), pp. 44–5.   [38] Svoronos (1956), pp. 325–35, and (1982), pp. 153–73.

also typical that most households were extended at some stage, usually while the older generation was alive. Laterally extended households, in which siblings with their own families form one fiscal unit, whether they reside together or not and own or exploit property together are also attested, with varying frequency. Their presence is undoubtedly connected to the system of inheritance and marriage, which divided the economic assets of a household with each generation, and restructured them, through marriage, to which the bride brought a dowry, and the bridegroom also brought property. Joint ownership and exploitation of landed resources, beneficial as it was in economic terms, held only for siblings and first cousins, breaking down after that.[39]

This peasant population, especially in Macedonia where the documents permit a close study, was experiencing an economic decline in the first half of the fourteenth century, visible above all in the reduction of the property of peasant households, especially the wealthier ones. There are clearly factors at work which act as barriers to the accumulation or even the conservation of peasant holdings, and these cannot include the system of inheritance, since its effects were countered by the reconcentration of property through marriage. The economic decline has been seen by some as a crisis resulting from the over-expansion, into marginal lands, of a population which had been, and was still, expanding.[40] According to this view, there was no demographic crisis in the countryside until the plague of the 1340s. A different interpretation suggests that the population had reached a demographic plateau around 1300, with a subsequent decline. We also find considerable mobility, with the migration both of entire families (among the poorer segment of the rural population) and of individuals (typically, among the wealthier peasants). There is, therefore, in the first half of the century, a crisis in rural society, whether only economic or both economic and demographic. Among its causes one must count the combined effects of wars, civil wars, plunder and pillage by troops both friendly and hostile to the state, all of which brought periodic high points to a crisis that was not yet acute.[41]

The Byzantine countryside was still a source of considerable wealth, as may be seen in the great fortunes that large proprietors were able to amass. The vitality and wealth of which this society was still capable are more evident in the cities, whose role and population underwent a true transformation. For one thing, although the capital retained its importance, a number of provincial cities, primarily in the European provinces, since Asia Minor was, for all intents and purposes, lost within the first three decades, emerged as centres

---

[39] Laiou (1992b), esp. pp. 167–70.

[40] Lefort (1991), pp. 77–8, and (1993), p. 105; for a different view, see Laiou-Thomadakis (1977), passim.

[41] John Kantakouzenos, writing on the first civil war, explained that, in 1322, the taxes could not be collected, both because of the war and because 'the peasants, from whom the taxes are primarily collected, have left their homes': IC, *Hist.*, I, pp. 136–7 = Bk I, 28.

of government. The defence of the cities by their inhabitants at the time of the Catalan attack and later undoubtedly contributed to the growing sense of independence of the urban populations.[42] Some cities acquired imperial privileges which guaranteed a certain degree of self-government in matters both administrative and fiscal. As for the population of the cities, we do not have firm numbers; Constantinople and Thessaloniki may have had 100,000 inhabitants each.[43] It included, as it had traditionally done, members of the aristocracy, but also groups that are much less visible in the sources: people with landed property, both urban and rural, who might be termed the local gentlefolk, who had some comfortable level of affluence and a certain political role, sometimes exercised through offices in the government of the city, including offices in the Church.[44] A third group includes merchants and artisans, whose existence is attested in a large number of cities, including Thessaloniki, Adrianople, Ainos, Raidestos, Serres, Ioannina, Arta, Mystras, Monemvasia and Sozopolis. The inhabitants of the coastal cities, in contact with Venetian and Genoese merchants, had commercial activities which were more developed than those of cities of the hinterland. However, the less visible commercial activities of cities and towns of the hinterland must not be neglected.

The role of the cities and urban populations in trade must be seen in conjunction with the larger economic realities of the period. Primary among them is the fact that, until the middle of the century, the cities of Venice and Genoa, as yet untouched by the crisis that affected northern Europe, had assumed a dominant position in a trade system which they had established, and which included the eastern Mediterranean, Italy and western Europe. For the countries of the eastern Mediterranean and above all for Byzantium which had given substantial commercial privileges to these cities, the result was that their exchange economy functioned within this larger system, and with a specific role: Byzantine exports to the west consisted primarily of foodstuffs and raw materials, and its imports consisted primarily of manufactured products, among which cloth was particularly important.

Nevertheless, it should be stressed that this set of economic relations created secondary systems of exchange, in which the native merchants participated actively: it was they, for the most part, who carried the merchandise

---

[42] The same is true of Philadelphia in 1304: Ahrweiler (1983), p. 184.

[43] Matschke (1971), pp. 106–7, n. 3.

[44] I use the term 'gentlefolk' to avoid the specifically English and country connotations of the term 'gentry'. This was an urban population but they were also landowners and their wealth came from land and minor office. The *ODB (s.v. archontopoulos)* defines the group as 'nobility of second rank', but since there was no nobility this seems inaccurate. The study of this group remains an important *desideratum.* As examples, I mention the families Mourmouras, Masgidas, Pothos from Thessaloniki and Serres.

along the land routes; they sailed from port to port in the Aegean, had active economic and financial relations with the Italians, and even, in the case of the Monemvasiots, a booming trade of their own. Secondary and dependent this role may have been, but it was significant. Thessaloniki, for example, was the hub of a trade network that included the Balkans west of the Strymon river, as well as Serbia, and reached the sea both in Thessaloniki itself and in Dubrovnik (Ragusa); an important part of the city population consisted of sailors and merchants. Other cities, like Adrianople, had merchants who were involved in a second subsystem, including Constantinople, Thrace and Bulgaria, and who had transactions with the Genoese in the towns of the Black Sea.[45] What the Byzantine merchants could not do was to engage in long-distance trade. The markets of Italy were almost closed to them.[46] As for the Black Sea, Byzantine traders probably had an uninterrupted presence here; that of the Monemvasiots should be particularly noted. The Byzantine presence became fairly massive in the 1340s, when the merchants of Constantinople profited from the conflict between Genoa, Venice and the khans of the Crimea, massive enough to provoke a war with Genoa, and a peace treaty (1352) that included a clause severely limiting the access of Byzantine merchants to Tana and the Sea of Azov. Merchants and bankers were an important group in Constantinople in the first half of the century.

Apart from the participation of the Byzantines in the regional trade which was connected with Italian commerce, there was trade between the city and its hinterland, fuelled partly by the fact that the peasants had to pay their taxes in coin, and partly by the commercialised production of landlords. There was also trade in foodstuffs between different parts of Macedonia.[47] Local production of woollen cloth is attested in Serres and Thessaloniki.[48] But this was small-scale production, for we hear mostly of imports of western cloth.

In those cities where commercial activity was most developed, the merchants (along with other urban inhabitants, including bankers and artisans) were, in this period, identified as a distinct social group. They were usually called the *mesoi*, literally, the 'middle group', being between the landowning aristocracy and the people.[49] They appear to have been conscious enough of their economic interests: they opposed vociferously Emperor John VI Kantakouzenos when, in 1347, he asked for contributions to rebuild the army and the fleet. While presumably a fleet would safeguard their commercial

---

[45] Laiou (1980–1) and (1985); Matschke (1970) and (1971); Oikonomidès (1979a), p. 46.

[46] Notice must be taken, however, of the presence of Byzantine sailors in Alexandria, in the late thirteenth century: *AASS*, Nov. IV, 676.   [47] Schreiner, *Texte*, no. 3.

[48] For Thessaloniki, see Matschke (1989). The evidence for production of cloth in significant quantities in this period is limited. For Serres, see Schreiner, *Texte*, no. 3.53.

[49] The most useful discussion is by Oikonomidès (1979a), pp. 114–20.

interests, especially in the Black Sea, it may be that their affairs were too deeply intertwined with those of the Italian merchants for them to wish to jeopardise them.[50] This is also the first time in Byzantine history where we find in literature mention of the merchants (or those who become rich through trade) in a way which juxtaposes them to the aristocracy, but certainly includes them among the rich, in the traditional division of rich and poor.[51]

The salient characteristics of the Byzantine city of this period, then, especially of the cities most involved with trade, are the following. They are the place of residence of members of the high aristocracy, who also hold political power. A segment of the population, involved in trade, is economically strong but does not participate in the governance of the city. There is in this relatively structured society a growing division between rich and poor, within the close confines of the city. There are, finally, times of insecurity, risk and stress, connected with political troubles. Thus, after 1328 Andronikos III had to give relief to creditors impoverished by the civil war, forgiving them the interest on loans. A number of people made a great deal of money, but social tensions were present, and obvious to contemporary observers, from Thomas Magister (Theodoulos Monachos) in the 1320s to Alexios Makremvolites in the early 1340s, who bitterly complained that the rich would have appropriated even the sun if they could, and deprived the poor of its light.[52]

Social tensions were to come to the forefront during the civil wars, most clearly during the second civil war, which started in October 1341, and is thus broadly speaking contemporary with other civic rebellions in western Europe. At first, this was a struggle for power at the centre: a dispute for the regency for the nine-year-old heir to the throne, John V (1341–91), between John Kantakouzenos on the one hand, and on the other John V's mother, Anne of Savoy, the patriarch and the *megas doux* Alexios Apokaukos. Before declaring himself emperor, Kantakouzenos had sent letters to the powerful and the military men of the cities, seeking their support; when his letter was read in Adrianople, on 27 October, three men, at least one of whom was almost certainly a merchant, aroused the people of the city, who attacked the aristocrats and burned their houses. Quickly, the civil war spread throughout the cities of Macedonia and Thrace. The most acute aspects of social conflict are visible in Thessaloniki where the opposition to Kantakouzenos was led by a group with radical tendencies, the Zealots. In some cities, like Serres, Kantakouzenos was opposed by members of the aristocracy, and it is certain that social alignments in this civil war were not more perfect than they were in western Europe. But

---

[50] Laiou (1987), p. 103.
[51] Ševčenko, 'Alexios Makrembolites', pp. 206–7. The author himself was of humble social origins: Ševčenko (1974), pp. 74, 86.   [52] Ševčenko (1974), p. 204.

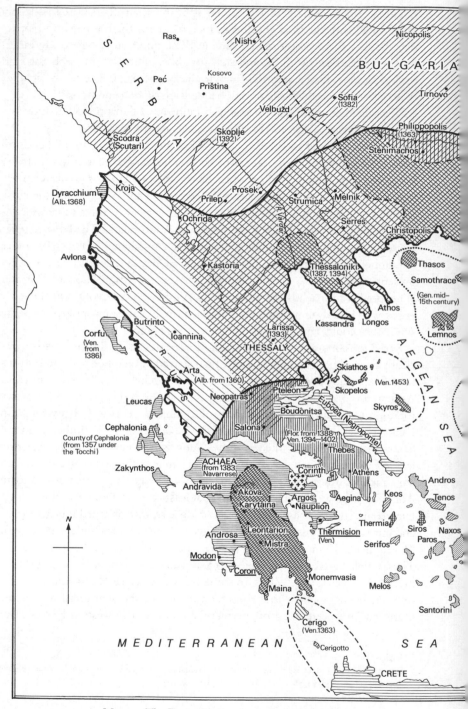

Map 17 The Byzantine empire in the 1340s

Varna

Mesembria
Anchialus
Sozopolis

B L A C K   S E A

Adrianople
(1362)

Didymoteichon
(1361)

Heraclea
(until 1360)

Selymbria Galata
Heraclea
Rhaedestus Constantinople Chrysopolis
Panidus (Scutari)
Nicomedeia

Sea of Marmara

Gallipoli Nicaea

bros

Brusa Ankara

nedos
til 1382)

Lesbos
(Gen. 1355)
Chios
(Gen. 1346) New Phocaea
(Gen. 1351)
Old Phocaea
(Gen. 1358) Philadelphia
(until 1390)
Smyrna
(from 1344)

Samos

Icaria

Amorgos
(¼ Ven. from 1370)

Astypalaia

Rhodes

	Byzantine territory *c.* 1340
	Byzantine territory *c.* 1350
	Byzantine territory *c.* 1402
	Dušan conquests after 1340
	Bulgarian conquests in 1344
	Turkish territory *c.* 1350
	Turkish conquests 1354–1402
	Venetian possessions
	Venetian fiefs
	Genoese possessions
	Angevin possessions
	Catalan possessions
	Possessions of the duchy of Naxos (archipelago)
	Fiefs of Naxos (Amorgos, Thermia)
	Possessions of the Hospitallers (Corinth 1400–4)

0   100 miles
0   150 km

the main lines of division are clear: the aristocracy, of whom Kantakouzenos was the richest and most powerful representative, rallied to his side, while in Constantinople, Thessaloniki, Didymoteichon, Adrianople and elsewhere the merchants, perhaps the bankers, certainly the sailors and, to a varying degree, the *mesoi* generally opposed Kantakouzenos, confiscated or destroyed the property of his supporters, and imprisoned many among them. In his *History*, Kantakouzenos described the civil war in self-serving statements. More telling than those is his discussion of the accession to power (in 1339) and the polity of Simone Boccanegra in Genoa. The revolution of 1339 is cast in terms of the Byzantine civil war, and he sees it as an opposition of the people to the nobles 'because they were better than they'. The story of Boccanegra is twisted, undoubtedly consciously, so that all the evils that befell Genoa can be ascribed to him, as the evils that resulted from the Byzantine civil war are ascribed to Apokaukos.[53] Although causal connections between the Genoese revolution and the revolution in Thessaloniki have been disproved, the similarities in the social aspects of the conflict are striking.

Since the forces of Kantakouzenos and his allies controlled the countryside, the civil war soon assumed the form of a struggle for the cities. Cities were difficult to take by assault but, with the countryside looted and in hostile hands, including the Turkish allies of Kantakouzenos, they began to surrender in 1344–5. In 1345, with the assassination of Alexios Apokaukos, the situation changed drastically, and in February 1346 Kantakouzenos entered Constantinople as co-emperor. Thessaloniki resisted until 1350, when, under pressure from the Serbs, it reluctantly accepted both John VI Kantakouzenos and John V Palaeologus. In 1354, John V forced the abdication of Kantakouzenos. This may be considered the end of the civil war.

The civil war was, among other things, an abortive effort to create a state quite different from what had existed in Byzantium, one where the interests of the commercial element would be paramount, while the resources of the landed aristocracy and the Church would be used for the needs of defence.[54] At exactly the same time, there was a conflict within the Church, between those who adopted a mystical attitude, that posited the possibility of experiencing the Divine Light through a special form of prayer (the Hesychasts), and those who believed that God may be experienced in his manifestations but not in his essence. The Hesychast controversy divided not only the Church but other

---

[53] IC, *Hist.*, III, pp. 197–8 = Bk IV, 26; 234–7 = Bk IV, 32.

[54] The discourse of Nicholas Kavasilas, written during the civil war, speaks of the confiscation of church property for the common good: Ševčenko, 'Nicolas Cabasisals's "Anti-Zealot" Discourse', pp. 92–4, par. 4, 6, 7. Most other sources of the period refer to the confiscation of the property of the aristocracy. On Apokaukos's plans to create a state that would be primarily maritime and dependent on trade, see IC, *Hist.*, II, p. 537 = Bk III, 87.

members of society, those who were interested in theological and religious questions. While political and social attitudes and theological positions did not entirely converge,[55] neither were they parallel. Hesychasm was practised on Mount Athos, and its most vocal proponent was St Gregory Palamas: Hesychasts were also staunch supporters of Kantakouzenos. The controversy ended with the political victory of Kantakouzenos. He presided over a Church council in 1351 which pronounced Hesychasm orthodox and its opponents heretical. No wonder that Palamas, appointed archbishop of Thessaloniki, was twice prevented by the city government from gaining his see, and was able to enter the city only in 1350, in the wake of Kantakouzenos's triumph.

In the end, Kantakouzenos and the aristocracy won a short-term political victory, but suffered a crushing long-term economic defeat. In order to win, Kantakouzenos had appealed to the Serbs in 1342, and to the Turks soon afterwards. The regency also made such appeals, unsuccessfully. Kantakouzenos, however, was successful. Stephen Dušan gave him help, but in the process he conquered much of Macedonia, Thessaly, Epiros and part of Greece, sometimes with the agreement of Kantakouzenos, but more frequently without it. In 1345, he took the large and important city of Serres, and thereafter he called himself emperor of the Serbs and the Romans. The state of Stephen Dušan was large but ephemeral, breaking down after his death, in 1355. His successors retained part of it, until the Ottomans conquered it after 1371. As for the Turks, both the emir of Aydın and, more ominously, the Ottomans, sent large forces into Europe to help Kantakouzenos; in 1354, they settled in Gallipoli, and from then onwards the Ottoman advance into European territory proceeded rapidly. As a result, the Byzantine state that emerged from the civil war was much smaller and much weaker than before.

Cultural life

The intellectual and artistic production of the fourteenth century is impressive in terms of quantity and in quality. Modern scholars have routinely contrasted these achievements to the weakness of the state; but we have seen that there was both strength and vitality, especially in the first half of the century, not surprisingly the period in which intellectual and artistic activity was at its highest. Whether one calls this a Renaissance or a revival,[56] the main traits are clear.

There were a considerable number of people whom one may term intellectuals. Many were acquainted with each other, corresponded with each other as the

---

[55] E.g. Nikephoros Gregoras was a supporter of Kantakouzenos in political matters, but a bitter opponent of Palamas and Hesychasm.

[56] The two opposing views may be found in Runciman (1970) and Ševčenko (1984).

voluminous epistolography of the period shows, were teachers of the next generation (as was the case, for example, for Theodore Metochites and Nikephoros
Gregoras). Most, though by no means all, of the intellectuals came from the ranks
of the clergy, the aristocracy, the officialdom as, more predictably, did their
patrons. These were people with a first-rate classical education in Greek; some,
like the monk Maximos Planoudes and Demetrios Kydones, also knew and translated Latin. They were polymaths, who wrote on a large number of subjects,
including theology, mathematics, astronomy, geography. The latter was of particular importance in the late thirteenth and early fourteenth centuries: Planoudes
is responsible for commissioning the first extant Ptolemaic *Geography* with the full
twenty-seven maps.[57] They were also editors and commentators of texts. Finally,
the period has considerable literary production, both in high Greek and in the
popular language. The great centres of intellectual life were Constantinople (until
the 1330s), Thessaloniki and Mystra. But smaller cities could also boast of intellectuals, and artistic production of high quality may be found in the provinces.

The causes of this revival are multiple. The recovery of Constantinople was in
itself a stimulus, although there were highly educated people in the empire of
Nicaea.[58] Political vicissitudes also influenced attitudes. The profound interest in
antiquity, responsible for classicising styles both in writing and in art, may well be
connected to new concepts of self-identification which included identification
with the Ancient Greeks, the Hellenes; this was already clearly evident in the late
twelfth century, when intellectuals posited a cultural identification with ancient
Greece, to contrast themselves to the westerners.[59] Patronage played an important role. Emperor Andronikos II was deeply interested in intellectual matters,
and his most important officials (Nikephoros Choumnos and Theodore
Metochites) were among the major scholars of the day. There was, also, still
sufficient money to permit intellectual and artistic production.

Until the end of the reign of Andronikos II the imperial court functioned
as an important patron. Michael VIII called himself a new Constantine, and
he was the first to invest in the rebuilding not only of the walls but of the city
which had greatly suffered during the Fourth Crusade and the Latin occupation. The Deesis mosaic in Haghia Sophia is thought to have been made just
after the reconquest.[60] Members of the highest aristocracy, relatives of this
emperor and his successor, participated in the rebuilding, primarily through
the restoration and expansion of monasteries and churches; women were

---

[57] This is the Cod. Urbinas Gr. 82, lavishly illustrated, perhaps for Andronikos II. The other two oldest
such manuscripts, Seragliensis 57 and Fragmentum Fabricianum Graecum 23, are also attributed to
Planoudes's activities: Harley and Woodward (1987), I, pp. 191–2, 269–70.
[58] E.g. George Pachymeres was educated both in Nicaea and in Constantinople, under George
Akropolites who was educated in Nicaea.   [59] Laiou (1991b), esp. pp. 77–81.
[60] On building activities in the early Palaeologan period, see Talbot (1993) and Ousterhout (1991).

important patrons. The mosaics and frescoes of the period, both in Constantinople and in Thessaloniki, were of the highest quality. Perhaps the best among them are the mosaics and frescoes in the church of the Chora monastery (Kariye Djami), the result of the patronage of Theodore Metochites. It seems that building churches and palaces was considered an important attribute of the aristocracy. The production of manuscripts also flourished, again with some women as patrons.

Aristocratic patronage was also important in other parts of the fourteenth-century Greek world, for example in Thessaly. By contrast, it has recently been pointed out that in Thessaloniki and Macedonia much of the building was due to ecclesiastical, especially episcopal, patronage.[61] The church of the Holy Apostles in Thessaloniki was built by the Patriarch Niphon, while the monasteries of Mount Athos were also important centres of artistic activity. Ecclesiastical patronage reflects the increasing economic and political power of the Church.

The period of the civil war and the crises of the mid-fourteenth century brought about changes and a significant reduction of activity, especially in the production of art. Characteristically, when the great eastern arch and part of the dome of Haghia Sophia collapsed (1346), the impoverished John VI sought money for its restoration from the Russians and from the inhabitants of the city.[62] In the despotate of the Morea, the patronage of the court of the despot was very active, and the superb frescoes of the Peribleptos date from the second half of the century. Monumental mosaics, a much more expensive medium, were not produced after the 1320s; the mosaics in the great eastern arch, the two eastern pendentives and the dome of Haghia Sophia, completed *c.* 1354–5, constitute an exception.

The cultural and artistic developments of the fourteenth century also serve as reminders of the fact that Byzantium of this period had an influence that far exceeded its political boundaries. Byzantine culture radiated both in the Orthodox world (the Slavs, the Georgians, the former Byzantine possessions under Italian occupation) and in the west, carried by artists (among them Theophanes the Greek) who worked in other Orthodox states and by intellectuals who began the migration to Italy that was to intensify in the fifteenth century.

THE COLLAPSE OF THE STATE AND THE REDISTRIBUTION
OF AUTHORITY (1354–1402)

In the second half of the fourteenth century, Byzantium was a tiny and disjointed state in a Mediterranean world that was undergoing its own crisis.

---

[61] Rautman (1991).   [62] Mango (1962), pp. 66ff.

Reduced economic circumstances exacerbated the antagonism of Venice and Genoa, which became involved in and fostered the virtually endemic Byzantine dynastic wars, while they also fought for possession of territory, such as the island of Tenedos, which eventually led to the War of Tenedos, otherwise known as the War of Chioggia (1378–81), in which the Byzantines became involved. After 1354, the Byzantine 'empire' consisted of Constantinople, Thrace, Thessaloniki (which by now could only be reached by sea) and its immediate hinterland, the islands of the northern Aegean and the despotate of the Morea in the Peloponnese. Even those possessions were insecure, since Thrace was being subjected by the Ottomans. Raids were soon followed by the conquest of cities, Didymoteichon falling in 1361, Philippopolis in 1363 and Adrianople in 1369. With the fall of the latter, the road to Macedonia and Bulgaria was open. In 1371 the Ottoman victory at the battle of the Maritsa destroyed the Serbian state of Serres; the city passed into Byzantine hands, but only until 1383. At the same time, the Byzantine and Serbian rulers became tributary to the Ottoman sultan; the emperor John V and later his son, Manuel II, were forced to follow the sultan on campaign.[63]

After 1371, the Byzantine emperors could rule only with the help or the forbearance of the Venetians, the Genoese and the Ottomans. The struggles for the throne among members of the imperial family only exacerbated their dependence, as each sought the help of one or another of these powers. True, there were some efforts to resist these trends. Thus Manuel Palaeologus, later emperor, at a time when he was at odds with his father, went secretly to Thessaloniki, where he established what Demetrios Kydones called 'a new authority'. For a short time he was able to launch expeditions against the Turks; but his successes, though heartening to Byzantines and western Europeans alike,[64] were short-lived, as may be seen by the fall of Serres to the Ottomans in 1383, and of Thessaloniki, after a four-year siege, in 1387. The city, cut off from its hinterland, suffered from lack of food, and its population was rent by social tensions and factional disagreements. Even its archbishop abandoned it in 1386–7, along with some of the clergy. Manuel, too, was forced to leave Thessaloniki. He eventually returned to Constantinople, where, in 1391, he succeeded his father on the throne (1391–1425). The first Turkish conquest of Thessaloniki lasted until 1403.

The other avenue of resistance that some Byzantines could contemplate was co-operation with and help from western Europe. There were sufficient economic and political ties to make such hopes possible, and furthermore by now

---

[63] In 1390–1, Manuel, who fought with the Ottomans in Asia Minor against the other Turkish emirates and the last Byzantine city, Philadelphia, gave, in his letters, a moving account of the decline of the former Byzantine possessions and the plight of the population: Dennis, *Letters*, nos. 16, 18.

[64] Barker (1969), pp. 47ff; *Démétrius Cydonès correspondance*, ed. Loenertz, 208, letter 264.80.

some of the leaders of western Europe, especially including the papacy, were considering the Ottoman advance a threat to Christendom. But Venice and Genoa, weakened by the crises of the mid century, were pursuing their own interests; France and England were engaged in the Hundred Years War, and the papacy made its help contingent upon a union of the Churches, on its own terms. But, although there were, in Byzantium, people who worked actively for the union, the Church generally and a large part of the population opposed it. Successive Byzantine emperors (John V, John VII, Manuel II) went to the west in search of aid, but in vain. John V even made a personal conversion to Catholicism; an official union was not proclaimed until the Council of Ferrara-Florence (1439) but by then it was much too late. Expeditions such as that of Count Amedeo VI of Savoy were mere palliatives, and the crusade of Nicopolis (1396) was a disaster.

The political crisis was attended by a general economic crisis, as well as a redistribution of dwindling resources and of political power. As in western Europe, there is a general reduction of the population, both in the countryside and in the cities. The picture of the countryside of Thrace and Macedonia is one of devastation and depopulation. The contribution of the Black Death remains an unknown factor. While there is evidence of plague in Constantinople, Macedonia, the Morea, the islands of the Aegean and Mount Athos, there are no particulars that might permit a study of its effects on various segments of the population. In 1384, the patriarch Neilos spoke of the flight of peasants from Church lands, attributing it to the invasions.[65]

The aristocracy as a group underwent significant changes in this period. The civil war had impoverished many among them, while the successive conquests of Macedonia by Serbs and Ottomans resulted in a redistribution of property into the hands either of the conquerors, or of those members of the aristocracy who were favourable to them, or of the Church. When Byzantine power was temporarily restored in such areas, there were long disputes for the recovery of lands lost by particular families or individuals.[66] Secondly, the aristocracy now became much more involved in trade than it had ever been before, a trend that was to continue into the fifteenth century.[67] Powerful men who bore aristocratic names invested in commercial and banking activities, closely tied to those of Genoese and Venetian merchants. Emperor John VII seems to have exported grain to Genoa in the 1380s, through his agents. Indeed, despite the great political uncertainty, and periodic acute crises in foodstuffs, the grain trade was an active one; some Greeks even brought grain to Caffa in 1386.

---

[65] Miklosich and Müller, *Acta et Diplomata*, II, pp. 61–2.

[66] See Oikonomidès (1980); Laiou (1985). John V issued an edict, probably in 1373, which declared that all lands illegally taken from their owners should be restored; but it did not have much effect.

[67] Oikonomidès (1979a), pp. 120–2; Laiou (1982b), pp. 105–9.

Moved by hardship, and also by the possibilities trade offered, aristocratic Constantinopolitan ladies invested in commerce with funds from dowry property, despite legal strictures on the use of dowry goods in risky ventures.

A third characteristic of the aristocracy is an increase in the importance of the local aristocracy or gentlefolk, the ἀρχοντόπουλοι or μικροί ἄρχοντες of the Greek sources, the *gentilhomeni picioli* of the Venetian sources.[68] In Serres, they formed part of the ecclesiastical and civil administration of the city under Serbian rule, and some reappear during the first stages of Ottoman rule; so also in Thessaloniki during the first Ottoman occupation. In Ioannina in 1411, they, along with the higher aristocracy, decide on the fate of the city. The emergence of the 'gentlefolk' may be connected with the final stages of decentralisation, which, by cutting the cities off from the capital, placed more decisions in the hands of their population;[69] it is also a further sign of the redistribution of power among the upper class. While the enhanced role of the gentlefolk is probably a long-term development (these are families with significant continuity, at least during the fourteenth century), the increased independence of the city populations took place in conditions of crisis, and was typically exercised in decisions to surrender the city to various conquerors.

The most enduring transfer of power of all kinds was to the Church collectively, and the monasteries of Mount Athos in particular. Long circumscribed by the existence of a strong central imperial power, the Church now expanded its authority and activities and in some ways supplanted the state. The resolution of the Hesychast controversy gave the conservative and fiercely Orthodox part of the Church spiritual and moral power. The weakness in imperial government can be seen in the increase of the Church's role in judicial matters and also in what may be termed relief functions, such as caring for the poor, the refugees or the inhabitants of cities in distress. As for economic resources, the monasteries of Mount Athos profited from donations by the Serbian kings and from privileges granted by the Ottomans; in return, Mount Athos accepted Ottoman overlordship early, perhaps before the conquest of Macedonia.[70] The monasteries also profited from transfers of landed property on the part of aristocratic lay landowners, who could no longer exploit their lands successfully. The state was well aware of the fact that the Church was now the only institution which had resources capable of being tapped. Several times in the course of the century, emperors tried to persuade either the patriarch or other churchmen to give or rent to them Church lands, so that soldiers could be compensated from the revenues. But this was usually refused, and Manuel Palaeologus's efforts to confiscate Church property in the first phases

---

[68] Mertzios (1947), p. 49. The document distinguishes three categories: *gentilhomeni e gentilhomeni picioli e stratioti*. Cf. Neçipoglu (1990). [69] Zachariadou (1989a), pp. 345–51. [70] Oikonomidès (1976).

of the siege of Thessaloniki occasioned a violent outburst on the part of the archbishop. In 1371 Manuel, in desperate straits, took away from the monasteries of Mount Athos and the Church of Thessaloniki half their properties, to turn them into *pronoiai* and give them to the soldiers, 'so as to avoid the complete loss of everything'. Part of these lands were restored to the monasteries after 1403. The Church, then, wealthy, powerful and with a moral and spiritual sphere of influence that was much larger than the Byzantine state, extending as it did to all the Orthodox world, was poised to play a primary role after the Ottoman conquest of Constantinople, in 1453.

As the century drew to a close, the only compact Byzantine possessions were in the Peloponnese, where Manuel, the son of John Kantakouzenos, had formed a small but viable state, the despotate of the Morea. Although it too was subject to Turkish raids, it was relatively prosperous, with a powerful and independent-minded aristocracy, and its capital, Mystra, had considerable intellectual and artistic achievements.[71] It was to survive the fall of Constantinople by seven years. Constantinople, on the other hand, was blockaded by the Sultan Bayezid for eight long years (1394–1402). Neither the efforts of Jean le Maingre, Marshal Boucicaut, who had been sent by Charles VI of France with 1,200 soldiers, nor the journey of Manuel II to western Europe, to seek aid, would have been sufficient to save the city from the siege and the attendant hunger and suffering. Many inhabitants fled the city, and some were ready to negotiate its surrender.[72] Only the defeat of the Ottoman forces by Timurlane at the battle of Ankara (28 July 1402) granted the Byzantine capital, the despotate of the Morea and the empire of Trebizond another half-century of life.

The economy, social structure and political orientation of the Byzantine state were all transformed through the crises of the fourteenth century. The decision to recover Constantinople in 1261 led, on the one hand, to a chimeric dream of reconstituting the old empire, thus negating the reality that, since the late twelfth century, the strongest forces in that area were those of decentralisation, which would have led to smaller, more homogeneous political entities with, perhaps, strong economic and cultural links with each other. The recapture of Constantinople led to another important choice; the orientation toward western Europe which Michael VIII followed almost single-mindedly. This choice, however, could not be retained at the political level. At the economic level, the Byzantine economy of exchange and manufacturing became inextricably connected with the Italian economy. Close cultural contacts with Italy

---

[71] On the despotate of the Morea, see Zakythinos (1953) and (1975).

[72] Schreiner, *Die Byzantinischen Kleinchroniken*, chronicle 22, paras. 28 and 30 = 1, pp. 184–5; Laonici Chalcocandylae, *Historiarum Demonstrationes*, 1, p. 77; *Ducae Istoria Turco-Byzantina (1341–1462)*, pp. 79, 81–3.

also existed. Internally, there were, in the course of the century, profound changes in the structure of the dominant classes, of the cities, the merchant class. Many of these developments were advantageous to new social groups and new structures just as they were detrimental to old ones; the great civil war resulted from such conflicts, but failed to resolve them. The most serious problem of the Byzantine empire in this period was that its internal development was thwarted and shaped under intense pressure from foreign and hostile powers, the Serbs for a short while, and the Ottomans. As a result, no viable units could coalesce from the process of decentralisation for surely individual cities, even with their hinterland, were not viable units. The despotate of the Morea was an exception, but its fate followed inexorably that of the rest of the empire and indeed of the Balkans, which eventually were reunited under a new imperial power, the Ottoman state.

CHAPTER 25

LATINS IN THE AEGEAN AND THE BALKANS IN THE FOURTEENTH CENTURY

Michel Balard

AT the beginning of the fourteenth century, the consequences of the Byzantine reconquest of 1261 on the expansion of Latins into the Aegean and the Balkans were clearly felt. Michael VIII Palaeologus had opened access to the Black Sea to the Genoese by the Treaty of Nymphaeum, and to the Venetians in the years that followed, and recognised the principal conquests made by the latter after the Fourth Crusade. A chain of ports of call and trading-posts stretched along the main sea routes, since Andronikos II had abandoned the maintenance of a Byzantine fleet as too costly. The Aegean Sea was thus at the heart of the great trade routes which led from Italy to Constantinople and the Black Sea, Cyprus and Lesser Armenia, Syria and Alexandria. Control of the islands and coasts became a vital necessity for the Italian maritime republics and the object of frantic competition between them: from this sprang the three 'colonial' wars between Genoa and Venice in the course of the fourteenth century. Their only result was a *de facto* sharing of the Aegean: Venice had the western and southern coasts, with Messenia, Crete and Negroponte, Genoa the eastern coasts with Chios and Mytilene, while the Catalans were to come to disturb Italian maritime and commercial hegemony through their domination over the duchy of Athens and the rapid development of piracy.[1]

As a result, the Aegean and the Balkans found themselves encompassed by a mercantile economy directed to the satisfaction of the needs of the west for foodstuffs and raw materials. They thus entered a colonial type of exchange system, receiving artisanal products from the west and in exchange supplying all that was required to manufacture them. Local and regional trade was subordinated to the fluctuations and rhythms of long-distance activities dominated by the Italians, before whom Greek businessmen stood aside.[2] These major trends were established in the course of the century which followed the

---

[1] Thiriet (1975); Balard (1978).   [2] Jacoby (1989b), pp. 1–44.

restoration of the eastern empire in 1261 in two successive phases which we need to examine before considering the structures of the mercantile economy, then the trade routes and commodities.

THE PHASES OF WESTERN EXPANSION

At the beginning of the fourteenth century, Genoa and Venice emerged from the war of Curzola, in the course of which Andronikos II had sided whole-heartedly with the Genoese. But the latter had abandoned the *basileus* by concluding the Treaty of Milan (25 September 1299) with their enemies. At the time of the conflict, Venice finally halted the Byzantine reconquest undertaken by Michael VIII in the Aegean and added a few islands to those already possessed. Henceforth, Venetian authority extended firmly over Crete, the partly reconquered Archipelago, Coron (Korone) and Modon (Methoni) in southern Messenia, Negroponte (shared with three Latin lords, the *terciers*). Venice retained considerable influence in the principality of the Morea, which Charles II of Anjou had just removed from the Villehardouin heiress to put it under the authority of his own son, Philip of Taranto. The Venetians enjoyed complete freedom to trade there and established themselves in the main ports, Clarence and Patras. As for the Genoese, they obtained the rich alum-pits of Phocaea on the coast of Asia Minor from the 1260s onwards; then their admiral Benedetto Zaccaria seized Chios in 1304 and succeeded in securing recognition of the occupation of the island from the *basileus*. At the same time, the Catalan Company, mercenaries rashly summoned by Andronikos II against the Turks, extended their influence in the Aegean, ravaging Thrace, then Macedonia, before going on to conquer the duchy of Athens in 1311, where the Catalans remained until 1388. As for the Angevins, they endeavoured to resist the Greeks of Mistra and began to favour some degree of Italianisation of the Moreot barony at the expense of the French element which had hitherto been preponderant under the Villehardouin.[3]

The first half of the fourteenth century, at least until 1348, was characterised by the consolidation of acquired positions. Venice refused to participate in Charles of Valois's plans for the reconquest of Constantinople and drew closer to Byzantium. In 1319 a treaty was made between Venice and the Catalans, who were threatening Venetian positions in Euboea where Venetian authority over the *terciers* was being strengthened. Venice did not succeed in totally subduing the Cretan revolts of 1332 and 1341, resulting from the excessive demands of the *dominante* on this colony. Above all, Venice engaged in the struggle against the Turks with whom the Catalans had no hesitation in allying:

---

[3] Topping (1975), pp. 104–66.

the 'Christian Union' of 1332, naval league of 1344–5 and the 'crusade' of the dauphin Humbert II of Viennois in 1345. In Greece, the Catalans strengthened the duchy of Athens under the control of the vicar-general Alfonso Fadrique (1318–30), seizing Neopatras and Siderokastron, and halting Walter of Brienne's attempt to recover his dukedom. But the infante Ferrante of Majorca failed in 1315 when he wished to exploit his rights over the principality of the Morea. The latter passed from the authority of Jean de Gravines to that of Robert of Taranto, whose mother, Catherine of Valois, titular Latin empress of Constantinople, promoted the fortune of Florentine bankers, the Acciaiuoli, compensated for the loans which they had granted her by substantial land concessions in the principality. The fate of Genoese possessions was more unsettled. Since Martino Zaccaria refused to recognise Byzantine sovereignty for his Aegean possessions, Andronikos III drove him out from Chios (1329), then Phocaea (1340), which both returned for a while to the eastern empire. But in 1346, exploiting the weak regency of Anne of Savoy and the hesitations of Humbert of Viennois in the conduct of his eastern crusade, the Genoese fleet of Simone Vignoso seized first Chios then Phocaea and installed there for two centuries the government of the *mahona*, derived from the shipowners who had financed the expedition.[4]

This brilliant feat, which was in addition to Genoese attempts to control traffic to Constantinople and the Black Sea, was the cause of the war of the Straits (1351–5) between Genoa and the coalition between Venice, the Catalans and the Byzantine empire. The conflict did not alter the situation in the Aegean, except in relation to the Turks, who reached the gates of Byzantium. In 1355, the Genoese family of Gattilusio obtained, through the friendship of John V Palaeologus, the concession of the island of Mytilene, then, at the beginning of the fifteenth century, of several islands in the northern Aegean. From this time onwards, Venice had to endeavour to keep the way free through the Straits to the Black Sea; the concession of Tenedos at the mouth of the Dardanelles was obtained from the *basileus*, but the effective occupation of the island in 1376 unleashed a fresh war with Genoa, the so-called 'War of Chioggia', in so far as it essentially took place in the Adriatic and, like the previous wars, ended in a 'white peace' (Treaty of Turin, August 1381). These confrontations prevented any Christian union against the Turks, who made inexorable progress in the Aegean: the capture of Thessaloniki in 1387, Neopatras and Salona in 1394, incessant raids on the Pelopponese coast and the encirclement of Constantinople which was fortunately delivered by the victory of Timur-Leng over Bayezid at Ankara (1402). To meet these pressing dangers, Venice strove to strengthen Greco-Latin Romania, by pursuing a

---

[4] Setton (1975); Bonn (1969); Housley (1992); Argenti (1958); Balard (1978).

policy of annexation: the purchase of Nauplia and Argos in 1388, increased authority over Negroponte and the islands of the Archipelago, enlargement of the territory of Coron and Modon in Messenia, temporary administration of Patras, finally direct aid to the Latin crusaders at Nicopolis. Crete was the only weak point, which was in revolt again from 1363 to 1367, under the leadership of Venetian feudatories rebelling against the *dominante*. Overall, Venice succeeded in preserving the cohesion of her possessions and protecting them from the Turkish advance, even though it might have aroused the hostility of the Greeks or the petty Latin lords of the Pelopponese.[5]

There were profound changes in mainland Greece in the second half of the fourteenth century. In 1348, at the time when the Greek despotate of the Morea was being established, Stephen Dušan annexed Thessaly and Epirus to his Serb dominions. Great Latin lordships were created; Niccolò Acciaiuoli, grand seneschal of the kingdom of Sicily, was the largest feudatory of the Morea, with lands in Messenia, Elis and Corinthia, while his cousin Giovanni was archbishop of Patras from 1360 to 1365. On Niccolò's death, his cousin Nerio inherited part of his Moreot possessions, lost them to the Navarrese Company, but took from the Catalans Megara and, above all, Athens in 1388, thus putting an end to eight decades of Catalan occupation. The Tocchi ruled Leucas, Cephalonia and Zante and sought to seize Corinth on the death of Nerio Acciaiuoli in 1394. We cannot ignore the remarkable good fortune of the Zaccaria, heirs of the Genoese Martino, former master of Chios: Centurione I was grand constable and three times *bailo* of the Morea; his grandson Centurione II dispossessed the heirs of the head of the Catalan Company, Pierre of Saint-Supéran, prince of Achaea since 1396, and was the last Latin prince of the Morea from 1402 to 1432. Thus the principality passed from Angevin domination in 1383 to that of the Navarrese in 1386, to end in the hands of the last descendant of an old Genoese family, in his turn dispossessed by his own son-in-law, the despot Theodore Palaeologus of Mistra.[6]

At the beginning of the fifteenth century, the Aegean was thus divided between several Latin sovereignties, little by little whittled away by the progress of the Turks and the Greeks of Mistra. The Venetians organised their possessions into several *regimina*: that of Candia, covering Crete and the island of Cerigo, that of Negroponte which extended over Euboea, Skyros, the Northern Sporades and Bodonitsa on the Thessalian coast, that of Corfu (island annexed in 1387) which also included Butrinto in Epirus and Naupaktos (Lepanto) on the gulf of Patras, that of Nauplia and Argos which encompassed the island of Aegina, finally Coron and Modon to which belonged the island of Sapienza. Furthermore, Venice extended her protectorate over the

---

[5] Thiriet (1975).   [6] Topping (1975), pp. 104–66; Bonn (1969); Zakythinos (1975).

islands of the Archipelago, administering Tenos and Mykonos directly and possessing several trading-posts in foreign territory, Thessaloniki in Macedonia, Ephesus and Palatia on the coast of Asia Minor. Since 1309 Rhodes had been in the hands of the Knights Hospitaller and served as a staging-post on the shipping routes to Cyprus and Syria.

The Genoese domain was more limited: in Chios, Samos and Old and New Phocaea held directly; a trading-post at Ephesus; Mytilene, Lemnos, Thasos, Imbros, Samothrace and Ainos held by members of the Gattilusio, but without great ties to the city. The duchy of Athens was in the hands of Antonio Acciaiuoli from 1403 to 1435, the principality of the Morea in those of Centurione II Zaccaria from 1404 to 1432, but this was reduced from year to year because of the reconquest by the despotate. It was within this territorial frame, but also in the Byzantine and Turkish domains, that the commercial activities of the Latins developed, which flooded the whole of the Aegean and the Balkans and whose structures are fairly well known today.

LONG-DISTANCE TRADE AND ITS INFRASTRUCTURE

These activities were encouraged by the concession of privileges which sometimes legalised earlier capture. Venice had obtained complete freedom to trade in Byzantine territories from 1082. By the agreement made in 1209 with Guillaume de Champlitte, Venice secured full ownership of Coron and Modon, possession of which was confirmed by the treaties concluded in 1268 and 1277 with Michael VIII Palaeologus. In the principality, Venice had also enjoyed privileges since the settlement of the Franks in the early thirteenth century. Finally, in 1394 an agreement with Theodore I Palaeologus restored the freedom to trade from which Venetian merchants benefited according to custom in the despotate. They were thus able to develop their business activities throughout the entire Aegean without any hindrance other than the daily harassment of the tax collectors and agents of the Byzantine fisc, ready to challenge imperial concessions, especially in relation to the export of wheat, subject to lengthy negotiations.

From 1261, the Genoese also benefited from a total exemption from the Byzantine *kommerkion* but they had to wait for the treaties of 1304 and 1317, concluded with Andronicus II Palaeologus, to export freely wheat produced in the empire. The attempts at reaction of John VI Kantakouzenos to free himself from the economic domination of the Genoese rapidly stopped short. From the reign of Michael VIII the Pisans also obtained exemption from all customs dues. This was not the case with the other Latin nations: the Catalans subject to a tax of 3 per cent obtained a reduction to 2 per cent in 1320 but never complete exemption. The Narbonnais paid a tax of 4 per cent throughout the fourteenth century, the Anconitans one of 2 per cent. The Florentines had to wait until 1422 to benefit from reduction of the *kommerkion* by half and the Ragusans until 1451 to see their duties reduced to 2 per cent. Even so, it is true that the Latins were generally, in varying degrees, in a more favoured position than the Greeks themselves, obliged to discharge the *kommerkion* at the full rate. This was one of the causes of their supremacy over their Byzantine counterparts.[7]

The second pillar of western trade was the network of colonies and trading-posts where a population of Latin origin settled permanently. This emigration naturally prolonged the vast *inurbamento* movement whereby the Italian mercantile republics drew from their *contado* the human resources necessary for their economic development. We shall leave to one side the islands of the Archipelago where the Venetians were no more than a handful of conquering families: Sanudo then Crispo at Naxos, Cornaro at Karpathos, Ghisi at Tenos, Mykonos and Amorgos, Venier at Cerigo and Barozzi at Santorini. Similarly, in ports of call such as Coron and Modon, the permanent Latin population was insignificant in comparison with passing merchants and mariners awaiting recruitment. The Latin population must be evaluated quite differently in territories of some importance. At Negroponte it would be difficult to exceed a figure of between 2,000 and 3,000 Latins in a total population estimated at 40,000 inhabitants in the fourteenth century. In Crete the first preserved census dating from 1576–7 only mentions 407 Venetian families settled in the *cavalerie* but makes no reckoning of the Latin *bourgeois* in the towns. It seems reasonable to estimate the number of Venetians on the island at some thousands – 10,000 according to Thiriet; 2,500 according to Jacoby. They divided into feudatories established in the *sergenteries* and *cavalerie* and the *bourgeois* in the towns. Among the feudatories were the greatest names of the Venetian aristocracy: Dandolo, Gradenigo, Morosini, Venier, Corner and Soranzo, all subject to heavy levies for the defence and exploitation of their domains, but concerned to exploit the products of their lands and obtaining from the *dominante* free trade in cereals. The Venetian *bourgeois* of Crete practised a profession or craft in the towns and shared above all in the profits of long-distance trade.[8]

Estimates for Genoese possessions in the Aegean are just as uncertain. The Gattilusio admittedly only attracted a handful of fellow-citizens at Mytilene, then in the islands of the northern Aegean which they occupied at the beginning of the fifteenth century. During the period of their domination at Chios, the Zaccaria had only a few companions and a garrison of 800 soldiers. Under

---

[7] Zakythinos (1975), p. 258; Laiou (1972); Laiou (1980–1), pp. 177–222; Balard (1978), II; Antoniadis Bibicou (1963), pp. 124–33; Giunta (1959), II, pp. 140–5; Magdalino (1993), pp. 142–50; Lilie (1984), for the Komnenoi period.

[8] Loenertz (1970); Koder (1973), pp. 170–3; Thiriet (1975), pp. 270–86; Jacoby (1989a), VI, p. 202.

the administration of the *mahona*, a report addressed to the doge of Genoa in 1395 by the *podestà* Niccolò Fatinanti makes it possible to estimate the Latin population at nearly 400 families, that is about 2,000 individuals. Among them, the most active participation in long-distance trade came from the *mahonesi* themselves, who had the monopoly of the sale of alum and mastic, the great products of Phocaea and Chios.[9]

Were the Latins settled in the trading-posts and colonies of the Aegean the sole actors in economic life? Were those from the eastern empire, Greeks and Jews, associated with them in trading activities? Looking at the only official texts, deliberations of the senate and other Venetian assemblies, it could be concluded that there was total mercantile *dirigisme* by the *dominante*, reserving the monopoly of trade between the *dominante* and its Romaniot colonies to the exclusive profit of its citizens and the Venetian fleet. The subject populations only participated in local and regional trade of minimal importance. It seems today that this rigid segregation of Venetian colonial societies, asserted by F. Thiriet, should be challenged. The study in progress of Cretan notarial acts of the fourteenth century shows the multiple associations formed between Latins, Greeks and Jews in the activities connected with long-distance trade. Did the community of interests between the various ethnic elites not come from the fact that the Venetian feudatories and old *archontes* (major landown-ers and dignitaries of the eastern empire) were found side by side at the head of the great Cretan revolt of 1363? At Chios, some Greeks and Jews played an equal role with Latins in long-distance trade: Antonius Argenti, the Rabbi Elias, Master Elixeus, invested capital in *societates* with Latins, participated in maritime insurances or the transport of cereals, to say nothing of local trade and the provisioning of small ships between the island and the nearby main-land. In this sense, the increase in maritime and mercantile activities in Latin Romania undoubtedly had an impact on the indigenous elite.[10]

However, the principal naval commissioning and the organisation of navi-gation were the work of the Latins alone. At Venice, the senate strictly regu-lated the system of *mudae*: the dates of bids and of the departure of the galleys, the ports of call, the merchandise to be loaded, the size of the crews, all was anticipated in the deliberations which were concerned with even the traffic of unarmed vessels, with the job of repatriating the surplus merchandise in transit in the Aegean ports of call. The *mudae* of Cyprus (before 1373), Syria and Alexandria made a compulsory port of call at Modon and Candia, while those of Romania necessarily put into port in Messenia and Negroponte. On the Genoese side, the organisation was more lax: it was only in 1330 that the *officium Gazarie*, responsible for navigation problems, forbade light galleys to sail alone

---

[9] Argenti (1958), 1; Balard (1978), 1; Pistarino (1990b).   [10] McKee (1993); Balard (1978), p. 336.

towards the Levant beyond Sicily. There was no regular convoy, but it was made compulsory for the owners of galleys to sail *in conserva*, in order to limit the risks and to ensure good conditions for the transport of the most precious commodities. Before 1300 the organisation of a double annual passage to Romania can be traced; after that date, it was reduced to just one. But Genoa had never been able to set afoot a system of bids comparable to that of the *incanti* at Venice, frequently leaving it to private initiative. The Catalans had not organised regular convoys to the east before the end of the fourteenth century. In addition to these regular sailings, there were unarmed ships practising coastal trade along the Aegean coasts: Negroponte and Thessaloniki were visited by the Venetians but also Ephesus and Palatia, while the Genoese ships provided the great shipments of alum from Phocaea and Chios to Flanders. Private commissionings, less well known than the galleys, should not be under-estimated.[11]

As in the west, the activity of Latin businessmen in the Aegean rested on contracts drawn up in the presence of a notary; *colleganze* and *commende, societates* and contracts of exchange, maritime insurances and procurations wove the periodic ties between merchants, associates for a voyage or longer periods. The Venetian notarial deeds from Crete, Coron and Modon, and those of the Genoese notaries of Chios, were not drawn up any differently from instruments drawn up at Genoa or Venice. Their object was to gather the necessary capital, insure ships and cargoes and create interdependencies capable of compensating for the absence of businessmen. In particular amongst them are contracts defining the conditions in which those from the *mahona* could exercise the monopoly of the sale of mastic in the three great geographical zones shared between the Giustiniani families which constituted the association.[12]

The totality of these contracts defined the actors in economic life, very diverse in origin and social level. Although the great majority of businessmen in the Venetian colonies came from the coasts of the Lagoon, and those of the Genoese trading-posts from Liguria, these documents also reveal the activity of many other entrepreneurs. Catalans, men from Languedoc and Provence, Pisans, Florentines, Lombards and Anconitans, those from southern Italy and Ragusa and former refugees from Syria-Palestine also participated in long-distance trade, either on their own account or in association with the representatives of the two great Italian maritime republics. The Aegean was truly a 'free trade community', in which rivalries could be exacerbated, but in which each

---

[11] Stöckly (1995); Balard (1978), pp. 576–85; del Treppo (1971); Ashtor (1983).
[12] Carbone (1978); Chiaudano and Lombardo (1960); Lombardo (1968); Morozzo dell Rocca (1950); Argenti (1958), iii, p. 3; Balard (1988).

man found his place, providing that he benefited from capital, opportunity and the spirit of enterprise.

ROUTES, PRODUCTS AND CONJUNCTURE

The great areas of Latin trade in the Aegean and the Balkans fell into three distinct zones: the Pelopponese, the Venetian insular domain and the Genoese possessions. The Pelopponese had long been considered the preserve of Venice which had obtained total freedom of trade there since the creation of the Frankish principality. At the end of the thirteenth century, the first known deliberations of Venetian assemblies refer to the trade of the people of the Lagoon between Clarence and Apulia. The Moreot port was in effect the most convenient of the routes between Italy and the principality, above all since the latter had passed into the Angevin domain. A Venetian consul saw to it that things ran smoothly, sometimes disturbed by people from the principality. The Venetians brought metals and cloth, loading there with salt, cereals, cotton, oil, raw silk and raisins: the *mudae* were authorised to make a stop there and unarmed ships to collect merchandise left in transit by the galleys. The Genoese also did business there, investing almost 4,620 *livres* in sixteen contracts between 1274 and 1345. On a smaller scale, the Ragusans were also interested in the ports of the principality from where they took wheat, hides, silk and linen, and where they imported woven cloth, wine and cheeses. The second half of the fourteenth century was less favourable: Clarence followed the decline of the principality and its port experienced some stagnation which Pero Tafur noted at the time of his journey *c.* 1435. Patras then appeared to have taken over: in 1400 the Venetian senate estimated the value of merchandise brought by their nationals at 80,000 ducats, at 60,000 to 70,000 ducats in 1401. It is understandable in these circumstances that Venice accepted the protection of the city in 1408, entrusted by its archbishop. Venice thought to find there a useful compensation for the decline of Clarence. In the despotate the Venetians played a role of the first significance until the beginning of the fifteenth century: they brought raw materials and manufactured goods and exported from it wheat, cotton, honey and raw silk. The conquests of Despot Constantine Palaeologus in 1428 (capture of Clarence and Patras) put an end to these good relations. In the absence of conclusive documents, it is difficult to evaluate the economic role of the Catalan duchies in this intra-Mediterranean exchange.[13]

To the south of Messenia, the two ports of Coron and Modon were of

---

[13] *Régestes*, ed. Thiriet; *Déliberations*; Krekic (1961); Bonn (1969), pp. 320–5; Zakythinos (1975), pp. 256–60.

major interest to Venice. They were, to use an expression of the senate, *oculi capitales* of the *dominante*. They were of the first strategic importance: they watched the movement of enemy fleets and served as a base for the reconquest of rebellious Crete in 1363–4. As staging-posts and warehouses, each year they received convoys of merchant galleys which were forced to call at Modon: the letters of loading preserved in the Datini archives of Prato give a list of the various merchandise, most often of eastern origin (cotton, sugar, spices), which the galleys would come to take. Backed by a rich agricultural region, Coron and Modon exported agricultural products, and above all the products of Messenian stock rearing. It is understandable that, in the face of Greek and Turkish incursions, Venice should have taken care to protect these two enclaves isolated from each other and to have reunited them in a continuous territory by a series of annexations carried out from 1390 to 1430.[14]

The insular Venetian domain was the place *par excellence* where the mercantile *dirigisme* of the *dominante* was exercised: the *dominante* hoped to develop agricultural production there to satisfy its own needs and create transit centres for merchandise coming from the Levant or exported there. Crete enjoyed an exceptional position in this respect. It was the point of departure for regional exchanges to the Turkish territories of Asia Minor, which supplied it with slaves, wheat, horses and alum, and to which Crete sent textiles, wine and soap; also to the islands of the Archipelago which suffered from a chronic shortage of cereals; to Negroponte, Coron and Modon. But above all its ports, and first amongst them Candia, played an essential role in Mediterranean trade. In effect, they saw two convoys of galleys pass each year: those of Cyprus, then Syria and those of Alexandria. Before 1373 (Genoese capture of Famagusta), trade with Cyprus was of prime importance: Crete received salt and sugar and sent cereals there; the Corner, with possessions in Crete and around Piskopi, dominated these exchanges. The galleys of Syria and Alexandria brought spices, silk and cotton, with the result that Crete became the warehouse for the most valuable products of Mediterranean trade. Finally, the island was regarded by the *dominante* as its granary for wheat, a product which was a state monopoly and which the great landowners could not export elsewhere without authorisation from the senate. Wine from Malvasia, dessert grapes, cotton, wood, cheeses and hides fostered important trade in the direction of Venice which dominated the entire Cretan economy with respect to its needs and interests, to such an extent that it provoked frequent revolts, even among the ranks of Venetian feudatories.[15]

The island of Negroponte, divided between Venice and the *terciers*, was a compulsory stop for the galleys of the *muda* of Romania which stopped there either

[14] Thiriet (1976–8), pp. 86–98.   [15] Thiriet (1975), pp. 328–37; Zachariadou (1983), pp. 159–73.

on the outward journey (at the end of August), or on the return from Constantinople (November). It was thus the pivot of Venetian trade in Lower Romania: it undertook the redistribution of the products of the west, woollen and linen cloth, which accumulated in the island's warehouses, and collected the products of Greece, wood, hides, vallania used for dyeing, wax, cotton, cereals, and raisins which the galleys took away to the west. Moreover, Chalkis, the island's principal port, was a stop for the trade linking Crete and Macedonia in wood, cereals, hides and cloth. But it was no longer a question of a trade organised by the state which left all initiative here to private commissionings, confining itself to coasting along the Thessalian coasts in spring and autumn. Thessaloniki was the culminating point of these voyages. The Venetians had a consul there and a small merchant colony which gathered wheat from Macedonia and the Bulgarian plains and distributed woollen and linen cloth from the west. Their trade continued, even after the Ottoman occupation of the town. Ragusan merchants had been active there since 1234, when the despot Manuel Comnenodukas had granted them a privilege. The Genoese had also attempted to establish themselves in Thessaloniki: they had a consul there in 1305 and, between the end of the thirteenth and the beginning of the fourteenth century, the town was the target of several commercial investments, but without common policy with those who headed for the eastern coasts of the Aegean, which was the heart of the Genoese domain from the end of the thirteenth century.[16]

Under the rule of the Zaccaria (1304–29), Chios witnessed the development of trade in mastic and alum. The latter acquired great importance after 1346, when the *mahonesi* secured its control. Alum, indispensable for fixing dye in cloth, came from the mines of the Old and New Phocaea on the coast of Asia Minor, but the Giustiniani also tried to control the production of alum from other sources in Ottoman territory, Koloneia (Sharki or Shebin Karahisar), Kütahya, Ulubad and Cyzicus. Chios was thus the great repository for alum which ships and cogs transported to Flanders for the textile industry. The transportation of such a heavy product undoubtedly lay at the root of the medieval 'nautical revolution', which saw square-rigged cogs substituted for the Latin ships in use in the thirteenth century, and which placed Genoa ahead of other maritime towns in the race for big tonnage. Until the loss of Phocaea in 1455, Genoese alum occupied a considerable place in the exchanges between east and west: it stimulated shipbuilding and an increase in the size of ships and dictated a regular rotation of shipping by means of a direct maritime link between Chios, Flanders and England.[17]

[16] Thiriet (1975), pp. 337–41; Krekic (1961), pp. 67–70; Balard (1978), p. 164.
[17] Argenti (1958), pp. 488–9; Heers (1971), pp. 274–84; Balard (1978), pp. 769–82; Pistarino (1990), pp. 243–80.

The island of the *mahona* also produced mastic, gum of the mastic tree (*lentiscus*), highly prized in the medieval world. The Giustiniani kept the monopoly to themselves, controlling production and distribution. They formed adjudicatory societies (farmers' societies) whose members shared the sales in the great spheres of commerce, the west, Romania and Turkey, and, finally, Syria, Egypt and Cyprus. Through this entire organisation, the *mahona* made Chios function like a 'plantation economy' in the modern sense of the term; half of the island's revenues came from mastic and it formed the basis of the members' wealth. Chios redistributed the products of international trade in Asia Minor, via Ephesus and Palatia, while at the same time drawing into its warehouses the resources of Anatolia. Finally, the island was at the axis of two shipping routes, one via the Straits as far as Constantinople and the Black Sea, the other leading to Syria and Alexandria by way of Rhodes and Famagusta. It was the hub of Genoese international trade in the west.[18]

Since 1355, the Genoese had had another base in the same region, the island of Mytilene, which had passed to the hands of the Gattilusio family. Apart from piracy, which seems to have added to the resources of the masters of the island, alum from Kallones, the port of Mytilene received Genoese trade going from Egypt to Constantinople, via Rhodes and Chios, a trade concerned first and foremost with trading in Pontic slaves transported to Egypt to increase the numbers of the Mamluk army. The seizure by the Gattilusio of the islands of the northern Aegean at the beginning of the fifteenth century, and of the port of Ainos, at the mouth of the Maritsa, gave the Genoese access to the cereal resources of Thrace and the Bulgarian plains.[19]

This picture of products and the western trade routes in the Aegean would not be complete without some reference to the fluctuations and hindrances which characterised these activities in the fourteenth century. Papal prohibitions on trade with the Saracens, effectively although variously followed until the years 1345–50 gave great significance to the sea routes to Rhodes, Cyprus and Lesser Armenia in the first half of the century; Crete then played a decisive role as a port of call and a warehouse for all Venetian shipping, while Negroponte was an essential staging-post for the galleys to Constantinople. In the second half of the century, the lawful return of the Latins to Syria and Egypt increased the number of trading links. Cyprus, partially dominated by the Genoese, was to a great extent abandoned by the Venetian merchant galleys, while Chios added to the great trade to the west the entrepot profits derived from north–south trade and that with Turkish Anatolia.

Despite everything, western trade in the Aegean suffered the setbacks which characterised the entire fourteenth century. Both the numbers of the *incanti* of

---

[18] Balard (1978), pp. 742–9; Heers (1971), pp. 276–7.   [19] Pistarino (1990b), pp. 383–420.

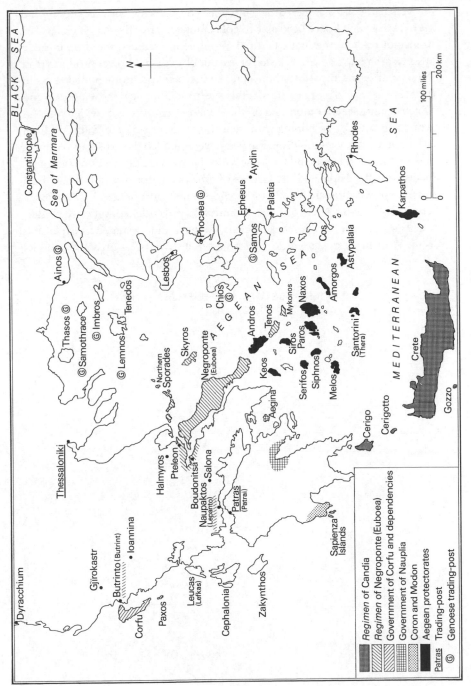

Map 18   The Aegean world

BLACK SEA

Constantinople

Sea of Marmara

Dyrracchium

Thessaloniki

Ainos Ⓖ

Thasos Ⓖ

Ⓖ Samothrace

Ⓖ Imbros

Ⓖ Lemnos   Tenedos

Lesbos

Phocaea Ⓖ

Ephesus

Ⓖ Samos   Palatia

Aydin

Halmyros
Pteleon

Skyros

Northern
Sporades

Negroponte
(Euboea)

A E G E A N   S E A

Chios

Andros

Tenos
Mykonos
Naxos

Amorgos

Astypalaia

Cos

Rhodes

Karpathos

Gijirokastr
Butrinto (Butrint)   Ioannina

Corfu
Paxos

Leucas
(Lefkas)

Cephalonia

Zakynthos

Boudonitsa
Naupaktos   Salona
(Lepanto)

Patras
(Patrai)

Aegina

Keos

Serifos
Siphnos

Melos

Sifos
Paros

Santorini
(Thera)

M E D I T E R R A N E A N   S E A

Crete

Gozzo

Cerigo

Cerigotto

Sapienza
Islands

N

100 miles

200 km

Regimen of Candia

Regimen of Negroponte (Euboea)

Government of Corfu and dependencies

Government of Nauplia

Coron and Modon

Aegean protectorates

Patras   Trading-post

Ⓖ   Genoese trading-post

the Venetian galleys gathered by Thiriet and Stöckly and the statistics of the *karati Peyre* which I have been able to collect reflect, after the very high level of Romaniot trade in the first half of the fourteenth century, the drop in trade after 1350, a recession which lasted at least until 1410–20. Lower production in the west after the Black Death in 1348, an increase in Ottoman incursions in the Aegean, the depopulation of their territories which the Genoese and Venetian authorities complained of, the development of piracy which finds an echo in all sources, beginning with the business letters of the Datini archive, all combine to explain this drop. But war never impeded the expansion of business for long: Venetians and Genoese were able to make the necessary arrangements with the Turks and the Greeks of Mistra. As for piracy, it would be a mistake to overestimate its effects: the goods misappropriated by the pirates returned sooner or later to the economic system burdened only by an additional tax. After several decades of crisis, western trade resumed its expansion in the Aegean after 1420, more diversified in its agents, its objectives and its results.[20]

[20] Thiriet (1977); Stöckly (1995); Balard (1978), pp. 683–4.

CHAPTER 26

THE RISE OF THE OTTOMANS

I. Metin Kunt

THE HISTORICAL SETTING

THE Ottomans emerged around 1300 and, after a century of continuous territorial enlargement and institutional development, their enterprise almost came to a premature end in 1402 when their army was defeated and their rule was shattered by Timur's (Tamerlane) formidable blow. Thus the fourteenth century exactly framed the first phase in the evolution of the Ottoman state when a small band of frontiersmen succeeded in establishing a sizeable regional state in Anatolia and in the Balkan peninsula.

The origins of the state are obscure because, at first, it was such an insignificant entity. Histories written in the cultural and political centres of the Islamic world, in Tabriz and Damascus and Cairo, did not take notice of the distant frontier zone in western Anatolia. Ottomans themselves did not put their own history in writing until the mid-fifteenth century, though there is evidence of a lively oral tradition.[1] Some modern historians, in fact, consider these later histories practically worthless in explaining Ottoman origins.[2] Archival evidence, too, is scant; few of the documents purporting to be from the fourteenth century but preserved as copies in later collections have been authenticated by rigorous scrutiny.[3] The historian's task, however, is not hopeless: recent research tends to corroborate the accounts of later Ottoman chronicles; modern historiography has also successfully integrated historical traditions with evidence from diverse sources, Byzantine and Islamic.[4]

Modern scholarly interest in the beginnings of the Ottoman state was stimulated by the dissolution and collapse of the empire in the aftermath of the First World War. The debate reached its culmination in the 1930s when Fuat

---

[1] Ménage (1962); Inalcık (1962); especially relevant is Kafadar (1995), ch. 2.
[2] Imber (1990), for example.   [3] Beldiceanu-Steinherr, *Recherches*, for the most thorough analysis.
[4] Zachariadou (1987) and (1993b) are very successful examples.

Köprülü in Paris and Paul Wittek in London delivered two seminal series of lectures both of which, in their own way, provided a larger historical picture as the setting for their depiction of the early Ottomans.[5] While Köprülü's canvas was much richer in social detail, Wittek's elegant yet bold masterstrokes provided a striking portrait: his Ottomans were now easily recognisable as *gazis* of the frontier, fighters for the glory of Islam. The scholarly audience, through Köprülü's explanation now much better informed on Anatolian social and political conditions in the thirteenth and fourteenth centuries, could see how for Wittek's *gazis* their religious zeal provided the life-force for large-scale conquest. So satisfying was the *gazi* theory of Ottoman origins that it remained the dominant explanation for close to half a century. Only in the last two decades has the debate been reopened, when Rudi Lindner questioned how *gazi* zeal, presumably implying Muslim exclusiveness, could be reconciled with the observable social, cultural and political inclusiveness of the Ottomans in the treatment of non-Muslim communities.[6] Lindner also introduced an anthropological understanding of early Ottoman society, both in the definition of an inclusive, newly formed 'tribe', and in his analysis of the declining fortunes of nomadic society while Ottoman leadership increasingly favoured their sedentary subjects. His theoretically informed analysis, convincing though it is, cannot yet be said to have gained currency but he has succeeded in stimulating comment.[7] Ottoman origins and the development of the Osmanlı tribe into a state are now better understood thanks to Cemal Kafadar's fresh and subtle study which successfully synthesises several strands of scholarship.[8] Kafadar gives new meaning to *gazis*, cutting down to size the purported Muslim zeal that was the hallmark of the Wittek thesis, especially as it came to be interpreted by non-specialist commentators. Kafadar's *gazis* emerged out of Osman Bey's 'tribe' and were properly inclusive in their dealings with non-Muslim neighbours. This new analysis is not, however, a forced marriage of Lindner's 'tribesmen' and Wittek's 'gazis' but it is a rich synthesis of literary and cultural history as well as of Byzantine, Islamic and later Ottoman historiography. After the re-examination of the last twenty years, the historiography of Ottoman origins seems now to have reached a new plateau.

Following the sound precedent set by modern historiography, we must consider general Anatolian conditions at the turn of the fourteenth century before we can view the small Ottoman community emerging to independence in Bithynia. For much of the thirteenth century a fairly stable frontier had been observed between Byzantium on the coastal plains of west and north Anatolia,

---

[5] Wittek (1938); Köprülü (1992).
[6] Lindner (1983); Heywood (1988) and (1989); Imber (1986), (1987) and (1993).
[7] Imber and Heywood (see n. 6); Inalcık (1981–2); Jennings (1986); Zachariadou (1993a).
[8] Kafadar (1995).

and the Seljuks of Rum on the central plateau.[9] From the mid century this balance was upset and the stability of the frontier zone disturbed because of changes in the fortunes and preoccupations of both these states. In the case of Byzantium, the return from Nicaean exile to Constantinople in 1261 served to increase involvement in the western reaches of the empire, with a relative neglect of the security of territories in Asia Minor. In any case, there seemed to be less cause for vigilance on Byzantium's Anatolian frontier. In 1243 the Rumi Seljuks were defeated in eastern Anatolia by a contingent of the world-conquering Mongol army. The Mongols did not immediately incorporate Seljuk lands into their vast domains. However, in 1258, with a renewed attack in west Asia they sacked Baghdad and, putting an end to any remaining semblance of a universal Islamic caliphate, they established a regional Mongol state, the Ilkhanid sultanate, ruling west Asia from their base in Azerbayjan. From then onwards the Rumi Seljuk kingdom was reduced to a satellite, its eastern zone more closely controlled by the Ilkhanids.

The Anatolian Seljuki society was not only an amalgam of Muslim Turks and local Greeks; its Muslim component was also made up of disparate elements. The state itself, in its capital in Konya (Iconium) and in other important cities such as Kayseri (Caesarea) and Sivas (Sebastea), reproduced in Anatolia the traditional urban culture of central Islamic lands. This meant that while the ruling dynasty was Turkish, the language of learning, religious as well as secular, was Arabic; Persian was the language and ethos of the scribes and financial bureaucrats, and also of refined literary culture. The *medrese* colleges and the court bureaucracy were staffed by Arab and Persian newcomers as well as by Anatolian Turks and Greeks who acquired these established languages of urban Islam for intellectual, cultural and administrative discourse. The military was mainly Turkish, but there too the Seljuk sultans followed long-established statecraft to create household armies composed of men from many ethnic groups. It was a basic principle for rulers not to depend exclusively on the Turkish tribal levies who had at first carried them to power, but to surround themselves with slave soldiers removed from their homes and families, no longer with any ethnic or tribal allegiance but loyal only to their master.

While this cosmopolitan urban society mixed Turkish and Greek in the market-place and Arabic and Persian in court and college circles, in the countryside different ethnic groups lived side by side but with less mingling. Some Turks settled down as peasants, but there were separate Greek and Armenian villages. Transhumance was the dominant mode of life for many Turks,

---

[9] 'Rum' is the Islamic term for the lands of Rome/Byzantium in Anatolia. 'Rum Seljuks' refers to the Anatolian branch and successor of the great Seljuk empire. The adjectival form 'Rumi' (Roman) continued to be used as the self-definition of Ottoman Turks, in former Byzantine territories in Anatolia and the Balkans, for many centuries.

especially in the mountainous zone of eastern Anatolia but also along the northern and southern rim of the central plateau, where the highland summer pastures were not too distant from sheltered wintering valleys. Rural Turks differed from their urban cousins not only in livelihood but also in maintaining an oral Turkish culture with both literary and religious implications. Bards sang Turkish epics and ballads; their sense of justice had more to do with tribal tradition than with Islamic *sheriat* law; their religious understanding owed more to the teachings of saintly men than to the prescriptions of *ulema* learned doctors; their practice involved ceremonies reminiscent of a perhaps not too distant shamanist past more than they resembled the correct procedures of the urban mosque. A version of Turkish folk Islam, expressed in the simple and sincerely fervent eulogies of the Turkistani saint Ahmed Yesevi, took hold in the Anatolian countryside.

Mongol expansion in Asia occasioned movement of central Asian peoples, some joining the conquest and some displaced by it. Of those who sought refuge in Asia Minor many were townsmen, Turks and Persians, but many more were Turkish tribesmen. With the rapid change in the population balance, the Rumi Seljuk state tried to contain social disruptions in the countryside but with difficulty and varying degrees of success. The state's efforts to control the incoming Turks caused resentment and resulted in a rift between the mutually suspicious cultures of town versus tribesmen. Eventually, state authority was able to steer some of this influx away from the central areas toward the frontier zones, but by then Mongol Ilkhanids had established suzerainty over Anatolia. Some of the Anatolian Turkmen tribesmen, especially those in the southern Taurus region, attempted to withstand Ilkhanid pressure by supporting the Mamluk armies in their confrontation with the Mongols. Even before Mamluk sultan Baybars's expedition into south-eastern Anatolia Karaman Mehmed Bey, chief of a large group of Taurus Turkmen, succeeded in occupying the Seljukid capital in 1273. He soon had to withdraw from the central plains to his mountain fastness, but during his brief time in Konya he demanded that business, both in the palace and in the market, be conducted in Turkish, that is, not in Arabic or Persian, an act equally as significant of the dichotomy of Anatolian Turkish-Muslim culture as were the tribal uprisings in mid century.

At about the same time other chiefs of the various frontier zones emerged to political prominence, all but independent of the Seljuk sultan's authority. While central power in Konya was dwindling in the face of Mongol pressure from the east, the tribesmen encouraged to leave the central lands and settle on the western frontiers increasingly threatened Byzantine defences. The influx of warlike Turkmen to the rim of the plateau, looking down the river valleys that reached the Aegean coast, pushed Byzantine administration back toward the sea. This expansion of the frontier zone was not accomplished, however, as conquest in the name of the Seljuk sultan who himself was by then an Ilkhanid puppet; the frontier chiefs saw no need to acknowledge him as anything more than a distant figurehead, if at all. The first to establish himself as a bey, an emir in his own right, was Menteshe in Caria in the extreme southwestern corner of Anatolia and therefore the farthest from Ilkhanid or Seljuk reach.[10] He was soon followed by the Karaman of the Taurus region, and by the end of the thirteenth century several more emirates were established along the Aegean coast: to the north of Menteshe there was Aydın in the Meander valley, Saruhan in the Hermus valley, and Karasi at Pergamum and Balıkesir. Germiyan, an earlier frontier command at Kütahya and Eskishehir, at the western edge of the central plateau, may indeed have sponsored the occupation of the coastal valleys, but the commanders who achieved the conquest acknowledged Germiyan suzerainty no more than they did Seljuk overlordship; instead, each became the eponymous founder of his own emirate. Among these territories there were even smaller groupings banded around a leader, not under the authority of any emir but not yet themselves sufficiently large to be termed an emirate. Osman Bey, the eponymous founder of the Ottomans, was one such chief in Bithynia, just to the north of Germiyan.

As a general historical problem, why it should have been the Ottoman state which rose to greatness is even more intriguing than why any state at all emerged out of this newly opened frontier zone. With the decline of Byzantium and of the Seljuk sultanate, and with the steady increase in tribal Turkmen population, it is not surprising that the frontier zone became the appropriate setting for a new power base in Anatolia, especially after Ilkhanid rule itself was fractured and dispersed by the mid-fourteenth century. Why the Ottoman state, rather than those of Menteshe, Karaman or Aydın rulers, should have become the pre-eminent frontier state is a question that necessitates a closer look at these emerging emirates. Indeed, later on we will have to face the further question of why Ottoman polity itself did not beget new emirates as the frontier moved farther away in time and in space.

We should note, first of all, the similarity between the various emirates. They all had an admixture of Turks and Byzantines: tribal Turkmen, sheep and horse breeders and fighters; Turkish agriculturalists and merchants displaced from the hinterland; and local Greeks, seamen, peasants, and townsmen. Turkish was the dominant language, but with intercourse in the market-place or in the village square, or even at latitudinarian gatherings at the dervish convent; with intermarriage, voluntary or otherwise, politically arranged in the case of leaders or more spontaneous for others, at least a number of Greeks and Turks

[10] Wittek (1934).

could understand each other's tongue and ways. Popular culture differed little, imbued as it was with heroic epics and ballads of divine love sung by the same dervishes and brethren circulating in the frontier society under whichever emir's rule. Other social groups, members of merchants' and craftsmen's *ahi* brotherhoods, were represented in all frontier towns. Political conceptions and institutions were shared as well, whatever the exact origins of a particular leader might have been. Furthermore, there was considerable movement, of groups and of individuals, in various directions. The predominant population movement was from the hinterland to the frontier, especially after the decline of Ilkhanid power and the resulting political upheaval to the east. In the frontier zone itself, volunteers for raids into Byzantine lands as well as tradesmen could seek their livelihood wherever opportunities seemed greater. Leaving the domains of one frontier emir and joining the banner of a more active leader was a simple matter. A floating population of *gazis* could be in Aydın service one year and turn up for an Osmanlı expedition the next.[11] As frontier raids increased in scale and exerted greater pressure, Byzantine peasants fleeing this harassment, not further away but into the relatively secure and tolerant conditions established under the emirates, also increased the manpower available to Turkish frontier lords, both as subjects and as fighters.[12] The relative prosperity of the frontier emirates, while inner Anatolia suffered from post-Ilkhanid power struggles in the east and Byzantine lands to the west were impoverished and rendered defenceless, set the stage for the rise of a new type of political entity.

EMERGENCE OF THE OTTOMAN EMIRATE

In the thirteenth century the Seljuk state had established frontier commands, the Germiyan to the west and Candar to the north. Some of the better-known frontier lords of the Aegean area were in fact sent forth by the Germiyan.[13] While such *gazi* lords as Menteshe and Aydın and Saruhan were engaged in a struggle against the Knights Hospitaller, now based on Rhodes, and the Byzantine navy in the Aegean, Osman Bey was trying to preserve the small band he had inherited from his father Ertughrul, both from Germiyan claims to suzerainty and from being incorporated into a more powerful neighbour's domains. He faced hostile local Byzantine lords of Bithynia, sometimes in weary mutual toleration and, at times, even in co-operation. Whatever the original name of the 'tribe' had been, whether they were called 'Ertughrullu' in his father's lifetime, Osman Bey's band earned its name when it achieved its first success of note in 1301 against a Byzantine army sent to defend the frontier.[14]

---

[11] Inalcık (1993).   [12] Zachariadou (1987).   [13] Inalcık (1985).   [14] Kafadar (1995), pp. 122–4.

This victory at Baphaeon (Koyulhisar) established his reputation among *gazis* beyond his immediate environment; from then on the 'Osmanlı', Osman's people, was a name heard and remembered in the frontier zone at large.[15]

Although Osman Bey remained the leader for more than two decades after this initial success, it appears that he spent most of this time consolidating his modest emirate rather than in expanding it. Within his 'tribe' he had far from absolute authority; he was the acknowledged leader of a group that included members of his family and other lieutenants, co-operating voluntarily to preserve the 'tribe' in a hostile environment: threats came from Byzantine lords and from Catalan mercenaries sent to the southern shores of the Marmara by the Byzantine government. Pressure from neighbouring emirates, especially from Germiyan, also continued.[16] At least during the first two decades of the fourteenth century Osman Bey accepted the reality of Ilkhanid power, if not quite submitting to it as a vassal, however distant it seemed to the frontier. Both to consolidate his position as leader and to ensure the survival of his 'Osmanlı' following he seems to have made alliances of marriage, for himself and for his sons, with Byzantine neighbours and with a well-respected *sheyh* of the frontier zone. In later Ottoman memory Osman Bey is remembered as an astute leader, though a fifteenth-century chronicler, Ashıkpashazade, representing the diminishing frontier ethos, portrayed him as a simple and direct man who resented the need for rules and regulations. When he acquired territory to govern, including towns and villages as well as the seasonally migrant Turkmen nucleus, scribes and learned men from the Anatolian hinterland came to keep accounts for him and to assist in collecting taxes. Osman Bey's supposed reluctance to impose market dues is more a reflection of the chronicler's reaction to the growing centralisation and bureaucratisation of Ottoman polity in his own age; nevertheless, the arrival in the newly expanding frontier zone of men from the hinterland more comfortable with the pen than with the sword is a familiar and plausible theme. As the frontier moved away from the original homebase and so the emirate's own inner core developed into a peaceful hinterland educational facilities came to be provided, but there were men well versed in bureaucratic forms and procedures in Osman Bey's entourage before the first Ottoman *medrese* was opened in Nicaea in his son's day, and such men continued to offer their services to the frontier lords throughout the fourteenth century.

Osman Bey's main accomplishment was not only to establish but also to maintain the independent existence of his followers, growing with the success of raids into Byzantine territories to the north and north-west. Given the fluidity of the frontier conditions, various of his captains with their own bands

---

[15] Inalcık (1993).   [16] Luttrell (1993); Varlık (1974).

might have joined other emirs were they to offer richer rewards in their own sectors. Osman Bey appears to have gained respect for his even-handed leadership while providing sufficient opportunity for the raiders under his command for booty to keep their support and loyalty. Towards the end of his life in 1324 he had gained enough followers to effect the blockade of Brusa (Bursa), the first sizeable Byzantine city in Bythinia to fall to Ottoman hands.

The pressure on Brusa may have been started by Osman but its capture was completed by his son and successor, Orhan Bey. The city provided Orhan's Ottomans with an important regional market and an obvious seat for the emir. On the other hand, with the environs of Brusa occupied, Orhan Bey became neighbours with the Karasi emirate further to the west. Expansion in this direction thus blocked, Orhan Bey turned north to follow his father's initial raiding route, toward Nicaea (Iznik) and Nicomedeia (Izmid). In 1328 Orhan Bey stopped the Byzantine imperial army at Pelekanon; the beleaguered cities, with no hope of succour, were captured in 1331 and 1337 in quick succession. Orhan Bey's raiders then moved west again, this time along the narrow neck of land between the Marmara and the Black Sea; their progress came to a halt only when they reached the Asian suburbs of Constantinople.

By this time, the mid 1330s, the Ilkhanid state was in the process of dissolution; eastern and central Anatolia became embroiled in the struggle for succession in the vacuum left with the demise of the dynasty. The disturbed political situation in the hinterland allowed western Anatolian frontier emirs greater freedom of action and also supplied them with reinforcements as more volunteers came to join their raids. Orhan Bey received his share of this influx although the more spectacular engagements were still in the lands of Aydın, pre-eminent sea raiders of the Aegean. During his visit to Anatolia the famed Iberian Muslim traveller Ibn Battuta was impressed by the prosperity and power of the emir of Aydın while noting that Orhan Bey too commanded considerable manpower and resources.[17] But in the next decade or so the Ottoman emirate remained hemmed in, until a four-way struggle that involved the Karasi emir and Orhan Bey supporting rival contenders for the Byzantine throne.[18] In his bid for power in Constantinople John Kantakouzenos had at first secured support from Umur Bey, the famous emir of Aydın, but after Umur Bey had been forced to defend his own lands in the Aegean, Kantakouzenos sought an Ottoman alliance, giving his daughter Theodora in marriage to Orhan Bey. The success of John Kantakouzenos in Constantinople was accompanied by his son-in-law Orhan Bey's ascendancy over the Karasi emirate. After a short while Karasi lands, Karasi commanders and Karasi people were all incorporated into Osmanlı domains.

---

[17] Gibb, *Travels.*   [18] Zachariadou (1993b).

Later Ottoman tradition describes this episode without reference to Byzantium, but as a struggle for the Karasi emir's seat. When the old emir died a fight broke out among his sons. One, popular among Karasi people but weaker than his elder brother, sought Orhan Bey's support in return for some of his territory. He died in the attempt; Orhan Bey then defeated the remaining Karasi prince and occupied much of Karasi lands. Voluntary submission of neighbouring beys to the rising fortunes of the house of Osman is a motif encountered repeatedly as the fourteenth century progressed. This device should not be taken as anything more than an effort on the part of later chroniclers to uphold the Muslim credentials of Ottoman emirs while explaining how Orhan Bey and his successors came to expand at the expense of Muslim neighbours as well as against the infidels. There may indeed have been a Karasi succession struggle just at the same time as the Byzantine throne was contested, but the decisive situation seems to have been that the alliance of Kantakouzenos and Orhan Bey won against John Palaeologus and his Karasi supporters. Their victory settled not only the Byzantine succession but allowed Orhan Bey to conquer his Karasi neighbours who had apparently been in difficulties, perhaps as a result of backing the wrong Byzantine claimant.

The significance of the Ottoman incorporation of the Karasi emirate is much more than simply doubling their territory and manpower. Just at a time when Aydın, the foremost Aegean emirate, was defeated by a Latin alliance and lost Smyrna/Izmir (1344), absorbing Karasi lands and people without much of a struggle, Orhan Bey emerged as the most formidable frontier emir. Even more important, Ottoman domains now stretched to the Dardanelles beyond which a new frontier beckoned. By the mid-fourteenth century the Anatolian frontier emirates had all settled within recognised and static boundaries for they had either become landlocked, as in the case of Germiyan, Hamid and Karaman, or they had reached the coasts. Menteshe, Aydın and Saruhan had attempted to carry the frontier fight to the Aegean islands; Aydın had conducted successful raids on mainland Greece.[19] The loss of Izmir in 1344, however, put a decisive end to any notions of new frontier conquest across the Aegean Sea. Now the only possible new frontier lay across the Dardanelles in Thrace, and when Orhan Bey overcame his Karasi neighbours he came to control the passage to this new frontier zone. In the 1350s any volunteer leaving behind the Anatolian hinterland to join the frontier enterprise, or any seasoned but now idle warrior from the maritime emirates eager to resume raiding, sought to enter Orhan Bey's service, to become Ottomans. With almost all of western and northern Anatolia turned into a hinterland, divided though these territories were among several emirates, the only frontier and the area of

[19] Inalcık (1985); Zhukov (1994).

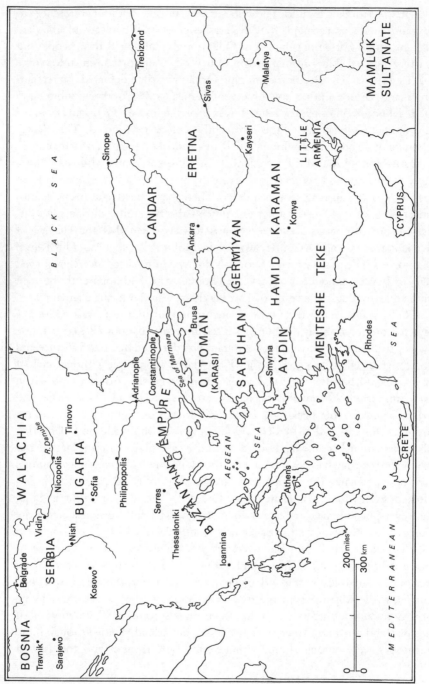

Map 19   Anatolia and the Balkans, c. 1350

further expansion lay in Europe, now termed Rumeli, Roman lands, by the Ottoman frontiersmen. The only passage to this new Rumeli from old Rum was now firmly in Ottoman control.

Orhan Bey entrusted the new territories to an older son Süleyman Bey who, now in command of former Karasi captains and troops, succeeded in capturing Gallipoli (Turkish, Gelibolu) Castle in 1354 when he was on the European shore of the straits once again aiding the Byzantine emperor against Stephen Dušan. Instead of returning to Anatolia after his mission he turned his new possession into a base for further frontier action in Thrace. Raids and expansion quickly ensued, east along the Marmara Sea, north up the Maritsa (Turkish, Meriç) valley toward Adrianople (Turkish, Edirne), and west along the Aegean shore. Süleyman Bey soon died (1359), in an accident, according to Ottoman tradition, and Orhan Bey did not live much longer (d. 1362); but Thracian expansion continued after Murad Bey succeeded to the emirate. Former Karasi commanders such as Hacı Ilbey and Evrenos Bey who had experience of the Thracian terrain while still serving their earlier masters were now the main leaders of this expansion across the Dardanelles, facilitated by the uncertainties resulting from the recent deaths of both the Serbian and the Bulgarian tsars and weak, sporadic Byzantine resistance. Murad Bey himself stayed in Anatolia, to finish the conquest of some Karasi territories still maintaining an independent existence to the south-west and to effect the definitive submission of Angora (Turkish, Ankara) which Orhan Bey had earlier captured from Eretna, an Ilkhanid successor state in central-eastern Anatolia. Lala Shahin Pasha, an Ottoman commander, was also sent to join the Thracian action to supervise the frontier lords of Karasi origin. Soon the Ottoman forces, frontiersmen and regular troops together, marched up the Maritsa to bring pressure to bear on Adrianople; the city was taken after a combined Serbian and Bulgarian army, possibly also aided by the Hungarian king Louis, was defeated on its way to relieve it.

The chronology of the early period of Murad Bey is still confused, with contradictory reports in various versions of Ottoman tradition and in local chronicles difficult to reconcile.[20] Hypotheses have been advanced to reduce uncertainties, but scholarly agreement, even on such basic dates as the capture of Adrianople and whether there was more than one battle against Balkan armies on that occasion, is not yet established. In later Ottoman sources some events are related twice, as in the case of the annexation of Ankara, once in

[20] Imber (1990).

the last years of Orhan Bey and again soon after Murad Bey took over as emir. Such repetition also occurs in the case of the first major Ottoman battle against Balkan forces. Quite possibly some recent Ottoman expansion was reversed upon the death of Orhan Bey while Murad Bey was still preoccupied with putting down challenges from his brothers, as mentioned briefly in some Ottoman accounts.[21] As Inalcık has suggested, not only Ankara but also Adrianople may have been first taken in Orhan Bey's last years (1361); it is possible that it reverted to Byzantine rule during the Ottoman succession struggle, to be recaptured several years later (?1369).[22] The Ottoman victory over Serb-Bulgarian forces may also have occurred twice, in the early 1360s and in 1371, each time in association with the taking of Adrianople.

The broad outlines are somewhat more clear. Ottoman action against Adrianople was followed up into the Balkans; Philippopolis (Plovdiv; Turkish Filibe) was taken soon after. The frontier route in the south into western Thrace also continued to proceed to Komotini (Turkish, Gümülcine) and beyond. A certain mutual suspicion not to say animosity can also be detected between the frontier commanders and their overlord, Murad Bey's deputy Lala Shahin Pasha. According to Ottoman tradition Hacı Ilbey, formerly of Karasi and the main figure in the victory over the Serbians that secured the Maritsa valley, soon died, said to have been assassinated by Shahin Pasha 'out of jealousy'.[23] Personal enmity is a possibility, but it is at least as likely that in Murad Bey's seat at Brusa there was genuine suspicion that successful frontier lords like Hacı Ilbey and Evrenos Bey may have been tempted to break away from the Ottomans to establish their own frontier emirates in Rumeli.

A crucial element in the vicissitudes of frontier life was that communication between the Anatolian hinterland and the European zone of activity was not always secure. The journey across the Dardanelles was a short one but Ottoman naval capacity was still curiously underdeveloped and the crossing remained vulnerable to hostile navies. This is surprising because even in earlier times the Ottomans are said to have had some ships on the Marmara. Furthermore, the Karasi beys possessed a much more developed navy, active on the Marmara as well as the Aegean, inherited by the Ottomans before they gained a foothold on the Gallipoli peninsula. Later developments indicate that the combined Ottoman–Karasi navy was not sufficient to the task. Ottomans needed Genoan galleys to transport fresh troops to reinforce the Rumeli frontiersmen and Anatolian Turkish clans to resettle in the newly opened lands; Thracian Greeks seem to have been brought back to Anatolia.[24] The need for

---

[21] Imber (1990), pp. 26–7; Uzunçarsılı (1947).
[22] Inalcık (1971); Beldiceanu-Steinherr (1965); Zachariadou (1970).
[23] Uzunçarsılı (1947); Sertoglu and Cezar (1957).   [24] Fleet, 'The Treaty of 1387'; Imber (1990).

Genoese co-operation was not only for special occasions of relatively large-scale movement of people to achieve a population balance between old Rum and new Rumeli. Even routine crossing became more precarious when Gelibolu fortress itself was captured by Amedeo of Savoy in 1366 and held by Byzantium for the next eleven years. Eventually Murad Bey wrested back this guardian of the Dardanelles; meanwhile, co-ordination of action was hampered, though obviously not halted. This period may have increased the tendency for independent action on the part of the frontier lords; but it must also have made it clear to them that their position in the hostile environment of Rumeli was as yet precarious, that they still needed reinforcements from Anatolia and the goodwill of Murad Bey who held their hinterland. They needed Anatolia not only as a source of manpower but also as the market for the booty they gained in their raids. Mutual suspicion there may have been, but there was also mutual dependence that pulled together Murad Bey's Anatolian hinterland and the frontier enterprise of the Rumeli lords.

Riches pouring into Brusa from across the Dardanelles allowed Murad Bey to expand into Anatolia as well. Around 1380 he acquired extensive territories to the south, in stages all the way to the Mediterranean at Satalia (Antalya). Expansion of the Ottoman state against its Muslim neighbours is related by Ottoman tradition as an inevitable and on the whole peaceful process. At that time Anatolia still had several well-established emirates, in addition to the east-central state governed by Kadı Burhaneddin, ultimately a survivor of the post-Ilkhanid power struggles. Karaman in the central plateau was still the largest of the emirates that had emerged at the collapse of the Seljuks of Rum, of course with the exception of the Ottoman state itself which had by then transcended its earlier limited nature. Others, especially those inland between Karaman and Ottoman lands, had become moribund for they were neither capable of expansion nor of survival as impoverished, land-locked statelets, under pressure from their more powerful neighbours. When dynastic ties were established between the house of Osman and the house of Karaman, the old emir of Germiyan must have feared for his own survival, for he offered his daughter in marriage to Murad's son Bayezid Bey with a sizeable portion of his lands as dowry, including his chief town, Kütahya. The rest of his emirate was to be incorporated into Ottoman lands at his death. Around the time of this wedding, made the more sumptuous by the rich presents from Evrenos Bey and other Rumeli lords, the emir of Hamid, to the south of Germiyan, agreed to sell his lands to Murad Bey. A few years later the Ottomans seized the emirate of Tekke and so gained access to the Mediterranean.

How voluntary was such secession of territory, whether as dowry, as bequest, or in return for money? We must note that giving away territory as dowry was not traditional at all. A few years earlier Murad Bey had married his daughter to the emir of Karaman, possibly to secure his rear while away on Rumeli conquest; there was no question of the Ottoman princess bringing a dowry of land to her intended husband. Purchase of an emirate, too, is unprecedented in Anatolian Turkish practice. The Germiyan and Hamid emirs may have felt helpless; however reluctantly, they must have concluded that it was preferable to end their years as respected and wealthy if small fish in the ever-growing Ottoman pond. The important point was that by then Ottoman expansion may have started to look irresistible, because they were so much more powerful and prosperous then their Anatolian neighbours. The source of this wealth and power was of course expansion in Rumeli, and controlling the only funnel-like crossing between Rum and Rumeli, sending fresh warriors west and bringing the frontier booty east. A second important point is that these political transactions between emirs seems not to have had any social implications. As far as the people were concerned they lost their own, local ruling families but became members of a much larger polity. In any case, there had traditionally been considerable mobility across political boundaries for merchants, *ahi* guildsmen, dervishes and members of mystic brotherhoods. Circulating scholars and poets had offered their services to various emirs; a learned or literary work originally intended or even dedicated to one emir was often presented to another by the time it was completed. Coinage bore the names of different emirs but it was comparable in weight and value from one emir's territory to the next.[25] Social and political institutions were similar, as were the ways of the market-place. Ottoman annexation, especially when it was effected without battle, did not occasion any social dislocation for the Anatolian population. Life went on as before; furthermore, there were greater opportunities in the energetic, expanding domains of the house of Osman, greater rewards for frontier raiders and richer patronage for scholars, poets and artists, busier markets and larger trade for merchants.

Not all Ottoman relations with Anatolian emirs were peaceful. The Karamanids resented this recent Ottoman expansion immediately to their west, or so Ottoman accounts relate, so that Murad Bey had to march against his son-in-law. The defeated Karamanid emir was allowed to rule in Konya, but Murad Bey extracted a promise that the Karamanids would keep the peace while he was busy in Rumeli where, toward the end of his life, he pursued a much more aggressive policy. Earlier in his emirate he had delegated the supervision of Rumeli territories to trusted commanders, first Shahin Pasha and then Timurtash Pasha; in the 1380s, with Gelibolu once again in Ottoman hands, he seems to have taken a more active role in the frontier zone. The raids of frontier lords had already weakened Bulgarian, Serbian and Byzantine

---

[25] Zhukov (1993).

defences; now Murad Bey, with his regular troops, proceeded to expand his holdings and incorporate the new territories within regularised administration. The Rumeli lords were sent forward into Macedonia and Albania to open new frontier zones as a hinterland with settled conditions evolved.

In the Balkans, as in Anatolia, dynastic disputes in neighbouring states provided opportunities for expansion. In Bulgaria, since the death of Tsar Alexander his two sons set up separate domains at Tarnovo and Vidin. After the (second?) conquest of Adrianople, frontier raiders and Lala Shahin Pasha's regular troops had already occupied southern and eastern Bulgaria. Sometime in the 1370s Murad Bey married the sister of Tsar Ivan Shishman of Tarnovo and henceforth considered him a vassal. But in 1387, perhaps in an attempt to take advantage of Murad Bey's dispute with Karaman, the tsar failed to respond to Murad Bey's call for auxiliary troops against Serbia. Before any action further west, Ottoman forces invaded much of Bulgaria; Shishman saved his life by handing over without resistance his last stronghold, Nicopolis (Turkish, Niğbolu) in northern Bulgaria on the Danube.

In the course of expansion west into Albania and north into Serbia pursued rigorously through the 1380s, it became clear that regional action was faltering. Nish was captured (1386) and the Serbian king Lazar had accepted Ottoman suzerainty, according to Ottoman tradition; Ottoman frontiersmen pushed north to raid Bosnian territory. But these successes were reversed soon after with a setback at Plochnik in 1387 and a more severe defeat in Bosnia in 1388. The successful alliance betwen the Bosnian king Tvrtko and Lazar attempted to push its advantage and a large-scale clash became inevitable. The following year, gathering all his troops from Anatolia and Rumeli, including contingents from independent emirates and Rumeli vassals, Murad Bey met and defeated the Bosnian-Serbian alliance at Kosovo at a grand-scale field battle. The Ottoman ruler was assassinated on the battlefield by a Serbian commander and the captured king Lazar was executed after Murad Bey's death, but gaining the upper hand in this great battle settled the future of the region in Ottoman favour.[26] Bayezid Bey, active in the battle, succeeded his father immediately. Lazar's son Stephan was recognised as the vassal ruler of Serbia, the marriage of his sister to Bayezid soon thereafter sealed Ottoman suzerainty.

THE RISE AND FALL OF BAYEZID'S EMPIRE

Bayezid's reign lasted only thirteen years after 1389, until his ignominious defeat at Ankara by Timur, the grand conqueror of Asia. During this short time, however, territorial expansion and establishment of the ruler's internal

---

[26] Reinert (1993) reconciles Ottoman, Serbian and other histories.

authority was accomplished at a much quickened pace. Bayezid was remembered in Ottoman tradition as Yıldırım, the 'Thunderbolt', a fame he gained in his lifetime for the swiftness of his campaigns and the decisiveness of his conquests and also for his ability to strike down opposition from former emirs and domestic challenges. He was equally impatient with equivocal vassals, threatening neighbours, and respected leaders of the Ottoman enterprise, learned *ulema* and powerful frontier *ghazi* lords. Both the problems and the opportunities for enhanced Ottoman power had been evident in the time of his father; now Bayezid took immediate action to secure and enhance his external and internal stature. His rapid rise was such that he was recognised as the first Ottoman sultan, the classical term for a substantial Islamic ruler. His father too had shed the simple title of bey and was known by the loftier if idiosyncratic title of *hüdtâvendigâr*, lord, but Bayezid truly achieved the sultanate.

Recently Colin Imber has questioned the Ottoman tradition that Bayezid seized power immediately upon the assassination of his father and, eliminating his brother Yakub soon after, established his unchallenged authority.[27] Noting that Bayezid's surviving coins were all struck at least six months after Kosovo, Imber raised the possibility that the power struggle between the brothers may have lasted months, rather than hours, after Murad's death. Stronger evidence indicates that some central Anatolian neighbours tried to take advantage of uncertainties upon Bayezid's accession, whether or not Yakub's challenge lasted any length of time. Imber quotes a non-Ottoman Anatolian source to this effect and also compares this account with Ottoman tradition on Yıldırım Bayezid's first campaign, directed against the still independent emirs of western Anatolia south from Karasi. Saruhan and Aydın succumbed quickly; Menteshe followed soon. Bayezid next turned north-east in 1391, annexing the lands of his erstwhile vassal Candaroghlu Süleyman and some petty emirates, until he reached the Kızılırmak (Halys) river across which he faced a more formidable foe, Kadı Burhaneddin, the ruler of Sivas (Sebastea). It is noteworthy that in this last campaign Bayezid was accompanied by the Byzantine Emperor Manuel II and by Serbian, Bulgarian and Albanian contingents, confirming their vassal status.[28] Furthermore, the Ottoman ruler's readiness to employ Balkan Christian troops for his conquests of Anatolian Muslim neighbours stood in contrast to the ideological motif of the *ghazi* warrior in the service of Islam. Whatever the role of religious sentiment had been in *ghazi* frontier enthusiasm earlier in the career of the Ottoman emirate, by Bayezid's time in the last decade of the fourteenth century his was a territorial state with ambitions in both directions, east as well as west, Muslim as well as Christian. As we have noted, even as a frontier *ghazi* emirate the

---

[27] Imber (1990), p. 37.   [28] Zachariadou (1980); Imber (1990).

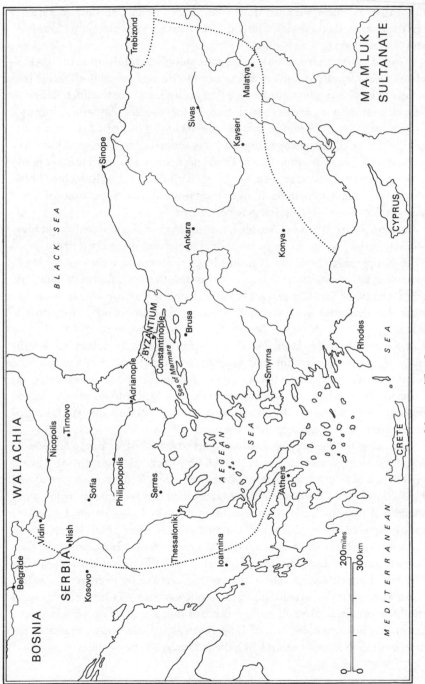

Map 20   The Ottoman state, c. 1400

Ottomans had never refrained from taking action against Muslim neighbours, but the confrontation in Anatolia had turned to open conflict only toward the end of the century.

Bayezid's programme of Anatolian annexation was interrupted by developments in Rumeli. In Murad's time the need to be vigilant on both fronts had necessitated the creation of a bey of beys, supreme commander, active in Rumeli while Murad personally took charge of Anatolian affairs. Now Bayezid, in his turn, created a second supreme commander, a bey of beys in Anatolia, to take charge of the newly conquered territories and to safeguard Ottoman rule. In both cases the immediate practical necessity was to curb the autonomy of local beys and to assure their loyalty, the frontier lords in Rumeli and now the former emirs of Anatolia. Longer-term institutional implications of these posts will also need to be separately considered.

As Bayezid was storming Anatolia, frontier lords had continued to put pressure on Serbia, where some commanders preferred Hungarian protection.[29] With campaigns in Serbia in 1392 and Bulgaria in 1393 Bayezid succeeded in extending his overlordship throughout the area, to the exclusion of Hungary. As in Anatolia, Bayezid may have thought that time was now ripe to seize outright the territories of his vassals: in 1394 he constructed a fort on the Anatolian shore of the Bosphorus for a long-term blockade of Constantinople. Following frontier raids further north, the sultan himself led his army across the Danube into Walachia and repulsed the Hungarian king Sigismund. The rivalry over Balkan supremacy thus settled in Ottoman favour, Bayezid annexed Bulgaria; the Shishman dynasty of Tarnovo came to an end when the son of the last Bulgarian tsar converted to Islam and was rewarded with a command in Anatolia as an Ottoman officer.

Sigismund had been trying for some years to recruit other European powers to reverse the Ottoman advance. In 1396 he succeeded in organising a grand coalition, a new 'crusade', against Bayezid. Securing Venetian support, joined by a considerable Burgundian force as well as warrior-knights from other western European lands, with Byzantium and Walachia as local allies, he marched once again along the Danube toward Nicopolis. Bayezid was, however, ready for the crusaders: he was able to raise a huge army from his Rumeli and Anatolian territories, supported by his Serbian vassal, and defeat Sigismund and his allies. The Ottoman victory was so decisive that, while Sigismund was trying to make his roundabout way back via Constantinople and the Mediterranean, Bayezid pushed forward into Hungary on a raiding campaign. The last remaining area of Bulgaria around Vidin was also taken in the aftermath of Nicopolis, completing the conquest of the country.

[29] Imber (1990).

Leaving the aged *ghazi* lord Evrenos Bey to press the raids into Albania and southern Greece, and continuing the blockade of Constantinople, Bayezid returned once again to Anatolian affairs. During the Ottoman preoccupation with Sigismund's invasion, Karaman had once again attempted to recover its territory. In 1397 Bayezid led a punitive campaign against Konya, determined this time to end the Karamanid emirate. The emir was defeated and executed, his lands incorporated into Ottoman domains. Further east, taking advantage of the confusion upon the death of Kadı Burhaneddin, Bayezid annexed Sivas and Malatya. By the end of the century, the Ottoman ruler had eliminated all former *gazi* emirates in western and central Anatolia, as well as the last remnants of post-Ilkhanid states. Lord of domains stretching from the Danube to the Euphrates, he was now a formidable neighbour to the two great states of west Asia, the Mamluk sultanate of Egypt and Syria, and Timur's (Tamerlane) all-conquering Asian empire. The Mamluk sultanate had no time to worry about Bayezid's rapid rise as it came under pressure when Timur invaded Syria. For Timur, however, reducing Bayezid soon became a more urgent task than conquering Mamluk lands. Bayezid's impatience with the Anatolian emirs, their forcible eviction and annexation of their lands caused some of them to seek justice from Timur the conqueror. Seen from Timur's splendid capital Samarkand, or even from nearer Islamic centres such as Damascus, Bayezid's Brusa and Adrianople were still minor and uncouth frontier towns. In Timur's eyes, Bayezid could be tolerated politically as a modest frontier emir, one among many, but not as an ambitious sultan bent on carving out a rival empire. In ideological terms, Bayezid might even be considered to be performing laudable service to the greater glory of Islam as a frontier lord, but not when he conquered Muslim emirs and turned further into Islamic heartlands, defying Timur's eminence as the supreme ruler in the Islamic world. Timur set out to crush the incipient Ottoman empire; his aim was not to conquer all of Bayezid's territories in Anatolia and in Rumeli but merely to restore these lands to what they had been only a generation earlier, a region of petty emirates preoccupied with frontier expansion more or less in fraternal relations with each other, but none of them too grand to contemplate extending conquest toward interior regions. For this purpose Timur invaded Anatolia but only after his earlier attempts to force Bayezid to submission were unsuccessful. He defeated Bayezid when the not yet coherent patchwork Ottoman army supported by Christian troops from Rumeli vassals and the soldiery of formerly independent Anatolian emirates dissolved in the face of the Timur's grand horde. Bayezid fell prisoner and died in Timur's captivity. The victor recreated the political map of the western frontier region annulling Bayezid's Anatolian conquests but allowing a much reduced Ottoman emirate to exist among the others. In the first decade of the fifteenth century Bayezid's sons fought each other to lead this patrimony; the relative ease with which a powerful Ottoman state was soon re-established indicates that the forces cohering near the Ottoman ruler were stronger than appeared to Timur and to other contemporaries.

DEVELOPMENT OF OTTOMAN POLITY

For a hundred years after its emergence the Ottoman state expanded from a tiny 'tribe' of Osman's followers on the Seljuk–Byzantine borderlands in Bythynia to a major sultanate in Anatolia and the Balkans. This territorial expansion meant that the frontier society of Osman's time moved on to new regions in south-eastern Europe, leaving behind a relatively peaceful and stable hinterland. A further aspect of change was the emergence of a political 'centre' distinct from the relatively loose organisation of frontier society. The expansion of the Ottoman state was, to a large extent, parallel to the elevation of the position of the ruler with sufficient central power to impose order on the periphery.

In the egalitarian days of Osman Bey's followers all members of the 'tribe' seem to have had their own livelihood, beys owning some flocks of sheep, common folk tilling the fields, artisans and small merchants active in the market-place. When the 'tribe' was threatened from the outside or when the beys called a raid shepherds and farmers, artisans and vendors took up arms. Sometime in Orhan Bey's long rule, as the frontier zone moved away from the original heartland there emerged a social differentiation between people who were essentially civilians as opposed to others who were fighters. The distinction was not rigid; there was always room for volunteers in frontier raids and also in the ruler's campaigns, but it was recognised that fighters should be given additional consideration. Land was given to soldier-farmers who could be called upon to take up arms by command, not simply as volunteers. The beys, captains and horsemen were allocated 'livings', *dirlik* in Turkish, made up of land rent from peasants and market dues in towns. The *dirlik* units were proportionate in size, both in terms of settlement and of revenue generated, to the rank or standing of the holder. A horseman might be given the revenues of a village, mostly in kind as a share of the agricultural produce; a captain or bey would be in charge of a town where the revenue was greater and more of it was generated by commercial activity and so in cash. The ruler, too, had a *dirlik*, concentrated around Brusa, which in time came to be known as the ruler's domain, and later also around Adrianople. The size of the ruler's *dirlik* was of course greater, but it was essentially a living as any other. Land as well as land revenues were also given to dervishes or to learned men, but these were in the form of *vakıf* endowments. It is interesting to note that all *dirlik* recipients and those who made their living out of *vakıf* revenues, whether warriors or men of religion, as a group were termed *askeri* which literally means 'military', an indication that early social differentiation was based on fighting ability, at least in concept. *Dirliks* were also known as *timars*, here meaning horse-grooming, implying a living for a horse warrior.

Small livings were of an amount of revenue sufficient to keep the holder, a cavalryman. Recipients of larger *dirliks* were expected, in addition, to keep a retinue proportionate to the level of their revenues. A town commander, for example, might have a *dirlik* ten times greater than a cavalryman's; in that case he would be expected to bring a retinue of ten men on campaign. He would be totally responsible for their keep, weapons, horses and any pocket money he might give them. The revenue grants supported not only the *dirlik* holders but also a number of fighters in their own households. Such fighters might be outsiders or local volunteers who offered their services to the commander, but these military households also included a number of bondsmen, perhaps captured in battle or in raids. Large households, those of the ruler or of leading beys, held a higher proportion of slave soldiers. The important point is that the *dirlik* grants supported household troops, whether free volunteers or slave retainers.

In the Islamic world it was an old tradition for rulers to maintain slave household troops. In early Ottoman society, when inner Asian steppe tribal traditions were still alive, some uprooted warriors bound themselves to beys, forming a band of fighters loyal to the person of the chief.[30] In an Islamic setting slave soldiers had to be of non-Muslim origin and from outside the domains, for neither Muslims nor protected *zimmi* non-Muslim subjects could legally be made into slaves. In Ottoman practice, too, slaves to serve as household troops were captured across the frontier. After the mid century when the frontier struggle moved across the Dardanelles, when there were very few non-Muslims in Anatolia who did not live under Muslim government in the domains of one *gazi* emirate or another, the Balkans became the only source of such captives. The frontier lords stocked their own households after raids, the surplus was transported for sale in Anatolia. At a time when the Ottoman bey himself no longer took part in raids, when he might as often lead campaigns in Anatolia against Muslim rivals as in the Balkans, the ruler might have been eclipsed by the frontier lords, each in command of many frontier raiders and with their own well-furnished and abundantly manned households, much larger than would have been possible solely on revenue grants. To redress the balance and establish his own eminence beyond challenge, Murad Bey claimed one fifth of the captives or of their cash value as well as of other plunder when

[30] Inalcık (1981–2).

they were brought to Anatolia. His claim was instituted as a customs point at Gelibolu; the frontiersmen resented what they considered an unjust appropriation, their bitterness at wily counsellors with their book-learning leading the Ottoman bey to injustice was long-remembered, though in the event they had little choice but to obey the ruler's command.[31]

This new ruling sometime in the 1370s increased the ruler's *dirlik* revenues and gave fresh impetus to the enlargement of his household much beyond those of leading commanders. He already furnished household cavalry regiments made up of wage-earning mercenaries and volunteers; with the suddenly increased flow of cash and captives from the Gelibolu customs Murad Bey was able to form several companies of foot soldiers called 'new troops', *yeniçeri* in Turkish (corrupted to janissary). Yet toward the end of the century the number of captives seems to have become insufficient for royal requirements, perhaps because there were more campaigns of conquest or field battles, including those in Anatolia, than raids for human or material booty. Whatever the original impetus, a new method of recruitment came into being: the forcible removal of men or boys from Christian peasantry, subjects of the Ottoman ruler. Both this cruel and unusual way of recruitment and the recruits themselves were known as *devshirme,* literally 'gathering' or 'hand-picking'. The plight of families losing their sons can be imagined, though the recruits might later attain high office and command. The method was also unknown in earlier Islamic practice, and almost certainly illegal from the point of view of *sheriat*, Islamic law.[32] Recently Demetriades has suggested that *devshirme* recruitment may have come about in the frontier zone, not in the pacified hinterland.[33] In the turbulent frontier conditions where the enemies were separated not by a line but confronted each other across the land it may have been difficult to tell what could be considered already in Ottoman domains and what was yet to be subdued, who was a subject and who was still the foe. Demetriades has also suggested that it may have been the old frontier lord Evrenos Bey who was responsible for such 'raiding' of his own territory. Was it that areas earlier plundered from the outside were required to provide recruits, human booty, even after they became subject to Ottoman rule? In any case, *devshirme* had the advantage over random captives in battle that recruits could be chosen at greater leisure for superior physical and mental ability. When the *devshirme* appears fully formed in Ottoman documentation it was a royal prerogative, but the possibility that Ottoman rulers took Evrenos Bey's lead and then monopolised his method cannot be disregarded.[34] However it may have come about, the *devshirme* in addition to the one fifth share of captives at Gelibolu provided

---

[31] Aşıkpasazade, *Tevârîh-i Âl-i Osmân*.   [32] Wittek (1955).   [33] Demetriades (1993).
[34] Vryonis (1971), pp. 240–4, for possible earlier versions of forced recruitment.

the means for the sultan to increase his household troops without cost, and Gelibolu customs revenues afforded the funds for the upkeep of the royal household. Holding Gelibolu seems to have increased Murad Bey's power over his lords by giving him the ability to control both the flow of *ghazi* volunteers to the Balkan frontiers and the shipment of captives and booty to Anatolia.[35]

In the enhancement of the power of the ruler the size of his household army may have been the crucial factor. Relatively smooth succession in the house of Osman, until Timur's blow, also assured that the royal household and royal authority were never disrupted, damaged and dissipated from generation to generation. The Ottomans were quick to take advantage of succession struggles in neighbouring states, Muslim or Christian. On the other hand, in their political conceptions and practices they seem to have been quite similar to other Muslim emirates of Anatolia. Was it simply coincidence that, while many neighbours suffered domestic discord, the house of Osman remained united? Kafadar has suggested otherwise: that the Ottomans deliberately avoided the danger of dissolution by a policy of 'unigeniture', keeping the patrimony intact and not dividing it among members of the ruling clan.[36] While it is true that we do not have instances of brothers of an Ottoman ruler holding different provinces, the more serious disruption to a ruling house usually happened at the death of a ruler. In the steppe tradition there was no set way of succession; not having a rule was itself the rule. Members of the ruling house were all potential successors; let them contest the succession and the best leader would emerge – success would be proof of his military and political ability. In this sense, the house of Osman was no different from their Muslim neighbours. The historian may not like the idea, but it *was* good fortune that Orhan succeeded his father apparently without much of a struggle and then remained the chief for almost forty years. By the time he died Gelibolu was already in Ottoman hands and the frontier had moved to Thrace. Murad in 1362 as well as Bayezid in 1389 may have had to fight for the bey's seat.[37] There is in Murad's time the curious episode of the challenge by his son, Savcı Bey: Savcı and a Byzantine prince unsuccessfully attempted a double revolt; he seems to have been eliminated soon after. Certainly there are many other challenges by real or 'false' princes in later Ottoman history, much better known and documented. If there was conscious unigeniture it was not unique to the house of Osman; nor was the house free from occasional trouble. Even if, in its first century, Ottoman succession was less disruptive than elsewhere both in 1362 and in 1389 the new emir apparently had to enforce the most recent conquests and treaties of his predecessor, to begin again in his own name.

---

[35] Kafadar (1995), p. 142.   [36] Ibid., pp. 136–7.   [37] See n. 27 above.

In political organisation, too, the Ottoman state at first followed earlier Islamic examples. Once the emir gained an elevated place and became a veritable ruler, a sultan, he appointed an *emir ül-ümera*, bey of beys, as the military chief. As in usual Islamic practice, the chief commander was balanced by a *kadiasker*, chief magistrate, from the learned profession, who acted as a civilian counsellor, a *vezir*. Already in Bayezid's short time in power, after the incorporation of Anatolian emirates, the Ottoman state departed from precedent by having two chief commanders, and possibly two chief magistrates as well, one for each territorial wing, Anatolia and Rumeli: the position of the sultan was now even grander. A further process was that among military commanders, men who had first served in the ruler's household as his bondsmen and so with greater loyalty to the person of the sultan came to take precedence. All these changes, unique to Ottoman organisation and designed to enhance the supremacy of the sultan, became much more definite in the decades following the disaster of 1402, but the direction and intent can be detected in the last quarter of the fourteenth century.

The internal power of the sultan made expansion more controlled, with the frontier lords obedient to a policy articulated by the sultan and his counsellors at the centre. Various practices at conquest lessened the shock for the populace: local dynasts were sometimes given the chance to become Ottoman officials as consolation for the loss of their own lands, usually to serve at a different corner of the Ottoman realm. Some Christian commanders were given Ottoman *dirliks*, as is evident from later land registers.[38] Local administrative practices were maintained so that daily life was relatively undisrupted. Taxation might in fact be lessened, sometimes only temporarily, to allow the area to recover its economic potential.[39] There were shifts in population; Turkish tribesmen moved to the Balkans both to reduce their unruliness in Anatolia and to achieve a swift presence in recently conquered Rumeli lands.[40] Certainty as to numbers is impossible, but changing demographic balance aided Ottoman expansion: while Byzantine lands were depopulated, sometimes because Christian folk crossed over to live in the secure conditions of Ottoman-held areas, Turkish-Muslim population was reinforced by fresh waves of westward movement.[41] Apparently the Black Death at mid century which devastated Arab as well as Byzantine cities had a lesser impact on Turkish people of central Asian stock: periodic outbreaks of plague are noted in Turkish sources but not as a single terrible blow, and there are indications that Anatolia was deemed safer during the great calamity.[42] To accompany the

---

[38] Inalcık (1952).   [39] Oikonomidès (1986).
[40] Gökbilgin, *Edirne ve Paşa Livası*, and *Rumeli'de Yürükler.*   [41] Zachariadou (1987).
[42] Dols (1977).

frontiersmen, Sufi dervishes too were encouraged to move to Rumeli by *vakıf* endowments; their convents served as social centres for the Muslims, their flexible and tolerant version of Islam also appealed to non-Muslims and facilitated conversion.[43] Religious attitudes confirmed the superiority of Islam without necessarily denigrating non-Muslim beliefs and practices.[44] Endowments in towns encouraged the market-place while providing social and religious services.[45] Murad Bey even joined the *ahi* guildsmen, recognising the social and even, at times, the political importance of the network they had created in Anatolian towns.[46]

These were all aspects of the remarkable rise of the Ottomans in the course of the fourteenth century, both in Anatolia and in Rumeli. Ottoman conquest and Ottomanisation was placed on firm foundations, sufficiently so that the state recovered from Timur's invasion with remarkable resilience. The Ottomans channelled the Turkish population of Anatolia to a new region of frontier opportunity and expansion, and they used the power gained in Rumeli to subjugate Turkish neighbours in Anatolia. This opportunity for expansion became possible only with the incorporation of the Karasi emirate and firm control of Gelibolu. At first it was, perhaps, an unexpected opportunity but the Ottomans knew well not to miss it.

---

[43] Barkan (1942).   [44] Kafadar (1995); Balivet (1993).   [45] Kiel (1989).
[46] Uzunçarsılı (1947), p. 530.

CHAPTER 27

CHRISTIANS AND MUSLIMS IN THE EASTERN MEDITERRANEAN

Peter Edbury

THE fall of Acre and the other Christian strongholds on the coast of Syria and Palestine to the Mamluk sultan in 1291 marked the end of the western military presence in the Holy Land which had begun at the time of the First Crusade. But the widespread conviction that Jerusalem and the other places associated with Christ's life on earth ought to be a part of Latin Christendom was by no means dead. The demise of the kingdom of Jerusalem did not signify the end of the crusading movement, though between 1291 and the end of the fourteenth century the question of whether the west should launch crusades to recapture the Holy Land came to be largely overshadowed by the more pressing question of how far the west could prevent the Muslims from occupying other Christian-held territories bordering the eastern Mediterranean. After 1291 the kingdom of Cyprus under its Lusignan dynasty remained as the sole western outpost in the Levant while to the north, in south-eastern Anatolia, the kingdom of Cilician Armenia provided the one Christian-controlled point of access to the Asiatic hinterland. Further west, in the former Byzantine lands in and around the Aegean, there were a number of European possessions, most of which had been won early in the thirteenth century as a result of the Fourth Crusade. The Hospitallers were to add significantly to these territories when between 1306 and 1310 they seized the island of Rhodes from the Byzantine Greeks. The Byzantine empire itself, though buoyed up by the reoccupation of Constantinople in 1261, lacked the resources necessary to defend its territory – now largely limited to Bithynia, Thrace and northern Greece – from the predatory designs of its neighbours, and the fourteenth century was to witness its decline into impotence (see above pp. 795–824).

Since the 1260s and indeed until the early sixteenth century the Cairo-based Mamluk sultanate ruled in Syria and Palestine. The regime was prone to periodic bouts of political crisis as rival military commanders jockeyed for power, but it was nevertheless able to provide a fair measure of internal stability. In 1299, 1301 and 1303 invading armies from the Mongol Ilkhanate of Persia briefly occupied Syria, but otherwise, apart from coastal raids from Cyprus in the 1360s, the region was largely free from external attack until Timur's invasion of 1400–1. Conflict between the Mongols and the Mamluks had begun in the mid-thirteenth century, and, as the Mamluks continued to consolidate their hold on Syria after 1291, so they strengthened their position by punitive attacks on the Mongols' allies, the Armenians of Cilicia. However, despite alarmist rumours of massive naval preparations, they lacked the capacity to strike at the island of Cyprus. In Asia Minor the political situation was more fluid. The Seljuk sultanate of Rum, which at the beginning of the thirteenth century had been a major force in the region, had dwindled in power and extent and by the early fourteenth century had ceased to matter. In its place had developed a number of smaller emirates or *beyliks*, and from the late thirteenth century forces from these principalities were able to seize cities and fortresses in the Byzantine lands in north-western Anatolia and prey on Christian shipping in the waters around the coast. By 1337 the Turks had almost entirely expelled the Byzantines from Asia Minor. Among their warrior-leaders, though by no means regarded as most important at the time, was a certain Osman (d. 1326) who in 1302 scored a notable victory over the Greeks at Baphaeon but whose chief claim to fame is as the ancestor of the dynasty known to posterity as the Osmanlı or Ottoman Turks (see above pp. 844–5).

Though the Muslims were dominant on land, the Christians retained their mastery of the sea. Merchant vessels from Italy and also from southern France and Catalonia traded regularly in the Aegean and Black Sea and in the Levant, calling at both Christian and Muslim ports. There can be no doubt that there were substantial rewards to be had from trade and shipping, and also that the regular presence of western merchant fleets did much to sustain the Christian bridgeheads and trading stations in the east. For their part, though they did possess a merchant marine, the Mamluks lacked an effective naval arm. Thus despite considerable provocation, there was no Mamluk expedition against Cyprus between 1271 and 1424, and no attack on Rhodes until 1440. More worrying for Christian seafarers were the Turkish emirates of western Asia Minor. In 1329 the emir of Aydın, who had controlled Ephesus since 1304, captured Smyrna, and corsairs based in these ports and also in the adjacent emirate of Menteshe in south-western Anatolia ranged widely across the Aegean raiding as far as Greece and Negroponte.

For Christians in the west at the beginning of the fourteenth century, the idea that the Holy Land should be recovered remained axiomatic. There can have been very few people who would have voiced opposition to the idea of a crusade to win back Jerusalem, and the papacy persevered in seeking ways to launch just such an expedition. But although the goal of Jerusalem retained its potency there was only limited agreement as to the practicalities, and for differing reasons the prospect of a major campaign gave rise to serious apprehensions and highlighted mutual tensions. For example, in France the mantle of St Louis hung heavily on the shoulders of his heirs and it was generally assumed that the Capetians would take the lead, but this in itself resulted in a certain tepidity towards a Holy Land crusade on the part of other monarchs, not least the kings of Aragon who had been locked in a struggle for control of Sicily with the cadet branch of the French royal family and successive popes since the 1280s. Problems of a different kind were presented by the mercantile interests. Crusading would entail the disruption of trade: the subsidiary aim of restoring the Latin empire of Constantinople would mean dislocation not only in the Levant but also around the Aegean and the Black Sea, and the merchants knew that they would be particularly vulnerable to reprisals should a crusade be less than totally successful. More immediately, it was widely accepted that as a preliminary to a successful assault, the Mamluk sultanate should be weakened by an extended trade embargo which would starve it of war materials and *mamluk* slaves and generally undermine the economy. But in view of the profits to be made, an embargo was the last thing the merchants wanted.

Directly after the fall of Acre the pope, Nicholas IV, took measures to send forces to defend Cyprus and Armenia, sought to organise the commercial blockade of Mamluk ports and proclaimed a general crusade for the summer of 1293. He also ordered the summoning of provincial Church councils to consider among other things the merging of the Templars and the Hospitallers, called on the bishops to engender peace within Europe and requested advice on crusading strategy. Not much came of the pope's efforts, since he died in the following year, but his activities set the tone for a generation. There was no shortage of advice: no fewer than twenty-six extant treatises on the theme *de recuperatione Terrae Sanctae* have been counted from the period 1274 to 1314.[1] Opinions varied on such issues as the numbers of men required, or whether a crusade should invade Syria via Cilicia or make a direct assault on Egypt, and not surprisingly some writers seem to have been more in touch with reality than others. Nicholas did manage to set the process in motion whereby a fleet brought aid to the Christian outposts in the east, but his crusading plans proved still-born. Peace in Europe was a forlorn hope, and further short-term measures to help Cyprus and Armenia were stymied by a war between Genoa and Venice which lasted from 1293 until 1299. The Templars and Hospitallers opposed the proposed merger of their Orders, though, when in 1312 the Templars were suppressed, the Hospitallers did acquire a substantial proportion of their former lands. The commercial blockade, with its automatic sentence of excommunication for those who transgressed, was never effective. It

---

[1] Schein (1991), pp. 269–70.

may well have deterred some, but too many merchants were prepared to risk the penalties. There could be no effective policing of the seas; in course of time release from excommunication in return for the payment of a fine became a matter of routine, and from the 1320s the popes began issuing licences to allow merchants to break the embargo and engage in trade within the Mamluks' lands.

Since the death of St Louis at Tunis in 1270 the contribution of the kings of France to crusading to the east had faltered. Concern for their Angevin kinsmen in southern Italy in their struggle against the Aragonese, and wars against the kings of England and the counts of Flanders, now took precedence over more distant campaigns. Acute awareness of the financial requirements for a major expedition overseas meant that they looked to the papacy to agree to assistance in the form of increasing clerical taxation. But for their part, churchmen were anxious that secular society should shoulder a substantial proportion of the burden of crusade finance and feared that monies raised from the Church would be put to other purposes. During the pontificate of Boniface VIII (1294–1303) relations between Philip the Fair of France and the papacy reached a new low, but subsequently, with the popes now choosing to live in or just outside the French kingdom, royal influence over the papacy increased. One direct result of this development was that Philip was able to bring pressure to bear on Clement V (1305–14) to suppress the Templars. Another was that he now professed his enthusiasm for crusading, and in 1312 at the Council of Vienne the king undertook to prepare for a crusade in the knowledge that a six-years' tithe from the beneficed income of the clergy throughout western Christendom would be raised to pay for it. The following year Philip, together with his sons and his son-in-law, Edward II of England, and many nobles, took the cross for an expedition that was supposed to start by the spring of 1319. Although in fact no fourteenth-century king of France ever led a crusade to the east, the commitment to crusading that Philip's actions in these years entailed left an indelible mark on French royal policy; for the next quarter of a century the crusade was never far from the forefront of affairs of state, and it continued to cast its shadow for long afterwards.

Philip's stated goal was Jerusalem. As early as 1297 he had secured the canonisation of his grandfather, that indefatigable crusader Louis IX, and in espousing the crusade he was not only seeking greater glory for himself and his dynasty but was also assuming the role that many people in Europe had come to expect of a French king. Philip had an additional interest, the re-establishment of the Latin empire of Constantinople. Since 1261, when the Greeks had reoccupied their capital, the papacy had vacillated between a policy of pressurising them into Church union with the west and one of encouraging moves to expel them once more. The failure of ecclesiastical union after the Council of Lyon of 1274 combined with the marriage in 1301 of the titular

Latin empress to Philip's own brother, Charles of Valois, put the idea of using a crusade to recapture Constantinople – a milestone on the road to Jerusalem – firmly back on the agenda.

There is no reason to doubt that Philip the Fair and his family were sincere in their intention to launch a crusade. But Philip himself died in 1314, and his death was followed by a period of dynastic uncertainty. His sons, Philip V (1316–22) and Charles IV (1322–8), both continued to plan crusading expeditions, but without achieving anything concrete. It was generally accepted that if an all-out assault by a crusading army from the west to regain the Holy Land was to be successful, there would have to be smaller preliminary expeditions to prepare the way and establish bridgeheads. In other words, there could be crusades to the east with specific goals which fell far short of the capture of Jerusalem. Philip V sought to organise a preliminary crusade, or, to use the current parlance, a *passagium particulare* or *primum passagium* to bring aid to the Armenians and enforce the trading embargo on Mamluk ports, but in 1319 the ships he had assembled became embroiled in Pope John XXII's Italian preoccupations and were lost in a naval battle near Genoa. In 1323 Charles IV began preparations for another fleet to be sent to the east, but disputes with the papacy over funding and then conflict with England over Gascony also brought his efforts to a halt. Philip VI (1328–50), however, found that circumstances were more favourable, and in 1334 he contributed to what he and the pope regarded as a *primum passagium* which was directed against Turkish shipping in the Aegean and which culminated in a victory over the Turks in the Gulf of Adramyttion.

At last the French monarchy and the papacy had something to show for all their efforts. The 1334 campaign signalled the start of a new chapter in European endeavours to bolster the Christian presence in the eastern Mediterranean, though not along the lines hitherto envisaged. With the benefit of hindsight it is clear that the inability of successive French kings to act had prevented other strategies for countering Muslim advance from gaining support, and the very fact that the 1334 expedition took place in itself reflects a change in atmosphere. The French had tacitly abandoned their ambition to re-establish the Latin empire of Constantinople; the Turkish conquest of the Byzantine areas of Asia Minor meant that western opinion had now swung firmly in favour of supporting the Byzantine regime against further Muslim losses and away from the idea of overthrowing it. More importantly, the 1334 campaign was not a French-led expedition but the product of a Christian league which both France and the papacy joined comparatively late and to which they contributed only a modest number of ships. The core of the league consisted of Venice, the Hospitallers, the Byzantine empire (which in the event failed to honour its pledge to participate) and Cyprus, and their alliance against

Turkish sea-borne depredations was spurred by a common self-interest rather than by the long-term goal of recovering the Holy Land. It was envisaged that there would be a follow-up campaign in 1335 with a larger French and papal contingent, but for a variety of reasons, not least the deteriorating relations between France and England, it was called off. With the outbreak of the Hundred Years War in 1337, further French involvement in the eastern Mediterranean was out of the question. But leagues involving the papacy, Venice, Cyprus and Rhodes were to have a long future.

Christian alliances directed against the Turks in the Aegean formed the focus for concerted action from the early 1330s until around 1360. Venice had the most ships to offer, and it was Venice's interests that were also the most vulnerable to Turkish corsairs. Since the early thirteenth century the Venetians had had control of Crete and Negroponte as well as a number of the smaller islands in the southern and western waters of the Aegean, and they were clearly anxious to defend these possessions against raids which might ultimately lead to conquest. More importantly, their ships traded regularly in Constantinople and the Black Sea, and the Turks posed a major threat to the security of their routes. Venetian rivalry with the Genoese added a further dimension to the situation, especially as the Genoese were more willing to reach accommodation with the Turks and had significant territorial and commercial interests of their own. Venice probably deserves most of the credit for getting the 1334 league started; the idea of an alliance with the Byzantines against the Turks can be traced back to the mid 1320s, but the political uncertainty that attended the last years of Andronikos II (1282–1328) and the accession of Andronikos III (1328–41) delayed matters. In the early 1330s, with the emir of Aydın now firmly in control of Smyrna, the threat to Venetian interests must have been greater than ever, and it would seem that it was they who managed to bring the Byzantines and the Knights of Rhodes together to form the nucleus of the league.

The Hospitallers had conquered Rhodes between 1306 and 1310 and had immediately made it their headquarters. Previously they had been based in Cyprus, and while there the Order had been beset by internal difficulties. Since the fall of Acre the knights' military activities had been sporadic and largely ineffective, but the initiative in acquiring a fortified base they could call their own, even if it was at the expense of the Greeks and not the Muslims, helped them find a fresh sense of purpose. In view of what was happening to the Templars at precisely the moment they were establishing themselves on Rhodes, this new enterprise would seem to have been very necessary. In 1309, with the active encouragement of Philip the Fair, the master, Fulk of Villaret, had led a crusading expedition which enabled him to consolidate his control over the island. Rhodes occupied a strategic point on the main shipping lanes to Cyprus and Armenia; it was also ideally suited for containing the Turks of south-western Asia Minor and maintaining Christian dominance in the southern approaches to the Aegean. A recurrent criticism of the Hospitallers was that they did not do as much as they might to stem Muslim advance, but during their early years in Rhodes debt and problems connected with transferring funds from their numerous estates in Europe to the east severely curtailed their ability to act. In 1319–20, however, a series of campaigns against the Turks and also against a Byzantine garrison on Leros inflicted heavy losses. The basic problem facing the Order was that their wealth, great as it was, paled when set against the costs of building fortifications, providing garrisons and maintaining a fleet.

In some respects the Knights of St John were more closely attuned to papal policy than the other Christian powers in the east. As members of an exempt Order of the Church they had a tradition of loyalty to the popes, who for their part expected them to execute their designs. For example, it would seem that besides trying to police the seas to prevent breaches of the trading embargo the Order followed papal instructions in bringing aid to Cilician Armenia. But they were also capable of thwarting papal intentions. In particular they fostered friendly relations with the kingdom of Aragon, promoting a marriage between King James II and a sister of Henry II of Cyprus in 1315 which could easily have led to Cyprus passing to the Aragonese crown, and at the same time they ignored a papal instruction to move against the Catalan Company in Athens. James II of Aragon (1291–1327) had a long record of defying the papacy. Not only had he sustained the Aragonese occupation of Sicily in the face of French and papal displeasure, he had maintained friendly diplomatic contacts with the Mamluk sultanate and his merchants were notorious for disregarding the papal ban on trade. Aragonese pragmatism in coming to terms with the sultanate, which during the third reign of al-Nasir Muhammad (1310–41) reached the height of its power, must have seemed more realistic than the papal crusading rhetoric and the distant and, as events were to show, insubstantial French sabre-rattling. There was no way the knights could challenge the Mamluks unaided, and unless and until a major European crusade became a genuine possibility it was much better to act with circumspection.

After the occupation of Rhodes, Hospitaller relations with Venice and also with Genoa were strained, partly because of competing territorial ambitions in the Aegean and partly because the Order made some attempt to enforce the papal embargo on trade with the Mamluks by intercepting ships coming from Egypt or Syria. But the Turks of Aydın and Menteshe posed the biggest threat to its activities, and the fact that despite their former differences the knights could make common cause with the Byzantines and Venetians against them is further evidence for the seriousness with which their depredations were now seen. The security of Rhodes and its environs was probably uppermost in their minds, but they would have accepted that it was part of their duty to protect Christian interests generally, and that meant safeguarding the other Christian-held territories in the Aegean and also the shipping lanes to Constantinople, Cyprus and Armenia.

By the early 1330s the Frankish rulers of Cyprus probably felt more secure than at any time since before the fall of Acre. A generation had passed and there had been no Mamluk attack on the island: rumours of large-scale preparations in the 1290s and 1300s had proved false. For their part, the Cypriots had attempted – ineffectually it is true – to join forces with the Mongols in their invasions of Syria in 1299 and 1301, and a Cyprus-based Templar force had briefly reoccupied the island of Ruad near Tortosa in 1301–2. But after 1303 there were no more Mongol campaigns into Syria, and the idea that the Holy Land might be recovered for Christendom by the Ilkhans of Persia, who in any case had by now adopted Islam, ceased to be taken seriously. But though Cyprus was secure behind its natural defence, the sea, Cilician Armenia lay open to Mamluk attrition. Devastating campaigns as in 1298, 1302 and 1304 or in 1320 and 1322 which resulted in cities being ravaged and fortresses ceded were interspersed by periods in which an uneasy peace could only be attained by the payment of heavy tribute. Western aid was limited – in the 1300s the popes sent financial help and the Hospitallers brought military assistance – and the situation was exacerbated by violence and bloodshed within the ruling family. The reign of King Oshin (1307–20) seems to have been comparatively untroubled, though it was characterised by bad relations with the king of Cyprus, Henry II (1285–1324), which on occasion appear to have led to armed conflict.[2]

What helped sustain both Cyprus and Armenia in these years was the wealth that accrued from international commerce. After 1291 the Armenian town of Ayas (Lajazzo) was the sole Levantine port through which western merchants could legitimately trade with Asia, while in Cyprus Famagusta flourished as a second major entrepot in the east. At both ports western merchants dealt in cloth, oriental spices and foodstuffs, and the surviving registers of the Genoese notary, Lamberto di Sambuceto, who was working in Famagusta in the 1290s and 1300s, well illustrate the vigour and importance of this trade. In 1322 the Mamluks briefly occupied Ayas, and it is likely that its trade never recovered. In 1335 it came under attack once more, and it was finally lost to the Muslims in 1337. Famagusta could offer far more security as a trading centre, and there the westerners could buy Asiatic goods from local merchants, many of them Syrian Christians who had taken refuge in Cyprus in 1291 or earlier, who in

[2] Edbury (1991), pp. 135–6.

their turn had acquired them in Cilicia or the smaller ports of northern Syria. Henry II's government seems to have tried to establish Famagusta as a staple for trade through the eastern Mediterranean, discouraging merchants from trading elsewhere in Cyprus, turning a blind eye to the activities of its own merchants who were acquiring eastern goods in the Mamluk sultanate for resale and trying to force the western merchants to trade in Cyprus by patrolling the sea to prevent them breaking the papal embargoes on trade with Egypt and Syria. It is, however, questionable how much the patrols actually achieved, although their activities undoubtedly soured relations with the Genoese and resulted in retaliatory raids on the Cypriot coast and threats of more serious attack.

The commercial importance of Cyprus had military implications. On the one hand, the kings were able to employ the money they raised from tolls and other dues for defence; on the other, the western merchants recognised that it was in their own interests that the island and the shipping lanes to the west should be safe from Muslim attack. No doubt it was awareness that the protection of the waters around Crete and Rhodes was vital to communications with the west that resulted in the kingdom of Cyprus becoming involved in the naval leagues. Hugh IV (1324–59) contributed six galleys in 1334, and in 1337 he won what would seem to have been an important victory over the Turks. A few years later a visitor from the west noted that the Turkish emirs of southern Anatolia paid him tribute. How the Cypriot kings viewed the prospect of a crusade to recover the Holy Land is more problematical. They themselves had a good claim to be the titular kings of Jerusalem, but since the 1270s their rights were disputed by the Sicilian Angevins, and they would have realised that in the event of a successful French-led crusade it would be unlikely that they would be restored to power. There were even voices in the west prepared to question the Lusignans' right to rule in Cyprus, although the marriage of Hugh's heir-presumptive to a kinswoman of the French king in 1330 must have laid that particular ghost to rest. There was also the problem of the form a crusade might take. A short-lived naval campaign would probably achieve little and only serve to antagonise the Mamluks with the result that after it was over Cyprus would be exposed to retaliation; in 1336 Hugh even had the pope order the cessation of crusade preaching in Cyprus. So far as he was concerned, military action against the Turks of Asia Minor and peaceful co-existence with the Mamluk sultanate was the order of the day.

On the whole Cyprus enjoyed good relations with both Venice and the Knights of St John in Rhodes. The Hospitallers had traditionally got on better with the Lusignans than had the Templars, and in 1310 they assisted in the counter-coup which re-established Henry II on his throne after four years of rule by his younger brother, Amaury. After the suppression of the Templars in

1312, the bulk of their estates in Cyprus passed to the Hospitallers, who thus became by far the wealthiest landholders on the island after the crown, and whose Cypriot preceptory in 1317 owed an annual responsion of 60,000 bezants to Rhodes. The Venetians too had for many years enjoyed much friendlier contacts with Cyprus than had their principal rivals, the Genoese, although at the beginning of Hugh IV's reign the king's refusal to confirm their privileges and deal with outstanding claims led to a period of strained relations. The other Christian power with growing interests in the east with which the kings of Cyprus sought close ties was Aragon. As mentioned already, in 1315 James II had married Henry II's sister, but the possibility that this union might prefigure the acquisition of Cyprus for the Crown of Aragon did not materialise. Shortly afterwards, Henry himself married into the cadet branch of the Aragonese royalty that held the throne of Sicily (Trinacria) and his cousin married a member of another cadet branch of the family which was ruling the kingdom of Majorca. Further marriage alliances followed a generation later when two of Hugh IV's sons, and one of his daughters, married Aragonese royalty. Of these unions, far and away the most important occurred in 1353 when the future King Peter I wed Eleanor of Aragon, a granddaughter of James II. Links with Aragon suited the Cypriots' own preference for peaceful co-existence with Egypt; Catalan merchants frequented Famagusta, and Aragon and Cyprus shared, though for different reasons, antipathy for both the Genoese and the Angevins of Naples.

The success of the 1334 naval league, though palpable, was limited. The Byzantines had failed to honour their undertaking to join in, and the victory in the Gulf of Adramyttion had left the most powerful of the Turkish rulers, Umur Bey of Aydın, unscathed. The fact that the projected 1335 expedition did not take place marked a further setback. Andronikos III came to an accommodation with Umur, whose power by the early 1340s was to reach alarming proportions. He is said to have been able to command a fleet of 350 ships for an expedition to the mouth of the Danube in 1341 and to have commanded a land army of 15,000 men two years later. It was not until 1341 that Hugh of Cyprus and the master of the Hospitallers sent their representatives to the papal court with proposals for a fresh round of concerted action. The new pope, Clement VI, responded positively. War between France and England had buried any hope of a major crusading campaign to the east, but the prospect of a more modest expedition to the Aegean appealed to Clement's own commitment to crusading. A league, comprising the papacy, Venice, Rhodes and Cyprus to last three years and to operate in the Aegean was eventually brought into being in 1343. In spring 1344 the participants assembled twenty galleys at Negroponte and won a substantial victory over a Turkish fleet off Pallene, the western prong of the Chalkidike peninsula. Then in October they surprised the garrison in Umur's principal port, Smyrna, seized the lower town, and burnt a large number of Turkish ships. The forces involved in the expedition had not been large, but the capture of Smyrna, which was to remain in Christian hands until 1402, stands out as the single most significant achievement of any collaborative Christian venture in the eastern Mediterranean during the fourteenth century.[3]

The capture of Smyrna caused a stir of excitement in the west even though the Turks retained control of the upper town and a Christian sortie at the beginning of 1345 ended with the deaths of a number of the Christian leaders. It was the cue for a wave of crusading fervour, particularly in Italy, and a crusade led by an oddly quixotic figure, Humbert II, dauphin of Viennois. Humbert sailed from Venice late in 1345, and although he won a victory at sea over the Turks, he proved inept as a commander. Having shown himself unable to prevent the Genoese from taking the important island of Chios from the Byzantines or drive the Turks from the upper town at Smyrna, his expedition fizzled out. In 1347, after his return to the west, the Christians were to win a further naval victory near Imbros, but by then it must have been apparent that they were not going to be able to expand inland from their toe-hold in Smyrna. Problems of finance as well as tension between the Hospitallers and the Venetians and between the Venetians and the Genoese jeopardised further activities, and the members of the league began to negotiate with the Turks for a truce. The onset of the Black Death in any case would probably have meant a cessation of hostilities.

Pope Clement worked hard to reverse the slackening of resolve which had set in after the successes of 1344, and in 1350, with the renewal of Turkish attacks, he managed to get the league renewed. Cyprus, Venice and Rhodes between them were to supply eight galleys to police the seas around the western coast of the Aegean, and together with the papacy they would share the costs of garrisoning Smyrna. But the Genoese occupation of Chios and also Old and New Phocaea in 1346 had caused alarm in Venice, and in 1350 tensions caused by the rivalry of the two trading republics in what remained of the war-torn Byzantine empire erupted into a full-scale war between them. Though Clement and his successor, Innocent VI (1352–62), struggled to salvage what they could and ensure that the Christian garrison remained in Smyrna, the new league was inoperable. Eventually in 1357, with peace now restored, it was revived yet again, this time for five years. The three participants were now committed to sending a mere two galleys each to police the seas and to contributing 3,000 florins annually for the defence of Smyrna. It is doubtful whether a squadron

---

[3] Luttrell (1958), p. 203.

of six galleys could achieve much in the face of Turkish sea-borne aggression, and in any case by the late 1350s the situation in Byzantium had changed dramatically for the worse.

Andronikos III had died in 1341. During his reign there had been signs that the Byzantines might yet consolidate their power in Thrace and northern Greece, but his death and the accession of his infant son, John V Palaeologos (1341–91), was the signal for the outbreak of a civil war in which the empress-mother, Anne of Savoy, was confronted by a leading associate of the late emperor, John Kantakouzenos. In 1347 Kantakouzenos entered Constantinople, and his opponents were obliged to accept that he should take power and reign as senior emperor with the young John V. His victory had been won at a huge price: he had introduced his Turkish allies, notably the Ottoman forces under Orhan son of Osman, into Thrace; the Serbian ruler, Stephen Dušan, had taken advantage of the war to conquer virtually all the Byzantine territory in northern Greece and Epirus for himself and had adopted the imperial title; and the imperial treasury was empty – Anne of Savoy had even raised money by pledging the crown-jewels to Venice. Kantakouzenos wanted to free Constantinople from the commercial stranglehold exerted by the Italians and at the same time rely on his alliances with the Turks, but he failed dismally. Far from deriving any benefit from the war between Genoa and Venice, his involvement only sapped his authority still further. Then in March 1354 the Ottomans seized Gallipoli, thus acquiring control of the Dardanelles and a base from which to extend their power into Thrace and beyond. Kantakouzenos himself was overthrown later in 1354 and John V restored. There was no power near at hand to whom John could turn for help other than the Italians whose self-interest had already done so much to weaken his empire. His only answer lay in the west, and in December 1355 he issued a chrysobull promising to secure the obedience of the Greek Church to the papacy in return for military aid against the Turks.

John's declaration showed the extent of his despair and took little account of reality. After generations of doctrinal and political bitterness, there was little prospect that the Orthodox clergy would kowtow to the pope. On the other hand there was no guarantee that the papacy could respond with anything like the amount of military resources that were needed; wars between France and England, between the Italian maritime powers and between pro- and anti-papal forces in Italy left little scope for switching substantial supplies of men and money to more distant theatres of conflict. Innocent VI's response was to reactivate the naval league, and in 1359 he sent a new legate, Pierre Thomas, to the east with the task of breathing fresh energy into western efforts to stem the Turkish advance. The legate, with the help of a naval squadron provided by the Venetians and the Hospitallers, led an attack on Lampsacus on the Asiatic side of the Dardanelles. His success seems not to have had any lasting effect, but the incident was the first occasion since before 1261 that a crusading venture had brought military aid with the specific intention of bolstering a ruler of Constantinople.[4] But then Pierre Thomas left for Cyprus, and with his departure western aid for Byzantium tailed off. The Turks extended their gains in Thrace, and in 1365 John V took the step, unprecedented for a Byzantine emperor, of going in person to the court of a foreign monarch, in this case the king of Hungary, to seek help. Not only did his pleas fall on deaf ears, on his way home he was taken prisoner by the Bulgars.

Western help, however, was on its way. The emperor's cousin, Count Amedeo of Savoy, had taken the cross in 1364, and Pope Urban V (1362–70) encouraged him to use his forces to aid Byzantium in the expectation that decisive action would pave the way for the promised subjection of the Greek Church to the papacy. But it was not until the summer of 1366 that Amedeo set out. In August his flotilla reached the Dardanelles, and there he led his crusaders in the capture of Gallipoli. It was a major achievement for it deprived the Turks of their foremost harbour in Europe, and its restoration to Byzantine control showed that crusades from the west might yet save the empire. Amedeo then moved on to Constantinople and thence to the Black Sea and the Bulgar ports of Mesembria and Sozopolis from where he was able to conduct the negotiations which led to the emperor's release. The campaign had demonstrated what a capable crusading leader could achieve, and in 1369, as a direct consequence of these events, John V journeyed to Rome and made his personal submission to the pope. But his gesture was largely in vain. There was to be no new crusade to aid Byzantium for another quarter of a century; meanwhile the Ottomans continued to advance.

One reason why so little western aid was directed to Constantinople in the 1360s was that Europe's interest in the east had turned elsewhere. The French monarchy revived its former schemes for a crusade to recover the Holy Land, and in 1365 Peter I of Cyprus (1359–69) began a war against the Mamluks with the sack of Alexandria, an event which must rank as the most spectacular Christian assault on the sultanate at any time in its history. With the benefit of hindsight it is clear that the Turkish penetration of Thrace meant that Byzantium needed military assistance more than ever, but it is by no means certain how far people in the west appreciated this point at the time. Nor is it clear how much credibility was accorded John V's undertaking to bring the Greek Church into obedience to the papacy. In any case, the issue was clouded by the rival ambitions of Serbia and Hungary, not to mention those of Venice

---

[4] Housley (1986), pp. 219–20.

and Genoa, and, given the conditions in Europe, it is difficult to see how the Catholic powers could sustain a viable anti-Turkish force for any length of time. What in fact happened in the 1360s was that a mixture of muddled thinking in the west and misguided ambition conspired to obscure the prior needs of the Byzantine empire and the Latin territories in the Aegean.

In May 1360 the French and English agreed the truce of Brétigny and thereby called a halt to the hostilities that had been in train since 1337. The difficulties facing John II of France (1350–64) were daunting. He needed to efface the humiliation he had suffered, restore his finances and clear France of the bands of unemployed mercenaries, the 'Free Companies', that were ravaging the countryside and even threatening the papal court at Avignon. A crusade to the east offered an opportunity for a general solution to these problems. It would enhance his reputation and that of the French monarchy; the pope would grant clerical taxes which would ease the financial strains, and the Free Companies could be drafted into the crusading army, their energies turned to the advantage of Christendom. It was only to be expected that John would concern himself with crusading. Every king of France since the time of Louis VII in the mid-twelfth century had taken the cross, and in the 1330s John's own father, Philip VI, had put forward ambitious proposals for a general passage to win back Jerusalem only to see them thwarted by the war with England. In November 1362 John II travelled to Villeneuve across the Rhône from Avignon and made contact with the newly elected Pope Urban V. Then, on the following Good Friday, he received the cross at his hands. Urban appointed him 'rector and captain-general' of a crusading expedition, the purpose of which was recovery of the Holy Land; he was to set off in March 1365, and the pope granted a six-year tenth together with the proceeds of various miscellaneous sources of papal income as the Church's contribution to the costs. Among those taking the cross at the same ceremony was Peter of Cyprus who had arrived at Avignon two days earlier.

Did John and Urban really think they could launch a crusade that would win back Jerusalem? John's record as a military leader was scarcely distinguished, and the condition of his kingdom meant that it would be even more difficult to get a crusade started than it had been earlier in the century. The pope seems to have had little idea about what the expedition would actually do once it had set sail. Maybe his chief concern was to help John regain his authority within France, promote peace in Europe and solve the problem of the Free Companies, and he saw the crusade in the first instance as a means to these ends. It was agreed that the Cypriot king should lead a preliminary expedition ahead of the main crusading army, and in the summer of 1363 Peter embarked on a tour of Europe designed to publicise the crusade and seek recruits. Attempts to enlist the Free Companies did not meet with much success, but there can be no doubting his enthusiasm for the task in hand. But when in April 1364 John II died, Peter was left as the undisputed leader of the whole enterprise.

Peter had inherited a crusade which had Jerusalem as its goal. He also had as his chancellor one of the most determined crusading publicists of the fourteenth century, Philippe de Mézières, and Philippe's *vita* of the legate who accompanied the 1365 expedition, Pierre Thomas, likewise emphasised the Holy City as the intended destination of the campaign. The rhetoric of the contemporary papal bulls combined with this work of hagiography have in the past led historians to view Peter as an unworldly dreamer whose chivalry and piety led him to embark on a holy war that in the mid-1360s was an anachronism, hopelessly adrift from reality. An alternative view, which tries to make allowance for the propagandist nature of these sources, suggests that Peter's crusading zeal was sublimated to self-interest: far from being out of touch with the real world, he used the crusade in an attempt to establish Cyprus as the pivotal power in the Levant and secure for his kingdom a larger share of the wealth that was then being generated in the east through international trade. If John II and Urban V can be accused of being vague and impractical in their crusading schemes, Peter's faults were those of a gambler whose optimism and over-ambition carried him way beyond the capacity of his resources.

According to Leontios Makhairas, the principal Cypriot chronicler of these events, Peter's arrival at Avignon at Easter 1363 had nothing to do with crusading. Rather, his intention in coming in person to the west was to settle a dispute over his accession to the throne. His rival was his nephew, Hugh, the son of his long-dead elder brother. Hugh had been living in the west and does not appear to have enjoyed any support within Cyprus itself. However, he did have powerful sympathisers in Europe including the French royal family and the pope, and so long as his claim remained unresolved there was always the possibility that he might destabilise Peter's rule. Since the death of Hugh IV in 1359 Peter had sent at least two embassies to the west to deal with the problem; the younger Hugh would need to be compensated if he were to be induced to relinquish his claim, and the king would have wanted the pope and the king of France to act as guarantors for the settlement. How far Peter was aware of the crusading plans that were afoot before his arrival at Avignon is not clear, but there can be no doubt that his enthusiastic espousal of them would have ingratiated him with his nephew's erstwhile supporters.

Hugh IV had helped secure the sea-routes to the west by participating in the leagues against the Turks in the Aegean and putting the emirates of southern Anatolia under tribute. At the beginning of his reign, before he came to Avignon, Peter had taken this policy one stage further. In 1360, in response to an appeal from its inhabitants, he placed a Cypriot garrison in the Armenian port of Gorhigos, and then the following year he took the city of Satalia (Antalya) by assault from the Turkish emir of Tekke. Satalia was a major port-of-call between Cyprus and Rhodes, and its capture was a significant achievement, comparable in importance to the capture of Smyrna in 1344. After his departure for the west towards the end of 1362, his brother and regent, John of Antioch, continued the work of clearing the seas of Turkish pirates. Peter's capture of Satalia meant that he had acquired a reputation as military leader in the struggle against Islam, and this too no doubt enhanced his standing at Avignon. It is likely that part of his intention in coming to the west was to recruit mercenaries and ships to enable him to continue these activities.

Peter's tour of Europe lasted from the summer of 1363 until November 1364 and included visits to Paris, where he spent Christmas and where in May 1364 he attended the funeral of John II and the coronation of his successor, England, Germany, Poland and Bohemia before ending in Venice. He was richly entertained but he did not recruit as many crusaders as he had hoped. The expedition departed from Venice in June 1365 and joined up with the Cypriot forces under John of Antioch at Rhodes in August. It is difficult to interpret the conflicting statistics furnished by our sources for the numbers of men and ships involved, but it would appear that the combined forces at Rhodes consisted in the main of Peter's own Cypriots together with the western mercenaries he had previously engaged and who were already in the east.[5] On 4 October the armada, which was certainly far larger than any previous fourteenth-century Christian fleet assembled in the eastern Mediterranean for war against the Muslims, set sail. Its destination was now for the first time revealed as the Egyptian port of Alexandria.

Why Peter should have challenged the military might of the Mamluk sultanate after decades of peaceful co-existence is a problem that admits no easy answer. While it is true that many crusade theorists believed that the way to win back the Holy Land was through an assault on Egypt, to explain Peter's choice of target in terms of crusading zeal or simply reckless adventurism would seem to underrate his political shrewdness. Commercial and material priorities had largely dictated the direction in which the Christian leagues in the Aegean had operated since the 1330s, and so it should not surprise us if similar considerations determined Peter's actions in the 1360s. Perhaps a clue to understanding his dramatic shift in policy is to be found in the peace proposals put forward in 1367 and 1368: Peter's chief concern then was to gain preferential commercial arrangements for the Cypriot merchants who traded in the Mamluk lands.

By the 1360s Cyprus's prosperity was in decline. As elsewhere, the economy

---

[5] Edbury (1991), p. 166.

would have contracted as a consequence of the Black Death; with fewer consumers and fewer producers, the volume of commerce and industrial and agrarian production would have dropped, and with it the income the king would have derived from tolls and other dues. The contraction in trade was made worse by a shift in international routes and the growing preparedness of western merchants to bypass the island and deal direct with Syria. On the one hand it may be that the proportion of Asiatic merchandise finding its way to the west through Cilicia and northern Syria and hence via Cyprus had fallen and more was going through the Black Sea or Egypt; on the other, the number of papal licences allowing westerners to traffic in the Mamluk sultanate had risen steadily since the 1330s, and there was no effective enforcement of the papal embargo. An example of how Cyprus was affected can be seen by an examination of Venice's state galley system. In the years 1334–45 the Venetians were regularly sending seven or eight galleys to the island. Then in 1346, taking advantage of papal licences, they began sending galleys to Alexandria. The number going to the east remained about the same, but fewer went to Cyprus. Thus in the three years 1357–9, a total of fourteen galleys were equipped for Alexandria but only nine for Famagusta.[6] If this change was symptomatic of the general trend – and there is no reason to suppose that it was not – then Peter had cause for serious concern. But how was it to be reversed? One solution was to acquire trading bases outside the island. The Italians had their stations in the Aegean and Black Sea as at Coron and Modon, Galata, Caffa and Tana, so why should Cyprus not have her stations around the Levant? Peter had already taken Satalia and Gorhigos and so had control of their trading activities and could tax their commercial wealth. Why not also acquire Alexandria and the profits of its commerce? A second solution lay in giving the Cypriot merchants a more central role in east–west trade. If the sultan could be induced to give them preferential status in his lands, they would have a competitive edge over the European business communities and so might be able to restore Cyprus to her position as one of the principal entrepots between Europe and Asia.

The 1365 Alexandria campaign went badly wrong. The crusaders began well enough, taking the garrison completely by surprise, and they had no difficulty in storming the city. But Peter was unable to stop his forces engaging in wanton pillage and destruction, and his men did so much damage to the fortifications and the city gates that the place was untenable. There was nothing for it but to withdraw to Cyprus. Any hopes he may have had of acquiring the key outlet for Egyptian commerce in the Mediterranean for himself were dashed, and Cyprus was now at war with the sultanate. Furthermore, the assault had infuriated the Italian mercantile republics whose citizens had not only lost merchandise in the

[6] Edbury (1977), pp. 96–7.

general mayhem but had been interned by the Mamluks by way of retaliation. The king hoped that news of the successful assault would encourage more crusaders to come to the east; the Italians did their best to prevent further hostilities and resume normal trading relations. In 1366 they managed to induce Peter to begin peace talks, but it would seem that he was only playing for time while he built up his strength for another assault. A second fleet, apparently not much smaller than the one that had conquered Alexandria, sailed belatedly from Famagusta in January 1367 only to be scattered in a winter storm. A group of galleys sacked the Syrian port of Tripoli, but the rest returned to Cyprus without, it seems, doing anything.

After that Peter was disposed to enter serious negotiations. He was under ever-increasing pressure from the western mercantile interests to make peace; the pope had made it clear that he could expect no more ecclesiastical taxes; failure and periods of inaction were making it increasingly difficult for him to keep his forces together, let alone attract fresh troops from the west; warfare was expensive and Cypriot resources were limited; a Turkish attack on Gorhigos and a mutiny in the Cypriot garrison in Satalia distracted his attention.

The talks broke down in the summer of 1367. It was increasingly apparent that Peter was in a weak position: he could neither maintain his aggression and win an outright victory nor compel the Mamluks to make peace. After leading further raids on the coast of Syria in September and October he travelled to the west in an attempt to find fresh support. Pope Urban, however, insisted that he allow the Venetians and Genoese to act on his behalf in negotiations with the Muslims. Peter was back in Cyprus in the closing months of 1368 with nothing to show for his visit. There his increasingly erratic behaviour brought him into conflict with his own vassals, and in January 1369 he was murdered in a palace coup. Peace with the Mamluks was eventually concluded in October 1370. So far as is known – the text of the treaty does not survive – the war had brought no advantage to Cyprus whatever. Instead, Peter had left a legacy of royal debt and sour relations with the western merchants on whom the economic well-being of his kingdom depended. In 1373–4 the Genoese invaded Cyprus and struck the island such a blow that never again was it in a position to contribute to Christian leagues against the Turks, still less challenge the power of the Mamluk sultanate. The Cypriots did however manage to retain Gorhigos until 1448, although the remnants of the Cilician kingdom of Armenia succumbed to Muslim conquest in 1375. But in 1373, rather than allow Satalia to fall into Genoese hands, they handed it back to the emir of Tekke.

Amedeo of Savoy's capture of Gallipoli in 1366 held out a promise for the future that western Europe could bring aid to the Byzantines. But once the

1365 attack on Alexandria had failed and Peter's assault on Syria had ended in fiasco in January 1367, it was clear little would be gained from conflict with the Mamluk sultanate. Apart from some small-scale piracy and a rather futile Genoese naval raid on the coast of Syria led by Marshal Boucicaut in 1403, the Christian powers henceforth left the sultanate largely in peace. The ideal of warfare against Muslims continued to appeal to those people in the west who were imbued with contemporary chivalric values, but the realities of war and the expense and difficulties of organising a worthwhile campaign, not to mention finding an appropriate theatre in which to operate, meant that little could be achieved. Part of the problem was that getting to the frontiers of Christendom and Islam in the eastern Mediterranean required naval transport, and this could only be provided by people whose trading interests called for accommodation and not confrontation with the Muslims. The Italians resorted to war to defend their markets and routes; they were less keen to go to war to defend their co-religionists. The military and economic power at the disposal of the Venetians and Genoese meant that rulers in the east such as the king of Cyprus or the master of the Hospitallers could not ignore them. It was one of Peter's greatest errors that he tried to break loose from the constraints they imposed.

In the 1370s the Genoese embarked on a particularly assertive phase in their history. The war with Cyprus of 1373–4 ended with their occupation of Famagusta which remained a Genoese possession until 1464. In 1376 they went to war with Venice once more, this time over control of the strategically placed Aegean island of Tenedos, and in the course of this conflict they blockaded Venice itself from their base at Chioggia. At the same time France and England had resumed hostilities. Not surprisingly, anti-Turkish activity languished. In 1372 the pope tried in vain to bring the Christian powers in the east together in a conference to be held at Thebes. He then turned to the Hungarians who failed to co-operate and to the Hospitallers who were induced to take sole responsibility for the defence of Smyrna but otherwise found themselves side-tracked in the intricate politics of Latin Greece. On the death of Gregory XI in 1378 the papacy itself entered an extended period of schism. Neither of the two rival popes was in a strong enough position to do much to galvanise the west into countering Ottoman expansion.

By the end of the 1360s the Ottomans had occupied the two key cities of Adrianople and Philippopolis. Thereafter Constantinople and its environs remained as an isolated Christian-held enclave in the rear as the Turks penetrated deeper into the Balkans. In 1371 the sultan Murad I won a major victory over the Serbs at Crnomen on the River Maritza. He recovered Gallipoli in 1377; Sofia fell to him in 1385, Nish in 1386 and Thessaloniki in 1387. In 1389 the Turks won an even more significant victory when they defeated the forces gathered by an alliance of the Christian rulers in the Balkans at Kosovo. Murad himself was killed in the battle, but his son and successor, Bayezid I, had no problem in continuing his advance. Bayezid also extended Ottoman control over the lands of the other emirates of western Asia Minor. In the 1390s he brought Ottoman rule as far as the Danube and set about making preparations to take Constantinople.

It was in response to these events that King Sigismund of Hungary (1387–1437) entered the fray. Hitherto, the Hungarians had done little in conjunction with other western efforts to stem Turkish advance. Now Sigismund tried to stiffen resistance in the Balkans and get aid from the west. He was fortunate that his efforts coincided with a truce in the war between France and England and in an upsurge in crusading zeal which had already led people as prominent as the duke of Bourbon to lead a crusade to al-Mahdiya in 1390 and the earl of Derby to join in the Teutonic Knights' *Reisen* into Lithuania in 1390 and 1392. Philippe de Mézières, the chancellor of Cyprus who had been living in the west since the death of Peter I, had been tireless in promoting crusades by appealing to the piety and chivalry of the aristocracy, and he more than any other individual publicist had prepared the ground for a crusade to the east. Planning went ahead for a large-scale Anglo-French expedition that would travel overland to Hungary and join forces with Sigismund's forces in a campaign intended to drive back the Turks. A fleet comprising Hospitaller, Venetian and Genoese warships would operate in the Black Sea in conjunction with the land army. In the event the crusading army consisted chiefly of Burgundians. It left for eastern Europe in April 1396 and advanced through Hungary to the Danubian fortress of Nicopolis. But there, on 25 September, the Christians were overwhelmingly defeated.

From the Christian perspective there were two positive aspects to the Nicopolis crusade. Despite the defeat, the ducal house of Burgundy had established its credentials as a focus for future crusading aspirations, and secondly the expedition had at least forced Bayezid to relax his blockade of Constantinople. In 1399 the famous French commander, Marshal Boucicaut, who himself had been captured at Nicopolis, was able to bring further relief to the Byzantine capital. However, what stopped the Turks in their tracks was not western intervention, but the appearance of Timur and his Mongols in Asia Minor. In 1402 Timur inflicted a crushing defeat on Bayezid at Ankara, and it was to take the Ottomans a generation before they could resume their conquests in the Balkans.

It is easy to write off western European attempts at stopping Muslim advance in the lands around the eastern Mediterranean in the fourteenth century as a sorry tale of incompetence, selfishness and unfulfilled dreams. The long periods of warfare that engulfed substantial parts of the west and the economic crises that punctuated the century prevented substantial armies waging any sustained campaigns against either the Turks or the Mamluks, and the best that can be said is that the Christians may have slowed Turkish advance. At least in the upper ranks of society enthusiasm for crusading remained undimmed, and holy war against the infidel was regarded as an essential part of chivalric culture. Crusading ideology and the belief that Christians shared a common responsibility for the defence of their brethren overseas continued to hold an important place in the fourteenth-century thought-world.

If military success was limited, and if the motivation of those powers that sponsored action against the Muslims was mixed, the same could equally be said for the twelfth or thirteenth centuries. However, the fact that one way or another Christian Europe expended so much effort over so long a period should warn against regarding this century as a time when crusading went into decline and people ceased to concern themselves with the defence of Christendom.

APPENDIX:

GENEALOGICAL TABLES

EDWARD III = Philippa of Hainault
(1327–77) (d. 1369)

Edward, the Black Prince (d. 1376) = (2) Joan of Kent (d. 1385) = (1) Thomas Holland 1st earl of Kent (d. 1360)

Lionel duke of Clarence (d. 1368) = Elizabeth de Burgh (d. 1363)

John of Gaunt duke of Lancaster, king of Castile (d. 1399) = (1) Blanche of Lancaster (d. 1369); = (2) Constanza of Castile (d. 1394); = (3) Katherine Swynford (d. 1403)

Edmund of Langley earl of Cambridge, duke of York (d. 1402) = Isabella of Castile (d. 1392)

Thomas of Woodstock earl of Buckingham, duke of Gloucester (d. 1397) = Eleanor Bohun (d. 1399)

RICHARD II (1377–99) = (1) Anne of Bohemia (d. 1394); = (2) Isabella of France

Philippa (d. 1382) = Edmund Mortimer 3rd earl of March (d. 1381)

Henry Bolingbroke earl of Derby HENRY IV (1399–1413) = Mary Bohun (d. 1394)

Catalina = Henry III of Castile

Beauforts →

Edward duke of York (d. 1415)

Richard earl of Cambridge (d. 1415)

Edward (d. 1371)

Thomas Holland 2nd earl of Kent (d. 1397)

John Holland earl of Huntingdon, duke of Exeter (d. 1400)

Thomas Holland 3rd earl of Kent, duke of Surrey (d. 1400)

Roger Mortimer 4th earl of March (d. 1398)

Sir Edmund Mortimer (d. 1409)

Edmund Mortimer 5th earl of March (d. 1425)

Table 1   The royal family in the reign of Richard II

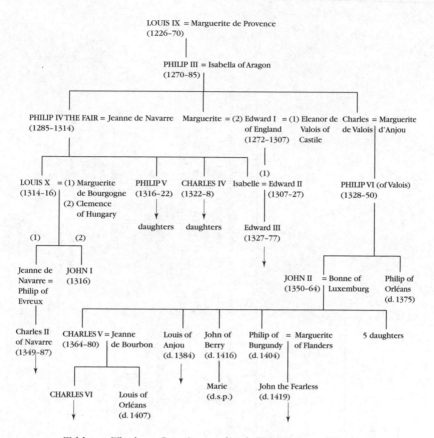

Table 2   The later Capetians and early Valois kings of France

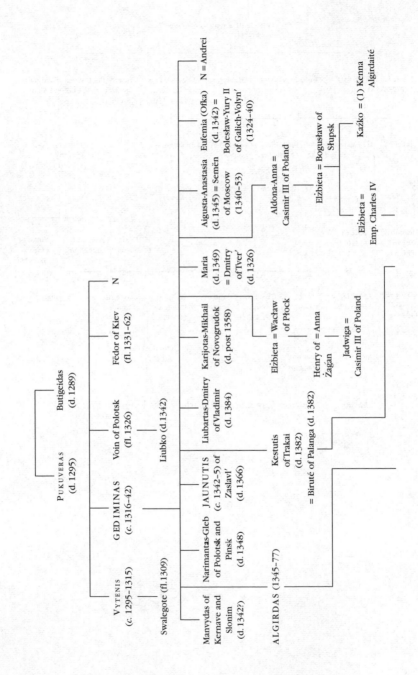

Anne = Richard II of England

Vaidotas-Butautas (Christian name: Henry, d. Prague, 1380)
Vytautas (Grand Duke 1392–1430)
Tauvilas (d. 1390)
Žygimantas (Grand Duke 1432–40)
Miklause-Maria = (1375) Ivan of Tver'
Danuté = (c. 1370) Janusz of Mazovia
Zingailé (d.1433) = (1390) (1) Henryk of Mazovia
                              (2) Aleksandr of Moldavia

= (1) ♀ (Maria?) of Vitebsk (= 1318?, d. c. 1349)

Andrei of Polotsk (d. 1399)
Dmitry of Briansk (d. 1399) = Anna
Konstantin of Czartorysk (d. 1390)
Vladimir of Kiev (d. 1398)
Fëdor of Ratno (d.1400)
Fëdora = Sviatoslav of Karachev
♀ = Ivan of Novosil'
Agrafena = (1354) Boris of Suzdal'

= (2) Ul'iana Aleksandrovna of Tver' (= 1350, d. 1392)

JOGAILA, Władysław II
KING OF POLAND (1386–1434)
Skirgaila-Ivan of Polotsk (d. 1397)
Lengvenis-Semën = (1) Maria Dmitrievna of Moscow (d. 1399) = (2) ♀ of Moscow
Korigaila-Casimir of Matislav (d. 1390)
Wigand-Aleksandr of Kernavė (d. 1392) =
Jadwiga of Opole
Koributas-Dmitry of Novgorod Seversky = Anastasia Olegovna of Riazan'
Svitrigaila-Bolesław (Grand Duke 1430–2)(d. 1452) = Anna Sofia Ivanovra of Tver'
Kenna-Joanna (d. 1368) = (c. 1359) Kaźko of Słupsk
Elena = (1372) Vladimir Khrobry of Serpukhov
Maria = (1) Vaidila (d. 1380) = (2) David of Gorodetsk
Wilheida-Katarzyna = (1388) Jan of Schwerin
Alexsandra (d. 1434) = (1387) Siemowit IV of Mazovia (d. 1426)
Jadwiga = (1394) Jan II of Oświęcim (d. 1405)
♀ = Oleg Ivanovich of Riazan' (1st wife)

CAPITALS – Grand Dukes of Gediminas's line
SMALL CAPITALS – Grand Dukes (father and brother of Gediminas)
N = name unknown

Table 3   The Gediminid Grand Dukes of Lithuania in the fourteenth century (simplified)

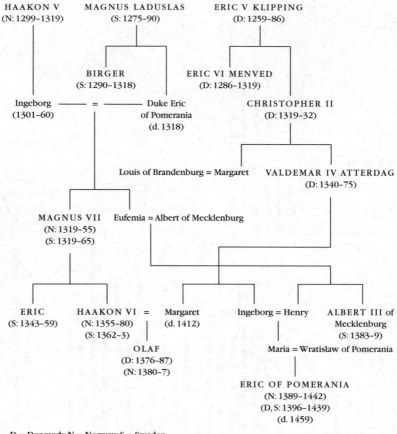

D = Denmark; N = Norway; S = Sweden

Table 4   The northern monarchies: the descent of Eric of Pomerania

Henry IV of Luxemburg (d. 1288)

Baldwin
archbishop
of Trier

Henry V of Luxemburg (d. 1313)
Emporer Henry VII (1308–13)

Albert of Habsburg (1255–1308)
emperor (1298–1308)

Wenceslas II (1271–1305)   (1) = Elizabeth   = (2) Rudolf of
king of Bohemia (1278–1305)   of Poland   Habsburg
king of Poland (1300–5)   (d. 1335)   king of
                                                             Bohemia
                                                             (1305–7)

Wenceslas III (1289–1306)
king of Bohemia (1305–6)
king of Hungary (1301–4)

Anne (1290–1313)
= Henry of Carinthia (d. 1335)
king of Bohemia (1307–10)

Beatrice (d. 1319)
= Charles-Robert
king of Hungary

Marie (d. 1324)
= Charles IV
king of France

John the Blind (1296–1346) = (1) Elizabeth (1292–1330)
king of Bohemia (1310–46)
= (2) Beatrice of Valois

(1) = Margaret Maultausch (d. 1359)
= (2) Lewis of Bavaria
margrave of Brandenburg

Charles IV (1315–78)
king of Bohemia (1346–78)
emperor (1355–78)

John-Henry (d. 1375)
margrave of Moravia

Bonne (1315–49)
= John the Good
king of France

Margaret (d. 1349)
= Louis the Great
king of Hungary (1342–82)

Wenceslas IV (1361–1419)
king of Bohemia (1378–1419)
emperor (1378–1400)

Jošt (d. 1411)
margrave of Moravia

Sigismund (1368–1437)
king of Bohemia (1419–37)
king of Hungary (1387–1437)
emperor (1433–7)
= (1) Mary (1370–95)
queen of Hungary (1382–95)
= (2) Barbara of Cilli

Table 5   The House of Luxemburg

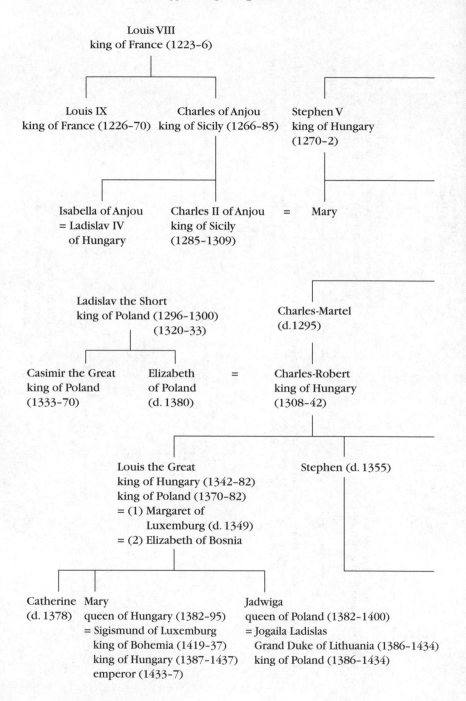

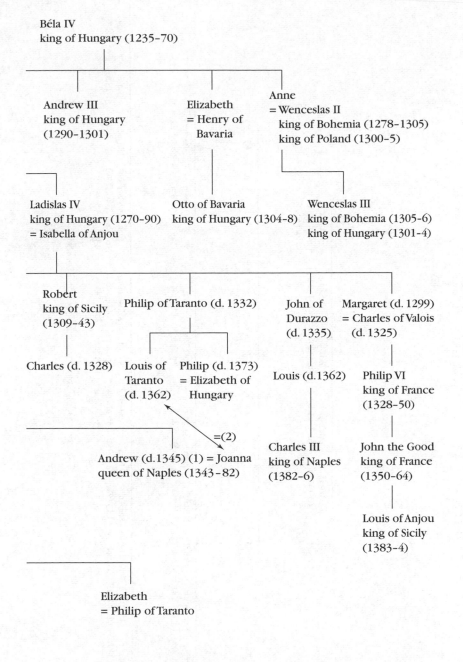

Table 6 The house of Anjou in Hungary and Naples

A genealogical chart showing the Daniilovich grand princes of Moscow.

DANIIL
(d. 1303)

Children of Daniil:
- **IURII** (d. 1325)
- Aleksandr (d. 1305/6)
- Boris (d. 1320)
- Afanasii (d. 1322/3)
- **IVAN KALITA** (d. 1340)

Children of Ivan Kalita:
- **SEMËN** (d. 1353)
- **IVAN** (d. 1359)
- **ANDREI** (d. 1353)

Children of Semën:
- Vasilii (d. 1338/9)
- Konstantin (d. 1341/2)
- Daniil (d. 1347)
- Miklaiil (d. 1349)
- Ivan (d. 1353)
- Semën (d. 1353)

Children of Ivan (d. 1359):
- **DMITRII** (d. 1389)
- Ivan (d. 1364)

Children of Andrei:
- Ivan (d. 1358/9)
- Vladimir of Serpukhov (d. 1410)

Children of Dmitrii:
- Daniil (d. by 1389)
- **VASILII** (d. 1425)
- Iurii of Galich (d. 1434)
- Semën (d. 1379)
- Ivan (d. 1393)
- Andrei of Mozhaisk (d. 1432)
- Petr of Dmitrov (d. 1428)
- Konstantin of Uglich (d. c. 1434)

Children of Vladimir of Serpukhov:
- Ivan (d. post-1401/2)
- Semën (d. 1426)
- Iaroslav (d. 1426)
- Andrei (d. 1426)
- Vasilii (d. 1427/8)

Table 7   Daniilovich grand princes of Moscow

PRIMARY SOURCES AND
SECONDARY WORKS ARRANGED
BY CHAPTER

I INTRODUCTION

Secondary works

Abu-Lughod, J.L. (1989), *Before European Hegemony. The World System A.D. 1250–1350*, Oxford

Aers, D. (1992), 'A Whisper in the Ear of Early Modernists: or, Reflections on Literary Critics writing the 'History of the Subject', *Culture and History 1350–1600. Essays on English Communities, Identities and Writing*, in D. Aers (ed.), New York, London, Toronto, Sydney, Tokyo and Singapore, pp. 177–202

Allmand, C.T. (1988), *The Hundred Years War. England and France at War c. 1300–c. 1450*, Cambridge

Blockmans, W. and Genet, J.-Ph. (1993), *Visions sur le développement des états européens. Théories et historiographie de l'état moderne*, Rome

Bulst, N., Descimon, R. and Guerreau, A. (1996), *L'Etat ou le roi. Les fondations de la modernité monarchique en France (XIVe–XVIIe siècles)*, Paris

Contamine, Ph. (1978), 'Les fortifications urbaines en France à la fin du moyen âge: aspects financières et économiques', *RH* 260: 23–47

Contamine, Ph. (1984), *War in the Middle Ages*, trans. M. Jones, Oxford

Coulet, N. and Genet, J.-Ph. (1990), *L'etat moderne: Le droit, l'espace et les formes de l'etat. Actes du colloque tenu à la Baume Les Aix, 11–12 octobre 1984*, Paris

Davies, N. (1996), *Europe. A History*, Oxford

Genet, J.-Ph. (1990), *L'Etat moderne. Genèse. Bilans et perspectives, Actes du colloque tenu au CNRS à Paris les 19–20 septembre 1989*, Paris

Herlihy, D. and Klapisch-Zuber, C. (1978), *Les Toscans et leurs familles. Une étude du Catasto florentin de 1427*, Paris; abbreviated in the English version, *Tuscans and their Families. A Study of the Florentine Catasto of 1427*, New Haven and London (1985)

Huizinga, J. (1924), *The Waning of the Middle Ages*, London

Hussey, J. M. (ed.) (1966–7), *The Byzantine Empire (Cambridge Medieval History, IV)*, part I, *Byzantium and its Neighbours*, Part II, *Government, Church and Civilisation*, Cambridge

Jones, Michael (1994), 'War and Fourteenth-Century France', in Anne Curry and Michael Hughes (eds.), *Arms, Armies and Fortifications in the Hundred Years War*, Woodbridge, pp. 103–20

Jones, Michael (1996), 'The Late Medieval State and Social Change: A View from the Duchy of Brittany', in Bulst, Descimon and Guerreau (1996), pp. 117–44

McLaughlin, M.L. (1988), 'Humanist Concepts of Renaissance and Middle Ages in the Trecento and Quattrocento', *RStds* 2: 131–42

Mollat du Jourdin, M. and La Roncière, M. de (1984), *Les Portulans. Cartes marines du XIIe au XVIIe siècle*, Paris

Moore, R.I. (1996), 'When did the Middle Ages begin', *Times Literary Supplement*, 7 June 1996, pp. 31–2 (review of *NCMH*, II, *c. 700–c. 900*, ed. Rosamond McKitterick, Cambridge (1995))

Nicholas, David (1997), *The Later Medieval City 1300–1500*, London

Prestwich, M. (1996), *Armies and Warfare in the Middle Ages. The English Experience*, New Haven and London

Previté-Orton, C. and Brooke, Z.N. (1932), *Cambridge Medieval History*, VII: *The Decline of Empire and Papacy*, Cambridge

Rigaudière, A. (1993), *Gouverner la ville au moyen âge*, Paris

Roberts, J.M. (1996), *A History of Europe*, Oxford

Southern, R.W. (1995), *Scholastic Humanism and the Unification of Europe*, I: *Foundations*, Oxford

Ullmann, W. (1949), 'The Development of the Medieval Idea of Sovereignty', *EHR* 64: 1–33

2 THE THEORY AND PRACTICE OF GOVERNMENT IN WESTERN EUROPE IN THE FOURTEENTH CENTURY

Secondary works

L'administration locale et le pouvoir central en France et en Russie (XIIIe–XVe siècle) (1989), Comité français des Sciences historiques. Actes du XIe colloque des historiens français et soviétiques, 18–21 septembre 1989, 1, Paris

Alessandro, V. d' (1963), *Politica e società nella Sicilia Aragonese*, Palermo

Allmand, C.T. (ed.) (1976), *War, Literature and Politics in the Late Middle Ages. Essays in Honour of G.W. Coopland*, Liverpool

Allmand, C.T. (1988), *The Hundred Years War*, Cambridge; French trans. *La guerre de cent ans*, Paris (1989)

Allmand, C.T. (ed.) (1989), *Power, Culture and Religion in France, c. 1350–c. 1550*, Woodbridge

Angermeier, H. (1966), *Königtum und Landfriede in deutschen Spätmittelalter*, Munich

Autrand, F. (1974), *Pouvoir et société en France, XIVe–XVe siècles*, Paris

Autrand, F. (1981), *Naissance d'un grand corps de l'état. Les gens du parlement de Paris 1345–1454*, Paris

Autrand, F. (1986), *Charles VI, la folie du roi*, Paris

Autrand, F. (1994), *Charles V le sage*, Paris

Babbitt, S.M. (1985), *Oresme's 'Livre de Politiques' and the France of Charles V*, Philadelphia

Baker, R.L. (1961), *The English Customs Service, 1307–1343. A Study of Medieval Administration*, Philadelphia

Bansa, H. (1968), *Studien zur Kanzlei Kaiser Ludwigs des Bayern vom Tag der Wahl bis zur Rückkehr aus Italien (1314–1329)*, Kallmünz

Barbey, J. (1983), *La fonction royale. Essence et légitimité d'après les 'Tractatus' de Jean de Terrevermeille*, Paris

Barbey, J. (1992), *Etre roi. Le roi et son gouvernement en France de Clovis à Louis XVI*, Paris

Barraclough, G. (1950), *The Medieval Empire. Idea and Reality*, London

Bautier, R.H. (1990), *Chartes, sceaux et chancelleries. Etudes de diplomatique et de sigillographie médiévales*, 2 vols., Paris

Bean, J.M.W. (1968), *The Decline of English Feudalism, 1215–1540*, Manchester

Beaune, C. (1985), *Naissance de la nation France*, Paris; augmented English trans. *The Birth of an Ideology*, ed. Frederic L. Cheyette, Berkeley, Calif. (1992)

Becker, M.B. (1967–8), *Florence in Transition*, 2 vols., Baltimore

Bellamy, J.G. (1970), *The Law of Treason in England in the Later Middle Ages*, Cambridge

Beneyto, J. (1949), *Los origenes de la ciencia politica en España*, Madrid

Benton, J.F. (1990), *Culture, Power and Personality in Medieval France*, ed. T.N. Bisson, London

Bisson, T.N. (1986), *The Medieval Crown of Aragon. A Short History*, Oxford

Blanchard, J. (ed.) (1995), *Représentation, pouvoir et royauté à la fin du moyen âge*, Paris

Bloch, M. (1923), *Les rois thaumaturges. Etude sur le caractère surnaturel attribué à la puissance royale particulièrement en France et Angleterre*, Strasburg and Paris; revised edn 1961

Blockmans, W. and Genet, J.-Ph. (eds.) (1993), *Visions sur le développement des états européens. Théories et historiographies de l'état moderne*, Rome

Bock, F. (1943), *Reichsidee und Nationalstaaten vom Untergang des alten Reiches bis zur Kündigung des deutsch-englischen Bündnisses im Jahre 1341*, Munich

Boockmann, H. (1975), *Johannes Falkenberg, der Deutsche Orden und die polnische Politik. Untersuchungen zur politischen Theorie des späteren Mittelalters, mit einem Anhang: Die 'Satira' des Johannes Falkenberg*, Göttingen

Boulton, D'A.J.D. (1985), *The Knights of the Crown. The Monarchical Orders of Knighthood in Later Medieval Europe, 1325–1520*, Woodbridge

Boureau, A. (1988), *Le simple corps du roi. L'impossible sacralité des souverains français, XVe–XVIIIe siècle*, Paris

Bresc, H. *et al.* (eds.) (1985), *Genèse de l'état moderne en Méditerranée. Approches historiques et anthropologiques des pratiques et représentations*, Rome

Brown, E.A.R. (1991a), *Politics and Institutions in Capetian France*, Aldershot

Brown, E.A.R. (1991b), *The Monarchy of Capetian France and Royal Ceremonial*, Aldershot

Brown, E.A.R. and Famiglietti, R.C. (1994), *The Lit de Justice. Semantics Ceremonials and the Parlement of Paris 1300–1600*, Sigmaringen

Brown, R.A., Colvin, H.M. and Taylor, A.J. (1963), *The History of the King's Works. The Middle Ages*, 2 vols. and plans, London

Brucker, G.A. (1962), *Florentine Politics and Society, 1343–1378*, Princeton, N.J.

Brunner, O. (1939), *Land und Herrschaft. Grundfragen der territorialen Verfassungsgeschichte Oesterreichs im Mittelalter*, Vienna and Wiesbaden; revised edn 1959

Buck, M. (1983), *Politics, Finance and the Church in the Reign of Edward II. Walter Stapeldon, Treasurer of England*, Cambridge

Cam, H.M. (1944), *Liberties and Communities in Medieval England. Collected Studies in Local Administration and Topography*, London and New York; 2nd edn 1963

Cambridge History of Medieval Political Thought, c. 350–c. 1450 (1988), ed. J.H. Burns, Cambridge

Carlyle, R.W. and A.J. (1903–36), *A History of Medieval Political Theory in the West*, 6 vols., London

Cauchies, J.M. (1982), *La législation princière pour le comté de Hainaut, ducs de Bourgogne et premiers Habsbourgs (1427–1506). Contribution à l'étude des rapports entre gouvernants et gouvernés dans les Pays-Bas à l'aube des temps modernes*, Brussels

Cazelles, R. (1958), *La société politique et la crise de la royauté sous Philippe de Valois*, Paris

Cazelles, R. (1982), *Société politique, noblesse et couronne sous Jean le Bon et Charles V*, Geneva and Paris

Cheney, C.R. (1972), *Notaries Public in England in the Thirteenth and Fourteenth Centuries*, Oxford

Chevalier, B. (1982), *Les bonnes villes de France du XIVe au XVIe siècle*, Paris

Chevalier, B. and Contamine, Ph. (eds.) (1985), *La France de la fin du XVe siècle. Renouveau et apogée. Economie, pouvoirs, arts, culture et conscience nationales*, Paris

Chittolini, G. (ed.) (1979a), *La crisi degli ordinamenti comunali e le origini dello stato del Rinascimento*, Bologna

Chittolini, G. (1979b), *La formazione dello stato regionale e le istituzioni del contado, secoli XIV–XV*, Turin

Chrimes, S.B. (1952), *An Introduction to the Administrative History of Mediaeval England*, Oxford: Blackwell; 3rd edn 1966

Clarke, M.V. (1936), *Medieval Representation and Consent. A Study of Early Parliaments in England and Ireland, with Special Reference to the 'Modus Tenendi Parliamentum'*, London and New York; 2nd edn 1964

Cockshaw, P. (1982), *Le personnel de la chancellerie de Bourgogne-Flandre sous les ducs de Bourgogne de la maison de Valois (1384–1477)*, Courtrai and Heule

Coelho, M.H. da Cruz and Homen, A.L. de Carvalho (eds.) (1995), *Portugal em definicão de fronteiras (1096–1325). Do condado portucalense à crise do século XIV*, in J. Serrão and A.H. de Oliviera Marques (eds.), *Nova História de Portugal*, vol. III, Lisbon

Colliva, P. (1977), *Il Cardinale Albornoz, lo stato della Chiesa, le 'Constitutiones Aegidianae' (1353–1357)*, Bologna

Contamine, Ph. (1972), *Guerre, état et société à la fin du moyen âge. Etudes sur les armées des rois de France (1337–1494)*, Paris

Contamine, Ph. (ed.) (1976), *La noblesse au moyen âge XIe–XVe siècles*, Paris

Contamine, Ph. (1980), *La guerre au moyen âge*, Paris; English trans. Michael Jones, *War in the Middle Ages*, Oxford: (1984); 2nd edn 1986; 3rd edn 1995

Contamine, Ph. (1989), *L'état et les aristocraties (France, Angleterre, Ecosse), XIIe–XVIIe siècle*, Paris.

Contamine, Ph. (1992), *Des pouvoirs en France. 1300–1500*, Paris

Las cortes de Castilla y Leon en la edad media (1988), Valladolid

Costa, P. (1969), *Jurisdictio. Semantica del potere politico nella pubblicistica medievale (1100–1433)*, Milan

Cuttino, G.P. (1940, 2nd ed. 1971), *English Diplomatic Administration, 1259–1339*, Oxford

Damiata, M. (1983), *'Plenitudo Potestatis' e 'Universitas Civium' in Marsilio da Padova*, Florence

David, M. (1950), 'Le serment du sacre du IXe au XVe siècle. Contribution à l'étude des limites juridiques de la souveraineté', *RMAL* 6: 5–272

David, M. (1954), *La souveraineté et les limites juridiques du pouvoir monarchique du IXe au XVe siècle*, Paris

Davies, R.G. and Denton, J.H. (eds.) (1981), *The English Parliament in the Middle Ages*, Manchester

Davies, R.R. (1978), *Lordship and Society in the March of Wales, 1282–1400*, Oxford

De Vergottini, G. (1959–60), *Lezioni di storia del diritto italiano. Il diritto publico italiano nei secoli XII–XV*, 2 vols., Milan

Dean, T. (1988), *Land and Power in Late Medieval Ferrara. The Rule of the Este, 1350–1450*, Cambridge

Demandt, K.E. (1981), *Der Personenstaat des Landgrafschaft Hessen im Mittelalter. Ein 'Staatshandbuch' Hessens vom Ende des 12. bis zum Anfang des 16. Jahrhunderts*, Marburg

Dempf, A. (1929; 3rd edn, 1962), *Sacrum Imperium. Geschichts und Staatsphilisophie des Mittelalters und der politischen Renaissance*, Munich

Denton, J.H. and Dooley, J.P. (1987), *Representatives of the Lower Clergy in Parliament, 1295–1340*, London

Dollinger, Ph. (1964), *La Hanse (XIIe–XVIIe siècles)*, Paris; English trans. D.S. Ault and S.H. Steinberg, *The German Hansa*, London (1970)

Dufourcq, Ch.-E. and Gautier Dalché, J. (1973), 'Economies, sociétés et institutions de l'Espagne chrétienne du moyen âge. Essai de bilan de la recherche d'après les travaux des quelques vingt dernières années. III. A travers les états de la couronne d'Aragon des origines au XVe siècle', *MA* 80: 285–319

Dupre Theseider, E. (1952), *Roma dal comune di popolo alla signoria pontificia (1252–1377)*, Bologna

Edwards, J.G. (1960), *Historians and the Medieval English Parliament*, Glasgow

Elias de Tejada, F. (1963–5), *Historia del pensiamento politico catalan*, 3 vols., Seville

The English Government at Work, 1327–1336 (1940–7), ed. J.F. Willard *et al.* 3 vols., Cambridge, Mass.

Erler, A. (1970), *Aegidius Albornoz als Gesetzgeber des Kirchenstaates*, Berlin

Favier, J. (1963), *Un conseiller de Philippe le Bel: Enguerran de Marigny*, Paris

Favier, J. (1966), *Les finances pontificales à l'époque du grand schisme d'occident, 1378–1409*, Paris

Favier, J. (1970), *Finance et fiscalité au bas moyen âge*, Paris

Favier, J. (1978), *Philippe le Bel*, Paris

Favier, J. (1980), *La guerre de cent ans*, Paris

Favier, J. (1984), *Le temps des principautés (1000–1515)*, in J. Favier (ed.), *Histoire de France*, II, Paris

Fedou, R. (1964), *Les hommes de loi lyonnais à la fin du moyen âge. Etude sur les origines de la classe de robe*, Paris

Ferguson, W.K. (1962), *Europe in Transition, 1300–1520*, Boston

Finances et comptabilité urbaines du XIIIe au XVIe siècle. Colloque international de Blankenberge, 1962, (1964), Brussels

Fisher, J.H., Richardson, M. and Fisher, J.L. (1984), *An Anthology of Chancery English*, Knoxville

Folz, R. (1953), *L'idée d'empire en Occident du Ve au XIVe siècle*, Paris

Folz, R. (1984), *Les saints rois du moyen âge en Occident, (VIe–XIIIe siècle)*, Brussels

Font Rius, J.M. (1949), *Institutiones Medievales Espanolas. La organizacion politica, economica y social de los reinos cristianos de la Reconquista*, Madrid

Font Rius, J.M. (1955), *Las instituciones de la coroña de Aragón en la primera mitad del siglo XV*, Palma da Mallorca

Fourquin, G. (1972), *Les soulèvements populaires au moyen âge*, Paris; English trans., A.L. Lytton-Sells, *The Anatomy of Popular Rebellion in the Middle Ages*, Amsterdam (1978)

Franca, E. d'Oliveira (1946), *O poder real em Portugal e as origens do absolutismo*, Sao Paulo

La 'France anglaise' au moyen âge (1988), *ACNSS*, CXIe session, Poitiers, 1986, section d'histoire médiévale et de philologie, 1, Paris

Fryde, E.B. and Miller, E. (eds.) (1970), *Historical Studies of the English Parliament*, 2 vols., Cambridge

Fryde, N. (1979), *The Tyranny and Fall of Edward II, 1321–1326*, Cambridge

Fügedi, E. (1986a), *Castle and Society in Medieval Hungary (1000–1437)*, Budapest

Fügedi, E. (1986b), *Kings, Bishops, Nobles and Burghers in Medieval Hungary*, ed. J.M. Bak, London

Gama Barros, H. de (1945–55), *Historia de administraçao publica em Portugal nos seculos XII a XV*, ed. T. de Souza Soares, 11 vols., Lisbon

Gandilhon, R. (1941), *Politique économique de Louis XI*, Rennes

Garcia Marin, J.M. (1974), *El oficio publico en Castilla durante la baja edad media*, Seville

Gaussin, P.R. (1976), *Louis XI, roi méconnu*, Paris

Gauvard, Cl. (1996), *La France au moyen âge du Ve au XVe siècle*, Paris

Genet, J.-Ph. (1990), *L'Etat moderne: Genèse. Bilans et perspectives, Actes du colloque tenu au CNRS à Paris les 19–20 septembre 1989*, Paris

Genet, J.-Ph. and Lottes, G. (1996), *L'Etat moderne et les élites, XIIIe–XVIIIe siècles. Apports et limites de la méthode prosopographique*, Paris

Giesey, R.E. (1960), *The Royal Funeral Ceremony in Renaissance France*, Geneva

Giesey, R.E. (1987), *Cérémonial et puissance souveraine. France, XVe–XVIIe siècle*, Paris

Gilmore, M. P. (1941), *Argument from Roman Law in Political Thought, 1200–1600*, Cambridge, Mass.

Gimeno Casalduero, J. (1972), *La imagen del monarca en la Castilla del siglo XIV. Pedro el Cruel, Enrique II y Juan I*, Madrid

Given-Wilson, C. (1987), *The English Nobility in the Late Middle Ages. The Fourteenth-Century Political Community*, London

Gorski, K. (1976), *Communitas, Princeps, Corona Regni. Studia selecta*, Warsaw, Poznań and Toruń

Gouron, A. and Rigaudière, A. (eds.) (1988), *Renaissance du pouvoir législatif et genèse de l'état*, Montpellier

Grant, A. (1984), *Independence and Nationhood. Scotland, 1306–1469*, London

Griffiths, R.A. (ed.) (1981), *Patronage, the Crown and the Provinces*, Gloucester

Griffiths, R.A. and Thomas, R.S. (1972), *The Principality of Wales in the Later Middle Ages. The Structure and Personnel of Government*, 1: *South Wales, 1277–1536*, Cardiff

Grohmann, A. (1981), *Città e territorio tra medioevo ed età moderna (Perugia, sec. XIII–XV)*, 2 vols., Perugia

Guenée, B. (1963), *Tribunaux et gens de justice dans le bailliage de Senlis à la fin du moyen âge (vers 1380–vers 1550)*, Paris

Guenée, B. (1980), *Histoire et culture historique dans l'Occident médiéval*, Paris

Guenée, B. (1981), *Politique et histoire au moyen âge. Recueil d'articles sur l'histoire politique et l'historiographie médiévales (1956–1981)*, Paris

Guenée, B. (1993), *L'occident aux XIVe et XVe siècles. Les états*, 5th edn, Paris; English trans. Juliet Vale, *States and Rulers in later Medieval Europe*, Oxford (1992)

Guenée, B. and Lehoux, F. (1968), *Les entrées royales françaises de 1328 à 1510,* Paris

Guillemain, B. (1962), *La cour pontificale d'Avignon, 1309–1376. Etude d'une société,* Paris; repr. 1966

Guillot, O., Rigaudière, A. and Sassier, Y. (1994), *Pouvoirs et institutions dans la France médiévale,* II: *Des temps féodaux aux temps de l'état,* Paris

Hale, J.R., Highfield, J.R.L. and Smalley, B. (eds.), *Europe in the Late Middle Ages,* London

Hanley, S. (1983), *The 'Lit de Justice' of the Kings of France. Constitutional Ideology in Legend, Ritual and Discourse,* Princeton, N.J.; French trans. *Le 'lit de justice' des rois de France. L'idéologie constitutionnelle dans la légende, le rituel et le discours,* Paris (1991)

Hassinger, E. (1959), *Das Werden des neuzeitlichen Europa, 1300–1600,* Brunswick

Heers, J. (1981), *Les partis et la vie politique dans l'occident médiéval,* Paris; English trans. David Nicholas, *Parties and Political Life in Medieval West,* Amsterdam (1977)

Hellmann, M. (ed.) (1961), *Corona regni. Studien über die Krone als Symbol des Staates im späteren Mittelalter,* Weimar

Hergemöller, B.U. (1983), *Fürsten, Herren und Städte zu Nürnberg, 1355–1356. Die Entstehung der Goldenen Bulle Karls IV.,* Cologne and Vienna

Hill, M.C. (1961), *The King's Messengers, 1199–1377. A Contribution to the History of the Royal Household,* London

Hlaváček, I. (1970), *Das Urkunden- und Kanzleiwesen des böhmischen und römischen Königs Wenzel (IV), 1376–1419. Ein Beitrag zur spätmittelalterlichen Diplomatik,* Stuttgart

Hödl, G. (1988), *Habsburg und Oesterreich, 1273–1493. Gestalten und Gestalt des österreichischen Spätmittelalters,* Vienna, Cologne and Graz

Hoffmann, E. (1976), *Königserhebung und Thronfolgeordnung in Dänemark bis zum Ausgang des Mittelalters,* Berlin

Homem, A.L. de Carvalho (1990a), *Portugal nos finais da idade média: estado instituições, sociedade política,* Lisbon

Homen, A.L. de Carvalho (1990b), *O desembargo régio (1320–1433),* Oporto

Hunnisett, R.F. (1961), *The Medieval Coroner,* Cambridge

Jewell, H.M. (1972), *English Local Administration in the Middle Ages,* Newton Abbot

Jones, M. (1970), *Ducal Brittany (1364–1399),* Oxford

Jones, M. (1988), *The Creation of Brittany. A Late Medieval State,* London

Jones, R.H. (1968), *The Royal Policy of Richard II. Absolutism in Later Middle Ages,* Oxford

Kaeuper, R.W. (1988), *War, Justice and Public Order. England and France in the Later Middle Ages,* Oxford

Kaminsky, H. (1967), *A History of the Hussite Revolution,* Berkeley, Ca.

Kantorowicz, E.H. (1957), *The King's Two Bodies. A Study in Medieval Political Theology,* Princeton, N.J.; French trans. *Les deux corps du roi,* Paris (1989); 2nd edn 1966

Kantorowicz, E.H. (1965), *Selected Studies,* New York

Kantorowicz, E.H. (1984), *Mourir pour la patrie et autres textes,* Paris

Kerhervé, J. (1987), *L'état breton aux XIVᵉ et XVᵉ siècles. Les ducs, l'argent et les hommes,* 2 vols., Paris

Kirby, J.L. (1970), *Henry IV of England,* London

Krieger, K. Fr. (1979), *Die Lehnshoheit der deutschen Könige im Spätmittelalter (ca. 1200–1437),* Aalen

Krynen, J. (1982), *Idéal du prince et pouvoir royal en France à la fin du moyen âge (1380–1440). Etude sur la littérature politique du temps,* Paris

Krynen, J. (1993), *L'empire du roi. Idées et croyances politiques en France, XIIIe–XVe siècle,* Paris

Krynen, J. and Rigaudière, A. (eds.), *Droits savants et pratiques françaises du pouvoir (XIe–XVe s.),* Bordeaux

Kubler, J. (1958), *Recherches sur la fonction publique sous l'ancien régime. L'origine de la perpétuité des offices royaux,* Nancy

Lagarde, G. de (1935–46, 1956–70), *La naissance de l'esprit laïque au déclin du moyen âge,* 5 vols., Louvain and Paris

Lalinde Abadia, J. (1967), *Las instituciones de la corona de Aragon en el siglo XIV,* Valencia

Lapsley, G.T. (1951), *Crown, Community and Parliament in the Later Middle Ages. Studies in English Constitutional History,* Oxford

Le Goff, J. (ed.) (1980), *Histoire de la France urbaine,* ed. Georges Duby, II: *La ville médiévale, des Carolingiens à la Renaissance* Paris

Le Goff, J. (ed.) (1989), *Histoire de la France. L'état et les pouvoirs,* Paris

Leist, W. (1975), *Landesherr und Landfrieden in Thüringen im Spätmittelalter, 1247–1349,* Cologne and Vienna

Leroy, B. (1983), *Seigneurs et bourgeois dans le gouvernement de Navarre sous les dynasties françaises (XIIIe–XIVe siècle),* Lille

Leroy, B. (1988), *L'Espagne au moyen âge,* Paris

Lewis, A.W. (1981), *Royal Succession in Capetian France. Studies on Familial Order and the State,* Cambridge, Mass.; French trans. *Le sang royal. La famille capétienne et l'état, France, Xe–XIVe siècle,* Paris (1986)

Lewis, P.S. (1968), *Later Medieval France. The polity,* London; French trans. *La France à la fin du moyen âge,* Paris (1977)

Lewis, P.S. (1985), *Essays in Later Medieval French History,* London

Lot, F. and Fawtier, R. (1957–62), *Histoire des institutions françaises au moyen âge,* 3 vols., Paris

Lydon, J.F. (1972), *The Lordship of Ireland in the Middle Ages,* Dublin

Lyon, B.D. (1957), *From Fief to Indenture. The Transition from Feudal to Non-Feudal Contract in Western Europe,* Cambridge, Mass.

Lyon, B.D. (1960), *A Constitutional and Legal History of Medieval England,* New York and London; 2nd edn 1980

McFarlane, K.B. (1973), *The Nobility of Later Medieval England. The Ford Lectures for 1953 and Related Studies,* Oxford

McGrade, A.S. (1974), *The Political Thought of William of Ockham. Personal and Institutional Principles,* Cambridge

MacIlwain, C.H. (1910), *The High Court of Parliament and its Supremacy. An Historical Essay on the Boundaries between Legislation and Adjudication in England,* Hamden; repr. 1962

MacIlwain, C.H. (1932), *The Growth of Political Thought in the West from the Greeks to the End of the Middle Ages,* New York

McKisack, M. (1932), *The Parliamentary Representation of the English Boroughs during the Middle Ages,* Oxford; repr. 1963

Maddicott, J.R.L. (1970), *Thomas of Lancaster, 1307–1322. A Study on the Reign of Edward II,* Oxford

Maddicott, J.R.L. (1978), *Law and Lordship. Royal Justices as Retainers in Thirteenth and Fourteenth Century England,* Oxford (*P&P,* Supplement 4)

Maiani, U. (1957), *Chiesa e stato nei teologi agostiniani del secolo XIV,* Rome

Maravall, J.A. (1954), *El concepto de España en el edad media,* Madrid

Marongiu, A. (1949), *Il parlamento in Italia nel medio evo e nell'età moderna,* Rome; 2nd edn, 1962

Marongiu, A. (1956), *Storia del diritto pubblico. Principi e instituti di governo in Italia dalla metà del IX alla metà del XIX secolo,* Milan

Marongiu, A. (1968), *Medieval Parliaments. A Comparative Study,* London

Menendez Pidal, R. *et al.* (1956, 1964, 1969), *Historia de España,* XIV, XV and XVII, Madrid

Menjot, D. (ed.) (1987), *Pouvoirs et sociétés politiques dans les royaumes ibériques. 1300–1450,* Nice

Menjot, D. (1996), *Les Espagnes médiévales 409–1474,* Paris

Meyer, B. (1972), *Die Bildung der Eidgenossenschaft im 14. Jahrhundert. Vom Zugerbund zum Pfaffenbrief,* Zurich

Mitre Fernandez, E. (1968), *Evolucion de la nobleza en Castilla bajo Enrique III (1396–1406),* Valladolid

Mitteis, H. (1938), *Die deutsche Königwahl und ihre Rechtsgrundlagen bis zur Goldenen Bulle,* Vienna; 2nd edn, 1944

Mochi Onory, S. (1951), *Fonti canonistiche dell'idea moderna dello stato (imperium spirituale, jurisdictio divisa, sovranità),* Milan

Moeglin, J.M. (1985), *Les ancêtres du prince. Propagande politique et naissance d'une histoire nationale en Bavière au moyen âge (1180–1500),* Geneva

Mohrmann, W.D. (1972), *Der Landfriede im Ostseeraum während des späten Mittelalters,* Kallmünz

Mollat, M. (1970), *Genèse médiévale de la France moderne XIVe–XVe siècles,* Paris; repr. 1977

Mollat, M. and Wolff, Ph. (1970), *Ongles bleus, Jacques et Ciompi. Les révolutions populaires en Europe aux XIVe et XVe siècles,* Paris; English trans. A. L. Lytton-Sells, *The Popular Revolutions of the Late Middle Ages,* London (1973)

Monahan, A.P. (1987), *Consent, Coercion and Limit. The Medieval Origins of Parliamentary Democracy,* Kingston and Montreal

Monier, R. (1943), *Les institutions centrales du comté de Flandre de la fin du IXe siècle à 1384,* Paris

Najemy, J.M. (1982), *Corporatism and Consensus in Florentine Electoral Politics, 1280–1400,* Chapel Hill

Nicholson, R. (1974), *Scotland. The Later Middle Ages,* Edinburgh

Nieto Soria, J.M. (1988), *Fundamentos ideologicos del poder real en Castilla (siglos XIII–XVI),* Madrid

O'Callaghan, J. F. (1989), *The cortes of Castile-León, 1188–1350,* Philadelphia

Palacios Martin, B. (1975), *La coronacion de los reyes de Aragon, 1204–1410. Aportación al studio de las estructuras politicas medievales,* Valencia

Paravicini, W. and Werner, K.F. (eds.) (1980), *Histoire comparée de l'administration (IVe–XVIIIe siècles). Actes du XIVe Colloque historique franco-allemand, Tours, 27 mars–1ᵉ avril 1977,* Beihefte der Francia, 9, Munich

Patze, H. (ed.) (1970–1), *Der deutsche Territorialstaat im 14. Jahrhundert,* 2 vols., Sigmaringen

Pegues, F.J. (1962), *The Lawyers of the Last Capetians,* Princeton, N.J.

Perez Bustamante, R. (1976), *El gobierno y la administracion territorial de Castilla (1230–1474),* 2 vols., Madrid

Perroy, E. (1945), *La guerre de cent ans,* Paris; English trans. W. B. Wells, *The Hundred Years War,* London (1951)

Peyer, H.C. (1955), *Stadt und Stadtpatron im mittelalterlichen Italien,* Zurich

Pollard, A.F. (1920), *The Evolution of Parliament,* London; 2nd edn, 1926

Polonio, V. (1977), *L'administrazione delle 'res publica' genovese fra tre e quattrocento. L'archivio 'antico comune',* Genoa

Post, G. (1964), *Studies in Medieval Legal Thought. Public Law and the State, 1100–1322,* Princeton, N.J.

Prestwich, M. (1972), *War, Politics and Finance under Edward I,* London

Les principautés au moyen âge (1979), Actes des Congrès de la Société des historiens médiévistes de l'enseignement supérieur public. Congrès de Bordeaux, 1973, Bordeaux

Quillet, J. (1970), *La philosophie politique de Marsile de Padoue,* Paris

Quillet, J. (1977), *La philosophie politique du 'Songe du Vergier' (1378). Sources doctrinales,* Paris

Rapp, F. (1989), *Les origines médiévales de l'Allemagne moderne. De Charles IV à Charles Quint (1346–1519),* Paris

Recherches sur les états généraux et les états provinciaux de la France médiévale (1986), *ACNSS,* CXe session, Montpellier, 1985. Histoire médiévale et philologie, III, Paris

Révolte et société (1988–9), *Actes du IVᵉ Colloque d'histoire au présent, Paris, mai 1988,* 2 vols., Paris

Richardson, H.G. and Sayles, G.O. (1952), *The Irish Parliament in the Middle Ages,* Philadelphia

Richardson, H.G. and Sayles, G.O. (1963), *The Administration of Ireland, 1172–1377,* Dublin

Richardson, H.G. and Sayles, G.O. (1981), *The English Parliament in the Middle Ages,* London

Riess, L. (1885), *Geschichte des Wahlrechts zum englischen Parlament im Mittelalter,* Leipzig; English trans. with notes by K.L. Wood-Legh, *The History of the English Electoral Law in the Middle Ages,* Cambridge (1940)

Rigaudière, A. (1993), *Gouverner la ville au moyen âge,* Paris

Riis, T. (1977), *Les institutions politiques centrales du Danemark, 1100–1332,* Odense

Roskell, J.S. (1965), *The Commons and their Speakers in English Parliaments, 1376–1523,* Manchester

Roskell, J.S. (1982), *Parliament and Politics in Late Medieval England,* 3 vols., London

Rotelli, E. and Schiera, P. (eds.) (1971), *Lo stato moderno,* I: *Dal medioevo all'età moderna,* Bologna

Royer, J.P. (1969), *L'église et le royaume de France au XIVe siècle, d'après le 'Songe du vergier' et la jurisprudence du Parlement,* Paris

Rucquoi, A. (1987a), *Valladolid en la edad media,* I: *Genesis de un poder,* II, *El mundo abreviado (1367–1474),* Valladolid

Rucquoi, A. (ed.) (1987b), *Genèse médiévale de l'état moderne. La Castille et la Navarre (1250–1370),* Valladolid

Rucquoi, A. (ed.) (1988), *Realidad e imágenes del poder. España a fines de la edad media,* Valladolid

Sayles, G.O. (1975), *The King's Parliament of England,* London

Sayles, G.O. (1988), *The Functions of the Medieval Parliament of England,* London

Schramm, P.E. (1937), *Geschichte des englischen Königtums im Lichte der Krönung,* Weimar; English trans. L.G. Wickham Legg, *A History of the English Coronation,* Oxford (1937)

Schramm, P.E. (1939), *Der König von Frankreich. Das Wesen der Monarchie vom 9. bis 16. Jahrhundert. Ein Kapitel aus der Geschichte des abendländischen Staates,* Darmstadt; 2nd edn, 2 vols., 1960

Schramm, P.E. (1954–6), *Herrschaftszeichen und Staatssymbolik,* 3 vols., Stuttgart

Schubert, E. (1979), *König und Reich. Studien zur spätmittelalterlichen deutschen Verfassungsgeschichte,* Göttingen

Schwarz, B. (1972), *Die Organisation kurialer Schreiberkollegien von ihrer Entstehung bis zur Mitte des 15. Jahrhunderts,* Tübingen

Segall, H. (1959), *Der 'Defensor Pacis' des Marsilius von Padua. Grundfragen der Interpretation,* Wiesbaden

Seibt, F. (1978), *Karl IV. Ein Kaiser in Europa, 1346–1378,* Munich

Shneidman, J.L. (1970), *The Rise of the Aragonese-Catalan Empire, 1200–1350,* 2 vols., New York

Spangenberg, H. (1912), *Vom Lehnstaat zum Ständestaat. Ein Beitrag zur Entstehung der landständischen Verfassung,* 1912, Aalen; new edn 1964

Strayer, J.R. (1970a), *Les gens de justice du Languedoc sous Philippe le Bel,* Toulouse

Strayer, J.R. (1970b), *On the Medieval Origins of the Modern State,* Princeton,N.J.; French trans., *Les origines médiévales de l'état moderne,* Paris (1979)

Tessier, G. (1962), *Diplomatique royale française,* Paris

Thomas, H. (1983), *Deutsche Geschichte des Spätmittelalters, 1250–1500,* Stuttgart, Berlin, Cologne and Mainz

Tierney, B. (1982), *Religion, Law and the Growth of Constitutional Thought 1150–1650,* Cambridge

Tierney, B. and Linehan, P. (eds.) (1980), *Authority and Power, Studies on Medieval Law and Government Presented to Walter Ullmann on his Seventieth Birthday,* Cambridge

Touchard, J. *et al.* (1959), *Histoire des idées politiques,* 1: *Des origines au XVIIIe siècle,* Paris

Tuck, A. (1986), *Crown and Nobility, 1272–1461. Political Conflict in Late Medieval England,* London

Ullmann, W. (1969), *Principles of Government and Politics in the Middle Ages,* 2nd edn, London

Ullmann, W. (1975), *Law and Politics in the Middle Ages. An Introduction to the Sources of Medieval Political Ideas,* London

Uytterbrouck, A. (1975), *Le gouvernement du duché de Brabant au bas moyen âge (1355–1430),* 2 vols., Brussels

Vale, Juliet (1982), *Edward III and Chivalry. Chivalric Society and its Context, 1270–1350,* Woodbridge

Vale, M. (1981), *War and Chivalry. Warfare and Aristocratic Culture in England, France and Burgundy at the End of the Middle Ages,* London

Valeri, N. (1949), *L'Italia nell'età dei principati dal 1343 al 1516,* Milan

Vaughan, R. (1962), *Philip the Bold. The Formation of the Burgundian State,* London; 2nd edn 1979

Vaughan, R. (1966), *John the Fearless. The Growth of Burgundian Power,* London; 2nd edn 1979

Vaughan, R. (1970), *Philip the Good. The Apogee of Burgundy*, London
Verger, J. (1973), *Les universités au moyen âge*, Paris
Violence et contestation au moyen âge (1990), *ACNSS*, CXIVe session, Paris, 1989, Section d'histoire médiévale et de philologie, Paris
Waley, D. (1988), *The Italian City Republics*, 3rd edn, London and New York
Walter, H. (1976), *Imperiales Königtum, Konziliarismus und Volkssouveränität. Studien zu den Grenzen des mittelalterlichen Souveränitätsgedankens*, Munich
Wellens, R. (1974), *Les états généraux des Pays-Bas des orgines à la fin du règne de Philippe le Beau (1464–1506)*, I, Heule
Wernli, Fr. (1972), *Die Entstehung der schweizerischen Eidgenosssenschaft. Verfassungsgeschichte und politische Geschichte in Wechselwirkung*, Uznach
Wilkinson, B. (1972), *The Creation of the Medieval Parliament*, New York
Wojciechowski, Z. (1949), *L'état polonais au moyen âge. Histoire des institutions*, Paris
Wright, J.R. (1980), *The Church and the English Crown, 1305–1334. A Study Based on the Register of Archbishop Walter Reynolds*, Leiden
Yardeni, M. (ed.) (1987), *Idéologie et propagande en France*, Paris
Zabalo Zabalegui, J. (1973), *La administracion del reino de Navarra en el siglo XIV*, Pamplona

3 CURRENTS OF RELIGIOUS THOUGHT AND EXPRESSION

Primary sources

Theology

Aureoli, Peter, *Scriptum super Primum Sententiarum*, ed. E.M. Buytaert, 2 vols., St Bonaventure, N.Y. (1953–6)
Bradwardine, Thomas, *De Causa Dei contra Pelagianos*, ed. H. Savile, Oxford (1618)
Campsall, Richard of, *Works*, ed. E.A. Synan, 2 vols., Toronto (1968–82)
Duns Scotus, John, *Opera Omnia*, ed. C. Balić *et al.*, Rome (1950)
Duns Scotus, John, *Scotus on the Will and Morality*, ed. A.B. Wolter, Washington, DC (1986)
Fitzralph, Richard, *De Pauperie Salvatoris*, ed. R.L. Poole in John Wyclif, *De Dominio*, Wyclif Society, London (1890)
Fitzralph, Richard, *De Questionibus Armenorum*, ed. J. Sudoris, Paris (1511)
Gerson, Jean, *Œuvres Complètes*, ed. P. Glorieux, 10 vols., Paris (1960–73)
Ghent, Henry of, *Opera Omnia*, ed. R. Macken *et al.*, 9 vols., Louvain (1979–)
Hus, Jan, *Opera Omnia*, ed. Czech Academy of Sciences, 8 vols., Prague (1959–)
Lull, Ramon, *Opera Latina*, ed. F. Stegmüller, 5 vols., Palma (1959–)
Malabranca de Orvieto, Hugolino, *Commentarius in Quattuor Libros Sententiarum*, 1, ed. W. Eckermann, Würzburg (1980)
Meyronnes, François de, *Commentarius in Libros Sententiarum*, Lyon (1579)
Mirecourt, John of, *Apologia Prima et Secunda*, ed. F. Stegmüller, *Recherches de théologie ancienne et médiévale*, 5 (1933), pp. 40–78, 192–204
Ockham, William of, *Opera Philosophica et Theologica*, ed. PP. Instituti Franciscani, 17 vols., St Bonaventure, N.Y. (1967–)
Ockham, William of, *Opera Politica*, ed. J.G. Sikes and H.S. Offler, 4 vols., Manchester and London (1940–)

Paris, John of (Quidort), *Commentary on the Sentences*, ed. J.-P. Mueller, 2 vols., Rome (1961–4)

Rimini, Gregory of, *Lectura super Primum et Secundum Sententiarum*, ed. D. Trapp and V. Marcolino, 6 vols., Berlin (1978–84)

Romanus, Aegidius (Giles of Rome), *Opera Omnia*, ed. F. del Punta and G. Fiorovati, 2 vols., Florence (1985–)

Woodham, Adam, *Super Quatuor Libros Sententiarum*, abbreviation of Henry Totting of Oyta, Paris (1512)

Wyclif, John, *De Universalibus*, ed. J. Mueller, Oxford (1985); trans. Anthony Kenny, *On Universals*, Oxford (1985)

Wyclif, John, *Works*, ed. J. Loserth, R. Buddensieg, *et al.*, Wyclif Society, 38 vols., London (1882–1914)

Canon law, exegesis and pastoral care

Andreae, Johannes, *Commentaria in Sextum*, Lyon (1550)

Andreae, Johannes, *Novella in Sextum*, Venice (1504; repr. 1963–6)

Butrio, Antonius de, *Consilia*, Frankfurt (1587)

Clamanges, Nicholas de, *Opera Omnia*, Leiden (1612; repr. 1967)

Corpus Iuris Canonici, ed. E. Friedburg, 2 vols., Leipzig (1879–81)

Ferrer, Vincent, *Textes choisis et présentés*, ed. B.H. Vanderberghe, Namur (1956)

Lyre, Nicholas of, *Postilla super Bibliam*, ed. in *Biblia Sacra cum Glossa Ordinaria et Postilla Nicholai Lyrani*, Douai and Antwerp (1617)

Niem, Dietrich of, *De Modis Uniendi et Reformandi Ecclesiae*, ed. H. Heimpel, Leipzig (1933)

Ubaldis, Baldus de, *Commentaria in Corpus Iuris Canonici*, Venice (1606)

Spirituality

Birgitta of Sweden, *Revelationes*, ed. E. and M. Wessen, 3 vols., Copenhagen (1949–56)

Catherine of Siena, *Dialogue*, trans. S. Noffke, London (1980)

Catherine of Siena, *Letters*, trans. S. Noffke, Binghamton, N.Y. (1988–)

The Cloud of Unknowing, ed. P. Hodgson, EETS, o.s. 218, London (1944)

Deonise Hid Divinite and Other Treatises, ed. P. Hodgson, EETS, o.s. 231, London (1955)

Eckhart, Meister, *Opera Latina*, ed. G. Théry and R. Klibansky, Rome (1934–)

Eckhart, Meister, *Werke* (Latin and German), ed. J. Quint, J. Koch, *et al.*, 5 vols., Stuttgart and Berlin (1936–)

Hilton, Walter, *Angels' Song*, ed. T. Takamiya, Studies in English Literature, Tokyo (1977)

Hilton, Walter, *Latin Works*, ed. J.P.H. Clark and C. Taylor, Analecta Cartusiana, CXXIV, 2 vols., London (1987)

Hilton, Walter, *Mixed Life*, ed. S.J. Ogilvie-Thomson, Salzburg Studies in English Literature, Salzburg (1986)

Hilton, Walter, *The Scale of Perfection,* ed. J.P.H. Clark and R. Derward, Salzburg (1991)

Kempe, Margery, *The Book of Margery Kempe*, ed. S.B. Meech and H.E. Allen, EETS, o.s. 212, London (1940)

Norwich, Julian of, *A Book of Showings to the Anchoress Julian of Norwich*, ed. E. Colledge and J. Walsh, 2 vols., Toronto (1978)

Porète, Marguerite, *Le miroir des simples âmes*, ed. R. Guarnieri, in *Il Movimento del Libero Spirito*, Archivio Italiano per la Storia della Pietà, Rome (1965)

Rolle, Richard, *English Writings*, ed. H.E. Allen, Oxford (1931)

Rolle, Richard, *Incendium Amoris*, ed. M. Deanesly, Manchester (1915); English trans. C. Wolters, *The Fire of Love*, Harmondsworth (1972)

Rolle, Richard, *Melos Amoris*, ed. E.J.F. Arnould, Oxford (1957)

Rolle, Richard *Prose and Verse*, ed. S.J. Ogilvie-Thomson, EETS, o.s. 293, London (1988)

Ruysbroeck, Jan, *Opera Omnia* (Latin with English translation), ed. G. de Baere, P. Crowley and H. Rolfson, 10 vols., Ruusbroecgenootschap, Tielt (1981–)

Suso, Henry, *Werke* (German), ed. K. Bihlmeyer, Stuttgart (1907)

Suso, Henry, *Horologium Sapientiae*, ed. P. Künzle, OP, Spicilegium Friburgense, XXIII, Freiburg (1977)

Tauler, Johann, *Die Predigten Taulers*, ed. F. Vetter, Deutsche Texte des Mittelalters, XI, Berlin (1910)

Secondary works

Theology, preaching and religious controversy

Avray, D. d' (1985), *The Preaching of the Friars*, Oxford

Balic, C. (1927), *Les commentaires de Jean Duns Scot sur les Quatre livres de sentences*, Louvain

Boehner, P. (1958), *Collected Articles on Ockham*, St Bonaventure, N.Y.

Boisset, L. (1973), *Un concile provincial au treizième siècle: Vienne 1289*, Paris

Catto, J.I. and Evans, T.A.R. (eds.) (1992), *History of the University of Oxford*, II: *Late Mediaeval Oxford*, Oxford

Combes, A. (1963–4), *La théologie mystique de Gerson*, 2 vols., Paris

Courtenay, W.J. (1974), 'Nominalism and Late Mediaeval Religion', in C. Trinkhaus and H.A. Oberman (eds.), *The Pursuit of Holiness*, Leiden, pp. 26–59

Courtenay, W.J. (1980), 'Augustinianism at Oxford in the Fourteenth Century', *Augustiniana* 30: 58–70

Courtenay, W.J. (1987a), 'Antiqui and Moderni in Late Mediaeval Thought', *JHI* 48: 1–8

Courtenay, W.J. (1987b), *Schools and Scholars in Fourteenth-Century England*, Princeton, N.J.

Delaruelle, E., Labande, E. R. and Ourliac, P. (1962–4), *L'église au temps du Grande Schisme et de la crise conciliaire*, 2 vols., Paris

Dobson, R.B. (1973), *Durham Priory, 1400–1450*, Cambridge

Dunbabin, J. (1991), *The Hound of God: Pierre de la Palud and the Fourteenth-Century Church*, Oxford

Ehrle, F. (1925), 'Der Sentenzenkommentar Peters von Candia', *Franziskanische Studien* 9

Kadlec, J. (1975), *Leben und Schriften des Prager Magisters Adalbert Ranconis de Ericinio*, Münster

Kaluza, Z. (1978), *Thomas de Cracovie*, Wrocław

Kaluza, Z. and Vignaux, P. (eds.) (1984), *Preuve et raisons à l'université de Paris*, Paris

Knowles, D. (1951), 'The Censured Opinions of Uthred of Boldon', *PBA* 37: 305–42

Lambert, M.D. (1961), *Franciscan Poverty. The Doctrine of the Absolute Poverty of Christ and the Apostles in the Franciscan Order 1210–1323*, London

Lambert, M.D. (1977), *Mediaeval Heresy,* London

Leff, G. (1957), *Bradwardine and the Pelagians,* Cambridge

Leff, G. (1961), *Gregory of Rimini. Tradition and Innovation in Fourteenth-Century Thought*, Manchester

Leff, G. (1967), *Heresy in the Later Middle Ages*, Manchester

Leff, G. (1975), *William of Ockham*, Manchester

Leff, G. (1976), *The Dissolution of the Medieval Outlook,* New York

Lerner, R.E. (1972), *The Heresy of the Free Spirit*, Portland, Oreg.

Michaud-Quantin, P. (1962), *Sommes de casuistique et manuels de confession au moyen âge,* Louvain

Mollat, M. (1965), *La vie et la pratique religieuse au XIVe et dans la première partie du XVe siècle*, Paris

Murdoch, J. and Sylla, E. (1975), *The Cultural Context of Mediaeval Learning*, Dordrecht

Pantin, W.A. (1955), *The English Church in the Fourteenth Century*, Cambridge

Rapp, F. (1971), *L'église et la vie religieuse en Occident au fin de la moyen âge*, Paris

Reeves, M. (1969), *The Influence of Prophecy in the Later Middle Ages*, Oxford

Robson, J.A. (1961), *Wyclif and the Oxford Schools*, Cambridge

Rubin, M. (1991), *Corpus Christi*, Cambridge

Scott, T.K. (1971), 'Nicholas of Autrecourt, Buridan, and Ockhamism', *JHP* 9: 15-41

Smalley, B. (1952), *The Study of the Bible in the Middle Ages*, Oxford

Smalley, B. (1960), *English Friars and Antiquity in the Early Fourteenth Century*, Oxford

Smalley, B. (1981), *Studies in Mediaeval Thought and Learning*, London

Southern, R.W. (1962), *Western Views of Islam in the Middle Ages*, Cambridge, Mass.

Swanson, R.N. (1979), *Universities, Academics and the Great Schism*, Cambridge

Trapp, D. (1956), 'Augustinian Theology of the Fourteenth Century', *Augustiniana* 6: 146–274

Walsh, K. (1981), *A Fourteenth-Century Scholar and Primate. Richard Fitzralph in Oxford, Avignon and Armagh*, Oxford

Zumkeller, A. (1941), *Dionysius de Montina*, Würzburg

Spirituality and the art of Contemplation

Allen, H.E. (1927), *Writings Ascribed to Richard Rolle*, New York

Ampe, A. (1950–7), *Kernproblemen uit de Leer van Ruusbroec*, 3 vols., Studien en Textuitgaven van Ons Geestelijk Erf, 11–13, Tielt

Axters, A. (1950–60), *Geschiedenis van de Vroomheid in de Nederlanden*, 4 vols., Antwerp

Baron, H. (1966), *The Crisis of the Early Italian Renaissance*, Princeton, N.J.

Brunn, E. zum and Libera, A. de (1984), *Maître Eckhart: metaphysique du verbe et théologie negative*, Paris

Clark, J.P.H. (1979), 'Action and Contemplation in Walter Hilton', *DR* 97: 258–74

Clark, J.P.H. (1980), 'Sources and Theology in the *Cloud of Unknowing*', *DR* 98: 83–109

Clark, J.P.H. (1986), 'Richard Rolle as a Biblical Commentator', *DR* 104: 165–213

Clark, J.P.H. (1991), 'Time and Eternity in Julian of Norwich', *DR* 109: 259–76

Colledge, E. (1962), *The Mediaeval Mystics of England*, London

Combes, A. (1945–59), *Essai sur la Critique de Ruysbroeck par Gerson*, I–III, Paris
Fawtier, R. and Canet, L. (1948), *Le double expérience de Catherine Benincasa*, Paris
Filthaut, E. (ed.) (1961), *Johannes Tauler, ein deutscher Mystiker*, Essen
Fogelqvist, I. (1993), *Apostasy and Reform in the Revelations of St Birgitta*, Bibliotheca Theologiae Practicae, LI, Uppsala
Glasscoe, M. (ed.) (1980–), *The Mediaeval Mystical Tradition in England,* Woodbridge
Grabmann, M. (1956), *Mittelalterliches Geistesleben*, I–III, Munich
Grundmann, H. (1961), *Religiöse Bewegungen im Mittelalter*, Hildesheim
Hogg, J. (ed.) (1981–2), *Kartäusermystik und -Mystiker*, I–V, Analecta Cartusiana, LXV, London
Hughes, J. (1988), *Pastors and Visionaries*, Woodbridge
Knowles, D. (1961), *The English Mystical Tradition*, London
Lossky, V. (1960), *Théologie negative et connaissance de Dieu chez Maître Eckhart*, Paris
Molinari, P., SJ (1959), *Julian of Norwich. The Teaching of a Fourteenth-Century English Mystic*, London
La mystique rhénane (1963), Paris
Nix, U. and Öchslin, R.L. *Meister Eckhart der Prediger. Festschrift zum Eckhart-Gedenkjahr*, Freiburg
Orcibal, J. (1966), *Saint Jean de la Croix et les mystiques rhéno-flamands*, Paris
Ozment, S.E. (1969), *Homo Spiritualis. A Comparative Study of the Anthropology of Johannes Tauler, Jean Gerson and Martin Luther in the Context of their Theological Thought*, Leiden
Palliser, M.A., OP (1992), *Christ our Mother of Mercy. Divine Mercy and Compassion in the Theology of the 'Showings' of Julian of Norwich*, Berlin and New York
Ruh, K. (ed.) (1964), *Altdeutsche und Altniederländische Mystik*, Darmstadt
Walsh, J., SJ (1965), *Pre-Reformation English Spirituality*, London
Warren, A.K. (1986), *Anchorites and their Patrons*, Berkeley
Watson, V. (1992), *Richard Rolle and the Invention of Authority*, Cambridge
Winkler, E. (1984), *Exegetische Methoden bei Meister Eckhart*, Tübingen

4 THE UNIVERSITIES

Primary sources

Auctarium Chartularii Universitatis Parisiensis, ed. H. Denifle and E. Châtelain, 2 vols., Paris (1894–7)
Beltran de Heredia, V., *Bulario de la universidad de Salamanca*, 3 vols., Salamanca (1966–7)
Beltran de Heredia, V., *Cartulario de la universidad de Salamanca*, 6 vols., Salamanca (1970–3)
Chartularium Studii Bononiensis. Documenti per dell'università di Bologna dalle origini fino al secolo XV, 15 vols., Bologna (1909–88)
Chartularium Universitatis Parisiensis, ed. H. Denifle and E. Châtelain, 4 vols., Paris (1889–97)
Chartularium Universitatis Portugalensis, ed. A. Moreira de Sà, 9 vols., and *Auctarium Universitatis Portulagensis*, ed. A. Moreira de Sà, 3 vols., Lisbon (1966–89)
Fournier, M., *Les statuts et privilèges des universités françaises depuis leur fondation jusqu'en 1789*, 4 vols., Paris (1890–4)

Gloria, A., *Monumenti della università di Padova*, 2 vols., Venice and Padua (1885–8)
Statuta Antiqua Universitatis Oxoniensis, ed. S. Gibson, Oxford (1931)

Secondary works

General works

Agrimi, J. and Crisciani, C. (1988), *Edocere medicos. Medicina scolastica nei secoli XIII–XV*, Naples

Brizzi, G.P. and Verger, J. (eds.) (1990), *Le università dell'Europa. La nascita dell'università*, Cinisello Balsamo

Bullough, V.L. (1966), *The Development of Medicine as a Profession. The Contribution of the Medieval University to Modern Medicine*, Basle and New York

Cobban, A.B. (1975), *The Medieval Universities. Their Development and Organization*, London

Denifle, H. (1885), *Die Entstehung der Universitäten des Mittelalters bis 1400*, Berlin

Fried, J. (ed.) (1986), *Schulen und Studium im sozialen Wandel des hohen und späten Mittelalters*, VF, 30, Sigmaringen

Gabriel, A.L. (1969), *Garlandia. Studies in the History of the Mediaeval Universities*, Notre Dame and Frankfurt am Main

History of Universities (one annual issue since 1981)

Ijsewijn, J. and Paquet, J. (eds.) (1978), *Universities in the Late Middle Ages*, Mediaevalia Lovaniensia, 1st series 6, Louvain; also published as J. Paquet and J. Ijsewijn (eds.) *Les Universités à la fin du moyen âge*, Publ. de l'Institut d'Etudes médiévales, 2nd series 2, Louvain (1978)

Kenny, A., Kretzmann, N. and Pinborg J. (eds.) (1982), *The Cambridge History of Later Medieval Philosophy*, Cambridge

Kibre, P. (1948), *The Nations in the Mediaeval Universities*, Cambridge, Mass.

Kibre, P. (1961), *Scholarly Privileges in the Middle Ages. The Rights, Privileges and Immunities of Scholars and Universities at Bologna – Padua – Paris – Oxford*, Cambridge, Mass.

Kittelson, J.M. and Transue, P.J. (eds.) (1984), *Rebirth, Reform and Resilience. Universities in Transition, 1300–1700*, Columbus, Ohio

Le Goff, J. (1985), *Les intellectuels au moyen âge*, 2nd edn, Paris

Leff, G. (1968), *Paris and Oxford Universities in the Thirteenth and Fourteenth Centuries. An Institutional and Intellectual History*, New York, London and Sydney

Piltz, A. (1981), *The World of Medieval Learning*, Oxford

Rashdall, H. (1936), *The Universities of Europe in the Middle Ages*, new edn by F.M. Powicke and A.B. Emden, 3 vols., Oxford

Ridder-Symoens, H. de (ed.) (1992), *A History of the University in Europe*, 1, *Universities in the Middle Ages*, Cambridge

Le scuole degli ordini mendicanti (secoli XIII–XIV) (1978), Convegni del Centro di Studi Sulla Spiritualità Medievale, XVII, Todi

Siraisi, N.G. (1990), *Medieval and Early Renaissance Medicine. An Introduction to Knowledge and Practice*, Chicago and London

Swanson, R.N. (1979), *Universities, Academics and the Great Schism*, Cambridge

Università e società nei secoli XII–XVI. Atti del nono convegno internazionale di studi tenuto a Pistoia nei giorni 20–25 settembre 1979 (1982), Pistoia

Les universités européennes du quatorzième au dix-huitième siècle. Aspects et problèmes. Actes du colloque international à l'occasion du VIe centenaire de l'université jagellone de Cracovie (1967), Geneva

Verger, J. (1973), *Les universités au moyen âge*, Paris

Zimmermann, A. (ed.) (1974), *Antiqui und Moderni. Traditionsbewusstsein und Fortschrittsbewusstsein im späten Mittelalter*, Miscellanea Mediaevalia, IX, Berlin and New York

Empire, northern and central Europe

Gabriel, A.L. (1969), *The Mediaeval Universities of Pécs and Pozsony*, Notre Dame and Frankfurt am Main

Meuthen, E. (1988), *Kölner Universitätsgeschichte*, I, *Die alte Universität*, Cologne and Vienna

Mornet, E. (1983), 'Le voyage d'études des jeunes nobles danois du XIVe siècle à la Réforme', *JS*: 287–318

Schwinges, R.C. (1986), *Deutsche Universitätsbesucher im 14. und 15. Jahrhundert. Studien zur Sozialgeschichte des alter Reiches*, Stuttgart

Die Universität zu Prag (1986), Schriften der Sudetendeutschen Akademie der Wissenschaften und Künste, 7, Munich

England

Aston, T.H. (1979), 'Oxford's Medieval Alumni', *P&P* 74: 3–40

Aston, T.H., Duncan, G.D., Evans, T.A.R. (1980), 'The Medieval Alumni of the University of Cambridge', *P&P* 86: 9–86

Cobban, A.B. (1988), *The Medieval English Universities. Oxford and Cambridge to 1500*, Berkeley and Los Angeles

Courtenay, W.J. (1987), *Schools and Scholars in Fourteenth-Century England*, Princeton, N.J.

Gabriel, A.L. (1974), *Summary Bibliography of the History of the Universities of Great Britain and Ireland up to 1800 Covering Publications between 1900 and 1968*, Texts and Studies in the History of Mediaeval Education, XIV, Notre Dame

A History of the University of Cambridge, I, Leader, D.R. (1988), *The University to 1546*, Cambridge

The History of the University of Oxford, I, Catto, J.I. (ed.) (1984), *The Early Oxford Schools*, Oxford, 1984; II, Catto, J.I. and Evans, G.R. (eds.) (1992), *Late Mediaeval Oxford*, Oxford

Orme, N. (1973), *English Schools in the Middle Ages*, London

Orme, N. (1976), *Education in the West of England*, Exeter

France

Bernstein, A.E. (1978), *Pierre d'Ailly and the Blanchard Affair. University and Chancellor of Paris at the Beginning of the Great Schism*, Leiden

Gabriel, A.L. (1992), *The Paris Studium. Robert of Sorbonne and his Legacy. Interuniversity Exchange between the German, Cracow, Louvain Universities and that of Paris in the Late Medieval and Humanistic Period. Selected Studies*, Texts and Studies in the History of Mediaeval Education, XIX, Notre Dame and Frankfurt am Main

Gouron, A. (1984), *La science du droit dans le Midi de la France au moyen âge*, London

Gouron, A. (1987), *Etude sur la diffusion des doctrines juridiques médiévales,* London

Guenée, S. (1978–81), *Bibliographie de l'histoire des universités françaises des origines à la Révolution,* 2 vols., Paris

Kaluza, Z. (1988), *Les querelles doctrinales à Paris. Nominalistes et réalistes aux confins du XIVe et du XVe siècle,* Bergamo

Meijers, E.M. (1938), *Responsa Doctorum Tholosanorum,* Haarlem

Tanaka, M. (1990), *La nation anglo-allemande de l'université de Paris à la fin du moyen âge,* Paris

Verger, J. (1970), 'Le recrutement géographique des universités françaises au début du XVe siècle d'après les suppliques de 1403', *MEFRA,* 82: 855–902

Verger, J. (ed.) (1986), *Histoire des universités en France,* Toulouse

Italy

Bellomo, M. (1979), *Saggio sull'università nell'età del diritto comune,* Catania

Capitani, O. (ed.) (1987), *L'università di Bologna. Personaggi, momenti e luoghi dalle origini al XVI secolo,* Bologna

Ermini, G. (1971), *Storia dell'università di Perugia,* 2 vols., Florence

Gargan, L. (1971), *Lo studio teologico e la biblioteca dei Domenicani a Padova nel tre e quattrocento,* Padua

Gargan L. and Limone O. (eds.) (1989), *Luoghi e metodi di insegnamento nell'Italia medioevale (secoli XII–XIV),* Galatina

Grendler, P.F. (1989), *Schooling in Renaissance Italy. Literacy and Learning, 1300–1600,* Baltimore and London

Pini, A.I. (1988), '*Discere turba volens.* Studenti e vita studentesca a Bologna dalle origini dello studio alla metà del trecento', in G.P. Brizzi and A.I. Pini (eds.), *Studenti e università degli studi a Bologna dal XII al XIX secolo, Studi e memorie per la storia dell'università di Bologna,* n.s., 7, Bologna, pp. 45-136

Quaderni per la storia dell'università di Padova (onc annual issue since 1968)

Siraisi, N.G. (1973), *Arts and Sciences at Padua. The Studium of Padua before 1350,* Pontifical Institute of Mediaeval Studies, Studies and Texts, 25, Toronto

Stelling-Michaud, S. (1955), *L'université de Bologne et la pénétration des droits romain et canonique en Suisse aux XIIIe et XIVe siècles,* Travaux d'Humanisme et Renaissance, 17, Geneva

Spain

Ajo Gonzalez de Rapariegos and Sainz de Zuñiga, C. M. (1957–77), *Historia de las universidades hispanicas. Origenes y desarrollo desde su aparicion a nuestros dias,* 11 vols., Madrid

Estudios sobre los origenes de las universidades españolas (1988), Valladolid

La universidad de Salamanca (1989–90), 3 vols., Salamanca

5 RURAL SOCIETY

Primary sources

The Anonimalle Chronicle, 1333–1381, ed. V.H. Galbraith, Manchester (1927)

The Black Death, ed. Rosemary Horrox, Manchester (1994)

Cartae Nativorum, ed. M.M. Postan and C.N.L. Brooke, Oxford (1960)

The Chronicle of Jean de Venette, ed. Richard A. Newhall, trans. Jean Birdsall, New York (1953)

La chronique de Jean le Bel, ed. Jules Viard and Eugène Déprez, 2 vols., Paris (1904–5)

La chronique des quatre premiers Valois, ed. Siméon Luce, Paris (1862)

'Documentos acerca de la peste negra en los dominios de la Corona de Aragón', ed. Amada López de Meneses, in *Estudios de edad media de la Corona de Aragón* 6 (1956), pp. 291–447

Essex and the Peasants' Revolt: A Selection of Evidence from Contemporary Chronicles, Court Rolls and Other Sources, ed. W.H. Liddell and R.G.E. Wood, Chelmsford (1981)

Froissart, Jean, *Œuvres*, ed. J.M.B.C. Kervyn de Lettenhove, 28 vols., Brussels (1867–77)

Knighton, Henry, *Chronicon Henrici Knighton*, ed. Joseph Rawson Lumby, RS 92, London (1895)

Knighton, Henry, *Chronicon Henrici Knighton*, ed. Geoffrey Martin, Oxford (1995)

The 'Liber Gersumarum' of Ramsey Abbey: A Calendar and Index, ed. Edwin B. DeWindt, Toronto (1976)

Libro Becerro de las Behetrías. Estudio y texto crítico, ed. Gonzalo Martínez Díez, 3 vols., León (1981)

The Peasants' Revolt of 1381, ed. R.B. Dobson, London (1970)

Quellen zur Geschichte des deutschen Bauernstandes im Mittelalter, ed. Günther Franz, Darmstadt (1974)

Walsingham, Thomas, *Chronicon Angliae*, ed. Edward Maunde Thompson, RS 64, London (1874)

Walsingham, Thomas, *Gesta Abbatum Monasterii Sancti Albani*, ed. Henry Thomas Riley, RS 28:3, London (1869)

Secondary works

Abel, Wilhelm (1976), *Die Wüstungen des ausgehenden Mittelalters* 3rd edn, Stuttgart

Abel, Wilhelm (1980), *Agricultural Fluctuations in Europe from the Thirteenth to the Twentieth Centuries*, trans. Olive Ordish, London

The Agrarian History of England and Wales, II, ed. H.R. Hallam, Cambridge (1988); III, ed. Edward Miller, Cambridge (1991)

Alvarez Borges, Ignacio (1987), *El feudalismo castellano y el libro Becerro de las Behetrías. La merindad de Burgos*, León

Anex, Danielle (1973), *Le servage au Pays de Vaud (XIII–XVI s.)*, Lausanne

Aston, Margaret (1994), 'Corpus Christi and Corpus Regni: Heresy and the Peasants' Revolt', *P&P* 143: 3–47

Aston, T.H. (ed.) (1987), *Landlords, Peasants, and Politics in Medieval England*, Cambridge

Aston, T.H. and Philpin, C.H.E. (eds.) (1985), *The Brenner Debate. Agrarian Class Structure and Economic Development in Pre-Industrial Europe*, Cambridge

Aventín i Puig, Mercè (1996), *La societat rural a Catalunya en temps feudals*, Barcelona

Backman, Clifford (1995), *The Decline and Fall of Medieval Sicily. Politics, Religion, and Economy in the Reign of Frederick III, 1296–1337*, Cambridge

Bader, Karl S. (1941), 'Bauernrecht und Bauernfreiheit in späteren Mittelalter', *HJb* 61: 51–87

Baratier, E. (1961), *La démographie provençale du XIIIe au XVIe siècle, avec chiffres de comparaison pour le XVIIIe siècle*, Paris

Bäuerliche Sachkultur des Spätmittelalters (1984), Veröffentlichungen des Instituts für mittelalterliche Realienkunde Österreichs, 7, Sitzungsberichte der österreichischen Akademie der Wissenschaften, phil.-hist. Kl., 439, Vienna

Bean, J.M.W. (1963), 'Plague, Population and Economic Decline in England in the Later Middle Ages', *EcHR* 2nd series 15: 423–37

Bennett, Judith (1984), 'The Tie that Binds: Peasant Marriages and Families in Late Medieval England', *JIH* 15: 111–29

Bennett, Judith (1986), 'The Village Ale-Wife: Women and Brewing in Fourteenth-Century England', in Barbara A. Hanawalt (ed.), *Women and Work in Preindustrial Europe*, Bloomington, pp. 20–36

Bennett, Judith (1987), *Women in the Medieval English Countryside. Gender and Household in Brigstock before the Plague*, New York

Beresford, Maurice (1954), *The Lost Villages of England*, London

Beresford, Maurice and Hurst, John G. (eds.) (1971), *Deserted Medieval Villages*, London

Berthe, Maurice (1984), *Famines et épidémies dans les campagnes navarraises à la fin du moyen âge*, Paris

Biddick, Kathleen (1987), 'Missing Links: Taxable Wealth, Markets and Stratification among Medieval English Peasants', *JIH* 18: 277–98

Biddick, Kathleen (1989), *The Other Economy. Pastoral Husbandry on a Medieval Estate*, Berkeley

Bierbrauer, Peter (1980), 'Bäuerliche Revolten im Alten Reich. Ein Forschungsbericht', in Peter Blickle *et al.* (eds.), *Aufruhr und Empörung? Studien zum bäuerlichen Widerstand im Alten Reich*, Munich, pp. 1–68

Blickle, Peter (ed.) (1975), *Revolte und Revolution in Europa*, HZ, Beiheft 4 (Munich)

Blickle, Peter (1992), *Communal Reformation. The Quest for Salvation in Sixteenth-Century Germany*, trans. Thomas Dunlop, Atlantic Highlands, N.J.

Bois, Guy (1984), *The Crisis of Feudalism. Economy and Society in Eastern Normandy, c. 1300–1550*, trans. Jean Birrell, Cambridge

Boyle, Leonard E. (1981), 'Montaillou Revisited: Mentalité and Methodology', in J. A. Raftis (ed.), *Pathways to Medieval Peasants*, Toronto, pp. 119–40

Brenner, Robert (1976), 'Agrarian Class Structure and Economic Development in Preindustrial Europe', *P&P* 70: 30–75; repr. in Aston and Philpin (1985)

Brenner, R. (1996), 'The Rises and Declines of Serfdom in Medieval and Early Modern Europe', in M.L. Bush (ed.), *Serfdom and Slavery. Studies in Legal Bondage* (1991), London and New York, pp. 247–76

Bridbury, A.R. (1981), 'Before the Black Death', *EcHR* 2nd series 34: 393–410

Britnell, R.H. (1966), 'Production for the Market on a Small Fourteenth-Century Estate', *EcHR* 2nd series 19: 380–7

Britnell, R.H. (1990), 'Feudal Reaction after the Black Death in the Palatinate of Durham', *P&P* 128: 28–47

Britton, Edward (1977), *The Community of the Vill. A Study in the History of the Family and Village Life in Fourteenth-Century England*, Toronto

Brunner, Otto (1992), *Land and Lordship. Structures of Governance in Medieval Austria*, Philadelphia

Bulst, Neithard (1987), '"Jacquerie" und "Peasants' Revolt" in der französischen und englischen Chronistik', in Hans Patze (ed.), *Geschichtsschreibung und Geschichtsbewusstsein im Spätmittelalter,* VF, XXXI, Sigmaringen, pp. 791–817

Burke, Peter (1978), *Popular Culture in Early Modern Europe,* New York

Cabrillana, Nicolás (1968), 'La crisis del siglo XIV en Castilla: la peste negra en el obispado de Palencia', *Hispania* 28: 245–58

Cabrillana, Nicolás (1971–2), 'Los despoblados en Castilla la Vieja', *Hispania* 119: 485–550; 120: 5–60

Campbell, Bruce M.S. (1984), 'Population Pressure, Inheritance and the Land Market in a Fourteenth-Century Peasant Community', in Smith (1984), pp. 87–134

Campbell, Bruce M.S. (ed.) (1991), *Before the Black Death. Studies in the 'Crisis' of the Early Fourteenth Century,* Manchester

Campbell, Bruce M.S. and Overton, M. (eds.) (1991), *Land Labour and Livestock. Historical Studies in European Agricultural Productivity,* Manchester

Cazelles, Raymond (1984), 'The Jacquerie', in Hilton and Aston (1984), pp. 74–83

Cechura, Jaroslav (1990), 'Die Bauernschaft im Böhmen während des Spätmittelalters Perspektiven neuer Orientierungen', *Bohemia* 31: 283–311

Cherubini, Giovanni (1985), *L'Italia rurale del basso medioevo,* Rome

David, Marcel (1959), 'Les laboratores du renouveau économique du XIIe siècle à la fin du XIVe siècle', *RHDFE,* 4th series 37: 174–95, 295–325

DeWindt, Edwin (1972), *Land and People in Holywell-cum-Needingworth. Structures of Tenure and Patterns of Social Organization in an East Midlands Village, 1252–1457,* Toronto

DeWindt, Edwin (1990), *The Court Rolls of Ramsey, Hepmangrove and Bury, 1280–1600,* Toronto

Dubuisson, R. (1930), *Etude sur la condition de personnes et des terres d'après les coutumes de Reims du XIIe au XVIe siècle,* Rome

Dyer, Christopher (1980), *Lords and Peasants in a Changing Society. The Estates of the Bishopric of Worcester 680–1540,* Cambridge

Dyer, Christopher (1989), *Standards of Living in the Later Middle Ages. Social Change in England c. 1200–1520,* Cambridge

Dyer, Christopher (1994), 'The English Medieval Village Community and its Decline', *JBS* 33: 407–29

Dyer, Christopher (1996), 'Memories of Freedom: Attitudes towards Serfdom in England, 1200–1350', in M.L. Bush (ed.), *Serfdom and Slavery. Studies in Legal Bondage,* Harlow, Essex, pp. 276–95

Faith, Rosamond (1984), 'The "Great Rumour" of 1377 and Peasant Ideology', in Hilton and Aston (1984), pp. 43–73

Flad, Max (1994), 'Zur Geschichte der oberschwäbischen Bauern im ausgehenden Mittelalter', *Zeitschrift für Agrargeschichte und Agrarsoziologie* 42: 142–59

Fossier, Robert (1973), 'Fortunes et infortunes paysannes au Cambrésis à la fin du XIIIe siècle', in *Economies et sociétés au moyen âge. Mélanges offerts à Edouard Perroy,* Paris, pp. 171–82

Fossier, Robert (1988), *Peasant Life in the Medieval West,* trans. Juliet Vale, Oxford

Fourquin, Guy (1978), *The Anatomy of Popular Rebellion in the Middle Ages,* Amsterdam; orig. pub. Paris (1972)

Franz, Günther (1984), *Der deutsche Bauernkrieg,* 12th edn, Darmstadt

Freedman, Paul (1991), *The Origins of Peasant Servitude in Medieval Catalonia*, Cambridge

Fryde, E.B. (1996), *Peasants and Landlords in Later Medieval England*, Stroud and New York

García de Cortázar, José Angel (1988), *La sociedad rural en la España medieval*, Madrid

Genicot, Léopold (1974–5), *L'économie rurale namuroise au bas moyen âge (1199–1429)*, 2 vols., Louvain

Genicot, Léopold (1990), *Rural Communities in the Medieval West*, Baltimore

Genicot, Léopold *et al.* (1970), *La crise agricole du bas moyen âge dans le Namurois*, Louvain

Gissel, Svend (1976), 'Agrarian Decline in Scandinavia', *SJH* 1: 43–54

Gràcia i Mont, Elisenda (1989), *Estructura agrària de la Plana de Vic al segle XIV*, Barcelona

Grava, Yves (1992), 'Seigneurs et paysans en Provence. La résistance paysanne à l'exploitation seigneuriale sur les rives de l'étang de Berre (XIe–XVe siècle)', *Histoire et société. Mélanges offerts à Georges Duby*, 2: 31–9

Die Grundherrschaft im späten Mittelalter (1983), ed. Hans Patze VF, xxvii, 2 vols., Sigmaringen

Hanawalt, Barbara (1986), *The Ties that Bound: Peasant Families in Medieval England*, New York

Harvey, B. (1991), 'Introduction: The "Crisis" of the Early Fourteenth Century', in Campbell (1991), pp. 1–24

Harvey, P.D.A. (1965), *A Medieval Oxfordshire Village. Cuxham 1200–1400*, Oxford

Harvey, P.D.A. (ed.) (1984), *The Peasant Land Market in Medieval England*, Oxford

Hatcher, John (1977), *Plague, Population and the English Economy, 1348–1530*, London

Hatcher, John (1981), 'English Serfdom and Villeinage: Towards a Reassessment', *P&P* 90: 3–39

Hatcher, John (1994), 'England in the Aftermath of the Black Death', *P&P* 144: 1–35

Herlihy, David (1967), *Medieval and Renaissance Pistoia. The Social History of an Italian Town, 1200–1430*, New Haven

Hilton, R.H. (1973), *Bondmen Made Free. Medieval Peasant Movements and the English Rising of 1381*, London

Hilton, R.H. (1974), 'Peasant Movements in England Before 1381', *Journal of Peasant Studies* 1: 207–19; repr. in R.H. Hilton, *Class Conflict and the Crisis of Feudalism. Essays in Medieval Social History*, London (1985), pp. 122–38

Hilton, R.H. (1975), *The English Peasantry in the Later Middle Ages*, Oxford

Hilton, R.H. (ed.) (1976), *Peasants, Knights and Heretics. Studies in Medieval English Social History*, Cambridge

Hilton, R.H. (1983), *The Decline of Serfdom in Medieval England*, London

Hilton, R.H. and Aston, T.H. (eds.) (1984), *The English Rising of 1381*, Cambridge

Hoffmann, Richard C. (1989), *Land, Liberties, and Lordship in a Late Medieval Countryside. Agrarian Structures and Change in the Duchy of Wroclaw*, Philadelphia

Hudson, Anne (1994), 'Piers Plowman and the Peasants' Revolt: A Problem Revisited', *Yearbook of Langland Studies* 8: 85–106

Hyams, Paul (1970), 'The Origins of a Peasant Land Market in England', *EcHR* 2nd series 23: 18–31

Hybel, Nils (1989), *Crisis or Change. The Concept of Crisis in the Light of Agrarian Structural Reorganization in Late Medieval England*, Aarhus

Jaritz, Gerhard (1989), *Zwischen Augenblick und Ewigkeit. Einführung in die Alltagsgeschichte des Mittelalters*, Vienna

Jordan, William Chester (1996), *The Great Famine: Northern Europe in the Early Fourteenth Century*, Princeton

Justice, Steven (1994), *Writing and Rebellion: England in 1381*, Berkeley

Kershaw, Ian (1973), 'The Great Famine and Agrarian Crisis in England, 1315–1322', *P&P* 59: 3–50

Klapisch-Zuber, C. and Herlihy, D. (1985), *Tuscans and their Families. A Study of the Florentine Catasto of 1427*, New Haven and London

Köhn, Rolf (1991), 'Freiheit als Forderung und Ziel bäuerlichen Widerstandes (Mittel- und Westeuropa, 11.–13. Jahrhundert), in J. Fried (ed.), *Die abendländische Freiheit vom 10. zum 14. Jahrhundert: der Wirkungszusammenhand von Idee und Wirklichkeit im europäischen Vergliech*, Sigmaringen (= *Vorträge und Forschungen*, 39), pp. 325–87

Kreidte, Peter (1981), 'Spätmittelalterliche Agrarkrise oder Krise des Feudalismus?', *GG* 7: 42–68

Langdon, John (1994), 'Lordship and Peasant Consumerism in the Milling Industry of Early Fourteenth-Century England', *P&P* 145: 3–46

Le Roy Ladurie, Emmanuel (1976), *Montaillou, village occitan de 1294 à 1324*, Paris; English trans. Barbara Bray, *Montaillou. Cathars and Catholics in a French Village 1294–1324*, London (1978)

Leclerq, Paulette (1985), 'Le régime de la terre aux XIVe–XVe siècles dans la region brignolaise', *Recueil de mémoires et travaux publié par la Société d'histoire du droit et des Institutions des Anciens Pays de Droit Ecrit* 13: 115–28

Luce, Siméon (1894), *Histoire de la Jacquerie*, 2nd edn, Paris

McIntosh, Marjorie (1986), *Autonomy and Community. The Royal Manor of Havering, 1200–1500*, Cambridge

Maddicott, J.R.L. (1975), *The English Peasantry and the Demands of the Crown, 1294–1341*, Oxford (*P&P*, Supplement 1)

Martín, José Luis (1983), *Economía y sociedad en los reinos hispánicos de la baja edad media*, 2 vols., Barcelona

Martínez Cea, Juan Carlos (1983), *El campesinado castellano de la cuenca del Deuero. Aproximaciones a su estudio durante los siglos XIII al XV*, n.p.

Mate, Mavis (1984), 'Agrarian Economy after the Black Death: the Manors of Canterbury Cathedral Priory, 1348–1391', *EcHR* 2nd series 37: 341–54

Mate, Mavis (1985), 'Medieval Agrarian Practices: The Determining Factors', *AgHR* 33: 22–31

Mate, Mavis (1991), 'The Agrarian Economy of South-East England before the Black Death: Depressed or Buoyant?', in Campbell (1991), pp. 79–109

Medeiros, Marie-Thérèse, de (1979), *Jacques et chroniqueurs. Une étude comparée de récits contemporains relatant la Jacquerie de 1358*, Paris

Miller, Edward and Hatcher, John (1978), *Medieval England. Rural Society and Economic Change 1086–1348*, London

Mollat, Michel and Wolff, Philippe (1973), *The Popular Revolutions of the Late Middle Ages*, trans. A.L. Lytton-Sells, London

Newman, Francis X. (ed.) (1986), *Social Unrest in the Late Middle Ages. Papers of the Fifteenth Annual Conference of the Center for Medieval and Early Renaissance Studies*, Binghamton

Nichols, John F. (1930), 'An Early Fourteenth Century Petition from the Tenants of Bocking to their Manorial Lord', *EcHR* 2: 300–7

Olson, Sherri (1991), 'Jurors of the Village Court: Local Leadership before and after the Plague in Ellington, Huntingdonshire', *JBS* 30: 237–56

Oman, Charles (1969), *The Great Revolt of 1381*, new edn with introduction and notes by E.B. Fryde, Oxford

Pastor, Reyna (1973), *Conflictos sociales y estancamiento económico en la España medieval*, Barcelona

Poos, L.R. (1985), 'The Rural Population of Essex in the Late Middle Ages', *EcHR* 2nd series 38: 515–30

Poos, L. R. (1991), *A Rural Society after the Black Death. Essex 1350–1525*, Cambridge

Portela Silva, Ermelindo (1976), *La region del obispado de Tuy en los siglos XII a XV. Una sociedad en expansion y en crisis*, Santiago de Compostela

Postan, M.M. (1966), 'Medieval Agrarian Society in its Prime', in *CEHE*, I, pp. 548–632

Postan, M.M. (1972), *The Medieval Economy and Society. An Economic History of Britain 1100–1500*, London

Postan, M.M. (1973), *Essays on Medieval Agriculture and General Problems of the Medieval Economy*, Cambridge

Postan, M.M. and Titow, J.Z. (1958–9), 'Heriots and Prices on Winchester Manors', *EcHR* 2nd series 11: 392–417; repr. in Postan (1973)

Putnam, Bertha Haven (1908), *The Enforcement of the Statutes of Labourers during the First Decade after the Black Death, 1349–1359*, New York

Raftis, J. Ambrose (1964), *Tenure and Mobility. Studies in the Social History of the Medieval English Village*, Toronto

Raftis, J. Ambrose (1967), 'Change in an English Village after the Black Death', *MS* 29: 156–77

Raftis, J. Ambrose (1974), *Warboys. Two Hundred Years in the Life of an English Mediaeval Village*, Toronto

Razi, Zvi (1980), *Life, Marriage and Death in a Medieval Parish. Economy, Society, and Demography in Halesowen, 1270–1400*, Cambridge

Razi, Zvi (1981), 'Family, Land and the Village Community in Later Medieval England', *P&P* 93: 3–36

Rösener, Werner (1992), *Peasants in the Middle Ages*, trans. Alexander Stützer, Urbana and Chicago; first publ. Munich (1985)

Rotelli, Claudio (1973), *Una campagna medievale. Storia agraria del Piemonte fra il 1250 e il 1450*, Turin

Ruiz, Teófilo (1987), 'La formazione del mercato della terra nella Castiglia del basso medioevo', *Quaderni storici*, n.s. 65, 2: 423–542

Ruiz, Teófilo (1994), *Crisis and Continuity. Land and Town in Late Medieval Castile*, Philadelphia

Searle, Eleanor (1979), 'Seigneurial Control of Women's Marriage: The Antecedents and Function of Merchet in England', *P&P* 82: 3–43

Seigneurs et seigneuries au moyen âge (1993), *Actes du 117e CNSS*, Clermont Ferrand, 1992, Paris

Sheehan, Michael M. (1971), 'The Formation and Stability of Marriage in Fourteenth-Century England: Evidence of an Ely Register', *MS* 33: 228–63

Sivéry, Gérard (1990), *Terroirs et communautés rurales dans l'Europe occidentale au moyen âge*, Lille

Smith, Richard (ed.) (1984), *Land, Kinship and the Life-Cycle*, Cambridge

Smith, Richard (1991), 'Demographic Developments in Rural England, 1300–1348', in Campbell (1991), pp. 25–77

Sweeney, Del (ed.) (1995), *Agriculture in the Middle Ages. Technology, Practice and Representation*, Philadelphia

TeBrake, William H. (1993), *A Plague of Insurrection. Popular Politics and Peasant Revolt in Flanders, 1323–1328*, Philadelphia

Tillotson, John H. (1974), 'Peasant Unrest in the England of Richard II: Some Evidence from Royal Records', *Historical Studies* (Melbourne) 16: 1–16

Titow, J.Z. (1969), *English Rural Society, 1200–1350*, London

Titow, J.Z. (1972), *Winchester Yields. A Study in Medieval Agricultural Productivity*, Cambridge

Toch, Michael (1991), 'Ethics, Emotions and Self-Interest: Rural Bavaria in the Later Middle Ages', *JMH* 17: 135–47

Valdeón Baruque, Julio (1969), 'Aspectos de la crisis castellana en la primera mitad del siglo XIV', *Hispania* 111: 5–24

Valdeón Baruque, Julio (1975), *Los conflictos sociales en el reino de Castilla en los siglos XIV y XV*, Madrid

Vicens Vives, J. (1978), *Historia de los Remensas*, 2nd edn, Barcelona

Zientara, Benedykt (1988), 'Die Bauern in mittelalterlichen Polen', *APH* 57: 5–42

6 URBAN LIFE

Primary sources

Froissart, Jean, *Chroniques*, ed. S. Luce *et al.*, 15 vols. (Paris, 1869–1975 continuing)

Secondary works

General

Barel, Y. (1975), *La ville médiévale, système social, système urbain*, Grenoble

Bennassar, B. (1985), *Histoire des Espagnols*, I: *VI–XVII siècle*, Paris

Bernard, G. (1998), *L'aventure des bastides. Villes nouvelles au Moyen Age*, Toulouse

Bois, G. (1976), *Crise du féodalisme*, Paris; English trans., Jean Birrell, *The Crisis of Feudalism. Economy and Society in Eastern Normandy c. 1300–1550*, Cambridge and Paris (1984)

Bourin, M. (ed.) (1989), *Villes, bonnes villes, cités et capitales. Mélanges offerts à Bernard Chevalier*, Tours

Bourin-Derruau, M. (1990), *Nouvelle histoire de la France médiévale: Temps d'équilibre, temps de ruptures*, Paris

Chevalier, B. (1982), *Les bonnes villes de France du XIVème au XVIème siècle*, Paris

Cuvillier, J.P. (1984), *L'Allemagne médiévale*, II: *1273–1525*, Paris

Dickinson, R.E. (1945), 'Morphology of the Medieval German Towns', *Geographical Review* 35: 74–97

Dollinger, Ph. (1988), *La Hanse*, new edn, Paris; English trans. D.S. Ault and S.H. Steinberg, *The German Hansa*, London (1970), from 1st edn, 1964

Duby, G. (gen. ed.) (1980), *Histoire de la France urbaine*, II: *La ville médiévale des Carolingiens à la Renaissance*, ed. A. Chédeville, J. Le Goff and J. Rossiaud, Paris

Dufourcq, Ch. E. and Gautier Dalché, J. (1976), *Histoire économique et sociale de l'Espagne chrétienne au moyen âge*, Paris

Dupâquier, J. (ed.) (1988), *Histoire de la population française*, 2 vols., Paris

Ennen, E. (1979), *The Medieval Town*, Amsterdam

Février, P.A. (1964), *Le développement urbain en Provence de l'époque romain à la fin du XVème siècle*, Paris

Fossier, R. (ed.) (1983), *Le moyen âge*, III: *Le temps des crises, 1250–1520*, Paris; English trans. Sarah Hanbury Tenison, *The Cambridge Illustrated History of the Middle Ages, 1250–1520*, Cambridge (1986)

Fournial, E. (1967), *Les villes et l'économie d'échange en Forez aux XIIIème et XIVème siècles*, Paris

Heers, J. (1973), *L'occident aux XIVème et XVème siècles. Aspects économiques et sociaux*, Paris

Heers, J. (1974), *Le clan familial au moyen âge*, Paris; English trans. Barry Herbert, *Family Clans in the Middle Ages*, Amsterdam (1977)

Heers, J. (1981), *Les partis et la vie politique dans l'Occident médiéval*, Paris; English trans. David Nicholas, *Parties and Political Life in the Medieval West*, Amsterdam (1977)

Heers, J. (1990), *La ville au moyen âge*, Paris

Higounet, Ch. (1989), *Les Allemands en Europe centrale et orientale au moyen âge*, Paris

Jehel, G. and Racinet, Ph. (1996), *La ville médiévale*, Paris

Le Goff, J. (1964), *La civilisation de l'Occident médiéval*, Paris

Le Goff, J. (1972), *Marchands et banquiers du moyen âge*, Paris

Le Mené, M. (1977), *L'économie médiévale*, Paris

Leguay, J.P. (1979), 'Un réseau urbain médiéval, les villes du comté puis du duché de Savoie', *Bulletin du Centre d'études franco-italien* (Turin-Chambéry), 4: 13–64

Leguay, J.P. (1981), *Un réseau urbain au moyen âge. Les villes du duché de Bretagne aux XIVème et XVème siècles*, Paris

Leguay, J.P. (1984), *La rue au moyen âge*, Rennes

Lestocquoy, J. (1952), *Les villes de Flandre et d'Italie sous le gouvernement des patriciens (XIème–XVème siècles)*, Paris

Mumford, L. (1964), *La cité à travers l'histoire*, Paris

Mundy, J.P. and Reisenberg, P. (1958), *The Medieval Town*, New York

Nicholas, David M. (1997), *The Later Medieval City 1300–1500*, London and New York

Oliveira Marques, A.H. de (1978), *Histoire du Portugal, des origines à nos jours*, Roanne

Oliveira Marques, A.H. de, Gonçalves, I. and Aguiar Andrade, A. (1990), *Atlas de Cidades Medievais Portuguesas (Séculos XII–XV)*, I, Lisbon

Les origines des libertés urbaines (1990), Actes du XVIème congrès des Historiens médiévistes de l'enseignement supérieur, Rouen

Le paysage urbain au moyen âge (1981), Actes du XIème congrès des Historiens médiévistes de l'enseignement supérieur, Lyon

Pirenne, H. (1971), *Les villes au moyen âge*, Paris

Planitz, H. (1954), *Die deutsche Stadt im Mittelalter*, Graz and Cologne

Platt, C. (1976), *The English Medieval Town*, London

Rapp, F. (1989), *Les origines médiévales de l'Allemagne moderne, de Charles IV à Charles Quint (1346 à 1519)*, Paris

Renouard, Y. (1969), *Les villes d'Italie de la fin du Xème siècle au début du XIVème siècle*, 2 vols., Paris

Reynolds, S. (1977), *An Introduction to the History of English Medieval Towns*, Oxford

Rörig, F. (1967), *The Medieval Town*, London (trans. from 4th German edn, 1964)

Roslanowski, T. (1964), *Recherches sur la vie urbaine dans les villes de la moyenne Rhénanie septentrionale, XIème–XVème siècles*, Warsaw

Roux, S. (1997), *Le monde des villes au Moyen Age (XIe–XVe siècle)*, Paris

Tuñon de Lara, J. (ed.), with Valdeon, J., Salrach, M. and Zabalo, J. (1989), *Historia de España*, IV: *Feudalismo y consolidacion de los Pueblos Hispanicos (siglos XI–XV)*, Madrid

Vicens Vives, J. (1959), *Historia economica de España*, Barcelona

Wolff, Ph. (1986), *Automne du moyen âge ou printemps des temps nouveaux*, Paris

Selected monographs

Collections

Editions Privat of Toulouse have produced in their series *Collection Univers de la France* scholarly collective histories of the following cities: Agen, Albi, Amiens, Angers, Angoulême, Annecy, Bordeaux, Brest, Caen, Carcassonne, Chartres, Dijon, Grenoble, La Rochelle, Le Mans, Lille, Lyon, Marseille, Montauban, Nantes, Narbonne, Nice, Perpignan, Rennes, Rodez, Rouen, Saint-Malo, Toulon, Toulouse, Vannes, Vendôme, Verdun and others. In the *Collection Histoire des Villes du Nord-Pas-de-Calais* (Presses Universitaires de Lille) there are histories of Boulogne, Calais, Douai, Dunkirk, Saint-Omer and Valenciennes.

Among atlases, the following may be noted: *Atlas of Historic Towns*, ed. M.D. Lobel *et al.* Oxford (1964–); *Atlas de Cidades Medievais Portuguesas (Séculos XII–XV)*, I, ed. A. H. de Oliveira Marques, I. Gonçalves and A. Aguiar Andrade, Lisbon (1990); *Atlas Historique des villes de France*, gen. eds. Ch. Higounet, J.B. Marquette and Ph. Wolff, Paris (1982–).

Monographs

Aguiar Andrade, A. (1990), *Um espaço medieval. Ponte de Lima*, Lisbon

Bargellini, P. (1977), *Florence*, 2nd edn, Paris

Becker, M.B. (1967–8), *Florence in Transition*, 2 vols., Baltimore

Billot, Cl. (1987), *Chartres à la fin du moyen âge*, Paris

Braunstein, Ph. and Delort, R. (1971), *Venise, portrait historique d'une cité*, Paris

Brondy, R. (1988), *Chambéry, histoire d'une capitale*, Lyon

Carrère, C. (1967), *Barcelone, centre économique à l'époque des difficultés, 1382–1462*, 2 vols., Paris

Cazelles, R. (1972), *Nouvelle histoire de Paris: Paris de la fin du règne de Philippe Auguste à la mort de Charles V*, Paris; 2nd edn 1996

Chevalier, B. (1975), *Tours, ville royale (1356–1520). Origine et développement d'une capitale à la fin du moyen âge*, Louvain/Paris

Clauzel, D. (1982), *Finances et politique à Lille pendant la période bourguignonne*, Paris

Costa Gomes, R. (1987), 'A Guarda Medieval 1200–1500', *Revista de Historia economica e social* 9-10: 1-226

Cuveiller, S. (1989), *Dunkerque, ville et port de Flandre à la fin du moyen âge à travers les comptes de bailliage de 1358 à 1407*, Lille

Desportes, P. (1979), *Reims et les Remois aux XIIIème et XIVème siècles*, Paris

Dollinger, Ph. and Rapp, F. (1981), *Strasbourg des grandes invasions au XVIème siècle*, 11, Strasburg

Duparc, P. (1973), *La formation d'une ville, Annecy jusqu'au début du XVIème siècle*, Annecy

Fabre, G. and Locard, Th. (1992), *Montpellier. La ville médiévale*, Paris

Favier, J. (1974), *Nouvelle histoire de Paris: Paris du XVème siècle*, Paris; 2nd edn 1996

Favreau, R. (1978), *La ville de Poitiers à la fin du moyen âge, une capitale régionale*, 2 vols., Poitiers

Fedou, R. (1964), *Les hommes de loi lyonnais à la fin du moyen âge, étude sur les origines de la classe de robe*, Paris

Fietier, R. (1978), *La cité de Besançon de la fin du XIIème siècle au milieu du XIVème siècle, étude d'une société urbaine*, Lille

Fourquin, G. (1962), *Les campagnes de la région parisienne à la fin du moyen âge, du milieu du XIIIème siècle au début du XVIème siècle*, Paris

Fourquin, G. (1970), *Des origines à l'avènement de Charles Quint* (vol. I of the *Histoire de Lille*, gen. ed. L. Trenard), Lille

Garrigou Grandchamp, P., Jones, Michael, Meirion-Jones, Gwyn I. and Salvèque, J.D. (1997), *La ville de Cluny et ses maisons, XIe–XVe siècles*, Paris

Heers, J. (1961), *Gênes au XVème siècle*, Paris

Herlihy, D. (1958), *Pisa in the Early Renaissance. A Study of Urban Growth*, New Haven

Higounet-Nadal, A. (1978), *Périgueux aux XIVème et XVème siècles, études de démographie historique*, Bordeaux

Lane, F.C. (1985), *Venise, une république maritime*, Paris

Miller, E. and Hatcher, J. (1995), *Medieval England. Towns, Commerce and Crafts 1066–1348*, London

Nicholas, David M. (1971), *Town and Countryside. Social, Economic and Political Tensions in Fourteenth-Century Flanders*, Bruges

Nicholas, David M. (1987), *The Metamorphosis of a Medieval City. Ghent in the Age of the Arteveldes 1302–1390*, Leiden

Renouard, Y. (ed.) (1965), *Bordeaux sous les Rois d'Angleterre* (*Histoire de Bordeaux*, gen. ed. Ch. Higounet, III), Bordeaux

Rigaudière, A. (1982), *Saint-Flour, ville d'Auvergne au bas moyen âge*, 2 vols., Paris

Schneider, J. (1950), *La ville de Metz aux XIIIème et XIVème siècles*, Nancy

Stouff, L. (1986), *Arles à la fin du moyen âge*, Aix-en-Provence

Van Houtte, J. A. (1967), *Bruges, essai d'histoire urbaine*, Brussels

Vercauteren, F. (1946), *Les luttes sociales à Liège, XIIIème–XIVème siècle*, Liège

Wolff, Ph. (1954), *Commerce et marchands de Toulouse, vers 1350–vers 1450*, Paris

Particular studies

Benoît, P. and Cailleaux, D. (eds.) (1988), *Hommes et travail du métal dans les villes médiévales*, Paris

Bibolet, Fr. (1974), 'Les métiers à Troyes aux XIVe et XVe siècles', *ACNSS 95e session, Reims, 1970*, 11, pp. 113–32

Biraben, J.N. (1975–6), *Les hommes et la peste en France et dans les pays européens et méditer-ranéens*, 2 vols., Paris and The Hague

Blumenkranz, B. (1972), *Histoire des Juifs en France*, Toulouse

Caille, J. (1978), *Hôpitaux et charité publique à Narbonne au moyen âge de la fin du XIème à la fin du XVème siècle*, Toulouse

Cazelles, R. (1984), *Etienne Marcel*, Paris

Chevalier, B. (1982), 'Corporations, conflits politiques et paix sociale en France aux XIVème et XVème siècles', *RH* 543: 17–44

Chiffoleau, J. (1980), 'La violence au quotidien, Avignon au XIVe siècle d'après les reg-istres de la cour temporelle, *Mélanges de l'Ecole française de Rome* 92: 325–71

Contamine, Ph. (1978), 'Les fortifications urbaines en France à la fin du moyen âge, aspects financiers et économiques', *RH* 527: 23–47; repr. in his *La France au XIVe et XVe s. Hommes, mentalités, guerre et paix*, London (1981)

Coornaert, E. (1941), *Les corporations en France avant 1789*, Paris

Croix, A. (1974), *Nantes et le pays nantais au XVIe siècle. Etude démographique*, Paris

Delumeau, J. and Lequin, Y. (eds.) (1987), *Les malheurs des temps, histoire des fléaux et des calamités en France*, Paris

Duby, G. and Perrot, M. (eds.) (1990), *Histoire des femmes, le moyen âge*, Paris

Emery, R.W. (1962), *The Friars in Medieval France. A Catalogue of French Mendicant Convents, 1200–1550*, New York and London

Falcao Ferreira, M. de Conceiçao (1989), *Uma rua de elite na Guimarâes medieval*, Guimarâes

Gaier, C. (1973), *L'industrie et le commerce des armes dans les anciennes principautés belges du XIIIème au XVème siècle*, Paris

Garrigou Grandchamp, P. (1992), *Demeures médiévales. Cœur de la Cité*, Paris

Geremek, B. (1969), *Le salariat dans l'artisanant parisien aux XIIIème–XVème siècles*, Paris

Geremek, B. (1976), *Les marginaux parisiens aux XIVème et XVème siècles*, Paris; English trans. Jean Birrell, *The Margins of Society in Late Medieval Paris*, Cambridge and Paris (1987)

Geremek, B. (1987), *La potence ou la pitié. L'Europe et les pauvres du moyen âge à nos jours*, Paris

Goglin, J.L. (1976), *Les misérables dans l'Occident médiéval*, Paris

Gonthier, N. (1978), *Lyon et ses pauvres au moyen âge, 1350–1500*, Lyon

Gouron, A. (1972), *Les métiers et l'organisation du travail dans la France médiévale*, Paris

Heers, J. (1972), *Fêtes, jeux et joutes dans les sociétés d'Occident à la fin du moyen âge*, Montreal

Heers, J. (1983), *Fêtes des fous et carnavals*, Paris

Heers, J. (ed.) (1984), *Espaces publics, espaces privés dans la ville, le liber terminorum de Bologne (1294)*, Paris

Heers, J. (ed.) (1985), *Fortifications, portes de villes, places publiques dans le monde méditerranéen*, Paris

Humbert, Fr. (1961), *Les finances municipales de Dijon du milieu du XIVème siècle à 1477*, Paris

Imbert, J. and Mollat, M. (1982), *Histoire des hôpitaux en France*, Toulouse

Kriegel, M. (1979), *Les Juifs à la fin du moyen âge dans l'Europe méditerranéenne*, Paris

Leguay, J.P. (1989), 'Un aspect essentiel de l'histoire urbaine: la propriété et le marché de l'immobilier à la fin du moyen âge en France et dans les grands fiefs', *MEFRA* 122: 135–99

Leguay, J.P. (1990), 'Les manœuvres des chantiers et de carrières en France et dans les pays voisins au moyen âge', *Atti del Convegno 'Il modo di costruire'*, Rome, pp. 29–48

Mehl, J.M. (1990), *Les jeux au royaume de France du XIIIème au début du XIVème siècle*, Paris

Mollat, M. and Wolff, P. (1970), *Ongles bleus, Jacques et Ciompi. Les révolutions populaires en Europe aux XIVème et XVème siècles*, Paris; English trans. A.L. Lytton-Sells, *The Popular Revolutions of the Late Middle Ages*, London (1973)

Mollat, M. (1978), *Les pauvres au moyen âge, étude sociale*, Paris; English trans. Arthur Goldhammer, *The Poor in the Middle Ages: An Essay in Social History*, Chicago (1986)

Oliviera, Marques, A.H. de (1987), *A sociedade medieval portuguesa, Aspectos de vida quotidiana*, Lisbon

Plaisse, A. and Plaisse, S. (1978), *La vie municipale à Evreux pendant la guerre de Cent Ans*, Evreux

Rigaudière, A. (1985), 'Le financement des fortifications urbaines en France du milieu du XIVème à la fin du XVème siècle', *RH*, 553: 19–95; repr. in his *Gouverner la ville au moyen âge*, Paris (1993), pp. 417–97

Rossiaud, J. (1988), *La prostitution médiévale*, Paris; English trans. Lydia G. Cochrane, *Medieval Prostitution*, Oxford (1988)

Roux, S. (1969), 'L'habitat urbain au moyen âge, le quartier de l'université de Paris', *AESC* 24: 1196–1219

Roux, S. (1976), *La maison dans l'histoire*, Paris

Schneider, J. (1956), 'Verdun au XIIIe siècle', in *Mélanges Félix Rousseau*, Brussels

Sosson, J.P. (1977), *Les travaux publics de la ville de Bruges, XIVème et XVème siècles. Les matériaux. Les hommes*, Brussels

Taylor, C.H. (1954), 'The Composition of Baronial Assemblies in France, 1315–1320', *Speculum* 29: 433–49

Touchard, H. (1967), *Le commerce maritime breton à la fin du moyen âge*, Paris

Wolff, Ph. (1977), 'Pouvoir et investissements urbains en Europe occidentale et centrale du treizième au dix-septième siècle', *RH* 524: 277–311

Wolff, Ph. and Mauro, F. (1960), *Histoire générale du travail*, II, Paris

7 PLAGUE AND FAMILY LIFE

Primary sources

Il libro del Biadaiolo. Carestia e annona a Firenze dalla metà del '200 al 1348, ed. G. Pinto, Florence (1978)

Villani, G., *Nuova Cronica*, ed. Giuseppe Porta, Parma (1990)

Villani, M., *Cronica*, Trieste (1857)

Secondary works

Albini, G. (1982), *Guerra, fame, peste. Crisi di mortalità e sistema sanitario nella Lombardia tardomedioevale*, Bologna

Baratier, E. (1961), *La démographie provençale du XIIIe au XIVe siècle*, Paris

Barbadoro, B. (1933), 'Finanza e demografia nei ruoli fiorentini d'imposta del 1352–55', *Atti del Congresso internazionale per gli studi sulla popolazione*, Rome, 11: 615–45

Bellettini, A. (1961), *La popolazione di Bologna dal secolo XV all'Unificazione italiana*, Bologna

Belletini, A. (1974), 'La populazione italiana dall'inizio dell'era volgare ai giorni nostri', in *Storia d'Italia*, v, Turin

Beloch, K.J. (1937–61), *Bevölkerungsgeschichte Italiens*, 3 vols., Berlin

Benedictow, O.J. (1992a), *Plague in the Late Medieval Nordic Countries, Epidemiological Studies*, Oslo

Benedictow, O.J. (1992b), *The Medieval Demographic System of the Nordic Countries*, Oslo

Berkner, L.K. (1972), 'The Stem Family and the Developmental Cycle of the Peasant Household. An Eighteenth-Century Austrian Example', *AmHR* 77: 398–418

Berkner, L.K. (1975), 'The Use and Misuse of Census Data for the Historical Analysis of Family Structure', *JIH* 5: 721–38

Berthe, M. (1984), *Famines et épidémies dans les campagnes navarraises à la fin du moyen âge*, 2 vols., Paris

Bideau, A. (1983), 'Les mécanismes autorégulateurs des populations traditionnelles', *AESC* 38: 1040–57

Bideau, A. and Perrenoud, A. (1981), 'Remariage et fécondité. Contribution à l'étude des mécanismes de récupération des populations anciennes', in J. Dupâquier *et al.* (eds.), *Marriage and Remarriage in Populations of the Past*, London and New York, pp. 547–59

Biget, J.-L. and Tricard, J. (1981), 'Livres de raison et démographie familiale en Limousin au XVe siècle', *ADH*: 321–63

Biraben, J.-N. (1975), *Les hommes et la peste en France et dans les pays européens et méditerranéens*, 2 vols., Paris and The Hague

Biraben, J.-N. (1988), 'L'hygiène, la maladie, la mort', in J. Dupâquier (ed.), *Histoire de la population française*, I: *Des origines à la Renaissance*, Paris, pp. 421–62

Blockmans, W.P. (1980), 'The Social and Economic Effects of Plague in the Low Countries (1349–1500)', *RBPH* 58: 833–63

Bois, G. (1976), *La crise du féodalisme. Recherches sur l'économie rurale et la démographie, du début du XIVe au milieu du XVIe s. en Normandie orientale*, Paris; English trans. Jean Birrell, *The Crisis of Feudalism, Economy and Society in Eastern Normandy, c. 1300–1550*, Cambridge (1982)

Bourin-Derruau, M. (1987), *Villages médiévaux en Bas Languedoc (Xe–XIVe s.)*, 2 vols., Paris

Bowsky, W. (1964), 'The Impact of the Black Death upon Sienese Government and Society', *Speculum* 39: 1–34

Britton, E. (1977), *The Community of the Vill. A Study in the History of the Family and Village Life in Fourteenth-Century England*, Toronto

Bulst, N. (1985), 'Vier Jahrhunderte Pest in niedersächsischen Städten. Vom Schwarzen Tod (1349–1351) bis in die erste Hälfte des 18. Jahrhunderts', in *Stadt im Wandel. Kunst und Kultur des Bürgertums in Norddeutschland, 1150–1650* (exhibition catalogue of the *Land* of Lower Saxony, 1985), Brunswick, pp. 251–70

Bulst, N. (1987), 'Zum Stand der spätmittelalterlichen demographischen Forschung in Frankreich', in P.-J. Schuler (ed.), *Die Familie als sozialer und historischer Verband. Untersuchungen zum Spätmittelalter und zur frühen Neuzeit*, Sigmaringen, pp. 3–22

Bulst, N. (1989), 'Krankheit und Gesellschaft in der Vormoderne. Das Beispiel der Pest', in *Maladies et société (XIIe–XVIIIe s.)*, Paris, pp. 17–47

Campbell, B.M.S. (1984), 'Population, Pressure, Inheritance and the Land Market in a Fourteenth-Century Peasant Community', in R.M. Smith (ed.), *Land, Kinship and Life-Cycle*, Cambridge, pp. 86–132

Campbell, B.M.S. (1991), *Before the Black Death. Studies in the 'Crisis' of the early Fourteenth Century*, Manchester

Carmichael, A.G. (1986), *Plague and the Poor in Renaissance Florence*, Cambridge

Carpentier, E. (1962a), *Une ville devant la peste. Orvieto et la peste noire de 1348*, Paris

Carpentier, E. (1962b), 'Autour de la peste noire: famines et épidémies dans l'histoire du XIVe siècle', *AESC* 17: 1062–92

Carpentier, E. and Glénisson, J. (1962), 'La démographie française au XIVe s.', *AESC* 17: 109–29

Cherubini, G. (1970), 'La carestia del 1346–47 nell'inventario dei beni di un monastero aretino', *Rivista di storia dell'agricoltura* 10: 178–93

Chevalier, B. (1975), *Tours, ville royale (1356–1520). Origine et développement d'une capitale à la fin du moyen âge*, Louvain and Paris

Comba, R. (1977), *La popolazione in Piemonte sul finire del medioevo: Ricerche di demografia storica*, Turin

Comba, R. (1984), 'Emigrare nel medioevo. Aspetti economico sociali della mobilità geografica nei secoli XI–XVI', in R. Comba, G. Piccinni and G. Pinto (eds.), *Strutture familiari, epidemie, migrazioni nell'Italia medievale*, Naples, pp. 45–74

Day, J. (1975), 'Malthus démenti? Sous-peuplement chronique et calamités démographiques en Sardaigne au bas moyen âge', *AESC* 30: 684–702

Del Panta, L. (1977), 'Cronologia e diffusione delle crisi di mortalità in Toscana', *Ricerche storiche*, 7: 293–343

Del Panta, L. (1980), *Le epidemie nella storia demografica italiana (XIV–XIX)*, Turin

Del Panta, L., Livi Bacci, M., Pinto, G. and Sonnino, E. (1996), *La popolazione italiana dal medioevo a oggi*, Rome and Bari

Delmaire, B. (1983), 'Le livre de famille des Le Borgne (Arras 1347–1538). Contribution à la démographie historique médiévale', *RN* 65: 301–26

La démographie médiévale. Sources et méthodes (1972), Nice

Desportes, P. (1966), 'La population de Reims au XVe siècle, d'après un dénombrement de 1422', *MA*: 463–509

Desportes, P. (1979), *Reims et les Rémois au XIIIe et XIVe s.*, Paris

DeWindt, E.B. (1972), *Land and People in Holywell-cum-Needingworth. Structures of Tenure and Patterns of Social Organization in an East Midlands Village, 1252–1457*, Toronto

Dobson, R. B. (1977), 'Urban Decline in Late Medieval England', *TRHS* 5th series 27: 1–22

Dollinger, P. (1972), 'Les recherches de démographie historique sur les villes allemandes au moyen âge', in *La démographie médiévale (1972)*, pp. 113–20

Dondarini, R. (1984), 'La famiglia contadina nel bolognese alla fine del trecento', in R. Comba, G. Piccinni and G. Pinto (eds.), *Strutture familiari, epidemie, migrazioni nell'Italia medievale*, Naples, pp. 201–18

Dubois, H. (1988a), 'La dépression (XIVe et XVe siècles)', in J. Dupâquier (ed.), *Histoire de la population française*, 1: *Des origines à la Renaissance*, Paris, pp. 313–66

Dubois, H. (1988b), 'L'essor médiéval', in J. Dupâquier (ed.), *Histoire de la population française*, 1, pp. 207–66

Dupâquier, J. (1972), 'De l'animal à l'homme: le mécanisme autorégulateur des populations traditionnelles', *Revue de l'Institut de sociologie*, 2: 177–211

Les Espagnes médiévales: Aspects économiques et sociaux. Mélanges offerts à J. Gautier Dalché (1983), Nice

Fiumi, E. (1962), 'La popolazione del territorio volterrano-sangimignanese ed il problema demografico dell'età comunale', in *Studi in onore di A. Fanfani*, 1, Milan, pp. 248–90

Fiumi, E. (1968), *Demografia, movimento urbanistico e classi sociali in Prato dall'età comunale ai tempi moderni*, Florence

Fossier, R. (1979), 'Peuplement de la France du nord entre le Xe et le XVIe siècles', *ADH*: 59–99

Franklin, P. (1986), 'Peasant Widows' "Liberation" and Remarriage before the Black Death', *EcHR* 2nd series 39: 186–204

Gauvard, C. (1991), *'De grace especial'. Crime, état et société en France à la fin du moyen âge*, 2 vols., Paris

Ginatempo, M. and Sandri, L. (1990), *L'Italia delle città. Il popolamento urbano tra medievo e rinascimento (secoli XIII–XVI)*, Florence

Goldberg, P.J.P. (1992), *Women, Work and Life Cycle in a Medieval Economy*, Oxford

Gottfried, R.S. (1982), *Bury St Edmunds and the Urban Crisis: 1290–1539*, Princeton

Gramain [Bourin-Derruau], M. (1972), 'Un exemple de démographie méridionale: la viguerie de Béziers dans la première moitié du XIVe s.', in *La démographie médiévale* (1972), Nice, pp. 33–8

Gras, P. (1939), 'Le registre paroissial de Givry (1334–1357) et la peste noire en Bourgogne', *BEC* 100: 295–308

Grundmann, J. (1970), 'Documenti umbri sulla carestia degli anni 1328–1330', *ASI* 128: 207–53

Guarducci, P. and Ottanelli, V. (1982), *I servitori domestici della casa borghese toscana nel basso medioevo*, Florence

Guenée, B. (1986), 'L'âge des personnes authentiques: ceux qui comptent dans la société médiévale sont-ils jeunes ou vieux?', in J-Ph. Genet and N. Bulst (eds.), *Prosopographie et genèse de l'Etat moderne*, Paris, pp. 249–79

Guilleré, C. (1984), 'La peste noire à Gérone (1348)', *Annale de l'Institut d'estudis gironins* 27: 87–161

Hajnal, J. (1965), 'European Marriage Patterns in Perspective', in D.V. Glass and D.E.C. Eversley (eds.), *Population in History*, London, pp. 101–43

Hajnal, J. (1982), 'Two Kinds of Preindustrial Household Formation', *Population and Development Review* 8: 449–94

Hallam, H.E. (1981), *Rural England, 1066–1348*, Glasgow

Hallam, H.E. (1985), 'Age at First Marriage and Age at Death in the Lincolnshire Fenland, 1252–1478', *PS* 39: 55 69

Hatcher, J. (1986), 'Mortality in the Fifteenth Century: Some New Evidence', *EcHR* 2nd series 39: 19–38

Heers, J. (1968), 'Les limites des méthodes statistiques pour les recherches de démographie médiévale', *ADH*: 43–72

Herlihy, D. (1967), *Medieval and Renaissance Pistoia. The Social History of an Italian Town, 1200–1430*, Newhaven and London

Herlihy, D. (1973), 'The Population of Verona in the First Century of Venetian Rule', in J.R. Hale (ed.), *Renaissance Venice*, London, pp. 91–120

Herlihy, D. (1985), *Medieval Households*, Cambridge, Mass.

Herlihy, D. and Klapisch-Zuber, C. (1978), *Les Toscans et leurs familles. Une étude du catasto florentin de 1427*, Paris; English trans. *Tuscans and their Families. A Study of the Florentine Catasto of 1427*, New Haven and London (1985)

Higounet, C. (1965), 'Villeneuves et bastides désertées', in *Villages désertés et histoire économique, XIe–XVIIIe siècle*, Paris, pp. 253–65

Higounet-Nadal, A. (1978), *Périgueux aux XIVe et XVe siècles. Etude de démographie historique*, Bordeaux

Higounet-Nadal, A. (1980), 'La démographie des villes françaises au moyen âge', *ADH*: 187–211

Higounet-Nadal, A. (1988), 'La croissance urbaine', in J. Dupâquier (ed.), *Histoire de la population française*, 1: *Des origines à la Renaissance*, Paris, pp. 267–312

Hollingsworth, T.H. (1957), 'A Demographic Study of the British Ducal Families', *PS* 11: 4–26

Hollingsworth, T.H. (1964), 'The Demography of the British Peerage', *PS* 18, 2 (Supplement, pp. 1–108)

Hollingsworth, T.H. (1977), 'Mortality in the British Peerage since 1600', *PS* (Supplement, pp. 323–52)

Kershaw, I. (1973), 'The Great Famine and Agrarian Crisis in England, 1315–22', *P&P* 59: 3–50

Klapisch-Zuber, C. (1983), 'Parents de sang, parents de lait. La mise en nourrice à Florence', *ADH*: 33–64

Klapisch-Zuber, C. (1988), 'La fécondité des Florentines', *ADH*: 41–57

Klapisch-Zuber, C. (1993), 'Le dernier enfant: fécondité et vieillissement chez les Florentines, XIVe–XVe s.', in J.-P. Bardet *et al.* (eds.), *Mesurer et comprendre. Mélanges offerts à Jacques Dupâquier*, Paris, pp. 277–90

Klapisch-Zuber, C. (1995), 'Les femmes et la mort à la fin du moyen âge', in *Ilaria del Carretto e il suo monumento nell'arte, la cultura e la società del '400*, Lucca, pp. 207–22

Klapisch-Zuber, C. (1998), 'L'enfant, la mémoire et la mort dans l'Italie des XIVe et XVe siècles', in E. Becchi and D. Julia (eds.), *Histoire de l'enfance en Occident*, 1: *De l'antiquité au XVIIe siècle*, Paris, pp. 200–30; orig. published in Italian, Rome and Bari (1996)

Kussmaul, A. (1981), *Servants in Husbandry in Early Modern England*, Cambridge

La Roncière, C.M. de (1974), 'Pauvres et pauvreté à Florence au XIVe siècle', in M. Mollat (ed.), *Etudes sur l'histoire de la pauvreté (moyen âge–XVIe siècle)*, Paris, II, 661–745

Laribière, G. (1967), 'Le mariage à Toulouse aux XIVe et XVe siècles', *AMi* 79: 334–61

Laslett, P. (1973), 'Characteristics of the Western Family Considered over Time', *Journal of Family and Marriage* 2: 53–80

Le Bras, H., and Dinet, D. (1980), 'Mortalité des laïcs et mortalité des religieux: les Bénédictins de St-Maur aux XVIIe et XVIIIe s.', *Population* 35: 347–83

Le Roy Ladurie, E. (1972), *Les paysans de Languedoc*, 2 vols., Paris

Le Roy Ladurie, E. (1975), *Montaillou, village occitan de 1284 à 1324*, Paris; English trans. Barbara Bray, *Montaillou. Cathars and Catholics in a French Village, 1284–1324*, London (1979)

Leverotti, F. (1984), 'La famiglia contadina lucchese all'inizio del '400', in R. Comba, G. Piccinni and G. Pinto (eds.), *Strutture familiari, epidemie, migrazioni nell'Italia medievale*, Naples, pp. 237–68

Livi Bacci, M. (1978a), 'Les répercussions d'une crise de mortalité sur la fécondité: une vérification empirique', *ADH*: 197–207

Livi Bacci, M. (1978b), *La société italienne devant les crises de mortalité*, Florence

Lorcin, M.-T. (1973), *Les campagnes de la région lyonnaise aux XIVe et XVe s.*, Lyon

Lot, F. (1929), 'L'état des paroisses et des feux de 1328', *BEC* 90: 51–107 and 256–315

Lucas, H.S. (1930), 'The Great European Famine of 1315, 1316 and 1317', *Speculum* 15: 343–77

McNeill, W.H. (1976), *Plagues and Peoples*, New York

Mazzi, M.S. (1978), *Salute e società nel medioevo*, Florence

Mazzi, M.S. (1982), 'Demografia, carestie, epidemie tra la fine del duecento e la metà del quattrocento', in G. Cherubini *et al.* (eds.), *Storia della società italiana*, VII, pt 2, Milan, pp. 11–37; 'Bibliography', pp. 426–8

Mazzi, M.S. (1984), 'La peste a Firenze 'nel quattrocento', in R. Comba, G. Piccinni and G. Pinto (eds.), *Strutture familiari, epidemie, migrazioni nell'Italia medievale*, Naples, pp. 91–115

Mols, R. (1954–6), *Introduction à la démographie historique des villes d'Europe du 14e au 18e siècle*, 3 vols., Louvain

Montanari, P. (1966), *Documenti su la popolazione di Bologna alla fine del trecento*, Bologna

Moxó, S. de (1979), *Repoblación y sociedad en la España cristiana medieval*, Madrid

Mueller, R.C. (1979), 'Aspetti sociali ed economici della peste a Venezia nel medioevo', in R.C. Mueller (ed.), *Venezia e la peste (1348–1797)*, Venice, pp. 71–6

Muzzi, O. (1984), 'Aspetti dell'evoluzione demografica della Valdelsa fiorentina nel tardo medioevo', in R. Comba, G. Piccinni and G. Pinto (eds.), *Strutture familiari, epidemie, migrazioni nell'Italia medievale*, Naples, pp. 135–52

Neveux, H. (1968), 'La mortalité des pauvres à Cambrai (1377–1473)', *ADH*: 73–97

Ottolenghi, D. (1903), 'Studi demografici sulla popolazione di Siena dal sec. XIV al XIX', *Bullettino senese di storia patria* 10: 297–358

Pesez, J.-M. and Le Roy Ladurie, E. (1965), 'Le cas français: vue d'ensemble', in *Villages désertés et histoire économique, XIe–XVIIIe siècle*, Paris, pp. 127–252

Phythian-Adams, C. (1978), 'Urban Decay in Late Medieval England', in P. Abrams and E.A. Wrigley (eds.), *Towns in Societies*, Cambridge, pp. 159–85

Phythian-Adams, C. (1979), *Desolation of a City. Coventry and the Urban Crisis of the Late Middle Ages*, Cambridge

Pini, A.I. (1969), 'Problemi di demografia bolognese del duecento', *Atti e memorie della deputazione di storia patria per la provincia di Romagna* n.s. 16–17: 147–222

Pini, A.I. (1976), *La popolazione di Imola e del suo territorio nel XIII e XIV secolo*, Bologna

Pini, A.I. and Greci, R. (1976), 'Una fonte per la demografia storica medievale: le "Venticinquine" bolognesi (1247–1404)', *Rassegna degli archivi di stato* 36: 337–417

Pinto, G. (1972), 'Firenze e la carestia del 1346–47. Aspetti e problemi delle crisi annonarie alla metà del trecento', *ASI* 130: 3–84

Pinto, G. (1984), 'La politica demografica della città', in R. Comba, G. Piccinni and G. Pinto (eds.), *Strutture familiari, epidemie, migrazioni nell'Italia medievale*, Naples, pp. 19–43

Poos, L.R. (1989), 'The Historical Demography of Renaissance Europe: Recent Research and Current Issues', *Renaissance Quarterly* 41: 794–811

Poos, L.R. (1991), *A Rural Society after the Black Death. Essex, 1350–1525*, Cambridge

Postan, M. M. (1950a), 'Histoire économique: moyen âge', *Rapports du IXe Congrès international des sciences historiques*, Section III, Histoire économique, sub-section, Moyen Age, Paris, pp. 225–41; revised as 'The Economic Foundations of Medieval Society', in his *Essays on Medieval Agriculture and General Problems of the Medieval Economy*, Cambridge (1973), pp. 1–27

Postan, M.M. (1950b), 'Some Agrarian Evidence of a Declining Population in the Later Middle Ages', *EcHR* 2nd series 2: 221–46; repr. in *Essays on . . . the Medieval Economy*, pp. 186–213

Postan, M.M. (1972), *The Medieval Economy and Society. An Economic History of Britain in the Middle Ages,* London

Prevenier, W. (1983), 'La démographie des villes du comté de Flandre aux XIVe et XVe siècles', *RN* 65: 255–75

Raftis, J.A. (1957), *The Estates of Ramsey Abbey. A Study in Economic Growth and Organization,* Toronto

Ravensdale, J. (1984), 'Population changes and transfer of Customary Land on a Cambridgeshire Manor in the 14th Century', in R.M. Smith (ed.), *Land, Kinship and Life-Cycle*, Cambridge, pp. 197–225

Razi, Z. (1980), *Life, Marriage and Death in a Medieval Parish*, Cambridge

Romano, D. (1991), 'The Regulation of Domestic Service in Renaissance Venice', *Sixteenth Century Journal* 22: 661–77

Rosenthal, J.T. (1973), 'Mediaeval Longevity and the Secular Peerage, 1350–1500', *PS* 27: 287–93

Rossiaud, J. (1976), 'Prostitution, jeunesse et société dans les villes du Sud-Est au XVe siècle', *AESC* 31: 289–325

Russell, J.C. (1948), *British Medieval Population*, Albuquerque

Russell, J.C. (1966), 'The Preplague Population of England', *JBS* 5: 1–21

Schofield, R. and Wrigley, E.A. (1981), 'Remarriage Intervals and the Effect of Marriage Order on Fertility', in J. Dupâquier et al. (eds.), *Marriage and Remarriage in Populations of the Past*, London and New York, pp. 211–28

Searle, E. (1979), 'Seigneurial Control of Women's Marriage: The Antecedents and Function of Merchet in England', *P&P* 82: 23–42

Shrewsbury, J.F.D. (1970), *A History of Bubonic Plague in the British Isles*, Cambridge

Smith, R.M. (1981), 'The People of Tuscany and their Families in the Fifteenth Century: Medieval or Mediterranean?', *Journal of Family History* 6: 107–28

Smith, R.M. (1983), 'Hypothèses sur la nuptialité en Angleterre aux XIIIe–XIVe siècles', *AESC* 38: 107–36

Smith, R.M. (1984), 'Families and their Land in an Area of Partible Inheritance: Redgrave, Suffolk, 1260–1320', in R.M. Smith (ed.), *Land, Kinship and Life-Cycle*, Cambridge, pp. 133–95

Stella, A. (1990), 'Les Ciompi et leurs familles', *Médiévales* 19: 65–70

Titow, J.Z. (1961), 'Some Evidence of the Thirteenth-Century Population Increase', *EcHR* 2nd series 14: 218–23

Trasselli, C. (1964), 'Sulla popolazione di Palermo nei secoli XIII–XIV', *Economia e storia,* 1: 329–44

Vandenbroucke, J.P. (1985), 'Survival and Expectation of Life from the 1400s to the Present: A Study of the Knighthood of the Golden Fleece', *American Journal of Epidemiology* 122: 1007–15

Venezia e la peste (1348–1797) (1979), ed. R.C. Mueller, Venice

Werveke, H. van (1959), 'La famine de l'an 1316 en Flandre et dans les régions voisines', *RN* 41: 5–8

Wrigley, E. A. (1969), *Société et population,* Paris

Wrigley, E.A. and Schofield, R.S. (1981), *The Population History of England, 1541–1871. A Reconstruction,* London

Ziegler, P. (1969), *The Black Death,* London

8 TRADE IN FOURTEENTH-CENTURY EUROPE

Primary sources

Dawson, C. (ed.), *The Mongol Mission. Narratives and Letters of the Franciscan Missionaries in Mongolia and China in the Thirteenth and Fourteenth Centuries,* trans. by a Nun of Stanbrook Abbey, London and New York (1955); repr. 1980

I libri di commercio dei Peruzzi, ed. Armando Sapori, Milan (1934)

I libri degli Alberti del Giudice, ed. Armando Sapori, Milan (1943)

Il libro del Biadaiolo. Carestia e annona a Firenze dalla metà del '200 al 1348, ed. Giuliano Pinto, Florence (1978)

Melis, Fedrigo, *Documenti per la storia economica dei secoli XIII–XVI,* Florence (1972).

Pegolotti, Francesco di Balducci, *La Pratica della Mercatura,* ed. Allan Evans, Medieval Academy of America, Cambridge, Mass. (1936)

Villani, Giovanni, *Nuova Cronica,* ed. Giuseppe Porta, 3 vols., Parma (1990–1)

Villani, Matteo, *Cronica,* ed. Giuseppe Porta, 2 vols., Parma (1995)

Zibaldone da Canal. Manoscritto mercantile del sec. XIV, ed. Alfredo Stussi, Venice (1967)

Secondary works

Abulafia, D. (1987), 'Asia, Africa and the Trade of Medieval Europe', in *CEHE,* II, 2nd edn, pp. 402–73

Abulafia, D. (1993), *Commerce and Conquest in the Mediterranean 1100–1500,* Aldershot

Abulafia, D. (1994), *A Mediterranean Emporium. The Catalan Kingdom of Majorca,* Cambridge

Abu-Lughod, Janet L. (1989), *Before European Hegemony. The World System A.D. 1250–1350,* Oxford

Aerts, Erik *et al.* (eds.) (1993), *Studia Historica Economica. Liber amicorum Herman Van der Wee,* Louvain

Ashtor, E. (1971), *Les métaux précieux et la balance des payements du proche-orient à la basse époque,* Paris

Ashtor, E. (1978), *Studies on the Levantine Trade in the Middle Ages,* Aldershot

Ashtor, E. (1983), *Levant Trade in the Later Middle Ages*, Princeton, N.J.

Ashtor, E. (1986), *East–West Trade in the Medieval Mediterranean*, Aldershot

Ashtor, E. and Cevidalli, G. (1983), 'Levantine Alkali Ashes and European Industries', *JEEH* 12: 475–522

Balard, M. (1978), *La Romanie génoise (XIIe–XVe siècle)*, 2 vols., Rome

Balard, M. (1989), *La Mer Noire et la Romanie génoise, XIIIe–XVe siècles*, Aldershot

Balard, M. (1991), 'I pisani in Oriente dalla guerra di Acri (1258) al 1406', *BSPS* 60: 1–16

Barron, Caroline M. (1995), 'Centres of Conspicuous Consumption: The Aristocratic Town House in London 1200–1550', *LJ* 20: 1–16

Bartlett, Robert (1993), *The Making of Europe. Conquest, Civilization and Cultural Change 950–1350*, Harmondsworth

Bautier, R.-H. (1953), 'Les foires de Champagne', in *La foire* (1953), 97–147; repr. in Bautier (1991), ch. 7

Bautier, R.-H. (1989), 'La circulation fluviale dans la France médiévale', in *Recherches sur l'économie de la France médiévale. ACNSS Lyon 1987. Les voies fluviales – la draperie*, Paris, pp. 7–36; repr. in Bautier (1991), ch. 5

Bautier, R.-H. (1991), *Sur l'histoire économique de la France médiévale*, Aldershot

Bautier, R.-H. (1992), *Commerce méditerranéen et banquiers italiens au moyen âge*, Aldershot

Beardwood, Alice (1931), *Alien Merchants in England 1350–77. Their Legal and Economic Position*, Cambridge, Mass.

Blockmans, W.P. (1982), 'The Social and Economic Effects of Plague in the Low Countries 1349–1500', *RBPH* 60: 833–63

Blockmans, W.P. (1991), 'Das westeuropäische Messenetz im 14 und 15 Jahrhundert', in R. Koch (ed.), *Brücke zwischen den Völkern. Zur Geschichte der Frankfurter Messe*, Frankfurt, 1, pp. 37–50

Blockmans, W. P. (1993), 'Aux origines des foires d'Anvers, in P. Contamine *et al.* (eds.), *Commerce, finances et société. Recueil de travaux d'histoire médiévale offert à M. le Prof. Henri Dubois*, Paris, pp. 21–6.

Bolton, J.L. (1980), *The Medieval English Economy*, London

Boutruche, Robert (1947), *La crise d'une société. Seigneurs et paysans du Bordelais pendant la guerre de cent ans*, Paris

Bresc, Henri (1986), *Un monde méditerranéen. Economie et société en Sicile, 1300–1450*, 2 vols., Rome

Bridbury, A.R. (1982), *Medieval English Clothmaking*, London

Britnell, R.H. (1989), 'England and Northern Italy in the Early Fourteenth Century: The Economic Contrasts', *TRHS* 5th series 39; 167–83

Britnell, R.H. (1993), *The Commercialisation of English Society 1000–1500*, Cambridge

Brunschvig, R. (1940), *La Berbérie orientale sous les Hafsides, des origines à la fin du XVe siècle*, 2 vols., Paris

Campbell, Bruce M.S. (ed.) (1991), *Before the Black Death. Studies in the 'Crisis' of the Early Fourteenth Century*, Manchester

Carrère, C. (1967), *Barcelone centre économique à l'époque des difficultés, 1380–1462*, 2 vols., Paris

Carsten, F. (1954), *The Origins of Prussia*, Oxford

Carus-Wilson, E.M. (1953), 'La guède française en Angleterre: un grand commerce du moyen âge', *RN* 35: 89–106

Carus-Wilson, E.M. (1950), 'Trends in the Export of English Woollens in the

Fourteenth Century', *EcHR* 2nd series 3: 162–79; repr. in *Medieval Merchant Venturers*, London (1954), pp. 239–64

Carus-Wilson, E.M. (1987), 'The Woollen Industry', in *CEHE*, II, 2nd edn, Cambridge, pp. 614–90

Carus-Wilson, E.M. and Coleman, Olive (1963), *England's Export Trade 1275–1547*, Oxford

Cavaciocchi, Simonetta (ed.) (1993), *La seta in Europa sec. XIII–XX*, Istituto Internazionale di Storia Economica 'F. Datini', Prato

Cazelles, Raymond (1972), *Histoire de Paris de Philippe Auguste à Charles V, 1223–1380*, Paris

Cazelles, Raymond (1976), 'La stabilisation de la monnaie par la création du franc (décembre 1360) – blocage d'une société', *Traditio* 32: 299–311

Chapin, E. (1937), *Les villes de foire de Champagne*, Paris

Childs, Wendy R. (1978), *Anglo-Castilian Trade in the Later Middle Ages*, Manchester

Chorley, Patrick (1987), 'The Cloth Exports of Flanders and Northern France during the Thirteenth Century: A Luxury Trade?', *EcHR* 2nd series 40: 349–79

Craeybeckx, J. (1958), *Un grand commerce d'importations: les vins de France aux anciens Pays-Bas (XIIIe–XVIe siècle)*, Paris

Davids, Karel and Lucassen, Jan (eds.) (1995), *A Miracle Mirrored. The Dutch Republic in its European Context*, Cambridge

Day, J. (1963), *Les douanes de Gênes 1376–7*, 2 vols., Paris

Day, J. (1978), 'The Great Bullion Famine of the Fifteenth Century', *P&P* 79: 3–54; repr. in Day (1987), ch. 1

Day, J. (1987), *The Medieval Market Economy*, Oxford

Day, J. (1996), *Monnaies et marchés au moyen âge*, Comité pour l'Histoire Economique et Financière de la France, Paris

Dini, Bruno (ed.) (1980), *Una pratica di mercatura in formazione 1394–5*, Florence

Doehaerd, Renée (1941), *Les relations commerciales entre Gênes, la Belgique, et l'Outremont au XIIIe et XIVe siècles*, Brussels and Rome

Dollinger, Philippe (1964), *La Hanse*, Paris; English trans. D.S. Ault and S.H. Steinberg, *The German Hansa*, London (1970)

Doumerc, Bernard (1991), 'Le galere da mercato', in Alberto Tenenti and Ugo Tucci (eds.), *Storia di Venezia*, XII: *Il Mare*, Venice pp. 357–95

Dubois, Henri (1976), *Les foires de Chalon et le commerce dans la vallée de la Saône à la fin du moyen âge (vers 1280–vers 1430)*, Paris

Dyer, Christopher (1989), *Standards of Living in the Later Middle Ages. Social Change in England c. 1200–1520*, Cambridge

Edler, Florence (1934), *Glossary of Medieval Terms of Business. Italian Series 1200–1600*, Medieval Academy of America, Cambridge, Mass.

Epstein, S.R. (1991), 'Cities, Regions and the Late Medieval Crisis. Sicily and Tuscany Compared', *P&P* 130: 3–50

Epstein, S.R. (1992), *An Island for Itself. Economic Development and Social Change in Late Medieval Sicily*, Cambridge

Epstein, S.R. (1994), 'Regional Fairs, Institutional Innovation, and Economic Growth in Late Medieval Europe', *EcHR* 2nd series 47: 459–82

Favier, Jean (1966), *Les finances pontificales à l'époque du grand schisme d'occident 1378–1419*, BEFAR, ccxi, Paris

Favier, Jean (1987), *De l'or et des épices. Naissance de l'homme d'affaires au moyen âge*, Paris

Felloni, Giuseppi (1984), 'Struttura e movimenti dell'economia genovese tra due e trecento: bilanci e prospettive di recerca', *Genova, Pisa e il Mediterraneo tra due e trecento*, Società Ligure di Storia Patria, Genoa, pp. 153–77

Fernandez-Armesto, Felipe (1987), *Before Columbus. Exploration and Colonisation from the Mediterranean to the Atlantic, 1229–1492*, London

La foire (1953), *RSJB*, v, Brussels

Fourquin, G. (1964), *Les campagnes de la région parisienne à la fin du moyen âge*, Paris

Fryde, E.B. (1951), 'The Deposits of Hugh Despenser the Younger with Italian Bankers', *EcHR* 2nd series 3: 344–62; repr. in Fryde (1983), III, with same pagination

Fryde, E.B. (1983), *Studies in Medieval Trade and Finance*, London

Fryde, E.B. (1988), *William de la Pole. Merchant and King's Banker (+1369)*, London

Gilchrist, John (1969), *The Church and Economic Activity in the Middle Ages*, London and New York

Hammel-Kiesow, Rolf (1993), 'Hansischer Seehandel und wirtschaftliche Wechsellagen. Der Umsatz im Lübecker Hafen in der zweiten Hälfte des 14. Jahrhundert, 1492–6 und 1680–2', in Stuart Jenks and Michael North (eds.), *Der hansische Sonderweg? Beiträge zur Sozial- unt Wirtschaftsgeschichte der Hanse*, QDHG, n.s., xxxxix, Cologne, pp. 77-94

Harrison, D.F. (1992), 'Bridges and Economic Development, 1300–1800', *EcHR* 2nd series 45: 240–61

Harte, N.B. and Ponting, K.G. (eds.) (1983), *Cloth and Clothing in Medieval Europe*, London

Hatcher, John (1973), *English Tin Production and Trade before 1550*, Oxford

Heers, Jacques (1966), *L'Occident aux XIVe et XVe siècles. Aspects économiques et sociaux*, 2nd edn, Paris

Heers, Jacques (1981), *Esclaves et domestiques au moyen âge dans le monde méditerranéen*, Paris

Herlihy, David J. (1958), *Pisa in the Early Renaissance. A Study of Urban Growth*, New Haven

Herlihy, David J. (1967), *Medieval and Renaissance Pistoia. The Social History of an Italian Town, 1200–1450*, New Haven

Heyd, W. (1885–6), *Histoire du commerce du Levant au moyen âge*, 2 vols., Leipzig

Hitzer, Hans (1971), *Der Straße*, Munich

Hocquet, Jean-Claude (1978–9), *Le sel et la fortune de Venise*, 2 vols., Lille

Hocquet, Jean-Claude (1985), *Le sel et le pouvoir*, Paris

Hocquet, Jean-Claude (ed.) (1987), *Le roi, le marchand et le sel*, Lille

Holmes, G. (1960), 'Florentine Merchants in England 1346–1436', *EcHR* 2nd series 13: 193–208

Hoshino, Hidetoshi (1980), *L'arte della lana in Firenze nel basso medioevo. Il commercio della lana e il mercato dei panni fiorentini nei secoli XIII–XV*, Biblioteca Storica Toscana, xxi, London

Hoshino, Hidetoshi (1983), 'The Rise of the Florentine Woollen Industry in the Fourteenth Century', in Harte and Ponting (1983), pp. 184–204

Houtte, J.A. van (1966), 'The Rise and Decline of the Market of Bruges', *EcHR* 2nd series 19: 29–47

Houtte, J.A. van (1977), *An Economic History of the Low Countries 800–1800*, London

Hunt, Edwin S. (1994), *The Medieval Super-Companies. A Study of the Peruzzi Company of Florence*, Cambridge

Irsigler, F. (1979), *Die Wirtschaftliche Stellung der Stadt Köln im 14. und 15. Jahrhundert*, *VSW*, Supplement 65

James, M.K. (1971), *Studies in the Medieval Wine Trade*, Oxford

Jenks S. (1992), *England, die Hanse und Preußen. Handel und Diplomatie; 1377–1474*, 3 vols., QDHG, n.s., xxxxviii, Cologne

Jordan, W.C. (1996), *The Great Famine. Northern Europe in the Early Fourteenth Century*, Princeton, N.J.

Kedar, Benjamin Z. (1976), *Merchants in Crisis. Genoese and Venetian Men of Affairs and the Fourteenth Century Depression*, New Haven

Keene, D. (1989), 'Medieval London and its Region', *LJ* 14: 99–111

King, D. (1993), 'Types of Silk Cloth Used in England, 1200–1500', in Simonetta Cavaciocchi (ed.), *La seta in Europa sec. XIII–XX*, Istituto Internazionale di Storia Economica 'F. Datini', Prato, pp. 457–64

Koch, R. (ed.) (1991), *Brücke zwischen den Völkern. Zur Geschichte der Frankfurter Messe*, 3 vols., Frankfurt

La Roncière, C.M. de (1973), *Un changeur florentin du trecento. Lippo di Fede del Sega (1285 env.–1363 env.)*, Paris

La Roncière, C.M. de (1976), *Florence, centre économique régional au XIVe siècle*, 5 vols., Paris (of which a compressed, and slightly revised version, is published as *Prix et salaires à Florence au XIVe siècle (1280–1380)*, Collection de l'Ecole Française de Rome, LIX, Rome (1982))

Lane, Frederic C. (1934), *Venetian Ships and Shipbuilders of the Renaissance*, Baltimore

Lane, Frederic C. (1963), 'Venetian Merchant Galleys, 1300–1334: Private and Communal Operations', *Speculum* 38: 179–203

Lane, Frederic C. (1966), *Venice and History*, Baltimore

Lane, Frederic C. (1973), *Venice. A Maritime Republic*, Baltimore

Lane, Frederic C. (1987), *Studies in Venetian Social and Economic History*, Aldershot

Lane, Frederic C. and Mueller, Reinhold C. (1985), *Money and Banking in Medieval and Renaissance Venice*, I, Baltimore

Laurent, H. (1935), *Un grand commerce d'exportation au moyen âge. La draperie des Pays-Bas en France et dans les pays méditerranéens (XIIe–XVe siècle)*, Paris

Le Goff, Jacques (1986), *Marchands et banquiers du moyen âge*, 7th edn, Paris

Liagre-de Sturler, Léone (1969), *Les relations commerciales entre Gênes, la Belgique, et l'Outremont d'après les archives notariales génoises (1320–1400)*, 2 vols., Brussels and Rome

Lloyd, T.H. (1977), *The English Wool Trade in the Middle Ages*, Cambridge

Lloyd, T.H. (1982), *Alien Merchants in England in the High Middle Ages*, Brighton

Lopez, Robert S. (1971), *The Commercial Revolution of the Middle Ages, 950–1350*, Englewood Cliffs

Lopez, Robert S. (1973), 'Une histoire à trois niveaux: la circulation monétaire', *Mélanges en l'honneur de Fernand Braudel*, II: *Méthodologie de l'histoire et des sciences humaines*, Paris, pp. 335–41

Lopez, Robert S. (1987), 'The Trade of Medieval Europe: The South', in *CEHE*, II, 2nd edn, pp. 306–401

Lopez, Robert S. and Raymond, Irving W. (1955), *Medieval Trade in the Mediterranean World. Illustrative Documents Translated with Introductions and Notes*, New York

Lucas, H.S. (1930), 'The Great European Famine of 1315, 1316, and 1317', *Speculum* 5: 343–77; repr. in E. Carus-Wilson (ed.), *Essays in Economic History*, II, London (1982), pp. 49–72

Luzzatto, Gino (1961), *An Economic History of Italy*, London

Malowist, Marian (1987), 'The Trade of Eastern Europe in the Later Middle Ages', in *CEHE*, II, 2nd edn, pp. 525–612

Mazzaoui, Maureen Fennell (1981), *The Italian Cotton Industry in the Later Middle Ages 1100–1600*, Cambridge

Melis, Federigo (1962), *Aspetti della vita economica medievale – studi nell'Archivio Datini di Prato*, Monte dei Paschi di Siena

Melis, Federigo (1973), 'Intensità e regolarità nella diffusione dell'informazione economica generale nel Mediterraneo e in Occidente alla fine del medioevo', in *Mélanges en l'honneur de Fernand Braudel. Histoire économique du monde méditerranéen 1450–1650*, I, Toulouse, pp. 389–424

Melis, Federigo (1974), 'La lana della Spagna mediterranea e della Barberia occidentale nei secoli XIV–XV', in Spallanzani (1974), pp. 241–51; also published in a slightly revised version in Melis (1990), pp. 233–50

Melis, Federigo (1975), *Origini e sviluppi delle assicurazioni in Italia (secoli XIV–XVI)*, Rome

Melis, Federigo (1984a), *I trasporti e le communicazioni nel medioevo*, Florence

Melis, Federigo (1984b), *I vini Italiani nel medioevo*, Florence

Melis, Fedrigo (1987), *La banca pisana e le origini della banca moderna*, Florence

Melis, Federigo (1989), *Industrie e commercie nella Toscana medievale*, Florence

Melis, Federigo (1990), *I mercanti italiani dell'Europa medievale e rinascimentale*, Florence

Miskimin, H. (1975), *The Economy of Early Renaissance Europe 1300–1460*, Cambridge

Miskimin, H. (1989), *Cash, Credit and Crisis in Europe, 1300–1600*, Aldershot

Mollat, Michel (1952), *Le commerce maritime normand à la fin du moyen âge*, Paris

Mollat, Michel (1968), *Le rôle du sel dans l'histoire*, Paris

Mueller, Reinhold C. (1995), 'The Spufford Thesis on Foreign Exchange: The Evidence of Exchange Rates', *JEEH* 24: 121–9

Munro, John H. (1973), *Wool, Cloth and Gold. The Struggle for Bullion in Anglo-Burgundian Trade 1340–1478*, Brussels and Toronto

Munro, John H. (1983), 'The Medieval Scarlet and the Economics of Sartorial Splendour', in Harte and Ponting (1983), pp. 13–70

Munro, John H. (1988), 'Textile Technology', in J.R. Strayer (ed.), *Dictionary of the Middle Ages*, New York, XI, pp. 693–715

Munro, John H. (1991), 'Industrial Transformations in the North-West European Textile Trades *c.* 1290–1340: Economic Progress or Economic Crisis?', in Bruce M.S. Campbell (ed.), *Before the Black Death. Studies in the 'Crisis' of the Early Fourteenth Century*, Manchester, pp. 110–48

Munro, John H. (1992), *Bullion Flows and Monetary Policies in England and the Low Countries, 1350–1500*, Aldershot

Munro, John H. (1994), *Textiles, Towns and Trade. Essays in the Economic History of Late-Medieval England and the Low Countries*, Aldershot

Nef, John U. (1987), 'Mining and Metallurgy in Medieval Civilisation', in *CEHE*, II, 2nd edn, pp. 693–761

Nicholas, David (1976), 'Economic Reorientation and Social Change in Fourteenth Century Flanders', *P&P* 70: 3–29; reprinted in his *Trade, Urbanisation and the Family. Studies in the History of Medieval Flanders*, Aldershot (1996)

Nicholas, David (1992), *Medieval Flanders*, London and New York

Nightingale, Pamela (1995), *A Medieval Mercantile Community. The Grocers' Company and the Politics and Trade of London, 1000–1485*, New Haven and London

Origo, Iris (1955), 'The Domestic Enemy: The Eastern Slaves in Tuscany in the Fourteenth and Fifteenth Centuries', *Speculum* 30: 321–66

Origo, Iris (1957), *The Merchant of Prato. Francesco di Marco Datini*, London

Peeters, J.P. (1988), 'De-Industrialization in the Small and Medium-Sized Towns in Brabant at the End of the Middle Ages', in Herman van der Wee (ed.), *The Rise and Decline of Urban Industries in Italy and in the Low Countries*, Louvain, pp. 165–86

Pinto, G. (1972), 'Firenze e la carestia del 1346–47, *ASI* 130: 3–84; repr. in Pinto (1982), pp. 338–98

Pinto, G. (1982), *La Toscana nel tardo medioevo*, Florence

Postan, M.M. (1987), 'The Trade of Europe: The North', in *CEHE*, II, 2nd edn, pp. 168–305

Pounds, N.J.G. (1973), 'Europe in the Early Fourteenth Century', in his *An Historical Geography of Europe 450 BC–AD 1330*, Cambridge

Power, Eileen (1941), *The Wool Trade in English Medieval History*, Oxford

Rawcliffe, C. (1978), *The Staffords, Earls of Stafford and Dukes of Buckingham, 1394–1521*, Cambridge

Renouard, Yves (1941), *Les relations des papes d'Avignon et des compagnies commerciales et bancaires de 1316 à 1378*, BEFAR, cli, Paris

Renouard, Yves (1968), *Les hommes d'affaires italiens du moyen âge*, Paris

Renouard, Yves (1969), *Les villes d'Italie de la fin du Xe siècle au debut du XIVe siècle*, II, 2nd edn, Paris

Reyerson, Kathryn L. (1982), 'Medieval Silks in Montpellier: The Silk Market ca.1250 – ca. 1350', *JEEH* 11: 117–40; repr. in her *Society, Law and Trade in Medieval Montpellier*, Aldershot (1995)

Reyerson, Kathryn L. (1985), *Business, Banking and Finance in Medieval Montpellier*, Toronto

Roover, Florence Edler de (1945), 'Early Examples of Marine Insurance', *JEH* 5: 172–200

Roover, Raymond de (1942), 'The Commercial Revolution of the Thirteenth Century', *BBHS* 16: 34–9; republished in Frederic C. Lane and Jelle C. Riemersma (eds.), *Enterprise and Secular Change*, Homewood, Ill. (1953), pp. 80–5

Roover, Raymond de (1948), *Money, Banking and Credit in Medieval Bruges: Italian Merchant-Bankers, Lombards and Money-Changers*, Cambridge, Mass.

Roover, Raymond de (1953), *L'évolution de la lettre de change (XIVe–XVIIIe siècles)*, Paris

Roover, Raymond de (1954), 'New Interpretations of the History of Banking', *JWH* 2: 38–76; repr. in Roover (1974), pp. 200–38

Roover, Raymond de (1956), 'The Development of Accounting Prior to Luca Pacioli According to the Account Books of Medieval Merchants', in A.C. Littleton and B.S. Yamey (eds.), *Studies in the History of Accounting*, London, pp. 114–74; repr. in Roover (1974), pp. 119–80

Roover, Raymond de (1963), 'The Organisation of Trade', in *CEHE*, III, pp. 42–118

Roover, Raymond de (1968), *The Bruges Money Market around 1400*, Brussels

Roover, Raymond de (1974), *Business, Banking, and Economic Thought in Late Medieval and Early Modern Europe*, ed. Julius Kirshner, Chicago

Ruddock, A.A. (1961), *Italian Merchants and Shipping in Southampton, 1270–1600*, Southampton

Sapori, Armando (1926), *La crisi delle compagnie mercantili dei Bardi e dei Peruzzi*, Florence

Sapori, Armando (1955), *Studi di storia economica, secoli XIII–XIV–XV*, 3rd edn, Florence

Sapori, Armando (1970), *The Italian Merchant in the Middle Ages*, London

Scammell, G.V. (1981), *The World Encompassed. The First European Maritime Empires c. 800–1650*, London and New York

Sosson, J.P. (1977), *Les travaux publics de la ville de Bruges, XIVe–XVe siècles. Les matériaux. Les hommes*, Brussels

Spallanzani, Marco (ed.) (1974), *La lana come materia prima. I fenomeni della sua produzione e circolazione nei secoli XIII–XVII*, Istituto Internazionale di Storia Economica 'F. Datini', Prato

Spallanzani, Marco (ed.) (1976), *Produzione commercio e consumo dei panna di lana (nei secoli XII–XVIII)*, Istituto Internazionale di Storia Economica 'F. Datini', Prato

Sprandel, Rolf (1968), *Das Eisengewerbe im Mittelalter*, Stuttgart

Sprandel, Rolf (1975), *Das mittelalterliche Zahlungsystem nach hansisch-nordischen Quellen des 13.-15. Jahrhunderts*, Stuttgart

Spufford, Margaret (1995), 'Literacy, Trade and Religion in the Commercial Centres of Europe', in Karel Davids and Jan Lucassen (eds.), *A Miracle Mirrored. The Dutch Republic in its European Context*, Cambridge, pp. 229–83

Spufford, Peter (1986), *Handbook of Medieval Exchange*, Royal Historical Society, Guides and Handbooks, 13, London

Spufford, Peter (1987a), 'Coinage and Currency', in *CEHE*, II, 2nd edn, pp. 788–873

Spufford, Peter (1987b), 'Mint Organisation in Late Medieval Europe' in Peter Spufford and N.J. Mayhew (eds.), *Later Medieval Mints. Organisation, Administration and Techniques*, BAR, International Series, Oxford, pp. 5–27

Spufford, Peter (1988), *Money and its Use in Medieval Europe*, Cambridge

Spufford, Peter (1991), 'Spätmittelalterliche Kaufmannsnotizbücher als Quelle zur Bankengeschichte. Ein Projektbericht', in Michael North (ed.), *Kredit im spätmittelalterlichen und frühneuzeitlichen Europa*, QDHG, n.s. xxxvii, Hansischen Geschichtsverein, Cologne, pp. 103–20

Spufford, Peter (1995), 'Access to Credit and Capital in the Dutch Republic and Other Leading Commercial Centres', in Karel Davids and Jan Lucassen (eds.), *A Miracle Mirrored. The Dutch Republic in its European Context*, Cambridge, pp. 303–37

Spufford, Peter (forthcoming), *The Trade of Medieval Europe*, Cambridge

Stefani, Giuseppi (ed.) (1958), *Insurance in Venice from the Origin to the End of the Serenissima*, London

Stromer, Wolfgang von (1970), *Oberdeutsche Hochfinanz 1380–1450*, 3 vols., Wiesbaden

Stromer, Wolfgang von (1978), *Die Gründung der Baumwollindustrie in Mitteleuropa. Wirtschaftspolitik im Spätmittelalter*, Stuttgart

Stuard, Susan Mosher (1995), 'Ancillary Evidence for the Decline of Medieval Slavery', *P&P* 149: 3–28

Tenenti, Alberto and Vivanti, Corrado (1961), 'Le film d'un grand système de navigation: les galères marchandes vénitiennes XIVe–XVIe siècles', *AESC* 16: 83–6 and
map

Touchard, Henri (1967), *Le commerce maritime breton à la fin du moyen âge*, Paris

Unger, Richard W. (1980), *The Ship in the Medieval Economy 600–1600*, Montreal

Veale, Elspeth M. (1966), *The English Fur Trade in the Later Middle Ages*, Oxford

Verlinden, Charles (1955–77), *L'esclavage dans l'Europe médievale*, 2 vols., Bruges and
Ghent

Verlinden, Charles (1963), 'Markets and Fairs', in *CEHE*, III, pp. 126–53

Wee, Herman van der (1963), *The Growth of the Antwerp Market and the European Economy
(Fourteenth–Sixteenth Centuries)*, 3 vols., The Hague

Wee, Herman van der (1975), 'Structural Changes and Specialisation in the Industry of
the Southern Netherlands, 1100–1660', *EcHR* 2nd series 28: 203–21; repr. in his
Low Countries in the Early Modern World (Aldershot), 1993, pp. 201–22

Wee, Herman van der (ed.) (1991), *La banque en Occident*, Antwerp

Werveke, Hans van (1947), 'De omvang van de Ieperse lakenproductie in de veertiende
eeuw', *MKVA, Klasse der Letteren,* IX, 2 (not included among papers on Flemish
trade and industry selected for his *Miscellanea Mediaevalia*, Ghent (1968))

Werveke, H. van (1959), 'La famine de l'an 1316 en Flandre et dans les régions voisines',
RN 41: 5–14

Werveke, Herman van der (1968), *Miscellanea Mediaevalia*, Ghent (1968)

Wolff, Philippe (1954), *Commerces et marchands de Toulouse (vers 1350–vers 1450)*, Paris

9 CHIVALRY AND THE ARISTOCRACY

Primary sources

The Black Book of the Admiralty, ed. T. Twiss, RS, 1, London (1872)

Chronica Adae Murimuth et Robert de Avesbury, ed. E. Maunde Thompson, London (1889)

Chronicas de los reyes de Castilla desde Don Alfonso el Sabio, ed. F. Cerda, 1, Madrid (1781)

Chronique des règnes de Jean II et Charles V, ed. R. Delachenal, 4 vols., Paris (1917–20)

De La Marche, O., *Mémoires*, ed. H. Beaune and J. d'Arbaumont, IV, Paris (1888)

Froissart, Jean, *Œuvres*, ed. J.M.B.C. Kervyn de Lettenhove, 28 vols., Brussels (1867–77)

'Private Indentures for Life Service in Peace and War 1278–1476', ed. Michael Jones
and Simon Walker, *Camden Miscellany* 33 (1994), pp. 1–190

Le songe du vergier, ed. M. Schnerb-Lièvre, 2 vols., Paris (1982)

Wapenboek ou Armorial de 1334 à 1372 par Gelre Héraut, ed. V. Bouton, 2 vols., Paris (1881)

Secondary works

Allmand, C.T. (ed.) (1976), *War, Literature and Politics in the Late Middle Ages*, Liverpool

Allmand, C.T. (1988), *The Hundred Years War. England and France at War c. 1300 to c. 1450*,
Cambridge

Artonne, A. (1912), *Le mouvement de 1314 et les chartes provinciales de 1315*, Paris

Ashmole, E. (1672), *The Institution, Laws and Ceremonies of the Most Noble Order of the
Garter*, London

Barber, R. (1970), *The Knight and Chivalry*, London

Barker, J.R.V. (1986), *The Tournament in England, 1100–1400*, Woodbridge

Barnie, J. (1974), *War in Medieval Society. Social Values and the Hundred Years War*, London

Boulton, D'A.J.D. (1987), *The Knights of the Crown: The Monarchical Orders of Knighthood in Later Medieval Europe*, Woodbridge

Boutrouche, R. (1963), *La crise d'une société. Seigneurs et paysans en Bordelais pendant la guerre de cent ans*, Paris

Bullough, D.A. (1974), 'Games People Played: Drama and Ritual as Propaganda in Medieval Europe', *TRHS* 5th series 24: 97–122

Cline, R. (1945), 'The Influence of Romances on Tournaments of the Middle Ages', *Speculum* 20: 204–11

Contamine, Ph. (1972), *Guerre, état et société. Etudes sur les armées des rois de France 1337–1494*, Paris and The Hague

Contamine, Ph. (ed.) (1976), *La noblesse au moyen âge*, Paris

Denholm-Young, N. (1961), 'The Song of Caerlaverock and the Parliamentary Roll of Arms', *PBA* 47: 451–62

Denholm-Young, N. (1965), *History and Heraldry*, Oxford

Denholm-Young, N. (1969), *The Country Gentry in the Fourteenth Century*, Oxford

Dravasa, E. (1965–6), 'Vivre noblement: recherches sur la dérogeance de la noblesse du quatorzième et quinzième siècles', *Revue juridique et économique du Sud-Ouest*, série juridique, 16: 135–93 and 17: 23–129

Dupont-Ferrier, G. (1930–2), *Etudes sur les institutions financières de la France à la fin du moyen âge*, 2 vols., Paris

Fleckenstein, J. (1977), *Herrschaft und Stand*, Göttingen

Fleckenstein, J. (1985), *Das Ritterliche Turnier im Mittelalter*, Göttingen

Gautier, L. (1884), *La chevalerie*, Paris

Given-Wilson, C. (1986), *The Royal Household and the King's Affinity. Service, Politics and Finance in England, 1360–1413*, New Haven

Green, R.F. (1983), 'The *Familia Regis* and the *Familia Cupidinis*', in Scattergood and Sherborne (1983), pp. 87–108

Hauptmann, F. (1896), *Das Wappenrecht*, Bonn

Huizinga, J. (1927), *The Waning of the Middle Ages*, London

Jones, Michael (1991), 'Les signes du pouvoir: l'ordre de l'Hermine, les devises et les hérauts des ducs de Bretagne au quinzième siècle', *MSHAB* 68: 141–73

Keen, M.H. (1965), *The Laws of War in the Late Middle Ages*, London

Keen, M.H. (1984), *Chivalry*, New Haven

Kilgour, R.L. (1937), *The Decline of Chivalry*, Cambridge, Mass.

Kruse, H., Paravicini, W. and Ranft, A. (eds.) (1991), *Ritterorden und Adelsgesellschaften im Spätmittelalterlichen Deutschland*, Frankfurt

La Curne de Ste. Palaye, J.B. (1759), *Mémoires de l'ancienne chevalerie*, Paris

Lewis, P.S. (1964), 'Decayed and Non-Feudalism in Later Medieval France', *BIHR* 37: 154–84

Lewis, P. S. (1968), *Later Medieval France. The Polity*, London

Linehan, P. (1987), 'Ideologie y liturgia en el reinado de Alfonso XI de Castilla', in A. Rucquoi (ed.), *Genesis medieval del estado moderno: Castilla y Navarra*, Valladolid, pp. 229–43

Lucas, R.H. (1977), 'Ennoblement in Late Medieval France', *MS* 39: 239–60

McFarlane, K.B. (1945), 'Bastard Feudalism', *BIHR* 20: 161–80

McFarlane, K.B. (1973), *The Nobility of Later Medieval England*, Oxford

Mertes, K. (1988), *The English Noble Household, 1250–1600*, Oxford

Palmer, J.J.N. (1972), *England, France and Christendom, 1377–99*, London

Palmer, J.J.N. (ed.) (1981), *Froissart: Historian*, Woodbridge

Paravicini, W. (1990), 'Verlorene Denkmäler europäischen Malereien des 14. Jahrhunderts im Dom zu Königsberg', in E. Böckler (ed.), *Kunst und Geschichte im Ostseeraum*, Keil, pp. 66–124 and plates 1–69

Pastoureau, M. (1979), *Traité d'héraldique*, Paris

Prestage, E. (1928), *Chivalry*, London

Renouard, Y. (1949), 'L'ordre de la Jarretière et l'ordre de l'Étoile: étude sur la gènese des ordres laics de chevalerie et sur le développement de leur caractère national', *MA* 4th series 4: 282–300

Scattergood, V.J. and Sherborne, J.W. (eds.) (1983), *English Court Culture in the Later Middle Ages*, London

Schäfer, K.F. (1911–40), *Deutsche Ritter und Edelknechte in Italien*, 3 vols., Paderborn

Schultz, A. (1892), *Deutsches Leben im Vierzehn und Fünfzehn Jahrhundert*, Leipzig

Seyler, G. (1885–9), *Geschichte der Heraldik*, 10 fasc. in 1 vol., Nuremberg

Vale, J. (1982), *Edward III and Chivalry*, Woodbridge

Vale, M. (1981), *War and Chivalry*, London

Wagner, A.R. (1956), *Heralds and Heraldry in the Middle Ages*, Oxford

10 COURT PATRONAGE AND INTERNATIONAL GOTHIC

Secondary works

Baltimore (1962), *The International Style. The Arts in Europe around 1400* (exhibition catalogue), Baltimore

Belting, H. (1981), *Das Bild und sein Publikum im Mittelalter. Form und Funktion Früher Bildtafeln der Passion*, Berlin

Belting, H. (1985), 'The New Role of Narrative in Public Painting of the Trecento: *Historia* and Allegory', in H.L. Kessler and M.S. Simpson (eds.), *Pictorial Narrative in Antiquity and the Middle Ages*, Studies in the History of Art, 16, Washington, pp. 151–68

Binski, P. (1995), *Westminster Abbey and the Plantagenets. Kingship and the Representation of Power 1200–1400*, New Haven and London

Bony, J. (1979), *The English Decorated Style. Gothic Architecture Transformed 1250–1350*, Oxford

Christiansen, K. (1982), *Gentile da Fabriano*, London

Cohen, K. (1973), *Metamorphosis of a Death Symbol. The Transi Tomb in the Late Middle Ages and the Renaissance*, Berkeley and Los Angeles

Enaud, F. (1971), 'Les fresques du Palais des Papes d'Avignon', *Les Monuments Historiques de la France*, 17/2–3: 1–139

Gardner, J. (1992), *The Tomb and the Tiara. Curial Tomb Sculpture in Rome and Avignon in the Later Middle Ages*, Oxford

Gibbs, R. (1989), *Tomaso da Modena*, Cambridge

Hamburger, J. (1990), *The Rothschild Canticles. Art and Mysticism in Flanders and the Rhineland circa 1300*, New Haven and London

Hedeman, A. D. (1991), *The Royal Image. Illustrations of the Grandes Chroniques de France 1274–1422*, Berkeley, Los Angeles and London

Huizinga, J. (1955), *The Waning of the Middle Ages*, Harmondsworth (orig. edn, 1924)

Keen, M. (1984), *Chivalry*, New Haven and London

Laclotte, M. and Thiébaut, D. (1983), *L'école d'Avignon*, Tours

Le Goff, J. (1984), *The Birth of Purgatory*, trans. A. Goldhammer, Chicago

Martindale, A. (1981), 'Painting for Pleasure – Some Lost Fifteenth Century Secular Decorations of Northern Italy', in A. Borg and A. Martindale (eds.), *The Vanishing Past. Studies in Medieval Art, Liturgy and Metrology presented to Christopher Hohler*, BAR International Series, 111, Oxford, 109–31

Martindale, A. (1988), *Simone Martini*, Oxford

Meiss, M. (1951), *Painting in Florence and Siena after the Black Death*, Princeton

Meiss, M. (1967), *French Painting in the Time of Jean de Berry. The Late Fourteenth Century and the Patronage of the Duke*, 2 vols., London

Morand, K. (1962), *Jean Pucelle*, Oxford

Morand, K. (1991), *Claus Sluter. Artist at the Court of Burgundy*, London

Munich (1978), *Kaiser Karl IV. Staatsmann und Mazen* (exhibition catalogue), Munich

Panofsky, E. (1953), *Early Netherlandish Painting*, 2 vols., Cambridge, Mass.

Paris (1981), *Les fastes du Gothique, le siècle de Charles V* (exhibition catalogue), Paris

Ringbom, S. (1965), *Icon to Narrative. The Rise of the Dramatic Close-Up in Fifteenth-Century Devotional Painting*, Acta Academiae Aboensis, ser. A, Humaniora 31, 2, Abo

Sherman, C. (1969), *The Portraits of Charles V of France*, New York

Sherman, C. (1995), *Imagining Aristotle. Verbal and Visual Representation in Fourteenth-Century France*, Berkeley, Los Angeles and London

Skinner, Q. (1986), 'Ambrogio Lorenzetti: The Artist as Political Philosopher', *PBA* 72: 1–56

Starn, R. and Partridge, L. (1992), *Arts of Power. Three Halls of State in Italy, 1300–1600*, University of California Press

Van Os, H. W. (1981), 'The Black Death and Sienese Painting: A Problem of Interpretation', *Art History* 4: 237–49

Van Os, H. W. (1994), *The Art of Devotion in the Late Middle Ages in Europe 1300–1500*, London and Amsterdam

White, J. (1966), *Art and Architecture in Italy 1250–1400*, Harmondsworth

11 ARCHITECTURE

Secondary works

Ackermann, James (1949), '"Ars sine Scientia nihil Est". Gothic Theory of Architecture at the Cathedral of Milan', *ArtB* 31: 84–111

Albrecht, Uwe (1986), *Von der Burg zum Schloss. Französische Schlossbaukunst im Spätmittelalter*, Worms

Albrecht, Uwe (1995), *Der Adelssitz im Mittelalter. Studien zum Verhältnis von Architektur und Lebensform in Nord- und Westeuropa*, Berlin and Munich

Białostocki, J. (1972), *Spätmittelalter und Beginnende Neuzeit*, Berlin (vol. VII Propyläen Kunstgeschichte, ed. K. Bittel, J. Fontein, H. Keller *et al.*, 8 vols.)

Binski, Paul (1995), *Westminster Abbey and the Plantagenets*, Yale

Bony, Jean (1979), *The English Decorated Style. Gothic Architecture Transformed 1250–1350*, Oxford

Boucher, François (1976), 'Micro-Architecture as the "Idea" of Gothic Theory and Style', *Gesta* 15: 71–89

Branner, Robert (1965), *St Louis and the Court Style*, London

Braunfels, W. (1953), *Mittelalterliche Stadtbaukunst in der Toskana*, 4th edn, Berlin

Braunfels, Wolfgang (1981), *Die Kunst im Heiligen Römischen Reich Deutscher Nation*, III, *Reichstädte, Grafschaften, Reichsklöster*, Munich

Clasen, Karl Heinz (1958), *Deutsche Gewölbe der Spätgotik*, Berlin

Colvin, Howard *et al.* (1963), *The History of the King's Works*, I: *The Middle Ages*, London

Crossley, Paul (1985), *Gothic Architecture in the Reign of Kasimir the Great*, Cracow

Durliat, Marcel (1962), *L'art dans le Royaume de Majorque*, Toulouse

Frankl, Paul (1962), *Gothic Architecture*, Pelican History of Art, Harmondsworth

Freigang, Christian (1992), *Imitare Ecclesias Nobiles: Die Kathedralen von Narbonne, Toulouse und Rodez und die Nordfranzösische Rayonnantgotik im Languedoc*, Worms

Frugoni, Chiara (1991), *A Distant City. Images of Urban Experience in the Medieval World*, Princeton

Gibbs, Robert (1989), *Tomaso de Modena, Painting in Emilia and the March of Treviso 1340–1380*, London

Górski, Karol (1973), *Dzieje Malborka*, Danzig

Gross, Werner (1948), *Die Abendländische Architektur um 1300*, Stuttgart

Harvey, John (1978), *The Perpendicular Style, 1330–1485*, London

Klotz, Heinz (1966), 'Deutsche und Italienische Baukunst im Trecento', *Mitteilungen des Kunsthistorischen Instituts in Florenz* 12: 171–206

Larner, John (1971), *Culture and Society in Italy 1290–1420*, London

Lavedan, Pierre (1935), *L'architecture religieuse en Catalogne, Valence et Baléares*, Paris

Leedy, Walter (1980), *Fan Vaulting. A Study of Form, Technology and Meaning*, Santa Monica

Lindley, Phillip (1986), 'The Imagery of the Octagon at Ely', *JBAA* 139: 75–99

Middeldorf-Kosegarten, Antje (1970), 'Zur Bedeutung der Sieneser Domkuppel', *Münchener Jahrbuch der bildenden Kunst* 21: 73–98

Middeldorf-Kosegarten, Antje (1984), *Sienesische Bildhauer am Duomo Vecchio. Studien zum Skulptur in Siena 1250–1330*, Munich

Nagel, G. (1971), *Das mittelalterliche Kaufhaus und seine Stellung in der Stadt*, Berlin

Nussbaum, Norbert (1994), *Deutsche Kirchenbaukunst der Gotik*, Darmstadt

Die Parler und der Schöne Stil 1350–1400. Europäische Kunst unter den Luxemburgern (1978), ed. A. Legner, 4 vols., Cologne

Platt, Colin (1982), *The Castle in Medieval England and Wales*, London

Romanini, A.M. (1973), 'Architettura', in *Il duomo di Milano*, Milan, pp. 97–232

Rubinstein, Nicolai (1995), *The Palazzo Vecchio, 1298–1532. Government, Architecture and Imagery in the Civic Palace of the Florentine Republic*, Oxford

Schenkluhn, Wolfgang (1985), *Ordines Studentes. Aspekte zur Kirchenarchitektur der Dominikener und Franziskaner im 13 Jahrhundert*, Berlin

Schürenberg, Lisa (1934), *Die kirchliche Baukunst in Frankreich zwischen 1270 und 1380*, Berlin

Skibiński, Szczęsny (1982), *Kaplice na Zamku Wysokim w Malborku*, Poznań

Stejskal, Karol (1978), *European Art in the Fourteenth Century*, Prague

Toker, Franklin (1978), 'Florence Cathedral: The Design Stage', *ArtB* 60: 214–31

Toker, Franklin (1983), 'Arnolfo's S. Maria de Fiore: A Working Hypothesis', *JSAH* 42: 101–20

Trachtenberg, Marvin (1971), *The Campanile of Florence Cathedral. 'Giotto's Tower'*, New York

Trachtenberg, Marvin (1988), 'What Brunelleschi Saw: Monument and Site at the Palazzo Vecchio in Florence', *JSAH* 47: 14–44

Trachtenberg, Marvin (1989), 'Archaeology, Merriment, and Murder, the First Cortile of the Palazzo Vecchio and its Transformations in the Late Florentine Republic', *ArtB* 71: 565–609

Trachtenberg, Marvin (1991), 'Gothic/Italian Gothic: Toward a Redefinition', *JSAH* 50: 22–37

Welch, Evelyn S. (1995), *Art and Authority in Renaissance Milan*, Yale

White, John (1966), *Art and Architecture in Italy: 1250–1400*, Pelican History of Art, Harmondsworth

Wilson, Christopher (1990), *The Gothic Cathedral. The Architecture of the Great Church 1130–1530*, London

12 LITERATURE IN ITALIAN, FRENCH AND ENGLISH: USES AND MUSES OF THE VERNACULAR

Primary sources

Boccaccio, Giovanni, *The Corbaccio*, ed. and trans. A.K. Cassell, Urbana, Chicago and London (1975)

Boccaccio, Giovanni, *Decameron*, ed. V. Branca, vol. IV in *Tutte le opere*, ed. Branca

Boccaccio, Giovanni, *Esposizioni sopra la Comedia di Dante*, ed. G. Padoan, vol VI in *Tutte le opere*, ed. Branca

Boccaccio, Giovanni, *Opere Minori in Volgare*, ed. M. Marti, 4 vols., Milan (1969–72)

Boccaccio, Giovanni, *Tutte le opere*, gen. ed. V. Branca, Milan (1967–)

Boethius, *Tractates and Consolation of Philosophy*, trans. H.F. Stewart *et al.*, London (1918)

Bonaventura, *Opera Omnia*, ed. Patres Collegii Sancti Bonaventurae, 10 vols., Quaracchi (1882–92)

Chaucer, Geoffrey, *The Riverside Chaucer*, gen. ed. L.D. Benson, 3rd edn, Oxford (1988)

Dante Alighieri, *Convivio*, ed. G. Busnelli and G. Vandelli, Florence (1957)

Dante Alighieri, *La divina commedia: testo critico della Società Dantesca Italiana*, ed. G.A. Scartazzini, Florence (1932), rev. G. Vandelli, 9th edn, Milan

Dante Alighieri, *La vita nuova*, ed. M. Barbi, Florence (1932)

Dante Alighieri, *De vulgari eloquentia*, ed. A. Marigo, 3rd edn, Florence (1957)

Deschamps, Eustache, *Œuvres complètes*, ed. A. Queux de Saint-Hilaire and G. Raynaud, 11 vols., Paris (1878–1904)

Dominici, Giovanni, *Lucula Noctis*, ed. E. Hunt, Notre Dame (1940)

Froissart, Jean, *Chroniques*, ed. S. Luce *et al.*, 15 vols., continuing, Paris (1869–1975)

Gower, John, *Complete Works*, ed. G. C. Macaulay, 4 vols., Oxford (1899–1902)

Langland, William, *Piers Plowman by William Langland: An Edition of the C-Text*, ed. D. A. Pearsall, London (1978)

Latini, Brunetto, *La rettorica*, ed. F. Maggini, Florence (repr. 1968)

Machaut, Guillaume de, *Le Jugement du Roy de Behaigne and Remède de Fortune*, ed. J.I. Wimsatt *et al.*, Athens, Ga., and London (1988)

Petrarch, Francesco, *Le familiari*, ed. V. Rossi and U. Bosco, 4 vols., Florence (1933–42)

Petrarch, Francesco, *Prose*, ed. G. Martellotti *et al.*, Milan and Naples (1955)

Pisan, Christine de, *Le livre du chemin de long estude*, ed. R. Püschel, Berlin and Paris (1883)

Pisan, Christine de, *Le livre de la Mutacion de Fortune*, ed. S. Solente, Paris (1959)

Polychronicon Ranulphi Higden, ed. C. Babington, II, RS 41b, London (1869)

Ruiz, Juan, *Libro de buen amor*, Princeton, N.J. (1965)

Secondary works

Antonelli, R. *et al.* (eds.), *Letteratura Italiana*, ed. A.A. Rosa, I: *L'età medievale*, Turin.

Auerbach, E. (1965), *Literary Language and its Public in Late Latin Antiquity and in the Middle Ages*, trans. R. Manheim, New York

Bahr, E. (ed.) (1987), *Geschichte der Deutschen Literatur*, I: *Mittelalter bis Barock*, Tübingen

Bennett, J.A.W. (1986), *Middle English Literature*, ed. D. Gray, Oxford

Blake, N.F. (1985), *The Textual Tradition of the Canterbury Tales*, London

Boitani, P. (1984), *Chaucer and the Imaginary World of Fame*, Cambridge and New York

Borgstädt, E. and McGinn, B. (1986), *Meister Eckhart, c.1260–1329*, New York

Bosco, U. (ed.) (1970–8), *Enciclopedia Dantesca*, 5 vols. and Appendix, Rome

Boyce, G.C. (1949), 'Erfurt Schools and Scholars in the Thirteenth Century', *Speculum* 24: 1–18

Brewer, D.S. (1978), *Chaucer. The Critical Heritage*, I: *1385–1837*, London

Brownlee, K. (1984), *Poetic Identity in Guillaume de Machaut*, Madison, Wisc.

Bühler, C. (1938), 'A Lollard Tract on Translating the Bible into English', *Medium Aevum* 7: 167–83

Burrow, J.A. (1982), *Medieval Writers and their Work. Middle English Literature and its Background 1100–1500*, Oxford

Burrow, J.A. and Turville-Petre, T. (eds.) (1992), *A Book of Middle English*, Oxford

Chartier, R. (1989), 'The Practical Impact of Writing', in R. Chartier (ed.), *Passions of the Renaissance* (*A History of Private Life*, III, gen. eds. P. Ariès and G. Duby), Cambridge, Mass., and London

Chaytor, H.J. (1966), *From Script to Print. An Introduction to Medieval Vernacular Literature*, repr., London

Clanchy, M.T. (1979), *From Memory to Written Record: England 1066–1307*, London; 2nd edn, Oxford (1993)

Clark, J.M. (1957), *Meister Eckhart. An Introduction . . . with an Anthology of his Sermons*, London

Coleman, J. (1981), *1350–1400. Medieval Readers and Writers*, London

Coleman, J. (1996), *Public Reading and the Reading Public in Late Medieval England and France*, Cambridge

Copeland, R. (1991), *Rhetoric, Hermeneutics and Translation in the Middle Ages. Academic Traditions and Vernacular Texts*, Cambridge

Coulter, C.C. (1944), 'The Library of the Angevin Kings at Naples', *Transactions and Proceedings of the American Philological Association* 75: 141–55

Cremona, J. (1965), 'Dante's Views on Language' in U. Limentani (ed.), *The Mind of Dante*, Cambridge, pp. 138–62

Crosby, R. (1936), 'Oral Delivery in the Middle Ages', *Speculum* 11: 88–110

Curtius, E.R. (1953), *European Literature and the Latin Middle Ages*, trans. W. Trask, New York

Davis, C.T. (1984), *Dante's Italy and Other Essays*, Philadelphia

Dazzi, M. (1964), *Il Mussato Preumanista (1261–1329). L'ambiente a l'opera*, Vicenza

Deanesly, M. (1920), *The Lollard Bible*, Cambridge

Deyermond, A. D. (1971), *A Literary History of Spain. The Middle Ages*, London and New York

Diller, G.T. (1982), 'Froissart: Patrons and Texts', in J.J.N. Palmer (ed.), *Froissart. Historian*, Woodbridge and Totowa, N.J., pp. 145–60

Eco, U. (1983), *The Name of the Rose*, trans. W. Weaver, London

Enciclopedia dantesca (1970–8), ed. U. Bosco, 5 vols. and Appendix, Rome

Fowler, D.C. (1960–1), 'John Trevisa and the English Bible', *Modern Philology* 58: 81–98

Fowler, D.C. (1977), *The Bible in Early English Literature*, London

Friederich, W.P. (1950), *Dante's Fame Abroad. 1350–1850*, Rome

Garland, H. and Garland, M. (1986), *The Oxford Companion to German Literature*, Oxford

Gibson, M.T. (ed.) (1981), *Boethius. His Life, Thought and Influence*, Oxford

Graff, H.J. (1987), *The Legacies of Literacy. Continuities and Contradictions in Western Culture and Society*, Bloomington and Indianapolis

Grande dizionario della lingua italiana (1961–), ed. G. Barberi Squarotti, Turin

Grayson, C. (1965), '*Nobilior est Vulgaris*: Latin and Vernacular in Dante's Thought', in *Centenary Essays on Dante*, Oxford, pp. 54–76

Grendler, P.F. (1989), *Schooling in Renaissance Italy. Literacy and Learning, 1300–1600*, Baltimore and London

Griffiths, J. and Pearsall, D.A. (1989), *Book Production and Publishing in Britain 1375–1475*, Cambridge

Haller, R.S. (ed. and trans.) (1973), *Literary Criticism of Dante Alighieri*, Lincoln, Nebr.

Haug, W., Jackson, T.R. and Janota, J. (eds.) (1983), *Zur deutschen Literatur und Sprache des 14. Jahrhunderts: Dubliner Colloquium 1981*, Heidelberg

Havely, N.R. (1980), *Chaucer's Boccaccio. Sources of 'Troilus' and the Knight's and Franklin's Tales*, Cambridge

Havely, N.R. (1983), 'Chaucer, Boccaccio and the Friars' in P. Boitani (ed.), *Chaucer and the Italian Trecento*, Cambridge, pp. 249–68

Hay, D. and Law, J.E. (1989), *Italy in the Age of the Renaissance, 1380–1530*, London

Hollander, R.M. (1993), *Dante's Epistle to Cangrande*, Ann Arbor, Mich.

Kelly, H.A. (1989), *Tragedy and Comedy from Dante to Pseudo-Dante*, Berkeley, Los Angeles and London

Kibre, P. (1946), 'The Intellectual Interests Reflected in Libraries of the Fourteenth Century', *JHI* 7: 257–97

Kukenheim, L. and Roussel, H. (1963), *Guide de la literature française du moyen âge*, Leiden

Lecoy de la Marche, A. (1886), *La chaire française au moyen âge*, Paris

Lesnick, D.R. (1989), *Preaching in Medieval Florence. The Social World of Franciscan and Dominican Spirituality*, Athens, Ga., and London

Levy, B.J. (ed.) (1981), *Nine Verse Sermons by Nicholas Bozon*, Oxford

Limentani, U. (1965), *The Mind of Dante*, Cambridge

McFarlane, K.B. (1973), *The Nobility of Later Medieval England. The Ford Lectures for 1953 and Related Studies*, Oxford

Marichal, R. (1964), 'Le Manuscrit', in *Dictionnaire des lettres françaises. Le moyen âge*, Paris

Matteini, N. (1958), *Il più antico oppositore politico di Dante: Guido Vernani da Rimini: testo critico del 'De reprobatione monarchiae'*, Padua

Mazzocco, A. (1993), *Linguistic Theories in Dante and the Humanists*, Leiden

Miller, J.T. (1986), *Poetic License. Authority and Authorship in Medieval and Renaissance Contexts*, New York and Oxford

Minnis, A.J. (1987), *The Medieval Boethius Studies*, Cambridge

Minnis, A.J. (1990), '*Amor* and *Auctoritas* in the Self-Commentary of Dante and Francesco da Barberino', *Poetica* 32: 25–42

Minnis, A.J. and Scott, A.B. (1991), *Medieval Literary Theory and Criticism, c. 1100–c. 1375. The Commentary Tradition*, rev. edn, Oxford

Moreno, S. (1991), 'Some Observations on the Date and Circumstances of the Fifteenth-Century Portuguese and Castilian Translations of John Gower's *Confessio Amantis*', *SELIM (Journal of the Spanish Society for Medieval English Language and Literature)* 1: 106–22

Olson, G. (1979), 'Making and Poetry in the Age of Chaucer', *Comparative Literature* 31: 272–90

Ong, W.J. (1982), *Orality and Literacy. The Technologizing of the Word*, London

Orme, N. (1973), *English Schools in the Middle Ages*, London

Osgood, C.G. (1956), *Boccaccio on Poetry*, repr., Indianapolis and New York

Owst, G.R. (1926), *Preaching in Medieval England. An Introduction to Sermon Manuscripts of the Period c. 1350–1450*, Cambridge

Palmer, J.J.N. (ed.) (1981), *Froissart. Historian*, Woodbridge

Paolazzi, C. (1989), *Dante e la Commedia nel trecento*, Milan

Parkes, M. B. (1973), 'The Literacy of the Laity', in D. Daiches and A. K. Thorlby (eds.), *The Medieval World*, Literature and Western Civilisation, II, London, pp. 555–77

Pearsall, D.A. (1988), 'Gower's Latin in the *Confessio Amantis*', in A.J. Minnis (ed.), *Latin and Vernacular. Studies in Late-Medieval Texts and Manuscripts*, York Manuscript Conferences: Proceedings Series, 1, Cambridge, pp. 12–26

Poirion, D. (1965), *Le poète et le prince. L'évolution du lyrisme courtois de Guillaume de Machaut à Charles d'Orléans*, Paris

Pratt, R.A. (1966), 'Chaucer and the Hand that Fed Him' *Speculum* 41: 619–42

Pullan, B. (1973), *A History of Early Renaissance Italy, from the Mid-Thirteenth to the Mid-Fifteenth Century*, London

Ramsay, L.C. (1983), *Chivalric Romances. Popular Literature in Medieval England*, Bloomington

Rusconi, R. (1981), *Predicazione e vita religiosa nella società italiana, da Carlo Magno alla contoriforma*, Turin

Russell, P.E. (1961), 'Robert Payn and Juan de Cuenca, Translators of the *Confessio Amantis*', *Medium Aevum* 30: 26–32

Saenger, P. (1982), 'Silent Reading: Its Impact on Late Medieval Script', *Viator* 53: 367–414

Sanchis y Sivera, J. (1932–4), *Sermons. Sant Vicent Ferrer*, 2 vols., Barcelona

Simon, E. (ed.) (1991), *The Theatre of Medieval Europe. New Research in Early Drama*, Cambridge

Smalley, B. (1960), *The English Friars and Antiquity in the Early Fourteenth Century*, Oxford

Smith, C. (1983), 'Juan Ruiz: The Book of Good Love', in B. Ford (ed.), *Medieval Literature. The European Inheritance*, Harmondsworth, pp. 275–86

Spencer, H.L. (1993), *English Preaching in the Late Middle Ages*, Oxford

Stevens, J. (1973), *Medieval Romance*, London

Taylor, P.B. and Bordier, S. (1992), 'Chaucer and the Latin Muses', *Traditio* 47: 215–32

Terry, A. (1972), *A Literary History of Spain. Catalan Literature*, London and New York

Trinkaus, C. and Oberman, H.A. (1974), *The Pursuit of Holiness*, Leiden

Vince, R.W. (ed.) (1989), *A Companion to the Medieval Theatre*, New York and London

Walker, R.M. (1971), 'Oral Delivery or Private Reading?', *Forum for Modern Language Studies* 7: 36–42

Weiss, J. (1990), *The Poet's Art. Literary Theory in Castile c.1400–60*, Oxford

Wenzel, S. (1986), *Preachers, Poets and the Early English Lyric*, Princeton, N.J.

Wicksteed, P.H. and Gardner, E.G. (1902), *Dante and Giovanni del Virgilio*, Westminster

Wilkins, H.J. (1915), *Was John Wycliffe a Negligent Pluralist? Also: John Trevisa, his Life and Work*, London

Williams, S.J. (1969), 'An Author's Role in Fourteenth-Century Book Production: Guillaume de Machaut's "Livre ou Je Met Toutes mes Choses"', *Romania* 90: 433–54

Wimsatt, J.I. (1968), *Chaucer and the French Love Poets. The Literary Background of the 'Book of the Duchess'*, Chapel Hill

Windeatt, B.A. (ed. and trans.) (1982), *Chaucer's Dream Poetry. Sources and Analogues*, Cambridge and Totowa, N.J.

Witt, R.G. (1977), 'Coluccio Salutati and the Conception of the *Poeta Theologus* in the Fourteenth Century', *RQly* 30: 538–63

Zahareas, A.N. (1965), *The Art of Juan Ruiz, Archpriest of Hita*, Madrid

Zeller, W. and Jaspert, B. (eds.) (1988), *Heinrich Seuse and Johannes Tauler. Mystiche Schriften*, Munich

13(a) ENGLAND: EDWARD II AND EDWARD III

Primary sources

le Bel, Jean, *Chronique*, ed. J. Viard and E. Déprez, 2 vols., SHF, Paris (1904–5)

Chrimes, S.B. and Brown, A.L., *Select Documents of English Constitutional History 1307–1485*, London (1964)

Higden, Ranulph, *Polychronicon*, ed. G. Babington and J.R. Lumby, RS, 41, 9 vols., London (1865–86)

Pronay, N. and Taylor, J., *Parliamentary Texts of the Later Middle Ages*, Oxford (1980)

Stubbs, W., *Select Charters and Other Illustrations of English Constitutional History*, 6th edn, Oxford (1913)

Walsingham, Thomas, *Historia Anglicana*, ed. H.T. Riley, 2 vols., RS, 28, London (1863–4)

Secondary works

Brown, A.L. (1989), *The Governance of Late Medieval England, 1272–1461*, London

Brown, R.A. (1963), 'The King's Works 1272–1485', in H.M. Colvin *et al.* (eds.), *The History of the King's Works. The Middle Ages*, 2 vols., London, 1, pp. 161–292

Buck, M.C. (1983), 'The Reform of the Exchequer, 1316–1326', *EHR* 98: 241–60

Burley, S.J. (1958), 'The Victualling of Calais', *BIHR* 31: 49–57

Cuttino, G.P. and Lyman, T.W. (1978), 'Where is Edward II?', *Speculum* 53: 522–44

Dunbabin, J. (1988), 'Government' in J.H. Burns (ed.), *The Cambridge History of Medieval Political Thought c. 350–c. 1450*, Cambridge, pp. 477–519

Duncan, A.A.M. (1988), '*Honi soit qui mal y pense*: David II and Edward III, 1346–52', *SHR* 67: 113–41

Fryde, N. (1979), *The Tyranny and Fall of Edward II 1321–1326*, Cambridge

Harriss, G.L. (1975), *King, Parliament and Public Finance in Medieval England to 1369*, Oxford

Holmes, G. (1975), *The Good Parliament*, Oxford

Jones, M. (1989), 'Relations with France, 1337–1399', in M. Jones and M. Vale (eds.), *England and her Neighbours 1066–1453. Essays in Honour of Pierre Chaplais*, London, pp. 239–58

Le Patourel, J. (1958), 'Edward III and the Kingdom of France', *History* 43: 173–89

Le Patourel, J. (1960), 'The Treaty of Brétigny, 1360', *TRHS* 5th series 10: 19–39

Maddicott, J.R. (1978), 'The County Community and the Making of Public Opinion in Fourteenth-Century England', *TRHS* 5th series 28: 27–43

Maddicott, J. R. (1987), 'The English Peasantry and the Demands of the Crown, 1294–1341', in T.H. Aston (ed.), *Landlords, Peasants and Politics in Medieval England*, Cambridge, pp. 285–359 (orig. published as *P&P*, Supplement 1, 1975)

Middleton, A.E. (1918), *Sir Gilbert de Middleton*, Newcastle upon Tyne

Ormrod, W.M. (1987a), 'Edward III and his Family', *JBS* 26: 398–442

Ormrod, W.M. (1987b), 'Edward III and the Recovery of Royal Authority in England, 1340–60', *History* 72: 4–19

Ormrod, W.M. (1990a), 'Agenda for Legislation, 1322–c. 1340', *EHR* 105: 1–33

Ormrod, W.M. (1990b), *The Reign of Edward III. Crown and Political Society in England, 1327–1377*, London

Ormrod, W.M. (1991), 'The Crown and the English Economy, 1290–1348', in B.M.S. Campbell (ed.), *Before the Black Death. Studies in the 'Crisis' of the Early Fourteenth Century*, Manchester, pp. 149–83

Phillips, J.R.S.(1986), 'Edward II and the Prophets', in W. M. Ormrod (ed.), *England in the Fourteenth Century. Proceedings of the 1985 Harlaxton Symposium*, Woodbridge, pp. 189–201

Pole-Stewart, E. (1926), 'The Interview between Philip V and Edward II at Amiens in 1320', *EHR* 41: 412–15

Postan, M.M. (1964), 'The Costs of the Hundred Years' War', *P&P* 27: 34–53; repr. in his *Essays in Medieval Agriculture and General Problems of the Medieval Economy*, Cambridge (1973), pp. 63–80

Powicke, M. (1962), *Military Obligation in Medieval England*, Oxford

Prestwich, M.C. (1972), *War, Politics and Finance under Edward I*, London

Prestwich, M.C. (1984), 'Cavalry Service in Early Fourteenth Century England', in J. Gillingham and J.C. Holt (eds.), *War and Government in the Middle Ages. Essays in Honour of J.O. Prestwich*, Woodbridge, pp. 147–58

Prestwich, M.C. (1992), 'Gilbert de Middleton and the Attack on the Cardinals 1317', in T. Reuter (ed.), *Warriors and Churchmen in the High Middle Ages. Essays Presented to Karl Leyser*, London, pp. 179–94

Putnam, B.H.(1929), 'The Transformation of the Keepers of the Peace into the Justices of the Peace, 1327–1380', *TRHS* 4th series 12: 19–48

Scammell, J. (1958), 'Robert I and the North of England', *EHR* 73: 385–403

Sherborne, J.W. (1977), 'The Costs of English Warfare with France in the Later Fourteenth Century', *BIHR* 50: 135–50

Thompson, A.H. (1933), 'Some Letters from the Register of William Zouche, Archbishop of York', in J.G. Edwards, V.H. Galbraith and E.F. Jacob (eds.), *Historical Essays in Honour of James Tait*, Manchester, pp. 327–43

Tuck, A. (1985), *Crown and Nobility 1272–1461*, London

Vale, M. (1990), *The Angevin Legacy and the Hundred Years War 1250–1340*, Oxford

Waugh, S.L. (1991), *England in the Reign of Edward III*, Cambridge

13(b): THE REIGN OF RICHARD II

The primary sources for this reign are numerous and the king himself, and the events of the years 1377–99, have attracted a great deal of historical attention. In this bibliography an attempt is made to indicate the main primary sources for the reign in their most recent and/or accessible editions and to list the most important secondary literature. The focus has been primarily on the political history of the reign and only the most obvious works dealing with Lollardy, the Peasants' Revolt, local history and Chaucerian studies have been selected. A more complete bibliography will be found in Saul (1997a) to which the author is much indebted.

Primary sources

The Ancient Kalendars and Inventories of the Treasury of His Majesty's Exchequer, ed. F. Palgrave, 3 vols, London (1836)

Annales Monasterii Sancti Albani a Johanne Amundesham, ed. H.T. Riley, 2 vols., RS, London (1870–1).

Annales Ricardi Secundi et Henrici Quarti, in J. de Trokelowe, *Chronica et Annales,* ed. H. T. Riley, RS, London (1866)

Anonimalle Chronicle 1333–81, ed. V.H. Galbraith, Manchester (1927)

A Book of London English 1384–1425, ed. R.W. Chambers and M. Daunt, Oxford (1931)

Calendar of the Cartularies of John Pyel and Adam Fraunceys, ed. S.J. O'Connor, Royal Historical Society, Camden 5th series 17, London (1993)

Calendar of Close Rolls 1377–1399, 6 vols., HMSO, London (1914–27)

Calendar of Fine Rolls 1377–1399, 3 vols., HMSO, London (1926–9)

Calendar of the Letter Books of the City of London . . . Letter Book H, ed. R. R. Sharpe, London (1907)

Calendar of Papal Registers, IV: *1362–1404,* HMSO, London (1904)

Calendar of Patent Rolls 1377–1399, 6 vols., HMSO, London (1895–1909)

Calendar of Select Plea and Memoranda Rolls of the City of London, 1381–1412, ed. A.H. Thomas, Cambridge (1932)

Chaucer Life Records, ed. M.M. Crow and C.C. Olson, Oxford (1966)

Chronicles of London, ed. C.L. Kingsford, Oxford (1905)

Chronicles of the Revolution, 1397–1400, ed. C. Given-Wilson, Manchester (1993)

Chronicon Adae de Usk, ed. E.M. Thompson, London (1904)

Chronicon Anglie 1328–1388, ed. E.M. Thompson, RS, London (1874)

Chronicon de la Traison et Mort de Richart II, ed. B. Williams, London (1846)

Chronique du Religieux de Saint-Denys, ed. L.F. Bellaguet, 6 vols., Paris (1839–52); repr. 1994, with introduction by B. Guenée

Chroniques de J. Froissart, ed. S. Luce *et al.,* 15 vols., SHF, Paris (1869–1975, continuing)

'The Dieulacres Chronicle', in M.V. Clarke and V.H. Galbraith, 'The Deposition of Richard II', *BJRL* 15 (1931), pp. 100–37

Diplomatic Correspondence of Richard II, ed. E. Perroy, Camden 3rd series, XLVIII, London (1933)

An English Chronicle of the Reigns of Richard II, Henry IV, Henry V and Henry VI, ed. J.S. Davies, Camden Soc., London (1856)

English Historical Documents 1327–1485, ed. A.R. Myers, London (1969)

Eulogium Historiarum sive Temporis, ed. F.S. Haydon, 3 vols., RS, London (1858–63)

Favent, Thomas, 'Historia sive Narracio Mirabilis Parliamenti', ed. M. McKisack, *Camden Miscellany* XIV, Camden 3rd series, XXXVII, London (1926)

Froissart, J., *Chronicles,* ed. T. Johnes, 2 vols., London (1862)

The Great Chronicle of London, ed. A.H. Thomas and I.D. Thornley, London (1938)

Historia Vitae et Regni Ricardi Secundi, ed. G.B. Stow, Philadelphia (1977)

Household Accounts from Medieval England, ed. C.M. Woolgar, 2 vols., London (1992–3)

Issues of the Exchequer, Henry III–Henry VI, ed. F. Devon, London (1847)

John of Gaunt's Register, 1372–1376, ed. S. Armitage-Smith, 2 vols., Camden 3rd series, XX–XXI, London (1911)

John of Gaunt's Register, 1379–1383, ed. E. C. Lodge and R. Somerville, 2 vols., Camden 3rd series, LVI-LVII, London (1937)

The Kirkstall Abbey Chronicles, ed. J. Taylor, Thoresby Soc., XLII, Leeds (1952)

Knighton's Chronicle 1337–1396, ed. G.H. Martin, Oxford (1995)

'A Metrical History of the Deposition of Richard II attributed to Jean Creton', ed. J. Webb, *Archaeologia* 20 (1814), pp. 1–423

Mézières, Philippe de, *Letter to King Richard II,* ed. G.W. Coopland, Liverpool (1975)

Munimenta Gildhallae, ed. H.T. Riley, 2 vols., RS, London (1858–62)

The Peasants' Revolt of 1381, ed. R.B. Dobson, 2nd edn, London (1983)

Proceedings and Ordinances of the Privy Council of England, ed. N.H. Nicolas, 7 vols., London (1834–7)

Rogeri Dymmok liber contra XII Errores et Hereses Lollardorum, ed. H.S. Cronin, London (1922)

Rotuli Parliamentorum, 7 vols., London (1767–1832)

Rymer, Thomas, *Foedera, Conventiones, Litterae etc.,* ed. G. Holmes, 20 vols., London (1704–35)

The Scrope and Grosvenor Controversy, ed. N.H. Nicolas, 2 vols., London (1832)

Select Cases in the Court of King's Bench under Richard II, Henry IV and Henry V, ed. G.O. Sayles, Selden Soc., LXXXVIII, London (1971)

Select Cases before the King's Council 1243–1482, ed. J.F. Baldwin, Selden Society, xxxv, London (1918)

Select Documents of English Constitutional History, 1307–1485, ed. S.B. Chrimes and A.L. Brown, London (1961)

Statutes of the Realm, 11 vols., London (1810–28)

Stow, John (1908), *Survey of London,* ed. C.L. Kingsford, London

Testamenta Vetusta, ed. N.H. Nicolas, 2 vols., London (1826)

The Treaty of Bayonne (1388), ed. J.J.N. Palmer and B. Powell, Exeter (1988)

Walsingham, Thomas, *Historia Anglicana,* ed. H.T. Riley, 2 vols., RS, 28, London (1863–4)

The Westminster Chronicle 1381–1394, ed. L.C. Hector and B.F. Harvey, Oxford (1982)

Secondary works

Alexander, J. and Binski P. (eds.) (1987), *The Age of Chivalry. Art in Plantagenet England, 1200–1400,* London

Alexander, J.G. (1998), 'The Portrait of Richard II in Westminster Abbey', in Gordon, Monnas and Elam (1998), pp. 197-222

Aston, M. (1960), 'Lollardy and Sedition, 1381–1431', *P&P* 17: 1–44; repr. in R. H. Hilton (ed.), *Peasants, Knights and Heretics,* Cambridge (1973), pp. 273–318

Aston, M. (1965), 'The Impeachment of Bishop Despenser', *BIHR* 38: 127–48

Aston, M. (1967), *Thomas Arundel,* Oxford

Aston, M. (1971), 'Richard II and the Wars of the Roses', in Du Boulay and Barron (1971), pp. 280–317

Aston, M. (1987), 'Wyclif and the Vernacular', in A. Hudson and M. Wilks (eds.), *From Ockham to Wyclif,* (*Studies in Church History,* Subsidia 5), pp. 281–330

Aston, M. and Richmond, C. (eds.) (1997), *Lollardy and the Gentry in the Later Middle Ages,* Stroud

Atkinson, R.L. (1923), 'Richard II and the Death of the Duke of Gloucester', *EHR* 38: 563–4

Baldwin, J.F. (1913), *The King's Council in England during the Middle Ages,* Oxford

Barker, J.R.V. (1986), *The Tournament in England 1100–1400,* Woodbridge

Barron, C.M. (1968), 'The Tyranny of Richard II', *BIHR* 41: 1–18

Barron, C.M. (1969), 'Richard Whittington: The Man behind the Myth', in A.E.J. Hollaender and W. Kellaway (eds.), *Studies in London History Presented to P.E. Jones,* London, pp. 197–248

Barron, C.M. (1971), 'The Quarrel of Richard II with London 1392–1397', in Du Boulay and Barron (1971), pp. 173–201

Barron, C.M. (1981), *Revolt in London. 11th to 14th June 1381*, London

Barron, C.M. (1985), 'The Art of Kingship: Richard II 1377–1399', *HT* 35: 30–7

Barron, C.M. (1990), 'The Deposition of Richard II', Taylor and Childs, (1990), pp. 132–49

Barron, C.M. (1993), 'Richard II: Image and Reality', in Gordon (1993), pp. 13–19

Barron, C.M. and Sutton, A. (eds.) (1994), *Medieval London Widows 1300–1500*, London

Bean, J.M.W. (1959), 'Henry IV and the Percies', *History* 44: 212–27

Bellamy, J.G. (1964–5), 'The Northern Rebellions of the Later Years of Richard II', *BJRL* 47: 254–74

Bennett, M.J. (1983), *Community, Class and Careerism. Cheshire and Lancashire Society in the Age of Sir Gawain and the Green Knight*, Cambridge

Bennett, M.J. (1998), 'Edward III's Entail and the Succession to the Crown, 1376–1471', *EHR* 113: 580–609

Binski, P. (1995), *Westminster Abbey and the Plantagenets. Kingship and the Representation of Power 1200–1400*, New Haven and London

Bird, R. (1949), *The Turbulent London of Richard II*, London

Brewer, D.S. (1973), *Chaucer*, 3rd edn, London

Brooks, N. (1985), 'The Organisation and Achievement of the Peasants of Kent and Essex in 1381', in H. Mayr-Harting and R.I. Moore (eds.), *Studies in Medieval History Presented to R.H.C. Davis*, London, pp. 247–70

Brown, R.A., Colvin, H.M. and Taylor, A.J. (eds.) (1963), *History of the King's Works. The Middle Ages*, 2 vols., London

Burrow, J.A. (1971), *Ricardian Poetry. Chaucer, Gower, Langland and the Gawain Poet*, London

Campbell, M. (1998), 'White Harts and Coronets: The Jewellery and Plate Collection of Richard II', in Gordon, Monnas and Elam (1998), pp. 95–114

Carey, H. (1992), *Courting Disaster*, London

Catto, J.I. (1981), 'Religion and the English Nobility in the Later Fourteenth century', in H. Lloyd-Jones, V. Pearl and B. Worden (eds.), *History and the Imagination. Essays in Honour of H.R. Trevor-Roper*, London, pp. 43–55

Catto, J.I. (1992), 'Wyclif and Wycliffism at Oxford, 1356–1403', in J.I. Catto and T.A.R. Evans (eds.), *The History of the University of Oxford*, II: *Late Mediaeval Oxford*, Oxford, pp. 175–261

Cavanaugh, S. (1988), 'Royal Books: King John to Richard II', *The Library* 10: 304–16

Chrimes, S.B. (1956), 'Richard II's Questions to the Judges', *Law Quarterly Review* 72: 365–90

Clarke, M.V. (1931), 'The Wilton Diptych', *Burlington Magazine* 68: 283–94; repr. in her *Fourteenth Century Studies*, ed. L.S. Sutherland and M. McKisack, Oxford (1968), pp. 272–92

Clarke, M.V (1932), 'Forfeitures and Treason in 1388', *TRHS* 4th series, 14: 65–94; repr. in ibid., pp. 115–45

Clarke, M.V. and Galbraith, V.H. (1930), 'The Deposition of Richard II', *BJRL* 14: 100–37; repr. in ibid., pp. 53–98

Clementi, D. (1971), 'Richard II's Ninth Question to the Judges', *EHR* 86: 96–113

Coleman, O. (1969), 'The Collectors of Customs in London under Richard II', in A.E.J.

Hollaender and W. Kellaway (eds.), *Studies in London History Presented to P.E. Jones,* London, pp. 181–94

Cosgrove, A. (1987), 'England and Ireland, 1399–1447', in A. Cosgrove (ed.), *A New History of Ireland,* II: *Medieval Ireland, 1169–1534,* Oxford, pp. 525–32

Crook, D. (1987), 'Derbyshire and the English Rising of 1381', *HR* 60: 9–23

Crook, D. (1991), 'Central England and the Revolt of the Earls', *HR* 64: 403–10

Curtis, E. (1927a), *Richard II in Ireland, 1394–5, and the Submission of the Irish Chiefs,* Oxford

Curtis, E. (1927b), 'Unpublished Letters from Richard II in Ireland', *PRIA* 37: 276–303

Dahmus, J. (1966), *William Courtenay, Archbishop of Canterbury, 1381–1396,* Philadelphia

Davies, R.G. (1971), 'Some Notes from the Register of Henry de Wakefield, Bishop of Worcester, on the Political Crisis of 1386–1388', *EHR* 86: 547–58

Davies, R.G. (1975a), 'Alexander Neville, Archbishop of York, 1374–1388', *Yorkshire Archaeological Journal* 47: 87–101

Davies, R.G. (1975b), 'Richard II and the Church in the Years of "Tyranny"', *JMH* 1: 329–62

Davies, R.G. (1976), 'The Episcopate and the Political Crisis in England of 1386–1388', *Speculum* 51: 659–93

Davies, R.R. (1971), 'Richard II and the Principality of Chester', in Du Boulay and Barron (1971), pp. 256–79

Dobson, R.B. (1989), 'Beverley in Conflict: Archbishop Alexander Neville and the Minster Clergy, 1381–8', in C. Wilson (ed.), *Medieval Art and Architecture in the East Riding of Yorkshire,* Brit. Arch. Assn., 9, London, pp. 149–64

Du Boulay, F.R.H. and Barron, C.M. (1971), *The Reign of Richard II. Essays in Honour of May McKisack,* London

Dyer, C. (1984), 'The Social and Economic Background to the Rural Revolt of 1381', in Hilton and Aston (1984), pp. 9–42

Eberle, P.J. (1985), 'The Politics of Courtly Style at the Court of Richard II', in G.S. Burgess and R.A. Taylor (eds.), *The Spirit of the Court. Selected proceedings of the Fourth Congress of the International Courtly Literature Society,* Woodbridge, pp. 168–78

Edwards, J.G. (1925), 'The Parliamentary Committee of 1398', *EHR* 40: 321–33; repr. in E.B. Fryde and E. Miller (eds.), *Historical Studies of the English Parliament,* I, Cambridge (1970), pp. 316–28

Emden, A.B. (1957–9), *A Biographical Register of the University of Oxford to AD 1500,* 3 vols., Oxford

Emden, A.B. (1963), *A Biographical Register of the University of Cambridge to 1500,* Cambridge

Faith, R. (1984), 'The "Great Rumour" of 1377 and Peasant Ideology', in Hilton and Aston (1984), pp. 43–75

Ferris, S. (1974), 'Chaucer, Richard II, Henry IV and 13 October', in B. Rowland (ed.), *Chaucer and Middle English Studies in Honour of Rossell Hope Robbins,* London, pp. 210–17

Fisher, J.H. (1965), *John Gower, Moral Philosopher and Friend of Chaucer,* London

Frame, R. (1975), 'English Officials and Irish Chiefs in the Fourteenth Century', *EHR* 90: 748–77

Fryde, E.B. (1981), *The Great Revolt of 1381,* Historical Association, London

Galbraith, V.H. (1942), 'A New Life of Richard II', *History* 26: 223–39

Galbraith, V.H. (1971), 'Thoughts about the Peasants' Revolt', in Du Boulay and Barron (1971), pp. 46–57

Gillespie, J.L. (1975), 'Thomas Mortimer and Thomas Molineux; Radcot Bridge and the Appeal of 1397', *Albion* 7: 161–73

Gillespie, J.L. (1985), 'Ladies of the Fraternity of St George and of the Society of the Garter', *Albion* 17: 259–78

Gillespie, J.L. (1987), 'Richard II's Knights: Chivalry and Patronage', *JMH* 13: 143–59

Gillespie, J.L. (ed.) (1997a), *The Age of Richard II*, Stroud

Gillespie, J.L. (1997b), 'Richard II: King of Battles?', in Gillespie (1997a), pp. 139–64

Gillingham, J. (1987), 'Crisis or Continuity? The Structure of Royal Authority in England 1396–1422', in R. Schneider (ed.), *Das Spätmittelalterliche Königtum im Europäischen Vergleich*, Sigmaringen, pp. 59–80

Given-Wilson, C. (1978), 'Richard II and his Grandfather's Will', *EHR* 93: 320–7

Given-Wilson, C. (1986), *The Royal Household and the King's Affinity. Service Politics and Finance in England 1360–1413*, New Haven and London

Given-Wilson, C. (1993a), 'Adam Usk, the Monk of Evesham and the Parliament of 1397–8', *HR* 66: 329–35

Given-Wilson, C. (1993b), 'The Manner of King Richard's Renunciation: A "Lancastrian Narrative"?', *EHR* 108: 365–70

Given-Wilson, C. (1994), 'Richard II, Edward II and the Lancastrian Inheritance', *EHR* 109: 553–71

Goodman, A. (1971), *The Loyal Conspiracy. The Lords Appellant under Richard II*, London

Goodman, A. (1992), *John of Gaunt. The Exercise of Princely Power in Fourteenth-Century Europe*, London

Goodman, A. and Gillespie, J.L. (1999), *Richard II: The Art of Kingship*, London

Gordon, D. (1992), 'A New Discovery in the Wilton Diptych', *Burlington Magazine* 134: 662–7

Gordon, D. (ed.) (1993), *Making and Meaning. The Wilton Diptych*, London

Gordon, D., Monnas, L. and Elam C. (eds.) (1998), *The Regal Image of Richard II and the Wilton Diptych*, London

Gransden, A. (1982), *Historical Writing in England*, II: *c.1307 to the Early Sixteenth Century*, London

Grant, A. (1992), 'The Otterburn War from the Scottish Point of View', in A. Tuck and A. Goodman (eds.), *War and Border Societies in the Middle Ages*, London, pp. 30–64

Green, R.F. (1976), 'King Richard II's Books Revisited', *The Library* 31: 235–9

Green, R.F. (1980), *Poets and Principleasers. Literature and the English Court in the Late Middle Ages*, Toronto

Hansen, H.M. (1980), 'The Peasants' Revolt of 1381 and the Chronicles', *JMH* 6: 393–415

Harvey, B.F. (1965), 'Draft Letters Patent of Manumission and Pardon for the Men of Somerset', *EHR* 80: 89–91

Harvey, J.H. (1961), 'The Wilton Diptych – a Re-Examination', *Archaeologia* 98: 1–28

Harvey, J.H. (1967), *The Plantagenets*, London

Harvey, J.H. (1971), 'Richard II and York', in Du Boulay and Barron (1971), pp. 202–17

Hector, L.C. (1953), 'An Alleged Hysterical Outburst of Richard II', *EHR* 68: 62–5

Hilton, R.H. (1962), 'Peasant Movements in England before 1381', *EcHR* 2nd series 2 (1949), reprinted in E.M. Carus-Wilson (ed.), *Essays in Economic History*, London II, pp. 73–90

Hilton, R.H. (1973), *Bond Men Made Free. Medieval Peasant Movements and the English Rising of 1381*, London

Hilton, R.H. and Aston, T.H. (1984), *The English Rising of 1381*, Cambridge

Holmes, G.A. (1957), *The Estates of the Higher Nobility in Fourteenth-Century England*, Cambridge

Holmes, G.A. (1975), *The Good Parliament of 1376*, Oxford

Holt, R. (1985), 'Thomas of Woodstock and Events at Gloucester in 1381', *BIHR* 58: 237–42

Housley, N. (1983), 'The Bishop of Norwich's Crusade, May 1383', *HT* 33: 15–20

Hudson, A. (1982), 'Lollardy: The English Heresy?', *SCH* 18: 261–83; repr. in her *Lollards and their Books*, London (1985), pp. 141–63

Hutchison, H.F. (1961), 'Shakespeare and Richard II', *HT* 11: 236–44

Ilg, U. (1994), 'Ein wiederentdecktes Inventar der Goldschmiedearbeiten Richards II von England und seine Bedeutung für die ikonographie des Wiltondiptychons', *Pantheon* 52: 10–16

James, M.K. (1956), 'Gilbert Maghfield, a London Merchant of the Fourteenth Century', *EcHR* 2nd series 8: 364–76

Johnston, D.B. (1980), 'Richard II and the Submissions of Gaelic Ireland', *IHS* 12: 1–20

Johnston, D.B. (1981), 'The Interim Years: Richard II and Ireland, 1395–1399', in J.F. Lydon (ed.), *England and Ireland in the Later Middle Ages. Essays in Honour of Jocelyn Otway-Ruthven*, Dublin, pp. 175–93

Johnston, D.B. (1983a), 'The Draft Indenture of Thomas Duke of Gloucester, as Lieutenant of Ireland, 1391', *Journal of the Society of Archivists* 7: 173–82

Johnston, D.B. (1983b), 'Richard II's Departure from Ireland, July 1399', *EHR* 98: 785–805

Jones, M. (1970), *Ducal Brittany 1364–1399*, Oxford

Jones, M. (1972), 'The Ransom of Jean de Bretagne, Count of Penthièvre: An Aspect of English Foreign Policy, 1386–8', *BIHR* 45: 7–26

Jones, R.H. (1968), *The Royal Policy of Richard II. Absolutism in the Later Middle Ages*, Oxford

Jones, S.R. (ed.) (1997), *The Government of Medieval York. Essays in Commemoration of the 1396 Royal Charter*, Borthwick Institute of Historical Research, York

Justice, S. (1994), *Writing and Rebellion. England in 1381*, Berkeley

Keen, M. (1973), *England in the Later Middle Ages*, London

Keen, M. (1986), 'Wyclif, the Bible and Transubstantiation', in A. Kenny (ed.), *Wyclif in his Times*, Oxford, pp. 1–16

Keen, M. (1998), 'The Wilton Diptych: the Case for a Crusading Context', in Gordon, Monnas and Elam (1998), pp. 189–96

Kipling, G. (1986), 'Richard II's "Sumptuous Pageants" and the Idea of the Civic Triumph', in D.M. Bergeron (ed.), *Pageantry in the Shakespearean Theater*, Athens, Ga., pp. 83–103

Kriehn, G. (1901–2), 'Studies in the Sources of the Society Revolt in 1381', *AmHR* 7: 254–85 and 458–84

Lancashire, I. (1984), *Dramatic Texts and Records*, Cambridge

Lewis, N.B. (1926), 'The "Continual Council" in the Early Years of Richard II, 1377–80', *EHR* 41: 241–51

Lindenbaum, S. (1990), 'The Smithfield Tournament of 1390', *JMRS* 20: 1–20

Lindley, P. (1998), 'Absolutism and Regal Image in Ricardian Sculpture', in Gordon, Monnas and Elam (1998), pp. 61–83

Loomis, R.S. (1969), 'The Library of Richard II', in E.B. Atwood and A.A. Hill (eds.), *Studies in Language Literature and Culture of the Middle Ages and Later*, Austin, Tex., pp. 273–8

Lydon, J.F. (1963), 'Richard II's Expeditions to Ireland', *Journal of the Royal Society of Antiquaries of Ireland* 93: 135–49

McFarlane, K.B. (1952), *John Wycliffe and the Beginnings of English Nonconformity*, London

McFarlane, K.B. (1972), *Lancastrian Kings and Lollard Knights*, Oxford

McFarlane, K.B. (1973), *The Nobility of Later Medieval England*, Oxford

McHardy, A. (1997), 'Haxey's Case, 1397: The Petition and Presenter Reconsidered', in Gillespie (1997a), pp. 93–114

McKisack, M. (1959), *The Fourteenth Century 1307–1399*, Oxford

McNiven, P. (1969–70), 'The Cheshire Rising of 1400', *BJRL* 52: 375–96

McNiven, P. (1994), 'Rebellion, Sedition and the Legend of Richard II's Survival in the Reigns of Henry IV and Henry V', *BJRL* 76: 93–117

Martin, G.H. (1997a), 'Narrative Sources for the Reign of Richard II', in Gillespie (1997a), pp. 51–69

Martin, G.H. (1997b), 'Knighton's Lollards', in Aston and Richmond (1997), pp. 28–40

Mathew, G. (1968), *The Court of Richard II*, London

Meyer, P. (1881), 'L'Entrevue d'Ardres', *ABSHF* 18: 211–24

Mitchell, S. (1998), 'Richard II and the Cult of Saints', in Gordon, Monnas and Elam (1998), pp. 115–24

Monnas, L. (1998), 'Fit for a King: Embroidered and Woven Silk Worn at the Court of Richard II', in Gordon, Monnas and Elam (1998), pp. 165–77

Morgan, P. (1987), *War and Society in Medieval Cheshire, 1277–1403*, Chetham Soc., 3rd series, XXXIV, Manchester

Morgan, P. (1995), 'Henry IV and the Shadow of Richard II', in R. Archer (ed.), *Crown, Government and People in the Fifteenth Century*, Stroud, pp. 1–31

Mott, R.A.K. (1974), 'A Study in the Distribution of Patronage, 1389–99', *Proceedings of Leeds Philosophical and Literary Society* 15: 113–33

Mott, R.A.K. (1991), 'Richard II and the Crisis of July 1397', in I. Wood and G.A. Loud (eds.), *Church and Chronicle in the Middle Ages. Essays presented to John Taylor*, London, pp. 165–77

Myers, A.R. (1969), 'The Wealth of Richard Lyons', in T.A. Sandquist and M.R. Powicke (eds.), *Essays in Medieval History Presented to Bertie Wilkinson*, Toronto, pp. 301–29

Myres, J.N.L. (1927), 'The Campaign of Radcot Bridge in December 1387', *EHR* 42: 20–33

Nightingale, P. (1989), 'Capitalists, Crafts and Constitutional Change in Late Fourteenth-Century London', *P&P* 124: 3–25

Nightingale, P. (1995), *A Medieval Mercantile Community: The Grocers' Company and the Politics and Trade of London 1000–1485*, New Haven and London

Norton, C. (1997), 'Richard II and York Minster', in Jones (1997), pp. 56–87

Oman, C. (1969), *The Great Revolt of 1381,* 2nd edn, ed. E.B. Fryde, Oxford

Ormrod, W.M. (1990), 'The Peasants' Revolt and the Government of England', *JBS* 29: 1–30

Otway-Ruthven, A.J. (1968), *A History of Medieval Ireland,* London

Palmer, J.J.N. (1966a), 'The Anglo-French Peace Negotiations, 1390–1396', *TRHS* 5th series 16: 81–94

Palmer, J.J.N. (1966b), 'Articles for a Final Peace between England and France, 16 June 1393', *BIHR* 39: 180–5

Palmer, J.J.N. (1968), 'England and the Great Western Schism, 1388–1399', *EHR* 83: 771–5

Palmer, J.J.N. (1969), 'The Impeachment of Michael de la Pole in 1386', *BIHR* 42: 96–101

Palmer, J.J.N. (1971a), 'The Background to Richard II's Marriage to Isabel of France, 1396', *BIHR* 44: 1–17

Palmer, J.J.N. (1971b), 'The Parliament of 1385 and the Constitutional Crisis of 1386', *Speculum* 46: 477–90

Palmer, J.J.N. (1971c), 'The War Aims of the Protagonists and the Negotiations for Peace', in K. Fowler (ed.), *The Hundred Years War,* London, pp. 51–74

Palmer, J.J.N. (1972), *England, France and Christendom, 1377–99,* London

Palmer, J.J.N. (1978–9), 'The Authorship, Date and Historical Value of the French Chronicles on the Lancastrian Revolution', *BJRL* 61: 145–81 and 398–421

Palmer, J.J.N. (ed.) (1981), *Froissart: Historian,* Woodbridge

Patterson, L. (1992), 'Court Politics and the Invention of Literature: The Case of Sir John Clanvowe', in D. Aers (ed.), *Culture and History, 1350–1600. Essays in English Communities, Identities and Writing,* Detroit, pp. 7–41

Pearsall, D. (1992), *The Life of Geoffrey Chaucer,* Oxford

Perroy, E. (1933), *L'Angleterre et le Grand Schisme d'Occident,* Paris

Philpotts, C.J. (1990), 'John of Gaunt and English Policy towards France, 1389–1395', *JMH* 16: 363–85

Plucknett, T.F.T. (1952), 'State Trials under Richard III', *TRHS* 5th series 2: 159–71

Pollard, A.F. (1938), 'The Authorship and Value of the Anonimalle Chronicle', *EHR* 53: 577–605

Post, J.B. (1981), 'The Obsequies of John of Gaunt', *Guildhall Studies in London History* 5: 1–12

Powell, E. (1896), *The Rising in East Anglia,* Cambridge

Prestwich, M. (1984), 'An Estimate by the Commons of Royal Revenue in England under Richard II', *Parliamentary History* 3: 147–55

Rawcliffe, C. (1994), 'Margaret Stodeye, Lady Philipot (d.1431)', in Barron and Sutton (1994), pp. 85–98

Richardson, H.G. (1936), 'Heresy and the Lay Power under Richard II', *EHR* 51: 1–25

Richmond, C.F. (1971), 'The War at Sea', in K. Fowler (ed.), *The Hundred Years War,* London, pp. 96–121

Richmond, C.F. (1990), *The Paston Family in the Fifteenth Century. The First Phase,* Cambridge

Rickert, E. (1926–7), 'Documents and Records: A Leaf from a Fourteenth-Century Letter Book', *Modern Philology* 24: 111–19

Rickert, E. (1933), 'Richard II's Books', *The Library* 4th series 13: 144–7

Rogers, A. (1964), 'Parliamentary Appeals of Treason in the Reign of Richard II', *American Journal of Legal History* 8: 95–124

Roskell, J.S. (1965), *The Commons and their Speakers in English Parliaments, 1376–1523,* Manchester

Roskell, J.S. (1984), *The Impeachment of Michael de la Pole, Earl of Suffolk, in 1386,* Manchester

Roskell, J.S., Clark, Linda and Rawcliffe, Carole (eds.) (1992), *The History of Parliament. The House of Commons 1386–1421,* 4 vols, Stroud

Ross, C.D. (1956), 'Forfeiture for Treason in the Reign of Richard II', *EHR* 71: 560–75

Royal Commission on Historical Monuments. An Inventory of the Historical Monuments in London, 1: *Westminster Abbey* (1924), London

Russell, P.E. (1955), *The English Intervention in Spain and Portugal in the Time of Edward III and Richard II,* Oxford

Sanderlin, S. (1987), 'Chaucer and Ricardian Politics', *Chaucer Review* 22: 171–84

Sandquist, T.A. (1969), 'The Holy Oil of St Thomas of Canterbury', in T.A. Sandquist and M.R. Powicke (eds.), *Essays in Medieval History Presented to Bertie Wilkinson,* Toronto, pp. 330–44

Saul, N. (1990), 'The Commons and the Abolition of Badges', *Parliamentary History* 9: 302–15

Saul, N. (1995), 'Richard II and the Vocabulary of Kingship', *EHR* 110: 854–77

Saul, N. (1996), 'Richard II and Westminster Abbey', in W.J. Blair and B. Golding (eds.), *The Cloister and the World: Essays in Medieval History in Honour of Barbara Harvey,* Oxford, pp. 196–218

Saul, N. (1997a), *Richard II,* New Haven and London

Saul, N. (1997b), 'Richard II, York and the Evidence of the King's Itinerary', in Gillespie (1997a), pp. 71–92

Saul, N. (1997c), 'Richard II and the City of York', in Jones (1997), pp. 1–13

Sayles, G.O. (1979), 'Richard II in 1381 and 1399', *EHR* 94: 820–9; repr. in Sayles (1982), pp. 291–300

Sayles, G.O. (1981), 'The Deposition of Richard II: Three Lancastrian Narratives', *BIHR* 54: 313–30; repr. in ibid., pp. 313–30

Sayles, G.O. (1982), 'King Richard II of England: A Fresh Look', in his *Scripta Diversa,* London, pp. 277–83

Scattergood, V.J. (1983), 'Literary Culture at the Court of Richard II', in Scattergood and Sherborne (1983), pp. 29–43

Scattergood, V.J. and Sherborne, J.W. (eds.) (1983), *English Court Culture in the Later Middle Ages,* London

Sherborne, J.W. (1967), 'The English Navy: Shipping and Manpower, 1369–89', *P&P* 37: 163–75; repr. in his *War, Politics and Culture in Fourteenth-Century England,* ed. A. Tuck, London (1994), pp. 29–39

Sherborne, J.W. (1975), 'Richard II's Return to Wales, July 1399', *WHR,* 7: 389–402; repr. in ibid., 119–29

Sherborne, J.W. (1977), 'The Cost of English Warfare with France in the Later Fourteenth Century', *BIHR* 50: 135–50; repr. in ibid., 55–70

Sherborne, J.W. (1981), 'Charles VI and Richard II', in Palmer (1981), pp. 50–63; repr. in ibid., 155–70

Sherborne, J.W. (1988), 'Perjury and the Lancastrian Revolution of 1399', *WHR* 14: 217–41; repr. in ibid., 131–53

Sherborne, J.W. (1990), 'The Defence of the Realm and the Impeachment of Michael de la Pole in 1386', in Taylor and Childs (1990), pp. 97–116; repr. in ibid., 97–117

Somerset, F. (1977), 'Answering the *Twelve Conclusions:* Dymmok's Halfhearted Gestures towards Publication', in Aston and Richmond (1997), pp. 52–76

Stamp, A.E. (1923), 'Richard II and the Death of the Duke of Gloucester', *EHR* 38: 249–51

Starkey, D. (1981), 'The Age of the Household: Politics, Society and the Arts, c. 1350–c. 1550', in S. Medcalf (ed.), *The Later Middle Ages,* London, pp. 225–305

Steel, A. (1934–5), 'The Sheriffs of Cambridgeshire and Huntingdonshire in the Reign of Richard II', *Proceedings of the Cambridgeshire Antiquarian Society* 36: 1–34

Steel, A. (1941), *Richard II,* Cambridge

Storey, R.L. (1957), 'The Wardens of the Marches of England towards Scotland, 1377–1489', *EHR* 72: 593–615

Storey, R.L. (1971), 'Liveries and Commissions of the Peace, 1388–90', in Du Boulay and Barron (1971), pp. 131–52

Stow, G.B. (1973), 'The *Vita Ricardi* as a Source for the Reign of Richard II', *Vale of Evesham Historical Society Research Papers* 4: 63–75

Stow, G.B. (1984), 'Richard II in Thomas Walsingham's Chronicles', *Speculum* 59: 68–102

Stow, G.B. (1985), 'Richard II in Jean Froissart's *Chroniques*', *JMH,* 11: 333–45

Stow, G.B. (1989), 'Chronicles versus Records: The Character of Richard II', in J.S. Hamilton and P. Bradley (eds.), *Documenting the Past. Essays in Medieval History Presented to G.P. Cuttino,* Woodbridge, pp. 155–76

Stow, G.B. (1993), 'Richard II in John Gower's *Confessio Amantis:* Some Historical Perspectives', *Medievalia* 16: 3–31

Stow, G.B. (1995), 'Richard II and the Invention of the Pocket Handkerchief, *Albion* 27: 221–35

Strohm, P. (1989), *Social Chaucer,* Cambridge, Mass.

Strohm, P. (1992), *Hochon's Arrow: The Social Imagination of Fourteenth-Century Texts,* Princeton, N.J.

Strohm, P. (1996), 'The Trouble with Richard: The Reburial of Richard II and Lancastrian Symbolic Strategy', *Speculum* 71: 87–111

Stubbs, W. (1875–8), *The Constitutional History of England,* 3 vols., Oxford

Suggett, H. (1947), 'A Letter Describing Richard II's Settlement with the City of London', *EHR* 72: 209–13

Tait, J. (1902), 'Did Richard II Murder the Duke of Gloucester?', in T.F. Tout and J. Tait (eds.), *Historical Essays by Members of the Owens College, Manchester,* Manchester, pp. 193–216

Taylor, J. (1971), 'Richard II's Views on Kingship', *Proceedings of the Leeds Philosophical and Literary Society* 14: 190–205

Taylor, J. (1987), *English Historical Literature in the Fourteenth Century*, Oxford

Taylor, J. (1990), 'The Good Parliament and its Sources', in Taylor and Childs (1990), pp. 81–96

Taylor, J. and Childs, W. (eds.) (1990), *Politics and Crisis in Fourteenth Century England*, Gloucester

Theilmann, J.M. (1976), 'Stubbs, Shakespeare and Recent Historians of Richard II', *Albion* 8: 107–24

Theilmann, J.M. (1990), 'Political Canonization and Political Symbolism in Medieval England', *JBS* 29: 241–66

Thomson, J.A.F. (1997), 'Knightly Piety and the Margins of Lollardy', in Aston and Richmond (1997), pp. 95–111

Tout, T.F. (1920–33), *Chapters in the Administrative History of Medieval England*, 6 vols., Manchester

Tuck, A. (1968), 'Richard II and the Border Magnates', *Northern History* 3: 27–52

Tuck, A. (1969), 'The Cambridge Parliament, 1388', *EHR* 84: 225–43

Tuck, A. (1970), 'Anglo-Irish Relations, 1382–1393', *PRIA* 69: 15–31

Tuck, A. (1971), 'Richard II's System of Patronage', in Du Boulay and Barron (1971), pp. 1–20

Tuck, A. (1973), *Richard II and the English Nobility*, London

Tuck, A. (1984), 'Nobles, Commons and the Great Revolt of 1381', in Hilton and Aston (1984), Cambridge, pp. 194–212

Tuck, A. (1990), 'Richard II and the Hundred Years War', in Taylor and Childs (1990), pp. 117–31

Tyerman, C. (1988), *England and the Crusades 1095–1588*, Chicago

Walker, S. (1983), 'Lancaster v. Dallingridge: A Franchisal Dispute in Fourteenth-Century Sussex', *Sussex Archaeological Collections* 121: 87–94

Walker, S. (1990), *The Lancastrian Affinity 1361–1399*, Oxford

Walker, S. (1991), 'Letters to the Dukes of Lancaster in 1381 and 1399', *EHR* 106: 68–79

Walker, S. (1995), 'Richard's II's Views on Kingship', in R.E. Archer and S. Walker (eds.), *Rulers and Ruled in Late Medieval England: Essays Presented to Gerald Harriss*, London, pp. 49–63

Wallon, H. (1864), *Richard II*, 2 vols, Paris

Warren, W.L. (1959), 'A Re-Appraisal of Simon Sudbury, Bishop of London (1361–1375) and Archbishop of Canterbury (1375–1381)', *JEH* 10: 139–52

Wathey, A. (1989), *Music in the Royal and Noble Households in Late Medieval England*, New York and London

Webster, B. (1984), 'The Community of Kent in the Reign of Richard II', *Archaeologia Cantiana* 99: 217–29

Whittingham, S. (1971), 'The Chronology of the Portraits of Richard II', *Burlington Magazine* 113: 12–21

Wilkins, N. (1983), 'Music and Poetry at Court: England and France in the Late Middle Ages', in Scattergood and Sherborne (1983), pp. 183–204

Wilkinson, B. (1940), 'The Peasants' Revolt of 1381', *Speculum* 15: 12–35

Wilson, C. (1990), 'The Tomb of Henry IV and the Holy Oil of St Thomas of Canterbury', in E. Fernie and P. Crossley (eds.), *Medieval Architecture in its Intellectual Context. Essays in Honour of Peter Kidson,* London, pp. 181–90

Wilson, C. (1998), 'Sacral Kingship and Shopping: The Hegemony of the Architect and Structural Pragmatics: Some Contexts of Richard II's Rebuilding of Westminster Hall 1393–1399', in Gordon, Monnas and Elam (1998), pp. 33–59

Wood, C.T. (1988), *Joan of Arc and Richard II. Sex, Saints and Government in the Middle Ages,* Oxford

Wright, H.G. (1939), 'The Protestation of Richard II in the Tower in September 1399', *BJRL* 23: 151–65

13(C) WALES

Secondary works

Carr, A.D. (1968–9), 'Welshmen and the Hundred Years War', *WHR* 4: 21–46

Carr, A.D. (1970–1), 'An Aristocracy in Decline: The Native Welsh Lords after the Edwardian Conquest', *WHR* 5: 103–29

Carr, A.D. (1982), *Medieval Anglesey,* Llangefni

Carr, A.D. (1991), *Owen of Wales. The End of the House of Gwynedd,* Cardiff

Carr, A.D. (1995), *Medieval Wales,* London

Cowley, F.G. (1977), *The Monastic Orders in South Wales, 1066–1349,* Cardiff

Davies, R.R. (1966), 'The Twilight of Welsh Law', *History* 51: 143–64

Davies, R.R. (1968), 'Owain Glyn Dŵr and the Welsh Squirearchy', *THSC,* pt 2: 150–69

Davies, R.R. (1969), 'The Survival of the Blood Feud in Medieval Wales', *History* 54: 338–57

Davies, R.R. (1974), 'Colonial Wales', *P&P* 65: 3–23

Davies, R.R. (1974–5), 'Race Relations in Post-Conquest Wales', *THSC:* 32–56

Davies, R.R. (1978), *Lordship and Society in the March of Wales, 1282–1400,* Oxford

Davies, R.R. (1987), *Conquest, Coexistence and Change. Wales, 1063–1415,* Oxford

Davies, R.R. (1995), *The Revolt of Owen Glyn D'r,* Oxford

Edwards, J.G. (1950), 'Edward I's Castle-Building in Wales', *PBA* 32: 15–81

Edwards, J.G. (1969), *The Principality of Wales, 1267–1967. A Study in Constitutional History,* Caernarfon

Given, J.B. (1990), *State and Society in Medieval Europe. Gwynedd and Languedoc under Outside Rule,* Ithaca, N.Y.

Glamorgan County History (1971), III, ed. T.B. Pugh, Cardiff

Griffiths, R.A. (1964–7), 'Gentlemen and Rebels in Later Medieval Cardiganshire', *Ceredigion* 5: 143–67

Griffiths, R.A. (1965), 'The Revolt of Llywelyn Bren', *Glamorgan Historian* 2: 186–96

Griffiths, R.A. (1966–7), 'The Revolt of Rhys ap Maredudd, 1287–8', *WHR* 3: 121–43

Griffiths, R.A. (ed.) (1978), *Boroughs of Medieval Wales,* Cardiff

Griffiths, R.A. (1994), *Conquerors and Conquered in Medieval Wales,* Stroud

Jarman, A.O.H. and Hughes, G.R. (eds.) (1997), *A Guide to Welsh Literature,* II, Cardiff

Lewis, E.A. (1902–3), 'The Decay of Tribalism in North Wales', *THSC*: 1–75

Lewis, E.A. (1903), 'The Development of Industry and Commerce in Wales during the Middle Ages', *TRHS* 2nd series 17: 121–75

Lewis, E.A. (1912), *The Mediaeval Boroughs of Snowdonia*, Cardiff

Lloyd, J.E. (1931), *Owen Glendower*, Oxford

Pierce, T.J. (1972), *Medieval Welsh Society*, ed. J.B. Smith, Cardiff

Rees, W. (1920), 'The Black Death in Wales', *TRHS* 4th series 3: 115–35

Rees, W. (1924), *South Wales and the March, 1284–1415. A Social and Agrarian Study*, Oxford

Rees, W. (1933), *Map of South Wales and the Border in the Fourteenth Century*, Ordnance Survey

Reeves, A.C. (1983), *The Marcher Lords*, Llandybie

Roberts, G. (1969), *Aspects of Welsh History*, Cardiff

Smith, J.B. (1966–7), 'Crown and Community in the Principality of North Wales in the Reign of Henry Tudor', *WHR* 3: 145–71

Smith, J.B. (1974–6), 'Gruffydd Llwyd and the Celtic Alliance', *BBCS* 26: 463–78

Smith, J.B. (1976–7), 'Edward II and the Allegiance of Wales', *WHR* 8: 139–71

Smith, L.B. (1976), 'The Gage and the Land Market in Late Medieval Wales', *EcHR* 2nd series 29: 537–50

Smith, L.B. (1976–8), '*Tir Prid*: Deeds of Gage of Land in Late Medieval Wales', *BBCS* 27: 263–77

Smith, L.B. (1978–80), 'Seignorial Income in the Fourteenth Century: The Arundels in Chirk', *BBCS* 28: 443–57

Soulsby, I.N. (1983), *The Towns of Medieval Wales. A Study in their History, Archaeology and Early Topography*, Chichester

Taylor, A.J. (1973), *A History of the King's Works in Wales, 1277–1330*, London

Walker, D. (1990), *Medieval Wales*, Cambridge

Williams, D.H. (1983–4), *The Welsh Cistercians*, 2 vols., Caldey Island, Tenby

Williams, G. (1966), *Owen Glendower*, Oxford

Williams, G. (1976), *The Welsh Church from Conquest to Reformation*, 2nd edn, Cardiff

Williams, G. (1979), 'Prophecy, Poetry and Politics in Medieval and Tudor Wales', in his, *Religion, Language and Nationality in Wales*, Cardiff, pp. 71–86

Williams, G.A. (1959), 'Owain Glyn Dŵr', in A.J. Roderick (ed.), *Wales through the Ages*, I, Llandybie

13(d) FOURTEENTH-CENTURY SCOTLAND

Primary sources

The Acts of the Parliaments of Scotland, ed. T. Thomson and C. Innes, 12 vols., Edinburgh (1814–75)

Bower, Walter, *Scotichronicon*, ed. D.E.R. Watt, 9 vols., Aberdeen (1987–98)

Calendar of Documents relating to Scotland in H.M. Public Record Office, ed. J. Bain *et al.*, 5 vols., Edinburgh (1881–1986)

The Exchequer Rolls of Scotland, ed. J. Stuart *et al.*, 15 vols., Edinburgh (1878–1908)

Fordun, John of, *Chronica Gentis Scotorum*, ed. W.F. Skene, 2 vols., Edinburgh (1871–2)

Regesta Regum Scottorum, v: *The Acts of Robert I, King of Scots, 1306–1329*, ed. A.A.M. Duncan, Edinburgh (1988)

Regesta Regum Scottorum, vi: *the Acts of David II, King of Scots, 1329–1371*, ed. B. Webster, Edinburgh (1982)

Wyntoun, Andrew of, *The Original Chronicle of Scotland*, ed. F.J. Amours, 6 vols., Scottish Text Society, Edinburgh (1903–14)

Secondary works

Bannerman, J.W.M. (1977),'The Lordship of the Isles', in J.M. Brown (ed.), *Scottish Society in the Fifteenth Century*, London, pp. 209–39

Barrow, G.W.S. (1973), 'The Highlands in the Lifetime of Robert Bruce', in G.W.S. Barrow, *The Kingdom of the Scots*, Edinburgh, pp. 62–83

Barrow, G.W.S. (1976), 'Lothian in the First War of Independence, 1296–1328', *SHR* 55: 151–71

Barrow, G.W.S. (1978), 'The Aftermath of War: Scotland and England in the Late Thirteenth and Early Fourteenth Centuries', *TRHS* 5th series 28: 103–25

Barrow, G.W.S. (1981), *Kingship and Unity. Scotland, 1000–1306*, London

Barrow, G.W.S. (1988), *Robert Bruce and the Community of the Realm of Scotland*, 3rd edn, Edinburgh

Barrow, G.W.S. (1990), 'The Army of Alexander III's Scotland', in N.H. Reid (ed.), *Scotland in the Reign of Alexander III*, Edinburgh, pp. 132–47

Boardman, S. (1992), 'The Man who would be King: The Lieutenancy and Death of David, Duke of Rothesay, 1399–1402', in R. Mason and N. Macdougall (eds.), *People and Power in Scotland. Essays in Honour of T.C. Smout*, Edinburgh, pp. 1–27

Boardman, S. (1996a), *The Early Stewart Kings. Robert II and Robert III*, East Linton

Boardman, S. (1996b), 'Lordship in the North-East: The Badenoch Stewarts, I. Alexander Stewart, Earl of Buchan, Lord of Badenoch', *Northern Scotland* 16: 1–30

Boardman, S. (1997), 'Chronicle Propaganda in Late Medieval Scotland: Robert the Steward, John of Fordun and the "Anonymous Chronicle"', *SHR* 76: 23–43

Brown, M. (1994a), *James I*, Edinburgh

Brown, M. (1994b), 'Scotland Tamed? Kings and Magnates in Late Medieval Scotland: A Review of Recent Work', *Innes Review* 55: 120–46

Brown, M. (1997a), 'The Development of Scottish Border Lordship, 1332–58', *HR* 70: 1–22

Brown, M. (1997b), '"Rejoice to Hear of Douglas": The House of Douglas and the Presentation of Magnate Power in Late Medieval Scotland', *SHR* 76: 161–87

Campbell, J. (1965), 'England, Scotland and the Hundred Years War in the Fourteenth Century', in J.R. Hale, J.R.L. Highfield and B. Smalley (eds.), *Europe in the Late Middle Ages*, London, pp. 184–216

Curry, A. (1993), *The Hundred Years War*, Basingstoke

Duncan, A.A.M. (1966), 'The Early Parliaments of Scotland', *SHR* 45: 36–58

Duncan, A.A.M. (1970), *The Nation of Scots and the Declaration of Arbroath*, Historical Association, pamphlet G. 75

Duncan, A.A.M. (1975), *Scotland. The Making of the Kingdom*, Edinburgh

Duncan, A.A.M. (1988), '*Honi soit qui mal y pense:* David II and Edward III, 1346–52', *SHR* 67: 113–41

Duncan, A.A.M. (1992), 'The War of the Scots, 1306–1323', *TRHS* 6th series 2: 125–51

Duncan, A.A.M. (1993), 'The "Laws of Malcolm MacKenneth"', in Grant and Stringer (1993), pp. 239–73

Duncan, A.A.M. (ed.) (1994), 'A Question about the Succession, 1364', in *Miscellany of the Scottish History Society,* XII, Scottish History Society, 5th series, 7, Edinburgh, pp. 1–57

Duncan, A.A.M. (1995), 'The Process of Norham', in P.R. Coss and S.D. Lloyd (eds.), *Thirteenth Century England,* v, Woodbridge, pp. 207–30

Gemmill, E. and Mayhew, N. (1995), *Changing Values in Medieval Scotland. A Study of Prices, Money, and Weights and Measures,* Cambridge

Goodman, A. (1987), 'The Anglo-Scottish Marches in the Fifteenth Century: A Frontier Society?', in Mason (1987), pp. 18–33

Goodman, A. (1992), 'Introduction', in A. Goodman and A. Tuck (eds.), *War and Border Societies in the Middle Ages,* London, pp. 1–29

Grant, A. (1984), *Independence and Nationhood. Scotland 1306–1469,* London

Grant, A. (1985), 'Extinction of Direct Male Lines among Scottish Noble Families in the Fourteenth and Fifteenth Centuries', in K.J. Stringer (ed.), *Essays on the Nobility of Medieval Scotland,* Edinburgh, pp. 210–31

Grant, A. (1987), 'Crown and Nobility in Late Medieval Britain', in Mason (1987), pp. 34–59

Grant, A. (1988), 'Scotland's "Celtic Fringe" in the Late Middle Ages: The MacDonald Lords of the Isles and the Kingdom of Scotland', in R.R. Davies (ed.), *The British Isles, 1100–1500. Comparisons, Contrasts and Connections,* Edinburgh, pp. 118–41

Grant, A. (1992), 'The Otterburn War from the Scottish Point of View', in A. Goodman and A. Tuck (eds.), *War and Border Societies in the Middle Ages,* London, pp. 30–64

Grant, A. (1993a), 'Thanes and Thanages, from the Eleventh to the Fourteenth Centuries', in Grant and Stringer (1993), pp. 39–81

Grant, A. (1993b), 'The Wolf of Badenoch', in W.D.H. Sellar (ed.), *Moray. Province and People,* Edinburgh, pp. 143–61

Grant, A. (1994), 'Aspects of National Consciousness in Medieval Scotland', in C. Bjørn, A. Grant and K. J. Stringer (eds.), *Nations, Nationalism and Patriotism in the European Past,* Copenhagen, pp. 68–95

Grant, A. and Stringer, K.J. (eds.) (1993), *Medieval Scotland. Crown, Lordship and Community. Essays Presented to G.W.S. Barrow,* Edinburgh

Keen, M.H. (1973), *England in the Later Middle Ages,* London

McDonald, R.A. (1997), *The Kingdom of the Isles. Scotland's Western Seaboard, c. 1100–c. 1336,* East Linton

McGladdery, C. (1990), *James II,* Edinburgh

McNamee, C. (1997), *The Wars of the Bruces. Scotland, England and Ireland, 1306–1328,* East Linton

McNeill, P.G.B. and MacQueen, H.L. (1997), *Atlas of Scottish History to 1707,* Edinburgh

Mackinnon, J. (1924), *The Constitutional History of Scotland,* London

MacQueen, H.L. (1993), *Common Law and Feudal Society in Medieval Scotland,* Edinburgh

Mason, R.A. (ed.) (1987), *Scotland and England 1286–1815*, Edinburgh

Munro, J. and Munro, R.W. (eds.) (1986), *The Acts of the Lords of the Isles*, Scottish History Society, 4th series, 22, Edinburgh

Nicholson, R. (1965), *Edward III and the Scots*, Oxford

Nicholson, R. (1974), *Scotland. The Later Middle Ages*, Edinburgh

Prestwich, M. (1972), *War, Politics and Finance under Edward I*, London

Prestwich, M. (1987), 'Colonial Scotland: The English in Scotland under Edward I', in Mason (1987), pp. 6–17

Rait, R.S. (1924), *The Parliaments of Scotland*, Glasgow

Reid, N.H. (1993), 'Crown and Community under Robert I', in Grant and Stringer (1993), pp. 203–22

Reynolds, S. (1984), *Kingdoms and Communities in Western Europe, 900–1300*, Oxford

Simms, K. (1987), *From Kings to Warlords. The Changing Political Structure of Gaelic Ireland in the Later Middle Ages*, Woodbridge

Simpson, G.G. (1977), 'The Declaration of Arbroath Revitalised', *SHR* 56: 11–33

Southern, R.W. (1970), *Medieval Humanism*, Oxford

Stones, E.L.G. and Simpson, G.G. (1978), *Edward I and the Throne of Scotland, 1290–1296. An Edition of the Record Sources for the Great Cause*, Oxford

Ullmann, W. (1978), *Principles of Government and Politics in the Middle Ages*, 4th edn, London

Watt, D.E.R. (1993), 'The Provincial Council of the Scottish Church, 1215–1472', in Grant and Stringer (1993), pp. 140–55

Webster, B. (1966), 'David II and the Government of Fourteenth-Century Scotland', *TRHS* 5th series 16: 115–30

Webster, B. (1975), *Scotland from the Eleventh Century to 1603*, London

Webster, B. (1993), 'Scotland without a King, 1329–1341', in Grant and Stringer (1993), pp. 223–38

Wormald, J. (1980), 'Bloodfeud, kindred and government in early modern Scotland', *P&P* 87: 54–97

13(e)   IRELAND

Primary sources

Berry, H. F., *Statutes, Ordinances and Acts of the Parliament of Ireland, King John to Henry V*, Dublin (1907)

Curtis, E., *Richard II in Ireland, 1394–5, and Submissions of the Irish Chiefs*, Oxford (1927)

Curtis, E., 'Unpublished Letters from Richard II in Ireland, 1394–5', *PRIA* section C 27 (1927), pp. 276–303

Graves, J., *A Roll of the Proceedings of the King's Council in Ireland, 1392–3*, RS 69, London (1877)

Mac Niocaill, G., *The Red Book of the Earls of Kildare*, Irish Manuscripts Commission, Dublin (1964)

O'Sullivan, A., *Poems on Marcher Lords*, Irish Texts Society 53, London (1987)

Richardson, H.G. and Sayles, G.O., *Parliaments and Councils of Mediaeval Ireland*, Irish Manuscripts Commission, Dublin (1947)

Sayles, G. O., *Documents on the Affairs of Ireland before the King's Council*, Irish Manuscripts Commission, Dublin (1979)

Secondary works

Barry, T.B., Frame, R. and Simms, K. (eds.) (1995), *Colony and Frontier in Medieval Ireland. Essays Presented to J. F. Lydon*, London

Bartlett, T. and Jeffery, K. (eds.) (1996), *A Military History of Ireland*, Cambridge

Childs, W. (1982), 'Ireland's Trade with England in the Later Middle Ages', *IESH* 9: 5–33

Connolly, P. (1981), 'The Financing of English Expeditions to Ireland, 1361–76', in Lydon (1981), pp. 104–21

Cosgrove, A. (1981), *Late Medieval Ireland 1370–1541*, The Helicon History of Ireland, 3, Dublin

Cosgrove, A. (ed.) (1987), *Medieval Ireland 1169–1534* (A New History of Ireland, 2), Oxford

Davies, R. R. (1984), 'Lordship or Colony?' in Lydon (1984), pp. 142–60

Down, K. (1987), 'Colonial Society and Economy in the High Middle Ages', in Cosgrove (1987), pp. 439–91

Duffy, S. (1991), 'The Bruce Brothers and the Irish Sea World, 1306–29', *CMCS* 21: 55–86

Empey, C.A. (1986), 'Conquest and Settlement: Patterns of Anglo-Norman Settlement in North Leinster and South Munster', *IESH* 13: 5–31

Frame, R. (1973), 'The Justiciarship of Ralph Ufford: Warfare and Politics in Fourteenth-Century Ireland', *SH* 13: 7–47

Frame, R. (1981), *Colonial Ireland 1169–1369*, The Helicon History of Ireland, 2, Dublin

Frame, R. (1982), *English Lordship in Ireland 1318–1361*, Oxford

Frame, R. (1990), *The Political Development of the British Isles 1100–1400*, Oxford

Frame, R. (1995), 'Two Kings in Leinster: The Crown and the MicMhurchadha in the Fourteenth Century', in Barry, Frame and Simms (1995), pp. 155–75

Frame, R. (1996a), 'The Defence of the English Lordship, 1250–1450', in Bartlett and Jeffery (1996), pp. 76–98

Frame, R. (1996b), 'Thomas Rokeby, Sheriff of Yorkshire, Justiciar of Ireland', *Peritia* 10: 274–96

Frame, R. (1998), *Ireland and Britain 1170–1450*, London

Gilbert, J.T. (1865), *A History of the Viceroys of Ireland*, Dublin

Hand, G.J. (1967), *English Law in Ireland 1290–1324*, Cambridge

Hogan, D. and Osborough, W. N. (eds.) (1991), *Brehons, Serjeants and Attorneys. Studies in the History of the Irish Legal Profession*, Dublin

Johnston, D. (1980), 'Richard II and the Submissions of Gaelic Ireland', *IHS* 22: 1–20

Lydon, J.F. (1963), 'Richard II's Expeditions to Ireland', *JRSAI* 93: 135–49

Lydon, J.F. (1964), 'Edward II and the Revenues of Ireland in 1311–12', *IHS* 14: 39–57

Lydon, J.F. (1965), 'William of Windsor and the Irish Parliament', *EHR* 80: 252–67

Lydon, J.F. (1972), *The Lordship of Ireland in the Middle Ages*, Dublin

Lydon, J.F. (1973), *Ireland in the Later Middle Ages*, The Gill History of Ireland, 6, Dublin

Lydon, J.F. (ed.) (1981), *England and Ireland in the Later Middle Ages. Essays in Honour of Jocelyn Otway-Ruthven*, Dublin

Lydon, J.F. (ed.) (1984), *The English in Medieval Ireland*, Dublin

Lydon, J.F. (ed.) (1997), *Law and Disorder in Thirteenth-Century Ireland: The Dublin Parliament of 1297*, Dublin

Lyons, M. C. (1989), 'Weather, Famine, Pestilence and Plague in Ireland, 900–1500', in E.M. Crawford (ed.), *Famine: The Irish Experience*, Edinburgh, pp. 31–74

McNamee, C. (1997), *The Wars of the Bruces. Scotland, England and Ireland 1306–1328*, East Linton

McNeill, T. E. (1980), *Anglo-Norman Ulster. The History and Archaeology of an Irish Barony, 1177–1400*, Edinburgh

Mac Niocaill, G. (1976), 'Aspects of Irish Law in the Late Thirteenth Century', *Historical Studies* (papers read before the Eleventh Irish Conference of Historians), ed. G.A. Hayes-McCoy, Galway, 10: 25–42

Mac Niocaill, G. (1984), 'The Interaction of Laws', in Lydon (1984), pp. 105–17

Matthew, E. (1984), 'The Financing of the Lordship of Ireland under Henry V and Henry VI', in A.J. Pollard (ed.), *Property and Politics: Essays in Later Medieval English History*, Gloucester, pp. 97–115

Nicholls, K. (1972), *Gaelic and Gaelicised Ireland in the Middle Ages*, The Gill History of Ireland, 4, Dublin

Nicholls, K. (1982), 'Anglo-French Ireland and After', *Peritia* 1: 370–403

Nicholls, K. (1987), 'Gaelic Society and Economy in the High Middle Ages', in Cosgrove (1987), pp. 397–438

Nicholls, K. (1993), 'The Development of Lordship in County Cork, 1300–1600', in O'Flanagan and Buttimer (1993), pp. 157–211

O'Brien, A. F. (1988), 'The Royal Boroughs, the Seaport Towns and Royal Revenue in Medieval Ireland', *JRSAI* 118: 13–26

O'Brien, A. F. (1993), 'Politics, Economy and Society: The Development of Cork and the Irish South-Coast Region, c. 1170–c. 1583', in O'Flanagan and Buttimer (1993), pp. 83–154

O'Flanagan, P. and Buttimer, C.G. (eds.) (1993), *Cork. History and Society*, Dublin

O'Neill, T. (1987), *Merchants and Mariners in Medieval Ireland*, Dublin

Otway-Ruthven, A.J. (1967), 'Ireland in the 1350s: Sir Thomas de Rokeby and his Successors', *JRSAI* 97: 47–59

Otway-Ruthven, A.J. (1968a), *A History of Medieval Ireland*, London

Otway-Ruthven, A.J. (1968b), 'The Partition of the De Verdon Lands in Ireland in 1332', *PRIA* section C 66: 401–55

Otway-Ruthven, A.J. (1980), 'The Background to the Arrest of Sir Christopher Preston in 1418', *Analecta Hibernica* 29: 73–94

Parker, C. (1995), 'The Internal Frontier: The Irish in County Waterford in the Later Middle Ages', in Barry, Frame and Simms (1995), pp. 139–54

Phillips, J.R.S. (1990), 'The Irish Remonstrance of 1317: An International Perspective', *IHS* 27: 112–29

Richardson, H.G. and Sayles, G.O. (1962), 'Irish Revenue, 1278–1384', *PRIA* section C 62: 87–100

Richardson, H.G. and Sayles, G.O. (1963), *The Administration of Ireland 1172–1377*, Irish Manuscripts Commission, Dublin

Richardson, H.G. and Sayles, G.O. (1964), *The Irish Parliament in the Middle Ages*, Etudes présentées à la Commission Internationale pour l'Histoire des Assemblées d'Etats, 10, Philadelphia

Saul, N. (1997), *Richard II*, New Haven

Sayles, G.O. (1982), *Scripta Diversa*, London

Simms, K. (1974), 'The Archbishops of Armagh and the O'Neills, 1347–1471', *IHS* 19: 38–55

Simms, K. (1986), 'Nomadry in Medieval Ireland: The Origins of the Creaght or *Caoraigheacht*', *Peritia* 5: 379–91

Simms, K. (1987), *From Kings to Warlords. The Changing Political Structure of Gaelic Ireland in the Later Middle Ages*, Woodbridge

Simms, K. (1989), 'Bards and Barons: The Anglo-Irish Aristocracy and the Native Culture', in R. Bartlett and A. Mackay (eds.), *Medieval Frontier Societies*, Oxford, pp. 177–97

Simms, K. (1996), 'Gaelic Warfare in the Middle Ages', in Bartlett and Jeffery (1996), pp. 99–115

Smith, B. (1993), 'A County Community in Early Fourteenth-Century Ireland: The Case of Louth', *EHR* 108: 561–88

Smith, B. (1999), *Colonisation and Conquest in Medieval Ireland. The English in Louth, 1170–1330*, Cambridge

Walsh, K. (1981), *A Fourteenth-Century Scholar and Primate. Richard FitzRalph in Oxford, Avignon and Armagh*, Oxford

Watt, J.A. (1970), *The Church and the Two Nations of Medieval Ireland*, Cambridge

Watt, J.A. (1972), *The Church in Medieval Ireland*, The Gill History of Ireland, 5, Dublin

Watt, J.A (1981), 'John Colton, Justiciar of Ireland (1382) and Archbishop of Armagh (1383–1404)', in Lydon (1981), pp. 196–213

14(a) FRANCE: THE LAST CAPETIANS AND EARLY VALOIS KINGS, 1314–1364

Primary sources

Bock, Friedrich, 'Some New Documents Illustrating the Early Years of the Hundred Years War, 1353–6', *BJRL* 15 (1931), pp. 60–99

Cazelles, Raymond, *Catalogue de comptes royaux des règnes de Philippe VI et de Jean II (1328–1364)*, Paris (1984)

Cazelles, Raymond, *Lettres closes, lettres 'de par le Roy' de Philippe de Valois*, Paris (1958)

Chaplais, Pierre, *The War of Saint-Sardos (1323–1325)*, Royal Hist. Soc., Camden 3rd series, LXXVII, London (1954)

Delachenal, Roland (ed.), 'Journal des états généraux réunis à Paris au mois d'octobre 1356', *NRHDFE* 24 (1900), pp. 415–65

Devic, Dom Cl. and Vaissete, Dom J., *Histoire générale de Languedoc*, ed. A. Molinier *et al.*, 16 vols., Toulouse (1872–1904)

Dupont-Ferrier, Gustave, *Gallia Regia, ou état des officiers royaux des bailliages et sénéchaussées de 1328 à 1515*, 7 vols., Paris (1942–65)

Durand de Maillane, P.-T., *Les libertés de l'église gallicane prouvées et commentées suivant l'ordre et la disposition des articles dressées par M. Pierre Pithou et sur les recueils de M. Pierre Dupuy*, 5 vols., Lyon (1771)

Fawtier, Robert, 'Un compte de menues dépenses de l'hôtel du roi Philippe VI de Valois pour le premier semestre de l'année 1337', *BPH (1715)*, 1928–9, pp. 1–57; repr. in Fawtier (1987), pp. 183–239

Fawtier, Robert (ed.), *Comptes du Trésor (1296, 1316, 1384, 1477)*, Paris (1930)

Finke, Heinrich (ed.), *Acta Aragonensia*, 3 vols., Basle (1966); orig. edn Berlin (1908–22), repr. with supplement of 1933

Froissart, Jean, *Œuvres*, ed. J.M.B.C. Kervyn de Lettenhove, 28 vols., Brussels (1867–79)

Hellot, A., 'Chronique parisienne anonyme de 1316 à 1339', *MSHP* 11 (1884), pp. 1–207

Higounet-Nadal, Arlette, 'Le journal des dépenses d'un notaire de Périgueux en mission à Paris (janvier–septembre 1337)', *AMi* 76 (1964), pp. 379–402

Jassemin, Henri, 'Les papiers de Mile de Noyers', *BPH (1715)*, 1918, pp. 174–226

Jones, Michael, 'Some Documents Relating to the Disputed Succession to the Duchy of Brittany, 1341', Royal Hist. Soc., *Camden Miscellany*, XXIV, London (1972), pp. 1–78

Maillard, François, *Comptes royaux (1314–1328)*, Paris (1961)

Merlin-Chazelas, Anne, *Documents relatifs au Clos des Galées de Rouen et aux armées de mer du roi de France de 1294 à 1418*, 2 vols., Paris (1977–8)

Miret y Sans, Joachim, 'Lettres closes des premiers Valois', *MA* 20 (1917–18), pp. 52–88

Moranvillé, Henri, 'Rapports à Philippe VI sur l'état de ses finances', *BEC* 48 (1887), pp. 380–95

Ordonnances des rois de la troisième race, ed. E.J. de Laurière *et al.*, 22 vols. and *Supplément*, Paris (1723–1849)

Petrarch, Francis, *Letters of Old Age. Rerum Senilium Libri I–XVIII*, trans. Aldo S. Bernardo, Saul Levin and Reta A. Bernardo, 2 vols., Baltimore and London (1992)

Recueil des actes de Charles de Blois et Jeanne de Penthièvre, duc et duchesse de Bretagne (1341–1364), suivi des Actes de Jeanne de Penthièvre (1364–1384), ed. Michael Jones, Rennes (1996)

Registres du trésor des chartes, II: *Règnes des fils de Philippe le Bel*, pt. 1: *Règnes de Louis X le Hutin et de Philippe V le Long*, ed. J. Guerout and Robert Fawtier, Paris (1966)

Registres du trésor des chartes, III: *Règne de Philippe de Valois*, pt. 1: *JJ 65A à 69*, ed. J. Viard, Aline Vallée and J. Favier, Paris (1978)

Registres du trésor des chartes, III: *Règne de Philippe de Valois*, pt. 2: *JJ 70 à 75*, ed. J. Viard, Aline Vallée and J. Favier, Paris (1979)

Registres du trésor des chartes, III: *Règne de Philippe de Valois*, pt. 3: *JJ 76 à 79B*, ed. Aline Vallée, Paris (1984)

Schnerb-Lièvre, Marion (ed.), *Le songe du vergier*, 2 vols., Paris (1982)

Viard, Jules, *Documents parisiens du règne de Philippe VI de Valois (1328–1350)*, 2 vols., Paris (1899–1900)

Webster, Bruce, *The Acts of David II, King of Scots, 1329–1371*, Edinburgh (1982)

Secondary works

Allmand, Christopher T. (1988), *The Hundred Years War*, Cambridge

Artonne, A. (1912), *Le mouvement de 1314 et les chartes provinciales de 1315*, Paris

Aubert, Félix (1886), *Le parlement de Paris de Philippe le Bel à Charles VII (1314–1422), son organisation*, Paris; repr. Geneva (1974)

Autrand, Françoise (1981), *Naissance d'un grand corps de l'état. Les gens du parlement de Paris, 1345–1454*, Paris

Balard, Michel (1991), *L'histoire médiévale en France. Bilan et perspectives*, Paris

Barber, Malcolm C. (1981), 'Lepers, Jews and Moslems: The Plot to Overthrow Christendom in 1321', *History* 66: 1–17

Baudon de Mony, Charles (1897), 'La mort et les funérailles de Philippe le Bel d'après un compte rendu à la cour de Majorque', *BEC* 58: 5–14

Bautier, Robert-Henri (1964, 1965), 'Recherches sur la chancellerie royale au temps de Philippe VI', *BEC* 122: 89–176; 123: 313–459

Bautier, Robert-Henri (1978), 'Introduction', to A. Lapeyre and Rémy Scheurer, *Les notaires et sécretaires du roi . . . 1461–1515*, 2 vols., Paris

Bautier, Robert-Henri (1986), 'Le personnel de la chancellerie royale sous les derniers Capétiens', *Prosopographie et genèse de l'état moderne. Actes de la Table ronde organisée par le C.R.N.S. et l'E.N.S.J.F., Paris 1984*, ed. Françoise Autrand, pp. 91–115; repr. in his *Chartres, sceaux et chancelleries*, 2 vols., Paris (1990), II, pp. 853–77

Bautier, Robert-Henri (1990), *Chartes, sceaux et chancelleries. Etudes de diplomatique et de sigillographie médiévales*, 2 vols., Paris

Beaune, Colette (1985), *Naissance de la nation France*, Paris; augmented English trans. Susan Ross Huston, *The Birth of an Ideology. Myths and Symbols of Nation in Late-Medieval France*, ed. Fredric L. Cheyette, Berkeley, Los Angeles and London (1991)

Beriac, Fr. (1987), 'La persécution des lépreux dans la France méridionale en 1321', *MA* 93: 203–21

Bois, Guy (1976), *La crise du féodalisme. Economie rurale et démographie en Normandie orientale du début du 14e siècle au milieu du 16e siècle*, Paris; English trans. Jean Birrell, *The Crisis of Feudalism. Economy and Society in Eastern Normandy, c. 1300–1500*, Cambridge (1984)

Borrelli de Serres, Léon-Louis (1895–1909), *Recherches sur divers services publics du XIIIe au XVIIe siècle*, 3 vols., Paris

Brown, E.A.R. (1971a), 'Subsidy and Reform in 1321: The Accounts of Najac and the Policies of Philip V', *Traditio* 27: 399–430

Brown, E.A.R. (1971b), 'Assemblies of French Towns in 1316: Some New Texts', *Speculum* 46: 282–301

Brown, E.A.R. (1972), 'Cessante Causa and the Taxes of the Last Capetians: The Political Applications of a Philosophical Maxim', *SG* 15: 565–87

Brown, E.A.R. (1973), 'Taxation and Morality in the Thirteenth and Fourteenth Centuries: Conscience and Political Power and the Kings of France', *FHS* 8: 1–28

Brown, E.A.R. (1974), 'Customary Aids and Royal Fiscal Policy under Philip VI of Valois', *Traditio* 30: 191–258

Brown, E.A.R. (1976a), 'Royal Necessity and Noble Service and Subsidy in Early Fourteenth-Century France: The Assembly of Bourges of November 1318', in H. G. Fletcher III and M.B. Schulte (eds.), *Paradosis. Studies in Memory of Edwin A. Quain*, New York, pp. 135–68

Brown, E.A.R. (1976b), 'Royal Salvation and Needs of State in Early-Fourteenth-Century France', in William C. Jordan, Bruce McNab and Teofilo F. Ruiz (eds.), *Order and Innovation in the Middle Ages. Essays in Honor of Joseph R. Strayer*, Princeton, pp. 365–83, 541–61; revised version in Brown (1991b)

Brown, E.A.R. (1978), 'The Ceremonial of Royal Succession in Capetian France: The Double Funeral of Louis X', *Traditio* 34: 227–71

Brown, E.A.R. (1980), 'The Ceremonial of Royal Succession in Capetian France. The Funeral of Philip V', *Speculum* 55: 266–93

Brown, E.A.R. (1981), 'Reform and Resistance to Royal Authority in Fourteenth-Century France: The Leagues of 1314–1315', *PER* 1: 109–37

Brown, E.A.R. (1988), 'The Case of Philip the Fair', *Viator* 19: 219–46

Brown, E.A.R. (1989), 'Diplomacy, Adultery and Domestic Politics at the Court of Philip the Fair: Queen Isabelle's Mission to the Court of France in 1314', in J.S. Hamilton & Patricia J. Bradley (eds.), *Documenting the Past: Essays in Medieval History Presented to George Peddy Cuttino*, London, pp. 53–84

Brown, E.A.R. (1991a), *Politics and Institutions in Capetian France*, Aldershot and Brookfield, Vt.

Brown, E.A.R. (1991b), *The Monarchy of Capetian France and Royal Ceremonial*, Aldershot and Brookfield, Vt.

Brown, E.A.R. (1991c), 'Philip V, Charles IV, and the Jews of France: The Alleged Expulsion of 1322', *Speculum* 66: 294–329

Brown, E.A.R. (1992), *Customary Aids and Royal Finance in Capetian France. The Marriage Aid of Philip the Fair*, Cambridge, Mass.

Campbell, James (1965), 'England, Scotland and the Hundred Years War in the Fourteenth Century', in J. R. Hale *et al.* (eds.), *Europe in the Late Middle Ages*, London, pp. 184–216

Capra, Pierre (1975), 'Les bases sociales du pouvoir anglo-gascon au milieu du XIVe siècle', *MA* 81: 273–99, 447–73

Cazelles, Raymond (1958), *La société politique et la crise du royauté sous Philippe de Valois*, Paris

Cazelles, Raymond (1962a), 'Pierre Becoud et la fondation du Collège de Boncourt', *BEC* 120: 55–103

Cazelles, Raymond (1962b), 'Les mouvements révolutionnaires du milieu du XIVe siècle et le cycle de l'action politique', *RH* 228: 279–312

Cazelles, Raymond (1962–3), 'Une exigence de l'opinion depuis saint Louis: la réformation du royaume', *ABSHF*: 91–9

Cazelles, Raymond (1966a), 'Une chancellerie privilégiée: celle de Philippe VI de Valois', *BEC* 124: 355–82

Cazelles, Raymond (1966b), 'Quelques reflexions à propos des mutations de la monnaie royale française (1295–1360)', *MA*: 83–105, 251–78

Cazelles, Raymond (1974), 'Jean II le Bon: Quel homme? Quel roi?', *RH* 251: 5–25

Cazelles, Raymond (1982), *Société politique, noblesse et couronne sous Jean le Bon et Charles V*, Paris and Geneva

Cazelles, Raymond (1984a), *Etienne Marcel, champion de l'unité française*, Paris

Cazelles, Raymond (1984b), 'The Jacquerie', in Rodney H. Hilton and T.H. Aston (eds.), *The English Rising of 1381*, Cambridge, pp. 74–83

Chaplais, Pierre (1981), *Essays in Medieval Diplomacy and Administration*, London

Chevalier, Bernard (1975), *Tours, ville royale (1356–1520)*, Paris and Louvain

Cheyette, Fredric L. (1970), 'The Sovereign and the Pirates, 1332', *Speculum* 45: 40–68

Cheyette, Fredric L. (1973), 'The Professional Papers of an English Ambassador on the Eve of the Hundred Years War', in *Economies et sociétés au moyen âge. Mélanges offerts à Edouard Perroy*, Paris, pp. 400–13

Contamine, Philippe (1972), *Guerre, état et société à la fin du moyen âge. Etudes sur les armées des rois de France, 1337–1494*, Paris and The Hague

Contamine, Philippe (1978), 'Les fortifications urbaines en France à la fin du moyen âge: aspects financières et économiques', *RH* 260: 23–47

Contamine, Philippe (1981), *La France au XIVe et XVe siècles. Hommes, mentalités, guerre et paix*, London

Contamine, Philippe (1992), *Des pouvoirs en France 1300/1500*, Paris

Contamine, Philippe (1994), 'The Norman "Nation" and the French "Nation" in the Fourteenth and Fifteenth Centuries', in David Bates and Anne Curry (eds.), *England and Normandy in the Middle Ages*, London, pp. 215–34

Cordey, Jean (1911), *Les comtes de Savoie et le rois de France pendant la guerre de Cent Ans (1329–1391)*, Paris

Couderc, Camille (1896), 'Le manuel d'histoire de Philippe VI de Valois', in Ernest Lavisse (ed.), *Etudes d'histoire du moyen âge dediées à Gabriel Monod*, Paris, pp. 415–44

Cuttino, George (1944), 'The Process of Agen', *Speculum* 19: 161–78

Cuttino, George (1956), 'Historical Revision: The Causes of the Hundred Years War', *Speculum* 31: 463–77

Cuttino, George (1971), *English Diplomatic Administration, 1259–1339*, 2nd edn, Oxford

Cuttler, Simon H. (1981), *The Law of Treason and Treason Trials in Later Medieval France*, Cambridge

Daumet, Georges (1898), *Etudes sur l'alliance de la France et de la Castille aux XIVe et XVe siècles*, Paris

Delachenal, Roland (1900), 'Premières négociations de Charles le Mauvais avec les Anglais (1354–1355)', *BEC*, 61: 253–82

Delachenal, Roland (1909–31), *Histoire de Charles V*, 5 vols., Paris

Delisle, Léopold (1894), 'Chronologie des baillis et des sénéchaux royaux depuis les origines jusqu'à l'avènement de Philippe de Valois', *RHGF* 24: 15*–368*

Déprez, Eugène (1902), *Les préliminaires de la guerre de Cent Ans (1328–1342)*, Paris

Déprez, Eugène (1908), 'Une conférence anglo-navarraise en 1358', *RH* 99; 34–9

Desportes, Pierre (1979), *Reims et les Rémois aux XIIIe et XIVe siècles*, Paris

Dieudonné, A. (1932), 'L'Ordonnance ou règlement de 1315 sur le monnayage des barons', *BEC* 93: 5–54

Dossat, Yves, 1978, 'L'Agenais vers 1325 après la campagne de Charles de Valois', in *La guerre et la paix au moyen âge, ACNSS*, 101, Paris, pp. 143–54

Douët d'Arcq, Louis (1840–1), 'Acte d'accusation contre Robert le Coq, évêque de Laon', *BEC* 2: 350–87

Duby, Georges (1991), *France in the Middle Ages, 987–1460*, trans. Juliet Vale, Oxford

Ducoudray, Gustave (1902), *Les origines du parlement de Paris et la justice aux XIIIe et XIVe siècles*, 2 vols., Paris; repr. 1970

Dunbabin, Jean (1988), 'Government', in J.H. Burns (ed.), *Cambridge History of Medieval Political Thought, c. 350–c. 1450*, Cambridge, pp. 477–519

Dunbabin, Jean (1991), *A Hound of God. Pierre de la Palud and the Fourteenth-Century Church*, Oxford

Dupâquier, Jacques (ed.) (1988), *Histoire de la population française*, 2 vols., Paris

Dupont-Ferrier, Gustave (1902), *Les officiers royaux des bailliages et sénéchaussées et les institutions monarchiques locales en France à la fin du moyen âge*, Paris

Faucon, Marcel (1879), 'Prêts faits aux rois de France par Clément VI, Innocent VI et le comte de Beaufort (1345–1360)', *BEC* 40: 570–80

Favier, Jean (1963), *Un conseiller de Philippe le Bel. Enguerran de Marigny*, Paris

Fawtier, Robert (1987), *Autour de la France capétienne*, London

Fournial, Etienne (1970), *Histoire monétaire de l'occident médiéval*, Paris

Fourquin, Guy (1956), 'La population de la région parisienne aux environs de 1328', *MA* 62: 63–91

Fourquin, Guy (1964), *Les campagnes de la région parisienne à la fin du moyen âge*, Paris

Fowler, Kenneth (1969), *The King's Lieutenant. Henry of Grosmont, First Duke of Lancaster, 1310–1361*, London

Fowler, Kenneth (1991), 'News from the Front: Letters and Despatches of the Fourteenth Century', in Philippe Contamine, Charles Giry-Deloison and Maurice H. Keen (eds.), *Guerre et société en France, en Angleterre et en Bourgogne, XIVe–XVe siècle*, Lille, pp. 63–92

Funk, Arthur Layton (1944), 'Robert le Coq and Etienne Marcel', *Speculum* 19: 470–87

Galliou, P. and Jones, Michael (1991), *The Bretons*, Oxford

Gavrilovitch, M. (1899), *Etude sur le traité de Paris de 1259*, Paris

Guenée, Bernard (1985), *States and Rulers in Later Medieval Europe*, trans. Juliet Vale, Oxford

Guenée, Bernard (1988), 'Le roi, ses parents et son royaume en France au XIVe siècle', *Bullettino dell'Istituto storico italiano per il medio evo e archivio muratoriano* 94: 439–70

Guessard, F. (1843–4), 'Etienne de Mornay, chancelier de France sous Louis Hutin', *BEC* 5: 373–96

Henneman, John Bell (1968), 'Taxation of Italians by the French Crown (1311–1363)', *MS* 31: 15–43

Henneman, John Bell (1971), *Royal Taxation in Fourteenth Century France. The Development of War Financing 1322–1356*, Princeton

Henneman, John Bell (1976), *Royal Taxation in Fourteenth-Century France. The Captivity and Ransom of John II, 1356–1370*, Philadelphia

Hewitt, H. J. (1958), *The Black Prince's Expedition of 1355–57*, Manchester

Hillgarth, J. N. (1971), *Ramon Lull and Lullism in Fourteenth-Century France*, Oxford

Housley, N. J. (1980), 'The Franco-Papal Crusade Negotiations of 1322–3', *PBSR* 48: 166–85

Housley, Norman (1986), *The Avignon Papacy and the Crusades, 1305–1378*, Oxford

Jones, Michael (1980), 'Sir Thomas Dagworth et la guerre civile en Bretagne au XIVe siècle: quelques documents inédits', *ABret* 87: 621–39

Jones, Michael (1987), 'Sir John de Hardreshull, king's lieutenant in Brittany, 1343–1345', *NMS* 31: 76–97

Jones, Michael (1988a), *The Creation of Brittany. A Late Medieval State*, London

Jones, Michael (1988b), 'Les capitaines anglo-bretons et les marches entre la Bretagne et le Poitou de 1342 à 1373', in *La France 'Anglaise' au moyen âge, ACNSS*, 111, Paris, pp. 357–75

Jones, Michael (1989), 'Relations with France, 1337–1399', in Michael Jones and

Malcolm Vale (eds.), *England and her Neighbours, 1066–1453. Essays in Honour of Pierre Chaplais*, London, pp. 239–58

Jones, Michael (1990), 'The Capetians and Brittany', *HR* 63: 1–16

Jones, Michael (1994), 'War and Fourteenth-Century France', in Anne Curry and Michael Hughes (eds.), *Arms, Armies and Fortifications in the Hundred Years War*, Woodbridge, pp. 103–20

Jones, Michael (1996). 'The Late Medieval State and Social Change: A View from the Duchy of Brittany', *L'Etat on le roi. Les fondations de la modernité monarchique en France*, ed. Neithard Bulst, Robert Descimon and Alain Guerreau, Paris, pp. 117–44

Jordan, William Chester (1989), *The French Monarchy and the Jews from Philip Augustus to the Last Capetians*, Philadelphia

Jordan, William Chester (1996), *The Great Famine. Northern Europe in the Early Fourteenth Century*, Princeton N.J.

Jugie, Pierre (1987), 'L'activité diplomatique du Cardinal Guy de Boulogne en France au milieu du XIVe siècle', *BEC* 145: 99–127

Jusselin, Maurice (1912), 'Comment la France se préparait à la guerre de Cent Ans', *BEC* 73: 209–36

Kaeuper, Richard W. (1988), *War, Justice and Public Order. England and France in the Later Middle Ages*, Oxford

Kicklighter, John (1990), 'Appeal Procedure in the Medieval Parlement of Paris', *BJRL* 72: 37–50

La Roncière, Charles de (1909), *Histoire de la marine française*, 3rd edn, 6 vols., Paris

Leguai, André (1969), *De la seigneurie à l'état. Le Bourbonnais pendant la guerre de cent ans*, Moulins

Lehoux, Françoise (1966–8), *Jean de France, duc de Berri, sa vie, son action politique (1340–1416)*, 4 vols., Paris

Lehugeur, Paul (1897–1931), *Histoire de Philippe le Long*, 2 vols., Paris

Lehugeur, Paul (1929), *Le conseil royal de Philippe le Long, 1316–1321*, Paris

Le Patourel, John (1984), *Feudal Empires Norman and Plantagenet*, ed. Michael Jones, London

Le Roy Ladurie, Emmanuel (1975), *Montaillou, village occitan de 1294 à 1324*, Paris; English trans. Barbara Bray, *Montaillou. Cathars and Catholics in a French Village 1294–1324*, London (1978)

Lewis, Andrew W. (1981), *Royal Succession in Capetian France. Studies on Familial Order and the State*, Cambridge, Mass., and London

Lewis, Peter S. (1968), *Later Medieval France. The Polity*, London

Lewis, Peter S. (1985), *Essays in Later Medieval French History*, London

Longnon, Auguste (1922), *La formation de l'unité française*, Paris

Lot, Ferdinand (1929), 'L'état des paroisses et des feux de 1328', *BEC* 90: 51–107, 256–315

Lot, Ferdinand and Fawtier, Robert (1957–62), *Histoire des institutions françaises au moyen âge*, 3 vols., Paris

Lucas, Henry S. (1929), *The Low Countries and the Hundred Years War 1326–1347*, Ann Arbor

Luce, Siméon (1894), *Histoire de la Jacquerie d'après des documents inédits*, revised edn, Paris

Lyon, Bryce D. (1957), *From Fief to Indenture*, Cambridge, Mass.

Mahn-Lot, M. (1939), 'Philippe d'Evreux roi de Navarre et un projet de croisade contre le royaume de Grenade (1329–1331), *BH*: 227–33

Mirot, Léon (1925), 'Dom Bévy et les comptes des trésoriers des guerres. Essai de restitution d'un fonds disparu de la chambre des comptes', *BEC* 86: 245–379

Mollat, Guillaume (1958), 'Philippe VI de Valois et son fils Jean, duc de Normandie', *BEC* 116: 209–10

Mornet, Elisabeth (ed.) (1995), *Campagnes médiévales: l'Homme et son espace. Etudes offertes à Robert Fossier*, Paris

Morel, Octave (1900), *La grande chancellerie royale (1328–1400)*, Paris

Nicholas, David M. (1971), *Town and Countryside. Social, Economic and Political Tensions in Fourteenth-Century Flanders*, Bruges

Nicholas, David M. (1992), *Medieval Flanders*, London and New York

Nicholson, Ranald (1965), *Edward III and the Scots*, Oxford

Olivier-Martin, F. (1909), *L'assemblée de Vincennes de 1329 et ses conséquences*, Paris

Pegues, Franklin J. (1962), *The Lawyers of the Last Capetians*, Princeton, N.J.

Perrot, E. (1910), *Les cas royaux*, Paris

Perroy, Edouard (1949), 'A l'origine d'une économie contractée: les crises du XIVe siècle', *AESC* 4: 167–82

Petit, Ernest (1885–1905), *Histoire des ducs de Bourgogne de la race capétienne*, 9 vols., Paris

Petit, Jean (1900), *Charles de Valois (1270–1325)*, Paris

Pocquet du Haut-Jussé, Barthélemy-Amadée (1925), 'Les faux états de Bretagne de 1315 et les premiers états de Bretagne', *BEC* 86: 388–406

Pocquet du Haut-Jussé, Barthélemy-Amadée (1928), *Les papes et les ducs de Bretagne*, 2 vols., Paris

Prestwich, Michael (1989), 'England and Scotland during the Wars of Independence', in Michael Jones and Malcolm Vale (eds.), *England and her Neighbours, 1066–1453. Essays in Honour of Pierre Chaplais*, London, pp. 181–97

Rogozinski, Jan (1969), 'The Counsellors of the Seneschals of Beaucaire and Nîmes, 1250–1350', *Speculum*, 44: 421–39

Rogozinski, Jan (1976), 'Ennoblement by the Crown and Social Stratification in France 1285–1322: A Prosopographical Survey', in William C. Jordan, Bruce McNab and Teofilo F. Ruiz (eds.), *Order and Innovation in the Middle Ages. Essays in Honor of Joseph R. Strayer*, New Jersey, pp. 273–91, 500–15

Russell, Major, John (1980), *Representative Government in Early Modern France*, New Haven and London

Small, Carola (1977), 'Appeals from the Duchy of Burgundy to the Parlement of Paris in the Early Fourteenth Century', *MS* 39: 350–68

Small, Carola (1979), 'Appeals to the Royal Courts from the County of Artois, 1328–46', in Joyce Duncan Falk (ed.), *Proceedings of the Sixth Annual Meeting of the Western Society for French History*, Santa Barbara, pp. 9–17

Spufford, Peter (1988), *Money and its Use in Medieval Europe*, Cambridge

Strayer, Joseph R. (1971), *Medieval Statecraft and the Perspectives of History*, Princeton, N.J.

Strayer, Joseph R. (1980), *The Reign of Philip the Fair*, Princeton, N.J.

Strayer, Joseph R. and Taylor, Charles H. (1939), *Studies in Early French Taxation*, Cambridge, Mass.

Sumption, Jonathan (1990), *The Hundred Years War*, I, *Trial by Battle*, London

Taylor, Charles H. (1938), 'An Assembly of French Towns in March 1318', *Speculum* 13: 295–303

Taylor, Charles H. (1939), 'Assemblies of French Towns in 1316', *Speculum* 15: 275–99

Taylor, Charles H. (1954), 'The Composition of Baronial Assemblies in France, 1315–1320', *Speculum* 29: 433–59

Taylor, Charles H. (1968), 'French Assemblies and Subsidy in 1321', *Speculum* 43: 217–44

TeBrake, William H. (1993), *A Plague of Insurrection. Popular Politics and Peasant Revolt in Flanders, 1323–1328*, Philadelphia

Tessier, Georges (1962), *Diplomatique royale française*, Paris

Timbal, Pierre (1961), *La guerre de cent ans vue à travers des registres du parlement de Paris (1337–1369)*, Paris

Trautz, Fritz (1961), *Die Könige von England und das Reich, 1272–1377*, Heidelberg

Tricard, Jean (1979), 'Jean, duc de Normandie et heritier de France, un double échec?', *ANo* 29: 23–44

Tucoo-Chala, Pierre (1960), *Gaston Fébus et la vicomté de Béarn, 1343–1391*, Bordeaux

Tucoo-Chala, Pierre (1961), *La vicomté de Béarn et le problème de sa souveraineté des origines à 1620*, Bordeaux

Tyerman, Christopher J. (1984a), 'Sed nihil fecit? The Last Capetians and the Recovery of the Holy Land', in John Gillingham and J.C. Holt (eds.), *War and Government in the Middle Ages. Essays in Honour of J.O. Prestwich*, Woodbridge, pp. 170–81

Tyerman, Christopher J. (1984b), 'Philip V of France, the Assemblies of 1319–20 and the Crusade', *BIHR* 57: 15–34

Tyerman, Christopher J. (1985), 'Philip VI and the Recovery of the Holy Land', *EHR* 100: 26–52

Vale, Malcolm (1989), 'England, France and the Origins of the Hundred Years War', in Michael Jones and Malcolm Vale (eds.), *England and her Neighbours, 1066–1453. Essays in honour of Pierre Chaplais*, London, pp. 199–216

Vale, Malcolm (1990), *The Angevin Legacy and the Hundred Years War, 1250–1340*, Oxford

Vale, Malcolm (1991), 'The Anglo-French Wars, 1294–1340: Allies and Alliances', in Philippe Contamine, Charles Giry-Deloison and Maurice H. Keen (eds.), *Guerre et société en France, en Angleterre et en Bourgogne, XIVe–XVe siècle*, Lille, pp. 15–35

Vaughan, Richard (1962), *Philip the Bold*, London

Viard, Jules (1888), 'Un chapitre d'histoire administrative. Les ressources extraordinaires de la royauté sous Philippe VI de Valois', *RQH* 44: 167–218

Viard, Jules (1890), 'Gages des officiers royaux vers 1329', *BEC* 51: 238–67

Viard, Jules (1894), 'L'Hôtel de Philippe VI de Valois', *BEC* 55: 465–87, 598–626

Viard, Jules (1896), 'La France sous Philippe VI de Valois. Etat géographique et militaire', *RQH* 59: 337–402

Viard, Jules (1921), 'Philippe VI de Valois: la succession au trône', *MA* 31: 218–22

Viard, Jules (1936), 'Les projets de croisade de Philippe VI de Valois', *BEC* 97: 305–16

Wood, Charles T. (1966), *The French Apanages and the Capetian Monarchy, 1224–1328*, Cambridge, Mass.

Wood, Diana (1989), *Clement VI. The Pontificate and Ideas of an Avignon Pope*, Cambridge

Wright, Nicholas (1998), *Knights and Peasants. Hundred Years War in the French Countryside*, Woodbridge

14(b) FRANCE UNDER CHARLES V AND CHARLES VI

Primary sources

Autrand, Fr., 'La prière de Charles V', *ABSHF, année 1995* (1996), pp. 37–61

Besse, G., *Recueil de diverses pièces servant à l'histoire du roi Charles VI*, Paris (1660)

Bock, F., 'Some New Documents Illustrating the Early Years of the Hundred Years War', *BJRL* 15 (1931), pp. 60–99

Boulet, M., *Questiones Johannis Galli*, Paris (1944)

Brun, R., 'Annales avignonnaises de 1382 à 1410, extraites des archives de Datini', *Mémoires de l'Institut historique de Provence* 12 (1935), pp. 17–142; 13 (1936), pp. 58–105; 14 (1937), pp. 5–57; 15 (1938), pp. 21–52; 16 (1939), pp. 154–92

Chaplais, P., 'Some Documents Regarding the Fulfilment and Interpretation of the Treaty of Brétigny (1361–1369)', *Camden Miscellany* 19 (1952), pp. 1–84

Chronique des règnes de Jean II et Charles V, ed. R. Delachenal, 4 vols., Paris (1917–20)

Chronique de la Pucelle ou chronique de Cousinot, followed by *Chronique normande de P. Cochon, relatives aux règnes de Charles VI et de Charles VII*, ed. A. Vallet de Viriville, Paris (1859)

Chronique des quatre premiers Valois (1327–1393), ed. S. Luce, Paris (1862)

La chronique du bon duc Loys de Bourbon, ed. A.-M. Chazaud, Paris (1876)

Chronique normande, ed. E. Molinier, Paris (1882)

Chroniques et annales de Gille le Muisit, abbé de Saint-Martin de Tournai (1272–1352), ed. H. Lemaître, Paris (1906)

Les chroniques du roi Charles VII par Gilles le Bouvier dit le Héraut Berry, ed. H.C. Courteault, L. Celier and M.-H. Julien de Pommerol, Paris (1979)

Chronographia Regum Francorum (1270–1405), ed. H. Moranvillé, 3 vols., Paris (1891–7)

Comptes du trésor (1296, 1316, 1384, 1477), ed. R. Fawtier, Paris (1930)

Contamine, P., 'Un traité politique du XVe siècle', *ABSHF, années 1983–4* (1986), pp. 139–71

Cosneau, E., *Les grands traités de la guerre de cent ans*, Paris (1889)

Cuvelier, Jean, *La chanson de Bertrand du Guesclin*, ed. J.-C. Faucon, 3 vols., Toulouse (1990–2)

Delisle, L., *Mandements et actes divers de Charles V (1364–1380)*, Paris (1874)

Delisle, L., *Recherches sur la librairie de Charles V*, 2 vols., Paris (1907)

Les demandes faites par le roi Charles VI, touchant son état et le gouvernement de sa personne, avec les réponses de Pierre Salmon, son secrétaire et familier, ed. G.-A. Crapelet, Paris (1833)

Deschamps, Eustache, *Oeuvres complètes*, ed. le marquis de Queux de Saint-Hilaire and G. Raynaud, 11 vols., Paris (1878–1904)

Devic, J. and Vaissette, C., *Histoire générale de Languedoc avec des notes et des pièces justificatives*, ed. A. Molinier, Toulouse, IX–XII (1885–9)

Douët d'Arcq, L., *Choix de pièces inédites relatives au règne de Charles VI*, 2 vols., Paris (1863–4)

Douët d'Arcq, L., *Comptes de l'Hôtel des rois de France aux XIVe et XVe siècles*, Paris (1865)

Douët d'Arcq, L., 'Document inédit sur l'assassinat de Louis, duc d'Orléans (23 novembre 1407)', *ABSHF, année 1864*, 2e partie, pp. 6–26

Douët d'Arcq, L., *Nouveaux recueil des comptes de l'Argenterie des rois de France*, Paris (1884)

Eder, R., 'Tignonvilla inedita', *RF* 33 (1975), pp. 851–1022

Fenin, Pierre de, *Mémoires*, ed. E. Dupont, Paris (1837)

le Fevre de Saint-Remy, Jean, *Chronique*, ed. F. Morand, 2 vols., Paris (1876–81)

Froissart, Jean, *Chroniques*, ed. S. Luce *et al.*, 15 vols., Paris (1869–1975 continuing)

Froissart, Jean, *Œuvres*, ed. J.M.B.C. Kervyn de Lettenhove, 28 vols., Brussels (1867–79)

Gerson, Jean, *Œuvres complètes*, ed. P. Glorieux, 10 vols., Paris, Tournai and Rome (1960–73)

Godefroy, D., *Le cérémonial françois*, Paris (1649)

Graves, F.-M., *Pièces relatives à la vie de Louis Ier duc d'Orléans et de Valentine Visconti, sa femme*, Paris (1913)

Guenée, B. and Lehoux, F., *Les entrées royales françaises de 1328 à 1515*, Paris (1968)

Guilhiermoz, Paul, *Enquêtes et procès. Etude sur la procédure et le fonctionnement du parlement au XIVème siècle, suivie du style de la chambre des enquêtes, du style des commissaires du parlement et autres*, Paris (1902)

'*L'honneur de la couronne de France*'. *Quatre libelles contre les Anglais (vers 1418–vers 1429)*, ed. N. Pons, Paris (1990)

Journal d'un bourgeois de Paris (1405–1449), ed. A. Tuetey, Paris (1881)

Journal de Clément de Fauquembergue, ed. A. Tuetey, 3 vols., Paris (1903–15)

Journal de Nicolas de Baye, greffier du parlement de Paris, 1400–1417, ed. A. Tuetey, 2 vols., Paris (1885–8)

'Journal des états généraux réunis à Paris au mois d'Octobre 1356', ed. R. Delachenal, *NRHDFE* 24 (1900), pp. 415–65

Juvénal des Ursins, Jean, *Ecrits politiques*, ed. P. S. Lewis, 3 vols., Paris (1978–92)

Juvénal des Ursins, Jean, 'Histoire de Charles VI, roy de France . . .', in Michaud et Poujoulat (ed.), *Nouvelle collection de mémoires pour servir à l'histoire de France . . .*, II, Paris (1836)

Labarte, J., *Inventaire du mobilier de Charles V, roi de France*, Paris (1879)

Le livre des fais du bon messire Jehan le Maingre, dit Bouciquaut, mareschal de France et gouverneur de Jennes, ed. D. Lalande, Paris and Geneva (1985)

Luce, S., *Histoire de la Jacquerie d'après les documents inédits*, 2nd edn, Paris (1894)

Machaut, Guillaume de, *Œuvres*, ed. E. Hoepffner, 3 vols., Paris (1908–21)

Mézières, Philippe de, *Le songe du vieil pélerin*, ed. G. W. Coopland, 2 vols., Cambridge (1969)

Mézières, Philippe de, *Letter to King Richard II. A Plea Made in 1395 for Peace Between England and France*, ed. G.W. Coopland, Liverpool (1975)

Monstrelet, Enguerrand de, *Chronique*, ed. L. Douët d'Arcq, 6 vols., Paris (1857–62)

Montebelluna, François de, '*Tragicum Argumentum de miserabili statu regni Francie (1357)*', ed. A. Vernet, *ABSHF, années 1962–1963* (1965), pp. 101–63

Montreuil, Jean de, *Opera*, ed. E. Ornato, G. Ouy and N. Pons, 4 vols., Turin and Paris (1966–86)

Morice, Dom P.-H., *Mémoires pour servir de preuves à l'histoire ecclésiastique et civile de la Bretagne*, 3 vols., Paris (1742–6)

L'ordonnance cabochienne (26–27 mai 1413), ed. A. Coville, Paris (1891)

Ordonnances des rois de France de la troisième race, ed. E.S. de Laurière *et al.*, 22 vols., Paris (1723–1849)

Oresme, Nicolas, *Le livre des éthiques d'Aristote*, ed. A. M. Menut, New York (1940)

Oresme, Nicolas, *Maistre Nicole Oresme. Le Livre de Politiques d'Aristote*, ed. A.M. Menut, Philadelphia (1970)

Oresme, Nicolas, *Traité des monnaies et autres écrits monétaires du XIVe siècle*, ed. and trans. C. Dupuy and F. Chartrain, Lyon (1989)

Partie inédite des Chroniques de Saint-Denys . . ., ed. J. Pichon, Paris (1864)

Le pastoralet, ed. J. Blanchard, Paris (1983)

Perroy, E., 'The Anglo-French Negotiations at Bruges, 1374–1377', *Camden Miscellany* 19 (1952), pp. I–XIX, 1–95

Pisan, Christine de, *Le livre des fais et bonnes meurs du sage roy Charles V*, ed. S. Solente, 2 vols., Paris (1936–40)

Plancher, Dom U., *Histoire générale et particulière de Bourgogne*, 4 vols., Dijon (1739–81)

Recueil des actes de Jean IV, duc de Bretagne (1357–1399), ed. Michael Jones, 2 vols., Paris (1980–3)

Registre criminel du châtelet de Paris du 6 septembre 1389 au 18 mai 1392, ed. H. Duplès-Agier, 2 vols., Paris (1861–4)

'Remontrances de l'université et de la ville de Paris à Charles VI', ed. H. Moranvillé, *BEC* 51 (1890), pp. 420–42

Secousse, D., *Recueil de pièces servant de preuves aux mémoires sur les troubles excités en France par Charles II, dit le Mauvais, roi de Navarre et comte d'Evreux*, Paris (1755)

Somnium viridarii, ed. M. Schnerb-Lièvre, I, Paris (1993)

'Le songe véritable. Pamphlet politique d'un Parisien du XVe siècle', ed. H. Moranvillé, *MSHP* 17 (1890), pp. 217–438

Le songe du vergier, ed. M. Schnerb-Lièvre, 2 vols., Paris (1982)

Timbal, P.C. *et al.*, *La guerre de cent ans vue à travers les registres du parlement (1337–1369)*, Paris (1961)

Venette, Jean de, *Continuationis chronici Guillelmi de Nangiaco pars tertia (1340–1368)*, ed. H. Géraud, 2 vols., Paris (1843); Eng. trans. Jean Birdsall, *The Chronicle of Jean de Venette*, ed. R.A. Newhall, New York (1953)

Secondary works

Allmand, C.T. (ed.) (1976), *War, Literature and Politics in the Late Middle-Ages. Essays in Honour of G.W. Coopland,* Liverpool

Allmand, C.T. (1988), *The Hundred Years War. England and France at War c. 1300–1450*, Cambridge

Autrand, Fr. (1969), 'Offices et officiers royaux en France sous Charles VI', *Revue historiques* 242: 285–338

Autrand, Fr. (1974), *Pouvoir et société en France*, Paris

Autrand, Fr. (1981), *Naissance d'un grand corps de l'état. Les gens du parlement de Paris, 1345–1454,* Paris

Autrand, Fr. (1986), *Charles VI. La folie du roi,* Paris

Autrand, Fr. (1994), *Charles V le sage*, Paris

Autrand, Fr. (1998), 'Les artisans de paix face à l'Etat. La diplomatie pontificale et le conflit franco-anglais au XIVe siècle', in Ph. Contamine (ed.), *Guerre et concurrence entre les états européens du XIVe au XVIIIe siècle*, Paris, pp. 305–37

Autrand, Fr. (1999), 'Aux origines de l'Europe moderne; l'alliance France-Ecosse au XIVe s.', in J.C. Laidlaw (ed.), *The Auld Alliance. France and Scotland over 700 years*, Edinburgh, pp. 33–46

Autrand, Fr. and Contamine, Ph. (1995), 'Les livres des hommes de pouvoir: de la pratique à la culture écrite', in M. Ornato and N. Pons (eds.), *Pratiques de la culture écrite en France au XVe siècle*, Louvain-la-Neuve, pp. 195–224

Autrand, Fr. and Le Maresquier, Y.-H. (1994), 'Vie sociale et municipale à Paris aux XIVe et XVe s.', *Franco-British Studies, Journal of the British Institute in Paris,* 17: 65-75

Autrand, Fr., Bournazel, E. and Riché, P. (1993), *Histoire de la fonction publique en France,* ed. M. Pinet, 1, *Des origines au XV siècle,* Paris

Avout, J. d' (1943), *La Querelle des Armagnacs et des Bourguignons. Histoire d'une crise d'autorité,* Paris

Avout, J. d' (1960), *31 juillet 1358. Le meurtre d'Etienne Marcel,* Paris

Babbit, S.M. (1985), *Oresme's 'Livre de Politiques' and the France of Charles V,* Philadelphia

Barber, R. (1978), *Edward, Prince of Wales and Aquitaine,* London

Barber, R. (1986), *The Life and Campaigns of the Black Prince,* Woodbridge

Barbey, J. (1983), *La fonction royale, essence et légitimité, d'après les 'tractatus' de Jean de Terrevermeille,* Paris

Beaune, C. (1981), 'Costume et pouvoir en France à la fin du moyen-âge. Les devises royales vers 1400', *Revue des sciences humaines* 183: 125–46

Beaune, C. (1985), *Naissance de la nation France,* Paris; augmented English trans. Susan Ross Huston, *The Birth of an Ideology. Myths and Symbols of Nation in Late-Medieval France,* ed. Fredric L. Cheyette, Berkeley, Los Angeles and London (1991)

Bell, D.-M. (1962), *L'idéal éthique de la royauté en France au moyen-âge d'après quelques moralistes de ce temps,* Geneva and Paris

Beltran E. (1989), *L'idéal de sagesse d'après Jacques Legrand,* Paris

Bonenfant, P. (1958), *Du meurtre de Montereau au traité de Troyes,* Brussels

Bozzolo, C. and Loyau, H. (1982–93), *La cour amoureuse dite de Charles VI,* 3 vols., Paris

Brachet, A. (1903), *Pathologie mentale des rois de France,* Paris

Calmette, J. and Déprez, E. (1937), *L'Europe occidentale de la fin du XIVe siècle aux guerres d'Italie,* 1: *La France et l'Angleterre en conflit,* Paris

Cazelles, R. (1972), *Nouvelle histoire de Paris. De la fin du règne de Philippe Auguste à la mort de Charles V (1223–1380),* Paris

Cazelles, R. (1982), *Société politique, noblesse et couronne sous les règnes de Jean II le Bon et Charles V,* Geneva and Paris

Cazelles, R. (1984), *Etienne Marcel, champion de l'unité française,* Paris

Chapelot, J. (1994), *Le château de Vincennes. Une résidence royale au moyen-âge,* Paris

Collas, E. (1911), *Valentine de Milan, duchesse d'Orléans,* Paris

Contamine, Ph. (1972), *Guerre, état et société à la fin du moyen-âge. Étude sur les armées des rois de France, 1337–1494,* Paris and The Hague

Contamine, Ph. (1980), *La guerre au moyen âge,* Paris; English trans. M. Jones, *War in the Middle Ages,* Oxford (1984); 2nd edn 1986; 3rd edn 1995

Contamine, Ph. (1981), *La France aux XIV et XVe siècles. Hommes, mentalités, guerre et paix,* London

Contamine, Ph. (1992a), *Des pouvoirs en France, 1300–1500,* Paris

Contamine, Ph. (1992b), *Histoire militaire de la France,* ed. A. Corvisier, 1. *Des origines à 1715,* Paris

Contamine, Ph. (1993), *La guerre de cent ans,* new edn, Paris

Contamine, Ph. (1997), *La noblesse au royaume de France de Philippe le Bel à Louis XII,* Paris

Coville, A. (1888), *Les Cabochiens et l'ordonnance de 1413,* Paris

Coville, A. (1932), *Jean Petit, la question du tyrannicide au commencement du XVe siècle,* Paris

Coville, A. (1941), *La vie intellectuelle dans les domaines d'Anjou-Provence de 1380 à 1435*, Paris

Cuttler, S.H. (1981), *The Law of Treason and Treason Trials in Later Medieval France*, Cambridge

Delachenal, R. (1909–31), *Histoire de Charles V,* 5 vols., Paris

Delaruelle, E., Labande, E.-R. and Ourliac, P. (1962–4), *L'église au temps du Grand Schisme et de la crise conciliaire (1378–1469)*, 2 vols., Paris

Demurger, A. (1978), 'Guerre civile et changement du personnel administratif dans le royaume de France de 1400 à 1418: l'exemple des baillis et sénéchaux', *Francia* 6: 151–258

Demurger, A. (1990), *Temps de crises, temps d'espoirs, XIVe–XV siècle*, Paris

Dubois, H. (1976), *Les foires de Chalon et le commerce dans la vallée de la Saône à la fin du moyen âge (vers 1280–vers 1430)*, Paris

Erlande-Brandenburg, A. (1988), *Le monde gothique. La conquête de l'Europe, 1260–1380*, Paris

Famiglietti, R. C. (1986), *Royal Intrigue. Crisis at the Court of Charles VI (1392–1420)*, New York

Les fastes du gothique. Le siècle de Charles V (1981) exhibition catalogue, Grand Palais, Paris

Favier, J. (1974), *Paris au XVe siècle, 1380–1500*, Paris

Favier, J. (1980), *La guerre de cent ans*, Paris

Fourquin, G. (1964), *Les campagnes de la région parisienne à la fin du moyen-âge*, Paris

Fowler, K.A. (ed.) (1971), *The Hundred Years War,* London

Gauvard, C. (1985), 'Le roi de France et l'opinion publique à l'époque de Charles VI', in *Culture et idéologie dans la genèse de l'état moderne*, Rome, pp. 353–66

Gauvard, C. (1992), *'De grace especial'. Crime, état et société en France à la fin du moyen âge*, 2 vols., Paris

Genèse et débuts du Grand Schisme d'Occident (1362–1394), Paris (1980)

Genet, J.-P. (ed.) (1990), *L'état moderne. Genèse, bilans et perspectives*, Paris

Gouron, A. and Rigaudière, A. (eds.) (1988), *Renaissance du pouvoir législatif et genèse de l'état*, Montpellier

Grandeau, Y. (1967), 'Itinéraires d'Isabeau de Bavière', *BPH, année 1964*, ii, pp. 569–670

Grandeau, Y. (1969), 'Les enfants de Charles VI. Essai sur la vie privée des princes et des princesses de la maison de France à la fin du moyen âge', *BPH, année 1967*, ii, pp. 809–50

Grandeau, Y. (1971), 'Le dauphin Jean, duc de Touraine, fils de Charles VI, (1398–1417)', *BPH, année 1968*, ii, pp. 665–728

Grandeau, Y. (1974), 'La mort et les obsèques de Charles VI', *BPH, année 1970*, ii, pp. 133–86

Grandeau, Y. (1977), 'De quelques dames qui ont servi la reine Isabeau de Bavière', *BPH, année 1975*, ii, pp. 129–238

Guenée, B. (1987), *Entre l'église et l'état. Quatre vies de prélats français à la fin du moyen âge*, Paris

Guenée, B. (1991), *L'Occident aux XIVe et XVe siècles. Les états*, new edn, Paris; English trans. Juliet Vale, *States and Rulers in Later Medieval Europe,*Oxford (1986)

Guenée, B. (1992), *Un meurtre, une société. L'assassinat du duc d'Orléans*, Paris

Guillemain, A. (1978), 'Le *Testament* de Philippe de Mézières', in *Mélanges de littérature . . . offerts à Mademoiselle Jeanne Lods . . .*, Paris, i, pp. 297–322

Henneman, J.B. (1971), *Royal Taxation in Fourteenth-Century France. The Development of War Financing, 1322–1356*, Princeton

Henneman, J.B. (1976), *Royal Taxation in Fourteenh-Century France. The Captivity and Ransom of John II, 1356–1370*, Philadephia

Henneman, J.B. (1996), *Olivier de Clisson and Political Society under Charles V and Charles VI*, Philadelphia

Henwood, P. (1979), 'Raymond du Temple, maître d'œuvre des rois Charles V et Charles VI', *Bull. Soc. hist. de Paris et de l'Ile de France, année 1978*, pp. 55–74

Jackson, R. (1984), *Vivat Rex. Histoire des sacres et des couronnements en France*, Strasburg and Paris

Jarry, E. (1889), *La vie politique de Louis de France, duc d'Orléans, 1372–1407*, Paris and Orléans

Jones, M. (1970), *Ducal Brittany, 1364–1399*, Oxford

Jones, M. (1988), *The Creation of Brittany. A Late Medieval State*, London

Jorga, N. (1896), *Philippe de Mézières 1327–1405 et la croisade au XIVe siècle*, Paris

Jugie, P. (1986), 'Le cardinal Gui de Boulogne (1316–1373). Biographie et étude d'une familia cardinalice', *PTEC*: 83–92

Jugie, P. (1987), 'L'activité diplomatique du cardinal Gui de Boulogne en France au milieu du XIVe siècle, *BEC* 145: 99–127

Kaminsky, H. (1983), *Simon de Cramaud and the Great Schism*, Rutgers

Kantorowicz, E.H. (1957), *The King's Two Bodies. A Study in Medieval Political Theology*, Princeton, N.J.

Kennedy, A.J. (1988), 'Christine de Pizan's *Epistre à la reine* (1405)', *RLR* 92: 253–64

Kerhervé, J. (1987), *L'état breton aux XIVe et XVe siècles. Les ducs, l'argent et les hommes*, 2 vols., Paris

Kimm, M.H. (1969), *Isabeau de Bavière, reine de France (1370–1435). Beitrag zur Geschichte einer bayerischen Herzogtochter und des französischen Königshauses*, Munich

Krynen, J. (1981), *Idéal du prince et pouvoir royal en France à la fin du moyen âge (1380–1440). Etude de la littérature politique du temps*, Paris

Krynen, J. (1993), *L'empire du roi. Idées et croyances politiques en France, XIIIe–XVe siècle*, Paris

Krynen, J. and Rigaudière, A. (eds.) (1992), *Droits savants et pratiques françaises du pouvoir*, Bordeaux

La Selle, X. de (1995), *Le service des âmes à la cour: confesseurs et aumôniers des rois de France du XIIIe au XVe siècle*, Paris

Lafaurie, J. (1951), *Les monnaies des rois de France*, i: *De Hugues Capet à Louis XII*, Paris and Basle

Le Roux de Lincy, A. and Tisserand, L.M. (1867), *Paris et ses historiens aux XIVe et XVe siècles*, Paris

Leguai, A. (1962), *Les ducs de Bourbon pendant la crise monarchique du XVe siècle*, Paris

Leguai, A. (1969), *De la seigneurie à l'état Le Bourbonnais pendant la guerre de cent ans*, Moulins

Lehoux, Fr. (1966–8), *Jean de France, duc de Berri. Sa vie. Son action politique (1340–1416)*, 4 vols., Paris

Lewis, P.S. (1968), *Late Medieval France. The Polity*, London

Lewis, P.S. (1985), *Essays in Later Medieval French History*, London

La librairie du roi (1968) (exhibition catalogue, Bibliothèque nationale), Paris

Lot, F. and Fawtier, R. (1957–62), *Histoire des institutions françaises au moyen âge*, 3 vols., Paris

'Le Louvre des rois. Les fouilles de la cour Carrée' (1986), *Dossiers histoire et archéologie*, no. 110

Maumené, Ch. and Harcourt, L. d' (1928), *Iconographie des rois de France*, 1: *De Louis IX à Louis XIII*, Paris

Millet, H. (1982), *Les Chanoines du chapitre cathédral de Laon, 1272–1412*, Rome

Millet, H. and Poulle, E. (1988), *Le vote de la soustraction d'obédience en 1398*, 1: Introduction. *Edition et fac-similés des bulletins du vote*, Paris

Minois, G. (1993), *Du Guesclin*, Paris

Mirot, L. (1905), *Les insurrections urbaines sous Charles VI (1380–1383), leurs causes, leurs conséquences*, Paris

Mirot, L. (1919), 'Lettres closes de Charles VI conservées aux archives de Reims et de Tournai', *MA* 30: 125–39

Mollat, M. and Wolff, Ph. (1970), *Ongles bleus, Jacques et Ciompi. Les révolutions populaires en Europe aux XIVe et XVe siècles*, Paris

Monfrin, J. (1964), 'Humanisme et traductions au moyen âge', in A. Fournier (ed.), *L'Humanisme médiéval dans les littératures romanes du XIIe au XIVe siècle*, Paris, pp. 217–46

Munro, J.H. (1973), *Wool, Cloth and Gold. The Struggle for Bullion in Anglo-Burgundian Trade (1340–1478)*, Toronto

Nordberg, M. (1964), *Les ducs et la royauté. Etude sur la rivalité des ducs d'Orléans et de Bourgogne, 1392–1407*, Uppsala

Ornato, E. (1969), *Jean Muret et ses amis Nicolas de Clamanges et Jean de Monteuil. Contribution à l'étude des rapports entre les humanistes de Paris et ceux d'Avignon (1394–1420)*, Geneva and Paris

Ouy, G. (1973), 'L'humanisme et les mutations politiques et sociales en France aux XIVe et XVe siècle', in *L'humanisme français au début de la Renaissance*, Paris, pp. 27–44

Ouy, G. (1974), 'Humanisme et propagande politique en France au début du XVe siècle: Ambrogio Migli et les ambitions impériales de Louis d'Orléans', in *Atti del Convegno su: 'Culture et politique en France à l'époque de l'Humanisme et de la Renaissance', Accademia delle Scienze di Torino, 29 marzo–3 aprile 1971*, Turin, pp. 13–42

Ouy, G. (1975), 'Le collège de Navarre, berceau de l'humanisme français', *ACNSS*, 95e Congrès, Reims, 1970, section phil. et hist., Paris, 1, pp. 275–99

Palmer, J.J.N. (1972), *England, France and Christendom (1377–1399)*, London

Phillpotts, C. (1984), 'The French Plan of Battle during the Agincourt Campaign', *EHR* 99: 59–66

Plaisse, A. (1972), *Charles dit le Mauvais, comte d'Evreux, roi de Navarre, capitaine de Paris*, Evreux

Pocquet du Haut-Jussé, B.-A. (1935), *Deux féodaux, Bourgogne et Bretagne (1363–1491)*, Paris

Pocquet du Haut-Jussé, B.-A. (1937), 'Le compte de Pierre de Gorremont, receveur général du royaume (1418–1420)', *BEC* 98: 66–98 and 234–82

Pocquet du Haut-Jussé, B.-A. (1959), *La France gouvernée par Jean sans Peur. Les dépenses du receveur général du Royaume*, Paris

Préludes à la Renaissance. Aspects de la vie intellectuelle en France au XVe siècle (1992), ed. C. Bozzolo and E. Ornato, Paris

Quillet, J. (1986), *Charles V. Essai sur la pensée politique d'un règne*, Paris

Rey, M. (1965a), *Le domaine du roi et les finances extraordinaires sous Charles VI, 1388–1413*, Paris

Rey, M. (1965b), *Les finances royales sous Charles VI. Les causes du déficit 1388–1413*, Paris

Rodinson, M. (1989), 'Le seigneur bourguignon et l'esclave sarrasin. De Charles VI à Alexandre Dumas', in M. Rodinson, *La fascination de l'Islam*, Paris, pp. 141–98

Royer, J.-P. (1969), *L'église et le royaume de France au XIVe siècle, d'après le 'Songe du vergier' et la jurisprudence du parlement*, Paris

Schnerb, B. (1986), *Les Armagnacs et les Bourguignons. La sale guerre*, Paris

Sherman, C.R. (1969), *The portraits of Charles V*, New York

Thibault, M. (1903), *Isabeau de Bavière, reine de France. La jeunesse, 1370–1405*, Paris

Tucoo-Chala, P. (1961), *La vicomté de Béarn et le problème de la souveraineté, des origines à 1620*, Bordeaux

Tucoo-Chala, P. (1976), *Gaston Fébus, un grand prince d'Occident*, Pau

Valois, N. (1888), *Le conseil du Roi aux XIVe, XVe et XVIe siècles*, Paris

Valois, N. (1896–1902), *La France et le Grand Schisme d'Occident*, 4 vols., Paris

Van Ossel, P. (1992), 'Nouvelles données sur l'enceinte de Charles V (XIVe–XVIe siècle) à Paris, d'après les fouilles du jardin du Carrousel au Louvre', *AIBL, comptes rendus*, pp. 337–51

Vaughan, R. (1962), *Philip the Bold. The Formation of the Burgundian State*, London

Vaughan, R. (1966), *John the Fearless. The Growth of Burgundian Power*, London

Vaughan, R. (1970), *Philip the Good. The Apogee of Burgundy*, London

Verger, J. (1987), 'Nouveaux fléaux, nouveaux recours', in J. Delumeau and Y. Lequin (eds.), *Les malheurs des temps. Histoire des fléaux et des calamités en France*, Paris, pp. 209–24

Whiteley, M. (1992), 'Le Louvre de Charles V; dispositions et fonctions d'une résidence royale', *Revue de l'art* 97: 60–75

15(a) THE ITALIAN NORTH

Primary sources

Annales Mediolanenses, *RIS*, XVI, Milan (1730)

Azario, Pietro, *Liber Gestorum in Lombardia*, ed. F. Cognasso, *RIS*, XVI/4, Bologna (1938)

Bartoli, A., *I Manuscritti Italiani della Biblioteca Nazionale di Firenze*, 3 vols., Florence (1883)

Chronicon Bergomense, ed. C. Capasso, *RIS*, XVI/2, Bologna (1926)

Chronicon Veronense, *RIS*, VIII, Milan (1726)

Cipolla, C. and Pellegrini, F. (eds.), 'Poesie minori riguardanti gli Scaligieri', *Bulletino del'Istituto storico italiana per il medio evo*, 24 (1902)

Conti, G., *Novellae inedite intorno a Bernabò Visconti*, Florence (1940)

Cortusi, Guigliclmo, *Cronica de Novitatibus Paduc et Lombardiae*, ed. B. Pagnin, *RIS*, XII/5, Bologna (1941)

Dati, G., *Istoria di Firenze*, ed. G. Manni, Florence (1735)

Liber de Laudibus Civitatis Ticinensis, ed. R. Maiocchi and F. Quintavalle, *RIS*, XVI/1, Città di Castello (1903)

Lünig, J.C., *Codex Italiae Diplomaticus*, I, Frankfurt and Leipzig (1725)

Medin, A., 'La letteratura poetica viscontea', *ASL* 2nd series 2 (1885), pp. 568–81

Miari, C., *Cronaca Bellunese*, ed. G. De Dona, Belluno (1873)

Musatti, M.P. (ed.), *Lamento di Bernabò Visconti*, Milan (1985)

Ordo funeris Joannis Galeatii Vicecomitis, RIS, XVI, Milan (1730)

Secondary works

Agnelli, G. (1901), 'Vertenze dei Visconti colla mensa vescovile di Lodi', *ASL* 3rd series, 16: 260–306

Assereto, U. (1900), 'Genova e la Corsica 1358–88', *Giornale storico-letterario della liguria* 1: 119–60

Avesani, R. (1988), 'Petrarca e Verona', in Varanini (1988b), pp. 505–10

Baron, H. (1955), *The Crisis of the Early Italian Renaissance*, Princeton; rev. edn, 1966

Benvenuti, G. (1977), *Storia della repubblica di Genova*, Milan

Berrigan, J.R. (1990), 'A Tale of Two Cities: Verona and Padua in the Late Middle Ages', in C.M. Rosenberg (ed.), *Art and Patronage in Late Medieval and Early Renaissance Italy*, Notre Dame, pp. 67–80

Besozzi, L. (1981), 'I processi canonici contro Galeazzo Visconti', *ASL* 10th series 6: 235–45

Biscaro, G. (1920), 'Dante Alighieri e i sortilegi di Matteo e Galeazzo Visconti contro papal Giovanni XXII', *ASL* 5th series 7: 446–81

Black, J.W. (1994), '*Natura Feudi Haec Est*: Lawyers and Feudatories in the Duchy of Milan', *EHR* 99: 1150–73

Bowsky, W.M. (1960), *Henry VII in Italy*, Lincoln

Brown, H. (1895), *Venice, an Historical Sketch*, London

Bueno da Mesquita, D.M. (1941), *Giangaleazzo Visconti*, Cambridge

Canning, J. (1987), *The Political Thought of Baldus Ubaldis*, Cambridge

Carlotto, N. (1993), *La città custodita. Politica e finanza a Vicenza dalla caduta di Ezzelino al vicariato imperiale*, Milan

Carrara, M. (1966), *Gli Scaligeri*, Varese

Cau, E. (1969–70), 'Lettere inedite Viscontee. Contributo alla diplomatica signorile', *Ricerche medievali* 4–5: 45–98

Ceriotti, G. (1972–3), 'Interpretazione storica di Fra Jacopo Bussulari', *BSPSP* n.s. 22–3: 3–34

Cessi, R. (1914), 'Venezia e le preparazioni della guerra friulana', *Memorie storiche Forogiuliesi* 10: 414–73

Chittolini, G. (1980), *La crisi delle Libertà Comunali e le origini dello stato del rinascimento*, Bologna

Chittolini, G. (1981), 'Signorie rurali e feudi alla fine del medioevo', *Storia d'Italia*, UTET, IV, Turin, pp. 591–676

Chojnacki, S. (1973), 'In Search of the Venetian Patriciate: Family and Faction in the Fourteenth Century', in J.R. Hale (ed.), *Renaissance Venice*, London, pp. 47–90

Chojnacki, S. (1994), 'Social Identity in Renaissance Venice: The Second *Serrata*', *RStds* 8: 341–58

Cipolla, C. (1881), *Storia delle signorie italiane*, Milan

Cognasso, F. (1922), 'Ricerche per la storia dello stato visconteo', *BSPSP* 22: 121–84

Cognasso, F. (1923), 'Note e documenti sulla formazione dello stato visconteo', *BSPSP* 23: 23–169

Cognasso, F. (1955), 'Le basi giuridiche della signoria di Matteo Visconti in Milano', *BSBS* 53: 79–89

Cognasso, F. (1971), *I Savoia*, Varese

Cogo, G. (1898), 'Il patriarcato di Aquileia e le aspirazioni dei Carraresi al possesso del Friuli', *NAV* 16: 223–320

Comani, F.E. (1900a), 'Usi cancellereschi viscontei', *ASL* 4th series 13: 385–412

Comani, F.E. (1900b), 'Prime informazioni sui documenti viscontei del R. Archivio di Stato a Reggio Emilia', *ASL* 3rd series 13: 221–9

Comani, F.E. (1902), 'Sui domini di Regina della Scala e dei sui figli', *ASL* 3rd series 18: 211–48

Corbanese, G.G. (1984), *Il Friuli, Trieste e l'Istria*, Bologna

Costa, A. (1977), *I vescovi di Trento*, Trent

Cox, E. (1967), *The Green Count of Savoy*, Princeton

Cozzi, G. and Knapton, M. (1986), *Storia della repubblica di Venezia dalla guerra di Chioggia alla riconquista della terraferma*, Storia d'Italia, UTET, xii/i, Turin

Crouzet-Pavan, E. (1992), *Espaces, pouvoir et société à Venise à la fin du moyen âge*, Rome

Crouzet-Pavan, E. (1994), 'Venice and Torcello: History and Oblivion', *RStds* 8: 416–27

Cusin, F. (1937), *Il confine orientale d'Italia*, I, Milan

De Marco, E. (1938–9), 'Crepusculo degli Scaligeri, la signoria di Antonio della Scala', *NAV* 22: 107–206 and 24: 1–20

De Negri, T. O. (1968), *Storia di Genova*, Milan

De Vergottini, G. (1941), 'Vicariati imperiali e signori', in *Studi di storia e diritto in onore di Arrigo Solmi*, Milan, pp. 41–64

Enciclopedia Italiana, 35 vols., Rome, Istituto della Enciclopedia Italiana (1949)

Ercole, F. (1910), 'Comuni e signorie nel veneto. Saggio storico-giuridico', *NAV* n.s. 19: 255–337

Ercole, F. (1929), *Dal comune al principato. Saggi sulla storia del diritto del rinascimento italiano*, Florence

Fondazione Treccani degli Alfieri (1954–5), *Storia di Milano*, iv and v, Milan

Fortuni Brown, P. (1988), *Venetian Narrative Painting in the Age of Carpaccio*, Newhaven and London

Gabotto, F. (1894), *Storia del Piemonte nella prima metà del sec. XIV*, Turin

Gabotto, F. (1895), 'L'eta del conte Verde', *Miscellanea di storia italiana* 3rd series 2: 75–324

Gabotto, F. (1896), 'Il "tuchinaggio" nel Canavese', *BSPS* 1: 81–95

Gabotto, F. (1897), *Gli ultimi principi di Acaia*, Pinerolo and Turin

Gianola, G. M. (1984), 'L'ecerinide di Ferreto Ferreti: *De Scaligerorum origine*', *SM* 3rd series 25: 201–36

Girgensohn, D. (1996), 'La crisi del patriarcato d'Aquileia', in Provincia di Pordenone (ed.), *Il quattrocento nel Friuli occidentale*, Pordenone, i, 53–68

Green, L. (1990), 'Galvano Fiamma, Azzone Visconti and the Revival of the Classical Theory of Magnificence', *JWCI* 53: 98–113

Green, L. (1993), 'The Image of Tyranny in Early Fourteenth Century Italian Historical Writing', *RStds* 7: 335–51

Hay, D. (1988), 'The Italian View of Renaissance Italy', and 'Italy and Barbarian Europe', in his *Renaissance Essays*, London, pp. 353–88

Hay, D. and Law, J.E. (1989), *Italy in the Age of the Renaissance*, London

Hyde, J.K. (1993), 'Contemporary Views on Faction and Civil Strife in Thirteenth and Fourteenth Century Italy', in his *Literacy and its Uses*, ed. D. Waley, Manchester, pp. 58–86

Ilardi, V. (1978), 'The Visconti–Sforza Regime of Milan; Recently Published Sources', *RQly* 31: 331–42

Istituto per gli Studi Storici Veronesi (1975), *Verona e il suo Territorio*, iii/1, Verona

Jarry, E. (1896), *Les origines de la domination française à Gênes*, Paris

Jones, P. (1997), *The Italian City-State from Commune to Signoria*, Oxford

Jones, P.J. (1965), 'Communes and Despots: The City-State in Late-Medieval Italy', *TRHS* 5th series 15: 71–96

Joppi, V. (1888), *I Carraresi ed il Friuli*, Udine

Kirsch, E.W. (1991), *Five Illuminated Manuscripts of Giangaleazzo Visconti*, University Park

Koenigsberger, H. (1978), 'The Italian Parliaments', *Journal of Italian History* 1: 40–6

Kohl, B.G. (1988), review article, *Speculum* 83: 707–9

Kohl, B.G. (1998), *Padua under the Carrara*, Baltimore

Lane, F.C. (1966), 'Medieval Political Ideas and the Venetian Constitution', in his *Venice and History*, Baltimore, pp. 285–308

Lane, F.C. (1971), 'The Enlargement of the Great Council of Venice', in J.C. Rowe and W.H. Stockdale (eds.), *Florilegium Historiale. Essays Presented to W.K. Ferguson*, Toronto, pp. 237–74

Lane, F.C. (1973), *Venice – a Maritime Republic*, Baltimore

Lanza, A. (1991), *Firenze contro Milano: gli intelletuali fiorentini nelle guerre con i Visconti*, Anzio

Law, J.E. (1974), 'The Commune of Verona under Venetian Rule from 1405 to 1455', DPhil thesis, University of Oxford

Law, J.E. (1981a), '"*Super Differentiis Agitatis Venetiis inter Districtuales et Civitatem*": Venezia, Verona e il contado nel '400', *AV* 5th series 116: 5–32

Law, J.E. (1981b), *The Lords of Renaissance Italy*, London

Law, J.E. (1988a), 'Venice and the Problem of Sovereignty in the *Patria del Friuli'*, in P. Denley and C. Elam (eds.), *Florence and Italy. Renaissance Studies in Honour of Nicolai Rubinstein*, London, pp. 135–48

Law, J.E. (1988b), 'La caduta degli Scaligeri', in G. Ortalli and M. Knapton (eds.), *Istituzioni, società e potere nella Marca Trevigiana e Veronese*, Rome, pp. 83–98

Law, J.E. (1996), 'L'autorità veneziana nella Patria del Friuli agli inizi del XV sec.', in Provincia di Pordenone (ed.), *Il quattrocento nel Friuli occidentale*, Pordenone, 1, pp. 35–52

Lazzarini, V. (1910), 'Un prestito di Francesco il Vecchio da Carrara al comune di Trieste, 1 aprile 1382', in *Miscellanea in Onore di A. Hortis*, 1, Trieste, pp. 229–36

Lazzarini, V. (1959), 'I titoli dei dogi di Venezia', in his *Scritti di paleografia e diplomazia*, Padua, pp. 195–226

Lazzarini, V. (1963), *Marino Falier*, Florence

Leicht, P.S. (1955), 'La giovenezza di Tristano Savorgnan', in *Studi di Storia Friulana*, Udine, pp. 3–40

Litta, P. (1819–99), *Famiglie celebri d'Italia*, Milan and Turin

Mallett, M. (1974), *Mercenaries and their Masters*, London

Marie-José (ex-queen of Italy) (1956), *La maison de Savoie*, Paris

Medin, A. (1891), 'I Visconti nella poesia contemporanea', *ASL* 18: 753–95

Mueller, R.C. (1992), 'Espressioni di *status* sociale a Venezia dopo la "serrata" del Maggior Consiglio', in G. Benzone *et al.* (eds.), *Studi Veneti Offerti a Gaetano Cozzi*, Venice, pp. 53–62

Nada Patrone, A.M. (1986), *Il Piemonte medioevale, Storia d'Italia,* UTET, v, Turin, pp. 61–86

Nasalli Rocca, E. (1968), 'La posizione politica del Pallavicini nell'eta dei comuni a quella delle signorie', *Archivio storico per le provincie parmensi* 4th series 20: 65–113

Novati, F. (1886), 'Le querele di Genova a Giangaleazzo Visconti', *Giornale ligustico* 13: 3–15

Novati, F. (1904), 'Il Petrarca e i Visconti', in *Francesco Petrarca e la Lombardia*, Milan, pp. 11–84

Ortalli, G. (1996), 'Le modalità di un passaggio: il Friuli occidentale e il dominio veneziana, in Provincia di Pordenone (ed.), *Il quattrocento nel Friuli occidentale*, Pordenone, I, pp. 13–34

Partner, P. (1972), *The Lands of St Peter*, London

Paschini, P. (1975), *Storia del Friuli*, Udine

Petti Balbi, G. (1981), 'I Maonesi e la Maona di Corsica', *MEFRM* 93: 147–70

Petti Balbi, G. (1991), *Simone Boccanegra e la Genova del '300,* Genoa

Prosdocimi, L. (1973), *Il diritto ecclesiastico*, Milan

Puncuh, D. (1978) 'Il governo genovese del Boucicaut', *MEFRM* 90: 657–87

Queller, D. E. (1986), *The Venetian Patriciate. Reality versus Myth*, Urbana and Chicago

Riedmann, J. (1991), 'L'area trevigiana e i poteri alpini', *Storia di Treviso* 2: 243–67

Robey, D. and Law, J.E. (1975), 'The Venetian Myth and the *De Republica Veneta* of Pier Paolo Vergerio', *Rinascimento* 2nd series 25: 3–59

Romano, G. (1894), 'Giangaleazzo Visconti avvelenatore', *ASL* 3rd series 1: 309–60

Romano, G. (1915), 'Un giudizio di A. Biglia sulla funzione storica dei Visconti e del ducato di Milano', *BSPSP* 15: 138–47

Rösch, G. (1989), *Der Venezianische Adel bis zur Schliessung der Grossen Rat*, Sigmaringen

Ruggiero, G. (1980), *Violence in Early Renaissance Venice*, New Brunswick

Ruggiero, M. (1979), *Storia del Piemonte,* Turin

Sandri, G. (1969), 'Il vicariate imperiale e gli inizi della signoria scaligera in Vicenza', in *Scritti di G. Sandri*, Verona, pp. 195–250

Seneca, F. (1952), 'L'intervento veneto-carrarese nella crisi friulana', *Miscellanea di studi e memorie della deputazione di storia patria per le Venezie*, 8/ii, 3–93

Scstan, E. (1961), 'Le origini delle signorie cittadine: un problema storico esaurito?', *Bulletino dell'Istituto storico italiano per il medio evo*, 73: 41–69

Simeoni, L. (1946), 'Signorie e principati', in E. Rota (ed.), *Questioni di storia medievale*, Milan, pp. 413–54

Simeoni, L. (1950), *Storia politica d'Italia. Le signorie*, 1, Milan

Soldi Rondinini (1984), 'Appunti per una nuova storia di Milano', in *Saggi di Storia e Storiografia Visconteo-Sforzesche*, Milan, pp. 9–37

Stella, A. (1979a), *I principati vescovile di Trento e Bressanone, Storia d'Italia,* UTET, xvii, Turin, pp. 510–18

Stella, A. (1979b), *Il comune di Trieste, Storia d'Italia,* UTET, xvii, Turin, pp. 619–35

Tosti Croce, M. (ed.) (1993), *Il viaggio di Enrico VII in Italia,* Città di Castello

Valeri, N. (1934), 'L'insegnamento di Giangaleazzo e i consigli al principe di Carlo Malatesta', *BSBS* 36: 452–87

Valeri, N. (1935a), 'Lo stato visconteo alla morte di Giangaleazzo', *NRS* 19: 461–73

Valeri, N. (1935b), 'Gli studi viscontei-sforzeschi fino all crisi della libertà nell'ultimo ventennio', *ASI* 93/iv: 101–32

Valeri, N. (1938), *L'eredità di Giangaleazzo Visconti,* Turin

Valeri, N. (1949), *Signorie e principati,* Verona

Valeri, N. (1959), *Storia d'Italia,* i, Turin

Varanini, G.M. (1988a), 'I dal Verme e le loro sprovincializzazione' in Varanini (1988b), pp. 198–203

Varanini, G.M. (ed.) (1988b), *Gli Scaligieri,* Verona

Varanini, G.M. (1988c), 'Pietro dal Verme podestà scaligero di Treviso', in G. Ortalli and M. Knapton (eds.), *Istituzioni, società e potere nella Marca Trevigiana e Veronese,* Rome, pp. 65–81

Varanini, G.M. (1991), 'Istituzioni e società a Treviso tra comune, signoria e poteri regionali', in *Storia di Treviso,* ii, Venice, pp. 135–211

Varanini, G.M. (1994), 'Propaganda dei regimi signorili: le esperienze venete del trecento', in P. Cammarosano (ed.), *Le forme della propaganda politica nel due e nel trecento,* Rome, pp. 311–43

Varanini, G.M. (1995), 'Istituzioni, politica e societa nel Veneto (1329–1403)', in A. Castagnetti and G.M. Varanini (eds.), *Il Veneto nel medioevo,* Verona, pp. 1–124

Vitale, V. (1955), *Brevario della storia di Genova,* i, Genoa

Waley, D. (1978), *The Italian City Republics,* 2nd edn, London, pp. 133–40

15(b) FLORENCE AND THE REPUBLICAN TRADITION

Primary sources

Compagni, D., *Cronica,* ed. I. Del Lungo, *RIS,* ix/2, Città di Castello (1916)

Stefani, Marchionne di Coppo, *Cronaca fiorentina,* ed. N. Rodolico, *RIS,* xxx/1, Città di Castello (1927)

Villani, G., *Cronica,* ed. F.G. Dragomanni, 4 vols., Florence (1844–5)

Villani, M., *Cronica,* ed. F.G. Dragomanni, 2 vols., Florence (1846)

Secondary works

Azzi, G. degli (1908), 'La dimora di Carlo figliuolo di Re Roberto a Firenze (1326–27)', *ASI* 5th series 42: 45–83, 259–305

Baldasseroni, F. (1906), 'Relazioni tra Firenze, la Chiesa, e Carlo IV (1353–55)', *ASI* 5th series 37: 3–60, 322–47

Balestracci, D. (1985), 'Una città nella crisi: Firenze (1280–1380). A proposito del recente volume di Charles Marie de la Roncière', *ASI* 143: 163–96

Barbadoro, B. (1929), *Le finanze della repubblica fiorentina. Imposta diretta e debito pubblico fino all'istituzione del Monte*, Florence

Barducci, R. (1979), 'Politica e speculazione finanziaria a Firenze dopo la crisi del primo Trecento (1343–1358)', *ASI* 137: 177–219

Barducci, R. (1981), 'Le riforme finanziarie nel Tumulto dei Ciompi', in *Il tumulto dei Ciompi: un momento di storia fiorentina ed europea*, Florence, pp. 95–102

Baron, H. (1966), *The Crisis of the Early Italian Renaissance. Civic Humanism and Republican Liberty in an Age of Classicism and Tyranny*, 2nd edn, Princeton

Becker, M.B. (1959), 'Some Economic Implications of the Conflict between Church and State in Trecento Florence', *MS* 21: 1–16

Becker, M.B. (1962), 'Florentine Popular Government (1343–1348)', *PrAPS* 106: 360–82

Becker, M.B. (1967–8), *Florence in Transition*, 2 vols., Baltimore

Becker, M.B. and Brucker, G.A. (1956). 'The Arti Minori in Florentine Politics', *MS* 18: 93–104

Bernocchi, M. (1979), *Il sistema monetario fiorentino e le leggi del governo popolare del 1378–1382*, Bologna

Bonolis, G. (1901), *La giurisdizione della mercanzia in Firenze nel secolo XIV*, Florence

Bowsky, W. M. (1958), 'Florence and Henry of Luxemburg, King of the Romans: The Re-Birth of Guelphism', *Speculum* 33: 177–203

Bowsky, W.M. (1960), *Henry VII in Italy. The Conflict of Empire and City-State (1310–1313)*, Lincoln, Neb.

Brucker, G.A. (1962), *Florentine Politics and Society 1343–1378*, Princeton

Brucker, G.A. (1968), 'The Ciompi Revolution', in N. Rubinstein (ed.), *Florentine Studies. Politics and Society in Renaissance Florence*, London, pp. 314–56

Brucker, G.A. (1977), *The Civic World of Early Renaissance Florence*, Princeton

Caggese, R. (1922–30), *Roberto d'Angiò e i suoi tempi*, 2 vols., Florence

Cipolla, C.M. (1982), *Il fiorino e il quattrino. La politica monetaria a Firenze nel 1300*, Bologna

Davidsohn, R. (1956–68), *Storia di Firenze* (Italian translation of *Geschichte von Florenz*, 4 vols., Berlin (1896–1927)), 8 vols., Florence

De Rosa, D. (1980), *Coluccio Salutati, il cancelliere e il pensatore politico*, Florence

Del Lungo, I. (1921), *I Bianchi e i Neri. Pagina di storia fiorentina da Bonifazio VIII ad Arrigo VII per la vita di Dante*, Milan

Dumontel, C. (1952), *L'impresa italiana di Giovanni di Lussemburgo, re di Boemia*, Turin

Falsini, A. B. (1971), 'Firenze dopo il 1348. Le conseguenze della peste nera', *ASI* 129: 425–503

Fiumi, E. (1977), *Fioritura e decadenza dell'economia fiorentina*, Florence

Franceschi, F. (1993a), 'Intervento del potere centrale e ruolo delle Arti nel governo dell'economia fiorentina del trecento e del primo quattrocento. Linee generali', *ASI* 151: 863–909

Franceschi, F. (1993b), *Oltre 'Il Tumulto': I lavoratori fiorentini dell'Arte della Lana fra tre e quattrocento*, Florence

Gherardi, A. (1867–8), 'La guerra dei Fiorentini con papa Gregorio XI, detta la guerra degli Otti Santi', *ASI* 5th series 5, ii: 35–131; 6, i: 208–32; 6, ii: 229–51; 7, i: 211–32; 7, ii: 235–48; 8, i: 260–96

Green, L. (1986), *Castruccio Castracani. A Study on the Origins and Character of a Fourteenth-Century Italian Despotism*, Oxford

Green, L. (1995), *Lucca under Many Masters: A Fourteenth-Century Italian Commune in Crisis (1328–1342)*, Florence

Guidi, G. (1972), 'I sistemi elettorali agli uffici del comune di Firenze nel primo Trecento (1300–1328)', *ASI* 130: 345–407

Guidi, G. (1977), 'I sistemi elettorali agli uffici della città-repubblica di Firenze nella prima metà del Trecento (1329–1349)', *ASI* 135: 373–424

Guimbart, C. (1992), 'Appunti sulla legislazione suntuaria a Firenze dal 1281 al 1384', *ASI*, 150: 57–82

Henderson, J. (1994), *Piety and Charity in Late Medieval Florence*, Oxford

Herde, P. (1965), 'Politik und Rhetorik in Florenz am Vorabend der Renaissance: die ideologische Rechtfertigung der Florentiner Aussenpolitik durch Coluccio Salutati', *AK* 47: 141–220

Herde, P. (1973), 'Politische Verhaltenweisen der Florentiner Oligarchie 1382–1402', *Geschichte und Verfassungsgefüge: Frankfurter Festgabe für Walter Schlesinger: Frankfurter Historische Abhandlungen* 5: 156–249

Holmes, G. (1986), *Florence, Rome and the Origins of the Renaissance*, Oxford

Hoshino, H. (1980), *L'Arte della Lana in Firenze in basso medioevo. Il commercio della lana e il mercato dei panni fiorentini nei secoli XIII–XV*, Florence

Jones, P.J. (1968), 'From Manor to Mezzadria: A Tuscan Case-Study in the Medieval Origins of Modern Agricultural Society', in N. Rubinstein (ed.), *Florentine Studies. Politics and Society in Renaissance Florence*, London, pp. 193–241

La Roncière, C.M. de (1968), 'Indirect Taxes or "Gabelles" at Florence in the Fourteenth Century', in N. Rubinstein (ed.), *Florentine Studies. Politics and Society in Renaissance Florence*, London, pp. 140–92

La Roncière, C.M. de (1981), 'La condition des salariés à Florence au XIVe siècle', in *Il tumulto dei Ciompi. Un momento di storia fiorentina ed europea*, Florence, pp. 13–40

La Roncière, C.M. de (1982), *Prix et salaires à Florence au XIVe siècle (1280–1380)*, Rome

Landogna, F. (1929), *La politica dei Visconti in Toscana*, Milan

Lesnick, D.R. (1989), *Preaching in Medieval Florence. The Social World of Franciscan and Dominican Spirituality*, Athens, Ga.

Mandich, G. (1988), 'Il fiorino di conto a Firenze nel 1294–1381', and 'Il fiorino di conto a Firenze nel 1382–1464', *ASI* 146: 23–48, 155–82

Mantini, S. (1995), 'Un ricinto di identificazione: le mura sacre della città. Riflessione su Firenze dall'età classica al medioevo', *ASI* 153: 211–61

Martin, A. von (1916), *Coluccio Salutati und das humanische Lebensideal. Ein Kapitel aus der Genesis der Renaissance*, Berlin and Leipzig

Mesquita, D.M. Bueno de (1941), *Giangaleazzo Visconti, Duke of Milan 1351–1402*, Cambridge

Molho, A. (1968a), 'The Florentine Oligarchy and the Balie of the Late Trecento', *Speculum* 43: 23–51

Molho, A. (1968b), 'Politics and the Ruling Class in Early Renaissance Florence', *NRS* 52: 401–31

Najemy, J.M. (1981), '"Audiant omnes artes": Corporate Origins of the Ciompi Revolution', in *Il Tumulto dei Ciompi. Un momento di storia fiorentina ed europea*, Florence, pp. 59–93

Najemy, J. M. (1982), *Corporatism and Consensus in Florentine Electoral Politics*, Chapel Hill, N.C.

Ninzi, R. (1992), 'Techniche e manipolazioni elettorali nel comune di Firenze tra XIV e XV secolo (1382–1434)', *ASI* 150: 735–74

Pampaloni, Giuseppe (1953), 'Gli organi della Repubblica fiorentina per le relazioni con l'Estero', *Rivista di studi politici internazionali* 20: 261–96

Pampaloni, Guido (1982), 'Un nuovo studio sulla produzione e commercio della lana a Firenze tra trecento e cinquecento', *ASI* 140: 197–213

Panella, A. (1913), 'Politica ecclesiastica del comune fiorentino dopo la cacciata del duca d'Atene', *ASI* 6th series 2: 271–370

Paoli, C. (1862), *Della signoria di Gualtieri, duca d'Atene in Firenze. Memoria compilata su documenti*, Florence; also published in *Giornale storico degli archivi toscani* 6: 86–286

Pardi, G. (1916), 'Disegno della storia demografica di Firenze', *ASI* 74: 3–84, 185–245

Perrens, F.-T. (1877–83), *Histoire de Florence depuis ses origines jusqu'à la domination des Médicis*, 6 vols., Paris

Petrucci, A. (1972), *Coluccio Salutati*, Rome

Pinto, G. (1972), 'Firenze e la carestia del 1346–7', *ASI* 130: 3–84

Pinto, G. (1973), 'Aspetti della guerra tra Firenze e Ludovico il Bavaro in alcune lettere della cancelleria fiorentina', *ASI* 131: 225–33

Rado, A. (1926), *Dalla repubblica fiorentina alla signoria medicea. Maso degli Albizzi e il partito oligarchico in Firenze dal 1382 al 1393*, Florence

Rodolico, N. (1899), *Il popolo minuto.. Note di storia fiorentina (1343–1378)*, Bologna

Rodolico, N. (1945), *I Ciompi. Una pagina di storia del proletario operaio*, Florence

Rubinstein, N. (1981), 'Il regime politico di Firenze dopo il Tumulto dei Ciompi', in *Il tumulto dei Ciompi. Un momento di storia fiorentina ed europea*, Florence, pp. 105–24

Rutenburg, V. (1971), *Popolo e movimenti popolari nell'Italia del '300 e '400*, Bologna

Sapori, A. (1926), *La crisi delle compagnie mercantili dei Bardi e dei Peruzzi*, Florence

Sapori, A. (1955–67), *Studi di storia economica (secoli XIII–XIV–XV)*, 3 vols., Florence

Stella, A. (1993), 'Fiscalità, topografia e società a Firenze nella seconda metà del Trecento', *ASI* 151: 797–862

Strocchia, S. T. (1992), *Death and Ritual in Renaissance Florence*, Baltimore

Szabó, T. (1992), *Comuni e politica stradale in Toscana e in Italia nel Medioevo*, Bologna

Tabacco, G. (1953), *La casa di Francia nell'azione politica di papa Giovanni XXII*, Rome

Tognetti, S. (1995), 'Prezzi e salari nella Firenze tardo-medievale: un profilo', *ASI* 153: 263–333

Trexler, R.C. (1974), *The Spiritual Power. Republican Florence under the Interdict*, Leiden

Trexler, R.C. (1985), 'Il parlamento fiorentino del 10 settembre 1378', *ASI* 143: 437–75

Vigo, P. (1879), *Uguccione della Faggiuola, podestà di Pisa e di Lucca 1313–1316*, Livorno

Witt, R.G. (1969), 'A Note on Guelfism in late Medieval Florence', *NRS* 53: 134–45

Witt, R.G. (1976), 'Florentine Politics and the Ruling Class', *JMRS* 6: 243–67

Witt, R.G. (1983), *Hercules at the Crossroads. The Life, Works and Thought of Coluccio Salutati*, Durham, N.C.

Zorzi, A. (1987), 'Aspetti e problemi dell'amministrazione della giustizia penale nella repubblica fiorentina I: la transizione dal XIV al XV secolo', *ASI* 145: 391–453

15(C) THE ITALIAN SOUTH

Primary sources

Davidsohn, R., *Forschungen zur Geschichte von Florenz*, III. Teil *XIII. und XIV. Jahrhundert*, I. *Register unedirter Urkunder zur Geschichte von Handel, Gewerbe und Zuftwesen*; II. *Die Schwarzen und die Weissen*, Berlin (1901)

Robert d'Anjou, *La vision bienheureuse. Traité envoyé au pape Jean XXII*, ed. M. Dykmans, Miscellanea Historiae Pontificiae, Rome (1970)

Secondary works

The literature is uneven, and some aspects are covered in far more detail than others. More extended treatment of most issues touched on in this chapter is found in Abulafia (1997).

The kingdom of Naples

Abulafia, D. (1980), 'Venice and the Kingdom of Naples in the Last Years of King Robert the Wise', *PBSR* 48: 186–204; repr. in Abulafia (1987)

Abulafia, D. (1981), 'Southern Italy and the Florentine Economy, 1256–1370', *EcHR* 2nd series 33: 377–88; repr. in Abulafia (1987)

Abulafia, D. (1987), *Italy, Sicily and the Mediterranean, 1100–1400*, London

Abulafia, D. (1994), 'Genova Angioina, 1318–35: gli inizi della Signoria di Roberto re di Napoli', in *La storia dei Genovesi*, XII: *Atti del Convegno internazionale di studi sui Ceti Dirigenti nelle Istituzioni della Repubblica di Genova, 12a Tornata, Genova, 11–14 giugno, 1991*, part 1, Genoa, pp. 15–24

Abulafia, D. (1997), *The Western Mediterranean Kingdoms, 1200–1500*, London

Boulton, D'A.J.D. (1987), *The Knights of the Crown. The Monarchical Orders of Knighthood in Later Medieval Europe, 1325–1520*, Woodbridge

Bowsky, W. M. (1960), *Henry VII in Italy*, Lincoln, Nebr.

Branca, V. (1976), *Boccaccio. The Man and his Works*, Hassocks, Sussex

Caggese, R. (1922–30), *Roberto d'Angiò*, 2 vols., Florence

Cole, B. (1976), *Giotto and Florentine Painting, 1280–1375*, New York

Cutolo, A. (1936), *Re Ladislao di Angio-Durazzo*, 2 vols., Milan

Ducellier, A. (1981), *La façade maritime de l'Albanie au moyen âge. Durazzo et Valona du XIe au XVe siècle*, Thessaloniki

Enderlein, L. (1997), *Die Grablegen des Hauses Anjou in Unteritalien. Totenkult und Monumente 1266–1343*, Worms

L'Etat Angevin. Ponvoir, culture et société entre XIIIe et XIVe siècle (1998), Collection de l'école française de Rome, 245, Rome

Galasso, G. (1992), *Il regno di Napoli. Il Mezzogiorno angioino e aragonese (1266–1494)*, UTET, Storia d'Italia, Turin

Gardner, J. (1975), 'Simone Martini's St Louis of Toulouse', *Reading Medieval Studies* 1: 16–29

Green, L. (1986), *Castruccio Castracani. A Study on the Origins and Character of a Fourteenth-Century Italian Despotism*, Oxford

Grierson, P. and Travaini, L. (1998), *Medieval European Coinage*, xiv: *Italy*, pt iii: *South Italy, Sicily, Sardinia*, Cambridge

Hilton, R.H. (1973), *Bond Men Made Free. Medieval Peasant Movements and the English Rising of 1381*, London

Housley, N.J. (1982), *The Italian Crusades. The Papal-Angevin alliance and the Crusades against Christian Lay Powers, 1254–1343*, Oxford

Housley, N.J. (1983), 'Pope Clement V and the Crusades of 1309–10', *JMH* 8: 29–43

Housley, N.J. (1986), *The Avignon Papacy and the Crusades, 1305–1378*, Oxford

Hunt, E.H. (1994), *The Medieval Super-Companies. A study of the Peruzzi Company of Florence*, Cambridge

La Roncière, C. M. de (1976), *Florence, centre économique régional*, 4 vols., Aix-en-Provence

Labande, E.R. (1957), 'La politique méditerranéenne de Louis Ier d'Anjou et le rôle qu'y joua la Sardaigne', *Atti del VI Congresso internazionale di studi sardi*, Cagliari, pp. 3–23; repr. in E.R. Labande, *Histoire de l'Europe occidentale, XIe–XIVe s.*, London (1973)

Léonard, E. (1932–6), *Le règne de Jeanne Ier de Naples*, 3 vols., Monaco and Paris

Léonard, E. (1954), *Les Angevins de Naples*, Paris

Léonard, E. (1967), *Gli Angioini di Napoli*, Milan (Italian version of Léonard (1954))

Mollat, G. (1965), *Les papes d'Avignon, 1305–1378*, 10th edn, Paris; English trans. Janet Love, of earlier edn (1963) as *The Popes at Avignon*, London (1963)

Pennington, K. (1993), *The Prince and the Law, 1200–1600. Sovereignty and Rights in the Western Legal Tradition*, Berkeley and Los Angeles

Pryor, J.H. (1980), 'Foreign Policy and Economic Policy: The Angevins of Sicily and the Economic Decline of Southern Italy', in L.O. Frappell (ed.), *Principalities, Powers and Estates. Studies in Medieval and Early Modern Government and Society*, Adelaide

Sapori, A. (1926), *La crisi delle compagnie mercantili dei Bardi e dei Peruzzi*, Florence

Tabacco, G. (1953), *La casa di Francia nell'azione politica di Giovanni XXII*, Rome

Trifone, A. (1921), *La legislazione angioina*, Naples

Ullmann, W. (1946), *The Medieval Idea of Law as Represented by Lucas de Penna*, London

Ullmann, W. (1948), *The Origins of the Great Schism*, London

Weiss, R. (1977), *Medieval and Humanist Greek*, Padua

Wood, D. (1989), *Clement VI. The Pontificate and Ideas of an Avignon Pope*, Cambridge

Yver, G. (1903), *Le commerce et les marchands dans l'Italie méridionale*, Paris

The island kingdom of Sicily

Abulafia, D. (1995), 'The Aragonese Kingdom of Albania. An Angevin Project of 1311–16', *MHR* 10: 1–13; repr. in Benjamin Arbel (ed.), *Intercultural Contacts in the Medieval Mediterranean. Studies in Honour of David Jacoby*, London (1996)

Backman, C. (1995), *The Decline and Fall of Medieval Sicily. Politics, Religion and Economy in the Reign of Frederick III, 1296–1337*, Cambridge

Benigno, F. and Torrisi C. (eds.) (1995), *Elites e potere in Sicilia dal medioevo ad oggi*, Catanzaro

Bresc, H. (1990), *Politique et société en Sicile, XIIe–XVe siècles*, Aldershot

Bresc, H. (1986), *Un monde méditerranéen. Economie et société en Sicile, 1300–1450*, 2 vols., Rome and Palermo

Corrao, P. (1991), *Governare un regno. Potere, società e istituzioni in Sicilia fra Trecento e Quattrocento*, Naples

D'Alessandro, V. (1963), *Politica e società nella Sicilia aragonese*, Palermo

D'Alessandro, V. (1994), *Terra, nobili e borghesi nella Sicilia medievale*, Palermo

Epstein, S.R. (1992), *An Island for Itself. Economic Development and Social Change in Late Medieval Sicily*, Cambridge

Fisber Polizzi, C. (1979), *Amministrazione della contea di Ventimiglia nella Sicilia aragonese*, Supplement to *Atti dell'Accademia Agrigentina di scienze lettere e arti*, 6, Padua

Kiesewetter, A. (1999), *Die Anfänge der Regierung Karls II. von Anjou (1278–1295)*, Husum

Luttrell, A.T. (ed.) (1975), *Medieval Malta. Studies on Malta before the Knights*, London

Mazzarese Fardella, E. (1974), *I Feudi comitali di Sicilia dai Normanni agli Aragonesi*, Milan and Palermo

Peri, I. (1981), *La Sicilia dopo il Vespro. Uomini, città e campagne, 1282–1376*, Bari

Peri, I. (1993), *Villani e cavalieri nella Sicilia medievale*, Bari

Romano, A. (ed.) (1992), *Istituzioni politiche e giuridiche e strutture del potere politico ed economico nelle città dell'Europa mediterranea medievale e moderna. La Sicilia*, Messina

Sciascia, L. (1993), *Le donne e i cavalier, gli affanni e gli agi. Famiglia e potere in Sicilia tra XII e XIV secolo*, Messina

16(a) THE EMPIRE: FROM ADOLF OF NASSAU TO LEWIS OF BAVARIA, 1292–1347

ADOLF OF NASSAU

Primary sources

MGH, Legum Sectio IV: Constitutiones et Acta Publica Imperatorum et Regum Tom. III, ed. Iacobus Schwalm, Hanover and Leipzig (1904–6), nos. 468–590, pp. 455–553

Die Regesten des Kaiserreiches unter Adolf von Nassau 1291–1298, ed. Vincenz Samanek (J. F. Böhmer, *Regesta Imperii* VI 2), Innsbruck (1948)

Historiographical sources

Lhotsky, Alphons, *Quellenkunde zur mittelalterlichen Geschichte Österreichs*, MIÖG, Ergänzungsband, XIX, Graz and Cologne, (1963), pp. 259ff

Lorenz, Ottokar, *Deutschlands Geschichtsquellen im Mittelalter seit der Mitte des dreizehnten Jahrhunderts*, I (3rd edn, Berlin (1886)); II (3rd edn, Berlin (1887)), esp. pp. 257ff

Secondary works

Baethgen, Friedrich (1956), 'Zur Geschichte der Wahl Adolfs von Nassau', *DA* 12: 536–43; repr. in his *Mediaevalia*, Stuttgart (1960), I, pp. 192–201

Barraclough, G. (1940), 'Edward I and Adolf of Nassau', *Cambridge Historical Journal* 6: 225–62

Gerlich, A. (1994), 'Adolf von Nassau (1292–8): Aufstieg und Sturz eines Königs, Herrscheramt und Kurfürstenfronde', *Nassauische Annalen* 105: 17–78

Gerlich, A. (1998), 'König Adolf von Nassau: Reichspolitik am Rhein und in Schwaben 1293 und 1294', *Nassauische Annalen* 109: 1–72

Patze, Hans (1963), 'Erzbischof Gerhard II. von Mainz und König Adolf von Nassau. Territorialpolitik und Finanzen', *Hessisches Jahrbuch für Landesgeschichte* 13: 83–140

Roth, F.W.K. (1879), *Geschichte des römischen Königs Adolf I. von Nassau*, Wiesbaden

Samanek, Vincenz (1930), *Studien zur Geschichte König Adolfs*, Akademie der Wissenschaften in Wien, philos.-histor. Klasse, Sitzungsberichte, 207.2, Vienna and Leipzig

Samanek, Vincenz (1932), *Neue Beiträge zu den Regesten König Adolfs*, Akademie der Wissenschaften in Wien, philos.-histor. Klasse, Sitzungsberichte, 214.2, Vienna and Leipzig

Trautz, Fritz (1961), *Die Könige von England und das Reich 1272–1377*, Heidelberg

Trautz, Fritz (1965), 'Studien zur Geschichte und Würdigung König Adolfs von Nassau', *Geschichtliche Landeskunde* 2, Veröffentlichungen des Instituts für geschichtliche Landeskunde an der Universität Mainz, Wiesbaden, pp. 1–45

ALBERT I OF HABSBURG

Primary sources

There is so far no new edition of the 'Regesta Imperii' for Albert's reign. The most important documents are in *MGH, Legum Sectio IV: Constitutiones et Acta Publica Imperatorum et Regum Tom. IV*, pt 1, ed. Iacobus Schwalm, Hanover and Leipzig (1906), nos. 1–236, pp. 1–199

Chronicon Ecclesiae Wimpinensis auct. Burcardo de Hallis et Dythero de Helmestat. MGH, Scriptores Tom, XXX, pt. I, Hanover (1896); repr. Stuttgart (1976)

Historiographical sources

See above under Adolf of Nassau

Secondary works

Baethgen, Friedrich (1928), 'Die Promissio Albrechts I. für Bonifaz VIII.', in *Aus Politik und Geschichte. Gedächtnisschrift für Georg von Below*, Berlin, pp. 75–90; repr. in his *Mediaevalia*, Stuttgart (1960), 1, pp. 202–17

Baethgen, Friedrich (1964), 'Zur Geschichte der Weltherrschaftsidee im späteren Mittelalter', in *Festschrift Percy Ernst Schramm*, Wiesbaden, 1, pp. 189–203

Hessel, Alfred (1931), *Jahrbücher des Deutschen Reiches unter König Albrecht I. von Habsburg*, Munich

Lhotsky, Alphons (1967), *Geschichte Österreichs seit der Mitte des 13. Jahrhunderts (1281–1358)*, Vienna

Lintzel, Martin (1935), 'Das Bündnis Albrechts I. mit Bonifaz VIII.', *HZ* 151: 457–85; repr. in Martin Lintzel, *Ausgewählte Schriften*, Berlin (1961), II, pp. 464–85

Lucas, H.S. (1934), 'Diplomatic Relations of Edward I and Albert of Austria', *Speculum* 9: 125–34

HENRY VII

Primary sources

So far there is no new edition of the 'Regesta Imperii' for the the reign of Henry VII. The most important documents are in *MGH, Legum Sectio IV: Constitutiones . . . Tom. IV*, pt 1, ed. Iacobus Schwalm, Hanover and Leipzig (1909–11), nos. 262–722, pp. 228–712; pt 2, ed. Iacobus Schwalm, Hanover and Leipzig (1909–11), nos. 723–1090, pp. 713–1090. This edition largely replaces two earlier ones: Doennigs, G[uillelmus], *Acta Henrici VII imperatoris Romanorum*, 2 vols., Berlin (1838), and Bonaini, Francesco, *Acta Henrici VII Romanorum imperatoris . . .*, 2 vols., Florence (1877)

Mommsen, Theodor E. and Hagemann, Wolfgang, *Italienische Analekten zur Reichsgeschichte des 14. Jahrhunderts (1310–1378)*, Schriften der MGH, 11, Stuttgart (1952), nos. 1–136, pp. 21–64

Le Opere di Dante Alighieri, a cura del Dr E. Moore, nuovamente rivedute nel testo dal Dr Paget Toynbee, 4th edn, Oxford (1924)

Stengel, Edmund E., *Nova Alamanniae. Urkunden, Briefe und andere Quellen besonders zur deutschen Geschichte des 14. Jahrhunderts*, 2 vols., Berlin and Hanover (1921–76)

Wampach, Camillo, *Urkunden- und Quellenbuch zur Geschichte der altluxemburgischen Territorien bis zur burgundischen Zeit*, 10 vols., Luxemburg (1935–55)

Secondary works

Bowsky, W.M. (1958a), 'Florence and Henry of Luxemburg, King of the Romans: The Rebirth of Guelfism', *Speculum* 33: 177–203

Bowsky, W.M. (1958b), 'Dante's Italy: A Political Dissection', *The Historian* 21: 82–100

Bowsky, W.M. (1958c), 'Clement V and the Emperor-Elect', *MH* 12: 52–69

Bowsky, W.M. (1960), *Henry VII in Italy. The Conflict of Empire and City-State, 1310–1313*, Lincoln, Nebr.

Dietmar, Carl D. (1983), *Die Beziehungen des Hauses Luxemburg zu Frankreich in den Jahren 1247–1346*, Cologne

Franke, Maria Elisabeth (1992), *Kaiser Heinrich VII. im Spiegel der Historiographie*, Cologne

Gade, John A. (1951), *Luxemburg in the Middle Ages*, Leiden

Heyen, Franz-Josef (1965), *Kaiser Heinrichs Romfahrt. Die Bilderchronik von Kaiser Heinrich VII. und Kurfürst Balduin von Luxemburg (1308–1313)*, Boppard; repr. Munich (1978)

Jäschke, Kurt-Ulrich (1988), *Imperator Heinricus. Ein spätmittelalterlicher Text über Kaiser Heinrich VII. in kritischer Beleuchtung*, Beiheft zu Hémecht, Luxemburg

Meltzer, Franz (1940), *Die Ostraumpolitik König Johanns von Böhmen*, Jena

Schneider, Friedrich (1924–8), *Kaiser Heinrich VII.*, 3 parts, Greiz and Leipzig

Schneider, Friedrich (1940), *Kaiser Heinrich VII. Dantes Kaiser*, Stuttgart and Berlin

Wenck, Carl (1882), *Clemens V. und Heinrich VII. Die Anfänge des französischen Papsttums*, Halle

LEWIS OF BAVARIA

Primary sources

A new edition of the 'Regesta Imperii' is under way, but so far only a few volumes have been published: *Regesten Kaiser Ludwigs des Bayern (1314–1347) nach Archiven und Bibliotheken geordnet*, ed. Peter Acht, pt 1: *Die Urkunden aus den Archiven und Bibliotheken Württembergs*, ed. Johannes Wetzel, Cologne (1991); pt 2: *Die Urkunden aus den Archiven und Bibliotheken Badens*, ed. Johannes Wetzel, Cologne (1994); pt 3: *Die Urkunden aus Kloster- und Stiftsarchiven im Bayerischen Haupstaatsarchiv und in der Bayerischen Staatsbibliothek München*, ed. Michael Menzel, Cologne (1996); pt 4: *Die Urkunden aus den Archiven und Bibliotheken des Elsasses (Département Haut- und Bas-Rhin)*, ed. Johannes Wetzel, Cologne (1998)

The most important documents of his reign to 1330 are published in *MGH, Legum Sectio IV: Constitutiones et Acta Publica Imperatorum et Regum Tom. V*, ed. Iacobus Schwalm, Hanover and Leipzig (1909–13), nos. 1–1027, pp. 1–851; *Tom. VI Pars I*, ed. Iacobus Schwalm, Hanover (1914–27), nos. 1–894, pp. 1–741

Das deutsch-englische Bündnis von 1335–1342, I, *Quellen*, ed. Friedrich Bock, Munich (1956)

Die Register der Kanzlei Ludwigs des Bayern, ed. Helmut Bansa, 2 vols., Munich (1971–4)

Vatikanische Akten zur deutschen Geschichte in der Zeit Kaiser Ludwigs des Bayern, ed. Sigmund Riezler, Innsbruck (1891)

Historiographical sources

Geschichte Ludwigs des Bayern. Nach der Übersetzung von Walter Friedensburg neu bearbeitet und herausgegeben von Christian Lohmer, 2 vols., Essen and Stuttgart (1987)

The Defensor Pacis of Marsilius of Padua, ed. C.W. Previté-Orton, Cambridge (1928)

Marsilius von Padua, Defensor Pacis, ed. Richard Scholz, *MGH, Fontes Iuris Germanici Antiqui* 7, Hanover (1932)

Marsile de Padoue, Œuvres mineures, Defensor minor – De translatione imperii, ed. Colette Jeudy and Jeannine Quillet, Paris (1979)

Guillelmi de Ockham, Opera politica, ed. H.S. Offler *et al.*, 3 vols., Manchester (1956–74)

Secondary works

Baethgen, Friedrich (1920), 'Der Anspruch des Papsttums auf das Reichsvikariat', *ZR kanonist. Abt.* 10: 168–268; repr. in his *Mediaevalia*, Stuttgart (1960), I, pp. 110–85

Bansa, Helmut (1968), *Studien zur Kanzlei Kaiser Ludwigs des Bayern vom Tag der Wahl bis zur Rückkehr aus Italien (1314–1329)*, Kallmünz

Barisch, Gerhard (1977), 'Lupold von Bebenburg', *Historischer Verein Bamberg* 113: 219–432

Benker, Gertrud (1980), *Ludwig der Bayer. Ein Wittelsbacher auf dem Kaiserthron 1282–1347*, Munich

Bock, Friedrich (1943), *Reichsidee und Nationalstaaten vom Untergang des alten Reiches bis zur Kündigung des deutsch-englischen Bündnisses in Jahre 1341*, Munich

Bornhak, Otto (1933), *Staatskirchliche Anschauungen und Handlungen am Hofe Kaiser Ludwigs des Bayern*, Weimar

Colberg, Katherina (1985), *Die deutsche Literatur des Mittelalters, Verfasserlexikon*, v, Berlin, cols. 1071–8

Gewirth, Alan (1951–6), *Marsilius of Padua. The Defender of Peace*, 2 vols., New York

Green, Louis (1986), *Castruccio Castracani. A Study on the Origins and Character of a Fourteenth-Century Italian Despotism*, Oxford

Heyen, Franz-Josef (ed.) (1985), *Balduin von Luxemburg. Erzbischof von Trier-Kurfürst des Reiches 1285–1354,* Mainz

Homann, Hans-Dieter (1974), *Kurkolleg und Königtum im Thronstreit von 1314–1330,* Munich

Huber, Alexander (1983), *Das Verhältnis Ludwigs des Bayern zu den Erzkanzlern von Mainz, Köln und Trier (1314–1347),* Kallmünz

Hundt, Barbara (1989), *Ludwig der Bayer. Der Kaiser aus dem Hause Wittelsbach 1282–1347,* Esslingen and Munich

McGrade, A.S. (1974), *The Political Thought of William of Ockham,* Cambridge

Meyer, Hermann (1909), *Lupold von Bebenburg. Studien zu seinen Schriften,* Freiburg im Breisgau

Miethke, J. (1969), *Ockhams Weg zur Sozialphilosophie,* Berlin

Moser, Peter (1985), *Das Kanzleipersonal Kaiser Ludwigs des Bayern in den Jahren 1330–1347,* Munich

Most, Rolf (1941), 'Der Reichsgedanke des Lupold von Bebenburg', *DA* 4: 444–85

Müller, Carl (1879–80), *Der Kampf Ludwigs des Bayern mit der römischen Kurie,* 2 vols., Tübingen

Offler, H.S. (1956), 'Empire and Papacy: The Last Struggle', *TRHS* 5th series 6: 21–47

Schlögl, Waldemar (1977), 'Beitrage zur Jugendgeschichte Ludwigs des Bayern', *DA* 33: 182–99

Scholz, Richard (1952), *Wilhelm von Ockham als politischer Denker und sein Breviloquium de principatu tyrannico,* Stuttgart

Schütz, Alois (1973), *Die Prokuratorien und Instruktionen Ludwigs des Bayern für die Kurie (1331–1345). Ein Beitrag zu seinen Absolutionsprozess,* Kallmünz

Schütz, Alois (1987), 'Ludwig der Bayer', *Neue Deutsche Biographie,* Munich, xv, cols. 334–47

Schwöbel, Hermann Otto (1968), *Der diplomatische Kampf zwischen Ludwig dem Bayern und der Römischen Kurie im Rahmen des kanonischen Absolutionsprozesses 1330–1346,* Weimar

Stengel, Edmund E. (1930), *Avignon und Rhens. Forschungen zur Geschichte des Kampfes um das Recht am Reich in der ersten Hälfte des 14.Jahrhunderts,* Weimar

Thomas, Heinz (1993), *Ludwig der Bayer (1282–1347). Kaiser und Ketzer,* Ratisbon, Graz, Vienna and Cologne

16(b) THE LUXEMBURGS AND RUPERT OF THE PALATINATE, 1347–1410

Primary sources

Battenberg, F. *Reichsacht und Anleite im Spätmittelalter. Ein Beitrag zur Geschichte der Höchsten Königlichen Gerichtsbarkeit im Alten Reich, besonders im 14. und 15. Jahrhundert,* Quellen und Forschungen zur Höchsten Gerichtsbarkeit im Alten Reich, Cologne and Vienna (1986)

Battenberg, F. *Urkundenregesten zur Tätigkeit des Deutschen Königs- und Hofgerichts bis 1451,* VI: *Die Königszeit Karls IV., 1346–1355 März,* Quellen und Forschungen zur Höchsten Gerichtsbarkeit im Alten Reich, 6, Cologne and Vienna (1990)

Brandl, V. *et al.* (eds.), *Codex Diplomaticus et Epistolaris Moraviae,* VII–XV, Brünn (1858–1903)

Chroniken der Deutschen Städte, Göttingen and Zurich, 1 – (repr.), (1965–)

Dahlmann, F.C. and Waitz, G., *Quellenkunde zur Deutschen Geschichte. Bibliographie der Quellen und der Litteratur zur Deutschen Geschichte*, 10th edn, Stuttgart (1969–)

Emler, J. *et al.* (eds.), *Fontes Rerum Bohemicarum*, IV and V, Prague (1884–93)

Fritz, W.D. (ed.), *Die Goldene Bulle Kaiser Karls IV. vom Jahre 1356*, Fontes Iuris Germanici Antiqui, 11, Weimar (1972)

Glafy, A.F., *Anecdotorum S.R.I. Historiam ac jus Publicum Illustrantium Collectio*, Dresden and Leipzig (1734)

Haas, A., *Archiv České Koruny, 1158–1935*, Prague (1961)

Haas, A., *Archiv Koruny České 5. Katalog Listin z let 1378–1437*, Prague (1947)

Hrub', V., *Archivum Coronae Regni Bohemiae*, II: *1346–1355*, Prague (1928)

Hubatsch, J.W. (ed.), *Regesta Historico-Diplomatica Ordinis S. Mariae Theutonicorum, 1193–1525*, I and II, Göttingen (1948–50)

Huber, A. (ed.), *Regesta Imperii*, VIII: *Die Regesten des Kaiserreiches unter Kaiser Karl IV., 1346–78*, Innsbruck (1877) and its supplement: A. Huber (ed.), *Regesta Imperii*, VIII: *Additamentum Primum*, Innsbruck (1889)

Janssen, W. *et al.* (eds.), *Regesten der Erzbischöfe von Köln im Mittelalter*, VII–X, Düsseldorf (1982–)

Koch, A. and Wille, J. (eds.), *Regesten der Pfalzgrafen am Rhein*, I and II, Innsbruck (1894–1939)

Kurze, D., *Quellen zur Ketzergeschichte Brandenburgs und Pommerns*, Veröffentlichungen der Historischen Kommission zu Berlin, 45, Berlin (1973)

Lüdicke, R., *Die Königs- und Kaiserurkunden der Königlich-Preussischen Staatsarchive und des Königlichen Hausarchiv bis 1439*, Mitteilungen d. kgl. Preuss. Archivverwaltung, 16, Leipzig (1910)

MGH Constitutiones, VIII: *Constitutiones et Acta Publica Imperatorum et Regum inde ab a. 1345 ad a. 1348*, ed. K. Zeumer and R. Saloman, Hanover (1982, repr. of 1910–26 edn)

MGH Constitutiones, IX: *Constitutiones et Acta Publica Imperatorum et Regum. Dokumente zur Geschichte des Deutschen Reiches und seiner Verfassung, 1349*, ed. M. Kühn, Hanover (1974–83)

MGH Constitutiones, X: *Constitutiones et Acta Publica Imperatorum et Regum. Dokumente zur Geschichte des Deutschen Reiches und seiner Verfassung, 1350–1353*, ed. M. Kühn, Hanover (1979–87)

MGH Constitutiones, XI: *Constitutiones et Acta Publica Imperatorum et Regum. Dokumente zur Geschichte des Deutschen Reiches und seiner Verfassung, 1354–1356*, ed. W.D. Fritz, Hanover (1978–92)

Patschovsky, A., *Quellen zur Böhmischen Inquisition im 14. Jahrhundert, MGH*, Quellen zur Geistesgeschichte des Mittelalters, 11, Weimar (1979)

Pfeiffer, G., *Quellen zur Geschichte der Fränkisch-Bayerischen Landfriedensorganisation*, Schriftenreihe zur Bayrischen Landgeschichte, 69, Munich (1975)

Repertorium Fontium Historiae Medii Aevi, I – Rome (1962–)

Ruser, K. (ed.), *Die Urkunden und Akten der Oberdeutschen Städtebünde vom 13. Jahrhundert bis 1519*, I: *Vom 13. Jahrhundert bis 1347*, and II: *Städte- und Landfriedensbündnisse von 1347 bis 1380*, Göttingen (1979–88)

Scholz, R. and Krüger, S. (eds.), *Die Werke des Konrad von Megenberg*, 2 vols., *MGH, Staatsschriften des Späteren Mittelalters*, 2 and 3, Berlin and Stuttgart (1941–84)

Steinherz, S. (ed.), *Ein Fürstenspiegel Karls IV*, Prague (1925)

Tadra, F. (ed.), *Summa Cancellariae: Cancellaria Caroli IV*, Prague (1895)
Weizsäcker, J., *Deutsche Reichstagsakten*, I-VI, Göttingen (1956, repr. of Munich 1867–88 edns)
Winkelmann, E., *Acta Imperii Saeculi XIII et XIV*, I and II, Innsbruck (1885)
Winkelmann, E. *et al.* (eds.), *Regesten der Pfalzgrafen am Rhein*, I and II, Innsbruck (1894–1939)
Wohlgemuth, H., *Das Urkundenwesen des Deutschen Reichshofgerichts 1273–1378*, Quellen und Forschungen zur Höchsten Gerichtsbarkeit im Alten Reich, I, Cologne and Vienna (1973)
Zeumer, K., *Die Goldene Bulle Kaiser Karls IV.*, I and II, Weimar (1908)

Secondary works

Angermeier, H. (1966), *Königtum und Landfriede im Deutschen Spätmittelalter*, Munich
Bartoš, F.M. (1947) *České Dějiny II-6, Čechy v Době Husově*, Prague
Battenberg, F. (1974), *Gerichtsschreiberamt und Kanzlei am Reichshofgericht, 1235–1451*, Quellen und Forschungen zur Höchsten Gerichtsbarkeit im Alten Reich, 2, Cologne and Vienna
Battenberg, F. (1979), *Das Hofgerichtssiegel der Deutschen Kaiser und Könige, 1235–1451*, Quellen und Forschungen zur Höchsten Gerichtsbarkeit im Alten Reich, 6, Cologne and Vienna
Battenberg, F. (1983), *Die Gerichtsstandsprivilegien der Deutschen Kaiser und Könige bis zum Jahre 1451*, I and II, Quellen und Forschungen zur Höchsten Gerichtsbarkeit im Alten Reich, 12, Cologne and Vienna
Blaschke, K. (1990), *Geschichte Sachsens im Mittelalter*, Munich
Bosl, K. and Seibt, F. (1967), *Handbuch der Geschichte der Böhmischen Länder*, I, Stuttgart
Burdach, K. *et al.* (eds.) (1893–1936), *Vom Mittelalter zur Reformation. Forschungen zur Geschichte der Deutschen Bildung*, Berlin
Conrad, H. (1962), *Deutsche Rechtsgeschichte*, 2nd edn, I, Karlsruhe
Demandt, K.A. (1972), *Geschichte des Landes Hessen*, 2nd edn, Kassel and Basle
Denifle, H. (1885), *Die Entstehung der Universitäten des Mittelalters bis 1400*, Berlin
Dirlmeyer, U. (1966), *Mittelalterliche Hoheitsträger im Wirtschaftlichen Wettbewerb*, Wiesbaden
Eisenhardt, U. (1980), *Die Kaiserlichen 'Privilegia de non Appellando'*, Quellen und Forschungen zur Höchsten Gerichtsbarkeit im Alten Reich, 7, Cologne
Engel, E. (ed.) (1982), *Karl IV. Politik und Ideologie im 14. Jahrhundert*, Weimar
Engel, E. and Holtz, E. (eds.) (1988), *Deutsche Könige und Kaiser des Mittelalters*, Berlin
Erler, A. and Kaufmann, E. (eds.) (1971–), *Handwörterbuch zur Deutschen Rechtsgeschichte*, I– , Berlin
Fahlbusch, F.B. and Johanek, P. (eds.) (1989), *Studia Luxemburgica. Festschrift Heinz Stoob zum 70. Geburtstag*, Warendorf
Franklin, O. (1967), *Das Reichshofgericht im Mittelalter*, I and II, Hildesheim (repr. of Weimar 1867 edns)
Fried, J. (ed.) (1986), *Schulen und Studium im Sozialen Wandel des Hohen und Späten Mittelalters*, VF, 30, Sigmaringen
Füchtner, J. (1970), *Die Bündnisse der Bodenseestädte bis zum Jahre 1390*, Veröffentlichungen des Max-Planck-Instituts für Geschichte, 8, Göttingen

Gebhardt, B. *et al.* (eds.) (1970), *Handbuch der Deutschen Geschichte*, 9th edn, I and II, Stuttgart

Gerlich, A. (1960), *Habsburg–Luxemburg–Wittelsbach im Kampf um die Deutsche Königskrone*, Wiesbaden

Graus, F. (1975), *Lebendige Vergangenheit. Überlieferung im Mittelalter und in den Vorstellungen vom Mittelalter*, Cologne and Vienna

Graus, F. (1987), *Pest-Geissler-Judenmorde*, Veröffentlichungen des Max-Planck-Instituts für Geschichte, 86, Göttingen

Handbuch der Historischen Stätten Deutschlands (1959–), various editors, I–XI, Stuttgart

Handbuch der Schweizer Geschichte (1972), I, Zurich

Hauck, A. (1954), *Kirchengeschichte Deutschlands*, Berlin and Leipzig, I and II, 8th edn

Heimpel, H. (1957), 'Deutschland in Späteren Mittelalter, 1200–1500', in O. Brandt *et al.* (eds.), *Handbuch der Deutschen Geschichte*, I–V, Constance,

Heimpel, H. (1982), *Die Vener von Gmünd und Strassburg, 1162–1447*, Veröffentlichungen des Max-Planck-Instituts für Geschichte, 52, I–III, Göttingen

Heinig, P.-J. (1983), *Reichsstädte, Freie Städte und Königtum, 1389–1450*, Veröffentlichungen des Instituts für Europäische Geschichte Mainz, Universalgeschichte, 108, Wiesbaden

Hergemöller, B.-U. (1983), *Fürsten, Herren und Städte zu Nürnberg 1355/1356. Die Entstehung der 'Goldenen Bulle', Karls IV.*, Städteforschung, ser. A, vol. 13, Cologne and Vienna

Hermkes, W. (1968), *Das Reichsvikariat in Deutschland. Reichsvikare nach dem Tode des Kaisers von der Goldenen Bulle bis zum Ende des Reiches*, Studien und Quellen zur Geschichte des Deutschen Verfassungsrechts, A 2, Karlsruhe

Hlaváček, I. (1970), *Das Urkunden- und Kanzleiwesen des Böhmischen und Römischen Königs Wenzel, 1376–1419*, Schriften der *MGH* 23, Stuttgart

Hlaváček, I. (1974), 'Konrad von Vechta', *Beiträge zur Geschichte der Stadt Vechta* 1: 5–35

Hlaváček, I. (1981), 'Studie k Dvoru Václava IV', *Folia Historica Bohemica* 3: 135–93

Hlaváček, I. (1991), *K Organizaci Státního Správního Syslému Václava IV. Dvě Studie o Jeho Itineráři a Radě*, Prague

Hödl, G. (1988), *Habsburg und Österreich 1273–1493: Gestalten und Gestalt des Österreichischen Spätmittelalters*, Vienna, Cologne and Graz

Hölscher, W. (1985), *Kirchenschutz als Herrschaftsinstrument. Personelle unde Funktionale Aspekte der Bistumspolitik Karls IV.*, Warendorf

Isenmann, E. (1988), *Die Deutsche Stadt im Spätmittelalter*, Stuttgart

Jahresberichte für Deutsche Geschichte, Berlin (1949–)

Jenks, S. (1992), *England, die Hanse und Preussen. Handel und Diplomatie 1377–1474*, Quellen und Darstellungen zur Hansischen Geschichte N.F. 38, I–III, Cologne and Vienna

Jeserich, K.G.A. *et al.* (eds.) (1983), *Deutsche Verwaltungsgeschichte*, I: *Vom Spätmittelalter bis zum Ende des Reiches*, Stuttgart

Kavka, F. (1989), *Am Hofe Karls IV.*, Leipzig

Kavka, F. (1993), *Vláda Karla IV. Za Jeho Císařství, 1355–1378*, Země České Koruny, Rodová, Říšská a Evrepská Politika, 1 and 2, Prague

Kellenbenz, H. (ed.) (1986), *Handbuch der Europäischen Wirtschafts- und Sozialgeschichte*, III, Stuttgart

Klare, W. (1990), *Die Wahl Wenzels von Luxemburg zum Römischen König 1376*, Münster

Kohl, W. (ed.) (1983), *Geschichte Westfalens*, I, Düsseldorf

Knott, R. (1899), 'Ein Mantuanischer Gesandtschaftsbericht aus Prag vom Jahre 1383', *Mitteilungen des Vereins für Geschichte der Deutschen in Böhmen* 37: 337–57

Krása, J. (1971), *Die Handschriften Wenzels IV.*, Prague

Kraus, T.R. (1987), 'Eine Unbekannte Quelle zur Ersten Gefangenschaft König Wenzels im Jahre 1394', *DA* 43: 135–59

Krieger, K.-F. (1979), *Die Lehenshoheit der Deutschen Könige im Spätmittelalter, c.1200–1437*, Untersuchungen zur Deutschen Staats und Rechtsgeschichte N.F. 23, Aalen

Krieger, K.-F. (1992), *König, Reich und Reichsreform im Spätmittelalter*, Enzyklopädie Deutscher Geschichte ,14, Munich

Kruse, H. *et al.* (eds.) (1991), *Ritterorden und Adelgesellschaften im Spätmittelalterlichen Deutschland. Ein Systematisches Verzeichnis*, Kieler Werkstücke Reihe D, 1, Frankfurt

Kühnel, H. (1985), *Alltag im Spätmittelalter*, 2nd edn, Graz, Vienna and Cologne

Lamprecht, K. (1885–6), *Deutsches Wirtschaftsleben im Mittelalter*, I–III, Leipzig

Landwehr, G. (1967), *Die Verpfändung der Deutschen Reichsstädte im Mittelalter*, Forschungen zur Deutschen Rechsgeschichte, 5, Cologne and Graz

Legner, A. (ed.) (1978–80), *Die Parler und der Schöne Stil 1350–1400*, 6 vols., Cologne

Lehmann, P. (1959–62), *Erforschung des Mittelalters*, I–V, Stuttgart

Leuschner, J. (1975), *Deutschland im Späten Mittelalter*, Göttingen

Lexikon des Mittelalters, 9 vols., Munich and Zurich (1980–98)

Lindner, T. (1875–80), *Geschichte des Deutschen Reiches unter König Wenzel in den Jahren 1378–1400*, I–II, Braunschweig

Lindner, T. (1882), *Das Urkundenwesen Karls IV. und Seiner Nachfolger, 1346–1437*, Stuttgart

Lorenz, O. (1887), *Deutschlands Geschichtsquellen im Mittelalter seit der Mitte des 13. Jahrhunderts*, 3rd edn, II, Berlin

Losher, G. (1985), *Königtum und Kirche zur Zeit Karls IV.*, Munich

Loyo, H. (1924), *Die Landfrieden unter Ruprecht von der Pfalz*, Giessen

Martin, T.M. (1993), *Auf dem Weg zum Reichstag, 1314–1410*, Schriftenreihe der Historischen Kommission bei der Bayer. Akademie der Wissenschaften, 44, Göttingen

Messerschmidt, W. (1907), *Der Rheinische Städtebund von 1381–1389*, Marburg

Meuthen, E. (1988), *Kölner Universitätsgeschichte*, I: *Die Alte Universität*, Cologne and Vienna

Mezník, J. (1990), *Praha Před Husitskou Revolucí*, Prague

Moraw, P. (1968a), 'Beamten und Rat König Ruprechts', *Zeitschrift für die Geschichte Oberrheins* 116: 59–126

Moraw, P. (1968b), 'Deutsches Königtum und Bürgerliche Geldwirtschaft um 1400', *VSW* 55: 289–328

Moraw, P. (1969), 'Kanzlei und Kanzleipersonal König Ruprechts', *DA* 15: 1–104

Moraw P. (1979), 'Reichsstadt, Reich und Königtum im Späten Mittelalter', *ZHF* 6: 385–424

Moraw, P. (1980), 'Zur Mittelpunktfunktion Prags im Zeitalter Karls IV', in *Europa Slavica, Europa Orientalis. Festschrift für Herbert Ludat*, Berlin, pp. 445–89

Moraw, P. (1982), 'Kaiser Karl IV., 1378–1978: Ertrag und Konsequenzen eines Gedenkjahres' in H. Ludat and R.C. Schwinges (eds.), *Politik, Gesellschaft, Geschichtsschreibung. Giessener Festgabe für František Graus zum 60. Geburtstag*, Cologne and Vienna, pp. 224–318

Moraw, P. (1985a), *Von Offener Verfassung zu Gestalteter Verdichtung 1250–1490. Das Reich im Späten Mittelalter*, Propyläen Geschichte Deutschlands, 3, Berlin

Moraw, P. (1985b), 'Grundzüge der Kanzleigeschichte Kaiser Karls IV., 1346–1378', *ZHF* 12: 11–42

Neitmann, K. (1986), *Die Staatsverträge des Deutschen Ordens in Preussen, 1230–1449*, Neue Forschungen zur Brandenburg-Preussischen Geschichte, 6, Cologne and Vienna

Paravicini, W. (1989), *Die Preussenreisen des Europäischen Adels 1*, Sigmaringen

Patschovsky, A. (1975), *Die Anfänge einer Ständigen Inquisition in Böhmen*, Beiträge zur Geschichte und Quellenkunde des Mittelalters, 3, Berlin

Patze, H. (ed.) (1970–1), *Der Deutsche Territorialstaat im 14. Jahrhundert*, VF, XIII and XIV, I and II, Sigmaringen

Patze, H. (ed.) (1978), *Kaiser Karl IV., 1316–1378: Forschungen über Kaiser und Reich*, Blätter für Deutsche Landesgeschichte, 114, Sigmaringen

Patze, H. and Paravicini, W. (eds.) (1991), *Fürstliche Residenzen im Spätmittelalterlichen Europa*, VF, XXXVI, Sigmaringen

Patze, H. and Schlesinger, W. (eds.) (1967–74), *Geschichte Thüringens*, II and III, Cologne and Vienna

Piattoli, R. (1976), *Miscellanea Diplomatica IV. Renati Piattoli in Memoriam*, Prato, pp. 77–203

Pirchan, G. (1930), *Italien und Kaiser Karl IV. in der Zeit seiner Zweiten Romfahrt*, I and II, Prague

Ritter, G. (1936), *Die Heidelberger Universität*, I, Heidelberg

Rüegg, W. (ed.) (1993), *Geschichte der Universität in Europa*, I, Munich

Růžek, V., 'Česka Znaková Galerie na Hradě Laufa u Norimberka z Roku 1361. Příspěvek Keskladbě Královského Dvora Karla IV', *Sborník Archivních Prací 38, 1*: 37–312

Samanek, V. (1910), *Kronrat und Reichsherrschaft im 13. und 14. Jahrhundert*, Abhandlungen zur Mittleren und Neueren Geschichte, 18, Berlin and Leipzig

Schneider, R. (ed.) (1987), *Das Mittelalterliche Königtum im Europäischen Vergleich*, VF, 32, Sigmaringen

Schramm, P.E. (1978), *Fillitz Herman mit Zus. von Florentine Mütherich*, Denkmale der Deutschen Könige und Kaiser, 2, Munich

Schröder, R. (1932), *Lehrbuch der Deutschen Rechtsgeschichte*, 7th edn, ed. E. Künssberg, Leipzig

Schubert, E. (1979), *König und Reich. Studien zur Spätmittelalterlichen Deutschen Verfassungsgeschichte*, Veröffentlichungen des Max-Plank-Institut für Geschichte, 63, Göttingen

Schubert, E. (1992), *Einfürung in die Grundprobleme der Deutschen Geschichte im Spätmittelalter*, Darmstadt

Schuchard, C. (1987), *Die Deutschen an der Päpstlichen Kurie im Späten Mittelalter, 1378–1447*, Bibliothek des Deutschen Historischen Instituts in Rom, 65, Tübingen

Schultze, J. (1961–), *Die Mark Brandenburg*, 1 – , Berlin

Schumann, S. (1974), *Die 'Nationes' an den Universitäten Prag, Leipzig und Wien*, Berlin

Schwinges, R.C. (1986), *Deutsche Universitätsbesucher im 14. und 15. Jahrhundert*, Stuttgart

Sedláček, A. (1914), *Zbytky Register Králův Římskýcha 'Českých z let 1361–1480*, Prague

Seeliger, G. (1885), *Das Deutsche Hofmeisteramt im Spaeteren Mittelalter*, Innsbruck

Seibt, F. (1978a), *Karl IV. Ein Kaiser in Europa 1346 bis 1378*, 2nd edn, Munich

Seibt, F. (ed.) (1978b), *Kaiser Karl IV. Staatsmann und Mäzen*, 2nd edn, Munich

Seibt, F. (1987), *Glanz und Elend des Mittelalters*, Berlin

Seibt, F. and Eberhard, W. (eds.) (1984), *Europa 1400. Die Krise des Spätmittelalters*, Stuttgart

Spěváček, J. (1980), *Karel IV. Život a Dílo, 1316–1378*, 2nd edn, Prague

Spěváček, J. (1986), *Václav IV., 1361–1419*, Prague

Spindler, M. (ed.) (1976–9), *Handbuch der Bayerischen Geschichte*, 2nd edn, II and III, Munich

Sprandel, R. (1975), *Verfassung und Gesellschaft im Mittelalter*, Paderborn

Sterken, M. (1989), *Königtum und Territorialgewalten in den Rheinmaasländishen Landfrieden des 14. Jahrhunderts*, Rheinishes Archiv, 124, Cologne and Vienna

Stoob, H. (1990), *Kaiser Karl IV. und seine Zeit*, Graz

Stromer, W. von (1970), *Oberdeutsche Hochfinanz 1350–1450*, Vierteljahrschrift für Sozial- und Wirtschaftsgeschichte, supplements, 55–7, I–III, Wiesbaden

Stromer, W. von (1971), 'Das Zusammenspiel Oberdeutscher und Florentiner Geldleute bei der Finanzierung von König Ruprechts Italienzug, 1401–2', in H. Kellenbenz (ed.), *Öffentliche Finanzen und Privates Kapital im Späten Mittelalter und in der Ersten Hälfte des 19. Jahrhunderts*, Stuttgart, pp. 50–86

Stromer, W. von (1978), *Die Gründung der Baumwollindustrie in Mitteleuropa. Wirtschaftspolitik im Spätmittelalters*, Monographien zur Geschichte des Mittelalters, 17, Stuttgart

Šusta, J. (1946–8), *České Dějiny*, II: 3 and 4, Prague

Thomas, H. (1973), *Zwischen Regnum und Imperium. Die Fürstentümer Bar und Lothringen zur Zeit Kaiser Karls IV.*, Bonner Historischen Forschungen, 40, Bonn

Thomas, H. (1983), *Deutsche Geschichte des Spätmittelalters, 1250–1500*, Stuttgart, Berlin, Cologne and Mainz

Uhlitz, K. and M. (1963), *Handbuch der Geschichte Österreich-Ungarns*, 2nd edn, I, Graz, Vienna and Cologne

Vaněček, V. (ed.) (1984), *Karolus Quartus*, Prague

Veldtrup, D. (1988), *Zwischen Eherecht und Familienpolitik. Studien zu den Dynastischen Heiratsprojekten Karls IV.*, Warendorf

Weigel, H. (1942), 'Männer um König Wenzel: Das Problem der Reichspolitik 1379–84', *Deutsches Archiv für Geschichte des Mittelalters* 5: 112–77

Weigel, H. (1944), 'König Wenzels Persönliche Politik: Reich und Hausmacht 1384–1389', *Deutsches Archiv für Geschichte des Mittelalters* 7: 133–99

Weller, K. and A. (1971), *Württembergische Geschichte*, Stuttgart and Aalen

Werunsky, K. (1880–92), *Geschichte Kaiser Karls IV. und seiner Zeit* (to 1368 only), I–III, Innsbruck

Winter, E. (1964), *Frühhumanismus. Seine Entwicklung in Böhmen und deren Bedeutung für die Kirchenreformbestrebungen im 14. Jahrhundert*, Berlin

Zöllner, E. (1984), *Geschichte Österreichs*, 7th edn, Vienna

17 THE LOW COUNTRIES, 1290–1415

Secondary works

Allmand, C. T. (1988), *The Hundred Years War. England and France at War, c. 1300–c. 1450*, Cambridge

Anrooij, W. van (ed.) (1991), *Holland in Wording. De ontstaansgeschiedenis van het graafschap Holland tot het begin van de vijftiende eeuw*, Hilversum

Arnould, M.A. (1969), 'Le Hainaut. Evolution historique d'un concept géographique', in *Le Hainaut français et belge*, Mons. pp. 15–42

Avonds, P. (1984), *Brabant tijdens de regering van hertog Jan III (1312–1356). De grote politieke crisissen*, VKAWLSKB, Brussels

Avonds, P. (1991), *Brabant tijdens de regering van hertog Jan III (1312–1356). Land en instellingen*, VKAWLSKB, Brussels

Avonds, P. and Janssen, J.D.(1989), *Politiek en literatuur. Brabant en de slag bij Woeringen, 1288*, Brussels

Baerten, J. (1969), *Het graafschap Loon (11de–14de eeuw)*, Assen

Berben, H. (1937), 'Une guerre économique au moyen âge. L'embargo sur l'exportation des laines anglaises (1270–1274)', in *Etudes d'histoire dediées à la mémoire de H. Pirenne par ses anciens élèves*, Brussels, pp. 1–17

Blockmans, F. (1938), *Het Gentsche Stadspatriciaat tot omstreeks 1302*, Antwerp

Blockmans, W.P. (1978), *De volksvertegenwoordiging in Vlaanderen in de overgang van Middeleeuwen naar Nieuwe Tijden (1384–1506)*, VKAWLSKB, Brussels

Blockmans, W.P. (1982), 'The Social and Economic Effects of Plague in the Low Countries 1349–1500', *RBPH* 60: 833–63

Blockmans, W.P. and Prevenier, W. (1978), 'Poverty in Flanders and Brabant from the Fourteenth to the Mid-Sixteenth Century', *Acta Historiae Neerlandicae* 10: 20–57

Blockmans, W.P. and Prevenier, W. (1997), *De Bourgondiërs. De Nederlanden op weg naar eenheid, 1384–1530*, Amsterdam and Louvain

Blok, D.P., Prevenier, W. *et al.* (1980), *Algemene Geschiedenis der Nederlanden*, IV: *(1384–1482)*, Haarlem

Blok, D.P., Prevenier, W. *et al.* (1982), *Algemene Geschiedenis der Nederlanden*, II: *(1100–1400)*, Haarlem

Boer, D. de (1978), *Graaf en grafiek. Sociale en economische ontwikkelingen in het middeleeuwse Noordholland tussen 1345 en 1415*, Leiden

Boer, D. de (1987), 'Een vorst trekt noordwaarts. De komst van Albrecht van Beieren naar de Nederlanden (1358)', in D. de Boer *et al.* (eds.), *De Nederlanden in de late middeleeuwen*, Utrecht, pp. 283–309

Boone, M. (1990a), *Geld en macht. De Gentse stadsfinanciën en de Bourgondische staatsvorming (1384–1453)*, VMGOG 15, Ghent

Boone, M. (1990b), *Gent en de Bourgondische hertogen*, VKAWLSKB, Brussels

Boone, M. and Prevenier, W. (eds.) (1993), *Drapery Production in the Late Medieval Low Countries. Markets and Strategies for Survival (11th–16th Centuries)*, Louvain and Apeldoorn

Bos-Rops, J.A.M.Y. (1993), *Graven op zoek naaar geld de inkomsten van de graven van Holland, 1389 1433*, Hilversum

Bovesse, J. (1949–50), 'Jean Ier, comte de Namur, *Annales de la société archéologique de Namur* 45: 1–66

Bovesse, J. (1958), 'La maison de Namur et les villes liègeoises au début du XIVe siècle', in *Mélanges F. Rousseau. Etudes sur l'histoire du pays mosan au moyen âge*, Brussels, pp. 121–43

Bovesse, J. (1966), 'Le comté de Namur, la France et l'empire en 1309–1310', *SL* 38: 65–95

Bragt, R. van (1956), *De Blijde Inkomst van de hertogen van Brabant Johanna en Wenceslas, SL,* 13, Louvain

Brokken, H. (1982), *Het ontstaan van de Hoekse en Kabeljauwse twisten,* Zutphen

Buntinx, J. (1949), *De Audiëntie van de graven van Vlaanderen. Studie over het centraal grafelijk gerecht c. 1330–c. 1409,* VKAWLSKB, Brussels

Byl, R. (1965), *Les juridictions scabinales dans le duché de Brabant (des origines à la fin du XVe siècle),* Brussels

Chorley, P. (1987), 'The Cloth Exports of Flanders and Northern France during the Thirteenth Century: A Luxury Trade?', *EcHR* 2nd series 40: 349–79

Coenen, J.M.A. (1986), *Graaf en grafelijkheid. Een onderzoek naar de graven van Holland en hun omgeving in de dertiende eeuw,* Utrecht

Cordfunke, E. (ed.) (1982), *Holland in de dertiende eeuw,* The Hague

Cordfunke, E. *et al.* (ed.) (1988), *De Hollandse stad in de dertiende eeuw,* Zutphen

Curry, A. (1993), *The Hundred Years War,* Basingstoke

Delcambre, F. (1938), *Les relations entre la France et le Hainaut depuis l'avènement de Jean II d'Avesnes jusqu'à la conclusion de l'alliance franco-hennuyère (1280–1297),* Paris

Demuynck, R. (1951), 'De Gentse Oorlog (1379–1385). Oorzaken en karakter, *HMGOG,* 5: 305–18

Déprez, E. (1902), *Les préliminaires de la guerre de Cent Ans. La papauté, la France et l'Angleterre, 1328–1342,* Paris

Derville, A. (1972), 'Les draperies flamandes et artésiennes vers 1250–1350. Quelques considérations critiques et problématiques', *RN* 54: 353–70

Dieperink, F.H.J. (ed.) (1953), *Studiën betreffende de geschiedenis van Oost-Nederland van de dertiende tot de vijftiende eeuw,* Groningen

Doudelez, G. (1974), 'La révolution communale de 1280 à Ypres', in O. Mus and J.A. van Houtte (eds.), *Prisma van de geschiedenis van Ieper,* Ypres, pp. 188–294

Ernsig, R. (1885), *Wilhelm III als Herzog von Geldern (1372–1393),* Paderborn and Münster

Fasel, W.A. (1980), 'De onlusten te Alkmaar tot aan het jaar 1500', in *Scrinium et Scriptura. Opstellen aangeboden aan J. L. van der Gouw,* Groningen, pp. 312–21

Favier, J. (1980), *La guerre de Cent Ans,* Poitiers

Favresse, F. (1932), *L'avènement du régime démocratique à Brussels pendant le moyen âge (1306–1423),* Brussels

Formsma, W.J. (1930), *De wording van de Staten van Stad en Lande tot 1536,* Assen

Formsma, W.J. (ed.) (1976), *Historie van Groningen. Stad en Land,* Groningen

Gaier, C. (1973), *L'industrie et le commerce des armes dans les anciennes principautés belges du XIIIe à la fin du XVe siècle,* Paris

Ganshof, F.L. (1938), *Brabant, Rheinland und Reich im 12., 13. und 14. Jahrhundert,* Bonn

Ganshof, F.L. (1957), 'La Flandre', in F. Lot and R. Fawtier (eds.), *Histoire des institutions françaises au moyen âge,* 3 vols., Paris, 1, pp. 343–426

Ganshof, F.L. and Verhulst, A. (1966), 'Medieval Agrarian Society in its Prime, I. France, The Low Countries, and Western Germany', in *CEHE,* 1, pp. 291–339

Genicot, L. (1943–82), *L'économie rurale namuroise au bas moyen âge (1199–1429),* 3 vols., Namur, Louvain and Brussels

Genicot, L. (1974), 'Sur le patriciat à Namur au XIVe siècle', in *Festschrift Karl Bosl,* Stuttgart, pp. 79–91

Gerven, J. van (1976), 'Nationaal gevoel en stedelijke politieke visies in het 14de eeuwse Brabant. Het voorbeeld van Jan van Boendale', *BG* 59: 145–64

Gorissen, P. (1956), *Het Parlement en de Raad van Kortenberg, SL*, 11, Louvain

Haegeman, M. (1988), *De anglofilie in het graafschap Vlaanderen tussen 1379 en 1435. Politieke en economische aspecten, SL*, 90, Kortrijk and Heule

Haepke, R. (1908), *Brügges Entwicklung zum mittelalterlichen Weltmarkt,* Berlin

Hardenberg, H. (1975), 'Het ontstaan van de Staten van Holland', in L. Brummel (ed.), *Driekwart eeuw historisch leven in Den Haag,* The Hague, pp. 104–20

Herwaarden, J. van (1986), 'Stedelijke rivaliteit in de middeleeuwen: Toscane, Vlaanderen, Holland', in P. Blaas and J. van Herwaarden (eds.), *Stedelijke naijver. De betekenis van interstedelijke conflicten in de geschiedenis,* The Hague, pp. 38–81

Houtte, J.A. van (1977), *An Economic History of the Low Countries 800-1800,* London

Hoven van Genderen, B. van den (1987), *Het kapittel-generaal en de Staten van het Nedersticht in de 15 de eeuw,* Utrecht

Howell, M. (1986), *Women, Production and Patriarchy in Late Medieval Cities,* Chicago

Hugenholtz, F.W.N. (1949), *Drie boerenopstanden uit de veertiende eeuw. Vlaanderen, 1323–1328. Frankrijk, 1358. Engeland, 1381,* Haarlem

Hugenholtz, F.W.N. (1966), *Floris V,* Bussum

Immink, P.W.A. (1942), *De wording van Staat en souvereiniteit in de middeleeuwen. Een rechts-historische studie in het bijzonder met betrekking tot het Nedersticht,* 1, Utrecht

Janse, A. (1993), *Grenzen aan de macht. De Friese oorlog van de graven van Holland omstreeks 1400,* The Hague

Jansen, H.P.H. (1966), *Hoekse en Kabeljauwse twisten,* Bussum

Janssen, W. (1981), 'Niederrheinische Territorialbildung', in E. Ennen and K. Flink (eds.), *Soziale und wirtschaftliche Bindungen im Mittelalter am Niederrhein,* Kleef, pp. 95–113

Janssen, W. (ed.) (1988), *Der Tag bei Worringen: 5. Juni 1288,* Düsseldorf

Jappe Alberts, W. (1950), *De Staten van Gelre en Zutphen tot 1459,* The Hague

Jappe Alberts, W. (1972), *Geschiedenis van de beide Limburgen,* Assen

Jappe Alberts, W. (1978), *Geschiedenis van Gelderland tot 1492,* Zutphen

Jappe Alberts, W. (1982), *Overzicht van de geschiedenis van de Nederrijnse territoria tussen Maas en Rijn,* II: *1288–c. 1500,* Assen

Jappe Alberts, W. (1984), *De graven en hertogen van Gelre op reis, 13 de-15 de eeuw,* Dieren

Joris, A. (1961), 'Der Handel der Maasstädte im Mittelalter, *HG* 79: 15–33

Joset, C.J. (1940), *Les villes au pays de Luxembourg (1196–1363),* Louvain

Kalma, J. (1968), *Geschiedenis van Friesland,* Drachten

Kan, F.J.W. van (1988), *Sleutels tot de macht. De ontwikkeling van het Leidse Patriciaat tot 1420,* Hilversum

Kastner, D. (1972), *Die Territorialpolitik der Grafen van Kleve,* Düsseldorf

Kerling, N.J.M. (1954), *Commercial Relations of Holland and Zeeland with England from the Late 13th Century to the Close of the Middle Ages,* Leiden

Kittell, E.E. (1991), *From Ad Hoc to Routine. A Case Study in Medieval Bureaucracy,* Philadelphia

Laet, M. de (1972), 'De Vlaamse aktieve handel op Engeland in de eerste helft van de 14de eeuw, aan de hand van de custom accounts', in *Economische Geschiedenis van Belgie. Behandeling van de bronnen en problematiek. Handelingen van het Colloquium te Brussel 17–19 nov. 1971, ARA,* Brussels, pp. 223–31

Laurent, H. (1933), *La loi de Gresham au moyen âge. Essai sur la circulation monétaire entre la Flandre et le Brabant à la fin du XIVe siècle,* Brussels

Lejeune, J. (1948), *Liège et son pays. Naissance d'une patrie (XIIIe–XIVe siècle)*, Liège

Lemmink, F.H.J. (1951), *Het ontstaan van de Staten van Zeeland en hun geschiedenis tot het jaar 1555*, Nijmegen

Lesger, C.M. (1990), *Hoorn als stedelijk knooppunt. Stedensystemen tijdens de late middeleeuwen en vroegmoderne tijd*, Hilversum

Lucas, H.S. (1929), *The Low Countries and the Hundred Years War (1326–1347)*, Ann Arbor

Luykx, Th. (1952), *Het grafelijk geslacht Dampierre en zijn strijd tegen Filips de Schone*, Louvain

Maertens, R. (1976), *Wertorientierungen und wirtschaftsliches Erfolgsstreben mittelalterlicher Grosskaufleute. Das Beispiel Gent im 13. Jahrhundert*, Cologne and Vienna

Maris, A.J. (1954), *Van voogdij tot maarschalkambt. Bijdrage tot de geschiedenis der Utrechts-bischoppelijke staatsinstellingen, voornamelijk in het Nedersticht*, Utrecht

Marsilje, J.W. (1985), *Het financiële beleid van Leiden in de laat-Beierse en Bourgondische periode, c. 1390–1477*, Hilversum

Meij, P.J. (1959), 'Over de lotgevallen van de Gelderse landsheerlijke privilegebrieven', *Bijdragen en Mededelingen van de Vereniging Gelre* 58: 141–55

Meilink, P.A. (1912), *De Nederlandsche hanzesteden tot het laatste kwartaal der XIVe eeuw*, Groningen

Monier, R. (1924), *Les institutions judiciaires des villes de Flandre des origines à la rédaction des coutumes*, Lille

Munro, J. H. (1991), 'Industrial Transformations in the North-West European Textile Trades, c. 1290–c. 1340: Economic Progress or Economic Crisis?', in B.M.S. Campbell (ed.), *Before the Black Death. Studies in the Crisis of the Early Fourteenth Century*, Manchester, pp. 110–48

Mus, O. and Houtte, J.A. van (1974), *Prisma van de Geschiedenis van Ieper*, Ypres

Neillands, R. (1990), *The Hundred Years War, 1337–1453*, London

Nicholas, D. (1971), *Town and Countryside. Social, Economic and Political Tensions in Fourteenth-Century Flanders*, Bruges

Nicholas, D. (1987), *The Metamorphosis of a Medieval City. Ghent in the Age of the Arteveldes, 1302–1390*, Lincoln, Nebr. and London

Nicholas, D. (1988), *The van Arteveldes of Ghent. The Varieties of Vendetta and the Hero in History*, Ithaca and New York

Nicholas, D. (1992), *Medieval Flanders*, London and New York

Nikolay, W. (1985), *Die Ausbildung der ständischen Verfassung in Geldern und Brabant während des 13. und 14. Jahrhunderts*, Bonn

Nüsse, K. (1958), *Die Entwicklung der Stände im Herzogtum Geldern bis zum Jahre 1418 nach den Stadtrechnungen von Arnheim*, Cologne

Oostrom, F. P. van (1992), *The Word of Honor. Literature at the Court of Holland in about 1350–1450*, Berkeley

Overvoorde, J. C. and Joosting, J.G.C. (1897), *De gilden van Utrecht tot 1528*, The Hague

Palmer, J.J.N. (1976), 'England, France, the Papacy and the Flemish Succession, 1361–9', *JMH* 2: 339–64

Pirenne, H. (1900), *Le soulèvement de la Flandre maritime de 1323–1328*, Brussels

Pirenne, H. (1963), *Early Democracies in the Low Countries. Urban Society and Political Conflict in the Middle Ages and the Renaissance*, New York

Pleij, H. (ed.) (1991), *Op belofte van profijt. Stadsliteratuur en burgermoraal in de Nederlandse letterkunde van de middeleeuwen*, Amsterdam

Pols, M.S. (1899), 'Graaf Jan I van Holland', *Bijdragen voor Geschiedenis en Oudheidkunde* 3rd series 10: 1–55

Posthumus, N. W. (1908), *De geschiedenis van de Leidsche lakenindustrie*, 1, The Hague

Prevenier, W. (1961), *De Leden en de Staten van Vlaanderen (1384–1405)*, VKAWLSKB, Brussels

Prevenier, W. (1973), 'Les perturbations dans les relations commerciales anglo-flamandes entre 1379 et 1407. Causes de désaccord et raisons d'une réconciliation', in *Economies et sociétés du moyen âge. Mélanges E. Perroy*, Paris, pp. 477–97

Prevenier, W. (1977), 'Motieven voor leliaardsgezindheid in Vlaanderen in de periode 1297–1305', *De Leiegouw* 19: 273–88

Prevenier, W. (1978), 'La bourgeoisie en Flandre au XIIIe siècle', *Revue de l'université de Brussels*: 407–28

Prevenier, W. (1983), 'La démographie des villes du comté de Flandre aux XIVe et XVe siècles', *RN* 65: 255–75

Prevenier, W. and Blockmans, W.P. (1985), *The Burgundian Netherlands,* Cambridge

Prevenier, W. and Boone, M. (1989), 'The "city-state" Dream. Fourteenth–Fifteenth Century', in J. Decavele (ed.), *Ghent. In Defence of a Rebellious City*, Antwerp, pp. 80–105

Quicke, F. (1947), *Les Pays-Bas à la veille de la période bourguignonne, 1356–1384,* Paris and Brussels

Ridder, P. de (1979), 'Brussel, residentie der hertogen van Brabant onder Jan I (1267–1294) en Jan II (1294–1312)', *RBPH* 57: 329–41

Rogghé, P. (1964), 'De politiek van graaf Lodewijk van Male', *Appeltjes van het Meetjesland* 15: 388–441

Roland, J. (1959), *Le comté et la province de Namur,* Namur

Rompaey, J. van (1977), 'De publiekrechterlijke achtergrond van de strijd tussen Gwijde van Dampierre en Filips de Schone', *De Leiegouw* 19: 337–59

Roover, R. de (1948), *Money, Banking, and Credit in Mediaeval Bruges*, Cambridge, Mass.

Rutgers, C.A. (1970), *Jan van Arkel. Bisschop van Utrecht,* Groningen

Rutgers, C.A. (ed.) (1978), *De Utrechtse bisschop in de middeleeuwen,* The Hague

Sabbe, J. (1951), 'De vijandelijkheden tussen de Avesnes en de Dampierres in Zeeland, Holland en Utrecht van 1303 tot 1305', *HMGOG* 5: 225–303

Schaefke, W. (ed.) (1988), *Der Name der Freiheit 1288–1968*, 2 vols., Cologne

Schaïk, R.W.M. van (1987), *Belasting, bevolking en bezit in Gelre en Zutphen (1350–1550),* Hilversum

Schmidt, H. (1975), *Politische Geschichte Ostfrieslands,* Leer

Schneider, F. (1913), *Herzog Johann von Baiern. Erwählter Bischof von Lüttich und Graf von Holland (1373–1425),* Berlin

Sivéry, G. (1977), *Structures agraires et vie rurale dans le Hainaut à la fin du moyen âge,* Villeneuve d'Ascq

Slicher van Bath, B.H. (ed.) (1970), *Geschiedenis van Overijssel,* Deventer

Slicher van Bath, B.H. (1977), *Een samenleving onder spanning, geschiedenis van het platteland in Overijssel,* Utrecht

Smit, J.G. (1995), *Vorst en onderdaan. Studies over Holland en Zeeland in de late middeleeuwen,* Louvain

Spading, K. (1973), *Holland und die Hanse im 15. Jahrhundert,* Weimar

Stabel, P. (1997), *Dwarfs among Giants. The Flemish Urban Network in the Late Middle Ages*, Louvain and Apeldoorn

Stercken, M. (1989), *Königtum und Territorialgewalten in den rheinmaasländischen Landfrieden des 14. Jahrhunderts*, Cologne and Vienna

Straeten, J. van der (1952), *Het Charter en de Raad van Kortenberg,* 2 vols., Brussels and Louvain

Stuip, R.E.V. and Vellekoop, C. (eds.) (1991), *Utrecht tussen kerk en staat*, Hilversum

Sturler, J. de (1936), *Les relations politiques et les échanges commerciaux entre le duché de Brabant et l'Angleterre au moyen âge*, Paris

Taal, G. (1965), 'Het graafschap Zeeland en zijn verhouding tot Holland in de landsheerlijke tijd', *Archief Zeeuwsch Genootschap der Wetenschappen*: 51–96

TeBrake, William H. (1993), *A Plague of Insurrection. Popular Politics and Peasant Revolt in Flanders, 1323–1328*, Philadelphia

Tihon, C. (1958), 'Le conflit des XVII villes entre Liège et Namur au XIVe siècle. Le procès en cour de Rome', in *Mélanges F. Rousseau. Etudes sur l'histoire du pays mosan au moyen âge*, Brussels, pp. 607–27

Töpfer, B. (1980), 'Die Rolle von Stadtebunden bei der Ausbildung der Ständeverfassung in den Fürstentümern Lüttich und Brabant', in B. Töpfer (ed.), *Städte und Ständestaat. Zur Rolle der Städte bei der Entwicklung der Ständeverfassung in europäischen Staaten vom 13. bis zum 15. Jahrhunderts*, Berlin, pp. 113–54

Uyttebrouck, A. (1975), *Le gouvernement du duché de Brabant au bas moyen âge (1355–1430)*, Brussels

Uytven, R. van (1962), 'Plutokratie in de 'oude demokratieën der Nederlanden', *Handelingen Koninklijke Zuidnederlandse Maatschappij voor Taal- en Letterkunde en Geschiedenis* 16: 373–409

Uytven, R. van (1963), 'Peter Couthereel en de troebelen te Leuven van 1350 tot 1363', *Mededelingen van de geschied- en oudheidkundige kring voor Leuven en omgeving* 3: 63–97

Uytven, R. van (1976a), 'Vorst, adel en steden: een driehoeksverhouding in Brabant van de twaalfde tot de zestiende eeuw', *BG* 59: 93–122

Uytven, R. van (1976b), 'La draperie brabançonne et malinoise du XIIe au XVIIe siècle', in *Produzione, commercio e consumo dei Panni di Lana*, Florence, pp. 85–97

Uytven, R. van and Blockmans, W. (1969), 'Constitutions and their Application in the Netherlands during the Middle Ages', *RBPH* 47: 399–424

Vandermaesen, M. (1971), 'Raadsheren en invloeden achter de grafelijke politiek in Vlaanderen in de 14de eeuw', in *Handelingen van het 14de Congres van de Federatie van Kringen voor Oudheidkunde en Geschiedenis van Belgie*, Mechelen, pp. 212–20

Vaughan, R. (1962), *Philip the Bold. The Formation of the Burgundian State*, London

Vaughan, R. (1966), *John the Fearless. The Growth of Burgundian Power*, London

Verbruggen, J.F. (1977), *1302 in Vlaanderen*, Brussels

Vercauteren, F. (1943), *Luttes sociales à Liège aux XIIIe et XIVe siècles*, Brussels

Verhulst, A. (1972), 'La laine indigène dans les anciens Pays-Bas entre le XIIe et le XVIIe siècle. Mise en oeuvre industrielle, production et commerce', *RH* 96: 281–322

Verhulst, A. (1990), *Précis d'histoire rurale de la Belgique*, Brussels

Verwijs, E. (1869), *De oorlogen van hertog Albrecht van Beieren met de Friezen in de laatste jaren der XIVe eeuw*, Utrecht

Vries, O. (1986), *Het Heilige Roomse Rijk en de Friese Vrijheid*, Leeuwarden

Waale, M.J. (1990), *De Arkelse oorlog, 1401–1412. Een politieke, krijgskundige en economische analyse*, Hilversum

Warlop, E. (1975), *The Flemish Nobility before 1300*, 4 vols., Courtrai

Wee, H. van der (1975), 'Structural Changes and Specialization in the Industry of the Southern Netherlands 1100–1600', *EcHR* 2nd series 27: 203–21

Werveke, H. van (1946), *Gand. Esquisse d'histoire sociale*, Brussels

Werveke, H. van (1954), 'Industrial Growth in the Middle Ages: The Cloth Industry in Flanders', *EcHR* 2nd series 6: 237–45

Werveke, H. van (1959), 'La famine de l'an 1316 en Flandre et dans les régions voisines', *RN* 41: 5–14

Wyffels, C. (1966), 'Nieuwe gegevens betreffende een XIIIde eeuwse "democratische" stedelijke opstand: de Brugse "Moerlemaye" (1280–1281)', *BCRH* 132: 37–142

Zeper, S.A. Waller (1914), *Jan van Henegouwen, heer van Beaumont. Bijdrage tot de geschiedenis der Nederlanden in de eerste helft der veertiende eeuw*, The Hague

Ziegler, J.E. (1983), 'Edward III and Low Country Finances: 1338–1340, with Particular Emphasis on the Dominant Position of Brabant', *RBPH* 61: 802–7

18(a) THE CROWN OF ARAGON

Primary sources

Cartas de población del reino de Aragón en los siglos medievales, ed. M.L. Ledesma Rubio, Zaragoza (1991)

Cartas de población y franquicia de Cataluña, ed. J.M. Font Rius, 3 vols., Madrid and Barcelona (1969–83)

Chronicle of Muntaner, trans. Lady Goodenough, 2 vols., London (1920–1)

Chronicle of San Juan de la Peña. A Fourteenth-Century Official History of the Crown of Aragon, trans. L.H. Nelson, Philadelphia (1991)

Cortes de los antiguos reinos de Aragón y de Valencia y principado de Cataluña, 26 vols., Madrid (1896–1922)

Pere III of Catalonia (Pedro IV of Aragon), *Chronicle,* trans. M. and J.N. Hillgarth, 2 vols., Toronto (1980)

Secondary works

Abadal i de Vinyals, R. d' (1966), 'Pedro el Ceremonioso y los comienzos de la decadencia política de Cataluña', in *HEMP*, XIV, pp. ix–ccii

Abulafia, D. (1994), *A Mediterranean Emporium. The Catalan Kingdom of Majorca,* Cambridge

Arribas Palau, A. (1952), *La conquista de Cerdeña por Jaime II de Aragón,* Barcelona

Ashtor, E. (1988), 'Catalan Cloth on the Late Medieval Mediterranean Markets', *JEEH* 17: 227–57

Assis, Y. T. (1987), 'The Papal Inquisition and Aragonese Jewry in the Early Fourteenth Century', *MS* 49: 391–410

Atiya, A. S. (1938), *Egypt and Aragon. Embassies and Diplomatic Correspondence between 1300 and 1330 A.D.*, Leipzig

Baer, Y. (1961–6), *History of the Jews in Christian Spain*, 2 vols., Philadelphia

Basáñez Villaluenga, M.B. (1989), *La aljama sarracena de Huesca en el siglo XIV*, Barcelona

Batlle, C. (1977), 'El municipio de Barcelona en el siglo XIV', *CH* 8: 203–11

Batlle, C. (1988), *L'expansió baixmedieval (segles XIII–XV)* (*Història de Catalunya*, III, ed. P. Vilar), Barcelona

Baucells i Reig, J. (1982), 'L'expansió peninsular en la política de Jaume II: el matrimoni de la seva filla gran Maria amb l'infant Pere de Castella', *AEM* 12: 491–535

Bisson, T.N. (1986), *The Medieval Crown of Aragon*, Oxford

Blasco Martínez, A. (1988), *La judería de Zaragoza en el siglo XIV*, Zaragoza

Boswell, J. (1977), *The Royal Treasure. Muslim Communities under the Crown of Aragon in the Fourteenth Century*, New Haven

Bramon, D. (1981), *Contra moros i jueus. Formació i estratègia d'unes discriminacions al País Valencià*, Valencia

Carrère, C. (1967), *Barcelone. Centre économique à l'époque des difficultés, 1380–1462*, 2 vols., Paris

Casula, F.C. (1990), *La Sardegna aragonese*, 2 vols., Sassari

Cateura Bennàsser, P. (1982), *Política y finanzas del reino de Mallorca bajo Pedro IV*, Palma de Mallorca

Chamberlin, C.L. (1992), '"Not all Martyrs or Saints": The Aragonese-Castilian Crusade against Granada, 1309–1310', *Comitatus* 23: 17–45

Doñate Sebastià, J. and Magdalena Nom de Déu, J.R. (1990), *Three Jewish Communities in Medieval Valencia. Castellón de la Plana, Burriana, Villareal*, Jerusalem

Dufourcq, C.-E. (1966), *L'Espagne catalane et le Maghrib aux XIIIe et XIVe siècles*, Paris

Estal, J.M. del (1982), *La conquista y anexión de las tierras de Alicante, Elche, Orihuela y Guardamar al reino de Valencia por Jaime II de Aragón (1296–1308)*, Alicante

Fernández-Armesto, F. (1987), *Before Columbus. Exploration and Colonisation from the Mediterranean to the Atlantic, 1229–1492*, London

Fernández-Armesto, F. (1992), *Barcelona. A Thousand Years of the City's Past*, Oxford

Ferrer i Mallol, M.T. (1970–1), 'El patrimoni reial i la recuperació dels senyorius juris-diccionals en els estats catalano-aragonesos a la fi del segle XIV', *AEM* 7: 351–491

Ferrer i Mallol, M.T. (1985), 'La redempció de captius a la Corona Catalano-Aragonesa (segle XIV)', *AEM*, 15: 237–97

Ferrer i Mallol, M.T. (1987), *Els sarraïns de la Corona Catalano-Aragonesa en el segle XIV: segregació i discriminació*, Barcelona

Ferrer i Mallol, M.T. (1988), *La frontera amb l'Islam en el segle XIV. Cristians i sarraïns al país Valencià*, Barcelona

Ferrer i Mallol, M.T. (1989), 'La frontera meridional valenciana durant la guerra amb Castella dita dels Dos Peres', in *Pere el Cerimoniós i la seva època*, Barcelona, pp. 245–357

Ferrer i Mallol, M.T. (1991), 'Origen i evolució de la Diputació del General de Catalunya', *Les corts a Catalunya*, Barcelona, pp. 152–9

Finke, H. (1907), *Papsttum und Untergang des Templerordens*, 2 vols., Münster

Forey, A.J. (1989), 'The Beginning of Proceedings against the Aragonese Templars', in D.W. Lomax and D. Mackenzie (eds.), *God and Man in Medieval Spain*, Warminster, pp. 81–96

Freedman, P. (1991), *The Origins of Peasant Servitude in Medieval Catalonia*, Cambridge

García Fernández, M. (1991) 'Jaime II y la minoría de Alfonso XI. Sus relaciones con la sociedad política castellana', *HID* 18: 143–81

Goñi Gaztambide, J. (1958), *Historia de la bula de la cruzada en España*, Vitoria

González Antón, L. (1975), *Las uniones aragonesas y las cortes del reino (1283–1301)*, 2 vols., Zaragoza

González Antón, L. (1977), 'Las cortes aragonesas en el reinado de Jaime II', *AHDE* 47: 523–682

González Antón, L. (1978), *Las cortes de Aragón*, Zaragoza

González Antón, L. and Lacarra y de Miguel, J. M. (1990), 'Consolidación de la Corona de Aragón como potencia mediterránea', *HEMP*, XIII, ii, pp. 255–316

Guilleré, C. (1982), 'Les finances royales à la fin du règne d'Alfonso IV el Benigno (1335–1336)', *MCV* 18: 33–60

Guilleré, C. (1984), 'Les finances publiques en Roussillon-Cerdagne au milieu du XIVe siècle', *AMi* 96: 357–84

Gutiérrez de Velasco, A. (1960), 'La conquista de Tarazona en la guerra de los dos Pedros (Año 1357)', *JZCH* 10–11: 69–98

Gutiérrez de Velasco, A. (1961), 'Las fortalezas aragonesas ante la gran ofensiva castellana en la guerra de los dos Pedros', *JZCH* 12–13: 7–39

Gutiérrez de Velasco, A. (1963), 'La contraofensiva aragonesa en la guerra de los dos Pedros', *JZCH* 14–15: 7–30

Gyug, R. (1983), 'The Effects and Extent of the Black Death of 1348: New Evidence for Clerical Mortality in Barcelona', *MS* 45: 385–98

Hamilton, E.J. (1936), *Money, Prices and Wages in Valencia, Aragon and Navarre, 1351–1500*, Cambridge, Mass.

Harvey, L.P. (1990), *Islamic Spain, 1250–1500*, Chicago

Hillgarth, J.N. (1975), *The Problem of a Catalan Mediterranean Empire, 1229–1327*, London

Hillgarth, J.N. (1976–8), *The Spanish Kingdoms, 1250–1516*, 2 vols., Oxford

Housley, N. (1982), 'Pope Clement V and the Crusades of 1309–10', *JMH* 8: 29–43

Jordá Fernández, A. (1990), 'Las remensas: evolución de un conflicto jurídico y social del campesinado catalán', *BRAH* 187: 217–97

Küchler, W. (1969), 'La influencia de la peste negra sobre la Hacienda Real', in *VIII CHCA*, Valencia, II.i, pp. 65–70

Laliena Corbera, C. (1987), *Sistema social, estructura agraria y organización del poder en el Bajo Aragón en la edad media (siglos XII–XV)*, Teruel

Laliena Corbera, C. and Iranzo Muñío, M.T. (1991), 'El grupo aristocrático en Huesca en la baja edad media: bases sociales y poder político', in *Les sociétés urbaines en France méridionale et en péninsule ibérique au moyen âge*, Paris, pp. 183–202

Lalinde Abadia, J. (1979), *La Corona de Aragón en el Mediterráneo medieval (1229–1479)*, Zaragoza

Lalinde Abadia, J. (1990), 'La ordenación política e institucional de la Corona de Aragón', *HEMP*, XIII, ii, pp. 319–416

López Bonet, J.F. (1989), 'La revolta de 1391: efectivament, crisi social', *XIII CHCA*, Palma de Mallorca, I, pp. 111–23

López de Meneses, A. (1959), 'Una consecuencia de la peste negra en Cataluña: el pogrom de 1348', *Sefarad* 19: 93–131, 321–64

Lourie, E. (1986), 'A Plot which Failed? The Case of the Corpse Found in the Jewish *Call* of Barcelona (1301)', *MHR* 1: 187–220

Lourie, E. (1990), 'Anatomy of Ambivalence: Muslims under the Crown of Aragon in the Late Thirteenth Century', in her *Crusade and Colonisation. Muslims, Christians and Jews in Medieval Aragon*, Aldershot, ch. vii, pp. 1–77

Luttrell, A.T. (1961), 'The Aragonese Crown and the Knights Hospitallers of Rhodes, 1291–1350', *EHR* 76: 1–19

Luttrell, A.T. (1966), 'Los Hospitalarios en Aragón y la peste negra', *AEM* 3: 499–514

Luttrell, A.T. (1969), 'La Corona de Aragón y la Grecia catalana: 1379–1394', *AEM* 6: 219–52

Martín, J.L. (1970), 'Las cortes catalanas en la guerra castellano-aragonesa (1356–1365)', *VIII CHCA*, Valencia, II, ii, pp. 79–90

Martín, J.L. (1991), 'La actividad de las cortes catalanas en el siglo XIV', in *Les corts a Catalunya*, Barcelona, pp. 146–51

Martínez Ferrando, J.E. (1948), *Jaime II de Aragón. Su vida familiar*, 2 vols., Barcelona

Masiá de Ros, A. (1951), *La Corona de Aragón y los estados del Norte de Africa*, Barcelona

Masiá de Ros, A. (1992), 'Las pretensiones de los infantes de la Cerda a la Corona de Castilla en tiempos de Sancho IV. El apoyo aragonés', *Medievalia* 10: 255–79

Motis Dolader, M.A. (1990), *Los judíos en Aragón en la edad media (siglos XIII–XV)*, Zaragoza

Moxó y Montoliu, F. de (1986), 'La política aragonesa de Alfonso XI y los hijos de Leonor de Guzmán', in *En la España medieval, V. Estudios en memoria del Profesor D. Claudio Sánchez-Albornoz*, Madrid, II, pp. 697–708

Nadal i Oller, J. (1983), 'La població', in J. Nadal Farreras and P. Wolff (eds.), *Història de Catalunya*, Barcelona, pp. 65–94

Palacios Martín, B. (1975), *La Coronación de los reyes de Aragón, 1204–1410*, Valencia

Reglá Campistol, J. (1951), *Francia, la Corona de Aragón y la frontera pirenaica. La lucha por el Valle de Arán (siglos XIII–XIV)*, 2 vols., Madrid

Reglá Campistol, J. (1966), 'La Corona de Aragón, 1336–1410', *HEMP*, XIV, pp. 439–605

Riera i Sans, J. (1977), 'Los tumultos contra las juderías de la Corona de Aragón en 1391', *CH* 8: 213–26

Riera Melis, A. (1986), *La Corona de Aragón y el reino de Mallorca en el primer cuarto del siglo XIV*, Madrid and Barcelona

Riu, M. (1983), 'The Woollen Industry in Catalonia in the Later Middle Ages', in N.B. Harte and K.G. Ponting (eds.), *Cloth and Clothing in Medieval Europe*, London, pp. 205–29

Robson, J.A. (1959), 'The Catalan Fleet and Moorish Sea-Power (1337–1344)', *EHR* 74: 386–408

Romano, D. (1989), 'Els jueus en temps de Pere el Cerimoniós (1336–1387)', in *Pere el Cerimoniós i la seva època*, Barcelona, pp. 113–31

Rubio Vela, A. (1987), 'Crisis agrarias y carestías en las primeras décadas del siglo XIV. El caso de Valencia', *Saitabi* 37: 131–47

Ruiz Doménec, J.E. (1977), 'La crisis económica de la Corona de Aragón: realidad o ficción historiográfica?', *CH* 8: 71–117

Russell, P.E. (1955), *The English Intervention in Spain and Portugal in the Time of Edward III and Richard II*, Oxford

Sáinz de la Maza Lasoli, R. (1984), 'La aljama judía de Montalbán (1307–1391)', *AEM* 14: 345–91

Salavert y Roca, V. (1956), *Cerdeña y la expansión mediterránea de la Corona de Aragón, 1297–1314*, 2 vols., Madrid

Salavert y Roca, V. (1959), 'Los motivos económicos en la conquista de Cerdeña', *VI CHCA*, Madrid, pp. 433–45

Salavert y Roca, V. (1973), 'La Corona de Aragón en el mundo mediterráneo del siglo XIV', *VIII CHCA*, Valencia, II, iii, pp. 31–64

Sánchez Martínez, M. (1982), 'La fiscalidad catalanoaragonesa y las aljamas de judíos en la época de Alfonso IV (1327–1336): los subsidios extraordinarios', *Acta Historica et Archaeologica Medievalia* 3: 93–141

Sánchez Martínez, M. (1989), 'Las relaciones de la Corona de Aragón con los países musulmanes en la época de Pedro el Ceremonioso', in *Pere el Cerimoniós i la seva època*, Barcelona, pp. 77–97

Sánchez Martínez, M. (1992), 'La fiscalidad real en Cataluña (siglo XIV)', *AEM* 22: 341–76

Sánchez Martínez, M., and Gassiot Pintori, S. (1991), 'La *Cort General* de Barcelona (1340) y la contribución catalana a la guerra del Estrecho', in *Les corts a Catalunya*, Barcelona, pp. 222–40

Sans i Travé, J.M. (1990), *El procés dels Templers catalans*, Lleida

Santamaría, A. (1982), 'Tensión Corona de Aragón–Corona de Mallorca. La sucesión de Sancho de Mallorca (1318–1326)', in *En la España medieval*, III: *Estudios en memoria del profesor D. Salvador de Moxó*, Madrid, pp. 423–95

Sarasa Sánchez, E. (n.d.), *Las cortes de Aragón en la edad media*, Zaragoza

Sarasa Sánchez, E. (1980), 'Notes sur la condition sociale des vassaux seigneuriaux dans le royaume d'Aragon aux XIVe et XVe siècles', *MA* 86: 5–47

Sarasa Sánchez, E. (1981), *Sociedad y conflictos sociales en Aragón, siglos XIII–XV: estructuras de poder y conflictos de clase*, Madrid

Sarasa Sánchez, E. and Orcástegui, C. (1985), 'El rechazo de la aventura mediterránea y la manifestación de las contradicciones internas: la consolidación del reino y los comienzos de la crisis (1276–1336)', and 'La recuperación del poder monárquico y el aislamiento de Aragón en sus límites territoriales: la plenitud de la crisis (1337–1410)', in A. Beltrán Martínez (ed.), *Historia de Aragón*, Zaragoza, VI, pp. 11–76

Sesma Muñoz, J.A. (1982), *Transformación social y revolución comercial en Aragón durante la baja edad media*, Madrid

Sesma Muñoz, J.A. (1983), 'La fijación de fronteras económicas entre los estados de la Corona de Aragón', *Aragón en la edad media* 5: 141–65

Setton, K.M. (1975), *Catalan Domination of Athens, 1311–1388*, London

Shirk, M.V. (1981), 'The Black Death in Aragon, 1348–51', *JMH* 7: 357–67

Shneidman, J.L. (1970), *The Rise of the Aragonese-Catalan Empire, 1200–1350*, 2 vols., New York

Sobrequés Callicó, J. (1970–1), 'La peste negra en la península ibérica', *AEM* 7: 67–102

Sobrequés Vidal, S. (1957), *Els barons de Catalunya*, Barcelona

Sobrequés Vidal, S. (1970–1), 'La nobleza catalana en el siglo XIV', *AEM* 7: 513–31

Soldevila, F. (1963), *Història de Catalunya*, Barcelona

Sturcken, H.T. (1979), 'The Unconsummated Marriage of Jaime of Aragon and Leonor of Castile (October 1319)', *JMH* 5: 185–201

Tasis i Marca, R. (1979), 'Le segle XIV. Pere el Ceremoniós i els seus fills', in *Història de Catalunya*, Barcelona, IV, pp. 7–215

Treppo, M. del (1972), *I mercanti catalani e l'espansione della Corona d'Aragona nel secolo XV*, Naples

Verlinden, C. (1955), *L'esclavage dans l'Europe médiévale*, I, Bruges

Verlinden, C. (1970–1), 'L'esclavage dans la péninsule ibérique au XIVe siècle', *AEM* 7: 577–91

Vicens Vives, J. (1969), *Economic History of Spain*, Princeton

Vicens Vives, J., Suárez Fernández, L. and Carrère, C. (1959), 'La economía de los países de la Corona de Aragón en la baja edad media', *VI CHCA*, Madrid, pp. 103–35

Vilar, P. (1962), *La Catalogne dans l'Espagne moderne*, 3 vols., Paris

Wolff, P. (1971), 'The 1391 Pogrom in Spain. Social Crisis or Not', *P&P* 50: 4–18

Zurita, J. (1967–85), *Anales de la Corona de Aragón*, ed. A. Canellas López, 9 vols., Zaragoza

18(b) CASTILE, NAVARRE AND PORTUGAL

Primary sources

[Alfonso X], *Las Siete Partidas*, ed. Real Academia de la Historia, 3 vols., Madrid (1807, repr. 1972)

As Gavetas da Torre do Tombo, II, Lisbon (1962)

Colmeiro, M., *Cortes de los antiguos reinos de León y de Castilla. Introducción*, Madrid (1883)

Cortes de los antiguos reinos de León y de Castilla, ed. Real Academia de la Historia, I, II, Madrid (1861–3)

Crónica de Alfonso XI, ed. C. Rosell, BAE, 66 (*Crónicas de los reyes de Castilla*, I), Madrid (1875), pp. 173–392

Crónica de Enrique III, ed. C. Rosell, BAE, 68 (*Crónicas de los reyes de Castilla*, II), Madrid (1877), pp. 161–257

Crónica de Fernando IV, ed. C. Rosell, BAE, 66 (*Crónicas de los reyes de Castilla*, I), Madrid (1875), pp. 93–170

Crónica de Juan I, ed. C. Rosell, BAE, 68 (*Crónicas de los reyes de Castilla*, II), Madrid (1877), pp. 65–159

Crónica de Pedro I, ed. C. Rosell, BAE, 66 (*Crónicas de los reyes de Castilla*, I), Madrid (1875), pp. 395–629

García y García, A., *Synodicon Hispanum*, 7 vols., to date, Madrid (1981–)

Gran Crónica de Alfonso XI, ed. D. Catalán, 2 vols., Madrid (1976)

Hechos de D. Berenguel de Landoria, arzobispo de Santiago, ed. M. Díaz y Díaz *et al.*, Santiago de Compostela (1983)

Jofré de Loaisa, *Crónica de los reyes de Castilla*, ed. A. García Martínez, Murcia (1982)

Lomax, D.W. and Oakley, R.J., *The English in Portugal 1367–87*, Warminster (1988)

Macchi, G. (ed.) and J. Steunou (trans.), *Fernão Lopes, Chronique du roi D. Pedro I*, Paris (1985)

O'Callaghan, J.F. (1986), 'Las cortes de Fernando IV: cuadernos inéditos de Valladolid 1300 y Burgos 1308', *HID* 13: 315–28

Peña Pérez, F.J., *Documentación del monasterio de San Juan de Burgos (1091–1400)*, Burgos (1983)

Pere III of Catalonia (Pedro IV of Aragon), Chronicle, trans. M. Hillgarth, with introduction and notes by J.N. Hillgarth, 2 vols., Toronto (1980)

Tanner, N.P. (ed.), *Decrees of the Ecumenical Councils*, 2 vols., London and Washington DC (1990)

Secondary works

Abadal i de Vinyals, R. d' (1976), in *España cristiana. Crisis de la Reconquista. Luchas civiles*, *HEMP*, xiv, ed. L. Suárez Fernández and J. Reglá Campistol, 2nd edn, Madrid

Almeida, F. de (1922), *História de Portugal*, i, Coimbra

Almeida, F. de (1967), *História da Igreja em Portugal*, ed. D. Peres, i, Oporto

Alonso Romero, M.P. (1990), in *La expansión peninsular y mediterránea (c. 1212–c. 1350)*, *HEMP*, xiii, i, *La corona de Castilla*, ed. J. Torres Fontes *et al.*, Madrid

Amasuno Sárraga, M.V. (1996), *La peste en la corona de Castilla durante la segunda mitad del siglo XIV*, Valladolid

Anasagasti Valderrama, A.M. and Sanz Fuentes, M.J. (1985), 'La hermandad de Andalucía durante la minoría de Alfonso XI: nueva aportación documental', *Saitabi* 35: 13–21

del Arco, R. (1954), *Sepulcros de la casa real de Castilla*, Madrid

Avezou, R. (1930), 'Un prince aragonais, archevêque de Tolède au XIVe siècle. D. Juan de Aragón y Anjou', *BH* 32: 326–71

Barros, H. da Gama (1945–54), *História da administração pública em Portugal*, 2nd edn, 11 vols., Lisbon

Beceiro Pita, I. (1987), 'Los dominios de la familia real castellana (1250–1350)', in Rucquoi (1987b), pp. 79–106

Benavides, A. (1860), *Memorias de D. Fernando IV de Castilla*, 2 vols., Madrid

Bermúdez Aznar, A. (1989), 'Los concejos y la administración del reino', in *Concejos y ciudades en la edad media hispánica. II Congreso de estudios medievales*, Avila, pp. 569–92

Boswell, J. (1977), *The Royal Treasure. Muslim Communities under the Crown of Aragon in the Fourteenth Century*, New Haven, Conn.

Brásio, A. (1958), 'As "razões" de João das Regras nas Cortes de Coimbra', *LS* 3: 7–40

Bueno Domínguez, M.L. (1991), 'El concejo de Zamora. Siglos XII–XIV', in *Primer congreso de historia de Zamora*, iii: *Medieval y moderna*, Zamora, pp. 119–36

Burns, J.H. (1992), *Lordship, Kingship, and Empire. The Idea of Monarchy, 1400–1525*, Oxford

Cabrillana, N. (1968), 'La crisis del siglo XIV en Castilla: la peste negra en el obispado de Palencia', *Hispania* 28: 246–58

Cactano, M. (1951), 'As Cortes de 1385', *RPH* 5: 5–86

Caetano, M. (1953), 'O concelho de Lisboa na crise de 1383–1385', *AAPH* 4: 179–247

Casado Alonso, H. (1987), 'Las relaciones poder real-ciudades en Castilla en la primera mitad del siglo XIV', in Rucquoi (1987b), pp. 193–215

Castro, J.R. (1967), *Carlos III el Noble, rey de Navarra*, Pamplona

Catalán Menéndez Pidal, D. (1962), *De Alfonso X al Conde de Barcelos. Cuatro estudios sobre el nacimiento de la historiografía romance en Castilla y Portugal*, Madrid

Coelho, A. Borges (1984), *A revolução de 1383*, 5th edn, Lisbon

Coelho, M.H. de Cruz and Homem, A.L. de Carvalho (1996), *Portugal em definição de fronteiras (1096–1325)*. *Do condado portucalense à crise do século XIV*, Lisbon

Costa, M.-M. (1981), 'Los reyes de Portugal en la frontera castellano-aragonesa (1304)', *Medievalia* 2: 27–50

David, P. (1943), 'Français du Midi dans les évêchés portugais (1279–1390)', *BEP* 9: 16–70

Delachenal, R. (1909–31), *Histoire de Charles V*, 5 vols., Paris

Díaz Martín, L. (1984), 'Le processus de fondation de Guadalupe sous Alfonso XI', *MA* 39: 233–56

Dupré Theseider, E. (1972), 'Egidio de Albornoz e la riconquista dello stato della Chiesa', in *El Cardenal Albornoz y el Colegio de España*, 1, Studia Albornotiana, 11, Bologna, pp. 433–59

Fernández Conde, F.J. (1978), *Gutierre de Toledo obispo de Oviedo (1377–1389)*, Oviedo

Fernández Conde, F.J. (ed.) (1980–2), *La iglesia en la España de los siglos VIII–XIV. Historia de la iglesia en Espana*, 2 vols., Madrid

Fita, F. (1908), 'El concilio nacional de Palencia en 1321', *BRAH* 52: 17–48

Gaibrois de Ballesteros, M. (1922–8), *Historia del reinado de Sancho IV de Castilla*, 3 vols., Madrid

Gaibrois de Ballesteros, M. (1967), *María de Molina, tres veces reina*, Madrid; originally publ. 1936

García de Cortázar, J.A. (1990), *La sociedad rural el la España medieval*, 2nd edn, Madrid

García Díaz, I. (1984), 'La política caballeresca de Alfonso XI', *Miscelánea medieval murciana* 11: 117–33

García Fernández, M. (1985), 'La hermandad general de Andalucía durante la minoría de Alfonso XI de Castilla: 1312–1325', *HID* 12: 351–75

García Fernández, M. (1991), 'Jaime II y la minoría de Alfonso XI. Sus relaciones con la sociedad política castellana', *HID* 18: 143–81

García y García, A. (1976), *Estudios sobre la canonística portuguesa medieval*, Madrid

García y García, A. (1988), 'Las constituciones del concilio legatino de Valladolid (1322)', in W. Brandmüller, H. Immenkötter and E. Iserloh (eds.), *Ecclesia Militans*, Paderborn, pp. 111–27

García y López, J.C. (1892–3), *Castilla y León durante los reinados de Pedro I, Enrique II, Juan I y Enrique III*, 2 vols., Madrid

Gautier-Dalché, J. (1970–1), 'L'histoire castillane dans la première moitié du XIVe siècle', *AEM* 7: 239–52

Gautier-Dalché, J. (1982), 'Alphonse XI a-t-il voulu la mort de D. Juan Manuel?', in *Don Juan Manuel. VII Centenario*, Murcia, pp. 135–47

Giménez Soler, A. (1932), *Don Juan Manuel. Biografía y estudio crítico*, Zaragoza

Goñi Gaztambide, J. (1958), *Historia de la Bula de la Cruzada en España*, Vitoria

Goñi Gaztambide, J. (1979), *Historia de los obispos de Pamplona*, II: *Siglos XIV–XV*, Pamplona

González Alonso, B. (1988), 'Poder regio, cortes y régimen político en la Castilla bajomedieval (1252–1474)', in *Las cortes de Castilla y León en la edad media*, Valladolid, II, pp. 201–54

González Mínguez, C. (1976), *Fernando IV de Castilla (1295–1312). La guerra civil y el predominio de la nobleza*, Vitoria

González Mínguez, C. (1983), 'Algunos datos sobre la población de Castilla durante el reinado de Fernando IV', in J. Crespo Redondo (ed.), *El pasado histórico de Castilla y Leön. Actas del I Congreso de historia de Castilla y León*, Burgos, 1, pp. 87–99

Grassotti, H. (1987), 'Novedad y tradición en las donaciones "con mero y mixto imperio" en León y Castilla', in *Homenaje al prof. Juan Torres Fontes*, Murcia, 1, pp. 723–36

Harvey, L.P. (1990), *Islamic Spain 1250 to 1500*, Chicago and London

Hernández, F.J. (1978), 'Ferrán Martínez, escrivano del rey, canónigo de Toledo, y autor del Libro del Cavallero Zifar', *Revista de archivos, bibliotecas y museos* 81: 289–325

Hillgarth, J. (1976), *The Spanish Kingdoms 1250–1516*, 1, Oxford

Kershaw, I. (1973), 'The Great Famine and Agrarian Crisis in England 1315–1322', *P&P* 59: 3–50

Lacarra, J.M. (1972, 1973), *Historia política del reino de Navarra desde sus orígenes hasta su incorporación a Castilla*, II, III, Pamplona

Leroy, B. (1984), 'Ruina y reconstrucción. Los campos y las ciudades de Navarra en la segunda mitad del siglo XIV', *Hispania* 44: 237–61

Leroy, B. (1988), 'La cour des rois Charles II et Charles III de Navarre (vers 1350–1425), lieu de rencontre, milieu de gouvernement', in A. Rucquoi (ed.), *Realidad e imágenes del poder. España a fines de la edad media*, Valladolid, pp. 233–48; repr. in Leroy, *Le royaume de Navarre à la fin du moyen âge*, Aldershot (1990)

Linehan, P. (1971), *The Spanish Church and the Papacy in the Thirteenth Century*, Cambridge

Linehan, P. (1983), 'The Church, the Economy and the *Reconquista* in Early Fourteenth-Century Castile', *Revista española de teología*, 43: 275–303; repr. in his *Past and Present in Medieval Spain*, Aldershot (1992)

Linehan, P. (1985), 'The Beginnings of Santa María de Guadalupe and the Direction of Fourteenth-Century Castile', *JEH* 36: 284–304; repr. in his *Past and Present in Medieval Spain*

Linehan, P. (1993a), *History and the Historians of Medieval Spain*, Oxford

Linehan, P. (1993b), 'The Mechanics of Monarchy. Knighting Castile's King, 1332', *HT* 43: 26–32

Lopes, F. Félix (1970a), 'Duas cartas inéditas da Rainha Santa Isabel sobre jóias empenhoradas', *RPH* 13: 61–72

Lopes, F. Félix (1970b), 'Santa Isabel na contenda entre D. Dinis e o filho, 1321–1322', *LS* 8: 57–80

López-Ibor Aliño, M. (1984), 'El "señorío apartado" de la cofradía de Arriaga y la incorporación de la tierra de Alava a la corona de Castilla en 1332', in *En la España medieval*, IV: *Estudios dedicados al prof. D. Angel Ferrari Núñez*, Madrid, 1, pp. 513–36

Martín Duque, A.J. (1970–1), 'El reino de Navarra cn cl siglo XIV', *AEM* 7: 153–64

Martínez Ferrando, J.E. (1948), *Jaime II de Aragón. Su vida familiar*, 2 vols., Barcelona

Mattoso, J. (1985), 'A nobreza e a revolução de 1383', in *1383–1385 e a crise geral dos séculos XIV/XV. Jornadas de história medieval, Lisboa, 20 a 22 de junho de 1985*, Lisbon, pp. 391–416

Mattoso, J. (1993), in *História de Portugal, direcção de José Mattoso*, II: *A monarquia feudal (1096–1480)*, Lisbon, pp. 8–309

Milhou, A. (1982), 'La chauve-souris, le Nouveau David et le roi caché (trois images de l'empereur des derniers temps dans le monde ibérique: XIIIe–XVIIe siècle', *MCV* 18: 61–78

Mínguez, J.M. (1989), 'Las hermandades generales de los concejos en la corona de Castilla', in *Concejos y ciudades en la edad media hispánica. II Congreso de estudios medievales*, Avila, pp. 537–67

Mitre Fernández, E. (1968), *Evolución de la nobleza en Castilla bajo Enrique III (1396–1406)*, Valladolid

Mitre Fernández, E. (1969), *La extensión del regimen de corregidores en el reinado de Enrique III de Castilla*, Valladolid

Moreta, S. (1978), *Malhechores-feudales. Violencia, antagonismos y alianzas de clases en Castilla, siglos XIII–XIV*, Madrid

Moxó, S. de (1969), 'De la nobleza vieja a la nobleza nueva. La transformación nobiliaria castellana en la baja edad media', *CH* 3: 1–210

Moxó, S. de (1975), 'La promoción política y social de los "letrados" en la corte de Alfonso XI', *Hispania* 35: 5–29

Moxó, S. de (1976), 'Relaciones entre la corona y las ordenes militares en el reinado de Alfonso XI', in *VII Centenario del Infante D. Fernando de la Cerda. Jornadas de estudio, Ciudad Real, abril 1975. Ponencias y comunicaciones*, Madrid, pp. 117–58

Moxó, S. de (1990), in *La expansión peninsular y mediterránea (c. 1212–c. 1350)*, *HEMP*, XIII, i, *La corona de Castilla*, ed. J. Torres Fontes *et al.*, Madrid

Nieto Soria, J.M. (1984), 'Abadengo episcopal y realengo en tiempos de Alfonso XI de Castilla', in *En la España medieval*, IV (*Estudios dedicados a A. Ferrari Núñez*), 2 vols., Madrid, pp. 707–36

Nieto Soria, J.M. (1988), *Fundamentos ideológicos del poder real en Castilla (siglos XIII–XVI)*, Madrid

Pérez-Prendes, J.M. (1974), *Cortes de Castilla*, Barcelona

Phillips, J.R.S. (1988), *The Medieval Expansion of Europe*, Oxford

Rashdall, H. (1936), *The Universities of Europe in the Middle Ages*, ed. F.M. Powicke and A.B. Emden, II, Oxford

Rau, V. *et al.* (1963), 'Para o estudo da peste negra em Portugal', in *Actas do Congresso histórico de Portugal medievo, Bracara Augusta*, 14–15, Lisbon, pp. 210–39

Rebelo, L. de Sousa (1981), 'The Idea of Kingship in the Chronicles of Fernão Lopes', in F.W. Hodcroft *et al.* (eds.), *Medieval and Renaissance Studies on Spain and Portugal in Honour of P. E. Russell*, Oxford

Rebelo, L. de Sousa (1983), *A concepção do poder em Fernão Lopes*, Lisbon

Rubio Vela, A. (1987), 'Crisis agrarias y carestías en las primeras décadas del siglo XIV. El caso de Valencia', *Saitabi* 37: 131–47

Rucquoi, A. (1987a), *Valladolid en la edad media*, 2 vols., Valladolid

Rucquoi, A. (ed.) (1987b), *Génesis medieval del estado moderno. Castilla y Navarra (1250–1370)*, Valladolid

Ruiz, T.F. (1977), 'The Transformation of the Castilian Municipalities: The Case of Burgos 1248–1350', *P&P* 77: 3–32

Ruiz, T.F. (1987), 'L'image du pouvoir à travers les sceaux de la monarchie castillane', in Rucquoi (1987b), pp. 217–27

Russell, P.E. (1955), *The English Intervention in Spain and Portugal in the Time of Edward III and Richard II*, Oxford

Serrão, J. Veríssimo (1979), *História de Portugal*, I: *Estado, pátria e nação (1080–1415)*, 3rd edn, 2 vols., n.p.

Sobrequés Callicó, J. (1970–1), 'La peste negra en la península ibérica', *AEM* 7: 67–101

Sousa, A. de (1993), in *História de Portugal, direcção de José Mattoso*, II: *A monarquia feudal (1096–1480)*, Lisbon, pp. 310–556

Sturcken, H.T. (1979), 'The Unconsummated Marriage of Jaime of Aragon and Leonor of Castile', *JMH* 5: 185–201

Suárez Fernández, L. (1951), 'Evolución histórica de las hermandades castellanas', *CH(E)* 16: 5–78

Suárez Fernández, L. (1953), 'Don Pedro Tenorio, arzobispo de Toledo (1375–1399)', *Estudios dedicados a Menéndez Pidal*, IV (Madrid), pp. 601–27

Suárez Fernández, L. (1955), *Juan I, rey de Castilla (1379–1390)*, Madrid

Suárez Fernández, L. (1959), *Nobleza y monarquía. Puntos de vista sobre la Historia castellana del siglo XV*, Valladolid

Suárez Fernández, L. (1960), *Castilla, el Cisma y la crisis conciliar (1378–1440)*, Madrid

Suárez Fernández (1976), in *España cristiana. Crisis de la Reconquista. Luchas civiles*, HEMP, XIV, ed. L. Suárez Fernández and J. Reglá Campistol, 2nd edn, Madrid

Suárez Fernández, L. (1977–82), *Historia del reinado de Juan I de Castilla*, 2 vols., to date, Madrid

Torres Fontes, J. (1953), 'El concejo murciano en el reinado de Alfonso XI', *AHDE* 23: 139–59

Torres Fontes, J. (1990), in *La expansión peninsular y mediterránea (c. 1212–c. 1350)*, HEMP, XIII, i, *La corona de Castilla*, ed. J. Torres Fontes *et al.*, Madrid

Vaca, A. (1977, 1979), 'La estructura socioeconómica de la Tierra de Campos a mediados del siglo XIV', *Institución Tello Téllez de Meneses* 39: 229–398, 42: 203–387

Valdeón Baruque, J. (1966), *Enrique II de Castilla. La guerra civil y la consolidación del regimen (1366–1371)*, Valladolid

Valdeón Baruque, J. (1969), 'Aspectos de la crisis castellana en la primera mitad del siglo XIV', *Hispania* 29: 5–24

Valdeón Baruque, J. (1975), 'Movimientos antiseñoriales en Castilla en el siglo XIV', *CH* 6: 357–90

Valdeón Baruque, J. *et al.* (eds.) (1980), *Feudalismo y consolidación de los pueblos hispánicos (siglos XI–XV)*, Historia de España dirigida por M. Tuñon de Lara, IV, Barcelona

Verlinden, C. (1938), 'La grande peste de 1348 en Espagne. Contribution à l'étude de ses conséquences économiques et sociales', *RBPH* 17: 103–46

Vones, L. (1993), *Geschichte der Iberischen Halbinsel im Mittelalter (711–1480). Reiche, Kronen, Regionen*, Sigmaringen

Wolff, P. (1971), 'The 1391 Pogrom in Spain. Social Crisis or Not?', *P&P* 50: 4–18

Zabalo Zabalegui, F. J. (1968), 'Algunos datos sobre la regresión demográfica causada por la Peste en la Navarra del siglo XIV', in *Miscellánea J. M. Lacarra y de Miguel*, Zaragoza, pp. 485–91

Zunzunegui, J. (1954), 'Para la historia del Concilio de Valladolid de 1322', *Scriptorium Victoriense* 1: 345–9

19 THE AVIGNON PAPACY

Primary sources

Baluze, E. (ed.), *Vitae Paparum Avenionensium*, new edn by G. Mollat, 4 vols., Paris (1914–27)

Barbiche, B., *Les actes pontificaux originaux des Archives nationales de Paris*, III, IARP, 3, Vatican City (1982)

Barraclough, G., *Public Notaries and the Papal Curia. A Calendar and a Study of a 'Formularium Notariorum Curie' from the Early Years of the Fourteenth Century*, London (1934)

Baumgarten, P.M., *Untersuchungen und Urkunden über die Camera Collegii Cardinalium für die Zeit von 1295 bis 1437*, Leipzig (1898)

Bresc, H. (ed.), *La correspondance de Pierre Ameilh, archevêque de Naples, puis d'Embrun (1363–1369)*, Paris (1972)

Coulon, A. and Clémencet, S., *Jean XXII (1316–1334). Lettres secrètes et curiales relatives à la France*, BEFAR, 3rd series, Paris (1900 ff)

Daumet, G., *Benoît XII (1334–1342). Lettres closes, patentes et curiales se rapportant à la France*, BEFAR, 3rd series, Paris (1899–1920)

Déprez, E. and Mollat, G., *Clément VI (1342–1352). Lettres closes, patentes et curiales intéressant les pays autres que la France*, BEFAR, 3rd series, Paris (1906–61)

Déprez, E., Glénisson, J. and Mollat, G., *Clément VI (1342–1352). Lettres closes, patentes et curiales se rapportant à la France*, 3 vols., BEFAR, 3rd series, Paris (1901–61)

Dykmans, M. (ed.), *Les sermons de Jean XXII sur la Vision béatifique*, Rome (1973)

Dykmans, M. (ed.), *Le cérémonial papal de la fin du moyen âge à la Renaissance*, II–III, Brussels and Rome (1981–3)

Finke, H. (1907), *Papsttum und Untergang des Templerordens*, 2 vols., Münster.

Finke, H. (ed.), *Acta Aragonensia*, 3 vols., Berlin (1908–22)

Finke, H., 'Nachträge und Ergänzungen zu den Acta Aragonensia (I–III)', *SFGG* 1, 4 (1933), pp. 355–536

Friedberg, E. (ed.), *Corpus Juris Canonici*, 2 vols., Leipzig (1879–82)

Gasnault, P. and Laurent, M.-H., *Innocent VI: lettres secrètes et curiales*, BEFAR, 3rd series, Paris (1959 ff)

Glénisson, J. and Mollat, G., *Correspondance des légats et des vicaires-généraux. Gil Albornoz et Androin de la Roche (1353–1367)*, Paris (1964)

Göller, E., *Die päpstliche Pönitentiarie von ihrem Ursprung bis zu ihrer Umgestaltung unter Pius V.*, I, 1–2, Rome (1907)

Göller, E., *Die Einnahmen der apostolischen Kammer unter Johann XXII.*, VQHF, 1, Paderborn (1910)

Göller, E., *Die Einnahmen der apostolischen Kammer unter Benedikt XII.*, VQHF, 4, Paderborn (1920)

Guillemain, B. (ed.), *Les recettes et les dépenses de la chambre apostolique pour la quatrième année du pontificat de Clément V (1308–1309)*, Rome (1978)

Hayez, M. *et al.*, *Urbain V (1362–1370). Lettres communes*, 12 vols., BEFAR, 3rd series, Paris (1954–89)

Herde, P., *Audientia Litterarum Contradictarum*, 2 vols., Tübingen (1970)

Hledíková, Z., *Raccolta Praghese di scritti di Luca Fieschi*, Prague (1985)

Hoberg, H. (ed.), *Die Inventare des päpstlichen Schatzes in Avignon 1314–1376*, Rome (1944)

Hoberg, H., *Die Einnahmen der apostolischen Kammer unter Innocenz VI.*, VQHF, 7–8, Paderborn (1955–72)

Lecacheux, P. and Mollat, G., *Lettres secrètes et curiales du pape Urbain V (1362–1370) se rapportant à la France*, BEFAR, 3rd series, Paris (1902–55)

Meyer, Matthäus (ed.), *Die Pönitentiarie-Formularsammlung des Walter Murner von Strassburg*, Freiburg (1979)

Mirot, L. *et al.*, *Lettres secrètes et curiales du pape Grégoire XI relatives à la France*, BEFAR, 3rd series, Paris (1935–57)

Mohler, L., *Die Einnahmen der apostolischen Kammer unter Klemens VI.*, VQHF, 5, Paderborn (1931)

Mollat, G., *Jean XXII (1316–1334). Lettres communes*, 16 vols., BEFAR, 3rd series, Paris (1904–33)

Mollat, G., *Lettres secrètes et curiales du pape Grégoire XI (1370–1378) intéressant les pays autres que la France*, BEFAR, 3rd series, Paris (1962–5)

Ottenthal, E. von (ed.), *Regulae Cancellariae Apostolicae. Die päpstlichen Kanzleiregeln von Johannes XXII. bis Nikolaus V.*, Innsbruck (1888)

Petrarca, Francesco, *Le Familiari*, ed. Vittorio Rossi, Edizione Nazionale delle Opere di Francesco Petrarca, 10–13, Florence (1933–42)

Regestum Clementis Papae V ex Vaticanis Archetypis . . . Cura et Studio Monachorum Ordinis Sancti Benedicti editum, 8 vols., Rome (1885–92); *Tables . . .*, ed. Y. Lanhers *et al.*, Paris (1948–57)

Rinaldi, O., *Caesaris S.R.E. Card. Baronii, Od. Raynaldi et Iac. Laderchii Annales Ecclesiastici*, ed. A. Theiner, 37 vols., Bar-le-Duc (1864–83)

Schäfer, K.H., *Die Ausgaben der apostolischen Kammer unter Johann XXII.*, VQHF, 2, Paderborn (1911)

Schäfer, K.H., *Die Ausgaben der apostolischen Kammer unter Benedikt XII., Klemens VI. und Innocenz VI.*, VQHF, 3, Paderborn (1914)

Schäfer, K.H., *Die Ausgaben der apostolischen Kammer unter den Päpsten Urban V. und Gregor XI.*, VQHF, 6, Paderborn (1937)

Schmidt, Tilmann (ed.), *Constitutiones Spoletani Ducatus a Petro de Castaneto Edite (a. 1333)*, Rome (1990)

Schröder, H., 'Die Protokollbücher der päpstlichen Kammerkleriker 1329–1347', *AK* 27 (1937), pp. 121–286

Segre, A., 'I dispacci di Cristoforo da Piacenza procuratore mantovano alla corte pontificia (1371–1383)', *ASI* 5th series 43 (1909), pp. 27–95; 44 (1909), pp. 253–326

Sella, P. (ed.), *Costituzioni Egidiane dell'anno MCCCLVII*, Corpus Statutorum Italicorum, 1, Rome (1912)

Tangl, M. (ed.), *Die päpstlichen Kanzleiordnungen von 1200–1500*, Innsbruck (1894)

Tarrant, J. (ed.), *Extravagantes Iohannis XXII*, Vatican City (1983)

Theiner, A. (ed.), *Codex Diplomaticus Dominii Temporalis S. Sedis*, 3 vols., Vatican City (1861–2)

Vidal, J.-M., *Benoît XII (1334–1342). Lettres communes et curiales analysées d'après les registres dits d'Avignon et du Vatican*, 3 vols., BEFAR, 3rd series, Paris (1903–11)

Vidal, J.-M. and Mollat, G., *Benoît XII (1334–42). Lettres closes et patentes intéressant les pays autres que la France*, 2 vols., BEFAR, 3rd series, Paris (1913–50)

Williman, D., 'Letters of Etienne Cambarou, camerarius apostolicus', *AHP* 15 (1977), pp. 195–215

Williman, D., *The Right of Spoil of the Popes of Avignon, 1316–1415*, Philadelphia (1988)

Zutshi, P.N.R., *Original Papal Letters in England, 1305–1415*, IARP, 5, Vatican City (1990)

Secondary works

General bibliographic note: Mollat (1965) contains full bibliographies, which are not present in the English translation (1963). Much of the more recent literature is cited in *Aux origines* (1990). The bibliography in Boyle (1972) is especially useful for publications of material in the Vatican Archives.

Aspetti culturali della società italiana nel periodo del papato avignonese (1981), Convegni del Centro di Studi sulla Spiritualità Medievale, 19, Todi

Aux origines de l'état moderne. Le fonctionnement administratif de la papauté d'Avignon (1990), CEFR, 138, Rome

Barraclough, G. (1935), *Papal Provisions*, Oxford

Barraclough, G. (1936), 'The Executors of Papal Provisions in the Canonical Theory of the Thirteenth and Fourteenth Centuries', in *Acta Congressus Iuridici Internationalis Romae 12–17 Novembris 1934*, III, Rome, pp. 109–53

Bernard, J. (1948–9), 'Le népotisme de Clément V et ses complaisances pour la Gascogne', *AMi* 61: 369–411

Bock, F. (1934), 'Die Geheimschrift in der Kanzlei Johanns XXII.', *RQ* 42: 279–303

Bock, F. (1935–7), 'Studien zum politischen Inquisitionsprozess Johanns XXII.', *QFIAB* 26: 20–142, 27: 109–34

Bock, F. (1941), *Einführung in das Registerwesen des Avignonesischen Papsttums*, QFIAB, 31, Ergbd.

Boehlke, F.J. (1966), *Pierre de Thomas. Scholar, Diplomat, and Crusader*, Philadelphia

Boyle, L.E. (1972), *A Survey of the Vatican Archives and of its Medieval Holdings*, Toronto

Bresslau, H. (1912–31), *Handbuch der Urkundenlehre für Deutschland und Italien*, 2nd edn, 2 vols., Berlin

Brucker, G. (1963), 'An Unpublished Source for the History of the Avignonese Papacy: The Letters of Francesco Bruni', *Traditio* 19: 351–70

Caillet, L. (1975), *La papauté d'Avignon et l'église de France. La politique bénéficial du Pape Jean XXII en France*, Paris

Chaplais, P. (1951), 'Règlement des conflits internationaux franco-anglais au XIVe siècle', *MA* 57: 269–302

Chiffoleau, J. (1984), *Les justices du pape. Délinquence et criminalité dans la région d'Avignon au XIVe siècle*, Paris

Coing, H. (ed.) (1973), *Handbuch der Quellen und Literatur der neueren europäischen Privatrechtsgeschichte*, 1, Munich

Colliva, P. (1977), *Il cardinale Albornoz, lo stato della Chiesa, le 'Constitutiones Aegidianae'*, Bologna

Courtel, A.-L. (1977), 'Les clientèles des cardinaux limousins en 1378', *MEFRM* 89: 889–944

Creytens, R. (1942), 'Le "Studium Romanae Curiae" et le maître du sacré palais', *AFP* 12: 5–83

Di Stefano, G. (1968), *La découverte de Plutarque en occident. Aspects de la vie intellectuelle en Avignon au XIVe siècle*, Turin

Duprè Theseider, E. (1939), *I papi d'Avignone e la questione Romana*, Florence

Dykmans, M. (1973), 'Le cardinal Annibal de Ceccano (c. 1282–1350)', *Bulletin de l'Institut historique belge de Rome* 43: 145–344

Ehrle, F. (1889), 'Der Nachlass Clemens' V. und der in Betreff desselben von Johann XXII. (1318–21) geführte Process', *ALKG* 5: 1–166

Ehrle, F. (1890), *Historia Bibliothecae Romanorum Pontificum*, 1, Rome

Frutaz, A.P. (1979), 'La famiglia pontificia in un documento dell'inizio del sec. XIV', in *Palaeografica Diplomatica Archivistica. Studi in onore di Giulio Battelli*, Rome, II, pp. 277–323

Glénisson, J. (1951), 'Les origines de la révolte de l'état pontifical en 1375', *RSCI* 5: 145–68

Göller, E. (1907), *Die päpstliche Pönitentiarie von ihrem Ursprung bis zu ihrer Umgestaltung unter Pius V.*, I, 1–2, Rome

Guillemain, B. (1952), *La politique bénéficiale du pape Benoît XII*, Paris

Guillemain, B. (1962), *La cour pontificale d'Avignon, 1309–1376*, Paris

Hale, J., Highfield, R. and Smalley, B. (eds.) (1965), *Europe in the Late Middle Ages*, London

Halecki, O. (1930), *Un empereur de Byzance à Rome*, Warsaw

Hayez, A.-M. (1978), 'Travaux à l'enceinte d'Avignon sous les pontificats d'Urbain V et Grégoire XI', in *ACNSS* 101, Paris, pp. 193–223

Hayez, A.-M. (1984), 'Les rotuli présentés au pape Urbain V durant la première année de son pontificat', *MEFRM* 96: 327–94

Hayez, A.-M. (1988), 'Préliminaires à une prosopographie avignonaise du XIVe siècle', *MEFRM* 100: 113–24

Hayez, M. (ed.) (1980), *Genèse et débuts du grand schisme d'occident* (1980), Colloques internationaux du CNRS, 586, Paris

Housley, N. (1986), *The Avignon Papacy and the Crusades*, Oxford

Jugie, P. (1991a), 'Un Quercynois à la cour pontificale d'Avignon: le cardinal Bertrand du Pouget', *CFan* 26: 69–95

Jugie, P. (1991b), 'Le vicariat impérial du cardinal Gui de Boulogne à Lucques en 1369–1370', *MEFRM* 103: 261–357

Luttrell, A.T. and Blagg, T.F.C. (1991), 'The Papal Palace and Other Fourteenth-Century Buildings at Sorgues near Avignon', *Archaeologia* 109: 161–92

Majic, T. (1955), 'Die Apostolische Pönitentiarie im 14. Jahrhundert', *RQ* 50: 129–77

Melville, G. (1982), 'Quellenkundliche Beiträge zum Pontifikat Benedikts XII. Teil 1', *HJb* 102: 144–82

Meyer, Andreas (1986), *Zürich und Rom. Ordentliche Kollatur und päpstliche Provisionen am Frau- und Grossmünster 1316–1523*, Tübingen

Meyer, Andreas (1990), *Arme Kleriker auf Pfründensuche. Eine Studie über das 'in forma pauperum'-Register Gregors XII. von 1407 und über päpstliche Anwartschaften im Spätmittelalter*, Cologne and Vienna

Mollat, G. (1921), *La collation des bénéfices ecclésiastiques à l'époque des papes d'Avignon*, Paris

Mollat, G. (1936), 'Contribution à l'histoire de l'administration judiciaire de l'église romaine au XIVe siècle', *RHE* 32: 877–928

Mollat, G. (1951), 'Contribution à l'histoire du Sacré Collège de Clément V à Eugène IV', *RHE* 46: 22–112, 566–94

Mollat, G. (1965), *Les papes d'Avignon*, 10th edn, Paris; English trans. Janet Love, *The Popes at Avignon, 1305–1378*, London (1963)

Mollat du Jourdin, M. and Vauchez, A. (eds.) (1990), *Histoire du Christianisme*, VI: *Un temps d'épreuves (1274–1449)*, Paris

Müller, E. (1934), *Das Konzil von Vienne 1311–1312*, Münster

Opitz, G. (1944), 'Die Sekretärsexpedition unter Urban V. und Gregor XI.', *QFIAB* 33: 158–98

Paravicini Bagliani, A. (1991), 'Der Papst auf Reisen im Mittelalter', in D. Altenburg *et al.* (eds.), *Feste und Ferien im Mittelalter*, Sigmaringen, pp. 501–14

Partner, P. (1953), 'Camera Papae: Problems of Papal Finance in the Later Middle Ages', *JEH* 4: 55–68

Partner, P. (1972), *The Lands of St Peter. The Papal State in the Middle Ages and the Early Renaissance*, London

Pelzer, A. (1947), *Addenda et Emendanda ad Francisci Ehrle Historiae Bibliothecae Romanorum Pontificum*, Vatican City

Piola Caselli, F. (1981), *La costruzione del Palazzo dei Papi di Avignone (1316–1367)*, Milan

Piola Caselli, F. (1984), *Un cantiere navale del trecento*, Milan

Piola Caselli, F. (1987), 'L'espansione delle fonti finanziarie della Chiesa nel XIV secolo', *Archivio della Società romana di storia patria* 110: 63–97

Renouard, Y. (1941), *Les relations des papes d'Avignon et des compagnies commerciales et bancaires de 1316 à 1378*, Paris

Renouard, Y. (1954), *La papauté à Avignon*, Paris; English trans. D. Bethell, *The Avignon Papacy*, London (1970)

Reydellet-Guttinger, C. (1975), *L'administration pontificale dans le duché de Spolète (1305–52)*, Florence

Richard, J. (1977), *La papauté et les missions d'orient au moyen âge*, Rome

Sade, J.F.P.A. de (1764–7), *Mémoires pour la vie de François Pétrarque*, 3 vols., Amsterdam

Samaran, Ch. and Mollat, G. (1905), *La fiscalité pontificale en France au XIVe siècle*, Paris

Schäfer, K.H. (1911–14), *Deutsche Ritter und Edelknechte in Italien während des 14. Jahrhunderts*, 3 vols., Paderborn

Schimmelpfennig, B. (1971), 'Die Organisation der päpstlichen Kapelle in Avignon', *QFIAB* 50: 80–111

Schimmelpfennig, B. (1973), *Die Zeremonienbücher der Römischen Kurie im Mittelalter*, Tübingen

Schimmelpfennig, B. (1976), 'Zisterzienserideal und Kirchenreform – Benedikt XII. (1334–1342) als Reformpapst', *Zisterzienser Studien* 3: 11–43

Schimmelpfennig, B. (1990), 'Papal Coronations in Avignon', in J.M. Bak (ed.), *Coronations. Medieval and Early Modern Monarchic Ritual*, Berkeley and Los Angeles, pp. 179–96

Schmidt, Tilmann (1989), *Der Bonifaz-Prozess. Verfahren der Papstanklage in der Zeit Bonifaz' VIII. und Clemens' V.*, Cologne and Vienna

Schneider, F.E. (1914), *Die Römische Rota*, I, Paderborn

Schwarz, B. (1972), *Die Organisation kurialer Schreiberkollegien von ihrer Entstehung bis zur Mitte des 15. Jahrhunderts*, Tübingen

Setton, K.M. (1953), 'Archbishop Pierre d'Ameil in Naples and the Affair of Aimon III of Geneva (1363–1364)', *Speculum* 28: 643–91

Setton, K.M. (ed.) (1975), *A History of the Crusades*, III, Wisconsin

Setton, K.M. (1976), *The Papacy and the Levant*, I, Philadelphia

Southern, R. W. (1987), 'The Changing Role of Universities in Medieval Europe', *HR* 60: 133–46

Tellenbach, G. (1932–3), 'Beiträge zur kurialen Verwaltungsgeschichte im 14. Jahrhundert', *QFIAB* 24: 150–87

Tomasello, A. (1983), *Music and Ritual at Papal Avignon, 1309–1403*, Epping

Ullmann, W. (1972), *The Origins of the Great Schism*, reprinted with a new preface, Hamden, Conn.

Vauchez, A. (1981), *La sainteté en occident aux derniers siècles du moyen âge*, Paris

Verdera y Tuells, E. (ed.) (1972–9), *El cardenal Albornoz y el Colegio de España*, 6 vols., Bologna

Verger, J. (1973), 'L'entourage du cardinal Pierre de Monteruc (1356–1385)', *MEFRM* 85: 515–46

Waley, D. (1974), 'Opinions of the Avignon Papacy: A Historiographical Sketch', in *Storiografia e storia. Studi in onore di Eugenio Duprè Theseider*, I, Rome, pp. 175–88

Waley, D. (1987), 'Lo stato papale dal periodo feudale a Martino V', in G. Galasso (ed.), *Storia d'Italia*, Turin, VII, 2, pp. 229–320,

Walsh, K. (1981), *A Fourteenth-Century Scholar and Primate. Richard FitzRalph in Oxford, Avignon and Armagh*, Oxford

Watt, D.E.R. (1959), 'University Clerks and Rolls of Petitions for Benefices', *Speculum* 24: 213–29

Weiss, R. (1977), 'Per la storia degli studi greci alla curia papale nel tardo duecento e nel trecento', in his *Medieval and Humanist Greek. Collected Essays*, Padua, pp. 193-203

Welkenhuysen, A. (1983), 'La peste en Avignon (1348) décrite par un témoin oculaire, Louis Sanctus de Beringen', in R. Lievens *et al.* (eds.), *Pascua Mediaevalia. Studien voor Prof. Dr. J. M. De Smet*, Louvain, pp. 452–92

Wilkins, E.H. (1955), *Studies in the Life and Works of Petrarch*, Cambridge, Mass.

Williman, D. (1985), 'Summary Justice in the Avignonese Camera' in S. Kuttner and K. Pennington (eds.), *Proceedings of the Sixth International Congress of Medieval Canon Law*, Vatican City, pp. 437–49

Wood, D. (1989), *Clement VI. The Pontificate and Ideas of an Avignon Pope*, Cambridge

Zacour, N.P. (1960), *Talleyrand. The Cardinal of Périgord*, Philadelphia

Zacour, N.P. (1975), 'Papal Regulation of Cardinals' Households in the Fourteenth Century', *Speculum* 50: 434–55

Zacour, N.P. (1979), 'Petrus de Braco and his Repudium Ambitionis', *MS* 41: 1–29

Zutshi, P.N.R. (1984), 'Proctors Acting for English Petitioners in the Chancery of the Avignon Popes', *JEH* 35: 15–29

Zutshi, P.N.R. (1989), 'The Letters of the Avignon popes (1305–1378). A Source for the Study of Anglo-Papal Relations and of English Ecclesiastical History', in Michael Jones and Malcolm Vale (eds.), *England and her Neighbours, 1066–1453. Essays in Honour of Pierre Chaplais*, London, pp. 259–75

20 THE GREAT SCHISM

General note

The bibliography is restricted, in principle, to works relevant – directly or at one or two removes – to the Schism as an integral historical subject; it omits works about particular phenomena of the Schism in a peripheral context, works dealing with other subjects that include the Schism by the way, and many older works that have been superseded by more recent studies of the same topics. Even within these limits it is only a selection intended to guide first approaches from various directions. With the same intention editions and studies of primary sources, noted according to more or less the same criteria, are listed under the appropriate subdivisions of the subject-matter; some standard repertories, however, are listed separately. Conciliarism and the Councils are covered only in so far as they figure in the history of the Schism, as the *via concilii generalis.*

Bibliographies and surveys of scholarship

Alberigo, Giuseppe (1978), 'Il movimento conciliare (XIV–XV sec.) nella ricerca storica recente', *SM* 3rd series 19: 913–50

Delaruelle, Etienne, Labande, E. and Ourliac, P. (1962–4), *L'Eglise au temps du grand schisme et la crise conciliaire (1378–1449),* 2 vols., Paris (Full bibliographical notes to each section.)

Institut d'Estudis Catalans (1979), *El cisma d'occident a Catalunya, les illes i el país Valencià. Repertori bibliogràfic,* Barcelona. (An exceptionally good list, with analyses and indexes, of more than 500 items, a great many of general, not just Catalan, relevance.)

Marini, A. (1982), 'Periodo Avignonese e scisma d'occidente alla luce de due convegni', *RSCI* 36: 426–36

Sieben, Hermann (1983), *Traktate und Theorien zum Konzil, vom Beginn des grossen Schismas bis zum Vorabend der Reformation (1378–1521),* Frankfurt a. M. (Pp. 11–30 survey the printed Schism tractates.)

Standard repertories of primary sources

Bourgeois du Chastenet, L., *Nouvelle histoire du concile de Constance,* Paris (1718) (Valuable documentary appendix.)

Bulaeus (Du Boulay, C.E.), *Historia Universitatis Parisiensis,* IV–VI, Paris (1668–73)

Denifle, H. and Chatelain, A., *Chartularium Universitatis Parisiensis,* III & IV, Paris (1894–7)

Deutsche Reichstagsakten unter König Ruprecht, ed. J. Weizsäcker, 3 vols., Gotha (1882–8)

Deutsche Reichstagsakten unter König Wenzel, ed. J. Weizsäcker, 3 vols., Munich (1867–77)

Documents relatifs au grand schisme, Textes et analyses (1924–73), I–VI, Analecta Vaticano-Belgica, 8, 13, 19, 26, 27, Brussels and Rome. (Letters, etc., of Clement VII and Benedict XIII concerning Belgium.)

Gerson, Jean, *Œuvres complètes,* ed. P. Glorieux, 10 vols., Paris (1960–73)

Mansi, J.D., *Sacrorum Conciliorum Nova et Amplissima Collectio*, XXII, XXVI, XXVII, Venice (1784)

Martène, E. and Durand, U., *Thesaurus Novus Anecdotorum*, I and II, Paris (1717)

Martène, E. and Durand, U., *Veterum Scriptorum et Monumentorum Historicorum, Dogmaticorum, Moralium Amplissima Collectio*, VII, Paris (1724)

Ordonnances des rois de France de la troisième race, ed. D. F. Secousse, VI–IX, Paris (1745–55)

1378 and after: the two elections and the ensuing polemics

Bliemetzrieder, Franz (1903), 'Zur Geschichte der großen abendländischen Kirchenspaltung. Die Kardinäle Peter Corsini, Simone de Borsano, Jakob Orsini und der Konzilsgedanke', *SMGBO* 24: 360–77, 625–52

Bliemetzrieder, F. (ed.) (1909a), *Literarische Polemik zu Beginn des großen abendländischen Schismas*, Vienna; repr. New York, 1967

Bliemetzrieder, F. (1909b), 'Le traité de Pierre Bohier, évêque d'Orvieto, sur le projet de concile général (1379)', *Questions ecclésiastiques* 2: 40–51

Brandmüller, W. (1974), 'Zur Frage nach der Gültigkeit der Wahl Urbans VI.' *AHC* 6: 78–120; repr. in *Papst und Konzil* (1990), pp. 3ff

Bresc, H. (1980), 'La genèse du schisme: les partis cardinalices et leurs ambitions dynastiques', in *GDGSO*, pp. 45–57

Colledge, E. (1956), 'Epistola Solitarii ad Reges: Alphonse of Pecha as Organizer of Birgittine and Urbanist Propaganda', *MS* 18: 19–49

Dykmans, Marc, S.J. (1975), 'Du conclave d'Urbain VI au grand schisme. Sur Pierre Corsini et Bindo Fesulani, écrivains florentins', *AHP* 13: 207–30

Dykmans, Marc, S.J. (1977a), 'La bulle de Grégoire XI à la veille du grand schisme', *MEFRM* 89: 485–95

Dykmans, Marc, S.J. (1977b), 'La troisième élection du pape Urbain VI', *AHP* 15: 17–64

Fink, K. A. (1962), 'Zur Beurteilung des Großen Abendländischen Schismas', *ZKG* 73: 335–43

Gayet, L. (1889), *Le grand schisme d'occident d'après les documents contemporains déposés aux archives secrètes du Vatican. Les origines*, 2 vols., Berlin, Florence and Paris (Important chiefly for its appendices of testimonies, etc., bearing on the events of 1378.)

Guillemain, B. (1980), 'Cardinaux et société curiale aux origines de la double élection de 1378', in *GDGSO*, pp. 19–30

Haller, J. (1941), review of Seidlmayer (1940), *HZ* 163: 595–7

Harvey, M. (1980), 'The Case for Urban VI in England to 1390', in *GDGSO*, pp. 541–60

Hayez, M. (ed.) (1980), *Genèse et débuts du grand schisme d'occident*, Colloques internationaux de CNRS, 586, Paris

MacFarlane, L. (1953), 'An English Account of the Election of Urban VI, 1378', *BIHR* 26: 75–85

Mirot, L. (1899), *La politique pontificale et le retour du Saint-Siège à Rome en 1376*, Paris

Mollat, M. (1980), 'Vie et sentiment religieux au début du grand schisme', in *GDGSO*, pp. 295–303

Moreau, E. de (1949), 'Une nouvelle théorie sur les origines du grand schisme d'occident', *Académie royale de Belgique. Bulletin de la classe des lettres* 35: 182–9

Ols, O. (1980), 'Sainte Catherine de Sienne et les débuts du grand schisme', in *GDGSO*, pp. 337–47

Pasztor, E. (1980), 'La curia romana all'inizio dello scisma d'occidente', in *GDGSO*, pp. 31–43

Petrucci, E. (1982), 'L'ecclesiologia alternativa alla vigilia e all'inizio del grande scisma: S. Caterina da Siena et Pietro Bohier vescovo di Orvieto', in *Atti del Simposio internazionale cateriniano-bernardiniano*, Siena, pp. 181–253

Přerovský, O. (1960), *L'elezione di Urbano VI e l'insorgere dello scisma d'occidente*, Rome

Re, N. del (1962), 'Il "consilium pro Urbano VI" di Bartolomeo da Saliceto (Vat. Lat. 5608)', *ST* 219: 213–63

Seidlmayer, M. (1933), 'Peter de Luna (Benedikt XIII.) und die Entstehung des großen abendländischen Schismas', *GAKGS*, *SFGG*, 1st series, 4: 206–47

Seidlmayer, M. (1940), *Die Anfänge des großen abendländischen Schismas. Studien zur Kirchenpolitik insbesondere der spanischen Staaten und zu den geistigen Kämpfen der Zeit*, *SFGG*, 2nd series, 5, Münster

Souchon, M. (1898–9), *Die Papstwahlen in der Zeit des Großen Schismas. Entwicklung und Verfassungskämpfe des Kardinalates von 1378 Bis 1417*, 2 vols., Braunschweig; repr. in one vol. Darmstadt, 1970

Steinherz, S. (1900), 'Das Schisma von 1378 und die Haltung Karls IV.', *MIÖG* 21: 599–639

Thibault, P.R. (1986), *Pope Gregory XI. The Failure of Tradition*, New York

Thomas, H. (1988), 'Frankreich, Karl IV. und das Große Schisma', in P. Moraw (ed.), '*Bundnissystem' und 'Außenpolitik' im späteren Mittelalter*, *ZHF*, Supplementary vol. 5, Berlin, pp. 69–104

Trexler, R. (1967), 'Rome on the Eve of the Great Schism', *Speculum* 42: 489–509

Ullmann, W. (1948), *The Origins of the Great Schism. A Study in Fourteenth-Century Ecclesiastical History*, London; repr. 1972

Williman, D. (1980), 'The Camerary and the Schism', in *GDGSO*, pp. 65–71

The Schism: general and miscellaneous

Bautier, R.-H. (1980), 'Aspects politiques du grand schisme', in *GDGSO*, pp. 457–81

Boüard, M. de (1936), *Les origines des guerres d'Italie. La France et l'Italie au temps du grand schisme d'occident*, Paris

Brandmüller, W. (1990), *Papst und Konzil im Großen Schisma (1378–1431). Studien und Quellen*, Paderborn

Engels, O. (1987), 'Die Obedienzen des Abendländischen Schismas', in H. Jedin *et al.* (eds.), *Atlas Zur Kirchengeschichte*, 2nd edn, Freiburg, pp. 48–52

Esch, A. (1966), 'Bankiers der Kirche im Großen Schisma', *QFIAB* 46: 277–398

Esch, A. (1969), review of Favier (1966), *Göttingische Gelehrte Anzeigen* 221: 133–59

Eubel, K. (1893), 'Die provisiones praelatorum während des großen Schismas', *RQ* 7: 405–46

Favier, J. (1966), *Les finances pontificales à l'époque du grand schisme d'occident, 1378–1409*, Paris

Fink, K.A. (1968), 'Das große Schisma bis zum Konzil von Pisa', in Hubert Jedin (ed.), *Handbuch der Kirchengeschichte. Die mittelalterliche Kirche*, II: *Vom kirchlichen*

Hochmittelalter bis zum Vorabend der Reformation, III, ed. H.-G. Beck et al., Freiburg, pp. 490–516

Finke, H. et al. (eds.) (1896–1928), Acta Concilii Constanciensis, 4 vols., Münster (esp. I: Akten zur Vorgeschichte des Konstanzer Konzils (1410–1414))

Haller, J. (1903), Papsttum und Kirchenreform, I, Berlin

Hefele, Ch.-J. and Leclercq, H. (1915–16), Histoire des conciles d'après les documents originaux. Nouvelle traduction française, VI, ii and VII, i, Paris

Herde, P. (1973), 'Politische Verhaltungsweisen der Florentiner Oligarchie 1382–1402', in Geschichte und Verfassungsgefüge, Walter Schlesinger Festschrift, Wiesbaden, pp. 156–249

Holmes, G. (1975), Europe. Hierarchy and Revolt, London

Jordan, G.J. (1930), The Inner History of the Great Schism of the West, London

Labande, E.-R. (1980), 'L'attitude de Florence dans la première phase du schisme' in GDGSO pp. 483–92

Landi, A. (1985), Il papa deposto (Pisa 1409). L'idea conciliare nel grande scisma, Turin

Largiadèr, A. (1961), 'Zum großen abendländischen schisma von 1378–1415', in Mélanges offerts à Paul E. Martin, Geneva, pp. 199–212

Manselli, R. (1980), 'Papes et papauté entre Christ et Antéchrist: approches religieuses du schisme', in GDGSO, pp. 591–8

Mercati, A. (1949), 'Un ignota missione francese nel 1401 presso Roberto de Palatino eletto re dei Romani', MAHEFR 61: 209–24

Millet, H. (1986), 'Le cardinal Martin de Zalba (m. 1403) face aux prophéties du grand schisme d'occident', MEFRM 98: 265–93

Millet, H. (1990), 'Ecoute et usage des prophéties par les prélats pendant le grand schisme d'occident', MEFRM 102: 425–55

Palmer, J.J.N. (1972), England, France and Christendom, 1377–1399, London

Pasztor, E. (1980), 'Funzione politico-culturale di una struttura della Chiesa: il Cardinalato', in GDGSO, pp. 197–226

Rusconi, R. (1979), L'attesa della fine. Crisi della società, profezia ed Apocalisse in Italia al tempo del grande scisma d'occidente (1378–1417), Rome

Salembier, L. (1921), Le grand schisme d'occident, 5th edn, Paris

Santa Teresa, G. di (1964), 'Contributi alla libellistica dello scisma occidentale (1378–1417)', Ephemerides Carmeliticae 15: 387–424

Scheuffgen, F.J. (1889), Beiträge zu der Geschichte des grossen Schismas, Freiburg im Br.

Smith, J. Holland (1970), The Great Schism 1378, London

Sorbelli, A. (1906), Il trattato di S. Vincento Ferrer intorno al grande scisma d'occidente, 2nd edn, Bologna

Steinherz, S. (1932), Dokumente zur Geschichte des großen abendländischen Schismas (1385–1395), QFGG, 11, Prague

Swanson, R.N. (1979), Universities, Academics and the Great Schism, Cambridge

Swanson, R.N. (1980), 'The Problem of the Cardinalate in the Great Schism', in P. Linehan and B. Tierney (eds.), Authority and Power, Cambridge, pp. 225–35

Swanson, R.N. (1983), 'A Survey of Views on the Great Schism, c. 1395', AHP 21: 79–103

Swanson, R.N. (1984), 'Obedience and Disobedients in the Great Schism', AHP 22: 377–87

Vauchez, A. (1990), 'Les théologiens face aux prophéties à l'époque des papes d'Avignon et du grand schisme', *MEFRM* 102: 578–88

The Avignon papacy and its obedience: French schism policy

Arnold, Ivar (ed.) (1926), *L'apparicion Maistre Jehan de Meun et le Somnium super materia Schismatis d'Honoré Bonet*, Paris

Bernstein, A. (1978), *Pierre d'Ailly and the Blanchard Affair, University and Chancellor of Paris at the Beginning of the Great Schism*, Leiden

Bess, B. (1890), *Johannes Gerson und die kirchenpolitischen Parteien Frankreichs vor dem Konzil zu Pisa*, Marburg

Bess, B. (1904), 'Frankreich und sein Papst von 1378 bis 1394: eine Skizze', *ZKG* 25: 48–89

Bliemetzrieder, F. (1903), 'Handschriftliches zur Geschichte des grossen abendländischen Schismas. I. Antwort der Universität in Wien an diejenige zu Paris, 12. Mai 1396, wegen der Zession der beiden Päpste', *SMGBO* 24: 100–5

Bossuat, A. (1949), 'Une relation inédite de l'ambassade française au pape Benoît XIII en 1407', *MA* 55: 77–101

Brun, R. (1935–8), 'Annales avignonnaises de 1382 à 1410, extraites des archives de Datini', *Mémoires de l'Institut historique de Provence* 12: 17–142; 13: 58–105; 14: 5–57; 15: 21–52; 16: 154–92

Cheyette, F. (1962), 'La justice et le pouvoir royal à la fin du moyen âge français', *RHDFE* 4th series 40: 373–94

Coopland, G.W. (ed.) (1969), Philippe de Mézières, *Le songe du vieil pélerin*, 2 vols., Paris

Coville, A. (ed.) (1936), *Le traité de la ruine de l'église de Nicolas de Clamanges*, Paris

Ehrle, F. (1889–1900), 'Aus den Akten des Afterkonzils von Perpignan 1408', *ALKG* 5: 387–487; 7: 576–696

Ehrle, F. (ed.) (1892–1900), 'Neue Materialien zur Geschichte Peters von Luna (Benedikts XIII.)', *ALKG* 6: 139–308; 7: 1–310

Ehrle, F. (1900), 'Die kirchenrechtlichen Schriften Peters von Luna (Benedikts XIII.)', *ALKG* 7: 515–75

Ehrle, F. (ed.) (1906), *Martin de Alpartils Chronica actitatorum temporibus domini Benedicti XIII.*, 1, Paderborn

Eubel, K. (1900), *Die avignonesische Obedienz der Mendikanten-Orden sowie der Orden der Mercedarier und Trinitarier zur Zeit des großen Schismas beleuchtet durch die von Clemens VII., und Benedikt XIII., an dieselben gerichteten Schreiben*, QFGG, 1, 2, Paderborn

Eubel, K. (1914), 'Die avignonesische Obedienz im Franziskanerorden zur Zeit des großen abendländischen Schismas', *FS* 1: 165–92, 312–27, 479–90

Favier, J. (1980), 'Le grand schisme dans l'histoire de France', in *GDGSO*, Paris, pp. 7–16

Goñi Gaztambide, J. (1962), 'Los obispos de Pamplona en el siglo XIV', *Principe de Viana* 23: 5–194, 309–400 (The second part is a monograph on Cardinal Martín de Zalba.)

Harvey, M. (1973), 'Papal Witchcraft: The Charges against Benedict XIII', *SCH* 10: 109–16

Immenkotter, H. (1976), 'Ein avignonesischer Bericht zur Unionspolitik Benedikts XIII.', *AHP* 8: 200–49

Jarry, E. (1892), 'La "voie de fait" et l'alliance franco-milanaise (1386–1395)', *BEC* 53: 213–53, 505–70

Kaminsky, Howard (1983), *Simon de Cramaud and the Great Schism*, New Brunswick, N.J.

Kehrmann, Carl (1890), *Frankreichs innere Kirchenpolitik von der Wahl Clemens VII., und dem Beginn des großen Schismas bis zum Pisaner Konzil und zur Wahl Alexanders V., 1378–1409*, Jena

Léman, A. (1929), 'Un traité inédit relatif au grand schisme d'occident, propositions de Chrétien Coq . . . au synode de Lille de 1384', *RHE* 29: 239–59

Léonard, E.-G. (1923), 'Négociations entre Clément VII et Charles VI au sujet des charges de l'Eglise de France et de l'ordonnance royale du 6 octobre 1385', *RHDFE* 4th series 2: 272–86

Logoz, R. (1974), *Clément VII (Robert de Genève), sa chancellerie et le clergé romand au début du grand schisme (1378–1394)*, Lausanne

Luc, P. (1938), 'Un complot contre le pape Benoît XIII (1406–1407)', *MAHEFR* 55: 374–402

Martin, V. (1939), *Les origines du Gallicanisme*, 2 vols., Paris

Millet, H. (1985), 'Du conseil au concile (1395–1408). Recherche sur la nature des assemblées du clergé en France pendant le grand schisme d'occident', *JS*: 137–59

Millet, H. (1986), 'Quels furent les bénéficiaires de la soustraction d'obédience de 1398 dans les chapitres cathédraux français?', in N. Bulst *et al.* (eds.), *Medieval Lives and the Historian*, Kalamazoo Mich., pp. 123–37

Millet, H. and Poulle, E. (eds.) (1988), *Le vote de la soustraction d'obédience en 1398*, 1, *Introduction, édition et fac-similés des bulletins du vote*, Paris

Millet, H. (1991), 'Les votes des évêques à l'assemblée du Clergé de 1398', *L'Ecrit dans la société Médiévale*, ed. C. Bourlet and A. Dufour, Paris, pp. 195–214

Mirot, L. (1934), *La politique française en Italie sous le règne de Charles VI, de 1380 à 1422*, Paris

Mollat, G. (1927), 'Episodes du siège du palais des papes au temps de Benoît XIII (1398–1399)', *RHE* 23: 489–501

Mollat, G. (1945), 'L'application en France de la soustraction d'obédience à Benoît XIII jusqu'au concile de Pise', *Revue du moyen âge latin* 1: 149–63

Mollat, G. (1948), 'Les origines du Gallicanisme parlementaire aux XIVe et XVe siècles', *RHE* 43: 90–147

Mollat, G. (1949), 'L'adhésion des Chartreux à Clément VII (1378–1380).' *Revue du moyen âge latin* 5: 35–42

Morrall, J. (1960), *Gerson and the Great Schism*, Manchester

Nélis, H. (1932), 'La collation des bénéfices ecclésiastiques en Belgique sous Clément VII (1378–1394)', *RHE* 28: 39–61

Ouy, G. (1970), 'Gerson et l'Angleterre. A propos d'un texte polémique retrouvé du chancelier de Paris contre l'université d'Oxford, 1396', in A. Levi (ed.), *Humanism in France*, Manchester, pp. 43–81

Pascoe, L.B. (1974), 'Jean Gerson: Mysticism, Conciliarism and Reform', *AHC* 6: 135–53

Puig y Puig, S. (1920), *Pedro de Luna, último papa de Aviñón*, Barcelona (Important documentary appendix.)

Renouard, Y. (1970), *The Avignon Papacy 1305–1403*, trans. D. Bethell, London, from *La papauté à Avignon*, Paris (1954)

Rubio, J.-A. (1926), *La politica de Benedicto XIII desde la substraccion de Aragón a su obedien-cia hasta su destitucion en el concilio de Constanza jenero de 1416 a julio de 1417*, Zamora

Salembier, L. (1931), *Le cardinal Pierre d'Ailly, chancelier de l'université de Paris, évêque du Puy et de Cambrai, 1350–1420*, Tourcoing

Schmitt, C. (1958), 'La position du cardinal Léonard de Giffoni, O.F.M. dans le conflit du grand schisme d'occident', *AFH* 50: 273–331; 51: 25–72, 410–72

Schmitt, C. (1962), 'Le parti clémentiste dans le province franciscain de Strasbourg', *AFH* 55: 82–102

Seidlmayer, M. (1940), 'Die spanischen "Libri de Schismate" des Vatikanischen Archivs', *GAKGS* 8: 199–262

Suárez Fernández, I. (1960), *Castilla, el cisma y la crisis conciliar (1378–1440)*, Madrid (Important documentary appendix.)

Swanson, R. N. (1975), 'The University of St. Andrews and the Great Schism, 1410–1419', *JEH* 26: 223–45

Tabbagh, V. (1996), 'Guy de Roye un évêque au temps du Grande Schisme', *RH* 296: 29–58

Tobin, M, (1986), 'Le "Livre des révélations" de Marie Robine (d. 1399), Etude et édition', *MEFRM* 98: 229–64

Tschackert, P. (1877), *Peter von Ailli (Petrus de Alliaco), Zur Geschichte des großen abendländis-chen Schisma und der Reformkonzilien von Pisa und Konstanz*, Gotha; repr. 1968

Valois, N. (1896–1902), *La France et le grand schisme d'occident*, 4 vols., Paris

Zunzunegui, J. (1942), *El reino de Navarra y su obispado de Pamplona durante la primera época del cisma de occidente, Pontificado de Clemente VII de Aviñon 1378–1394*, San Sebastián

Zunzunegui, J. (1943), 'La legación en España del cardinal Pedro de Luna 1379–1390', *Miscellanea Historiae Pontificiae* 7: 83–137

The Roman (Urbanist) papacy

Brezzi, P. (1944), 'Lo scisma d'occidente come problema italiano (La funzione italiana del papato nel periodo del grande scisma)', *Deputazione Romana di storia patria, Archivio*, 67 (n.s. 10): 391–450

Brown, E. (ed.) (1690), 'Speculum Aureum de Titulis Beneficiorum', *Fasciculus Rerum Expetendarum et Fugiendarum*, London

Cutolo, A. (1969), *Re Ladislao d'Angiò-Durazzo*, 2nd edn, Naples

Erler, Georg (ed.) (1890), *Theoderici de Nyem, De schismate libri tres*, Leipzig

Esch, A. (1969), *Bonifaz IX. und der Kirchenstaat*, Tübingen

Esch, A. (1972), 'Das Papsttum unter der Herrschaft der Neapolitaner. Die führende Gruppe Neapolitaner Familien an der Kurie während des Schismas 1378–1415', in *Festschrift für Hermann Heimpel*, Göttingen, II, pp. 713–800 (a French abridge-ment in *GDGSO*, pp. 493–506)

Esch, A. (1974), 'Simonie-Geschäft in Rom 1400: Kein Papst wird das tun, was dieser tut', *VSW* 61: 433–57

Esch, A. (1976–7), 'La fine del libero comune di Roma nel giudizio dei mercati fiorentini . . . 1395–98', *Bolletino dell'Istituto storico italiano per il medio evo*, 86: 235–77

Fodale, S. (1973), *La politica napoletana di Urbano VI*, Palermo

Frankl, K. (1977), 'Papstschisma und Frömmigkeit. Die "Ad instar-Ablässe"', *RQ* 72: 57–124, 184–247

Graf, T. (1916), *Papst Urban VI. Untersuchungen über die römische Kurie während seines Pontifikates (1378–1389)*, Berlin

Heimpel, H. (1932), *Dietrich von Niem (c. 1340–1418)*, Münster

Heimpel, H. (1974), *Studien zur Kirchen- und Reichsreform des 15, Jahrhunderts, 2, Zu zwei Kirchenreform-Traktaten des beginnenden 15, Jahrhunderts: Die Reformschrift 'De praxi curiae Romanae' ('Squalores Romanae curiae', 1403) des Matthäus von Krakau und ihr Bearbeiter – Das 'Speculum aureum de titulis beneficiorum' (1404/05 und sein Verfasser)*, Heidelberg

Jansen, M. (1904), *Papst Bonifaz IX. (1389–1404) und seine Beziehungen zur deutschen Kirche*, Freiburg i. Br.

Jones, P. (1974), *The Malatesta of Rimini and the Papal States. A Political History*, London

Rothbart, M. (1913), *Urban VI. und Neapel*, Berlin

Sauerland, H. (1893), 'Aktenstücke zur Geschichte des Papstes Urban VI.', *HJb* 14: 820–932

Stacul, P. (1957), *Il cardinale Pileo di Prata*, Rome

Tachella, L. (1976), *Il pontificato di Urbano VI a Genova (1385–1386) e l'eccidio dei cardinali*, Genoa

The Schism and various princes, polities, regions, corporations

Baptista, J.C. (1956), 'Portugal e o cisma de occidente', *LS* 1: 65–203

Binz, L. (1973), *Vie religieuse et réforme ecclésiastique dans le diocèse de Genève pendant le grand schisme et la crise conciliaire (1378–1450)*, 1, Geneva

Bliemetzrieder, F. (1904), 'Der Zisterzienserorden im großen abendländischen Schisma', *SMGBO* 25: 62–82

Bliemetzrieder, F. (1908), 'Herzog Leopold III, von Österreich und das große abendländische Schisma', *MIÖG* 29: 662–72

Boüard, M. de (1931), 'L'empereur Robert et le grand schisme d'occident 1400–1403', *MAHEFR*, 48: 215–32

Diener, H. (1980), 'Die Anhänger Clemens' VII. in Deutschland', in *GDGSO*, pp. 521–31

Ehlen, L. (1910–13), 'Das Schisma im Metzer Sprengel . . . bis zur Niederlage der Urbanisten', *Jahrbuch der Gesellschaft für lothringische Geschichte und Altertumskunde* 21: 1–69; 25: 380–477

Erler, G. (1889), 'Florenz, Neapel und das päpstliche Schisma', *Historisches Taschenbuch* 6: 179–230

Eschbach, P. (1887), *Die kirchliche Frage auf den deutschen Reichstagen von 1378–1380*, Gotha

Gerlich, A. (1956), 'Die Anfänge des großen abendländischen Schismas und der Mainzer Bistumsstreit', *Hessisches Jahrbuch für Landesgeschichte* 6: 25–76

Graham, R. (1929), 'The Great Schism and the English Monasteries of the Cistercian Order', *EHR* 44: 373–87

Guggenberger, K. (1907), *Die Legation des Kardinals Pileus in Deutschland 1378–1382*, Munich

Hauck, A. (1958), *Kirchengeschichte Deutschlands*, v, ii, Berlin; orig. publ. 1920

Hennig, E. (1909), *Die päpstlichen Zehnten aus Deutschland im Zeitalter des avignonesischen Papsttums und während des großen Schismas*, Halle

Ivars, A. (1928), 'La "indiferencia" de Pedro IV de Aragón en el gran cisma de occidente (1378–1382)', *Archivo ibero-americano* 29: 21–97, 161–86

Jank, D. (1983), *Das Erzbistum Trier während des Großen Abendländischen Schismas (1378–1417/18)*, QAMK, 47, Mainz

Junghanns, H. (1915), *Zur Geschichte der englischen Kirchenpolitik von 1399–1413*, Freiburg i. Br.

Komarek, H.P. (1970), *Das große abendländische Schisma in der Sicht der öffentlichen Meinung und der Universitäten des Deutschen Reichs 1378–1400*, Salzburg

Machilek, F. (1977), 'Das Große Abendländische Schisma in der Sicht des Ludolf von Sagan', in Remigius Bäumer (ed.), *Das Konstanzer Konzil*, WF, 415, Darmstadt, pp. 37–95

Miebach, A. (1912), *Die Politik Wenzels und der rheinischen Kurfürsten in der Frage des Schismas von der Thronbesteigung bis zum Jahre 1380*, Münster

Palmer, J.J.N. (1966), 'The Anglo-French Peace Negotiations, 1390–1396', *TRHS* 5th series 16: 81–94

Palmer, J.J.N. (1968), 'England and the Great Western Schism, 1388–1399', *EHR* 83: 516–22

Palmer, J.J.N. (1971), 'The Background to Richard II's Marriage to Isabel of France (1396)', *BIHR* 44: 1–16

Paquet, J. (1964), 'Le schisme d'occident à Louvain', *RHE* 59: 401–36

Pauw, N. de (1904), 'L'adhésion du clergé de Flandre au pape Urbain VI et les évêques urbanistes de Gand (1379–1395)', *BCRH* 73: 671–702

Perroy, E. (1933), *L'Angleterre et le grand schisme d'occident. Etude sur la politique religieuse de l'Angleterre sous Richard II (1378–1399)*, Paris

Roth, F. (1958), 'The Great Schism and the Augustinian Order', *Augustiniana* 8: 281–98

Rott, J. (1935), 'Le grand schisme d'occident et le diocèse de Strasburg (1378–1415)', *MAHEFR* 52: 366–95

Schönenberger, K. (1926), 'Das Bistum Konstanz während des großen Schismas 1378–1415', *Zeitschrift für Schweizerische Kirchengeschichte* 20: 1–31, 81–110, 185–222, 241–81

Schönenberger, K. (1927–8), 'Das Bistum Basel während des großen Schismas 1378–1415', *Basler Zeitschrift für Geschichte und Altertumskunde* 26: 73–145; 27: 115–89

Segre, A. (1906–7), 'I conti di Savoia e lo scisma d'occidente', *Atti dell'Accademia delle scienze di Torino* 42: 575–610

Shank, M. (1981), 'Academic Benefices and German Universities during the Great Schism: Three Letters from Johannes of Stralen, Arnold of Emelisse and Gerard of Kalkar to Henry of Langenstein, 1387–1388', *Codices manuscripti* 7: 33–47

Stewart, A.F. (1907), 'Scotland and the Papacy during the Great Schism', *SHR* 4: 144–58

Swanson, R.N. (1977), 'The University of Cologne and the Great Schism', *JEH* 28: 1–15

Tipton, Charles L. (1967), 'The English Hospitallers during the Great Schism', *SMRT* 4: 91–124

Torrisi, N. (1954), 'I riflessi dello scisma d'occidente in Sicilia', *Siculorum gymnasium* 7: 129–37

Ullmann, W. (1958), 'The University of Cambridge and the Great Schism', *JThS* n.s. 9: 53–77

Vincke, J. (1938), 'Der König von Aragón und die Camera apostolica in den Anfängen des Großen Schismas', *GAKGS* 7: 84–126

Vincke, J. (1972), 'Ruprecht von der Pfalz und Martín von Aragón', in *Festschrift für Hermann Heimpel*, Göttingen, II, pp. 500–30

Weltsch, R. (1968), *Archbishop John of Jenstein (1348–1400), Papalism, Humanism and Reform in Pre-Hussite Prague*, The Hague

Wriedt, K. (1972), *Die deutschen Universitäten in den Auseinandersetzungen des Schismas und der Reformkonzilien. Kirchenpolitische Ziele und korporative Interessen (1378–1449)*, I. *Vom Ausbruch des Schismas bis zum Beginn des Basler Konzils*, Kiel

Ending the Schism: theory, politics, publicistics, 'viae'

Angermeier, H. (1961), 'Das Reich und der Konziliarismus', *HZ* 192: 529–83

Bäumer, R. (1977a), 'Konrad von Soest und seine Konzilsappellation 1409 in Pisa', in Bäumer (1977b), pp. 96–118; orig. publ. 1973

Bäumer, R. (ed.) (1977b), *Das Konstanzer Konzil*, WF, 415, Darmstadt

Bliemetzrieder, F. (1903), 'Handschriftliches zur Geschichte des grossen abendländischen Schismas. II. Zwei kanonistische Traktate aus Bologna (Ende 1408) wegen des Pisanerkonziles', *SMGBO* 24: 106–14

Bliemetzrieder, F. (1904a), *Das Generalkonzil im großen abendländischen Schisma*, Paderborn

Bliemetzrieder, F. (1904b), 'Konrad von Gelnhausen und Heinrich von Langenstein auf dem Konzile zu Pisa (1409)', *HJb* 25: 536–41

Bliemetzrieder, F. (ed.) (1905), 'Abt Ludolfs von Sagan Traktat "Soliloquium scismatis"'[early 1409], *SMGBO* 26: 29–47, 226–38, 434–92

Bliemetzrieder, F. (1908–9), 'Traktat des Minoritenprovincials von England Fr. Nikolaus de Fakenham (1395) über das grosse abendländische Schisma', *AFH* 1: 577–600; 2: 79–91

Boockmann, H. (1974), 'Zur politischen Geschichte des Konstanzer Konzils', *ZKG* 85: 45–63

Brandmüller, W. (1975a), 'Die Gesandtschaft Benedikts XIII., an das Konzil von Pisa', in G. Schwaiger (ed.), *Konzil und Papst (H. Tüchle Festschrift)*, Munich, pp. 169–205; repr. in *Papst und Konzil* (1990), pp. 42ff

Brandmüller, W. (1975b), 'Sieneser Korrespondenzen zum Konzil von Pisa 1409', *AHC* 7: 166–278; repr. in *Papst und Konzil*, Munich (1990), pp. 171ff

Culley, D. (1913), *Konrad von Gelnhausen. Sein Leben, seine Werke und seine Quellen*, Halle

Finke, H. (1889), *Forschungen und Quellen zur Geschichte des Konstanzer Konzils*, Paderborn

Girgensohn, D. (1984), 'Kardinal Antonio Caetani und Gregor XII., in den Jahren 1406–1408: vom Papstmacher zum Papstgegner', *QFIAB* 64: 116–226

Girgensohn, D. (1987), 'Antonio Loschi und Baldassarre Cossa vor dem Pisaner Konzil von 1409 (mit der 'Oratio pro unione ecclesiae')', *IMU* 30: 1–93

Girgensohn, D. (1989), 'Ein Schisma ist nicht zu beenden ohne die Zustimmung der konkurrierenden Päpste. Die juristische Argumentation Benedikts XIII. (Pedro de Lunas)', *AHP* 27: 197–247

Harvey, M. (1970), 'England and the Council of Pisa: Some New Information', *AHC* 2: 263–83

Harvey, M. (1972), 'A Sermon by John Luke on the Ending of the Great Schism, 1409', *SCH* 9: 159–69

Harvey, M. (1974), 'The Letter of Oxford University on the Schism, 5 February 1399', *AHC* 6: 121–34

Harvey, M. (1975), 'The Letters of the University of Oxford on Withdrawal of Obedience from Pope Boniface IX', *SCH* 11: 187–98

Harvey, M. (1977), 'Two "Quaestiones" on the Great Schism by Nicholas Fakenham, O.F.M.', *AFH* 7 (1977): 97–127

Harvey, M. (1983), *Solutions to the Schism. A Study of Some English Attitudes, 1378–1409*, KQS, 12, St Ottilien

Heimpel, Hermann (ed.) (1933), *Dialog über Union und Reform der Kirche, 1410* (Dietrich von Niem, *De modis uniendi et reformandi ecclesiam in concilio universali*), Leipzig and Berlin

Kaminsky, H. (ed.) (1984), Simon de Cramaud, *De substraccione obediencie*, Cambridge, Mass.

Kreuzer, G. (1987), *Heinrich von Langenstein. Studien zur Biographie und zu den Schismatraktaten unter besonderer Berücksichtigung der Epistola pacis und der Epistola concilii pacis*, QFGG, NF, 6, Paderborn

Machilek, F. (1967), *Ludolf von Sagan und seine Stellung in der Auseinandersetzung um Konziliarismus und Hussitismus*, Munich

Morrissey, T. (1981), 'Franciscus Zabarella (1360–1417): Papacy, Community and Limitations upon Authority', in G. Lytle (ed.), *Reform and Authority in the Medieval and Reformation Church*, Washington, pp. 37–54

Oakley, F. (1960), 'The "Propositiones utiles" of Pierre d'Ailly: an Epitome of Conciliar Theory', *Church History* 29: 398–403

Oakley, F. (1964), *The Political Thought of Pierre d'Ailly. The Voluntarist Tradition*, New Haven. (Includes edition of 'Tractatus de materia concilii generalis', pp. 252–342.)

Oakley, F. (1978), 'The "Tractatus de fide et ecclesia, romano pontifice et concilio generali" of Johannes Breviscoxe', *AHC* 10: 99–130

Swanson, R.N. (1983) 'The Way of Action: Pierre D'Ailly and the Military Solution to the Great Schism', *SCH* 20: 191–200

Thomson, J.A.F. (1980), *Popes and Princes, 1417–1517*, London

Tierney, B. (1955), *Foundations of the Conciliar Theory. The Contribution of the Medieval Canonists from Gratian to the Great Schism*, Cambridge; repr. 1968

Vincke, J. (ed.) (1938), 'Acta Concilii Pisani', *RQ* 46: 81–331

Vincke, J. (ed.) (1940), *Briefe zum Pisaner Konzil*, Bonn

Vincke, J. (ed.) (1942), *Schriftstücke zum Pisaner Konzil. Ein Kampf um die öffentliche Meinung*, Bonn

Vincke, J. (1955), 'Zu den Konzilien von Perpignan und Pisa', *RQ* 50: 89–94

Wenck, K. (1896), 'Konrad von Gelnhausen und die Quellen der konziliaren Theorie', *HZ* 76: 6–61

21 BALTIC EUROPE

A history of the Baltic region requires a familiarity with several different cultures and language groups (Slavonic, Germanic and Baltic) but the general reader should not be disheartened. This bibliography serves two functions: to guide the reader through selected primary and secondary material (first and second sections) and to indicate other works used for this chapter (third section).

Primary sources

The main national collections of medieval documents and chronicles have been under way since the nineteenth century.

Acta

Bullarium Franciscanum, ed. K. Eubel, 7 vols., Rome (1759–1904)

Bullarium Poloniae, ed. I. Sułkowska-Kuraś and S. Kuraś, 3 vols., Rome (1982–)

Chartularium Lithuaniae Res Gestas Magni Ducis Gedeminne illustrans, seu/ arba Gedimino Laiškai, ed. S.C. Rowell, Vilnius (1999)

Codex Diplomaticus Prussicus, ed. J. Voigt, 6 vols., Königsberg (1836–61); 2nd edn, Osnabrück (1965)

Codex Epistolaris Vitoldi Magni Ducis Lithuaniae 1376–1430, ed. A. Prochaska, Cracow (1882)

Diplomatarium Danicum, ed. Danske Sprog og Litteraturselskab, Copenhagen (1938–)

Gedimino Laiškai, ed. V.T. Pashuto and I. Shtal, Vilnius (1966)

Gramoty Velikogo Novgoroda i Pskova, ed. S.N. Valk, Moscow and Leningrad (1949)

Hansisches Urkundenbuch, ed. K. Höhlbaum *et al.*, 11 vols., Halle, Leipzig and Weimar (1876–1939)

Liv-, Esth-, und Kurländisches Urkundenbuch nebst Regesten, ed. F.G. von Bunge, part 1, I–VI, Reval and Riga (1853–71); Aalen (1967–74)

Das Marienburger Tresslerbuch der Jahre 1399–1409, ed. E. Joachim, Königsberg (1896)

Preussisches Urkundenbuch, ed. M. Hein, E. Maschke, K. Conrad *et al.*, 6 vols., Königsberg and Marburg (1882–1986)

Die Recesse und andere Akten der Hansetage von 1256–1430, ed. K. Koppmann, 8 vols., Leipzig (1870–97); 2nd edn, Hildesheim and New York (1975)

Les regestes du patriarcat de Constantinople, 1: *Les actes des patriarches,* parts 4–6, ed. J. Darrouzès, 6 vols., Paris (1977–9)

Scriptores rerum svecicarum medii aevi, ed. E.M. Fant *et al.*, 3 vols., Uppsala (1818–76)

Belles lettres

Chaucer, Geoffrey, *The Canterbury Tales,* ed. F.N. Robinson, London (1966)

Deschamps, Eustache, *Œuvres complètes,* ed. G. Raynaud, 11 vols., Paris (1878–1903)

Machaut, Guillaume de, 'Confort d'ami', in his *Oeuvres,* ed. E. Hoepffner, 3 vols., Paris (1911–21), III, pp. 1–142

Mézières, Philippe de, *Songe du vieil pélerin,* ed. G.W. Coopland, 2 vols., Cambridge (1969)

Chronicles

Annales Danici Medii Aevi, ed. E. Jorgensen, Copenhagen (1920)
Danmarks Middelalderlige Annaler, ed. E. Kroman, Copenhagen (1980)
Długosz, Jan [Dlugossius, Iohannes], *Annales seu cronicae incliti regni Poloniae*, ed. J. Dąbrowski, D. Turkowska *et al.*, Warsaw (1964–)
Dusburg, Peter von, *Cronica terrae Prussiae*, in *SRP*, 1, pp. 3–219; German trans. and ed. K. Scholz and D. Wojtecki, *Die Peters von Dusburg Chronik des Preussenlandes*, Darmstadt (1984)
Erikskrönikan, ed. S.-B. Jansson, Stockholm (1985)
Livländische Reimchronik, ed. L. Meyer, Paderborn (1876); 2nd edn, Hildesheim (1963); English trans. with an historical introduction and appendices, J.C. Smith and W.L. Urban, *The Livonian Rhymed Chronicle*, Bloomington (1977)
Mannhardt, W., *Letto-preussiches Götterlehre*, Riga (1936); 2nd edn, Hanover and Döhren (1971)
Monumenta Poloniae Historicae, 6 vols., Lwów and Cracow (1864–93)
Novgorodskaia Pervaia Letopis', ed. M.N. Tikhomirov, Moscow and Leningrad (1950); [Unreliable] English trans. R. Mitchell and N. Forbes, *The Chronicle of Novgorod, 1016–1471*, London (1914)
Scriptores Rerum Prussicarum, ed. T. Hirsch *et al.*, 5 vols., Leipzig (1861–74); repr. with a sixth vol. Frankfurt am Main (1965)
Wartberge, Hermann von, *Chronicon Livoniae*, in *SRP*, II, pp. 21–116

Debt registers, lawbooks, etc.

Iura Prutenorum, ed. J. Matuszewski, Toruń (1963)
Kammerei-Register der Stadt Riga 1348–1361 und 1405–1474, ed. A. von Bulmerincq, Leipzig (1909)
Das Rigische Schuldbuch (1285–1352), ed. H. Hildebrand, St Petersburg (1872)
Der Stralsunder Liber Memorialis, ed. H.-D. Schroeder, Leipzig (1964)
Tabliczki woskowe, miasta Torunia, ok. 1350–I poł. XVI w. [Tabulae cereae civitatis Torunensis], ed. K. Górski and W. Szczuczko, Warsaw, Poznań and Toruń (1980)

Secondary works

A general history of the medieval Baltic is unavailable and studies in English are particularly rare. Much can be said for E. Christiansen, *The Northern Crusades. The Baltic and the Catholic Frontier, 1100–1525*, London (1980), which owes a great deal to continental historians but is readable and usually accurate. Periodical literature is recorded annually in the *International Medieval Bibliography* (Leeds) by region and by subject.

Scandinavia

A satisfactory history of medieval Scandinavia has yet to be written covering the gap between the Vikings and the Vasas which has been so little to the taste of both Lutherans and socialists. B. and P. Sawyer, *Medieval Scandinavia. From Conversion to Reformation, circa 800–1500*, Minneapolis and London (1993), is an excellent starting place for those who cannot manage L. Musset, *Les peuples scandinaves au moyen âge*, Paris (1951), which is still valuable. *Danish Medieval History. New Currents*, ed. N. Skyum Nielsen and N. Lund, Copenhagen (1981) is good. A good demographic and plague study is O.J. Benedictow, *Plague in the Late Medieval Nordic Countries. Epidemiological Studies*, Oslo (1992). For short informative articles see *Medieval Scandinavia. An Encyclopaedia*, New York (1993). Periodical literature includes *Medieval Scandinavia* (Odense); *Scandinavian Journal of History; Scandinavian Studies.*

Lithuania

Surprisingly, perhaps, medieval Lithuania is much better served by historians than is Scandinavia. The pagan grand duchy is viewed as a golden age in Lithuanian history. Much has been written in Russian (V.T. Pashuto, *Obrazovanie litovskogo gosudarstva*, Moscow (1958), with bibliography, pp. 429–64), Polish (see especially H. Paszkiewicz (below) and more recently the works of J. Ochmański and M. Kosman) and Lithuanian (Z. Ivinskis, *Lietuvos istorija*, Rome, and Vilnius (1978, 1991) – bibliography up to 1971, E. Gudavičius and A. Nikžentaitis (see below)). German historians have tended to write only about the Baltic Germans and their colonies. In western European languages, including English, see *La Cristianizzazione della Lituania,* ed. P. Rabikauskas (*Atti e documenti*, 2), Vatican City (1989); M. Giedroyć, 'The Arrival of Christianity in Lithuania . . .', *OSP* n.s. 18 (1985–9), pp. 1–30; 20, pp. 1–33; 22, pp. 34–57; R.J. Mažeika, 'Of Cabbages and Knights: Trade and Trade Treaties with the Infidel on the Northern Frontier, 1200–1390', *JMH* 20 (1994), pp. 63–76, and 'Bargaining for Baptism: Lithuanian Negotiations for Conversion 1250–1358', in J. Muldoon (ed.), *Religious Conversion. The Spiritual Transformation of the Old World and the New*, Florida University Press (1996). Mažeika provided a bibliographical article on Baltic history in 'The Grand Duchy Rejoins Europe: Post-Soviet Developments in the Historiography of Pagan Lithuania', *JMH* 21 (1995), pp. 289–303. See also the valuable chapters on Lithuania in H. Paszkiewicz, *The Origin of Russia*, London (1954), a misleading title since Lithuania was not a part of Russia, but vice versa. His *Jagiellonowie a Moskwa*, Warsaw (1933) remains the best coverage of pre-1385 Lithuania, thanks to clear reliance on primary sources and extensive critical apparatus. Most recently see S.C. Rowell, *Lithuania Ascending. A Pagan Empire within East-Central Europe 1295–1345,* Cambridge (1994) – bibliography pp. 318–60.

Volumes in the series *Acta Historica Universitatis Klaipedensis*, Klaipèda (1993–   ) have up-to-date articles by Lithuanian and foreign scholars and include summaries or whole pieces in English or German: *Žalgirio laiku Lietuva ir jos kaimynai* (Lithuania and her neighbours in the time of Grunwald/Tannenberg), Vilnius (1992). The *Encyclopedia Lituanica*, 6 vols., Boston (1970) contains generally reliable historical entries in English.

For the European context of the *Preussenreisen* see the excellent catalogue and analysis in W. Paravicini, *Die Preussenreisen des europäischen Adels,* 2 vols., (of three) Sigmaringen (1989–95)

The Teutonic Order

The best general history is H. Boockmann, *Der Deutsche Orden. Zwölf Kapitel aus seiner Geschichte*, Munich (1985). This should be complemented by M. Biskup and G. Labuda,

Dzieje zakonu krzyżackiego w Prusach, Danzig (1986). For a general background to the crusades in north-eastern Europe, see N. Housley, *The Later Crusades. From Lyons to Alcazar 1274–1580,* Oxford (1992); on soldier-monks see A. Forey, *The Military Orders. From the Twelfth to the Early Fourteenth Centuries,* London (1992). F.L. Carsten, *The Origins of Prussia,* Oxford (1954), remains useful. For a splendid study of the Ordensstaat in the fifteenth century see M. Burleigh, *Prussian Society and the German Order. An Aristocratic Corporation in Crisis c. 1410–1466,* Cambridge (1984). Those interested in closer scholarship should take note of *Zeitschrift für Ostmitteleuropa,* now *Zeitschrift für Ostmitteleuropa-Forschung,* and *Jahrbücher für Geschichte Osteuropas;* the former has summaries in English, the latter publishes in English as well as German. For the Polish littoral see *Zapiski Historyczne,* Toruń.

Rus'

J.L.I. Fennell, *The Emergence of Moscow 1304–1359,* London (1968), remains the best English study, carefully delineating the Lithuanian invasions from the Russian point of view. General histories available in idem, *The Crisis of Medieval Russia 1200–1304,* London and New York (1983) and R.O. Crummey, *The Formation of Muscovy 1304–1613,* London and New York (1987).

Other works consulted

Those who read only English may still find the references and quotations in foreign articles a useful springboard to further studies.

800 Jahre Deutscher Orden (1990), ed. U. Arnold *et al.*, Gütersloh and Munich (A large, well-illustrated exhibition catalogue.)

Balticum. Studia z dziejów polityki, gospodarki i kultury XII–XVII w. (1992), ed. Z.H. Nowak, Toruń

Batūra, R. (1975), *Lietuva tautų kovoje prieš Aukso Ordą* (Lithuania in the nations' struggle against the Golden Horde), Vilnius

Birgitta hendes værk og hendes klostre i Norden (1991), ed. T. Nyberg, Odense

Birkhan, H. (1989), 'Les croisades contre les paiens de Lituanie et de Prusse. Idéologie et réalité', in D. Buschinger (ed.), *La croisade. Réalités et fictions. Actes du colloque d'Amiens 18–22 mars 1987,* Göttingen, pp. 31–50

Ekdahl, S. (1994), 'The Treatment of Prisoners of War during the Fighting between the Teutonic Order and Lithuania', in M. Barber (ed.), *The Military Orders. Fighting for the Faith and Caring for the Sick,* London, pp. 263–9

Fenske, E. and Militzer, K. (1993), *Ritterbrüder im livländischen Zweig des Deutschen Ordens,* QSBG, 12, Cologne and Vienna

Friedland, K. (1991), *Die Hanse,* Stuttgart

Geschichte der Deutschbaltischen Geschichtsschreibung (1986), ed. G. von Rauch, Cologne and Vienna

Giedroyć, M. (1992), 'The Ruthenian-Lithuanian metropolitanates and the progress of Christianisation (1300–1458)', *Nuovi studi storici,* 17: 315–42

Gudavičius, E. (1991), *Miestų atsiradimas Lietuvoje* (The development of towns in Lithuania), Vilnius

Gudavičius, E. (1992), 'Lietuvių pašauktinės kariuomenės organizacijos bruožai'

(Aspects of the organisation of Lithuanian conscript forces), *Karo archyvas* 13: 43–118

Hartknoch, C. (1679), *Selectae dissertations historicae de variis rebus prussicus*

Higounet, C. (1986), *Die deutsche Ostsiedlung im Mittelalter,* Berlin (trans. from the French)

Jensen, J.S. (1973), 'Danish Money in the Fourteenth Century', *Mediaeval Scandinavia,* 6: 161–71

Jogaila (1935), ed. A. Šapoka, Kaunas; 2nd edn, 1991

Johnsen, P. and Mühlen, H. von zur (1973), *Deutsch und Undeutsch im mittelalterlichen und frühneuzeitlichen Reval,* Cologne and Vienna

Jungbluth, G. (1969), 'Literarisches Leben in Deutschen Ritterorden', *Studien zum Deutschtum in Osten* 5: 27–51

Kłoczowski, J. (1980), 'The Mendicant Orders between the Baltic and Adriatic Seas in the Middle Ages', in S. Bylina (ed.), *La Pologne au XVe Congrès International des sciences historiques à Bucarest,* Wrocław, Warsaw, Cracow and Gdańsk, pp. 95–110

Kosman, M. (1992), *Orzeł i pogoń. Z dziejów polsko-litewskich XIV–XXw.,* Warsaw

Kričinskis, [Kryczynski], S. (1993), *Lietovos totoriari. Istorinės ir etnografinės monografijos bandymas,* trans. T. Bairasauskaitė, Vilnius

Das Kriegswesen der Ritterorden in Mittelalter (1991), ed. Z.H. Nowak, OMCTH, 6, Toruń

Kunst und Geschichte im Ostseeraum (1990), ed. E. Böckler, Homburger Gespräche, 12, Kiel

Lerdam, H. (1996). *Danske len og lensmænd 1370–1443,* Copenhagen

Lloyd, T.H. (1991), *England and the German Hanse 1157–1611. A Study of their Trade and Commercial Diplomacy,* Cambridge

Mažeika, R.J. (1987), 'Was Grand Prince Algirdas a Greek Orthodox Christian?', *Lituanus* 33, 4: 35–55

Mažeika, R.J. (1997), 'Bargaining for Baptism: Lithuanian Negotiations for Conversion, 1250–1358', in J. Muldoon (ed.), *Religious Conversion in the Middle Ages,* Gainsville, pp. 131-45

Mažeika, R.J. and Rowell, S. C. (1993), '*Zelatores Maximi:* Pope John XXII, Archbishop Frederick of Riga and the Baltic Mission 1305–1340', *AHP* 31: 33–68

Mažiulis, V. (1981), *Prūsų kalbos paminklai,* Vilnius

Nikžentaitis, A. (1989), *Gediminas,* Vilnius

Nikžentaitis, A. (1992), 'XIII–XV a. lietuvių kariuomenės bruožai (organizacija, taktika, papročiai)', *Karo archyvas* 13: 3–33

Nikžentaitis, A. (1993), 'Die friedliche Periode in den Beziehungen zwischen dem Deutschen Orden und dem Grossfürstentum Litauen (1345–1360) und das Problem der Christianisierung Litauens', *JGO* n.s. 41: 1–22

Nowak, Z.H. (1996), *Współpraca polityczna państw unii Polsko-Litewskiej i unii Kalmarskiej w latach 1411–1425* (Political cooperation between the states of the Polono-Lithuanian and Kalmar Unions, 1411–25), Toruń (German summary)

Ochmamński, J. (1986), *Dawna Litwa. Studia historyczne,* Olsztyn

Der Ost- und Nordseeraum, Politik, Ideologie, Kultur vom 12. bis zum 17. Jahrhundert (1986), ed. K. Fritze *et al.,* Hansische Studien, 7, Weimar

Pounds, N.J.G. (1974), *An Economic History of Medieval Europe,* London and New York

Riis, T. (1977), *Les institutions politiques centrales du Danemark 1100–1332,* Odense

Rowell, S.C. (1993), 'Of Men and Monsters: Sources for the History of Lithuania in the Time of Gediminas (ca. 1315–42)', *JBaS* 24: 73–112

Rowell, S.C. (1994), 'Pious Princesses or the Daughters of Belial: Pagan Lithuanian Dynastic Diplomacy 1279–1423', *Medieval Prosopography* 15: 1–77

Rowell, S. C. (1996), 'Unexpected Contacts: Lithuanians at Western Courts, c. 1316–c. 1400', *EHR* III: 557–77

Smith, J. and Urban, W. (1985), 'Peter von Suchenvirt', *Lituanus* 31, 2: 5–26

Varakauskas, R. (1982), *Lietuvos ir Livonijos santykiai XIII–XVI a.,* Vilnius

W kregu stanowych i kulturowych przeobrażeń Europy północnej w XIV–XVIII wieku (1988), ed. Z.H. Nowak, Toruń

Werkstatt des Historikers der mittelalterlichen Ritterordens, Quellenkundliche Probleme und Forschungsmethoden (1987), ed. Z.H. Nowak, OMCTH, 41, Toruń

Zur Wirtschaftsentwicklung des Deutschen Ordens im Mittelalter (1987), ed. U. Arnold, QSGDO, 38, Marburg

Zernack, K. (1993), *Nordosteuropa, Skizzen und Beiträge zu einer Geschichte der Ostseeländer,* Lüneburg

22 THE KINGDOMS OF CENTRAL EUROPE IN THE FOURTEENTH CENTURY

Primary sources

Bak, J.M. *et al.* (eds.), *The Laws of the Medieval Kingdom of Hungary, 1000–1301,* The Laws of Hungary, ser. 1, 1, Bakersfield (1989)

Döry, F. *et al.* (eds.), *Decreta Regni Hungariae: Gesetze und Verordnungen Ungarns, 1301–1457,* Budapest (1976)

Secondary works

Bak, J. (1973), *Königstum und Stände in Ungarn in 14–16. Jahrhundert,* Wiesbaden

Bak, J.M. (1987), 'Das Königreich Ungarn in Hochmittelalter 1060–1444', in F. Seibt (ed.), *Europa im Hoch- und Spätmittelalter,* Handbuch des Europäischen Geschichte, Stuttgart, II, pp. 507–32

Bardach, J. (1965), 'Gouvernants et gouvernés en Pologne au moyen âge et aux temps modernes', *APAE* 36: 255–85

Bónis, G. (1965), 'The Hungarian Feudal Diet (13th-18th Centuries)', *APAE* 36: 287–307

Bosl, K. (ed.) (1967), *Handbuch der Geschichte der Böhmischen Länder,* I: *Die Böhmischen Länder von der Archaischen Zeit bis zum Ausgang der Hussitischen Revolution;* II: *Die Böhmischen Länder von der Hochblüte der Ständeherrschaft bis zum Erwachsen eines Modernen Nationalbewusstseins,* Stuttgart

Boulton, D'A. J.D. (1987), *The Knights of the Crown. The Monarchical Orders of Knighthood in Later Medieval Europe, 1365–1520,* Woodbridge

Carter, F.W. (1987), 'Cracow's Wine Trade (Fourteenth to Eighteenth Centuries)', *SEER* 65: 537–78

Cazelles, R. (1947), *Jean l'Aveugle, comte de Luxembourg, roi de Bohême*, Bourges

Csernus, S. (1990), 'Quelques aspects européens du conflit Armagnac-Bourguignon: Sigismond et la France des partis', *114e Congrès national des Sociétés savantes, Paris 1989*, pp. 305–18

Dąbrowski, J. (1928), 'Jean de Czarnkow et sa chronique', *Bulletin international de l'Académie polonaise des sciences et des lettres. Classe de philologie-classe d'histoire et de philosophie* 7–10: 101–12

Dąbrowski, J. (1953), 'Corona Regni Poloniae au XIVe siècle', *Bulletin international de l'Académie polonaise des sciences et des lettres. Classe de philologie-classe d'histoire et de philosophie*, n° sup. 7: 41–64

David, P. (1934), *Les sources de l'histoire de Pologne à l'époque des Piast 963–1386*, Paris

Davies, N. (1981), *God's Playground, a History of Poland*, Oxford

Deletant, D. (1986), 'Moldavia between Hungary and Poland 1347–1412', *SEER* 64: 189–211

D'Eszlary, C. (1959), *Histoire des institutions publiques hongroises*, Paris

Domonkos, L.S. (1983), 'The Problem of Hungarian University Foundations in the Middle Ages', in S.B. and A.H. Vardy (eds.), *Society and Change. Studies in Honor of Béla K. Kiraly*, Boulder and New York, pp. 371–90

Dumontel, C. (1952), *L'impresa italiana di Giovanni di Lussemburgo, re di Boemia*, Turin

Dvornik, F. (1970), *Les Slaves. Histoire et civilisation de l'Antiquité aux débuts de l'époque contemporaire*, Paris

L'Eglise et le peuple chrétien dans les pays de l'Europe du Centre-Est et du Nord (XIVe–XVe siècle) (1990), Actes du Colloque organisé par l'Ecole française de Rome, les 27–29 janvier 1986, Paris and Rome

Fedorowicz, J.K. *et al.* (1982), *A Republic of Nobles. Studies in Polish History to 1864*, Cambridge

Fiala, Z. (1978), *Před-Husitské Čechy. Český Stát pod Vládou Lucemburků 1310–1419*, Prague

Fine Jr., J.V.A. (1975), *The Bosnian Church. A New Interpretation*, Boulder and New York

Fügedi, E (1986a), *Kings, Bishops, Nobles and Burghers in Medieval Hungary*, London

Fügedi, E. (1986b), *Castles and Society in Medieval Hungary (1000–1437)*, Studia Historica Academiae Scientarum Hungaricae, 187, Budapest

Gabriel, A. (1944), *Les Rapports dynastiques Franco-Hongrois au moyen âge*, Budapest

Gabriel, A. (1969), *The Medieval Universities of Pécs and Pozsony*, Notre-Dame, Ind., and Frankfurt am Main

Gazi, S. (1973), *A History of Croatia*, New York

Gerlich, A. (1960), *Hapsburg–Luxemburg–Wittelsbach im Kampf um die Deutsche Königskrone*, Wiesbaden

Giedroyć, M. (1989), 'The Arrival of Christianity in Lithuania: Baptism and Survival (1341–1386)', *OSP* n.s. 22: 34–57

Gieysztor, A. (1970), 'Economie, société et civilisation polonaises aux XIVe et XVe siècles. Essai de synthèse, état des recherches', in L. di Rosa (ed.), *Ricerche storiche ed economiche in memoria di Corrado Barbagallo*, Naples, II, pp. 199–210

Górski, K. (1966), 'The Origins of the Polish Seym', *SEER* 44: 122–38

Górski, K. (1968), 'Les débuts de la représentation de la "Communitas Nobilium" dans les assemblées d'état de l'Est européen', *APAE* 47: 37–55

Graus, F. (1960), 'Die Handelbeziehungen Böhmens zu Deutschland und Österreich im 14. und zu Beginn des 15. Jahrhunderts', *Historica* 2: 77-110

Graus, F. (1965), 'Die Entstehung des Mittelalterlichen Staaten in Mitteleuropa', *Historica* 10: 5-65

Graus, F. (1966), 'Die Bildung eines Nationalbewusstseins im Mittelalterlichen Böhmen', *Historica* 13: 5–49

Graus, F. (1980), *Die Nationenbildung der Westslawen im Mittelalter*, Sigmaringen

Guldescu, S. (1964), *History of Medieval Croatia*, The Hague

Halecki, O. (1952), *Borderlands of Western Civilization. A History of East Central Europe*, New York

Higounet, C. (1986), *Die Deutsche Ostsiedlung im Mittelalter*, Berlin

Holub, J. (1958), 'La représentation politique en Hongrie au moyen âge', *APAE* 18: 77–121

Housley, N. (1984), 'King Louis the Great of Hungary and the Crusades, 1342–1382', *SEER* 62: 192–208

Janáček, J. (1973), 'L'Argent tchèque et la Méditerranée (XIVe et XVe siècles)', in *Histoire économique du monde méditerranéen. Mélanges en l'honneur de Fernand Braudel*, Paris, 1, pp. 245–61

Joris, A. (1971), 'Documents concernant la commune de Huy avec la Bohême et la Haute-Meuse (XIIIe–XIVe siècles)', *BCRH* 137: 1–37

Kejř, J. (1966), 'Les impôts dans les villes médiévales de Bohême', in *L'Impôt dans le cadre de la ville et de l'état*, Historische Uitgaven, 13, pp. 208–31

Kejř, J. (1968), 'Les privilèges des villes de Bohême depuis les origines jusqu'aux guerres hussites (1419)', in *Les Libertés urbaines et rurales du XIIe au XIVe siècles*, Brussels, pp. 79–90

Kejř, J. (1969), 'Zwei Studien über die Anfänge der Städteverfassung in den Böhmischen Ländern', *Historica* 16: 81–142

Kejř, J. (1972), 'Organisation und Verwaltung des Königlichen Städtewesens in Böhmen zur Zeit der Luxemburger', in W. Rausch (ed.), *Stadt und Stadtherr im 14. Jahrhundert*, Linz, pp. 79–90

Kieniewicz, S. (ed.) (1971), *Histoire de Pologne*, Warsaw

Kłoczowski, J. (1967), 'Les ordres mendiants en Pologne à la fin du moyen âge', *APH* 15: 5–38

Kłoczowski, J. (1987), *Histoire religieuse de la Pologne*, Paris

Knoll, P.W. (1972), *The Rise of the Polish Monarchy. Piast Poland in East-Central Europe, 1320–1370*, London

Köpeczi, B. (ed.) (1992), *Histoire de Transylvanie*, Budapest

Kozlowska-Budkowa, S. (1985), 'The Foundation of the University of Cracow', in *Poland in Christian Civilisation*, London, pp. 165–79

Kubinyi, A. (1972), *Der Ungarische König und seine Städte im 14. und am Beginn des 15. Jahrhunderts*, Linz

Labuda, G. (1970), 'Die Entstehung des Mittelalterlichen Staats und die Entwicklung des Polnischen Kultur', *APH* 21: 93–107

Lalik, T. (1976), 'La génèse du réseau urbain en Pologne médiévale', *APH* 34: 97–120

Ludwig, M. (1984), *Besteuerung und Verpfandung Königlicher Städte im Spätmittelalterlichen Polen*, Osteuropastudien der Hochschulen des Landes Hessens, Reihe I. Giessener Abhandlungen zur Agrar- und Wirtschaftforschung des Europäischen Ostens, 126, Berlin

Macek, J. (1984), *Histoire de la Bohême des origines à 1918*, Paris

Magocsi, P.R. (1985a), *Galicia. A Historical Survey and Bibliographic Guide*, Toronto, Buffalo and London

Magocsi, P.R. (1985b), *Ukraine. A Historical Atlas*, Toronto, Buffalo and London

Makkai, L. (1946), *Histoire de Transylvanie*, Paris

Małowist, M. (1972), *Croissance et régression en Europe XIVe–XVIIIe siècles*, Paris

Mályusz, E. (1965), 'Les débuts du vote de la taxe par les ordres dans la Hongrie féodale', *Nouvelles études historiques* 1: 55–82

Mályusz, E. (1980), 'Die Entstehung der Ständischen Schichten im Mittelalterlichen Ungarn', *EHH* 1: 101–32

Mályusz, E. (1990), *Kaiser Sigismond in Ungarn 1387–1437*, Budapest

Matuszewski, J.S. (1985), 'La signification des privilèges fiscaux de Louis de Hongrie en Pologne', *APH* 51: 33–50

Mezník, J. (1969), 'Der Ökonomische Charakter Prags im 14. Jahrhundert', *Historica* 17: 43–91

Molenda, D. (1976), 'Mining Towns in Central-Eastern Europe in Feudal Time: Problem Outline', *APH* 34: 165–88

Pach, Zs. P. (1975), 'Levantine Trade and Hungary in the Middle Ages (Theses, Controversies, Arguments)', *EHH* 1: 283–307

Pamlényi, E. (ed.) (1974), *Histoire de la Hongrie des origines à nos jours*, Budapest

Preveden, F.R. (1955), *A History of the Croatian People*, 1: *Prehistory and Early Period until 1397*, New York

Pustejovsky, O. (1965–7), 'Zur Geschichte der Böhmischen Länder im 14. Jahrhundert. 30 Jahre Tschechischer und Slowakischer Forschung, 1935–64, 1967', *JGO* 13: 65–106; 15: 99–130 and 251–76

Pustejovsky, O. (1975), *Schlesiens Übergang an die Böhmische Krone. Machtpolitik Böhmens im Zeichen von Herrschaft und Frieden*, Forschungen und Quellen zur Kirche- und Kulturgeschichte Ostdeutschlands, 13, Cologne and Vienna

Reddaway, W.F. *et al.* (eds.) (1950), *The Cambridge History of Poland. From the Origins to Sobieski (to 1696)*, Cambridge

Russocki, S. (1974), 'Les assemblées préreprésentatives en Europe centrale. Préliminaire d'une analyse comparative', *APH* 30: 33–52

Schlesinger, W. (ed.) (1975), *Die Deutsche Ostsiedlung des Mittelalters als Problem der Europäischen Geschichte*, VF, XVIII, Sigmaringen

Seibt, F. (ed.) (1974), *Bohemia Sacra. Das Christentum in Böhmen, 973–1973*, Düsseldorf

Seibt, F. (1987), 'Polen von der Jahrhundertwende bis 1444', in F. Seibt (ed.), *Europa im Hoch- und Spätmittelalter,* Handbuch der Europäischen Geschichte, Stuttgart, II, pp. 1042–79

Šmahel, F. (1969), 'The Idea of the "Nation" in Hussite Bohemia. An Analytical Study of the Ideological and Political Aspects of the National Question in Hussite Bohemia from the End of the 14th Century to the Eighties of the 15th Century', *Historica* 16: 143–247

Šmahel, F. (1987), 'Die Böhmischen Länder im Hoch- und Spätmittelalter c. 1050–1452' in F. Seibt (ed.), *Europa im Hoch- und Spätmittelalter*, Handbuch der Europäischen Geschichte, Stuttgart, II, pp. 507–32

Spěváček, J. (1971), 'Statuts luxembourgeois donnés en 1333 à la ville de Lucques', *Historica* 18: 59–104

Spěváček, J. (1982), *Král Diplomat Jan Lucemburský 1296–1346*, Prague

Spieralski, Z. (1980), 'Die Jagiellonische Verbundenheit bis zum Ende des 15. Jahrhunderts', *APH* 41: 51–83

Sułkowska-Kurasiowa, I. (1980), 'Les conseillers de Ladislas Jagellon (1386–1434)', *APH* 42: 27–40

Troubert, O. (1988), 'Beatrix de Bourbon, reine de Bohême', *AE* 5th series 40: 252–80

Vardy, S.B., Grosschmid, G. and Domonkos, L.S. (eds.) (1986), *Louis the Great. King of Hungary and Poland*, New York

Weczerka, H. (1982), 'Les routes terrestres de la Hanse', *Flaran 2. L'homme et la route en Europe occidentale au moyen âge et aux temps modernes*, Auch, pp. 85–105

Wiesiołowski, J. (1981), 'Le réseau urbain en Grande-Pologne aux XIIIe–XVIe siècles. L'espace et la société', *APH* 43: 5–29

Wyrozumski, J. (1978a), 'La société úrbaine en Pologne au bas moyen âge', *RN* 60: 31–41

Wyrozumski, J. (1978b), 'Le sel dans la vie économique de la Pologne médiévale', *Studi in memoria di Frederigo Melis*, Naples, II, pp. 497–506

Zientara, B. (1974), 'Foreigners in Poland in the 10th–15th Centuries: Their Role in the Opinion of the Polish Medieval Community', *APH* 24: 5–28

23 THE PRINCIPALITIES OF RUS' IN THE FOURTEENTH CENTURY

Selected primary sources

Akty feodal'nogo zemlevladeniia i khoziaistva XIV–XVI vekov, 3 vols., Moscow (1951–61)

Akty istoricheskie, 5 vols., St Petersburg (1841–2). *Dopolneniia k Aktam istoricheskim*, 12 vols., St Petersburg (1846–72)

Akty istoricheskie, otn. k Rossii, izvlechennye iz inostrannykh arkhivov i bibliotek . . . A.K. Turgenevym, 3 vols., St Petersburg (1841–8). *Dopolneniia k Aktam istoricheskim . . . Turgenevym*, St Petersburg (1848)

Akty, otnosiashchiesia k istorii Iuzhnoi i Zapadnoi Rossii, 15 vols., St Petersburg (1863–92)

Akty, otnosiashchiesia k istorii Zapadnoi Rossii, 5 vols., St Petersburg (1846–53)

Akty, sobrannye v bibliotekakh i arkhivakh Rossiiskoi imperii Arkheograficheskoiu ekspeditsieiu . . ., 4 vols., St Petersburg (1836)

Akty sotsial'no-ekonomicheskoi istorii severo-vostochnoi Rusi kontsa XIV–nachala XVI v., 3 vols., Moscow (1952–6)

Drevnerusskaia slavianskaia kormchaia XIV titulov bez tolkovanii, ed. A.V. Beneshevich, St Petersburg (1906)

Drevnerusskie kniazheskie ustavy. XI–XV vv., ed. Ia. N. Shchapov, Moscow (1976)

Dukhovnye i dogovornye gramoty velikikh i udel'nykh kniazei XIV–XVI vv., Moscow and Leningrad (1950)

Gramoty Velikogo Novgoroda i Pskova, Moscow (1949)

Merilo pravednoe, ed. M.N. Tikhomirov and L.V. Milov, Moscow (1961)
Novgorodskaia pervaia letopis' starshego i mladshego izvodov, ed. A.N. Nasonov and M.N. Tikhomirov, Moscow and Leningrad (1950)
Novgorodskie gramoty na bereste: iz raskopok 1951–, ed. A.V. Artsikhovskii, 6 vols., Moscow (1953–)
Pamiatniki literatury drevnei Rusi. XIV–seredina XV veka, Moscow (1981)
Pamiatniki russkogo prava, 8 vols., Moscow (1952–63)
Polnoe sobranie russkikh letopisei, 41 vols., to date, St Petersburg and Moscow (1841–)
Pskovskie letopisi, ed. A.N. Nasonov, 2 fascs., Moscow (1941–51)
Rossiiskoe zakonodatel'stvo X–XX vekov v deviati tomakh, 9 vols., to date, Moscow (1984–94)
Sobranie gosudarstvennykh gramot i dogovorov, 5 vols., Moscow (1813–94)
Troitskaia letopis'. Rekonstruktsiia teksta, ed. M.D. Priselkov, Moscow (1950)
Zakon sudnyi liudem kratkoi redaktsii, ed. M.N. Tikhomirov, Moscow (1961)
Zakonodatel'nye akty Velikogo kniazhestva litovskogo XV–XVI vv., Leningrad (1936)

Secondary works

Chronicle writing

Kuzmin, A.G. (1965), *Riazanskoe letopisanie*, Moscow
Likhachev, D.S. (1947), *Russkie letopisi i ikh kul'turnoi-storicheskoe znachenie*, Moscow and Leningrad
Lur'e, Ia. S. (1976), *Obshcherusskie letopisi XIV–XV vv.*, Leningrad
Murav'eva, L.L. (1983), *Letopisanie severo-vostochnoi Rusi kontsa XIII-nachala XV veka*, Moscow
Nasonov, A.N. (1930), 'Letopisnye pamiatniki Tver'skogo kniazhestva', *Izvestiia Akademii nauk SSSR. Seriia 7: Otdelenie gumanitarnykh nauk* 9–10: 709–73
Nasonov, A.N. (1969), *Istoriia russkogo letopisaniia XI–nachala XVIII veka*, Moscow
Priselkov, M.D. (1940a), *Istoriia russkogo letopisaniia XI–XV vv.*, Leningrad
Priselkov, M.D. (1940b), 'Letopisanie Zapadnoi Ukrainy i Belorussii', *Uchenye zapiski Leningradskogo gosudarstvennogo universiteta. Seriia istoricheskikh nauk* 7 67: 5–24
Shakhmatov, A.A. (1908), *Razyskaniia o drevneishikh russkikh letopisnykh svodakh*, St Petersburg
Shakhmatov, A.A. (1938), *Obozrenie russkikh letopisnykh svodov XIV–XVI vv.*, Moscow and Leningrad
Ulashchik, N.N. (1985), *Vvedenie v izuchenie belorusskogo-litovskogo letopisaniia*, Moscow

Political history of north-east Rus'

Antonovich, V.B. (1885), *Monografii po istorii zapadnoi i iugo-zapadnoi Rossii*, 1, Kiev
Bardach, Juliusz (1970), *Studia z ustroju i prawa Wielkiego księstwa litewskiego, XIV–XVII w.*, Warsaw
Bernadskii, V.N. (1961), *Novgorod i novgorodskaia zemlia v XV veke*, Moscow and Leningrad
Birnbaum, Henrik (1981), *Lord Novgorod the Great*, 1, Columbus, Ohio
Borzakovskii, V.S. (1876), *Istoriia tverskogo kniazhestva*, St Petersburg

Cherepnin, L.V. (1948–51), *Russkie feodal'nye arkhivy XIV–XV vekov*, 2 vols., Moscow and Leningrad

Cherepnin, L. V. (1960), *Obrazovanie russkogo tsentralizovannogo gosudarstva v XIV–XV vekakh*, Moscow

Crummey, Robert O. (1987), *The Formation of Muscovy, 1304–1613*, London and New York

Dollinger, Philippe (1970), *The German Hansa*, London and Stanford, Calif.

Ekzempliarskii, A.V. (1889–91), *Velikie i udel'nye kniazia severnoi Rusi v tatarskoi period, s 1238 po 1505 g.*, 2 vols., St Petersburg

Fennell, J.L.I. (1968), *The Emergence of Moscow, 1304–1359*, Berkeley

Floria, B.N. (1992), *Otnosheniia gosudarstva i tserkvi u vostochnykh i zapadykh slavian*, Moscow

Grekov, B.D. and Iakubovskii, A. Iu. (1950), *Zolotaia orda i ee padenie*, Moscow

Grekov, I.B. (1975), *Vostochnaia Evropa i upadok Zolotoi Ordy*, Moscow

Grekov, I.B. and Shakhmagonov, F.F. (1986), *Mir istorii. Russkie zemli v XIII–XV vekakh*, Moscow

Halperin, Charles (1985), *Russia and the Golden Horde. The Mongol Impact on Medieval Russian History*, Bloomington, Ind.

Hrushevsky, Mykhailo (1941), *A History of Ukraine*, New Haven

Hrushevsky, Mykhailo (1952), 'The Traditional Scheme of "Russian" History and the Problem of a Rational Organization of the History of Eastern Slavs', *The Annals of the Ukrainian Academy of Arts and Sciences in the U.S.* 2: 355–64

Ianin, V.L. (1962), *Novgorodskie posadniki*, Moscow

Ianin, V.L. (1970), *Aktovye pechati drevnei Rusi X–XV vv.*, Moscow

Istoriia Kieva (1982–6), 3 vols., in 4 bks, Kiev

Istoriia Moskvy (1952–9), 6 vols., in 7 pts, Moscow

Kafengauz, B.B. (1969), *Drevnii Pskov. Ocherki po istorii feodal'noi respubliki*, Moscow

Karamzin, N.M. (1842–3), *Istoriia gosudarstva rossiiskogo*, 5th edn, 12 vols., in 3 bks, St Petersburg

Karger, M.K. (1973), *Novgorod the Great*, Moscow

Kashtanov, S.M. (1988), *Finansy srednevekovoi Rusi*, Moscow

Kazakova, N.A. (1975), *Russko-livonskie i russko-ganzeiskie otnosheniia. Konets XIV–nachalo XVI v.*, Leningrad

Khoroshev, A.S. (1980), *Tserkov' v sotsial'no-politicheskoi sisteme novgorodskoi feodal'noi respubliki*, Moscow

Khoroshkevich, A.L. (1982), 'Istoricheskie sud'by belorusskikh i ukrainskikh zemel' v XIV–nachale XVI v.', in V.T. Pashuto, B.N. Floria and A.L. Khoroshkevich, *Drevnerusskoe nasledie i istoricheskie sud'by vostochnogo slavianstva*, Moscow, pp. 69–150

Kireevskii, I.V. (1966), 'On the Nature of European Culture and its Relation to the Culture of Russia', in Marc Raeff (ed.), *Russian Intellectual History. An Anthology*, New York, pp. 174–207

Kizilov, Iu. A. (1984), *Zemli i narody Rossii v XIII–XV vv.*, Moscow

Kliuchevskii, V.O. (1956–8), *Kurs russkoi istorii*, I–V, of Kiuchevskii (1956–9)

Kliuchevskii, V.O. (1956–9), *Sochineniia*, 8 vols., Moscow

Klug, Ekkehard (1985), 'Das Fürstentum Tver'. 1247–1485', *FOG* 37: 7–355

Kolankowski, Ludwig (1930), *Dzieje wielkiego ksiestwa litewskiego za Jagiełłonów*, Warsaw

Kolankowski, Ludwig (1936), *Polska Jagiełłonów. Dzieje polityczne*, Lwów

Kostomarov, N.I. (1903–6), *Sobranie sochinenii. Istoricheskie monografii i issledovaniia*, 8 vols., St Petersburg

Kuchkin, V.A. (1984), *Formirovanie gosudarstvennoi territorii severo-vostochnoi Rusi v X–XIV vv.*, Moscow

Langer, Lawrence (1974), 'V.L. Ianin and the History of Novgorod', *SR* 33: 114–19

Langer, Lawrence (1984), 'The Posadnichestvo of Pskov: Some Aspects of Urban Administration in Medieval Russia', *SR* 43: 46–62

Leontovich, F.I. (1893–4), *Ocherki istorii litovsko-russkogo prava*, St Petersburg

Liubavskii, M.K. (1910), *Ocherki istorii litovsko-russkogo gosudarstva do Liublinskoi unii vkliuchitel'no*, Moscow

Liubavskii, M.K. (1918), *Lektsii po drevnei russkoi istorii do kontsa XVI veka*, 3rd edn, Moscow

Liubavskii, M.K. (1929), *Obrazovanie osnovnoi gosudarstvennoi territorii velikorusskoi narodnosti*, Leningrad

Martin, Janet (1983), 'Muscovy's Northeastern Expansion: The Context and a Cause', *CMRS* 24: 459–70

Meyendorff, John (1980), *Byzantium and the Rise of Russia. A Study of Byzantino-Russian Relations in the Fourteenth Century*, Cambridge

Miliukov, P.N. (1930–64), *Ocherki po istorii russkoi kul'tury*, 3 vols., Paris

Nasonov, A.N. (1940), *Mongoly i Rus'. Istoriia tatarskoi politiki na Rusi*, Moscow

Nasonov, A.N. (1951), '*Russkaia zemlia' i obrazovanie territorii drevnerusskogo gosudarstva. Istoriko-geograficheskoe issledovanie*, Moscow

Ocherki istorii SSSR. Period feodalizma IX–XV vv. (1953), ed. B.D. Grekov *et al.*, 2 pts, Moscow

Ochmański, Jerzy (1967), *Historia Litwy*, Wrocław

Ostrowski, Donald (1990), 'The Mongol Origins of Muscovite Political Institutions', *SR* 49: 525–42

Pashuto, B.T. (1959), *Obrazovanie litovskogo gosudarstva*, Moscow

Pickhan, G. (1992), *Gospodin Pskov. Entstehung und Entwicklung eines städtischen Herrschaftszentrums in Altrussland*, *FOG* 47

Presniakov, A.E. (1918a), *Moskovskoe tsarstvo*, Petrograd

Presniakov, A.E. (1918b), *Obrazovanie velikorusskogo gosudarstva*, Petrograd

Presniakov, A.E. (1938–2), *Lektsii po russkoi istorii*, 2 vols., Moscow

Rowell, S.C. (1993), 'Of Men and Monsters: Sources for the History of Lithuania in the Time of Gediminas (ca. 1315–1342)', *JBaS* 24: 73–112

Rowell, S.C. (1994), *Lithuania Ascending. A Pagan Empire within East-Central Europe, 1295–1345*, Cambridge

Russ, Hartmut (1975), *Adel und Adelsoppositionen im Moskauer Staat*, Wiesbaden

Sergeevich, V.I. (1902), *Russkie iuridicheskie drevnosti*, 1, *Territoriia i naselenie*, 2nd edn, St Petersburg

Sergeevich, V.I. (1903–9), *Drevnosti russkogo prava*, 3 vols., 3rd edn, St Petersburg

Solov'ev, S.M. (1959–62), *Istoriia Rossii s drevneishikh vremen*, 29 vols., in 15 bks, Moscow

Subtelny, Orest (1988), *Ukraine. A History*, Toronto

Thompson, Michael W. (1967), *Novgorod the Great*, New York

Tikhomirov, M.N. (1947), *Drevniaia Moskva (XII–XV vv.)*, Moscow

Tikhomirov, M.N. (1952), 'Moskva – stolitsa Moskovskogo velikogo kniazhestva XIV v. – vtoraia polovina XV v.', in *Istoriia Moskvy* (1952–9), 1, pp. 26–64

Tikhomirov, M.N. (1957), *Srednevekovaia Moskva v XIV–XV vekakh,* Moscow

Tikhomirov, M.N. (1966), *Srednevekovaia Rossiia na mezhdunarodnykh putiakh (XIV–XV vv.),* Moscow

Vernadsky, George (1953), *The Mongols and Russia,* New Haven and London

Culture and ideology

Andreyev, Nikolay (1977), 'Literature in the Muscovite Period (1300–1700)', in Robert Auty and Dimitri Obolensky (eds.), *An Introduction to Russian Language and Literature,* Cambridge, pp. 90–110

Birnbaum, Henrik (1977), 'Lord Novgorod the Great: Its Place in Medieval Culture', *Viator* 8: 215–54

Borisov, N.S. (1986), *Russkaia tserkov' v politicheskoi bor'be XIV–XV vekov,* Moscow

Budovnits, I.U. (1960), *Obshchestvenno-politicheskaia mysl' drevnei Rusi (XI–XIV vv.),* Moscow

D'iakonov, M.A. (1889), *Vlast' moskovskikh gosudarei: Ocherki iz istorii politicheskikh idei drevnei Rusi do kontsa XVI veka,* St Petersburg

Fedotov, G.P. (1966), *The Russian Religious Mind,* II: *The Middle Ages. The Thirteenth to the Fifteenth Centuries,* Cambridge, Mass.

Floria, B.N. (1993), 'Istoricheskie sud'by Rusi i etnicheskoe samosoznanie vostochnykh slavian v XII–XV vekakh (k voprosu o zarozhdenii vostochnoslavianskikh narodnostei)', *Slavianovedenie* 2: 42–66

Gol'dberg, A.L. (1975), 'Istoriko-politicheskie idei russkoi knizhnosti XV–XVII vekov', *Istoriia SSSR* 5: 60–77

Golubinskii, E.E. (1901–10), *Istoriia russkoi tserkvi,* 2 vols. in 4 pts, Moscow

Halperin, Charles (1976), 'The Russian Land and the Russian Tsar: The Emergence of Muscovite Ideology, 1380–1408', *FOG* 23: 7–103

Karger, M.K. (1973), *Novgorod the Great. Architectural Guidebook,* Moscow

Kartashev, A.V. (1959), *Ocherki po istorii russkoi tserkvi,* 2 vols., Paris

Kazakova, N.A., and Lur'e, Ia. S. (1955), *Antifeodal'nye ereticheskie dvizheniia na Rusi XIV–nachala XVI veka,* Moscow and Leningrad

Khoroshev, A.S. (1986), *Politicheskaia istoriia russkoi kanonizatsii (XI–XVI vv.),* Moscow

Kliuchevskii, V.O. (1871), *Drevnerusskie zhitiia kak istoricheskii istochnik,* Moscow

Lazarev, V.N. (1966), *Old Russian Murals and Mosaics from the XI to the XVI Century,* London

Lazarev, V.N. (1976), *Novgorodskaia ikonopisi,* 2nd edn, Moscow

Lazarev, V.N. (1980), *Moskovskaia shkola ikonopis',* Moscow

Likhachev, D.S. (1958), *Chelovek v literature drevnei Rusi,* Leningrad

Likhachev, D.S. (1967), *Poetika drevnerusskoi literatury,* Leningrad

Likhachev, D.S. (1973), *Razvitie russkoi literatury X–XVII vekov. Epokhi i stili,* Leningrad

Likhachev, D.S. (1987), *Velikii put'. Stanovlenie russkoi literatury XI–XVII vekov,* Moscow

Makarii, metropolitan of Moscow (1857–87), *Istoriia russkoi tserkvi,* 12 vols., St Petersburg

Miller, David E. (1979), 'The "Velikie Minei Chetii" and the "Stepennaia kniga" of Metropolitan Makarii and the Origins of Russian National Consciousness', *FOG* 26: 263–382

Ocherki russkoi kul'tury XIII–XV vekov (1969), 2 pts, Moscow

Okinshevich, Leo (1953), *The Law of the Grand Duchy of Lithuania. Background and Bibliography*, New York

Pautkin, A.A. (1989), 'Kharakteristika lichnosti v letopis'nykh kniazheskikh nekrologakh', in *Germenevtika drevnerusskoi literatury. XI–XVI veka*, Moscow, pp. 231–46

Pelenski, Jaroslaw (1977), 'The Origins of the Official Muscovite Claim to the "Kievan Inheritance"', *HUS* 1: 29–52

Pelenski, Jaroslaw (1983), 'The Emergence of the Muscovite Claims to the Byzantine-Kievan "Imperial Inheritance"', *HUS* 7: 520–31

Philipp, Werner (1983), 'Die religiöse Begründung der altrussischen Hauptstadt', *FOG* 33: 227–38

Rowland, Daniel (1979), 'The Problem of Advice in Muscovite Tales of the Time of Troubles', *RuH* 6: 259–83

Salmina, M.A. (1966), '"Letopisnaia povest'" o Kulikovskoi bitve i "Zadonshchina"', in *'Slovo o polku Igoreve', i pamiatniki Kulikovskogo tsikla. K voprosu o vremeni napisaniia Slova'*, Moscow and Leningrad, pp. 344–84

Salmina, M.A. (1970), 'Slovo o zhitii i o prestavlenii velikogo kniazia Dmitriia Ivanovicha, tsaria Rus'kogo', *TODL* 25: 81–104

Salmina, M.A. (1974), 'K voprosu o datirovke "Skazaniia o Mamaevom poboishche"', *TODL* 29: 98–124

Salmina, M.A. (1977), 'Eshche raz o datirovke "Letopisnoi povesti" o Kulikovskoi bitve', *TODL* 32: 3–39

Slovar' knizhnikov i knizhnosti drevnei Rusi (1987–9), 3 vols., in 5 pts to date, Leningrad

Smirnova, E.E. (1989), *Moscow Icons*, Oxford

Stökl, Günther (1981), 'Staat und Kirche im Moskauer Russland. Die vier Moskauer Wundertäter', *JGO* 29: 481–93

Szeftel, Marc (1979), 'The Title of the Muscovite Monarch up to the End of the Seventeenth Century', *Canadian-American Slavic Studies* 13: 59–81

Tikhomirov, M.N. (1968), *Russkaia kul'tura X–XVIII vekov*, Moscow

Tikhomirov, N. Ia. and Ivanov, V.N. (1967), *Moskovskii kreml'. Istoriia arkhitektury*, Moscow

Val'denberg, Vladimir (1916), *Drevnerusskie ucheniia o predelakh tsarskoi vlasti*, Petrograd

Zimin, A.A. (1972), 'Antichnye motivy v russkoi publitsistike kontsa XV v.', in *Feodal'naia Rossiia vo vsemirnom istoricheskom protsesse*, Moscow, pp. 128–38

Governance

Baron, Samuel H. (1977), 'Feudalism or the Asiatic Mode of Production: Alternative Interpretations of Russian History', in Samuel H. Baron and Nancy W. Heer (eds.), *Windows on the Russian Past*, Columbus, Ohio, pp. 24–41

Bloch, Marc (1970), *Feudal Society*, trans. L. A. Manyon, 2 vols. Chicago

Blum, Jerome (1961), *Lord and Peasant in Russia from the Ninth to the Nineteenth Century*, New York

Brown, Elizabeth A.R. (1974), 'The Tyranny of a Construct: Feudalism and Historians of Medieval Europe', *AmHR*, 79: 1063–88

Cherepnin, L.V. (1940), 'Iz istorii drevnerusskikh feodal'nykh otnoshenii XIV–XVI vv.', *IZ* 9: 31–78

Crummey, Robert O. (1984), 'Periodizing "Feudal" Russian History', in R.C. Elwood (ed.), *Russian and East European History. Selected Papers*, Berkeley, pp. 17–41

D'iakonov, M. A. (1908), *Ocherki obshchestvennogo i gosudarstvennogo stroia drevnei Rusi*, 2nd edn, St Petersburg

Eck, Alexandre (1933), *Le moyen âge russe*, Paris

Gorskii, A.D. (1982), 'O votchinnom sude na Rusi v XIV–XV vv.', in *Rossiia na putiakh tsentralizatsii. Sbornik statei*, Moscow, pp. 25–35

Halbach, Uwe (1985), *Der russische Fürstenhof vor dem 16. Jahrhundert*, Stuttgart

Howes, Robert Craig (trans. and ed.) (1967), *The Testaments of the Grand Princes of Moscow*, Ithaca, N.Y.

Kaiser, Daniel H. (1980), *The Growth of the Law in Medieval Russia*, Princeton, N.J.

Kashtanov, S. M. (1982), 'Finansovoe ustroistvo Moskovskogo kniazhestva v seredine XIV v. po dannym dukhovnykh gramot', in *Issledovaniia po istorii i istoriografii feodalizma*, Moscow, pp. 173–89

Kliuchevskii, V.O. (1919), *Boiarskaia duma drevnei Rusi*, 5th edn, St Petersburg

Kliuchevskii, V.O. (1959), *Istoriia soslovii v Rossii*, VI, of Kliuchevskii (1956–9)

Kollmann, Nancy Shields (1987), *Kinship and Politics. The Making of the Muscovite Political System. 1345–1547*, Stanford, Calif.

Kollmann, Nancy Shields (1990), 'Collateral Succession in Kievan Rus'', *HUS* 14: 377–87

Kotliarov, A.N. (1985), 'Boiarskii "gorod" v XIV veke', in *Feodalizm v Rossii*, Moscow, pp. 84–7

Levin, Eve (1983), 'The Role and Status of Women in Medieval Novgorod', PhD dissertation, Indiana University

Limonov, Iu. A. (1987), *Vladimiro-Suzdal'skaia Rus'. Ocherki sotsial'no-politicheskoi istorii*, Moscow

Nazarov, V.D. (1978), '"Dvor" i "dvoriane" po dannym novgorodskogo i severo-vostochnogo letopisaniia (XII–XIV vv.)', in *Vostochnaia Evropa v drevnosti i srednevekov'e. Sbornik statei*, Moscow, pp. 104–23

Pavlov-Sil'vanskii, N.P. (1988), *Feodalizm v Rossii*, Moscow

Phillip, Werner (1980), 'Zur Frage nach der Existenz altrussischer Stände', *FOG* 27: 64–76

Pipes, Richard (1974), *Russia under the Old Regime*, New York

Poe, Marshall (1993), '"Russian Despotism": The Origins and Dissemination of an Early Modern Commonplace', PhD dissertation, University of California, Berkeley

Sergeevich, V.I. (1887), 'Vol'nye i nevol'nye slugi moskovskikh gosudarei', *Nabliudatel'*, 6: 58–89

Sergeevich, V.I. (1904), *Lektsii i issledovaniia po drevnei istorii russkogo prava*, 3rd edn, St Petersburg

Szeftel, Marc (1965), 'Aspects of Feudalism in Russian History', in Rushton Coulborn (ed.), *Feudalism in History*, Hamden, Conn., pp. 167–82

Vernadsky, George (1939), 'Feudalism in Russia', *Speculum* 14: 300–23

Veselovskii, S.B. (1926), *K voprosu o proiskhozhdenii votchinnogo rezhima*, Moscow

Veselovskii, S.B. (1936), *Selo i derevnia v severo-vostochnoi Rusi XIV–XVI vv.*, Moscow and Leningrad

Veselovskii, S.B. (1947), *Feodal'noe zemlevladenie v severo-vostochnoi Rusi*, 1 vol. in 2 pts, Moscow and Leningrad

Veselovskii, S.B. (1969), *Issledovaniia po istorii klassa sluzhilykh zemlevladel'tsev,* Moscow

Vladimirskii-Budanov, M.F. (1909), *Obzor istorii russkogo prava*, 6th edn, St Petersburg

Zimin, A. A. (1973), *Kholopy na Rusi (s drevneishikh vremen do kontsa XV v.)*, Moscow

Trade and agrarian life

Bater, James H. and French, R.A. (eds.) (1983), *Studies in Russian Historical Geography*, 2 vols., London

Budovnits, I.U. (1966), *Monastyri na Rusi i bor'ba s nimi krest'ian v XIV–XVI v.*, Moscow

Cherepnin, L.V. and Nazarov, V.D. (1986), 'Krest'ianstvo na Rusi v seredine XII–kontse XV v.', in *Istoriia krest'ianstva v Evrope*, II: *Epokha feodalizma*, Moscow, pp. 250–86

Danilova, L.V. (1955), *Ocherki po istorii zemlevladenii i khoziaistva v Novgorodskoi zemle v XIV–XV vv.*, Moscow

Gorskii, A.D. (1966), *Ocherki ekonomicheskogo polozheniia krest'ian severo-vostochnoi Rusi XIV–XV vv.*, Moscow

Grekov, B.D. (1952–4), *Krest'iane na Rusi s drevneishikh vremen do XVII veka*, 2 vols., 2nd edn, Moscow

Kazakova, N.A. (1945), *Rus' i Pribaltika. IX–XVII vv.*, Leningrad

Khoroshkevich, A.L. (1963), *Torgovlia Velikogo Novgoroda s Pribaltikoi i Zapadnoi Evropoi v XIV–XV vekakh*, Moscow

Kochin, G.E. (1965), *Sel'skoe khoziaistvo na Rusi v period obrazovaniia Russkogo tsentralizovannogo gosudarstva konets XIII–nachalo XVI v.*, Moscow and Leningrad

Martin, Janet (1975), 'Les uškujniki de Novgorod: marchands ou pirates?', *Cahiers du monde russe et soviétique* 16: 5–18

Martin, Janet (1986), *Treasure of the Land of Darkness. The Fur Trade and its Significance for Medieval Russia*, Cambridge

Sakharov, A.M. (1959), *Goroda severo-vostochnoi Rusi XIV–XV vekov*, Moscow

Shapiro, A.L. (1977), *Problemy sotsial'no-ekonomicheskoi istorii Rusi XIV–XVI vv.*, Leningrad

Shapiro, L. (1987), *Russkoe krestianstvo pered zakreposhcheniem XIV–XVI vv.*, Leningrad

Smirnov, P.P. (1947–8), *Posadskie liudi i ikh klassovaia bor'ba do serediny XVII v.*, 2 vols., Moscow and Leningrad

Smith, R.E.F. (1966), 'Medieval Agrarian Society in its Prime: Russia', in *CEHE*, I, pp. 507–47

Syroechkovskii, V.E. (1936), *Gosti surozhanie*, Moscow and Leningrad

24 THE BYZANTINE EMPIRE IN THE FOURTEENTH CENTURY

Primary sources

Actes de Chilander (= *Actes de l'Athos*, v), ed. L. Petit, St Petersburg (1911); repr. Amsterdam (1975)

Akindynos, Gregory, *Letters of Gregory Akendynos*, ed. A. Hero, Washington, DC (1983)

Archives de l'Athos, ed. P. Lemerle, N. Oikonomidès, J. Lefort *et al.*, Paris (1937–)

Cantacuzeni, Iohannis, *Eximperatoris Historiarum Libri IV*, ed. L. Schopen, 3 vols., *CSHB*, Bonn (1828–32)

Chrysostomides, J., *Manuel II Palaeologus. Funeral Oration on his Brother Theodore*, Thessaloniki (1985)

Démétrius Cydonès correspondance, ed. G. Cammelli, Paris (1930)

Démétrius Cydonès correspondance, ed. R.J. Loenertz, ST, 186, 208, Vatican City (1956–60)

Dennis, G.T., *The Letters of Manuel II Palaeologus*, Washington, DC (1977)

Diplomatarium Veneto-Levantinum, I: *1300–1350*; II: *1351–1454*, ed. G.M. Thomas, Venice (1880–99)

Dölger, F., *Aus den Schatzkammern des Heiligen Berges*, Munich (1948)

Dölger, F., *Sechs byzantinische Praktika des 14. Jahrhunderts für das Athoskloster Iberon*, Munich (1949)

Ducae Istoria Turco-Byzantina (1341–1462), ed. B. Grecu, Bucharest (1958)

Ducas, *Historia Byzantina*, ed. I. Bekker, *CSHB*, Bonn (1830)

Ducas, *Istorija Turco-Bizantina 1341–1462*, ed. V. Grecu, Bucharest (1958)

Faturos, G., *Die Briefe des Michael Gabras (ca. 1290–nach 1350)*, 2 vols., Vienna (1973)

Grégoire, H. (ed.) (1959–60), 'Imperatoris Michaelis Palaeologi "De Vita Sua"', *Byzantion* 29–30 (1959–60), pp. 447–76

Gregoras, Nicephorus, *Byzantina historia*, I–III, ed. L. Schopen and I. Bekker, *CSHB*, Bonn (1829–55)

Guillou, André, *Les archives de Saint-Jean-Prodrome sur le mont Ménécée*, Paris (1955)

Hero, A., *A Woman's Quest for Spiritual Guidance. The Correspondence of Princess Irene Eulogia Choumnaina Palaiologina*, Brookline, Mass. (1986)

Hopf, C., *Chroniques gréco-romanes inédites ou peu connues*, Berlin (1873)

Kodinos (Pseudo-), George, *Traité des offices*, ed. J. Verpeaux, Paris (1976)

Laonici Chalcocandylae, *Historiarum Demonstrationes*, ed. E. Darkó, 2 vols., Budapest (1922–3)

Martini, A., *Manuelis Philae carmina inedita*, Naples (1900)

Mercati, A., *Notizie di Procoro e Demetrio Cidone, Manuele Caleca e Teodoro Meliteniota, ed altri appunti per la storia della teologia e della litteratura bizantina del secolo XIV*, ST, 56, Vatican City (1931)

Miklosich, F. and Müller, J., *Acta et Diplomata Graeca Medii Aevi Sacra et Profana*, 6 vols., Vienna (1860–90)

Miller, E., *Manuelis Philae Carmina*, 2 vols., Paris (1855–7)

Pachymeres, George, *De Michaele et Andronico Palaeologis Libri Tredecim*, ed. I. Bekkerus, 2 vols., *CSHB*, Bonn (1835)

Pachymeres, George, *Relations historiques*, ed. A. Failler, 2 vols., Paris (1984)

Sathas, K., Μεσαιωνικὴ Βιβλιοθήκη, 7 vols., Venice (1841–1914)

Schreiner, P., *Die Byzantinischen Kleinchroniken*, *CSHB*, 12, 3 vols., Vienna (1975–9)

Schreiner, P., *Texte zur spätbyzantinischen Finanz- und Wirtschaftsgeschichte in Handschriften der Biblioteca Vaticana*, Vatican City (1991)

Ševčenko, I., 'Nicolas Cabasilas' "Anti-Zealot" Discourse: A Reinterpretation', *DOP* 11 (1957), pp. 79–171

Ševčenko, I., 'Alexios Makrembolites and his "Dialogue between the Rich and the Poor"', *ZRVI* 6 (1960), pp. 187–228

Talbot, A.-M., *The Correspondence of Athanasius I Patriarch of Constantinople. Letters to the Emperor Andronicus II, Members of the Imperial Family, and Officials*, Washington, DC (1975)

Theodoulos Magistos, Λόγος περὶ Βασιλείας, *MPG* 145 (1965), pp. 447–96

Theodoulos Magistos, Λόγος περὶ πολιτείας, *MPG* 145 (1965), pp. 496–548

Treu, M., *Dichtungen des Grosslogotheten Theodoros Metochites*, Potsdam (1895)

Treu, M., *Maximi Monachi Planudis Epistulae*, Breslau (1890)

Zepos, J. and Zepos, P., *Jus Graecoromanum*, 1, Athens (1931)

Secondary works

Ahrweiler, Hélène (1983), 'La région de Philadelphie au XIVe siècle (1290–1390), dernier bastion de l'hellénisme en Asie Mineure', *AIBL*: 175–97

Angelov, D. (1956), 'Certains aspects de la conquête des peuples balkaniques par les Turcs', *Byzantinoslavica* 17: 220–75

Atiya, A.S. (1934), *The Crusade of Nicopolis*, London

Barker, J.W. (1969), *Manuel II Palaeologus, 1391–1425*, New Brunswick

Bartusis, M. (1992), *The Late Byzantine Army. Arms and Society, 1204–1453*, Philadelphia

Beck, H.-G. (1952), *Theodoros Metochites. Die Krise des byzantinischen Weltbildes im 14. Jahrhundert*, Munich

Beck, H.-G. (1974), 'Die griechische volkstümliche Literatur des 14. Jahrhunderts', *Actes du XIVe congrès international des études byzantines, Bucarest, 1971*, Bucharest, pp. 125–38

Belting, H., Mango, C. and Mouriki, D. (1978), *The Mosaics and Frescoes of St Mary Pammakaristos (Fethiye Camii) at Istanbul*, Washington, DC

Bernicolas-Hatzopoulos, D. (1983), 'The First Siege of Constantinople by the Ottomans (1394–1402), and its Repercussions on the Civilian Population of the City', *BS* 10: 39–51

Bertelé, T. (1962), 'I gioelli della corona bizantina dati in pegno alla repubblica veneta nel sec. XIV e Marino della Scala', *Studi in onore di Amintore Fanfani*, Milan, II, pp. 87–188

Bertelé, T. (1978), *Numismatique Byzantine*, Wetteren; ed. and reissued by Cecile Morrisson

Bosch, U.V. (1965), *Andronikos III. Palaiologos. Versuch einer Darstellung der byzantinischen Geschichte in den Jahren 1321–1341*, Amsterdam

Brătianu, G.I. (1929), *Recherches sur le commerce génois dans la mer noire au XIIIe siècle*, Paris

Brătianu, G.I. (1936), *Privilèges et franchises municipales dans l'empire byzantin*, Paris and Bucharest

Bryer, A.A.M. (1986), 'Late Byzantine Rural Society in Matzouka', in A. Bryer and H. Lowry (eds.), *Continuity and Change in Late Byzantine and Early Ottoman Society*, Birmingham and Washington, DC, pp. 53–95

Buchthal, H. and Belting, H. (1978), *Patronage in Thirteenth-Century Constantinople. An Atelier of Late Byzantine Book Illumination and Calligraphy*, Washington, DC

Canard, M. (1937), 'Un traité entre Byzance et l'Egypte au XIIIe siècle et les relations diplomatiques de Michel VIII Paléologue avec les sultans Mamluks Baibars et Quala'un', in *Mélanges GaudefroyDemombynes*, Cairo, pp. 197–224

Charanis, P. (1941), 'Internal Strife in Byzantium during the Fourteenth Century', *Byzantion* 15: 208–30

Charanis, P. (1942/3), 'The Strife among the Palaeologi and the Ottoman Turks, 1370–1402', *Byzantion* 16: 286–314

Charanis, P. (1948), 'The Monastic Properties and the State in the Byzantine Empire', *DOP* 4: 51–119

Charanis, P. (1951), 'On the Social Structure and Economic Organization of the Byzantine Empire in the Thirteenth Century and Later', *BS* 12: 94–153

Chatzidakis, M. (1955), 'Rapports entre la peinture de la Macédoine et de la Créte au XIVe siècle', in Πεπραγμένα τοῦ θ' Διεθνοῦς Βυζαντινολογικοῦ Συνεδρίου, Athens, pp. 136–49

Chatzidakis, M. (1974), 'Classicisme et tendances populaires au XIVe siècle. Les recherches sur l'évolution du style', *Actes du XIVe congrès international des études Byzantines, Bucarest, 1971*, Bucharest, pp. 153–88

Chrysostomides, J. (1965), 'John V Palaeologus in Venice (1370–71) and the Chronicle of Caroldo: A Reinterpretation', *OCP* 31: 76–84

Dade, E. (1938), *Versuche zur Wiedererrichtung der lateinischen Herrschaft in Konstantinopel im Rahmen der abendländischen Politik (1261 bis etwa 1310)*, Jena

Dennis, G.T. (1960), *The Reign of Manuel II Palaeologus in Thessalonica, 1382–1387*, *OCA*, LIX, Rome

Dölger, F. (1931), 'Johannes VII., Kaiser des Rhomäer', *BZ* 31: 21–36

Dölger, F. (1938), 'Johannes VI. Kantakuzenos als dynastischer Legitimist', *Annales de l'Institut Kondakov*, 10: 19–30; repr. in ΠΑΡΑΣΠΟΡΑ, Ettal (1961), pp. 194–207

Dölger, F. (1940), 'Die dynastische Familienpolitik des Kaisers Michael VIII. Palaiologos', in *Festschrift Eichmann*, n.p. pp. 179–90 ; repr. in ΠΑΡΑΣΠΟΡΑ, Ettal (1961), pp. 178–88

Dölger, F. (1949), 'Einiges über Theodora, die Griechin, Zarin der Bulgaren (1308–1330)', in *Mélanges H. Grégoire*, 1, n.p., = *AIPHO* 9: 211–21; repr. in ΠΑΡΑ-ΣΠΟΡΑ, Ettal (1961), pp. 222–30

Dölger, F. (1952), 'Der Vertrag des Sultans Quala'un von Agypten mit dem Kaiser Michael VIII. Palaiologos (1281)', in *Serta Monacensia. Festschrift Babinger*, Leiden, pp. 60–79; repr. in *Byzantinische Diplomatik*, Ettal (1956), pp. 225–44

Dujčev, I. (1972), 'Contribution à l'histoire de la conquête turque en Thrace aux dernières décades du XIV siècle', *EB* 9: 80–92

Ferjančič, B. (1974), *Tesalija u XIII i XIV veku*, Belgrade

Fögen, M.-Th. (1982), 'Zeugnisse byzantischer Rechtspraxis', *Fontes Minores* 5: 215–80

Francès, E. (1962), 'La féodalité byzantine et la conquête turque', *Studia et Acta Orientalia* 4: 69–90

Geanakoplos, D. (1959), *Emperor Michael Palaeologus and the West 1258–1282. A Study in Byzantine–Latin Relations*, Cambridge, Mass.

Gouma-Peterson, T. (1991), 'The Frescoes of the Parekklesion of St Euthymios in Thessaloniki: Patrons, Workshop, and Style', in S. Čurčič and D. Mouriki (eds.), *The Twilight of Byzantium*, Princeton, pp. 111–60

Guilland, R. (1922), 'Le palais de Métochite', *REG* 35: 82–95

Guilland, R. (1926a), *Essai sur Nicéphore Grégoras*, Paris

Guilland, R. (1926b), 'Les poésies inédites de Théodore Métochite', *Byzantion* 3: 265–302

Haldon, J. (1986), 'Limnos, Monastic Holdings and the Byzantine State: ca. 1261–1453', in A. Bryer and H. Lowry (eds.), *Continuity and Change in Late Byzantine and Early Ottoman Society*, Birmingham and Washington, DC, pp. 161–215

Halecki, O. (1930), *Un empereur de Byzance à Rome. Vingt ans de travail pour l'union des églises et pour la défense de l'empire d'orient, 1355–1375*, Warsaw

Harley, J.B. and Woodward D. (eds.) (1987), *The History of Cartography*, 1, Chicago and London

Heisenberg, A. (1920), *Aus der Geschichte und Literatur der Palaiologenzeit*, Munich

Hero, A. (1991), 'Theoleptos of Philadelphia (ca. 1250–1322): From Solitary to Activist', in S. Ćurčić and D. Mouriki (eds.), *The Twilight of Byzantium*, Princeton, pp. 27–38

Hrochova, V. (1967), 'Le commerce vénitien et les changements dans l'importance des centres de commerce en Grèce du 13e au 15e siècles', *SVen* 9: 3–34

Hrochova, V. (1972), 'Aspects sociaux et économiques de la décadence des villes byzantines à l'époque des Paléologues', *Actes du IIe congrès international des études du sud-est européen*, Athens, 11, *Histoire*, pp. 435–40

Hrochova, V. (1989), *Aspects des Balkans médiévaux*, Prague

Hunger, H. (1974), 'Klassizistische Tendenzen in der byzantinischen Literatur des 14. Jh.', *Actes du XIVe congrès international des études byzantines, Bucarest, 1971*, Bucharest, pp. 139–52

Jacoby, D. (1973), 'The Encounter of Two Societies: Western Conquerors and Byzantines in the Pelopennesus after the Fourth Crusade', *AmHR* 78: 873–906

Jacoby, D. (1974), 'Catalans, Turcs et Vénitiens en Romanie (1305–1322): un nouveau témoignage de Marino Sanudo Torsello', *SM* 3rd series 15: 217–61

Jugie, M. (1928), 'Démetrius Cydonès et la théologie latine à Byzance aux XIVe et XVe siècles', *EO* 27: 385–402

Kalligas, H. (1990), *Byzantine Monemvasia. The Sources*, Monemvasia

Kazhdan, A.P. (1980), 'L'histoire de Cantacuzène en tant qu'œuvre littéraire', *Byzantion* 50: 279–335

Kazhdan, A.P. (1982), 'The Fate of the Intellectual in Byzantium', *Greek Orthodox Theological Review* 27: 83–97

Kazhdan, A.P. (1993), 'State, Feudal, and Private Economy in Byzantium', *DOP* 47: 83–100

Kravari, V. (1989), *Villes et villages de Macédoine occidentale*, Paris

Kyrris, K.P. (1982), *Το Βυζάντιον κατά τον ΙΔ αἰῶνα*, 1, Nicosia

Laiou, A.E. (1970), 'Marino Sanudo Torsello, Byzantium and the Turks; the Background to the Anti-Turkish League of 1332–1334', *Speculum* 41: 374–92

Laiou, A.E. (1972), *Constantinople and the Latins. The Foreign Policy of Andronicus II (1282–1328)*, Cambridge, Mass.

Laiou, A.E. (1973), 'The Byzantine Aristocracy in the Palaeologan Period: A Story of Arrested Development', *Viator* 4: 131–51

Laiou, A.E. (1978), 'Some Observations on Alexios Philanthropenos and Maximos Planoudes', *Byzantine and Modern Greek Studies* 4: 88–99

Laiou, A.E. (1980–1), 'The Byzantine Economy in the Mediterranean Trade System, 13th-15th Centuries', *DOP* 34–5: 177–222

Laiou, A.E. (1981), 'The Role of Women in Byzantine Society', *JÖB* 31: 233–60

Laiou, A.E. (1982a), 'L'économie et la société de Crète vénitienne (ca. 1270–ca. 1310)', in *Bisanzio e l'Italia, Raccoita di studi in de Agostino Pertusi. Vita e Pensiero*, Milan, pp. 177–298

Laiou, A.E. (1982b), 'The Greek Merchant of the Palaeologan Period: A Collective Portrait', *The Proceedings of the Academy of Athens*: 97–132

Laiou, A.E. (1984), 'Observations on the Results of the Fourth Crusade: Greeks and Latins in Port and Market', *MH* n.s. 12: 47–60

Laiou, A.E. (1985), 'In the Medieval Balkans: Economic Pressures and Conflicts in the Fourteenth Century', in S. Vryonis Jr (ed.), *Byzantine Studies in Honor of Milton V. Anastos (Byzantina kai Metabyzantina,* 4), Malibu, Calif., pp. 137–62

Laiou, A.E. (1987), 'Un notaire vénitien à Constantinople: Antonio Bresciano et le commerce international en 1350', in M. Balard, A. Laiou, C. Otten Froux (eds.), *Les Italiens à Byzance*, Paris, pp. 79–151

Laiou, A.E. (1991a), Στὸ Βυζάντιο τῶν Παλαιολόγων: Οἰκονομικὰ καὶ πολιτιστικὰ φαινόμενα, *Eufrosynon. Festschrift für M. Chatzidakis,* Athens, pp. 283–96

Laiou, A.E. (1991b), 'The Foreigner and the Stranger in 12th-Century Byzantium: Means of Propitiation and Acculturation', in M.-Th. Fögen (ed.), *Fremde des Gesellschaft*, Frankfurt, pp. 71–98

Laiou, A.E. (1992a), 'Venetians and Byzantines: Investigation of Forms of Contact in the Fourteenth Century', *Thesaurismata* 22: 29–43

Laiou, A.E. (1992b), *Mariage, amour et parenté à Byzance aux XIe–XIIIe siècles*, Paris

Laiou, A.E. (1993), 'On Political Geography: The Black Sea of Pachymeres', in R. Beaton and C. Roueché (eds.), *The Making of Byzantine History. Studies dedicated to Donald M. Nicol*, Aldershot and London, pp. 94–121

Laiou, A.E. (1995a), 'Italy and the Italians in the Political Geography of the Byzantines (14th Century)', *DOP* 49: 73–98

Laiou, A.E. (1995b), 'Peasant Rebellion: Notes on its Vocabulary and Typology', in M.-Th. Fögen (ed.), *Ordnung und Aufruhr im Mittelalter*, Frankfurt, pp. 99–117

Laiou, A.E. (1995c), 'Thessaloniki, its Hinterland and its Economic Space', *Vyzantine Makedonie*, Thessaloniki, pp. 183–94

Laiou, A.E. and Simon, D. (1992), 'Eine Geschichte von Mühlen und Mönchen: der Fall der Mühlen von Chantax', *Bolletino dell'Istituto di diritto romano* 3rd series 30: 619–76

Laiou-Thomadakis, A.E. (1977), *Peasant Society in the Late Byzantine Empire. A Social and Demographic Study*, Princeton

Lampros, S. (ed.) (1912), 'Ἰσιδώρου ἐπισκόπου Θεσσαλονίκης ὀκτὼ ἐπιστολαὶ ἀνέκδοται, *Νέος Ἑλληνομνήμων* 9: 343–414

Laourdas, B. (ed.) (1954), 'Ἰσιδώρου ἀρχιεπισκόπου Θεσσαλονίκης ὅμιλίαι εἰς τὰς ἑορτὰς τοῦ ἁγίου Δημητρίου, *Ἑλληνικά Παράρτημα,* v, Thessaloniki

Laurent, V. (1938), 'Grégoire X (1271–1276) et un projet de ligue antiturque', *EO* 37: 257–73

Laurent, V. (1945), 'Les grandes crises religieuses à Byzance. La fin du schisme arsénite', *Acad. Roum. Bull. Sect. Hist.* 26: 225–313

Lefort, J. (1982), *Villages de Macédoine*, I: *La Chalcidique occidentale*, Paris

Lefort, J. (1985), 'Radolibus: populations et paysage', *TM* 9: 195–234

Lefort, J. (1986a), 'The Village of Radolibos, XIIth–XIVth Centuries', in A. Bryer and H. Lowry (eds.), *Continuity and Change in Late Byzantine and Early Ottoman Society*, Birmingham and Washington, DC, pp. 11–21

Lefort, J. (1986b), *Paysages de Macédoine*, Paris

Lefort, J. (1986c), 'Une exploitation de taille moyenne au XIIIe siècle en Chalcidique', in Ἀφιέρωμα στό Νίκο Σβορῶνο, Rethymon, pp. 362–72

Lefort, J. (1991), 'Population et peuplement en Macédoine orientale, IXe–XVe siècles', in V. Kravari, J. Lefort and C. Morrisson (eds.), *Hommes et richesses dans l'empire byzantin*, 2 vols., Paris, II: *VIIIe–XVe siècle*, pp. 63–82

Lefort, J. (1993), 'Rural Economy and Social Relations in the Countryside', *DOP* 47: 101–13

Lemerle, P. (1945), *Philippes et le Macédoine orientale à l'époque chrétienne et byzantine*, Paris

Lemerle, P. (1948), 'Le juge général des Grecs et la réforme judiciaire d'Andronic III', in *Mémorial L. Petit*, Bucharest, pp. 292–316

Lemerle, P. (1949), 'Recherches sur les institutions judiciaires à l'époque des Paléologues I: le tribunal impérial', *Mélanges H. Grégoire*, I = *AIPHO* 9: 369–84

Lemerle, P. (1950), 'Recherches sur les institutions judiciaires à l'époque des Paléologues II: le tribunal du patriarcat ou tribunal synodal', *Mélanges P. Peeters*, II = *AB* 68: 318–33

Lemerle, P. (1957), *L'émirat d'Aydin. Byzance et l'occident*, Paris

Lemerle, P. (1964), 'Documents et problèmes nouveaux concernant les juges généraux', Δελτίον χριστιανικῆς ἀρχαιολογικῆς ἑταιρείας 4: 29–44

Loenertz, R.J. (1937–8), 'Manuel Paléologue et Démétrius Cydonès. Remarques sur leurs correspondences', *EO* 36: 271–87, 474–87; 37: 107–24

Loenertz, R.J. (1938), 'Démétrius Cydonès citoyen de Venise', *EO* 37: 125–6

Loenertz, R.J. (1939), 'La première insurrection d'Andronic IV Paléologue (1373)', *EO* 38: 334–45

Loenertz, R.J. (1958), 'Jean V Paléologue à Venise (1370–1371)', *REB* 16: 217–32

Maksimović, L. (1973), 'Geneza i karakter apanaža u Vizantiji', *ZRVI* 14/15: 103–54

Maksimović, L. (1981), 'Charakter der sozial-wirtschaftlichen Struktur d. spätbyzantinischen Stadt', *JÖB* 31: 149–88

Maksimović, L. (1988), *The Byzantine Provincial Administration under the Palaiologoi*, Amsterdam

Mango, C. (1962), *Materials for the Study of the Mosaics of St Sophia at Istanbul*, Washington, DC

Matschke, K.P. (1969), 'Rolle und Aufgaben des Gouverneurs von Konstantinopel in der Palaiologenzeit', *Byzantino-Bulgarica* 3: 81–101

Matschke, K.P. (1970), 'Zum Charakter des byzantinischen Schwarzmeerhandels in XIII. bis XV. Jh.', *Wiss. Zeitschrift Univ. Leipzig* 19: 447–58

Matschke, K.P. (1971), *Fortschritt und Reaktion in Byzanz im 14. Jahrhundert. Konstantinopel in der Bürgerkriegsperiode von 1341 bis 1354*, Berlin

Matschke, K.P. (1973), 'Bemerkungen zum spätbyzantinischen Salzmonopol', *SB* 2: 37–60

Matschke, K.P. (1975), 'Johannes Kantakuzenos, Alexios Apokaukos und die byzantinische Flotte in der Bürgerkriegsperiode 1340–1355', *Actes du XIVe congrés international des études byzantines, Bucarest, 1971*, Bucharest, pp. 193–205

Matschke, K.P. (1979), 'Geldgeschäfte, Handel und Gewerbe in spätbyzantinischen Rechenbüchern und in der spätbyzantinischen Wirklichkeit', *JGF* 3: 181–204

Matschke, K.P. (1981a), 'Bemerkungen zu den sozialen Trägern des spätbyzantinischen Seehandels', *Byzantino-bulgarica* 7: 253–61

Matschke, K.P. (1981b), 'Sozialschichten und Geisteshaltungen', *JÖB* 31: 189–212

Matschke, K.P. (1984a), 'Byzantinische Politiker und byzantinische Kaufleute im Ringen um die Beteiligung am Schwarzmeerhandel in der Mitte des 14. Jh.', *Mitteilungen des Bülgarischen Forschungsinstitutes in Österreich* 6: 75–90

Matschke, K.P. (1984b), 'Grund-und Hauseigentum in und um Konstantinopel in spätbyzantinischer Zeit', *Jahrb. für Wirtschaftgeschichte* 4: 103–28

Matschke, K.P. (1989), 'Tuchproduktion und Tuchproduzenten in Thessalonike und in anderen Städten und Regionen des späten Byzanz', *Βυζαντιακά* 9: 47–87

Matschke, K.P. (1991), 'Bemerkungen zu den Mikro- und Makrostrukturen der spätbyzantinischen Gesellschaft', *XVIIIth International Congress of Byzantine Studies, Major Papers*, Moscow, pp. 152–95

Matschke, K.P. (1993), 'Die spätbyzantinische Offentlichkeit', in S. Tanz (ed.), *Mentalität und Gesellschaft in Mittelalter: Gedenksschrift für Ernst Weiner*, Frankfurt, pp. 155–223

Mavromatis, L. (1978), *La fondation de l'empire serbe. Le Kralj Milutin*, Thessaloniki

Mertzios, K. (1947), *Μνημεῖα Μακεδονικῆς Ἱστορίας*, Thessaloniki

Meyendorff, J. (1959), *Introduction à l'étude de Grégoire Palamas* (Patristica Sorbonensia, 31), Paris

Meyendorff, J. (1960a), 'Projets de concile oecuménique en 1367', *DOP* 14: 147–77

Meyendorff, J. (1960b), 'Jean-Joasaph Cantacuzène et le projet de concile oecuménique en 1347', in *Akten des XI. Internat, Byz.Kongresses: Munich, 1958*, Munich, pp. 363–9

Meyendorff, J. (1974), 'Society and Culture in the Fourteenth Century: Religious Problems', *Actes du XIVe congrès international des études byzantines, Bucarest, 1971*, Bucharest, pp. 111–24

Miller, W. (1908), *The Latins in the Levant. A History of Frankish Greece, 1204–1566*, London

Miller, W. (1921), *Essays on the Latin Orient*, Cambridge

Morrisson, C. (1991), 'Monnaie et finances dans l'empire byzantin, Xe–XVe siècle', in V. Kravari, J. Lefort and C. Morrisson (eds.), *Hommes et richesses dans l'empire byzantin*, Paris, II, pp. 291–315

Mouriki, D. (1991), 'The Wall Paintings of the Pantanassa at Mistra: Models of a Painter's Workshop in the Fifteenth Century', in S. Ćurčić and D. Mouriki (eds.), *The Twilight of Byzantium*, Princeton, pp. 217–50

Neçipoglu, N. (1990), 'Byzantium between the Ottomans and the Latins: A Study of Political Attitudes in the Late Palaeologan Period 1370–1460', dissertation, Harvard University

Nelson, R. and Lowden, J. (1991), 'The Palaeologina Group: Additional Manuscripts and New Questions', *DOP* 45: 59–68

Nicol, D.M. (1968), *The Byzantine Family of Kantakouzenos (Cantacuzenus) ca. 1100–1460. A Genealogical and Prosopographical Study*, Washington, DC

Nicol, D.M. (1972), *The Last Centuries of Byzantium, 1261–1453*, London

Nicol, D.M. (1979), *Church and Society in the Last Centuries of Byzantium*, Cambridge

Nicol, D. M. (1982), 'Thessalonica as a Cultural Center in the Fourteenth Century', in *Ἡ Θεσσαλονίκη μεταξὺ ᾽Ανατολῆς καὶ Δύσεως*, Thessaloniki, pp. 122–31

Nicol, D.M. (1984), *The Despotate of Epiros 1267–1479*, Cambridge

Oikonomidès, N. (1964), 'Contribution à l'étude de la pronoia au XIIIe siècle: une formule d'attribution de parèques à un pronoiaire', *REB* 22: 158–75

Oikonomidès, N. (1968), *Σημείωμα γιά τόν Ανδρόνικο Εύ Παλαιολόγο* (1390), *Θησαυρίσματα*, 5: 23–31

Oikonomidès, N. (1969), 'Le haradj dans l'empire byzantin du XVe siècle', *Actes du 1er congrès international des études Balkanique et sud-est européennes*, Sofia, III, pp. 681–8

Oikonomidès, N. (1973), 'Notes sur un praktikon de pronoiaire (juin 1325)', *TM* 5: 335–46

Oikonomidès, N. (1976), 'Monastères et moines lors de la conquête ottomane', *SF* 35: 1–10

Oikonomidès, N. (1977), 'John VII Palaeologus and the Ivory Pyxis at Dumbarton Oaks', *DOP* 31: 329–37

Oikonomidès, N. (1979a), *Hommes d'affaires grecs et latins à Constantinople (XIIIe–XVe siècles)*, Paris and Montreal

Oikonomidès, N. (1979b), *῎Ενα πρόσταγμα τοῦ Ματθαίου Καντακουζηνοῦ* (4 *Δεκεμβρίου* 1353), *Σύμμεικτα* 3: 53–62

Oikonomidès, N. (1980), 'The Properties of the Deblitzenoi in the Fourteenth and Fifteenth Centuries', in A.E. Laiou-Thomadakis (ed.), *Charanis Studies: Essays in Honor of Peter Charanis*, New Brunswick, pp. 176–98

Oikonomidès, N. (1980–1), *Οἱ δύο Σερβικές κατακτήσεις τῆς Χαλκιδικῆς τόν ΙΔ', αἰώναῦ, Δίπτυχα* B: 294–9

Oikonomidès, N. (1981), 'A propos des armées des premiers Paléologues et des compagnies de soldats', *TM* 8: 353–71

Oikonomidès, N. (1985), 'La chancellerie impériale de Byzance du 13e au 15e siècle', *REB* 42: 167–95

Oikonomidès, N. (1986), 'Ottoman Influences on Late Byzantine Fiscal Practice', *SF* 45: 1–24

Oikonomidès, N. (1988), 'Byzantium and the Western Powers in the Thirteenth to Fifteenth Centuries', in J.D. Howard-Johnston (ed.), *Byzantium and the West, c. 850–c. 1200*, Amsterdam, pp. 319–32

Oikonomidès, N. (1992), 'Byzantine Diplomacy, A.D. 1204–1453: Means and Ends', in J. Shephard and S. Franklin (eds.), *Byzantine Diplomacy*, London, pp. 73–88

Ostrogorsky, G. (1954), *Pour l'histoire de la féodalité byzantine*, Subsidia, CBHB, 1, Brussels

Ostrogorsky, G. (1956), *Quelques problèmes d'histoire de la paysannerie byzantine*, CBHB, Subsidia, 11, Brussels

Ostrogorsky, G. (1958), 'Byzance, état tributaire de l'Empire turc', *ZRVI* 5: 49–58

Ostrogorsky, G. (1965a), *Serska Oblast posle Dušanove smrti*, Belgrade

Ostrogorsky, G. (1965b), 'La prise de Serrès par les Turcs', *Byzantion* 35: 302–19

Ousterhout, R. (1987), *The Architecture of the Kariye Camii in Istanbul*, Washington, DC

Ousterhout, R. (1991), 'Constantinople, Bithynia, and Regional Developments in Later Palaeologan Architecture', in S. Čurčič and D. Mouriki (eds.), *The Twilight of Byzantium*, Princeton, pp. 75–110

Oxford Dictionary of Byzantium (1991), 3 vols., Oxford

Parisot, V. (1845), *Cantacuzène homme d'état et historien*, Paris

Radojčič, S. (1974), 'Der Klassizismus und ihm entgegengesetzte Tendenzen in der Malerei des 14. Jahrhunderts bei den orthodoxen Balkanslawen und den Rumänen', *Actes du XIVe congrès international des études byzantines, Bucarest, 1971*, Bucharest, pp. 189–205

Rautman, M. (1991), 'Aspects of Monastic Patronage in Palaeologan Macedonia', in S. Čurčič and D. Mouriki (eds.), *The Twilight of Byzantium*, Princeton, pp. 53–74

Rubió y Lluch, A. (1883), *La expedición y dominación de los catalanes en oriente*, Barcelona

Runciman, Steven (1970), *The Last Byzantine Renaissance,*Cambridge

Schlumberger, G. (1902), *Expéditions des 'Almugavares' ou routiers catalans en orient*, Paris

Schreiner, P. (1978), 'Ein Prostagma Andronikos' III. für die Monembasioten in Pegai (1328) une das gefälschte Chrysobull Andronikos' II für die Monembasioten im byzantinischen Reich', *JÖB*: 203–28

Schreiner, P. (1981–2), Παρατηρήσεις διὰ τὰ προνόμια τῆς Μονεμβασίας, Πρακτικά Β'Συνεδρίου Πελοποννησιακῶν Σπουδῶν, Athens

Setton, K. (1948), *Catalan Domination of Athens 1311–1388*, Cambridge, Mass.

Setton, K. (1976–84), *The Papacy and the Levant 1204–1571*, 4 vols. Philadelphia

Ševčenko, I. (1962), *Etudes sur la polémique entre Théodore Métochite et Nicéphore Choumnos*, Brussels

Ševčenko, I. (1974), 'Society and Intellectual Life in the Fourteenth Century', *Actes du XIVe congrès international des études byzantines, Bucarest, 1971*, Bucharest, pp. 69–92

Ševčenko, I. (1984), 'The Palaeologan Renaissance', in W.J. Treadgold (ed.), *Renaissances Before the Renaissance: Cultural Revivals of Late Antiquity and the Middle Ages*, Stanford, pp. 144–71

Skržinskaja, E.C. (1947), 'Genuezcy v Konstantinople v XIV veke', *VV* n.s. 1: 213–34

Sokolov, J. (1923–6), 'Krupnye i meikiie vlasteli v Fessalii v epochu Paleologov', *VV* 24: 35–44

Solovjev, A. (1932), 'Fessalijskie archonty v XIV veke', *BS* 3: 159–74

Soulis, G.C. (1984), *The Serbs and Byzantium during the Reign of Tsar Stephen Du'an (1331–1355) and his Successors*, Washington, DC

Svoronos, N. (1956), 'Sur quelques formes de la vie rurale à Byzance: petite et grande exploitation', *AESC* 11: 325–35

Svoronos, N. (1982), 'Le domaine de Lavra sous les Paléologues', in P. Lemerle, A. Guillou, N. Svoronos and D. Papachryssanthou (eds.), *Actes de Lavra*, Paris, IV, pp. 65–173

Tafrali, O. (1913), *Thessalonique au XIVe siècle*, Paris

Talbot, A.-M. (1992), 'Empress Theodora Palaiologina, Wife of Michael VIII', *DOP* 46: 295–303

Talbot, A.-M. (1993), 'The Restoration of Constantinople under Michael VIII', *DOP* 47: 243–61

Theocharides, G.I. (1963), Οἱ Τζαμπλάκωνες. συμβολὴ εἰς τὴν Βυζαντινὴν Μακεδονικὴν προσωπογραφίαν τοῦ ΙΔ' αἰῶνος, *Makedonika* 5: 125–83

Underwood, P. (1966), *The Kariye Djami*, 3 vols., New York

Vakalopoulos, A.E. (1955–60), Οἱ δημοσιευμένες ὁμιλίες τοῦ ἀρχιεπισκόπου Θεσσα-λονίκης Ἰσιδώρου ὡς ἱστορικὴ πηγὴ γιὰ τὴ γνώση τῆς πρώτης Τουρκοκρατίας στὴ Θεσσαλονίκη, *Μακεδονικά*, 4: 20–34

Vakalopoulos, A.E. (1962), 'Les limites de l'empire byzantin depuis la fin du XIVe siècle jusqu'à sa chute (1453)', *BZ* 55: 56–65

Verpeaux, J. (1959), *Nicéphore Choumnos, homme d'état et humaniste byzantin, 1255–1327*, Paris

Vryonis, Jr, S. (1971), *The Decline of Medieval Hellenism in Asia Minor and the Process of Islamization from the Eleventh through the Fifteenth Century*, Berkeley and London

Weiss, G. (1969), *Joannes Kantakuzenos – Aristokrat, Staatsman, Kaiser und Mönch – in der Gesellschaftsentwicklung von Byzanz im 14. Jahrhundert*, Wiesbaden

Werner, E. (1965), 'Johannes Kantakuzenos, Umur Pasha und Orchan', *Byzantinoslavica* 26: 255–76

Werner, E. (1974), 'Gesellschaft und Kultur im XIV. Jahrhundert: sozial-ökonomische Fragen', *Actes du XIVe congrès international des études byzantines, Bucarest, 1971*, Bucharest, pp. 93–110

Wirth, P. (1965), 'Zum Geschichtsbild Kaiser Johannes' VII. Palaiologos', *Byzantion* 35: 592–600

Xyngopoulos, A. (1953), Ἡ ψηφιδωτὴ διακόσμηση τοῦ ναοῦ τῶν ʽΑγίων ʼΑποστόλων Θεσσαλονίκης, Thessaloniki

Zachariadou, E.A. (1970), 'The Conquest of Adrianople by the Turks', *SV* 12: 211–17

Zachariadou, E.A. (1977), 'John VII (alias Andronicus) Palaeologus', *DOP* 31: 339–42

Zachariadou, E.A. (1980), 'The Catalans of Athens and the Beginning of the Turkish Expansion in the Aegean Area', *SM* n.s. 3: 821–38

Zachariadou, E.A. (1983), *Trade and Crusade. Venetian Crete and the Emirates of Menteshe and Aydin (1300–1415)*, Venice

Zachariadou, E.A. (1987), 'Notes sur la population de l'Asie Mineure turque au XIVe siècle', *BF* 12: 223–31

Zachariadou, E.A. (1989a), Ἐφήμερες ἀπόπειρες γιά αὐτοδιοίκηση στίς ἑλληνικές πόλεις κατά τόν ΙΔ΄και ΙΕ΄ αἰῶνα, ʼΑριάδνη 5: 345–51

Zachariadou, E.A. (1989b), 'Holy War in the Aegean during the Fourteenth Century', *MHR* 4: 212–25

Zakythinos, D.A. (1953), *Le despotat grec de Morée*, II: *Vie et institutions*, Athens

Zakythinos, D. A. (1975), *Le despotat grec de Morée (1262–1460)*, I: *Histoire politique*, London (reissue of the same work published in Paris in 1932, with revisions and additions by Chryssa Maitezou)

Zakythinos, D.A. (1948), *Crise monétaire et crise économique à Byzance du XIIIe au XVe siècle*, Athens

25 LATINS IN THE AEGEAN AND BALKANS IN THE FOURTEENTH CENTURY

Primary sources

Balard, M. (ed.), *Notai genovesi in Oltremare. Atti rogati a Chio da Donato di Chiavari, 17 febbraio – 12 novembre 1394*, Genoa (1988)

Carbone, S. (ed.), *Pietro Pizolo, notaio in Candia*, I: *1300*, Venice (1978)

Chiaudano, M. and Lombardo, A. (eds.), *Leonardo Marcello, notaio in Candia, 1278–1281*, Venice (1960)

Délibérations des assemblées vénitiennes concernant la Romanie, ed. F. Thiriet, 2 vols., Paris and The Hague (1966–71)

Documents sur le régime des terres dans la principauté de Morée au XIVe siècle, ed. J. Longnon and P. Topping, Paris and The Hague (1969)

Duca di Candia. Quaternus consilorum (1340–1350), ed. P. Ratti Vidulich, Venice (1976)

Duca di Candia. Ducali e lettere ricuvete (1358–1360; 1403–1405), ed. F. Thiriet, Venice (1978)

Libra delle uxanzo e statuti delo Imperio de Romania, ed. A. Parmeggiani, Spoleto (1998)

Lombardo, A. (ed.), *Zaccaria de Fredo, notaio in Candia, 1352–1357*, Venice (1968)

Monumenta Peloponnesiaca. Documents for the History of the Peloponnese in the 14th and 15th Centuries, ed. J. Chrysostomides, Camberley (1995)

Morozzo della Rocca, R. (ed.), *Benvenuto de Brixano, notaio in Candia, 1301–1302*, Venice (1950)

Notai genovesi in Oltremare. Atti rogati a Chio da Giuliano da Canella (2 Novembre 1380–31 Marzo 1381), ed. E. Basso, Athens (1993)

Notai genovesi in Oltremare. Atti rogati a Chio da Gregorio di Panissaro (1403–1405), ed. P. Toniolo, Genoa (1995)

Régestes des délibérations du Sénat de Venise concernant la Romanie, ed. F. Thiriet, 3 vols. Paris and The Hague (1958–61)

Secondary works

Antoniadis Bibicou, H. (1963), *Recherches sur les douanes à Byzance*, Paris

Arbel, B. (ed.) (1996), *Intercultural Contacts in the Medieval Mediterranean*, London

Argenti, P.P. (1958), *The Occupation of Chios by the Genoese and their Administration of the Island, 1340–1566*, 3 vols., Cambridge

Ashtor, E. (1983), *Levant Trade in the Later Middle Ages*, Princeton

Balard, M. (1978), *La Romanie génoise, XIIe – début du XVe siècle*, 2 vols., Genoa and Rome

Balard, M. and Ducelier, A. (1995), *Coloniser au Moyen Age*, Paris

Balard, M. and Ducelier, A. (eds.) (1998), *Le partage du monde. Echanges et colonisation dans la Mediterrannée médiévale*, Paris

Bon, A. (1969), *La Morée franque. Recherches historiques, topographiques et archéologiques sur la principauté d'Achaïe, 1205–1430*, 2 vols., Paris

Gallina, M. (1989), *Una società coloniale del Trecento. Creta fra Venezia e Bisanzio*, Venice

Giunta, F. (1959), *Aragonesi e Catalani nel Mediterraneo*, II: *La presenza catalana nel Levante dalle origini a Giacomo II*, Palermo

Heers, J. (1961), *Gênes au XVe siècle. Activité économique et problèmes socieaux*, Paris

Housley, N. (1992), *From Lyons to Alcazar. The Later Crusades, 1274–1580*, Oxford

Ilieva, A. (1991), *Frankish Morea (1205–1262). Socio-Cultural Interactions between the Franks and the Local Population*, Athens

Jacoby, D. (1989a), 'Social Evolution in Latin Greece', in K. M. Setton, *A History of the Crusades*, VI, Madison

Jacoby, D. (1989b), 'From Byzantium to Latin Romania: Continuity and Change', *MHR* 4: 1–44

Jacoby, D. (1997), *Trade, Commodities and Shipping in the Medieval Mediterranean*, Aldershot

Koder, J. (1973), *Negroponte. Untersuchungen zur Topographie und Siedlungsgeschichte der Insel Euboioa während der Zeit der Venezianerherrschaft*, Vienna

Krekic, B. (1961), *Dubrovnik (Raguse) et le Levant au moyen âge*, Paris and The Hague

Laiou, A. (1972), *Constantinople and the Latins. The Foreign Policy of Andronicus II, 1282–1328*, Cambridge, Mass.

Laiou, A. (1980–1), 'The Byzantine Economy in the Mediterranean Trade System, Thirteenth–Fifteenth Centuries', *DOP* 34–5: 177–222

Lilie, R.J. (1984), *Handel und Politik zwischen dem byzantinischen Reich und den italienischen Kommunen Venedig, Pisa und Genua in der Epoche der Komneni und der Angeloi, 1081–1204*, Amsterdam

Lock, P. (1995), *The Franks in the Aegean 1204–1500*, London and New York

Loenertz, R.J. (1970), *Byzantina et Franco-Graeca*, ed. P. Schreiner, Rome

McKee, S. (1993), 'Uncommon Dominion: The Latins, Greeks and Jews of Venetian Crete in the Fourteenth Century', PhD thesis, University of Toronto

Magdalino, P. (1993), *The Empire of Manuel I Komnenos, 1143–50*, Cambridge

Pistarino, G. (1990a), *Genovesi d'Oriente*, Genoa

Pistarino, G. (1990b), 'Duecentocinquant'anni dei Genovesi a Chio', in Pistarino (1990a), pp. 243–80

Pistarino, G. (1990c), 'I Gattilusio di Lesbo e di'Enos signori nell'Egeo', in Pistarino (1990a), pp. 383–420

Setton, K.M. (1975), *Catalan Domination of Athens*, 2nd edn, London

Stöckly, D. (1995), *Le système de l'Incanto des galées du Marché à Venise (fin XIIIe–milieu XVe siècle)*, Leiden

Thiriet, F. (1975), *La Romanie vénitienne au moyen âge. Le développement et l'exploitation du domaine colonial vénitien, XIIe–XVe siècles*, 2nd edn, Paris

Thiriet, F. (1976–8), 'La Messénie méridionale dans le système colonial des Vénitiens en Romanie', in *Praktika tou I Diethnous Synedriou Peleponnesiakon Spoudon*, Athens

Thiriet, F. (1977), 'Quelques observations sur le trafic des galées vénitiennes d'après les chiffres des *incanti*, XIVe–XVe siècles', in *Etudes sur la Romanie gréco-vénitienne, Xe–XVe siècles*, VIII, London

Topping, P.W. (1949), *Feudal Institutions as Revealed in the Assizes of Romania, the Law Code of Frankish Greece*, London

Topping, P. (1975), 'The Morea, 1311–1364' and 'The Morea, 1364–1460', in *A History of the Crusades*, ed. K.M. Setton, Madison, Wisconsin, III, pp. 104–66

Treppo, M. del (1971), *I mercanti catalani e l'espansione delle corona d'Aragona nel Mediterraneo*, Naples

Zachariadou, E.A. (1983), *Trade and Crusade. Venetian Crete and the Emirates of Menteshe and Aydin, 1300–1415*, Venice

Zakythinos, D. (1975), *Le despotat grec de Morée*, 2nd edn, London

26 THE RISE OF THE OTTOMANS

Primary sources

Azıkpasazade, Ç. N. Atsış (ed.), *Tevârîh-i Âl-i Osmân*, Istanbul (1949)

Beldiceanu-Steinherr, Irène, *Recherches sur les actes des règnes des Sultans Osman, Orhan et Murad I*, Munich (1967)

Fleet, Kate, 'The Treaty of 1387 between Murad I and the Genoese', *BSOAS* 56 (1993), pp. 13–33

Gibb, H.A.R., *Travels of Ibn Battuta*, II, Cambridge (1962)

Gökbilgin, Tayyib, *Edirne ve Paşa Livası*, Istanbul (1952)

Gökbilgin, Tayyib, *Rumeli'de Yürükler, Tatarlar ve Evlâd-ı Fâtihân*, Istanbul (1957)

Secondary works

Balivet, Michel (1993), 'Culture ouverte et échanges inter-religieux dans les villes ottomanes du XIVe siècle', in Zachariadou (1993a), pp. 1–6

Barkan, Ömer Lütfi (1942), 'Kolonizatör Türk Dervişleri', *Vakıflar* 2: 279–386

Beldiceanu-Steinherr, Irène (1965), 'La conquête d'Adrianople par les Turcs', *TM* 1: 439–61

Demetriades, Vassilis (1993), 'Some Thoughts on the Origins of the Devsirme', in Zachariadou (1993a), pp. 23–33

Dols, Michael (1977), *The Black Death in the Middle East*, Princeton, N.J.

Emecen, Feridun (1993), 'Ottoman Policy of Conquest of the Turcoman Principalities of Western Anatolia', in Zachariadou (1993a), pp. 35–40

Heywood, Colin (1988), 'Wittek and the Austrian Tradition', *JRAS*: 7–25

Heywood, Colin (1989), 'Boundless Dreams of the Levant: Paul Wittek, the *George-Kreis*, and the Writing of Ottoman History', *JRAS*: 30–50

Imber, Colin (1986), 'Paul Wittek's "De la défaite d'Ankara à la prise de Constantinople"', *Osmanlı Araştırmaları* 5: 65–81

Imber, Colin (1987), 'The Ottoman Dynastic Myth', *Turcica* 19: 7–27

Imber, Colin (1990), *The Ottoman Empire, 1300–1481*, Istanbul

Imber, Colin (1993), 'The Legend of Osman Gazi', in Zachariadou (1993a), pp. 67–75

Inalcık, Halil (1952), 'Timariotes chrétiens en Albanie au XVe siècle', *Mitteilungen des Österreichischen Staatsarchivs* 4: 118–38

Inalcık, Halil (1954), 'Ottoman Methods of Conquest', *Studia Islamica*, 2: 104–29

Inalcık, Halil (1962), 'The Rise of Ottoman Historiography', in B. Lewis and P.M. Holt (eds.), *Historians of the Middle East*, London, pp. 152–67

Inalcık, Halil (1971), 'The Conquest of Edirne (1361)', *Archivum Ottomanicum*, 3: 185–210

Inalcık, Halil (1981–2), 'The Question of the Emergence of the Ottoman State', *IJTS* 2: 71–9

Inalcık, Halil (1985), 'The Rise of the Turcoman Maritime Principalities in Anatolia', *BF* 9: 179–217

Inalcık, Halil (1993), 'Osman Gazi's Siege of Nicea and the Battle of Bapheus', in Zachariadou (1993a), pp. 77–100

Jennings, Ronald C. (1986), 'Some Thoughts on the Gazi-thesis', *Wiener Zeitschrift für die Kunde des Morgenlandes*, 76: 151–61

Kafadar, Cemal (1995), *Between Two Worlds. The Construction of the Ottoman State*, Berkeley, Los Angeles and London

Kiel, Machiel (1989), 'Urban development in Bulgaria in the Turkish Period', *IJTS* 4/2: 79–159

Köprülü, Mehmed Fuad (1992), *The Origins of the Ottoman Empire*, London; trans. and ed. Gary Leiser, Albany (from the 1935 French original and the 1959 expanded Turkish version)

Lindner, Rudi Paul (1983), *Nomads and Ottomans in Medieval Anatolia,* Bloomington

Luttrell, Anthony (1993), 'Latin Responses to Ottoman Expansion before 1389', in Zachariadou (1993a), pp. 119–34

Mantran, Robert (ed.) (1989), *Histoire de l'empire ottoman,* Paris

Ménage, V.L. (1962), 'The Beginnings of Ottoman Historiography', in B. Lewis and P.M. Holt (eds.), *Historians of the Middle East,* London, pp. 168–79

Oikonomidès, Nicolas (1986), 'Ottoman Influences on Late Byzantine Fiscal Practice', *SF* 45: 1–24

Reinert, Stephen (1993), 'From Nis to Kosovo Polje: Reflections on Murad I's Final Years', in Zachariadou (1993a), pp. 169–211

Sertoğlu, M. and Cezar, M. (1957), *Mufassal Osmanlı Tarihi,* 1, Istanbul

Uzunçarşılı, I.H. (1947), *Osmanlı Tarihi,* 1, Ankara

Varlık, Mustafa Çetin (1974), *Germiyanoğulları Tarihi,* Ankara

Vryonis, Speros (1971), *The Decline of Medieval Hellenism in Asia Minor and the Process of Islamisation from the Eleventh through the Fifteenth Century,* Berkeley and Los Angeles

Wittek, Paul (1934), *Das Fürstentum Mentesche,* Istanbul

Wittek, Paul (1938), *The Rise of the Ottoman Empire,* London

Wittek, Paul (1955), 'Devshirme and shari'a', *BSOAS* 17: 271–8

Zachariadou, Elizabeth (1970), 'The Conquest of Adrianople by the Turks', *SV* 12: 211–17

Zachariadou, Elizabeth (1980) 'Manuel II Paleologus on the Strife between Bayezid I and Kadi Burhan al-Din Ahmad', *BSOAS* 43: 471–81

Zachariadou, Elizabeth (1987), 'Notes sur la population de l'Asie Mineure turque au XIVe siècle', *BF* 12: 223–31

Zachariadou, Elizabeth (ed.) (1993a), *The Ottoman Emirate,* Rethyninon

Zachariadou, Elizabeth (1993b), 'The Emirate of Karasi and that of the Ottomans: Two Rival States', in Zachariadou (1993a), pp. 225–36

Zhukov, Konstantin (1993), 'Ottoman, Karasid and Sarukhanid Coinages and the Problem of Currency Community in Turkish Western Anatolia ('40s–'80s of the 14th Century)', in Zachariadou (1993a), pp. 237–43

Zhukov, Konstantin (1994), 'The "Destan of Umur Pasha"', *Proceedings of the 11th Turkish Congress of History,* Ankara

27 CHRISTIANS AND MUSLIMS IN THE EASTERN MEDITERRANEAN

Primary sources

Argenti, P., *The Occupation of Chios by the Genoese and their Administration of the Island, 1346–1566,* Cambridge (1958)

Atiya, A.S., *Egypt and Aragon. Embassies and Diplomatic Correspondence between 1300 and 1330 A.D.,* Leipzig (1938)

Housley, N.J., *Documents on the Later Crusades, 1274–1580,* London (1996)

Martínez Ferrando, J.E., *Jaime II de Aragón. Su vida familiar,* Barcelona (1948)

Mas Latrie, L. de, *Histoire de l'île de Chypre sous le règne des princes de la maison de Lusignan*, 3 vols., Paris (1852–61)

Richard, J., *Chypre sous les Lusignans. Documents chypriotes des archives du Vatican (XIVe et XVe siècles)*, Paris (1962)

Secondary works

Ahrweiler, H. (1966), *Byzance et la mer: la marine de guerre, la politique et les institutions maritimes de Byzance aux VIIe–XVe siècles*, Paris

Arbel B., Hamilton B. and Jacoby, D. (eds.) (1989), *Latins and Greeks in the Eastern Mediterranean after 1204*, London

Ashtor, E. (1983), *Levant Trade in the Later Middle Ages*, Princeton, N.J.

Atiya, A.S. (1934), *The Crusade of Nicopolis*, London

Atiya, A.S. (1938), *The Crusade in the Later Middle Ages*, London

Ayalon, D. (1965), 'The Mamluks and Naval Power – a Phase of the Struggle between Islam and Christian Europe', *Proceedings of the Israel Academy of Sciences and Humanities* 1: 1–12

Balard, M. (1978), *La Romanie génoise (XIIe–début du XVe siècle)*, 2 vols., Genoa and Rome

Balard, M. (1985), 'L'activité commerciale en Chypre dans les années 1300', in Edbury (1985), pp. 251–63

Balard, M. (1994), 'La place de Famagouste génoise dans le royaume des Lusignan', in *Les Lusignans et l'Outre Mer: Actes du Colloque*, Poitiers, pp. 16–27

Balard, M. (1995a), 'Chypre, les républiques maritimes Italiennes et les plans des croisades (1274–1370)', in Coureas and Riley-Smith (1995), pp. 97–106

Balard, M. (1995b), 'The Urban Landscape of Rhodes as Perceived by Fourteenth- and Fifteenth-Century Travellers', *MHR* 10: 24–34

Balard, M. and Ducellier, A. (eds.) (1995), *Coloniser au Moyen Age*, Paris

Barber, M. (1978), *The Trial of the Templars*, Cambridge

Barber, M. (1994), *The New Knighthood. A History of the Order of the Temple*, Cambridge

Boase, T.S.R. (ed.) (1978), *The Cilician Kingdom of Armenia*, Edinburgh

Boehke, F.J. (1966), *Pierre de Thomas. Scholar, Diplomat and Crusader*, Philadelphia

Boulton, D'A.J.D. (1987), *The Knights of the Crown. The Monarchical Orders of Knighthood in Later Medieval Europe, 1325–1520*, Woodbridge

Coureas, N. (1994), 'The Papacy's Relations with the Kings and the Nobility of Armenia in the Period 1300–1350', in *Les Lusignans et l'outre mer. Actes du colloque*, Poitiers, pp. 99–108

Coureas, N. (1995), 'Cyprus and the Naval Leagues, 1333–1358', in Coureas and Riley-Smith (1995), pp. 107–24

Coureas, N. and Riley-Smith, J. (eds.) (1995), *Cyprus and the Crusades*, Nicosia

Cox, E.L. (1967), *The Green Count of Savoy. Amadeus and Transalpine Savoy in the Fourteenth Century*, Princeton, N. J.

Delaville Le Roulx, J. (1886), *La France en orient au XIVe siècle*, Paris

Delaville Le Roulx, J. (1913), *Les Hospitaliers à Rhodes jusqu'à la mort de Philibert de Naillac (1310–1421)*, Paris

Der Nersessian, S. (1962), 'The Kingdom of Cilician Armenia', in Setton (1955–89), II, pp. 630–59

Edbury, P.W. (1977), 'The Crusading Policy of King Peter I of Cyprus, 1359–1369', in Holt (1977), pp. 90–105

Edbury, P.W. (1980), 'The Murder of King Peter I of Cyprus (1359–1369)', *JMH* 6: 219–33

Edbury, P.W. (ed.) (1985), *Crusade and Settlement. Papers Read at the First Conference of the Society for the Study of the Crusades and the Latin East and Presented to R.C. Smail*, Cardiff

Edbury, P.W. (1986), 'Cyprus and Genoa: The Origins of the War of 1373–1374', in T. Papadopoullos and V. Englezakis (eds.), Πρακτικα τοῦ Δευτέρου Διεθνοῦζ Κυπριολογικοῦ Συνεδίου, Nicosia, II, pp. 109–26

Edbury, P.W. (1991), *The Kingdom of Cyprus and the Crusades*, Cambridge

Edbury, P.W. (1993), *The Lusignan Kingdom of Cyprus and its Muslim Neighbours*, Nicosia

Edbury, P.W. (1994), 'The Aftermath of Defeat: Lusignan Cyprus and the Genoese, 1374–1382', in *Les Lusignans et l'outre mer. Actes du Colloque*, Poitiers, pp. 132–40

Forey, A.J. (1980), 'The Military Orders in the Crusading Proposals of the Late-Thirteenth and Early-Fourteenth Centuries', *Traditio* 36: 317–45

Gill, J. (1979), *Byzantium and the Papacy, 1198–1400*, Brunswick, N.J.

Halecki, O. (1930), *Un empereur de Byzance à Rome: vingt ans de travail pour l'union des églises et pour la défense de l'empire d'orient, 1355–1375*, Warsaw

Hill, G. (1940–52), *A History of Cyprus*, 4 vols., Cambridge

Hillgarth, J.N. (1971), *Ramon Lull and Lullism in Fourteenth-Century France*, Oxford

Holt, P.M. (ed.) (1977), *The Eastern Mediterranean Lands in the Period of the Crusades*, Warminster

Holt, P.M. (1986), *The Age of the Crusades*, London and New York

Housley, N.J. (1980), 'The Franco-Papal Crusade Negotiations of 1322–3', *PBSR* 48: 166–85

Housley, N.J. (1982a), 'The Mercenary Companies, the Papacy and the Crusades, 1356–1378', *Traditio* 38: 253–80

Housley, N.J. (1982b), 'Pope Clement V and the Crusades of 1309–10', *JMH* 8: 29–43

Housley, N.J. (1982c), *The Italian Crusades*, Oxford

Housley, N.J. (1986), *The Avignon Papacy and the Crusades, 1305–1378*, Oxford

Housley, N.J. (1992), *From Lyons to Alcazar. The Later Crusades, 1274–1580*, Oxford

Housley, N.J. (1995), 'Cyprus and the Crusades, 1291–1571', in Coureas and Riley-Smith (1995), pp. 187–206

Irwin, R. (1986), *The Middle East in the Middle Ages. The Early Mamluk Sultanate*, London and Sydney

Irwin, R. (1994), 'How Many Miles to Babylon? The *Devise des chemins de Babiloine* Redated', in M. Barber (ed.), *The Military Orders. Fighting for the Faith and Caring for the Sick*, Aldershot, pp. 57–63

Jacoby, D. (1968), 'Jean Lascaris Calophéros, Chypre et La Morée', *REB* 26: 189–228

Jacoby, D. (1977), 'Citoyens, sujets et protégés de Venise et de Gênes en Chypre de XIIIe au XVe siècle, *BF* 5: 159–88

Jacoby, D. (1984), 'The Rise of a New Emporium in the Eastern Mediterranean: Famagusta in the Late Thirteenth Century', Μελέται καὶ Ὑπομνήματα I: 143–79

Jorga, N. (1896), *Philippe de Mézières (1327–1405) et la croisade au XIVe siècle*, Paris

Kedar, B.Z. (1976), *Merchants in Crisis. Genoese and Venetian Men of Affairs and the Fourteenth-Century Depression*, New Haven and London

Kedar, B.Z. and Schein, S. (1979), 'Un projet de "passage particulier" proposé par l'Ordre de l'Hôpital 1306–1307', *BEC* 137: 211–26

Keen, M.H. (1984), *Chivalry*, New Haven and London

Laiou, A.E. (1970), 'Marino Sanudo Torsello, Byzantium and the Turks: The Background to the Anti-Turkish League of 1332–1334', *Speculum* 45: 374–92

Laiou, A.E. (1972), *Constantinople and the Latins. The Foreign Policy of Andronicus II, 1282–1328*, Cambridge, Mass.

Lemerle, P. (1957), *L'émirat d'Aydin. Byzance et l'Occident. Recherches sur 'La geste d'Umur Pacha'*, Paris

Lock, P. (1995), *The Franks in the Aegean, 1204–1500*, London and New York

Luttrell, A.T. (1958), 'Venice and the Knights Hospitallers of Rhodes in the Fourteenth Century', *PBSR* 26: 195–212

Luttrell, A.T. (1965), 'The Crusade in the Fourteenth Century', in J.R. Hale, J.R.L. Highfield and B. Smalley (eds.), *Europe in the Late Middle Ages*, London, pp. 122–54

Luttrell, A.T. (1975), 'The Hospitallers at Rhodes, 1306–1421', in Setton (1955–89), III, pp. 278–313

Luttrell, A.T. (1978a), *The Hospitallers in Cyprus, Rhodes, Greece and the West, 1291–1400*, London

Luttrell, A.T. (1978b), 'The Hospitallers' Interventions in Cilician Armenia: 1291–1375', in Boase (1978), pp. 118–44

Luttrell, A.T. (1980a), 'Gregory XI and the Turks, 1370–1378', *OCP* 46: 391–417

Luttrell, A.T. (1980b), 'Popes and Crusaders: 1362–1394', in *Genèse et débuts du grand schisme d'occident: 1362–1394*, Paris, pp. 575–85

Luttrell, A.T. (1982), *Latin Greece, the Hospitallers and the Crusades, 1291–1400*, London

Luttrell, A.T. (1988), 'English Levantine Crusaders, 1363–1367', *RStds* 2: 143–53

Luttrell, A.T. (1992), *The Hospitallers of Rhodes and their Mediterranean World*, Aldershot

Luttrell, A.T. (1995), 'Rhodes: base militaire, colonie, métropole de 1306 à 1440', in Balard and Ducellier (1995), pp. 235–40, 244–5

Metcalf, D.M. (1996), *The Silver Coinage of Cyprus, 1285–1382*, Nicosia

Nicol, D.M. (1972), *The Last Centuries of Byzantium, 1261–1453*, London

Nicol, D.M. (1988), *Byzantium and Venice*, Cambridge

Otten-Froux, C. (1994), 'Le retour manqué de Jacques Ier en Chypre', in *Les Lusignans et l'outre mer. Actes du colloque*, Poitiers, pp. 228–40

Otten-Froux, C. (1995), 'Les relations politico-financière de Gênes avec le royaume des Lusignan (1374–1460)', in Balard and Ducellier (1995), pp. 61–75

Palmer, J.J.N. (1972), *England, France and Christendom, 1377–99*, London

Papacostea, S. (1995), 'De la guerre du Bosphore à la guerre de Ténédos: rivalités commerciales et alignements politiques dans le sud-est de l'Europe dans la seconde moitié du XIVe siècle', in Balard and Ducellier (1995), pp. 341–7, 350–52

Petti Balbi, G. (1974), 'La maona di Cipro del 1373', *Rassegna storica della Liguria* 1: 269–85

Pryor, J.H. (1988), *Geography, Technology and War. Studies in the Maritime History of the Mediterranean 649–1571*, Cambridge

Racine, P. (1977), 'Note sur le trafic Veneto-Chypriote à la fin du moyen âge', *BF* 5: 307–29

Richard, J. (1952), 'La révolution de 1369 dans le royaume de Chypre', *BEC* 110: 108–23

Richard, J. (1984), 'Le royaume de Chypre et l'embargo sur le commerce avec l'Egypte (fin XIIIe–début XIVe siècle)', *AIBL, comptes rendus*, pp. 120–34

Richard, J. (1995), 'L'état de guerre avec l'Egypte et le royaume de Chypre', in Coureas and Riley-Smith (1995), pp. 83–95

Riley-Smith, J. (1967), *The Knights of St John in Jerusalem and Cyprus c. 1050–1310*, London

Riley-Smith, J. (1987), *The Crusades. A Short History*, London

Riley-Smith, J. (ed.) (1991), *The Atlas of the Crusades*, London

Riley-Smith, J. (ed.) (1995), *The Oxford Illustrated History of the Crusades*, Oxford

Rudt de Collenberg, W.H. (1963), *The Rupenides, Hethumides and Lusignans. The Structure of the Armeno-Cilician Dynasties*, Paris

Rudt de Collenberg, W.H. (1986), 'Les *Bullae* et *Litterae* adressées par les papes d'Avignon à l'Arménie cilicienne, 1305–1375 (d'après les Registres de l'Archivio Segreto Vaticano)', in D. Kouymjian (ed.), *Armenian Studies in Memoriam Haïg Berbérian*, Lisbon, pp. 697–725

Sáez Pomés, M. (1952), 'Los Aragoneses en la conquista saqueo de Alejandria por Pedro I de Chipre', *Estudios de edad media de la corona de Aragón* 5: 361–405

Schein, S. (1979), '*Gesta Dei per Mongolos* 1300. The Genesis of a Non-Event', *EHR* 94: 805–19

Schein, S. (1991), *Fideles Crucis. The Papacy, the West, and the Recovery of the Holy Land, 1274–1314*, Oxford

Setton, K.M. (ed.) (1955–89), *A History of the Crusades*, 6 vols., Philadelphia and Madison

Setton, K.M. (1976–84), *The Papacy and the Levant (1204–1571)*, 4 vols., Philadelphia

Thiriet, F. (1959), *La Romanie vénitienne au moyen âge*, Paris

Trenchs Odena, J. (1980), '"De Alexandrinis" (el comercio prohibido con los musl- manes y el papado de Aviñón durante la primera mitad de siglo XIV)', *AEM* 10: 237–320

Tyerman, C.J. (1984a), 'Philip V of France, the Assemblies of 1319–20 and the Crusade', *BIHR* 57: 15–34

Tyerman, C.J. (1984b), 'Sed Nihil Fecit? The Last Capetians and the Recovery of the Holy Land', in J. Gillingham and J.C. Holt (eds.), *War and Government in the Middle Ages*, Woodbridge, pp. 170–81

Tyerman, C.J. (1985), 'Philip VI and the Recovery of the Holy Land', *EHR* 100: 25–52

Tyerman, C.J. (1988), *England and the Crusades, 1095–1588*, Chicago

Zachariadou, E.A. (1983), *Trade and Crusade. Venetian Crete and the Emirates of Menteshe and Aydin (1300–1415)*, Venice

Zachariadou, E.A. (1989), 'Holy War in the Aegean during the Fourteenth Century', in Arbel *et al.* (1989), pp. 212–25

Zachariadou, E.A. (1993), 'The Early Years of Ibrahim I. Karamanoglu', in A.A.M. Bryer and G.S. Georghallides (eds.), *The Sweet Land of Cyprus*, Nicosia, pp. 147–56

INDEX